International Relations
Since 1945

International Relations Since 1945

A Global History

JOHN YOUNG and JOHN KENT

OXFORD
UNIVERSITY PRESS

Great Clarendon Street, Oxford OX2 6DP

Oxford University Press is a department of the University of Oxford.
It furthers the University's objective of excellence in research, scholarship,
and education by publishing worldwide in

Oxford New York

Auckland Bangkok Buenos Aires Cape Town Chennai
Dar es Salaam Delhi Hong Kong Istanbul Karachi Kolkata
Kuala Lumpur Madrid Melbourne Mexico City Mumbai Nairobi
São Paulo Shanghai Taipei Tokyo Toronto

Oxford is a registered trade mark of Oxford University Press
in the UK and in certain other countries

Published in the United States
by Oxford University Press Inc., New York

British Library Cataloguing in Publication Data

Data available

Library of Congress Cataloging in Publication Data

Data available

ISBN 0–19–878164–4

10 9 8 7 6 5 4 3 2 1

Typeset in Stone Serif and Stone Sans
by RefineCatch Limited, Bungay, Suffolk
Printed in Great Britain by
Antony Rowe Limited, Chippenham, Wiltshire

Preface

This book is an attempt to provide a general account of the nature and development of the post-war international system with the origins, nature, and end of the Cold War at its centre. The approach is a historical one but one which hopes to offer something of value to general International Relations students interested in the development and interpretation of the post-1945 international system from a sounder empirical foundation. In particular the book seeks to examine Cold War controversies in a way which will stimulate debate and produce some reinterpretations. It implicitly challenges the importance of realism and suggests that realism is an unsuitable tool for understanding and explaining the Cold War and its end because it ignores the importance of domestic influences on foreign policy. The book makes no claim to contribute to historical sociology but it does attempt to suggest that domestic affairs, ideologies, and culture have significant connections to international events and are influences on the events described and analysed here. In particular that it is inappropriate to consider the post-war international system in isolation from the nature of the domestic state, the role of elites, and their use of ideas and ideologies.

Although world politics will be examined throughout from an essentially historical perspective rather than in terms of any particular theory of international relations the aim is not simply to tell what happened but to provide overall analysis and broad interpretations of events. Theories rest more securely on detailed empirical understanding, and good historical methodology does not neglect theoretical concepts or fail to deal with causation. Yet we recognise that it may not be possible to explain fully the causes of the changes in the international system after 1945, either in general or specific terms.

Given the work available on the post-1945 period we set out specifically to provide a book which incorporates some new ways of synthesizing complicated material and which also adds new and controversial interpretations for consideration while attempting to define the Cold War more precisely. For those teachers eager to get students thinking for themselves and contributing ideas to seminars and tutorials this should be a provocative book which outlines different ideas as well as providing basic information. As such it should offer something to students seeking to discover and reflect on new interpretations rather than simply discovering the facts and the so-called 'correct' explanations. Special attention is placed on new interpretations of the Cold War and its various phases while trying to link its development to a number of military and economic themes. Not least because a feature of the Cold War on both sides of the Iron Curtain has been the expenditure of vast resources on making people think in particular ways about many aspects of international relations; new interpretations of the Cold War's development are especially needed now it has ended. It is only by reflecting more fundamentally about the ascribed nature of the Cold War that we can begin to understand just why it ended so dramatically.

By placing more emphasis on controversies and challenging some conventional interpretations, the book hopes to offer a basis for debate and discussion in courses associated with the nature and development of the post-Second World War international system. A more analytical overview defining key issues precedes the more detailed coverage in the six chronological sections. This is intended to reinforce some of the key questions for debate which are also featured in much of the main text. Where there is repetition of interpretation it is hoped that students will benefit from being able to consider again some of the key issues raised. Both general and more specifically focused chronologies are included along with considerable cross-referencing. Where terms are used which may be unfamiliar and require explanation we hope to have provided this. Interpretations are not usually presented as definitive and the intention is often to present alternative views especially where detailed evidence cannot be produced. Text boxes will be found throughout, especially in the earlier sections, to provide details of important documents, interesting meetings and memoranda, summaries of debates, or interpretations and brief biographies of key figures. They will also be used to provide glimpses of the kind of ideas which are unusual, less well known and hopefully interesting and revealing.

As with the interpretations there will be some variety in the way specific themes are treated in different chronological periods which inevitably produce different issues and more or less debate. The variety should again serve to encourage the use of a general text as a means of thinking about the post-war world while discovering what happened. Some aspects of it will be covered in more detail than others and the constraints of space inevitably require that some topics which others might deem important will not be featured at all. The changes in the international economic order, the importance of the end of the European and Soviet empires, and links between the developed and less developed worlds will be touched on. And we hope to provide glimpses of all areas of the world and of the effects of international changes in and after the Cold War which have for many years been felt in both global and regional contexts.

We would like to express our thanks in helping to prepare this manuscript for publication to Lindsey Kent and Martine Langer and especially to Janet Smith for her extensive and excellent typing and to Helen Adams for having to confront a very demanding manuscript.

Outline contents

Part III: The Cold War of Peaceful Coexistence and the Rise of Multipolarity, 1963–1971

Part IV: The Détente Era, 1972–1980

Part V: From Confrontation to Communist Collapse, 1981–1989

Part VI: **The Post-Cold War World, 1990–2000**

Detailed contents

Part II: Cold War: Crises and Change, 1953–1963

Part III: The Cold War of Peaceful Coexistence and the Rise of Multipolarity, 1963–1971

Part IV: The Détente Era, 1972–1980

List of Abbreviations

ABM	Anti-Ballistic Missile
AFPL	(Burmese) Anti-Fascist People's Freedom League
ALCM	Air-Launched Cruise Missile
ANC	African National Congress (South Africa)
ANF	Atlantic Nuclear Force
ANSOM	(French) National Archives Overseas Section
ANZUS	Australian–New Zealand–US alliance
APEC	Asia–Pacific Economic Co-operation
ARAMCO	Arabian–American Oil Company
ARENA	(El Salvador) National Republican Alliance
ARVN	Army of the Republic of Vietnam
ASEAN	Association of South-East Asian Nations
CAP	Common Agricultural Policy (of EEC)
CCP	Chinese Communist Party
CDU	(German) Christian Democratic Union
CFCs	Chloro-Fluoro-Carbons
CFE	Conventional Forces in Europe treaty
CFSP	(EU) Common Foreign and Security Policy
CIA	(American) Central Intelligence Agency
CIS	Commonwealth of Independent States (in former USSR)
COCOM	Co-ordinating Committee (on East–West trade)
COMECON	Council for Mutual Economic Aid
Cominform	Communist Information Bureau
CPP	(Gold Coast) Convention People's Party
CPSU	Communist Party of the Soviet Union
CSCE	Conference on Security and Co-operation in Europe
CTBT	Comprehensive Test Ban Treaty
DBPO	Documents on British Policy Overseas
DEFCON	(US) Defence Condition
DMZ	De-Militarized Zone
EDC	European Defence Community
EC	European Community
ECOWAS	Economic Community of West African States
ECSC	European Coal-Steel Community
EEC	European Economic Community
EFTA	European Free Trade Association
ERM	(EC) Exchange Rate Mechanism
EMU	Economic Monetary Union
EU	European Union
Euratom	European Atomic Energy Authority

Ex Comm	Executive Committee of the NSC
FBI	(US) Federal Bureau of Investigation
FBS	Forward Based Systems (of nuclear weapons in Europe)
FIDES	(French) Funds for Economic and Social Investment
FLN	(Algerian) National Liberation Front
FLSN	(Nicaraguan) National Sandinista Liberation Front
FNLA	Front for the National Liberation of Angola
FPR	Rwandan Popular Front
FRELIMO	Front for the Liberation of Mozambique
FRUS	Foreign Relations of the United States
FTAA	Free Trade Area of the Americas
GATT	General Agreement on Tariffs and Trade
GDP	Gross Domestic Product
GDR	(East) German Democratic Republic
GLCM	Ground-Launched Cruise Missile
ICBM	Inter-Continental Ballistic Missile
IDF	Israeli Defence Forces
IGC	(EC and EU) Inter-Governmental Conference
IMF	International Monetary Fund
INF	Intermediate-range Nuclear Forces
KGB	(Soviet) State Security Committee (1954–91)
KI	(Soviet) Small Committee of Information
KHAD	Afghan secret police
KLA	Kosovan Liberation Army
KMT	Kuomintang (Chinese Nationalist Party)
KPD	German Communist Party
LDC	Less Developed Country
LNM	Lebanese National Movement
MAD	Mutual Assured Destruction
MBFR	Mutual Balanced Force Reduction talks
MERCUSOR	Common Market of the South (South America)
MGB	(Soviet) Ministry for State Security (1946–54)
MI5	British counter-intelligence and counter-subversion service
MIRV	Multiple Independent Re-entry Vehicle
MLF	(NATO) Multilateral Force
MNC	Multi-National Company
MPLA	Popular Movement for the Liberation of Angola
MX	(US) Missile Experimental
NA	(US) National Archives
NAFTA	North American Free Trade Area
NATO	North Atlantic Treaty Organization
NGO	Non-Governmental Organization
NIE	(US) National Intelligence Estimate
NKVD	Soviet secret police apparatus (1934–46)
NLF	(South Vietnam) National Liberation Front
NPT	Non-Proliferation Treaty
NSC	(US) National Security Council

NVA	North Vietnamese Army
OAS	Organization of American States
OAU	Organization of African Unity
OECD	Organization for Economic Co-operation and Development
OEEC	Organization of European Economic Co-operation
OPC	(US) Office of Policy Co-ordination
OPEC	Organization of Petroleum Exporting Companies
OSCE	Organization for Security and Co-operation in Europe
PAIGC	African Independence Party of Guinea and Cape Verde
PAP	(Singapore) People's Action Party
PCF	French Communist Party
PD	(US) Presidential Directive
PDG	Guinea Democratic Party
PDPA	People's Democratic Party of Afghanistan
PFLP	Popular Front for the Liberation of Palestine
PKI	Indonesian Communist Party
PLO	Palestinian Liberation Organization
PRO	Public Record Office
RDA	African Democratic Rally
RENAMO	Mozambique National Resistance
RSA	Non-UK Sterling Area
SAC	(US) Strategic Air Command
SAVAK	Iranian secret police
SALT	Strategic Arms Limitation talks and treaty
SCAP	Supreme Commander Allied Powers (Japan)
SDI	(US) Strategic Defense Initiative
SEATO	Southeast Asian Treaty Organization
SED	East German Communist Party
SLBM	Submarine-Launched Ballistic Missile
SLCM	Sea-Launched Cruise Missile
SPD	(German) Social Democratic Party
START	Strategic Arms Reduction Treaty
SWAPO	South-West African People's Organization
TBT	Test Ban Treaty
UAR	United Arab Republic
UDSR	(French) Social Democratic Resistance Union
UGCC	United Gold Coast Convention
UK	United Kingdom
UN	United Nations
UNIFIL	UN Interim Force in Lebanon
UNITA	National Union for the Total Independence of Angola
UNLU	(Palestinian) United National Leadership of the Uprising
UNO	(Nicaraguan) National Opposition Union
UNOSOM	UN Operation in Somalia
UNPROFOR	UN Protection Force (former Yugoslavia)
UNSCOP	UN Special Committee on Palestine
UPA	Union of Angolan Peoples
UPNA	Union of Peoples of Northern Angola

US   United States
USSR   Union of Soviet Socialist Republics
WTO   World Trade Organization

Introduction

The history of international politics since 1945, has been dominated by the origins, development, and sudden end of the Cold War. Although defined in a number of radically different ways, the Cold War fundamentally distinguishes the post-Second World War period from the earlier years of the twentieth century. The change it produced following the most destructive interstate global conflict in history fundamentally altered the international system after 1945. Arguably it was the Cold War which the Second World War helped produce that formed the most important legacy of the twentieth century. It dominated the international system for nearly fifty years and its effects are still present. The transition from World War to Cold War provided the key foundations for the post-war international order with its rapid and unprecedented social and technological change. Other international developments, including the growing importance of the mass media, the role of international and trans-national non-governmental organizations (NGOs), and the impact of globalization have eroded the power and significance of sovereign states. They are all important changes to the international system in their own right although many have been produced or affected by the Cold War. In a single work it is not possible to examine all these developments in detail and in this book they will be subordinated to an examination of relations between states in a global and regional context during and after the Cold War and to an explanation of what the Cold War meant for the development and understanding of the state system.

The Antecedents of the 1945 International System

The new post-war system that emerged in 1945 was now for the first time in history dominated by two extra-European powers. Relations between the European states had been destabilized by the unification of Germany in 1871. Prior to this a balance of power within the continent had preserved stability only as long as the manpower and resources of Germany were not united. The problem of Germany after its unification was a problem that could not be solved without the intervention of non-European powers—the United States and the Soviet Union (partly a European and partly an Asian power). Europe could no longer resolve its own problems and assistance from outside was required to overcome Germany in the last two years of the First World War when the US became involved. American reluctance to shoulder the burdens of maintaining peace in the inter-war years became the key element which permitted the re-emergence of a powerful Germany. Containing the German threat required in the 1920s the kind of commitment the US was not prepared to make until the 1940s. The role of the United States as either a hegemonic power or as a key global player in a bipolar world was by then a dramatic new feature of international politics after 1945. It had only one obvious challenger in the form of the Soviet Union whose land-based Empire extended into Asia but whose victory in the great land battles against the Third Reich provided the opportunity for it to play an important if not dominant European role.

It is easy to portray the decline of European nation states as a direct result of two European wars and the enormous shift in the global balance of economic and military power. After the violent power struggles between 1939 and 1945 the divisions in Europe became part of a global power struggle in which the continent's position was fundamentally altered. Whatever the significance of Europe in terms of the peace settlement and the rise of international tensions, the continent was now only one part of a new global power political equation. Disagreements soon began to appear as the victors in the war struggled to come to terms with a new global system of power and influence which was far from a predominantly European one. One purpose of this book is try and portray a Cold War developing out of the Second World War not because there were post-war differences in and over Europe but because the world as a whole had radically changed. It is a strange paradox of European and North American pre-occupations that while the Cold War has been interpreted as beginning in Europe and spreading to Asia and the rest of the world, the peacemakers were attempting to create a new world order partly because in the 1940s the power of European nation states was rapidly draining away from those areas to which the Cold War was allegedly spreading from Europe.

The onset of the Cold War conflict has been given a number of different historical roots and chronological starting points. The development of two large land-based empires, particularly in the nineteenth century, could have paved the way for what has been seen as an inevitable clash. The economic and human resources they possessed were likely to produce growing inter-national power and influence and a greater sense of rivalry. This certainly fits with a realist explanation of international relations but ignores the ideological conflict between communism and capitalism which is thus subordinated to geopolitical rivalries and a competition for resources. Yet the two land-based empires with rival ideologies had coexisted since 1917 and the relations which developed after 1945 were clearly different from those existing before the First and Second World Wars. Whatever the role of geopolitics and ideology, and both are important, the timing of the Cold War was connected to radical changes in the global power balance produced by the Second World War *and* to a new sense of ideological rivalry. In Western Europe elite fears of domestic instability and the destruction of the social and economic status quo which the Second World War produced were particularly important.

General theories do not serve to explain the timing of the Cold War and, for those not primarily focused on power, realism serves no purpose as it takes no account of ideas or ideologies. The Cold War's origins for them are better located in the success of the Russian Revolution and the irreconcilable ideo-logical conflict it produced. As better communications made the transmission of ideas on a global basis easier and cheaper, the conflict between two ideological

---

Realism

The realist school of international relations theorists was born out of the failure of liberal thinkers in the inter-war period to attach sufficient weight to the importance of power as a determinant of international relations. And in particular to Hitler's aggressive desire to maximize the territorial expansion and military power of the Third Reich. In contrast to liberals who put their faith in international cooperation and the importance of states working together realists, noting the lack of any single international authority and the anarchical nature of the international system, point to the necessity of survival through self-help. States are seen as competing with one another to achieve security from external threats which can be achieved only through relative gains in military and economic power. As states pursue this goal they are defined by realists as unitary actors competing to maximize their power in ways determined by the nature of the international system. Hence there is little or no linkage between domestic and foreign policy with the latter determined exclusively by external considerations. As regards the Cold War, realists see it as a power political competition between two competing power systems led by the US and the USSR with their development of new and more powerful weapons. Hence the ideological and domestic considerations are not seen as important determinants of the Cold War.

---

state systems assumed global proportions. The Cold War was therefore about competing ideologies, which for the first time threatened the social and economic status quo on which national ruling elites in capitalist countries depended. Thus domestic interests and the pursuit of ideological goals superseded the old international rivalries and alliances that had been geared to the competing interests of all sovereign states. In such an analysis the domestic social and economic systems and their political philosophies assume significance in shaping the global conflict, and explanations of the Cold War have to define the relationships between power political and ideological requirements. Economic development and the maintenance or prevention of social mobility in Latin America, Africa as well as in the developed states of Europe then become crucial in the origins and development of the conflict.

The Origins of the Cold War

The rivalries which emerged in 1945 were produced, at least in part, by the problems arising from the wartime shift in the global balance of economic and military power. However, the importance of the initial failure to agree on how to resolve them and the concomitant increase in international tensions owed much to domestic economic and political forces. It was not simply the existence of rival ideologies but the fact that the challenge to the pre-war social order in much of Western Europe was strengthened by the war itself and the forces for change it had unleashed. By the end of the Second World War it was clear that states would have to assume responsibilities for more than the maintenance of territorial integrity and the external pursuit of economic and military interests. Citizens throughout the globe expected improvements in their social and economic welfare and that governments would directly or indirectly promote these goals. Demands for social reform with better conditions for the lower classes had been feared and foreseen by those appeasers who sought to avoid war like the British prime minister Neville Chamberlain. In 1945 their wartime ally in the East had been strengthened by the war and threatened revolution rather than reform. For the first time since the French Revolution a movement for radical social change was accompanied and supported by a powerful state. The Cold War was in fact a battle for the domestic and international survival of states, social elites, and ways of life. In such circumstances students should be aware of how much elites on both sides have been prepared to invest in distorting the truth. In terms of strengthening their position and attracting mass support, it has always been vital to blame their opponents for instigating the conflict and to portray the actions of their own states as defensive and reactive. This has led to all sorts of distortions and misunderstandings of the nature of the global struggle and the ways in which regional conflicts have been linked to it.

The quest for international power and influence both contributed to the breakdown of the victorious wartime alliance in 1945 and assumed greater importance in the disagreements over the new world order because of the combination of the domestic and the international. Global status and prestige could influence the balance of domestic forces and the appeal of radical ideologies more so than in the inter-war years. Power politics and ideologies were always interlinked. While Europe may well have been seen as the most valuable region where these were played out, it was as much the failure to agree on how to allocate power, influence, and responsibility on a global basis between three main areas (Asia, Europe, and the Middle East) that was central to the power political disagreements in 1945.

The Decline of Europe and Global Economic Relations

The end of a Europe-dominated world was indicated during the war by the, albeit temporary, loss of many parts of its Empire. The European states system had been central to great power relations in the first half of the century (and, indeed, for long before that) as well as to the development of international relations theory. After 1945 it was the nature of Europe's relationship to the broader global balance of power that was crucial. Whatever the significance of the continent in terms of the rise of international tensions, it was now only one part of a new power political equation. The ending of European control over large areas of the globe, often referred to as decolonization, was one indication of the increasing shift of the focus of international politics. Large numbers of newly independent states were to change the nature of the newly formed United Nations and focus attention on the relationship between the industrialized world and the less developed areas which relied on the production for export of raw materials and foodstuffs. At the same time new regional power configurations had to be considered in Asia, Africa, and the Middle East and these assumed significance for the global Cold War conflict because some were seen as increasingly significant in global terms.

Important questions emerged about the economic and trade relations between these areas, with newly independent states emerging in the twenty years after the war and the developed world, including the former imperial or colonial powers. The debate about the structural nature of these relations remains unresolved. Some see economic problems being created in the developing nations because of the alleged failure to give free rein to market forces. Others claim that capitalism in the developed world operates to the increasing detriment of the less developed world through its control over raw material prices and investment capital flows. At the same time the terms of trade of the rich countries improved at the expense of the poor ones. Whether this was linked to the effect of colonialism is another unresolved but highly charged debate about global economic relations which is being subsumed within the increasing controversies over the nature and effect of globalization and the emergence of problems which require global cooperation to solve. Environmental pollution and climate change, along with international crime and disease, are phenomena outside the control of individual nation states and can be seen as eroding their power.

The process by which European rule over much of the world came to an end was accompanied by political and economic changes within Europe. It was these changes which indicated the end of the nation state or at least its exclusive role in international relations. The European colonial powers began to construct economic and institutional links between themselves which undermined sovereignty and began the process of defining a common European approach to international and domestic affairs. The current study will discuss these European developments, which began with economic integration in Western Europe, and the expanding international economy, but will focus more on the nature of the new regional conflicts and the role of the US and USSR in influencing them. European integration and the increasing contact between elites with loyalties not centred solely on the nation state may signify the beginning of a new era in international affairs, again with a legacy from the Second World War, but the focus will largely be on the Cold War and its end. Equally important outside Europe is the continued existence of global inequality and the extreme poverty experienced by millions of people in the less developed world. The debates about economic development will be briefly touched upon in parts of the book to indicate that world politics do not simply take place between the rich nations with the power to dominate international affairs.

Bipolarity or Hegemony?

The post-1945 world is normally defined as bipolar because of the disparity between the military capabilities and economic resources of the world's two most powerful states and the lesser powers, and because of the alignment of many states with one of the opposing ideological blocs before 1989. Yet the concept of bipolarity does require some qualification. At the end of the Second World War only Britain and the US had the ability to act militarily in large areas of the world, but only the US had escaped the problems caused by the devastation of war and only the US had the economic strength to dominate the global economy and its institutions. Thus it is possible to argue that the world after 1945 can be seen in terms of the exercise of hegemonic power by the US. After emerging from a relatively isolationist position and its regional dominance in the Western Hemisphere, the US arguably began to extend that dominance to many other areas of the globe and the Cold War was not defined by a bipolar world but by the attempts to preserve or terminate US hegemony.

The original US desire to end isolationism was based on a belief in a set of universal values which American wartime planners hoped to see established on a global basis. Non-discriminatory trade, the end of power political arrangements, the removal of imperial trade blocs, and the political values of self-determination and democratic government were seen as necessary for the preservation of peace; they were also seen as important for the successful development of American capitalism and the maintenance of national prosperity. These American ideals and traditions helped define and justify the goals of post-1945 American foreign policy in ways which would otherwise be more meaningfully interpreted as a quest for hegemony. United States wartime planners put forward ideas which claimed to favour a principled world order based on universal values that have been seen as benign and beneficial especially when placed alongside the more brutal regimes which emerged under the ideological auspices of fascism and communism. Yet the exercise of American power was not far below the surface of liberal ideals and values based on freedom and democracy and considerably distant from the goals of internationalism first heralded as the reason for American attempts to influence the world. The blend of international concerns and national self-assertion became a potent ideological mix as what was best for the world was juxtaposed with what was best for America.

The challenge of the Soviet Union has been from the start portrayed as a dynamic force driven by a crusading ideology linked to global expansion which the United States sought to resist in the name of universal values rather than specific interests associated with the preservation of its hegemony. It may be more plausible to see the Soviet challenge as born not from an assertive ideological triumphalism but from a sense of weakness and a desire to achieve bipolarity and equality. And the US must also be judged in the context of a triumphalist ideology which it has sought to extend far beyond American shores. The picture of a hegemonic power and those it assists by bankrolling them and upholding rules and institutions within its hegemonic sphere may well have had a positive impact on the preservation of order. Yet seeing two hegemonic powers battling it out for primacy with the outcome of such an equal contest uncertain until the last is a highly questionable portrayal of the post-1945 world and one possible explanation of why the Cold War's end surprised so many with its suddenness. The disparity between the two powers' capabilities was at times considerable and if one interprets the Cold War world as a series of challenges to American hegemony it is possible to find greater continuity between the twenty-first century and the Cold War period.

In analysing the world of the two Cold War protagonists there is also a need to take account of the emergence of the non-aligned movement, the

impact of a powerful, communist China, and the tendency of newly independent states to try and manipulate the superpowers to help secure
their own regional goals. All such things run counter to simplistic notions of
bipolarity and from the end of the 1960s onwards, as the Soviets mounted
a military challenge, the dominance of the two so-called superpowers was
consistently eroded. Even before that the control and influence exerted by
the US and the USSR over their respective blocs was facing a number of
challenges and relations within their blocs which form another important
feature of the Cold War world. Nevertheless it was a world in which domestic
interests, as well as foreign policy goals, often dictated support for one of the
two main rivals and one where the need to attract global support for the
values and social and economic systems each held dear assumed unprecedented
international importance

Cold War, as Distinct from Hot War, and the Role of Armaments

Central to the prospect of hot war arising from alleged military threats was the
role of nuclear weapons which revolutionized thinking about war. As global war
(referred to as hot war as opposed to Cold War or limited, regional conflicts)
became potentially ever more horrific, the use of force by the nuclear powers
against each other threatened to have disastrous consequences. One problem,
which was never solved, was to try and integrate the use of nuclear weapons into
a rational military strategy which did not risk large-scale national destruction. As
strategists wrestled with this dilemma, military power became less useful as a
means of forcing smaller states to comply with the wishes of the great powers.
Combined with the Cold War need to win over international opinion this
placed greater emphasis on prestige, status, the appearance of strength, and the
preservation of credibility. While economic resources and key strategic areas
remained of some significance, particularly in the 1940s and early 1950s,
unlike in the inter-war years competition in areas of no economic or strategic
importance became a feature of Cold War international politics and the
ideological battle for credibility.

At the same time it was necessary to find ways of fighting the Cold War which
did not run too great a risk of developing into hot war. This distinction between
measures short of international armed conflict (Cold War) and preparations to
fight a hot war is an important one which needs to be borne in mind particularly
when analysing the nature of and reasons for the arms race. Yet the Cold War
cannot be fully isolated from military conflict because the deployment of armed
forces was seen as necessary to deal with internal conflicts or to prevent the
emergence of unfriendly governments. And also because the militarization of
an essentially ideological threat was perceived as vital for the mobilization of
popular support for the Cold War struggle. In order to do this, governments were
prepared to exaggerate or invent an actual and immediate military threat when
what they really feared was an ideological challenge or a potential, long-term
military danger. This was particularly significant in the 1940s when the Soviet

leadership had most reason to fear the greater material wealth of the United States, and when the American and particularly Western European elites had most reason to fear the strength of left-wing political movements whose credibility had been enhanced by active resistance to fascism from 1942 onwards.

Military alliances such as NATO, SEATO, and the Baghdad Pact were important manifestations of the Cold War. Yet they have seen from the start as military alliances geared to hot war when they were actually far more important as political symbols of a will to resist communism, just as the Warsaw Pact in the East symbolized the resistance to capitalism and particularly to German capitalism. NATO was not an alliance preparing to attack the Soviet Union or one seen as capable of winning a conventional war in the defence of Western Europe; nor was the Warsaw Pact an organization geared to the expansion of Soviet power through the use of military force, yet they were both portrayed as such. The fact was that threat perception in the military sense did not drive force deployments or the level of armaments. More specifically the strategic need to defend a particular area did not lead to consideration of the ways in which this could be done effectively by military means. Nor did the requirements of Western European defence, for example, produce the force levels needed, or the rationale for foreign-policy-makers to act on. Rather it was political considerations (the need to keep Western Europe together) which dictated the development of military strategy. The latter was then used to provide and justify the rationale for the political needs which had produced the strategy in the first place. The result was that the actual military requirements to carry out the strategy were never met (as in all three Western military alliances mentioned above).

In such a situation the role of armaments and the concept of security have to be carefully considered in a Cold War context. Negotiations and discussions on arms levels formed a constant feature of Soviet–American relations and they consumed a vast amount of resources. Nuclear weapons in particular and the strategies behind their development and possible use were continually in the public eye. They had, and have, an obvious deterrent role (although the exact nature of such a role is highly debatable). In many ways armaments can be seen in the context of global conflict as predominantly symbolic of the role of the military and of the technological dynamism characteristic of the contrasting economic systems. Arms negotiations became protracted and detailed but were often designed to secure advantages which, like the weapons themselves, would serve the appearance of greater strength or power. Equally and crucially, the political pressure from public opinion for governments to become involved in them was intense. The need to prevent hot war was a continued feature of the Cold War and the need to appear committed to disarmament, peace, and stability a vital component of the battle for hearts and minds even if the timing and nature of the process was up for debate and the commitment to it not always genuine.

The Nature of the Cold War World

The military threat and danger presented by the Cold War have generally been exaggerated both at the time and in the literature. The military threat was and has been often proclaimed as the crucial element in the origins and development of the conflict even though power has arguably become more associated with prestige and influence. The control of resources and the development of military capabilities, in practical terms, have perhaps become less important in the nuclear age especially in relation to a global war increasingly hard to contemplate. Instead the Cold War brought a perceived need for states to control their citizens and ensure that their perceptions of the outside world reinforced the legitimacy of a totalitarian communist or a democratic capitalist state. In this new situation, the very existence of an ideological rival was for a time seen as an unacceptable threat. The refusal to accept the long-term existence of rival sovereign states was a feature of the early period of Cold War which strengthened or helped produce highly secret government agencies. Intelligence organizations also began to play more significant roles in overseas espionage and subversion. They were designed to operate covertly and to subvert or overthrow hostile or potentially hostile regimes in ways which could be denied by the governments ostensibly controlling them.

At the same time propaganda became more extensive and significant in relation to domestic as well as foreign affairs. More effort was devoted to providing 'information' to citizens and to ensuring that 'subversives' were marginalized or eliminated. It was important, for example, for Stalin to try and convince Soviet citizens that domestic opponents of his brutal and tyrannical regime were imperialist spies who deserved exile or death. At the same time it was important for Western governments, not only to play on the horrors of the Soviet regime, but to present it as a threat in ways which would win support for a policy of confrontation and the pursuit of ambitious foreign policy goals. As a result there is a need to examine if such dangers were exaggerated in both quantitative and qualitative terms largely in order to achieve maximum domestic effect.

The Use of Terminology in Western Interpretations of the Cold War

The initial increase in rivalries and tensions in and after 1945 produced a new international vocabulary which itself is a feature of a particular Cold War mindset. In the West many of these words display a subtle condemnation of the ideological opponent and reinforce a world-view in which Cold War confrontation stems from the activities of the communist states rather than from their counterparts in the capitalist world. Moreover, this itself produces justifications for policies which assume a fundamental sense of righteousness in international as well as domestic terms. To produce an objective international analysis of the Cold War it is necessary to question some of the standard Cold War terminology used in the West and to relate the conflict to the more traditional goals of great powers. And at the same time to look more closely at the changes that occurred in the Cold War international system and their links to domestic forces and ideational influences. Thus the two rival systems can be assessed more objectively and without the ascription of blame to the ideological opponent. When blame is given to one side it is often done as part of fighting rather than explaining the Cold War.

The use of the word 'security' by both sides has provided Cold War justifications for actions and policies that would have been previously interpreted differently. It has come to mean much more than protection from invasion and the avoidance of war. The fine dividing line between 'security' and imperial expansion needs to be carefully considered in relation to the Soviet Empire in Asia and to its satellites in Eastern and Central Europe. More importantly the American use of the term 'national security' involves the merging of a number of old concepts into a radically new one which has underpinned much of Western Cold War rhetoric after 1947. Essential to this is the belief that any state controlling large geographical areas containing significant quantities of natural resources in a way unacceptable to the US presents a threat to the 'national security' of the United States. This means that rather than having to deal with a specific military danger in a vital area (as Germany presented to Britain's essential maritime trade routes before the First World War), US 'national security' is threatened by a more general global menace. In part this is a reflection of a shrinking world in which more rapid aircraft and the arrival of the missile age have brought all members of the global community closer together. Without unrestricted access to the world's resources, the United States could be forced to impose domestic controls over raw materials and production which would threaten free enterprise, the American way of life, and thus 'national security'. Also, the adoption of communist or capitalist ideologies by newly independent states, or changes from one system to the other in any part of the globe, would have implications for Western or Soviet credibility and, in conventional Cold War terms, constitute a threat to 'national security'. In the pre-Cold War era, attempts to control access to important overseas resources and the installation of, or influence over, a particular foreign government would normally have been referred to as 'imperialism' not as a threat to national security.

Another feature of historical and social science writing in the West is the way in which phrases such as 'Soviet expansion(ism)' and 'Soviet behaviour' flow freely from the pages of many books on international politics after 1945. In the US the Soviet Union came to be regarded as a revolutionary state not prepared to accept the norms governing international relations. The attribution of traits reflecting abnormal human actions is used in many different situations to demonize an enemy to whom rational analysis is not then applied. The term 'American expansion', which was arguably far more extensive than that achieved by the Soviets after the end of the War, is hard to find, while the United States and its Western European allies hardly ever suffer from international behavioural problems. In addition, although as will be seen, the Soviet Union expected additional post-war rewards from its wartime efforts, what it did secure came directly from the War. It acquired territory and satellites not from post-war expansion but from its unscrupulous wartime deal with the Nazis and from the accepted military need to defeat Germany. Many general works on international politics imply that the Soviets 'behaved' in expansionist ways which aroused Allied disapproval after the War and neglect to point out that the Nazi–Soviet deal was subsequently endorsed by Britain or that during the war the main Allied fear was of the Soviets *not* expanding and defeating the Germans.

Of course, the lack of evidence from Soviet archives, despite greater access to them over the last decade, precludes any definitive judgements about Moscow's goals and ambitions. And it is quite clear that not only did the Soviet Union have imperialist ambitions to expand its power and influence but its treatment of its own citizens and of those under Soviet occupation was quite appalling. Nevertheless it should not be assumed that the United States and Britain were simply reacting to Russian 'behaviour' in occupied Europe or to ambitious Soviet diplomacy. Nor should it be assumed that the United States and Britain did not have expansionist goals themselves, as both countries, like the Soviets, planned to extend their influence after 1945 and gain new military bases from which to project their power on an increasingly global basis. Indeed the United States military planned to acquire bases in Western Europe, the Middle East, North Africa, South, South-East and East Asia, including China, as well as large numbers of island bases in the Atlantic and Pacific Oceans.

One way around the problem of Cold War terminology is to view all the great powers, particularly the wartime Big Three (Britain, the Soviet Union, and the United States), as seeking to maintain or enhance their influence. This projection of power and influence into new areas is one way of broadly defining imperialism and it is no bad thing for students of international politics to approach the post-war world from the perspective of imperial rivalries. This removes the need to consider ideological differences as a cause of the initial breakdown of co-operation and only requires that they be considered, along with the other changes brought about after the War, as defining elements of a Cold War world that later emerged from the initial international competition for control and influence in the 1945–6 period.

The use of the word 'containment' is another misleading term in standard Western historiography because it is often applied to American policy through-out the Cold War period. In fact while 'containment' can be deemed to contrib-ute to the first stage of any offensive strategy, the idea that it was a consistent US policy employed as the ultimate response to Soviet power throughout the period is misleading. US policy went through a number of stages related to changing perceptions of how best to deal with the Soviet challenge. The period from 1946 to 1948 may be seen as a defensive response but from 1948 until at least the mid-1950s, if not the early 1960s, the US moved to an offensive strategy designed to destroy the Soviet satellite empire not to contain it.

Periodization

The chronological divisions in the book correspond to changes in the nature of the Cold War or in Soviet–American relations (and the two things are not synonymous). The first period up to 1953 was the period in which the Cold War developed from the tensions and mistrust arising out of the early attempts to agree on the nature of the post-war order and the peace treaties with Germany's allies. In the first and very intense phase of the Cold War, from 1947 to 1953, the ideological commitment of the Soviet Union and the capitalist states to differing economic and political systems was reinforced by the demands of post-war reconstruction. Survival in the short term was deemed to depend either on the success of Western democracy and free enterprise or on the maintenance of totalitarian, communist controls. In addition, the ability directly to control and exploit certain areas of the globe was seen as vital by both British and Soviet policy-makers who both initially feared the adoption of US principles was a recipe for maintaining or increasing US power and influence at their expense. Thus there emerged a mix of old-fashioned imperialism and new ideological imperatives. The former helped prevent cooperation while the latter subsequently gave an entirely new meaning to imperial and interstate rivalries. It was a period in which confrontation, fuelled by competing, universal ideologies, then developed to such an extent that some on both sides saw the other's long-term existence as an unacceptable threat. However, there was a fear of another war and a reluctance to prepare for one on both sides, with the Western powers privately convinced that the Soviets would not deliberately start a major conflict (even though they did not reveal this publicly). War was only deemed possible through accident or miscalculation. In effect this meant the extension of control or influence by one side without any realization that it would be so unacceptable to the other side that war would be preferable. In the West the Cold War was nevertheless deemed to be winnable by means short of hot war (international armed conflict)

By the early 1950s the fighting of the Cold War was perhaps at its most aggressive. In the West, German rearmament (deemed most likely to provoke armed Soviet aggression) was planned and attempts were made to devise more aggressive means of undermining Soviet control within its satellite empire. In the East Stalin finally agreed to endorse and support a North Korean attack on South Korea. Western Cold War strategists then had to consider the implications of fighting a limited war. Along with the death of Stalin in 1953, and Churchill's idea of encouraging more Western contacts with the Soviet bloc as a means of sapping the strength and appeal of communism, this led to what became known as a 'thaw' in East–West relations. However, the 'thaw' was an attempt to stabilize relations and avoid armed conflict rather than a 'thaw' in the Cold War of propaganda and subversion. The need to avoid armed conflict increased steadily once the US and the Soviet Union exploded their first thermonuclear weapons in 1952 and 1953. The hydrogen bomb was thousands of times more powerful than the atomic bomb and used the fusion of atoms rather than their fission to create energy. It made the prospect of global war more fearsome and eventually made the pursuit of peace and arms agreements more necessary. More urgent consideration had now to be given to ways of preventing the aggressive fighting of the Cold War leading to a hot war. The fears that an offensive strategy might lead to a thermonuclear confrontation eventually contributed to the modification of the American policy of undermining and ultimately destroying the Soviet system (often referred to as 'roll back') as did the realization that changes would be difficult to achieve without a major war.

The Soviets had ostensibly also accepted the idea of peaceful coexistence in the mid-1950s but ideological competition remained acute. In fact in some ways the

Cold War was extended after the death of Stalin because of his successors' heightened interest in Asia, Africa, and regions of the less developed world. This increased the importance of competition for hearts and minds in these largely neglected areas and took the Cold War into a new era. Soviet–American Cold War competition now extended to all parts of the globe. By the end of the 1950s this competition for influence between the communist and capitalist world was further intensified by the emergence of the newly independent nations in Africa and Asia and the importance of the future alignment of those non-self-governing territories earmarked for independence. The issue now was less the control of important resources or political stability, as initially it had been in Europe, than the need to claim ideological successes in terms of the progress of socialism or capitalist democracy. This did not remove the need for the power and status of the Soviet and American states to be enhanced. It meant that the success of one protagonist whether in terms of greater influence in Africa, Europe, or even outer space was an integral part of great power competition.

However, the 1960s saw the competition to preserve or gain ideological allies come near to military confrontation in Cuba in 1962. The Cuban missile crisis, when some US policy-makers were prepared to attack Soviet missiles, was a head-to-head Soviet–American confrontation that contributed to what some have argued was the end of the first Cold War. By that it was meant that the risk of hot war was such that both sides were now prepared to accept long-term peaceful coexistence. Fighting the Cold War to eliminate their rival's control over its allies, satellites, or dependencies in order to undermine their position as a great world power arguably now finally ceased to be the ultimate aim of the superpowers. What mattered was a more traditional competition for greater global influence. In these circumstances the arms race, conducted under the banner of deterring war, became even more of a battle for status and influence rather than serious preparation for global war.

However, in the 1960s when the Soviets began for the first time to approach nuclear parity with their American rivals, the nature of the apparently bipolar world began to change. The United States faced serious challenges to its economic and military supremacy while the growing split between the Soviets and their communist Chinese allies became a permanent rupture and resulted in border clashes. The Americans, having embarked on a massive programme of military expansion at the start of the decade, found themselves in a less advantageous position at the end of it. For the first time their military supremacy was threatened by the expansion of Soviet nuclear arms and the development of an ocean-going navy which further increased perceptions of the Soviet Union as a world power equal to the United States. American economic dominance was also challenged from within the Western world particularly by the rapidly expanding German and Japanese economies and by the French attempt to win greater independence from the American-dominated international economic order. From 1963 onwards international politics thus became a more general competitive battleground with alliances and regional power blocs assuming greater importance in a less bipolar world.

The emergence of a more multipolar world in the 1970s meant that new ways of attempting to manage Soviet–American relations within the changed international system had to be found. China's emergence, and the growing economic strength of Western Europe and Japan, presented new challenges to US hegemony. As the hegemonic power was defeated in Vietnam new social forces appeared to be challenging the supremacy of democratic capitalism within the Western world. In the 1970s, faced with this new situation and with economic problems exacerbated by the oil price rises, greater efforts were made to maintain international stability. Détente offered the prospect of regulating the Cold War by agreement. For the Americans it could prevent further erosion of their military superiority and maintain their general credibility which was being damaged by the continuation of the Vietnam War. Henry Kissinger, Nixon's National Security Adviser and later Secretary of State, was eager to take up the challenge to American power from an increasingly multipolar world by the use of détente. Traditional power political goals were incorporated into a process of détente designed to control Cold War competition in order to retain maximum American influence and prevent further communist successes. The Soviets were also attracted to détente because it offered economic benefits and the prospect of encouraging revolutionary change in the Third World with less risk of hostile Western responses or intervention.

Yet at the end of the 1970s—a decade of revolutionary change in many parts of the less developed world—the conflicting expectations of détente produced Soviet–American dissatisfaction and led to return to greater confrontation. Often referred to as a second Cold War, the 1979–85 period saw tensions in Europe over the deployment of more advanced nuclear missiles and continuing crises in the less developed world which involved one or both of the superpowers. As in 1945, this eventually produced both domestic and international reactions which produced another major Cold War confrontation despite the more multipolar world. The rise of a more socially conservative and individualist Right in the West was matched in the mid-1980s by the emergence of a new generation of leaders in the Soviet Union who were prepared to embark on a programme of radical reform and foreign policy reorientation. It was precisely when these forces were both encouraging international confrontation and redefining economic and social policy that the Cold War ended, or perhaps more accurately was ignored or transcended by Gorbachev. While designed to preserve the basis of the communist state and its influence over the constituent parts of the Soviet Empire, reform unleashed forces which Gorbachev could not control. The book hopes to shed light on all these developments which produced the collapse of the Soviet Union and the end of the Cold War.

Why precisely this process occurred can, as yet, only lead to tentative and controversial conclusions. Equally controversial is the nature of the new world order that emerged in the 1990s. Again, as in 1945, the question arises as to why this new international order did not give way to an era of cooperation. Why was there not a new world order encompassing the end of confrontation and employing technological and scientific advances to increase the well-being and prosperity of all? Why was there a new era of conflict now that the state was playing a decreasing role? The removal of an all-encompassing enemy has made it more difficult for governments to mobilize domestic opinion behind military expenditure and foreign policy goals. Yet there is no apparent shortage of conflicts or of enemies that are referred to in the West as terrorists or rogue states.

More fundamentally the end of the Cold War may not have significantly altered the goals of the remaining superpower if these are expressed, as in US wartime planning for the post-war world, through an international order based only on American principles which serve American interests. Just as at the end of War which marks the start of this book, the Cold War's unexpected termination did not produce international agreements on how best to cooperate in the maintenance of peace. The nature of war has dramatically changed but it has not been eradicated. In the midst of new challenges in the form of pollution, disease, international terrorism, and climate change the triumph of liberal democracy has resulted in many countries experiencing greater inequality, greater conflict, and greater insecurity.

Part I

The Origins and Development of the Cold War

1945–1953

INTRODUCTION

The debate on the nature and origins of the early Cold War has had an enormous impact on the way historians and social scientists have interpreted the nature of the international system in the years up to 1989. Realists seeking confirmation of their emphasis on power, represented through economic and military strength, have maintained that the Cold War with its associated expansion of weapons, vindicated their ideas. Yet the realist refusal to associate domestic factors with foreign policy and to consider ideology, domestic, social, and economic factors as key features of the Cold War have left an enormous void in many attempts to understand the conflict and its origins. The latter can only be fully understood if the linkage between power politics and the social and economic upheavals of war, which threatened a revolutionary change in the dominant capitalist status quo, is understood in historical terms.

The Historiographical Debate on the Origins of the Cold War

In theoretical terms the conflicting explanations by historians and political scientists as to the reasons for this unique Cold War period in the history of international relations are no nearer resolution. The origins of the Cold War remain a matter of long-standing historical dispute and the arguments, generally not mutually exclusive, are linked to ideas about the nature of the Cold War international system. Was it a bipolar world whose systemic characteristics dictated the power struggle between the two protagonists? Was it a world dominated by exogenous concerns about inter-state rivalries or was it a world in which internal battles over economic power and political influence had a significant effect on external ideological and power political rivalries?

The initial attempts to explain the Cold War in the West focused on the actions of the Soviet Union as the key factor in producing confrontation. These so-called orthodox theories assume that alleged Soviet aggression, or more usually, alleged Soviet expansionism, dictated American reactions. In essence the Cold War became a battle for global power and influence because Stalin and/or the Soviet system made cooperation impossible. The reason for this in orthodox accounts rests with the paranoid and ruthless leader of an expansionist and ideologically driven Soviet state. Stalin and Soviet communism had to be confronted and contained by Western capitalist states for the sake of international peace and security and the survival of liberal democratic values. Or in other Western Cold War words an allegedly expansionist Soviet Union threatened the so-called national security of the United States and Western Europe which required an economic and military response. The historical focus on security from external threats links with realist, and more importantly, neo-realist explanations of superpower rivalry. Power and security thus have a more significant explanatory role than ideology or the internal make-up of capitalist and communist states and their respective external requirements.

In the 1960s the crude orthodox approach was challenged by revisionist historians focusing less on the international state system and the struggle to gain greater power and influence than on the alleged requirements of international (and in 1945 largely American) capitalism. Revisionists interpret the foreign policy of the United States as designed to meet the expansionist requirements of capitalism. The Soviets therefore sought security in the form of resisting the expansion of capitalism into areas that would threaten the continuation of Soviet communism. For the revisionists, the blame for the Cold War lies with aggressive United States policies to which the Soviets had to respond. Rather than Soviet expansionism creating American insecurity, the US commitment to the expansion of capitalism created Soviet insecurity.

Since the economic challenge by revisionists, other Cold War historians and political scientists who allegedly reject the stark interpretations of the opposing schools have been labelled post-revisionists. This term can refer to a number of very different authors but is commonly based on interpretations that allegedly adopt a more balanced and research-orientated approach. Thus ascribing responsibility exclusively to one side is often avoided and criticism of both powers is generally made on the basis of more archival evidence. While this approach can embody attempts to reach consensus, and an acknowledgement that both sides may have misperceived the policies of the other, it should also be remembered that some post-revisionists still attribute blame to the Soviet Union rather than to the United States or to both powers equally. In addition a significant part of the Cold War took the form of a massive state-influenced campaign on both sides of the Iron Curtain to justify military policies and expenditures in order to gain popular support for them. Thus, despite the greater sophistication of the various arguments and emphases of the post-revisionist historians and social scientists in the 1980s and 1990s, they may still have been participating in or justifying the Cold War rather than explaining it.

The leading exponent of post-revisionism, John Lewis Gaddis, has claimed that the best ideas from both schools are subsumed in an emerging post-revisionist consensus. In addition to the emphasis on national security, Gaddis's book *The Long Peace* sees the alleged Cold War bipolar system as a basis for stability and gives support to the neo-realist approach in general and to the work of Kenneth Waltz in particular. Here security concerns and the nature of the international system are portrayed as explanatory tools for understanding the nature of the early Cold War. While accepting that United States policy-makers may have exaggerated the Soviet threat and failed to appreciate the impact of their own policies, Gaddis nevertheless portrays the United States as reacting to an expansionist Soviet state in justifiable ways. For

Gaddis, particularly in his most recent work, the essential responsibility for the Cold War lies with Stalin whose policies created the need for defensive resistance. This despite the fact that the geopolitical position of the United States had always provided more security than any of the other great powers in the years before intercontinental missiles. The reaction to this by Warren Kimball, for example, has been to dismiss the Gaddis version of post-revisionism as 'orthodoxy with archives'.

Other post-revisionist historians who share the emphasis on so-called security/ national security issues have taken a different line to Gaddis's ascription of blame to Stalin. Post-revisionist historians less inclined to justify American policy, most notably Melvyn Leffler, still locate Cold War explanations primarily within a national security framework of power politics. Yet from Leffler's work it is not at all clear that US policy can be justified simply as a response to the Soviets. The quest for what he terms a preponderance of power sometimes involved excessive efforts to project US power and influence. At best therefore this was an overreaction to Soviet policies. However, it also involved the formulation and implementation of policies defined in terms of American goals and interests that existed independently of Soviet aims and ambitions. Thus to some extent Leffler moves away from portraying a reactive, defensive strategy of national security to describing a more expansionist US strategy based on American global interests. These interests remain largely defined in terms of state power and actual or potential threats to the American exercise of this within a framework of international relations clearly dominated by military power, geo-politics, and foreign economic policy. Another example of post-revisionism which is compatible with realist theory.

It has been suggested by Howard Jones and Randolph Woods that national security concerns provide the basis for a post-revisionist consensus on the origins of the Cold War in general and the reasons for United States policy in particular. This has been criticized on a number of grounds and has led to a debate on the role of ideology and ideas in foreign policy as opposed to state concerns about power, survival, competition, and, in Cold War parlance, security. Anders Stephanson has noted that, in line with realist thinking, security removes ideology and class an explanations of and influences on foreign policy. In addition there are the vital questions of security for whom and for what purpose. In the West does this mean security for elite groups in the United States, security for the Western hemisphere or security for US capitalism and its foreign markets? Emily Rosenberg has questioned the very meaning of 'national security', as it is itself a product of the Cold War, and its increasingly broad usage can serve the needs of 'advocates of almost everything and anything'. Thus Randall and Woods define it as 'the relation between domestic and foreign elements affecting a country's safety and to include the social, economic, political and military considerations that influence strategy'. The implication being that external policy is geared to securing all aspects of social, economic, and political life on the basis of resisting threats to values or interest groups as well as threats to territory and physical safety. Such ideas prepare the ground for conceptions of common national interests in the face of external powers who may not pose a direct military threat, but who do represent an ideological danger particularly to elite groups on both sides of the Iron Curtain.

More generally the attempts to build a Cold War consensus on 'national security' issues sidestep the ideological and domestic conflicts which were central to the Cold War's origins and nature. They serve the realist cause by disconnecting foreign policy from domestic problems and issues and by emphasizing state/national concerns about security and military power. Finally, such ideas disguise descriptions of Cold War thinking and strategy on how to win the conflict (building a domestic consensus on resisting the 'other' by portraying it as a dangerous military threat to national security) as explanations of the Cold War. As Emily Rosenberg notes, some historians make the same 'discursive turn that Cold War policy-makers themselves made: conflating a wide variety of contexts and complexities into a symbolically powerful but increasingly diffuse phrase—national security.' The subordination of internal forces, in the sense that their dynamics are not of significance in determining, as opposed to justifying foreign policy, is a key feature of realist and orthodox accounts of the Cold War's origins and nature.

Other historians have rejected the basic national security approach and the idea of a bipolar systemic analysis as central to a Cold War dominated by issues of power and security. Anders Stephanson has challenged the idea that the Cold War was essentially systemic in nature. Thus the concept of a bipolar world from 1945 to the collapse of the Soviet Union, dictated by a relative equilibrium of forces, is in his view erroneous. It ignores the distinctive time periods which reflect the different character of the Cold War and of course the changing nature of the threat to the internal social and economic order, particularly in Europe. Thus the elimination of dissidents within the Soviet bloc and the McCarthyist persecution within the United States cannot 'be reduced in origins and development, to geopolitics and strategy'.[1] Nor can be determined efforts to overthrow governments throughout the world be explained solely in terms of strategy or economic resources.

Ideology thus becomes an important element in the Cold War but in ways which are more complex than most Cold War accounts assume. In orthodox terms, and as seen by some policy-makers at the time, the ideology of Soviet communism promoted worldwide revolution which in foreign policy terms became a quest for Soviet world domination. More sophisticated explanations look at the general ways in which ideas are employed by elites to serve domestic political purposes. In more specific Cold War terms it means examining how ideology, linked to foreign policy success or failure, can have a damaging impact on the internal social and political order which maintains the privileged position of elite groups. Thus foreign policy goals reflect elite ambitions in the form of state preoccupations with power and expansion as linked to status rather than security. Domestic goals reflect elite needs to preserve the socio-economic order that secures their position and secures its acceptance through the portrayal of ideological challenges as external threats. This provides a key to an accurate understanding of the early Cold War as more a political battle for domestic dominance than a military conflict over national security. This is certainly how elites in Britain and the United States perceived it at the time although the conflict was, and still is, often justified in terms of security and its military requirements.

There are of course always connections between foreign economic policy, geo-politics, territorial security, and ideology in any analysis of the Cold War. Those who question the alleged post-revisionist national security consensus and the explanatory value of 'national security' simply place more emphasis on economics and ideology. Or in theoretical terms they attach greater significance to internal non-state actors, their connections with the state, and the linkages between domestic affairs and foreign policy. Thus corporatism is a post-revisionist approach which places less emphasis on power politics and security and more on the need to ensure the spread of liberal capitalism as a means of securing a stable world order. In the model put forward by Michael Hogan corporatism embodies capitalist cooperation between government, non-governmental organizations (NGOs), and business corporations in an attempt to establish a 'corporative world order'. Thus there was an economic need to rebuild Western Europe, which served private interests as well as producing overall benefits for the US economy. This need dovetailed with, and provided the basis for, maintaining and preserving the socio-economic status quo in democratic capitalist states that was under acute electoral threat in Western Europe in the immediate post-war years. It also complemented a broader global strategy of building a new economic world order on the expansion of multilateral trade which required the reconstruction of Western Europe and the elimination of imperial and communist economic blocs.

For those post-revisionists concerned with the relations between public and private interests and between foreign economic policy and military strategy, alleged external threats served more to justify than to explain policies linked to the domestic needs of the state and the position of its ruling elites. It seems that the Cold War developed at a time when there was a conjunction of external and internal threats to the stability of capitalist states and their communist rivals, which had not existed to the same extent in the inter-war years. In Western Europe the experiences of the Second World War produced more awareness of class divisions and privilege from which the Left gained new strength. Significant social reform, as predicted by appeasers like Chamberlain, was now unavoidable, but post-war economic difficulties might open the door to more radical challenges to the capitalist status quo. In the East the Soviet regime had been weakened by the destruction of the Second World War in which traditional ideas about the nation had again proved more powerful than the ideology of communism in rallying the people. Consideration of these issues and their links to foreign policy is important if the nature of the early Cold War is to be properly understood.

More difficult to determine is the degree of responsibility for the Cold War, given the extent to which explanations of the conflict have been put forward as part of the strategy of fighting and winning the Cold War rather than as determinants of policy or as analyses of the nature of the struggle. In this situation where all govern-ments were involved in overt and covert propaganda campaigns, often aimed primarily at their own citizens, it is difficult to disentangle the genuine perceptions of policy-makers from the perceptions they wanted the public to have in order to succeed in their various Cold War aims. How far, for example, did the military measures adopted reflect genuine fears of attack or how far were they put forward in order to unite domestic opinion against an ideological and political challenge to elite values and interests?

Attempts to allocate blame by portraying the policies of one state as essentially free from desires to maintain and expand power and influence and as geared only to countering the aggressive intentions of others are not convincing. Far better to start from the position of all major states seeking to expand their power and influence in proactive as well as reactive ways for whatever combination of reasons. The Cold War was not essentially a reaction by one side to the actions of the other and its origins need explaining in terms of conflicting ambitions and the differing perceptions of what kind of post-war order was necessary to reconcile such ambitions and interests with order and stability. In addition foreign policy in the immediate post-war years has to be connected to the dynamics of internal and external socio-economic relations. The issue then becomes how the external quest for power and the internal attempt to preserve the social and economic status quo, combined to produce a unique Cold War era in international relations. In other words how and why did the desires for two very different domestic political and economic orders prove internationally irreconcilable. In this context aims and perceptions have to be explained, and these historical details linked to broader theories locating the Cold War within an interpretative international relations framework.

Specific Issues regarding the Causes and Nature of the Early Cold War

The Power Political Issue of Confrontation replacing Cooperation

The first stage of any effort to explain why three great victorious powers, all initially committed to the maintenance of cooperation in order to prevent a future global conflict embarked on the Cold War, is to define the different stages by which attempts at cooperation and compromise were replaced by confrontation and conflict. These stages are vital to any understanding of how and why the determination to ensure that recently defeated enemies should never again have the power to disturb world peace was replaced by an equal determination on the part of one bloc to rebuild them in opposition to a former ally. In essence the prime commitment to cooperation was replaced in the first three months of 1946 (although the British had reached this stage by September 1945) by an emphasis on confrontation followed by the definition of requirements which had to be accepted by the other parties if continued cooperation was to be successful.

Initially in 1945 power politics dominated the disagreements but ideology became increasingly more evident in the development of the conflict in 1946 and 1947. By the beginning of 1948 confrontation and hostility was accepted and a new phase of Cold War conflict began. Yet both sides still justified actions and policies directed

The Orthodox/Revisionist Debate on the Origins of the Cold War Realism

Initial orthodox works in the West on the origins of the Cold War blamed the expansionist ambitions of the Soviet Union for causing the conflict. They argued that with the Soviet Union failing to keep to the agreements made at the wartime conferences the Western Allies simply responded to aggressive Soviet demands and actions. The imposition of communist regimes in Eastern and Central Europe and the Balkans, which were controlled by Moscow, and demands in the Middle East and Mediterranean, justified a firm response based on the idea of containment. Revisionist historians argued that the expansionist requirements of capitalism and the demands of the US Government for markets, investment opportunities, and non-discriminatory trade threatened the Soviet scoio-economic system and inclined the Russians to establish a communist-dominated bloc in Europe. In both orthodox and revisionist interpretations blame is ascribed to one side and linked to the universal ambitions of Soviet communism or US capitalism. Post-revisionist accounts ostensibly adopt a more balanced and sophisticated explanation and are based more on archival research. However, the leading post-revisionist, John Lewis Gaddis, essentially adopts an orthodox position in emphasizing the ambitions of the Soviet state and communist ideology which justified a defensive American response and the confrontation with Stalin. On occasion the nature of the menace may have been exaggerated by American policy-makers and misperceptions on both sides are factored into the explanation. Other post-revisionists attach more weight to American ambitions and paint US policy in a more proactive light.

against ideological enemies in terms of traditional interstate threats and challenges (geopolitical or geostrategic).

The Issue of the Second World War's Impact

The world from which the Cold War was born was one in which popular expectations of social reform and international cooperation were high in the wake of the Second World War. Leaders in the allied states doubted whether such goals could be easily fulfilled partly because of the enormous difficulties of economic reconstruction and the failure to fashion a peaceful world order in 1919. Moreover, there was no consensus as to how international peace and stability could best be preserved. In addition, the lessons of the past and the needs of the present were seen differently in the Soviet Union, in Western Europe, and in the United States. In part these differences can be explained by short-term self-interest, particularly in those countries which had suffered most from the War. In terms of insecurity and potential threats (usually deemed to be important causes of Cold War tensions) it is necessary to consider the contrasting impact of the War on the allies. The Soviet Union suffered enormous economic losses. Its industries were moved eastwards and its population was reduced by up to 29 million in a war of extermination on the Eastern European front. Britain too was hit economically although it had neither the huge armed forces nor the massive problems of reconstruction which characterized the Soviet Union in

1945. The Soviet Union was desperate for economic aid and the British, eager to regain great power status, were determined not to sacrifice the short-term needs of recovery for the sake of free trade and international economic cooperation. Only the United States could wield military and economic strength and this has to be considered in any objective assessment of tensions stemming from so-called concerns about power and threats to security.

The Issue of Reconciling Vital Interests and Idealistic Rhetoric

However, rather than so-called national security problems it was the failure to reconcile the maintenance of expanding vital interests with the preservation of the vital interests of others that was the initial source of disagreement and tension in 1945.

The Soviet Union certainly had the greater territorial ambitions but tensions also stemmed from the failure to implement the new principles of international political and economic cooperation which were expounded most forcefully in the United States. In the 1940s the principle of mutually beneficial international goals proclaimed by many American policy-makers did not square with their own practices let alone gain universal acceptance. Despite much American rhetoric, idealism did not override American self-interest, even though it became an important element in US domestic politics.

Post-Revisionism and the Geopolitics/Revisionist Debate on the Origins of the Cold War

Those post-revisionist writers who reject the orthodox idea that American policy was essentially reacting to Soviet actions also reject the revisionist idea that American policy was deliberately geared to confronting the Soviets. Instead they have sought to focus on factors such as geopolitics, cultural traits and elite perceptions, on psychology, bureaucratic politics, security requirements, misunderstandings and misperceptions none of which are mutually exclusive.

Geopolitics. At its most basic level this view is linked to the pre 1917 development of two great land-based empires in Eurasia and the Western Hemisphere. Inevitably these two exploitative land-based systems would come into conflict. Another explanation, based on the post-1945 period is the clash of three imperial powers seeking to expand their influence who were unable to agree on a cooperative strategy for so doing. Thus ideology

is largely removed from the analytical framework and issues of power and security are, in the realist tradition, central to the conflict. However, the different geopolitical situations of the great powers and the different traditions and socio-economic systems provided different perspectives on 'security'.

Security. The emphasis many writers place on 'security' (or in the West particularly after 1947 'national security') often fails to distinguish between security and imperial requirements. In the Soviet case territorial vulnerability, the fear of another war of extermination, and more twentieth-century attacks from the West were undoubtedly real, but whether they justified the kind of repressive measures taken against the Soviet population and the peoples of Eastern and Central Europe is more questionable. In the US, 'national security' clearly came to involve factors other than military power and territorial defence. Even if the extension of a Soviet-controlled Eurasian empire constituted a threat to the US did it justify the acquisition of a vast array of military bases and the determination to project a 'preponderance' of power? The US drive for 'security' on a global basis ironically ignored the more limited Soviet security/imperial requirements, largely confined to areas neighbouring the Soviet Union, and emphasized the universal, revolutionary rhetoric of Marxism-Leninism. Was this a misperception or a calculated strategy to protect state and elite interests?

In the West the most commonly used Cold War terms are 'national security' and 'containment' with threats to the former from an expansionist Soviet Union allegedly leading to the latter. The importance of both terms as explanations of the Cold War have recently been questioned. National security has become so broad in its usage that it can be used to justify virtually any internal or external policies pursued by the US government whether related to national or sectional interests. Moreover, its emphasis on the Soviet threat excludes many of the economic and social requirements of elite groups whose interests were most threatened by left-wing ideologies in the West or by opposition to communism in the East. Thus two

questions arise. How important were the influences of internal economic and political factors in producing external policy in the US and the Soviet Union and were the alleged requirements of security policy, defined in terms of military power and inter-state struggles for influence, justified as defensive measures prompted by genuine fears? Barton Bernstein has argued that to use national security as an explanation of the Cold War makes more sense in relation to Soviet policy than it does to that of the United States. Indeed, given the relative geopolitical positions of the two powers it is the US that has historically been secure and the Soviet Union that has been vulnerable. Moreover, given the ability of the US to project all forms of military power in 1945, (including the only nuclear capable forces), in ways which no other state could match, and the enormously superior American economic powers, it does seem odd that the quest for national security has been attributed more to the US than to a Soviet state subjected to numerous twentieth-century invasions, suffering from human and economic devastation on an almost unimaginable scale and lacking initially atomic weapons. It is however for readers to justify the distinction between security and imperialism as determinants of policy.

The Cold War may therefore have been born out of the failure by both sides to reconcile old practices with new principles. The West needed to proclaim the end of power politics, but if such policies were still pursued, such hypocrisy had to be concealed from domestic opinion for political reasons. One way to do this was to attack Soviet power political ambitions in Europe while pretending that Britain and the US had no such goals in the Middle East or the Pacific. Thus even if an imperialist deal with the Soviet Union, based on vital interests, had been acceptable on a global basis to Stalin it would not have been acceptable in the West.

The Issue of Ideology and Legitimate Expansion

Such tripartite explanations of the Cold War have never satisfied most historians in the West. For them, conceptions of competing national interests, of conflicting rhetoric and practice, of equally crusading ideologies, or different understandings of democracy and security are less important than the allegedly in-built motivation of a communist state assuming the mantle of a traditional imperialist power. They do not see post-war leaders having to reconcile competing power political ambitions— Soviet control of Eastern Europe, the maintenance and extension of exclusive British influence in the Middle East, or the acquisition of new US bases and control of Japan to ensure domination of the Pacific—but as facing the same situation as in the 1930s. Then the issue was not how to reconcile great power differences but whether it would have been better to resist an inherently expansionist German power sooner rather than later. Thus the Cold War can be attributed to the West's lack of realization that Stalin had unlimited ambitions, albeit with no timetable for achieving them, and its consequent failure to confront the Soviet dictator soon enough.[2]

Fundamental to these explanations is the belief that Western ambitions were legitimate and limited whereas, because of the ideological and repressive nature of the Soviet regime, its ambitions were neither. While there can be no doubt that the Soviet Union did have imperialist ambitions after 1945, the question is the extent to which, in foreign policy terms, they were fundamentally different from those that Britain and the United States saw as essential to their post-war roles as great powers. To portray them in terms of an unlimited drive for global domination by Moscow means excluding the possibility that some, such as the demand for a trusteeship in Tripolitania, may have been put forward in order to win acceptance of limited gains in areas more important to the Soviets. It also means ignoring the substantial evidence that Stalin, like his Western counterparts, was not only extremely cautious but initially committed to the maintenance of great power cooperation and the concessions this would require. Thus he was prepared to compromise over the nature of the new-world organization and to accept the position of Greece in the percentages agreement. And the main motivation for this cooperation was the self-interested need to prevent the revival of a strong Germany. More importantly it means accepting that the United States did not have a crusading ideology whose aim was to shape the world in ways which would reconcile ideological principles with the expansion and success of American political and economic interests. Given the substantial, detailed evidence of the specific ways in which American post-war planners intended to create a world dominated by US values and interests, and while there is as yet no evidence of similar Soviet planning, the idea of a one-sided Soviet effort to gear a crusading ideology to world domination remains difficult to swallow.

The Issue of Geographical Focus and the Regional or Global Origins of the Cold War

Those who take the line of unlimited Soviet ambitions, which forced the West to confront Stalin, tend to focus more on European issues and on the aims of the Soviet Union and the US within a new a bipolar framework. For some, France and Britain allegedly played subordinate roles to the dominant forces of Soviet–American rivalry, roots of which have been traced back to before the 1917 revolution. In this clash between the two land-based empires of the Western hemisphere and Eurasia, European problems served to arouse or exacerbate Soviet–American disagreements.

It was in Europe that the Soviet Union carried out its most repressive and exploitative acts in defiance of the Yalta agreements on Liberated Europe pertaining to the formation of broadly based provisional governments and the ultimate holding of free elections. This focus on Eastern Europe has normally been accompanied by an ideological condemnation of the ruthless and undemocratic nature of Soviet power. In emphasizing European developments, historians have ensured that areas of vital interest to the Soviet Union became the centre of attention. The post-war aims and ambitions of Britain and the United States in areas of vital interest to them (the Middle East and Pacific, for example) receive relatively less attention and the imperialist mantle of repression is placed squarely and solely on the Soviets. A full understanding of the Cold War's origins requires a closer examination of the Middle East and Pacific regions and the interaction between great power goals outside Europe and the Soviet attempts to maintain and strengthen their control within it.

The efforts of the Western powers to preserve areas of exclusive influence outside Europe may well have been seen by Soviet leaders as comparable to their determination to have an exclusive sphere of influence over the territories adjoining the Soviet Union. We can be more certain that while many Americans, then and in subsequent historical accounts, have seen Soviet imperialism as part of an ideological crusade for global domination, their Soviet counterparts have seen US power and ideology in precisely the same light. The messages from the Soviet embassy in Washington in 1946 and 1947 portrayed the United States as keen to ensure global domination based on a crusading capitalist ideology and on the economic hegemony of the United States at the end of the Second World War. And in addition it was believed that the Americans were even prepared to embark on global war to bring it about.

These perceptions, an almost mirror image of the threat presented by the other, had clearly developed by 1947 despite the perceived self-interest of both sides in maintaining cooperation. The most plausible power political explanation of the Cold War lies in the failure to reconcile great power imperialist goals, *in areas outside Europe as well as within it*. The implications of this failure became more serious because of ideological concerns and the possible challenges to the domestic status quo that all elites faced in the wake of the Second World War's upheavals.

The Issue of the Early Cold War's Portrayal and its Link to the Importance of Domestic Factors

Both sides now faced a situation which was unique in the previous history of international relations since the French Revolution. Internal opposition threatened the socio-economic dominance of European ruling elites through a political ideology with mass appeal, that was more dangerous because it was backed by a powerful state. In the East Stalin could contemplate, in the light of invasion and external intervention in the Russian Civil War, the threat presented by capitalist powers hostile to communism or the Soviet Union or both. External enemies could unite national sentiments and pre-empt opposition to oppression more effectively if they were presented as military and territorial threats. In the West, communism was now linked to the victorious and most powerful continental European state that was prepared to confront the Western Allies with its own imperial demands. And it was now a more potent ideological threat because of the post-1941 increase in support for the Left in much of Western Europe, which was driven by its important role in resistance movements and by the increased demand for significant social reform. Again far safer to present this as a military danger to the nation than an ideological threat to elites even if it meant transforming wartime friends into post-war enemies. The military focus, portrayed in terms of containing a military or imperialist threat, has been subsequently emphasized but the problems and challenges of reconstruction and the preservation of the political and economic status quo were now even more important in defining the developing Cold War.[3]

The Issue of Defining US Early Cold War Policy

Territorial security was much less of a direct concern for American policy-makers (unlike the Germans, the Soviets in 1945 had no powerful surface fleet to threaten US naval supremacy). American aims have been frequently explained in terms of the invented concept of 'national security' and in terms of a defensive reaction defined as 'containment' which has been associated with the diplomat George Kennan. National security came to encompass much more than the need to defend the boundaries or home waters of the state and has been used to explain US policy in terms of the geopolitical and strategic nature of the Soviet threat. Based on the fear, as in the Second World War, of one single power dominating the European land-mass, the possibility of a hostile power dominating Eurasia was allegedly a much bigger threat to US national security than the prospect of a German-dominated Europe. Soviet–American hostilities are then explained in terms not of a failure of three powers to accept a new power political world order but on containing Soviet expansionism to preserve national security. Thus economic and ideological factors are reduced in importance which is difficult to justify in 1947.

The Debate on the Role of Ideology and Perceptions on the Origins of the Cold War

Ideology has generally figured in the debate on the Cold War in terms of policy-makers assessing its influence on the policies of the opponent. Communism was perceived as innately hostile to capitalism just as the contradictions of capitalism were deemed in Moscow to produce war and conflict. Were these the most important influences of ideology or did ideology play a different role in the origins of the Cold War? And was ideology linked to misperception rather than misrepresentation.

Perception and Misperception. The importance of misperceiving the aims of the opponent and particularly of misperceiving ideology's influence on policy has featured strongly in the accounts of those post-revisionists who believe the Cold War could have been avoided. For such authors the US view of Marxism-Leninism producing policies aimed at world domination misperceives the role of Soviet ideology and ignores such factors as differences within Soviet political elites and the historical traditions which shaped Russia's geopolitical fears and ambitions. The Soviet analysis of capitalist contradictions exaggerates the inevitability of US actions and ignores the various influences on US policy decisions. It also distorts the relations of capitalist powers by assuming rivalries and divisions arising from the contradictions of capitalism. Ideology is thus connected to misperceptions of its influence on the foreign policy of the other, but it is normally assumed that as only the Soviets had a crusading ideology the issue is the impact of communism on foreign policy and US (mis)perceptions of this. In the West the unstated assumption has been that liberal, democratic, free-market capitalism is not a crusading ideology or an ideological determinant of foreign policy. The focus is therefore on how the ideology of communism influences (mis)-perceptions of Soviet foreign policy rather than on how the West's own ideology influences (mis)perceptions of Soviet foreign policy. Moreover such assessments ignore the ideological influences which shaped US and Soviet elites' perceptions of the role their own state was to play and the extent to which these influenced (mis)perceptions or misrepre-

sentations of the other's policies and actions. Ideology may well be most important in producing a particular conception of the kind of world role the perceiver's own state should play. This in turn produces a perception of what is required from the other and when the other fails to play the required role ideology can serve as an explanation for this. Few studies have looked at the possible impact of a Western crusading ideology and the links to Western policy or on Soviet (mis)perceptions of this. Perceptions of one's own role may determine expectations of the other's role and the actions or ideology of the other may not shape perceptions of the other's policy as much as considerations of one's own world role with its ideological justifications. Hence the importance of each side's crusading ideology and its ideological relationship to foreign policy and the real world may be linked more to Cold War misrepresentations than misperceptions. Moreover these misrepresentations may have formed a vital part of a coordinated propaganda campaign to persuade the masses that the Cold War was more to do with power and military capabilities than it was to do with ideology. In the West ideology is thus relegated to the simple question of freedom versus tyranny posed in political terms, with the fundamental nature of the social and economic order played down and divorced from the Cold War.

The Acceptance of an Ideological Cold War

By the end of 1947 imperial ambitions and geopolitical rivalries were accompanied by a greater sense of ideological differences, which reflected genuine fears about domestic stability and the nature of the international economic order. If the period prior to the first quarter of 1946 was dominated by the desire for cooperation, but with growing tension that resulted from the failure to reconcile or compromise over imperial rivalries, 1946 and especially 1947 were dominated by ideological confrontation. This led to the real onset of Cold War by the beginning of 1948.

In early 1947, tensions increased with the Truman Doctrine and the economic problems brought by the winter hardships in many parts of Europe. However, it was the Marshall Plan which subordinated rhetoric to the economic reality of whether capitalism or communism could survive in Europe. The Soviets saw in the Marshall Plan an economic threat to communist ideology and to their need to dominate Eastern Europe. In reality the Americans were initially more concerned to keep Western Europe within the democratic camp while serving the interests of the US economy than to attract the countries of Eastern Europe into an American economic bloc. By alleviating the economic difficulties that could have been portrayed as the failure of democratic capitalism, the spread of communism in Western Europe could be prevented. But by including Eastern Europe in the offer of benefits to those prepared to accept the expansion of non-discriminatory trade and economic integration, Soviet fears were heightened. Thus the Marshall Plan signalled the creation of a divided Europe in which the consolidation of confrontational capitalist and communist blocs became a priority on both sides.

The German Problem

The confrontation which developed during 1947 was formalized by the December failure of the Council of Foreign Ministers to reach agreement on the German peace treaty and the decision not to arrange a further meeting. The more that suspicion and confrontation developed the more difficult it became to reach a decision on the

Joseph Vissarionovich Stalin (1879–1953)

Born in Gori, Georgia Stalin joined the Social Democratic Party in 1898 and the Bolsheviks in 1903. He founded *Pravda* in 1911 and was the Bolshevik leader in the Duma until exiled to Siberia in 1913. On his return after the October revolution of 1917 he became Commissar for Nationalities and General Secretary of the Communist Party in 1922 a position he held to his death. It was this position and the patronage it provided that enabled Stalin to succeed Lenin as Chairman of the Politburo on Lenin's death in 1924. Stalin then changed his ideological stance in order to defeat all his rivals, including Trotsky, and become the all-powerful leader of the party and the government in 1927. At enormous human cost Stalin embarked on the modernization of the Soviet Union transforming it into a major industrial power by the Second World War. Millions died in the process with the collectivization of agriculture and the inefficient expropriation of rural surpluses for urban development. Stalin also moved to eliminate all potential rivals within the party and the military through show trials, and he created a regime of fear and terror in which families and neighbours were prepared to denounce each other to the secret police. In 1939 in a futile attempt to ward off an attack by Hitler and to secure territory in Poland he signed an agreement with the Nazi leader. Reluctant to accept he had been duped when the Germans attacked in 1941, Stalin then embarked on a brutal war of survival in which millions died because of the extermination policies of the invaders or because of the sacrifices demanded by Stalin. Preferring to work and hold meetings at night, Stalin continued as the undisputed but highly suspicious head of a brutal and tyrannical regime until his death.

future of Germany. As past German actions and future military potential were considered in an atmosphere of confrontation both sides came to realize that a divided Germany offered the safest bet. The risk of a revived united Germany allying with the opposing bloc was too great. However, as was evident from 1945, there were economic difficulties inherent in a divided Germany that was unable to use its agricultural surpluses in the East to provide for the industrial population in the West. To avoid expenditure on foreign exchange it was inevitable that the British and the Americans would support the revival of West German industry and attempt to limit the Soviet desire for reparations. Thus a combination of power political concerns and the economic needs of reconstruction places Germany at the centre of the confrontation. However, because the final breakdown of the attempts to find an acceptable German solution did not occur until the end of 1947, it is hard to ascribe a causal role to the German question in the origins, as opposed to the development, of the Cold War. This is all the more significant when it is realized that initially there was a general assumption that self-interest in preventing the revival of Germany would facilitate agreement. At the same time the economic difficulties and potential sacrifices created further antagonism and made it more likely that German industry would have to be rebuilt which in turn would create further insecurity. This was the context from which the Berlin crisis was born. It was a conflict which is often deemed to herald the birth of NATO and another phase in the Cold War where the preparations for military conflict loomed much larger. However, this depends on the type of analysis of the Cold War, and in particular of the nature of its development, that is adopted.

The Myth of Containment?

In the West the early Cold War has been described and justified in terms of the development of containment on which Western strategy was allegedly based. However, there are a number of basic problems associated with this idea, particularly regarding the stages that Western policies went through. A frequently encountered sketch of these developments, before and after 1947, is that in Europe a more or less expansionist and militaristic Soviet Union was eager to increase the pressure on the free world. This was allegedly indicated by the expansionist takeover of Eastern Europe, the 1947 actions of Western communist parties, and then by the more serious 1948–9 Berlin Blockade, which necessitated a firm Western response. Thus the militarization of containment in the form of NATO was required to deter an aggressive Soviet attack on Western Europe. Then in 1949 the focus of the Cold War allegedly moved to Asia with the success of the communists in China and the growing left-wing insurgencies in Burma, Indo-China, and Malaya. As the Americans began to consider these new challenges in the spring of 1950 with the production of a lengthy National Security Council Memorandum (NSC 68), the communist threat culminated in armed aggression in Korea. The Korean War allegedly produced further modifications of containment. Not only did the war serve to prove the aggressive intentions of the Soviet Union, but it signified that the Cold War had become a global conflict with an active military dimension that required rearmament on a gigantic scale. Most notably it required the arming of the recent German enemy to contain Soviet expansionism and ensure the defence of freedom in Western Europe.

The first problem with such a scenario is that the Soviets had in fact not expanded into areas outside their control after 1945. They simply kept control of the areas occupied during the war while attempting expansion at the expense of Turkey and Iran in 1945 and 1946. They drew back there out of fear of provoking hostilities with the United States, but Soviet ambitions justifiably aroused mistrust in the West. Secondly, there is the issue of whether US policy can accurately be represented by the idea of containment by 1948. Interestingly, a common view in the West has been that during the period from 1946 and beyond containment was the ultimate goal of US policy but this is now under question for the period after 1947. Of course in order to defeat an enemy one would need to adopt an initial strategy of containment before a more aggressive strategy could be implemented. Preventing the spread of Soviet control or influence from areas like Western Europe, to which the United States attached particular significance, was an important consideration in 1946 and 1947.

However, from the end of 1947 onwards the US also aimed, for the rest of the

Kennan's Pre-War Views on US–Soviet Coexistence

[It is my belief] that the present system of Soviet Russia is unalterably opposed to our present system, that there can be no possible middle ground or compromise between the two, that any attempt to find such a middle ground, by the resumption of diplomatic relations or otherwise, are bound to be unsuccessful, that the two systems cannot even exist together in the same world unless an economic cordon is put around one or other of them, and that within twenty or thirty years either Russia will be capitalist or we shall become communist.

George Kennan to Walt Ferris, 12 Jan. 1931

Source: Anders Stephanson *Kennan and the Art of Foreign Policy* (Harvard University Press, Cambridge, 1989), 7. Stephanson is quoting from the unpublished Ph. D. thesis by C. Ben Wright *George F. Kennan, Scholar-Diplomat: 1926–1946* (University of Wisconsin, 1972).

Kennan's Post-War Views on US–Soviet Coexistence

A defensive policy cannot be considered an effective means of checking the momentum of communist expansion and inducing the Kremlin to relinquish its aggressive designs . . . it leaves the initiative to the Kremlin, enabling it to strike at the time and place most suitable to its purpose and to effect tactical withdrawals and diversions. It permits the Kremlin to hold what it has already gained and leaves its power potential intact.

NSC 7 'The Position of the US with Respect to Soviet Directed World Communism', 30 March 1948

Source: Scott Lucas, *Freedom's War. The US Crusade against the Soviet Union 1945–56* (Manchester University Press, Manchester, 1999), 58.

period covered here, at the destruction of the Soviet satellite empire in Eastern Europe not at containing it there by preventing its expansion westward. Indeed, the crusading American ideology had no place for the existence of communism or socialism, and Kennan himself, despite the Cold War label as the architect of containment, had not envisaged any long-term coexistence with the Soviet Union. Thus, as the Soviets directed communists in Western Europe to undermine bourgeois governments there, the United States began its campaign not just to contain communism and Soviet power, but to weaken the Soviet hold on Eastern Europe. New agencies were created within the US government, initially the Office of Policy Coordination, whose aim was to prepare for the undermining of the Soviet system by weakening and ultimately eliminating Soviet control over its satellites in Eastern Europe. It was already not just a question of containing Soviet power but reducing it. The activities of American agencies within Eastern Europe generally remain classified but they were the other side of the 1948 coin of assisting Western Europe. The strategy was more than just containment and reflected Kennan's earlier beliefs that coexistence between capitalism and communism was impossible: one or the other had to be destroyed. We do not know so much about the aggressive aims of the Soviets in destabilizing the democratic capitalist world, but in Marxist doctrine the existence of bourgeois governments can be accepted as part of the ultimate transition to communism. Yet it seems more accurate to portray the Cold War in 1948, not in terms of coexistence or containment, but as a determined effort by both sides to develop offensive means of weakening the other in order to achieve outright victory (as in any military conflict where coexistence is ruled out). The idea of containment then serves more to indicate how, during the Cold War, the means of explaining and fighting it were subordinated in the West to the need to justify it and to build support for the attempts to win it. More than an attempt to explain American policy and long-term strategy, the idea of containment became a part of the Cold War battle itself.

Bloc Consolidation

Whatever the nature of the two sides' strategies in 1948 there can be no doubt that one consequence was the attempt, in various ways, to consolidate influence or control over their respective blocs in Eastern and Western Europe. The Soviet Union began this process with a ruthless policy of economic exploitation based on the extraction of raw materials and machinery from Eastern Europe to serve the needs of Soviet reconstruction. Whether the influence of Moscow was gradually extended from an initial post-war position in which Stalin was determined never to allow any socialist popular front independence; or whether Stalin was reacting more to growing concerns about the Marshall Plan and the revival of Germany, there can be no doubt that one by one Romania, Bulgaria, Poland, Hungary, and Czechoslovakia were, by 1948, denied the right to choose their own governments or their form of socialist development. The fact that in Yugoslavia Tito was reluctantly allowed to develop his own form of communism only reinforced Stalin's determination to clamp down on any deviation from Moscow's control elsewhere in Eastern Europe. As the attempts of both sides to subvert the other began in earnest, control and influence over the respective blocs became more important for the future of the European continent.

In the West, American influence and US dominance of the economic and political reconstruction of Western Europe has been deemed 'Empire by invitation' or 'Empire by inspiration'.[4] Certainly there was a desire on the part of European elites to achieve stability and reconstruction even if it meant accepting American terms. Suppressing the Left was both a short- and long-term goal given its strength in much of post-war Western Europe. At the same time short-term US assistance offered the prospect of eventually charting a more independent domestic and foreign policy course between raw, free-market American capitalism and the harsh and oppressive practices of Soviet communism. In the event, by 1949 the Western bloc was established voluntarily under US dominance as a permanent feature for the foreseeable future. More importantly because the ideological competition was part of a broader battle over the nature and success of European economies and societies, Western European economic recovery was vital. It was firmly believed that such recovery was dependent not just on American aid to overcome the dollar gap but on a revived West German economy contributing to the recovery of Western Europe as a whole. And as in other areas there was a clear linkage between economic and political requirements. Fears of an economically powerful Germany, which were widespread in Western Europe and generally under-represented in Cold War historiography, meant the incorporation of Germany into a cohesive Western bloc was essential as part of a policy of containment. Indeed, containment can be seen as a more accurate description of the goals of Western policy to Germany in 1948 than the goals of Western policy to the Soviet Union.

The Cold War and European Integration

In 1948 the first moves to closer European cooperation coincided with the implementation of the Western European Recovery programme, talks on military alliances, and the attempts of both sides to undermine the opposing bloc. Like the process of decolonization, which was beginning to gather pace outside the European continent, European integration was linked to the dynamics of the Cold War as well as to the prevention of any further threat from Germany. Behind the process lay the vision of integrationists like Jean Monnet, who had a broad political agenda for the development of European integration as well as a more narrow economic agenda defined by the national needs of French recovery. Yet Monnet's political vision of a more united federal Europe was always present and driven by the need to pursue Franco-German reconciliation within a framework which limited Germany's ability to embark once again on a path of confrontational nationalism.

The debate over the goals and achievements of European economic cooperation and integration has focused on whether this was an abandonment or strengthening of the nation state. On the one hand the French in particular have been perceived as driven by nationalism and the process of integration interpreted as the salvation rather than the demise of the nation state in Europe.[5] On the other hand liberal institutionalists like Joseph Nye and Robert Keohane do not see the creation of institutions like the Coal and Steel Community as mere tools of the nation state but as significant in their own right and capable of producing greater international cooperation. Similarly functionalists and neo-functionalists in the tradition of David Mitrany and Ernst Haas see European integration as promoting a transfer of allegiance away from the nation state by European elites and then the mass of the population.

In the early days of integration, the minds of both these groups were certainly focused more on the practical problems of recovery and German containment than on changing the nature of the international system. By 1946 the idea of a divided Germany had its attractions particularly for those in the West even though the Russians made a number of proposals for a neutral but united Germany. The most famous of these occurred in March 1952 and debate has subsequently raged over whether Stalin's proposal was a serious one or one merely designed to prevent a rearmed Western Germany becoming a more important American partner. In a sense some of the arguments are not mutually exclusive. On the one hand is the idea that Stalin was always driven by the idea of creating a united but communist Germany which would form part of the Eastern bloc. All his proposals for a united Germany therefore had that goal in mind, which was why it was important to prevent an economically revived West Germany from being incorporated into the capitalist bloc. Thus talking to Stalin on such matters was deemed be disadvantageous to the West given Stalin's allegedly spurious appeals to the German people that would only arouse sympathy and undermine Western solidarity. On the other hand Stalin may have genuinely been seeking a settlement, without aiming to dominate a united Germany, in ways which would bring greater German stability. It seems clear from Soviet sources that Stalin hoped to use the 12 March note as a means to thwart German disarmament, but that does not necessarily mean he was motivated by a quest for gain as opposed to genuine fears about a rearmed West Germany. In the latter case he would be sharing the same fears as many in the West and his attempts to mitigate them were to be geared to modelling East Germany more on Soviet lines.

The Militarization of the Cold War?

It was the Berlin Blockade which allegedly made a major contribution to the creation of NATO. A strong response to Soviet actions was perceived as necessary by Western governments for the sake of credibility, but explained and justified in terms of the risk of war and resisting Soviet expansion. Here was the point, it is claimed, when the military dangers presented by the Soviet Union became clearer, presaging the limited warfare that the Soviets were to authorize and support in Korea two years later. Not normally mentioned are the first American moves in 1948 in what was to become a significant campaign to undermine Soviet control over Eastern Europe. Nor is it often mentioned that military opinion in Britain and the United States in 1948 deemed it unlikely that the Soviets would deliberately start a major war. In other words that the US and British military believed that there was no immediate *military* threat to Western Europe. Their assessments were borne out by what was another example of Stalin's cautious nature and his fear of a direct clash with the United States when the blockade was terminated in humiliating circumstances in 1949.

The reasons for creating what became known as the North Atlantic Treaty Organization were not primarily geared to hostile Soviet actions in Berlin nor to perceptions of an imminent Soviet military attack in Europe. In the West, while Soviet moves over Berlin were seen as increasing the risk of war by accident, NATO was essentially conceived to meet political not military threats and requirements. Indeed the military role for NATO in operational terms has always been subordinated to its political importance. The fear in 1948–9 was of further communist political successes, and NATO's creation was seen as a political boost to the morale of the people of Western Europe. Put another way it was deemed better to present the threat in military terms to encourage popular resistance to left-wing ideologies expounded by political parties some of which were effectively dominated by a foreign power. NATO had little chance in the immediate future of providing a military defence of Europe but its political impact could be considerable. Unlike the military, the public and academics would come to accept that the Soviets were geared to attacking Western Europe rather than spreading communism or increasing Soviet power and influence peacefully. This deception was a vital part of Cold War strategy in the West. It developed against a post-war background of what has been described as an exaggeration of Soviet military strength in order to maximize the need for strong American armed forces.[6]

In the Soviet Union the creation of a confrontational military bloc also influenced the domestic aspects of Stalin's Cold War strategy. Paranoid and insecure, imagining internal and external threats to his personal power, the Soviet leader, although he would have known from spies within the British government that NATO was not planning to attack the Soviets, could, as in the West, use an invented short-term military threat for domestic purposes. Imperialist spies could be linked to armed aggressors seeking to destroy the Soviet Union and thus provide the excuse for the brutal elimination of political rivals and opponents alike. In a sense by 1948–9 the three former allies were manipulating public perceptions of the external world for domestic as well as foreign policy reasons, and the US and the Soviet Union, were consolidating influence or control over their respective European spheres.

Empire, Decolonization, and the Impact of Colonialism

In 1948 when the Cold War began in earnest there were conflicts within the Asian possessions of Holland, Britain, and France, and in South Asia Britain had abandoned India and was about to concede independence to Burma and Ceylon. European rule was on the retreat in an area where it had never recovered from military defeat in the Second World War and the consequent loss of belief in the innate superiority of the white man. The term 'decolonization', itself somewhat problematic, has thus been applied to the beginning of a process which was to transform the world in the next twenty years by the creation of a large number of new states and signify the decline of Europe in the post-war world. The impact of decolonization, or the end of the European empires, affected the workings of international organizations, had important implications for state formation and for the relationship between political and economic freedom. The process was closely tied up with the development of nationalist or anti-colonial movements, the specific cultures and ideologies of the colonial powers, and the impact of international developments, most notably the Cold War.

To provide an overall interpretation for developments in such disparate countries as India the Windward Islands, Algeria, Fiji, and Angola is a difficult task, as the circumstances in each former colony reflected differences in everything from geography to the political structures of colonial rule. Moreover, the perceptions and policies of the imperialists in the metropoles and the colonial capitals also reflected different ideas on the meaning of empire and the nature of colonialism. These stemmed from, amongst other things, European perceptions of how colonies contributed to an imperial system that was designed to fulfil an economic, strategic, cultural, or even symbolic role indicating international status and prestige. It was precisely because European colonies reflected metropolitan perceptions of national roles as great world powers that the transformations during and after the Second World War helped produce the violent nature of the conflicts between colonial rulers and their subjects. Had the issue been simply the nature of the administrative, judicial, or cooperative arrangements between parts of Europe and large areas of the non-European world, then transferring power would not have been so burdened by such disputes. Nor would it have become so closely entwined with the developing Cold War if the only issues were how best to control, influence, or be involved with some of the poorest and most inhospitable places on the planet.

Central to the progress of decolonization were a number of interrelated factors, all influenced by the Second World War and the Cold War. They ranged from the crucial mobilization of Asian and African political movements in opposition to colonial rule to the emotive attachment of Europeans to their own perceptions of superiority. For some in Britain this reflected a concern for and knowledge of what is often referred to as the developing world, and came to be embodied in a sense of duty or mission to prepare what were perceived as more backward peoples for the modern world. For other policy-makers it reflected a belief in their country's position within a global community that was defined in the same terms of exclusiveness, status, and sense of superiority that had characterized their upbringing in English public schools and Oxbridge. Thus for some, by the late 1930s it was desirable to transfer power as soon as the colonies were sufficiently developed politically, once progress had also been made in providing the necessary infrastructure and social welfare. For others, even in the mid-1950s they found the very idea of independence, as opposed to self-government, hard to swallow. And in the case of the mandated territory of Togoland, some of whose people were also inhabitants of the Gold Coast, the thought of uniting them in French territory was ruled out by the unbearable prospect of part of the British Empire being given to the French. The sense of importance and prestige associated with Britain's international role, in comparison with France, would be compromised by such actions whatever the situation in Africa. Hence the governmental debates on colonial policy were influenced by international perceptions as well as by the demands of the anti-colonial movements that grew in strength and number after 1945.

The historical debate on decolonization has developed over the years within the tripartite framework of nationalist challenges to colonial rule, the European colonial policies which confronted them, and the international influences which all parties had to take into account. The rise of what are generally deemed to be nationalist movements began in nineteenth-century India but did not emerge in parts of Black Africa until after the Second World War. Whether they were nationalist in terms of civic or ethnic nationalism is a matter of debate. It is true that the Western-educated elites who tended to dominate political movements in the colonies sought to build popular mass-based parties in support of independence. Yet some would argue that the lack of a civic tradition in many African cultures weakened any sense of identification with newly created states based on externally imposed boundaries. And while nationalist parties sought to transcend ethnic divisions and attract support on policies and issues, in both Africa and Asia, parties tended to divide on ethnic or religious grounds, particularly with the approach or attainment of independence. This lack of a civic or political culture has led some to conclude that nationalism in the era of decolonization constituted a set of elite groups whose supporters were united by anti-colonialism and then divided by competition over who should wield power with the achievement of independence. Others have seen the failure of nationalist movements to create successful post-independence states as rooted in the allegedly divisive nature of colonial rule and the corruption and weakness of some African and Asian elites. The causes of state instability may be primarily social and political, with their internal roots in colonialism, or they may be primarily economic, with their roots in the nature of the developing world's links with the international economy. What is certain, however, is whatever the success of nationalist or anti-colonial movements, the political freedom gained by decolonization was generally not matched by the gaining of economic freedom.

Whether this was due to some form of neocolonialism is again a matter of dispute, but a uniform analysis of international capital's development that supposedly produced neocolonial links of dependence is difficult to reconcile with the different economic and political policies of the various colonial powers. In political terms the aims of Britain can be linked to the tradition of granting independence to the white Dominions of Australia, New Zealand, Canada, and South Africa. The British were certainly committed to eventual self-government for parts of their colonial Empire before the Second World War, but the crucial factor was the timing of it and independence. The French and Portuguese, on the other hand, found such a concept anathema, and after the Second World War initially preferred a policy of assimilation into the culture and political structure of the metropolitan state. Thus in the face of indigenous opposition they argued that there were no longer any colonies or nationalist movements. In the French case their overseas territories were portrayed as part of the one and indivisible Fourth Republic with their inhabitants granted political rights according to the same principles as metropolitan Frenchmen. Such claims ignored the unstated premiss that on a constitutional and on an individual basis overseas Frenchmen and their territories would not achieve full political equality with their metropolitan counterparts. However, both France and Portugal claimed that all overseas citizens were part of the metropolitan nation or on the way to being assimilated into it so there could be no internally inspired nationalism. Protests against colonial rule were therefore seen as examples of external forces at work, whether they be communist-inspired or a consequence of American imperialism. This remained the case for the period in question and it was only the British and the Dutch who were prepared to grant independence before 1953.

In economic terms the benefits or burdens of colonialism remain as controversial as neocolonialism. The first Colonial Development Act, enacted by the British in 1929, was designed to provide outlets for the goods of British firms hit by the Depression. However, by 1946 Britain, and especially France, began to provide funds aimed at assisting the colonies. In Overseas France this gave metropolitan producers with overpriced goods that were unable to complete on world markets privileged access to protected colonial markets. On the other hand it could be argued that French colonial producers also benefited from produce prices which in the franc zone were fixed above world market prices. Jacques Marseille has argued that the economics of the French imperial trading bloc influenced the process of decolonization. As the French economy changed in the 1950s with the modernization of French industry reducing the numbers of small producers dependent on the markets of Overseas France, so the resistance to ending French rule was weakened.

Portugal also adopted a system of imperial preference, which maintained close economic ties with its overseas possessions, and this trade was certainly important for the Portuguese economy. Moreover, in Portugal's African colonies, where many Portuguese settlers sought to escape the high levels of unemployment back home, as in French Algeria racial tensions were high as white settlers competed with Black Africans for menial employment. The situation was made worse by the post-war continuation of forced labour which the British and French no longer used for such tasks as road-building. In Portuguese Africa exploitation was not to be mitigated by even minimal social and economic reforms until the 1960s.

In the rest of colonial Africa development was more evident but of limited effect. The hopes of the British Colonial Office that economic measures could be taken to assist African producers in achieving higher and more stable prices for their tropical produce were dashed by 1947. The demands of the imperial state for post-war recovery centred on increased colonial production without any compensation in the form of increased imports of consumer goods. The latter were in short supply as wartime industry in Britain struggled to revert to peacetime production. The priority given to metropolitan consumers meant at the very least the short-term exploitation of colonial producers in the interests of overcoming the dollar gap and assisting an ailing metropolitan economy. These pressures were never fully removed in this period and the chances of making a significant impact in a vast continent lacking in infrastructure were always remote. Despite the acceptance by some policy-makers of the principle of colonial development for the colonies it remained of marginal importance both from the point of view of benefiting the metropole and for producing significant changes in the colonies.

Moreover, as the urgency of economic requirements was reduced in the early 1950s, international pressures on colonial rule began to grow. They had been significant in the 1930s when the British response to disturbances in some colonies, most notably in the West Indies and Palestine, was clearly influenced by he impending war. It was particularly important then to avoid deploying troops, not just for the obvious military reasons but also to avoid international criticism of British colonialism, which would have been damaging to Britain's international reputation at a crucial time. After 1939 international pressures came to be associated with the anti-colonialism of Britain's two main wartime allies, particularly the United States. However, this American criticism was almost immediately reduced as the war ended due initially to the demand of the American military for an extensive network of overseas bases, particularly in the Pacific and E Asia.

With the establishment of the United Nations and the influence of its Latin American, Middle Eastern, and Asian members who had once been former colonies, a new source of international pressure for the end of colonial rule emerged by the 1950s. The developing anti-colonialism in the United Nations had an important Cold War dimension in terms of winning support for the West in the non-European world. This gave the United States, which saw colonialism and its end as part of the East–West conflict, a number of dilemmas. It was not simply a question of avoiding NATO divisions which would jeopardize American strategic requirements. The broader Cold War dilemma stemmed from the disadvantages of fighting a Cold War for freedom with large areas of the Western world denied this right. The Soviets could point to the Western idea of freedom in the context of formal subjugation making colonialism a serious handicap in the propaganda battle. It therefore appeared to make sense to terminate colonial rule as soon as possible. If this did not happen, unrest would mount and the conditions would be ripe for communist exploitation even if growing numbers of colonial people did not look to the Soviets for support in their battle for independence. Unfortunately the problem was that if the European powers granted independence too soon, without adequate preparation, then the new states would be unstable and open to subversion if they proved unable to provide law and order and a stable political environment. From a Western Cold War perspective there were dangers in transferring power too soon as well as in delaying it.

In 1953 John Foster Dulles tried to get round the dilemmas of Cold War and colonialism by portraying the latter as a lesser evil in terms of the denial of freedom than Soviet communism, thus overcoming the disadvantages colonialism presented to the West. It was a dubious ploy to excuse one denial of freedom by pointing to the existence of a greater loss of liberty. Moreover, colonial people did not accept that their freedom should be delayed merely because it was denied to Soviet citizens so the American dilemma remained. Even though they accepted the British strategy of granting independence to 'responsible' leaders when their countries were ready for it, the issue was whether that would be sooner rather than later.

The question of timing was a key one and remains so for any understanding of the transfers of power which ended formal European rule. If anti-colonial movements were the *sine qua non* in producing change is it plausible to say that they determined the timing of the transfers of power? Did the colonial powers change their policies or speed them up simply because they grew more aware of the strength of indigenous opposition to their continued presence? Or was the international situation important in determining precisely when power was transferred? And how important were considerations of preserving economic interests as opposed to establishing new collaborators who would look to their colonial masters for advice and guidance? Were Cold War considerations vital in efforts to ensure that power was transferred at appropriate times to those elites whose allegiances would be to the Western rather than to the communist world and who were deemed likely to provide the necessary stability in viable new states?

Some ideas on these and other questions arising from the complex process of decolonization will be suggested in the following sections. For the period from 1945 until 1953 it is clear that Cold War requirements were mixed up with the perceived need to retain influence on a regional and global basis while dealing with challenges to European rule. And to some extent the nature of the international environment can be used to explain why in 1947 power was transferred in India but not in what are often regarded as less important parts of the British Empire. Some explanations for this have focused exclusively on the strength of the Indian nationalist movements which forced the British hand. Subsequently it can therefore be argued that with the jewel in the British Crown abandoned it was inevitable that the rest of the dependencies would achieve independence as and when nationalist movements were strong enough to demand it. This does not explain why the British were so keen to resist any loss of influence in the Middle East during this period nor why there was resistance in London to the transfer of power in parts of Black Africa. To some extent explanations for this can be located in the different circumstances in the colonies including their economic viability, political awareness, and educational development, but also such things as their racial mix, particularly when there was a significant white-settler minority. Thus in many ways it can be argued India was ripe for independence when most parts of the British Empire were not. Another argument which ignores the influence of international factors is that by the end of the Second World War India was much less important to the British economy and therefore it was abandoned as it had outlived its usefulness. By contrast, the fact that Prime Minister Attlee had an intimate involvement with India through his work on the Simon Commission (which drew up the devolved 1935 Constitution), and a personal commitment to Indian independence, has been portrayed as another significant factor.

What the above have in common is that to a greater or lesser extent they made it easier to concede to the demands of the nationalists and for Attlee easier to convince his reluctant colleagues of the need to leave India. The international situation had a similar effect, as did the fact that opponents such as the foreign secretary Ernest Bevin could offer no practical alternative, although the conflict between the practical and the desirable in imperial policy-making did not always favour the former in the process of decolonization. In 1945 and 1946 before the growing international tensions fully gave way to confrontation and Cold War, the spirit of internationalism, characterized by the commitment to freedom for which the War had allegedly been fought ran through the newly established United Nations and into all corners of the globe. The expression of that spirit and plans for its implementation dominated the immediate post-war years in which the key decisions on India's future were taken. Britain's status in the international community could be enhanced by embracing that principle of freedom and offering it to Indian subjects as well as to those deprived of it by Nazi rule.

The United Nations and the ideas it embodied, in terms of the rhetoric, if not the reality, was important before the Cold War really began to impact on international politics. The new Prime Minister was someone who embraced internationalism as something which would be a new addition to the post-war international order which could be used effectively by Britain as a tool for crafting a new and more affordable world role. Attlee did not see internationalism as something which would supersede the old order and replace empire and interstate rivalry but as something which would modify the latter and which therefore had to be taken into account. Such ideas have proved easy to misrepresent and easier to dismiss once the Cold War world was established at the end of 1947. By then of course India was independent and the idea that Britain would gain kudos from transferring power as part of her quest to regain her status as one of the Big Three powers was less plausible. Moreover, the glib assumption that Britain would recover economically from the war was under threat from the harsh winter of 1947 and the growing dollar gap. Empire thus came to be seen not only in the different light of the Cold War but as something which would have to be employed to regain British economic strength and great power status. Thus Colonial Office efforts to develop the colonies in ways which would prepare them for self-government now coincided with the attempts of the Treasury and the Board of Trade, backed by the Foreign Office, to increase colonial production. Produce and raw materials could then help British industry and consumers or be sold to the dollar area. As a result, the second colonial occupation, as it has been termed, also involved increasing exploitation, through production without economic incentives which in turn would influence anti-colonial movements and the nature of the British response. Increased exploitation was difficult to reconcile with increased cooperation the Cold War notwithstanding.

Ideology and Power Politics in East Asia

It has been suggested that the tensions that developed in the Grand Alliance in 1945 stemmed from disagreements over power and influence on a global basis with the Middle East and East Asia contributing as much as Europe to the failure to agree on the distribution of formal and informal influence. As such the idea of a Cold War developing separately in Asia is a misperception despite the fact that the establishment of a new, unified China in October 1949 was the result of the particular circumstances that produced a communist victory over the Nationalists in the Chinese Civil War. In order to understand Soviet and American reactions to this one has to take into account the regional circumstances and the way in which East Asian events interacted with broader international considerations. Such interactions have to be seen in terms of the Cold War's ideological nature and in terms of the impact on the regional power balance which cannot simply be defined by analyses of Soviet–American relations based on the assumption that a gain for one was a loss for the other. China's emergence in particular was a threat to both powers and both were uncertain about how best to respond.

The more powerful Mao and communist China became the more they became a threat to Stalin who had ambitions to achieve in East Asia, particularly with regard to a warm-water port and the extension of Soviet influence. The success of Mao effectively put a brake on these ambitions especially the agreement which, with American help, had effectively been foisted upon Chiang Kai-shek's Chinese Nationalist opponents of the communists. Arguably Stalin's ambitions would have been achieved more easily with American support. It was logical for the Soviet leader to assume that the price would be paid by the Nationalists with whom ideological sympathy was lacking, and therefore power political goals would be easier to achieve at their expense. An ideologically friendly regime, while it might enhance the global communist movement, would not be so easy to reconcile with Stalin's power political goals.

The conflict in Korea and the communist takeover in China were far more than an extension of a European confrontation into a more global one centred on Soviet–American rivalry. They involved a mixture of ambitions with purely Asian elements as well as the confrontation between the capitalist and communist worlds. The Chinese communist success was long seen as inevitable by those in the West with knowledge of the region but this did not remove old Chinese fears and ambitions in East Asia. On the other hand power politics did not mean Mao would turn to the Americans. Just as the prospect of the US saving China was a forlorn hope so was the prospect of Mao, disillusioned with Stalin, turning to the United States. Whatever Mao's disillusion and suspicion of the Soviets or his ideological affinities with Moscow there was the American attitude to the Nationalists to consider. This major obstacle required a massive shift in American policy to surmount and to take into account the importance for Mao of unifying China. This fundamental Chinese communist goal was far more important than ideology or long-term regional ambitions. It was always to constrain Sino–American relations and rule out any Sino–American cooperation in the 1980s.[7]

In a sense the Korean War for the Soviets, given the closer links with the Chinese communists, was part of the attempt to reconcile ideological support with Stalin's particular ambitions in East Asia. As has been argued by Shen Zhihua this could be achieved by returning the port of Darien and replacing it with warm-water ports in Korea once the peninsular was united under communist control. Unfortunately for Stalin his fears of taking on the Americans made him disinclined to risk such actions, and until early 1950 he refused to accede to the North Korean leader Kim Il Sung's requests to support a proposed invasion of the South. Only when the Chinese were on board and it seemed the Americans were unwilling to fight for an area they deemed strategically unimportant did Stalin finally give Kim Il Sung the green light. It was a grave miscalculation on Stalin's part and another example of his lack of understanding of the West manifesting itself in serious consequences for the Soviets who emerged the only real loser from the war, despite playing a back seat and only providing trained military personnel and equipment.

The Korean War can be characterized and assessed in a number of contrasting ways. A war which enhanced the status of the United Nations and which saw a firm stand being taken against armed aggression on the part of the North. A war which saw a further extension of Soviet–American hostility and which clearly played a major role in the global conflict and added a new armed dimension. The Korean War can thus be seen as a Cold War which became hot but which was limited to a regional conflict. This indicated the fears in the communist camp about the military power of the US and the fact that those in the latter country who favoured an extension of the war were finally defeated with Truman's sacking of General MacArthur in April 1951. Nevertheless the war was enormously destructive and the aggression perpetuated by the North Koreans brought no reward. Yet the Chinese gained in status enormously through the war because of their proven capabilities against the Americans in a military stalemate. The Americans managed to prevent the loss of South Korea and, as they perceived it, the loss of credibility for their leadership and defence of the free world. They also concluded that communist aggression in Korea was instigated by Moscow and led them to dramatically overstate the scale and ambitions of the Soviet Union and the closeness of its ties with China. Stalin was the loser because the Americans acted on this exaggerated perception and reinforced their commitment to the kind of aggressive Cold War actions that Stalin feared. It was therefore a war which intensified the Cold War in the short term and reinforced Stalin's paranoid perceptions while bringing him no power political gains.

NOTES

1. H. Jones and R. B. Woods *et al.* 'The Origins of the Cold War: A Symposium', *Diplomatic History* 2 (1993), and the commentaries by E. Rosenberg, A. Stephanson and B. Bernstein, 251–311.

2. John Lewis Gaddis, *We Now Know, Rethinking Cold War History* (Clarendon Press, New York, 1997), 31.

3. V. Zubok and C. Pleshakov, *Inside the Kremlin's Cold War: From Stalin to Khrushchev* (Harvard University Press, Cambridge, 1996), 102–3.

4. By Geir Lundestad and John Lewis Gaddis respectively.

5. Argued in Alan Milward, *The European Rescue of the Nation-State* (Routledge, New York, 2nd edn., 1992).

6. M. Evangelista 'The "Soviet Threat": Intentions, Capabilities and Context', *Diplomatic History* 3 (1998).

7. O. A. Westad 'Losses, Chances and Myths: the United States and the Creation of the Sino–Soviet Alliance, 1946–1950', *Diplomatic History* 2 (1997).

PART I CHRONOLOGY: THE ORIGINS AND DEVELOPMENT OF THE COLD WAR, 1944–1953

1944

October	Percentages Agreement between Stalin and Churchill over Greece, Romania, Hungary, Yugoslavia, and Bulgaria.

1945

January	USSR requests American loan.
February	Yalta conference of Big Three leaders.
	Ceasefire in Greek Civil War.
March	British Foreign Office discusses value of a tougher stance against and showdown with the Soviets.
	Some Anglo-American concern over Soviet installation of puppet Romanian government (27 Feb.) and failure to broaden Lublin governments in Poland in breach of Yalta agreement.
	Soviets denounce Turkish treaty and refuse to sign another one unless Turkey returns provinces of Kars and Ardahan.
April	President Roosevelt dies.
	Truman confronts Molotov over Soviet failure to stick to all the Yalta agreements.
May	German surrender ends the war in Europe.
May–June	Hopkins mision to Moscow succeeds in securing agreement on Poland with Stalin broadening the Polish government.
June	Soviets inform Turkey of their desire for bases in the Straits of the Dardanelles.
	State Department report on international communism concludes it poses a serious challenge to the US.
	UN Charter agreed at San Francisco.
	Soviet request for say in the international administration of Tangier.
	James Byrnes becomes US Secretary of State.
	George Kennan reports that the end of the Comintern has not weakened Moscow's control over international communism.
July	Potsdam conference of Big Three leaders.
	British Foreign Office debating value of concentrating on protecting vital interests in the Mediterranean, Middle East, and Germany at the expense of endeavouring to retain a say in areas such as Poland and Romania where no interests were at stake.
6 August	Atomic bomb dropped on Hiroshima.
8 August	USSR declares war on Japan.
9 August	Atomic bomb dropped on Nagasaki.
14 August	Japanese cease fighting.
September	54 per cent of US public opinion trusts Soviets to cooperate.

September–October	London Council of Foreign Ministers (UK, US, China, France, and USSR attend).
November	Communists are defeated in Hungarian elections.
	Marshall leaves for China to mediate between communists and Nationalists.
	44 per cent of US public opinion trusts Soviets to cooperate.
December	Ethridge report on Soviet policy in Romania and Bulgaria concludes that to concede Soviet sphere of influence in Eastern Europe would be to invite its extension.
16–26 December	Moscow Council of Foreign Ministers.

1946

January	UN meeting where Iran complains about alleged Soviet interference in its internal affairs.
	Truman tells Byrnes he is tired of babying the Soviets.
	Secret Yalta agreement on Soviet acquisition of South Sakhalin and the Kurile Islands made public in the United States.
February	US warship sent to Istanbul to signal support for Turkey.
9 February	Stalin speech calling for new 5-year plan to prepare for the inevitable conflict between communism and capitalism.
February	35 per cent of US public opinion trusts the Soviets to cooperate.
	Reports on Soviet spy ring providing information on US atomic bomb.
22 February	Kennan's Long Telegram from Moscow.
March	Soviets fail to withdraw troops from Iran in accordance with agreement.
5 March	Churchill's Fulton speech describing an Iron Curtain across Europe from Stettin in the Baltic to Trieste in the Adriatic.
March	US send a note complaining of the Soviet troops present in Iran which violated the Soviet–Iranian treaty.
	70 per cent of Americans disapprove of Soviet actions.
April	Soviets agree to withdraw troops from Iran in May.
	Fighting begins again in Manchuria between Chinese Nationalists and communists.
April–May	First Paris Council of Foreign Ministers takes place.
June–July	Second Paris Council of Foreign Ministers.
July–October	Paris Peace Conference (all Allied nations attend).
November–December	New York Council of Foreign Ministers takes place.
December	The Bi-Zone agreement fuses US and British occupation zones in Germany.

1947

January	Polish elections are rigged.
12 March	Truman makes his Doctrine speech.
March–April	Moscow Council of Foreign Ministers on Germany.
June	The Marshall Plan is launched.
July	Kennan's Mr X article in *Foreign Affairs*.
August	Elections in Hungary are rigged.
September	Rio Treaty of Latin American states signed.
November	UN partition plan for Palestine.

1948

February	Communist coup in Czechoslovakia.
March	Brussels Treaty signed.
May	British leave Palestine and Israel established.
June	The Berlin blockade begins as the Soviets block the surface access to West Berlin. Yugoslavia is expelled from Cominform.

1949

April	The North Atlantic Treaty is signed.
May	Berlin blockade is ended.
August	Soviets explode their first atomic bomb.
September	The Chinese People's Republic is proclaimed by Mao Tse-tung.

1950

January	Acheson speech withdraws Korea from US defensive perimeter. Stalin decides to authorize N. Korean plan to attack S. Korea.
February	The Sino–Soviet Alliance is signed.
April	The National Security Council memorandum number 68 (NSC 68) proposes a large arms build up.
May	Schuman Plan launched for a European Coal and Steel Community.
June	North Korean forces invade South Korea.
October	Pleven plan for a European army launched.
November	The Chinese intervene by using force in Korea.

1951

June	Establishment of Psychological Strategy Board.
July	Ceasefire talks concerning Korea begin.
September	US Japanese defence treaty is signed.
November	An agreement on the ceasefire line is reached in Armistice Talks in Korea.

1952

May	The occupation of West Germany is ended.
November	US explodes first hydrogen bomb.

1 Tensions in the Grand Alliance and the Growing Confrontation, 1945–1947

A. The Yalta Conference

The Context

The Yalta Conference of February 1945 was the second of the three wartime summits between the leaders of Britain, the US, and the Soviet Union. Unlike the first meeting between Churchill, Roosevelt, and Stalin at Tehran in the autumn of 1943, a significant part of the proceedings in the Crimea involved discussions on the post-war settlement. Yet the military situation was bound to overshadow the Conference. The conduct of operations in various parts of the globe could not be divorced from the attempts of the Big Three allies to maintain or increase influence. As the talks took place, the

Soviet armies had crossed the Vistula and reached the Oder–Neisse river, while in the West, although the December 1944 German offensive in the Ardennes had been repulsed, Allied armies were not making the progress expected when the invasion of France began in June 1944.

By 1945 a number of military decisions and developments had helped produce mutual suspicion. The Soviets had long been concerned about the delay in establishing the second front in Western Europe. Roosevelt and Churchill were aware that the Soviet military position in Europe was extremely strong and that in the lands east of Germany there was little influence that could be brought to bear.

Franklin Delano Roosevelt, 1882–1945

Born in New York Roosevelt (FDR) attended Harvard University and Colombia University Law School and qualified as a lawyer in 1907. In 1910 he was elected to the New York state senate and came up against the infamous Tammany Hall machine. Roosevelt's political instincts were such that he survived the encounter and after a spell as assistant secretary to the Navy in Woodrow Wilson's administration he ran unsuccessfully as vice-presidential candidate in democrat James Cox's bid for the White House in 1920. The following year FDR contracted polio and remained partially paralysed as a result. Nevertheless he returned to public life in 1928 when he was elected governor of New York. In 1932 he was elected president and served three successive terms in the White House. His programme of reform to counter the economic and social problems of the Depression, known as the New Deal, was a landmark in government intervention in the US and was bitterly resented by the right. FDR however remained an immensely popular president whose 'fireside radio chats' charmed the American public and added to his enormous political abilities. Always preferring to use personal relations rather than political principles to retain his hold on the levers of power, FDR remains an enigma whose beliefs are difficult to define. In foreign affairs, while keen to play a leading role in international conferences and the affairs of Latin America, he was nervous of the public's reaction to any US involvement in alliances that would remove America's freedom to act. This kind of isolation helped keep the US out of the Second World War until the Japanese attacked Pearl Harbor in December 1941. Significantly, FDR agreed with Churchill that wartime military strategy should give priority to the defeat of Germany. Roosevelt, who has been unfairly accused of selling out to the Soviets at Yalta, died in April 1945 creating much subsequent speculation as to whether cooperation with Stalin would have continued had he remained alive.

There were fears that the Russians might eventually occupy the whole of Germany, which would increase the influence that the Soviet Union could exert on the peace process. At the same time it was realized that without cooperation with the Soviets and the continuation of the offensive in the East, the defeat of Germany would be difficult and costly. There was a common interest in securing Germany's unconditional surrender and in maintaining postwar cooperation to prevent a re-emergence of the German threat. But there was also a concern in both East and West that a separate peace could have unfortunate consequences by enabling German forces to be focused on a single front.

As the Red Army advanced westward Stalin appeared determined to eliminate as far as possible those organized groups opposed to the Soviet Union and/or to the ideology of communism. In keeping with the ruthless and inhumane character of the Stalinist regime, this applied not only to the former enemy states but also to Poland, which had always fought on the Allied side. The most glaring example of Stalin's desire to eliminate potential sources of opposition, even if they were anti-German, occurred in Warsaw. In August 1944 members of the Polish resistance, known as the Home Army, rose against the Germans in an effort to seize the city before the arrival of the Red Army. The rebellion was ruthlessly put down by the Germans, as Soviet forces refused to cross the Vistula to assist the rebels despite Anglo-American requests. This sign that Stalin supported the German destruction of independently minded or anti-Soviet Poles was matched at the start of 1945 by the deportations in Romania, the other nation with long-standing territorial disputes with Russia; these were also designed to make control from Moscow easier. It was never likely that the Soviets would even agree to semi-independent governments for their two most important regional enemies.

Roosevelt and Churchill were fully aware of the appalling nature of the Soviet regime, and if anything, had fallen over backwards to avoid condemnation of some of Stalin's wartime actions. It is easy to argue that the domestic policy of totalitarian regimes and the evil nature of men prepared, like Stalin, to send thousands of their fellow citizens to their deaths precludes effective international cooperation. Yet there is no evidence at the end of 1944 that the British or Americans saw this as a barrier to future cooperation with Moscow. The Russians were bound to be interested in cooperating to control Germany. To do this would require the maintenance of Allied cooperation and the formalization of a new international order dedicated to the preservation of peace. One key question was whether this could be achieved if the Soviets insisted on a tightly controlled sphere of influence containing Poland and Romania and possibly other parts of Eastern and Central Europe.

The US Approach to Yalta

Roosevelt had always been a supporter of the kind of world order and international cooperation advocated by President Woodrow Wilson. At the end of the First World War, Wilson had failed to win the approval of the American Congress for US participation in the League of Nations and this had fatally damaged the new organization. For Roosevelt it was vitally important not to repeat the same mistake in 1945. A prime goal for the US president when he went to Yalta was therefore to win his allies' support for the kind of world order and international organization which would be acceptable to Congress and public opinion in the US.

In addition to these requirements and general principles, Roosevelt, like the other leaders, had also to consider vital US defence and economic interests which were deemed essential for US influence and prosperity. The US had always had what was seen as a sphere of influence in Latin America, although the State Department was keen to emphasize the difference between the US position in the Western hemisphere and the Soviet position that eventually emerged in Eastern and Central Europe. Charles Bohlen of the State Department claimed the US right 'to have a guiding voice in a certain limited sphere of the foreign relations' of Latin America but that the US did 'not attempt on the basis of that right to dictate their internal national life or to restrict their intercourse with foreign nations except in a limited sphere' which he defined as 'the politico-strategic sphere of their foreign relations'.[1]

While maintaining US influence and vital interests Roosevelt had to establish a basis for cooperation with two other powers that did not share American views on the underlying principles of a new world order. In so doing he had to convince opinion in the US that any post-war settlement was in line with American ideals and justify to international opinion the continuation of exclusive US influence in Latin America. At the same time he had to take account of the military and political realities of the situation in early 1945. In the Pacific, where the Japanese were still fighting, the US was clearly the controlling Allied influence, but in Europe the Soviets had done most of the fighting against the German armies and were therefore likely to exercise dominance. The US had no vital economic or political interests in much of Central and Eastern Europe, and the issue was simply whether the post-war arrangements there would conform to American principles of democracy and non-discriminatory trading blocs. Here the only card the Americans had to play was the Soviet need for support in the containment of Germany, which might ensure that Russian desires to expand their power and influence would be limited. Roosevelt had to deal with this problem while maintaining the cooperation needed to establish an international organization that could preserve peace. Despite the dominant economic and military position which the US had obtained on a global basis (the Soviet Union had no significant navy and no real ability to project power beyond the areas adjacent to its borders) the president had a difficult task. The difficulties would have been there irrespective of the political or ideological stance of America's allies.

The Soviet Approach to Yalta

It is more difficult to assess Soviets ideas on the nature of the settlement and the new international order or the problems they had in realizing them. Historians, like some Western policy-makers who had to fight the Cold War, have sometimes attributed unlimited expansionist goals to Stalin and other Soviet leaders. For some, Stalin had a clearly worked out a plan to take control of Eastern and Central Europe with the possible extension of such dominance to Western Europe if little resistance were met. Other historians have emphasized the important security requirements of a Soviet state whose short history had continually borne witness to frequent foreign invasions.[2] Recent research in Soviet archives, while still at an early stage, has helped cast doubts on such simple interpretations. From Stalin's statements at Tehran it was clear that he favoured a world order based on spheres of influence with each of the three great powers being responsible for peace and security within their respective spheres. It was also clear from the Soviet leader's unprincipled cooperation with the Nazis that his ambitions/security requirements in Eastern and Central Europe were considerable (see Chapter 2, B). Restoration of the borders of the old Tsarist empire and full access to the warm waters of the Mediterranean were also important Soviet goals. The latter could be secured by ending the restrictions on Soviet shipping passing through Straits of the Dardanelles which had been imposed by the 1936 Montreux Convention. Such ambitions would likely to have been present even under a capitalist Russian regime, and to some extent the peacemakers had to consider whether such aims were acceptable within the framework of the new world order. More generally a desire to increase the world standing of the Soviet Union, given the importance of the Russian war effort to the Allied cause, was another unsurprising Soviet aim which had to be reckoned with.

With regard to Soviet desires for spheres of influence, the extent of the domination imposed on the lesser states was an important issue given the ideological differences between the Soviets and the Western Allies. In the wake of the Tehran meeting and subsequent events in Poland it should have been clear that Stalin was not going to accept a Polish regime which had the political freedom to oppose the Soviet Union.[3] It was likely that the Poles would only be independent in the cultural and linguistic sense. A free and democratic Poland, in the Western sense of the term, was not going to be achievable, given the long-standing hostility between the Russians and many sections of the Polish population. This was bound to cause problems in both Britain and the US despite the fact that neither the British nor the Americans had any vital interests in Poland. Many Poles had fought in the British armed forces and there would certainly be awkward questions in Parliament if the Poles were fully subjected to Russian domination. In the US, not only would the establishment of Soviet control over Poland be at odds with the principle of all peoples being allowed to choose the form of government under which they lived, but it would particularly affect the large Polish-American community.

The British Approach to Yalta

The British went to Yalta as the weakest of the three allies but with an equal determination to protect what they saw as vital interests. As an imperial power with formal control over subject peoples they had something in common with the Russians, despite the different nature of the controls pertaining in the Soviet Empire. The British Empire had certainly aroused hostility amongst sections of the American government during the war. Its existence clashed with American principles in the same way as the Soviet Empire and was more threatening to US economic interests. Yet the British shared the same ideology and political system as the US and were committed to the same kind of new economic order once British post-war recovery had been achieved.

British post-war planning was therefore torn between acceptance of a set of principles and a system of cooperation based on spheres of influence. The former might threaten the future of the British Empire but would ensure the support of the world's leading economic and military power. The latter would be more conducive to the maintenance of formal empire and the prevention of German domination of Europe, but might threaten the unusually close Anglo-American cooperation established during the War. British policy-makers went some way towards the latter in October 1944 with the spheres of influence deal arranged by Churchill and Stalin in Moscow. In order to gain freedom of action in Greece, Churchill had proposed giving the Soviets the same licence in Romania on the basis of 90 per cent influence for both powers in their respective spheres. In addition, influence in Bulgaria would be divided 75–25 in the Soviets' favour with Hungary and Yugoslavia shared on a 50 per cent basis. In essence this kind of arrangement was designed to maintain Anglo-Soviet cooperation in Europe: Churchill did not see any need in late 1944 to construct, as the military desired, a British-led Western bloc (of France, Benelux, and part or all of Germany), with a view to containing the Russians. As it turned out the Yalta Conference was to undermine Churchill's arrangements rather than to reinforce them and claims that Yalta divided Europe are not compatible with the records of the conference.

Record of Conversations between Edgar Snow and Maxime Litvinov (Soviet Foreign Minister), 6 October 1944 (Summarized by authors)

Edgar Snow asked Litvinov if he thought the war was going to end the elimination of all anti-Soviet forces. Litvinov said there were plenty of fascists in England and the worst fascists in France will be left untouched. He had no faith in de Gaulle and France needed a real purge. Churchill would insist on Franco staying. Snow asked whether this meant that Western Europe would be reorganized as a potential anti-Soviet bloc and that suspicions of Anglo-American policy in Moscow would continue. Litvinov replied in the affirmative. He said look at Poland as Britain and the United States don't even want to throw out the old crowd there. He disagreed with the Soviet government on many issues but on Poland they were absolutely right and if anything too lenient. The Poles are fixed on a mirage of sixteenth-century Poland when it was a great power and Russia was weak. Anti-Soviet Poles, he claimed, aimed to make Poland a great power and a gate barring Russian from Europe. Beck wanted a five-power council after the war constituting Britain, Germany, France, Italy, and Poland. Litvinov was adamant that Poland had to be friendly towards the Soviet Union and must abandon the idea that she could be a springboard against Russia and thereby get back her sixteenth-century empire. Before the war Beck and Sosnhowsky had offered their services to Germany for this end and now they were offering themselves to Britain and the United States. Litvinov went on to suggest that if the Allies could agree on how to reconstruct Germany and to re-educate the Germans to make them harmless and peaceful maybe we could get a small but united Germany. However, the Allies he claimed would be unable to agree on a common programme. And if the three-power combination were to break down over Germany, everything would break down. Cooperation would be threatened by the revival of traditional British diplomacy in Europe and their inability to think in new terms. Britain only understood the idea of the balance of power in Europe and would never be willing to see a strong power on the European continent without organizing a counterforce against it. The idea of collaboration with the strong power in Europe was alien to Britain. Diplomacy might have been able to maintain cooperation if the Soviet Union had made its limits clear to Britain. Now it was too late and suspicion was rife on both sides.

Source: Franklin D. Roosevelt Presidential Library, PSF Box 49, Record of Conversations, 6 Oct. 1944.

The Conference Proceedings

The atmosphere at Yalta, the first crucial inter-allied meeting primarily on the post-war world, was one of hope that a new era of peace and cooperation could be fashioned from the rubble of war; the participants were also conscious of their responsibilities in the face of such an enormous task. There was no Anglo-American alliance partly because Roosevelt had no desire to confront the Soviet Union. The US President was also disinclined to support an unreformed British imperial system which was a threat to US economic interests. Although it has been suggested that Roosevelt, whose health was failing, was duped by Stalin at Yalta, it appears that the US President was fully aware of the problems of peace-making. It would be difficult if not impossible to reconcile Stalin's requirements with the appearance of a new world order. US principles were never likely to override the Red Army's domination of Eastern and Central Europe, but this problem dictated Roosevelt's tactics in the Crimea. It led the US President to attempt to fool American opinion, at least until Congress had accepted the new United Nations organization, by pretending that the Yalta agreements embodied American principles.

One element of Roosevelt's plan at Yalta involved James Byrnes, a leading Southern democrat. Byrnes was excluded from certain sessions and sent home before the conclusion of the conference in order that he could quite genuinely portray a version of events which was incomplete but in line with American expectations. Meanwhile Roosevelt was free to make agreements which suited great power interests and military realities rather than American principles. Byrnes was instrumental in leading the American public to believe that Yalta marked the end of old-fashioned power politics and the beginning of international cooperation based on American principles. On his return from Yalta, Roosevelt

Extracts from the Yalta Conference

Meeting between Marshal Stalin and President Roosevelt

MARSHAL STALIN replied that he had not found de Gaulle a very complicated person, but he felt he was unrealistic in the sense that France had not done very much fighting in this war and de Gaulle demanded full rights with the Americans, British, and Russians who had done the burden of the fighting.

THE PRESIDENT then described his conversation with de Gaulle in Casablanca two years ago when de Gaulle compared himself with Joan of Arc as the spiritual leader of France and with Clemenceau as the political leader . . .

THE PRESIDENT said he would now tell the Marshal something indiscreet, since he would not wish to say it in front of Prime Minister Churchill, namely that the British for two years have had the idea of artificially building up France into a strong power which would have 200,000 troops on the eastern border of France to hold the line for the period required to assemble a strong British army. He said the British were a peculiar people and wished to have their cake and eat it too.

Source: FRUS, 1945: *The Conferences of Malta and Yalta* (Dept. of State, Washington, DC, 1955, 571).

himself attempted to reinforce the message by telling Congress that 'The Crimean Conference ought to spell the end of the system of unilateral action, the exclusive alliance, the spheres of influence, the balance of power and all the other expedients that have been tried for centuries, and have always failed.'[4]

By contrast some historians have portrayed Yalta as an American betrayal of moral principles, which were sacrificed by an acceptance of a Soviet sphere of influence in Eastern Europe that effectively divided the continent. Both interpretations are wide of the mark. Yalta marked the first attempt to reconcile principles with power politics and to devise arrangements which protected vital Allied interests. One historian has noted: 'Because FDR could not concede portions of Eastern Europe to Stalin or deny them to him he would in effect do both—the former through implicit understandings, the latter through the promulgation of principles that were interpreted differently by the Soviets and by the American people.'[5] As such few specific agreements

were finalized, much remained to be clarified and little progress was made on the more difficult issues.

The most important, if not the most difficult issue, was the future of Germany. Germany had already been divided into agreed zones of occupation by the three main Allies, and would be governed by an Allied Control Council. But there was disagreement on whether Germany should remain a single state. A united Germany would again be in a position to wield economic and military power, which could not be contained by its neighbours in the West or the small states to the East. On the other hand the dismemberment of Germany into a number of separate states, or the detachment of important economic areas, would run the risk of arousing the kind of German resentment that Hitler had exploited in the inter-war years. The feeling at Tehran had been in favour of dismemberment but nothing had been decided. At Yalta the principle was accepted by all three Allies, but the method was deferred for further study and, despite the existence of separate occupation zones, Germany was to be treated as a single administrative unit by the Control Council. Similarly the question of German reparations was referred to a commission in Moscow, directives to which would be given by the foreign ministers who would report back to the conference. What was decided (without consulting the inhabitants) was the position of Poland's eastern frontier. Poland would cede territory to the Soviet Union by following the Curzon Line with a digression from it in some regions of 5–8 kilometres in favour of Poland.[6] Poland would then gain German territory in the west as compensation for the territory lost in the east. Crucially, the western frontier on the Oder–Neisse river was not finally agreed upon. The Soviet proposal clearly referred to the Western Neisse rather than the Eastern Neisse, a difference which was to prove significant later.

With the future of Germany and its boundaries still undecided, the other European issue was the treatment of Germany's allies and the governance of other areas liberated from German control. In Greece the British had been the arbiters between the competing political factions, while in Italy, a former German ally, the British and the Americans had decided to give control to the military commanders on the spot; this was exercised through an Allied

Extracts from the Yalta Conference, 3rd and 4th Plenary Meetings

3rd Plenary Meeting, 6 February

MARSHAL STALIN then gave the following summary of his views on the Polish question: Mr Churchill had said that for Great Britain the Polish question was one of honor and that he understood, but for the Russians it was a question of both honour and security. It was one of honour because Russia had many past grievances against Poland and desired to see them eliminated. It was a question of strategic security not only because Poland was a bordering country but because throughout history Poland had been the corridor for attack on Russia. We have to mention that during the last thirty years Germany twice passed through this corridor. The reason for this was that Poland was weak. Russia wants a strong, independent, and democratic Poland. Since it was impossible by the force of Russian armies alone to close from outside this corridor, it could be done only by Poland's own forces. It was very important, therefore, to have Poland independent, strong, and democratic. It is not only a question of honour for Russia, but one of life and death.

4th Plenary Meeting, 7 February

THE PRIME MINISTER . . . said in regard to the second point of Mr Molotov's proposals [the moving of the western frontier of Poland to the Oder–western Neisse rivers] he would always support the movement of Polish frontiers to the west since he felt they should receive compensation [for the loss of territory in the east], but not more than they could handle. He said it would be a pity to stuff the Polish goose so full of German food it got indigestion. . . . He said he felt if it were confined to East Prussia, six million Germans probably could be handled quite aside from moral grounds, but the addition of the line west of the Neisse would create quite a problem in this respect.

MARSHAL STALIN remarked that most Germans in those areas had already run away from the Red Army.

Source: FRUS, 1945, *The Conferences of Malta and Yalta* (Dept. of State, Washington, DC, 1955, 669).

Control Council, thereby excluding the Soviets, who had no military commanders in Italy where a right-wing government under Badoglio was left in place. In Poland Stalin had imposed a provisional government, the Lublin Committee, which excluded representatives of the Polish resistance (including local communists) and members of the London-based government-in-exile. In addition the Soviets had supervised the installation of a communist-dominated Popular Front government in Bulgaria.

At Yalta the discussions focused on the arrangements to be made for the provisional governments in the liberated areas and for the people eventually to choose, in line with the Atlantic Charter, the form of government under which they would live. The outcome was a formal agreement, the Declaration on Liberated Europe, supplemented by an additional agreement on the formation of a Polish Provisional government. The latter seemed necessary given the particular interest in Poland as an ally and as the country for whom Britain had gone to war and over which Stalin had previously come to an arrangement with Hitler.

The Declaration on Liberated Europe made specific reference to the Atlantic Charter and required the signatories to 'form interim governmental authorities broadly representative of all democratic elements in the population and pledged to the earliest possible establishment through free elections of governments responsive to the will of the people . . . and to facilitate where possible the holding of such elections.' The agreement on Poland was that the Lublin government should be 'reorganized on a broader democratic basis with the inclusion of democratic leaders from Poland itself and from Poles abroad'. Perhaps even more surprisingly Stalin informed Churchill and Roosevelt that elections would be held in Poland in a month provided there were no military disasters.[7]

This agreement on applying the principles of the Atlantic Charter in Europe was accompanied by an agreement to break them in Asia. In return for Soviet entry into the war with Japan it was agreed that, again without consulting the inhabitants, the Soviet Union would receive Southern Sakahlin and the Kurile Islands from the Japanese. Here was the mix

Extracts from the Yalta Conference

Tripartite Dinner Meeting, 8 February

The atmosphere of the dinner was most cordial and forty five toasts in all were drunk . . .

MARSHAL STALIN proposed a toast to the health of the Prime Minister, who he characterized as the bravest governmental figure in the world. He said that due in large measure to Mr Churchill's courage and staunchness, England, when she stood alone, had divided the might of Hitlerite Germany at a time when the rest of Europe was falling flat on its face before Hitler. . . . He drank a toast to Mr Churchill, his fighting friend and a brave man.

THE PRIME MINISTER, in his reply, toasted Marshal Stalin as the mighty leader of a mighty country, which had taken the full shock of the German war machine, had broken its back, and driven the tyrants from her soil. He said that in peace no less than in war Marshal Stalin would continue to lead his people from success to success.

MARSHAL STALIN then proposed the health of the President of the United States. He said that he and Mr Churchill . . . had been fighting for their very existence against Hitlerite Germany but there was a third man whose country had not been seriously threatened with invasion but who had . . . been the chief forger of the instruments which had lead to the mobilization of the world against Hitler.

THE PRESIDENT, in reply to this toast, said he felt the atmosphere at the dinner was as that of a family, and it was in those words that he liked to characterize the relations that existed between our three countries. . . . He said that fifty years ago there were areas of the world where people had little opportunity and no hope, but much had been accomplished, although there were still great areas where people had little opportunity and little hope, and their objectives here were to give every man, woman, and child on this earth the possibility of security and well-being.

In a subsequent toast to the alliance between the three great powers, MARSHAL STALIN remarked that it was not so difficult to keep unity in time of war since there was a joint aim to defeat the common enemy which was clear to everyone. He said the difficulty came after the war when diverse interests tended to divide the allies. He said he was confident the present alliance would met this test also and it was our duty to see that it would

THE PRIME MINISTER then said he felt we were all standing on the crest of a hill with the glories of future possibilities stretching before us. He said that in the modern world the function of leadership was to lead the people out from the forests into the broad sunlit plains of peace and happiness. He felt that this prize was nearer our grasp than any time before in history and it would be a tragedy for which history would never forgive us if we let this prize slip from our grasp through inertia or carelessness.

Source: FRUS, 1945, *The Conferences of Malta and Yalta* (Dept. of State, Washington, DC, 1955, 717).

Extracts from the Yalta Conference, 6th Plenary Meeting

THE PRESIDENT said he would like to add one word. He felt that the elections was [sic] the crux of the whole matter, and since it was true, as Marshal Stalin had said, not only at home but also abroad, he would like to have some assurance for the six million Poles in the United States that these elections would be freely held, and he was sure if such assurance were present that elections would be held by the Poles there would be no doubt as to the sincerity of the agreement reached here . . .

THE PRESIDENT pointed out that the Declaration [on Liberated Europe] would of course apply to any areas or countries where needed as well as Poland.

THE PRIME MINISTER said he did not dissent from the President's proposed Declaration as long as it was clearly understood that the reference to the Atlantic Charter* did not apply to the British Empire. He said he had already made plain in the House of Commons that as far as the British Empire was concerned the principles already applied. He said he had given Mr Willkie [sic] [Wendell Wilkie, Republican presidential candidate 1940 and author of *One World*] a copy of his statement on the subject.

THE PRESIDENT inquired if that was what had killed Mr Willkie [sic].

Source: FRUS, 1945, *The Conferences of Malta and Yalta* (Dept. of State, Washington, DC, 1955, 848).

* Declaration on war aims issued by Churchill and Roosevelt in 1941 affirming the right of peoples to choose their form of government.

Sir Winston Leonard Spencer Churchill (1874–1965)

Son of Sir Randolph Churchill and an American mother Churchill was committed to a world characterized by cooperation between English speaking peoples. He saw nineteenth-century military service in the Sudan and India before being elected to Parliament as a Conservative in 1900. Opposed to Balfour and the party leadership he joined the Liberals in 1904 over the tariff reform issue and served as President of the Board of Trade, Home Secretary, First Lord of the Admiralty, and Minister for Munitions before the end of the First World War. When the war ended he became Colonial Secretary but lost his seat in 1922. In 1924 he effectively rejoined the Conservatives and returned to Parliament serving as Chancellor of the Exchequer where he alienated many workers with his stance over the 1926 General Strike. In 1931 Churchill resigned from the Shadow Cabinet over his opposition to Indian self-government and remained free to speak in opposition to the government's appeasement of Nazi Germany. In 1939 he was again appointed to the Admiralty until a Conservative revolt led to him becoming Prime Minister of a coalition government in 1940. An unconventional but brilliant wartime leader Churchill aroused fear and respect in large measure. Despite some unrealistic ideas he galvanized the war effort in all its aspects and, unlike some members of his party, realized the importance of cooperation with the Soviets and the necessity of involving the Americans in the war if Hitler was to be defeated. Defeated in the election of 1945 he returned victorious in 1951 and served as prime minister until 1955.

of power politics and high-minded rhetoric which lay at the heart of Yalta and subsequent attempts to reconcile two conflicting approaches to the new world order.

Yalta did see some progress towards Roosevelt's beloved United Nations Organization. Stalin's acceptance of American views on voting procedures produced agreement on the calling of a conference at San Francisco. It would prepare a charter for a general international organization for the maintenance of peace and security based on a Security Council of five permanent members (Britain, China, France, the Soviet Union, and the United States). This concession by Stalin matched a number of other concessions made by the Soviet leader: the acceptance of the Western request for French membership of the German Control Council, the commitment (particularly in Poland) to representative government and free elections in Europe, and the postponement of the reparations issue along with the issue of revising the Montreux Convention. No wonder that the British believed that Stalin had never been so obliging. In fact the issues discussed at Yalta were related much more to the vital interests of the Soviet Union than they were to the interests of Britain or the United States. In return for his concessions (although not part of an explicit bargain) Stalin had received territory on the Polish border in addition to that agreed with Hitler in the Baltic States and Bukovina (Romania) and in Asia. Part of this territory agreed at Yalta was in return for committing Soviet forces to the war against Japan and the rest was territory the British had long felt was rightly part of the Soviet Union. Subsequent dissatisfaction with Yalta came because of the large number of unresolved issues and, as was to be revealed, the fact that Stalin failed to abide by the Yalta agreements whenever their rhetoric clashed with the interests of the Soviet state, whether defined in terms of security or imperial ambitions.

B. From Yalta to Potsdam

From the point of view of the British and the Soviets the Yalta agreements were at odds with the agreements reached in October 1944 at Moscow regarding the exercise of British and Soviet influence in parts of Eastern and South-Eastern Europe. When, on 27 February 1945, the Soviets intervened in Romania to install a puppet regime under cover of a 'democratic front' government, the British could either regard this as a breach of Yalta or the implementation of the percentages agreement. It was an act, which bypassed the Allied Control Council and confirmed that, as in Italy, the occupying power was going to exercise effective control. If Britain were to dispute this, it would mean that the Soviets might challenge the exercise of British control in Greece. Romania did not thus become an issue in the early spring, unlike Poland, which had not been a subject of the Anglo–Soviet deal.

In the United States at the beginning of March, Roosevelt was proclaiming that Yalta had reversed the trend to a spheres of influence arrangement and provided hope for a free, independent, and prosperous Poland. It began to look as if Poland might provide an initial test case of whether the Soviets would abide by the rhetoric of the Yalta declarations or impose controls on parts of Central and Eastern Europe in line with an exclusive spheres of influence arrangement.

Stalin may have believed that a gesture to Western opinion would be sufficient to maintain the great power cooperation to which all three allies attached importance. Roosevelt may have believed that he could convince the American people that accepting the realities of military power and political influence was all part of a new idealistic world order. That was never tested due to the president's death in April 1945, and it is not possible to determine whether or not Roosevelt was set on a collision course with Stalin over the Soviet leader's initial refusal to abide by the Yalta agreements on Poland. Roosevelt's successor, the former Vice President, Harry Truman, had little or no knowledge of foreign affairs. He also lacked Roosevelt's chameleon-like character, which could represent different things to different people, and his political sleight of hand, which enabled him to keep abreast of public opinion and to manipulate supporters and opponents alike.

In stark contrast to Roosevelt, Truman's inexperience led him to give more weight to advisers within the State Department for whom his predecessor had little time. Thus the influence of those more inclined to confront the Soviet Union as an ideological opponent began to grow. Truman was more inclined to join the British in challenging the Soviets over Yalta. On 23 April Truman told the Soviet foreign minister in a famous confrontation that the Russians should stick to their agreements and, with the

German surrender in May, Lend Lease aid to Moscow was terminated. Yet Truman too was torn between an inclination to confront the Soviets and a desire to maintain cooperation and good relations. At the end of May the new president sent a close confidant of Roosevelt's, Harry Hopkins, to Moscow in an attempt to get agreement with Stalin over Poland. In defiance of what was said at Yalta, Stalin had neither held elections nor broadened the provisional government, but in response to the Hopkins mission (26 May–6 June) on 21 June the Soviet leader gave four non-Lublin Poles ministerial office. The letter of Yalta was now adhered to in terms of the composition of the Polish government and although the actual impact was negligible, for the Americans the problems of Poland no longer assumed centre stage. The Western democracies could hardly insist on elections in Eastern Europe when they had been unable to hold any in Western Europe.

However, it was not only in Europe that there was a clash between US principles and the Yalta agreements on the one hand, and Soviet desires to expand influence and control through spheres of influence arrangements on the other. The area of contention that emerged after the Hopkins mission was the Mediterranean where the British and Soviet empires had long competed for influence. Having given up exclusive control (but not effective domination) in Poland, the Soviets began to press for greater involvement in what had previously been an area of exclusive British influence. In June 1945 the Soviets expressed a desire to share in the international administration of Tangier, an important port in North-West Africa, and informed the Turks of their desire to have bases in the Straits of the Dardanelles. In the run up to the Potsdam Conference, the focus was not, as at Yalta, largely on Germany and those European areas of greatest concern to the Soviets, but other regions where British vital interests, as well as American principles, were at stake.

The Potsdam Conference Proceedings

At Potsdam, where Churchill was replaced towards the end of the conference by the newly elected Labour prime minister, Clement Attlee, there was

Harry S. Truman (1884–1972)

The son of a Missouri farmer Truman served in France during the First World War before starting a clothing business in Kansas City. After his business failed Truman entered politics in 1922 under the auspices of Kansas Party boss Thomas J. Prendergast and was chosen by him to stand for the Senate in 1934. On election Truman became a committed New Dealer and achieved fame as head of a Committee to investigate waste in military expenditure in 1940. Roosevelt manipulated his vice-presidential nomination as a compromise candidate between Henry Wallace, a northern liberal and James Byrnes, a southern conservative. On succeeding to the presidency Truman had little or no knowledge of foreign affairs and his greater reliance on the State Department officials shunned by Roosevelt has led some to conclude that Truman followed a more hard line policy towards the Soviets. Certainly this was the case by 1946 and the greater emphasis on confrontation produced the Truman Doctrine of March 1947. As a down-to-earth president with a tendency to 'shoot from the hip' Truman's Cold War policies in Europe with the Marshall Plan and the Berlin airlift are seen as great successes in contrast to his China policies which failed to prevent the loss of China to communism. Truman's unexpected electoral victory in 1948 was overshadowed by the triumph of Mao Tse-tung's forces, and his domestic Fair Deal programme of social reform was largely blocked by Congress. His determination to prevent a communist triumph in Korea led to the involvement of US forces in a bloody conflict with the Chinese and he remained committed to confronting the Soviets in both Europe and Asia.

more discussion of specific questions such as the resumption of diplomatic relations with the provisional governments of Germany's allies. Consequently more difficulties emerged. Sometimes the British and Americans agreed and sometimes the Americans and the Soviets agreed, but the British and the Soviets, almost always disagreed. The diplomatic conflict was initially an Anglo-Soviet one.[8] Significantly Stalin pointed out that while Britain and the United States were refusing to resume diplomatic relations with the non-elected governments of the former German satellites in the East, they had re-established relations with the unelected government in Italy. He was also unhappy about the lack of action against the extreme right-wing regime of General Franco in Spain.

The Western allies were naturally disturbed by the unilateral Soviet actions in East-Central Europe. The wartime brutality, economic devastation, and mass murder perpetuated by the Germans were followed by the reprisals of a Soviet regime whose recent history was steeped in atrocities and repression. The Russians were beginning the post-war economic subjugation of the Eastern European economies to Soviet recovery and removing industrial plant, notably oil equipment from Romania. More significant was the unilateral Soviet action in handing over to the Polish government responsibility for the administration of the newly acquired territory in the West up to the boundaries of the Western Neisse river.

Although this was a contentious issue at Potsdam and stored up trouble for the future, Allied disagreements in the second half of 1945 centred neither on Germany nor Poland. In order to avoid an open breach, differences on Germany were papered over with a firm agreement on reparations and on the principles of denazification, decentralization, and disarmament in governing Germany under the Allied Control Council. Decisions on the frontier between Germany and Poland were postponed until the final peace settlement, but it was accepted by all three powers that the territory up to the Western Neisse should in the meantime be administered as part of Poland. This added to the problems of transferring populations, and with these lands effectively removed from Germany it would not be possible, as initially assumed, to use their agricultural production to feed Germans. The administration of Germany as a single economic unit—a principle continued at Potsdam—would have to be done with a smaller food supply for the inhabitants of Germany's cities. In the event this was to force the British to pay for the importation of wheat to feed the starving inhabitants of their occupation zone which contained Germany's prime industrial region of the Ruhr.

No agreement could be reached on a number of other issues in addition to the acceptance of provisional governments in Romania and Bulgaria. The Soviets claimed a trusteeship, or involvement in a joint trusteeship, over Tripolitania, the western part of the Italian colony of Libya; this aroused British fears about Soviet ambitions in the Mediterranean which was seen as a vital part of Britain's imperial communications. Decisions on trusteeship and the fate of the Italian colonies (in Libya and the Horn of Africa) were to be taken by a Council of Foreign Ministers which was to be established to draw up peace treaties with Germany and its allies. The future of Tangier was to be considered by representatives of the three governments at a special conference. The third Mediterranean issue also failed to produce full agreement. It was accepted that the Montreux Convention should be revised, but Soviet claims for bases in the Straits, put forward on the grounds that the British had a base in Egypt in order to protect the Suez Canal, another important international waterway, were rejected. The British maintained that, because of the supreme importance of the Middle East and the Eastern Mediterranean to their empire, they could not accept an increase in Soviet influence in the region or allow their responsibilities for its defence to be replaced by arrangements of an international character.

The Potsdam Conference was longer and more troublesome than Yalta. Although all the participants remained keen to reach agreement, there were more disputes, more problems with detail, and more areas of the world discussed. While there was still no united Anglo-American front it was clear that, for the Soviets and the British, concerns about their post-war positions were going to make confrontation difficult to avoid. Soviet economic recovery was not going to be helped directly by America, the only solvent capitalist power. It could only be secured indirectly through the exploitation of the Soviet zone in Germany and the lands to the east of it. This in turn was likely to produce difficulties and require sacrifices by the Western allies if Germany were to be treated as a single economic unit.

The problems of reconciling American principles embodied in the rhetoric of Yalta with Soviet spheres of influence and territorial adjustments epitomized in the secret Yalta deal on the Far East remained. They were complicated by the British determination to preserve what they regarded as an exclusive sphere of influence in the Eastern Mediterranean and the Middle East. British officials debated whether it would be desirable to accept a Soviet sphere in areas of Eastern Europe in return for Soviet recognition of a British sphere in the Mediterranean and Middle East. These issues pertaining to the great powers' vital interests, prestige, and status were to become more acute at the first Council of Foreign Ministers held in London in September 1945 when US vital interests were first seriously challenged. By then the impact of the first atomic explosion, which took place during the Potsdam Conference, was a new factor in Allied relations.

C. **Atomic Diplomacy and the Councils of Foreign Ministers, 1945**

The first atomic test took place in the deserts of New Mexico on 16 July 1945. It was followed by the dropping of an atomic bomb on the Japanese city of Hiroshima on 6 August with a second bomb dropped three days later on Nagasaki. Accusations have been levelled against the Truman administration that the bombs were dropped for political rather than military reasons. The surrender of Japan, it is alleged, would have taken place anyway because of the terrible destructive power of the conventional carpet bombing being undertaken by the US Air Force. The Japanese economy was in tatters and an invasion of Japan was not planned to take place until November —so that the dropping of the atom bombs did not save many American lives. Therefore, it is argued, Truman dropped the bombs in order to impress the Soviet Union with the destructive power of the United States. Yet the fear of large-scale losses if the United States had to invade Japan was clearly present in the minds of US policy-makers. On the other hand,[9] it is certainly likely that Truman's secretary of state, James Byrnes, believed at Potsdam and at the London Council of Foreign Ministers that the bomb would enable the United States to pressure its allies into greater compliance with American post-war aims. It has also been suggested that the timing of the atomic attack on Japan was influenced by the Yalta agreement on the Far East according to which the Soviets had to enter the war against Japan by 8 August. If Japan surrendered before the Soviets entered the war, then there would be no grounds for implementing Roosevelt's old-fashioned territorial deal by which the Soviets acquired Southern Sakahlin and the Kurile Islands. And even if the Soviets did enter the war, an early Japanese surrender would reduce the impact the Red Army could make in the Far East and thereby reduce future Soviet influence.

There were both political and military arguments for the use of the bomb, but if the Americans were influenced by a desire to strengthen their diplomatic hand it proved at best ineffective. With Stalin an overtly suspicious, paranoid character, and all Soviet leaders inevitably insecure in the wake of the German assault, a US monopoly of the bomb was only likely to create more distrust. This distrust could feed on ideological differences, geopolitical rivalries, and the increasing problem, more in evidence at Potsdam than at Yalta, of universal acceptance of what each of the Allies regarded as their vital interests. These interests were reflected in general approaches to the post-war settlement and in the particular aspects of it which, along with Germany's future, they regarded as most important to their world roles.

The first indication of the US approach to an area it regarded as vital to American interests came when Japan offered to surrender on 11 August. In Germany as in other parts of Europe, Allied Control Councils had been set up to provide at least for the nominal involvement of the Big Three (and in Germany's case, France). In Japan, the United States, which had fought the Pacific War without British participation

in an Allied Command, initially refused to consider an Allied occupation agreement for Japan. This was a key area for the Americans because of Japan's industrial power, its strategic position in relation to access to the Pacific, and its large, highly educated population. Determined to secure a dominant post-war position there, they were reluctant to consider even the token involvement of the British or the Russians. A willingness to reject cooperation in order to protect what were seen as vital interests was shared by all members of the alliance. The more it was done, the more mistrust was created, which in turn reinforced the tendency to seek security on a unilateral basis rather than through compromise and cooperation.

The London Council of Foreign Ministers

From Potsdam onwards, while it is not possible to make any confident judgements on Soviet strategy, the British were no longer prepared to compromise for fear of jeopardizing their vital interests. This British concern was heightened by the growing consciousness of their weakness in economic and political terms compared to their Allies. To make concessions and compromises would threaten their position as one of the three great powers particularly if it increased the influence and importance of the Soviet Union. The Americans had not yet moved away from attempting to resolve issues through tripartite arrangements, but the British now believed their interests would be best protected by gaining the support of the United States in a common front against the Soviets. This was especially important with regard to the Mediterranean.

These problems became more evident at the first meeting of the Council of Foreign Ministers, which broke up in disagreement and revealed the first significant failure of post-war Allied cooperation. The Council of Foreign Ministers met under the terms and conditions laid down at Potsdam. It was to consist of the representatives of Britain, China, France, the Soviet Union, and the United States and was charged with drawing up the peace treaties with Germany's allies (Italy, Romania, Bulgaria, Hungary, and Finland) and preparing a peace settlement for a future German government. In discussing a particular peace treaty, the Council would be composed of members of those states which had signed the surrender agreement with the enemy state in question. The exception was Italy where France was to be regarded as a signatory of the surrender terms. In order to exclude China from European affairs, other members would only be invited to take part when matters directly concerning them were under discussion. But at the first meeting, the British foreign secretary, Ernest Bevin, requested a change to enable all powers to be present and to participate in the discussions but with only the signatories to the surrender terms having voting rights.

This having been agreed, there followed a wrangle over the agenda with the Americans not wanting to discuss Japan and the British not wanting to discuss Greece. If Romania was going to be on the agenda, the Soviet Foreign Minister, Vyacheslav Molotov, could see no reason why the situation in Japan and Greece should not be addressed, although under the terms of the Potsdam agreement they were outside the Council's remit. The French, who now entered high-level Great Power discussions for the first time since 1940, also wanted to discuss Germany, intending to press for territorial changes on Germany's western border. But the Big Three, who had discussed Germany quite fully at Potsdam, wished to leave discussions on the German peace treaty until other less complex treaties were signed. Unhappy at this situation, the French were to veto all measures by the Allied Control Council to treat Germany as a single unit and this called into question an important element of the Potsdam agreements. After this inauspicious start Italy was the first state to be dealt with and the first item on the agenda was the future of the Italian colonies. Libya was seen as vital by the British, who occupied most of the colony. They wanted not only the trusteeship of Cyrenaica (Eastern Libya) but to establish a new military base there and prevent the Soviet Union from being involved in the trusteeship arrangements for Tripolitania (Western Libya). After lengthy discussions no progress was made and the issue was passed to the foreign ministers' deputies and eventually to the United Nations. It was finally resolved with the independence of Libya in 1952. The conference then turned to Finland and Romania which the

Soviets saw as vital interests. Again no progress was made, with the Americans refusing to recognize the Romanian government as being broadly representative of all democratic elements.

If spheres of influence were ruled out and the Yalta agreements adhered to, it was perfectly understandable for the Americans, British, and French to complain about Soviet actions in Romania. However, if that was the case, then there was no sound argument for excluding the Soviets from Japan or from a trusteeship of an Italian colony. Soviet diplomacy seemed to have little room for manoeuvre. In this situation Molotov claimed that progress had been too slow and raised a procedural issue on which the Council broke down: the Soviets would no longer attend the Council unless the Potsdam agreements on Council procedure, which would exclude the French from discussing most peace treaties, were reverted to. From the Soviet point of view they had been outmanoeuvred, having agreed to change the Potsdam agreement in one case while the British and Americans were determined to stick by it in others.

The breakdown of the London Council revealed the determination of all the Allies to pursue their own power political interests even if they involved confrontation. The commitment to cooperation, whether out of principle or self-interest, was weakening and priority was being given to protecting vital interests. Trust was being eroded and suspicions developing. Crucially, the idea that the Allies could accept an international framework which met all their requirements and ambitions as great powers was proving unrealistic. The diplomatic battleground which was to become a Cold War was thus being laid out in power political terms.

However, the attempts at cooperation did not end at the London Council and some Western concessions were to be forthcoming, largely at the instigation of James Byrnes. American opinion had been upset by the London failure and Byrnes may have decided that the attempts to pressure the Soviets under the shadow of the atomic bomb had not worked and that it would still be possible to make progress with a more conciliatory stance. He instigated another Council in Moscow, confined to the Big Three, and offered the prospects of international cooperation over the use of atomic energy.

Bevin was not keen on such a meeting, preferring to build an Anglo-American front to convince the Soviets to modify their stance. He had now rejected any deal with the Soviets on spheres of influence because it would be damaging to Britain's international position: exclusion from large areas of East-Central Europe was deemed by the Foreign Office to be incompatible with great power status even if Britain's vital interests in the Middle East and Mediterranean were secured. The British foreign secretary argued that the Soviets had no need for a substantial European sphere of influence to offset the British position in the Mediterranean and Middle East because the Soviets had gained territory as a result of the war. Byrnes however was keen to compromise with the Soviets whatever the British view.

The Moscow Council in effect witnessed the last serious attempt at compromise between the Big Three but one which did not fundamentally alter power political realities. It thus proved possible, as in Poland, to achieve an agreement on the broadening of the provisional governments. In Romania a joint commission was to arrange for the inclusion of additional ministers which was duly done in February 1946. Bulgaria was trickier because elections had been held in the autumn of 1945 which were not regarded in the West as entirely free. The agreement therefore was to *advise* the Bulgarian government to include some members of the opposition. In return the United States accepted an Allied Control Council for Japan. When the conference ended, a proposal was also accepted for a United Nations Commission on the international control of atomic energy and on the resumption of peace negotiations in the full Council of Foreign Ministers. The desire for compromise had prevented the collapse of cooperation but by the end of 1945 the atmosphere was very different from Yalta.

The London and Moscow Councils clearly revealed that the issues which divided the Big Three, and which would lie at the heart of the Cold War, were of a global nature. Each power had vital interests to preserve: the US in Latin America and the Far East, the Soviets in Eastern Europe, and the British in the Mediterranean and Middle East. The principles and practices which were to be applied to the post-war world affected those interests which were linked to perceptions of global power and influence. The alliance experienced tensions because it proved difficult to reconcile vital interests within an agreed international framework. Principles and power politics were clashing and undermining cooperation; this was to assume much greater significance than previous great power rivalries because of the importance of ideology at the end of the Second World War.

At the end of 1945 the Soviets clearly saw the British as more antagonistic than the Americans despite the American position on the Romanian and Bulgarian governments. Cooperation with the Americans could be combined with attempting to drive a wedge between the two capitalist powers which Marxist ideology deemed in any case to be inevitable. Molotov complained bitterly about British actions in Greece and reasserted Soviet claims for bases in the Straits and for the return of two Turkish provinces (Kars and Ardahan) which had once been part of the Russian empire. From the Soviet point of view, it was vital for them to move forward with post-war economic recovery, and while the Americans agreed to assist the British, they were not prepared to treat the Soviets, or indeed the French in the same way. This was one factor which was to encourage assertive, unilateral action rather than tripartite cooperation. There was also the Soviet concern that backed by the atomic bomb the Americans were attempting to dictate the post-war settlement. The Soviets may have put forward claims for involvement in Tripolitania and Turkey in order to convince their Allies that a spheres of influence deal would be desirable. They may have been seeking recognition of their newly acquired importance as a great power. Or they may have been determined to extend their influence outside Eastern and Central Europe in an attempt to undermine British vital interests and hasten conflict within the capitalist world. Whatever Soviet aims may have been, and despite the American concessions in Moscow, their realization through cooperation was going to be difficult.

From the American perspective, the Soviets were failing to carry out the Yalta agreements that had been sold as the embodiment of a New World Order in which old-fashioned power politics were to be removed. Already by the autumn of 1945 serious questions were being raised in the US following the Soviet occupation of Southern Sakhalin and the Kuriles in line with the Yalta agreements. Senators and members of Congress were questioning the Democrats' role in appeasing the Soviets through the abandonment of American principles. James Byrnes was called to account before a Senate investigatory committee. Both Republicans and Democrats were concerned about policies they regarded as too soft on communism. At the end of November ambassador Patrick Hurley, an eccentric Republican right-winger, resigned over policy to China, calling the diplomats on his staff 'communist supporters'. Opinion polls were indicating that more and more Americans were less sympathetic to cooperation with the Soviets and supportive of a more assertive policy. The Soviets had reneged on some of the Yalta agreements and criticism of their ruthless and self-serving actions in Eastern Europe was mounting. Although the United States had no vital interests there, an American mission under Ethridge was sent to determine the facts in Romania and Bulgaria. The report was critical of Soviet actions and argued that representative government was necessary if peace was to be secured.

Spheres of influence would invite further conflict and encourage Soviet ambitions.

Truman had to confront his growing domestic difficulties from a weak position because of his lack of experience in foreign affairs. In addition he was in the unfortunate position of being a former protégé of his Secretary of State. He had tried the tough approach with the ending of Lend Lease and harsh criticism of Soviet bad faith and he had tried the conciliatory approach through the Hopkins mission. His decisions on which line to take after Potsdam were not helped by Byrnes's tendency to keep him in the dark about diplomatic moves and in particular about the concessions made at Moscow. With the criticism of the US role at Moscow mounting, Truman declared in early 1946 that he was 'tired of babying the Soviets'. The president appeared ready to embark on a more confrontational approach as public opinion became less willing to trust the Soviets. And it was in early 1946 that a crisis in Iran was to provide a basis for a confrontation that, for the first time, was firmly to unite the British and the Americans in open opposition to Soviet ambitions.

D. Growing Confrontation: The Near East and the Mediterranean

The Iranian Crisis 1946

As President Truman tired of babying the Soviets, a crisis was developing in Iran. From the Western perspective this would confirm the perception of the Soviet Union as an ambitious imperialist power. The Iranians were increasingly unhappy about the Soviet occupation of northern Iran which they feared would encourage Azerbaijani separatism and create pressure for oil concessions. Like the British, who occupied the southern part of the country, the Soviets were required, under the terms of the 1942 treaty, to end their occupation six months after the termination of hostilities. Based on the Japanese surrender, this would be on 2 March 1946. Before then, however, the Iranians complained to the

United Nations about Soviet interference in their internal affairs.

The British were keen to provide support and encouragement to the Iranians. They hoped to demonstrate to the Americans the need to resist a Soviet threat to an independent state, which also presented a threat to Britain's own imperial position in the Middle East and Mediterranean. Soviet imperialism in Iran was justified in Stalin's eyes by the alleged danger of Iranian sabotage of the Baku oilfields, by the fact that the British were refusing to withdraw troops from Greece and were occupying Egypt with more troops than permitted by the Anglo-Egyptian treaty. The fact that the British refused to discuss the Greek situation at the Moscow Conference in December 1945 may have reinforced the Soviet desire to retain the influence stemming from a military presence in Iran.

When the Soviets broke the 1942 agreement in March 1946, by not withdrawing their troops from Iran, both the British and the Americans urged the Iranians to renew their complaint to the UN Security Council. The Soviet Union was thus placed in an unfavourable international light. Moreover it had succeeded in uniting the British and the Americans against Soviet imperialism in a region where, unlike in Eastern and Central Europe, Soviet influence was bound to threaten Britain's imperial position. Stalin's ambitions had led the Americans, who had been genuinely suspicious of British imperialism, to support a common stance against the Soviet Union in a clash of rival imperialisms. This diplomatic blunder became more evident when the Soviets backed down in the face of British and American opposition and agreed to withdraw from Iran on 20 March. The reasons for this Soviet retreat remain unclear. The prospect of confrontation with a more powerful adversary possessing atomic weapons may have been a factor, as may have Stalin's fear of destroying future prospects of cooperation. Alternatively, Stalin may have assumed that his ambitions in Iran, including the securing of oil concessions, could be achieved at less cost through the creation of a separate state in Azerbaijan which the Russians were actively encouraging. Either way it was clear that the Soviets were averse to a serious international confrontation with the British and the Americans.

The Turkish Crisis 1946

In early 1946, Soviet ambitions presented another challenge to the Western powers. As in Iran the issue centred not on those European areas, which the Soviets had inevitably come to dominate as part of the effort to defeat Germany, but on areas outside Europe. Nothing had been heard from the Soviets since the summer of 1945 about their claims for bases in the Straits and the return of the former Russian provinces of Kars and Ardahan. Western concerns about Turkey therefore centred on the presence of Soviet troops in Bulgaria and the Trans-Caucasus, but as 1946 began there were fears in the US of a possible Soviet attempt to use military force to seize the Straits. The Soviet press was unremittingly hostile to Turkey and as a gesture of support, in February 1946, the United States sent the battleship *Missouri* to return the body of the Turkish ambassador. The situation remained tense throughout the spring as conflicting reports of Soviet troop movements were received in Washington. It is clear that Stalin, by a combination of military and non-military means, was seeking to exert pressure on the Turks before in August 1946 calling for a revision of Montreux and joint Soviet–Turkish defence of the Straits. This prompted a determined stand by the Truman administration, which, while accepting the need for the revision of Montreux warned against Soviet aggression against Turkey.

In Cold War terms the United States determination to assist Turkey (probably communicated to the Russians by the British spy Donald MacLean) was a reflection and reinforcement of a developing strategy, usually referred to as containment, that involved greater determination to confront the Soviets. Politically it was important to avoid further expansion of Soviet influence. Militarily it was believed that the Soviets could be stopped without risking a major conflict because Stalin was not in a position to wage a war in 1946. It was therefore necessary to make clear the importance attached by the American government to defending Turkey from Soviet encroachment. If the Soviets were convinced that their attempts to make gains in the Near East would be resisted, then it was likely, as proved to be the case with both Turkey and Iran, that the status quo would be maintained and the Soviets would back down. Thus the issue was the prevention of Soviet expansion into areas not already dominated by the Russians as a result of the war. Unfortunately this was not a line which could easily be sold to the Western public who were more concerned about predominantly European issues and who therefore had to be convinced that the Soviet Union expanded after, not during, the war.

E. Containment, Confrontation, and the Truman Doctrine, 1946–1947

During the Iranian crisis in the first two months of 1946, other developments revealed the increasingly confrontational approach adopted by the three former allies. In January and February, Soviet attacks on British policy became more hostile. The idea that cooperation was impossible with capitalist powers was reinforced in Stalin's 9 February address to the Supreme Soviet which claimed that economic competition under capitalism made war inevitable. The British Foreign Office's response was to create the Russia Committee to examine how best to reply to what was seen as a Soviet propaganda offensive. Britain and the Soviet Union, like the Truman administration, were beginning to put confrontation, propaganda, and the protection of vital interests before cooperation and compromise.

Developments in the United States centred on the famous Long Telegram sent from Moscow by George Kennan two weeks after Stalin's speech. By then opinion polls showed that the numbers of Americans who believed in the possibility of co-operation with the Soviet Union had fallen, from the 54 per cent of September 1945 to 34 per cent. Kennan had been a long-time critic of Roosevelt's policy of cooperation with the Soviet Union because he believed the nature of the Soviet system demanded a hostile approach to the outside world. In other words Soviet foreign policy would essentially be dictated not by external developments but by ideological imperatives geared to promoting what Moscow believed would be the inevitable collapse of capitalism.

As early as February 1945, Kennan had urged the division of Europe into spheres of influence based on a line beyond which the expansion of Soviet power would not be permitted. Now, one year later, Kennan urged firm action on the part of the Western powers to confront and contain a Soviet state deemed ideologically averse to cooperation with the capitalist West. Kennan believed containment was necessary because cooperation with a state ideologically committed to the destruction of capitalist democracy

was impossible. Thus at the beginning of March 1946, US domestic opinion, Soviet defiance of its treaty agreements in Iran, and an extensive analysis of Soviet attitudes to the West all pointed America to a policy of greater confrontation. In the British embassy in Moscow Frank Roberts, who had always favoured a spheres-of-influence deal in 1945, now became concerned about the implications of any such arrangements. With the Soviets more and more interested in areas outside Europe, especially the Mediterranean and Middle East, any concessions there, even to legitimate Soviet aims, would be interpreted as a severe setback to Britain throughout the Arab world. Roberts saw prestige and security considerations intermingling in the Middle East and Soviet security could not be achieved without damaging British or American interests.[10] In early 1946 both Kennan and Roberts saw advantages in containment through confrontation rather than a spheres-of-influence deal involving concessions to the Soviets. For the Truman administration, while attempts at cooperation were not to be abandoned in 1946, from now on, cooperation was only desirable on American terms. US policy to the Soviets was now in line with that advocated by the British in 1945 and again it was Middle Eastern rather than European issues which had had the most important influence on policy.

Kennan's idea on the implementation of containment was based on securing the world's important industrial areas. The advance of Soviet communism at the expense of capitalism could be prevented if this could be achieved. Kennan, like most policy-makers in the US, was not afraid of the Soviet Union deliberately starting a global war. What most concerned the Americans and British was the spread of Soviet influence and control on the basis of communist political successes. Churchill, who reinforced the moves to confrontation/containment in early March 1946 with his Iron Curtain speech in Fulton Missouri, emphasized this point. While criticizing the nature and extent of

Soviet actions in Eastern and Central Europe, the former British prime minister, in Truman's presence, referred to the Soviet desire to achieve the fruits of war while avoiding military conflict.

The condemnation of Soviet actions in Central and Eastern Europe was linked to the growing realization of the ruthless nature of the persecution and economic exploitation they entailed. A satellite empire had not yet been fully consolidated as the strict Soviet controls that were eventually to be imposed were not in evidence outside Romania. The prospect of such an empire presented a threat to the British position as a great power with European-wide interests and to American perceptions of the new European order. Yet fear of the extension of Soviet military power and/or political influence into areas like the Mediterranean and Middle East remained more important in 1946 than developments in Eastern Europe, as it would constitute Soviet post-war expansion rather than wartime gains. However, by April when the next session of the Council of Foreign Ministers met in Paris, Soviet demands were reduced when Molotov supported the French idea of returning the Italian colonies to Italy as compensation for its proposed loss of Trieste. Again the Soviets appeared willing to bargain in the Mediterranean while the British were adamant that no concessions should be contemplated that might threaten their vital interests and great power status. It still proved impossible to reach agreement at the first session of the Paris Council prior to the formal opening of the actual Paris Peace Conference. A second Council had to meet in Paris and a further one in New York before peace treaties with Germany's allies could be finalized at the end of 1946.

British interests continued to centre on the Mediterranean and Middle East where, over the issue of the Dardanelles, they now had American support. The Soviets were aware that in that region Britain believed it had vital interests and were prepared to back down. In areas of Central and Eastern Europe, however, where the Soviets believed they had vital interests, there was to be no retreat in the face of Anglo-American pressure. This growing confrontation was exacerbated by the failure to secure agreement on future international controls over the use of atomic energy. In March 1946 the Acheson–Lilienthal proposal provided for a transition period

to international control during which the United States would retain its advantageous position as the only power with nuclear weapons. The American proposals seemed to be based on a determination to preserve the dominant US position until international arrangements were in place which would prevent the Soviets securing any advantage. Moscow's position was that existing stocks of weapons should be dealt with as a precursor to future controls. In 1946 suspicion and mistrust were gathering pace even though there were still some signs of a willingness to compromise on both sides. In 1947, this willingness was to disappear and confrontation was eventually to lead to the end of efforts at cooperation.

One element in this scenario was the importance of propaganda. If both sides were, in effect, to insist that the maintenance of cooperation could only be on their terms, it was important to convince the rest of the world that the other side was to blame if cooperation proved impossible. Thus when the attempts to produce a post-war settlement at the Paris Peace Conference became public, the propaganda battle was joined in earnest and by the end of 1947 was to become of much greater significance in the conduct of the Cold War. For both the United States and the Soviet Union 1947 was to be a crucial year when fears of losing control over their respective European satellites or areas of influence reached such an extent that priority was accorded to the consolidation of Europe into two opposing blocs. The key events in the abandonment of cooperation and the start of an unremitting propaganda campaign were the failure to reach agreement on the future of Germany and the discussions on the Marshall Plan to provide American economic aid to Europe. They were to lead to an extension of Soviet control in Eastern Europe and to the modification of the doctrine of containment in the United States.

The Truman Doctrine

Often portrayed as the defining moment for the American strategy of containment, Truman's famous speech delivered in March 1947 can also be seen as a substantial modification of a previously defensive doctrine, which eventually opened the door to all kinds of proactive US actions throughout the globe. Its origins lay in the general sense of economic crisis in Europe which developed during the winter of 1946–7, but also in the specific problems faced by Turkey and Greece. While the Soviets had been unsuccessfully endeavouring to intimidate the former in 1945, Stalin had largely ignored Greece, despite the initial opportunity presented by a large communist-dominated left-wing opposition and a civil war. The conflict which began in 1944 and led to armed British intervention was renewed in 1946, when the Left reacted to the persecution of opposition groups by the British-backed government, and was to continue until 1949. The lack of Soviet interference prior to 1947 reflected a desire to appease the British and uphold the percentages agreement which would increase the prospects for continued cooperation on the basis of agreed spheres of influence. Nevertheless, the cost of the British efforts to contain the conflict and create long-term stability was becoming too high to bear by the end of 1946.

The difficulties facing Greece and other areas of Western Europe were part of the general problem of post-war reconstruction, made more difficult by the failure to cooperate over the economic future of Germany. The Soviet desire to maximize the exploitation of all of Eastern Europe, ended the pre-war East to West trade in agricultural produce. The problem was made worse by the Soviets handing over to Polish administration the agricultural lands between the Eastern and Western Neisse. Thus there was less food to feed the Germans in the West than the British and Americans had anticipated. A poor harvest in 1946 was followed by a desperately harsh winter and it became clear that the post-war US loans to individual countries in Western Europe would not meet the needs of recovery. Fears of an economic collapse were exacerbated by the probability that already strong communist movements in the West would seize the opportunity presented by the apparent failure of capitalism. The link between economic hardship and greater opportunities for the spread of communism was to remain central to the worldview of Western elites for many years after 1945.

If economic hardship was to be mitigated, two immediate problems had to be confronted. One was the general imbalance in world markets resulting from the wartime disruption of previous global trade patterns and the consequent dominance of the United States as a supplier of industrial goods and foodstuffs. The other was the economic revival of Germany which was deemed necessary for the recovery of the rest of Western Europe. With German production levels only a third of what they were in 1936, and with no food supplies from the territory in the east now controlled by Poland, basic foodstuffs were having to be imported into the Western zones. This not only exacerbated the trade imbalance and contributed to a serious dollar gap[11] by the end of 1946, but imposed further economic hardship on the occupying powers. These problems contributed to the British decision, communicated to Washington in February 1947, to end their economic and military assistance to Greece and Turkey.

The United States were than faced with a number of difficulties. The future of the capitalist world economy was in doubt and with it the capacity of the United States to ensure that the economic expansion of the wartime years was maintained. If there was a serious trade imbalance, a worldwide recession could ensue, as many countries would not have the dollars to purchase American goods and foodstuffs. The serious crisis in Europe, particularly Germany, would threaten the successful implementation of George Kennan's strategy of preserving important areas of economic strength for the capitalist, as opposed to the communist, world. Finally, Turkey and Greece would be left more exposed to Soviet pressure and interference if British assistance was not replaced. One way in which all these problems could be tackled was the provision of US economic aid on a large scale. Unfortunately these problems came to a head just after a Republican Congress had been elected and was committed to a policy of tax-cutting and retrenchment.

On the international front, although some progress had been made with the treaties with Germany's allies tensions continued to grow as confrontation made compromise unlikely. These tensions and problems made it more difficult to draw up a German peace treaty, which had yet to be tackled in detail by the Council of Foreign Ministers. The West, because of the economic difficulties in running their zones, was already moving towards the division of Germany and the consolidation of the Western zones (see Chapter 2, D). It was an option which offered the largest economic advantages and the smallest geopolitical risks. Both sides were fully aware that if cooperation could not be maintained it was far better to extend control over their own spheres in Germany than to risk a united Germany coming under the influence of a potentially hostile power or bloc.

From the American perspective, if Germany was to be divided there was little prospect of eventually securing the kind of European settlement in line with their ideals. The Soviets had indicated in 1945, as before, that there was little chance of democratic governments in the Western sense emerging in Romania, Bulgaria, or Poland. What was now at issue were the future prospects of Western Germany and Western Europe which might fall prey to a political ideology that would threaten the socio-economic system on which Western elites depended. Consolidating influence and control in the West therefore became more important than applying principles in the East. In these circumstances the disadvantages of escalating confrontation were much less than the risks of standing aside from the specific crises in Greece and Turkey and the more general crisis in Western Europe. (Similar considerations about the risk of not taking action in parts of Eastern Europe were likely to have influenced Stalin in 1947.) By then a more determined stance against communism also offered domestic political benefits for the Truman administration, because the more the threat was played up, the more likely it was that Congress would provide the money to aid Western Europe.

The result was a speech by Truman on 12 March 1947, which universalized the conflict then confronting the free world in Greece and Turkey. In the Greek case a civil war was represented as part of a global struggle. Moreover, the speech portrayed the struggle in a general manner without specifying whether it emanated from the military threat of a rival state, a political ideology connected to a rival great power, or an economic threat to American business. Unlike any previous conflict in history between competing states, dynastic rivals, or other forms of government, according to Truman, the United States was engaged in a worldwide battle between two different ways of life. What became known as the Truman Doctrine proclaimed that 'One way of life is based on the will of the majority, and is distinguished by free institutions, representative government, free elections, guarantees of individual liberty, freedom of speech and religion and freedom from political oppression. The second way of life is based upon the will of a minority forcibly imposed upon the majority. It relies upon terror and oppression, a controlled press and radio, fixed elections and the suppression of personal freedoms.' The United States therefore had 'to support free peoples who are resisting attempted subjugation by armed minorities or by outside pressures'.

The Truman Doctrine was not a response to an unforeseen or new situation as the United States had already sent $260 million dollars of aid into Greece in 1946. Moreover concern over Greece increased after the Truman Doctrine because of Yugoslav involvement and the greater Soviet commitment to support communist subversion in the West from the autumn of 1947. It was more a calculated attempt to instil fear into the American population and their representatives in order to procure aid on a much larger scale.[12] In this aim it was astonishingly successful in the short term but it sowed the seeds of a policy which would have unfortunate long-term consequences. By implying that the United States had unlimited responsibilities to assist all those who were allegedly resisting a challenge to the American way of life, the Truman Doctrine opened the door to intervention in any civil war. As long as one of the participants could be portrayed as sympathetic to communism, then an internal conflict would become part of a global struggle against the Soviets and require US involvement. In addition, threats to the American way of life could emanate from within the United States and the invocation of such threats, however far-fetched and imaginary, could be exploited for political benefit. In the long term the United States was to pay a heavy price abroad for the development of an ideology of global dimensions which defined security in extremely broad terms. In the short term the impact of the Truman Doctrine was much more significant within the United States than it was on Soviet foreign policy. Stalin seemed unperturbed by the US president's proclamation.

Actions rather than words always meant more to Stalin, and the forthcoming Moscow Conference still offered the prospect of an advantageous agreement on Germany. It was not until the Moscow Conference proved fruitless and the Americans produced the Marshall Plan to aid Europe as a whole, that Soviet policy underwent a decisive shift which effectively meant the abandonment of cooperation. It was to be replaced not just by confrontation and a significant tightening of Soviet political control over Eastern Europe, but by increasing efforts to weaken the Western hold over the other half of the continent. Particular attention was to be given to preventing the rebuilding of the Western zones of Germany as part of an anti-Soviet bloc. Similarly, by the end of the year the United States, having devised a strategy for aiding the recovery of Western Europe in line with American economic interests, had begun the construction of a national security state. This was to be followed by policies to weaken the Soviet position in its sphere of influence in Eastern Europe. Whether such strategies can best be seen as the beginning or the end of containment remains a debatable Cold War question.

NOTES

1. US National Archives, Charles Papers, Box 4, memorandum 18 Oct. 1945. Cited in W. LaFeber, *Inevitable Revolutions. The United States and Central America* (New York, W.W. Norton, 1984), 89.

2. The distinction between genuine military security requirements and the requirements of expansionist imperial states is often impossible to make. To approach such matters objectively it is safest to assume that all great powers are seeking to maximize their power and influence through territorial means or by direct or indirect control over the governments of less powerful states.

3. See Foreign Relations of the United States (FRUS), 1943, *The Conferences at Cairo and Tehran* (Dept. of State, Washington, DC, 1961).

4. *New York Times*, 3 March 1945.

5. B. Kuniholm, *The Origins of the Cold War in the Near East* (Princeton University Press, Princeton, 1980), 129.

6. The Curzon line was drawn up on general ethnic lines, with some inevitable exceptions, by Lord Curzon and the French prime minister, Clemenceau, after the First World War.

7. FRUS, 1945, *The Conferences at Malta and Yalta* (Dept. of State, Washington, DC, 1955, 781).

8. Fraser J. Harbutt, *The Iron Curtain: Churchill, America, and the Origins of the Cold War* (Oxford University Press, New York, 1986), 115.

9. R. L. Messer, *The End of an Alliance: James F. Byrnes, Roosevelt, Truman and the Origins of the Cold War* (University of North Carolina Press, Chapel Hill, 1982), 127.

10. Robert's views can be found in FO 371/47882, Roberts to Warner, 13 May 1945; FO 371/47856, Roberts to FO, 28 Sept. 1945; FO371/52327, Roberts to Bevin 16 Jan. 1946.

11. The dollar gap was the result of a devastated Europe being unable to produce sufficient goods to sell to the dollar zone to gain the currency to purchase much needed imports.

12. W. LaFeber, *America, Russia and the Cold War 1945–2000* (McGraw-Hill, New York, 9th edn., 2002), 52–3.

2 Two Worlds East and West, 1945–1948

By the end of 1947 the establishment of two opposing blocs was largely in place. Whether this was essentially an ideological, economic, or military confrontation is still a matter of contention. Moreover, historical understanding of this confrontation has been made more difficult by the Cold War itself. It has produced worst-case assumptions of the threats each side faced and claims that only one side had reason to be concerned. The evidence suggests that both sides had reason to be concerned and that in private these concerns were often genuine but they were not predominantly military ones. The historical explanation of the emergence of the two blocs needs to be removed from the linear, aggressive action/defensive response model that ultimately produced military confrontation. If we want fully to understand the ambitions, and particularly after 1947, the concerns of both sides, we need to look beyond arms build ups and the military dimension of power politics.

Traditional concepts of power in the economic and military sense were combined with ideologies and their translation into a world order based on liberal or socialist values. These were in tune with the deeper currents and traditions of elite culture including the general preservation of domestic status and not just the specific economic interests which helped realize and preserve it. In this sense Soviet elites lacked the historical memories of their Western counterparts and a clear conception of how the world could be moulded to reflect both their country's status and their own values and privileges. For elites in the West who felt threatened in 1947, a way of life at home was firmly linked, particularly in the United States, to an international order embodying values (however self-interested) as well as power.

At the heart of these values in 1947 was the establishment of a liberal order which would involve the global dominance of a capitalist economy based on multilateral trade. If this failed, a liberal international order would not win mass acceptance. With Western Europe unable to generate the means to recover, a free and unregulated market economy was more likely to create chaos than prosperity. Action was therefore required by the United States, not just in American economic interests, but in the interest of a new international liberal order which had been planned for by the United States in universal terms even before the attack on Pearl Harbor. Crucially events propelled the United States into a position to link its power with a crusading ideology at the appropriate historical moment. In the Soviet Union the events of the 1940s, and particularly the wartime devastation, inclined elites to concentrate less on the global and the universal than on the domestic and the regional. In ideology as in most other things the Soviets were on the back foot and while the Marshall Plan could offer both ideological and practical advantages the Soviets could offer nothing of the latter.

A. The Marshall Plan and the Western Economic System

The Origins of the Marshall Plan

The Marshall Plan was without doubt a key turning point in the development of the two blocs and the origins of the Cold War although some historians see it more as a watershed than others. On the political level it was both a cause and a consequence of growing fears and tensions. On the economic level its origins can be traced to long-held American perceptions of the kind of international economy that would bring prosperity and avoid war. Its consequences stemmed from the threat it presented to Soviet status and influence and to the maintenance of a rival socio-economic system to capitalism. This unprecedented American aid package sought to ward off the threat of communism in Western Europe and to ensure that the post-war American economy was not sent into recession by unfavourable economic conditions. The Marshall Plan was thus partially geared to the requirements of US businesses and to the problems facing the American economy which had expanded dramatically during the Second World War.

The American planners, who began their attempts to define a new international order even before the United States entered the War, were clearly influenced by ideas that war in general developed from unfair economic competition. Both Cordell Hull, the US Secretary of State until late 1944 and Sumner Welles, Roosevelt's key foreign policy adviser until the autumn of 1943, believed that state power should not be used to exercise control over resources. Imperial trading blocs were deemed to lead to military confrontations and war. Hull and Welles were not advocates of free trade but of the elimination of discriminatory tariffs and quotas which allowed some nations privileged access to markets and resources. They sought ways to promote greater commercial access to all areas of the globe and to facilitate multilateral trade. During the War, at Bretton Woods in New Hampshire in July 1944, a system was put in place to do just that. The Bretton Woods agreements were endorsed by forty-four nations and led to the establishment of an International Bank for Reconstruction and Development (the World Bank) and an International Monetary Fund (IMF). The former was designed to provide reconstruction loans and to promote private investment, while the latter was designed to prevent currency difficulties hampering international trade. Thus if a nation found itself suffering from temporary balance of payments difficulties, the IMF would provide the requisite currency loans which would encourage and facilitate multilateral rather than bilateral trade. The system was effectively underpinned by the strength of the dollar, which was exchangeable for gold, and by the economic power of the United States, which as the main provider of funds was able to dominate both institutions. The World Bank has always had an American president and one-third of the World Bank's money and one-third of the votes in both institutions are exercised by the United States.[1]

Despite this, the World Bank and the IMF, like the Marshall Plan which followed them, were not without opponents in the United States. All were seen as embodying the New Deal ideology of government controls and interference. It was the influence

European Integration and the Origins of the Marshall Plan

The MARSHALL PLAN rested squarely on American conviction that European economic recovery was essential to the long-term interests of the United States. These interests were interdependent and mutually reinforcing, so much so that public officials saw little need to rank them in the order that subsequent historians have tried to establish. They included economic interests. Policy-makers in the Truman administration were convinced that a 'dynamic economy' at home required American trade and investment abroad, which in turn required the reconstruction of major trading partners in Europe and their reintegration into a multilateral system of world trade. Those requirements summed up a world-view rooted in political convictions as well as economic interests. American leaders envisioned an open international economy founded on the principles of liberal capitalism, such as free trade and equal opportunity. But they also equated these principles with democratic forms of government, associated autarkic economic policies with totalitarian regimes, and assumed that 'enemies in the market place' could not be 'friends at the council table.' 'The political line up followed the economic line up,' as Cordell Hull once put it.

Source: Michael J. Hogan. *The Marshall Plan: America, Britain and the Reconstruction of Western Europe, 1947–1952* (Cambridge University Press, Cambridge, 1987), 26. Citing US, Office of the Federal Register, *Public Papers of the Presidents of the United States: Harry S. Truman, 1947* (Washington, 1963), 37; Thomas G. Paterson, *Soviet-American Confrontation: Post-War Reconstruction and the Origins of the Cold War* (Johns Hopkins University Press, Baltimore, 1973), 4 (for the second quotation); and Cordell Hull, *The Memoirs of Cordell Hull*, 2 vols. (Hodder & Stoughton, New York, 1948), I: 364.

of what the leading Marshall Plan historian has called the 'New Deal coalition' which was central to American attempts to define a new economic order at home and abroad. 'A bloc of capital-intensive firms and their allies amongst labour, farm, financial and professional groups' desired a new, world economic system. This would be founded on 'self-governing economic groups integrated by institutional coordinators and normal market mechanisms, led by cooperating public and private elites, nourished by limited but positive government power, and geared to an economic growth in which all could share.'[2] These ideals and interest groups linked the Bretton Woods system and the American efforts to rebuild Western Europe. They would have influenced American policy irrespective of the existence or ideology of the Soviet Union.

However, the ideological challenge mounted by the Soviets, especially if presented as a more sinister military threat, was a useful weapon for those wishing to use American economic power to create an integrated market for European goods that would serve the interests of US exporters. The fear that the American recovery from the Depression of the 1930s would be thwarted if new world markets were not secured was a real if largely groundless one. The vast expansion of the US economy, in which the trade surplus at the end of the War was greater than the total of US exports in the Depression, fuelled these fears. When it became obvious by the end of 1946 that the European dollar shortage had not been solved by the initial American loans, short-term self-interest reinforced the long-term goals of remodelling Western European economies as part of a new international economic order.

Whether the primary aim of the Marshall Plan was to enable the American economy to dominate Western Europe as part of a multilateral trading system, whether it was geared to the long-held views of specific interest groups on a new economic world order, or whether it was a reaction to growing fears about the spread of communism, all such aims and concerns were mutually reinforcing. Republican opponents of the New Deal were more likely to swallow the government expenditure involved if the Marshall Plan had a political goal, vividly represented in the Truman Doctrine, of defeating Soviet communism. Fighting communism and Soviet ambitions were more likely to be supported if American exporters and the US economy in general would benefit as a result.

Whatever the motivation, it has been argued that Western Europe did not need large-scale American aid and that certain countries were well on the road to recovery.[3] The American drive for European integration may have contained elements of self-interest and economic imperialism. However, any US attempt to consolidate Western Europe under its auspices at least offered something to attract European governments into a voluntary association. In contrast the further consolidation of a Soviet sphere in Eastern Europe, which followed the Marshall Plan, offered economic asset-stripping and political repression as a means of preserving Soviet dominance. It was only later that Soviet imperialism achieved the unique distinction of an Empire in which many inhabitants of the periphery were generally better off than their metropolitan equivalents.

The Implementation of the Marshall Plan and its Consequences

A US plan to provide economic aid to Europe was announced by the American Secretary of State, George Marshall, in a speech on 5 June 1947. It was followed by a conference in Paris later in the month of the British, French, and Soviet Foreign Ministers. It was expected in Washington that the Europeans would take the initiative in coordinating a more specific response to Marshall's general proposal. The Soviets attended because they saw the prospect of capital for much needed reconstruction and initially encouraged Eastern European countries to respond positively. There were, however, those in the Soviet government who saw the Plan as an attempt to undermine their position in Germany and Eastern Europe. Confronted with firm British and French intentions (which they never fully carried out) to produce a combined set of aid requirements rather than a series of country-based proposals, Molotov became more convinced that the main American aim was the creation of an anti-Soviet bloc including the revived Western zones of Germany. As a result, and much to the relief of the Truman administration, the Soviets walked out of the Paris meeting and subsequently exerted sufficient pressure on Eastern European countries for them not to become involved. The Plan was never designed by the United States to encompass all of Europe *and* the Soviet Union, but for domestic political reasons it would have been difficult to deny particular countries the opportunity to participate. Had the offer been taken up by the Soviet bloc, it is unlikely that Congress could have been persuaded to vote the necessary

funds. As it was a $4 million aid package for sixteen Western European nations was approved in March 1948 when the Economic Co-operation Act was passed.

The Cold War consequences of the Marshall Plan were momentous. It reflected the American belief that the economic rebuilding of Western Europe, which required an economic contribution from Western Germany, was more important than attempting to maintain cooperation with the Soviets. Exactly the same conclusions were drawn in Moscow where it was assumed that the Plan was designed to draw Western and Eastern Europe into the American economic orbit thereby isolating the Soviet Union and creating a revived, united Germany. Stalin believed that even limited co-operation with the West was now impossible because the Marshall Plan was seen as a serious threat. Unlike the restrained Soviet response to the Truman Doctrine, after which the Soviets had agreed to Americans proposals to speed the work of a commission to form an interim German government, there was now a very different reaction.[4] The response was to end cooperation in the commission and prepare to strengthen the Soviet hold over Eastern Europe which by February 1948 was to extend to Czechoslovakia, the only country in which Western-style democracy had been preserved in the inter-war years.

According to one historian, the Soviet response to the Marshall Plan was essentially defensive. Soviet leaders saw their war-devastated country as weak, and were therefore unwilling to embark on a confrontation with the West.[5] It may well have been the case that this confrontation was inevitable given the obstacles to agreement on the future of Europe, and that at some point the Soviet attempt to preserve token coalition governments in Eastern Europe for the sake of appearances would have ended and rigid controls been imposed from Moscow (see Chapter 2, B). Nevertheless it was the Marshall Plan that influenced the timing of these developments. In July the Molotov Plan, a series of bilateral agreements linking the Soviet Union with Eastern European countries, became the economic response to Marshall's offer and the forerunner of the Council for Mutual Economic Assistance (COMECON) established in 1949

The political response was coordinated at a meeting of communist leaders at Szlarska Poreba in September 1947. Here the Communist Information Bureau (COMINFORM) was established to provide Moscow with the institutional means to control foreign communist parties and formally to end co-operation with other non-fascist parties. Zhdanov spoke of the creation of two camps, and although there was one last attempt at cooperation at the London Council of Foreign Ministers in November and December 1947, the Marshall Plan was the decisive catalyst for the division of Europe. Both sides had concluded that it was more important to maintain their preferred economic and political systems in one-half of a divided Europe than to co-operate in creating a united Europe that would risk a reunited Germany siding with their ideological rival.

A satisfactory resolution of the German problem was another goal of the Marshall Plan and European economic integration. Tying the western zones of Germany into a system of economic cooperation would help prevent the revival of German economic power (see Chapters 2, D and 4, C). Although the Organization of European Economic Cooperation (OEEC), which was established in March 1948 to deal with Marshall Aid, was not a supra-national body, it was the first stage of a process that ultimately aimed to revive the German economy while limiting German economic independence. The OEEC lacked the power to make policy independently of the sixteen national governments it represented, but it provided institutional evidence of the West's commitment to European economic recovery.

For the US administration, the Marshall Plan at one stroke offered a way to bring the long-held New Deal vision of a new international economic order a step nearer realization, a way to reduce the security risks of German recovery, and a way to make it more difficult for communists to take control of Western European governments. For the Soviet Politburo the Marshall Plan was seen as an American attempt 'to restore the economy of Germany and Japan pro-

vided it is subordinated to the interests of American capital'. As a result Germany would be linked to the 'forces of capitalist encirclement'. In the United States George Kennan published an article in *Foreign Affairs* in July 1947 under the pseudonym Mr X which claimed that Stalin was determined to overthrow all Western governments, and that the only counter to this would be the 'adroit and vigilant application of counterforce at a series of constantly shifting geographical and political points'.[6]

It is difficult to assess how far these interpretations stemmed from genuine fears or from a perceived propaganda need to maximize the threat of the other side. The rooting out of Stalin's internal opponents could be justified on the grounds that they were linked to Western imperialist forces encircling the Soviet Union. In the West, by the end of the decade the Truman administration was under fire for not rooting out alleged communist sympathizers, particularly those in the government service. By early 1950, Senator Joe McCarthy of Wisconsin was conducting a campaign of hate and vilification based on lies and accusations that would not have been out of place in Stalin's regime. McCarthyism was to lead to a loss of livelihood for a number of American officials and to an atmosphere in the United States in which any contact with left-wing ideologies or governments was deemed unacceptable. Even moderate US opinion tended to regard Marxist-based political opposition to capitalism as undermining the security of the state. Overseas, in parts of the French and British empires after 1947 (see Chapter 3, A and B), as in Soviet controlled Eastern Europe, the alleged aims of the new enemy were used to justify repressive measures to maintain internal stability or to win support for the status quo. And this stability was seen to be important precisely because the attempts by both sides to maintain it were interpreted as an attempt to undermine the other's ability to do so in its areas of control. This is what national security (or old and new imperialisms), the Truman Doctrine, the Marshall Plan, and the COMINFORM had produced by the end of 1947.

B. The Soviet Takeover of Eastern and Central Europe

The origins of Soviet policy towards Eastern Europe can be traced back to before the Second World War but its nature and motivation remain intense sources of controversy. Newly released documents from the former Soviet Union have not lessened the arguments. At the heart of the debate is the extent to which Stalin sought remorselessly to extend Soviet controls as part of a grand scheme for European or even world domination. Views on this are bound to influence explanations of the Cold War, for the more determined and coherent Stalin's ambitions were, the more justifiable it becomes to see Western actions as a response to Soviet ambitions or, to employ the most common term, Soviet expansionism. Those who favour such explanations can point to the Nazi–Soviet pact of 1939 and the subsequent Soviet occupation of Eastern Poland and seizure of

Northern Bukovina (part of Romania). These actions were then followed by attempts to win Nazi approval for further territorial gains and influence. Stalin vainly endeavoured to secure greater influence over Finland, to make Bulgaria part of a Russian security zone, to acquire military bases in the Dardanelles, to establish a Russo–Danish condominium over the Baltic Straits, and to annex southern Bukovina while securing a special interest in Hungary, Yugoslavia, and Greece.

Such goals bear some resemblance to the kind of situation created at the end of the War by Soviet arms, but in 1940 they were the product of desperate Soviet diplomacy in the face of gathering German power. What Stalin would have liked, what he could obtain, and what he saw as bargaining counters, have always to be carefully distinguished as elements

---

Soviet Reaction to the Marshall Plan

There is little evidence that before the Marshall Plan Stalin had any master plan for immediate expansion. He had to digest what he had already gained during the War. But later, when the Americans were aiming at the whole of Europe, how did Stalin's foreign policy change? Did he want first of all to organize Eastern Europe? Or did he seriously expect to use the Cominform to revive 'party foreign policy' and to take advantage of the political and economic chaos in Western Europe to get the Americans out of there?

The newly available Russian sources suggest the emphasis was on the former: building up the Soviet-led bloc. This was the practical thrust of the 'Six-Points' formulated by Zhdanov in his memorandum to Stalin in early September for the upcoming conference in Poland. Zhdanov suggested that a report on the international situation should be 'devoted primarily to':

1. an analysis of the post-war situation and the unmasking of the American plan for the political

and economic subjugation of Europe (the Truman–Marshall plan);

2. the tasks of organizing forces for counteraction to new plans of imperialist expansion and for the further strengthening of socialism and democracy on both a national and international scale;

3. the increased role of communist parties in the struggle against American serfdom;

4. the decisive significance of the USSR as the most powerful force and a reliable bulwark of the workers of all countries in their struggle for peace, socialism, and real democracy;

5. a critique of errors committed by some communist parties (French, Italian, Czechoslovak, and so on), in part because of a lack of communication and cooperation;

6. the urgent necessity of coordinating the actions of communist parties on the modern international situation.

Source: Vladislav Zubok and Constantine Pleshakov, *Inside the Kremlin's Cold War: From Stalin to Khruschchev* (Harvard University Press, Cambridge, 1996) 130. Citing Zhdanov to Stalin (On the probable agenda of the conference of the nine communist parties in Poland), RTsKhIDNI, f. 77, op. 3, d. 90, 12.

of Soviet foreign policy throughout the 1940s. The lack of evidence and the contradictory policies also make it difficult to assess what Soviet aims actually were. The Soviet exploitation of German and Eastern European resources did not bode well if the aim was to enhance the appeal of Soviet communism. If the aim was to impose the Soviet model of political control and economic development, this was not initially attempted in all areas occupied by the Red Army and was not systematically imposed at any time during Stalin's rule. It may well have been that Stalin was proceeding cautiously in order to avoid taking on too much too soon. On the other hand, the Soviet leader may have had limited ambitions in Eastern Europe in the expectation that these could be reconciled with Allied cooperation over the containment of Germany.

The motivation for Stalin's Eastern European policies is a further source of controversy. Were they born out of traditional Russian imperialism, out of Marxist-Leninism which predicted the inevitable collapse of capitalism and the triumph of communism, or out of the specific needs of the Soviet state? Whatever the role of ideology it can hardly be denied that the Soviet Union still remained an essentially imperialist power seeking to enhance its power and influence. Yet it should not be forgotten that all great powers, including the Western allies, have had similar imperial goals. Their precise nature, and of course the means of their implementation, varied according to the type of regime and its geopolitical situation. It is also the case that prior to 1942 the Soviet Union faced more serious threats to its territorial security than either Britain or the United States. Its enemies in Europe were not only the Germans, who had twice attacked and destroyed large parts of Russia and the Soviet Union in the twentieth century. There were also the Poles and the Romanians, long embroiled in territorial disputes with Moscow, and under German pressure the Hungarians who had all recently been engaged in hostilities against the Soviets. On the other hand, it is clearly inappropriate to attempt to justify Soviet policy purely as a response to security needs. Stalin's ambitions extended to the restoration of those parts of the Russian empire lost in the First World War and the Russo–Japanese war of 1904–5. The Soviet leader also sought to extend Soviet influence into Iran

and into areas like the Eastern Mediterranean from which hitherto it had largely been excluded. Soviet foreign policy at the end of the Second World War was geared very much to a crude pursuit of control and influence, and only after Stalin's death in 1953 to more sophisticated attempts at achieving greater status as a world power.

Much of this has subsequently been justified in terms of Soviet security needs. Territorial security in the traditional sense of protection against military aggression was something that must have played heavily on Stalin's mind. However, it cannot justify or explain all Soviet actions in Europe, let alone those in Asia and the Middle East. Nor can the control of Eastern European communist parties imposed by Moscow. Security and imperialism can be very similar concepts and the same issues apply to defining US goals and policies about which much more evidence is available.

Stalin's own personality remains a key factor in any analysis of Soviet actions, not least because foreign policy was always his policy rather than that of the Soviet foreign ministry or the communist party. A brutal and secretive leader whose personal habits reflected a deeply disturbed personality, Stalin and his murderous regime have sometimes been portrayed as incapable of conducting a cooperative foreign policy. It seems unlikely, however, from Western records of meetings with the Soviet leader that he was unwilling to compromise, or that he was irrational and unable to make judgements about Soviet interests in Eastern Europe or elsewhere. Nor was he regarded during the War by Western leaders as someone with whom a cooperative relationship was impossible.

The Pattern at the End of the War

In 1944 and early 1945, as the Red Army moved closer to Berlin, there was no evidence of Stalin deploying Soviet forces with an eye to the post-war settlement, other than allowing the Germans to eliminate anti-Soviet elements in Poland. Priority was given to the most expeditious way of defeating the Germans, at least until after the Yalta Conference in the spring of 1945 when it has been suggested that Soviet policy then began to change.[7] What may have influenced this was the British response to the Soviet-sponsored coup in Romania which breached the Yalta agreements. Stalin's failure to include in the Polish provisional government democratic elements from abroad or to hold the elections he had promised within about one month (see Chapter 1, A) also flew in the face of the Yalta agreements.[8] Yet Yalta itself contradicted the 1944 percentages agreements.

The Romanian coup was the only Soviet-imposed government in Eastern Europe after Yalta and before the end of the War. Having led the efforts to remove the pro-German Romanian government in 1944, King Michael was faced in February 1945 with Soviet demands for a communist government. The decision had been taken by the Red Army to move Romanian units out of Bucharest in January 1945, prior to the Yalta conference. On February 27, with Soviet tanks in the streets of Bucharest, King Michael, on Vyshinski's insistence, appointed a Cabinet sub-servient to Moscow although four of its members were non-communists.

As British protests, more over Poland than Romania, were being voiced, Stalin became increasingly fearful that a separate peace, if not collaboration with the Germans, was being sought. To the Russians it was difficult to explain why German troops fought a desperate rearguard action in Czechoslovakia while offering only token resistance on the Rhine. Thus it has been claimed that in April and May the Soviets began to view military operations with an eye to future bargaining counters in preparation for what was termed the strategies of occupation.[9]

It seems that Stalin had not however abandoned his commitment to cooperation with the West. Rather, in keeping with his character, he was increasingly suspicious and uncertain. While Zhdanov argued for encouraging socialism in Eastern Europe, others such as Malenkov, were more concerned with grabbing what was possible from Germany and Eastern Europe and retreating into isolation without becoming too concerned over cooperation with the West or Eastern European socialism. Whether cooperation remained Stalin's priority would depend on the extent to which any such cooperation satisfied Soviet interests. Unfortunately it is not possible to be sure which Soviet interests Stalin regarded as vital and worth ending cooperation for.

Litvinov defined the maximum aims in 1944 in terms of a Soviet sphere of influence including Sweden, Finland, Poland, Hungary, Czechoslovakia, Romania, and the Slav Balkan countries. A minimum set of aims would clearly have included Poland and Romania, both containing traditional Russian enemies, and more than in a traditional sphere of influence the latter countries would have required tight controls in order to ensure the necessary pro-Soviet regimes.

The imposition of Soviet control over Eastern Europe made little progress in 1945. In November free elections in Hungary in which the Communist Party won only 17 per cent of the vote were followed by elections in Bulgaria, which were suspect but not rigged as blatantly as some later ones in areas less favourably disposed to the Russians. The unilateral search for the best means of maintaining Soviet interests in Eastern Europe, including Soviet security, may not have begun until early 1946[10] or even later. As 1946 began the Polish elections were postponed while elections in Czechoslovakia proved favourable to the communists who gained 38 per cent of the vote. On the other hand, the elections in Romania in November 1946 were rigged. Disagreement rages on the significance of all this. Was Stalin playing for time to deter Western intervention if moves were made to impose communist rule throughout Eastern and Central Europe? Did Stalin believe that it was possible for communists to be freely voted into power? Did he still believe that cooperation with the West was desirable to contain Germany and therefore strict Soviet control would have to be minimized?

The communists throughout the region were certainly aware of the likely need to undermine opposition parties if their position was to be strengthened. In 1946 efforts were made in Hungary to ensure that the opponents of communism were weakened and the party strong enough to prevent anti-Soviet groups effectively controlling the state. Yet there was clearly no imposition of total Soviet control over most of Eastern and Central Europe in the face of majority opposition until 1947. The tightening of Soviet control began in Poland before the Truman Doctrine and the Marshall Plan, with the rigged elections of January 1947. However it was the latter which increased the need, from a Soviet perspective, to preserve the communist system and maintain Soviet domination of the region. Nothing had yet happened before the late spring of 1947, brutality and exploitation notwithstanding, which would not have been clear to perceptive Western officials in 1943 and 1944—namely that the Soviets would not permit anti-Soviet political movements in Poland and Romania.

It was the defeat of Germany by the Red Army which put the Soviets in a position to control Eastern Europe and the issue after 1945 was less whether there would be further European expansion than whether there would be any contraction. With regard to political domination of provisional governments, even in Romania there was no certainty before 1947 that the Soviet economic and political model would be fully imposed. In Hungary and Czechoslovakia, Stalin had clearly not implemented a policy of strict Soviet control by the end of 1946 and even in Poland there were still opposition elements who had not yet been crushed. Indeed, Vojtech Mastny has argued that Stalin had no real desire for a tightly controlled system in Eastern let alone Western Europe. Rather than a formally divided Europe, with half under communist domination, a Europe made pliable by internal conflict may have been the Soviet leader's preferred option.[11] Ideologically, communist leaders had to believe in the eventual demise of capitalism and therefore Stalin's natural preference could have been a system of political inefficiency and economic chaos for most of Europe which would lead to that demise. Communist parties in both Eastern and Western Europe could contribute to this instability which would serve an ideological purpose as well as satisfying the interests of the Soviet state, not least through preventing the re-emergence of a powerful Germany.

Such a scenario offered the prospect of maintaining cooperation with the British and the Americans, and avoiding the kind of confrontation in Europe that Stalin had engendered over Turkey and Iran before hurriedly backing down. Before 1947 there was always a need for Stalin to balance his heightened ambitions against the advantages of maintaining some form of cooperation with the West. The latter could not only solve the problem of German revival but also offer the possibility of economic assistance to help Soviet recovery. It is possible that the Soviet abandonment of any hope of cooperation with the West came as early as 1946. The strongest evidence indicates, however, that this important shift came between the failure of the Moscow Council of Foreign Ministers on the future of Germany, in March 1947, and the Paris meeting on Marshall Aid for Europe, in June of the same year. Prior to Moscow, Stalin retained the hope that he could extract concessions over German reparations, which was a more important consideration than the rhetoric of the Truman Doctrine. After the failure of the Moscow Council and after reflecting on the Marshall Plan, there seemed no advantage for the Soviets in maintaining cooperation. The Marshall Plan was seen as an attempt to build a Western economic bloc in opposition to the Soviet Union and as a scheme to bring Eastern Europe into the orbit of American capitalism (see above). It therefore became vital for the Soviets to prevent this and to secure control over their half of a divided Europe.

The Extension of the Soviet System in Eastern Europe

Soviet interference with the political process in Eastern Europe had been considerable, but far from uniform, prior to the genesis of the Marshall Plan in the spring of 1947, after which it became much more repressive, with the exclusion of all non-communist parties and the imposition of the Soviet system without any consideration of local needs or wishes. Yet it remains uncertain as to the extent to which fear of Western interference embodied in the Marshall Plan affected the nature and timing of Stalinist rule in Eastern Europe as steps towards this were taken both before and after June 1947. In Romania the non-communist minority members of the government who had been installed as part of the Moscow Council agreement of January 1946 had been removed by fraudulent elections in November that year. But it was a year later, following the Marshall Plan and the creation of COMINFORM, that all opposition parties were finally repressed. In Hungary, some allegedly undesirable non-communists had been removed from the government in May 1947. Then in August, rigged elections, which still gave non-communist groups 35 per cent of the vote, were followed by the exclusion of all such groups from power. Hungary therefore followed Romania, Bulgaria, and Poland down the road of one-party governments subordinate to Moscow and committed to the imposition of the Stalinist approach to economic development. However, it was not until 1948 that the most significant events for the future of the Soviet bloc were to come in Czechoslovakia and Yugoslavia.

In the former it appears possible that until the events of 1947 Stalin was happy to let the Czechs develop their own socialist model in their own time. The fear after 1947 was that Czechoslovakia would ally itself with the West or that the West would interfere in Czechoslovakia thereby threatening Soviet dominance. The coup, which took place at the end of February 1948 and installed a communist government under Gottwald, was precipitated by the elections scheduled to take place in the spring of 1948 in which the communists were likely to do badly.[12] It is not clear whether Stalin was the instigator of the coup or whether the initiative came from within the Czech communist party and was welcomed by Stalin. However it raised the prospect of communist governments coming to power without the Red Army playing a direct role and in countries with a significant democratic past. Czechoslovakia thus symbolized the worst fears of Western governments who were primarily concerned about the spread of communism by political means rather than the expansion of Soviet power by military means. Indeed, the State Department, as far as foreign policy was concerned, had already assigned Czechoslovakia a role as a Soviet satellite. However, the need to unite Western Europe against communism, which was now more closely directed by Moscow, contributed to an attempt, if not to promote a war scare, at least to portray what was viewed as a short-term political danger as an immediate military one.[13]

The Tito–Stalin Split

Yugoslavia, like Czechoslovakia, had been relatively free of direct control from Moscow, not least because the liberating role of the Yugoslav resistance reduced the Red Army's influence. With Stalin's and Zhdanov's belief that the United States now sought to extend capitalism to Eastern Europe, the relative autonomy of Yugoslavia was seen as a greater threat in Moscow. Ironically, but with significance for any understanding of the role of ideology as opposed to state interests in Stalin's foreign policy, the Yugoslavs were the leading proponents of Zhdanov's revolutionary line. Tito was the COMINFORM's strongest supporter and one who, in ideological terms, was 'following Stalin out of conviction rather than fear'.[14]

Now that Stalin was determined to control what was perceived as a communist Eastern Europe any lack of subservience on Tito's part was deemed a threat in itself. The threat loomed larger because there were a number of power political differences to sour Soviet–Yugoslav relations and override ideological convictions. Tito had clashed with Stalin over military strategy during the War, and in the immediate post-war period Tito resented Stalin's refusal to give firm backing to Yugoslavia in its dispute with Italy over Trieste. By December 1947 when treaties were signed between Yugoslavia and Bulgaria, Romania, and Hungary respectively, Stalin feared that Yugoslavia could become a rival for the allegiance of Eastern European states. Such fears were confirmed by the announcement in January 1948 of a customs union between Bulgaria and Yugoslavia. Talks between Tito and Bulgaria's Dmitrov were geared to the formation of a Balkan federation which could even be extended to states outside the Balkans. The Yugoslavs and the Bulgarians were therefore informed that 'relations between people's democracies which exceeded the interests of the Soviet government and which did not have its approval . . . were inadmissable' and that the Soviet Union had the right to interfere in the internal affairs of the People's Democracies.[15]

This was particularly galling to Tito, who had been persuaded to establish joint Soviet–Yugoslav economic enterprises on disadvantageous terms. The Yugoslav leader now faced continued economic exploitation by Moscow, more interference in Yugoslav Party affairs, and demands for special privileges for Soviet personnel. As a particularly strong personality with a high self-regard Tito was not prepared to accept Soviet economic or political domination.

Rather than follow the Bulgarian leader to Moscow to accept a dressing down from Stalin, Tito only sent representatives. In March Stalin therefore withdrew Soviet economic experts from Yugoslavia. With backing from the majority of the Yugoslav central committee, Tito was able to resist Stalin's efforts to orchestrate an internal pro-Soviet coup. On 28 June 1948, four days after the Berlin blockade (see Chapter 2, D) began in earnest, a special Cominform meeting expelled Yugoslavia. Thus began the final consolidation of the Soviet bloc.

As problems appeared to threaten Stalin's control, the necessity to install loyal followers and prevent the emergence of other Titos increased. Trade and friendship agreements between Yugoslavia and the other communist states were cancelled as part of the strategy of punishing Tito. Such actions served to open the door to economic and military cooperation between Yugoslavia and the West and the Yugoslav regime was to survive. Elsewhere in Eastern Europe the Tito–Stalin split was followed by purges of alleged 'deviators' from the Soviet revolutionary path. In all the communist countries of the Eastern bloc except East Germany, arrests and show trials took place. Some ministers were executed, while others such as the Polish leader, Gomulka, faced imprisonment.[16] Yet as Stalinist tactics were succeeding in creating an atmosphere of terror and in imposing rigid controls over a Soviet satellite empire (with the exception of Yugoslavia), they were failing to resolve the German question to Moscow's satisfaction (see Section 2, D).

C. **The Struggle for Influence in East Asia**

One central argument of this text is that the Cold War was born out of a global conflict over the nature of the post-war international order which was conceived, particularly in the West, as embodying principles which would enable power, domestically and internationally, to be exercised and preserved. It was not a conflict born out of actions and reactions in Europe which then spread to Asia or which can be portrayed predominantly in power political terms without reference to principles and the ideologies which produced and justified them. Thus as Western concern over the economic condition of the defeated enemy in Europe became acute in 1947 so did concern about the economic condition of Japan in Asia. In both cases there were fears that a failure to rehabilitate the two countries would play into the hands of the opponents of capitalism. It was not just that the worsening economic conditions would produce unrest, but that the failure to rebuild the important German and Japanese economies would prevent regional recovery and undermine the global vision of a new liberal order. Moreover, failure would vindicate Soviet ideology as it predicted that the contradictions of capitalism would produce conflict and divisions in the West. Such expectations on the part of Stalin and other communist leaders were to be proved wrong in both Europe and East Asia.

Japan and the Reverse Course

In Japan the Americans, having abandoned their 1945 attempt to exclude their wartime allies from any formal role in the occupation of Japan, had to rely on all effective authority being exercised by the military commander. Thus the situation in Italy and Eastern Europe was repeated in Japan except that the American commander, General Douglas MacArthur, considered himself more than capable of running Japan single-handedly. Strong-willed and not amenable to control or even advice, MacArthur as Supreme Commander Allied Powers (SCAP) began a programme of decentralization and the break up of large economic groupings (zaibatsus) while purging those associated with the aggressive policies of expansion and war. In line with the American system of federalism and anti-trust laws MacArthur believed he was reforming Japan in ways which would involve reparations and the destruction of a society which did not conform to the American model. While this might have succeeded in the long term, in the short term it did little or nothing to solve the pressing problems of preventing Japanese economic collapse. As in Germany, the War had destroyed the regional patterns of trade and by 1946 there were to be increasing signs of acute hardship amongst a population whose economic viability was soon to become more important than their social or economic structures.

MacArthur was however disinclined to be deflected from his chosen course when in 1946 the State Department, as in Germany, became concerned about the dangers of economic hardship. In early 1947 SCAP ordered the purge of business executives who could be linked to ultranationalist groups or who had supported military aggression. MacArthur was attacking the industrial-banking system without concern for the means by which the economy could attract foreign investment and earn the means to import food and avoid inflation and shortages. Moreover, in Japan the cost to the United States of preventing hardship by supplying food and other essentials would be even greater than in Europe unless the Japanese themselves could make a contribution. In the middle of 1948 the non-military cost of supplying food, fuel, and medicine had almost reached $1 billion.[17] The State Department argued, at the moment the Truman Doctrine was launched, that a 'positive economic programme' must quickly 'create a viable Japanese economy' which would be 'self-sustaining' by 1950.[18]

In the late spring of 1947 criticism of MacArthur's policies was intensified by George Kennan's appointment to the newly created Policy Planning Staff in the State Department. Kennan saw the main problems as political, economic, and psychological, rather than military in both Europe and Japan. He also conceived the Soviet ideological challenge in global terms in 1947. In other words it was not just important to keep communism from gaining control and influence in Europe but in all areas, including Japan, which had developed strong industrial economies. Kennan linked these economic and political factors to a concept of a non-military balance of power in Eurasia with a rebuilt Japan and Germany countering Soviet power but not threatening Western interests. Rebuilding Germany and Japan would 'immunize them and their regions against communism'.[19] He had support for a change

of course and the abandonment of MacArthur's policies from an increasing number of sources, including former President Hoover and the War Department. Opposition to MacArthur was strengthened with the establishment of the Department of Defence in July 1947, which made it more difficult for MacArthur to portray himself as above the individual services. A more concerted effort was now to be made to produce what became known as the 'reverse course' in Japan that would end reparations and the decentralization programme with its attacks on the zaibatsus.

In the summer of 1947 the State Department produced a paper on Japanese recovery which contained similar ideas to those in the Marshall Plan and which aimed to provide $500 million to produce Japanese self-sufficiency by 1950. In September 1947 General William Draper, the recently appointed undersecretary, visited Japan and took on the role of coordinating the State-Army assault on MacArthur. The crunch came in the first two months of 1948 when the State-War-Navy Coordinating Committee[20] approved a Japanese recovery programme thereby accepting the State Department line. But then came proposals from Tokyo earmarking over 300 companies for possible dissolution. Kennan regarded this as a greater threat to Japan than Soviet military strength and departed for Tokyo determined to persuade MacArthur of the need to use the economic potential of Japan in the Cold War rather than undermine it by a post-war reform programme.[21] As in Europe, what had been earmarked for destruction now had to be utilized in a new battle for salvation.

Kennan's visit coincided with that of Draper who had been lobbying Congress to win support for a Japanese recovery programme. Kennan produced arguments for reversing course which portrayed Japan as more important than China in the struggle against Soviet communism. Draper got support from businessmen whom he brought to Tokyo and put the economic arguments in regional terms. The Japanese situation was portrayed as a regional problem which jeopardized the future of multilateral trade in Asia and with it the creation of an open international economic system. Even if Japan could successfully rebuild its manufacturing export sector, markets in Asia remained problematic. A full-scale civil war was underway in China and cheap sources of raw materials were no longer available because of the collapse of the pre-war Japanese empire. Japanese self-sufficiency would have to depend on access to Asian raw materials and markets with less dependency on obtaining them from the dollar zone. These were the official conclusions of the report drawn up by Draper and his aides which was followed by the Army under-secretary's establishment of a Deconcentration Review Board to make final recommendations to MacArthur on the policies to be adopted with regard to Japanese business and financial institutions.

By June Congress had voted funds for the economic recovery of Japan as part of a programme laid out in June 1948 in National Security Council (NSC) memorandum 13 which proposed terminating the reform programme and seeking stability by siding with business against organized labour. Japan, like Europe was being rebuilt not reformed in order to integrate it into an American-dominated economic world order, with the cooperation of traditional elites, in opposition to Soviet communism. And its recovery was to be accompanied by attempts to link Japan with other Asian economies, most notably South Korea, which had previously been a victim of Japanese imperialism. The fact that Japan's war machine was seen as having been run by the country's most able businessmen now mattered little.[22]

Thus Japan moved further to the Right in 1948 as China moved further to the Left with the prospect of a communist victory in the Civil War appearing increasingly likely. A new Japanese government was formed by the conservative Democratic Liberal Party leader, Yoshida Shigeru, and at the end of 1948 President Truman issued a new stabilization directive and appointed Joseph Dodge as a special emissary charged with overseeing the Japanese economy. MacArthur, who had suffered a crushing defeat in the Republican primaries, was no longer the powerful political force he had been in the immediate post-war years. The Kennan–Draper policy could now be implemented along with renewed efforts to integrate Japan successfully into an Asian regional economy as outlined in NSC 48. With China about to fall to communism this assumed greater importance, but it was not until the disturbing events of 1950 that its success would be achieved.

The Emergence of Communist China

China entered the Sino–Japanese War in 1937 without a central government and having suffered a long period of internal weakness and chaos after the collapse of the Manchu dynasty. In the nineteenth and twentieth centuries its independence was continually compromised with the great powers interfering in Chinese affairs and winning extraterritorial privileges. The failure of the Boxer rebellion in 1900 indicated the futility of attempting to resist without using external alliances as a means of regaining greater independence. Thus Michael Hunt has argued that China was torn between the need for support from friends and the dependence that this could produce. The conflict between dependency and autonomy was deeply embedded in the Chinese psyche and remained there after the Second World War when China became one of the victorious allies.[23]

It was not, however, a unified or powerful China which emerged from the War in 1945. Sun Yat-sen had led a united nationalist party into the inter-war period but divisions had appeared in 1927 as the split with the communists was formalized. Following the collapse of the united front, during the next decade the nationalist leader Chiang Kai-shek failed to establish a central government over all of China and found himself facing Japanese attacks on Chinese territory. Chiang had abandoned any attempt to win over the masses and preferred to bargain for support with local strongmen and warlords. Fighting the Japanese enemy led to a brief reconciliation with the communists, but when the Sino–Japanese war began in earnest in 1937 this further reduced the prospects of Chiang creating a united China.

The wartime problems stemmed from the Japanese invasion and their takeover of China's coastal cities, which provided a significant amount of government revenue through customs duties. Deprived of this resource Chiang's KMT had resorted to printing money which created high inflation and discontent amongst government employees and manual workers. Things became more serious when the Japanese left and the KMT proved to be incapable of providing an effective, corruption-free administration. With labour unrest and student demonstrations taking place even the KMT's traditional

Mao Tse-tung (1893–1976)

Born in Shaoshan, Hunan province, Mao enlisted in 1911 for the revolutionary army in Hunan during the first rebellion against the Manchu dynasty. Influenced by the nationalistic ideas of Sun Yat-sen, Mao converted to Marxism and became involved in political activity as a student at Peking University. In 1921 he co-founded the Chinese Communist Party. He also organized communist guerrilla army units as part of the revolutionary forces between 1924 and 1925. Mao was appointed chief of propaganda and publicity under Sun Yat-sen and he also supported a united front with the Kuomintang (Nationalist Party) under Chang Kai-shek until 1927, when the two parties split and he was dismissed from office. Mao, now leader of the communists, retreated to south-eastern China where he established the Chinese Soviet Republic in a section of Kiangsi province. In 1934, Kuomintang troops forced Mao to leave Kiangsi and he led his army on the 'long march' of 6000 miles to Shensi in northern China. During the Second World War an alliance was negotiated between the communists and the Kuomintang against the Japanese during which time Mao wrote major works on Marxist-Leninism. In 1945 the Civil War resumed and resulted in eventual victory for the communists. In 1949 Mao became leader of the newly established People's Republic of China. During the 1950s Mao abandoned the Soviet economic model and began to introduce his own reforms to rejuvenate the economy. In 1958 he initiated the Great Leap Forward. However, these new policies disrupted Chinese industry and opposition mounted and in 1959 Mao resigned as leader of the republic but continued to influence policy as leader of the Communist Party. He launched the Cultural Revolution of 1966 to 1969 during which revolutionary attitudes were encouraged, officials dismissed and all aspects of culture destroyed. Schools and universities were closed and students were organized into Red Guards who attacked nonconformists and destroyed property. Mao's thoughts in the 'Little Red Book' provided a doctrine for the mass of Chinese people, inspiring a cult based on his own personality that lasted until his death.

supporters were alienated when the administration acceded to workers' wage demands. In the rural areas not controlled by the communists the KMT foolishly reimposed the land tax in 1946 and caused further hostility by compulsory purchases of grain at below market prices. In addition their poorly paid troops were ill-disciplined and aroused resentment both during and after the conflict with Japan.

The experiences of recent Chinese history were imprinted on the mind of the communist leader Mao Tse-tung who in the 1930s began a struggle to unite the country under a single central authority and carve out a more independent and prestigious role for China in international affairs. They were to influence Mao's perception of how the international community could both strengthen and weaken his domestic position as he sought to re-establish China as a regional power. Like any other revolutionary movement the Chinese communists were in need of domestic legitimacy but the Cold War situation in 1949 would complicate this and significantly influence international reactions to the new state. In part this was connected to the nature of the achievement of Mao. He ensured that for the urban middle classes and rural peasants who were equally

opposed to the KMT in the years after 1945 the communists were the only viable alternative. While the urban middle classes were thoroughly disillusioned with Chiang Kai-shek they had little positive commitment to a communist regime. Mao was conscious of the need to preserve this fragile alliance which could require external help to overcome the enormous problems left by the demands of the War and the corruption and incompetence of the KMT administration. The weaknesses of the KMT clearly contributed to the communist victory but the military and political strategies of Mao's forces were also significant.

In 1945 few expected the communist forces that were outnumbered by five to one to emerge victorious and Stalin was particularly doubtful of such an eventuality. In part this was because, with Soviet influence in East Asia very much in mind, Stalin had gained concessions from the Nationalists, albeit with British and American support, regarding the warm-water port of Lushun and the control over the Chinese Eastern Railway. As a result it is argued, Stalin was prepared to restrict communist activities in Manchuria when the Soviets entered the War against Japan in August 1945 and even to try and expel them from Manchurian cities. At the time of the Soviet involvement in the war against Japan Stalin was more interested in possible territorial and economic gains than he was in the prospects of a communist revolution in China. This was one of the reasons why he was initially reluctant to offer aid to Mao and preferred to avoid a confrontation with the Americans over China. In 1945 and 1946 when cooperation with the Americans seemed possible and desirable ideology was not a sufficient incentive for Stalin to give full backing to Mao. Moreover Stalin, as in Europe, was suspicious of communists who might show independence from Moscow and Mao's revolution had always been free of Moscow's control. This could sow the seeds of rivalry in East Asia especially if China began to play a more important regional role.

In the West the orthodox Cold War tendency has been to play down the impact of power politics and history as influences on Stalin's and Mao Tse-tung's foreign policy and emphasize Marxist-Leninism and global revolution as the dominant influences shaping Chinese and Soviet approaches to the external world. It may be more meaningful to see the ideological forces as justifying rather than determining foreign policy which retained at least some of the traditional Chinese and Russian imperial influences. These gave priority to the pursuit of power and influence for the state and its rulers and for a quest for domestic legitimacy through international means.

As the Civil War intensified in 1945, and with US and Soviet forces in China, the Americans initially attempted to reconcile the Nationalists and the communists through the Marshall Mission. Led by General George Marshall the initiative seemed to produce results in the form of a ceasefire in February 1946 but it collapsed by April. By then the Soviets were withdrawing from Manchuria leaving behind considerable quantities of confiscated Japanese arms which were seized by the communists. One month later the communists, in the rural areas they controlled, shifted from a policy of rent reduction to a more radical one of land reform. Their policies in terms of winning support from the peasants were sensible and flexible. As they moved south and faced counter-attacks by the KMT they would revert to rent reduction in areas where control was difficult,

realizing that land reform could not be implemented without effective military control. All that was necessary at this stage was the overthrow of existing rural elites.[24]

In 1946 Stalin could feel confident enough to begin small-scale military aid to the communists if only to mitigate future recriminations. Cautious as ever, he was unwilling to make a bigger commitment out of fear of an American military response. Nevertheless for Mao this was a crucial turning point as it was the first concrete signs of the support which he desired from the Soviets. Recent research indicates that Mao was more desirous of close relations with the Soviets than had previously been thought. While it is true that there was little reason for Mao to trust Stalin, especially as Stalin was still attempting to maintain links with Chiang Kai-shek in1946, he had even less reason to turn towards the Americans. Mao was preoccupied with what he perceived as the long-term hostility of the United States to the communist revolution in China. He saw the prospects of renewed US intervention as a significant possibility, if only in the form of encouraging resistance on the part of the urban bourgeoisie to his attempts to forge a new China through the heat of revolution. Consequently he needed backing from Stalin.

It has been argued that in 1946 Mao had the basis of the Soviet alliance he had been seeking in place.[25] The Chinese communists were given free rein in Manchuria as the Soviet forces withdrew, and the contacts were certainly closer than has generally been assumed in the West.[26] For Mao the fact that the Soviets gave the communists an increasing amount of military assistance and civilian aid as time progressed was more important than Stalin's subsequent attempts to reopen contacts with the Nationalists.[27]

As the KMT continued to display incompetence and corruption more members of the Truman administration became convinced that aid to the KMT would not rescue an increasingly unpopular organization which by 1948 was clearly losing the war. Spreading forces too thinly had made the KMT army vulnerable to more concentrated communist deployments, and in 1948 Marshall, now Secretary of State, had finally decided that the communists were going to win. By the end of that year Stalin too was convinced that victory for Mao was in sight and that the United States was unlikely to prevent it. Soviet attention now moved more towards influencing future relations with the Chinese Communist Party (CCP) within an East Asian context. One option was to act as a mediator in the final days of the conflict in order to win international acclaim as a peacemaker and to make the Chinese communists more beholden to Moscow. In the event Mao was having none of it but remained determined to look to the Soviets for fear of malign American influence in China although it was not until 1950 that a firm alliance was concluded.

D. **The Division of Germany**

The German question was perhaps the most important single problem facing the Allies at the end of the war. It was not, however, the source of immediate conflict in 1945 when issues about it were either resolved or more usually postponed. Talks on a German peace treaty—always seen as the most difficult to achieve—were delayed until 1947 after treaties with Germany's allies were concluded. It was more the case that as tensions increased during 1946, and particularly in 1947, they made an acceptable German peace settlement harder to achieve; this in turn produced more tension and more unilateral actions in the Eastern and Western zones. The initial agreements on Germany resulted partly from the importance both sides attached to containing the principal enemy state. The fact that there might be different views on how to do this did not imply that failure to reach a final agreement was impossible. Yet, as the costs of various options became clearer, who should pay for them formed one irresolvable problem. To that extent the Cold War role of Germany had an economic dimension linked to ideology as well as to the strategic interests of the great powers. The latter, but particularly the Soviet Union, had reasons to be concerned about such a potentially powerful state at the heart of Europe which formed the link between East and West.

During the War a number of conflicting ideas had arisen about how finally to prevent a resurgence of German militarism. The US Morgenthau Plan effectively proposed a pastoral state deprived of the industrial capacity to make war. From the Soviet point of view the best way to ensure that a capitalist Germany was prevented from making war on its Eastern boundaries was to create a communist state. Given that it had been agreed during the War to establish an Allied Control Council this was not a short-term option. There was also the possibility of the dismemberment of Germany and of demilitarizing the country with international controls to prevent its industrial capacity being used to produce military equipment. All this would require cooperation and joint control which might have been why Stalin was not averse at the end of the war to American troops remaining in Europe. Finally, there was the issue of German reparations which the Soviets, who had suffered most from German aggression, were desperately keen to impose.

From the Western perspective it was important to prevent the revival of German militarism within a powerful centralized state. How best to do this was seen as more problematic given that excessively harsh treatment (as some believed the Germans had received at the end of the First World War), was likely to foster resentment; this in turn could produce a determination to overturn any post-war settlement. There was a further consideration, which soon became important to the West, and that was Germany's role in European recovery. Stalin was not only unperturbed by the prospect of starving Germans but had no interest in the revival of European capitalism, especially as this would require German resources, particularly coal. For the West, capitalism's ability to produce European prosperity was an important consideration and for that Germany's role was crucial. The cost of preventing starvation in Germany also required some form of controlled German recovery in which the Soviets had less short- or long-term interest.

The future treatment of the country and the particular issues of dismemberment and reparations had been broached at Yalta (see Chapter 1, A). It had been decided to 'take such steps including the complete disarmament, demilitarization, and dismemberment of Germany' as was deemed necessary for peace and security.[28] The specific issue of dismemberment, strongly favoured by the Soviets, was to be considered by a committee. On reparations it was agreed by the Soviets and Americans that a commission would examine this on the basis of a figure of $20 million half of which would go to the Soviet Union. When the leaders next met at Potsdam, decentralization had replaced dismemberment as the accompaniment of disarmament and demilitarization, but during the period of occupation Germany was to be administered as a single economic unit. The occupying powers were to extract reparations from their own zones, but in addition the Soviets would be entitled to receive from the Western zones '10 per cent of industrial capital equipment as is unnecessary for the German peace economy', and '15 per cent of such usable and complete industrial capital equipment … as is unnecessary for the German peace economy' in return for an equivalent value of food and raw materials.[29]

The potential for conflict in such arrangements was enormous. For a start, there was a conflict between zonal reparations and Germany's administration as a single economic unit. This problem was made worse by the fact that the Russians gave over a sizeable part of the agricultural lands of Eastern Germany to the Poles. This increased the food shortages within Germany making it more necessary to bring in food from outside, which in turn required German industries to be brought back into production to pay for it. The Russians remained determined that German industry and coal should primarily be used for reparations even though they had handed over the German coalfields in Silesia to the Poles. The Western Allies were disturbed that they were being expected to pay for the loss to Germany of dismantled industry, coal and one-quarter of its agricultural land. The deputy American military governor, General Lucius Clay, was emphasizing the need to increase productive capacity in the Western zones even before the Potsdam meeting. The Western desire to use and develop German industrial resources was bound to increase in importance and to disturb the Soviets. If the people of a united Germany were to be fed, there would be costs to

be met either by importing food or by increased industrial production and reduced dismantling for reparations.

These short-term economic costs had more serious political implications once it became clear by early 1946 that the arguments on the Mediterranean, Eastern Europe, and Japan had produced confrontational speeches and increased tension. If control over Bulgaria and Cyrenaica were such difficult issues to agree on, how would control over Germany be resolved? If it was a battle between two rival economic and political systems which one would prevail in a united Germany? If economic hardship could not be averted by increased production was that not likely to increase support for communism? If it was averted would that not only strengthen capitalism but raise the spectre of German revival?

For General Clay the practical difficulties in the Allied Control Council stemmed in early 1946 more from the French than from the Soviets. The French were demanding the right to take reparations from their own zone and the restitution of goods taken by the Germans during the War (something the Soviets were not interested in because of the scorched earth policy on the Eastern front). They were determined to keep Germany weak, but in contrast to other powers, wanted to do this by severing areas from Western Germany (including the industrial Ruhr) and decentralizing the country. While there were Soviet–American arguments over the level of German industrial production, the nature of a German import–export programme and reparations from current production, the French were determined to sabotage any form of central planning. One vital issue was the standard of living to be accorded to the German population. The Americans were keen to bring it up to the European average, which understandably upset the Russians whose post-war living standards were well below that average. It took until March 1946 to agree on a Level of Industry plan but the Russians stalled on an export–import programme claiming this was a zonal issue that could not be addressed by the Control Council before reparations had been settled and a trade surplus produced. The Russians who had higher productivity levels in the east in both agriculture and industry realized that they would be making economic sacrifices over imports and exports and were in effect postponing indefinitely a single import–export programme. With the Eastern zone the most self-sufficient, there were grounds for the Soviets to believe that a single import–export programme would result in them subsidizing the Western zones. On 3 May 1946 General Clay therefore suspended reparations deliveries from the Western zones believing that zonal reparations had to be linked to a single export–import programme.[30]

At the same time the Russians were alienating the West by extending controls over their zone, including in April 1946 the forced merger of the Social Democratic Party with the German Communist Party (KPD). This move could have been part of Soviet preparations for the communization of all Germany—an indication of Soviet ambitions rather than Soviet security concerns, although a communist Germany would have been the best security option. It was in an endeavour to allay Soviet fears that a few days later on 29 April the US Secretary of State, James Byrnes, had proposed a demilitarization treaty for Germany. The Soviets, whose priority remained dismantling for reparations and reparations from current production, rejected the idea. In the United States it was assumed that this indicated the Soviets were interested in more than just security.

However, there is an alternative explanation stemming from Soviet ideology and fears. German Nazism, as other forms of fascism was, in communist eyes, a structural feature of capitalism. To prevent it re-emerging fundamental changes in the German economy and society were needed. Demilitarization was not enough. Moreover, for security reasons it would be better, from the Soviet point of view, to ensure that the factories were dismantled to limit German war potential than to sign a disarmament treaty. For suspicious Soviet leaders, if the West were reluctant to dismantle German industry to the extent desired by Moscow, it would be important, as Molotov told Byrnes, to have inspections to ensure that disarmament measures were being enforced. Otherwise German resources could ultimately be used against the Soviets. If the Americans were prepared to allow inspections, then the rebuilding of German industry would be less of a threat; and disarmament agreements would be more appropriate after the occupation had ended.

Also, this would enable the Soviets to have a role in the more important industrial areas of Western Germany. None of this could be done by a demilitarization treaty and nor would the alternative of division provide the Soviets with any influence over the resources of the Ruhr.[31]

The value of a united or a divided Germany to the respective allies was related to security *and* economic requirements. The dismantling of German industry was linked not only to how much industrial production would enable the needs of the population to be met, but also to security and reparations. In 1946 there were advantages to the Soviets in a united Germany, whether one interprets their motives as defensive or expansionist (influence over the Ruhr and changes in, or controls over, German capitalism and society). For some Americans like George Kennan, who discounted Soviet fears of Germany against the aggressive designs of communism and Russian imperialism, Stalin would succeed in his aim of creating a communist Germany if the country remained united. As early as March 1946 Kennan was already of the view that it would therefore be preferable to integrate the Western zones into a Western bloc. By contrast Clay and his American associates in Germany did not believe in Soviet aggression and pointed out that the Russians had 'been meticulous in their observance of Potsdam'. There were thus clear divisions within the US administration over the desirability of a divided Germany which emerged in 1946.[32]

Whether or not Stalin had a long-term aim of dominating Germany, there were a number of possible benefits from posing as champions of German unity, which the Soviets continued to do in the summer of 1946. The British, on the other hand, who were faced with the largest zonal costs and who had little to gain but much to lose from a united Germany, were beginning to favour permanent division by May 1946. This would either enable them to exploit the Ruhr's resources more for their own benefit or ensure that the Ruhr was merged with the other Western zones to alleviate British costs. One reason for British support of zonal merger, which the Americans came out in favour of in July 1946, was to relieve the economic burdens of occupation. It was becoming more evident that for the West, German recovery, in whatever ultimate form, was an integral part of European recovery and therefore, as Byrnes outlined in his Stuttgart speech in September 1946, Germany would not be bled dry or dismembered.

The issue of European, as opposed to German, recovery was increasingly to be at the centre of the disagreements. With the growing need for a European recovery programme in 1947, it made the implementation of the relatively harsh Potsdam agreement more difficult for some Americans to swallow. By the time the next step towards division was taken with the creation of the bi-zone (the fusion of the British and American zones) in January 1947, Byrnes, it is claimed, had abandoned the idea of a united Germany out of fear it would fall prey to Soviet influence.[33] However, as the pro-'containment' group of officials in Washington favoured integrating the Western zones of Germany into a Western bloc, the Soviets made substantial concessions which suggested that they were not primarily motivated by the desire to produce a Soviet-controlled Germany.

In October 1946 the Kolpakov proposal offered an upwards revision of the level of German industry and, once the Control Council had set the levels of current production reparations taking into account the capital removal, to institute a balanced export–import programme. In the same month the East Germans went to the polls in free elections and inflicted major losses on the Soviet-sponsored SED. The idea of communist successes through political integration would therefore depend on subversion not elections, but the Soviets seemed to be backing away from this and emphasizing economic requirements. This gave credence to the idea, held by Clay, that it would be possible to gain influence in the Soviet zone as part of the price the Soviets were prepared to pay for the maintenance of acceptable cooperation in determining the economic future of all Germany. In particular, Clay believed that in exchange for reparations from current production the Soviets might permit democracy to develop in East Germany.[34]

In the run up to the March Council of Foreign Ministers in Moscow, which began talks on a German peace treaty, the key issue was reparations from current production. Could these be used to secure agreement on Germany or would it be

---

Marshall's Medicine

The difficulty under which we labor is that in spite of our announced position we really do not want nor intend to accept German unification in any terms that the Russians might agree to, even though they seemed to meet most of our requirements, since as they have declared war on European recovery, we know . . . that they would . . . prevent the resources of Germany from contributing.

Source: Carolyn Eisenberg, *Drawing The Line: The American Decision to Divide Germany, 1944–1949* (Cambridge University Press, New York, 1996), 318. Citing: Dwight D. Eisenhower Presidential Library, Bedell Smith Papers 162, Box 101, Walter Bedell Smith to Eisenhower, 10 December 1947.

It is now known that there is an intention to make Germany, or at least western Germany, the object of a definite American plan in Europe. . . . Germany's affairs are judged and decided by American Senators and American Businessmen of every description who boss it in the Western zones and help the American monopolists to penetrate ever deeper into the industries and banks of Western Germany.

Source: Carolyn Eisenberg, *Drawing The Line: The American Decision to Divide Germany, 1944–1949* (Cambridge University Press, New York, 1996), 318. Citing: V. Molotov, Statement to Soviet Press, 31 December, 1947 in V. Molotov *Problems of Foreign Policy*, 551.

---

preferable to exclude the idea and use the resources of the Western zones for the rebuilding of Western Germany and Western Europe? Some in Washington were opposed to the former strategy and argued that a German settlement with the Soviets might not be in America's best interests. Others simply assumed that a united Germany would inevitably become communist. And by the start of 1947 the British were keen to push ahead with the bi-zone in order to produce self-sufficiency there. In the United States, even before the Moscow Council, the importance of European recovery as a means of countering communism and assisting the American and Western European economies meant that German resources in the Western zones were increasingly earmarked for that end. By March 1947, as the Moscow Council got underway, for Marshall, the Potsdam agreement to limit German industrial production to meeting German subsistence needs was no longer appropriate. Nor, for the same reasons, would it be desirable to accept reparations from current production even though the Soviets were now prepared to accept a combined import–export programme. The bottom line was that for the United States, German reparations for the Soviets had to be sacrificed in order to meet the needs of Western European recovery, which particularly required German coal, and the avoidance of starvation and unrest in Western Germany. The only compensation would be a disarmament treaty. The Soviets on the other hand wanted the economic benefits of reparations from current production, while, for reasons of security and influence, maintaining joint controls over German industrial production. To achieve this they were apparently prepared to accept a German Constitution based on the Weimar model with reduced executive powers, and nationwide elections to decide the future governmental structure. Stalin may ultimately have been hoping for a united communist Germany at the expense of Allied co-operation, but the British and the Americans were already committed to the division of Germany in the interests of European recovery. In that sense whether Stalin was seeking to control a communist Germany, embark on world revolution, or achieve security from right-wing German aggression made little difference. Western concessions to the Soviets would hamper German and Western European recovery, boost communism, and weaken the American and British economies.[35]

By the time the Council of Foreign Ministers met again in London in November 1947, the State Department was affirming that there were no terms under which the US would accept Germany's economic unification.[36] As in other areas of Cold War policy in the West, the approach to the German question was based on perceptions of economic and political advantages, not simply on responding to what the Soviets were doing. Even before the March 1947 meeting, many British and American policy-makers were determined to proceed with the integration of the Western zones of Germany into the Western European capitalist economy. After London this could go ahead without further constraints and led in September 1949 to the creation of a West German state.

The Berlin Blockade

In the meantime Western policy in Germany and Stalin's fears of a strong German capitalist state, with American aid (denied to the Soviets at the end of the War) going to the rebuilding of West Germany, contributed to a crisis between the embryonic blocs in June 1948. Arguably, one of the key moments in the Cold War resulted from the determination of the Western powers to continue the economic rebuilding of the Western zones with a view to the creation of a West German state.

In February 1948 the Western powers convened a conference in London from February to June 1948 to discuss zonal policy in Germany, including control of the Ruhr, with a view to establishing a West German state. The decision to exclude the Soviets came after Stalin's objections to the currency reforms which had been broached in the Control Council. The London Conference and its published proposal on 6 March to incorporate the Western zones within the European recovery programme led the Soviet Control Council representative, Marshal Sokolovsky, to walk out two weeks later. From this point on Stalin produced a mix of coercion and diplomacy in an endeavour to prevent the formation of a West German state strengthened by Marshall aid. The initial coercion took the form of restricting the movement of Allied personnel entering Berlin by rail and road from 1 April. The diplomacy included offers to discuss the disputed German issues on a Soviet–American basis and an attempt to encourage French doubts about the creation of a West German state. By June, as it seemed that a new currency would be introduced in the Western zones, the Soviets walked out of the Berlin Kommandatura. The following day when the new currency was introduced in the Western zones of Germany, but not in Berlin, the Soviet response was to close all surface routes into West Berlin on 24 June.

It could have been a desperate Soviet act to prevent the creation of a potentially threatening West German state or a calculated attempt to drive the West out of Berlin. It was more likely to have been Stalin's attempt to prevent the former and to reopen talks on the future of Germany as a whole. If the Western Allies could be forced to reopen talks on Germany, the possibility of an economically strong

West German state might be averted. Whatever interpretation is favoured, if the blockade failed to prevent a new German state it would at least enhance the prospects of a Soviet-controlled East German state. In the West this form of Soviet intimidation was seen as a challenge which had to be met and an airlift was mounted to get supplies into the city of Berlin. Stalin offered to lift the blockade in August 1948 in return for a Council of Foreign Ministers on the future of Germany, and in January 1949 to end it if the establishment of a West German state was postponed. In the event beating the blockade became a major operation which lasted 324 days and airlifted 13,000 tonnes of supplies per day

Western leaders were determined to show resolve when, with European communist parties subverting elected governments, the morale of a war-weary European public might have fallen. An ability to retain credibility and resist pressure was important in resisting communism. On the other hand, if the crisis escalated a war-weary public might not have seen the value of an armed clash with what had been a key ally only three years before. The airlift challenged the Soviets to start a military conflict by shooting down the planes and that was something Stalin was unprepared to contemplate in 1948. Consequently, the means chosen by the Soviet leader to try and stop the rebuilding of a capitalist Western Germany led to humiliation and to further measures which proved disadvantageous to the Soviet Union there.

The Berlin crisis was in many ways a symbolic crisis in a city which came to epitomize Cold War tensions until 1989. It has also been regarded as an important cause of the militarization of the Cold War and the formation of NATO, although it is more plausible to see the crisis as a justification for, rather than a cause of, the formation of a Western military alliance. The crisis itself has also been interpreted as another indication of aggressive Soviet moves designed to win control of a communist Germany, but it probably stemmed from Soviet fears of a capitalist Germany being used as part of an anti-Soviet bloc. What is certain is that Stalin's ill-conceived actions, the risks they entailed, and the hardships they produced in Berlin, provided justification for those in the West who *were* seeking to construct an anti-Soviet bloc.

The airlift was ultimately successful as the Berlin blockade was lifted in May 1949 but Western resolve to see it through without concessions was not always firm. Both British and American representatives proposed compromise and a retreat from the London Conference proposals. Ultimately those who saw the importance of Berlin as a symbol of Western resistance to communism prevailed. They feared a retreat from Berlin would drain confidence in the American commitment to Europe and lead to a withdrawal from Germany as a whole.[37] Thus Berlin became an island of resistance to communism and a symbol of Western determination, not to defend Europe militarily against the Soviets (West Berlin was always indefensible), but to prevent the spread of communism as a political force. In addition the crisis gave the West Germans confidence in American support and led opinion in the West to become more sympathetic to Germans only three years after the end of the Second World War. The adoption of communism was now less likely in Western Europe and Stalin's blunder had undermined Moscow's influence. This was the crux of what had become a Cold War and explains the true significance of Berlin. Berlin was more important politically in terms of its resistance to Soviet attempts to extend communism or weaken capitalism than it was militarily in producing a Western alliance. The latter developed for reasons which were evident before the 1948–9 crisis over Berlin and were linked to a mix of fear and ambition concerning the political and economic future of Western Europe and to the links to non-European areas (see Chapter 4, B). None of this could be explained to the Western public for whom it was now easier and more advantageous to depict the Cold War, not primarily as a political or economic conflict, but as a military confrontation.

NOTES

1. Thomas G. Paterson and J. Garry Clifford, *America Ascendant US Foreign Relations since 1939* (D.C. Heath & Co., Lexington, 1995), 34.

2. M. J. Hogan, *The Marshall Plan. America, Britain and the Reconstruction of Western Europe 1947–1952* (Cambridge University Press, Cambridge, 1987), 2–3, 427.

3. Alan Milward, *The Reconstruction of Western Europe, 1945–1951* (Methuen, London, 1984), 483 and Milward 'Was the Marshall Plan Really Necessary', *Diplomatic History* 2 (1989).

4. Scott D. Parrish. 'New Evidence on the Soviet Rejection of the Marshall Plan, 1947', *Cold War International History Project*, Working Paper no. 9 (1994).

5. Ibid.

6. W. LaFeber, op. cit. 63–4, 69 citing *Foreign Affairs*, 1947 and a telegram from the Moscow embassy to Washington, 26 May 1947 in the Papers of Joseph Jones, Truman Library.

7. Caroline Kennedy-Pipe, *Stalin's Cold War. Soviet Strategies in Europe 1943–1956* (Manchester University Press, Manchester, 1995), 59–66.

8. The time period was not in the protocols but had been stated by Stalin at the 5th Plenary Meeting at Yalta. FRUS, 1945, *Conferences of Malta and Yalta* (Dept. of State, Washington, DC, 1955, 79407).

9. Kennedy-Pipe, op. cit., 60.

10. V. Zubok and C. Pleshakov, *Inside the Kremlin's Cold War from Stalin to Khrushchev* (Harvard University Press, Cambridge, 1996), 54.

11. V. Mastny, *The Cold War and Soviet Insecurity: The Stalin Years* (Oxford University Press, New York, 1996), 20.

12. Kennedy-Pipe, op. cit., 123.

13. Several historians have claimed that in 1948 the West promoted a war scare including Caroline Kennedy-Pipe and Walter LaFeber

14. V. Mastny, op. cit., 45.

15. W. Loth, *The Division of the World 1941–1955* (Routledge, London, 1988), 169 citing Milovan Djilas, *Gespräche with Stalin* (Hart Davis, London, 1962), 217–20.

16. Ibid., 170–1.

17. M. Schaller, *The American Occupation of Japan* (Oxford University Press, New York, 1985), 82–5.

18. FRUS, 1947, VI, 159,184. Cited in W. LaFeber, *The Clash: A History of US–Japan Relations* (W.W. Norton & Co., New York, 1997), 270–1.

19. W. LaFeber, op. cit., 273.

20. A wartime body which continued its endeavours to coordinate policy in areas of interest to the State Department and the Services.

21. M. Schaller, op. cit., 109–25.

22. W. LaFeber, op. cit., 272; M. Schaller, op. cit., 132–3.

23. Michael H. Hunt, *The Genesis of Chinese Communist Foreign Policy* (Columbia University Press, New York, 1996), ch. 1.

24. Suzanne Pepper, *Civil War in China: The Political Struggle 1945–1949* (University of California Press, Berkeley, 2nd edn., 1999), 423–25.

25. On the above points see O. A. Westad, 'Losses, Chances and Myths: the United States and the Creation of the Sino-Soviet Alliance, 1946–1950', *Diplomatic History* 2 (1997).

26. Chen Jian, 'The Myth of America's Lost Chance in China', *Diplomatic History* 2 (1997).

27. Westad, op. cit.

28. FRUS, 1945, *The Conferences of Malta and Yalta* (Dept. of State, Washington, DC, 1955).

29. FRUS, 1945, *The Conference of Berlin* (State Dept., Washington, DC, 1960), 1485–6.

30. Carolyn Eisenberg, *Drawing the Line: The American Decision to Divide Germany* (Cambridge University Press, New York, 1996), 210–12, 230.

31. Ibid., 298, 228–30.

32. Ibid., 224–5, citing Kennan Papers, Kennan to Secretary of State, 6 Mar. 1946; RG 59 State Department Office of European Affairs, Box 146, Murphy to Matthews, 3 Apr. 1946 and Matthews to Murphy 18 Apr. 1946.

33. W. Loth, *The Division of the World 1941–1955* (Routledge, London, 1988), 124.

34. Eisenberg, op. cit., 249–50, 252–4, 288.

35. Ibid., 291, 293, 314–15, 352–3.

36. FO 371/624207, FO to Lord Strang, 22 Oct. 1947. Cited in Eisenberg, op. cit., 353.

37. W. Loth, op. cit., 244–5.

CHRONOLOGY: THE GERMAN PROBLEM, 1945–1949

1945

February	Agreed at Yalta by the Big Three that (1) reparations would be considered by a commission sitting in Moscow on the basis of (a) removals to eliminate war potential, (b) deliveries of goods from current production, (c) use of German labour. (2) in principle the dismemberment of Germany was desirable and the means to achieve it should be considered by a three-man committee. (3) Naziism and German militarism would be destroyed.
July–August	Agreed at Potsdam by the Big Three that reparations would be extracted from the zones of the occupying powers and the Soviets would also receive 10 per cent of industrial capital equipment not needed for the peacetime economy and 15 per cent of usable and complete industrial equipment.

1946

Early	French cause problems in Allied Control Council by demanding the right to take reparations from the French-controlled zone.
March	Level of Industry plan is agreed; however the Russians stall on the import–export programme, claiming it is a zonal issue.
April	The forced merger of the Social Democratic Party with the German communist party takes place, indicating a Russian attempt to extend control and alienate the West.
	Byrnes call for Four Power Treaty guaranteeing the disarmament of Germany for 25 years.
3 May	General Clay suspends reparations deliveries from the Western zones.
May	Britain becomes more favourable to a permanent division of Germany.
Summer	Soviets are in favour of uniting Germany.
July	The US favour a zonal merger of Germany.
September	Byrnes' Stuttgart speech arguing that zonal boundaries should be regarded as defining areas of occupation for security purposes only and not seen as self-contained economic or political units.
October	The Kolpakov programme offers an extension of the levels of German industry and favours an introduction of a balanced export–import programme.

1947

January	British keen to push ahead with the bi-zone.
	Byrnes completely abandons the idea of a united Germany, fearing it would fall under Soviet control.
March	Moscow Council begins, and for Marshall the Potsdam agreement is no longer appropriate.

| November | Council of Foreign Ministers meets in London and the US State Department make it clear that they will not accept the unification of Germany on any terms. |

1948

February	Western powers have a conference in London to discus zonal policy in Germany, including the control of the Ruhr. The Soviets are excluded from this meeting.
6 March	London Conference leads to the proposal of an incorporated West Germany. Proposals lead to the Soviet Control Council representative walking out two weeks later.
1 April	Stalin restricts the movement of Allied personal entering Berlin by road and rail.
June	Soviets walk out of the Kommandatura when it became clear a new currency would be introduced in West Germany.
24 June	The introduction of the new currency (in Western zones but not in Berlin) leads to the Soviets closing surface routes into the city.
August	Stalin offers to lift the 'Berlin Blockade' if a Council of Foreign Ministers meets to discuss the future of Germany.

1949

January	Stalin offers to lift the blockade if the establishment of a West German state is postponed.
May	Berlin Blockade is lifted. Airlifts to the city proved successful for the Allies
September	The West German state is created.

3 Empire, Cold War, and Decolonization, 1945–1953

A. Asia

The changes that took place within the European empires during the early years of the Cold War constituted another crucial element of the new international order after the Second World War. Often referred to as decolonization (a vague term which here is not meant to imply that the process was devised and implemented by the colonial powers or that the colonial regions were the only components of empires) these changes formed part of the broader shift in the global balance of power. This shift produced by the War marked the end of the European-dominated system of nation states and was followed by the decline of the major European powers and the international dominance for a quarter of a century of the United States challenged only by the Soviet Union. For many policy-makers in the European capitals, the loss of their overseas possessions was not simply about ending the formal administrative and judicial arrangements which constituted colonial rule. It was also about adjusting to the Cold War and the new forces of anti-colonialism in ways which would enhance their positions as great powers.

The challenges to colonial rule were evident in both Africa and Asia during the inter-war years. In the Indian subcontinent a mass-based anti-colonial movement, the Congress Party, had emerged by the end of the First World War and the British had responded with a mix of concessions and repression. The economic changes which influenced the nature and development of anti-British movements in India also had an impact in Africa. British rule everywhere depended to an enormous extent on the collaboration of important social groups. Particularly in West Africa the increasing commercialization of cash crop production, a process which began in the nineteenth century, brought to the fore producers whose economic power was not reflected in their social and political standing within native societies. In short, the chiefs on whom the British depended were facing challenges from within that were to have implications for their British masters. During the Depression when the role of foreign trading firms was resented more and more by African producers, who had little control over marketing, solutions to economic problems were seen as requiring the removal of the social and political obstacles that were blamed for economic difficulties. Chiefs who tried to use traditional powers to control land or the marketing of such crops as cocoa could be removed, but ultimately greater opportunities were seen only in a new political order; this would undermine the basis of British rule by giving greater political control to emerging economic groups, keen to exclude foreign and traditional influence.

The economic changes brought by the Second World War and production for the war effort added new difficulties to some already unstable situations. Moreover, the War brought a radically new political challenge to European colonialism. While its impact was not always immediate, and certainly not uniform, the importance of the War as a precursor of political change is difficult to exaggerate. In the first place, by 1942 the disastrous defeats suffered by the British, French, and Dutch in South-East Asia at the hands of a non-white people, the Japanese, dealt a massive international blow to the standing of European colonialism. If, as was the case, the indigenous people did not resist the Japanese invasion, the benefits of colonial rule had to be questioned. This was particularly so for the British, who were increasingly keen to point to the alleged value of colonial rule in nurturing and encouraging the advancement of native societies. The British Colonial Office was keen to emphasize the enlightened and liberal nature of their rule and the loss of their Asian colonies significantly undermined this. The worst British military defeat of modern times at Singapore in 1942 has to be placed in the context of their position as rulers in South-East Asia. The indigenous inhabitants were generally not prepared to fight to preserve British colonialism and were generally indifferent as to who should rule them. The European defeats at the hands of the Japanese destroyed the myth of white supremacy, which had always underpinned colonial rule.

In the second place the Second World War was fought by the Allies as a war for freedom from Nazi oppression. The occupation of conquered territory by the Nazis was something that could not be tolerated, not just because of the inhumane nature of the new regimes, but because it denied people what was increasingly perceived as their legitimate right of self-determination. The publicity surrounding the Anglo-American signing of the Atlantic Charter in 1941, with its statement of the right of all peoples to choose their own governments, was a significant blow to colonialism. The war for freedom and for a new world order became exactly that, although its precise effects manifested themselves in different ways to what many at the time expected.

To comprehend the nature of the subsequent large-scale termination of colonial rule remains a complex undertaking and explanations for the timing of the transformations are particularly difficult. Why was power transferred quickly in Sri Lanka but not in Malaya? Why was India given up when efforts were made to cling to influence in Egypt and to maintain control in East Africa? Why were so many territories granted independence in the early 1960s? Obviously a key factor was the strength of those anti-colonial movements that were demanding the transfer of power and the establishment, often in very difficult economic circumstances, of independent nation states. The colonial powers had always to respond to these demands. Yet at the same time they were devising policies to place relationships with their overseas possessions on new footings and however much these were influenced by the colonial peoples' demands they clearly had an effect on the nature and timing of independence. Moreover, these policies and the reaction to anti-colonial movements were to some extent determined by the nature of the Cold War and by broader perceptions of the European powers' own roles in the international system.

India

Organized political opposition to British rule in India had begun in the nineteenth century with the founding of the Congress Party in 1888. Congress was the first political organization to pose a threat to the continuation of British rule in the non-white Empire. Although dominated by educated, westernized Indians, Congress became a broad-based mass party by the end of the First World War. It was then open to both Hindus and Muslims and could accommodate the radical, non-violent protests of Gandhi. The latter's emphasis on traditional, as opposed to Western values, was a marked contrast with the English-educated intellectual Nehru, Jawaharlal who became the party's leader in 1929 and the first Indian prime minister on independence in 1947. The inclusive nature of the Indian National Congress Party was not to survive the Second World War and the religious divisions which were to scar India in the late 1940s were already significant in the 1930s.

The British have to assume some responsibility for the increasing conflict and bitterness which began to affect Hindu and Muslim communities that had happily coexisted for hundreds of years. The key point in the politicization of religious differences came with the enactment of the Government of India Act in 1935. The act applied to those Indian provinces directly administered by the British and was designed to take the sting out of the opposition to British rule by devolving local power to the provinces while maintaining effective national control at the centre. The measure was never likely to quench the desire for independence and it

Jawaharlal Nehru, 1889–1964

Born in Allahabad, Nehru began his education in England at Harrow School and later attended Trinity College, Cambridge. He then qualified as a barrister at the Inner Temple, London. After his return to India in 1912, Nehru became involved in the India nationalist movement. He joined the Indian National Congress, led by Mahatma Gandhi, after the massacre at Armistar in 1919. In 1929, Nehru was elected leader of the Congress Party, succeeding his father, (Pandit) Motilal Nehru. Despite being imprisoned nine times by the British during the 1930s, Nehru worked closely with Gandhi in the campaign for Indian independence, even entering into negotiations with the British authorities. In 1947, when India and Pakistan became separate nations, Nehru was elected as India's first Prime Minister. An early act of Nehru in his new office was his decision to keep India as an independent republic within the continent, which helped it to evolve into a multiracial society of equals. He was also responsible for India's foreign policy, based on non-alignment. Nehru was popular with his people and remained in office until his death at the age of 74. His daughter, Indira Gandhi, was elected Prime Minister in 1966.

enormously complicated the process of achieving it. After 1935 political power in the provinces was up for grabs and this and the attempts to secure representation for both Hindus and Muslims provided the reason for greater competition and conflict between the two communities. And it eventually encouraged Congress to become a Hindu Party as the various Muslim political groupings came to be effectively dominated by Mohammed Ali Jinnah's Muslim League.

The Second World War reinforced the politicization of these religious differences as the Muslim League grew in importance assisted by the British. The latter perceived the Muslims as more reliable wartime partners in the wake of Gandhi's Quit India civil disobedience campaign. Both parties in the wartime coalition in London saw this attempt to force the British to leave as a major threat to the war effort and in 1942 most of the leading members of the Congress movement were imprisoned. With the way clear for the Muslim League to strengthen its position as a political force, and therefore as a participant in any transfer of power, problems began to mount for any attempt to move India closer to independence.

By 1945 there was little doubt that India would soon become independent despite the fact that die-hard imperialists in the Conservative and Labour parties had an emotive aversion to such a step. The issue was simply when and how. During the War, India had been offered Dominion status largely because of its importance to the war effort. In addition the new Prime Minister of the first post-war Labour government, Clement Attlee, had been a long-time advocate of Indian independence. As a member of the Simon Commission, which looked at constitutional change in the 1930s, and which was responsible for the 1935 Government of India Act, Attlee had advocated Indian independence then and was the author of the Commission's minority report. The War could only have reinforced his support for Indian independence, although neither Attlee nor the Labour Party had any clear plans as to how this was to be achieved except that the Indians should somehow be made to decide their own future.

Unfortunately a Constitutional Assembly to do just this raised a number of difficulties. The position of the princely states, ruled indirectly by the British through the medium of residents at the royal courts, was now overshadowed by the political/religious divisions in India. In order to ensure that Muslims and Hindus were fairly represented in any Constituent Assembly to determine an independent India's future, how was such a body to be elected? With Jinnah determined on a separate Muslim state it was difficult to see a way forward to a united India. In 1946 a Cabinet mission was despatched to India to negotiate with Congress and the Muslim League on the basis of the provinces combining into three groups one for Hindu majority provinces, one for Muslim majority ones and one for Bengal and Assam. These groups would thus provide a third tier of government which would be placed between the provinces and the central administration that would still deal with foreign affairs and defence.

Unfortunately both sides feared that accepting such a proposal would weaken their position in the constitutional battle. In the wake of the failure of the Cabinet mission, communal tensions between Muslims and Hindus erupted into large-scale violence in August 1946. The number of deaths in Calcutta ran into the thousands and to make matters worse there were growing doubts about the desirability of withdrawal within the government. In February 1947 in an attempt to put pressure on the Indians to agree on the mechanism by which to achieve independence, Attlee made a firm commitment of British withdrawal by June 1948.

At the forefront of those averse to Indian independence were the military who were keen to retain bases in what was to become Pakistan. They were supported by the foreign secretary, Ernest Bevin, for broader reasons of foreign policy and Britain's international standing. In essence these were related to the problems of re-establishing Britain as a great world power but the development of the Cold War by 1947 was also a factor. When the decision to plan for Britain's departure was taken there were still expectations that a new world order guided by the spirit of internationalism and based on the cooperation of independent states in the United Nations would emerge. Even in February 1947 the Cold War had not been fully accepted and there was still the possibility that the proclamation of Indian independence would be seen in a positive way as a great power contribution to the new international order.

By then there was an urgent need to convince the Indians to work together by giving a date on which Britain would withdraw, hence the statement of 18 February 1947. Yet the situation in India was so troublesome and the cost of attempting to resolve it by the continuation of British rule so enormous that avoiding future involvement with India's problems was a key consideration. Even so in January 1947 Bevin urged the prime minister to resist pressure for withdrawal from India fearing the consequences for Britain's position as a great world power and the subsequent loss of electoral support. Attlee, however, pointed to the lack of any viable plans to remain in India and appointed Mountbatten as the viceroy charged with securing Indian independence.

By the time Mountbatten arrived in the subcontinent in March 1947 the withdrawal date of June 1948 appeared too much like a costly dragging of British feet. Ignoring the desirability both of defence agreements before independence and of a united India, Mountbatten brought the date for the transfer of power forward to August 1947. While this helped to secure agreement between Congress and the Muslim League it did so on the basis of two separate independent states. Congress's acceptance of partition was out of fear of even greater divisions which would lead to the Balkanization of the subcontinent. Thus the independence of India was created in an unseemly rush and managed by a British plenipotentiary rather than ministers or officials in London. It brought the British little credit because population transfers between India and Pakistan were accompanied by large-scale bloodshed. Yet for all parties there was the saving grace that the creation of two new states within the British Commonwealth had spared everyone from something much less acceptable. In that respect the transfer of power in India, *faute de mieux*, had revealed an important rationale for the end of empire which was to figure in future European decolonization.

Ceylon, Burma, and Indo-China

The loss of what was generally perceived as the jewel in the British imperial crown helped produce the transfer of power in the rest of south Asia. During the war both Burma and Ceylon had been promised self-government or Dominion status in a short space of time. For Ceylon in particular, having conceded independence for India, there seemed little reason to resist demands from moderate leaders for similar treatment when a defence agreement and membership of the Commonwealth were part of the package. Moreover, the elections of September 1946 confirmed Senanayake's United National Party as the leading political force, but in the face of a strong challenge from the communists. In 1947 strikes and disturbances in the wake of the elections only reinforced the British desire to work with the moderates in strengthening their position. There was thus every reason for the British to cooperate in the achievement of independence. Such a strategy offered the best prospects of replacing British control with British influence and avoiding the coming to power of radical leaders as the Cold War became an accepted fact of international life. Ceylon duly became the independent state of Sri Lanka in February 1948

Burma was more problematic, and here it was less a question of working out a process with nationalist leaders than accepting the inevitable however unpleasant. As in India British weakness in the face of Burmese opposition was significant in determining the timing of the transfer of power. Burmese leaders were generally more distrustful of their British rulers than their Sri Lankan counterparts and Aung San, the most influential who was head of the Anti-Fascist Peoples's Freedom League (AFPL), could call on the Burmese 'national army' which had been created under Japanese rule. Aung San was determined to gain control of the administration without delay and to avoid any return of the old socio-economic order based on British commercial interests and Indian migrant labour. Reluctantly the British accepted the rapid speed of constitutional change despite the fact that the Burmese were refusing to join the Commonwealth. The means to resist Burmese demands were simply not there and an additional concern in 1947 was the strength of the Burmese communist party. With the old order destroyed in all its aspects there was no middle way for the British to pursue in Burma between armed resistance to political change or a rapid unconditional retreat from power which was completed by January 1948.

While the British chose the path of retreat in Burma and India, the French chose to fight in Indo-China. These contrasting choices owed much to the perceptions of policy-makers in London and Paris as well as to the situation on the ground and the strength of the opposition to colonial rule. Whereas in India a strong political movement seeking independence was already in existence before the onset of the great Depression and the Second World War, in Indo-China, Malaya, and Indonesia it was the dramatic social and economic changes in the 1930s and early 1940s which helped produce significant challenges to the continuation of European rule. Whether the extent of the change in socio-economic relations made it more likely that the colonial power would refuse to fight, as in Burma, or to embark on a bloody conflict as in Indo-China, is a moot point.

Indo-China proved to be the longest and bloodiest of the conflicts born out of the quest for independence in Asia, and regional divisions exacerbated the subsequent struggle to control Vietnam. Tonkin, later to be known as North Vietnam, was a predominantly rural society of smallholding peasants, increasingly exploited on a sharecropping basis by absentee landlords. As population pressures mounted those who escaped to the plantations of the south in Cochin China found themselves victims of an unregulated labour market. In South Vietnam, where the pattern of landholding was more varied, the existence of French and Chinese plantation owners provided another focus for Vietnamese discontent. When the Second World War began, the level of rural discontent in many parts of Vietnam made the situation ripe for the development of a mass-based movement opposed to foreign rule.

The leader of such a movement, created in 1941 and known as the Viet Minh, was Ho Chi Minh, a charismatic communist figure with experience of both China and the Soviet Union. Emphasizing the nationalist characteristics of the organization, Ho maintained communist control and established strongholds in many parts of Vietnam during the War. The Japanese left a puppet French Vichy administration in control until March 1945, which further eroded the legitimacy of the French regime in the eyes of many Vietnamese peasants who retained a strong sense of hierarchy and authority. Food

Ho Chi Minh, 1890–1969

Born in Kim-lien, North Vietnam, Ho Chi Minh was educated at a Franco-Annamite school. He worked as a teacher and a seaman before moving to England in 1915 and France in 1917. He became a founder member of the French Communist Party in 1920. Three years later Ho Chi Minh moved to Moscow and studied at the East University. In 1924 he travelled to China as a translator with the Soviet consulate in Canton and began to organize the Vietnamese nationalist movement. However, in 1927, Ho Chi Minh returned to Moscow after the split between the Chinese Nationalists and the communists. In 1930 he founded the Indo-Chinese Communist Party. He then escaped to Moscow in 1932, after being arrested as a revolutionary by the French, only to return to China five years later. In 1941 he formed the communist-dominated Vietnam League for Independence, the Viet Minh. During the Second World War he organized the Viet Minh in guerrilla raids against the Japanese. When the Japanese were defeated by the Allies in 1945, Ho Chi Minh entered Hanoi and declared Vietnam an independent republic with himself as the first President. When the French returned to Vietnam after the war they refused to accept independence for Vietnam and a military struggle followed between 1946 and 1954, until the French were finally defeated at Dien Bien Phu. At the Geneva conference in 1954, Ho Chi Minh agreed to the partition of Vietnam along the 17th parallel and assumed the presidency of North Vietnam. He supported the Viet Cong guerrilla movement in South Vietnam during the second Indo-China war. When Saigon fell to the communists in 1975 it was renamed Ho Chi Minh City in his honour.

shortages added to the loss of French acceptability as rulers and produced growing internal support for the Viet Minh. Externally Ho Chi Minh and his supporters received encouragement from the wartime Roosevelt administration and the Office of Strategic Services, the predecessor of the Central Intelligence Agency, because they were initially viewed predominantly as an anti-colonial nationalist movement. More significant were the military supplies that Ho and his forces were able to obtain from the Chinese. Thus in the North the Viet Minh established a viable government in Hanoi by August 1945. In the South, where the British, with some assistance from their former Japanese enemies, began to re-establish control in September the situation was rather different. French settlers and the provisional French government in Paris had no intention of allowing a nationalist movement to control a united Vietnam. As the French began to pour forces into Indo-China the stage was set for confrontation despite the weakening of colonialism that the War had brought.

The weak French position did however contribute to the attempts to negotiate an agreement with Ho Chi Minh in 1946. The discussions took place as the constitution of the Fourth Republic was being drawn up. Central to the new republic's constitution was the Union Française, or French Union, which in imperial terms was designed to reconcile the irreconcilable. It was made up of the indivisible French Republic, which along with metropolitan France included what was termed Overseas Territories and a number of Associated States, like those in Indo-China which would achieve internal autonomy. Colonialism was therefore in theory abolished because within the republic one and indivisible its individual citizens would eventually all be assimilated as equals with the same rights as metropolitan Frenchmen. Associated states would, the French claimed, willingly accept their new constitutional position. One contradiction was that if all the citizens of the French Empire were equal within a single republic, then those of metropolitan France would be outnumbered and the former Empire's subservience would be ended. Hence the structure of the Union, while proclaiming equality, had to ensure the dominance of metropolitan France, 'freely consented to', not least through the power granted to the French president as head of the Union Française. Another contradiction emerged in Indo-China where the essence of the problem was that Ho Chi Minh, while prepared to consent freely to membership of some form of union, would only do so on the basis of an independent state first having the freedom to consent. For the French the indivisibility of the French Union meant that no state could exist independently outside the Union and then subsequently join on the lines of the British Commonwealth. On this barrier the talks broke down while in Indo-China the determination of the French military and the settlers to reimpose control soon led to confrontation. In November 1946 the French bombardment of Haiphong marked the beginning of what was to become a protracted military struggle for control over a united Vietnam.

By 1947 the Viet Minh had become a guerrilla force and the French were seeking viable collaborators whom they could use to attract support away from Ho Chi Minh and his campaign for independence. The first figure to play such a role was the titular emperor Bao Dai who, despite his Catholic religion, did have some credibility as a supporter of Vietnamese nationalism. The problem was that if the French were to increase his standing they would have to offer the kind of meaningful concessions on independence that they had refused to offer to Ho Chi Minh. Catholic or communist made no difference to this fundamental issue, although the French were subsequently to emphasize the importance of combating the latter particularly to the Americans. What mattered to the French was the impact of the loss of Vietnam to their position as a global power. It was a position constructed on the basis of a French Union which embodied the formal end of colonialism but retained French domination under a new guise and refused to consider either independence or self-government. And unlike the British the constraints and contradictions it embodied made political concessions in the overseas territories to even the most pro-Western indigenous leaders extremely difficult to make.

B. **Africa**

French West Africa

In order to win African support for the Fourth Republic at the end of the War the French, given the political constraints imposed by the Union Française, chose to rely on social and economic reform combined with greater representation in Paris for increased numbers of Africans. Those Africans who were deemed to have the required attributes of French civilization could qualify for the same rights as metropolitan Frenchmen and send significantly more representatives to the French parliament. This still meant, however, that even educated Africans with full voting rights could wield no effective power in Paris or the local capitals. In French West Africa, prior to 1956, the right to vote did not enable Africans to elect members of local representative bodies with any executive or administrative functions. In Paris the effective domination of the legislative assembly was difficult enough for metropolitan parties let alone a limited number of African representatives. The growing African realization of this fact during the late 1940s was to change the focus of African political parties. It was also eventually to contribute significantly to the acceptance by the Ministry of Overseas France that neither social and economic reform nor the ending of some of the worst abuses of pre-war French colonialism would satisfy the demands of Africans. Meaningful political change would eventually be needed if the French were to continue to exert influence in Africa.

The impact of social and economic changes in the post-war African colonies should not however be dismissed entirely. The French in particular spent large sums of money under the Fonds d'Investissement Economiques et Socials (FIDES) programme especially in the 1950s. If the effects were minimal this was largely due to the nature and scale of the African developmental problem. Geography and demography along with the linkages to the international capitalist economy, which were established before as well as during colonialism and which were far from dependent on the continuation of European rule, made significant economic progress difficult to achieve. The principle of metropolitan taxpayers contributing to the benefit of colonial subjects through the development of the colonial economies was nevertheless accepted by both the

British and the French by the end of the Second World War. Unfortunately in the immediate post-war period the practice was to a large extent compromised by the economic needs of European recovery.

In the French case it was the conference of colonial governors which met in Brazzaville in January 1944 that produced the commitment to provide public money for social and economic development. Africans were also to be wooed by the ending of forced labour and the *indegénat*, a system of justice whereby the French colonial authorities could imprison Africans without trial. Political reforms which might lead to independence were firmly excluded although the tradition of assimilation[1] was questioned at Brazzaville where there was some support for decentralization. In the end these issues were left to the drafters of the new constitution to resolve and here the interests of metropolitan France were clearly paramount. The wartime importance of French Equatorial and later West Africa as a base for the Gaullist opponents of Vichy did not produce a desire to provide political benefits to Africans in Africa. There was to be no form of independence or equality in the foreseeable future and there were no Africans at Brazzaville even for consultation. Imperial questions of France's world role meant that France's African territories and the majority of their inhabitants would only receive greater freedom and status within a political structure still dominated by metropolitan France.

This was in contrast not only to British actions in South Asia but to the thrust of their West African policy which was galvanized by events in the Gold Coast that began in 1948 with serious disturbances in Accra. As the War drew to a close the French had sought to cooperate with the British over colonial policy in West Africa partly so that in technical matters mutual benefits for Africans might occur, but primarily to keep out what they saw as American imperialism and the involvement of international bodies. Such proposed bodies would operate on a regional basis and would be accountable to the new United Nations organization. The French hoped that by an association with the British such bodies could be pre-empted. In the event nothing came of the proposed regional commissions under international auspices, but the French and to a lesser extent the

British became concerned to avoid any UN involvement in the affairs of non-self-governing territories other than the former mandates which were now placed under Trusteeship.

By the beginning of the 1950s international pressures through the United Nations were on the increase and the very basis of the French Union was under threat in Africa from new internal and external forces. With the Cold War after 1947 those concerned with maintaining France's international standing could portray the nationalist challenges more as ones directed by the forces of international communism. These were certainly influential in Indo-China but were much weaker in Black Africa and the Magreb. However, the fact that the Rassemblement Démocratique Africain (RDA), an interterritorial political grouping established in 1946, was associated with the French Communist Party (PCF) clearly offered the possibility of communist advances. Africans had initially been attracted to the communists prior to May 1947 when they were part of the coalition government. After that date when the communists left the French government and adopted a strategy of subversion rather than co-operation, the threat they presented was more menacing. This coincided with serious disturbances in Madagascar, which began in March 1947 and which remained out of control until July.[2] They were partly inspired by a general process in much of the French Empire stemming from reactions to reform and the nationalist/communist challenge. In broad terms, as the process of reform began French settlers and merchant firms, fearing their economic and political interests threatened, began to react to the changes in the colonies and the metropole. They and those focused on the general issue of French status in the post-war world were given a fresh impetus by the Cold War, which in turn was to produce a reaction in Africa. In Madagascar this reaction was expressed in the attacks on settlers by indigenous groups based on the wartime growth of secret societies. By August, the socialist Minister of Overseas France, Marius Moutet, wondered, after reading some intelligence reports on Africa, whether the problems were 'premonitory symptoms of a vast disintegration in our Overseas Territories, which is tending, following Indo-China and Madagascar to create new fronts of agitation and conflict.'[3] As the Cold War became firmly linked to disturbances in the colonies and the possible disintegration of France's overseas territories, the need for French resistance was strengthened. Support could be garnered on a mix of international and colonial fronts for repressive policies in Black Africa. In the Ivory Coast where the RDA was strong the French attempted to smash the party in 1949 and a series of violent incidents provoked or encouraged by the administration occurred between the RDA and its local African opponents. Strikes and boycotts created a serious situation which led to the banning in February 1950 of RDA meetings throughout French Africa. However, the dangers inherent in this policy of confrontation, which contrasted with the British response to the disturbances in Accra, were soon obvious.

The French were now dealing with a major war in Indo-China that was increasingly dependent on American assistance. When René Pleven, one of the architects of the Brazzaville reforms, became prime minister in July 1950 it was clear that the French lacked the ability to cope with a multitude of conflicts through the use of force. Pleven therefore sought, as in 1944, to mollify African opinion, which was now more politicized, and isolate the communists by a combination of social and now political reforms based on electoral changes. François Mitterand was sent to persuade the Ivory Coast leader of the RDA, Félix Houphouet-Boigny, to break with the PCF and affiliate to his Union Démocratique et Sociale de la Résistance (UDSR) party. Measures against the colour bar were introduced along with greater African involvement in elections, but while the French had extended the hand of collaboration it contained nothing of substance.[4] The problem remained that whoever was elected by whom, African deputies in the French parliament remained essentially as supplicants to or dependent on French political parties. In Black Africa progress towards self-government or even *s'administrer eux-mêmes* remained dead in the water as long as local assemblies were given no administrative or legislative powers and remained advisory bodies.

International pressures were now stemming more from the UN and from the greater American interest in Black Africa, which was apparent from 1950 with the conference in Lourenço Marques in January and February of consular and diplomatic representatives.

It was followed by the reorganization of the State Department, which allowed for the creation of regional bureaus. Conflicts, as in Indo-China might be avoided and opportunities denied to communists if the French were to move more towards the kind of political concessions made by the British in their West African territories of Nigeria and the Gold Coast. To some extent this view was shared by the French Foreign Ministry in the early 1950s who had a very different view from the Ministry of Overseas France on how to deal with African political movements and build up resistance to communism. In essence by 1951 the Quai was in favour of greater cooperation with Britain on colonial matters concerned with political change. The ultimate aim was to create a West African Federation, which would be one of a number of federations linking European colonial territories with France and Britain in a new and close association. In part this stemmed from the Quai d'Orsay's disillusionment with the French Union which they believed was unacceptable to international opinion and less attractive to Africans than the British policy of granting self-government. Cooperating with the British in a West African federation would involve granting greater autonomy to French territories and Anglo-French joint policies on constitutional change and the problem of anti-colonial and anti-Western movements.[5] Regionalism and autonomy would provide an alternative attraction to nationalism and the centralism associated with assimilation. The Ministry of Overseas France was firmly opposed to such suggestions and it was to be several more years before the republic one and indivisible ceased to be a barrier to moves to grant powers to local bodies in French West Africa.

British West Africa

The British granting of local powers to elected African representatives began in the 1940s and accelerated after the War. It was a process which involved social and economic development as well as political change, but it was influenced by broader imperial and international requirements. In this mix of conflicting intergovernmental pressures Britain's post-war economic needs ran counter to the desire to use political concessions to attract pro-Western

Africans who would cooperate in the process of handing over power. Again there was a blend of Cold War goals to ensure that left-wing, 'irresponsible' Africans were excluded and traditional desires to maintain British as well as Western influence under a new guise could be met. The ultimate aim was to use new links with the colonies to reflect and preserve the world power status that was deemed the *sine qua non* by British elites. More specifically in Africa the aim was the 'substitution of a relationship of friendly association for that of benevolent domination' in order that Britain could emerge as a 'leader of free associates rather than a commander of a band of subordinates'. To achieve this it was necessary to devise machinery to 'substitute links of consultation for links of control' to avoid 'the very real danger of the ultimate dissolution of the colonial part of the British Commonwealth'.[6] The Colonial Office therefore became committed to

taking initiatives to control and manage the process of political and constitutional change, but after the riots in Accra the British were always playing catch up in terms of pre-empting African protests. Political concessions never bought the hoped-for time which was deemed necessary to provide greater social and economic benefits for Britain's African subjects.

The riots in the Gold Coast stemmed from economic dissatisfaction with the post-war regime as much as from a desire for independence from Britain. Having lost out in the battle to benefit colonial producers, the Colonial Office had to rely on political means to appease African dissatisfaction. In a sense the concessions stimulated further African political awareness and indicated that the best way of securing more economic benefits would be to escape external controls through the achievement of independence.

A process of constitutional change designed to

Colonial Office Draft Report on Disturbances in the Gold Coast

The background

From the end of the war until the appointment of the Watson Commission in March 1948, there was a deterioration of public confidence in government. This was due mainly to five immediate causes, namely, the tide of nationalism that was flooding over many dependent territories, serious inflation, the inability of government, through lack of qualified staff and materials, to carry development projects beyond the planning stage, the commercial struggle between an independent and ambitious Greek firm, A. G. Leventis & Co., and the main European importing firms forming the Association of W. A. Merchants and, finally, the bitterness of the group of politicians, led by Dr J. B. Danquah, over the hanging of the Kibi murderers. Of these the last two were purely local and require a short explanation.

2. At a time when imports were controlled by Government, Leventis organized and sustained a vitriolic press campaign against the Association of W. A. Merchants, the Gold Coast government and the Colonial Office both of which, he alleged, supported the Association. This campaign was waged through a period of acute inflation, when it was easy to inflame popular feelings against European importing firms on the grounds that they were responsible for the high prices. The accusations of racial discrimination and the exploitation of Africans by the concerted action of government and European firms,

bedevilled hitherto good relations and stirred up racial suspicions and hatred of government. It culminated in the boycott of imported goods that immediately preceded the 1948 disturbances.

The disturbances of 1948

7. In February and March 1948, the constant inflaming of public opinion against government fanned by the passions aroused over the boycott, led to disturbances and an attempt by the UGCC to seize power. The outbreak of violence was sudden and unexpected. The shooting by the police on an unruly mob of demonstrators, including ex-servicemen who were marching on Government House, allowed the extremists to work up anti-government and anti-European feelings into the wildest excesses of mob violence, bloodshed, looting, and arson. This outbreak, which lasted for several days before it was brought under control, shook the public's confidence in the ability of the government to maintain its authority and to protect person and property.

8. The UGCC claimed that the existing government was paralysed and had so lost the confidence of the people that the only solution for the Gold Coast was the immediate grant of self-government. The convention cabled to the Secretary of State that it was prepared to take over the interim government of the country, pending the calling of a constituent assembly.

9. A Commission of Enquiry was appointed in April and in August its report (Colonial No. 231) was published together with a statement on it by His Majesty's Government (Colonial No. 232). The leaders of the UGCC, who were widely believed to be responsible for the disturbances and were held to blame by the Commission, were allowed to go unpunished, except for their removal to the Northern Territories for six weeks immediately after the disturbances, and a far-reaching plan for political advance emerged. These two facts helped to convince large sections of the urban public that government was on the run and that violence brought great political concessions.

Proposals for constitutional reform

10. The proposals for rapid political advance gave the politicians and the country much to think about and overshadowed the blame attached to the UGCC leaders. As a result, political tension was greatly reduced. There followed a political lull which lasted until November. This was due partly to the absence of many prominent politicians, including Dr Danquah, in the United Kingdom at the Colonial Conference, and partly to the fact that the public was slow to digest the Watson Report.

11. At the end of December 1948, the appointment of the widely representative and all-African Coussey Committee, which included several of the leaders of the UGCC, to work out the detailed application to the Gold Coast of the plan for political advance set out in His Majesty's Government's statement on the Watson Report, lowered tension still further, except among the extremists, and brought constitutional questions back from the realms of heady nationalist slogans to constructive discussions round a conference table. Moderate opinion began to express its views.

Nkrumah builds up his own extremist party

12. In the meantime, however, in the middle of 1948, the struggle for power within the Convention between the general secretary, Mr Nkrumah, and the rest of the working committee, led by Dr Danquah, had reached a climax. Nkrumah had been relived of his key post and, in order to avoid an open split in the Convention just before the publication of the Watson Report, had been given the sinecure post of treasurer.

13. From that time onwards Nkrumah began to build up within the UGCC a personal following organized largely as youth groups. Into these he attracted supporters both from the rank and file of the UGCC partly by wild promises, and partly by threats against those who stood aloof. Many of the younger literates and some older people who were failures and hoped for rapid advancement under a new regime were attracted by his exciting nationalist propaganda, which was anti-imperialist and anti-European, and painted a colourful picture of the people of 'Ghana', freed from the shackles of imperialism, building a paradise of jobs and high pay for all. Many members of the junior civil service joined his ranks: many schoolteachers all over the country gave him support and carried the teaching of his slogans into their schools. To these were added the growing hooligan element from among the young unemployed in the urban areas.

14. In September 1948, with the help of Convention funds, Nkrumah started his own press and built up through his paper, 'The Accra Evening News', a violent campaign for immediate self-government, the early course of which was outlined in Mr Scott's secret despatch of the 10 March 1949. He started calling for a 'constituent assembly' to decide the future Constitution. He began to attack in advance the appointment of a local representative committee on constitutional reform on the grounds that it would not be able to achieve the full and immediate self-government which he demanded.

Source: CO 537/5812, 1950, reproduced in Richard Rathbone (ed.), *Ghana Part I, 1941–1952* (1992), 384–7 *British Documents on the End of Empire, Series B, vol. 1, pt. 1* (1992).

head off nationalist demands and the predicted agitation when the War ended began, and in 1946 a new constitution was introduced essentially to give the Legislative Council an unofficial majority of Africans. By then Africans had been appointed as assistant district officers in the colonial administration and town councils with elected majorities established in Accra, Cape Coast, and Sekondi. The reforms had at first been welcomed but then resented. By 1947, cocoa growers were being badly hit by swollen shoot disease and food prices in the rural areas were affected by low rainfall, while the loss of the wartime American air-staging base in Accra had increased unemployment.[7] Import prices had also been rising as the British throughout the empire restricted imports to the colonies to preserve dollar resources for the United Kingdom itself.

In the same year the United Gold Coast Convention Party was founded demanding 'self-government in the shortest possible time'. Discontent was on the verge of combining with organized anti-colonialism when the riots erupted in Accra in February 1948. Coming at a crucial time in the Cold War and when the Colonial Office assumption was that anti-colonial forces were being contained and pre-empted, the scale of the disturbances caused a mixture of shock and outrage. New security measures involving MI5 and the Gold Coast police reflected the belief that the riots, while inspired by social and economic discontent, must have been organized by communists or those who were influenced by communism. A commission of enquiry was soon set up which reported within four months. Rather than identifying the communist problem, the Watson Report, although exceeding its remit, was extremely critical of the colonial government. Described by one historian as 'one of the most important documents produced in the colonial period of not only Ghanaian history but also of modern African history.'[8] From then on, even though the British believed they could control developments, they were often taken by surprise by events which outstripped their expectations. The British failed to appreciate the growth of political consciousness and its translation into a movement for national independence. If, unlike in India, the British were not desperately seeking an avenue of escape, the pace of their retreat in the Gold Coast, however cooperative was much more rapid than they expected.

The constitutional criticisms of the Watson Report were addressed by a British-appointed committee composed entirely of Africans, who were expected to produce the necessary constitutional remedies. The Coussey Committee contained members of the United Gold Coast Convention Party who were deemed sufficiently 'responsible' to cooperate on essentially British terms in the transfer of power. The thrust of the recommendations was generally in line with Colonial Office thinking as, unlike their French counterparts, British officials were prepared to accept the transfer of power and the self-government that went with it. The issues were how, when, and to whom.

The British hope was that the Coussey proposals would enable them to control the pace of change.

Kwame Nkrumah

Born in Nekroful, Western Gold Coast (now Ghana) and educated at Catholic mission schools, Nkrumah trained to be a teacher in Accra in 1926. Later he travelled to the United States and took degrees at Lincoln and Pennsylvania Universities. Nkrumah then moved to London in 1945 and studied law. Nkrumah was active in the West African Students Union and when he returned to the Gold Coast in 1947 he became leader of the United Gold Coast Convention Party. After being forced to resign in 1949 over his 'Positive Action' campaign which included widespread agitation and civil disobedience, Nkrumah formed his own political party called the Convention People's Party. In 1950 he was imprisoned by the British as a subversive but was released in 1951 following a landslide victory by the CPP. He was elected the first Prime Minister of the Gold Coast in 1952 and five years later the Gold Coast became the first black African colony to achieve independence and took the name of Ghana. Nkrumah declared Ghana a republic in 1960 and decreed himself president for life in 1964 and banned all opposition parties. In 1966 he was deposed while on a visit in Peking and the Ghanaian people reacted with jubilation. Nkrumah died in exile.

In 1948 a Committee on Youth Organization had been established within the UGCC by Kwame Nkrumah an American-educated former school-teacher. Nkrumah was a radical nationalist with left-wing beliefs and associations who was sometimes unfairly depicted as a communist detainee but who was less inclined to accept the gradualism with which the Colonial Office wished to approach self-government. In June 1949 Nkrumah formed his Committee into the Convention Peoples Party, which soon wrested the initiative from the British and the United Gold Coast Convention. Campaigning on the slogan of 'Self-Government Now' Nkrumah, to British surprise, quickly built support and established a political machine, which was more dynamic and had greater mass appeal than that of the UGCC. The reforms which were introduced included ministerial government and a legislative assembly with representatives from the whole of the Gold Coast. But they were measures which were seen as limiting the kind of radicalism Nkrumah represented. Crucially, ministers were responsible to the executive council and therefore to the governor who retained reserve powers over the whole constitution. It was a long way from 'Self-Government Now'.

In January 1950 Nkrumah launched 'Positive Action' in the form of a general strike but the colonial government prevented any serious violence and most of the leaders of the protest, including Nkrumah, were arrested, charged, and convicted. If there were expectations that this was another stage in containing radicalism and ensuring that the elections in early 1951 would be won by moderates, they were again to be mistaken. One leading member of the CPP, K. A. Gbedemah, had remained at large and was able to maintain the party organization. When municipal elections were held later in 1950 the CPP swept the board. As the registration for the assembly elections got under way it became clear that the CPP was better equipped to assist in this process than the chiefs. When the CPP repeated their electoral success in 1951 and even managed to gain twenty-nine seats from the collegiate electoral system it was clear that a mass-based political party demanding independence had to be reckoned with.

The next stage of the transfer of power was facilitated by the approach of the post-Accra riots governor, Sir Charles Arden-Clarke, who had never believed in the idea that the Cold War involved African communists hiding under every bush. He was also aware that neither a commitment to democracy nor to the retention of British influence could be secured with the leader of the largest political party in gaol. Nkrumah was therefore released and persuaded to cooperate with Arden-Clarke and the British in transferring power to himself and the CPP. In the Gold Coast this was to be a straightforward democratic process and the Africanization of government at all levels continued apace.

The smooth transfer of power was still dependent to some extent on the close cooperation between Nkrumah and the governor, which would avoid conflict and hopefully establish the kind of good post-independence relations that the British valued as a means of preserving influence. Arden-Clarke was able to persuade Oliver Lyttelton, the new Colonial Secretary under the 1951 Churchill government, of the value of this strategy even though there were many in the Conservative Party who fought shy of the idea of independence. Thus Britain kept control of foreign and defence policy, along with the police, while in 1952 Nkrumah assumed the title of prime minister as the executive council became the Cabinet. In 1953 the British accepted that the legislative assembly should be directly elected and after fresh elections in June 1954 the CPP again emerged victorious.

The only cloud on the horizon was the emergence in Ashanti of an opposition party seeking independence on the basis of a federal system. Eventually Nkrumah and the CPP were forced to undergo another electoral trial before the Gold Coast became independent in March 1957. In a sense the importance of the process in the Gold Coast seemed a model success but although Ghana joined the Commonwealth it contained the seeds of failure that were to sprout in other areas of British Africa. The model was applied, as much out of necessity as choice in Nigeria, which also received a new Constitution in 1946 in order to remain in step with the Gold Coast. The same process of Britain reacting to events, perhaps in ways which accelerated the development of anti-colonialism, was to be evident in Nigeria.

East and Central Africa

In 1952 a rebellion broke out amongst the Kikuyu of Kenya which was to bedevil the transfer of power in a colony that had to confront the interests of white settlers. The latter were more in evidence in Central Africa where in 1953 the British created the Central African Federation that ultimately presented an even bigger problem. It was not resolved until 1980 when the last significant act in Britain's imperial retreat (the Falklands War notwithstanding) took place. The Federation contained the territories of Nyasaland and Northern and Southern Rhodesia, but the latter had achieved an anomalous position under the Crown in 1923 as a self-governing territory. This enabled its settlers to benefit from the allocation of most of the land to white farmers while promoting pass laws and colour bars. After the war the Colonial Office feared that the Rhodesian settlers might turn to the exponents of a similar and even more pernicious and exploitative system in South Africa. Broader imperial concerns about the spread of South African economic power and influence also provided an incentive for the creation of an economically strong federation. Whites in Northern Rhodesia would be united with their more numerous equivalents in the south, providing an alternative to joining with the Union of South Africa. Pressure for federation came from their leader, Roy Welensky, who had risen through the trade union ranks and from the old-fashioned reactionary, Sir Godfrey Huggins, prime minister of Southern Rhodesia and later Lord Malvern. In 1960 he continued to believe the African was a 'decent fellow' provided things were explained to him. Unfortunately 'he is being carried away by people who have been to Britain and America and have come back with left wing-ideas in their heads.'[9] What was established with ease in 1953 was to prove far more difficult to unravel in the early 1960s and had to confront the problems and dilemmas of a multiracial society which were largely absent from West Africa.

By the time they became urgent in the late 1950s there was more pressure from external sources to respond to the alleged needs of a changing Cold War world. These needs reflected the importance of regional and global requirements as opposed to the needs of individual colonies. In essence this meant transferring power to the right people at the right time generally on the basis of negative, short-term goals (out of fear of more instability or outside interference) and the formality of Commonwealth membership. The Colonial Office's hope of building Western-orientated states with sound economic prospects and adequate education and welfare was even more difficult to attain. In East and Central Africa settlers were able to influence governments in the colonial capitals as well as in London. As a result there was to be less opportunity for establishing a basis for cooperation and compromise over the nature and timing of the end of British rule. Racial problems had already contributed to a guerrilla war in 1952 in Kenya and were eventually to become a key factor in the abrupt ending of British rule in Central Africa.

C. **The Middle East**

The Middle East, perhaps more than any other region has suffered from a multitude of conflicts and rivalry. Imperialism and the struggles against it have formed part of a post-war landscape that has also witnessed disputes over oil and water, superpower competition for influence, inter-Arab rivalry, and the conflict over Palestine and the fate of its peoples. It is an area which, particularly in the immediate post-war world, had a geopolitical and strategic significance because of its position at the meeting of three continents and the scene of large-scale battles between European powers. Yet colonialism in its purest form was largely absent by the end of the Second World War. French influence was no longer significant and apart from the mandated territory and the colonies of Aden and Cyprus British rule did not formally exist. Even in the Gulf in 1945 responsibility remained that of the India Office until 1947 while the Anglo–Egyptian condominium

of the Sudan was the responsibility of the Foreign Office.

What existed in the region, dominated by the British, were less formal means of projecting and symbolizing power. In the inter-war years this informal empire had involved considerable power and influence. In the 1920s Britain exercised its mandatory responsibilities in Iraq by bombing its peoples; in Egypt before 1945 it overthrew governments by both direct and indirect means, and was able to manipulate the king, the notables, and the nationalist party of the pashas, the Wafd, to maintain significant influence over the government. Informal empire no longer was able to operate in such ways after the war as British power declined just as the importance of the region to the British increased.

This did not involve a process of decolonization but an abandonment of an ability to project power which was seen at the time, if not since, as a much more significant retreat than the abandonment of India or the moves towards self-government in South Asia and Africa. What was at issue in the Middle East was not nation-building nor the exercise of paternalism, but the future of the British Empire as a world system and the kind of world role Britain should play. Here there was no prospect of replacing control with influence even if British domination had been more benevolent. It was a question of acknowledging to the world that Britain no longer had the power to exercise dominance in the Middle East and for that there was no substitute; no Commonwealth finesse could disguise this impotence, and if it was accepted the implications were perceived as disastrous for Britain's status and prestige as a world power. British elites, always keen to maintain an international position, which reflected their superior social status at home, could not willingly accept such a loss of power. Therefore it became vital to maintain the symbols of power in the hope that what little real power did remain would be buttressed by the Americans.

Palestine

Before that a British failure occurred in Palestine which was reminiscent of the retreat from India, but without an agreement to go with the bloodshed. Palestine had become a major problem in the wake of the Balfour Declaration of 1917 and the establishment of the mandate six years later. The Palestine question was complicated by disputes over what constitutes Palestine, as the administrative units of the Roman and Ottoman empires had different boundaries from those established by the European powers after the defeat of Turkey in the First World War. Yet at one level the issue was very simple: a dispute over land between two people who believe their claims are justified. The Balfour Declaration gave British support to the establishment of a Jewish national home in Palestine and the mandate confirmed this on the understanding that it was not prejudicial to the welfare of the native inhabitants. There was of course no inherent reason why two people could not coexist side by side within the same territory, but the Zionist movement which had

---

Foreign Office Opinion of Egypt

Thinking over our difficulties in Egypt, it seems to me that the essential difficulty arises from the very obvious fact that we lack some power. The Egyptians know this, and that accounts for their intransigence.

On a strictly realistic view we ought to recognize that our lack of power must limit what we can do, and should lead us to a policy of surrender or near surrender imposed by necessity.

But the basic and fundamental aim of British policy is to build up our lost power. Once we despair of doing so, we shall never attain this aim. Power, of course, is not to be measured in terms alone of money and troops: a third ingredient is prestige, or in other words what the rest of the world thinks of us.

Here the dilemma arises. We are not physically strong enough to carry out policies needed if we are to retain out position in the world; if we show weakness our position in the world diminishes with repercussions on our world wide position.

The broad conclusion I am driven to is therefore that we ought to make every conceivable effort to avoid a policy of surrender or near surrender. Ideally we should persuade the Americans of the disaster which such a policy would entail for us and for them, and seek their backing, moral, financial, and if possible, military, in carrying out a strong policy in Egypt.

Source: FO371/90152 Minute by Sir Pierson Dixon, 23 January 1952.

---

developed since the end of the nineteenth century wanted the establishment of a Jewish state rather than the creation of a Jewish homeland. Almost immediately this produced difficulties as by 1920 Jewish immigration into Palestine had increased nearly five-fold and in 1921 Palestinian Arabs took to the streets of Jaffa in protest. The British subsequently made a number of efforts to deal with the rights of Arabs and Jews in Palestine and the issues arising from significant Jewish immigration. They were attempts to reconcile the irreconcilable. A serious outbreak of communal violence in 1929 led to two commissions under Sir William Shaw and Sir John Hope-Simpson, which examined the causes of the riots and the problems they presented. The conclusions were that the attacks stemmed from 'Arab feelings of animosity and hostility to the

Jews consequent upon the disappointment of their political and national aspirations and fear for their economic future.' The latter was understandable given Hope-Simpson's assessment that there was 'no margin of land available for agricultural settlement by new immigrants'. However, the British could only ban further immigration at the expense of the commitment to a Jewish national home and so the fundamental contradiction of the Palestine mandate was to remain. In the wake of the Arab revolt in 1936, which required significant numbers of British troops to put down, the Peel Commission in 1937 recommended the partition of Palestine. However, this solution was unacceptable to the Arabs and as the Second World War approached the prospect of further disturbances, which would require the deployment of troops, led the British government to abandon the idea. As a further gesture to the Arab world the British also imposed Jewish immigration quotas of 10,000 per year for five years plus 25,000 refugees. This coincided with the rise of Nazis persecution and genocide, which many European Jews were to experience as a result.[10]

The British were therefore in a tricky situation as the War drew to a close and boat loads of refugees made desperate attempts to obtain sanctuary in

---

David Ben-Gurion (1886–1973)

Born in Plonsk, Poland, Ben-Gurion attended local Jewish schools in Poland before emigrating to Palestine in 1906. He worked as a farm labourer and became an active Zionist. At the Universities of Salonika and Constantinople he studied law but was forced to leave Turkey in 1915 because of his Zionist activities. During the First World War I he fought against the Turks in Palestine. Ben-Gurion became secretary-general of the Jewish Labour Federation from 1921 to 1930, when he was elected leader of the Mapai Party. In 1935 he was appointed chairman of the Jewish Agency, the executive body of the World Zionist Organisation. When the state of Israel was proclaimed in 1948, he became the first prime minister and minister for defence. He held these positions until 1953 and then again from 1955 to 1963, when he retired. He briefly returned to politics from 1965 to 1967 to lead the breakaway Labour (Rafi) Party but resigned his seat in parliament in 1970.

Palestine. Their attempts to escape from it were based less on a solution acceptable to both parties (which did not exist) but on getting the United States to assist in determining and then imposing one, which would be least hated. An Anglo-American Committee of Inquiry was set up in 1945 and in 1946 proposed the establishment of a bi-national state still under the supervision of the mandatory power and the entry of 100,000 Jews. The British government was not happy with the immigration proposals nor with still being left with sole responsibility for Palestine. Further discussions by British and American officials to resolve these issues produced the Morrison–Grady report, named after the participants. The modified proposals it contained placed a new emphasis on partition with separate and autonomous political units that would be both under international supervision. As the solutions of partition or a bi-national state were debated within the British government the American president, Harry Truman, decided to make a statement in support of the immediate entry of 100,000 Jews. This would affect decisions on the actual divisions in Palestine which had not yet been determined and effectively killed off the idea of Anglo-American cooperation in a solution to the Palestine problem. In the autumn of 1946 the British brought Zionist representatives together with those from Arab states in a final attempt to reach a settlement but the effort was counter-productive in that Arab leaders competed with each other to champion the Palestinian cause which made any compromise even more unlikely.

Meanwhile the situation on the ground was continuing to worsen from the British point of view. Despite the Arab Mufti of Jerusalem's support for the Germans, the British were reluctant to create distinct Jewish forces for the war effort. Their concerns about their position in the broader Middle East created strong support for policies which were acceptable to Arab leaders and delayed the formation of a separate Jewish army thereby hampering the creation of well-trained Jewish forces except those who were incorporated individually into the British Army. The War in that sense increased the incentives to establish a Jewish organization which would be in place to wage a campaign against Palestinian Arabs to establish a Jewish state. It also encouraged the development of underground Jewish forces in the Hagana, which had been created in 1920. Given the lack of Palestinian unity and the persistence of different political groupings the British were the only organized force in the way of Zionist ambitions at the end of the War and some Jews were prepared to use all means to remove them. As a result Arab nationalism and the Palestinian revolt were now accompanied by an anti-British Jewish campaign from 1942 onwards. Between 1944 and 1946 the Stern Gang and the Irgun, Jewish terrorist groups, carried out a number of operations against British forces. With the involvement of two future Israeli prime ministers they also assassinated the Minister of State in the Middle East, Lord Moyne, and blew up the British military HQ at the King David Hotel in Jerusalem killing ninety-one people including Jewish and Arab civilians.

With violence on the increase by 1947 the British were reluctant to try and hold the ring in Palestine even though in 1946 the military had argued that the retention of Palestine was vital for their position in the region. Consequently in the same month, February 1947, that Attlee announced the date of the British withdrawal from India, the government agreed to place the Palestine problem in the hands of the United Nations. The United Nations set up a Special Committee on Palestine (UNSCOP) which in August 1947 duly came out in favour of the partition of Palestine and the creation of a Jewish state. The partition solution was accepted by the Zionists and endorsed by the UN General Assembly in November 1947. It was a settlement which gave the Jews 56 per cent of the land when they constituted less than one-third of the population. The Arabs who had never accepted the principle that they should give up their land to save significant numbers of Jewish refugees from the holocaust when the vast areas of Europe and North America were reluctant to share any of the burden. Neither were the British prepared to take up the burden of implementing the UN-devised settlement and in the wake of the partition plan announced in September that all British forces would be withdrawn by May 1948.

The hanging of murdered and booby-trapped British soldiers had caused bitter feelings in post-war Britain but the reasons for the withdrawal were more complex. They were partly financial, partly inherent

in the realization that there was no settlement that both parties could accept, and partly because Britain's position could be maintained through a military presence in Egypt. In addition there was a sense that Palestine was going to continue to be a source of trouble and it might therefore pay the British to wash their hands of the matter. It was believed that if a Jewish state were established blame would be focused on the Americans with the British able to claim to the Arab world that they had done their best to work out a solution. Once partition was agreed they could claim, on the back of an abstention in the UN, that they had not supported partition. By then refusing to be involved with its imposition they would preserve some kudos in he Arab world. In that sense it was not the first stage of a planned retreat from the Middle East but the cause of a renewed commitment to stay and to attempt to get Arab support for that presence.

Unfortunately that support was far from guaranteed. Already in 1945 the Egyptians had requested that the British withdraw in peacetime from Egypt. Concerned as always with their military position within the region as a whole, the British military agreed to do so in the spring of 1946 when they still assumed it would be possible to retain Palestine. Unfortunately an agreement was never ratified because the rest of 1946 was taken up with arguments over the conditions under which the base would be maintained and reoccupied in times of conflict. By the start of 1947 the position in Palestine was rather different and the year saw Britain facing the prospect of a military withdrawal. The military then claimed that large numbers of troops were necessary in Egypt in peacetime in order to defend the Middle East, which by 1951 was to bring them into serious conflict with the Egyptians.

With the UN acceptance of the partition in Palestine conditions there deteriorated rapidly. British forces were no longer concerned with efforts to maintain law and order as they were preoccupied with a safe and dignified withdrawal by May 1948. From November 1947 onwards Palestine became the location for a civil war as Arabs and Jews battled for position and strategic advantage. Initial Arab attacks on Jews in Haifa, Tel Aviv, and other cities and the formation of a Palestinian force to resist partition, were followed by an attempted siege of Jerusalem.

As spring broke, however, Jewish forces broke out and by March 1948 had gained control of the areas allocated to the Jews by the UN and began to seize Arab territory in Palestine. By the time the state of Israel was established on the departure of the British on 14 May 1948 the Palestine army was in disarray and many thousands of Arabs were fleeing their homes. The following day Israel was attacked by the armed forces of Egypt, Jordan, Syria, and Iraq thereby beginning the first Arab–Israeli War which, in three phases was to last until early 1949.

The first phase ended in June 1948 with a truce that was broken briefly in July. By September the United Nations mediator Count Bernadotte from Sweden had produced a plan for the repartition of Palestine. Bernadotte proposed to attach Arab Palestine to Transjordan but the Arabs refused again to accept the principle of partition and a Jewish state. The Israelis were also unhappy because the Negev, which had enormous symbolic importance to Jews like the Israeli leader, David Ben Gurion, was now given to the Arabs. The peace process was abruptly halted by terrorists from the Stern Gang who assassinated the peacemaker in September 1948. To all intents and purposes the first Arab–Israeli War ended with the Egyptian–Israeli armistice in February 1949. Israel had now extended its territory by one-third and further gains were to follow. The peace process continued in earnest, encouraged by the great powers and was to remain in progress (or without it) until the next century.

After the Lausanne Conference in 1949 when both sides accepted the UN partition as a framework for discussion, Britain, France, and the United States signed the tripartite declaration in May 1950 which was an attempt to prevent further armed conflict in the region. The declaration indicated their opposition to the use of force, restricted the sale of arms to the region, and promised consultation over the action to take if either side breached the armistice lines. The Cold War now had a new dimension in the Middle East because the Soviet Union had been an important backer of Israel and enabled it to receive vital arms supplies. The Russians had previously tried to gain greater influence in the Middle East on the basis of specific demands on Turkey and Iran. Now they were supporting Israel because the British in particular were seen as firmly

linked to the Arab world which was a necessary means of retaining their regional predominance. Soviet–Israeli links were broken when the Korean War broke out and Israel sided firmly with the West, but Soviet influence presented a prospect that would worry their policy-makers for years to come. As Western support for Israel became firmer there was always the risk that the Soviets would be able to establish close links with the Arab states that would greatly enhance their regional influence.

Egypt, the Cold War, and Middle Eastern Defence

Thus the Cold War in the Middle East became a battle for influence rather than a battle to prevent Soviet territorial or military gains in the form of bases. As in Europe, however this political and ideological battle for hearts and minds was connected to, but in reality separate from, the military issue of defence. The British and the Americans held talks on defence in the autumn of 1947 and in essence the United States was prepared to support the importance that the British attached to the defence of the region. American aircraft and troops were to join with the British in attempting to defend the region within one month of D-Day. Similarly the State Department defined US policy in the 1940s in terms of supporting the British as the leading Western power.

However, by 1950 things were beginning to change as American economic interests and Cold War concerns began to increase as their support for defending the region lessened. The growth of Middle Eastern oil production in response to increasing demand produced a new agreement between the Saudi monarchy and the Arabian–American Oil Company (ARAMCO). British firms, receiving no Treasury backing, were unable to match this agreement which gave greater benefits to the producing country by replacing the existing royalties arrangement with a more generous profit-sharing agreement. Interestingly, as the American stake in oil development grew, its commitment to defending the region declined in the wake of the changes to the short-term global war plan in 1949. With a new commitment to defend a bridgehead in southern

Spain and to build up reinforcements in North Africa, the Americans were no longer prepared to commit forces to the defence of the Middle East, which they deemed a British responsibility. Unfortunately the British lacked the resources to do this and their first plan to defend the region in 1948 (Plan Sandown) took a line from Tel Aviv to Ramallah as the main defence line. Not only did this not defend the Middle East, it did not even defend Israel. The British were in the position of insisting on retaining peacetime base facilities in Egypt in order to defend the Middle East. But the reality was that they needed a base in Egypt, as a symbol of power and prestige, and the military plans were to defend that base not the Middle East. Moreover, what resources they did have were progressively to be reduced especially in the wake of the 1952 global strategy paper.

All hot war defence plans of course were not concerned with the Cold War use of military force, which the Global Strategy Paper gave priority to, in ways that would assist in the battle for the hearts and minds of the region's people. The British argument was that their military presence was necessary to quell internal unrest and to promote confidence by convincing the indigenous people that they would protect them from the Soviet threat. The argument was disingenuous in a number of ways, in addition to the lack of British capability, and simply reflected the British need to avoid being seen as a declining global power when formal imperial responsibilities were abandoned. For one thing it was not going to be easy to convince Arabs and Jews of the need to defend the region from an external threat when they saw the real threat as emanating from within. For another thing, as the Americans began to realize, the British presence was more a threat to stability than a promoter of it. They were then influenced by two events in the early 1950s, which were important in the end of the British Empire and in terms of the Cold War.

The Iranian Crisis and the Coup in Egypt

In March 1951 the Iranian parliament passed a decree nationalizing the Anglo-Iranian Oil Company which was implemented in May by the party of Mohammed Mussadiq the only bourgeois nationalist party in Iran. Mussadiq was striking at the greatest symbol of foreign domination as the Anglo-Iranian Oil Company ran the biggest refinery in the world at Abadan. By October the issues of personnel and management within the newly nationalized company were still not resolved and resulted in the expulsion of British workers from Abadan. This 'scuttle' was regarded as a deep British humiliation by the Conservative government, which came to power in the same month eager to persuade the Americans that Mussadiq and his supporters were anti-Western. Attacks on Britain were claimed to be damaging to the Western cause and the irresponsible nationalism of Mussadiq deemed likely to produce the kind of instability that would be exploited by the communist party. As the British sought support in the overthrow of Mussadiq the Truman administration were reluctant to accept the picture that the British were portraying. For them Mussadiq represented a progressive form of nationalism which was needed to create a more modern and democratic Middle East no longer subject to European, as opposed to American, imperialism.

More importantly, the State Department came to believe that because Britain no longer had the power to impose itself in the region and in so doing dictate to the Arab states in the Cold War, the United States would have to take a greater interest in the region. It was assumed that that would essentially involve developing their own policies in conjunction with the British but by 1951 that was becoming difficult to do. Seeing the corruption and inefficiency which characterized the rule of King Farouk in Egypt and the landowning notables who formed the palace cliques, the CIA had begun to foster contacts with young Egyptian officers who it was hoped would end the corruption of the monarchy which the British continued to rely on. Once these 'free officers' led by Gamal Abdul Nasser had overthrown Farouk in July 1952, the Americans were particularly keen to play the role of mediators in the conflict between Britain and Egypt over the Suez base. This was not welcomed by the British, who had used tanks in January 1952, after a campaign of terror had begun in 1951, with the aim of expelling the British from the Suez base and which culminated in the burning of the

European district of Cairo. The British believed that strong American backing for their stance would be the way to obtain an agreement on the base, but this became less and less likely as the Americans struggled to keep a foot in both camps without alienating the British. A new phase in the Middle East battleground began in June 1953 when the new Republican administration's Secretary of State, John Foster Dulles, visited the region. In addition to the conflict between the Arab states and Israel which involved cross-border incidents and an Arab blockade, there was the Anglo–Egyptian conflict and the Anglo–Iranian dispute which were adding to the divisions in the region and diverting attention from resolving the Arab–Israeli dispute. Dulles returned shocked by the extent of anti-British feeling in the region and convinced that the United States would have to take the initiative in the Middle East even if it meant pursuing policies which the British were unwilling to back.

This was to contribute to the subsequent disaster which befell the British in the Suez Crisis of 1956, but in the short term new American policies led to cooperation over Iran. Dulles, as part of the new Cold War American initiatives, was seeking to inaugurate a Middle East regional defence grouping. Unlike previous attempts such as the Middle East Command, it would not be based on Egypt but based on the northern tier of countries from Turkey down through Iraq, Iran, and Pakistan. It would aim to prevent Soviet expansion into the Gulf but in reality such geopolitical ideas made little strategic sense. Apart from the lack of direct US military involvement in the Middle East and the lack of British and indigenous forces there was the fact the natural defence line of the Zagros Mountains ran through rather than between Iran and Iraq. This may have influenced American thinking in so much as it made

it more difficult to ensure Iranian involvement and therefore it was important to have a ruler there who could be relied on to put US interests first. As a result, as H. W. Brands has suggested,[11] the Americans now changed their position on Iran. Mussadiq, whatever his value in relation to nationalism and anti-communism, could not be relied on whereas the Shah would be happier to play the role defined for him by the Americans. Thus the CIA cooperated with MI6 in creating the right conditions for a coup to bring the Shah back to power which took place in July 1953. As a result the possibility of a modern, secular political movement as a unifying force in Iran was sacrificed for the prospect of a political encirclement of the Soviet Union. The means was a defence grouping which would have little strategic benefit and a lot of political disadvantages to offset any Cold War political gains.

One of the main tensions between a global Cold War and regional instability and conflict was that measures deemed likely to assist in the Cold War would contribute to regional conflicts. This was particularly true in the Middle East where the Soviet desire for more influence was made clear in 1945 and 1946. Economic concessions and territorial gains were regarded as completely unacceptable by the British who were able to persuade the Americans that Soviet imperialism was more threatening than their own. By the time these regional power political crises had contributed to the global Cold War by 1948, the Middle East was the scene of internal hot war over territory that was linked to the retreat of British power. If, as suggested by Ronald Hyam,[12] decolonization was merely a footnote to the Cold War, there can be no doubt that in the Middle East the Cold War and its connections to rival imperialisms and regional conflicts were to produce a deadly mix of irreconcilable aims.

NOTES

1. The policy of assimilating Africans into French culture and political life.
2. John D. Hargreaves, *Decolonization in Africa* (Longman, New York, 2nd edn., 1996), 98–9.
3. Ibid. Citing Archives National Section d'Outre-Mer (ANSOM), *Affaires Politiques* 2255/1, Moutet to Ramadier, 1 Aug. 1947.
4. Hargreaves, op. cit., 154–5.

CHRONOLOGY: DECOLONIZATION, 1945–1953

1944

August   National Council of Nigeria and Cameroons is created.

1945

8 May   Sétif massacre in Algeria.

1946

February   Indian elections confirm Congress and Muslim League as main parties.
March   New Gold Coast Constitution published.
March–June   Failure of Cabinet Mission to India.
October   Bamako Congress founds the Rassemblement Démocratique Africain (RDA).
                Bengal massacres.

1947

February   Cabinet statement on Britain's decision to hand over power in India.
March   Riots in Madagascar.
August   India and Pakistan independent.
November   Nkrumah is made Secretary of the United Gold Coast Convention (UGCC).

1948

January   Burma and Ceylon become independent.
28 February   Riots in Accra.
June   Watson report on the Gold Coast published.
                Malayan Emergency begins.

1949

June   Nkrumah forms the Convention People's Party (CPP) in Ghana.
October   Britain accepts the Coussey report on the Gold Coast.
December   Northern Peoples' Congress is established in Nigeria.
December–January Disorder in the Ivory Coast.

1950

January	'Positive Action' in the Gold Coast.
September	René Pleven makes overtures to Félix Houphouet-Boigny.

1951

February	The CPP is elected in the Gold Coast.
June	The Macpherson Constitution is enacted for Nigeria.
September	Victoria Falls Conference on the Central African Federation takes place.

1952

20 October	Mau Mau Emergency begins.

1953

30 July	Nigerian Constitutional Conference takes place in London.
August	Sultan of Morocco deported.

The Cold War Intensifies: Containment Superseded, 1948–1953

A. Covert Operations and the Origins of Cold War Fighting

By 1948 the dominant relationship between the Soviet Union and Britain and the United States had moved from one of cooperation to confrontation and then to hostility and conflict. In this situation the Cold War had not only begun but required a clearly defined strategy for fighting it. In the West interpretations of this strategy have been largely based on the idea of containment and therefore much of the argument has been about the form of containment that should be chosen or subsequently deemed most appropriate. Did it require military strength and a preponderance of power or should it concentrate on economic success with the provision of full employment, growth, and consumer goods? Should it focus on the important economic areas of the world or should it be a truly global struggle? The idea that, as confrontation gradually replaced cooperation from 1946, containment too was superseded by a Cold War aimed at destroying the enemy or fatally undermining its strength is a relatively new idea that has received little attention. For one thing containment implies an expansionist power (in orthodox interpretations the Soviet Union) which provokes a defensive response (the United States and its European allies). Yet, as with the origins of the Cold War, by 1948 fighting the Cold

War needs to be seen more in terms of competing powers each prepared to go beyond preserving the status quo and to reject the form of coexistence implied by a Cold War of containment as too defensive.

One neglected and murky area, which came to the fore of the Cold War confrontation in 1948, is the area of covert operations and propaganda, an area geared to aggressive subversion rather than defensive containment. The Soviets had of course many agents in the West during the inter-war years, which was a reflection of their Civil War experiences in which fear of the capitalist West was rooted. Fear was easily converted into paranoia by Stalin who saw most things in terms of threats to his personal position of power and to the ruthless, tyrannical system which sustained it. This in turn required that every effort be made to discover internal and external enemies, and if possible eradicate or weaken them.

Soviet intelligence activities at home and abroad in the inter-war years were geared to the detection and elimination of these 'enemies of the people' like Trotsky and those foreigners who were prepared to work against the revolution. Stalin never trusted the Americans and the British to refrain from their early efforts to destroy the Bolshevik regime and the Soviet intelligence services had agents operating in both the US and Britain. Western communists working for the Soviet Union often had the naïve idea that working for the NKVD (People's Commissariat for Internal Affairs which incorporated state security) would make a significant contribution to the struggle against fascism. In Britain five recruits successfully infiltrated the British Foreign and Intelligence Services (Burgess, Blunt, Cairncross, Philby, and MacLean). During the War Stalin devoted considerable resources to spying on his allies (221 agents in the US) and was never free from the paranoid suspicion that the British and the Americans would be prepared to do a deal with the Germans to the detriment of Moscow. When the War ended some of the numerous agents that were operating in the West (most successfully in Britain) were compromised by an American code-breaking success known as VENONA. Along with defectors' testimonies, VENONA enabled some agents to be identified and the extent of the Soviet espionage system to be revealed.[1]

The Soviet secret services did however have the advantage of knowing about the British position prior to the negotiations at some of the wartime conferences and about British attitudes to the Soviets in the 1940s, as well as the nature of British and American operations against the Soviet Union.[2] It is not possible to tell what information went to Stalin and there are doubts about how effectively the Soviets could deal with the vast amount of information coming from Philby, Burgess, and MacLean.[3] Papers of the Post Hostilities Planning Committee reflecting military hostility to the Soviet Union and its perceived wartime status as the next enemy or only potential enemy were sent to Moscow. Whether this, as the Foreign Office feared, encouraged Soviet suspicion and resentment remains a matter for speculation.[4] As in most areas, the impact of intelligence remains uncertain, but for Stalin it is at least arguable that what mattered was less the undermining of the capitalist system than the preservation of a Soviet state from enemies, some of whom were imaginary, but some of whom were very real and hostile to it. This state embodied his own personal power and its protection required concentrating on enemies, and eliminating or monitoring them whether they were individuals or governments, real or imaginary. The desire to infiltrate Soviet agents into Western governments in order to acquire military and technical information and learn about Western policy and strategy (which after 1917 was often aimed against the Soviets) could also be reasonably interpreted as a desire to control or manipulate policy and enhance the aggressive desires of the Soviet Union. When the network of Soviet spies continued to operate during the Second World War and after, its exposure was something which cast doubt about Soviet desires to cooperate and could be used to portray Moscow in a negative light from 1946 onwards. On the other hand, it could be interpreted as a means of manipulating Western policy (along with foreign communist parties) with the goal of simply reducing the threat from hostile powers opposed to cooperation. Once cooperation was no longer a realistic option for either side the issue of whether Stalin was a cautious or a reckless leader becomes more important.

Soviet spies became important weapons at the start of the propaganda war, which was beginning in 1946 as confrontation loomed larger between the wartime allies. As another illustration of the similarity of both sides' perceptions of being under threat each was concerned about the hostile propaganda of the other and each claimed to be reacting to the hostility of the other. In 1945 Russian diplomatic representatives claimed the 'Anglo-Americans have not curtailed but enhanced their propaganda apparatus' and redirected it to the 'ideological struggle against the USSR'. As the issue became more important, organizations in Moscow debated how propaganda could be improved to counter the West's 'global and reckless ideological offensive'. It led to conflict and bureaucratic in-fighting as well as repeated assertions of the need for propaganda to be more 'offensive' and 'penetrating'. Of course the justification of Stalin's regime, which lacked the political freedom and economic success of Western Europe and North America, was always going to be difficult but the idea of a vast and well-organized Soviet propaganda offensive clearly needs revising.[5]

In the West the secret services in the inter-war years were, like their Russian counterparts, con-cerned with a historic and ideological enemy. Once the Cold War began at the end of 1947, a significant campaign of psychological warfare was mounted which involved more than propaganda and the gathering of intelligence. 'Instead it encompassed any initiative which might affect the position of a foreign regime.'[6] From the start this involved the mounting of covert operations against the Soviet Union and its satellite regimes by organizations like the Special Operations Executive, whose operatives had remained in place since the War and who had occasionally contributed even before 1948 to measures taken against the Soviet regime. This was a different kind of threat from that posed by Soviet spies infiltrating the West and it reflected a certainty amongst the personnel of the Special Operations Executive and the Secret Intelligence Service that the Soviet Union should be undermined whatever, whether it was an ally or an enemy. Throughout the war MI5 (responsible for counter-subversion) maintained extensive surveillance on Bolsheviks in Britain.[7]

To some extent the different roles of covert operatives stemmed from the great advantage enjoyed by the West in having a socio-economic and political system which was based largely on elements of popular support. As a result there was less opportunity for communist agents to work with dis-affected national minorities or opponents of a harsh repressive regime, but greater prospects of gathering information. Soviet oppression made it harder for spies to operate within the Soviet Union and this was always to be a problem for Western intelligence. However, the existence of groups opposed to Russian communism had had secret contacts with Western operatives as early as 1946. In December some of the 25,000 Ukrainian guerrillas assassinated the head of the Odessa MGB (the successor to the NKVD and the predecessor of the KGB). What precise role the West played in relation to these opponents of Stalin remains obscure both then and subsequently, but the responsibility for managing Ukrainian exiles lay with the British Secret Service until 1953 when the CIA took over.[8] The Soviet support for communist parties in the West was geared to electoral success until 1947 after which Moscow demanded that greater emphasis be given to extra-parliamentary action, although the popularity of the French and Italian communists remained a cause of concern in Britain and the US. However, by 1948 the communists' initial post-war electoral successes were effectively being countered by the vast resources that the Central Intelligence Agency could deploy to influence elections. The two situations in which Eastern European opponents of communism were assisted in undermining it and Western opponents assisted in preventing its spread reveal quite nicely the distinction between a policy of containment and a policy of rollback or liberation.

In 1948, while CIA money was working to reduce the prospect of communist electoral successes in Italy, the various branches of the Truman adminis-tration, most particularly the newly established National Security Council, were devising the best ways of fighting the Cold War against the Soviet Union. Drawing on all means at their disposal the NSC first attempted to devise an overall strategy in March 1948 which in orthodox post-revisionist accounts would be referred to as the development or implementation of containment.[9] One key con-sideration in the establishment of the National Security Council was the need to link the military with the foreign-policy-makers in the State Department, but there were to be divisions within and between the various civilian and military sections of the government over Cold War strategy. NSC memorandum 7, 'The Position of the US with Respect to Soviet Directed World Communism', called for a worldwide counter-offensive against Soviet-directed world communism. It concluded that

The defeat of the forces of Soviet-directed world communism is vital to the security of the United States. This objective cannot be achieved by a defensive policy. The United States should therefore take the lead in organizing a worldwide counter-offensive aimed at mobilizing and strengthening our own and anti-communist forces in the non-Soviet world, and at undermining the strength of the communist forces in the Soviet world ... Develop, and at the appropriate time carry out, a coordinated programme to support underground resistance movements in countries behind the iron curtain, including the USSR.[10]

From March 1948, although details of the covert operations conducted by Western intelligence services are sparse, it seems that Western strategy for fighting the Cold War involved more than containment. It was based not just on making Western Europe economically strong and politically resistant to Soviet communism (containment) but undermining communism and terminating the Soviet satellite-empire in Eastern Europe (roll-back/liberation). Roll-back would thus have started earlier than the 1950s and the idea of a Cold War beginning as one side defensively responded to the aggressive moves of the other (containment) becomes even more implausible.

Those who do not accept this would argue that the West's response was to the February 1948 communist coup in Czechoslovakia but they find it more difficult to claim that the response was purely defensive. John Lewis Gaddis's attempt is based on the fact that some members of the State Department were not happy with NSC 7. While this is true (although the Joint Chiefs of Staff endorsed it), the State Department's one criticism was that the memorandum and its recommendations, most of which were deemed worthy of support, lacked one general theme. In April this criticism of one Assistant Secretary in the State Department was based on the lack of any measures to 'eliminate communism at its roots' by solving the problems that many considered could be cured by communism. If the right kind of economic and political programmes were put in place, there would be no need to suppress communist activities in the West because they would have no impact.[11] It was an important point, but separate from the undermining of communism in Eastern Europe. A policy of containment would have involved keeping communism in Eastern Europe and preventing its spread westwards by assisting Western Europe economically (the Marshall Plan line of the previous year) and if necessary interfering in the electoral process. Gaddis, however, takes the worldwide offensive as applying only to the suppression of communism in the West, and ignores the explicit linkage to subversion in Eastern Europe and the inappropriateness of a purely defensive strategy.[12]

When NSC 7 was replaced by NSC 20/4 in November 1948 this latter memorandum was drawn up by the State Department's Policy Planning Staff and was the culmination of the process begun in the summer of defining 'US Objectives with Respect to Russia'. The objectives of both countries were now laid out in more specific terms. The references to Soviet aims of world domination were accompanied by assessments that the Soviets would seek to achieve this by 'endeavouring to insert Soviet-controlled groups into positions of power and influence everywhere, seizing every opportunity presented by weakness and instability in other states and exploiting to the utmost the techniques of infiltration and propaganda, as well as the coercive power of preponderant military strength.' Yet

While the possibility of planned Soviet armed actions which would involve this country cannot be ruled out, a careful weighing of the various factors points to the probability that the Soviet government is not now planning any deliberate armed action calculated to involve the United States and is still seeking to achieve its aims primarily by political means, accompanied by military intimidation.

In this light the US should 'encourage and promote the gradual retraction of undue Russian power and influence from the present perimeter areas around traditional Russian boundaries and the emergence of the satellite countries as independent of the USSR.' To achieve this aim the US should 'place the maximum strain on the Soviet structure of power and particularly on the relationships between Moscow and the satellite countries'.[13] This further reinforced the need for measures, which were not defensive in nature, and which, according to Kennan, should constitute 'Organized Political Warfare' meaning 'the employment of all the means at a nation's command, short of war, to achieve its national objectives.' The machinery which this required was deemed to be a 'covert operations directorate within the government'. This naturally raised the question of who such a directorate would be accountable to and Kennan was determined to ensure State Department control rather than, for example, leaving it to the CIA. What emerged was the Office of Special Projects which was supervised by the Secretaries of State and Defence and which would be responsible for operations

Conducted or sponsored by this government against hostile foreign states or groups or in support of friendly foreign states or groups but which are so planned and executed that any US government responsibility for them is not evident to unauthorized persons and that, if uncovered, the US government can plausibly disclaim any responsibility for them. Specifically, such operations shall include any covert activities related to: propaganda; economic warfare; preventive direct action, including sabotage, anti-sabotage, demolition, and evacuation measures; subversion against hostile states, including assistance to underground resistance movements, guerrillas and refugee liberation groups, and support of indigenous anti-Communist elements in threatened countries of the Free World.[14]

As a result the CIA was removed from special operations and the gathering of intelligence separated from the covert fighting of the Cold War until 1950.

The Office of Special Projects soon became the Office of Policy Coordination responsible for all US covert operations behind the Iron Curtain as defined in NSC 20/4. It is hard to see how this could be seen as containment although it was not the overthrow of the Soviet government either but the weakening and rolling back of Soviet power by all means short of war. It was, however, crucial to the Cold War, and from a staff of 302 with a budget of

$4.7 million in 1949 the OPC had expanded by 1952 to 2,812 personnel with 3,142 contract staff and a budget of $82 million. This of course was what many in Moscow expected as part of the effort to extend US-backed capitalism to Eastern Europe and ultimately to the rest of the world, just as many in Washington expected the expansion of communism to be geared to world domination by the Soviet Union.

By 1948 many people in the US administration were convinced that they were in a war. It was not a hot one in the sense that it involved international armed conflict, but it was a crucial struggle in which, as in a hot war, there could be only one winner. The Soviet Union with its numerous spies in North America had shown that it was keen, like Britain and the United States, to acquire and maintain global influence and to promote a rival ideology through groups who were answerable to Moscow. It thus presented a power political and an ideological threat of great potency, which was a combination not seen since the French Revolution. Moreover, it threatened the fundamental allegiance to capitalist democracy and the new international order, planning for which had occupied so much more attention in the United States.

This has been described as a liberal order, which the liberal moment in 1945 prompted the US to seek to bring about as a goal and consequence of hegemony.[15] Once this order was seen as threatened, rather like the Bolsheviks and Stalin saw their order as under threat, the inauguration of political warfare became necessary in 1948. It has been suggested above (see Part I, Introduction) that this competition for the survival or destruction of two incompatible world-orders was initially born from the power political turbulence of 1945 which then exacerbated the mistrust and confrontation inherent in two conflicting ideologies. In the West, American policy has almost universally been described as containment either because it was necessary to keep the evils of Stalin's totalitarian regime at bay and/or because the expansionist aims of the Soviet state as allegedly developed in Eastern Europe had to be contained. The possibility of the Cold War breaking out, because of competition over power, influence, and the establishment of incompatible global orders is rarely discussed. Nor are the implications of the US being involved in an ideological crusade to impose an economic or political order, rather than contain a Soviet one.

Such possibilities further undermine the standard orthodox and post-revisionist justification of the West's role in the first 20 years of the Cold War but without giving support to the revisionist emphasis on economics, the importance of the latter notwithstanding, or attributing blame to the US. Further evidence on the idea of containment is presented by Scott Lucas, referring to correspondence sent to

the Psychological Strategy Board.[16] 'Though it seems to be widely believed inside the Government as well as by the public that our policy is simply "containment", it may be doubted whether it is or has been, except for public consumption.'[17] Military strategy and the need for Western rearmament may have also been defined in terms that were geared to public consumption, but the reason why the Cold War came to involve the expansion of armaments, largely required for hot war, requires more explanation.

B. Armaments and Militarization

The first stage in the rearmament of the West began at a time when the military in Britain and the United States did not believe it likely that the Soviet Union would start a major war. The initial steps were political in nature and designed to create military alliances for political purposes. Furthering the Cold War in this way was, however, not the whole story and the first alliances in Europe, the Treaty of Dunkirk between Britain and France and the Brussels Treaty between Britain, France, Holland, Belgium, and Luxembourg had their roots in European concerns which were separate from the Cold War. The attempts to create a Third Force and to seek the containment of Germany instigated a process of European integration which became tangled with and taken over by the demands of the Cold War. The second stage of the process stemmed from NSC 68 and involved the significant expansion of Western armed forces. This was not, however, a response to the aggression in Korea: it came from the internal debate about fighting the Cold War which began in 1948 and was to continue after the Korean War enabled the supporters of military strength and rearmament to carry the day. While the war made this policy more acceptable to public opinion and legislatures on both sides of the Atlantic, it did not provide the original rationale for Western rearmament any more than the Berlin crisis provided the original rationale for NATO.

The Third World Power Idea

The involvement of the United States in a European military alliance has been portrayed as a centre point of Western involvement in the Cold War. It has almost invariably been described by politicians as the key provider of deterrence and security, which they deemed necessary because of the developing Soviet threat to Western Europe. In reality NATO's origins, like its role in the Cold War, were more complex. As with other features of East-West relations, NATO was born out of a mix of fear and ambition and in Cold War terms was designed to serve political more than military goals. None of this was to be explained to the Western public for whom it was now easier and more advantageous to depict the Cold War, not primarily as a political or economic conflict, but as a military confrontation

The broader value of a Western military alliance, linked only partially to the military threat of the Soviet Union, initially reflected different priorities in Washington, Paris, and London. For the Truman administration, having made an economic commitment to Europe, it seemed logical to make a military commitment if only to defend a significant investment. In Europe there was not only the communist danger to consider but also how best to deal with an economically strong West German state. Some kind of control, either economic or military, would be needed to calm Western European nerves.

NSC 68 (extract)

US Intentions and Capabilities—Actual and Potential

Political and Psychological

Our overall policy at the present time may be described as one designed to foster a world environment in which the American system can survive and flourish. It therefore rejects the concept of isolation and affirms the necessity of our positive participation in the world community.

This broad intention embraces two subsidiary policies. One is a policy which we would probably pursue even if there was no Soviet threat. It is a policy of attempting to develop a healthy international community. The other is the policy of 'containing' the Soviet system. These two policies are closely interrelated and interact on one another. Nevertheless the distinction between them is basically valid and contributes to a clearer understanding of what we are trying to do.

The policy of trying to develop a healthy international community is the long-term constructive effort we are engaged in. It was this policy which gave rise to our vigorous sponsorship of the United Nations. It is of course the principal reason for our long continuing endeavours to create and now develop the Inter-American system. It, as much as containment, underlay our efforts to rehabilitate Western Europe. Most of our international economic activities can likewise be explained in terms of this policy.

In a world of polarized power, the policies designed to develop a healthy international community are more than ever necessary to our own strength. As for the policy of 'containment', it is one which seeks by all means short of war to (1) block further expansion of Soviet power, (2) expose the falsities of Soviet pretensions, (3) induce a retraction of the Kremlin's control and influence, and (4) in general, so foster the seeds of destruction of the Soviet system that the Kremlin is brought at last to the point of modifying its behaviour to conform to generally accepted international standards. It was and continues to be cardinal in this policy that we possess superior overall power (1) as an ultimate guarantee of our national security and as (2) as an indispensable backdrop to the conduct of the policy of 'containment'. Without superior aggregate military strength, in being and readily mobilizable'—a policy of 'containment'—which in effect is a policy of calculated and gradual coercion—is no more than a policy of bluff.

Source: FRUS, 1950, 1 (State Dept., Washington, DC, 1977) NSC 68, 14 April 1950, 252–3.

Concern was understandably most evident in Paris, although there were those in the Foreign Office in London who were worried about, and distrustful, of Germans having unrestricted control over their economic and military resources. The continued presence of American forces on European soil would help allay fears of a revived German state.

For Britain, the move towards a Western alliance initially formed part of a broader scheme for economic cooperation aimed at the creation of a British-led Third Force or Third World Power. By combining the manpower and resources of Western Europe, the Middle East, and the African continent with those of the Dominions, the Foreign Office hoped that this would provide the necessary economic strength, once Marshall Aid had stimulated European recovery, for a British-led bloc to stand on equal terms with the United States and the Soviet Union. In 1948 Britain was clearly the leading European power and the Foreign Office had been making plans to develop this role further. The ultimate aim of achieving equality in terms of military and economic power with the United States and the Soviet Union was part of a global strategy to which Western Europe could contribute. It was believed (incorrectly) that the resources of the colonies and the Dominions would also be necessary as Europe could not manufacture enough goods to sell to the dollar zone in order to finance the purchase of what Western Europe needed. Raw materials and primary produce, particularly from Africa, were thought to be needed both as exports to the Western hemisphere and as substitutes for imports from America. For the Foreign Secretary, Ernest Bevin, this would represent a spiritual union of the West in which the anti-communist forces of social democracy, backed by the United States, could provide an alternative ideological focus to communism and unrestrained capitalism. More importantly, it would enable Britain to remain a world power as one of the Big Three by assuming leadership of this Third Force.

The Foreign Office gave wholehearted support to

the idea of Euro-Africa (which by the end of the year was proving increasingly unrealizable) and in January 1948 advocated the creation of a European Customs Union or Common Market which Britain would join and lead to full economic integration.[18] They met opposition from the Treasury and the Board of Trade and these economic differences proved important as the prospects of using European economic cooperation to strengthen Britain's economic position relative to the United States were reduced in 1948 and 1949. In April 1948 even a European Customs Union was seen as damaging to British interests in the short term. Military co-operation with Western Europe seemed to offer more prospects for mutual benefits, but given Britain's lack of resources and the military's distrust of their European counterparts this made an American involvement essential. Fears of communists in the French government and the desire of recreating an exclusive Anglo-American military relationship also made the military less keen on purely European cooperation than the Foreign Office. The more European cooperation was orientated to military matters the more likely it was to involve the Americans.

In the meantime there were also those in the State Department who were attracted by the idea of a successful anti-communist Third Force.

Some form of political, military, and economic union in Europe will be necessary if the free nations of Europe are to hold their own against the people of the east united under Moscow rule . . . The only way in which a European union, embracing Britain but excluding eastern Europe, could become economically healthy would be to develop the closest sort of trading relationships either with this hemisphere or with Africa.[19]

If it were to provide for permanent European recovery and the resolution of the dollar-gap problem, then it could serve American interests without incurring continued costs to the US taxpayer.

In early 1948 as Bevin worked to bring the idea of a Third Force to fruition, the first steps towards Western Union were taken with the signing of the Brussels Treaty on 17 March. The Brussels Treaty was not simply designed to create a security organiza-tion. It had important economic clauses, inspired by

ideas on future economic integration, as well as pro-viding an indication that military issues were now a consideration. Clearly the timing of the signature was influenced by the Czech coup but, as has been noted, the main short-term fear was a political not a military one. To some extent Bevin was striving to get some form of European cooperation established for the Americans to support *before* the nature of that support or involvement was defined. Unfortunately it proved difficult to find economic advantages for Britain to support the perceived political ones and impossible to get European military collaboration without involving the Americans.

By the end of 1948 any form of European inte-gration was seen as involving short-term sacrifices that could restrict British recovery and weaken the sterling area. Thus the Foreign Office conducted an assessment of the advantages and disadvantages of proceeding with the Third World Power idea or accepting a subordinate but special place in an American-dominated alliance. It argued that now the prospects of creating an independent economic bloc was not viable, and, if Europe failed to recover, Britain would be dragged down by the devastated economies of Western Europe. The devaluation crisis of October 1949 reinforced the argument and the Cabinet decided in favour of the special place in the American-dominated alliance, which had by then been partly established through the creation of NATO. The Third World Power was now dead and Britain was retreating from European economic cooperation which was to be dominated by very different goals.

The Creation of NATO

The reasons for creating what became known as the North Atlantic Treaty Organization were not primarily geared to hostile Soviet actions in Berlin nor to perceptions of an imminent Soviet military attack in Europe. Indeed, NATO was essentially con-ceived to meet political not military threats and requirements and these were as evident to the Americans as they were to the British. What mat-tered was how an alliance could build the confidence to strengthen the political will to resist communism. Reluctance to accept a paper treaty, rather than military aid or a joint military strategy as the basis for a defence agreement, came from the French not the Americans. Britain's main contribution to the creation of NATO was to persuade the French that only through the political gains of signing a paper treaty would they get the military benefits of an American commitment to provide the resources to defend Western Europe. In that they were to be proved wrong but the political value of the American commitment was to assume enormous importance in the years to come.

The military situation was such in March 1948 that neither the British nor the Americans had drawn up an emergency global war plan to determine what should be done with existing forces if a war against the Soviets should occur. Now that the Europeans had signed a defence pact it became more necessary to examine military strategy for future cooperation involving the Americans; and with the Berlin crisis there seemed a greater possibility of war by accident. The first emergency plans were produced in the early summer of 1948 before the blockade began, but it transpired that the military requirements of retreating from Western Europe clashed with the political ones of encouraging cooperation and resistance to communism. The latter depended on the political not the military effectiveness of NATO. A military alliance would inspire confidence as part of a political Cold War strategy, which at the same time was also being vigorously pursued with financial assistance to the electoral opponents of the Italian Communist Party prior to the April 1948 elections. With the Soviets not expected to attack, the British Chiefs of Staff even believed that if war did break out the Soviets would retreat eastwards rather than attack westwards. If they did attack westwards, in the short term neither European nor US forces were expected to be able to halt them.[20]

The discussions on Western military strategy, which were held in March 1948, featured only the British, the Americans, and the Canadians. In part this was because of political concerns that strategic assumptions about global war in Europe were premised on the evacuation of or retreat from the continent. Preparing for hot war against the Soviets was perceived as distinct from Cold War measures and in the short term even at odds with what was

seen as the best way of defeating communism. It thus became more convenient for this distinction to be blurred and for defence agreements to be regarded as central to defeating a Soviet military attack rather than part of a political strategy to prevent the spread of communism. This was in many ways inevitable given the clear attraction of left-wing ideas during and immediately after the War and the fact that many converts to communism in the West had been duped into believing that the Stalinist regime was something other than a murderous dictatorship. It was, however, all part of the Cold War in which militarization was not seen as necessary to prevent an imminent Soviet attack but as a necessary tool to fighting an ideological war.

In the spring of 1948, there was general agreement on some arrangement linking the United States to Western Europe involving military cooperation but not on its precise nature. Once it became clear that the Americans preferred to concentrate on an Atlantic Pact, as they feared Soviet pressure on Norway, this received priority. In the summer the political and constitutional obstacles in the United States to military ties with Europe had then to be negotiated. It soon became clear that the main French interest was not in the political aspect of military cooperation but in the practical aspects of military assistance from the Americans. By September 1948 the main framework of an agreement was in place. NATO embodied the need to portray the West's willingness to resist even if any military successes were unachievable in the medium term due to the numerical superiority of Soviet conventional forces. Political alliances with defence commitments would achieve that aim, and most importantly indicate that the Western European powers were going to stand together and not allow themselves to fall prey to communist parties beholden to Moscow. The Atlantic Pact, which established NATO, was formally signed in April 1949 and clearly directed against the Soviet Union.

The military dimension of the struggle against communism had been encouraged by the Truman Doctrine which was part of the distortion of the nature of the Soviet threat and also part of the process whereby political success in the Cold War was to become part of a zero-sum game. Gains and losses for either side in terms of governmental converts to the ideological cause were to come to have significance because of political credibility not because of the economic or strategic value of the states in question. Yet already by early 1949 the West was portraying an ideological conflict over the political and economic basis of the new world order as a military effort to defend economic and strategically important territory. The irony was not just that the idea of power blocs defining territorial areas to defend had been rejected in the immediate aftermath of the War, but that the Soviets appeared to have no desire to attack the area in Europe which in 1949 the West proclaimed was so important but which it lacked the resources to defend. NATO had contributed to a process which, largely because of the Cold War, was not what it seemed and has subsequently been made out to be.

Military Considerations for Hot War

Throughout Europe the initial military developments after the end of the War were not surprisingly ones of demobilization. The United States had a monopoly, but limited numbers of atomic weapons (13 in 1947 and 56 in 1948) and reduced its forces from 10 million in 1945 to 1.4 million in 1947. The Soviets reduced their forces from 12 million to 2.8 million in the same period.[21] At the same time the latter were taking up railway lines in Eastern Europe because of the shortage of steel in the Soviet Union. In early 1947 the 'Plan for the active defence of the territory of the Soviet Union' envisioned three main tasks for the armed forces. The first was to repel aggression and maintain the integrity of the frontiers agreed at the end of the War. The second task, for the Soviet air force, was to repel an air offensive, including one involving nuclear weapons. The third role, for the navy, was to repel a sea-borne assault and to operate in coastal waters in support of Soviet land forces. As in previous campaigns these defensive operations to halt an invasion of Soviet territory would pave the way for a counter-offensive, but the details of the planned offensive operations have not yet been disclosed. The Soviet posture in Europe after the War, concludes one historian who has examined Soviet sources, 'was the posture of a state determined to consolidate its power on the

territory it now occupied, rather than expand that territory'.[22]

Significantly the so-called militarization of the confrontation began at a time when neither side expected the other deliberately to start a major conflict. In the immediate aftermath of the War the Soviet leadership saw the atomic bomb more as a political than a military threat. Nevertheless the explosion and then the use of the first atomic weapons in the summer of 1945 clearly had momentous implications for the future nature of warfare. However, the implications were slow to produce new military ideas about warfare, and in the 1940s the concept of deterrence was not immediately embraced in Western military circles. In fact, while civilian strategists like Bernard Brodie began to think through the implications of weapons that might make war too horrible to contemplate, military thinkers remained either uncertain about the role of atomic weapons or perceived them as merely an extension of conventional warfare based on strategic bombing. Nor did the Americans believe that atomic weapons would prove decisive. In late 1948 a study of the likely outcome of dropping all their existing atomic bombs on the Soviets concluded that while it would result in 2.7 million deaths and the destruction of 30–40 per cent of Soviet industrial capacity, it would not defeat the Soviet Union and not stop Soviet forces advancing into Western Europe or the Middle East.

In the West, as the Soviet military planned how best to deal with an invasion, the subsequent rationale for NATO, based on deterring a Soviet military attack, was not one put forward by the military in 1948. First, the belief in the United States and in Britain was that the Soviets did not have the ability, due to the needs of economic reconstruction, effectively to put the nation on a war footing again. There was of course the possibility of war breaking out by accident[23] for which by 1948 preparations were being made (see below). Secondly, the importance of nuclear weapons as a deterrent was not so readily accepted by the military as is often assumed. There were those, like Air Force General Curtis LeMay who was to become head of the Strategic Air Command (which controlled US nuclear bombs) in 1948, who saw nuclear weapons as the ultimate means of ensuring the supremacy of air power. For LeMay nuclear devastation was an extension of war fighting by the kind of carpet-bombing he had employed against Japan when head of XXI Bomber Command at the end of the Second World War. Total destruction was the way LeMay believed wars would be won and for him the advent of nuclear weapons simply removed any doubts about this.[24] Yet not everyone in the US air force accepted the kind of indiscriminate nuclear targeting of cities that LeMay had in mind. And once it became a question of resources for nuclear and conventional war there were more serious doubts raised about the value of nuclear weapons in the army and navy who did not yet have them. Thus in the early 1950s there were major disputes within the American services about the role of nuclear weapons which, because of the resource implications, paralysed the drawing up of detailed global war plans on an interservice basis. Nuclear weapons did not immediately change the approach to war fighting or instantly inaugurate an age dominated by deterrence. It was a change that came gradually but one which was given more impetus by the development of the immensely more powerful hydrogen bomb than by the first atomic weapons.

Attempts were repeatedly to be made to incorporate weapons of mass destruction into a war fighting capacity, usually on the basis of their tactical use in limited war. Yet, in the Clausewitz tradition, nobody advocating their use could provide convincing reasons for limiting such use in global warfare once the other side also had the capacity to inflict mass destruction with similar weapons. If you were going to use them, it made sense to use them all as quickly as possible to minimize the opponent's capacity to retaliate and thereby to guarantee that the extent of the destruction wrought by the enemy would be as small as possible. However, once the hydrogen bomb was successfully developed by the United States in 1952 (although not then in a form which was deliverable), the likely retaliatory destruction was bound to be unacceptable for any civilized society.

The hydrogen bomb used the fusion of atoms, not just their fission or break-up, to release energy thousands of times more powerful than the atomic bomb. The threat to civilization itself was now real but it did not prevent the efforts to incorporate nuclear weapons into an active military role as well

as into a more passive one in the form of deterrence. The Soviets exploded their first hydrogen weapon in 1953, which again was more symbolic of power than of its practical, military realization as a usable weapon in a given situation. The remark of the British Foreign Secretary, Ernest Bevin, in 1947 that Britain would have to have the atomic bomb with 'the bloody Union Jack flying on top of it' was an early sign that nuclear weapons would be more of an asset in terms of status and prestige than in the wars that were to be fought. Even when such weapons could be made small enough to deliver, their political and symbolic importance remained, particularly with regard to their possession in numbers far in excess of what was likely to serve as an effective deterrence. In addition to providing the ultimate symbols of power and a source of bitter interservice rivalry, they served as a measurement of great power status.

Weapons and Strategy v. Politics and Ideology

The difficulties with the Soviets, even by 1947, had not produced unity in the West on a military plan of how best to respond were war to break out by accident. When discussions on a Western military alliance began in 1948 the Soviets did not possess nuclear weapons (their first test was in August 1949) and it was not expected that they would deliberately start a major war in the immediate future. It was believed that such a war would be likely at some point between 1954 and 1957 when Soviet capability to wage one successfully was restored. Thus there was a need to prepare for such an eventuality (although in the eyes of the military, due to developments in the early 1950s, this eventuality of the Soviets being likely to start a major war never materialized). In addition, by the end of the 1940s when an offensive Cold War campaign of political and psychological warfare got under way it began to be argued that a policy of rearmament to deter a Soviet attack was more necessary, particularly after the Soviets acquired the bomb in August 1949. The key factor here was that the Soviets would feel sufficiently provoked and threatened to resort to war out of desperation now that they too had nuclear weapons. In other words an aggressive Cold War strategy could lead to the outbreak of a hot war and this idea was to lead both to Western rearmament and to divisions between and within the British and American governments.

The relationship between military strategy, weapons, and defence policy on the one hand, and foreign policy and the politics of international relations on the other, is a somewhat neglected field. The reason for this neglect relates to the vague assumptions about the Cold War as encompassing the general aspects of Soviet–American rivalry within the newly invented framework of national security. It thus affects the debate on the importance of security and power politics, as opposed to ideology and culture, as determinants and characteristics of the Cold War. The issue can be partly unravelled by an analysis of whether foreign policy had to adapt to the requirements of strategy and operational plans (the means of implementing power to secure influence internationally), or whether these military elements had to take second place to politics and ideology (the means of creating perceptions of power to secure influence domestically and internationally). And by a more precise understanding of the Cold War and how weapons and their acquisition, along with strategies for the prevention or fighting of hot war, was influenced by and related to the Cold War struggle.

Orthodox accounts point to the heightening of the Cold War between 1940 and 1953 with a subsequent thaw on the death of Stalin. They tend to blame the Soviet leader for threatening war in Europe followed by his use of armed conflict in Korea to attempt to achieve his expansionist goals. Korea allegedly led to German rearmament and the increasingly military nature of the conflict. While correctly highlighting the attempts to expand Soviet influence, there is again a neglect of Western goals particularly in terms of how they defined fighting the Cold War. At the end of the 1940s the Cold War was not seen as all the various forms Soviet–American relations took but was a particular form of conflict, which like other wars, was expected to have winners and losers. It was defined by the British military (almost certainly with American approval) as a war fought by all means short of international armed conflict. The kind of force deployments for

this kind of war, which included civil wars, were quite different from what was required to fight a major hot war and eventually had an impact on the British military's approach to defence and global strategy.

The British and the Americans first began to draw up military plans after the March 1948 meetings on the nature of US support for Western Europe but there were soon differences of approach both between them and between the three US services. In 1949 the Americans changed their strategy for emergency war plans, preferring to give priority in global war to the maintenance of a beachhead in southern Spain which could be reinforced from North Africa rather than concentrating on defending the Middle East as the British wanted. In the United States planning for global war was a complex and difficult process within the extensive military bureaucracy. Outline plans for global war, such as plan Pincher, were different from emergency plans pertaining to meeting an attack on Western Europe with existing resources. The former were geared to a broad strategic concept and the latter having to focus on the actual availability of forces as a determinant of strategy. Each service within the Pentagon was prepared to produce plans even though there was a structure for producing the various types of combined plans which would have the approval of all three services. Because of differences between the services over what was most important to achieve in any future global war, the production of joint plans got into difficulties after 1949 despite Truman's attempts to reform the organizational planning structure. Truman tried to establish machinery that would provide for effective interservice coordination but with little success. Indeed, if global war had broken out in the early 1950s the United States' armed services would have fought three separate wars against the Soviet Union.

At the heart of the matter was the relative importance that should be attached to the strategic air offensive and thus to the role of nuclear weapons. The emphasis or lack of it would influence mobilization priorities and the ability of all the services to make significant contributions to the war effort. This was a political battle for interservice influence in the wake of the possible changes to warfare that nuclear weapons heralded. The fear was that nuclear war planning might enable one service to steal a march on the others and become the major military player. This was especially true at a time when not all the services had the same nuclear capacity and had to justify their roles in other areas. Here again was a political dimension driving attitudes to armaments and weapons and the strategy and dangers for which they were needed. It was therefore fortunate for the non-nuclear US services, but ironic, that in 1950 the Korean War produced a rearmament effort focused on conventional forces. These would be required for global war when the military in both Britain and the United States believed that the Soviets did not want a global conflict and would not deliberately start one.

This rearmament drive in the West was part of the attempt to make the NATO alliance into an effective defence organization that could repulse a Soviet attack in Western Europe without inflicting a nuclear holocaust on much of the continent. For this ninety-six divisions were deemed necessary. Almost as soon as these force goals were discussed at Lisbon in February 1952, it became clear, given the experience of the Korean War-inspired rearmament drive, that such goals would be impossible to meet without major economic and social dislocation in Europe. Thus NATO strategy had to depend on deterring a Soviet attack, which the British and the Americans believed would not take place anyway, or using nuclear weapons with devastating, almost suicidal consequences, unless of course a rational way was found to incorporate them into conventional warfare in a limited capacity. These kinds of military realities in terms of hot war were, however, distinct from the Cold War conflict about a particular social and economic order and the relative political and economic merits of capitalism and communism, democracy and totalitarianism. No sooner were the Lisbon force goals effectively abandoned (although the US military refused to countenance any formal acknowledgement of that fact) than the British military had revised their global strategy in June 1952 for the first time since 1947. Gone was the prime commitment to the winning of a global war, partly because of resource constraints, partly because of the effect of nuclear weapons, and partly because of the Cold War. Priority now was to be given to the latter in terms of the kind of global deployments

that would deter armed subversion and civil war, with nuclear weapons as a deterrent taking second priority and preparations for hot war relegated to third place. It was a good indication of the way Cold War was distinct from, but linked, to military forces rather than being part of a bipolar Soviet–American competition for power in which military developments threatened to bring further instability and conflict. Conventional forces could inspire confidence and strength and provide unity in the West while continuing to serve a purpose in convincing domestic public opinion of the imminent danger they faced in terms of armed conflict with an expansionist enemy. Nuclear weapons would also serve a particular Cold War function in terms of justifying the technological merits of capitalism or communism and serving to attract states seeking protection (more specifically nuclear umbrellas) in order to escape the military threat that Cold War participants had invented or exaggerated on both sides of the Iron Curtain. In the US they had a particular role in the development of a strategy of fighting the Cold War in NSC 68.

Whatever the neglect of the relationship between the Cold War and hot war, between power politics and ideology, there is general agreement that developments in Asia were focusing more Cold War attention on that region. With the stabilization of Western Europe through Marshall Aid and NATO the battle for hearts and minds and support for the values of democratic capitalism and totalitarian communism was now centred in East and South-East Asia. The national security memorandum NSC 68 drafted by contemporary advocates of a more comprehensive (i.e. linked to preparations for hot war) and global US Cold War strategy formulated a response to the new situation in April 1950 *before* the hostilities began on the Korean peninsular. This American document, the implementation of which by a cost-conscious US administration and Congress was facilitated by the Korean War, is generally regarded as a document which emphasized the need to meet the communist challenge by military means (because of Korea). And it is also portrayed as extending the Cold War into a universal or global struggle with containment no longer confined to Europe. It certainly indicated a new concern with military force, an extension of the conflict to areas which were not economically vital, and a belief that the world was not big enough for two ideologically conflicting power systems. Containment was called for, not as an end but as the means of ultimately undermining the Soviet system because totalitarianism and freedom were locked into a struggle for existence: one would dominate and the other would at best play a subordinate role. NSC 68 also contained some potent examples of a crusading American ideology as justifications of the modified Cold War strategy. However, it was the war in Korea and the opportunity to portray the Soviet Union as willing to change the status quo by military means that confirmed US acceptance of a new and more aggressive Cold War strategy while providing a more effective deterrent. This strategy stemmed from the American crusade against the Soviet satellites and the Asian challenges to the West before Korea which gave rise to NSC 68.

C. The Cold War and Integration in Europe

When European leaders surveyed the situation in Europe when the failure to produce a German settlement had been formalized at the end of 1947, they faced a number of problems and challenges. There was the dollar shortage which it was hoped the Marshall Plan would address and thereby provide the impetus for European economic recovery. But there was also the problem of rebuilding Germany as a necessary part of that economic progress without recreating the dangers associated with previous manifestations of German strength. There was the need for the right to prevent the kind of left-wing or communist movement which would threaten the status quo or offer Moscow the prospect of either greater control or influence or the prospect of encouraging chaos. Many were far from sanguine about achieving any of these goals, but in the various European capitals ruling elites were identifying national goals in terms of Europe's future. These produced the first steps towards the integration of Western Europe, but the motives stemmed from different national priorities: the political need to resist communism; the need to protect national economic interests and ensure recovery; the need to find a way to rebuild Germany without reviving German nationalism; the need to use influence in Europe to maximize the importance of a world role, and the need to move towards federalism to end the conflicts between European nation states. It is still far from clear therefore whether European integration represented an erosion of the nation state or merely its adaption to a new role.

By 1948 the French government, if not the French public, was reconciled to the economic rebuilding of West Germany and the creation of a new West German state. The concern was over how to achieve this without risking the consequences that would flow from an independent, economically powerful West Germany. The answer seemed to lie in integrating Germany into a Europe which would have some supranational bodies to curtail independent German development. Thus while the British saw European developments as part of a solution to their global weakness the French gave more emphasis to initiatives that would solve their problems within Europe. In September 1948 the French proposed that the Ministerial Council of the Brussels Treaty Organization study the idea of a European parliament which was the start of their attempts to create European institutions. The result was a European Assembly that would serve as a consultative body and a Council of Europe with a wider membership than the Brussels Treaty Organization but with no independent powers, as these remained with ministers to exercise at the intergovernmental level. France was now taking the lead in Europe as British ideas of the third force (see Chapter 4, B) were seen as less viable.

In 1948 the first moves to closer European co-operation coincided with the implementation of the Western European Recovery programme, talks on military alliances, and the attempts of both sides to undermine the opposing bloc. Like the process of decolonization, which was beginning to gather pace outside the European continent, European integration was linked to the dynamics of the Cold War as well as to the prevention of any further threat from West Germany. Sometimes examined independently from broader issues, the economic and political initiatives taken by the French in 1948 and 1949 stemmed from a combination of national economic needs, political idealism, and the preservation of European capitalism. Old fears about Germany combined with, and to some extent were softened by, new fears about Soviet communism. The recipe for dealing with the communist threat by strengthening capitalism through the European Recovery programme could be neatly combined with cementing West Germany into a prosperous European economic and military bloc designed to prevent another German attempt at European domination.

This was particularly important for the French and the first stage of the process began with the Schuman Plan for a European Coal and Steel Community outlined in 1950 and implemented in 1952. The military process, which was necessary to provide Germany with the status of reacceptance as an equal member of the post-war international community, was embodied in the 1952 agreement to establish a European Defence Community. Again this was another French initiative (by René Pleven) in 1950, but it proved somewhat more controversial than the Schuman Plan. Behind such plans lay the vision of integrationists like Jean Monnet who had a broad political agenda for the development of European integration as well as a more narrow economic agenda defined by the national needs of French recovery.

The debate over the goals and achievements of European economic cooperation and integration has focused on whether this was an abandonment or strengthening of the nation state. On the one hand, the French in particular have been perceived as driven by nationalism and the process of integration interpreted as the salvation rather than the demise of the nation state in Europe.[25] On the other hand, liberal institutionalists like Joseph Nye and Robert Keohane do not see the creation of institutions like the Coal and Steel Community as mere tools of the nation state but as significant in their own right and capable of producing greater international co-operation. Similarly functionalists and neofunction-

alists in the tradition of David Mitrany and Ernst Haas see European integration as promoting a transfer of allegiance away from the nation state by European elites and then the mass of the population.

The Schuman Plan and the European Coal and Steel Community

The architect of post-war French recovery through a national plan was Jean Monnet, and it was Monnet who devised the plan for a European Coal and Steel Community which was announced by French Foreign Minister Robert Schuman on 8 May 1950. Schuman was born in Luxembourg to a family from Lorraine, which had been part of Germany from 1871 to 1919. Having that background made him ideally suited to develop European institutions even if they were clearly geared to serving French national interests. The Schuman Plan was part of Franco–German reconciliation but in ways which would bind Germany into Western Europe and serve the needs of French coal and steel producers. The more closely the German economy was integrated into the Western European one the less likely it would be that aggressive German nationalism could again emerge backed by independent economic strength.

At the same time French recovery needs would be more easily met in ways which would be to the advantage of French producers. West German steel producers were much larger than their French counterparts and had significant cost advantages over them with the input price of coke being the most important. Coal costs were higher in France, which in the post-war years was heavily dependent on supplies from the Ruhr. Price negotiations were therefore necessary if French industry was not to be disadvantaged or unless the entire Franco–German coal and steel production was controlled by a single authority. In announcing his proposals for such a High Authority, Schuman also pointed out that this would 'create the first concrete foundation for a European federation which is so indispensable for the preservation of peace'. The threat to peace, which the Germans represented, would be reduced by federal controls while the threat to peace, which the Soviets represented, would be reduced by the Western European nations uniting together.

While the French saw important economic and political advantages in the Schuman plan the British saw significant dangers. Britain was keen to support the efforts of its European allies in the early 1950s but not inclined to become part of any supranational organization. The impact of the proposed Coal and Steel Community on Britain's nationalized industries was not seen as favourable nor was greater economic cooperation after 1948 seen as bringing benefits. Quite the reverse, as the resources of the sterling area, which was seen as a support for Britain's recovery, were seen as having to be mobilized more effectively for the benefit of Western Europe.

After the Organization for European Economic Cooperation (OEEC) was established in April 1948 to supervise the Marshall Aid programme the question arose as to how and on what basis dollars would be granted to cover trade deficits between the European powers and with the United States. The British position was complicated by the existence of the rest of the sterling area (RSA) outside the United Kingdom and by its large sterling balances (sterling that was held in London as wartime debts for goods received by Britain). Only the colonial part of the RSA was running a surplus with the dollar zone whereas the whole of it was running a surplus with Western Europe at a time when there were large deficits and surpluses in intra-European trade. Coordinating payments arrangements to deal with this situation and with dollar aid was not going to be easy. One answer would be to provide dollars to cover each European nation's dollar deficit minus the European surplus, thereby encouraging European creditors to buy more in Europe. In the event the Intra-European Payments and Compensation Scheme that was established was based on estimated bilateral surpluses and deficits which provided drawing rights from prospective creditors who would then receive conditional aid for dollar imports. This was less damaging to Britain especially as the Americans agreed to finance the RSA deficit but on condition that the RSA countries agreed to curtail non-essential imports from the Western hemisphere. This would give Britain political difficulties with the independent members of the sterling area. Moreover, further cooperation with Europe was at best likely to

involve Britain, as the strongest European economy, in short-term sacrifices over payment arrangements while the United States alone was in a position to help or undermine the sterling area.

What also had to be considered was the prospect of Marshall Aid not bringing about a successful economic recovery, and this was what primarily conditioned Britain's response to the Schuman Plan in 1950. The year before, an official committee (the Permanent Under-Secretary's Committee) had been set up to consider long-term policy and had examined the Third World Power concept (see Chapter 4, B). It expressed grave reservations about the success of the Marshall Plan, which added to the government's perception in 1949 that the payments situation would involve British sacrifices. In 1948 the British had been required to allow OEEC countries to draw $209 million from balances in sterling (in effect unrequited exports when goods were needed for consumption or dollar exports) in order to receive $312 million. Even if Britain received goods in return once Europe recovered, it was likely that the Europeans would argue that any sterling surplus they had with Britain should be offset by their deficit with the RSA. This pointed to the incompatibility of Europe with Britain and the sterling area except at Britain's expense. But if Britain became more integrated into Europe and gave up its economic sovereignty it would suffer the same as the Europeans.

French concerns, however, remained with their emerging political leadership of Western Europe and with the establishment of common Franco–German arrangements over coal and steel as quickly as possible. The Germans too saw political advantages despite the short-term economic disadvantages, and the new West German chancellor, Konrad Adenauer, who assumed office in August 1949, was particularly keen to tie Germany to the West. He believed strongly in the cause of liberal democracy, as opposed to communism and Naziism; in hastening the removal of occupation controls, and in ultimately achieving German reunification. These crucial Franco–German goals could be achieved without British involvement and although Monnet preferred that Britain join in discussions on the plan he was not prepared for Britain to delay the process. The French therefore issued invitations to discussions in Paris on the basis that acceptance required also accepting the principle of supranationality. The British were naturally reluctant to do this as they required to know in advance what degree of control they would be surrendering. Attempts were made to find a formula to enable Britain to participate but none could be found before the French imposed a deadline on the talks. It was not the principle of giving up some sovereignty that the British drew back from but the open-ended commitment in advance. As such the loss of sovereignty or control was something that was essential for the French plan but essential for the British to avoid without precise knowledge of what was involved.

There were other reasons why the British had doubts. The lack of political stability in France remained a cause for concern, while in military terms the tendency to look to the Americans had been strengthened by the acceptance of NATO and the abandonment of the Third Force. The priority now was the creation of a special place in an American-dominated alliance and Britain's relations with Europe were henceforth to be geared towards that goal. At times it was believed that Britain would carry more weight in Washington by serving as a bridge across the Atlantic (with the corollary that Western Europeans could not speak for themselves) if Britain had strong intergovernmental ties with its European allies. Britain was therefore keen to encourage European integration, not least because the Americans were strongly in favour of it, as long as Britain did not participate fully in the process of giving up economic controls to European bodies. Nevertheless the fact remained that the first step to European integration had been taken at French behest, with strong German support and without British participation.

The establishment of the Coal and Steel Community the following year, with which Britain became formally associated, was something the British had doubted would come to pass and its significance remains a matter of debate. Whether it marked a decisive moment in Britain's relations with Europe, which for half a century and more would leave Britain half in and half out of Europe with less ability to exercise important influence is difficult to judge. What is certain is that this was not a matter of oversight but part of a more fundamental plan to avoid being seen as primarily a European power. The

Third Force and equality with the Americans may have been an impossible dream but the harsh reality of a Europe still struggling economically was too risky and demeaning for the British to contemplate.

The Pleven Plan and the European Defence Community

The mixture of new Cold War concerns and old fears about Germany that had influenced the political rationale for the Schuman Plan were soon to combine in another significant European initiative by the French. Although the military dimensions of the Brussels Pact and NATO had been less important than the political cooperation they embodied, the military naturally wished to add some military clout to them once NATO was formed. Not least was the aim to develop conventional forces sufficient to defend most of the western part of the continent from a future attack when the Soviets might have the desire and the necessary preparations in place. When this was examined both London and Washington concluded that some military contribution from West Germany would be necessary. At the same time they were aware of the opposition this would produce given that it was only four years since many had made the ultimate sacrifice to destroy Germany's armed might. The British seemed less concerned than the Americans, particularly the military, who in late 1949 began arguing for an armed gendarmerie in the face of Foreign Office opposition. Adenauer also urged the creation of a gendarmerie which aroused French and American opposition. However, the main opposition was likely to come from the Soviets who it was feared would be so hostile to the idea of rearming Germans that they might be prepared to fight a preventive war. The British military, however, looking to try and defend Western Europe further east than the Rhine were convinced that this required a German contribution. The gendarmerie was designed to be the equivalent of the East German Bereitschaften, which was more a miniature army than a police force, and to lead to German troops being deployed within the forces of Western Europe. As early as April 1950 the Joint Planning Staff, in a rejected paper, had proposed that this West German force should be one of thirty divisions.

In May 1950, Bevin approved the creation of a gendarmerie of 25,000 men in line with Adenauer's proposals.[26]

The following month the Korean War broke out and the prospect of hot war loomed larger even before the Chinese entry into the conflict. Events in East Asia thus gave the German rearmament question a new importance and gave a great boost to its proponents. By September, the American Secretary of State Dean Acheson, had been won over and proposed the creation of a West German army to Bevin and Schuman which would be linked to a greater American commitment to European defence. The British accepted this idea in principle although they were increasingly cooler to the idea of German rearmament now that the Korean War had raised the stakes. The dust had hardly settled on Acheson's proposals than the French came up with a different but essentially federal idea for involving German forces in Western European defence. Again it was an idea of Jean Monnet's presented this time by René Pleven. The Pleven Plan was not for a German army integrated into NATO but for the creation of a European army into which German and other forces would be integrated and hereby remove the spectre of independent German forces with their own general staff. The plan posed a threat to NATO cohesion and to basic British military values and traditions. Even though their commitment to the importance of the Middle East was being eroded because of the attention given to Europe they still lacked enthusiasm for a continental commitment and cooperation with European partners who were regarded as somewhat inferior. Economic and power political interests remained important considerations for Britain and other European states but these have tended to be underestimated by historians concentrating on the alleged security problem which they claim arose from the Cold War and the Soviet threat to Western Europe.

D. Developing a Strategy for Fighting the Cold War: NSC 68, Rearmament, and the Cold War Offensive Controversy

The rearmament issue was closely connected to security and to the future development of the Cold War as involving a nuclear confrontation which began with the Soviet testing of an atomic bomb in 1949. The linking of the two separate issues of preparing for a possible hot war in the future and fighting the Cold War in the present now became more closely connected in the minds of some American policy-makers. In hot war terms the Soviet bomb presented greater risks for the West because they would be more fearful of using atomic weapons. In the short term the threat of retaliation would be faced only by the Europeans but there was a medium-term threat to the US. As Paul Nitze, a member of Kennan's Policy Planning Staff in the State department pointed out, the fact that there might be no resort to nuclear weapons made conventional forces much more important. Consequently, in order to devote resources to increasing conventional forces in Western Europe it might be necessary to lower rather than raise civilian standards of living there.[27] These kinds of ideas were to give a boost to advocates of West German rearmament but they were at odds with a key component of Cold War strategy. The Marshall Plan involved the reconstruction of Western Europe in order to remove the conditions of poverty and austerity which were deemed to give root to communism. For those like George Kennan who had argued for containment in this way between 1946 and 1948 rearmament and the militarization of the Cold War made no sense. However, once communism had been contained in Eastern Europe by 1948 and seemed unlikely to spread westwards,

Kennan had also advocated the Cold War strategy of liberation of the Soviet satellites in order to win the Cold War by the rolling back of communism. Now if this Cold War fighting was to act as a provocation to the Soviets, their reluctance to risk a hot war rather than capitulate would actually be increased if the West rearmed to gain a clear preponderance of power.

Rearming for Cold War—NSC 68

The whole American approach to the Cold War was debated in 1949 and the famous NSC 68 memorandum was the culmination of that debate, which signalled a victory for the aggressive Cold War fighters and rearmers. A leading advocate of this group was Paul Nitze even though he continued to believe that 'a total war started deliberately by the Soviets is a tertiary risk.'[28] The question was not whether the United States should prepare for such an eventuality but how it should prepare for the prevention of hot war while fighting an offensive Cold War. For some the answer was that hot war could only or best be avoided by winning the Cold War which meant the fall of the Soviet government and the collapse of its satellite-empire which was what covert operations were seen by many of their advocates as designed to achieve.

Although Western support for Ukrainian rebels and anti-communist groups in Romania and Bulgaria began in 1946, by 1949 covert operations involved significant support for armed rebels and dissidents in the Soviet bloc, the infiltration of agents, the development of underground resistance, and the facilitation of guerrilla operations in strategic areas. Unmarked American aircraft were used to send supplies, dollars, and gold into the Baltic states, Czechoslovakia, Romania, and Yugoslavia and the Ukraine. Propaganda was broadcast through the voice of America and Radio Free Europe.[29] As outlined in a secret annex to NSC 68 there was a substantial attempt to implement what was termed 'The Ring Plan'. Powerful transmitters were to surround the Soviet satellites in order to prevent the Russians jamming the propaganda broadcast by American radio stations. Ukraine, Poland, and Hungary were the three main targets.[30]

The efforts to promote psychological warfare and subversion were not however confined to Europe. The success of the Chinese communists created new opportunities for the United States to use the troops of the defeated Chinese Nationalists in order to fight an aggressive Cold War in Asia. These efforts to assist armed incursions by the Nationalists into mainland China took several forms and became increasingly important with Chinese involvement in the Korean War in 1950. General Li Mi, the Chinese Nationalist warlord from Yunnan province, had retreated into Burma after the communist victory. Supported by the CIA through its running of front companies such as Civil Air Transport, Western Enterprises, in Taiwan, and the Sea Supply Company in Thailand, in 1951 Mi Li attempted an invasion of Yunnan which was repeated the following year with around 10,000 troops. The force advanced 60 miles into China before being repulsed. At the same time in the early 1950s the CIA was parachuting Nationalists into communist China to build up opposition in the remote areas and to conduct sabotage missions on important installations.[31]

It is most unlikely that the Chinese and the Russians saw such actions as the implementation of containment rather than an attempt to destroy communism and to bring their subjects under the umbrella of capitalism. Could then the Cold War be described as an attempt to bring down communist regimes and liberate their subjects? Richard Aldrich, in a brilliantly researched book, has argued that within a year of coming to power in 1953 the Republican administration under President Dwight D. Eisenhower abandoned liberation but he never makes clear when liberation began. This is part of the controversy of whether the problem can be avoided by legitimately describing liberation and the overthrow of the Soviet government or its satellite regimes as part of containment.

In addition there are different interpretations of the ultimate purpose of the new offensive Cold War policy of the United States. The central issue is whether the Americans were keen to use their support for dissidents and rebels to overthrow the regimes in Moscow and Beijing and thereby win Cold War, or whether their aims were less ambitious and more limited. A number of reasons have been put forward to justify the latter explanation. The

British Russia Committee thought the goal of these policies was the stirring up of trouble in the Soviet empire and George Kennan argued that covert operations were to maintain pressure on the Soviets in order to make them less likely to probe Western weak spots. William Donovan, head of the Office of Strategic Services, the wartime equivalent of the CIA, was clear that the aim of Cold War fighting was not liberation but 'keeping the communists off balance'. It has also been suggested that covert operations were means of 'venting frustration against the intractability of Cold War problems and a means of finding ideological expression, rather than realistic plans to overturn communist rule'. Or 'a form of ideological aggression, the only honest expression of America as a freedom-loving nation'.[32]

On the other hand, when the Foreign Office became concerned at some of the American operations, because of a fear of hot war, they argued that instead of encouraging risings and revolts more specific operations should be launched against particular targets.[33] This clearly points to the difference between a policy of 'pinpricks' to keep the Soviets preoccupied and a policy designed to seriously threaten regimes behind the Iron Curtain. Lloyd Berkner, the director of Project Troy,[34] told Secretary of State Dean Acheson that 'it is possible to organize an aggressive political war of sufficient effectiveness to bring the Soviet Union to its knees in a relatively short time without resorting to widespread military action.' And the guidelines for Radio Free Europe defined its purpose as contributing 'to the liberation of nations imprisoned behind the Iron Curtain by sustaining their morale and stimulating in them a spirit of non-cooperation with the Soviet-dominated regimes'. According to its handbook, speakers should assert that there was 'no possibility of an enduring peace anywhere in the world until the Moscow-dominated regimes have been overthrown'. Kennan in 1948 had advocated not merely the liberation of the satellites but attempts to change boundaries and thereby break up the Soviet Union by encouraging minority groups to split. Moreover, a member of the Psychological Strategy Board, which was established in 1951 in a vain attempt to coordinate all activity related to the fighting of the Cold War, called for an all-out psychological counter-offensive. This was deemed to require

less an official change of policy than a frank recognition of what is really explicit in our existing policy objectives, i.e.

(a) abandoning 'containment' and openly espousing 'liberation';

(b) scrapping—not necessarily in public but in our strategic planning—the passive wishful thinking of 'coexistence' and adopting a positive approach that acknowledges the vital necessity of overthrowing the Kremlin regime;

(c) discarding our present strategy of fighting a defensive delaying action in the Cold War while we prepare to defend ourselves in a hot one, and substitute, therefore, a fully planned and phased global strategy of offensive underground fighting.

Others would go further in their suggestions, and consultants advising the Psychological Strategy Board proposed in November 1951 that

US power and interests require continuation of the present hostilities in Korea, either on an active or standby basis until such time as the Japanese can be infiltrated on to the Asian land base. This concept requires control of a resurgent rearmed Japan with a major drive towards the Manchurian complex.

In Europe the United States was to work with Western Europeans, including the West Germans, to bring about 'the break-up of the USSR into separate national component states so that, in effect, the emissaries of the Grand Dukes of Moscovy are sent back to Moscow'.[35]

These different views do indicate that American policy-makers had different perceptions of what the goals of Cold War fighting should be, of what they actually were, and of what their consequences might involve. It thus makes it difficult to define precisely when liberation replaced containment because of these differences over the desirability of an offensive strategy and what it involved. What can be said is that the military on both sides of the Atlantic were generally more in favour of trying to win the Cold War than officials in the Foreign Office or the State Department. In the United States this was reflected in the bureaucratic wrangling, which, according to the CIA, meant it was impossible 'to arrive at a definitive answer for the fundamental question of whether it is possible to live with the Kremlin or whether it must be destroyed'. In Britain Air Vice-Marshal Slessor had argued as early as the beginning of 1948 that the way to avoid hot war was to win the Cold War. By the end of the year the desirability of winning the Cold War was endorsed by the Chief of the Air Staff Lord Tedder, who defined it as the over-throwing of the Soviet regime within five years.[36] Once the Korean War had begun the British Chiefs of Staff were to argue that an offensive strategy of fighting the Cold War was even more necessary. If the West failed to win the Cold War, they would be increasingly embroiled in limited hot wars like Korea which Britain's defence budget could ill afford to bear. As yet there has been nothing found in the limited number of archival resources available in the former Soviet Union to indicate any discussions about the desirability of destroying Western regimes by winning the Cold War. It may be that it was never considered feasible and that some historians researching Russian archives are right in their assessment that the emphasis in the Kremlin was on building up the Soviet bloc rather than undermining the Americans in Western Europe.[37]

Some in the American military were not only considering how to destroy the Kremlin by Cold War but the possibility of doing so by resorting to hot war. To a large extent this reflected the views of those who believed that there could be no coexistence with the Soviets. Either Moscow would start a war once they were ready or else they would force the West to take military action to prevent the spread of communism. For those thinking along those lines, especially in the US air force, war with the Soviet Union was inevitable in the not too distant future, and the issue was when it would be best to fight it. In 1951 the British Director of Naval Intelligence noted that 'there is a clear danger of the USA becoming involved in a preventive war against Russia, however firmly their NATO allies object.'[38] Obviously, like the consequences of Cold War fighting, this was very much linked to a rearmament drive, which would provide for clear American military superiority in the light of the post-Soviet atom bomb danger that the Russian conventional forces would become relatively stronger.

The commitment to rearmament was clearly a feature of NSC 68 and the reasons for it can be linked to allegedly far-sighted people understanding the nature of the growing Soviet menace soon to be con-firmed by Moscow-supported North Korean aggres-

sion. Yet NSC 68 was not just about rearmament and its origins can also be traced to ideas about American perceptions of how best to achieve US goals in the East–West conflict, which were related more to the very existence of communist states than to a response to particular Chinese and Soviet actions. It was the general threat that was highlighted at the start of NSC 68 and portrayed in universal terms. The issues involved the 'fulfilment or destruction' not only of the American Republic, whose 'fundamental purpose is to assure the integrity and vitality of our free society' but of 'civilisation itself'. The Soviets were deemed to have universal goals aimed at domination of the world, or civilization (the free American society), in a negation of freedom through a 'quest for total power over all men'. Consequently

In a shrinking world which now faces the threat of atomic warfare, it is not an adequate objective merely to check the Kremlin design, for the absence of war among nations is becoming less and less tolerable. This fact imposes on us, in our own interests, the responsibility of world leadership. It demands that we make the attempt, and accept the risks inherent in it, to bring about order and justice by means consistent with the principles of freedom and democracy.

Here was reflected a perception of the temporary nature of peace and a desire to avoid a military stalemate and pursue American hegemony. Yet in an apparent compromise between the drive for Cold War victory and liberation on the one hand and containment or coexistence on the other,

[I]t might be possible to create a situation which will induce the Soviet Union to accommodate itself, with or without the conscious abandonment of its design, to coexistence on tolerable terms with the non-Soviet world. . . . The objectives outlined in NSC 20/4. . . . Are fully consistent with the objectives stated in this paper and they remain valid. The growing intensity of the conflict which has been imposed on us, however, requires the changes of emphasis and the additions that are apparent. Coupled with the probable fission bomb capability and possible thermo-nuclear capability of the Soviet Union, the intensifying struggle requires us to face the fact that we can expect no lasting abatement of the crisis unless and until a change occurs in the nature of the Soviet system.[39]

Central to NSC 68 therefore was consideration of how best to destroy the Soviet satellite empire and ultimately to win the Cold War. The Soviet Union itself could be transformed or destroyed, and the appeal of a free and healthy capitalist society could be relied on to contain the spread of communism. The reality was that the Soviets did not and could not use the kind of covert actions and support for rebel groups to endeavour to undermine the West, and many still believed that such a situation was likely to lead to an undesirable hot war. The Soviets could only manipulate Western communist parties to endeavour to bring about change and therefore would need to rely on military force. In this situation it made sense to go for massive rearmament to deter the Soviets from resorting to war either as a means of dominating the globe or as a reaction to their imminent demise brought on by a successful Western strategy of fighting the Cold War.

NSC 68 made clear the importance of the connection between rearmament and a more proactive and offensive fighting of the Cold War rather than simply preparing for a Soviet hot war offensive. 'If such a course of increasing our military power is adopted now, the United States would have the capability of eliminating the disparity between its military strength and the exigencies of the situation we face; eventually of gaining the initiative in the "cold" war and of materially delaying if not stopping the Soviet offensives in war itself.' And there was a third pillar to the NSC 68 strategy derived from the idea that rearmament would make the US appear resolute and determined which would encourage its friends in Europe. Without the sense of purpose provided by the mobilization of greater military power the free world for some unexplained reason would become demoralized. It was an interesting feature of the early Cold War that both sides were appealing for support for a particular ideology and way of life and both had doubts about their ability to attract such support without other Cold War measures.[40]

Time and again NSC 68 would come back to the connection between winning the Cold War while using rearmament to reduce the risk of hot war.

The risk of having no better choice than to capitulate or precipitate a global war at any number of pressure points is bad enough in itself, but it is multiplied by the weakness it imparts to our position in the cold war. Instead of appearing strong and resolute we are continually at the verge of appearing and being alternately irresolute and desperate; yet it is the Cold War which we must win, because both the

Kremlin design, and our fundamental purpose give it the first priority.

For those assuming that the Soviets would attack when they believed they could win, rearmament would buy time for the fighting of the Cold War to at least produce some results.

Such a build up of strength could safeguard and increase our retaliatory power, and thus might put off for some time the date when the Soviet Union could calculate that a surprise blow would be advantageous. This would provide additional time for the effects of our policies to produce a modification of the Soviet system.

Without the build-up of strength, the writers of NSC envisaged (without producing any evidence other than the Soviet atom bomb) the balance of strength would continue to change to the advantage of the Russians. The American possession of nuclear weapons while it could 'open the road to victory in a long conflict, it is not sufficient by itself to advance the position of the United States in the cold war'. Consequently, 'a build-up of the military capabilities of the United States and the free world is a precondition to the achievement of the objectives outlined in this report and to the protection of the United States against disaster.'[41] Whether disaster would be less likely with some different objectives was not considered.

What was considered was persevering with what was deemed the existing programmes, war, isolation, or a military build up as part of meeting Cold War objectives. The first scenario was criticized because the

military capabilities, actual and potential, of the United States and the rest of the free world, together with the apparent determination of the free world to resist further Soviet expansion, have not induced the Kremlin to relax its pressures generally or to give up the initiative in the cold war. On the contrary the Soviet Union has consistently pursued a bold foreign policy modified only when its probing revealed a determination and an ability of the free world to resist encroachment upon it.

Crucially the resistance of encroachment was not deemed sufficient as 'a continuation of present trends will mean that the United States and especially other free countries will tend to shift to the defensive, or to follow a dangerous policy of bluff, because the maintenance of a firm initiative in the Cold War is closely related to aggregate strength in being and readily available.' Nor were economic programmes designed to remove the causes of communism regarded as sufficient. Finally, NSC 68 while ruling out negotiation at the present time suggested that without a build-up of American military strength any attempt to negotiate a general settlement on US terms would probably be long drawn out and ineffective.[42] In a sense NSC 68 had rejected the very concept of containment but was struggling to define an acceptable way to move beyond that and specify the precise nature and objectives of roll-back and Cold War victory.

Isolation, as an alternative to the present policies, was ruled out because the abandonment of the European allies was deemed likely to result in the Soviet domination of most of Eurasia. And many Americans 'would feel a deep sense of responsibility and guilt for having abandoned their former friends and allies'. More importantly, with the resources of Eurasia the Soviet's relative military capabilities would increase and the United States government would find itself facing a number of unpalatable options. There would be those advocating 'peace' on Soviet terms while others 'would seek to defend the United States by creating a regimented system which would permit the assignment of a tremendous part of our resources to defence. Under such a state of affairs our national morale would be corrupted and the integrity and vitality of our system subverted.'[43]

The prospect of war which some favoured was rejected on the grounds that it would not be supported by the American people, and would give the US enormous problems in re-establishing some sort of order. Even a victory would bring the US

little if at all closer to victory in the fundamental ideological conflict . . . and that the only sure victory lies in the frustration of the Kremlin design by the steady development of the moral and material strength of the free world and its projection into the Soviet world in such a way as to bring about an internal change in the Soviet system. . . . A more rapid build-up of political, economic, and military strength and thereby of confidence in the free world than is now contemplated is the only course which is consistent with progress toward achieving our political purpose. The frustration of the Kremlin's design requires the free world to develop a successfully functioning political and economic system and a vigorous political offensive against the Soviet

Union. These, in turn, require an adequate military shield under which they can develop.

In other words a military victory was of little value in securing a way of life and the global triumph of capitalism and democracy over alternative economic and political systems.[44]

Rearming for Hot War and the Questioning of NSC 68

NSC 68 and its rearmament strategy, like NATO, were initially designed more to create the conditions for a strong foreign policy geared to fighting the Cold War and strengthening allies, than to providing the resources for a military victory over the Soviet Union.

The immediate objectives—to the achievement of which such a build-up of strength is a necessary but not sufficient condition—are a renewed initiative in the Cold War and a situation to which the Kremlin would find it expedient to accommodate itself, first by relaxing tensions and pressures and then by gradual withdrawal'.[45]

Yet the Kremlin had not embarked on any new initiatives. Rather the triumph of communism in China, combined with the Soviet atomic bomb, had created a fear that the American way of life, while secure in Western Europe, would not be universally emulated. The power of the Soviet Union was seen as sufficiently dangerous, despite its wartime losses, to detract from American achievements and as the source of a way of life which could become universal, by imposition if not emulation. Ultimately, therefore, the successes of communism would have to be reversed and NSC 68 was a clarion call for more military power that would enable cold warfare to triumph without a global conflict even though it was unclear how this triumph would be achieved. The global conflict was something the Soviet Union, according to NSC 68, might now contemplate within the next 4 to 5 years when it would posses sufficient capability to deliver a significant surprise atomic attack. As with the Cold War situation this too required greater military strength for defence and deterrence rather than the offensive covert measures generally referred to in NSC 20/4 and reaffirmed in NSC 68. The needs of hot war began to assume

NSC 68

NSC 68 is based on the assumption that the military power of the USSR and its satellites is increasing in relation to that of the US and its allies. In view of the vast preponderance of US and allied assets in every respect except that of manpower that assumption needs more documentation than is contained in NSC 68. In particular no attention seems to have been given to the question of the possible drain which recent developments may have been placed on Soviet military strength. Tightening of controls at home and in particular in the satellites would tie down military manpower and equipment. The furnishing of military technicians to China in any number would constitute an important drain on the USSR whose supply is relatively limited. Put another way, it is hard to accept a conclusion that the USSR is approaching a straight-out military superiority over us when, for example, (1) our air force is vastly superior qualitatively, is greatly superior numerically in the bombers, trained crews and other facilities necessary for offensive warfare; (2) our supply of fission bombs is much greater than that of the USSR, as is our thermonuclear potential; (3) our navy is so much stronger than that of the USSR that they should not be mentioned in the same breath; (4) the economic health and military potential of our allies is, with our help, growing daily; and (5) while we have treaties of alliance with and are furnishing arms to countries bordering the USSR, the USSR has none with countries within thousands of miles of us.

Source: FRUS, 1950 (State Dept., Washington, DC, 1977); Comments by the Bureau of the Budget on NSC 68, 8 May 1950.

greater importance after the outbreak of the Korean War which convinced some in the US that Moscow was now prepared to risk a major conflict to achieve its goals.

The planned military expansion set out in NSC 68/4 and approved after the outbreak of the Korean War was on an unprecedented scale. The force goals for the 1952 financial year were 18 divisions, 397 combat vessels, and 95 air wings compared with the previously planned goals for 1954 of 10 divisions, 281 naval vessels, and 58 air wings. In all the numbers of military personnel were to double to 3,211,000. By the beginning of the summer of 1951 the US army had 18 divisions, the navy 342 combat ships, and the air force 87 wings.[46] Ironically just as the military build-up was taking place the US armed services were so riven by rivalry that they were unable to agree how these forces should be used if the Soviets were to launch a surprise attack within the next 12 months. This rivalry bedevilled the planning process which had always suffered from the fact that war plans, for example a plan for a strategic offensive, could be drawn up by the individual services for a particular year and would then have to be incorporated into a joint planning process. The initial process could constitute outline plans as well as those geared to existing circumstances or long- and medium-term plans. In the wake of difficulties over agreement to approve the 1951–52 joint emergency plan (for fighting a war within twelve months with existing resources), related to the agreed outline plan, Truman attempted to systemize the planning process.

From the summer of 1952 long, medium- and short-term objectives would be defined for a ten-year period as a Joint Long Range Strategic Exercise, a Joint Strategic Objectives Plan, and a Joint Capabilities Plan, with the latter covering the forthcoming year. The Strategic Objectives Plan was to cover three different types or phases of conflict ranging from the peacetime conflict short of global war to the emergency phase of general war and the additional forces needed for a mobilization base along with the US and allied requirements in the first four years of general war. Objective and Capability plans would dictate priorities for resources and mobilization, which in turn would influence the relative importance of the services' roles. In this context the main differences were over the importance of the strategic nuclear offensive with the army and the navy rejecting the overwhelming importance which the air force wished to attach to it. The result was that it took until March 1953 to draft a Joint Capabilities Plan which the Joint Strategic Plans Committee spent three months arguing over without agreement. By the time the Joint Chiefs of Staff began debating it the time period it was supposed to apply to had ended. The Joint Operations Plans ran into even greater difficulties and if global war had occurred there was no combined plan for dealing with it.[47]

The fact that an enormous programme of military expansion was implemented owed less to the cogent arguments of the military strategists and the drafters of NSC 68 than to the outbreak of the Korean War, which increased the sense of insecurity in Washington. The fact was that NSC 68 rested on a number of general and questionable assessments that were disputed by other members of the administration and remain unproven to this day. The first, which was questioned by a leading State Department Soviet expert, Charles Bohlen, concerned Soviet aims. Bohlen took issue, not with the idea of rearmament, but with the depiction of the Soviets as hell bent on world domination. If that were the case, then war would be inevitable unless the Soviet regime was brought down. Here was the crux of the argument before and after NSC 68. The acceptance of the Soviets as determined on world domination ruled out the possibility of coexistence and the only issue, if that were the case, was whether the Soviet Union should be destroyed by cold or hot war. Bohlen, however, was to become an advocate of containment and coexistence and was therefore repeatedly to challenge some of the NSC 68 assessments of the goals of the Soviet regime. In 1952 he became responsible for coordinating the first major attempt at re-evaluating the goals of the Soviet Union and the implications for the national security of the US in the Cold War.

In the meantime there were critics of other dubious assumptions contained in NSC 68. The Bureau of the Budget took exception to the idea that the Cold War was a conflict over the future of civilization between the 'slave world' and the 'free world'. While the Soviet Union, it argued, could properly be called a slave state it was not true that the US and its friends constituted a free world. There were those living under the corrupt Quirino government in the Philippines and those in Indo-China who could not be termed free and vast numbers of people who were in neither Cold War camp. The fact was that this simplistic and inaccurate approach to freedom obscured the important point that many people were attracted to communism precisely because they were experiencing despotic and/or corrupt governments.[48]

Despite these important question marks about the assumptions underlying NSC 68 the Korean War made it difficult to question not only the conclusion that more rearmament was necessary but that a new phase in Moscow's quest for world domination had begun. When changes in the world situation in the light of the Korean War were examined in NSC 114 the conclusion was that the Soviet willingness to accept the risk of global war was greater than envisaged in NSC 68. Moreover, Moscow was now deemed to be preparing the Russian people for war with the United States to achieve global domination. Whereas in April 1950 it was assumed that 1954 was the year when this would be most likely, by August 1951 it was argued in NSC 114 that this time of maximum danger already existed and would continue to do so until rearmament was complete.[49]

Bohlen continued to take issue with this interpretation of Soviet strategy as, like Kennan and the US ambassador in Moscow, he believed that the Soviets had no desire to start a global war. This did not mean that Bohlen and others in the State Department were averse to some degree of rearmament; it meant that they did not view rearmament as part of a crusade against an enemy that was committed to world domination and prepared to go to war to bring it about because of its revolutionary ideology. They tended to see Soviet ambitions as limited ones that had to be checked, which in a sense was a reversion to something like containment without any aggressive US Cold War attempts at roll-back that required greater strength to deter the Soviets from acting to prevent their demise. For Bohlen 'In the eyes of Soviet rulers, they are in a constant state of warfare with all non-Soviet powers and organizations. However, the chief purpose of the Soviet Union is not the worldwide extension of communism to which all other considerations are subordinated, but rather the reverse. The world revolutionary movement is since the inception of Stalin's dictatorship in Russia the servant and not the master of the Soviet Union. Ever since his accession to power the guiding thought of the Stalinist Group has been that under no circumstances and for no revolutionary gains must the Soviet State be involved in risks to the maintenance of Soviet power in Russia. The process of imperialistic expansion will always take place when opportunities for such expansion exist without serious risk to the maintenance of Soviet power in Russia, but will not be undertaken if in the eyes of the Kremlin the acquisition of any positions for communism involve a serious risk to the Soviet system.

Soviet actions since the end of the Second World War confirm in every respect the accuracy of this judgement. It has been for the last six years within the power of the Soviet Union to acquire by overt force virtually all of continental Western Europe and the Middle East since there has been no force even remotely comparable to that which the Soviets could bring to bear in those areas. The reason why the Soviet Union has not capitalized on these opportunities is clearly the fear of world war or rather war with the United States which would inevitably risk the continued existence of the system in Russia. The case of the armed aggression in Korea, according to available evidence, is not a departure from traditional Soviet caution in this respect but appears to have been based on a very profound miscalculation on the part of the Kremlin as to what US reaction would be.'[50]

E. The Growing Importance of Communist China and the Conflict in Korea

It has been suggested that (see Chapter 2, C) the idea of a Cold War developing separately in Asia is a misperception despite the fact that the establishment of a new, unified China in October 1949 was the result of the particular circumstances that produced a communist victory over the nationalists in the Chinese civil war (see Chapter 2, C). In order to understand Soviet and American reactions to this one has to take into account the regional circumstances and the way in which East Asian events interacted with broader international considerations in the 1940s. Such interactions have to be seen in terms of the Cold War's ideological nature and in terms of the impact on the regional power balance. The latter cannot simply be incorporated into analyses of Soviet–American relations based on the assumption that a gain for one was a loss for the other. To some extent communist China's emergence was a threat to both powers and both were uncertain about how best to respond.

The 'Who Lost China' Debate

In the West, both at the time and in the historiography, controversy has arisen over how the emergence of another communist state was allowed to happen. Was there any possibility of preventing the alliance between the Soviet Union and communist China, which was formalized through the Sino–Soviet Treaty of February 1950? These issues became part of an American debate, which centred on the allocation of blame for the communist victory and played a key role in US politics. Based on the theme of 'Who lost China' it contributed to the witch-hunts in the early 1950s of Senator Joseph McCarthy that led to many people being accused of communist sympathies. The degree of intolerance and persecution which this represented is a matter of debate but many lost their jobs and careers on the basis of false allegations that stoked up anti-communism and contributed to the Cold War crusade in the United States.

The idea that somebody in the US could have lost such a vast and populous country as China is an extraordinary example of the Americancentric worldview. It assumes that in the wake of developments in, or actions by, foreign states, the United States could have done something to improve what in this instance was a Cold War situation. And it goes counter to the views of all US policy-makers who believed by 1948, if not before, that nothing could be done to prevent a communist success, not least because of the incompetence and corruption of the Nationalist forces. The idea of the United States being able to play a decisive role against the communists in a country where there was substantial mass support for their political and economic programme is now generally rejected. The rejection has been helped by the experiences in Vietnam where, with the lack of a viable indigenous alternative to the communists, no amount of money could prevent the latter's success even when backed by the use of considerable military force.

This idea that the world can be shaped by American actions underlies the more interesting academic debate about what the United States could have done once the communist victory in China was assured. 'The Last Chance' debate concerns the possibility of whether the United States threw away an opportunity in 1949 for establishing better relations with China and preventing the 'lean to one side' embodied in the Sino–Soviet alliance of February 1950. It implies that the opportunity was lost because of the state of US domestic politics with Republicans criticizing the Truman administration for being soft on communism. Proponents of the missed opportunity interpretation argue that China was in need of aid for reconstruction after the devastation of the war with Japan and the 4-year civil war which followed it. Therefore economic assistance and trade links could have mitigated the ideological ties with the Soviet Union and encouraged divisions between them. Even if Mao was not inclined to turn to the US there may have been a prospect of him preserving some links to avoid any possible dependence on the Soviet Union.

Along with this incentive there went the assumed Chinese communist dislike and suspicion of Stalin's reluctance to give unequivocal support to Mao. This was evident in the inter-war years when Stalin sought to reconcile the communists and Nationalists and after the war as Stalin showed a reluctance to abandon Chiang Kai-shek. In part this was because, with Soviet influence in East Asia very much in mind, Stalin had gained concessions from the Nationalists, albeit with British and American support, regarding the warm-water port of Lushun and the control over the Chinese Eastern Railway. At the same time as these were secured in the Yalta agreements of 1945, Stalin remained doubtful about the communists' prospects for ultimate, military victory. As a result it is argued, Stalin was prepared to restrict communist activities in Manchuria when the Soviets entered the war against Japan in August 1945 and even to try and expel them from Manchurian cities.

While it is true that there was little reason for Mao to trust Stalin there was less reason for him to trust the Americans and the thesis which rejects the idea of a lost American opportunity has been supported by new evidence from Chinese and Soviet sources. As early as the summer of 1946 when Stalin's attempts to maintain links with Chiang Kai-shek had collapsed, it has been argued that Mao had the basis of the Soviet alliance he had been seeking in place.[51] The communists were not only given free rein in Manchuria but active support, and the contacts were certainly closer during the subsequent period than has generally been assumed in the West.[52] For Mao the fact that the Soviets gave the communists an increasing amount of military assistance and civilian aid was more important than Stalin's subsequent attempts to reopen contacts with the Nationalists and to pressure him to seek a negotiated settlement. Moreover, Mao was preoccupied with the long-term hostility of the United States to the communist revolution in China. He saw the prospects of renewed US intervention as a significant possibility, if only in the form of encouraging resistance on the part of the urban bourgeoisie to his attempts to forge a new China through an ideological campaign to maintain a revolutionary momentum. As a consequence by 1948 Mao was speaking of squeezing out Western diplomats and firmly committed to seeking a Soviet alliance whatever its flaws. Even though there is some evidence the US sought to build some links with China such links were never a possibility. Only by abandoning Chiang Kai-shek and treating the communists as equals could the door to China be even partially opened.[53] This more than any chance of a partial rapprochement was what was ruled out by US domestic politics and the 'Who Lost China' lobby.

Stalin, the Establishment of Communist China, and the Origins of the Korean War

If Mao was committed to building cooperation with Stalin to meet his domestic, if not his international requirements, the question arises as to Stalin's attitudes to Mao and the emergence of a communist state on the Soviet Union's eastern border. Why was the Soviet leader reluctant to embrace a like-minded revolutionary? There were of course differences between Mao's vision of a revolutionary communist state and Stalin's. However, the motives for Stalin's China policies can also be explained by his concern with the implications of a strong China for Soviet leadership of the international communist movement and more importantly for Soviet influence in East Asia. In addition, because the Cold War was a global issue, Soviet–American relations in one part of the world were affected by events in another. After the Council of Foreign Ministers in September perhaps options were best left open for preserving the Soviet gains from Yalta and more generally the idea of the Soviet Union playing a role in the resolution of the civil war. In both cases an outright victory or defeat for Mao Tse-tung would not be the most desirable option. As has been suggested in Eastern Europe, divisions may have been seen as desirable as a means of maximizing Stalin's ability to exploit the situation. Stalin in August 1945 may have also have been influenced by his expectation that cooperation with the British and Americans involved not supporting Mao strongly. On the other hand, when in 1948 all doubts about a communist victory in China were removed it paid to move closer to Mao provided Soviet leadership and influence were not threatened.

In Mao's case Michael Hunt has argued that China was torn between the need for support from friends and the dependence that this could produce. This conflict between dependency and autonomy was deeply embedded in the Chinese psyche. These experiences from recent Chinese history were imprinted on the mind of the communist leader Mao Tse-tung as he began a struggle to unite China under a single central authority and carve out a more independent and prestigious role for China in international affairs. They were to influence Mao's perception of how the international community could both strengthen and weaken his domestic position as he sought to re-establish China as a regional power. Like any other revolutionary regime the Chinese communist state was in need of domestic legitimacy but the Cold War situation in 1949 would complicate this and significantly influence international reactions to the new state. In the West

the Cold War tendency has been to play down the impact of history and culture as influences on Mao Tse-tung's foreign policy and emphasize Marxist-Leninism and global revolution as the dominant influences shaping Chinese approaches to the external world. It may be more meaningful, as with the Soviet Union, to see the ideological forces as justifying rather than determining foreign policy which retained at least some of traditional Chinese and Russian imperial influences. These gave priority to the pursuit of power and influence for the state and its rulers and for the quest for domestic legitimacy through international means. On the other hand, Mao may have initially been inclined to turn more to Stalin out of fear and dislike of the Americans and to meet his domestic reconstruction needs. Yet this did not suppress power political rivalries between Moscow and Beijing and these need to be examined along with the ideological pressures of the Cold War.

It would not be surprising that the strengthening of the communist bloc, which the Americans saw as a Cold War reversal, was also perceived by Stalin as a reversal, if of a different type. Assuming the Cold War is distinct from traditional power political rivalries, Stalin may have seen Mao's success more in terms of regional power politics than in terms of his Cold War conflict with the West. This argument is supported by the work of Shen Zhihua, in his interpretation of Stalin's Korean policy and in particular of Stalin's change of mind in January 1950 which led to him authorize and support a North Korean attack on the South which he had resisted in 1949.[54] From Stalin's point of view there was a need to build up China and use her as an ally in the Cold War, but this would have a number of adverse regional consequences. It would mean a new treaty with the Chinese communists replacing Yalta and the loss of the port and railway concessions, which would deprive Stalin of a warm-water port in Asia. On the other hand, if North Korea controlled the whole peninsula that could well provide Stalin with access to the warm-water port he desired. These former Russian imperialist goals were the advantages of a quick success, which was deemed likely if the US did not become involved. On the other hand, Stalin made it clear to the North Korean leader Kim Il Sung that Mao's agreement was an essential condition for his approval of the invasion and to Mao that the Soviets would not intervene directly in Korea. Therefore if there was no quick success, provided the Chinese gave direct support, then the disadvantages would be offset by the Chinese inability to launch an invasion of Taiwan and by making China more dependent on Soviet assistance.

The prospect of direct confrontation with the United States always haunted Stalin. It seems that the US Secretary of State Dean Acheson's speech of January 1950 in which Korea and Taiwan were excluded from the Asian-Pacific defence perimeter of the United States led him to believe a confrontation with the US was unlikely in the wake of North Korean aggression. At the same time Stalin may have been concerned by the prospect of another strong communist power in Asia. This would threaten his control over international communism and would create competition in parts of East Asia that were areas of traditional strategic concern to the Soviet Union. Thus it may be that the emergence of China, the Korean War, and the rebuilding of Japan (see Chapter 2, C) were seen as regional problems as much as new aspects of the global confrontation with the United States. Certainly there is reason to believe that Stalin was attempting to balance these considerations with the aim of increasing Soviet influence in East Asia rather than in the hope of furthering a revolutionary ideology aiming at world domination. The Chinese Revolution and the Korean War may therefore constitute more complex international phenomena than when seen simply through the Cold War lens of the communist world versus the capitalist world.

However, bipolarity, where the focus is on the influences of the global conflict on regional and domestic events remains the dominant image. A contrasting perception downplays the international dimension and seeks to locate the causes of the Korean War and the Chinese Revolution predominantly in the domestic circumstances of each country. A third interpretation assesses the interaction of the international and the domestic within a framework that was not exclusively defined by Soviet–American relations. It would take account of the regional situation and distinguish hot war from Cold War and the ideological struggle from the struggle to enhance and maintain traditional interests. The emphasis

on international bipolarity as both cause and consequence tends to be accompanied by a belief that Soviet–American relations are all about power politics and military force and *are* the Cold War because they are accompanied by an ideological confrontation. A more sophisticated approach to regional dynamics may open up a greater understanding of the global Cold War.

The West and the Korean War

The events in China and Korea, whatever their domestic and international significance, have come to be seen in the West as landmarks in the development of a Cold War defined primarily and perhaps misleadingly by bipolar Soviet–American relations. In Western historiography there are two accompanying assessments of the emergence of China and the conflict in Korea's significance in the developing Cold War. First, the events in East Asia allegedly embody the globalization of the Cold War in so much as containment was extended to Asia with the emergence of the Chinese communist threat and the Soviet-sponsored aggression in Korea. Secondly, they allegedly signify the militarization of the conflict as Korea indicated Stalin's intention to use force and limited war to realize his expansionist aims. As such the Cold War was escalated to another level requiring the kind of military response defined in NSC 68 and justifying the claims made when NATO was created that the free world was in imminent danger of military attack. Such interpretations justify the West as again simply responding to an aggressive Soviet Union and the portrayal of Stalin as determined to march towards new communist successes even at the expense of military conflict.

These standard interpretations may well contain some truth but fail to consider a number of facts as well as the evidence available from sources in the Soviet Union. A more aggressive American Cold War strategy was suggested before NSC 68, the communist triumph in China, and the Korean War. The latter had a double-edged impact on this proactive American policy. While it could serve to vindicate it, it also led to worries that an aggressive strategy aimed at undermining the Soviet satellites might increase the risk of hot war. Rearmament was advocated to reduce that risk. On the other hand, as the British military argued, if a more aggressive Cold War strategy was not pursued and the Cold War thereby won, the West could find itself facing more Koreas which the British at least could ill afford. As far as the globalization of the conflict is concerned, it has been argued that the Cold War developed from disagreements about the nature of the post-Second World War global changes not because of events in a particular region. While the Cold War can be portrayed as a series of events stemming from Soviet actions that had European and then worldwide implications, this argument based on reactions to Soviet initiatives is not convincing. It ignores the ambitions of the Western powers in areas of special concern to them outside Europe and the events in Indo-China and Malaya which occurred in 1946 and 1948. These had international implications but also domestic roots which preceded the Cold War.

The Korean War and its Internal Origins

The Korean War was an important Cold War watershed for a number of reasons. It massively increased tension, provided a new regional focus in Asia, which became the new danger area in Western eyes, and ensured that armaments and preparing for hot war began to figure more prominently in plans to deal with the Soviets. Its origins and development are still surrounded in controversy despite the recent revelations from communist sources about the actions and thoughts of Stalin and Mao Tse-tung. The war provides a remarkable example of how internal conflicts can interact with the broader international situation to determine the nature and development of a military struggle. In particular Korea provided an example of how a Cold War, which raged as a civil war from June 1950 until October of that year, developed into a regional hot one once the United States, acting on behalf of the United Nations, then became engaged in a major war with China.

When the Second World War ended, Korea, as a territory under former Japanese control, was divided at the 38th parallel for occupation purposes between the Americans and the Soviets. Although a Joint

Commission was set up at the Moscow Council of Foreign Ministers, leaders in both zones were not happy with the division and the drive for unification was to figure strongly in the political programmes of Korean political parties who were split ideologically as well as geographically. In the North the Soviets, whose zone comprised only one-third of the population, initially permitted all political groupings but restricted movement across the border which would make the imposition of tighter controls easier if it was deemed necessary. In the South the American commander refused to cooperate with the self-proclaimed Korean People's Republic and maintained the Japanese bureaucratic structure.

By early 1946 when Allied relations began to deteriorate, non-communist elements in the North were purged. The Soviets supported Korea being placed under trusteeship but the Americans campaigned against it with non-communists in the South, and the Joint Commission, having failed to produce proposals for the unification of Korea, was suspended in May 1946. Political turmoil and Soviet–American disagreement was accompanied in 1946 by bad economic conditions that produced riots and strikes in rural and urban areas in the South. There was support in Washington for building a non-communist coalition of moderates in the South but the man on the spot, General John Hodge, favoured the forces of the Right.

Polarization accompanied factionalism on the Korean peninsular with the communists in the North attempting to build support in the South. Their leader, Kim Il Sung, was keen not only to reunite the peninsular but to end the splits in the North. An invasion was one way of doing this but its success proved to be more difficult than expected because of American intervention. The invasion was only launched because of Stalin's change of mind in early 1950 and the expectation that the US would not fight for Korea. Despite Soviet support in terms of equipment and trained personnel, the fact that the Americans were able to launch a counter-attack under UN auspices led to a bloody and destructive conflict. The counter-attack, spearheaded by a surprise landing behind enemy lines at Inchon, led to the recrossing of the 38th parallel and the pushing back of the communist forces to the brink of defeat. The opportunity to reunify Korea under Western auspices appeared too good to miss but after much consultation between Moscow and Beijing, and warnings to the Americans, the Chinese intervened on a large scale in November 1950.

The war had now become a fully fledged regional conflict as the opposing forces recrossed the 38th parallel for the third time. Pressure began to mount for a negotiated peace but the Chinese were determined that the talks should be on regional issues concerning peace and security including the issue of Taiwan (Formosa). The British had been pressing for a negotiated settlement before Chinese intervention, not least because of the fear that the war would escalate into a global conflict involving the use of nuclear weapons. By the end of the year some Americans, including the military commander General MacArthur, wanted to take the war to China either by blockading Chinese territory or by bombing the Chinese mainland. In the event escalation by the Americans was avoided by Truman sacking General MacArthur and General Ridgeway preserving a foothold on the peninsular to prevent a Chinese victory. Once again in 1951 the opposing forces battled up the Korean peninsular until in June 1951 a stalemate was reached very close to the old dividing-line on the 38th parallel.

The question was whether this stalemate could produce an armistice as what might have been a simple process dragged on in a lengthy and protracted wrangle for two years. Military pressure applied by the Americans in 1953 may have contributed to the ending of the conflict as might the death of Stalin who had his own reasons for keeping the Chinese and the Americans embroiled in a struggle. The fact that Eisenhower was threatening to escalate the war might have combined with Stalin's death to increase the communist desire to reach an agreement over an armistice. The difficulties arose primarily over the issue of prisoners of war. The Americans were reluctant to return to the communists those prisoners who did not wish to return to the oppressive societies they had come from, whereas the communists preferred the exchange and return of all prisoners. Elaborate efforts were made by both sides and through third parties to ensure that prisoners were persuaded to take the option of return or express a desire to stay. In the end the problem was partly resolved by the establishment in

May 1953 of a repatriation commission to supervise prisoners of war inside Korea to prevent intimidation during the time permitted for the exercise of a free choice. In addition the five-member commission would allow representations to be made for non-repatriated prisoners for four months which was shorter than the communists wanted but longer than the West would have liked.

At the end of the day the Korean War was a war which affected all aspects of Cold War and East–West relations. Propaganda and psychological warfare were promoted to fight the Cold War and win the propaganda battle over the repatriation of prisoners of war. A clear connection was made between Cold War and the fact that it could lead to regional military conflicts which made global war more likely. However, the lessons that were drawn both at the time and with hindsight have proved to be flawed. It was a war with domestic and international causes and consequences and to portray it simply as an internal struggle which developed into an international one is akin to seeing the Cold War as a European conflict which became a global one. The two were always intertwined. The West saw it not just as a test of how effectively they would resist communist aggression but how they could remain united in the carrying out of military action in a regional context that always threatened to become a global one. It was a war which set regional issues firmly within a global context and one in which the West for the first, but not the only time, confused Stalin's regional ambitions with ascribed global ones. Their determination to act firmly against the communist menace was now combined with some clear justification for military measures to deal with the Soviets and their new allies, and in the wake of NSC 68 for taking Cold War measures to avoid the outbreak of hot war.

As far as Stalin was concerned, the Korean War confirmed the idea suggested here (see Chapter 1, D) that in 1946 he was keen to extend Soviet power and influence along the same lines as Russian imperialism. Yet it also suggests that Stalin's imperialism was characterized by caution, fear, and paranoia rather than by revolutionary fervour and risk-taking. What was crucial was the need to avoid confrontation and military conflict with the United States, which, nevertheless, it has been claimed, was likely to occur without American vigilance and rearmament. Stalin's ambitions were held in check by fear and caution until the beginning of 1950 when he saw the opportunity to benefit from Kim Il Sung's proposed aggression in Korea. It is unlikely, however, that he sought simply to strike a Cold War blow against the United States. His concerns were also with the regional power and influence that stemmed from old imperial ambitions and with his new requirements as the leader of international communism. As such this was a reflection of all the wartime allies' concerns about old power political requirements and their new post-war roles. When combined with the fears that new power alignments could threaten the domestic position of elites in new ways, the tensions became acute. The Cold War was the result of these ideological concerns but had to be painted as

a military struggle in order to win the ideological battle and preserve the economic and social status quo, which was what in 1948 the Cold War was primarily about. At least this was what distinguished it from a traditional battle between rival imperialisms. If the above analysis of Stalin's policies in East Asia is to be accepted, it may mean that although both sides were keen to give this conflict a predominantly military appearance, the West was the more concerned about imposing a particular ideology onto the rest of the world. Stalin, in East Asia and elsewhere, had the power political concerns of the Soviet state foremost in his mind and thus neglected the international ideological battle. If so, this has important implications for interpretations of Soviet approaches to the Cold War conflict in general.

NOTES

1. Christopher Andrew and Vasili Mitrokhin, *The Mitrokhin Archive* (Allen Lane, London, 1999), 73–207.

2. In Britain the Foreign Office was largely in favour of trying to maintain cooperation with the Soviets not because they were under any illusions about the nature of Stalin's regime but because they believed Britain and the Soviet Union would have certain common interests. The military and the intelligence services were uniformly hostile to the Soviet Union and eager to adopt anti-Soviet policies long before the War ended. Questions remain as to the impact this had on Soviet assessments of Britain and whether the military view essentially reflected a humanitarian rejection of Soviet brutality and oppression, a hard-headed calculation of British interests or an ideological aversion to left-wing policies. However, what converted the Foreign Office were calculations about British interests not the fact that the Soviet regime was 'nasty' or 'left wing'.

3. Ibid., 73–207.

4. Richard J. Aldrich, *The Hidden Hand Britain, America and Cold War Secret Intelligence* (John Murray, London, 2001), 110–11. For differing accounts of the PHP and the conflicting attitudes to and actions to be taken against the Soviets see Aldrich, op. cit.; J. Lewis, *Changing Direction: British Military Planing for Post-War Strategic Defence 1942–1947* (Sherwood, London, 1987), and J. Kent, *British Imperial Strategy and the Origins of the Cold War 1944–1949* (Leicester University Press, Leicester, 1993).

5. V. Pechatnov, 'Exercise in Frustration: Soviet Foreign Propaganda in the Early Cold War 1945–1947', *Cold War History* 1 (2001).

6. Scott Lucas, *Freedom's War: The US Crusade against the Soviet Union 1945–56* (Manchester University Press, Manchester, 1999), 47.

7. Aldrich, op. cit., 41.

8. Ibid., 142–3.

9. See John L. Gaddis, *Strategies of Containment* (Oxford, Oxford University Press, 1982), Chs. 2 and 3.

10. Foreign Relations of the United States (FRUS), 1948, I, NSC 7, 30 March 1948, 548–9.

11. FRUS 1948, I, Memorandum by Thorp (Assistant Secretary of State for Economic Affairs), 7 Apr. 1948, 557–60.

12. Gaddis, op. cit., 155. Readers should form their own judgements about the interpretation of the two documents

13. FRUS 1948, I, NSC 20/4, 'Notes on US Objectives with Respect to the USSR to Counter Soviet Threats to US Security', 23 Nov. 1948, 663–9.

14. Scott Lucas, *Freedom's War: The US Crusade against the Soviet Union 1945–56* (Manchester University Press, Manchester, 1999), 58–61. Citing USNA Department of State Lot Files, 64 D 563, Records of the Policy Planning Staff 1947–1953, Subject Files, Box 11A, Political and Psychological Warfare 1947–1950; Policy Planning Staff Report 'The Inauguration of Organized Political Warfare', 30 Apr. 1948 and US Declassified Documents 1978 189C, Memorandum by S. W. Souers, 15 June 1948.

15. Robert Latham, *Modernity, Security and the Making of Postwar International Order*, 36–41. Liberal order is used to indicate that international relations have been ordered in the context of liberal modernity which is constructed from 'shifts in social forces, ruptures in discourse and inventions in practices and institutions'. Latham argues that there was a convergence of liberalism, modernity, and international order at the end of the Second World War.

16. The Psychological Strategy Board, an inter-departmental/agency Cold War body, was established by a presidential directive of 4 Apr. 1951 to provide for more effective planning, coordination, and conduct, within nationally approved policies, of psychological operations.

17. Scott Lucas, op. cit., 145. Citing US Declassified Documents 1991, 1693, Morgan to Allen, 10 April 1952.

18. A FO circular produced universal approval from the relevant departments. See FO371/62555, minutes by R. B. Stevens, R. M. A. Hankey, W. G. Hayter, F. B. A. Rundall, and G. Jebb, Dec. 1947 and Jan. 1948.

19. FRUS, 1948, I, Report by the Policy Planning Staff, 'Review of Current Trends US Foreign Policy', 24 Feb. 1948, 510.

20. DEFE 4/11, COS (48) 37th, 17 Mar. 1948.

21. David Holloway, *Stalin and the Bomb* (Yale University Press, New York, 1994), 152, 228; W. LaFeber, op. cit., 49.

22. David Holloway, op. cit., 231–3.

23. What appears to have been meant by this is a miscalculation by the Soviets of what actions they could take without provoking a significant response from the West. Stalin might not want war with the West but he might fail to understand that his actions in support of communist movements would require the West to resort to force. Preventing another European state or the western sector of Berlin, for example, becoming communist was such an important Cold War goal in 1948 that it might have been necessary to resort to hot war.

24. Fred Kaplan, *The Wizards of Armageddon* (Simon & Schuster, New York, 1983), 43.

25. See Alan Milward, *The European Rescue of the Nation-State* (Routledge, London, 1992).

26. Spencer Mawby, *Containing the German Threat: Britain and the Arming of the Federal Republic* (St Martin's Press, New York, 1999), 20–35.

27. FRUS, 1949, 1, Minutes of the Policy Planning Staff, 11 Oct. 1949, 402.

28. Ibid., 16 Dec. 1949, 414.

29. Lucas, op. cit., 65–6, 134.

30. Aldrich, op. cit., 320.

31. Ibid., 296–8; Lucas, op. cit., 88.

32. Aldrich, op. cit., 173, 178, 294, 297.

33. Ibid., 324.

34. Troy was a 1951 project to look at how Soviet jamming of American propaganda broadcasts could be overcome and then to examine other ways of penetrating the Iron Curtain and developing a concept of political warfare.

35. Lucas, op. cit., 128. Citing USNA, Dept of State, Records Relating to Project Troy, Box 1, Berkner to Acheson, 27 Dec. 1950; 100–1. Citing Harry S. Truman Library (HST) Staff Memoranda and Office Files, PSB Files, Box 1, 001 Rand Corporation Structure, Curtin to Gray 9 Oct. 1951; US Declassified Documents, 1986, 1974, Radio Free Europe Handbook 30 Nov. 1951; G. Mitrovich, *Undermining the Kremlin: America's Strategy to Subvert the Soviet Bloc 1947–1956* (Cornell University Press, Ithaca, 2000), 20–34; Lucas, 146. Citing HST, Staff Memoranda and Office Files, PSB Files, Box 15, 091.412 The Field and Role of Psychological Strategy in Cold War Planning, PSB Staff Study, 'Overall Strategic Concept for our Psychological Operations', 7 May 1952, 135. Citing HST, Staff Memoranda and Office Files, Box 23, 334 Director's group, Planning Framework, 12 Nov. 1951.

36. Lucas, op. cit., 144; Aldrich, op. cit., 145, 154.

37. V. Zubok and C. Pleshakov, *Inside the Kremlin's Cold War from Stalin to Khrushchev* (Harvard University Press, Cambridge, 1996), 130.

38. Aldrich, op. cit., 327. Citing PREM 11/159, NID 7956 Memo by Longley-Cook, 6 July 1951.

39. FRUS 1950, 1, NSC 68, 14 Apr. 1950, 238–42.

40. Ibid., 262, 255.

41. Ibid., 264, 267, 272, 277.

42. Ibid., 276–9.

43. Ibid., 280.

44. Ibid., 281–2.

45. Ibid., 284.

46. Robert R. Bowie and Richard H. Immerman, *Waging Peace: How Eisenhower Shaped an Enduring Cold War Strategy* (Oxford University Press, Oxford, 1998), 23.

47. See W. F. Poole and R. J. Watson, *The History of the Joint Chiefs of Staff, IV and V, 1950–1952 and 1953–1954* (1977) and (1986).

48. FRUS, 1950, 1, Memo by the Chief of the Division of Estimates, Bureau of the Budget (Schaub) to NSC, 8 May 1950, 300–1.

49. FRUS, 1951, 1, NSC 114/1, 'Preliminary report by the NSC on Status and Timing of Current US Programs for National Security', 8 Aug. 1951, 129–32.

50. FRUS, 1951, 1. Memo by C. Bohlen, 22 August 1951, p. 165.

51. O. A. Westad, 'Losses, Chances and Myths: the United States and the Creation of the Sino-Soviet Alliance, 1946–1950', *Diplomatic History* 2 (1997).

52. Chen Jian, 'The Myth of America's Lost Chance in China', *Diplomatic History* 2 (1997).

53. Ibid.; Westad, op. cit.

54. Shen Zhihua, 'Sino–Soviet Relations and the Origins of the Korean War: Stalin's Strategic Goals in the Far East', *Journal of Cold War Studies* 2 (2000).

CHRONOLOGY: THE KOREAN WAR

1945

August   US and USSR agree on division of Korea along 38th parallel.

1948

August   South Korea established.
December   Russian troops leave the peninsular.

1949

June   US troops withdraw from Korea.

1950

January   Stalin concedes to Kim Il Sung's request to use military force against the South.
25 June   Kim Il Sung attacks South Korea.
27 June   UN Security Council in the absence of USSR calls for members to assist Korea.
7 July   UN command established under General MacArthur.
15 September   US/UN landing at Inchon.
9 October   US troops cross 38th parallel.
25 October   Chinese make contact with US forces and retreat after pushing South Koreans back from River Yalu.
24 November   MacArthur launches assault towards the Chinese border on the Yalu.
26 November   Chinese forces begin counter-attack and push US troops south.

1951

4 January   Chinese capture Seoul.
Mid-January   US begin a counter-offensive.
15 March   Seoul recaptured as Chinese and N. Koreans retreat.
July   First meeting to discuss conditions for an armistice at Kaesong.

1952

May   Talks deadlocked over the voluntary repatriation of prisoners.
8 October   Americans suspend armistice talks.
3 December   UN General Assembly adopts the modified Indian plan for the release of prisoners.

1953

26 April	Armistice talks resume.
27 August	Armistice signed.
April–June	Geneva Conference fails to reach agreement on Korean reunification.

Part II

Cold War:
Crises and Change
1953–1963

INTRODUCTION

Soviet–American Approaches to Cold War and Peaceful Coexistence

The beginning of a new Cold War era with the death of Stalin and a new Republican administration in Washington has generally been analysed in terms of a quest for peace and a 'thaw' in Cold War relations. One cause of debate is whether the new rulers in Moscow were genuinely prepared to introduce new policies and to change the foreign policy approach of the Soviet Union. Policy under Stalin was based on promoting a climate of Western hostility in order that this could assist the regime's repression of dissent. The question was whether the death of Stalin would change this climate and lead to a new era of accommodation. In other words, was there any prospect of a real change in Soviet policy and a real possibility for accommodation and agreement on issues such as Germany or the control of nuclear weapons?

The debate has been framed in the West with the usual onus on Soviet actions and policy. Therefore issues tend to be defined in terms of whether the United States missed an opportunity for real accommodation or whether the actions of the Soviet Union continued to reflect the ascribed goals of expansion and conflict while employing different means to achieve them. As with other issues the questions about Soviet motivation could be applied equally pertinently to American policy. Were the policies of Eisenhower such as 'atoms for peace' and 'open skies' genuine attempts to reach accommodation with the Soviet Union or were they gestures to reassure Western opinion that the United States was prepared to deal constructively with the Soviet Union? With the advent of the hydrogen bomb it was clear that any resort to military conflict was now likely to have catastrophic consequences for the future of civilization and public concerns about future war were to grow in the second half of the 1950s. We also know that there were those in the US administration who believed that it was not possible to reach agreement with Moscow which would use any negotiating process to score propaganda points and raise false optimism in the West about the prospects for peace in the hope that the United States would get the blame when this did not materialize. On the other hand, Churchill was set on trying to reach agreement with the Soviets and reduce Cold War tension through summit meetings, albeit as part of a grand exit from politics in the form of a peacemaking role.

The issue both then and now of whether the Soviets would genuinely participate in a process of détente has been defined within a Cold War framework which, as suggested in Part I, has tended to down play both the offensive policy of the United States and the extent to which it was defined not by what the Soviets were doing but by assessments of what they might do. When the extent of the American move away from containment is taken into account, and despite the opposition in 1952 to plans to subvert the Soviet regime and/or its control over the satellite regimes of Eastern Europe, the focus on peace initiatives becomes questionable. There are those who see the changes between 1953 and the Geneva summit of 1955 as constituting a 'thaw' in the Cold War. The issue of the extent to which the Soviets were genuine in trying to reduce tensions after Stalin's death or how far Eisenhower's proposals were designed for propaganda purposes are then transformed into the idea that the Cold War atmosphere was changing for the better.

The Changing Cold War

This concept of a 'thaw' in the Cold War depends on a definition of the conflict which encompasses all aspects of Soviet–American relations and does not distinguish between those policies aimed at the destruction of the Soviet bloc short of war and those policies designed to use diplomacy to lessen the chance of a major hot war breaking out. In the United States the new administration contained a number of ardent supporters of psychological warfare including covert operations to undermine the Soviet bloc. Moreover, the Eisenhower administration and the new Secretary of State, John Foster Dulles, became associated with ideas expressed publicly that communism could be rolled back unlike during the Truman administration which was criticized for not doing enough in the battle against the Soviets. At the same time the Americans were becoming more concerned with the possibility of war and the vulnerability of the United States to future Soviet attack with nuclear weapons. Similarly with the Soviet Union it is possible to distinguish between the encourage- ment given to communist parties to oppose Western governments by action outside the political process, and the desire to seek accommodation and reduce the possible threat from American military might and a revived Germany. Thus it is possible to see a 'thaw' not in the Cold War but in the concerns to stabilize Soviet–American relations and to mitigate the danger of Cold War becoming hot. Moreover, this Cold War could be intensified in the hope that the Soviet Union might collapse while efforts were at the same time made to maintain an equilibrium that along with greater American military strength might reduce the risk of hot war. The post-Stalin period could there- fore be interpreted as an intensification of the Cold War while improving relations to reduce the risk of hot war breaking out if the Cold War was not won. Even with the impact of the hydrogen bomb it took some time before the obvious point seemed to sink in that offensive Cold War policies would almost inevitably lead to greater risks of hot war in several important respects.

In addition from the American point of view there were growing doubts about the effectiveness of subversive measures. These were seen as unlikely to have an impact on the Soviet Union or its hold over the satellites without a major war that would be increasingly destructive. On the other hand, there were those in the military who did not want to abandon the Cold War attempts at roll back. The debate between the civilian and the military formed a growing division in the US between advocates of coexistence and those in favour of the ultimate roll-back of the Soviet satellite Empire or the transformation of the Soviet Union itself. Different Cold War measures would be needed for either strategy but the US tried to keep both options open. Instead of going all out with an offensive Cold War strategy or accepting peaceful co–existence and the pursuit of US interests by trying to reach agreements with Moscow, Eisenhower avoided that choice. In the end it faded away in the early 1960s as the Soviet Union continued to exist and as Cold War attention moved away from Eastern Europe to the less developed world (see below) and the Cuban Missile Crisis provided more of an incentive for trying to reach agreements to avoid hot war.

Whatever the outcome of the debate on this there are three separate areas which need to be distinguished in order to provide a more meaningful analysis of the Cold War in this period. On the one hand, there are the specific points of disagreement between the United States and the Soviet Union, such as the failure to agree on peace treaties for Austria and Germany and the problem of reaching a settlement to the war in Korea. Linked to these are the more general attempt to put East–West relations on a better footing whether it be through summit meetings or through proposals to grant overflying rights so that military developments were not secret

Another way in which the Cold War might be said to have intensified was the growing concern on both sides of the Iron Curtain about events in the colonial or less developed world. Stalin had little or no interest in areas of the world not adjacent to the Soviet Union and had not attempted to compete with the West in such regions by providing economic or military aid. However, with the new regime of Malenkov, Khrushchev, and Bulganin, who were less stricken with the siege mentality of Stalin and keener to see the Soviet Union compete as a superpower, the idea of competing with the West on a global basis held more attraction. In addition Soviet attacks on Western imperialism and the continuation of colonialism would appeal not just to the people of Asia, Africa, and the Middle East who were still denied the freedom to choose the form of government under which they lived, but to those newly independent countries keen to oppose Western colonialism.

Cold War and Colonialism

The degree of Soviet hypocrisy on this could be hidden by the armed struggles against colonial rule that were taking place in Malaya, Kenya, Vietnam, and Algeria by 1954 along with disturbances in Egypt and Morocco. On the one hand, the demonstrations and armed rebellions could be portrayed by Britain and France as instigated by communists or as opening the door to communism and there-fore as something for the Americans to oppose. On the other hand, the continued imposition of foreign rule against the wishes of so many people made the West appear guilty of hypocrisy in trumpeting the virtues of freedom and democracy which were lacking in colonial situations as much as in the countries of the communist bloc. Dulles was keenly aware of the damage this did to the West's propaganda campaign against communism as well as making it extremely difficult to balance the needs of strengthening the Western Alliance with the needs of increasing American and Western influence in the non-European world. Initially Dulles tried to transcend these conflicting needs by shifting the NATO alliance away from the practical needs of military defence cooperation to the reasons why these were needed in the first place. At the end of 1953 Dulles suggested a moral crusade against the 'root evil' of communism which he claimed was a far bigger obstacle to freedom than Western colonialism. By no longer contrasting the military importance of NATO with the political importance of sympathy for those struggling, as the United States once had, against colonialism, the moral crusade against the enormity of the portrayed communist threat could unite the Western and non-Western worlds.

Unfortunately the moral crusade meant little to those seeking political freedom and can only have encouraged those worried about the implications of a world where everyone was roped into a conflict between two systems represented by military blocs. Even though the Warsaw Pact was not created in response to NATO until 1955 Dulles can only have encouraged those like Nehru who believed in non-alignment and the avoidance of blocs. The leaders of those countries who initiated the non-aligned movement in 1955 at Bandung rejected any idea of crusades with the world divided into two groups. Bandung was an attempt to do just what Dulles was trying to avoid and associate non-alignment with the efforts to end colonialism.

Latin America and the Cold War

Dulles's initial failure to devise a means of removing the conflict between support for colonial powers and support for the Western bloc in opposition to communism was only part of a bigger failure of American policy outside Europe. In the important region of Latin America, which was now dominated economically and politically by the United States, fear of communism was growing. In Europe 'the empire by invitation' which had produced enormous American influence was built on economic aid that Latin America never received. After the War it soon became clear that the United States was going to extend a large measure of political as well as economic control over the region but without the benefits given to Europe. Post-war American hegemony was more overt and less rewarding. The United States involvement in the overthrow of the Guatemalan government in 1954 has provoked a debate as to whether this was done out of Cold War concerns or because of a need to protect American economic interests in the particular form of the United Fruit Company. What is certain is that the Eisenhower administration was not acting against the forces of communism which barely existed in Guatemala or elsewhere in Latin America in the first half of the 1950s. Even small communist parties were, like Soviet diplomatic missions, few and far between in South and Central America and although there were communists associated with the Guatemalan leader, Jacob Arbenz, it was the belief that left-wing governments would prepare the way for communism that was crucial. The pressures exerted by the United Fruit Company which had connections to the Dulles brothers, who were Secretary of State and Director of the Central Intelligence

Agency, undoubtedly made the overthrow of Arbenz easier but it was the Cold War and Eisenhower's belief in the value of covert operations that probably proved more important. The early success in Guatemala followed that in Iran the previous year but United States attempts to mould the Third World to its economic and political requirements were not always to be successful. Even in Latin America where the policy of the first Eisenhower administration to leave development and aid in the hands of the private sector began to change in 1958 the results were not good. They did not prevent the Cold War's key development in the Western hemisphere which was the emergence of a communist Cuba in the wake of Castro's successful 1959 revolution.

The Cuban revolution reflected the difficulties of the United States in reconciling capitalism with the need for welfare and development in those non-industrialized countries which lacked the resources that could command high world market prices. Such countries, especially those countries exporting tropical produce, were usually characterized in Latin America by gross inequality, corruption, and a landowning class whose economic interests were tied, as in pre-revolutionary Cuba, to the United States economy. The dictatorial regime of General Batista had not tackled agrarian reform, modernization in the sugar industry, or low investment. Castro's attempts to do so soon fell foul of those middle-class supporters who had welcomed the overthrow of Batista along with the Eisenhower administration. As Castro's links to Moscow and communism became more influential the United States then began to take action to subvert the communist regime. This was to provoke enormous controversy as the Kennedy administration became obsessed with the removal of the Cuban dictator. How far the measures taken to bring down Castro can be linked to the Soviet decision in 1962 to deploy nuclear armed missiles is still being debated. The fact that Castro remained in power in Cuba and implemented health and education policies which generally improved the lot of the population was a source of concern to US governments after the revolution. The fear was that alternative paths of development, if they were successful, would be a boost to left-wing ideologies and to Soviet communism. Kennedy embarked on a significant attempt to use federal funds to promote the kind of liberal economic development that he associated with the American democratic system. The problem was that without any form of social change or redistribution of wealth the social and economic system was unlikely to be acceptable to a majority of the population. Kennedy's attempt to assist Latin America with what was known as the Alliance for Progress and provide an acceptable alternative to Castro were unsuccessful in promoting democracy or bringing broad-based development to the region.

Regional Defence Pacts and their Political and Military Roles

American policy was equally unsuccessful in producing positive results in areas of the world where either US economic interests were less prevalent or where political control was deemed less of a requirement. In the Middle East and South-East Asia, which bordered on the Soviet Union, and where the negative achievement of preventing the spread of communism was the goal, the Eisenhower administration sought to build defence organizations like NATO which would encircle the Soviet Union and in theory prevent Soviet military expansion which it was assumed lay behind the Korean War. More importantly they would, like NATO, be deemed have a political effect in promoting the confidence to resist communism. The South-East Asia Treaty Organization (SEATO) and the Baghdad Pact seemed to confirm that the United States and other Western powers would come to the signatories' assistance if the Soviets were to use force to impose their political ideas. Both organizations remained militarily weak and the Baghdad Pact never came near to achieving the force levels that were deemed necessary to defend the Middle East.

In the Middle East by 1953 Dulles had decided to pursue policies independent of the British including the creation of the Baghdad Pact. Based on the Northern tier which followed a line across Turkey and the Zagros mountains down through Iraq and Iran to the Persian Gulf its political consequences were extremely destabilizing in both the Middle East and South Asia. With a membership of Pakistan, Iran, Iraq, Britain, and Turkey the Baghdad Pact was probably the most useless and hated military organization of the Cold War. The shortfall of forces to meet a Soviet invasion was in some respects greater than those in the area and the Pact only became plausible as a military organization when the British promised to use nuclear weapons to defend the Zagros passes. Unfortunately these could not be made available in the region until 1959. Militarily the British thus invented a new meaning for deception plans based on deceiving your allies as well as your enemies. Politically the Israelis hated it because it allied an Arab state with a Western organization backed by the United States and thereby reduced the likelihood of American aid and assistance. The Egyptians and Saudis hated it because it appeared to elevate their arch enemies in Iraq towards leadership of the Arab world. Colonel Nasser, the Egyptian prime minister, particularly hated it because his attempts to become the clear leader of the Arab world were linked to his success in 1954 in reaching an agreement by which the British agreed to remove their troops from the Suez base. The French hated it because it signified the end of their last remaining influence in the Middle East. And even the Americans became luke-warm towards it after its creation in early 1955 because it reinjected anti-Western sentiments into the region and alienated Nasser, whom the Americans hoped would play the leading role in achieving an Arab–Israeli settlement. Moreover, because it placed Pakistan in an alliance backed by the United States, it alienated the Indians who were in dispute with their neighbour over the territory of Kashmir. Ultimately it alienated the Pakistanis because it failed to give them the means to get help in their conflict with the Indians and eventually contributed to their links to the Chinese.

The Cold War in Asia and Africa

In South-East Asia the disastrous American involvement in the renewed Vietnam conflict after the Geneva settlement of 1955 was built on the perceived need to prevent the spread of communism. The motives for providing aid and military 'advisers' to South Vietnam during this period have been located in the so-called domino theory whereby the fall of one part of the region would lead to the collapse of the other parts. Thus even though Vietnam had little or no strategic or economic importance the United States had to prevent its takeover by the communist North whether through the elections for a unified Vietnam, promised in the 1955 agreement which the United States refused to sign, or through an armed rebellion. By the end of the 1950s when the Chinese began assisting the insurgents in their campaign against the Saigon government the Cold War had become a battle of wills in the developing world where communist successes would undermine the prestige and credibility of the United States and the Western world. Would communism be able to surpass capitalism as the best means of development and progress or would capitalism prove more able to satisfy the needs of non-Western people and offer them greater economic and technological benefits? This was the question that could only be answered by the allegiance and support of those in the world not yet associated with either bloc who could still exercise a choice.

Africa was the continent where most nations still had choices to make once they achieved independence for the first time. Hence the interest taken in the continent by both sides as the transfer of power moved closer in a large number of former colonies. The issue for the Americans became not so much how to reconcile the interests of the metropolitan powers and the unity of NATO with attracting support and allegiance from Africans, but how to ensure that power was transferred at the right time and to the right people. To delay might encourage the leaders of anti-colonial movements to become more radical and to turn to the Soviets for support. Or it might lead to their replacement by new and more radical leaders not prepared to cooperate with the West. On the other hand, to transfer power too soon in Africa might produce unstable non-viable regimes which would be prone to collapse and therefore were seen as offering opportunities to communist parties or other radical left-wing groups. This was the dilemma for the British and eventually the French, if not the Portuguese, and the way in which American support came to be offered was on the basis of providing a specific commitment to self-government in return for US support in the United Nations while efforts were made to arrange the appropriate moment for the transfer of power.

This approach, modelled on British policy for transferring power, eventually worked with the French in that it helped produce a commitment in 1953 for Moroccan self-government and thereby sounded the death-knell for the French Union. Yet it failed with the Portuguese in Angola. Portugal under the fascist dictator Salazar was determined to hang on to Angola at all costs even, as their foreign minister told the Americans, if it meant the start of a Third World War. Once a rebellion in Angola broke out in February 1961 the issue became vital as over the border in the former Belgian Congo, which became an independent state (later Zaire) in June 1960, chaos reigned and the possibility of Soviet intervention loomed. To the east of the Congo the British were faced with a delicate situation as the Central African Federation of Northern and Southern Rhodesia and Nyasaland was on the verge of breaking up. Thus in Central Africa all the complexities of African decolonization were in evidence. The United Nations was involved, the Soviets were being asked to support the Congo's first Prime Minister Patrice Lumumba, and the British policy of creating a multiracial society in which political representation would be based on racial affiliation rather than the will of the majority was collapsing. Fighting and internal conflict became serious in the Congo as Moshe Tshombe established a breakaway kingdom in the mineral-rich province of Katanga. The intervention of Belgian troops further complicated a situation comprising a failed transfer of power, the problems of multiracialism, important European economic interests, the Cold War implications of Soviet involvement, the responsibilities of the United Nations, and the determination of the Kennedy administration to give support to Africans.

The first thing to be aware of in this extraordinary tangle of the Cold War with the end of Empire and multiracialism is that the Cold War did not simply involve Soviet–American competition over giving aid to some of the groups competing for control over the central government or those in Katanga seeking to escape from it. The issue was a broader one, particularly with regard to newly independent West African states. Kennedy was determined that Africa should be at the centre of American foreign policy and the allegiance of the newly independent states, such as Nkrumah's Ghana was deemed crucial. The concern within Africa about the possible collapse of the Congo or the secession of Katanga was based on a determination that the gaining of independence should not be seen as a failure. In particular that Belgian or other European forces should not create what was expected to be a blatant form of neocolonialism based on Katangan secession. If Lumumba, whose position was under threat from internal enemies and from the CIA who were working towards his assassination, could not unite the country and Katanga succeeded, then the transfer of power would be seen as a failure. The role of Belgian troops and the assets of the Union Minière Co. in Katanga would be interpreted as economic neocolonialism. On the other hand, to have a united Congo courtesy of Soviet help to Lumumba was another disaster for the West to avoid.

One of the lessons to emerge from the crisis was the extent to which the United States and the UN Secretary-General, Dag Hammarskjold, shared the common goal of preventing Soviet involvement in the Congo. Over time, and well before Hammerskjold's death in September 1961, there were disputes about the best means to achieve this but the fact that the UN worked closely with the American government is undeniable. Once Lumumba's murder became public knowledge in February 1961 the Americans had to provide a 'moderate' alternative for the leadership of an increasingly divided Congo. The struggle to win support for the former trade unionist, Cyrille Adoula, whose election as Congo premier was secured by American money in August 1961, meant defeating Lumumba's left-wing successor, Antoine Gizenga, and ending Katanga's secession. More importantly for US policy it meant fighting British, Belgian, and French reluctance to involve the UN in the forcible termination of Tshombe's regime in Katanga. Not only were there links between European governments and the financial interests of the Union Minière du Haut Katanga and its associated companies, but neither the British nor the Belgians were keen to eject the anti-communist Tshombe in such a fluid and unpredictable situation. Interestingly, in ending Katangan secession the Kennedy administration opted for a policy which would win African support in the Cold War. In avoiding the easy option of preferring the devil they knew who would be pro-European and anti-communist (Tshombe) to a devil with an uncertain future (Adoula) the Kennedy administration showed its commitment to a liberal Cold War political strategy which was to be repeated in Angola after the 1961 revolt began. Sadly as the dangers of African instability seemed to increase, as in other areas, the Johnson administration was to abandon the efforts to win over the less developed world by liberal policies and to rely on dictators like the military leader Joseph Mobutu who took over the Congo in 1965. African decolonization did not always equate with political freedom let alone economic opportunity.

The End of European Empires

The end of French rule in Africa was almost as rapid as that of Belgian rule in the Congo, although the consequences are of less significance than the little that has been written on the causes. The Algerian War, which began in 1954, was obviously a key moment in post-war French history, not least because it led to the return of Charles de Gaulle as president of the new Fifth Republic in 1958. In the same year de Gaulle established the French Community which served to replace the defunct Fourth Republic's French Union and provided a new constitutional framework for the territories of Overseas France. This framework was more in line with the British Commonwealth in terms of being a friendly association rather than a manifestation of the French Republic 'one and indivisible'. To explain why this change took place is a matter of juggling the various changes that occurred from 1953 onwards. At the top of the list are pressures from the developing anti-French nationalist movements in North Africa. The Istiqlal in Morocco, the Neo-Destour in Tunisia, and the FLN in Algeria were more willing to use more violent means than their equivalents in French West and Equatorial Africa in the first half of the 1950s. Faced with riots, disturbances, and a full-scale war in Algeria the French in one sense had little alternative. Yet there were other pressures from within France given the Quai d'Orsay's dislike of the French Union as an acceptable means of preserving influence over Overseas France which may have influenced the Minister for Overseas France, P.-H. Teitgen, when in 1955 he began to prepare for real devolution. The French equivalent of this British process involved constitutional change that required a *loi cadre* or enabling law which came into force in 1956.

Before then, however, the process of moving towards internal self-government was well advanced in Morocco and Tunisia which were associated territories of the French

Union. Again it is easy to attribute this simply to the French conceding to the demands of the Istiqlal and the Neo-Destour. Yet the American role may have also been important. Given their economic interests and the existence of important American air bases in Morocco it was clear that American concerns about French policy were at a much higher level than in Black Africa. Active American involvement had to take the form of a quest for stability that depended on preserving good relations with the nationalists and their allies in the Asian and Arab worlds without alienating the French. After 1951 when riots occurred in Casablanca and efforts began to bring the North African situation before the United Nations General Assembly, American involvement may have prevented the French from refusing to devolve power in ways which would damage the interests of French settlers. American support in moderating UN resolutions may have led the French to contemplate bringing Morocco to self-government. Once the French had acknowledged this possibility progress towards it could not be delayed and the ultimate fate of the French Union was sealed.

The deposition of the Sultan of Morocco in August 1953 where traditional leaders were more in favour of the French than the Istiqlal or the Sultan, and the Algerian revolt in 1954, made progress easier in Tunisia where the principle of internal self-government was conceded that same year. Thus by the time de Gaulle was faced with the problem of solving the Algerian mess a pragmatic approach would not require principles to be conceded other than those emotive ones inherent in Algeria's constitutional position as part of France. De Gaulle had of course always given consideration to how French greatness could be best pursued on the international stage. It may be argued that de Gaulle had rapidly concluded that the drain of a bloody and bitter conflict in Algeria was the last thing that would rebuild French prestige and status as a leading world power. Moreover, that power in political and economic terms could only be exercised through an emphasis on a modern Europe centred on France rather than on an outmoded collection of undeveloped colonial territories. Hence the establishment of the French Community, a federal organization whose president, elected primarily by metropolitan Frenchmen would retain control over foreign and defence policy and certain aspects of economic policy. Membership was voluntary and although most African leaders accepted the argument on what today would be considered the advantages of an increasingly interdependent world, the people of Guinea chose independence. The French did what they could to make life difficult for the newly independent state but when they failed to cajole Sekou Touré, the radical Guinean leader, the attractiveness of African independence received a massive boost. For de Gaulle, who was seeking to base European cooperation on a union of nation states, endeavouring to hold a reluctant group of African federalists together was singularly unattractive. Close bilateral links could be created which would preserve French influence on the African continent more effectively.[1]

The British, having led the way with the Gold Coast, now found themselves having to catch up with the French as eleven French territories in Black Africa became independent in 1960. Difficulties for Britain were growing at the end of the decade as troubles in Nyasaland and Kenya added to the political problems of creating a federal structure in Nigeria which was facing division and conflict. In a sense the final phase of Britain's African Empire was not finally given up after careful calculations about costs of resisting nationalists, or because of a strategic choice between Africa and Europe, but because it was the easiest way to resolve a growing list of problems. Plans that Britain had for transferring power were hardly ever implemented on the basis of social and economic infrastructure, multiracialism, or strategic requirements for bases. As particular plans ran into difficulty whether in Africa or in smaller colonies like Malta and Cyprus, political change was concocted on an ad hoc basis that would encounter the least resistance. These plans could involve increasing British control, as in the Aden Protectorates, and not just relinquishing it by bowing to the inevitable. In many respects Britain was slow to realize what was necessary let alone inevitable particularly in terms of timing. In places like the Central African Federation settler interests were still seen in 1959 as protectable under the guise of multiracialism. In the last moments of Empire, rather than transferring power reluctantly under pressure from Africans, the latter were suddenly pushing at an open door through which the British government was only too happy to go if only it could find a way to do so without bringing greater disasters upon itself.

The disasters that befell the French in South-East Asia and North Africa in the form of long and bloody wars were largely avoided by the British whose conflicts were of a much smaller scale and significance except in areas where most British control and influence was exercised informally. A major crisis erupted in 1956 in independent Egypt, which has been seen by some as a milestone in the history of British decolonization. In defiance of the US and Arab world Britain invaded Suez in November in collusion with the French and the Israelis. This infamous moment in British history, when some members of the Eden government and the Foreign Office tried to hide from the world the true nature of the military aggression perpetrated against Egypt has engendered debate and controversy ever since.

There are those who maintain that the disgrace and humiliation experienced at Suez destroyed any claim that might have been made for the liberal, progressive nature of the British Empire. Moreover the limited nature of the British ability to project power by using military force was exposed to the world. Without the backing of the United States the British imperial lion was powerless and with the use of force now ruled out in 'colonial' situations the increasing pace of decolonization was inevitable. On the other hand, there are those who do not see Suez as a watershed in British imperial history. Suez was essentially about power and the end of British dominance in the Middle East, as expressed in the ability to deploy military forces in strategic positions overseas. They were to be used in global or regional conflicts as befitting the world-power status desired by British elites. The humiliation of no longer being able to use forces to depose independent governments had little to do with the formal transfer of power on a basis of cooperation. In terms of power, and particularly world-power status, Suez simply affected the means by which this was now to be exercised. Military power and the occupation of bases now became more symbolic and totally dependent on American support. Yet the pursuit of world-power status and the preservation of overseas commitments remained at the heart of British policy at least between the fiasco at Suez and the retreat from East of Suez over a decade later.

Moreover, while the strategic importance of the Suez crisis was great in terms of the loss of overflying rights, the British continued to fight for their position in the Gulf and South Arabia by sending troops to Kuwait in 1961 and by trying to tighten its control over the Aden Protectorates in the 1950s. Even in the heart of the Middle East the British sent troops to the region as part of an effort to react to the problems presented by the Iraqi revolution in 1958. In a sense the British pleaded for the Americans to allow them to send troops to Jordan, allegedly to stabilize the situation in the same way as the Americans were allegedly deploying forces to stabilize the situation in Lebanon. As result the British perception was very much that their continued involvement in the Middle East was important for their world status and as a means of protecting the region from Soviet influence. The latter was seen as increasingly likely as more radical Arab regimes came to power.

What was certain was that the United States was now the dominant regional power in the Middle East that was given formal expression through the Eisenhower Doctrine in January 1957 which basically offered aid to countries threatened by the forces of international communism. The subsequent issue has been whether the stability of Middle Eastern states was threatened by international communism or whether, as in Lebanon in 1958, the instability was internally engendered. By then the only significant external influence in the Middle East came from the United States.

The Years of Crisis, 1958–1962: Soviet Challenges to US Hegemony

The second half of the 1950s witnessed for some the true emergence of bipolarity when the old European empires were crumbling, China was suffering the internal convulsions of the Great Leap Forward and its economic disasters, and the economic strength of Western Europe and Japan was not yet in evidence. Others see merely the zenith of American hegemony as the Soviet Union's military and economic strength was well below that of the United States. The debate over this challenge concerns the post-1956 degree of Soviet commitment to their proclaimed policy of peaceful coexistence and the seriousness of Khrushchev's attempt to bully the West over Berlin and Cuba.

The Russian leader made a number of claims about the success and future of socialism in the wake of sputnik's launch. His provocative boasting was probably born from a sense of weakness but helped feed the rhetoric of John F. Kennedy who promised a more dynamic America both at home and abroad. The two leading powers both sought more and more adherents to their cause as the global community expanded and more newly independent states joined the United Nations. The Cold War became acute as a result and a number of crises occurred in the early 1960s in Laos and Berlin as well as the escalation of the Vietnam conflict, and culminated in the Cuban Missile Crisis. Their roots may be traced back to the late 1950s and to 1958 in particular when the Soviets began their challenge to the Western position in Berlin soon after the Sino–American confrontation over the Chinese nationalist hold on a number of islands a few miles off the Chinese coast.

Clearly designed to intimidate, this breast-beating and grandiose claims about the success of socialism in military and economic terms did not translate into determined attempts to secure Soviet changes to the post-war order by force if necessary. Given the parlous state of the Soviet economy, the true nature of which was not fully understood at the time, and the clear Soviet inferiority in nuclear weapons, it is more convincing to see Khrushchev's policies as nothing more than bluff. Equally Mao Tse-tung's desire to unify China was never posited on plans to tackle the military might of the US again, at least in a situation where US naval and air forces were likely to be decisive. This is not to say that the crises over Berlin, the Offshore Islands, and Cuba were mere communist gestures as there were some specific aims for them to achieve. In Europe the position of Berlin was increasingly causing problems to the Soviets and the East Germans, and a change in the status quo was both logical and necessary from Moscow's perspective. The need to strengthen a hold on a key component in the Eastern bloc was made more important by the need to prove that the proclaimed policy of peaceful coexistence could bring concrete benefits to Moscow. In the West the German problem had been solved with the integration of the Federal Republic into NATO and the establishment of the European Economic Community. The unity of the Western bloc was only problematic from the American point of view in that it might become too much of a rival if the EEC's policies deviated too far from those serving US interests as well. The 1950s ended with Western unity preserved at the failed Paris summit where the Soviets produced embarrassment by shooting down an American spy plane and proving that Eisenhower had lied about its true nature and mission.

However, divisions in the communist bloc were becoming serious as the Sino–Soviet split grew wider in the late 1950s. Some of Khrushchev's harsh words and threats of action against the West may have been designed to impress hardliners in Moscow. But it was also necessary to take the sting out of Chinese claims to be the true inheritors of revolutionary Marxism-Leninsm. The Offshore Islands crisis indicated more differences between Moscow and Beijing. And the Cuban crisis was in part exacerbated by Khrushchev's fears of losing Castro and his own reputation as the leader of global communism. Preserving the Cuban revolution would serve to prove that the progress of revolutionary socialism could take place without the revolutionary wars that Mao still deemed necessary. For the Americans bloc divisions were to become more of a problem with the challenge mounted by de Gaulle which was to grow during the 1960s. But in essence victory for them in the early 1960s Cold War now meant preserving the status quo by resisting the communist challenge wherever it occurred and their ideological friends never broke with them like the Chinese broke with the Russians.

The Soviet rift with the Chinese which began in the wake of Khrushchev's rejection of Stalinism in 1956 has been linked to ideological differences, competition for geopolitical rivalries in East Asia, the quest for leadership of the communist world, the re-emergence of China as a leading Asian power, and the personalities of Mao Tse-tung and Khrushchev. The Sino–Soviet split was a shock to those who saw the communist challenge as monolithic but it had little impact on American Cold War strategy in this period. Subversive operations were carried out against China as well as in Eastern Europe and while the determination to subvert and destroy the Soviet Union waned in Eisenhower's second term the activities were not abandoned. The focus was much less on destroying the Soviet Union than on preventing the spread of communism in the less developed world as part of a struggle for hearts and minds. Khrushchev and others could claim to offer a better way towards economic and national development free from the shackles of Western imperialism and exploitation by vaunting the socialist model but people were fleeing from it in Berlin. Some had been taken in by such claims, as the Soviets sent the first satellite into space in 1957 and produced fears that socialist technology might outstrip the West as the sense of American insecurity had not gone away.

Part of this Soviet attempt to claim superiority was linked to military power and the development of nuclear weapons with intercontinental delivery systems which promised to bring instant destruction on an opponent. The Soviets' desire to claim far greater military strength than they actually possessed could have been linked to fears that their inferiority would make them vulnerable to diplomatic pressure. Ironically it was not their actual inferiority but their imagined superiority that was emphasized by the Democratic opponents of President Eisenhower. They claimed a missile gap in favour of the Soviet Union caused by the neglect of the Republican administration. In a sense the accusations about Eisenhower letting things slip and handing an advantage to the Soviets have been replicated in the subsequent historical controversy. Initially historians portrayed Eisenhower as a lack-lustre president lacking in assertiveness who let things drift by neglecting to keep a firm grip on government. Eisenhower revisionists have claimed that the reality was that Eisenhower was a hands-on president who calmly and carefully defended American interests without getting carried away by Soviet posturing and rushing into excessive and unnecessary military spending. Now, as in the Cold War, we are seeing the emergence of post-revisionists who constitute the equivalent of the re-emergence of orthodoxy in the form of portraying Eisenhower as an indecisive and ineffective president.

At the time the arguments about missile gaps proved to be bad for both Eisenhower and Khrushchev with the American president's age and apparent neglect of American defence needs contributing to his party's defeat at the hands of the younger and apparently more dynamic John F. Kennedy. Problems began for Khrushchev when the Americans finally revealed the reality of Soviet weakness in missile development in 1961. Soviet prestige was badly dented and may have contributed to Khrushchev's decision to install MRBMs and IRBMs in Cuba in 1962 in an attempt at least to gain the appearance of overcoming the advantages enjoyed by the United States.

It is certainly important to view the development of the arms race in the 1950s and early 1960s in terms of the political advantages which the appearance of strength offered. The Cold War was less about the actual military balance, effective deterrence or nuclear conflict than about the attractiveness or advantages of socialism and capitalism. The arms race was not the essence of the Cold War or even central to its pursuit but something which was linked to it and which thereby threatened international stability. The growing importance of nuclear weapons and armaments had originally stemmed from the perceived American need to have them in order to deter a military reaction to the aggressive fighting of the Cold War, as in NSC 68. Then, particularly after the hydrogen bomb, there developed on the one hand attempts to integrate nuclear weapons into the conventional conduct of warfare and diplomacy and on the other hand efforts to devise meaningful strategies of deterrence to avoid their use. These conflicting aims were to affect Soviet and American approaches to a number of crises particularly in the early 1960s. By then the number of newly independent states had grown and the battles in the less developed world were increasingly being won by the West.

The result was an increasing Soviet attempt to challenge the United States by a greater emphasis on world power status and to hope that revolutionary movements would develop and build on the communist success in Cuba. Hence the need to exploit the impact of the sputnik and to install missiles in Cuba when power in tangible terms, as opposed to its appearance, was weighted in favour of the United States. The prospect of changes in the East–West status quo were much greater outside Europe where the long-running crisis over Berlin reflected the Soviet desire to do precisely that either by removing the Western powers from the city or achieving the recognition of East Germany. For the Soviets and for Khrushchev's own personal position the need to achieve something from the proclaimed policy of peaceful coexistence that could at least appear to change the status quo became increasingly urgent as the 1960s began. It was not enough to preserve Soviet control of their area of influence by repression in Hungary or to forge links with what began as a broad-based revolutionary movement in Cuba. Credibility in global terms was now more of an issue, hence by 1962 the so-called long peace was increasingly unstable—because of instability outside Europe and challenges to the status quo within it. As the Cold War came to focus more on Asia and Africa and as the Americans, inspired by the rhetoric of the young President Kennedy, became more determined to resist the Soviet challenge everywhere, the risk of Cold War becoming hot war increased. Then came the crisis over Cuba and the subsequent realization that the risk of nuclear war had to be prevented from being gambled with again. As 1963 began the Cold War might be said to have been entering a new phase.

NOTE

1. John D. Hargreaves, *Decolonization in Africa* (Longman, New York, 2nd edn., 1999), 189.

PART II CHRONOLOGY: COLD WAR: CRISES AND CHANGE, 1953–1963

1953

January	Eisenhower becomes President of the US.
March	Death of Stalin.
April	Eisenhower's Chance for Peace Speech.
May	Malenkov's peace offensive.
June	Riots in East Germany.
July	An Armistice agreement ends the Korean war.
August	Soviets explode their first hydrogen bomb.
October	'New Look' doctrine laid down in the NSC.
December	Eisenhower makes his 'Atoms for Peace' speech.

1954

January–February	Berlin Foreign Ministers' Conference on Germany.
January	Dulles makes Massive Retaliation Speech.
April	Eisenhower talks of the 'falling dominoes' in South-East Asia.
April–July	Geneva Conference on Korea and Indo-China takes place.
May	The French are defeated in Vietnam at Dien bien phu.
June	The Central Intelligence Agency (CIA) backed coup takes place in Guatemala.
July	Geneva Accords on Vietnam.
August	French refusal to ratify EDC treaty.
September	The South-East Asia Treaty Organisation (SEATO) is created.
	Chinese Offshore islands crisis begins as Chinese communists begin shelling Jinmen.

1955

January	Malenkov's speech on the necessity of peaceful coexistence.
	Formosa Doctrine announced authorising US troops to defend Formosa.
February	Khrushchev assumes sole effective leadership of USSR.
April	The Baghdad Pact is created.
	Bandung conference of developing nations takes place.
	First Chinese Offshore Islands Crisis ends.
May	Austrian peace treaty signed.
	West Germany joins NATO.
	Creation of the Warsaw pact.
June	Jawarahal Nehru visits the USSR.

July	Geneva Summit takes place (US, Britain, France, and the Soviet Union attend).
	Eisenhower's Open Skies speech.
September	Chancellor Adenauer goes to Moscow.
October–November	Geneva Foreign Ministers' Conference takes place.

1956

February	Khrushchev denounces Stalin at 20th Party Congress.
April	The Cominform is dissolved.
October	Polish crisis resolved peacefully.
October–November	Suez Crisis.
	Soviets suppress the Hungarian anti-Communist revolt.
November	Eisenhower is re-elected.

1957

January	Eisenhower doctrine for the Middle East is created.
March	Agreement to establish the European Economic Community.
May	Gaither Committee formed.
August	US and Canada begin a Distant Early Warning (DEW) system against nuclear attack.
October	First sputnik is launched by the Soviets.
	Rapacki Plan.
November	Mao's visit to Moscow forms watershed in ending Sino-Soviet cooperation.

1958

January	First US intercontinental missile launched.
May	Vice-President Nixon encounters strong anti-American feeling during a trip to Latin America.
July	Iraq coup overthrows monarchy.
August	Second Chinese offshore islands crisis begins with shelling of Jinmen.
November	Khrushchev delivers an ultimatum over Berlin. and calls for it to become a free city.

1959

January	Castro takes power in Cuba.
July	Nixon visits the USSR and takes part in the 'Kitchen Debate'.
September	Khrushchev visits the US.

1960

February	The French perform their first atomic bomb test.
	Soviet-Cuban trade agreement.
May	An American U2 spy plane is shot down over Soviet territory.

May	Khrushchev storms out of the Paris summit.
November	John F. Kennedy is elected to be the President of the US.
December	Organisation for Economic Co-operation and Development (OECD) is founded.

1961

January	Eisenhower's farewell speech condemns military industrial complex.
	Kennedy is inaugurated as President.
March	Alliance for Progress announced.
April	The Bay of Pigs invasion takes place.
	Yuri Gagarin becomes the first human in space.
	Hundreds of US military advisers in Laos.
May	Alan Shepard becomes the first American in space.
June	The Vienna Summit, involving Khrushchev and Kennedy, takes place.
August	Berlin Wall is constructed.
October	Taylor-Rostow mission to Vietnam starts a massive build up of American advisers in Vietnam.

1962

January	Cuba is excluded from the Organisation of American States (OAS).
June	Laos becomes neutral.
October	Cuban Missile Crisis.
December	Kennedy–Macmillan Nassau meeting takes place.

5 Soviet–American Relations: Avoiding Hot War and the Search for Stability

Soviet–American relations in the wake of Stalin's death were generally more complex than standard accounts of the Cold War allow for. There was the basic distinction between Cold War and hot war and how to conduct them both. And there was the conduct of conventional diplomacy to resolve disputed issues, including a number of summit meetings. Fighting a major hot war was transformed by the destructive power of the hydrogen bomb. Fighting the Cold War thus became more risky because of the possibility of hot war breaking out especially if the survival of the other was under severe threat in a military or ideological sense. There were some ways in which the United States and the Soviet Union began a more concerted period of competition as great powers seeking global influence or the destruction of the other's area of influence or control. The desire to prove that their domestic socio-economic and political systems were superior was linked to covert Cold War measures on an increasing scale as the period began. At the same time particular problems and traditional disputes in and outside Europe had to be addressed by attempting to resolve them through agreement. If only to appease public opinion by apparently reducing tension, such efforts could be used to reap Cold War propaganda benefits. Having inspired fear in their populations it was incumbent on Western politicians to appear to be endeavouring to reach an overt *modus vivendi* with the Soviets when the destructive powers of the hydrogen bomb could threaten the very existence of human civilization. Efforts had therefore to be made to avert this and achieve some form of détente either to reduce the danger of nuclear war or to cultivate an image of searching for peace more determinedly than the other side; or to attempt to gain a particular advantage through negotiating an agreement. The question of the genuineness of both sides' efforts to achieve disarmament and resolve troublesome disputes is an important one to consider in Cold War interpretations.

A. **The German Question**

How to approach the future position of Germany had been under consideration since the latter years of the Second World War and was vital to the future of Europe and a particular concern of the Soviet Union. The Soviet attitude at the time of Stalin's death has been often explained in terms of imposing communist control over all of a united Germany. There is no doubt that Stalin would have considered such a possibility but he may have concluded that the problems this presented were such that a better option would be to formalize the division of Germany. This would provide some measure of relief from the possibility of a revived, expansionist state bent on another conflict with the Soviet Union. On the other hand, there were two main worries inherent in such a scenario and both were associated with the future of West Germany. The rapid economic reconstruction of a viable West German state under Western auspices was accompanied by the 1952 agreement, which was never in fact ratified, to create a European Defence Community incorporating a rearmed West German state. The prospect of Germans in the West being rearmed and eventually even having nuclear weapons made the situation far more dangerous from the Soviet point of view. Hence it is reasonable to conclude that the Soviets had an interest in the possibility of a neutral and permanently disarmed Germany whether it became capitalist or communist. The dilemmas of rearmament, or neutralization and division, or unity over maximizing security may well have accounted for the Kremlin's interest in proposals for the reunification of Germany if there were guarantees that no part of it would again figure as a potential armed aggressor.

The same basic dilemma was evident to Western leaders but their fundamental concerns over Germany's future incorporated a clear strategy for dealing with the German problem. Initially, as with the Soviets, they saw advantages in the creation of a divided Germany which reduced the potential risks. Western writers focusing on the idea of a Cold War which deemed it necessary to reduce the risk of an expansionist Soviet Union have tended to underplay the continuing fears, particularly in Western Europe, about a revived Germany. The extent to which this influenced policy on the German question, even after Eisenhower became president, has also been neglected. One key element in the economic and military moves to integrate West Germany into Western Europe was to minimize this risk. It was a very different approach to control from that followed by the Soviets with regard to their enemies. Division for them in the spring of 1953 still meant control and domination not integration, even if this was seen as becoming less oppressive. Therefore a united Germany could present a more attractive option, provided it produced security, than it did to the West where integration rather than direct control was the prime means of containing Germany. The greater the emphasis (see Chapter 6, A) on reducing direct Soviet dictation over the internal policies of the Eastern bloc countries the more this was so. In a sense, as John Lewis Gaddis has pointed out, both sides wanted to rely on and contain Germany.[1]

The Death of Stalin

When Stalin died Western policy was defined through the response to the Stalin note of March 1952 and subsequent exchanges with Moscow over the unification and demilitarization of Germany. The Western position was in essence based on two principles. In the first place unification must not mean the denial of the right of a united Germany to join any alliance and in the second that free elections, monitored by the UN, should precede unification. Stalin's proposal may well have been posited on the possibility of disrupting German rearmament by winning the propaganda war and putting the Soviet Union in a favourable position to appeal to the German people to support unity under communism. The Western response, also disingenuous, was clearly designed to be rejected by Moscow without arousing too much criticism. Once Stalin was dead the new regime and Malenkov put forward another idea in April 1953 which was part of the so-called peace offensive (see Chapter 5, B) and which has not been taken seriously by Western leaders or historians who have portrayed it as something purely designed to disrupt the Western alliance. The new proposal called for the immediate formation of a provisional government for the whole of Germany thus sidestepping the obstacle to progress on unification constituted by the disagreement over whether to form a government before or after elections under UN auspices. It also reduced the risk of such elections producing results which threatened the Soviets with the loss of all Germany to the capitalist world. The fact that this proposal might have reflected a genuine desire for the neutralization of Germany and might be associated with the policies that came to be adopted for loosening controls over the Eastern bloc in the next three months deserves more consideration. In particular its links with the particular strategy of Beria and its emphasis on security and economic needs, as opposed to ideology deserve more consideration despite Beria's fall from grace and elimination in June 1953 (see Chapter 6, A).

Reunification or Rearmament

In the West those prepared to take the possibility of German unification seriously were led by the British Prime Minister, Winston Churchill. Churchill regarded German reunification at some point in the future as inevitable and thus was prepared to consider the terms under which it might be implemented. Against this were Dulles and Eisenhower who were focused on the economic and military strengthening of the Western bloc as the main requirement of German policy, just as Adenauer, from a different perspective, saw reunification as something that should follow but not precede West Germany's full restoration to independent statehood through its incorporation into the Western world. When the NSC examined the problem in August 1953 they defined the goal of German policy as:

Firm association of a united Germany, or, at a minimum the Federal Republic with the West, preferably through an integrated European community, to enable Germany to participate in the defence of the West and make the greatest contribution to the strength of the Free World, with the least danger of its becoming a threat.[2]

As Moscow began its efforts to strengthen the diplomatic status of the German Democratic Republic (GDR), the possibility of summit meetings, as desired by Churchill in 1953, receded and the prospects grew of division becoming more permanent. Eisenhower had reluctantly agreed to Churchill's contacts with Moscow partly because he feared the impact on Western public opinion if he appeared, in the age of the hydrogen bomb, as the obstacle to progress on resolving key issues such as the future of Germany or disarmament. The American president, however, saw any summits on Germany or other issues as first requiring Soviet concessions to prove that they were changing their approach to relations with the West. The Russians did not however respond positively to Churchill's ideas and their proposal for a Foreign Ministers Conference instead led to a four-power meeting in Berlin in January–February 1954 where the future of Germany was again discussed.

The West produced what became known as the Eden Plan which represented a change from their 1952 position. It proposed that elections would now take place for an all-German constituent assembly supervised by the four powers. Decisions it took would be based on a majority vote and any future government would be given the right to take over the existing international obligations of the West German government. Molotov responded by proposing that the elections should only take place after the withdrawal of occupation forces apart from those supervising the elections. From the propaganda perspective, the West was helped by the crushing of the East German revolt in the summer of 1953 (see Chapter 6, A) and Molotov's offer lacked sufficient appeal to compensate for the dislike and distrust of the Soviets. His last attempt at agreement was based on a security treaty for the whole of Europe which would of course have the advantage from the Soviet perspective of excluding the Americans.[3] The Western allies however preferred to continue with the existing policy of incorporating a rearmed Federal Republic into an integrated Western Europe to counter future threats from both the Germans and the Soviets. In the event the EDC collapse because of the French National Assembly's refusal in August

1954 to ratify the treaty appeared to undermine this strategy. Western policy on Germany was then thrown into disarray until agreement was quickly reached on the incorporation of West Germany into NATO and the creation of the Western European Union (see Chapter 6, B). The extent of the Soviet fear of a revived West Germany, and its importance in influencing their policy on reunification, may be gauged from the fact that the next Soviet proposal did not come until the very day the Treaties of Paris ratifying the new arrangements were signed in January 1955.

The Soviets now indicated their willingness to accept the Eden Plan for the holding of elections for the whole of Germany as a basis for discussion. It was shutting the stable door after the horse of German rearmament had definitely bolted. The next Soviet move, perhaps to emphasize their seriousness about the neutralization of Germany, offered Austria the state of armed neutrality without the condition that this would have to be linked to the resolution of the German question. In May 1955 a treaty was signed followed by the withdrawal of Soviet troops. Moscow could now claim that there was no reason why the same thing could not happen in Germany. Indeed, from the Soviet point of view there would be great advantages in a peace treaty with or without German reunification. Western recognition of a divided Germany would at least formalize the division of the country and thereby at least attain the Soviet goal of consolidating East Germany's position in the Eastern bloc after the 1953 riots.

Whether this was the secondary aim and German reunification the main aim will continue to arouse controversy but it was certainly a significant one. The problems of 1953 and the failure to prevent the rearmament in the West indicate that Khrushchev's preference by 1955 was to consolidate the position of Walter Ulbricht and the East German state of which he was leader. The whole question was linked to the three issues of security and disarmament arrangements in Europe (see Chapter 5, B), to the nature of the Eastern bloc and Soviet controls (see Chapter 6, A and B), and to the general development of the Cold War (see Chapter 7, A and Chapter 5, C). Some Americans saw the latter as still requiring the weakening of the Soviet hold over Eastern Europe. But by 1955 the Soviet approach was beginning to

be defined in terms of the peaceful coexistence of two European blocs. Certainly for Moscow there was less reason to pursue a reunification policy after 1955 and even less after more problems in the Eastern bloc in 1956 (see Chapter 6, A). The importance of preserving the Soviet and Western blocs began to reduce the importance of proposals for German reunification and neutrality. Rather than the potential threat from a revived Germany being reduced by reunification and neutrality, it became linked to broader proposals for European security based on disarmament and neutral zones.

During this transition period, in 1955–6 the British proposed that reunification could be furthered by creating a zone between the blocs in which armaments would be limited. In response to Adenauer's concerns, this area was defined as lying to the east and west of the demarcation line between a united Germany and the Eastern bloc and was thus never likely to be acceptable to Moscow.[4] In fact it can only have reinforced the need for the Soviets to consolidate East Germany's position in the Eastern bloc just as Adenauer did not want to rule out reunification through Western integration. Thus on the one side of the Iron Curtain a treaty between the GDR and the Soviet Union in 1955 guaranteed the presence of Soviet troops on East German soil and in 1956 the People's Army's (the rearmament of East Germany) incorporation into the military forces of the Eastern bloc. On the other side the Hallstein Doctrine was formulated whereby the Federal Republic would not establish diplomatic relations with any state (the Soviet Union had a special position) that had formal ties to the GDR.

As the Soviet moves towards bloc consolidation increased, a summit conference took place in Geneva in July 1955, which attempted in vain to make progress on Germany and has traditionally been associated with détente despite its notable lack of achievement. The signing of the Austrian Treaty in May 1955 marked a Soviet concession and thus made the conference difficult for the Eisenhower administration to continue to oppose. The 'spirit of Geneva' lacked substance but did focus attention on arms control from a broader European perspective rather than as a means to bring about German reunification. In the West progress was to continue towards integration with West Germany very much central to the process and now restored to full independent statehood in 1955. Moscow then suddenly experienced a new set of major Eastern European challenges to its control born from the attempts to change the nature of Soviet domination (see Chapter 6, A and B). For the rest of the period attention would be concerned with the nature of these controls and the relationships within and between the two sides of the Iron Curtain.

Konrad Adenauer (1876–1976)

Adenauer was born in the city of Cologne in 1876. He was widely educated, studying at universities in Freiburg, Munich, and Bonn. He then studied law at Cologne. In 1906 he entered the arena of politics and later became deputy mayor of Cologne in 1909 and finally the lord mayor in 1917. Also in 1917, Adenauer became a member of the Centre Party of the Provincial Diet and the Prussian State Council. He was chairman of these councils from 1920 to 1933. However, he was dismissed from all the posts for opposing the Nazi regime and imprisoned on the same grounds. During Allied occupation in 1945, Adenauer was once more installed as the mayor of Cologne. In 1946 he established the Christian Democrat Party and also became the first chancellor of the Federal Republic in 1949. He was re-elected in 1953, 1957, and 1961 but retired in 1963 at the age of 87. Adenauer was renowned for his part in transforming post-war Germany, both politically and economically.

John Foster Dulles (1888–1959)

Dulles was born in 1888 in Washington, DC and was the grandson of two former secretaries of state. He was educated at Princeton and George Washington universities and at the Sorbonne. He joined a New York Law firm after attaining acceptance to the bar, and specialized in international law. Dulles enjoyed an early career in diplomacy as he attended The Hague Conference in 1907 as secretary to his grandfather. He also performed the role of legal adviser to United States' delegates at the Versailles Peace Conference in 1919. In 1945, after having helped prepare the United Nations charter, Dulles became a consultant to the US delegation which took part in the San Francisco UN conference. He was also appointed by President Truman to negotiate the 1952 peace treaty with Japan. In 1953 he finally filled the role of secretary of state when appointed by President Eisenhower. His main goal in his new position was to better the position of the USA in the Cold War, being as he was a strong anti-Communist who was against any negotiation with the Soviet Union. Dulles was also responsible for the policy of 'brinkmanship' due to confrontations with China and the Soviet Union. He famously described the possible US response to Soviet aggression as 'massive retaliation', which referred to the large-scale use of nuclear weapons. Dulles remained in power as secretary of state until his resignation on the grounds of ill health in April 1959. He died of cancer only 6 weeks later.

B. The Progress of Arms Control and Peace Efforts

The impact of the hydrogen bomb cannot be exaggerated, both for strategies for hot war and for a Cold War 'fought by all means short of international armed conflict'. Moves towards controlling or restricting the deployment of these thermonuclear weapons were inevitable. Even if many in government and in the military were opposed to the idea, there was bound to be pressure to reduce the risks of nuclear conflict. The role of nuclear weapons in the Cold War and disarmament talks then lay partly in convincing the public on both sides of the Iron Curtain that their side was engaged in a quest for peace but hampered by the aggressive designs of the other. Yet whether or not responses to these concerns with disarmament proposals were genuine and designed to secure an agreement, their advocates also had to consider ways in which armaments might best be deployed and integrated into a military strategy for hot war.

Nikita Sergeevich Khrushchev (1894–1971)

Khrushchev was born in 1894 in the province of Kursk. He later moved to Yuzovka (later Stalino, later Donetsk) in Donbas region, Ukraine where he trained as a metal fitter. In 1917, Khrushchev first became involved in politics when he represented miners at political meetings. In 1918 he became a communist, and a year later joined the Red Army. In 1921 his first wife died, and he returned from the front in 1922. He then became deputy director of the Ruchenkov mines as well as a student and political leader at Yuzovka Workers' Faculty. In 1925 he was appointed Party Secretary of Petrovsko-Marinsk District of Stalino (formerly Yuzovka) Region. A year later he made his first political speech at the Ukrainian Party Conference in Kharkov. He was then promoted to regional politics in 1926 and became the Deputy Chief of the Organizational Section of the Ukrainian Central Committee in Kharkov. His rapid rise through the political ranks continued when he was appointed to the Moscow City Party Committee and then promoted to be First Secretary of Red Presnya District in 1931. In 1934 Khrushchev became the first secretary on the Moscow City Party Committee. He took an active role in the construction of the Moscow metro. Also in this year he was elected to the Central Committee at the 17th Party Congress.

Khrushchev's rise continued as Stalin's career went on and when he was made the First Secretary of the Ukrainian Central Committee he announced that he would annihilate 'all agents of fascism, Trotskyites, Bukharinites, and all those despicable bourgeois nationalists on our free Ukrainian soil'. As a full member of the Politburo, Khrushchev supervised the occupation and sovietization of Western (Polish) Ukraine from 1939 to 1940. In 1944,

after Ukraine was liberated, he took up the position of Chairman of Ukrainian Soviet of Ministers. In 1945 he had his first meeting with Eisenhower, in Moscow. After 1945, however, Khrushchev suffered some political setbacks. He was accused of not effectively ridding Ukraine of nationalist agitation and was removed as First Secretary. However, Khrushchev was reinstated as First Secretary of the Ukraine in 1948. In 1953, following the death of Stalin, Khrushchev was named as a possible First Secretary of the Supreme Soviet. In 1954, he toured the Soviet Union and also brought 32 million acres of previously uncultivated land in Kazakhstan and south-western Siberia into cultivation. By 1955, he had consolidated his power by ridding the Party of those opposed to him. In 1956 he continued this process by creating a Central Committee bureau for the Russian Union Republic, which he headed and also filled with his supporters. He escaped an assassination attempt the same year. In 1957, three members of the Party attempted to have Khrushchev dismissed. However, he refused to accept the vote, and had the Central Committee consider the matter and overturn it. In 1958 Khrushchev became Premier and party leader. In 1959 he visited the US and addressed the UN in New York in 1960. In 1961 he met Kennedy in Vienna during the Berlin Crisis. Khrushchev was responsible for erecting the Berlin wall during this period. In April 1962 Khrushchev decided to place missiles in Cuba, and began the Cuban missile crisis. Following the end of the crisis, in which he withdrew the missiles, he signed a Nuclear Test Ban Treaty in 1963 but was overthrown in 1964 and died in 1971.

It may be argued that the level of armaments generally has no decisive impact on the reasons for going to war and their control or limitation has an equally small impact on the maintenance of peace. Weapons do not automatically produce conflict or tension. However, it was seen as desirable for public consumption at least to seek ways of using agreements on weapons to indicate the decreasing likelihood of war. At the same time the simplistic idea that the Cold War reflected the likelihood of a military conflict developing from bloc confrontation, which was conditioned by levels of armaments, was convenient for governments to have the public believe.

A more realistic analysis focuses on how the covert means and ideological ends at the heart of the Cold War interacted with other elements of inter-state relations and their power political requirements, including the role of armaments.

Peace Proposals

The arrival in the White House of the Eisenhower administration coincided with the death of Stalin and the Soviet 'peace offensive'. There was a need to respond and also a need to counter the expressed desire of the British Prime Minister for détente with the Soviets. In addition, a United Nations Disarmament Commission, established in 1951, the conclusions of which were to be dealt with at the 1953 General Assembly, was also an issue. The initial Eisenhower approach was to link progress on disarmament and the control of nuclear energy to the way in which Soviet stances on important international concerns developed. However, pressure grew for the definition of a disarmament policy in 1953 even though many in the West claimed the same aggressive policies were being followed by Moscow but different means were being employed. As part of the so-called 'peace offensive' the Soviets announced that they were ready to settle all unresolved differences and suggested a new approach to disarmament involving a discussion of 'detailed proposals for an international control organ which could put into effect and supervise a comprehensive disarmament program'. Eisenhower himself was clear that the US would now have to do something to demonstrate its desire for comprehensive disarmament. Hence his Chance for Peace Speech in April 1953.[5]

There was already a five-point programme for the 'reduction in the burden of armaments' in the British and the American submission to the UN Disarmament Commission and the speech was generally vague and non-specific. Its first part was directed to the situation in East Asia and the efforts to achieve an armistice in Korea; then it turned to the German and Austrian questions left by the postwar failure to agree on peace treaties. The speech has been interpreted either as reflecting Eisenhower's genuine belief that the Soviets should 'choose between war and peace, fear and security and hunger and prosperity'. Or as 'not intended to promote a starting for negotiation but had the opposite aim'.[6] Eisenhower noted that 'Every gun that is made, every warship launched, every rocket fired signifies in the final sense, a theft from those who hunger and are not fed, those who are cold and not clothed.' However, disarmament was consciously placed after the resolution of important problems which would involve a change in Soviet policies. It was the creation through this of the right atmosphere which was deemed to be decisive in the efforts to reduce the risk of nuclear war. The president did not make any

firm disarmament proposals because he remained determined that the Soviet Union most show some sign of being more accommodating and changing its ways over Austria, a Korean settlement, Indo-China, or Malaya. Only then, he believed, could the control of nuclear energy and arms limitations be considered.[7]

The speech therefore provided very little of substance and this was partly because the administration could not agree on an approach to disarmament or the reduction of the nuclear threat. The State Department was supportive of the idea of attempting to make some progress in arms negotiations while the Defence Department was opposed to holding any such talks. The issues were discussed in the National Security Council as part of the 1953 attempt to redefine national security policy. The latter now in essence encompassed anything that might pose problems or dangers to the US and how best to alleviate such threats within the general Cold War context. One problem, which was to reoccur in disarmament talks for much of the Cold War, was the problem of inspection. The Pentagon doubted whether any safe system of inspection to prevent cheating was feasible, whereas the State Department wanted such issues explored fully on the grounds that some limited safeguards were less risky than no limitation of nuclear weapons. In 1954 the military were still arguing that 'Soviet bad faith, evasion, and outright violation would render any disarmament agreement sterile, except as a means to advance Soviet objectives.'[8] Eisenhower clearly rejected the idea that the US could always say 'No' to talks and so the crux of the issue came back to the conditions required to make it advisable to hold them or impossible not to.[9]

The situation that Eisenhower was in has been described as the 'Disarmament Dilemma' in that there were a number of reasons why disarmament could be detrimental to American interests, but it was impossible to say so and therefore something had to be done to show willing to push the process forward. Thus a debate has emerged between those, notably Eisenhower revisionists, who see the president committed to disarmament and trying through a series of speeches to promote progress towards an effective means of preserving peace, and those who see the proposals being geared to a Cold War strategy of attempting to appear more committed to peace than the Soviets but never really desiring an agreement with them. Interpretations range from those who put disarmament and reducing the nuclear danger at the top of Eisenhower's agenda to those who regard it as something which Eisenhower had to avoid without giving that impression. In the latter case it has been argued that Eisenhower subordinated his disarmament efforts to psychological warfare and the maintenance of Western strategic superiority. Their purpose was thus to discourage neutralism, satisfy Western opinion, discredit Soviet initiatives, and to expose Soviet intransigence.[10] Rather than agreement Eisenhower opted for a policy of half-heartedly attempting to win the Cold War by undermining the Soviet satellite empire while failing to accept fully that it might promote hot war.

There is evidence for both arguments just as there are reasons for taking Soviet proposals for German neutralization at face value or dismissing them as attempts to divide the West. It is easy to point to American concerns, expressed privately, about the dangers of nuclear war and the need for some form of disarmament—for example Eisenhower's conversation with Senator Knowland in 1956. He told Knowland there would be no reason for staying here if he had to give up the objective of getting a disarmament agreement. He believed a decent disarmament treaty was an absolute must.[11] Eisenhower revisionists are particularly clear that the president was therefore committed to disarmament and attached importance to American efforts for peace.[12] Yet a case can also be made for Eisenhower being reluctant to accept disarmament, and certainly the attempt to redefine national security policy produced unequivocal opposition to the idea. Whether based on a principled aversion to the holding of talks or on the need for the Soviet Union first to change its approach to international affairs, there was disquiet about disarmament (see Chapter 7, A).

Internationally the settlement of the Korean War affected the claim that the Soviets first had to prove their behaviour was changing before meaningful talks could take place, but for some it was not enough. In any case US interpretations of change could have been related to the US Cold War strategy of eliminating or altering the Soviet Union as a communist state in control of satellites (see Chapter 4, D and Chapter 7, A). Only then would talks be valuable. In September Dulles came out with the suggestion of linking disarmament to the creation of a broad zone of restricted armaments in Europe and to a Soviet withdrawal from Eastern Europe accompanying a US withdrawal from the West. Withdrawal could well mean liberalization in the satellite states which would effectively achieve US goals and at the same time could produce international control of nuclear weapons to accompany an end to the revolutionary mission of the Soviet Communist Party. In such a scenario disarmament again appeared to be linked to the end of the Soviet system. Other proponents in the NSC of an American initiative on a more modest scale pointed to the increased Allied pressure for disarmament proposals given the Soviet testing of a hydrogen bomb in August 1953. They suggested something on the lines of A Chance for Peace which did not introduce 'new major substantive proposals on disarmament'.[13]

The next attempt or gesture for peace and reconciliation therefore came in December 1953 with Eisenhower's 'Atoms for Peace' speech. The Atoms for Peace idea involved the transfer of a certain amount of fissionable materials to an atomic energy agency where they would be used for peaceful purposes. The proposal was vague enough to avoid any basis for concrete disarmament discussions and has been described as 'deliberately not a disarmament proposal'. It emerged against the background of the administration's failure to agree on the way forward on such matters. The ratification by the French of the European Defence Community Treaty which integrated a rearmed West Germany into the Western bloc was still in the balance and the concern still present that disarmament talks would encourage its failure.

Immediately after, and in the wake of the US New Look policy (see Chapter 5, C), the Soviets announced that Atoms for Peace did not address the two fundamental problems of acquiring the capacity to produce nuclear weapons and the actual use of them in war. The Soviet response was the idea of a 'no first use' agreement and they therefore proposed an agreement not to undertake the use of weapons of mass destruction. This move towards the possible renunciation of the use of nuclear weapons was rejected by the US in January 1954. Eisenhower remarked that 'In the present state of world affairs, it is impossible that any effective agreement toward [disarmament] could be worked out which could provide the necessary safeguards.' Nothing would undermine the New Look policy more than an agreement banning the first use of nuclear weapons. Dulles and Secretary of Defence Charles Wilson commented in the same NSC meeting that there had to be an 'opening up of the iron curtain'.[14] In other words disarmament was not something that could bring about the end of the Cold War but something that could occur when the Cold War had ended. The Soviet response in April 1954 was to reject any discussion on Atoms for Peace until the two powers had first agreed on renouncing the use of atomic weapons.[15]

Unfortunately waiting for that day without some meaningful disarmament was rendered more difficult for the Americans by the contamination of a Japanese fishing vessel by nuclear fall-out from an American thermonuclear test in March 1954. Renewed demands for a summit meeting were made in 1954 by Churchill, although this had to wait until Eden became prime minister in April 1955. By then more pressure was mounting on the US as a result of the French and British disarmament proposals and the signing of the Austrian peace treaty. Britain, France, and the US finally agreed on the desirability of a summit on 10 May, the same day as the Russians made detailed disarmament proposals including the means of on-site inspection. The lack of any inspection had been one key reason for Eisenhower claiming that disarmament agreements might not be safe given Soviet secrecy. Now he changed course somewhat and stated in a press conference 'Are we going to open up every one of our factories, every place that something might be going on that could be inimical to the interests of someone else?'[16]

Earlier in 1955 Eisenhower had received a report advocating a different type of inspection regime, in some ways more comprehensive, than the Soviets were to produce and this now became the basis of his Geneva 'Open Skies' speech. That speech of 21 July 1955 referred again to the dangers of disarmament without proper inspection and he therefore proposed the exchange of full information on military establishments, and the provision of facilities for aerial photography to the other country thereby producing transparency on all military issues. Both the Soviets and the US Joint Chiefs of Staff were horrified and so initially was Dulles.

If the proposal had been accepted by Moscow, it might have produced an important breakthrough in arms control and could thus be described as a reflection of the priority Eisenhower gave to disarmament. The Soviets therefore have to take the blame for its failure. It is certainly the case that the Soviet commitment to disarmament was questionable. When Malenkov spoke in January 1955 about the hydrogen bomb making peaceful coexistence both necessary and possible this was used against him shortly after by Khrushchev as part of the discrediting of Malenkov which was necessary for his own rise to power. Such ideas were deemed to be detrimental to the proletarian revolution but were promptly adopted by Khrushchev when he emerged as leader. Whatever the Soviets were, being strong on principles was not among them. It does seem, however, that there are many reasons to suspect the Americans did not want disarmament or peaceful coexistence. Their Cold War strategy aimed at undermining the Soviet empire might, for instance, have been more important than any perceptions about the untrustworthiness of Soviet leaders especially given their reluctance to test the latter. Open Skies can be seen as an attempt to benefit the US given that it already had an open society and the Soviets could thus acquire the information relatively easily. Or the speech could be interpreted as an attempt to legitimize the U2 programme of illegal spy flights which was about to get underway. Perhaps the most meaningful conclusions to draw from the failure of disarmament by the mid-1950s was that it was never accepted by the Americans as something which could create détente. They saw it as something which was irrelevant to the course of the Cold War or which could be produced by its end. For the Soviets it might have had value in furthering revolution because it could reduce the prospects of American military intervention and create the impression of military equality which Khrushchev pursued by other means in the second half of the decade.

European Disarmament and Arms Control

By the mid-1950s the German question's link to disarmament was changing. In 1956 Adenauer developed the idea that rather than link reunification to German neutrality the latter should be linked to the withdrawal of all troops from Europe. This would sidestep in the short term the growing problem of East Germany's consolidation in the Eastern bloc (see Chapter 5, A) and was similar to a proposal made in 1957 by the Polish Foreign Minister, Adam Rapacki. Adenauer's proposal was put to Eisenhower in January 1957 and was more comprehensive than Rapacki's which was put to the UN in October 1957. Rapacki's idea, endorsed by the Soviet government, was based on a zone free of nuclear weapons encompassing the two Germanies and Poland. Given the lengthy discussions on the Rapacki Plan, Soviet documents suggest it was less a genuine arms reduction plan than an attempt to undercut the West German government.[17] More particularly it may have been influenced by Adenauer's decision about the dilemma he faced in 1956 over removing or acquiring weapons on German soil. If because of the 'New Look' in 1953 and the American policy of less reliance on conventional forces it embodied (see below), US troops were to be reduced in Europe, both political and military benefits might accrue to West Germany. The prospect of using the opportunity to acquire American battlefield nuclear weapons rather than to produce demilitarization was possible. Even the prospect of nuclear weapons in German hands was regarded with horror in Moscow. Something therefore had to be done if it seemed to the Soviets that Adenauer's proposal could produce such an outcome. For West Germany the dilemma over conventional forces was only resolved with the Berlin crisis if 1958 (see Chapter 7, B).

Another set of disarmament proposals came from France and Britain in February 1955 and called for a total ban on the manufacture of nuclear weapons and reductions in all nuclear and conventional forces with the establishment of a control organ to guarantee the agreed prohibitions and reductions. The Soviets then produced their programme for arms reduction and the banning of nuclear weapons to be implemented in stages according to a precise timetable with an international body which would operate through the 'inspection of large ports, railroad junctions, highways and airports', which was not an outright rejection of inspection.[18]

The Geneva Summit Conference then followed in the summer of 1955 despite Eisenhower's reluctance and Dulles's attempt to exclude disarmament from the agenda. The future of Germany remained an issue. It is easy to portray the summit as a summit of appearances for appearances' sake as there was little or no substantive agreement. The Soviets might have been prepared to take a more cooperative line in order effectively to gain time for the consolidation of East Germany's position now that rearmament was going ahead in the West, or, as Dulles thought, seeking more international prestige by demonstrating equality with the West.[19] The Soviets were certainly losing interest in a neutral Germany as the prospect of a rearmed and united Germany in NATO loomed larger. Disturbances in Eastern Europe (see Chapter 6, A) followed in 1956 and prevented contacts on disarmament as the East–West atmosphere worsened as the decade progressed. In 1957 the Soviet achievement of putting a satellite (sputnik) into orbit (see Chapter 5, C) and the 1958 Berlin crisis were other disincentives to disarmament talks. The crisis provided the Europeans with the need or opportunity to install American medium-range missiles in Europe although no members of NATO were given independent control over them. Khrushchev emphasized the importance of disarmament in his 1959 meeting with Eisenhower but the president was approaching the end of his term. Moreover, as tensions appeared it was if there was a greater need to preserve the appearance of seeking peace. Preparing for war and seeking peace were not contradictory and linked to the argument of negotiation from strength.

The Paris Summit and the U2 Incident

The Paris summit proved an even bigger fiasco than the Geneva one and was effectively sunk by the U2 incident and the reactions of both sides to it. The Soviets had been watching these high-altitude American spy planes flying 70,000 feet above them for nearly five years. When they finally managed to shoot one down the pilot, Gary Powers, chose to allow himself to be captured and Khrushchev decided to exploit this flagrant violation of Soviet airspace. Assuming that the pilot would not have allowed himself to be taken alive the Americans claimed that the plane was a weather plane which had gone off course when flying near the Iranian border. The Soviets then produced the pilot and pictures of the crash site which was thousands of miles from where the Americans claimed the plane had inexplicably entered Soviet airspace. Khrushchev insisted that Eisenhower apologize at Paris but the President refused and the summit was abandoned in acrimony. It could be that neither side wanted the summit to succeed. Apart from the general reluctance to agree on concrete measures Khrushchev may have been keen to pander to the hardliners and opponents of peaceful coexistence. On the other hand, Khrushchev may have believed that Eisenhower knew little about the flights and was being manipulated by imperialists in the US administration. At all events the summits of Geneva and Paris, like all the disarmament and peace proposals, achieved nothing, and Germany remained divided.

When Kennedy became president in January 1961 a new era began. There would be no more summits involving second-rate powers like France and Britain. In order to give the impression of seizing the initiative and playing a more positive world role the Americans began a massive rearmament programme while arms control attention focused on a Test Ban Treaty. Abandoning tests would have the effect of making it difficult to develop new nuclear weapons although it took the Cuban missile crisis to bring concrete results (see Part III on the Test Ban Treaty

> ### Dwight D. Eisenhower (1890–1969)
>
> Dwight D. Eisenhower was born in Texas in 1890 but grew up in Kansas. He joined the army and was a second-lieutenant stationed in Texas when he married Mamie Geneva Doud in 1916. He enjoyed a successful army career, serving under General Pershing and Douglas MacArthur. In 1942, Eisenhower commanded the landing of Allied forces in North Africa. On D-Day 1944 he was the supreme commander of the troops invading France. Following the war he took up the post of President of Columbia University but left in 1951 in order to take up command of the newly assembled NATO forces. In 1952 he was persuaded by the Republican Party to run for president of the US and won a large victory. Eisenhower made a number of vague proposals for peace and control of atomic energy between 1953 and 1955. In 1955 he had a heart attack but in 1956 he was elected for his second-term. Eisenhower was a believer in equal rights and was keen to desegregate the army and also enforce (albeit slowly) the Federal decision to desegregate schools. Some have portrayed him as a weak and indecisive president who lacked a firm grip on his administration; he has been praised by others as bringing a steady but firm hand to government but without the rhetoric that many other leaders have been handicapped by. He left office in January 1961, and died after a long illness in 1969.

and Chapter 8, D on the missile crisis) in the form of a Test Ban Treaty. Kennedy focused on the world of ideas and the changing nature of technology in the expectation that American achievements, not least the quest to put a man on the moon, would outshine the Soviet sputnik. The rhetoric of the early 1960s was soon to have a destabilizing effect.

C. Cold War, Armaments, and Preparations for Hot War

The West's commitment to disarmament or controls on nuclear weapons has to be evaluated against the need to prepare for hot war *and* the contribution these made to the Cold War. The political impression given by the attempts to reduce the risk of a major armed conflict may have been the most important Western consideration in analysing the motivations of US leaders for the arms control proposals they made. The proposals themselves have already been outlined in terms of a possible improvement in Soviet–American relations. The arguments about the value of disarmament and other agreements for different American groups in the context of a changing national security strategy have also been referred to. The relationship of arms control to the use of weapons in hot war and to some aspects of fighting the Cold War now need to be examined.

The New Look

When Eisenhower became president one key aspect of preparing for hot war was the role of nuclear weapons and how to integrate them into a strategy for so doing. The use of nuclear weapons, particularly in global war, was becoming unthinkable for many, especially in Europe, but for Eisenhower with the lesson of the end of the Korean War (see Chapter 4, E) very fresh in his mind there was a different conclusion to be drawn. The conflict was perceived to have ended because of the threat of using nuclear weapons and therefore Dulles in particular saw value in using the retaliatory threat they presented as a means of deterring the kind of aggression which had produced the Korean War in the first place. The ending of a bloody and costly war with threats about the possible use of nuclear weapons may have been an inaccurate interpretation but a policy of massive retaliation through the nuclear threat now seemed a distinct option. Eisenhower's inclination to look to nuclear weapons was reinforced by the savings they offered as compared to the costs of conventional forces. The implications of this were considerable because Eisenhower was reluctant to except some of the arguments of NSC 68. The massive increase in armaments it proposed seemed to contain dangers for the US economy. Its desire to maintain high levels of defence expenditure was not welcomed by Eisenhower because he feared that this could threaten the American way of life. In the worst-case scenario the role of the state in an economy geared primarily to production for a possible war was likely to increase government controls and deprive Americans of the individual freedoms they had been used to. Alternatives therefore had to be found to acquiring the overwhelming all-round military

strength allegedly required to deter the Soviet Union everywhere in the world. In that sense the New Look was a combination of attempts to redefine US national security taking account of military *and* economic needs. And it emphasized the importance of defending a way of life as well as a territory, and as such figured in Cold War thinking and in particular in the role of covert operations and psychological warfare[20] (see Chapter 7, A).

How this would be done was very much related to the tasks of Project Solarium which was set up to determine the best ways of dealing with the Soviet Union. In May 1953 a panel of military and civilian dignatories was established to define the precise terms of reference under which three task forces would consider what was required to meet three alternative scenarios in the development of a Cold War strategy and its implications for hot war (see Chapter 7, A). One general requirement for all task forces would be the forces needed and the costs that would be incurred, although equally important were the various assessments of the nature of the Soviet threat. In subsequent discussions Eisenhower ruled out policies which would be opposed by America's allies, or which would cost too much or increase the risk of general war by, for example, arguing that the US could survive a nuclear one. These discussions influenced the formulation of the New Look, which in policy-making terms was one element of US national security strategy because it determined the role of US military forces. While the precise circumstances in which nuclear weapons were to be used remained vague, with the New Look there was now a much greater inclination to use them.

Thrashed out in the autumn of 1953 the New Look was not intended to mean that because nuclear weapons would now be relied upon a conflict would involve the ultimate commitment of US nuclear strike forces. What it meant was that nuclear weapons were now an integral part of American military deployments and would enable the US to make conventional force reductions. Nuclear weapons used on the battlefield would thus be like any other weapon and serve to give the US an advantage as and when needed. This point was then developed by Dulles into what became known as massive retaliation in a speech in January 1954.

Rather than wait and react to any Soviet or communist aggression Dulles argued that the best way to deter any such actions was to be willing to respond at a time and in a place of the West's own choosing. The forces of local allies would be backed by the nuclear power of the US.[21] The credibility of such an idea was always questionable as the idea of risking annihilation over a localized conflict was never likely to be convincing. The New Look was also designed to make the use of, and crucially the threat of using, nuclear weapons more meaningful and the provision of conventional forces less costly by using covert operations. And it would place particular emphasis on the roles of America's allies as vital players in any conflict. Implicit was the hope that as the Americans provided the nuclear components in Western strategy their European partners might become more involved in the provision of conventional forces.[22]

Thus there was little change in the US acquisition of more nuclear weapons or the development of a NATO strategy based on the first use of them because of the advantage enjoyed at the time by the Eastern bloc's conventional forces. It therefore became necessary for the Eisenhower administration to work out a strategy for the preparations for hot war in a situation where the Europeans did not believe that they could provide sufficient conventional forces for the defence of Western Europe (see Chapter 4, B). The connections between the use of nuclear weapons, conventional force strategy, and deterrence were to preoccupy Eisenhower during his first administration. Historians who see Eisenhower as genuinely committed to a process of disarmament produced by the fears of nuclear weapons downplay the subsequent development of the New Look.

Whatever the president's views there were those who regarded disarmament as largely irrelevant to the real problem of two opposing ideological blocs. More importantly, there were those who were committed to policies aimed at undermining the Eastern bloc or the Soviet Union or both. For them disarmament and cooperation ran counter to the ultimate goal of US Cold War policy and its undermining or destruction of the Soviet Union And there were those who wanted to seize the opportunity of Stalin's death to further these Cold War goals such as

the president's Cold War adviser C. D. Jackson. He wanted a speech from Eisenhower to produce divisions between Soviet leaders and allies such as China, and which would combine elements of a serious policy proposal with elements of Cold War psychological strategy. Dulles for his part simply believed that nothing could be achieved and that dealing with the Soviets would encounter delays and handicap the efforts to incorporate West Germany into a united Western European bloc. Hence the importance of an aggressive Cold War strategy and of the New Look and massive retaliation.

Sputnik and the Gaither Report

In 1957 thinking about nuclear weapons was transformed with the Russian development of a missile which could leave and re-enter the atmosphere and therefore pass over the US or descend to earth there. Even though the Eisenhower administration had seen a massive expansion of American nuclear weapons the reaction in the US was dramatic. Edward Teller who was associated with the development of the H-bomb and who later became a nuclear expert, stated on television that the US 'had lost a battle more important and greater than Pearl Harbor'. There was a suggestion that the Russians would reach the moon within a week and an aide to Senator Lyndon B. Johnson wrote in a memorandum. 'It is unpleasant to feel that there is something floating around in the air which the Russians can put up and we can't. . . . It doesn't really matter whether the satellite has any military value. The important thing is that the Russians have left the earth and the race for control of the universe has started.'[23] In this kind of Cold War atmosphere the politics of disarmament were unlikely to have much of an impact.

The situation was not improved by the establishment of a special presidential commission to examine the implication of the hydrogen bomb for civil defence measures that some saw as essential to deter the enemy. Formally established on 8 May 1957 under H. Rowan Gaither, the committee of industrialists, academics, and engineers ended up with a remit broadened into considering the question of civil defence in a wider security context especially that of maintaining second-strike capability by preventing a surprise attack. Assisted by researchers and an advisory panel largely of former government experts, the committee was effectively led by Robert Sprague of the Sprague Electric Company. Sprague had a number of conversations with Curtis Le May, the head of the Strategic Air Command which was responsible for US nuclear bombers. Le May initially told him that B52s would solve any problems and there would be no missile threat in his lifetime. A few weeks later on 4 October the sputnik was launched but Sprague was unhappy before then and returned to talk with Le May. As a result a nuclear alert was staged and it turned out that it would take nearly 6 hours for nuclear bombers to be loaded and take off. Even if the bombers were on alert the early warning detection of an incoming Soviet attack would not allow them to be loaded even though they could get of the ground unloaded. Le May was unruffled and told Sprague about the U2 spy planes that were making frequent spying missions over the Soviet Union at altitudes so high it made it extremely difficult for them to be shot down by ground-to-air missiles. As a result Le May claimed he would know when there was activity on Soviet bases and when he saw planes gathered for an attack he was 'going to knock the shit out of them before they take off the ground'.

This was not government policy and it is unlikely that Eisenhower knew about it, but it was indicative of military thinking especially in the air force and Strategic Air Command. The determining factor was that the most sensible thing to do was to fire nuclear weapons first and with as much force as possible—at least if the aim was to have any chance of partial survival or to inflict the most damage on an enemy as a result of a nuclear exchange. If this was one disconcerting element in the US approach to hot war, then it was similar to the Soviet strategy of using massive force as the mainstay of strategy in a major conflict. There was another worry about US thinking in relation to preparing for hot war which had Cold War implications. In the wake of the sputnik one thing the Gaither Committee did favour was the installation of nuclear weapons in Europe as part of a call for more rearmament in the face of what seemed a major Soviet military success. The drafting of the final Gaither Committee report presented in

November 1957 was entrusted to an academic James Baxter III who called on none other than Paul Nitze for advice and assistance. Nitze it will be recalled had been involved in the drafting of NSC 68 and its revision in NSC 141 (see Chapter 4, D). Its call for more arms to enable the US to fight the Cold War from a position of strength that would deter hot war had led to a massive increase in defence spending of nearly 300 per cent. Eisenhower had rejected NSC 141, and slightly reduced defence spending which was reinforced by the development of the New Look. Nitze was able to return to the charge through his significant contribution to the drafting of the Gaither report. The report claimed that the Soviets now had the material to produce 1,500 nuclear bombs and that their GNP was growing. The Soviet Union's long-range air force, intermediate range missiles, air defence system and intercontinental rockets in which it 'probably surpasses us' were all described. These assets were deemed to be particularly dangerous given the vulnerability of the SAC to surprise attack especially when international tension was low.[24] We now know that the claims of Soviet strength were wide of the mark but attention was fixed again on rearming and matching the Soviets when the US was in fact still way ahead especially with regard to nuclear weapons.

Eisenhower may have been reluctant to listen to the calls for disarmament but he was definitely loath to commit himself to more rearmament. If he is not to be praised for his commitment to reducing the risks of war with the Soviets he must at least gain credit for not exaggerating them. Eisenhower refused to give in to pressure from Congressmen and Senators who began to claim that the US was falling behind in the nuclear race. He also reasoned that there could not be a war without international tension first and therefore there need be no panic over warning times. The claims of a possible bomber gap and then a missile gap also failed to change Eisenhower's approach. In the run up to the 1960 election the Democrats tried to make political capital out of the missile gap as it indicated weakness in the face of post-sputnik Soviet strength. John F. Kennedy, who was running against Richard Nixon in 1960, hoped to win support by his claims that the Republicans had neglected American defence needs. 'We are facing a gap on which we are gambling with our survival' was one of his campaign lines.[25]

The various estimates made by the different intelligence organizations all saw the US falling behind but the estimates of how far the Soviets were in front varied. The National Intelligence Estimate (NIE) of February 1960 was full of footnotes referring to service disagreements with the estimates. By mid-1961 the NIE claimed the Soviets would have between 170 and 270 missiles and by mid-1963 between 450 and 650. The higher number reflected the air force view and the lower number that of the CIA. Army and navy estimates were about one-fifth to one-quarter of those figures. The difference in part stemmed from the estimates of how far the Soviets would increase the rate of production and from guesses about what lay in the Plesetsk region of northern Russia which the U2s had not reached. They can also be explained by the roles the respective services would have in dealing with the Soviet nuclear threat and the money that could be justified for such purposes in the defence budget.

As more became known from satellites it appeared that in 1961 the Soviets had 3.5 per cent of the NIE estimates and in 1960 may only have had three ICBMs. Kennedy was to emphasize the importance of Americans making a commitment and moving forward to tackle the danger. Eisenhower on the other hand was not prepared to use the danger of hot war to make commitments which were too costly and too threatening to the American way of life that the Cold War was seeking to preserve. Unlike Kennedy he was prepared to play down the risk of nuclear war whatever the political costs.

NOTES

1. John Lewis Gaddis, *We Now Know Rethinking Cold War History* (Clarendon Press, Oxford, 1997), 135.

2. FRUS, 1952–4, VII, NSC 160/1, 'United States Position with Respect to Germany', 17 Aug. 1953, 518. Cited in ibid., 132.

3. Wilfred Loth, *Overcoming the Cold War: A History of Détente* (Palgrave, New York, 2001), 26–8.

4. Ibid. 37.

5. Ibid., 179–82.

6. Robert Bowie and Richard H. Immerman, *Waging Peace: How Eisenhower Shaped an Enduring Cold War Strategy* (Oxford University Press, Oxford, 1998), 120; Tal, 182.

7. Stephen E. Ambrose, *Eisenhower the President 1952–1969, 2* (Allen & Unwin, London, 1984), 94–5.

8. Bowie and Immerman, 229, citing FRUS, 1952–4, II, part II, 680–6.

9. Bowie and Immerman, 227–30.

10. David Tal defines the dilemma in 'Eisenhower's Disarmament Dilemma: From Chance for Peace to Open Skies Proposal' in *Diplomacy and Statecraft* 2 (2001), 175–7; on disarmament's relationship to the needs of psychological warfare see Kenneth A. Osgood 'Form before Substance: Eisenhower's Commitment to Psychological Warfare and Negotiations with the Enemy', *Diplomatic History* 3 (2000).

11. Ambrose, op. cit., 343.

12. In addition to Ambrose above see Bowie and Immerman, 120 and S. Dockrill *Eisenhower's New Look National Security Policy* (Macmillan, Basingstoke, 1996), 132.

13. Tal, op. cit., 183–4; John Lewis Gaddis, op. cit., 132.

14. Tal, op. cit., 185.

15. David Tal, op. cit., 182–5.

16. Stephen E. Ambrose, op. cit., 247.

17. John Lewis Gaddis, op. cit., 138, Citing Beate Ihme-Tuchel 'The Soviet Union and the Politics of the Rapacki Plan', CWIHP Conference Paper Essen, (1994).

18. Ibid., 186.

19. Saki Dockrilll and Gunter Bischof (eds) 'Geneva: the Fleeting Opportunity for Détente' in *Cold War Respite* (Louisiana University Press, Baton Rouge, 2000).

20. Psychological warfare as described by Kenneth Osgood as 'Planned use of propaganda and other actions designed to influence the opinions, emotions, actions, attitudes and behaviour of enemies, neutrals and friendly foreign groups to support the accomplishment of national aims and objectives' (Introduction), 13.

21. Fred Kaplan, *The Wizards of Armageddon* (Simon & Schuster, New York, 1983), 175.

22. Andreas Wenger, *Living with Peril Eisenhower Kennedy and Nuclear Weapons* (Rowman Littlefield Publishers, Lanham, 1997), 38–47; Robert R. Bowie and Richard H. Immerman, *Waging Peace* (Oxford University Press, Oxford, 1998), 125–36, 227–30.

23. Kaplan, op. cit., 135.

24. Ibid., 136–8, 141–2.

25. Richard Reeves, *President Kennedy* (Papermac, London, 1993), 58.

6 Maintaining the Spheres of Influence

A. Eastern Europe

The Stalinist period of bloc consolidation had been based on a combination of terror and strict adherence to Soviet models of political and economic development. It was justified by Cold War concerns and the 'enemies', internal and external, that the Soviet Union allegedly faced. Moreover the atmosphere of threat, danger, and sacrifice was accompanied in Eastern Europe by the economic exploitation and plunder of territory for the benefit of post-war Soviet recovery. With the death of Stalin and the assumption of power by the triumvirate of Beria, Khrushchev, and Malenkov a fresh approach to domestic issues and to the nature of Soviet control over its European satellites soon emerged. The change was partly out of necessity and partly out of the desire to get away from the type of system associated with the Stalinist state. The apparent change produced a new Soviet approach to East–West relations, if not to the fighting of the Cold War by covert means, as well as having a dramatic impact in East Germany, Poland, and most significantly in Hungary.

The New Leadership and the Crisis in East Germany

The full horror and paranoia of the latter days of Stalin's rule experienced by those members of the party and governmental elite only gradually became evident. Yet it was something that the three leaders were very much conscious of and an important consideration in deciding to change Stalin's approach to domestic policy that, like most things in the Cold War, as this book argues, was intimately linked to foreign policy. One way to begin the process of change was to remove the central role that Stalin had played by emphasizing the idea of joint leadership and undermining the cult of personality which Stalin had encouraged. Another was to reduce the degree of repressive interference carried out by the security services. This posed difficulties for Beria who had been responsible for state security under Stalin. It was therefore easier for Beria to distance himself from Stalin by proposing foreign, rather than domestic, policy initiatives, and he therefore came up with a new policy towards Germany which was the key problem for the Soviets in Europe (see Chapter 5, A).

This, like other initiatives failed to secure any fundamental changes in foreign policy as the perceptions of the new Soviet leaders, stemming in part from the 'small Committee of Information' (KI), ultimately remained unchanged. The KI was an autonomous intelligence body affiliated to the Ministry of Foreign Affairs which was imbued with Stalinist assumptions about the dangers presented by the West. It was the attempt to define new responses to such beliefs that led to the idea of change in Soviet foreign policy. What the new leadership wanted above all was to avoid giving any impression of Soviet weakness which might encourage more aggressive Western policies, including the campaign of subversion,[1] which had been waged against the Soviets since 1948. This may have required some commitment to better relations and preventing hot war but the ultimate goal was the interests of the Soviet Union in terms of defence (security) and, unlike under Stalin, its status as a superpower capable of competing on equal terms with the leading capitalist power.

In a sense this was the beginning of the attempt to introduce peaceful coexistence which, for the Soviets, involved the idea of competition between two equal powers representing two different socio-economic systems. Both Malenkov and Khrushchev may have seen things in terms of better relations with the West which would reduce the Soviet fear of attack and overcome the sense of military and economic inferiority. The latter was seen to require reform of the domestic structures in order to provide for the people of the Soviet Union and its satellite empire in Eastern Europe in the same way that American capitalism, through the Marshall Plan, had provided for the people of Western Europe. Khrushchev was to pursue both the foreign and domestic aspects of such a strategy more effectively than Malenkov and certainly more effectively than Beria. Arguing for radical new projects like the 'Virgin Lands Scheme' in Soviet Central Asia and against the 'anti-party' bureaucrats in the Soviet establishment, Khrushchev sought greater popular legitimacy which, as in the West, required success

relative to the ideological adversary. Whether or not this was a means to achieve personal power more than an aversion to the horrors of Stalinism, Khrushchev succeeded between 1953 and February 1955 in removing both of his rivals for power and assuming complete control.

Beria was the first to fall as a result of attempts to portray himself as a reformer with regard to the future of East and West Germany. According to Sudoplatov then head of the First Directorate of the MGB (Ministry for State Security) which was incorporated into what officially became the KGB in March 1954 (the term KGB is often used to denote the security and intelligence apparatus of the whole Soviet era), Beria wanted to link solving the German question (see Chapter 5, A) to the solution to Soviet economic difficulties.

He cited the following points for exploratory talks: 1. extending German reparations to the Soviet Union; 2. a reconstruction programme for Russia, the Ukraine, White Russia, and the Baltic states; the costs were to be borne by Western sponsors, mainly the Germans. New industrial works were to be built as well as a large network of railroad lines and highways. Beria contemplated technical help with German participation in the range of $10 million. As he argued, if the Soviets wanted to support the illusory construction of Socialism in the GDR, they must invest no less than £20 billion within ten years, which would include deliveries of raw materials and food to East Germany and Poland. He wanted to be rid of that heavy burden. In its place, he sought a wide-ranging economic agreement with the West. He wanted to have this agreement with the West. He wanted to have this agreement blessed by the UN after arranging things with America, England, and France.[2]

Beria thus wished for a treaty guaranteeing a neutral Germany in which the issue of socialism came second to the issue of Soviet economic recovery even if the latter involved capitalist help. As Molotov recalled, for Beria, if Germany became a peaceful state, it mattered little whether it was socialist or not. The extent to which this turned the Soviet leadership against Beria or the extent to which they seized upon this as a reason for his removal and death remains unclear. Whatever the views on this, the situation regarding the East Germans in 1952–3 does indicate the importance of power over ideology. In 1952 East Germany began to witness a programme of forced collectivization and industrialization, subsidized by the Soviet Union, which had an important ideological component. However, in early 1953 when it produced the understandable reactions with over 100,000 fleeing to West Germany via crossing from East to West Berlin in the first four months of the year things began to change.[3] The new leadership now had to address the possibility of an East German economic collapse in addition to the other concerns. Worse, in 1953 they faced the prospect of revived, rearmed West Germany and in such a situation ideology eventually went out of the window.

What to do about the problems resulting from collectivization and industrialization still favoured by the East German leader, Walter Ulbricht, seemed to have caused some initial disagreement in Moscow. After a meeting on 27 May 1953 the Presidium did however condemn the forced construction of socialism and the intensified collectivization. The broad issue was how best to ensure some control over East Germany while preventing a powerful West Germany attracting more and more people to the West or, even worse, incorporating the East into a rearmed capitalist state. As Beria's arguments were heard, Molotov argued for a relaxing of the military occupation in order to increase the popularity of the East German government.[4] If Beria, possibly with some support from Malenkov, was ready to give up the GDR for German neutralization and economic cooperation with the West it shows the enormous differences to Stalin's regime, especially if Stalin, as late as March 1952, was committed to the creation of a communist Germany as part of the westward advance of the Soviet revolutionary state. The proposals discussed in 1953 now suggest a picture in which communist revolution and the expansion of Soviet power in Germany were definitely not at the top of the agenda or even in the debate. The murderous nature of the Soviet regime would still be in evidence, albeit in a reduced form, but its concerns, if they had ever been anything else, were the maintenance of controls in Eastern Europe. The preservation of the East German state remained vital to some and emerged as the main requirement. But it was now to be achieved by means other than Stalinist controls and ideological development. Hence 1953 was an important milestone for con-

sidering how the Soviets viewed the maintenance of their control and influence east of the Iron Curtain.

The Soviet leadership opted to reduce Soviet subsidies while the East Germans slowed the pace of change in order to attract more support within the GDR. The aim was to obtain more popular acceptance of the East German state by relaxing the kind of controls associated with Stalin. Such a policy might also bring dividends if Germany was unified again. Consequently, the politburo of the East German communists (technically the East German Socialist Unity Party) rescinded all measures against the existence of private farmers and artisans along with new measures pertaining to cultural and religious freedoms. The alterations were justified on the basis of 'securing and expanding a mass movement for the creation of a unified, peace-loving, independent Germany'.[5] Yet they contained some obvious risks. To introduce economic measures which would impoverish and alienate people and then to follow it by the lifting of some forms of economic and political repression was a potentially explosive mix. Within a week of the announcements workers in East Berlin and elsewhere took to the streets in open revolt. The uprisings were quelled throughout East Germany with the help of Soviet troops and tanks. They did, however, see the end of Beria and the salvation of Ulbricht, yet it was no clear victory for the hardliners in Moscow. The problems created by liberalization had to be compared to those created by forced collectivization and industrialization and the new leadership faced a dilemma irrespective of the German problem. Was it now better to move towards liberalization or away from it? It was a key issue awaiting resolution.

Hungary and Poland

The troubles faced by the Soviets in 1953 were a taste of things to come and the crunch came after the 20th Party Congress in February 1956. Khrushchev's famous speech attacking Stalin heralded a series of events that now indicated a definite change of approach by the Soviets under Khrushchev and which was seen as an opportunity by many in Hungary and Poland. Apart from confessing to the crimes of Stalin and suggesting that conflict with capitalism was not inevitable, the speech claimed that Moscow could no longer tell communist parties in other countries what to do but should encourage them to adapt to local conditions. The change since Stalin, with the prospect of peaceful coexistence and greater independence, seemed to be confirmed by the disbanding of the Cominform in April and the unilateral reduction in Soviet troop numbers by over 1 million in May. It was reasonable to conclude that bloc ties were loosening and greater freedom and reduced militarization were on the way.

For Khrushchev, the worries that unrest of the East German variety would spread to the rest of the bloc, encouraged by American psychological warfare, had not disappeared. There were those in Moscow disinclined to pursue a more relaxed approach which Khrushchev favoured as they drew the opposite conclusions about the cause of dissent and its remedies. In Poland the Communist Party leader Bierut died in 1956 and deStalinization was in progress accompanied by the release of political prisoners. As news of Khrushchev's speech was leaked in the ensuing months a series of strikes helped strengthen the demands for the return of Wladyslaw Gomulka, one of Stalin's leading victims. By August Gomulka's rehabilitation was complete and the final step for his supporters was to bring him back to power in October on the back of massed rallies. In response Soviet troops in Poland were put on alert and a Soviet tank division moved towards Warsaw, but the Soviets could not guarantee effective control over the Polish army. A worried Khrushchev flew to Warsaw on 19 October as Gomulka was about to be elected and halted the Soviet advance towards the capital. The Poles and Gomulka refused to back down but Gomulka combined assurances that Poland would not leave the Warsaw Pact (the NATO equivalent formed in response to West Germany joining the Atlantic Pact) with threats of arming workers to resist. Khrushchev compromised, Gomulka was returned to power, and communism in Poland was given a more nationalist leader demanding a more equal relationship with Moscow.

Hungary was a different story where protests were more rooted in the mass of the population, including the workers. The demands were thus more threatening to the increasingly fragile nature of bloc solidarity in the East. In the wake of the East

German riots Prime Minister Imre Nagy had rejected greater concentration on heavy industry. He had placed more emphasis on the production of consumer goods and by 1955 had released a number of political prisoners. His departure from government meant that opposition to Prime Minister Rakosi after Khrushchev's 20th party Congress speech began to focus on Nagy's return. Student protest groups called for this, but unlike in Poland it was not just changes in the party hierarchy but in Hungarian politics and society that they demanded. The immediate withdrawal of Soviet troops from Hungary was a demand that reflected deep-rooted Hungarian resentments at control by Moscow, but the reformers also demanded the introduction of a multi-party system and free elections to the National Assembly. In addition they wanted Rakosi and another leading figure in the Hungarian Workers Party (the ruling Communist Party) be put on trial for past crimes. The students in Budapest planned a massive demonstration in the capital for 23 October 1956 and won the backing of workers there to the extent that the latter had to be persuaded not to call a political strike in support of the demonstration.[6] The protests in Hungary were based on a more radical and wide-ranging programme than in Poland and were developing a much greater focus on political reform than those in East Germany. The role of workers was also to assume greater significance in trying to wrest control from the Workers Party and place it directly in the hands of those in the factories. Hungarian workers on whose behalf the Communist Party allegedly acted were at the forefront of opposition in 1956.

The Budapest demonstration had grown in size during 23 October and unrest had spread outside the capital with four people shot dead in Debreccen. This brought home to the Soviets that the Hungarian crisis was becoming more serious than the Polish problem and a delegation from the Hungarian Workers Party was summoned to Moscow. As Nagy returned to the parliament building to speak the decision was taken in Moscow to send in troops. Ironically Nagy, who was sworn in as prime minister in the morning, was calling for the demonstrators to return home and allow the government to deal with Hungary's problems. Ironically, dealing with Hungary's problems on the basis of the 1953–5 reforms made by Nagy was not enough and his speech to the demonstrators damaged his credibility and reinforced the support for radical change.

Soviet troops arrived in Budapest on the morning of 24 October with the task of turning the rebels over to the police, but their presence initially added fuel to the flames of nationalist protest and made the demonstration more one in favour of national liberation. By the end of the morning as the situation deteriorated and organized resistance groups began to form at key points in the city, the Soviet troops were ordered to open fire when attacked while Hungarian troops proved unreliable. As the Soviet army began to establish control over Budapest, Nagy, whose return the Soviets were now backing, lost further credibility when he referred to the organized resistance as fascist, and martial law was declared. Armed resistance grew with young workers playing a leading role and the numbers of deaths at the hands of Soviet troops was well into three figures by 25 October. Two Soviet emissaries, Mikoyan and Suslov, began to call for compromise and a political solution as a means to win back the mass of the workers by implying that bloody repression was undesirable.

By 28 October it appeared that peace could be restored by the new government's proclamation of a general ceasefire and the introduction of some radical changes. The State Security Authority was dissolved and the government reorganized on a multi-party basis. Its new programme retained socialist control over the 'commanding heights' of the economy but announced a more nationalist-oriented foreign policy. The government in Moscow examined the options it faced in the light of the Polish situation where it had opted for a less obedient but more populist government rather than maintaining a puppet regime in the face of a possible revolt. In Hungary the armed revolt was already happening with workers groups to the fore, the Hungarian army in disarray, and the collapse of the old government system in the capital and the regions well advanced. It was decided on 28 October to support the Nagy government and comply with its demand for the withdrawal of Soviet troops. Therefore the following day tank units began leaving Budapest and the withdrawal was complete on 30 October. *Pravda* then published a declaration

outlining the need for more equality between the socialist countries of Europe. The inclination to reconsider the kind of controls Moscow exercised over the Eastern bloc continued at the Presidium meeting. Foreign Minister Shepilov talked about widespread anti-Soviet sentiments in Eastern Europe and in order to overcome them it was necessary to remove 'elements of direct control'. Significant evidence existed that things were leading to a revision of relations within the Eastern bloc.[7]

The following day things changed and the decision to redeploy troops and use force was taken. The reasons for this sudden shift have always been speculated on but in terms of the local situation, the requirements of socialism, or the Soviet position in the region. Now that we have archival evidence it seems that more attention needs to be given to the international context and the global rivalries. For the Soviets, a key element of the Cold War now involved a determined quest for greater equality with, or the surpassing of, the achievements of Western capitalism and the acquisition of global status. In the mid-1950s the best means of doing this were being considered in two ways—the maintenance of the socialist bloc of states in Europe and also the development of Soviet relations with the non-European states and colonial territories of the Western powers. The cohesion of the satellite states and the position of Germany were central to the first issue, and particularly so given the determination of the West to incorporate a rearmed West Germany into the anti-Soviet alliance. In addition, the decisions of the Truman and Eisenhower administrations to embark on measures designed at least to undermine the Soviet position there must have been another influence. The second issue was how the Soviets could win kudos in the less developed world by playing on its own anti-imperialism or at least its opposition to Western colonialism and in this instance by developing a more active role in the Middle East.

The importance of these international considerations for the Kremlin and its Hungarian policy lies in the fact that on 31 October, as the Soviet forces were leaving Budapest, British bombers began attacking Egypt a possible Soviet ally and recipient of Czech arms. Their express but secret purpose of bringing down the Nasser regime was being implemented in collusion with the French and the Israelis who on 29 October had launched an unprovoked attack on Sinai (see Chapter 8, C). Moreover, by the end of the first week of the revolt in Hungary it was clear that the Americans were not going to use force to assist the rebels there. Soviet control was not therefore under threat from American military intervention. The first action taken by the Soviet military supplied convincing proof of US inaction, but on 31 October Eisenhower announced that the US was pursuing a policy of non-intervention in the affairs of other countries. This statement was addressed as much to the British and their French and Israeli allies as to anyone else but it provided some final reassurance for Moscow. Khrushchev had initially expressed concerns on 28 October about the need to avoid getting into the same company as the British who he believed were stirring up trouble in Egypt. However, the Soviets had little confidence in Egyptian resistance and were expecting the attack on Suez to result in a significant loss of Soviet influence in the Middle East which might be combined with a loss of Soviet influence in Eastern Europe.[8] It was exactly the same scenario as in 1945 (see Chapter 1, D) when the Soviets were faced with the possibility of losing out in Eastern Europe while the British gained in the Middle East. As Khrushchev noted 'If we withdraw from Hungary, it will inspire the British, French, and American imperialists. They will regard it as our weakness and go on the offensive. . . . Then we will add Hungary to Egypt. We have no other choice.' Soviet global influence was deemed to be on the line. The Chinese had also become concerned by 30 October. After initially being in favour of more equal relations between East European states and Moscow, they then became worried about a 'capitalist restoration' in Hungary.[9]

The emphasis on Eastern Europe and the idea that Soviet concern was about Hungary's proposed withdrawal from the Warsaw Pact precipitating a wholesale crisis in the Eastern European states now seems less credible.[10] The announcement of the Hungarian withdrawal from the Pact was made on 1 November when Soviet forces had redeployed around Budapest. The decisions on the use of force

were taken after meetings with other European Communist Party leaders in the last days of October and therefore before the Hungarian announcement on the Warsaw Pact, although the troops did not immediately move into Budapest. It was only the visit to Belgrade to consult the Yugoslavs, with whom a post-Stalin reconciliation had been made that took place after the announcement. The reasons given by Khrushchev for the invasion were very similar to those motivating the British Prime Minister Anthony Eden in the attack on Suez—fear of communist advances in Egypt combined with concern over Britain's position in the region. The consequences were far more serious in Hungary where the Soviets were battling for global status and facing an ideological struggle for influence against the advances of capitalism. As the British Cabinet voted to go ahead with the airborne landings in Egypt on 4 November Soviet troops were in Budapest where 25,000 people were killed and 200,000 fled.[11] The rebels fought alongside some regular Hungarian troops but their resistance was ended by the following week. The relaxation of controls in Poland was therefore followed by a clampdown in Hungary. Khrushchev's speech rejecting Stalinism and allowing different forms of socialism was rendered meaningless by a crisis which threatened to highlight apparent Soviet weakness. It coincided with events in the Middle East which threatened to reinforce Western imperialism. The possibility of the Soviet Union relaxing controls and eschewing the use of force was rendered less likely by the international conditions prevailing at the time. The Soviet Union again resorted to repression and coercion with little or no consideration for the consequent large-scale loss of life. For the Americans the events in Hungary proved that the liberation concept inherent in the attempts to subvert the Eastern bloc were not going to lead to anything other than the death of local insurgents unless considerable military force was deployed. The aversion to this in the thermonuclear age was part of the re-evaluation of the aggressive Cold War strategy pursued in Washington in the first half of the decade.

B. Western Europe

The Western bloc, which arguably came to be dominated, if not controlled, by the US, was first conceived during the War in Britain as an organization which would assist in dealing with a future German threat. It later came to be seen as a counter to the communist challenge mounted by Moscow (see Chapter 4, B). By 1952 a European Coal and Steel Community and a European Defence Community had been agreed which provided for closer Western European ties (see Chapter 4, C), but an important setback to European integration occurred in 1954 with the refusal of the French National Assembly to ratify the EDC treaty. The setback was overcome in 1955 (see Chapter 5, A), the year that further steps were taken towards European economic integration and which were soon to create the European Economic Community (EEC). The progress towards integration within Europe was closely watched by the United States because of a number of important factors influencing its support for the movement. As Europe recovered, the prospect of a powerful economic bloc appeared to present a possible threat to American interests and the Kennedy administration began to seek more effective ways of 'influencing' European economic developments. Although American influence was exerted very differently from Soviet control, in essence both powers were to some extent concerned with ensuring that the members of the respective blocs followed their wishes. In the East there were a number of popular revolts against Soviet domination while in the West disquiet about American domination took the form of intergovernmental tensions. These were largely confined to economic policy and nuclear weapons—two things the US was particularly concerned to influence—and led by the French president Charles de Gaulle.

Western European Union

The collapse of the European Defence Community (EDC) was produced by French reluctance to give up a national military role for some of its army in order to absorb a German army into a European force and by the British refusal, repeatedly expressed, to become part of, rather than associated with, Western Europe. From the French point of view nationalists feared both the equality a European army gave to the Germans and the prospect of that equality being replaced by German domination especially if the British were refusing to act as a possible counterweight. There had been a lot of effort expended in trying to ensure the EDC's ratification but there seemed to have been much less thought given to its possible failure. The exception was in Britain where doubts about its success and viability had always been strong. The Americans were particularly annoyed as the idea of the Europeans contributing more conventional forces to the defence of the continent was an integral part of the New Look (see Chapter 5, C). It was the British foreign secretary, Anthony Eden, who embarked on a tour of European capitals in order to get the framework of an agreement for Western European Union in place. It had to meet the requirements of a rearmed West Germany, integrated into the Western Alliance, without presenting the same kind of threat to the French as a European army with West Germany as an equal partner and unrestrained by Britain's refusal to participate in a supranational military organization. The agreement involved all the key parties, the British, French, and Germans making some concessions at a conference in London for the sake of taking Western unity further. The Brussels Treaty Organization was expanded by adding West Germany and Italy and it became Western European Union, while West Germany was also admitted as a full member of NATO into which a West German army would be incorporated. Giving a rearmed West Germany equality in NATO had been rejected by the French at the time of the Pleven Plan in 1950 (see Chapter 4, C). Now there was a much greater fear of French isolation and the prospect of facing a US reassessment of its commitment to Western Europe. The French acceptance was made easier by the West German agreement not to manufacture its own nuclear armaments or any other weapons of mass destruction. And by the British acceptance of a

United Kingdom Participation in the European Defence Community

Disadvantages

3. We consider that there are the following disadvantages in UK participation:

   (a) An EDC is a step towards Federation. HMG do not wish to become part of a federalist Europe, as this would:

      (i) involve a derogation of sovereignty,

      (ii) weaken the ties between the UK and the rest of the Commonwealth, and consequently

      (iii) impair our international standing, particularly vis-à-vis the United States.

   (b) We should be handicapped in adapting ourselves, politically or strategically, to any change in international affairs.

   (c) When the European Defence Zone is defined there will be pressure to include the UK within it. This would involve placing forces for the defence of the UK in the EDC.

   (d) We should not be able to maintain larger forces outside the EDC than those we contribute to it.

   (e) UK forces committed to the Continent could only be withdrawn in the event of national emergency with the consent of the Commissioner, Supreme Commander, and Council of Ministers

   (f) In the short term there would be a risk that the high efficiency of a British contribution would be impaired by inclusion in a new and inexperienced organization.

   (g) The morale of British units in the European Defence Forces would be likely to suffer as a result of being 'European' instead of 'British' and this might have a serious effect on recruiting.

   (h) Owing to the necessity for periodical changeovers between UK forces allocated to the EDC and those retained in our national army, there would be grave administrative difficulties connected with:

      (i) discipline and pay;

      (ii) training and the supply of equipment (until such time as complete standardization were achieved).

Source: DEFE 4/49, COS(51)42nd, 28 Nov., Annex to JP(51)196, 23 Nov. 1951.

commitment to provide and maintain four divisions in Europe along with the 2nd tactical air force or its equivalent. Thus the French desire to involve the British in a continental commitment was designed to reduce the threat from a rearmed West Germany. The whole agreement was embodied in the Treaty of Paris and from the Western point of view the incorporation of the Federal Republic into the Western bloc had survived another setback and the German danger was therefore reduced.

The Messina Conference and its Aftermath

The economic integration of the Western bloc took another step forward with a conference at Messina in 1955, to get agreement on the next stage of the process. A key decision had to be made over whether economic integration would proceed on a piecemeal basis or whether there would be a more comprehensive approach through the creation of a Customs Union or Common Market. In a sense the success of Western European Union had inspired the proponents of integration. Yet the failure of the more federal EDC had strengthened the British view that Western Europe's future should be based on intergovernmental cooperation in which Britain, basking in the glory of Eden's diplomatic successes, would have a key role to play. At Messina the ECSC ministers confronted a memorandum from the Dutch putting the case for a full-blown Customs Union and a committee was established in Brussels, under the chairmanship of Paul Henri Spaak, to assess the merits of the sector-by-sector approach associated with Jean Monnet and the Common Market idea of the Dutch foreign minister Jan Beyen

With the setting up of the Spaak Committee Britain was again confronted with a choice about Europe that as before affected perceptions of its role as a world power as opposed to a European one (see Chapter 4, B). The six countries at Messina (Italy, France, Belgium, Luxembourg, West Germany, and Holland) decided to invite Britain, as a member of the Western European Union, to send a representative to the Spaak Committee and join in the work as a member. The six asked for no commitment to the supranational principle in advance, unlike in 1950 before the negotiations for the ECSC. The British government instinctively wanted, as in the past, to be associated with the European move towards the extension of the supranational ideal and the new prime minister, Anthony Eden, was a supporter of the idea that Britain should encourage the movement towards greater European integration. By continuing to support and associate Britain with such developments Eden believed Britain would remain in a position to serve as a link between Western Europe and the United States while remaining a world power with important links to the Empire/Commonwealth. Macmillan, foreign secretary in 1955, saw things rather differently in that he regarded the strengthening of economic ties between the states of Western Europe *without* Britain's involvement as a dangerous development. Western Europe could emerge as a powerful economic force which the United States would eventually relate to independently of Britain. In other words Britain had to do more than be associated with the European integration movement.

Macmillan was not, however, in favour of Britain becoming involved in a supranational Europe where it could be regarded as on a par with countries like France and West Germany. The general lack of any enthusiasm for anything which would detract from Britain's perceived status as a world power different from its Western European allies was reflected in the fact that Britain sent a representative to the Spaak Committee in the form of a Board of Trade official Russell Bretherton. He was sent 'without prior commitment' and with a wish that consideration be given to the significance of existing intergovernmental organizations for cooperation like the Organization for European Economic Cooperation (OEEC).[12] In that sense the British were making a half-hearted attempt to steer the discussions along lines away from supranationalism but without any coherent alternative. The vision that Macmillan had

articulated several years earlier was that of a confederal Europe. Such ideas, like many of Macmillan's, remained grandiose but vague, and apart from being something akin to the Commonwealth with a ministerial committee and a consultative assembly the concept of a confederal Europe offered no real alternative to the stark choice between a supranational Europe or an intergovernmental Europe.

Bretherton was initially able to report that there was little emphasis in the Spaak Committee on supranational authority but it eventually became clear that if Britain were to remain a member of the committee it would be drawn into unacceptable decisions.[13] Bretherton therefore asked Spaak to draw up the final report without reference to Britain's position. Britain had avoided any possibility of being committed to a supranational outcome of the committee's deliberations. However, there was a growing belief in the idea that the establishment of a common market might be damaging to Britain's interests and that rather than simply encouraging the development of a supranational Western Europe Britain should provide an alternative and one which did not suffer from the vagueness of Macmillan's confederal proposals. The idea was to be based on a free trade area rather than a customs union but the extent of support for Britain's approach and the enthusiasm for a common market was badly misjudged by Whitehall.

In the first place the failure of the EDC was given too much emphasis in Britain and led too easily to the mistaken conclusion that the Germans in particular were against the idea of a common market. The idea that such a union would not work was particularly misplaced as it was generally accepted that if a common market were established the long-term economic outcome would be disadvantageous for Britain as long as it remained excluded. Hence the importance of the belief that this next stage in European integration would not work. It was true that the German economics minister, Ludwig Erfurt, would have preferred the looser arrangements involved in a free trade area but Adenauer came out in favour of a common market. Moreover, the Americans were very much in favour of continued European integration and were to work hard for such an outcome by covert and overt means. How determined the British were to sabotage the work of the Six is a matter of debate but the announcement that Britain would not join with them certainly came before the publication of the Spaak Committee's report.

It was at Venice in May 1956 that the Spaak Committee's report was finally considered and it was agreed to draw up two treaties to establish a European Atomic Energy Authority (EURATOM) and a European Economic Community (EEC). There were a number of difficulties to be overcome—the reconciliation of high French tariff barriers with the German and Dutch preference for low ones, also favoured by the British for a future free trade area. The differences were eased by the British failure to produce their proposals for a free trade area, Plan G, until July 1956 and by the British and French fall out over the ending of the Anglo–French–Israeli invasion of Egypt (see Chapter 8, C). Plan G incorporated a free trade area to be run through the OEEC, all of whose members were to be eligible, with the Six EEC countries joining as a single bloc. In other words, it was not an alternative to the EEC, which even the British accepted would now be created, and can therefore be interpreted less as an attempt to frustrate the kind of economic integration born from Messina and the Spaak Committee than an attempt to forge closer ties with the Six as Britain had originally envisaged at the start of the decade.[14]

In a way the situation embodied the reluctance of British elites to compromise their perception of themselves as a force in the world that would be affected by accepting an 'ordinary' European role. Whatever the dictates of future economic success or American conceptions of a united Europe that included Britain, there is a case for arguing that such perceptions of status mattered more than the economic issues. In a sense Britain was aware that it could not afford to be excluded from Europe but there were some economic, as well as the more emotive, reasons indicating that Britain could not afford to be included either. The Commonwealth still accounted for over 40 per cent of Britain's trade and while this was shifting to a more European and North American focus the Commonwealth still offered advantages in the way of cheap food imports. The dilemma over the advantages of being out or in was also reflected in the creation of a free trade

area which would enable Britain to benefit from important low-cost food imports while gaining access to the European industrial market where cheap food would allow British industrialists to pay their workers less and benefit from comparative cost advantages. Britain wanted the best of both worlds.

Sixes and Sevens and the First British Application

It can hardly have been a surprise that the Six were both distrustful and unenthusiastic about the creation of a European Free Trade Area especially once their own difficulties had been resolved with the signing of the Treaties of Rome in March 1957. For a time it seemed that the French insistence on special arrangements being made for the overseas territories of the French Union and another French dispute over social policies would produce failure. However, the treaties were implemented in January 1958, eighteen months before the creation of the European Free Trade Area (EFTA) comprising Britain, Austria, Denmark, Norway, Portugal, Sweden, and Switzerland. Before the creation of the EEC and EFTA Britain had proposed a Grand Design outlined by Selwyn Lloyd, Macmillan's foreign secretary. It was a proposal for joining the various European institutions which had developed in the Western bloc during the Cold War—Western European Union, NATO, the European Coal and Steel Community, the EEC, and the Council of Europe—through representation in a single assembly. It was of course a recipe for strengthening intergovernmental links at the expense of supranational ones, but Europe was prepared for a future without Britain if necessary and London seemed slow to realize that it was no longer powerful enough to act as a restraining influence. There was a further problem in that following the Anglo–American divisions over Suez and the attack on Egypt, Macmillan was determined to rebuild relations with Washington. While Washington was in favour of European integration the problem of British exclusion would be exacerbated if there appeared to be two competing economic blocs (the Six and the Seven) within the Western alliance.

Macmillan was certainly conscious that influence

in Washington would be harder to achieve in terms of Britain's special position as a link to Europe if there was no way of reconciling a free trade area with the EEC. Attempts were certainly made within an OEEC framework, but with de Gaulle's return to power in 1958 French interests were now asserted more powerfully and the new French leader had no desire to open up French markets to OEEC states. If anything, as Miriam Camps has argued, the talks between the Six and the FTA countries forced the EEC countries to define their own policies and speeded up their integration.[15] The British favoured a low-tariff system, with loose ties and maximum access to world markets while the French wanted a common market surrounded by high tariffs to protect French industry. More generally the British were concerned that their exclusion from a politico-economic bloc would, especially in the long term, harm British economic interests and result in the EEC becoming the key American partner within the Western alliance. 'The French feared that the EEC, carefully constructed to protect French political and economic interests, and to limit German power would be dissolved within a wider FTA.'[16] With Adenauer again prepared to support the basic French position there was to be no agreement on links between the EEC and a free trade area in 1958 which forced Britain to become one of the seven members outside the EEC.

The Americans had no love for EFTA, which they regarded as economically and politically divisive, and US support and encouragement were to become an important factor in Britain's decision to apply for EEC membership in 1961. The American attitude highlighted the growing British fear of being overtaken by the EEC with regard to its importance as a major actor in international affairs. At the end of 1959, just after the first meeting between Eisenhower and Khrushchev took place and just before the last summit meeting in which the British and French were to participate collapsed in acrimony, the EEC foreign ministers agreed to hold quarterly meetings to discuss international affairs. It is relatively easy to point to the imminent loss of the colonial Empire as a further international consideration requiring a reordering of Britain's international priorities and a move to Europe. However, there are alternative explanations based more firmly on Macmillan's own

personal predilections and assessments of Britain's difficulties in redefining its world role. There were also domestic factors, which as in many instances, impinged on international considerations and policies. In the spring of 1960 economic problems seemed to reinforce a sense of national unease and the economy appeared unable to match the growth rates in much of Western Europe. Some in Whitehall began to argue that EEC membership would stimulate growth, attract US investment, and make the British economy more competitive. Internationally the Congo crisis began in June 1960 as Britain's policy of multiracialism was under severe challenges in Central Africa (see Chapter 8, B and D). It began to look as if the last days of Empire would be filled with difficulties if not loss of life. Nor did the Commonwealth appear to offer an attractive way forward. The 1958 Commonwealth Economic Conference appeared to confirm that any prospects of making the organization into an effective economic or trading bloc stood no chance of success. The Americans were likely to look more and more to Europe and less and less to Britain if the success of the EEC and the relative failures of EFTA and the Commonwealth were to continue.

There were thus a great variety of reasons for Britain to join Europe and be more positive about economic integration. Yet Macmillan was first and foremost an Empire/Commonwealth man with considerable governmental experience of several aspects of Empire life. It might therefore be possible to argue that Europe and the application to join the Common Market was supported for extra-European reasons. The Americans were very much in favour of British entry because they believed the EEC was then more likely to develop along lines favoured by the US as a low-tariff, lightly regulated organization with Britain supporting such goals inside the organization (see below). And if the EEC could revive the British economy then Britain could strengthen its Commonwealth ties through aid and economic development programmes which, in the existing circumstances, it could ill afford. If so, a strengthened Commonwealth could continue to bolster Britain's position as a global power, carry weight in Washington, and lessen the apparent risk of becoming just another European state as long the EEC provided the means to achieve economic success. The idea of an old imperialist like Macmillan becoming converted to the idea of Europe helping Britain reinvigorate the Commonwealth is certainly no more implausible than the idea that Britain made a strategic choice between a shrinking empire with its decreasing trade importance and an expanding Europe with its economic potential and political importance. If that was such a clear-cut case, the great debates within Britain at the turn of the decade over the relative importance of NATO or defence commitments 'out of' the European area would not have been so prolonged within the corridors of power. And Britain would have easily strengthened its European forces rather than argue for the need to keep an East of Suez presence during most of the 1960s.

Nuclear Cooperation and the Role of the US

Much of the development within the Western bloc focused on the nature and extent of its members' roles within Europe. However, the guiding hand of Washington was always there even if only to supply support and encouragement in the economic sphere and it was certainly ever present in the area of nuclear cooperation. In part this indicated a more controlling hand or at least the attempt to try and exercise one. In economic terms the fact that, for instance, the US exported such a small amount of its total steel production led it to believe there was little inherent in the creation of a strong Western European economic unit that would pose a threat. The Eisenhower administration consistently supported integration from the sidelines but was more interested in the nuclear aspect of cooperation which began with the establishment of EURATOM by the treaties of Rome. Under Kennedy nuclear issues continued to be important and potentially more divisive in alliance terms. Within the American administration there was more of a split between the 'Europeanists' who wholeheartedly supported integration and the 'Atlanticists' who preferred to reduce the importance of integration and accept a much broader and less regulated framework which would be more acceptable to Britain.

Initially EURATOM seemed to many on both sides of the Atlantic a more manageable project than the creation of a common market. The idea was that there should be common European ownership of all raw materials used in the production of nuclear energy. By emphasizing the peaceful use of energy the French were enabled to go ahead with their production of nuclear weapons. And the Americans could be satisfied that they were not assisting European powers with their own weapons programmes. On the other hand, the launch of sputnik justified the Eisenhower administration's move some way towards this with the amendment of the McMahon Act. Under the terms of the act, passed in 1946, supplying nuclear technology or information to foreign parties was outlawed, but in 1957, the year Britain exploded its first hydrogen bomb, Eisenhower directed that the 'exchange of information on the design and production of warheads and the transfer of fissionable materials' be permitted with those nations that had made 'substantial progress' in nuclear weapons development.[17]

In effect this meant Britain, but while the Eisenhower administration was seeking to provide help and ensure greater cooperation it was done in a way that could preserve American control over European, including Britain's nuclear weapons. As fears grew under Kennedy that the Germans might develop their own nuclear programme and the French faced pressure to submit to US desires to prevent national weapons programmes, the British position remained ambivalent. To a large extent American policy reflected the Europeanist v. Atlanticist divisions in Washington and the key issue came to be the creation of a Multilateral Nuclear Force (MLF). There were those 'Europeanists' eager to integrate nuclear weapons in Europe into a European force in NATO outside national control. This would include British and future French warheads and the British abandonment of their missile programme in 1960 coincided with the first MLF ideas. The term itself contained an in-built ambiguity over whether any European MLF would be based on a pool of national contributions or require the creation of a mixed manned force.

Kennedy himself was unclear about this and about the precise importance of a MLF. He was however committed to the principle of a more united Europe, perhaps because he believed it would be the best way to secure American influence. On the other hand, he did look favourably on the British as in a different or even special position to the states of mainland Europe even if he was prepared to use them to serve American interests. The question of US hegemony again has to be considered in this Western European context. Was it the case that policy in Washington was driven by the idea of maintaining influence and continued hegemonic control as Western Europe became more powerful economically and a possible nuclear rival? Was it a non-hegemonic relationship based on partnership or as Macmillan would have had it 'interdependence'? The question has to be asked in terms of relations with Britain and with the Six EEC states to determine the extent of shared US interests and a special relationship with Britain. By that is meant a relationship based on a common culture and language which was significantly different from that with other members of the Alliance and influenced the American approach to Europe.

One example of the alleged special British relationship has been the nuclear cooperation between London and Washington which culminated at the Nassau conference of 1962. Here the Kennedy administration agreed to supply the British with Polaris missiles that gave the appearance of preserving Britain's 'independent' nuclear deterrent. This was the end of a long-running saga involving a commitment, never formalized by Eisenhower, to supply an air-launched missile, Skybolt, to the British. With the Americans developing a sea launched missile, Polaris, Macmillan tried and failed to establish Anglo–American cooperation and 'interdependence' in nuclear submarines and sea-launched missiles by trading the granting of base rights to the Americans at Holy Loch Scotland for such 'interdependence'. The Americans regarded Holy Loch as the *quid pro quo* for Skybolt but when the Skybolt programme was abandoned the British were left with nothing.[18] Hence Macmillan's determination to remain a nuclear power by obtaining Polaris from the Americans while blurring the nature of the commitment of a British Polaris force to an MLF. Polaris would have been made available to the French too but de Gaulle was determined on an independent French deterrent and the French leader chafed at the prospect of US domi-

nation of Europe with exclusive control of nuclear weapons.

This is precisely how the aims of Kennedy's policy can be defined in relation to his Grand Design which embodied the American president's ideas for the future of US–Western European relations. Britain would gain entry into the EEC, which was applied for in 1961, Europe would bear more of the defence burden, its nuclear aspirations would be channelled into the MLF, and US exports would be enhanced by the reduction of trans-Atlantic tariff barriers. It was all designed to bolster the US position, which was becoming relatively weaker in economic terms with a growing US trade deficit. Hence the idea of creating a willing but largely subservient partner. In specific terms, Adenauer was told that good relations with Washington depended on Britain in the EEC and the creation of the MLF rather than on Franco–German nuclear cooperation. It has all been termed a quest for greater US influence in Western Europe and NATO with Britain, as one official put it, acting as America's lieutenant, but it was marketed under the auspices of a more equal Atlantic community.[19]

Fear of Britain as an American lieutenant was precisely what de Gaulle wanted to avoid as France began its own quest to shape Western Europe to its own advantage. Once de Gaulle realized that neither Britain nor America were keen to follow his idea of a tripartite global directorate he looked more to Western Europe and Germany to realize his plans of regaining France's position of leadership in the world which he believed had not been attained since Waterloo. The first attempt, through the Fouchet plan, involved the creation of a political community of the Six EEC nations forming an inter-governmental organization to coordinate foreign and defence policy. The Dutch in particular were opposed to a political union of such a type without Britain, whereas for de Gaulle, who vetoed Britain's entry into the EEC in 1963, the exclusion of the British and their American backers was vital to ensure French leadership in Europe.[20]

The Fouchet plan had failed by 1962 but de Gaulle was later to pursue other means to challenge US leadership (see Part III, Introduction) and permit France a more prominent European role. The unrealized aim was a change in the nature of inter-bloc relations as well as intra-Western European links. Kennedy's Grand Design was no more successful, and the MLF never got off the ground, hence preserving the British illusion of an independent nuclear deterrent even though the warheads and delivery systems were dependent on American know-how and equipment. Although the EEC did in fact develop broadly along the lines desired by the Americans the degree of US influence remained less than many would have liked. The integrationists amongst the Kennedy 'Europeanists' were somewhat disappointed by the failure of Britain to join the EEC which was to remain both a challenge and an opportunity to Washington. While for Europeans, not just de Gaulle, the US remained an essential support for the Continent but had to be prevented from becoming a determinant of the kind of Europe it was having to back. It is difficult to claim that the Americans controlled Western Europe, but equally difficult to avoid the impression of them trying in rather uncoordinated ways to do so without appearing as engaged in such a quest.

C. Latin America

US relations with Latin America had long been characterized by intervention and a determination, evidenced as soon as the 1890s, to exclude other powers from the region. US marines in the years before and after the First World War were constantly landing in South and Central America to protect US economic interests and to attempt to produce stable regimes. When Roosevelt became president he aimed to replace the use of military force with a 'Good Neighbour' policy, but the problems remained and US intervention was not entirely ruled out. Dictators like the Somozas in Nicaragua tended to wield force in a brutal manner and without any hint of democracy yet still win support from Washington. In 1944 dictators were ousted in Guatemala and El Salvador, but the war for democracy did not bring elected governments to much of Latin America. Indeed, when in 1949 Uruguay proposed that the Organization of American States (OAS) consider action against those regimes like the Somozas who violated human rights the idea was rejected by the US.[21] In terms of political freedoms Latin America was more akin to Eastern Europe than the US sphere in the Western half of the Continent. The problem for many in Latin America lay in the lack of economic development in the region, which some thought had to be overcome if democracy were to take root, while others believed that democracy could provide the means to encourage economic development.

There were significant differences between countries such as Argentina and Uruguay who produced primarily temperate-zone produce and those, especially in Central America, who were reliant on tropical produce. Prices for the latter were far more volatile and the chances of agricultural improvements providing surpluses for investment in other economic activities, as in Europe, were much fewer. In Argentina the standard of living of the lowest 20 per cent of the population was three times higher than in Brazil in the 1960s where there was particular attention given to externally promoted development and foreign investment capital was encouraged with incentives and by wages being kept low.[22] Another handicap was faced by countries with high population densities, such as Guatemala, as compared to those like Nicaragua, where on paper fewer people should have led to easier access to land. In the event this proved to be less important than the social relations which determined the use of and access to that land. Finally, in trade terms dependency for some countries was reflected in trade with the US which took up to 80 or 90 per cent of crops such as coffee produced in countries like Nicaragua. The producer country was inescapably dependent on the US for earnings from its exports which formed a small fraction of US imports and which could be easily obtained elsewhere. An alternative to the large US market was not readily available for most Latin American producers.

Economic Development, US Policy, and the Early Cold War

At the heart of the debate about US policy lies the issue of development and the US role in hindering or supporting the diversification of many Latin American economies. Were the activities of US companies promoting wealth creation to benefit the local population or extracting resources for the benefit of their shareholders and/or US consumers? What form of dependency dominated the economic relationship between the two parts of the Western hemisphere and how was this affected by the actions of the US government? In terms of the Cold War the important question is whether policy in Washington was dictated primarily by the need to protect economic interests or by the need to defeat communism. It is easy to link the two together in the sense that free trade and respect for private property were associated with the development of free societies. Yet in Latin America for much of the time this did not involve the exercise of political freedom but the maximization of the opportunities for the wealthy and powerful to operate freely in economic terms.

At the end of the Second World War all Latin American countries, apart from Mexico, still had in place colonial agrarian structures where the ownership of land, with the exception of Chile, dictated the basic institutions of social organization. As one State Department analysis had noted at the end of the 1940s: 'the economic development of these countries, adapted to the shifting market of the industrial countries of the Northern hemisphere and handicapped by a system of large landed estates, was so unbalanced as to prevent the emergence of an economically strong and politically conscious middle class.' During the Eisenhower and Kennedy administrations it was certainly the case that the US would have been delighted to welcome a strong middle class on which to build a democratic capitalist society, and it tried various ways to encourage the economic development to achieve this. Unfortunately these efforts proved a failure because the existing social structures were never tackled and the distribution of the economic surplus they produced was never altered. Change would not have accorded with the political and economic

principles which were based on very different economic conditions in North America and which the US government was fighting a Cold War to preserve.

In terms of the power political relations between the US and its southern neighbours the State Department, like the British with regard to the Middle East at the end of the War, wanted the UN kept out of the region which they regarded as an exclusive US zone, or sphere of influence. The difference between Latin America and Eastern Europe was described as 'While we do claim the right to have a guiding voice in a certain limited sphere of the foreign relations of Latin America we do not attempt to dictate the internal national life or to restrict their intercourse with foreign nations except in that limited sphere.'[23] A sphere that was defined as the politico-strategic aspect of their foreign relations. The importance of the region increased with the Korean War and the need for raw materials. George Kennan believed that US policy must be directed to their protection, to preventing the enemy gaining any military benefits from the region, and to preventing any mobilization of the region under a banner of anti-Americanism directed at the US.[24]

Dulles shared the concern about the loss of raw materials if revolutionary movements seized power, and Eisenhower saw dangers of changes in the region being exploited by communists. The first National Security Council paper on inter-American affairs analysed everything in terms of the global struggle against communism and emphasized the US concern about respecting property rights and guaranteeing security which would require consideration of unilateral intervention.[25] The development of the New Look formalized Eisenhower's preference for intervention in the form of covert operations that could be developed from the activities being considered in Eastern Europe. What concerned the US in this area of large economic interests and important foreign policy requirements were often explained by policy-makers within a Cold War framework and associated with security. Yet there was no real military threat and with regard to the distinction between the ideology of communism and Soviet power political goals, there were only three countries in the whole of the region with which Moscow had diplomatic relations in 1952.[26] In addition the post-war concerns in America about the possibility of European economic weakness or collapse did not apply in Latin America under Truman. Despite its problems Truman did not provide government aid in the form of a Marshall Plan and during Eisenhower's first term the new president continued the policy of relying on private capital to serve the region's financial needs. If communism appeared, it could be dealt with by cheap covert means.

The 1954 Coup in Guatemala

In 1944 the rich landowners constituting around 2 per cent of the population owned nearly three-quarters of the cultivatable land in Guatemala most of which was left fallow because it was more profitable for large landowners to limit production and maintain higher price levels. The election of President Arevalo began to change this and other iniquities in Guatemala. The franchise was extended and forced labour ended. In March 1951 a more radical impetus was given to the reform programme by Jacob Arbenz, who was elected president in 1950 with 60 per cent of the vote. Arbenz introduced income tax, poured money into building ports and roads, and worryingly for American companies such as United Fruit, in 1952 he expropriated uncultivated land over 670 acres. 85 per cent of the United Fruit Company's land was uncultivated and the compensation payment in the form of government bonds was disputed by them as the figure decided on by the government was based on the company's tax valuation which turned out to be considerably lower than the company's market valuation.

United Fruit looked to the American government for help as it had influential contacts in the Eisenhower administration. Both the Dulles brothers had represented the company (Allen Dulles was now Deputy Director of the Central Intelligence Agency until February 1953 when he became the head of the CIA and John Foster Dulles was Secretary of State). The alarm cry of communism in Guatemala was soon heard and encouraged by US officials in the region. Yet while communists figured in the parliamentary coalition under Arbenz they numbered only four out of fifty-one and none of them was in the cabinet. According to US intelligence there were only 500 Communist Party members in Guatemala in 1952 who had become 1,000 by 1953 when the new administration took office. The US commitment to covert operations could now be tested in terms of removing undesirable governments that were tainted with the communist brush. It would clearly be inaccurate to portray the Arbenz government as communist rather than left-wing or reformist, but in this context it was not that such governments were communist or not that was crucial for Dulles. The Secretary of State abhorred the Arbenz government not because it was a communist-regime controlled or largely influenced by Moscow, which it clearly was not, but because it could easily become so. Dulles believed that all left-wing Popular Front governments, as in Eastern Europe or in the pre-Second World War years in the West, faced an uphill struggle to avoid being taken over by the more ruthless communist parties. The government had thus already defined Latin American problems in global not regional or country-specific terms. And those at the highest level did not fail to understand what constituted a communist government but were opposed to any left-wing regimes of a radical nature because they might open the door to communism. How much this was influenced by the need to protect US economic interests remains an unresolved question.

On his own admission Dulles had no evidence of

The Duck Test

Many times it is impossible to prove legally that a certain individual is a communist; but for cases of this sort I recommend a practical method of detection—the 'duck test'. The duck test works this way: suppose you see a bird walking around in a farm yard. This bird wears no label that says 'duck'. But the bird certainly looks like a duck. Also he goes to the pond and you notice he swims like a duck. Then he opens his beak and quacks like a duck. Well, by this time you have probably reached the conclusion that the bird is a duck, whether he's wearing a label or not.

Source: Walter LaFeber, *Inevitable Revolutions: The United States in Central America* (W.W. Norton, New York, 2nd edn., 1993), 114.

Arbenz's links to Moscow but it was decided to take action against his regime. The catalyst was provided by a shipment of Czech arms in May 1954 and a small force numbering no more than those in the Communist Party was assembled by Colonel Castillo Armas. The following month the CIA flew planes over the capital with leaflets, bombed shipping, and dropped explosive devices in the form of dynamite. As Armas marched towards the capital the CIA's aim was to create the impression of a large force of rebels preparing to overthrow the government. Arbenz then made a fatal mistake by distributing arms and trying to create a peasant militia only to alienate the army. It was this which produced Arbenz's demise and Guatemala abandoned efforts at reform to face a period when the economy was dominated by foreign enterprises operating without labour legislation. Death squads appeared and the United Fruit Company was able to acquire more land. It was brought about, according to Dulles, by the action taken against the evil designs of the Kremlin and their manipulation of Arbenz.[27] And the success of the attempts to overthrow Arbenz, along with the overthrow of Mossadeq in Iran, were to reinforce the American commitment to covert operations.

The Change of Policy under Eisenhower and the Initial Response to the Cuban Revolution

The end of democracy and reform in Guatemala did not mean that the Eisenhower administration became convinced that a successful Latin American policy had to be based on dictators rather than democrats nor that the status quo had to be preserved at all costs. Eisenhower himself preferred democracy of a non-left-wing kind and he became more committed to its promotion in the second half of the decade as dictators failed to provide stability and were more frequently opposed or overthrown by popular movements. In 1954 there were thirteen out of twenty Latin American countries under the thumb of dictators but as economic conditions deteriorated, with the terms of trade moving against Latin American countries and producers of primary

produce and raw materials generally things began to change. Ironically the Soviet Union under Khrushchev became more interested in the less developed world and in building aid and trade links with it, but Latin American consumers found Soviet goods singularly unattractive. The Soviet diplomatic presence in the region remained low key and at the end of the 1950s there were still representatives only in Argentina, Mexico, and Uruguay. There were contacts made between Latin America and Soviet satellites like Bulgaria but in general there was little 1950's interference in what the Soviets may have regarded as an American sphere of influence.

It was certainly more likely that problems which appeared had nothing to do with Soviet influence and everything to do with the economic conditions in the region. At all events the situation led to a change in Eisenhower's thinking as dictators were overthrown and the vice-president, Richard Nixon, narrowly escaped serious injury or worse on a 1958 visit to Venezuala. Between 1956 and 1960 ten dictators fell from power and as early as 1957 Eisenhower, for the first time, asked Congress for more economic than military aid. Dictators apparently had not provided the hoped-for political and economic stability. Nor had the private sector, on which Eisenhower had earlier placed so much reliance, produced successful, self-sustaining development. In 1958 the US supported the establishment of a regional development bank as the economic turmoil produced the overthrow of one of America's leading, dictatorial friends President Jimenez of Venezuela. Nixon attributed the stone-throwing demonstrators in Caracas to communist infiltration into the region but his reaction to the experience was part of a US shift to a more state interventionist economic policy that culminated with John F. Kennedy's Alliance for Progress.

Significant elements of this were in place by 1960 and partly connected to the progress of the Cuban Revolution that brought Fidel Castro to power in 1959 (see below). The economic problems were now reflected by the fact that in 1960 Latin American interest payments were almost equal to the foreign loans and investments provided. Brazil made a trade and aid agreement with the Soviet Union the same year so there was the danger that capitalism's increasing failure in the Latin American context could lead to the adoption of more radical solutions and closer links to Moscow. In order to pre-empt this, Eisenhower established a Social Progress Fund while the Inter-American Development Bank was now to focus on loans to those who imposed progressive income taxes. The US even supported the more progressive regimes like those of Frondizi in Argentina and Betancourt in Venezuala who had earlier been frowned upon when dictators like Jimenez were seen as preferable. They were regimes which, in the words of the NSC, favoured 'rising living standards and a more equitable distribution of national income within the general framework of a free enterprise system'.[28]

Part of this concern came from what later drove John F. Kennedy in his obsessive campaign against Fidel Castro. In essence it was a fear that the Cuban Revolution might provide an example of alternative ways to develop under a different social and economic system. Castro came to power on the sugar-growing island of Cuba, where US investors controlled 40 per cent of the sugar production, by leading a popular uprising against the former US-backed dictator Fulgencio Batista. The rebellion was initially supported by a broad-based coalition of reformers from the middle classes as well as by peasants and workers. But Castro, and particularly his brother Raoul, had close links with Moscow and in 1959 he legalized the Communist Party and began to move towards the establishment of a left-wing dictatorship. Farmland over 1,000 acres was expropriated in 1960 and he became more determined to abandon the US connection. But as early as January of that year Allen Dulles was calling for Castro's overthrow and in March 1960 Eisenhower approved a covert operation to achieve this. Castro proceeded with his radical reform programme which, as he embraced nationalization, produced debates as to whether anti-Castro US actions actually encouraged this radicalization and ultimate ties to the Soviet Union. Only in December 1961 did Castro publicly announce his conversion to Marxist-Leninism, but his sympathies lay in that direction long before 1961 and even if the Americans had not been so obsessed with the global communist challenge the outcome in Cuba was likely to have been the same.

The Cuban Revolution produced someone who could be painted as a dictator of the wrong political kind, i.e. left-wing. It reinforced Eisenhower's belief that communism had to be stopped and dictators like Batista were probably not the kind of leader to do it but the kind who produced revolutionaries like Castro. Eisenhower's policies provided the initial impetus for those that the Kennedy administration became well known for. These reflected an intense dislike of Castro and his ideas and a belief in a more interventionist approach to produce the kind of political and economic conditions that would suit both US ideals and interests. Such policies laid out the contradictions between attempts to prevent another Castro and protect American interests, and attempts to bring about economic and political change. The latter might claim to be in tune with US ideals but they threatened to damage American economic interests. Put another way, changes were needed in Latin America to ensure the kind of stability that did not depend on brutal dictators, but without brutal dictators Castro's influence could spread along with Marxist-Leninism.

The Bay of Pigs and the Alliance for Progress

When John F. Kennedy became president there was a belief in America and in his administration that all problems could be tackled by applying fresh new ideas and moving away from what seemed to be those of the old, outmoded Republican administration. In Latin America Kennedy saw the problems of poverty and instability that had not been solved by Eisenhower. His belief that US government money could make a difference to the plight of the Latin American poor and produce development and stability was enhanced by the growing difficulties he faced over Cuba.

Kennedy inherited a covert operational plan from the Eisenhower administration which resembled the overthrow of Arbenz in Guatemala. A small force of exiles would land in Cuba in April 1961, gain support from the populace and overthrow the regime. The president failed to realize the flaws in the operation which were not pointed out to him by the military or the CIA. The chosen landing place was completely unsuitable and led into swamps which were not easy for any invading force to escape through if under air attack. Intelligence was poor and secrecy not well kept with the result that the belief that Castro's forces would take two days to respond proved wrong. To make matters worse, considerable numbers were lost in the initial invasion as some landing craft were sunk on reefs in the bay while the Cuban air force sank two ships. The remaining force soon faced surrender if overt US intervention with increased air support was not forthcoming. Kennedy refused to deploy regular US air crews to add to the small number of CIA pilots flying unmarked planes and the *débâcle* therefore ran its course. There was little support from the general population anyway and the idea that the population would defect to the US once an invasion had established itself was wishful thinking.[29] Both the miscalculations and the refusal of Kennedy to authorize what would have amounted to a full-scale invasion of Cuba had lasting effects. The president became reluctant to accept advice from those he did not trust and grew more concerned about any appearance of weakness. Castro became for Kennedy a figure associated with his failure and therefore an enemy of supreme importance.

The response to the Bay of Pigs failure came in the form of a series of covert operations designed to help Cubans overthrow the Castro regime by using psychological warfare, sabotage, diplomacy, economic and if necessary military action. The type of activities considered under what became known as Operation Mongoose were often extremely bizarre. The Pentagon suggested dropping one-way air tickets onto Cuba, using high-powered transmitters in Florida to override Cuban TV, putting chemical agents into fuel storage tanks, introducing corrosive materials to cause aircraft, boat or vehicle accidents, and issuing fake photos of an obese Castro surrounded by food and beautiful women with a caption referring to his different rations.[30]

The need to destroy Castro was accompanied by a need to ensure that there was some alternative attraction to the promises of Marxist-Leninism. In keeping with the general desire to demonstrate the benefits of capitalism and prove its superiority over communism, Kennedy sought to promote the development of Latin America through an ambitious programme of government aid. The Alliance for Progress, announced in March 1961, was what resulted. The hope was that dollars and freedom would prove more attractive than Castro and communism who would be unable to provide what the US could offer. The new administration would bring to bear American drive and money and produce their own form of revolution in Latin America. Unfortunately in the long run Kennedy did more than Castro to provide the kind of revolution he feared and Castro would have wanted.

One explanation for the failure of the Alliance for Progress was that Kennedy concentrated too much effort on the Castro side of the equation. Stopping Castro began to loom too large in his thinking. Thus the aid and development programme became subordinated to the efforts to remove Castro and to the need to encourage measures that would quell any unrest which was deemed to be exploitable by Cuba. The result was expenditure on internal security and counter-insurgency measures in Latin America which encouraged the military to promote repression rather than freedom and democracy. And there was more expenditure on security measures than on health and sanitation programmes. By October 1963 Kennedy's Assistant Secretary of State for Latin American affairs was admitting that the goals of development and democracy could not be attained in every country in the near future. The US had promised change through another democratic revolution while training the armies to prevent it.[31] And even that was to some extent a failure as in the wake of the Alliance for Progress there were seventeen coups in a nine year period.

Another reason for the failure of the Alliance can be illustrated by Nicaragua which in the 1980s was to produce exactly the kind of mass-based left-wing government Kennedy was keen to prevent. In many ways Nicaragua can be seen as a good prospect for development as it had a low population density. Therefore in theory land should have been more readily available than in countries such as Guatemala where the population density was much higher. The ownership of land was of course crucial and the fact was that most of the population lived on less than 5 per cent of the land. In 1962 when the Sandinistas, the National Sandinista Liberation Front (FLSN), were founded in opposition to the American-backed General Anastasio Somoza the US took 40 per cent of Nicaraguan exports and supplied 50 per cent of its imports.

What the Alliance for Progress did do was to achieve economic growth in this situation of dependency but put starkly it was growth without development. In the Nicaraguan case the country used the injection of resources to export more cotton and more coffee as more land was brought into production and the country's GNP grew. In fact exports rose by 20 per cent in the first half of the 1960s but in order to achieve this more peasants were thrown off their land and more recruits from a growing class of landless labourers joined the Sandinistas over the next 15 years. The Alliance for Progress failed to instigate land reform and therefore simply made the old system and its enormous inequalities more effective. It was an alliance with the old landholding elite who received US money to increase production and maintain the existing social system without progress. The efforts to bring stability on occasions proved counter-productive and created more developmental problems than they solved. With

Jacob Guzman Arbenz (1913–1971)

The son of a Swiss pharmacist Arbenz was born in Quezaltenango in September 1913. He was educated at the national military academy. From 1951 to 1954 Arbenz held the position of Guatemalan president, with the support of the military and members of the Left, including the Communist Party. The Right opposed Arbenz as he let communists hold positions in labour unions and also in the government itself. His radical policies upset the United States greatly, especially the confiscation of United Fruit Company's (a major US interest) land not under cultivation. Due to this, there was a US instigated coup in 1954. Arbenz left for Mexico and died in 1971 in Mexico City.

coups again taking place on a regular basis and unrest increasing, this time the cure would be what was once seen as the problem—military dictators. The circle of unrest and brutal repression would begin again even if Americans were to become increasingly indifferent to it.

NOTES

1. Vladislav M. Zubok, CWIHP Working Paper 4 'Soviet Intelligence and the Cold War: the "Small" Committee on Information, 1952–53' (1992), 11.

2. Wilfred Loth, *Overcoming the Cold War: A History of Détente* (Palgreave Macmillan, Basingstoke, 2002), 20, citing Lev Besymenski in '1953—Beria will die DDR beseitigen' in *Die Zeit* 15 Oct. 1993.

3. John Lewis Gaddis, *We Now Know Rethinking Cold War History* (Clarendon Press, Oxford, 1997), 130.

4. Vladislav Zubok and Constantine Pleshakov, *Inside the Kremlin's Cold War from Stalin to Khrushchev* (Harvard University Press, Cambridge, 1996), 160–1.

5. Loth, op. cit. 22–3.

6. Alexsandr Stykalin, 'The Hungarian Crisis of 1956: the Soviet Role in the Light of New Archival Documents' *Cold War History*, 1 (2001), 114, 118–20.

7. The above paragraphs are based on ibid., 121–34.

8. Ibid., 136.

9. Ibid., 137.

10. Caroline Kennedy-Pipe *Russia and the World 1917–1991* (Arnold, London, 1998).

11. Raymond Pearson, *The Rise and Fall of the Soviet Empire* (Macmillan, Basingstoke, 1998).

12. John W. Young, *Britain and European Unity 1945–1999* (Macmillan, Basingstoke, 2nd edn., 2000), 41.

13. Sean Greenwood, *Britain and European Co-operation since 1945* (Blackwell, Oxford, 1992), 65.

14. Young, op. cit., 46–8.

15. M. Camps, *Britain and the European Community, 1955–63* (Princeton University Press, Princeton, 1964), 508–9.

16. Young, op. cit., 53–60.

17. Pascaline Winand, *Eisenhower, Kennedy and the United States of Europe* (Macmillan, Basingstoke, 1993) 83–8, 211.

18. See Michael Middeke, 'Britain's Interdependence Policy and Anglo-American Co-operation on Nuclear and Conventional Force Provision, 1957–1964', Unpublished PhD thesis, LSE, 1999 from where this argument is taken.

19. F. Costigliola, 'The Pursuit of Atlantic Community: Nuclear Arms, Dollars and Berlin' in T. G. Paterson (ed.), *Kennedy's Quest for Victory: American Foreign Policy, 1961–63* (Oxford University Press, New York, 1989), 24–56.

20. Jeffrey W. Vanke, 'An Impossible Union: Dutch Objections to the Fouchet Plan 1959–1962', *Cold War History*, 1 (2001).

21. Stephen G. Rabe, *Eisenhower and Latin America: the Foreign Policy of Anti-Communism* (Chapel Hill, London, 1988), 14.

22. C. Furtado, *The Economic Development of Latin America* (Cambridge University Press, Cambridge, 1976).

23. Walter LaFeber, *Inevitable Revolutions* (W.W. Norton, New York, 2nd edn., 1993), 89.

24. Ibid., 107.

25. FRUS, 1952–4, 4 (Dept. of State, Washington, DC, 1979), NSC 144/1, 18 Mar. 1953.

26. Rabe, op. cit. 21.

27. LaFeber, op. cit.

28. Stephen G. Rabe, *The Most Dangerous Area in the World: John F. Kennedy Confronts Communist Revolution in Latin America* (Chapel Hill, London, 1999), 11.

29. Peter Wyden, *Bay of Pigs the Untold Story* (Cape, London, 1979), 327.

30. Mark J. White (ed.), *The Kennedy's and Cuba: the Declassified Documentary History* (1999), 88–95, 100–5.

31. Stephen G. Rabe, 'Controlling Revolutions: Latin America, the Alliance for Progress and Cold War Anti-Communism' in T. J. Paterson (ed.), *Kennedy's Quest for Victory* (Oxford University Press, New York, 1983), 115; LaFeber.

7 Fighting the Cold War: The Offensive Strategies

A. US Covert Operations and the Revised National Security Strategy

When the Eisenhower administration took office it confronted the need to examine the effectiveness of the offensive Cold War strategy developed by the Truman administration and the machinery put in place to implement it, most notably the Psychological Strategy Board. However, there was also the questioning of NSC 68 and some of its assumptions which had been begun by the State Department and Charles Bohlen in particular (see Chapter 4, D). NSC 68 and its proposals might no longer be accepted as contributing to national security. Given also the president's concern over economic policy and the need to control defence expenditure to maintain the kind of low tax, sound economy deemed to be essential to the American way of life, NSC 68 might require considerable revision. The other obvious concern was the danger of hot war which increased the importance of a Cold War successfully destroying

or weakening the Soviet Union while increasing the risks inherent in attempting to do so.

Operation Solarium and the Basis of a New Strategy

Stalin's death further encouraged the reassessment of Truman's Cold War/national security policy with Nitze posing the question as to whether the US would find itself committed to the overthrow of the regime in the Kremlin or be willing to reach a *modus vivendi*, which was better than the present uncertainty. The first formal reassessment came with Robert Cutler's critical examination of Truman's aims which was produced in mid-March. Its criticism was in many ways based on an unrepresentative account of Truman's policy but it belittled its effectiveness and was contemptuous of its limited and defensive objectives. NSC 20/4 and NSC 68 were described as merely policies of coexistence with the objective of a military build-up being only to deter the Soviets from hot war and live with them until they changed their ways.[1] This criticism was very much in accordance with the initial thinking of Eisenhower and Dulles who, after Stalin's death, saw inducing the disintegration of Soviet power as a means of ending the danger presented by Moscow. If psychological and other pressure were maintained, the Soviet Union would either collapse or be transformed into a satellite system geared only to defence.[2] The issue was clearly whether NSC 68 was good enough to deter the Soviets from hot war *and* to enable psychological pressure to wear down and eventually bring about the collapse or transformation of the communist regime. Roll-back over the long term, in effect.

Those who believed in the value of making a determined effort to overthrow the Soviet regime because of the opportunity presented by Stalin's death, such as C. D. Jackson,[3] favoured roll-back in the short term and with much greater determination than under Truman. Jackson produced a psychological war plan, PSB D 43, which is still classified, but according to another memo its objectives were 'to induce the Soviet armed forces to overthrow the Soviet regime at a propitious future time . . ., and to weaken Soviet power by psychological exploitation of the vulnerabilities of the Soviet armed forces.' The push for success in destroying the Soviet regime was encouraged by the East German revolt (see Chapter 6, A) and Jackson produced another paper on the exploitation of satellite unrest in Eastern Europe which was approved as NSC 158 in June 1953. That NSC meeting remains closed although NSC 158 was released in late 1996 and its first objective was to 'nourish resistance to communist oppression throughout satellite Europe, short of mass rebellion in areas under Soviet military control, and without compromising its spontaneous nature'.[4]

The rapidity of the East German uprising and its end indicated one of the problems the Americans faced with such policies but the issue of how to proceed further with undermining the Soviet Union or its satellites, while avoiding hot war, remained. Operation Solarium was in essence directed to this

question as part of a review of national security policy which would examine the key assumption of NSC 68—the need for rearmament to deter hot war while the Cold War was fought in ways which would bring about the collapse or transformation of the Soviet satellites or the Soviet regime itself. As has been seen Eisenhower had concerns about the H-bomb and about the cost of the rearmament programme which was accompanied by an interest in covert operations (see Chapter 5, B and C). Solarium consisted of three teams or task forces examining a set of assumptions pertaining to the mix of pursuing Cold War and avoiding hot war. Teams A and C reflected alternatives for policy towards the Soviet Union as a whole in this context, while Team B looked at the relationship of US nuclear weapons to deterring Soviet aggression. Team A, as has been pointed out by Gregory Mitrovich, has commonly been considered as the containment option but was really aimed at the liberation of the satellites and changing Soviet behaviour. And along with Team C it reflected the divisions in the State Department between just how far to pursue an aggressive policy in order 'to induce the disintegration of Soviet power', as Dulles put it.

The report of Task Force A thus proposed a dual strategy of roll-back in Eastern Europe and some element, at least in the short term, of peaceful coexistence with a changed Soviet Union. Greater emphasis on the latter would be somewhat contradicted by the US assumption of the strategic offensive in the ideological Cold War conflict. Containment, unlike covert operations, was not in the picture whereas concern to prevent a hot war definitely was.[5]

The fundamental difference between Task Force A and Task Force C was that while A advocated roll-back of the Soviet satellite empire in Eastern Europe, but was prepared for possible coexistence with the Soviets, Task Force C aimed at the destruction of the Soviet Union itself and peaceful coexistence was rejected in the medium term.[6] It made clear that the US must face up to 'the lack of a national strategy to end the Cold War by winning it'. The general goals were the removal of the Iron Curtain, reducing the strength of any communist elements left in the USSR, and the overthrow of the Soviet leadership. More specifically, Task Force C proposed that the US should ensure that in five years the unification of Germany and Korea and a nationalist stronghold in

Solarium Project Report of Task Force A

With the assistance of allies to achieve through progressive steps and without undue risk of war, but recognizing that the threat of war must not inhibit our unfolding courses of action, a stop to Soviet expansion; the diminution and progressive retraction of Soviet control over its east European satellites and Red China; the discrediting of Soviet power and Communist ideology as effective instruments of Soviet foreign policy; and a maximum contribution to the increase in internal stresses and conflicts within the Soviet system; to the end that the Soviet rulers will be forced to accept the necessity of adjusting their objectives to those of peaceful coexistence with the Free World ... a new approach to the problem of German reunification can ... exploit and intensify present Soviet internal stresses and achieve, in due time, the first major roll-back of Soviet hegemony over Eastern Europe.

Source: Dwight D. Eisenhower Library, White House Office Files 1952–1961, Office of the Special Assistant for National Security Affairs, NSC Series-Subject Sub-Series, Box 9, Project Solarium cited in G. Mitrovich *Undermining the Kremlin America's Strategy to Subvert the Soviet Bloc, 1947–1956*, 137, 139.

The Search for a Post-Solarium National Security Policy with a Strategy for Fighting the Cold War

The fact that the emerging policy after Solarium came to contain more of Task Force A than C was an indication that the acceptance of peaceful co-existence was coming closer. For one thing, the aim of destroying the Soviet Union was no longer to be the aim of US covert activities. The lesser goal of undermining the Soviet bloc seemed less dangerous but not necessarily any more realistic unless it provided for direct involvement by the US. As NSC 162/2 pointed out, while there were strains evident within the Eastern bloc, as evidenced by the June 53 East German uprising (see Chapter 6, A), the Soviet ability to exercise control had not been appreciably reduced and was unlikely to be so while Moscow maintained adequate military forces. Detachment of satellites was therefore not feasible except by war or Soviet acquiescence.[8]

Hence the continuing doubts of the efficacy of an aggressive Cold War strategy which were to produce disagreements between the Joint Chiefs and the more cautious State Department in the post-Solarium attempts to produce a new national security strategy involving the fighting of the Cold War. Initially, in forming a new policy, consideration was to be given of to how to boost the strength of the free world while putting the Soviet bloc on the defensive, but what this would involve and at what risk remained vague. Consequently, the immediate impact of Solarium was to produce indecision and conflicting views about the future development of any national security strategy centred on fighting the Cold War. The outcome, as it emerged during the first half of Eisenhower's presidency, was to prove a key moment in the American approach to the Cold War even though there was an absence of agreement or decisive presidential leadership. The eventual shift in emphasis came largely as a result of three other factors: the reassessment of Soviet capabilities with regard to hot war and which related in particular to the communist acquisition of nuclear weapons; the fact that as more interest was taken in areas outside Europe the success of a Cold War strategy came to be defined less in terms of

mainland China were achieved. And in the next phase up to 1965 the satellite governments would be overthrown by an all-out political offensive. How all this could have been done without a major war remains unclear.[7]

The Cold War strategy defined by Task Force A was one that envisaged the possibility of coexistence if or when roll-back proved undesirable because of the difficulty of achieving it without resorting to hot war. The problem which Eisenhower never fully came to terms with was that aggressively fighting the Cold War risked disaster through hot war, yet accepting the continued existence of the Soviet Union could require such strong military forces over a long period and such large defence expenditures as to threaten the American way of life and ultimately lead to Cold War defeat. Aggressive moves against the communists were not therefore abandoned but merely reduced in importance. And the choice between doing whatever it took to win the Cold War or accepting peaceful coexistence because the Cold War could not be won was consequently fudged.

the eradication of communism in Eastern Europe through an aggressive strategy and more in terms of preventing communism spreading to other areas of the world; and finally the concern, particularly in 1954 as divisions seemed to be appearing within the Western Alliance (see Chapter 4, C on the problem of German rearmament), that the unity of the Western bloc would be difficult to maintain unless efforts to reach an agreement with the Soviets were made while avoiding aggressive acts which might provoke war.

However, despite the problems and reservations about the success of an aggressive strategy in Eastern Europe, the American reluctance to accept the continued existence of the Soviet Union led to importance still being attached to the conduct of covert operations and psychological warfare some of which were included in the formal paper on overall national security policy NSC 162/2. The paper referred to measures to impose pressure on the Soviet bloc which should take account of the desirability of creating conditions to induce the Soviet leadership to be more receptive to negotiated settlements. Covert measures in particular should be taken to create and exploit problems for the USSR and eliminate its control over its satellites. Thus although the aim of destroying the Soviet regime was removed as the goal of US policy, the means to achieve this still included similar measures and left scope for the kind of secret actions which were risky and provocative. The change was that the possibility of peaceful coexistence was now more acceptable and was likely to involve attempts at reaching negotiated settlements beneficial to the US.[9]

In a sense Eisenhower was presented with two options (A and C) in the wake of Solarium and could not decide which to choose. The decision was made worse by the growing realization that the Soviets had the H-bomb and would at some point in the future be likely to achieve nuclear parity. If under Truman, and especially in the wake of NSC 68, coexistence was not in the interests of the US, would not a preemptive strike in 1953–4 be better than waiting for parity or bankrupting the US? The question then reverted to that raised by Charles Bohlen as to whether the Soviets aimed at world domination by all means including the use of force (see Chapter 4, D). If they did, as the military claimed, then there was no real choice other than the destruction of

the Soviets, but if they did not coexistence was an option. It was another dilemma which Eisenhower considered but never decisively resolved. What was certain was the destruction of the assumptions behind NSC 68. If rearmament was to enable the US to fight an aggressive Cold War to destroy or weaken the Soviets without risking hot war because of the deterrence provide by America's overwhelming nuclear and conventional strength, this policy was no longer an option once the Soviets achieved nuclear parity.

Subversion and Intelligence Gathering

The contrast between, on the one hand, policies of negotiation and peaceful coexistence and, on the other, covert actions to weaken the Soviet Union and its control over the satellites (subversion) was to remain a feature of US policy under Eisenhower. As Dulles and the State Department favoured the former, the military remained committed to more aggressive Cold War policies. The scope and value of covert operations and psychological operations remained part of US Cold War policy and helped produce a number of risky operations against the Soviet Union. If the Soviet Union had to be destroyed or its behaviour radically altered, there was no real need to limit the risk of war. Or as fears of war grew (again as in earlier periods there was a belief that the Soviets were unlikely to deliberately start a war) more attention was paid to how the US would be best able to cope with Soviet capabilities in defensive and offensive hot war terms. The need to consider how best to assess and cope with Soviet hot war capabilities, combined with the underlying offensive and aggressive strategy in the Cold War of the US military, led to dangerous risk-taking. The former need also helped produce much more NSC attention to such matters in its reviews of national security. By the time Kennedy radically changed the whole NSC approach and reduced the importance of the National Security Council, it dealt with such issues as civil defence, early warning, Soviet air defence systems, and relative nuclear and conventional capabilities including joint war plans which would be important in hot war.

One of the most secretive US operations involving the clearest most direct risk of hot war was Operation Home Run about which a lot less is known than the illegal overflying of Soviet airspace by U2 spy planes. Staged from Greenland fifty US bombers were sent into Soviet airspace carrying eavesdropping equipment and cameras as opposed to nuclear weapons. Most of Northern Russia was penetrated over a period of seven to eight weeks in the spring of 1956, and 156 missions over Russian airspace were flown. Part of the aim was to acquire information about Russian radar, which may be considered in relation to the mysterious and disastrous overflight of the Korean civilian airliner under President Reagan (see Chapter 16, A). US reconnaissance overflights of the Soviet Union began in 1954[10] and the US military were not just concerned about hot war intelligence as they also wanted to use air power and technological supremacy for Cold War purposes. They initially proposed Project Control in 1953 which was based on the political use of air power. The reconnaissance offensive could lead to the use of US nuclear weapons to resolve key problems with the USSR. In other words US technological supremacy in the air could be used as a bargaining tool with the Soviets to urge, for example, the withdrawal from Eastern Europe. If concessions were not given by Moscow and there were attempts to stop the reconnaissance planes, the US would respond with a nuclear attack.[11]

Whatever may have come of such a plan, Soviet espionage and subversion appear, from what we know, to have been of a very different kind in the 1950s to those of the US. Soviet spies operated in an environment where it was easier for agents to escape detection. Developing their agents to follow on from the wartime defectors to the cause of Soviet communism was now more difficult because of recruitment problems in the Cold War. Recruits would have to come from members of the Soviet intelligence services and become illegal entrants to the West. In the US VENONA (see Chapter 4, A) had revealed such knowledge of Soviet agents that the network in the US had to be almost entirely rebuilt. The essence of Soviet espionage and subversion was a legacy of Stalinist paranoia and wartime mistrust which produced a need to discover what the West was planning to do against the Soviet Union. Fears in

the Cold War may have been better grounded in reality but they were based on perceptions that the Soviets needed to know more about the nature of what was being planned against them. Hence, probably their most successful agent, apart form the ones recruited in the inter-war years, was George Blake[12] who betrayed Western agents to his Soviet masters.

Counter-subversion for the Soviets and for Blake was also directed at the secret Western tunnel in Berlin. Approved in 1953 the tunnel was begun in the late summer of 1954 and completed in 1955; 1,600-ft. long it ran from West Berlin underground into East Berlin in order that the West could intercept land-lines running from the Soviet military and intelligence HQ at Karlshorst. The Soviets learned of the planned tunnel through Blake in January 1954 but were unable to 'discover' it until 1956 for fear of compromising their British agent.[13] The Berlin tunnel and the Blake spy case came to symbolize some of the similarities and differences between Soviet espionage and subversion and the Western variety. Both sides were keen to use agents to provide knowledge of what the other side was doing, to compromise officials, and to prevent the efficient conduct of intelligence operations. The different features of the two societies (see Chapter 4, A) made it easier for the Soviets to use agents inside the US or Europe. This meant in the 1950s that the West used more devious means, like the Berlin tunnel, to obtain information on Soviet intelligence and military activities; and in the military case this made risky exercises to assess Soviet capabilities more likely (see below). In the case of subversion it meant that because the degree of underground resistance was less in the West, it was therefore more difficult for the communists to encourage the use of illegitimate means (uprisings) to overthrow the regime. The result was that while 'illegals' were sent by Moscow with the aim of disrupting Western governments' policies and obtaining secrets, the West was able to use tactics based on encouraging insurrection of the people against the communist governments. Actions to disrupt economic planning, to highlight the relative lack of consumer goods with food and leaflet drops, to establish contacts with dissidents, and to continue broadcasting propaganda were not part of Soviet subversion. This was irrespective of whether there were those individuals and agencies who linked their activities to a strategy based on the ultimate destruction of the other side. Here we must wait for evidence from the Soviet side that this was ever considered as part of a Cold War strategy at the centre of which was the issue of eventual coexistence, which was what the Americans considered.

At the same time what each side understood by subversion was clearly similar but also partly influenced by the different possibilities that were made available by the nature and location of the two opposing societies. Subversion to the Americans was not just action authorized and controlled by the Soviet state and its agents which aimed at the destruction or weakening of the US, but any left-wing communist political activity. Because such activities were, in theory at least, permitted in free societies, any such group, whether controlled or influenced by the Soviets or largely independent of them, was labelled subversive. Moreover, in some societies it was possible for groups to emerge which had different variants of interests and ideology, as in Vietnam, which by 1954 was the key US example of Soviet subversion. The confusion then and now arose over the analysis of these movements as both ideological and power political opponents controlled by Moscow when some were not.

The advantage for the communists was the ease of encouragement of ideological opposition to capitalism that the existence of communist parties provided. It is arguable, however, that the Soviets were never fundamentally interested in ideology but were aware of its importance to justify and explain actions which were always primarily geared to the power political goals of the Soviet state. Naturally the old debate over whether Soviet expansion, world domination, the survival of the satellite Empire, the needs of state security, the achievement and enhancement of world power status was the dominant goal remains crucial, as does the role of ideology in Soviet foreign policy. Yet the Americans arguably used ideology not as a power political state tool but as a universal principle of international well-being. In other words, communist/socialist ideology was interpreted in the same way as, and often juxtaposed or confused with, the advancement of Soviet state power as a threat to US national security. Communist ideology was not a threat because it was seen as a tool of another state but because it was deemed a threat to international well-being and American interests and values. The result in the 1950s was that the US perceived threats on a broader front and propaganda became more important. Moreover, to a significant extent it was prepared to run greater risks to remove or counter them.

Defining an Overall Cold War National Security Strategy

However, the fact that at the end of the 1940s (see Chapter 4, D) the US decided on an aggressive Cold War policy which then required much greater hot war capabilities to deter the Soviets by maintaining superior US military strength had to be reconsidered in the light of increased Soviet nuclear capabilities. While there was some reluctance to abandon an aggressive strategy the voices of moderation continued to gather strength in late 1953 and 1954. They were boosted by the destructive power of the H-bomb, the prospect of Soviet nuclear sufficiency or equality, and the futility of the immediate Cold War destruction of the enemy. In one sense American policy-makers can be seen as attempting to justify and reconcile the two somewhat contradictory tracks in US policy and to modify NSC 162. By 1954 this modification was deemed necessary because of the increasing likelihood of Soviet subversion now that North Vietnam had been lost to the West, the increased Soviet nuclear capability, and the growing signs of divisions between the Western allies. As NSC 5440 put it in December 1954 the hostile policies of the Soviet Union could only be resolved in accordance with US security interests either through the overthrow of the Soviet regime and its replacement by a government with no expansionist policies 'or any other objectives inconsistent with US security'. Or the problem could be resolved by the modification of the Soviet system so that its leaders 'abandon expansionist policies and accept arrangements in accordance with US national security interests'.[14] Thus covert measures could be continued with the aim of encouraging the modification of the Soviet regime or the withdrawal from Eastern Europe and the end of Soviet expansion which most Americans wrongly believed had caused, rather than encouraged, the events in Korea and Vietnam.

Dulles to his credit had tried to define the limits to which the Operations CoOrdinating Board (the replacement for the Psychological Strategy Board in September 1953) could go in covert operations by arguing in September 1954 that no actions should be taken which would impair a negotiated settlement.[15] The statement proved to be ironic in that it was the covert U2 spy flights in 1960 which effectively sabotaged the Paris summit negotiations (see Chapter 5, B). Moreover, the crux of the controversy was over the acceptance or rejection of peaceful coexistence and negotiation as the best strategy for ending Soviet hostility. The debate was formalized in NSC 5440 in terms of the JCS and State Department views. The former argued that it was dangerous to try and solve problems with the Soviets through negotiations which should be therefore be rejected until Soviet behaviour changed. The latter sought from a position of strength to achieve a *modus vivendi*.[16] Thus the dilemma posed by the NSC committee in June 1954 under Robert Cutler remained unresolved. Cutler noted that

As it has been formulated, NSC policy towards the USSR has not provided a 'strategic concept' adequate for operational guidance in the exploitation of Soviet vulnerabilities. . . . There is no clear guidance in NSC policies for determining the balance and relationship between measures taken within the context of a policy of coexistence and measures to be taken within a context which postulates the destruction of the Soviet system and regime.[17]

The problem of linking subversion and covert operations to the destruction of the Soviet regime with a policy based on coexistence and reducing the Soviet threat by negotiation was to remain during the Eisenhower administration. In 1954 the JCS continued to argue that for a change in Soviet attitudes to occur communists had to be convinced that their policies would produce countermeasures that would threaten their continued existence.[18] Dulles, however, believed that while he could sympathize with the military desire for a more dynamic Cold War policy, which he himself had called for in 1952, it was not easy to go beyond the point the Eisenhower administration had reached in translating policy

into action. If strong pressure were applied to change the Soviet system or overthrow the Chinese communist regime, general war was likely. And even if this did not occur the problem of Soviet atomic plenty (which had ended the NSC 68 strategy of being able to apply Cold War pressure from a position of hot war superiority) would remain. Finally, to continue with an aggressive Cold War policy was likely to destroy the unity of the free world.[19] When the next review of national security gave rise in 1955 to NSC 5501 the outline national security strategy was defined as a choice between meeting the Soviet threat by 'destroying the power of the Soviet-communist bloc or modifying the policies of the Soviet government along lines more compatible with US security interests'. The means to implement this were not addressed; instead it was merely stated that 'Either policy could include action to disrupt or neutralize the international Communist apparatus *in the free world*'.[20]

The emphasis on the free world effectively meant counter-subversion not subverting or destroying the Soviet system but protecting the Western one. Yet it took more time before the aggressive Cold War policy disappeared. The basic reviews of national security policy in 1956, 1957, 1958, and 1959 (NSC 5602, NSC 5707, NSC 5810, NSC 5906 memoranda) changed little in terms of strategy and still contained sections on 'Means of Directly Influencing the Soviet bloc', including the exploitation of Soviet vulnerabilities as part of a Cold War strategy which encouraged bureaucratic and popular pressures inside the bloc. Thus the scope was there for the continuation of measures originally designed as part of a strategy of undermining the Soviet Union or its satellites. However, negotiations and the exploitation of Soviet vulnerabilities now went hand in hand.

Throughout the 1950s the contradictions in the two elements of Cold War strategy were not totally resolved in the context of national security strategy. What happened was that new things were added to it, again stemming from the attempts to define such a strategy in the wake of Solarium in 1953 and 1954. In the first place more emphasis was given to hot war now that the Soviets were approaching nuclear plenty meaning that they could deliver by the second half of the decade an immensely damaging strike on the US. More emphasis was placed on deterring this and analysing ways in which it might be prevented by military and techno-logical means. Secondly, the growing importance of the less developed world had enormous implications by the end of the decade. Rather than concentrate on destroying the Soviet bloc it now became more necessary to strengthen the free world against the spread of communism. Aid and other measures to do this, including counter-subversion had to be an integral part of such a strategy and under Kennedy the whole emphasis was placed there. Covert operations would no longer be organized as part of a general Cold War strategy of peaceful coexistence or roll-back, or both, as it had become for much of Eisenhower's administration.

The implications of this Cold War shift away from Europe as fear of hot war grew and peaceful co-existence became something of a fact, as well as a more desirable State Department goal, have enormous implications for interpretations of US national security and Cold War strategy. The dif-ference between policies geared to hot war and to those pertaining to all other forms of conflict short of an international armed one are again vital for coming to grips with the Cold War. Yet understand-ing that the whole process was never fully centred on containment is even more important. The old idea of containing Soviet power in Europe in a Cold War that then became for the US a global form of containment is in need of challenge. In the 1950s the issues were coexistence and negotiation with the communists or destroying or radically changing the Soviet regimes Moscow imposed on the Eastern bloc. As Dulles pointed out if the US was going to accept coexistence, it would be important to deter-mine which areas of the world it should hold. One can only contain something which exists. Practising a policy of coexistence, as Secretary of the Treasury Humphrey pointed out in 1954, would be the result of abandoning roll-back. Containment was arguably more in evidence after roll-back was being abandoned than before it. The difficulties and unlikely success of a policy of removing the com-munist problem by weakening and/or removing the regime in Moscow were rightly seen as greater in the wake of Solarium. Coexistence and peaceful negotiations, arguably leading to containment, then became more attractive. Eisenhower never made the choice and the implementation of a policy never went beyond what Dulles had defined as a problem in 1954.

B. The Berlin Crises

Berlin was at the heart of the Cold War, the heart of the German question, and on several occasions became the focus of tension between the two blocs in Europe. The airlift of 1948–9 to preserve the Western position in the city which was surrounded by East Germany (GDR) had become a potent Cold War symbol. Berlin could be portrayed as a beacon of freedom in a land devoid of democracy where com-munist aggressors were poised to strike once Western vigilance relaxed. It also symbolized the division of Germany but was a city that offered a gateway to the West for people who could move between the Soviet sector and the British, French, and American sectors. Thus it became a focal point for East German citizens seeking a better life in the West.

In the early 1950s the scale of the exodus was fast becoming a problem for the East German authorities and a massive disadvantage in propaganda terms as people began to vote with their feet on the success of communism. Nevertheless, the roots of the crises which began in 1958 and 1961 were not simply communist designs on the city because of a need to ease the political and economic difficulties faced by Walter Ulbricht's regime in the GDR. Nor was the American response based on a reaction to the crises provoked by Khrushchev. American policy was defined by two key considerations before the first crisis broke, at the Russian leader's instigation, in 1958. One was related to the pressure the Soviets could bring to bear on the US position by a repeat of the blockade strategy and the other was the pressure the US could put on the Soviets through covert operations and psychological warfare conducted from West Berlin.

The Background to the 1958 Crisis

The West was very much aware of the virtual impossibility of defending West Berlin in the wake of a determined Soviet attack. The Eisenhower administration considered this and concluded by 1954 that the Western position was sufficiently important to retain even at the risk of general war. This raised the stakes by changing Truman's policy of threatening war only when the Western position was unsustainable. Eisenhower saw that as too defensive, and while the defence of West Berlin was impossible he wanted to use the US position in the city to wrest the Cold War initiative away from Moscow. The president believed West Berlin could be used to implement a 'dynamic programme of penetration to bring freedom to those who want it'.

The covert operations programme comprised disinformation and radio broadcasts to encourage Eastern Europeans to revolt against communist rule even though its effectiveness had been put into question by the collapse of the East German uprising in the summer of 1953. By then West Berlin had become the centre of anti-Soviet activities in Europe including eavesdropping projects in a secret Berlin underground tunnel. One particularly embarrassing Western campaign for the East Germans and Soviets was the provision of food parcels. This forced the East Germans to impose restrictions on travel into West Berlin and to penalize East Berliners who were found to be participating in the programme. Eisenhower also adopted a more assertive Cold War policy with new defensive measures and believed that the blockade relief option, despite stockpiling in West Berlin, was no longer desirable. Whatever the increased difficulties of implementing a repeat of the 1948 airlift in response to a new blockade, there might come a time when the US, by finally threatening military action, would be placed on the back foot. There would then be the possibility of a humiliating climbdown after losing a battle to save West Berlin without resorting to general war. Of course the threat of general war was inevitable if the Soviets were determined enough, given the relative strengths of the opposing forces, but Eisenhower wanted to resort to the threat of military action at the *beginning* of any future crisis.[21]

Khrushchev was aware of East German weakness, and particularly after the incorporation of West Germany into the Western alliance he became more committed to strengthening the GDR as a firm member of the Eastern bloc. The fear of losing a satellite to capitalism was accompanied by a desire to prevent any Eastern European state collapsing especially in the second half of the decade. The failure to make any progress on a German settlement which could be portrayed as a success was also something that Khrushchev became concerned about. His failure to secure peace presented a possible threat to the Soviet Union, yet after 1956 Khrushchev had embarked on a policy of peaceful coexistence and cut Soviet conventional forces considerably. If this continued to fail to bring results in the form of increased security and status for the Soviets, then domestic criticism would grow. Some analysts told Khrushchev that Adenauer could soon force Washington to support the 'implementation of German reunification on a bourgeois basis'. And there were other fears of a West German rapprochement with Poland which would force Russian troops back inside the Soviet borders. There was particular concern about the Germans getting their hands on nuclear weapons.[22]

In addition pressure on Khrushchev came from Walter Ulbricht and the East Germans who reminded him of the subversive activities of the Americans and the continued flow of East Germans to the West. Ulbricht urged Moscow to take measures which would enhance the international status of the largely unrecognized GDR. The East Germans were increasingly seeing the need to gain sovereignty over the whole of Berlin which otherwise would remain an open sore inside the GDR.

In Berlin, as elsewhere, US subversion policy (see Chapter 7, A) moved to one of supporting passive resistance rather than armed rebellion in the Eastern bloc. The Americans also made it clear that they would not tolerate interference with Western access to the city and based their response to any such interference on 'immediate and forceful action to counter the Soviet challenge even though such countermeasures might lead to general war'. Berlin was also placed under the NATO nuclear umbrella, and fearing that the Russians might relinquish some of their administrative officials to the East Germans, a decision was made in 1954 to accept GDR officials as representatives of the Soviet Union.[23] But the crux of the developing crisis was Soviet concerns over nuclear developments in West Germany and the increasing need to strengthen the East German state when the US attached enormous symbolic and Cold War importance to West Berlin as the centre of psychological warfare against the Eastern bloc.

The Crisis of 1958

The attempts to strengthen East Germany had led in 1954 to a Soviet announcement that it regarded the GDR as a sovereign state and to Ulbricht's statement in 1955 that East Berlin was its capital and that he was prepared to restrict traffic between the zones. As economic conditions in West Berlin began to improve the attractions of the Western sector only increased and Khrushchev's domestic credibility became increasingly threatened. Internationally there was the impact of a massive increase in 1958 of the numbers of escaping East Germans. The victory of socialism as an economic force could not be reconciled with the growing desire to escape from its clutches in East Germany in order to share in the economic success of capitalism. Nor could the security benefits of peaceful coexistence be squared with a West German state apparently on the verge of controlling nuclear weapons. In the spring of 1957 Adenauer did not deny to the Soviet ambassador that West Germany might become a nuclear power and Heinrich Brentano, the West German foreign minister, asked if other West European powers had nuclear weapons why should the Germans not too. Khrushchev suspended high-level contacts with the West Germans for a year as a result. In 1958 Ulbricht sent Khrushchev alarming reports about American nuclear weapons in Berlin and at the end of the summer the Soviet leader devised a way to strengthen his and East Germany's position. Berlin would be declared a free, demilitarized city and he would threaten to transfer control over West Berlin

access routes to the East Germans. The ultimate aim was to use this threat to persuade the West to recognize the GDR, and with it the formal division of Germany, preferably with both states renouncing nuclear weapons. Khrushchev was confident he could reduce the rights of the West in Berlin bit by bit without giving a real justification for war.

On 10 November 1958 he therefore announced that the Soviet Union would transfer its Berlin occupation rights to the GDR so that the West would have to discuss all Berlin questions with the East Germans. He then informed the West Germans that talks in Bonn would only continue on the basis of the West Germans not acquiring nuclear weapons and acknowledging the GDR as a negotiating partner. Finally, on 27 November he presented a large memo to the Western powers demanding an agreement to transform Berlin into a free, demilitarized city and an understanding with the GDR on unhindered travel between the city and the rest of the world. If no such agreement was reached within six months, the Soviet Union would make its own agreement with the GDR, giving the latter full sovereignty over East Berlin. This ultimatum occurred, coincidentally or not, at the same time in 1958 as German bomber units were trained so that they might have a nuclear capability and at the same time that the construction of German nuclear storage facilities was completed.[24] The NATO powers rejected Khrushchev's demands the following month.[25]

In early 1959 Khrushchev tried to take the heat out of the stalemate by claiming the speech was not intended to be an ultimatum, an assurance repeated to the British prime minister, Harold Macmillan, when he visited Moscow in February 1959. The Russian leader also accepted Eisenhower's suggestion for another foreign ministers conference on the German question which began in Geneva in May 1959. By then the possibilities for agreement on disarmament had been exhausted (see Chapter 5, B and C) and the conference made no progress but it effectively ended the ultimatum. It also led to another formal process of meetings designed to reduce tension through more summits and other high-level discussions, but Khrushchev's motives for this have not been made clear. The most logical one seems a desire, born from a genuine fear, to reduce the German military threat. What particularly concerned Khrushchev was the possibility of West German forces being used against a weak East Germany backed by the threat of nuclear weapons. When Khrushchev visited the United States in September 1959 to meet Eisenhower tensions over Berlin were further reduced as the American president seemed willing to discuss the partial withdrawal of US troops from West Berlin. Thus Berlin for the moment was subsumed in the general round of meetings on bigger and broader issues and the crisis would not re-emerge in acute form until a new American president was in the White House. There would then be another opportunity for Khrushchev to try again to improve the Soviet position relative to Germany as the Western half continued to prosper and difficulties in the Eastern half continued to increase.

The Crisis of 1961

The importance of Berlin was likely to render any agreement difficult as the real question was whether the Soviets would take any military action to change the status quo and if they did would the Americans go to war in response. It was a cat-and-mouse game of bluff for the two protagonists, which in 1961 involved their respective allies much more than in 1958. It has been suggested that Ulbricht not Khrushchev drove the 1961 crisis because of the desperate situation in East Germany. Something had to be done irrespective of Khrushchev's domestic problems or any Soviet desire to avoid confrontation with the US. For Ulbricht the general questions of West Germany obtaining nuclear weapons and the creation of two neutral Germanies were also less important. 200,000 inhabitants of East Germany fled into West Berlin in 1960, many of them qualified professional people most needed by the country as the East German economy could not afford the salaries needed to retain them. When the two communist leaders met in the last months of 1960 they agreed on what their priorities would be in seeking a settlement that would solve East Germany's problem. Top of the list was West Berlin becoming a free city and the recognition of both Germanies in the form of a four-power peace treaty. If not, the communist aim was to get an interim four-power

agreement pending the negotiation of a peace treaty based, for example, on the withdrawal of troops. Finally, there was the possibility of a separate peace treaty between the Soviet Union and its allies that would give the East Germans control over the access routes to Berlin.[26]

The real problem was that there was no possible resolution of the situation that would satisfy both sides. From the communist perspective the status quo had to change whereas from the American perspective it was vital to preserve it. As 1961 came, the exodus from East Germany increased, as did the numbers of Westerners taking advantage of buying basic subsidized goods in the East at cheaper prices. The failed Paris summit of 1960 (see Chapter 5, B) also made peaceful coexistence less attractive and increased pressures for more confrontational policies. Thus in January 1961 Khrushchev told the West German ambassador that the Berlin problem must be solved within a year. And at Vienna he threatened Kennedy with signing a separate treaty with the GDR if the problem was not resolved by December.[27] The problem with the American determination to preserve the status quo remained— that a US conventional response to any Soviet actions was bound to be ineffectual while the threat of nuclear war, simply because the Soviets signed a peace treaty with the GDR, seemed way out of proportion. On the other hand, the abandoning of American rights or any real alteration of the West's position was deemed likely to reduce international confidence in any form of US guarantee.

The scene was set for Berlin and a German peace treaty to form an important part of the summit between Kennedy and Khrushchev planned for June 1961 in Vienna. The meeting has become notorious for Khrushchev's attempts to bully the young and inexperienced president. There is no doubt that Kennedy was taken aback by Khrushchev's attempts at intimidation and his crude and stark portrayals of US–Soviet disagreements but there was no caving in to Khrushchev's demands, especially on Berlin. The Soviet leader proposed his ideal solution already agreed with Ulbricht, but Kennedy likened West Berlin to Western Europe in an attempt to get across the importance the US attached to Berlin. He told Khrushchev he was determined to avoiding anything which would appear as a change in the global balance to the benefit of the communists. Khrushchev emphasized that the Soviets could not afford a long delay and if there were no agreement by the end of the year they would sign a separate peace treaty with East Germany. The young American president repeated the importance the US attached to Berlin and to American occupation rights which would be infringed if the status quo were changed. He hoped that the two states would not end up confronting each other in a situation where other's vital interests were at stake. The Soviet leader put the responsibility for choosing war on the Americans if war was what they wanted over Berlin.[28]

The prospect of war was of particular concern to the British, who would have preferred a negotiated settlement even if it involved changing the status quo at some yet to be specified date. Surprisingly de Gaulle was more firmly behind Kennedy in 1961 as the French leader believed (correctly) that Khrushchev was bluffing. De Gaulle was in favour of facing the Soviets down at the risk of general war. When the Soviets made the ultimatum public on 10 June 1961, Kennedy pushed though a conventional arms build-up with the aim of giving US forces more flexibility and announced the call up of reservists. It was little more than a token gesture but it forced Khrushchev, already under pressure from the military, to cancel his proposed cutbacks in the Red Army (see Chapter 6, A).[29] And it was designed to indicate the seriousness of Western intent. As tension rose the Americans began to examine what exactly had to be preserved in West Berlin at all costs. The bottom line was the freedom and survival of the Western sector, but how to ensure this except by deterring Soviet action was less clear. As Khrushchev told John McLoy, the president's disarmament adviser, a German peace treaty would be signed no matter what and as the Soviet leader increased the defence budget by one-third the game of cat and mouse reached its peak at the end of July. On 31 July

Kennedy himself acknowledged that Khrushchev would have to stop the refugee flow with perhaps the building of a wall.[30]

Despite Ulbricht's June denial that a wall was not anyone's intention, one had already been discussed on the basis of a well-prepared East German plan given the Soviet reluctance to act and then see if the US would start a major war to preserve West Berlin. On the other hand, the KGB chief, Shelepin, advocated a far-reaching programme of covert operations and psychological warfare, like those favoured by Eisenhower, but on a global scale. It would be something to tie American forces down in various parts of the world while the attempts to secure a German peace treaty were pursued. The aim was to convince the Americans that if they unleashed a military conflict they could lose influence in many parts of the less developed world as KGB armed uprisings against reactionary pro-Western governments took place. When the Cuban missile crisis broke in 1962 this was one of the things Kennedy believed the Soviets aimed to achieve by exerting pressure from Cuba (see Chapter 7, D). Shelepin also suggested a campaign of deception which would exaggerate the Soviet nuclear arsenal (see Chapter 5, C). The KGB was then instructed to present more specific measures for consideration by the Presidium.[31]

For Berlin the worst part of the crisis was over when on 13 August the two halves of Berlin were separated by barbed wire, followed a month later by the building of a wall to divide Khrushchev's free city into two inaccessible parts for most Berliners. Ulbricht's problems were solved and although Soviet and American tanks confronted each other for a time across the sector boundary in Berlin, the possibility of war over the city no longer seemed likely. The Soviets had failed again to change the status quo and the Western alliance had held firm despite doubts from some of its members. Yet the West did nothing, effectively accepting the Soviet sphere of influence in Eastern Europe.

John F. Kennedy (29 May 1917–22 November 1963)

John F. Kennedy was born in Brookline, in the state of Massachusetts. He was educated at the University of Harvard and upon graduating in 1940 he joined the US navy. During his naval career Kennedy became somewhat of a hero in 1943 when after a Japanese attack he led many survivors to safety despite his own serious injuries. After the War, Kennedy became a Democratic congressman for Massachusetts in November 1946 and was re-elected in 1948 and 1950. He entered the Senate in 1953 and in September of the same year he married Jacqueline Bouvier. In 1958 and 1959 Kennedy gave much of his time to labour reform legislation. In 1960, he became the first ballot nominee for president which was the culmination of a career planned out for him by his ruthless and domineering father, Joe Kennedy. John F. Kennedy, or Jack as he was known, won the presidential election by a narrow margin, following televised debates with Richard Nixon, and became the first Roman Catholic to enter the White House. At the age of 43 he was also the youngest man to take up the office of president. It was in his inaugural address that Kennedy's famous phrase was first used: 'Ask not what your country can do for you—ask what you can do for your country.' As president, Kennedy launched many economic programmes designed to push forward US expansion. Kennedy was a president who eventually backed the cause of Civil Rights, and he pledged to rid the country of persistent areas of poverty. Kennedy set up the Alliance for Progress in 1961, to attempt to alleviate much of the poverty in Latin American countries. The Peace Corps were also established by the administration in 1961. Then, in April 1961, Kennedy faced his first international challenge as president, when he allowed the unsuccessful Bay of Pigs invasion of Cuba to take place. The failure of the invasion became a large setback for the Kennedy administration, resulting in criticism and anti-American feeling abroad. In 1961 and 1962 Kennedy also had to deal with the Soviet leader Nikita Khrushchev over the Berlin crisis. This proved a difficult period in Kennedy's political career, as he was forced to emphasize US strength and determination during talks in which Khrushchev repeatedly threatened the president not least over the crisis in Berlin. A crisis over Cuba also emerged in 1962, with the discovery that Soviet missiles had been positioned on the island. Kennedy announced a naval quarantine on all Soviet shipments to Cuba and readied US armed forces. In October of 1962, after a number of exchanges between the US and Soviet leaders, it was announced that the Soviets would remove the missiles. Kennedy was credited with this success and gained great international support. Following the crisis, Kennedy urged other world leaders to join him in preventing any further nuclear testing in the atmosphere and on 5 August 1963, British, Soviet, and US leaders signed a tentative Nuclear Test Ban Treaty. Tragically, on the 22 of November 1963, Kennedy was shot by an assassin in Dallas, Texas. He died in hospital, shortly after the attack.

CHRONOLOGY: THE BERLIN CRISIS

1954

Eisenhower decides that maintaining the Western position in Berlin was very important, even at the risk of a war. The threat of military action, he decided, would always be a possibility.

The Soviets announce that they feel the German Democratic Republic is a sovereign state.

Walter Ulbricht declares that East Germany is the capital of the GDR.

1957

In the spring, Konrad Adenauer does not deny to the Soviet ambassador that West Germany might become a nuclear power.

1958

Ulbricht sends Khrushchev reports on nuclear weapons in Berlin. Khrushchev plots ways to strengthen the Soviet position.

10 November — Khrushchev announces that the Soviet Union would give its occupational rights in East Berlin to the GDR so that the West will have to discuss all Berlin matters with the East Germans. He also stated that talks in Bonn would only continue if no nuclear weapons were allowed in Western Germany and also only if the GDR were acknowledged as a negotiating partner.

27 November — Khrushchev sends a memo to Washington demanding that Berlin be transformed into a free, demilitarized city. If this was not agreed to, Khrushchev would make his own agreement with the GDR, giving it sovereignty over East Berlin.

December — NATO rejects Khrushchev's memo.

1959

February — Khrushchev claims to Harold Macmillan that his memo was never an ultimatum.

March — Selwyn Lloyd hints UK willing to recognize GDR.

May–August — Geneva Foreign Ministers' Conference concerning the German question.

September — Khrushchev visits Eisenhower in the US, who was willing to discuss the possibilities of a limited withdrawal of US troops. Crisis seems to have been averted.

1960

200,000 people, many of them professionals, flee from East to West Berlin.

1961

January	Khrushchev tells the West German ambassador that the problem of Berlin and of fleeing citizens must be solved within a year. Robert McNamara identifies US over-reliance on nuclear weapons.
February	Adenauer visits London.
May	The Soviets threaten to sign a separate treaty with the GDR if the problem is not resolved by October.
June	Summit between Kennedy and Khrushchev. Kennedy finds the Soviet leader intimidating.
	Macmillan says West would be willing to talk on Berlin if no Khrushchev duress.
10 June	Soviets make their ultimatum public. In response Kennedy calls up the reserves and begins arms build up.
8 July	Soviet increase in military spending.
13 July	Pentagon demands increase in US defence expenditure.
17 July	Ambassador Kohler suggests recognizing East Germany in return for guarantees on Berlin.
July	US says Berlin only defensible in nuclear war but conventional increases ordered.
	Bundy tells Kennedy that contingency planning for Berlin is too rigid. Kennedy tells Adenauer and de Gaulle that the Western Alliance has to convince the Soviet Union that it would meet its challenge over Berlin. The Alliance must demonstrate measures to increase military preparations whilst accepting the need for talks.
31 July	Kennedy admits that Khrushchev may have to stop refugees by building a wall.
August	Kennedy sends 1,500 troops to Berlin. Soviets announce the resumption of nuclear testing.
13 August	The two sides of Berlin are separated by barbed wire, followed a month later by a wall. US commanders in Berlin want a show of force in response to the building of the wall.
September	Nuclear contingency plans predicting 2.3 million US casualties.
	Rusk and Gromyko meet for talks.
October	Western and Soviet tanks face each other in Berlin.
	Khrushchev withdraws time limit for resolving the Berlin question and GDR peace treaty.

c. **The Offshore Islands Crises**

The Formosa Situation

The numerous small islands in the Formosa Strait between Mao's forces on mainland China and the forces of Chiang Kai-shek on the island of Formosa (now Taiwan) came close to producing a major war in the 1950s. They formed an essential element in the conflict between the US and communist China after the Korean War as they could serve as a stepping stone for the Nationalist Chinese to invade the Chinese mainland. On the other hand the island groups of Jinmen (Quemoy), Mazu (Matsu), and Dachen could be used to put pressure on the Nationalists and to weaken their hold on Formosa. The shelling which the communists began in 1954 was certainly tied to the issue of the 'two Chinas' and the battle over the right to control Formosa.

The Chinese island of Formosa had been taken by the Japanese in the Sino–Japanese War of 1895. During the Second World War in the Cairo Declaration signed by China, Britain, and the US stated that 'all the Chinese territories Japan has stolen from the Chinese, such as Manchuria, Formosa and the Pescadores, shall be returned to the republic of China.' This was reaffirmed at the Potsdam Conference which resolved to implement the terms of the Cairo Declaration.[32] The US thus formally acknowledged that there should be one Chinese authority governing mainland China and the islands lost to the Japanese. The fact that as a result of the civil war the rump of the defeated Nationalists were in possession of Formosa and the communists in possession of the mainland led the Americans to renege on their commitment as soon as this fact became evident in 1949. By 1950 it became clear that unless the US was to invoke military force the agreement it had made would be implemented and thus Truman placed the US 7th Fleet in the Strait of Formosa as the Korean War began.

The offshore Chinese islands are very much on the mainland side of the Straits adjacent to the Chinese coast but were controlled by Nationalist forces. The Dachen islands are nearer to Shanghai than to Taipei

and naturally of great concern to the government in Beijing while Mazu is also much nearer to mainland China and the city of Fuzhou than to Formosa. Quemoy is the southernmost group of islands and at its nearest is a mere four miles from the Chinese coast. They are all in effect like the Hebrides or the Orkneys—effectively islands in mainland China's coastal waters. The actions taken by the Chinese against the islands have been interpreted as part of the general communist attempts to test Western resolve, as part of the Chinese geostrategic quest to become the dominant power in East Asia, as the attempt to complete the unification of China, and as the need to preclude an invasion from Formosa which it was feared would be aided by American imperialists. The most probable explanation relates to Mao's determination to avoid the long-term potential threat from a rival seat of Chinese government and the need to reduce the military difficulties of having islands within a few miles of the coast in the hands of Chiang's troops. Some interpretations depend on accepting a belief by American policy-makers that the communists in Beijing were the puppets of Moscow. Not only was this not the case but we can be almost certain that in private US leaders did not believe it either. They were under more pressure in public to justify their policies in the face of political opponents and this frequently involved simplifications and stark portrayals of the unity of purpose which US enemies allegedly possessed. Hence the interference in China's internal conflict was influenced by domestic Cold War politics.

The Chinese Approach

The islands are vital for Chinese defence but above all else they, along with the Pescadores and Formosa, both islands of greater size and distance from the Chinese coast, were part of the emotive desire for the restoration of complete Chinese sovereignty. Mao saw American imperialism in terms of its efforts to undermine China by interfering in the internal affairs of its civil war. His opposition to that imperialism was not yet fully formulated into a broader regional strategy which was to be based on confronting the US and to bring conflict with the Soviet Union. In 1954–5 when the first offshore islands crisis developed, it was the specifics of the Formosa question which preoccupied Mao. The fact that the United States had, since 1950, forced the postponement of communist attempts to reclaim Formosa by force, intervened in Chinese affairs, and provided military aid to Chiang Kai-shek was both annoying and disturbing for Mao. The importance of the Formosa issue was highlighted by the ceasefire in Korea in 1953 and by military manoeuvres between the American and Formosan forces. They were followed one month later in September 1953 by an Agreement on Mutual Military Understanding. The fact that the US was now training and equipping Chiang's army, ensuring consultation over the movement of Nationalist troops and then discussing in early 1954 a Mutual Defence Treaty seemed to foreshadow a military front in the Strait of Formosa as Chiang built up troops on the offshore islands. By July 1954 Mao's response was to launch a propaganda campaign in which the importance of 'liberating' Formosa was emphasized along with the prevention of external interference in Chinese affairs.

The political offensive, related to sovereignty and outside interference more so than to the Cold War, was extended to the military sphere in August 1954 when the Central Committee of the Chinese Communist Party issued instructions for the shelling of Jinmen which began on 3 September. It was unlikely that Mao had any intention of provoking the United States but he was seeking to focus world attention on what he believed was a situation in which imperialists were opposing China's determination to reclaim full sovereignty over its territory. The shelling of Jinmen would also 'puncture the arrogance' of the Kuomintang army and enable forces to be concentrated on parts of the coast especially Zhejiang. Mao may well have been determined both to express resolve over and to make some progress towards regaining Formosa, or at least to reduce the threat from the Nationalists and their imperialist backers. On the other hand, he may have been seeking to test US resolve or to probe for any possibility of settling the Formosan question in the communists' favour

through diplomacy. Either way the issue was becoming increasingly urgent with the moves towards greater military cooperation between Taipei and Washington.

There is evidence that in the months after the Korean War's end and the beginning of the shelling of Jinmen the Chinese made considerable efforts at establishing contacts with US diplomats and offering to negotiate on the Formosan issue. It is also likely that Mao did not see any inconsistency between the strategy of friendly approaches to the US in pursuit of negotiations and the strategy of using force against the offshore islands. In a sense if the United States continued to pursue its fundamental policy of maintaining 'two Chinas', he was indicating a determination to resist and that relations could deteriorate significantly. Yet he was also offering cooperation if the Americans were prepared to stop supporting Chiang.[33]

Mao was probably looking for ways to put pressure on Chiang and the Americans as part of an attempt to end the division of China. With the Korean War only a year away and with communist China still seeking to consolidate the revolution there was little incentive to take on the US in another major conflict. The communist emphasis was on rebuilding the country economically and seeking national unity rather than regional influence. On the other hand, the links between the Americans and Chiang were very worrying. The prospect of regaining some at least of the offshore islands was another reason why Mao was keen to combine pressure and a show of force with the prospect of cooperation rather than war. This strategy made cooperation with the Soviets easy to maintain. Good relations with Moscow were still seen as important despite Mao's reservations which had been heightened by his Korean War contacts with Stalin. Hence the first offshore island crisis brought little tension between Moscow and Beijing as Khrushchev was largely informed of Chinese actions and had little reason to fear that Mao was prepared for a war with the US.

The American Approach

Much more information is available on the various approaches of US policy-makers and the difference of views between the military and civilian policy-makers. More interestingly the crises reveal the apparently different approaches of both Eisenhower and Dulles as they seemed to vacillate between moderation and compromise and an unrelenting determinism and extremism. This is in part related to the debate on Eisenhower revisionism (see Part II, Introduction) and whether Eisenhower exercised a calm, controlling influence over US policy or was a victim of indecision sometimes imposed on an irrational anti-communism. In part it is also related to the different ways Americans could conceive of the crisis and which perceptions were most useful to emphasize as a way of undermining domestic critics of US foreign policy. Was the issue of 'two Chinas' fundamentally related to the international communist conspiracy with its alleged commitment to expansion or was it related to the more traditional US battle for influence in East Asia and the Western Pacific?

The domestic factor had traditionally been important in terms of America's China policy and the roles of the China lobby and the Republican Right. It may have been these domestic influences that produced the kind of description of the crisis that figured in Dulles's first public statement after the shelling had begun. The Secretary of State referred to the 'danger that stems from international communism and its insatiable ambition'. However, the records now available reveal not only a less stark US analysis in private but also a tendency to see Chinese actions as part of its geopolitical ambitions in Asia. The US had itself long regarded influence in East Asia and the Pacific as an important component of American foreign policy before the communist takeover in Beijing. The traditional ambitions of China were often mixed with US references to China as a dangerous and ambitious state such as the analysis in NSC 5429 in December 1954. It was the mix of geopolitical rivalries with the ideological framework of the Cold War which is particularly relevant in Asia. Did the ideology force an exaggeration of the threat power political challenges represented or did they help produce them? In the American case it is difficult to believe that they did anything other than exacerbate hostility to China and to distort geostrategic perceptions. Hence the judgement of Senator Wiley that 'we can defend the US in the Formosa Straits now, or we can defend it later in San Francisco Bay.'[34]

The divisions between US policy-makers and between the Americans and their allies over China were considerable. As Eisenhower noted in his memoirs:

The administration heard the counsel of Attlee (liquidate Chiang), Eden (neutralize Jinmen and Mazu), [Democraric Senators] (abandon Jinmen and Mazu), Lewis Douglas (avoid entry into a civil war, on legal principles), Radford (fight for Dachen, bomb the mainland), Knowland (blockade the Chinese coast), and Rhee (join him and Chiang in a holy war of liberation).[35]

The main differences were between the military who were keen to fight for the offshore islands and Eisenhower and Dulles who were not. Some civilians, notably outside the administration, were happy to support the Chairman of the Joint Chiefs of Staff, Admiral Radford, who was suspected by the US ambassador in Taipei of encouraging Chiang to step up his attacks on the mainland in response to the shelling. NSC 5429 of December 1954 also urged the provision of a commitment to defend all the offshore islands as it portrayed Beijing as the key source of the challenges to American power and influence in Asia. Moreover, this strategy was part of the broader offensive Cold War strategy that was advocated especially during the early years of the Eisenhower presidency. NSC 5429 advocated an expanded programme of 'psychological activities and the use of all feasible covert means against the communists'.[36]

One cause of concern was the possible role for nuclear weapons and the crisis was instrumental in producing presidential statements about the acceptance of the use of tactical nuclear weapons in the same way as conventional ones. Nevertheless, according to one historian, in early 1955 the US came closer to using nuclear weapons than at any other time under Eisenhower.[37] There is no doubt that the president was determined to fight for Formosa: the question was whether the communist pressure on the offshore islands constituted the build-up to an assault on Formosa or not. Eisenhower, as with other alleged dominoes, was initially keen to draw the line against communist successes but then came to see the problems this would cause by letting the communists know precisely what actions the US would resist by force. How could some islands be deemed more important than others? Would it be better to keep the communists guessing?

The fact that Eisenhower declined to respond except in vague tones has been used by Eisenhower revisionists to demonstrate the president's calm, calculated, and responsible handling of a crisis in the face of communist provocation. By saying that he would only take action if the attacks on the offshore islands constituted a threat to Formosa he produced the maximum deterrence and the minimum danger of global war. At the same time he remained true to the policy of recognizing and supporting Chiang as the legitimate ruler of China. He could not ignore communist actions or abandon the offshore islands for fear of undermining Nationalist morale by creating the impression that the US was abandoning hope of restoring Chiang as ruler of mainland China.

This kind of analysis largely depends on the need to deter the Chinese from starting a major war or achieving significant gains through pressure and intimidation. If the Chinese were simply trying to produce talks on the future of Formosa and not inclined to go to war over the islands or even Formosa, then Eisenhower's strategy may have been irrelevant. On the other hand, Eisenhower can be portrayed as locked into an unreasonable and dangerous policy which did not produce unfortunate consequences because of the lack of any serious Chinese wish to go to war. Thus while there may be a good deal of truth in the Eisenhower assessment, it depends on the Western assumption about the threat of Chinese expansion (as in the Korean War) as opposed to the securing of islands close to the Chinese coast.

The First Offshore Island Crisis

As has been noted, the shelling was related to Mao's attempts to encourage the full exercise of Beijing's sovereignty and the US attempts to prevent it by increasing support for Chiang Kai-shek's claim to exercise sovereignty over the whole of China. As international cooperation increased so did the communist fears and the need to display some capacity to resist the West. This only increased US perceptions of the aggressive nature of communist regimes

and focused attention on what the Nationalists should be assisted in defending apart from Formosa and the Pescadores. As Admiral Radford urged the bombing of the mainland and the deployment of American forces on the offshore islands, Eisenhower informed the Joint Chiefs in October 1954 that there would be no retaliation and no war with China unless Formosa was attacked. In that case the US would deploy naval forces to assist in its defence and Congress would be consulted.[38]

As American military cooperation with the Nationalists developed further and the prospect of a defence treaty loomed, Mao increased the tension and the stakes. While the attention was focused on Jinmen the communists began shelling Dachen on 1 November and sunk a Formosan destroyer off the Zhejiang coast. The short-term tactical aim was probably to seize Yijiangshan, an offshore base of the Dachen Islands, without a major confrontation with the United States. On 23 November the Chinese sentenced US airmen taken prisoner after being shot down in the Korean War to terms in jail, some on the basis of espionage charges. Not surprisingly this brought no response in the form of offers to negotiate but the signing on 2 December 1954 of a Mutual Defence Treaty between Formosa and the US.

Mao's response was to have Zhou Enlai denounce the treaty and order the People's Liberation Army to consider an opportune moment to seize Yijiangshan. On 10 January the Chinese air force raided Dachen and 8 days later Yijiangshen was attacked by Chinese forces who wiped out about 1,000 Nationalist troops stationed there and threatened Dachen which was now in range of PLA fire. Eisenhower was thus forced to consider a suitable response if the morale of the Nationalists and their commitment to return to the mainland were to be maintained. The result was the Formosa Doctrine asking Congress to authorize the use of American troops to defend Formosa but not to defend Jinmen and Mazu as Dulles preferred. The resolution went through the Senate on 28 January 1955 and in effect Eisenhower was given carte blanche to take military action to defend either Formosa or the Pescadores but not to be involved with Dachen. In early February, however, the escalation of the crisis stopped. The US announced that the 7th Fleet would help the

Nationalist forces on Dachen evacuate and Mao issued orders not to fire on withdrawing troops with or without the presence of US naval forces. By April 1955 the crisis was effectively over as talks were agreed to. There was thus no confrontation or renewed Sino–American war, but Mao had re-affirmed China's 'commitment to liberating Taiwan, reduced the KMT's dangerous strongholds along the coast and tested the resolve of the US.'[39] The Americans had preserved Chiang in Formosa and demonstrated their commitment to a 'two China' policy.

Sino–Soviet Relations and China's New Anti-Imperialist Strategy

In 1955 the Chinese made efforts to produce talks that would resolve the Formosa issue peacefully, most notably at the Afro-Asian conference at Bandung in April 1955. In July eleven Americans detained in China were released and talks then began at the ambassadorial level which Beijing hoped would lead to higher-level conversations focused on the future of Formosa. This was exactly what the Americans did not want, preferring only to secure a guarantee from the communists that they would not use force against Chiang. The lengthy ambassadorial talks merely produced an agreement on the rights of citizens to return to their own countries. Mao was to become increasingly frustrated by the attempts to work with the Americans and to bring about the peaceful liberation of Formosa. Yet in July 1956 Chou Enlai proposed another period of cooperation between the communists and the Nationalists as had taken place in the inter-war years. In 1957 Taipei dismissed the concept as a ploy which aimed at the seizure of Formosa, and from the autumn of 1957 the Nationalist raids and sabotage on the Chinese coast intensified.[40]

The years 1956 and 1957 witnessed broad changes in the nature of Chinese foreign policy which were reflected in another offshore islands crisis in 1958. In part this was produced by a belief that American imperialism was determined to interfere in Chinese affairs; in part it stemmed from a different assessment of the Soviet Union that followed Khrushchev's

denunciation of Stalin in February 1956; and in part it reflected Mao's analysis of the changing international situation. The turning point in relations with the Americans over Formosa came at the end of 1956. In August Mao told the Eighth Party Congress that he was still willing to pursue friendly relations with the United States. But as the American commitment to its 'two China' policy remained firm in 1957, in September of that year with a renewed threat from Chiang, Mao stated that China's policy towards Western countries was now 'to fight against them'.[41]

Mao's visit to Moscow in November 1957 has also been described by one historian as a watershed in Sino–Soviet relations and the last time that the Sino–Soviet alliance functioned well. The background to this was the collectivization which began in 1955 and marked for Mao an intensification of socialist transformation. The denunciation of Stalin by Khrushchev, on which Mao had not been consulted, made the Chinese leader more committed to finding his own version of socialist development. At the same time the problems that Khrushchev had had to confront in Eastern Europe gave Mao food for thought about the policies of deStalinization pursued by the Soviet leader. The apparent successes of socialism in 1957, including the launch of the first sputnik, led Mao to doubt the wisdom of the whole idea of peaceful coexistence as socialism seemed to be emerging as a stronger force than capitalism. As Mao put it the east wind was prevailing over the west wind and thus it should now be possible for the communist world to 'confront the Americans with confidence in their own strength and without fearing war'. Khrushchev on the other hand, wanted 'to redirect Soviet policy towards a relaxation of tension with the West'.[42]

By 1957 Mao had decided on a far more assertive foreign policy. It may have been motivated primarily by the need to confront the Americans over their determination to maintain a 'two China' policy. It may have been based on an ideological commitment to revolution in which the growing strength of China was important both as a regional power and as a key member of the world communist movement. It may have been linked essentially to the perceived need to take the Chinese revolution further through the Great Leap Forward and a greater commitment to socialist transformation. Either way the change had an impact on relations with the US and with the Soviet Union and produced a second offshore islands crisis which was different from the first despite obvious similarities.

The Second Offshore Islands Crisis

The second offshore islands crisis began with the shelling of Jinmen on 23 August 1958. Attitudes on all sides had hardened as Mao was now committed to confrontation and Chiang more determined to cling to the hope of returning to the mainland with American help. Eisenhower and Dulles were more determined to protect Formosa from what they saw as Chinese attempts to drive the US from Asia in accordance with the well-known domino theory of one state falling to communism and precipitating a total collapse. Hence their commitment to Chiang to assist in the defence of the islands, unlike in 1954–5. As early as December 1957 Dulles told the NSC that the defence of the offshore islands was now an integral part of the defence of Formosa (over 100 miles away) and that their loss to the communists could not be accepted.[43] The islands had now become a symbol to Dulles as well as Chiang because it was overall US military sea and air power which were important to the defence of Formosa not islands adjacent to the Chinese coast.

Yet in this situation in 1958 the main American concerns were to maintain the morale of the Nationalists and their determination to resist communism by not abandoning the prospect of returning to the mainland and preserving the territorial integrity of Formosa. As Dulles claimed a few days before the shelling began, if the Offshore Islands were taken by the communists 'morale [on Formosa] would crumble and Chiang's control would be lost'. And as Eisenhower noted 'the key point is the evaluation of morale, since physically the islands would not help the Chinese Communists against Formosa.' Initially the Americans faced two major problems in the form of firstly restraining Chiang and preventing him from dragging them into a war with China; and secondly of convincing world and Western opinion that it was worth risking a major war to prevent communist China retaking islands some 4 miles

from its coast. The first scenario was more likely to arise if Chiang attacked Chinese airfields on the mainland. If the communists retaliated this would serve as the means by which he might secure the American support he needed to re-establish himself on mainland China. The second problem related to perceptions of what was at stake. The Americans saw everything in terms of assisting Chiang and maintaining the morale of the Nationalists which was vital for their 'two China' policy. But many saw the cause of defending the Nationalist claim to the islands as being unjustifiable and Chiang as a dangerous and untrustworthy partner. Moreover, there was something contradictory in both trying to restrain Chiang and prevent American involvement in a war with China, and perhaps the Soviet Union, while maintaining a commitment to the very person most likely to bring this about. Sustaining the morale of the Nationalists might eventually have come to mean endorsing the very offensive operations the Americans feared Chiang wanted to involve them in.

The Chinese were now not only confronting the Americans but prepared to go against Moscow. Khrushchev had recently embarked on what became known as his 'peace offensive' towards the Americans and had visited Beijing in July 1958. Mao may still have been nervous of war with the US but he had no time for peace offensives and did not tell Khrushchev that the shelling of Jinmen would soon begin. Instead he concentrated on acquiring more Soviet aid and establishing closer military co-operation.[44] Khrushchev, while warning the Americans against an attack on China, was now prepared to be critical of Mao over his more aggressive approach to international relations. Khrushchev now believed in coexistence and developing a more peaceful Cold War strategy. The Sino–Soviet split which was now beginning was to be characterized by moves to develop cooperation juxtaposed with disagreements and denunciations often as the international situation seemed to require one approach or the other.

One issue for the American president to face was the nature of a White House statement on the islands. With more importance attached to their defence, pressure for an unambiguous statement was greater than in 1954, but again Eisenhower refused to give a clear public commitment to the defence of Jinmen as opposed to indicating a willingness to take military action. In private a three-stage plan was devised in which the US would convoy ships resupplying Nationalist forces. Then if a major assault was mounted on any of the islands the Americans would join in their defence and, finally, if China extended the action to international waters 'appropriate' action, would be taken which almost certainly would involve the use of tactical nuclear weapons favoured by the Joint Chiefs.[45]

Despite the more confrontational position taken by Mao in terms of the global struggle between communism and capitalism, it seems unlikely that he was prepared for a major confrontation with the US. Yet the perceptions of the Americans did not indicate an appreciation of this possibility. The emphasis was on preventing or deterring the communist capture of the offshore islands because it represented the alleged communist challenge aimed at driving the US from Asia and which was epitomized by the possible destruction the pro-Western regime of Chiang Kai-shek in Formosa. Moreover, this anti-communist stance over the importance of a a few offshore Chinese islands was justified with reference to the Munich crisis of 1938 even though neither Eisenhower nor Dulles were keen on a war with China. By September Eisenhower was seeking a way out and considered an offer to Chiang to withdraw his forces in exchange for an amphibious capability to make an assault on the mainland more feasible. The only bright spot was the effectiveness of the convoys which, by the end of the month were bringing sufficient quantities of supplies to Jinmen.[46]

The stalemate at the end of September did not alter the American position of using direct military intervention in publicly unspecified circumstances to preserve Chiang and the 'two China' policy. In private these circumstances were defined as preventing the offshore islands falling to the communists. Yet the prospect of nuclear war remained equally unpalatable and Eisenhower in particular continued to look for ways out. This was made easier by the Chinese proclaiming a seven-day ceasefire on 6 October provided the Americans agreed to stop convoying supplies which they did. Dulles then pressured Chiang to announce that the liberation of China would be achieved principally by the application of Sun Yat-sen's[47] three principles of nationalism, democracy, and socialism/social well-being rather than by the use of force. As in 1954, talks offered by the Chinese at ambassadorial level were taken up by the United States and the crisis was virtually over in October. Even though the communists resumed the bombardment on 25 October this indicated the islands' importance as propaganda and political symbols rather than serious Chinese military intent. Tension was further reduced by Chiang agreeing to remove 15,000 men in November 1958.

The Aftermath

The Sino–American confrontation in 1958 also had an impact on Sino–Soviet relations. The lack of consultation with Moscow worried Khrushchev, not least because of the nuclear implications, while Mao believed the Soviets were lessening their commitment to the defence of China. Although Mao did not criticize Soviet policies towards the US in the immediate aftermath of the crisis in June 1959, the Soviets told the Chinese they were abandoning the programme of nuclear cooperation. From this point on it has been argued, as the Great Leap Forward ran into difficulties, Mao began to see the Soviets as more of a handicap than a benefit in the development of China and the pursuit of revolutionary goals at home and abroad. Therefore he began to distance China from the Soviet Union while still preserving the basic commitment to the alliance. Then came the border incidents with India in the summer of 1959 directed against the Soviet's main non-aligned contact and could have produced a bigger rupture had it not been for Mao's weak domestic position. It was Mao's stronger position at the time of the Sino–Indian War in 1962 that finally produced an unbridgeable gap between the two former communist allies.[48]

The Sino–Soviet split featured ideological disputes which had implications for domestic and foreign policy, particularly with regard to relations with the Western world and non-aligned nations. The latter had implications for straightforward power political influence especially in Asia as well as for the development of Cold War policies. The relationship between domestic weakness and the commitment to a cooperative relationship with Moscow was evident in Chinese policy and the progress of the split. For the Soviets the need to avoid being dragged into a confrontation with the Americans was a key factor in their relationship with Beijing. The offshore islands crises could be seen from the Chinese perspective as originating in the civil war and the fundamental struggle to achieve a united China to which Chiang presented a threat irrespective of ideological differences.

The role of the Cold War in American policy during the offshore islands crises is clearer and unequivocally influenced more by Cold War considerations than traditional state goals in terms of vital interests. The second crisis was extremely revealing of American attitudes which were hard-line in political Cold War terms. There was a determination for reasons of morale and credibility to defy the communists however absurd or trivial the economic and strategic issues at stake. At the same time it is evident that leading policy-makers in the US were reluctant to risk a major war which might well involve the use of tactical nuclear weapons. Mao was also exercising restraint, despite his desire to confront the Americans, as he was still unprepared for a major military confrontation with the nuclear power of the US. The crisis should be compared to the Cuban missile crisis (see Chapter 7, D) for despite the differences the American conceptions of the

geostrategic importance of the islands in relation to security provides an interesting example of how the US failed to consider the perceptions of the other side.

One interesting question is the role of national security. Then and now the concept of US national security being dependent on the preservation of an alien military presence on an island 4 miles from China and thousands of miles from the US has been stated without any sense of the absurd. Nor do Western writers normally attempt any analysis of what might constitute Chinese national security by a comparison based on similar criteria. What can be stated very simply in terms of understanding the Cold War is that the islands, which the Americans were reluctantly prepared to defend with nuclear weapons, had no military or strategic significance. Their significance was as symbols representing the preservation of a political and ideological position that was under challenge. The particular policies followed by the US on the basis of this general perception required the preservation of the Nationalists' position and their determination to return to the mainland. The irony was in providing them with support while persuading them not to act. It is worth speculating as to whether, subconsciously or not, the development of the link to the preservation of the US position in Asia and the Western Pacific was to justify the importance attached to the island's symbolism or whether it produced it.

D. **The Cuban Missile Crisis**

Origins

The crisis which resulted from Khrushchev's decision secretly to install intermediate and medium-range nuclear missiles in Cuba in 1962 has frequently been portrayed as the only time that the world stood on the brink of nuclear war between the superpowers. The latest research has tended to downplay the risk of war, but the crisis continues to engender controversy despite detailed records of the American decision making process becoming avail-

able. Explanations of why Khrushchev decided to risk the deployment of surface-to-surface missiles which could threaten cities in most of the United States have varied while, many in the United States have retained a mix of outrage and incomprehension. Some analysts have located Khrushchev's motives in the situation in Cuba where the Castro regime appeared to be under threat from an American determination to bring it down by covert means or even by an outright invasion. Others have seen Khrushchev's motives stemming from his penchant for bullying and intimidation and his perception of Kennedy as a weak president whom he could take advantage of to further the strategic ambitions of the Soviet Union. A third explanation stems not from the local or the international situation but from the domestic situation in the Soviet Union which may have forced Khrushchev to be more adventurous in order to appease domestic critics. None of the interpretations are mutually exclusive and all may have acted as influences on the Soviet leader.[49]

The first idea that Khrushchev was concerned about the threat to Castro is undoubtedly true to some extent. As the only country to have turned to communism in this period Castro's symbolic importance to the credibility of the communist world was considerable and Khrushchev could ill afford the deposition of the Cuban leader. The damage to the Soviet claim to leadership of the alleged progressive socialist countries would be great, particularly as this was under threat from communist China in the early 1960s. Moreover, Khrushchev knew that the CIA was hatching a number of plots to take Castro's life and may well have been aware of US plans (unapproved) for an invasion of the island. However, if the Soviet leader was merely concerned with the defence of the Cuban revolution, it is difficult to see why MRBMs and IRBMs served a better defence than tactical nuclear weapons or even conventional forces.

The military/strategic value of these weapons remains a matter of dispute as it did at the time when the Executive Committee was established to advise President Kennedy on how best to respond to the installation of the missiles. The American military saw them as giving the Soviets an important advantage, which changed the strategic balance in their favour. The secretary of defence, Robert McNamara, believed they had no real effect on the strategic balance, but gave the Soviets the *appearance* of a significant gain, a view which the president seemed largely to share. It is likely that Khrushchev was attracted by the idea of appearing to gain greater military strength relative to the United States particularly as he was desperately concerned to cover up the military and economic weakness of the Soviet Union. Such things were crucial in terms of convincing the rest of the world that the Soviets, as demonstrated by the success of sputnik, were in

fact outstripping the United States because of the superiority of socialism. Khrushchev was particularly concerned about apparent Soviet weakness in nuclear terms and the reality was less important than the perceptions of it. This was particularly the case for those Americans who had been arguing with the Democrats in the 1960 election that there was a missile gap encapsulating Soviet superiority. There was indeed an enormous missile gap but one in favour of the United States, which was duly indicated by the U2 spy flights and finally revealed by the assistant secretary of defence, Roswell Gilpatric, in August 1961.

Khrushchev was almost certainly embarrassed by this revelation even though it was done in a relatively unobtrusive manner. From Khrushchev's perspective not only was it bad Cold War news for the world to learn how far the Soviet Union was behind the United States in missile production, but the Soviet leader was under considerable domestic pressure. Those who wanted a more hard-line assertive policy towards the West, which was certainly the line being taken by the Chinese, were keen to increase military expenditure and were generally unhappy about the adoption of peaceful coexistence with the West. In addition Khrushchev, rather like Gorbachev, was keen to restructure the ailing Soviet economy, particularly the agricultural sector, by reducing military expenditure. His hope had been that by using Berlin as a pressure point on the West he could gain concessions that would be regarded as Soviet achievements and a justification for his foreign policy. Unfortunately, his Berlin policy had led to the passing of two Soviet deadlines without changes in the status quo in Berlin or in the position of East Germany.

In these circumstances there was a desperate need for a successful Soviet initiative which would silence domestic critics by enhancing the Soviet position as a great world power and leader of the communist movement. The temptation of attempting to score a nuclear success over the Americans was therefore enormous even if it was more apparent than real. Moreover, Khrushchev could justify his Cuban policy by the fact that the Americans had similar Jupiter missiles in position right on the Soviet doorstep in Turkey. On these grounds it might have been reasonable to conclude that the Americans would find it hard to take a strong line in opposition to the arrivals of missiles in Cuba.

And then there was the final point concerning the idea of Kennedy as a weak and uncertain president lacking in experience and guile. Such perceptions could have been based on Kennedy's handling of the Bay of Pigs crisis in 1961 (see Chapter 6, C) just months after he took office. The Bay of Pigs was an ill-conceived plan to launch an invasion of Cuban exiles to depose Castro. Kennedy was quickly faced with the choice between using American air power or accepting the failure of the assault and he chose the latter with the consequent sacrifice of the exiled forces. Subsequently, Kennedy had been some-what intimidated by Khrushchev at their summit meeting in Vienna in June 1961 and rather than give unconditional support to the anti-communist forces engaged in a civil war in Laos had sought a compromise. Rather than sending the 10,000 troops requested by the Joint Chiefs of Staff to Laos, Kennedy sent Averell Harriman to negotiate an agree-ment at the May 1961 Geneva Conference. Why therefore should the American president react by confronting the Soviets over nuclear weapons in Cuba? After all when in July 1960 Khrushchev had spoken of Soviet missiles perhaps one day being used to defend Cuba he had received no response, unlike over Berlin where the United States had always made its position clear.

The Crisis

The crisis began in earnest on 16 October 1962 when Kennedy and his advisers first saw U2 pictures of Soviet missile sites on Cuba that had been taken two days before. However, the immediate origins of the crisis and the explanation of the installation's impact on the Americans goes back to April 1962, the date when Khrushchev decided on their deployment. The deployment was not only to be done in secret, but the Americans were subsequently lied to about Soviet intentions, which was naturally disturbing to the Kennedy administration. What made the situation worse were the leaks about the concerns of some, like the CIA Director John McCone, that produced a series of questions and accusations regarding the role of the Soviets in Cuba.

It was only two days before the president examined the photos of the site that McGeorge Bundy had asserted there was no likelihood of the Soviets acquiring a major offensive capability in Cuba. This was the last statement by the administration based on Khrushchev's denying the Soviets had any intention to install surface-to-surface missiles and equip Cuba as an offensive base, which the president had warned against.

When the reality was revealed, whatever US assessments of the strategic or symbolic importance, the sense of resentment was enhanced by an aware-ness of Khrushchev's deception. Not surprisingly Kennedy's initial reaction was along the lines that the United States would have to do something in response. The determination to take some action was reinforced by Kennedy's sense of his own domestic position and the belief that he was vulnerable to accusations of weakness in terms of anti-communism and American defences. The president from the start was also convinced that the crisis was connected to the situation in Berlin where the Soviets held the military cards and could well be using the missiles in Cuba as a further means of putting pressure on the Americans in Berlin. At all events the question now was what kind of response the United States should make.

The essential requirement of any action was that it would lead to the removal of the missiles, even though Kennedy and McNamara believed their presence did not alter the strategic nuclear balance. One option was an air strike to take out the missiles but the USAF would not guarantee 100 per cent success and this raised the question of whether the missiles had nuclear warheads in place. In the event we now know that they *did* and such warheads could in fact have been fired at US cities. Decision-makers at the time, some of whom changed their minds over the days, were not of course to know this. Other military options were a nuclear attack on, or a full-scale invasion of, Cuba. Those members of the executive who had been in power during the days when the US enjoyed a nuclear monopoly tended to believe that the nuclear advantage held by the Americans in 1962 would enable them to get their demands for the withdrawal of the weapons met. Yet if the Soviets refused, then some form of military action seemed inevitable. It was Robert McNamara on 18 October who came up with the idea of a quarantine on further Soviet shipments to Cuba as a means of exerting pressure for the removal of the missiles.

Such action would have no basis in international law but it would place the Soviets in a difficult position where they might have to be the first to use force to beat the naval quarantine. When the first ExCom vote was taken on 18 October, 11 members were in favour of the quarantine option while 6 voted for an air strike. Three days later opinion had hardened with 9 members in favour of the air attack and only 6 for quarantine. By then, however, Kennedy had given up on the idea of an air strike, and when he addressed the American people on the 22 October it was to tell them that in order to halt the offensive military preparations in Cuba he had ordered a strict quarantine on the shipment of military equipment to Cuba. If necessary further military action would be taken and the US armed forces had been instructed to prepare for any eventuality. He would regard any military attack on the United States from Cuba as an attack by the Soviet Union that would require a full retaliatory strike. The quarantine would begin on the morning of 24 October.

The United States response was essentially dictated by the need not to look weak in the face of Khrushchev's challenge to the status quo in the Western hemisphere. Accepting the missiles as a *fait accompli* would give the impression of growing Soviet strength and increasing American vulnerability, although as Kennedy had said it mattered little whether nuclear warheads were fired on the United States from 50 or 500 miles. For domestic and Cold War reasons Kennedy had to respond. The method he initially chose was the most reasoned and restrained of the ones available to him. Khrushchev initially responded by denouncing the interference with vessels on the high seas as unjustified, and an action which constituted a threat to peace, but Kennedy had wrested the initiative away from the Soviet leader. When the crunch came some Soviet ships stopped and one tanker carrying a non-military cargo was allowed through. However, the following morning Kennedy received another message from Khrushchev accusing the president of banditry and pushing mankind to the brink of

nuclear war. In it he stated that the Soviet government could not give instructions to the captains of Soviet vessels to obey the instructions of American ships blockading Cuba.

As Khrushchev continued to refuse concessions on the missiles, the American press published a column by Walter Lippmann in effect suggesting a trade-off between Soviet missiles in Cuba and American missiles in Turkey. Such a deal while eminently sensible had the disadvantage of appearing to give concessions to the Soviets. On the other hand, as Kennedy realized, to start a nuclear war for the sake of preserving some obsolete missiles in Turkey might not be the most popular action either. The world continued to wait as ships bound for Cuba were intercepted on 26 October and the US navy forced six Soviet submarines to the surface but there were no signs of the missiles being removed from Cuba. On 27 October Kennedy received another letter from Khrushchev in which the Soviet leader accused the US of threatening him with war, which he believed could only be done by lunatics or suicides. More importantly Khrushchev suggested that if the US would guarantee not to invade Cuba and recall its navy, the question of armaments would disappear because if there was no threat they would simply be a burden to maintain. Almost immediately after the contents had been digested by the ExCom news came to the White House of another letter from Khrushchev, this time a public one. The Soviet leader was now offering a deal: he would remove the missiles from Cuba if the United States did the same for those in Turkey and pledged not to invade Cuba.

The United States faced a new difficulty because if they accepted the public deal Khrushchev would have gained the removal of the missiles in Turkey. On the other hand, if the deal was rejected what could the United States reasonably do if Khrushchev went ahead with developing the missile sites with material already in Cuba? Would it mean that an invasion of Cuba would have to be launched as the Joint Chiefs were suggesting? The president then came to two key decisions. The first was that the US could not invade Cuba to remove missiles that they could have had taken out by agreeing to remove obsolete weapons from Turkey. The second was to follow McGeorge Bundy's suggestion of replying to the first private letter from Khrushchev rather than to the second public one. In other words the basis of the public deal would be that the Soviets would remove the missiles if the US gave a guarantee not to invade Cuba. Khrushchev would not have gained anything at the expense of the Americans but could save face by claiming to have protected Cuba from invasion.

This in fact formed the public basis of the agreement although it was buttressed by a private commitment made to the Soviet ambassador by the president's brother, Attorney-General Robert Kennedy. This involved an assurance that the Jupiter missiles in Turkey would be withdrawn in the near future. This commitment could not be part of a public deal because of how it would reflect on the United States which emerged from the crisis having apparently been successful in resisting Khrushchev's brinkmanship. It appeared to have stood firm and prevented any advantages accruing to the Soviets whether apparent or real. Yet while Kennedy resisted the options which presented the greater threat to peace he also engaged in brinkmanship in order to avoid the impression of weakness or conceding any advantage to the Soviets. In terms of credibility and the assertion of US nuclear power in the face of a Soviet challenge, the United States in a sense had preserved its superiority and made clear that Khrushchev's intimidation was essentially bluff and bluster.

The risks that were run, and indeed the reasons for running them, have probably both been overstated. At the end of the day neither leader was likely to have ordered a major nuclear strike for the sake of what was more apparent than actual strategic benefits. Yet there were risks and not just from those in Washington who were prepared to be more assertive than the president. There was the danger of local commanders seizing the initiative and dragging their superiors into a conflict they would have wanted at all costs to avoid. Not only did the US navy clash with the Soviets but a local commander in Cuba, acting on his own authority, shot down an American U2 on 25 October. In addition, General Tommy Power, the head of the Strategic Air Command placed his forces on DEFCON 2 and prepared for immediate action without consulting the White House. The flaws in the decision-making process and the chain of command could have led to a

nuclear clash because of the level of brinkmanship and despite the politicians' desire to avoid any such conflict.

Consequences

The consequences of the crisis were felt at both local and international levels and had a profound impact on the future nature of the Cold War. The impression that a catastrophe had only just been avoided made the need to prevent the Cold War turning into a hot one all the more urgent. Arguably, the Cuban missile crisis made the United States accept for the first time that no longer should American foreign policy aim at the eventual removal of the Soviet Union or even seek to prevent the Soviets being fully accepted as a great-power. It was now more a question of learning to cope with a world in which the United States was unable to exercise hegemony and adapting to a world in which the United States had to coexist with communism. Peaceful coexistence certainly now meant more to both Moscow and Washington and efforts were made, like the hot line between the Kremlin and the White House, to prevent any more direct confrontations in which it was difficult for either side to back down. None of this made the winning of hearts and minds in the less developed world any less important but now the battles had to be fought more carefully. For the Americans there was a hope that in the future such less developed world confrontations could eventually be removed if the status quo was accepted by the communists, but this was never likely given that the status quo would only serve to maintain American hegemony.

As to the practical reasons for the fears provoked by the Cuban crisis, namely the existence of growing numbers of nuclear weapons, it is tempting to argue that after 1962 there began the process to control and limit them starting with the Test Ban Treaty in 1963 (see Chapter 9, A) and leading via the 1968 Non-Proliferation Treaty to SALT 1 in 1972 (see Chapter 12, B). However, other lessons were undoubtedly drawn at the time. For the Americans the crisis reinforced the value of nuclear superiority whereas for the Soviets the need to achieve nuclear parity became a *sine qua non* of equality with the

Americans in order to avoid another humiliating climbdown. Thus while in the early 1960s it was the Americans that led the way in producing more armaments in the late 1960s the Soviets outpaced them in the acquisition of arms. More weapons rather than fewer remained the order of the day even if this could be justified in the name of deterrence which must at best remain questionable. Whether this was responsible for the disastrous long-term decline of the already weak Soviet economy is a moot point. More immediately Khrushchev's position within the Soviet Communist Party and government was certainly weakened, although his removal from power would take another two years and follow the Chinese acquisition of nuclear weapons.

With regard to the local situation the effect was not what the Americans would have desired. In effect they had placed the Cold War goal of appearing as more powerful and credible than the Soviet Union on a nuclear issue above the Cold War goal of preventing the spread of left-wing revolutionary ideas in the Western hemisphere. By guaranteeing not to remove Castro by overt means they had limited their ability to cut off the source of communist propaganda and assistance. Of course that did not stop some of the covert efforts to remove Castro under the Mongoose programme but it could no longer be backed up with any overt involvement of US forces. As a result while Castro was furious with Moscow for agreeing to the removal of the weapons he probably emerged slightly more secure as a result.

Whether the changes after the Cuban missile crisis were sufficient to warrant describing 1962 as the end of the first Cold War remains contentious, but the relations between the two superpowers certainly entered a new phase. Even if the idea of peaceful coexistence was now generally accepted within the US, the aftermath of the crisis was not the first time that the United States and the Soviet Union

---

Fidel Castro (1926–   )

Castro was born in Biran in the year 1926. He went on to be educated at a Jesuit school and completed his legal studies at the University of Havana. Graduating with a law degree in 1950 he began work with the poor. In 1953, Castro attempted to overthrow the Cuban dictator, Batista. The attempt failed and Castro was imprisoned but his movement would be known as the 26th of July Movement and achieve lasting recognition. Upon his release in 1955 Castro organized more guerrilla campaigns and after another unsuccessful revolt in 1956, Castro and his men fled into the Sierra Maestra mountains and began a three-year-long guerrilla campaign. In 1959, Castro finally overthrew Batista and became the leader of a socialist government. The United States were quick to enforce economic sanctions and also instigated the Bay of Pigs invasion. This merely reinforced Castro's desire to look to the Soviet Union for help and support. Cuba's dependence on the Soviet Union eventually led to the Cuban missile crisis, as Khrushchev was able to install missile bases on Cuba. Castro later created a new Constitution in which he took the role of president and secretary-general of the Communist Party and commander-in-chief of the army. Castro refused to liberalize Cuban society and criticized the reforms of Mikhail Gorbachev. This resulted in an increasingly isolated position for Cuba in the international community.

---

can be regarded as having made an effort to improve relations. Nor was it the time when consideration was first given to the advantages of peaceful coexistence. However, the issue after 1962 was whether the existence of nuclear weapons had combined with the realization that in the climate of unrestricted competition new approaches *had* to be adopted to the Cold War and Soviet–American relations. If so, these would have to be based on a greater acceptance of the other side as a power with whom coexistence was desirable.

NOTES

1. Gregory Mitrovich, *Undermining the Kremlin. America's Policy to Subvert the Soviet Bloc, 1947–1956* (Cornell University Press, Ithaca, 2000), 123, 127.

2. FRUS, 1952–54, II, Pt II (Dept. of State, Washington, DC, 1979), Record of Discussion at NSC Special Meeting, 31 Mar. 1953, 266–7.

3. Former Head of the Psychology Strategy Board until its dissolution in Sept 1953 and a member of the Operations Coordinating Board.

4. Mitrovich, op. cit. 128–9, 133.

5. Ibid., 134–40.

6. Mitrovich points out that this was not apparent from the sanitized version of the Task Force reports declassified in 1991 but emerged in a synopsis of the reports declassified in 1996.

7. US National Archives, Dept. of State Records Lot Files 66 D 148. Records pertaining to State Dept. participation in OCB and NSC 1947–63, box 129. Report by Task Force C 16 July 1953, quoted in Scott Lucas, *Freedom's War: The US Crusade against the Soviet Union 1945–1956* (Manchester University Press, Manchester, 1999), 179; Mitrovich, op. cit., 141–2.

8. FRUS, 1952–4, II, Pt. II (Dept. of State, Washington, DC, 1979) NSC 162/2, 30 Sept. 1953, 491–514.

9. Ibid.

10. James Bamford, *Body of Secrets* (Arrow, London, 2002), 35–8.

11. Scott Lucas, op. cit., 190.

12. Blake was an SIS agent whom the Soviets recruited in 1951 after the dismissal of the notorious spy Kim Philby who betrayed Western agents in the Eastern bloc and alerted the Soviets to the Berlin tunnel.

13. Christopher Andrew and Vasili Mitrokhin, *The Mitrokhin Archive* (Allen Lane, Penguin Press, London, 1995), 521; David E. Murphy, Sergai A. Kondrashev, and George Bailey, *Battleground Berlin* (Yale University Press, New Haven, 1997), Ch. 11.

14. FRUS, 1952–54, II, Pt. II, (Dept. of State, Washington, DC, 1979) NSC 5440, 13 Dec. 1954, 806–22.

15. Mitrovich, op cit., 147.

16. NSC 5440, op. cit., 806–22.

17. Report on US Policy for the Exploitation of Soviet Vulnerabilities in Box 18 of the Papers of the Office of the Special Assistant for National Security Affairs, NSC Series 1952–61, Briefing Notes Subseries, White House Office Files, Dwight D. Eisenhower Library, cited in Mitrovich, op. cit., 161

18. FRUS, 1952–4, II, Pt. II (Dept. of State, Washington, DC, 1979), Memo by the JCS, 17 Dec. 1954, 828–30.

19. Ibid,

20. FRUS, XIX, 1955–7 (Dept. of State, Washington, DC, 1985), NSC 5501, 7 Jan. 1955, 24–9, emphasis added.

21. David G. Coleman, 'Eisenhower and the Berlin Problem 1953–54', *Journal of Cold War Studies* 2 (2000), 13–17.

22. Vladislav Zubok and Constantine Pleshakov, *Inside the Kremlin's Cold War from Stalin to Khrushchev* (Harvard University Press, Cambridge, 1996), 195.

23. Coleman, op. cit., 25, 32, citing NSC 5401, 29 Dec. 1954.

24. Marc Trachtenberg, *A Constructed Peace. The Making of the European Settlement 1945–1963* (Princeton University Press, Princeton, 1999), 253.

25. Wilfred Loth, *Overcoming the Cold War* (Palgreave Macmillan, Basingstoke, 2002), 47–50; Zubok and Pleshakov, op. cit., 194–8.

26. John Lewis Gaddis, *We Now Know Rethinking Cold War History* (Clarendon Press, New York, 1997), 143–4.

27. Michael R. Beschloss, *Kennedy v Khrushchev: the Crisis Years 1960–63* (Faber & Faber, Boston, 1991), 216, 221, 224.

28. Ibid.

29. Loth, op. cit., 60–1.

30. Beschloss, op. cit., 223.

31. David E. Murphy, Sergei A. Kondrashev, George Bailey, *Battleground Berlin CIA v. KGB in the Cold War* (Yale University Press, New Haven, 1997), 371–3; Zubok and Pleshakov, op. cit., 253–5.

32. Cited in Gong Li, 'Tension across the Taiwan Strait in the 1950s. Chinese Strategy and Tactics' in Robert S. Ross and Jiang Changbin (eds), *Re-examining the Cold War. US–China Diplomacy 1954–1973* (Harvard University Press, Cambridge, 2001), 142.

33. Zhang Bajia, 'The Changing International Scene and Chinese Policy towards the United States, 1954–1970' in Ross and Changbin, op. cit., 50.

34. Ronald W, Pruessen, 'Over the Volcano. The United States and the Taiwan Strait Crisis, 1954–1955', in Ross and Changbin, op. cit., 80; Stephen E. Ambrose, *Eisenhower the President 1952–1969* (Allen & Unwin, London, 1984), 239.

35. Cited in Ambrose, op. cit., 244.

36. Pruessen, op. cit., 94–7.

37. Ambrose, op. cit., 231.

38. Ibid., 213.

39. Gong Li, op. cit., 148–51. Ambrose, op. cit., 231.

40. Ibid., 151–6.

41. Ziang Baijia, op. cit., 50–2.

42. Odd Arne Westad in the Introduction to Westad (ed.), *Brothers in Arms: The Rise and Fall of the Sino–Soviet Alliance 1945–1963* (Stanford University Press, Stanford, 1998), 18–20.

43. Robert Accinelli, ' "A Thorn in the Side of Peace": The Eisenhower Administration and the 1958 Offshore Islands Crisis' in Ross and Changbin, op. cit., 112.

44. Odd Arne Westad, 'The Sino-Soviet Alliance and the United States' in Westad (ed.), op. cit. 176.

45. Accinelli, op. cit., 114, 118.

46. Ibid., 120–8.

47. Sun Yat-sen was the first Chinese Nationalist leader who died in 1925 and who is often referred to as the father of modern China.

48. Westad (ed.), op. cit., 22, 28.

49. The following is a synthesis of the ideas from many of the vast array of articles on the Crisis and a large selection of important articles can be found in the Bibliography.

CHRONOLOGY: THE CUBAN MISSILE CRISIS

1961

May	Summit between Kennedy and Khrushchev, during which Kennedy was intimidated by the Russian leader due to the failure of the Bay of Pigs invasion and the American president's refusal to act.
August	Missile gap between the US and Soviet Union is revealed by the assistant secretary of defence, Roswell Gilpatric.

1962

April	Khrushchev decides on the secret deployment of missiles to Cuba.
16 October	Crisis begins as Kennedy sees U2 pictures of Soviet missiles on Cuba, taken 2 days before. A discussion on possible responses ensues, with the emphasis on action.
18 October	Robert McNamara has the idea of a quarantine on Soviet shipments to Cuba. The idea of air strikes is also considered. In the first ExCom vote on the same day, 11 vote for quarantine and 6 for air strikes.
21 October	Second ExCom vote and opinions have changed: 9 vote for air strikes and 6 for quarantine.
22 October	Kennedy informs US citizens of the missile presence in Cuba and also of his quarantine on Soviet shipments. He also warns of possible military action.
24 October	Quarantine begins on Soviet shipments to Cuba.
25 October	U2 shot down over Cuba.
26 October	Ships are intercepted and Soviet submarines are forced to surface.
27 October	Kennedy receives private letter from Khrushchev. Contents state that if the US promise not to attack Cuba and withdraw its navy then the issue of armaments would disappear. On the same day a public letter arrives from Khrushchev announcing that if the US remove its missiles from Turkey and promise not to invade Cuba, then the Soviet missiles would be withdrawn from the island. This emphasized the danger of the large powers being forced into a conflict they wished to avoid due to brinkmanship tactics and a poor chain of command. Kennedy decides to reply to the first letter buttressed by a private guarantee from Robert Kennedy that the obsolete Jupiters will be withdrawn.

8 Collapsing Empires: The Cold War Battle for Hearts and Minds, 1953–1963

A. The End of the French Empire

The war between the French and the Vietnamese nationalists led by Ho Chi Minh, the influential communist, became a long and bloody affair which received substantial American financial backing from 1949. Despite this it ended with much controversy and calls for military intervention with the French defeat at Dien Bien Phu in May 1954. The Geneva Conference which followed saw agreement on the neutralization of an independent Laos and Cambodia, whilst Vietnam was divided in two, along the seventeenth parallel, with French forces regrouping in the South before their eventual withdrawal and a communist government being set up in the North under Ho Chi Minh. The Americans were not happy about the partial loss of a former French

possession to communism and what was worse was that the division between North and South was not meant to last: under the terms of Geneva, all-Vietnamese elections were meant to reunite the country within two years. Such elections however were never held, mainly because their outcome was mostly likely to be a victory for Ho. Instead, as French power disintegrated, the United States backed the South Vietnamese government of Ngo Dinh Diem in its refusal to deal with the North and got involved in what became the most bloody of post-colonial conflicts.

In Africa the French approached their empire after the Second World War in fundamentally different ways from the British. Black Africa had been the only part of the empire loyal to the 'true' French republic, and had enabled de Gaulle and the Free French to emerge as an important source of opposition to the collaborators in Vichy. Empire and its preservation was thus totally tied up with French greatness and world power status. Moreover, unlike in Britain where those on the Left were thinking about which colonies might follow the Dominions, the Popular Front government in Paris during the 1930s saw reforms not as leading the empire to self-government but tying it closer to metropolitan France. This signified what was soon an important fact of French political life in the 1940s that those on the Left as well as the Right were committed to an imperial future. Yet by the early 1950s the French Union had ceased to attract Africans by its offer of associating them with the exercise of power in metropolitan France (see Chapter 3, B). The issue was thus becoming whether the French Union would survive or whether and under what conditions the French would accept a transfer of power in Africa.

The Loss of French Indo-China and the Start of American Involvement in Vietnam

Ngo Dinh Diem had been appointed prime minister of South Vietnam by the French-selected head of state, Emperor Bao Dai, in June 1954, when the days of French rule were already numbered. Born in 1901, the son of a mandarin official, Diem had already served as a regional governor and, in 1932–3, as a government minister. But then he had retired to private life, exasperated by France's failure to reform its methods of colonial rule. Diem became increasingly reclusive but in 1945–6 his anti-communist convictions were hardened when he was imprisoned for a time by the Viet Minh. In 1950 he went into exile, living for some time in the US where his pious Catholicism helped him establish links with, among others, the Kennedy family. By late 1954 the US government, unhappy with the prospect of an all-communist Vietnam, saw Diem as a potential saviour. In particular, the CIA counter-insurgency expert, Edward G. Lansdale, fresh from defeating a rebellion by the communist 'Hukbalahup' move-

ment in the Philippines, took it upon himself to groom Diem as an ally, whilst also providing the South with advice on covert military operations. Diem appealed to Americans because his background made him both anti-French and anti-communist, so that he could pose as a defender of South Vietnamese independence from both colonial rule and Marxist-Leninism. The only serious doubt about him concerned his ability to face up to dissident elements. But in March–May 1955, aided by Lansdale, he proved his worth on this front by ruthlessly securing control of Saigon, driving out armed groups who were opposed to him. In October 1955 he was able to depose Bao Dai and establish a republic, being approved as president by a 98 per cent majority in a rigged poll. To US satisfaction, he also refused to prepare for all-Vietnamese elections on the grounds that his government had not been party to the Geneva Accords.

Diem's overwhelming triumph in the 1955 referendum disguised the fact that South Vietnam was a complex society, in which his support was severely restricted, a legacy partly of French colonial tactics of 'divide and rule'. His military victory in May 1955 was essentially over three groups, each with its own private army: two were Buddhist sects, the Hoa Hao and the Cao Dai; the other—and the most serious threat—was a criminal group, the Binh Xuyen who effectively ran the police force in the capital, Saigon. The victory gave Diem some respite from serious opposition, as did the withdrawal of the last French troops in September 1956. A 'mixture of monk and mandarin, he was honest, courageous and fervent in his fidelity to Vietnam's national cause' but he was also 'distrustful of everyone outside his family, he declined to delegate authority, nor was he able to build a constituency ... beyond his fellow Catholics.'[1] Buddhist opposition to his Catholic-dominated regime continued and even intensified, as Northern Catholics fled to the South in the wake of Geneva and were shown favouritism in terms of landholdings and official appointments. Catholics were always a minority in the country numbering up to one-and-a-half million, out of a total population of 13 million, in the mid-1950s, and they were identified by many with French colonial rule. Other groups in the country, particularly ethnic minorities such as the Chinese, Cambodians, and Montagnards (the last living in the sparsely populated highland areas) were also alienated, in their case by Diem's practice of favouring the majority Viets. Neither did the president try to tackle the problems of government corruption, grasping landlords, and peasant debt which had become widespread. Instead, as with religious and ethnic issues, he tended to compound problems, by relying on rich landlords (who controlled about three-quarters of the land) and government officials for support. In 1957, Lansdale left South Vietnam, disappointed that Diem had failed to reform the country on liberal democratic lines which the US would have welcomed. Instead the president, personally aloof from his people, insisted on an authoritarian form of rule, appointed members of his family to leading positions, and especially relied for advice, not on American representatives, but his corrupt brother Nhu, who dreamt up the vague doctrine of 'personalism', as justification for a system dominated by one individual.

Despite the weaknesses of his regime, Diem seemed to succeed until 1959 in limiting the threat from the Communist Viet Minh and South Vietnam's position was far from hopeless. His determined campaign after 1956 to arrest or execute any suspected communists helped reduce their active numbers markedly, as well as claiming thousands of innocent lives. Alongside the defeat of the 'Huks' in the Philippines (1946–54) and of the Malayan communists (1948–60), South Vietnam seemed part of a pattern of Western victories against leftist subversion in South-East Asia. However, Diem never succeeded in completely destroying the Viet Minh and neither was the Vietnam situation without costs for the US, even if they avoided a direct commitment of troops there. The Eisenhower administration had provided about $1 billion worth of military aid to South Vietnam by 1961, as well as a lesser amount of economic assistance, and the first American casualties occurred in July 1959, when two military advisers were killed. Furthermore, there were already signs that American involvement carried its own problems: Diem became ever more reliant on US money, the circulation of which created inflationary pressures and oiled the wheels of corruption among officials. The Army of the Republic of Vietnam (ARVN) was resentful of the patronizing and bullying approach of many Americans, and

US advice took the form, not of anti-insurgency expertise (which was what was needed), but of help in creating a 150,000 strong conventional army that could meet an all-out North Vietnamese invasion (which never came). The ARVN was in any case poorly led, largely by Catholic officers promoted more for loyalty to Diem than for ability, and was another element identified in the popular mind with French rule. Neither did its supposed loyalty prevent one group of officers from attempting a coup in November 1960, suggesting that not all was well, even at the heart of Diem's regime. This was doubly worrying because the ARVN was about to face a resuscitated communist campaign, backed by the North.

Ho Chi Minh and North Vietnam, 1954–1961

Ho Chi Minh, who had led the Viet Minh to victory over the French, accepted the idea of elections at the 1954 Geneva Conference as the best way to remove French troops from the North. It was in northern Vietnam that the colonial war had been at its most intense, where the physical destruction was greatest, and where he wished to secure control first. But, supported by the USSR and China, he expected that North and South Vietnam would soon be united, especially since it seemed improbable in 1954 that anyone like Diem might emerge, who could forge a separate state in the South. Reunification was an economic as well as a political imperative because the North had a higher population, yet the South the most productive areas for growing the staple food, rice. In 1954–6, therefore, Ho pursued a peaceful strategy for securing the reunification of Vietnam, based on the fulfilment of the Geneva Accords, and concentrated on setting up a classless society and a centralized government in the North. The latter did not prove an easy task, and it was accompanied by considerable violence. He succeeded in collectivizing agriculture, but only by wiping out anyone suspected of being a 'landlord', a process which involved executing or imprisoning tens of thousands of people. Many were not real landlords at all (the real ones had often joined the refugee trail to the South), but fell victim to local feuds or the overenthusiasm of Ho's officials. Another practice was the extensive use of forced labour to help the reconstruction efforts. Small wonder that more than a million people fled to the South in the mid-1950s. In November 1956 such policies had become so unpopular that there was serious peasant unrest in Ho's native province of Nghe An.

The events in Nghe An were salutary in a number of ways: they led Ho's government to backtrack on certain policies, especially collectivization; they created the impression that life in the North was no better (and for some was far worse) than in the South; and they underlined the need to strengthen communist rule in the North before beginning any serious armed campaign to reunite the country, now that it was clear that peaceful reunification was unlikely. In any case, the ability of the Viet Minh to mount such a campaign was limited in 1956. Although they had numbered perhaps 100,000 in the South in 1954, and had controlled large swathes of the countryside, most communists had moved to the North in the wake of the General Accords and those who remained were mainly prepared for self-defence, not major offensive operations. One Viet Minh leader from the South was Ho's deputy, Le Duan, who was increasingly exasperated at the situation. A limited guerrilla war was revived in 1957, mainly marked by assassinations of government officials, but by 1959 there were perhaps as few as 5,000 active Viet Minh in the South, repressed by Diem's secret police and demoralized by the apparent lack of support from the North. There was still widespread sympathy for the communists among the peasantry, to whom they promised land reform, lower taxes, and an end to corrupt officialdom. But such support was latent not active. Furthermore, despite religious, ethnic, and political opposition to Diem, this too was difficult for the communists to exploit. Buddhists, criminal gangs, and would-be liberals were naturally unsympathetic to Marxism.

Despite this unpromising situation, in January the 15th plenum of the Vietnamese Communist Party decided to back military action and revolutionary violence in the South, meeting Le Duan's pleas and hoping to expose the weakness of Diem's regime. In part this was linked to the greater Chinese commitment to support revolutionary movements throughout Indo-China. Little was initially forth-coming in practical terms for the Vietnamese and their 'momentous decision did not lead immediately to war ... attention was instead directed towards strategic and logistical preparation'.[2] The foundations of a supply route to the South—the 'Ho Chi Minh Trail'—were laid and Viet Minh attacks on local officials, government offices, and the army were intensified, so that some country areas again came under communist rule, especially in the Central Highlands. Only in 1960 did the Chinese begin to back the armed struggle in South Vietnam. One way in which Diem responded was to draw some peasants into fortified 'agrovilles', but these were hated by the peasantry who were torn from their ancestral villages. In any case, the number of 'agrovilles' was limited: more significant in alienating the peasantry—the bulk of the population—from Diem was his destruction of village autonomy in creating a centralized state. Even the French had respected village rights. By September 1960 the North Vietnamese leadership was convinced that a revolution was in sight in the South, a conviction probably helped by Ho's success in creating a strong, united North Vietnam in the wake of the 1956 troubles. Ho's Politburo now presided over a stable, one-party state, financially supported by both the USSR and China, with a (largely) centrally planned economy that was approaching self-sufficiency. Industrial production was expanding, although from a very narrow base. The communists could also be confident that, in aiming above all at national reunification, they had one cause which appealed to most Vietnamese whilst paradoxically, by promising to respect ethnic minorities, they could win sympathy among the Chinese and Montagnard minorities. On 20 December 1960 Ho's government finally confirmed the primacy of the armed struggle in the South over consolidation in the North, when it set up the National Liberation Front as a government-in-exile for the South, designed to win the widest possible political sympathy there, including non-communist groups, but under communist leadership. 'After six years of trying to reunify the country through political means alone, the (North Vietnamese leaders) accepted a combination of political and military struggle movements to overthrow the Diem regime.'[3] The NLF quickly expanded its number of recognized sympathisers in the South to over a quarter of a million, although only about 20,000 were Viet Minh activists and even fewer could be termed guerrillas. Also, in February 1961 it formally created a military wing, the People's Liberation Armed Forces, although Northern leaders hoped that it might be possible to undermine Diem and create a coalition government (as a step to communist domination) without a drawn out, costly conflict. These important developments made Vietnam a challenging situation for the incoming American administration of John F. Kennedy.

Kennedy, the Viet Cong Menace, and the Fall of Diem, 1961–1963

Kennedy arrived in office as a critic of the supposed weakness of the Eisenhower regime in the face of the communist menace, keen to resist the 'wars of national liberation' (about which Khrushchev first publicly spoke on 6 January 1961, promising Soviet support and specifically mentioning Vietnam) and already personally allied to his fellow Catholic, Ngo Dinh Diem. Viet Cong activity continued to intensify, and Kennedy immediately came under pressure to increase the 685 military advisers who Eisenhower had despatched to South Vietnam. Despite the evident discontent with Diem and the genuine desire of Vietnamese nationalists for reunification, it was easy for Americans to see the NLF as a puppet movement of North Vietnam, itself seen as part of a monolithic communist menace which would spread throughout South-East Asia if it was not resisted. The crisis in Laos actually dominated US thinking about South-East Asia at this time however, and its peaceful outcome in 1962, when a neutralist coalition was formed, suggested that an armed conflict involving the US was not inevitable. Kennedy, with plenty of problems elsewhere in the world, was warned soon after coming into office, in a report by Edward Lansdale, about the weaknesses of the anti-communist position in South Vietnam. Diem's failure to reform, together with the unreliability of the ARVN, led the US to follow a dual policy of providing greater military assistance to South Vietnam while trying to win Diem over to the wisdom of change. Discussions of military requests to send US combat troops led to Kennedy opposing

any mention of the possibility of such a policy and to subsequent speculation that he would never have got embroiled in the later conflict. The aim was to contain the communists militarily in the short term while broadening political support for the South's government in the long term. By such means Kennedy apparently hoped to prevent any communist advance without the need for direct US involvement, a policy which essentially built on Eisenhower's, albeit with a greater commitment of advisers and money.

By the end of 1961 there were 3,200 US military advisers in Vietnam and the Defense Department had effectively replaced the State Department as the prime factor in policy-making on Vietnam. A number of senior officials in the administration, including Walt Rostow (Deputy National Security Adviser) were becoming sympathetic to a deployment of American combat troops. Although Kennedy always ruled out the combat option his support for Diem remained undiminished, despite the latter's continued failure to carry out land reform or legalize opposition groups. By late 1963 US personnel in South Vietnam had climbed to 16,000. The 1961 Bay of Pigs fiasco and the need to compromise on Laos, may have strengthened the desire to 'win' in Vietnam and such alternatives as negotiation with the communists, or making further aid to Diem conditional on reform, were not properly considered. Arguably, the Americans were already becoming trapped in a situation where their anti-communism tied them to an unpopular regime fighting an unwinnable war. Even those who feared an escalation of the US commitment, like George Ball, the under-secretary of state, did not speak out strongly at this time. In any case, during 1962, over-optimistic reports from US representatives in Vietnam, created the impression that the 'Viet Cong', as the communists were now described by Americans, were being contained. One development, backed by the US at this time and inspired by British policy in Malaya, was the US 'strategic hamlets' programme which, like Diem's 'agrovilles', tried to move peasants away from communist influence. The programme at least showed a recognition of the need for a proper counter-insurgency programme, winning the peasantry to the government side, but it was carried out overhastily and proved as unpopular with the peasants as had the 'agrovilles', although its failure took some time to become evident. Even the celebrated battle of Ap Bac in January 1963, when 1,400 heavily armed ARVN troops were held at bay by about 350 Viet Cong, failed to destroy American optimism about the war and in 1963 Kennedy was hopeful that the US presence in Vietnam might soon be reduced. The weaknesses of Diem's position—his reliance on repression rather than reform, an ill-disciplined badly led army and widespread alienation of the countryside—were not yet fully exposed by a Viet Cong movement which still numbered only several thousand guerrillas. Nor was the extent and nature of the South Vietnamese support for the communist-led resistance movement perceived accurately by American leaders preoccupied with communism as the explanation for anti-Western revolts.

US confidence in Diem was finally, fatally questioned in mid-1963 not by any communist action but by dissatisfaction among the Buddhist majority. There were widespread disturbances in May following a new law which gave the national flag precedence over all other symbols, even religious banners carried during celebrations. Then, on 11 June, in front of Saigon press cameras, one Buddhist priest burnt himself to death as a protest against Diem. Several similar cases followed, increasing doubts about Diem's leadership among the American media and further emphasizing his failure to reform. The situation was made worse by remarks from his sister-in-law, Madam Nhu, that she was quite happy to have monks 'barbecue' themselves. By mid-August, Diem felt so threatened that he introduced martial law, as well as raiding Buddhist pagodas in key cities, imprisoning hundreds. The US was shocked and, in Washington, the issue of replacing Diem was seriously considered. There was a major problem with any such step: he had no obvious successor. But his opponents among the army were confident, by late October, that the US government would welcome his replacement. Certainly the American ambassador, Henry Cabot Lodge, did not discourage this belief and on 1 November after trying to flee, Diem was captured by an army unit and murdered along with the much despised Nhu. Kennedy, who had known that a coup was possible, but who did not want Diem dead, was stunned by the news.

Only three weeks later Kennedy too was assassinated, leaving the problems of South Vietnam to be tackled by his successor, Lyndon Johnson. The question of what Kennedy would have done about Vietnam, had he lived, is one which continues to exercise historians. Some are sympathetic. William Post, for example, believes that the President 'would not have bombed North Vietnam, and would not have committed US ground troops' in the way Johnson later did. But even this claim is qualified by the admission that there was an 'absence of clear direction to Kennedy's policy'.[4] The President had spoken privately on several occasions of his desire to reduce US personnel levels in South Vietnam; yet, on the very day he died, he was planning to give an address which confirmed his commitment to fighting communism in South-East Asia. The contradiction is probably best explained by Gary Hess who argues that by late 1963, Kennedy 'was thinking on two levels: the commitment to South-Vietnam was integral to US national security, but the price of upholding it seemed less controllable.'[5] He did not live long enough to focus upon, or resolve this dilemma and, as another study of Kennedy's policy concludes, he 'bequeathed to Johnson a failing counter-insurgency programme and a deepened commitment to the war in South Vietnam.'[6] From this commitment Johnson found no easy escape.

The Collapse of French Rule in Morocco and Tunisia

In North Africa the French faced, as in Indo-China, a number of nationalist movements that grew in strength after 1945 and were causing major problems by 1953–4. The existence of French settlers created additional political problems in dealing with them, even for those ministers who came to accept the idea of self-government if not independence. The region, particularly Algeria, had significant numbers of French settlers along the coastal plain many of whom were competing for menial jobs with the local population. In addition, while Morocco and Tunisia had originally been French protectorates that were the responsibility of the Quai d'Orsay and became associated states of the French Union, Algeria provided a much bigger constitutional and

Ngo Dinh Diem (1901–1963)

Diem was born into an important Roman Catholic family in South Vietnam in 1901. In the years before the Second World War he was a civil servant. In 1954, Diem became the prime minister of South Vietnam after having previously refused any position in Bao Dai's government. A year later he became the president of his country after controlling the 1955 referendum which abolished the royal family. The United States supported Diem but there were problems within Vietnam due to his favouring Roman Catholics over the Buddhist population. This, combined with his arbitrary and dictatorial rule, resulted in much dissatisfaction. Opposition to Diem also increased by 1960 as his attempt to root out opponents in the civil war in the South became less effectual with help to the rebels coming from the North. In 1963 Diem was murdered during a takeover by unhappy generals, in which the CIA was involved, and to which the American government gave tacit approval.

emotive problem. Technically part of metropolitan France, and like French départements, it was technically the responsibility of the French Ministry of the Interior. This produced, amongst certain French elites, an absolute refusal to give up a part of French soil to nationalists who began a campaign of violent resistance in November 1954. Thus strong Gaullists and former members of the resistance, including Georges Bidault who had been both prime minister and foreign minister under the post-war Fourth Republic, were prepared to abandon loyalty to de Gaulle and to the French state over the issue of Algeria.

The events in Sétif, Algeria in 1945 which involved serious loss of life with over 100 settlers massacred, followed by large-scale reprisals, seriously damaged relations between the European and Muslim communities. When the hoped for reforms never materialized the already significant nationalist groups throughout North Africa became more and more disillusioned with French promises. As the 1950s began the French were facing increasingly radical nationalists. In Algeria these were grouped in the Front de Libération National (FLN); in Morocco the nationalist focus was provided by the Istaqlal

(Independence) Party, founded in 1943 and supported since 1947 by the Sultan of Morocco, Mohammed V; and in Tunisia the Neo-Destour (New Constitutional) Party was created as early as 1934 although, like many nationalist groups it first sought better links with France and easier access to French citizenship. Its leader was Habib Bourgiba who after 1949 returned to Tunisia to lead the campaign for independence.

The French hope was to head off any political reform which would undermine the French Union or damage the privileged position of the French settlers. In Morocco, Sultan Mohammed V came to seek the renegotiation of the 1912 Treaty of Fez, which defined the protectorate status, in order to gain greater influence for himself, as opposed to the traditional pashas and caids, and then to end French controls. Troubles began when the proposed reforms of General Juin were revealed by 1951 to be a sham. The Istaqlal used demonstrations and riots, most notably in Casablanca in 1952, and attempted to exploit American and international concern to demand realistic reforms leading to self-government. In the face of these pressures and the inscription of Morocco on the security council agenda, the French position became increasingly difficult. Their attempts to introduce local assemblies with equal representation for settlers and the indigenous population were patently inadequate but consistent with avoiding any commitment to the devolution of local power which would have implications for the future of the French Union. They were those in the Quai who had never believed that the French Union would gain international acceptance and the writing was on the wall for the centralization it embodied from the early 1950s. The need for American support at the UN may well have been a decisive factor in influencing the eventual French acceptance of meaningful self-government by 1954.

Paying lip-service to political change which would temporarily satisfy the Americans had ultimately to be followed by meaningful actions to start the process of change. In Morocco this was more easily said than done, as in September 1953, when traditional dislike of the Sultan's commitment to the Istaqlal led to the armed followers of the reactionary leader El Glaoui preparing to overthrow the Sultan. The French, rather than be seen as lacking the will to maintain law and order, took action themselves and deposed Mohammed V.[7] As in many other cases nationalist opposition to European rule was not uniform and this complication led to greater progress to self-government in cooperation with the French being made in Tunisia. Pierre Mendès-France, the new radical prime minister in June 1954, was instrumental in this acceptance of self-government just as he sensed the impossibility of successfully continuing the war in Indo-China. In July 1954 he promised Tunisia full internal self-government, but by then the demand was for independence and control over foreign and defence policy. The French were now simply reacting to events. To make matters worse an armed insurrection had broken out in Algeria in November 1954, and although by the following year El Glaoui was prepared to accept the return of Mohammed V in Morocco, there was no respite from French difficulties. After Minister of Overseas France, Pierre-Henri Teitgen, had begun its preparation in 1955, the passing of the enabling law (*loi cadre*) to permit the constitutional changes that rendered the French Union inoperable was achieved in 1956. Tunisia and Morocco gained independence the same year and there was now the prospect of a meaningful process of transferring power in France's Black African territories. Algeria, however, was a different kettle of fish.

Algeria

The crisis in Algeria became an acute crisis for the French Republic and one which was to threaten the very basis of civilian government. Unlike the other territories in North Africa, the abandonment of Algeria was seen by many establishment figures as akin to the abandonment of Brittany or any other French *département*. The war itself had become a brutal and very bloody affair with atrocities on both sides and emotions were running extremely high. In 1957 fierce fighting in the Muslim quarters of Algiers was accompanied by the extensive use of torture. The French army could win control of the urban areas, albeit at significant cost, but it was in no position to extend that control into the mountainous rural regions despite the deployment of 400,000 troops. The war also assumed an important inter-

national dimension, not least because Gamal Abdul Nasser was supplying the rebels and the French could not seal the Algerian borders. When the Tunisia border town of Sakiet was bombed in 1958 the French also incurred widespread international condemnation. As the burden of the war fell more heavily on metropolitan France and opposition to it grew, the army in Algeria became increasingly frustrated. Believing that they were winning the military battle and concerned with another loss of political will they joined with a settler protest in May 1958 that resulted in the proclamation of a Committee of Public Safety in Algiers. A military coup in Paris was becoming a real possibility when agreement was reached on the return of the French wartime hero Charles de Gaulle with increased presidential authority.

In a famous outdoor speech de Gaulle told a cheering mass of settlers *je vous ai compris*, but in fact he had understood what he believed were more important issues pertaining to the future of France. Always confident in his ability to both understand and personify France, de Gaulle looked to the continued transformation of the country with a view to playing a more important world role, not on the back of an increasingly burdensome empire, but through a reinvigorated Europe under French leadership. Moreover, he also understood that the Algerian settlers, when France last faced a crisis, had, to a man, supported the collaborationist regime of Marshall Pétain not de Gaulle's Free French. There could be no reason for de Gaulle being reluctant to sacrifice the interests of such people in order to further the true interests of France if this required escaping from the millstone of Algeria. Once this could be accomplished the economic modernization of France could be continued and foreign policy refocused on Europe and building links with West Germany.

The Algerian embroglio like many other key elements in decolonization became something from which de Gaulle had to find the best way out. It was not a question of planning a strategy but of finding one which would be a acceptable to nationalist leaders and to at least some of the French governing elite. In 1959 de Gaulle spoke of an Algerian Algeria as something in line with the self-government idea embodied in the *loi cadre*, but it was February 1961 before secret negotiations began with the FLN. One obstacle in the way of any agreement to end the fighting was the French army, or at least some of its former generals who launched a failed coup in April 1961. Another was the French determination to obtain a special regime for the Sahara in the south of the country which was rich in oil and gas. In the end it took over a year before French concessions secured an agreement in which the settlers were to be given three years in which to choose whether or not to remain in an independent Algeria. If they left, their goods and capital could go with them while the French retained their atomic test site in the Sahara and the naval base at Mers el Kebir for limited periods. The war had cost hundreds of thousands of lives and nearly brought down the French government on two occasions. The loss perceived by some as the loss of a part of France was another seminal moment in French history with its bitter internal divisions at all levels of French society and politics.

Black Africa

By 1953 the divisions between French and British colonial policy in Black Africa were still starkly evident as the French idea was to avoid political change leading to self-government. The French Union continued to define the constitutional process whereby French overseas territories were to be incorporated into the single and indivisible French Republic and the Black African empire's importance for metropolitan France's regaining world power was still generally accepted by both the Right and the Left. Divisions were soon to appear with the Algerian War and colonial policy became an important distinguishing feature between parties of the Right.[8] In Black Africa the wars in Indo-China and Algeria were not, however, to be repeated except in the Cameroon where the Union des Peuples Camerounais launched an armed struggle in 1956.

The prospect of fighting a major war in Black Africa seemed to be largely irrelevant by 1958 when de Gaulle was committed to the giving up of Algeria. Therefore the struggle for independence in Africa was concluded quickly between the establishment of the French Community in 1958 and its dissolution in 1960 when independence was largely conceded.

From the French side the years until de Gaulle's return to power began the process, formalized in 1956 where by power was devolved at the local level to 'responsible' African leaders. For the Africans the obtaining of this power was the inevitable result of their abandonment in the early 1950s of the policy of associating themselves with the power exercised in Paris by French politicians. By 1956 the French were effectively following the same path as the British even if their expectations and planning remained somewhat different.

The *loi cadre* encouraged the development of territorially based political movements and the weakening of the French regional and semi-federal structures in place in French West and Equatorial Africa. Critics of the process refer to the Balkanization of West Africa and the determination of the richer territories, like Ivory Coast, to divest themselves of any sacrifices inherent in regional structures with supranational powers. In fact there were important changes undermining the very idea of African unity, which was embodied in the Organization of African Unity, established in 1963, even before the African states themselves had been formally created with the end of French colonial rule. It is true that from the French perspective the idea of centralization in the French Union was replaced by the goal of creating structures which would tie the former overseas territories closer to France. Hence the French determination to include their African territories in the economic provisions of the Treaty of Rome so that the creation of the European Common Market would not disadvantage them. Hence the need, particularly with the end of the French Empire, to distinguish the struggle for political independence from the achievement of economic independence.[9]

There are obviously links between the two and it has been argued that the economic changes in France enabled political changes to accompany economic developments in the empire.[10] Jacques Marseille points to the importance of the modernization of French industry and claims that this process weakened the role of small businesses who benefited from protected empire markets. Once greater competitiveness became more necessary, as French trade and industrial expansion took place, smaller less efficient or cost-effective enterprises, traditionally empire supporters, were displaced by those with equivalent economic ideas to the political ideas on France's future being developed by de Gaulle.

For de Gaulle the problems of Black Africa in 1958 were much less than those of Algeria. The Constitution of the Fifth Republic effectively committed Black African territories to a new federal structure but on the principle of decentralization. Africans would elect leaders to the French Community whose president, de Gaulle, would retain responsibility for foreign and defence policy and large areas of economic policy. Leaders would emerge from the territorial assemblies constituted in 1957, after the *loi cadre*, and membership of the Community would be determined by the individual territories on the basis of plebiscites. Those in favour would be the recipients of continued French aid and assistance while those choosing independence would be left to fend for themselves. While most countries were prepared to join, Guinea, where the radical former trades unionist Sékou Touré had established a large following, the voters chose independence by a large majority. Once de Gaulle had tried and failed to prevent the establishment of a viable state by withdrawing French equipment and administrators he realized that French ties could best be preserved by a series of bilateral agreements with suitable African leaders. Consequently in 1960 most French African territories secured new Constitutions as internationally sovereign states within the Community. As the French Community was, like its predecessor, never intended to be a community of equals, pressure

Sékou Touré (1922–1984)

Touré was born in 1922, the son of a Muslim peasant farmer. He completed his education at a French technical school and following his expulsion worked at a variety of different jobs. He first caught the attention of the public in his younger years during his time in the Labour Union, where he became Secretary-General. He was very critical of colonialism but became Mayor of Conakry (the capital of Guinea) in 1956 and Guinea's deputy to the French national assembly. In 1958, when Guinea gained its independence under Touré, he became its first president. His leadership of the sole political Party, the Parti Démocratique de Guinée marked him as a radical Leftist. During his presidency, Touré received aid from the USSR but at the same time tried to improve relations with the Western world. He died in 1984 and a week later a military coup took over governance and banned the PDG.

for formal independence was bound to build up quickly. Between June and November 1960 seven new states came into being and the final vestiges of the federation inherent in French West Africa also disappeared. What was left was a mix of French education and culture, military agreements based on the stationing of the modern day equivalent of rapid reaction forces, and economic assistance programmes.[11] The *loi cadre*, for good or ill, had failed to produce a Commonwealth and arguably left a different perspective to that of the British on the meaning of great power status.

B. The Crises in the Congo and Angola

The Zenith of the Cold War in Black Africa

The two crises which began in Central Africa in 1960 and 1961 illustrate the importance that was attached to the Cold War in Black Africa at the turn of the decade. They both involved the Americans in situations where the French and the British were playing

minor roles and roles generally at odds with what the Americans desired. The situation in the Congo raised issues of neocolonialism, important European economic interests, Soviet involvement, regional conflict with racial overtones, and the importance of Cold War issues for Africa as a whole. In Angola Portuguese–American relations over the future direction of colonial policy combined with strategic issues centred on the continued American use of the Portuguese airbase in the Azores. It was an unprecedented mix of Cold War and colonialism. As has been seen, in the US the questioning of covert operations and propaganda directed at the Soviet bloc in Europe, combined with the increasing importance of the less developed world as European rule was ending to shift the focus of Cold War attention more to Asia and Africa. The idea that the Cold War was a battle for hearts and minds was indicated by an examination of the Congo and Angolan issues and their importance for many members of the Kennedy administration.

To some extent there was a battle between those who still saw Western Europe as the mainstay of the Cold War front and the important economic partner or competitor with the United States. Others like Chester Bowles and the assistant secretary of state for African affairs, G. Mennen Williams, believed that the US could not afford to alienate African opinion. It was certainly the case that as in the 1940s and 1950s in Europe there was an exaggeration of Africa's importance in both economic and political terms. It took a few years for the Americans to realize this but it does not lessen the Kennedy administration's commitment to the less developed world or to the ideals of freedom and self-determination even when other interests were at risk. Cynics might argue that progressive policies regarding Black Africans were easier to endorse and brought greater political dividends in the US than progressive policies towards Afro-Americans. Or it might be argued that there was no genuine concern for the welfare of Africans but merely a sign that they were important pawns in the latest Cold War game. Either way the fact that such policies were followed at all provides a contrast with many other American administrations.[12]

The Congo Crisis

The crisis in the Congo, which sprang from the speed with which the Belgians transferred power to a large, unprepared colony lacking trained personnel and indigenous administrators, began on 8 July 1960 just over a week after independence. The lack of any provisions for political transition or the effective functioning of public services without trained

Belgian personnel made the loss of discipline in the army and subsequent rioting more serious. Rivalries between different ethnic groups in Leopoldville province and Luluaburg added to the difficulties of maintaining order which was only restored by reinforcements of Belgian troops. The initial crisis was then compounded on 11 July when Katanga province under Moshe Tshombe proclaimed its independence from the government of Patrice Lumumba in Leopoldville. The Belgian presence led Lumumba to appeal first to the UN for assistance in what his government termed a state of war with Belgium and then to the Soviets.

UN troops soon arrived in Leopoldville but without a mandate to end Katangan secession which Lumumba and his important African supporters, particularly Kwame Nkrumah in Ghana, saw as vital for a united Congo. In fact the UN secretary-general Dag Hammarskjöld began to liaise with the United States, not the Congo government, on the best way of dealing with the crisis while keeping the Soviets out of the region. They could not, however, stop the supply of Soviet aid or remove the risk of direct Soviet military involvement or assistance. The longer the Belgian troops stayed the greater the risk of increasing Soviet influence as there was the danger that Belgian or other European forces would continue to assist what would be perceived as a blatant form of neocolonialism based on Katangan secession. The issue was crucial for the newly independent African states and those colonies which were about to gain independence. Kennedy, if not Eisenhower, was determined that Africa should now be at the centre of American Cold War policy and the allegiance of the newly independent states, such as Nkrumah's Ghana, was deemed crucial. The concern within Africa about the possible collapse of the Congo or the continuing secession of Katanga was based on a determination that the gaining of independence should not be seen as a failure. If Lumumba could not unite the country and Katanga was allowed to secede, then the transfer of power would be seen as a failure. On the other hand, the success of Lumumba was seen by the Americans as opening the door to pro-Soviet or other radical left-wing groups in Africa.

One obvious way to ease the difficulty was to eliminate Lumumba. On 5 September 1960 President

Kasavubu, in a move of dubious constitutional legitimacy, dismissed Lumumba from his position as prime minister, but Lumumba then set up a rival government until on 14 September General Mobutu announced a temporary army takeover. Mobutu dismissed both governments and the parliament and placed Lumumba under house arrest in the light of the growing violence in the Congo. The number of UN troops in the Congo, including those from Ghana and Guinea who backed Lumumba, was now growing. The long-term issues were whether they would be used to end Katangan secession and restore the territorial integrity of the new state and whether or not Lumumba would remain as the elected leader of a reunited Congo. The latter outcome was not acceptable to the Americans who in September 1960 split with Nkrumah over this issue. When Nkrumah attended Khrushchev's speech in the UN the Eisenhower administration portrayed Nkrumah as being pro-Soviet rather than pro-Lumumba. The reality was that for Eisenhower the idea of a radical African leader in the Congo was more than problematic and in fact completely beyond the pale. The new Kennedy administration did not have to deal with the uncomfortable fact of Lumumba being for many Africans the legitimate Congo leader and was more able, with an eye to the future Cold War position of the West in Africa, to pursue a more pro-African independence policy. The short-term problem in the Congo was the maintenance of order and governmental authority as Lumumba's supporters, led by Antoine Gizenga, were firmly established in Stanleyville. Along with the capital in Leopoldville, and the Katangan capital Elizabethville there were thus three rival power centres with an additional secessionist movement based in South Kasai and ethnic divisions and violence in most provinces.

As acrimonious disputes occurred in the General Assembly and the UN secretary-general, Hammerskjöld, worked closely with the Eisenhower administration to pre-empt Soviet involvement in the region, the divisions were made worse by Lumumba's escape and recapture. The problem was that the government in Leopoldville lacked the legitimacy which it could only get through the reconvening of parliament which would offer opportunities to Lumumba and his supporters. As the United States devised various plans for the liquidation of the Congo's first leader, in January 1961 Lumumba was moved to Katanga. At some point during or after the journey he was beaten to death by his captors, although his death was not announced until 13 February. The United States was thus relieved of the Lumumba problem but still had to find and legitimize a Congo leader who would be acceptable to African opinion. They settled on Cyrille Adoula, a former trades unionist, and when parliament was reconvened on 19 July 1961 CIA bribes effectively ensured that Adoula was elected prime minister.

The first priority for the new leader was to reunite the country, which above all required the ending of Katangan secession. Unfortunately this was easier said than done despite the support of the new Kennedy administration. For one thing the Belgians, the French, and the British did not share American confidence in the future stability of a united Congo run from Leopoldville. Any regime led by Lumumba's supporters was seen as capable of again appealing to the Soviets and irresponsible enough to provide opportunities for the spread of radical left-wing ideas. A radical regime would affect significant European financial interests in the copper-rich Katanga represented by the Union Minière du Haut Katanga and its subsidiaries. The British were also nervous of the political risk of alienating the right-wing Empire supporters in the Conservative Party who were keen to preserve white-dominated regimes particularly that in the Central African Federation (see Chapter 8, D) which had close links with Moshe Tshombe. Therefore the last thing they wanted to see was a beacon of pro-Western anti-communism removed from power by United Nations forces consisting largely of Asian and African troops operating with American logistic support. As time went on the British became more keen to escape from any responsibility for Central Africa which might involve them in a racial conflict. The Americans with their determination to end Katangan secession were seen as stirring up trouble that would threaten British economic interests and cause conflict involving the Central African Federation whose leader, Roy Welensky, was supplying arms to Tshombe via Northern Rhodesia.

In September Adoula announced that Gizenga would become vice-premier in the Leopoldville government, and UN forces engaged Tshombe's troops and mercenaries in Elizabethville. A ceasefire was announced the following month but by then the agreement between Adoula and Gizenga had collapsed and the former's supporters were becoming increasingly incensed by the prime minister's failure to end Katangan secession. The Americans were determined to bring the two governments together and reunite the former Congo territory. If they failed, and independence was seen to have failed, the aim of ensuring that power should be transferred peacefully to new African states as part of the Western world would have received a serious blow. Ironically, the British were less concerned with that kind of successful outcome in the Congo than with being dragged into a civil war which could spread to British territories especially after a rebellion broke out in neighbouring Angola in the spring of 1961. In November, as renewed incidents took place between the white mercenaries making up Katangan forces and the UN and other Congolese troops, a UN resolution was passed authorizing the use of force to remove the mercenaries.

Hammarskjöld was now dead, killed in a plane crash in September 1961, and had anyway been less receptive to US desires once the threat of direct Soviet involvement was lifted. His replacement, U Thant, was now threatening to use force on a large-scale basis, while Gizenga was waiting in Stanleyville as a potential radical successor to Lumumba. In this situation the British feared that law and order could completely collapse if Tshombe was attacked by UN forces, while valuable economic assets would be lost and the white community endangered even if the war did not spread. They therefore preferred the preservation of Tshombe as a form of stability rather than the use of UN force to remove him if negotiations ultimately failed between Adoula and Tshombe. However, in December 1961 the Kitona accords brought success and agreement on the reincorporation of Katanga into the new state of Zaire.

Unfortunately Tshombe, playing for time, declined to take any steps to implement the agreement and the supporters of Adoula became more and more disillusioned. The only bright spot for the Western powers was the collapse of the Stanleyville regime in January 1962. As the British, like Tshombe,

took refuge in inaction, the Americans began to support the idea of sanctions and to put pressure on the Union Minière to withhold tax revenue from the Katangan government. The Kennedy administration was so determined to bring about reunification that in the face of Tshombe's refusal to act they eventually decided to instigate the use of UN force. In this situation at the end of 1962 the UN were in the hands of the Americans who alone could provide the necessary support for the ground forces who finally forced Tshombe to flee in December 1962. The UN military operation was in effect illegal under the terms of the UN resolutions and the British still remained opposed to the use of force. Kennedy, however, had support from the Belgians in the form of Paul Henri Spaak, and a reunited Congo symbolized the US commitment to African independence and the attempt to win the support of the emerging African states.

The triumph was short-lived and like elsewhere, particularly in Latin America, the idealistic commitment displayed by the Kennedy administration either did not produce the desired long-lasting effects or was soon changed under the Johnson and Nixon administrations (see Chapter 11, A) In the Congo Tshombe returned as president of the reunited state in 1964, whereupon the fighting resumed and renewed intervention by Belgian troops fuelled African resentment. It was only when General Mobutu returned to power in 1965 with a military coup backed by the Americans that stability returned, not under the banner of freedom and independence, but as a result of brutal repression. It was characteristic of changing American policy in the less developed world where the importance of promoting support for the West was replaced by imposing values of the Western world whether indigenous people liked them or not. In this situation the Cold War became more about the values of capitalism than the spread of democracy.

The Angolan Crisis

Over the border from the Congo in north-western Angola a rebellion broke out in the spring of 1961 which has been associated with the Union of Angolan Peoples (UPA) established and led by Holden

Roberto. Roberto had come to prominence though the Union of the Peoples of Northern Angola (UPNA) which was based on Bakongo nationalism and on the idea of restoring the old Kongo kingdom. The UPA was an attempt to establish an Angolan nationalist movement as Roberto appeared at the 1958 All African Conference in Accra. It was, however, just one of the fifty or more Angolan political movements operating from Leopoldville when the Congo became independent in 1960. Those in the UPA seeking to make alliances were initially opposed by Roberto who was determined to establish himself as leader, which he only achieved in 1961.[13] The fact that the UPA then, unlike its main rival the Popular Movement for the Liberation of Angola (MPLA), became more committed to armed struggle, means it is easy to interpret the revolt in Northern Angola as stemming from the growth of nationalism through the UPA.[14] However, there is evidence from missionaries in the region that the outbreak of violence was more spontaneous and due less to political organization than to the economic grievances associated with peasants being removed for forced labour and unable to tend to their own crops, particularly coffee. In any event it is likely that the UPA benefited from being able to develop and further politicize the rebels.

The anti-communist Roberto was a frequent visitor to the US and met with President Kennedy. His ideological opponents, the MPLA, did not initially favour violence, until the revolt effectively forced their hand, and by the end of 1961 they too were established in Leopoldville under the leadership of Mario de Andrade, the founder of the movement, and Viriato da Cruz. The fact that the rebellion occurred only a few months after the UN resolution of December 1960, supported by the US, influenced Portuguese perceptions of the rebellion which, while it was eventually brutally suppressed and largely contained, was never totally extinguished. The UN resolution referred to colonialism as alien domination and a denial of human rights and called for immediate steps to be taken to transfer power. It was followed by one in March 1961 calling for Portugal to introduce reforms and allow the exercise of the right of self-determination. The Portuguese therefore began to assume that it was the Americans who were responsible for the troubles in Angola and

who were thereby providing opportunities for communism to advance.

The State Department rightly concluded early on that in order to avoid jeopardizing American standing with the African states and in the UN, it would be necessary to maintain a position unpalatable to the Portuguese. It was certainly unpalatable to the Portuguese foreign minister Nogueira who warned the Americans that if their undermining of the Portuguese empire continued the communists could take over the whole of the Iberian peninsular. He also claimed that the Angolan crisis was more important than the Berlin one and that if necessary the Portuguese were prepared to go to the bitter end and face a Third World War rather than give up their empire. The argument of the Africanists was that it would be important to champion African self-determination even if Portugal withdrew from NATO—a good example of the extent to which Cold War considerations were Africa-based.

The point is particularly relevant to the question of the Azores base which was used by the Americans under an agreement due to expire at the end of 1962. The fact was that the agreement was neither renewed nor the Americans thrown out, and while there were changes in the way the Kennedy administration dealt with the Angolan issue at the UN, the essential nature of the policy remained unchanged. Public criticism to win Afro-Asian support accompanied private criticism and persuasive pressure. The problem was that the resolutions put forward at the UN became more radical and the US feared not just their effect on Portugal but on their relations with more moderate Afro-Asian states. It thus became more reluctant to support them especially when sanctions were involved. However, the commitment to Africans still remained and while Kennedy was aware of the importance the military attached to the Azores and was keen not to lose the base, it did not mean that there was a move to preserve better relations with Portugal at the expense of the commitment to African self-determination. As late as December 1963 the US was supporting resolutions calling for self-determination and no arms supply to Portugal.

The problem was that the Portuguese would not tolerate the concepts of independence and self-government and would not introduce political change in any meaningful form. The Kennedy administration at the very highest levels of Dean Rusk and even Kennedy himself tried in meetings with high-level Portuguese representatives to change these attitudes but failed. Thus the revolt simmered beneath the surface in Angola and the anti-colonial movements continued without establishing a single unified movement. The MPLA with its *mestico* domination was at odds with the Black African UPA which in March 1962 merged with the Democratic party of Angola (PDA), another largely Kikongo-speaking group, to form the National Liberation Front of Angola (FNLA). The purpose was to broaden the ethnic base and aspire to become a national

party and in April an Angolan revolutionary government in exile (GRAE) was formed with an anti-communist message. Later in the year in December 1962 Agostinho Neto became leader of the MPLA after escaping from prison in Portugal and the seeds of future conflict were sown. Although the MPLA tried to play down its socialist links until 1964,[15] there was now an ideological division in Angolan anti-colonialism which could be interpreted in Cold War terms. Ultimately the Cold War achieved little for Angolans except contributing to their divisions, despite the commitment of the Kennedy administration to promote African nationalism of a 'responsible' kind.

C. Crises in the Middle East

The mid-1950s produced a number of crises during the transition from the period of British domination to the era of superpower competition in which the Soviets posed a challenge to Western dominance in the area. Outside interference was a feature of the post-1953 period which focused on the conflict between the Arabs and the new Jewish state of Israel that dominated the region after the armistice of 1949 brought the first round of fighting to a close. The second Arab–Israeli War in 1956, or Suez Crisis, stemmed from a number of interconnected international, regional, and national problems. In essence these involved the maintenance of power, which as one senior British official pointed out, in terms that could also apply to the Cold War, is to be measured not only in terms of money and military forces but in prestige. What the world thinks about the status of a great power is in other words extremely important. In the Middle East by the middle of the decade there was one power, Britain, which was clearly declining in hard power terms as measured by military and economic strength, was desperate to preserve its power in terms of status and prestige. As the British saw it this had to be done in the face of threats from both friends, notably the United States, and enemies whether the Soviet Union or emerging radical Arab states. This British determination to remain the leading external power

was accompanied by regional rivalries which embodied not just the Arab–Israeli dispute but also serious rivalries within the Arab world. And finally there were the problems and conflicts within individual states in the Middle East. It was the combination of all three that produced the Suez Crisis in 1956.

Britain's Declining Power

The collapse of Britain's informal Empire in the Middle East, which was the clear result of the Suez Crisis, has formed a central part of the debate on decolonization. Having abandoned its position in India and other parts of South Asia, as well as Palestine, it can be argued that Britain was also engaged in planning its withdrawal from the Middle East. It therefore ran into difficulties over the nature and timing of this process. Britain was allegedly seeking to preserve some degree of influence and to resist the spread of Soviet communism by selecting pro-Western leaders as its successors. Equally it can be argued that the Middle East was radically different from Asia in that the development of the Cold War and the growing need for oil made Britain reluctant to abandon the Middle East until the Suez Crisis made Britain's departure inevitable. Thus Suez can fit the model of the planned transfer of power, with the occasional aberration, or the model of radical nationalists demanding the end of external control whether exercised formally or informally as in pre-1945 Egypt.

However, Suez has been interpreted as a much more important milestone in the history of British imperialism and deocolonization. The Suez Canal was probably the most well-known symbol of the British Empire and the vain efforts to retain control of it in 1956, for some, signified Britain's imperial demise.[16] The decolonization of the rest of Britain's Empire was inevitable after the 'lion's last roar' had been muffled on the banks of the Canal. Suez was a watershed because force had failed and Britain could no longer fight to hold its Empire. Opponents of that view argue that Suez was not a watershed because it failed to change the fundamental goals of British policy overseas.[17] This argument rests in part on the assumption that Suez was not part of decolonization in the sense that it did not involve the formal transfer of power. It is much more accurate to see Suez as the loss of influence that was supposed to remain *after* power had been transferred. In the Middle East this was particularly important because of the region's geopolitical importance and its association, not with colonies, but with Britain's status as a great world power by virtue of its responsibility for the defence of the area. Thus the policy of maintaining the status of a great world power remained unaltered

by the Suez fiasco which had little effect on decolonization except to undermine the idea of Britain as a liberal colonial power. What it did do was to reveal that Britain could only exercise influence and employ force in a regional context with the approval and support of the United States.

The Regional Crises

The first crisis which the British and the Americans began to address at the end of 1955 was the Arab–Israeli conflict which was centred now on Egyptian organized raids of *fedayeen* into Israel. Originally such raids were largely the result of local grievances over the position of the border but by 1955 their organization by Egypt and the scale of the Israeli reprisals had made the situation more inflammatory. If the British, or even the Americans, were to pose as the region's protectors against the Soviet threat, they would need a united Middle East in which such internal conflicts were no longer more important than an external threat. This meant securing an Arab–Israeli peace settlement. The plan to do this, code-named Alpha, involved the creation of a link between Egypt and Jordan to symbolize Arab unity, the right of Palestinian refugees to return to their homes or to receive compensation, which would be financed by the West, and the provision of guarantees of Israeli security. The Egyptian leader,

---

Abdul Gamal Nasser (1918–1970)

This future Egyptian statesman was born in Alexandria in 1918. He completed his education at the Cairo Military Academy, which he joined in 1936. While there, Nasser contributed to the establishment of a nationalist movement known as the Free Officers or the El-Dhobatt El-Ahrar. Nasser fought and was wounded in the 1948–9 war against Israel. Following this conflict there was increased support for the Free Officers Movement because of the King's corrupt involvement in the procurement of inadequate weapons. In 1952 Nasser led a military coup against the King Farouk regime. A new Egyptian republic was born and Nasser became minister of the interior under General Neguib. Neguib was always a figurehead and Nasser formally assumed power as president and

prime minister in 1954. Nasser caught the world's attention by announcing the nationalization of the Suez Canal Company in 1956 after a covert Anglo–American attempt to undermine his regime. The Suez crisis ensued which only enhanced Nasser's popularity in the Arab world. Although he attempted many reforms including land redistribution, expansion of public works schemes, and improving educational opportunities, his domestic policies were a failure. Nasser used Arab nationalism to win support in Egypt but lost the 1967 war against Israel. Nasser resigned for a short period following that defeat but he returned to power until his death in 1970, which left the Arab world in deep mourning.

Sensitive Subjects: The Baghdad Pact

United Kingdom aims

1. The United Kingdom aims in the Baghdad pact are:

   (a) to bolster up resistance to communism in the area in cold war;

   (b) to build up an effective defence organization in the Middle East under British command;

   (c) to achieve (a) and (b) above with the minimum financial expenditure and without incurring any increased British military commitment in the theatre, but at the same time to maintain the momentum of the Pact.

4. The United Kingdom representatives should not disclose HMG's reluctance to become financially involved. Any questions involving financial obligation should be parried on the grounds that agreement on details must await agreement on the overall plan and consequent requirements.

The strategic air plan

5. Due to the very high secrecy accorded to the Allied strategic air plan, no information, other than that included in the Appreciation of the Military Situations, should be disclosed.

Theatre nuclear effort

6. Since no United Kingdom nuclear weapons are expected to be available in the Middle East before 1959 and since no agreement has yet been reached for the employment of the United States Sixth Fleet or other United States forces with nuclear capability in support of the Baghdad Pact area even our interim concept could not be substantiated if subjected to detailed examination. It is the primary concern of existing deception plans for the Middle East to cover up this nuclear deficiency by portraying a nuclear capability for our forces in the theatre now.

7. The present lack of nuclear capability must therefore on no account be revealed. When this question arises the United Kingdom representatives should state that neither HMG nor the United States government is prepared to release information on the quantity, deployment, or detailed plans for using nuclear weapons. However, the United Kingdom representatives are authorized to state that the existing United Kingdom plans for the theatre in war are based on the availability of nuclear weapons from H-hour, and that these would be available in support of operations under the Baghdad Pact.

Source: DEFE 6/34, JP (56) 10 (Final) 18 Jan. 1956 'The Baghdad Pact: background brief': JPS report to COS Committee. *Annex*. Reproduced in: John Kent (ed.), *British Documents on the End of Empire Series B, 4. Egypt and the Defence of the Middle East, Part III, 1953–1956* (Stationery Office, London,1998), 481–2.

Colonel Gamal Abdul Nasser, was chosen by the US to convince the Arab world of the plan's desirability before the Americans would begin to pressure the Israelis to accept.

There were some obvious difficulties in that the Israelis would have to give up the Negev and accept the right of refugees to return, albeit in a controlled fashion. No amount of American pressure was likely to do that even without the Jewish lobby in the US. Moreover, even if Nasser was personally willing to accept the existence of an Israeli state, his chances of persuading other Arab leaders to do the same, while recognizing his leadership, were almost as low. To some extent the idea of Arab nationalism and anti-imperialism which Nasser had promoted raised more Arab divisions. He had deposed a monarch in Egypt and his rivals for leadership in Iraq and Saudi Arabia were both conservative monarchs.[18] Yet Nasser's

radical Arab nationalism, while certain to upset the old Arab landowning elites, was also unacceptable to the masses if it was combined with the recognition of Israel.

In the Middle East after 1955 Nasser was to emerge as the key challenger to the idea that Britain had a special regional role as military protector, and it was Nasser, who in effect, challenged the British for the right to exert predominant influence in the Arab parts of the region. In 1954 the Anglo–Egyptian agreement on the withdrawal of British troops from the Suez Canal Zone, was based on the maintenance of the base in peacetime and on its reactivation in war, and offered the prospect of a new era of Anglo–Egyptian cooperation. However, such hopes were dashed in April 1955 with the creation of the Baghdad Pact, an extension of the Turco–Iraqi Pact which would by the end of the year incorporate

Pakistan and Iran as well as Britain. Almost immediately the Baghdad Pact became a hated military alliance, symbolizing again British attempts at domination, even though this dislike was inversely proportional to the Pact's military value. Its main achievement was to sour Anglo–Egyptian relations and exacerbate the major conflicts which were bedevilling the Middle East. First, it involved the Iraqis who were the main challengers to Nasser's claim to leadership of the Arab world. Secondly, Nasser's standing after the 1954 agreement depended to a significant extent on his claims to be an anti-imperialist leader who had finally got rid of the peacetime British military presence in Egypt. He could hardly therefore welcome his main rival's almost immediate conclusion of a new defence agreement with the imperialist power from whose clutches Egypt had finally been delivered. The result was that Nasser embarked on a campaign to denounce the Pact and to prevent any other Arab members from joining. This in turn made it less likely that he would cooperate with the British and the Americans in implementing Alpha.

The British became keener to promote the Pact by getting other, particularly Arab states, to join. In December 1955 they approached Jordan in order to isolate Nasser in the Arab world and emphasize British leadership of the defence organization deemed necessary for the Middle East. The Baghdad Pact was proclaimed as the vehicle for this even though the shortfall in the forces in the region that the British and Americans deemed necessary to do this was greater than the number of forces that could be made available. The British efforts to secure Jordanian accession led to riots and disturbances which threatened King Hussein's government and had to be abandoned in January 1956.

In the meantime Nasser, fearing his domestic position would be undermined by his apparent inability to defend Egypt from large-scale Israeli reprisals against *fedayeen* raids, turned to the Soviets for arms in September 1955. This deal between Egypt and Czechoslovakia raised the spectre of growing Soviet influence in the Middle East and was likely to lead to questions about the value of the Baghdad Pact. It was falsely claimed that the region from Turkey through Iraq and Iran to the Persian Gulf (the Northern tier) could be protected by defending the

passes through the Zagros mountains. In any case what good was that if the Soviets were already in Egypt? A further element of concern stemmed from the fact that once the new arms were absorbed into the Egyptian armed forces in about a year's time, the military superiority which the British and Americans believed the Israelis enjoyed over the combined forces of the Arab states, would be lost. Consequently, there was a fear in Britain that Israel would attack Egypt in the near future to avoid such an eventuality.

The defence issue could more readily be turned to British advantage in that they could claim that, rather than the reality of competing with Nasser for influence in the Middle East, they were in fact serving Western interests by leading the struggle against the Soviets. This theme of portraying the preservation of Britain's imperial interests as part of fighting the Cold War was one with which the Americans were already closely acquainted. And they regarded it understandably with a certain scepticism, as it could be argued that the unwelcome presence of British forces in the region actually contributed to the instability which the Soviets might be able to exploit. But that presence was a vital symbol of Britain's influence in a region where, if it was lost, the country's status as a world power would be at risk. Now that Britain had given up its peacetime presence in Egypt it was even more important to emphasize the crucial role its forces in Iraq and Jordan might play in defence terms. This was in fact why they had joined the Baghdad Pact in the first place because it was through that organization that they would secure their continued peacetime presence in Iraq. The consequences of the other problem created by the Czech arms deal would only become apparent in 1956.

With the failure to get Jordan into the Baghdad Pact it began to look as if Nasser was winning the battle with Britain for influence in the Middle East. In this situation, and encouraged by British intelligence assessments, prime minister Eden began to see the only way of saving face was the removal of Nasser. Yet the Egyptian leader was still regarded as essential to the realization of Alpha and an Arab–Israeli agreement, which in turn was necessary for a united Middle East to focus on the threat of the Soviet Union for which a British military presence

Sir Anthony Eden (1897–1977)

Sir Anthony Eden was born in 1897 at Windlestone Hall, Bishop Auckland and was educated at Eton. After fighting in the First World War, where he reached the rank of Major, Eden won the seat of Warwick and Leamington in 1923 as a Conservative candidate. In 1935 he became the secretary of state for foreign affairs but resigned in 1938 ostensibly due to his opposition to Neville Chamberlain's ideas on appeasing Mussolini. However, in 1939 he was back in the Cabinet, taking up the role of secretary of state for dominion affairs. When Winston Churchill took power in 1940, Eden briefly became secretary of war, before returning to the foreign office in December 1940. He had an important role in helping create the United Nations and in concluding the wartime Anglo–Soviet Alliance. During the Labour government, from 1945 to 1951, Eden remained in parliament. Following the Conservative victory in 1951 he once again became foreign minister and in 1954, at the Geneva Conference, he helped to negotiate a temporary settlement of the conflict in Indo-China. In the same year, Eden received a knighthood and in 1955 he became prime minister upon the resignation of Churchill. Eden was in charge during the Suez Crisis, when he controversially used armed intervention in collusion with the French and Israelis. He resigned as prime minister in 1957, ostensibly due to bad health but essentially due to his role in the Suez Crisis and lack of support from the Americans. In 1961 he was made the Earl of Avon. Eden died in 1977.

was ostensibly needed. It was the dismissal of General Glubb, who led the British-officered Arab Legion in Jordan, and the American realization that, despite the despatch of a presidential envoy, Nasser was not going sell Alpha to Arab leaders that gave credence to Eden's arguments in Washington. The result was an American plan, codenamed Omega, with which the British were to cooperate and which sought to remove Nasser by a combination of measures designed to weaken his internal position and isolate him in the Arab world. A number of economic measures were to be taken against Egypt including the withdrawal of the promised aid to build a dam on the River Nile at Aswam. Externally the Americans would try to turn King Saud of Saudi Arabia against Nasser, and the CIA and MI6 would sponsor a coup, code-named Straggle, against the left-wing Syrian regime which was Nasser's other important Middle Eastern friend.

However, once Nasser realized that British and American policy had changed and become hostile to Egypt, he looked for a way to strike back which would increase his support in the Arab world. In the wake of the announcement, based on Omega, that Aswam Dam aid would be withdrawn Nasser decided on 26 July 1956 that the nationalization of the Suez Canal Company would best serve his needs of striking back at the British.

The Suez Crisis

The nationalization of the Suez Canal Company, which was largely owned by the French and British governments, was a massive blow to British prestige as the dominant regional power. It was, however, an Egyptian registered company and as Nasser offered compensation he was in fact acting perfectly legally and simply buying out the shareholders. It was, nevertheless, a hugely symbolic moment, encapsulating the decline of British influence and belittling Britain in the eyes of the world, that was too much for Eden to swallow. He immediately ordered the Chiefs of Staff to prepare plans for an invasion of Egypt and began a long series of efforts to convince the Americans that Nasser would now use the nationalized company's control of the Canal to strangle Britain's supply of Middle Eastern oil. Eisenhower and Dulles were not impressed, but extremely worried about the reactions in the Middle East and elsewhere to a naked show of what would be regarded as imperialist force by the British. With Omega the Americans had shown a willingness to seek Nasser's removal but were reluctant to jeopardize the West's position by an act of overt aggression for which there was no justification. Both Eisenhower and Dulles instantly realized that they would need to persuade Eden against using force, but to confront the British by ruling out military options in all circumstances, including the closure of the

Canal to international shipping, would be counter-productive: the British might resent American opposition, unless qualified, and be encouraged to use force. The strategy therefore became one of playing for time by convincing the British that regaining control of the Canal could be achieved by peaceful methods or that military force required further action by Nasser. The longer the attempts at negotiation went on the less likely it would be that force would be used. In the event a London Conference of Users and signatories to the 1888 Suez Canal Convention establishing the Canal as an international waterway and governing its use reached a majority agreement in August 1956 on the principles of a new international regime for the Canal. Nasser, however, refused to go along with the agreement which did not specify how international control was to be exercised over a waterway that was part of sovereign Egyptian territory. With another American proposal to establish a Users Group that would assert the rights given under the Suez Canal Convention, the issue again came down to whether the Egyptian company would oversee the Canal through an international supervisory board or whether an international body would actually run the Canal. The crux of the matter for Eden was whether the international body operating the Canal would have the power to impose sanctions and humiliate Nasser or not. If it did, it would be unacceptable to the Egyptians. When the British went to the United Nations with the problem the two countries were nevertheless coming close to a deal because the power to humiliate could not easily be portrayed as an international requirement. It was then that Eden had some unexpected French visitors.

General Challe and General Gazier visited London on 26 October and produced a plan which would avoid any need for a settlement and thereby spare Eden being pilloried by the right-wing imperialist wing of the Tory Party for appeasing Egypt during its annual conference. Eden had every reason to believe that his party would find it difficult to live with a settlement that did not provide for the humiliation of Nasser and reassert British prestige in the Middle East. The French generals had been in close contact with the Israelis who were keen to destroy any possible advantage the Egyptians might gain from the Czech arms deal. The French were also keen to

strike at Nasser because he was supplying the rebels in Algeria fighting for independence from France. The plan put to Eden was that Israel would attack Egypt, rather than Jordan where large-scale Israeli raids were causing serious concern given that Britain was obligated by treaty to assist Jordan in the event of an Israeli attack. As Israel invaded Egypt, Britain and France would issue an ultimatum to cease fighting and when this was refused would send forces to Egypt, allegedly to protect the Canal from the warring parties. It would have been a strange irony if, having accused Nasser of wishing to take over the Middle East on behalf of the Soviet Union, and having suffered from Egyptian propaganda against imperialism and the Baghdad Pact, Eden had ended up assisting Jordan alongside Nasser. On the other hand, to collude with the French and the Israelis was even more bizarre and based on the illusion that the collusion with the Israelis could be kept secret.

One immediate reason for Eden's actions may have been the feeling at the Tory Party conference, but the roots of Eden's decision go back before this. Eden himself has argued that the decision helped prevent the spread of Soviet influence in the Middle East, while the strategic importance of the region and the existence of large quantities of oil also made action necessary. However, the more emotive perceptions of the prime minister and some of his Cabinet colleagues and officials reflected a world-view of Britain as a global power with exclusive responsibilities in the Middle East. These perceptions and belief systems were broadly comparable to the ways in which the United States and the Soviet Union saw their credibility in terms of competing in a Cold War. To lose status was seen as disastrous and while all sorts of reasons could be brought forth to justify this view, at the end of the day it reflected a sense of prestige derived from emotive belief systems more than interests. Reason was thus cast aside, and Eden's failure to take account of the true extent of American opposition to the use of force is one example of how rationality could be overridden. The idea of collusion being kept secret is another.

The final agreement was reached with the French and Israelis after a number of secret meetings at Sèvres: it involved an Israeli attack on 29 October followed by a 24-hour ultimatum. This would demand a withdrawal to ten miles from each bank of the Canal which, when refused, would be followed by a British attack on Egyptian airfields after midnight on 30/31 October. The reason for this was the Israeli fear of Egyptian planes bombing their cities, but in the event the bombing was postponed until after all American citizens were evacuated from Cairo. Unfortunately, by the time the ultimatum was delivered the Israelis were still a long way from the Canal. In effect it demanded that the aggressor advance into Egyptian territory while the victim of the aggression fell back. In addition the latest British military plan called for an extended period of psychological warfare including the bombing of important civilian installations. This was clearly incompatible with the type of quick operation that would have been over before international and especially American opinion had time to mobilize.

By early November the United Nations passed two resolutions calling for a ceasefire and on 4 November the British were in a position of being morally unable to condemn the Soviet assault on the civilians of Budapest (see Chapter 6, A) while they themselves were bombing Cairo. A United Nations peacekeeping force was then agreed on by the General Assembly and as a result further pressure mounted for military action to be halted. The emotive nature of the Suez crisis is epitomized by the majority decision of the Cabinet on 4 November when it was believed (incorrectly) that both the Egyptians and the Israelis had accepted a ceasefire. When asked whether to go ahead with the airborne landings, to postpone them, or to abandon them altogether, the Cabinet voted to go ahead. In a sense it was the final futile attempt to assert British power in the Middle East that had already evaporated. Twenty-four hours later when the Canal was half in British hands, but useless as the Egyptians had sunk block ships in it, the British government called the fighting to a halt. As the Americans refused to consider any action to stop the run on the pound the British were facing a balance of payments crisis and criticism from the entire world apart from the antipodean Dominions. The pressure from the Americans and the disapproval of the United Nations where the United States and the Soviet Union were essentially in agreement finally brought home to the British the disastrous

consequences were they to continue. The collusion always suspected by the Americans was soon obvious despite the British denials, and having lied to parliament the prime minister was forced to resign in January 1957 to be succeeded by the American-backed Harold Macmillan.

The Aftermath of Suez

For the British, Suez meant that they could no longer operate militarily in old imperial areas without the tacit support of the United States. Eden's efforts to maintain a dominant regional role as the leading representative of the Western Alliance was a futile attempt to cling to a world role of significance. Britain would have to accept American leadership in the Middle East as well as in East and South-East Asia, Latin America, and even Africa. However, this did not mean that Britain was suddenly willing to decolonize and abandon Africa. Unlike the French who, under de Gaulle were prepared to abandon an empire which was becoming increasingly costly and an impediment to the modernization of French agriculture and industry, the British did not suddenly decide to abandon their African empire. The quest to retain some world status to distinguish Britain from the other European powers was to remain an almost constant theme of British foreign policy. Indeed, Macmillan was to see it as a means of embodying Britain's 'special' position as America's leading partner.

The most obvious consequence of Suez was the reduction of British status in the Middle East, although the British still continued to try and preserve what influence did remain. As with the loss of empire in general, Suez did not mark a decisive watershed in British Middle East policy. British influence was to decline over a further period of years as Nasser's success contributed to the rise of radical Arab nationalism if not in a united and coherent form. However, from 1957 onwards it was the United States which had to face that challenge under the Cold War umbrella. What amounted to a formal expression of US policy came in January 1957 with the Eisenhower Doctrine. The Doctrine stated that US would provide military and economic aid to those nations who were prepared to resist the forces of international communism. It was misleading in terms of Middle Eastern problems which did not centre on communism but on radical Arab movements. The Americans, because of the Cold War, believed they were likely to be taken over by Soviet communism or would produce the kind of instability that communists could exploit. It was to lead very quickly to American involvement in what were local Middle East problems that, however they were depicted, had nothing to do with communism or Soviet interference.

The Eisenhower Doctrine was the second in the line of anti-communist doctrines that all American presidents would have, apart from Kennedy and Ford, until George Bush entered the White House with the end of the Cold War. It led to US marines landing in Lebanon in 1958 while British troops were sent into Jordan inspired less by fear of communism than by fear of the spread of Arab movements unfriendly to the West. And in particular by the overthrow and murder of the Iraqi king and his pro-Western prime minister Nuri Said. Many Arabs disliked Western imperialism *and* Soviet commu-

nism and it became a bone of contention between London and some in Washington as to whether the leaders of radical nationalism in Egypt and Iraq could become a useful counter to communism. Ultimately it was the Americans who would carry the clout and the Eisenhower Doctrine symbolized the end of British domination more than a new element in the Cold War. Nasser was to remain relatively favoured by some in Washington while totally anathema to all in London, but in the end he was unable to unite the Arab world. Despite Egypt joining with Syria to form the United Arab Republic for three years between 1958 and 1961, the lure of controlling their own nation state proved too compelling for territorial civil and military elites. The rivalry between Egypt and Iraq was also to continue despite the end of their respective monarchies. Arab leaders remained more willing to use the nationalism of the masses to build support for their positions as head of particular groups competing for power than to promote political union, or even co-operation, despite the existence of the common Israeli threat.

CHRONOLOGY: THE SUEZ CRISIS

1954

Anglo–Egyptian Base Agreement is signed. British troops must be withdrawn from the Canal Zone by June 1956.

1955

June	Project Alpha accepted by the British Cabinet.
September	Egyptian–Czech arms deal signed.

1956

January	Project Alpha stalls.
1 March	King Hussein of Jordan dismisses the British Commander of the Arab Legion, General Glubb.
April–May	Anglo–American discussions on Egypt and the Middle East lead to the decision under plan Omega that Aswan Dam funding should not be provided in the immediate future.
10 May	Egypt recognizes the People's Republic of China.
19 July	US announces the removal of funding for the Aswan High Dam.
26 July	Abdul Gamal Nasser nationalizes the Suez Canal Company.
31 July	John Foster Dulles travels to London for talks. Eisenhower warns Eden against the employment of force.
2 August	British government announces recall of selected groups of reservists.
3 August	The US, Britain, and France call for a conference to be held in London.
8 August	Treasury delivers first economic warning to Macmillan.
16–23 August	Dates of first London Conference.
3 September	Eisenhower again warns Eden against the use of force.
3–9 September	Nasser in talks with Menzies mission in Cairo as a result of the London Conference.
4 September	Dulles proposes the idea of a Suez Canal Users Association (SCUA).
7 September	Treasury issues second economic warning to Macmillan.
8 September	Eisenhower once more warns Eden against employing force.
12 September	SCUA publicly announced.
19 September	Second London Conference begins.
21 September	Second London Conference approves the Users Association. Treasury issues further warnings on economy to Macmillan.
23 September	Britain and France refer dispute to the United Nations.

29 September	Treasury warnings received by British government on the economic front.
30 September– 1 October	Golda Meir and Moshe Dayan meet the French for high-level talks.
5 October	Selwyn Lloyd meets Christian Pineau and Dulles before the Security Council debate.
10–11 October	The Israelis carry out a raid on Qualqilya in Jordan.
13 October	Six principles for a negotiated agreement are passed by the Security Council.
14 October	Albert Gazier and General Maurice Challe discuss Israeli participation with Eden at Chequers.
16 October	Eden and Lloyd fly to France for talks with Guy Mollet and Pineau.
18 October	In Cabinet there is the first mention of possible Israeli action against Egypt.
22 October	Lloyd travels to Sèvres to meet representatives from France and Israel.
24 October	Patrick Dean signs the Sèvres protocol.
25 Ocober	Cabinet discusses the plans for 'collusion'.
26 October– 2 November	Treasury discusses drain on reserves and emergency action to stop this.
29 October	Israelis attack Egypt.
30 October	Britain and France send ultimatums to both Israel and Egypt and the two countries also veto American and Soviet resolutions calling for a ceasefire. Eisenhower once again warns Eden about using force.
31 October	Anglo–French air attacks begin against Egyptian targets. The UN security council calls an emergency meeting of the General Assembly. Lloyd denies any collusion in the Commons.
1 November	Egyptian forces in Sinai are defeated by the Israelis. The countries of the Commonwealth denounce British actions at the General Assembly meeting. The General Assembly also passes the American ceasefire resolution.
2 November	A call for ceasefire is made by the General Assembly.
3 November	Israel seemingly accepts the ceasefire, on the condition that Egypt does the same.
4 November	The Suez Canal is blocked, Israel also rejects the ceasefire. The Cabinet is divided on whether to launch an invasion. Majority are in favour even though they believe Israel has accepted the ceasefire.
5 November	Britain and France launch their paratroop invasion. Nikolai Bulganin sends a note referring to rocket attacks. Israel accepts the ceasefire.
6 November	British and French seaborne landings are begun, despite the sterling currency being in crisis. Macmillan counsels Eden to accept the ceasefire, which he does at midnight.
7 November	UN expeditionary forces to be sent to Egypt are authorized by the General Assembly. The Treasury reports that $85 million has been lost from the sterling reserves in the week before.
15 November	The US inform the Egypt Committee that it will receive no US aid until French and British troops are withdrawn from the Canal Zone.
20 November	Macmillan informs colleagues of the bad economic situation.
22 November	Cabinet agrees to a small withdrawal of troops from the area, pending the results of negotiations on the clearance and operation of the Canal.
23 November	Eden travels to Jamaica to rest.
30 November	Cabinet accepts total withdrawal from Egypt.
1 December	Public announcement of withdrawal of troops.

20 December	Eden lies to the Commons about collusion.
22 December	The removal of British troops from Egypt is finished.

1957

9 January	Eden resigns as prime minister and is succeeded by Macmillan.

D. The End of the British Empire in Africa

The British Empire in Black Africa also came to an end with a rush, if not quite such a precipitate one as its French and Belgian counterparts. The Gold Coast had already been irrevocably set on the road to independence by 1954 and the Sudan soon followed, thereby effectively following in the footsteps of the Dominions. Central to any analysis of the end of the British Empire in the early 1960s is accounting for its timing and for the lack of any long-term planning in that timing. The basic principles may well have been lurking in the minds of policy-makers, and if there was any impact of initiatives in the colonies they had more of an immediate effect on policy than on planning in the Colonial Office. If there was a key rationale behind the decisions that were taken in the latter half of the 1950s and the first half of the 1960s, it was based on the principle of whatever was necessary, or could be made acceptable, in order to transfer power while minimizing the international and domestic problems that would result from satisfying the demands of African political leaders.

Originally the plan was to prepare each of the larger colonies for independence by assisting in the social, economic, and political development that would make them viable states. Despite the lack of resources the Colonial Office still professed to believe in this, but by the middle of the decade other factors were coming into play. The Foreign Office became increasingly worried that the task of keeping Africa loyal to the West could not be trusted to a Colonial Office concerned with the particular issues of a number of fragmented territories. A regional or continental policy would be more suitable to deal with Cold War needs. Then there was the broader difficulty of transferring power too slowly which, perhaps in the face of Colonial Office claims that some colonies were not ready for independence, might produce the radicalization of independence movements in British Africa. There was the example of the Mau Mau rebellion in Kenya (1952–9), even though it did not fit the Cold War model and was produced by the changing nature of land use with people being excluded from using land traditionally available to them. Then there was the opposite problem of moving too fast to independence which would create unstable states that could of course be deemed exploitable by Soviet communism.

Multiracialism and its Demise

What was worse was the existence in East and Central Africa (in Kenya, Northern and Southern Rhodesia in particular) of significant minorities of white settlers. The problem was further complicated by the creation of the Central African Federation of the two Rhodesias and Nyasaland in 1953 largely in order to prevent the influence of South Africa spreading northwards under the banner of apartheid. In effect this united a white-dominated Southern Rhodesia, having effective internal self-government and the dominant economy with two colonies still under Colonial Office tutelage. In Kenya, where the Mau Mau rebellion continued to smoulder beneath the surface, there was no courting of Black African parties as there was in West Africa and it was difficult to see by 1957 how the British were going to find native collaborators. There was a particular problem in Kenya where African leaders, like Jomo Kenyatta, who were suspected of association with Mau Mau terrorism, could not be trusted by the British as 'responsible' leaders of African parties. The problem in the largest West African colony, Nigeria, was of keeping the disparate three main regions together in the establishment of a modern state—divide and rule but unite and decolonize in order to move from control to influence. The Gold Coast model of working cooperatively with the leaders of the largest African Party in return for early independence seemed inapplicable to many other territories. Problems of regional differences or the politicization of ethnic diversity were formidable obstacles to the creation of viable pro-Western nations in East, West, and Central Africa.

One solution that the British came up with was the idea of multiracialism in which the idea of African majority rule with one man one vote would be superseded by the idea of racial groups working in separate electoral colleges to produce governments based on racial cooperation, although not of a proportional kind. It was designed to give representation on a 'community' or ethnic basis which would clearly benefit the European and Indian minorities. It was encouraged by a mistaken belief that white settlers brought added expertise to African farming and crop cultivation, and by the need to try and reconcile the racial groups in Central Africa to make the Federation work. As the 1950s wore on it became increasingly less likely that the British would be able to get away with the avoidance of one man one vote.

The Americans were much quicker to realize this even though they had long worried about too rapid a transfer of power leaving badly prepared and unstable states prone to communism. In 1959 they saw that the British were slow and rather too complacent because they believed that the transfer of power could be delayed and major conflict avoided, whether by multiracialism or anything else. In essence this concern was based on the British paper 'Africa the Next Ten Tears', an official report begun in early 1959 and presented in June of that year. The report explicitly defined the dilemma between moving too fast and moving too slowly, but as the Americans noted, there was a lack of concrete proposals for avoiding this conundrum. Instead, there was some criticism, which the prime minister endorsed, along the lines that Britain still wielded influence in Africa. It was a strange illusion and one which was to be tested in East and Central Africa by a series of events which brought the idea of moulding Africa in line with British designs into question, and was to lead by the end of 1960 into a much greater commitment to the abandonment of responsibilities as soon as was reasonably possible.[19]

In those territories away from the troubled racial mix in Kenya and the Central Africa Federation early 1959 saw the continuation of what was still a medium-term goal to transfer power by the Colonial Office, albeit without any coherent or precise timeframe. It was true that after Suez doubts were cast, if largely ignored, about the continuance of Britain's world role but this goal was to be maintained in changed form and in the long term without colonies. Resources for defence expenditure were less in relative terms, economic problems continued

to mount, and strategic conceptions changed as the Suez-induced air barrier across much of the Arab world refocused attention on the Persian Gulf and East African regions. In the Gulf it is arguable that attempts were made to strengthen British involvement in ways other than the mere retention of influence that was being sought in the largest West African territory of Nigeria as it approached independence. In Nigeria the goal was to bring the new nation together under the banner of independence, but the latter was desired more by the educated and Westernized people of the Eastern and Western regions than by the more populated but less politically aware Muslim north. British policy aimed to concede independence, demanded by the southern provinces, through the creation of a federal entity which would include a 'modernized' north that was somewhat reluctant to embark on such a process. In one sense Britain was attempting to create nationalism in the north in order to comply with the wishes of the 'nationalists' in the south for the sake of a larger, more powerful state. Post-colonial British influence would then be stronger than in a divided set of newly independent small provinces. The main concern of the British was that the backward north would refuse to participate in a unitary state geared to the demands of a Christian, capitalist elite in the south. The Willink Report and constitutional conference in 1957 had set a precedent in so much as resolving difficulties by offering independence was seen as a way to avoid further problems. If the different parties in Nigeria could agree on the nature of a federal government, independence could be granted and the role of the colonial power was to encourage in the north what the south was clamouring for.[20] As the Cold War began to focus more on the less developed world in the second half of the decade, and Africa in particular by 1959–60, the getting out of difficult situations assumed greater importance and meant that less attention was paid to the preparation for independence which had dominated Colonial Office thinking in the first post-war decade.

In a sense progress was easier in the less developed territory of Tanganyika where independence was not expected to be achieved rapidly and the dangers of 'irresponsible' elements inheriting power was less of a consideration. The idea put forward in 'Africa the Next Ten Years' that Kenya would not achieve independence until at least 1970 was even more true of Tanganyika, although for different reasons. While there was a united nationalist Party, the country was deemed to be educationally backward and therefore not ready for even internal self-government until 1970. The fact that events moved much quicker resulted from the crises which emerged in Central Africa from 1959 onwards, although the first sign came in 1958 with the Southern Rhodesian rejection of Garfield Todd's liberal commitment to African advancement. Much worse was to follow in 1959 and eventually it was to make a significant impact on the approach to the transfer of power. In a sense the realization of the internal and international difficulties, and more importantly the dangers, Britain faced in clinging on to power provided an incentive to speed up the process. Power was thus transferred much quicker than anticipated when 'Africa the Next Ten Years' was first drafted in the crisis year of 1959. Transferring power rapidly was encouraged by the need to retain the initiative and control the basis of present and future cooperation and because as a last resort it increasingly seemed the only way of avoiding embroiling Britain in the kind of scenarios that were emerging in the Congo (see Chapter 8, B).

The riots that broke out in that country in January 1959 were accompanied by a state of emergency in Southern Rhodesia in February. Fears amongst the whites in the Federation of wide-ranging disturbances led to Southern Rhodesian troops being sent to Nyasaland which further increased tensions and produced clashes in which around fifty Africans died. In March a state of emergency was declared and Hastings Banda, the leader of the Nyasaland Congress Party, was arrested. This provoked further demonstrations in which twenty Africans were shot dead. A Commission of Enquiry under Lord Devlin, a distinguished high court judge, was then established and the Devlin report, delivered in July 1959, was scathing in its criticism of the colonial administration. The latter was accused of reacting to the widespread growth of African political consciousness by the creation of a 'police state'.

Extract from the Conclusion of 'Africa the Next Ten Years'

(a) *Racial relations and constitutional development.* The pace of the advance towards independence has become rapid in much of Africa. France has granted all her colonies internal self-government, with the right, at least in theory to opt for self-government at anytime; and the Belgian Congo is likely to reach the same position in a short period. We ourselves have moved even faster in West Africa. But in the east and south the position is different. If, on the one hand, we retreat there too rapidly before the rising tide of Pan-Africanism, we shall run the risk of transferring power to local governments before they are competent to exercize authority or to maintain stable and viable administration. We shall expose volatile and unsophisticated peoples to the insidious dangers of communist penetration. And we shall endanger European interests and investments, which have made the major contribution to the development of large parts of Africa and can claim the main credit for the gradual improvement in the African standard of living. This danger is particularly acute for the United Kingdom in relation to East Africa. If, on the other hand, we are too intransigent in opposing African aspirations, or, where European minorities are dominant, are too ready to appease these, we run the risk of being identified with the extreme racial doctrines of the Union of South Africa, or exacerbating African hostility towards the European and of provoking the African States, when they finally achieve independence—as in the end they must—to turn more readily towards the Soviet Union. This danger arises with particular urgency for the United Kingdom in relation to Central Africa. The West must therefore seek to steer a middle course between these extremes, bearing well in mind that, while the Soviet Union will be alert to seize every opportunity to exploit our dilemma. Pan-Africanism in itself is not necessarily a force which we need regard with fear or suspicion. On the contrary, if we can avoid alienating it and can guide it on lines generally sympathetic with the free world, it may well prove in the longer term a strong, independent barrier to the penetration of Africa by the Soviet Union and the United Arab Republic.

Source: FO 371/137972, Memorandum 'Africa the Next Ten Years', June 1959 reproduced in BDEEP, Series A, 4, pt. I, Ronald Hyam and Wm Roger Louis (eds), *The Conservative Government and the End of Empire 1957–1964*, 131–2.

On the same day as Banda's arrest, at a remote camp in Kenya where terrorist suspects were detained (without a formal conviction), a number of African prisoners refused to carry out their forced labour. In response their guards carried out beatings and eleven were beaten to death with twenty more badly injured. The deaths at Hola became part of an attempted cover-up based on stomach illnesses that unsurprisingly failed and questions were asked in the British parliament. The veil of liberalism, always somewhat threadbare since Suez, was now being unceremoniously lifted from British colonialism. Multiracialism, clearly a difficult if not an impossible goal, was also dramatically seen to be worthless as a liberal veneer when the Southern Rhodesian government interned some 500 people including a white missionary farmer, Guy Clutton Brook, whose case was taken up in parliament by Barbara Castle, MP. Clutton Brook was described as 'subversive' by the native commissioner, who was unaware in the bush of the concept of multiracialism. Regarded as an 'odious and harmful influence' because he allowed Africans to eat at his table and even sleep in his own house Brook was accused of neglecting to require them to stand up if a European entered the room.[21]

The End Comes Quickly

The failure of multiracialism, the granting of independence by the French (see Chapter 8, A), and the atrocities in East and Central Africa contributed to a growing desire to avoid yet more difficulties and ridicule by solving problems as rapidly as possible whenever the easiest way to do so seemed an early transfer of power. Where this could be done in ways uncomplicated by multiracialism, as in Tanganyika, it stemmed from a desire to retain the initiative, as was vainly hoped in the 1940s, if not to slow down the African drive for independence but to ensure that the process ran smoothly. In Tanganyika Governor Richard Turnbull presented proposals for rapidly increasing the pace of political advancement in 1959. His plan was 'to tame Nyerere', the leading African politician, and prevent the 'wild men' coming into positions of power, as appeared to be the case in other parts of eastern and central Africa. Turnbull therefore immediately introduced an unofficial

majority (African representatives as opposed to British officials) on the legislative council. He envisaged an African majority on the Council of Ministers by 1965, some 5 years earlier than planned and the new colonial secretary Iain Macleod, who came to office in October 1959, was more easily reconciled to such a rapid transfer of power. In the event the Cabinet moved even faster, won over by the perceived need to retain confidence in Britain and ensure 'peaceful development'. The result was independence in December 1961.

Kenya, with its significant minority of white settlers was more difficult to keep on the narrow road of peaceful development given settler opposition to African majority rule. It was even more difficult in the Central African Federation where African politicians seeking political advancement in Northern Rhodesia and Nyasaland were up against the white-dominated Federation. When government in the newly independent Congo effectively collapsed in 1960 the problem appeared even worse as Europeans were attacked. In both cases the options of Britain not giving independence seemed to present more problems and presage African disturbances, and even racial violence, with Europeans rallying to the regime in Pretoria. In January 1960 Macleod devised a new Constitution for Kenya, which, by extending the electoral roll, effectively guaranteed an African legislative majority and an important watershed was crossed. The Americans, worried as 1959 began, at British reluctance to embrace the inevitable quickly enough, now had renewed confidence in the implementation of the British transfer of power in Africa. Of course the acceptance of African majority rule still left the problem of compensation for white farmers and the rehabilitation from jail of Jomo Kenyatta the only claimant for leading Kenyans on a national basis. As with Nkrumah in the Gold Coast, Banda in Nyasaland, and others, the inside of a British-run jail was the precursor to national leadership. What produced the change for the British were perceptions of the difficulties of slowing down, never mind preventing, change. Rapid change was easier to accept because of the mounting strength of African political movements combined with a growing fear of turning a difficult situation into something worse. In Kenya it was fear of reviving the Mau Mau rebellion which had largely ended in 1959 and the general breakdown of law and order in the middle of a Cold War for the hearts and minds of Africans. By December 1963 Kenya was independent.[22]

The real problem was speeding up change in the Central African Federation where independence for Nyasaland and Northern Rhodesia could herald the break-up of the Federation. In the crisis summer of 1959 the government decided to appoint a commission of enquiry under the former opponent of his government's handling of the Suez affair (see Chapter 8, C), Sir Walter Monckton, to examine the Federation's constitutional future. The Monckton Commission began work in February 1960 and in September eight of its twenty-five members submitted an agreed report. The rest had reservations and the two African members submitted a minority report. With the recommendations including an African majority on the Northern Rhodesian legislative council and the conclusion that the Federation could not continue in its present form, Macleod decided to bite the bullet and attempt to move forward on these lines. Kaunda, another African political leader released from gaol in Northern Rhodesia, had acted to restrain his followers and channel their protests along peaceful lines. Yet, given the complications of the Federation and the white opposition to its break-up, forcefully led by the former Union leader Sir Roy Welensky, there were serious obstacles to change.

Back home white settlers had considerable support within the Conservative Party while many in the government were loathe to abandon the Federation and risk sending Southern Rhodesia into the arms of the South Africans. Macleod may have hoped that moving forward to African majority rule was a way of preserving the Federation by placing it on a new footing, but the whole of 1961, before and after Macleod's departure from the Colonial Office, was taken up with wrangling over the future of the Federation and the precise arithmetic to be applied to the Northern Rhodesian Constitution. White opposition to Macleod's proposal for the minimum impact and maximum concealment of an African majority produced protests in Africa and the Conservative Party but the real menace lay in the prospect of large-scale African violence if it was not implemented. From the collapse of the Federation's constitutional review conference in December 1960

Sir Roy Welensky (1907–1991)

Welensky was born in Salisbury (now known as Harare) in 1907. He was educated in his town of birth until he later joined the railways as a driver and fireman in 1924. He also became the Rhodesian heavyweight boxing champion between the years 1926 and 1928. In 1933, after having moved to Broken Hill (now Kabwe), he was elected chairman of the Railway Workers' Union. He remained chairman until 1953. Welensky became further involved in politics when he joined the Northern Rhodesian Legislative Council in 1938. He was later given promotion to the executive council in 1946. A year later he became the leader of the unofficial opposition. He cooperated with Huggins, prime minister of Southern Rhodesia and the first head of the Central Africa Federation in 1953. In the same year he was elected to the federal legislature and was deputy prime minister to Huggins, as well as being knighted. Welensky became prime minister in 1956 following the retirement of Huggins. He was now the leader of the United Federal Party, a position he held until its break-up in 1963. Welensky retired from politics in 1964 after failing to win the seat of Arundel in Southern Rhodesia.

---

to the final decision on the Northern Rhodesian Constitution in February 1962, with its African majority built in, deceit, recrimination and bitterness grew on all sides. Responsibility for planning the final denouement in the Federation in the worst possible situation was given in April 1962 to R.A. Butler as head of a new government department. Inevitably it resulted in the secession of Northern Rhodesia and Nyasaland who achieved independence in 1964 as Zambia and Malawi after the dissolution of the Central African Federation in December 1963.[23]

The extremely rapid end to the process of transferring power requires some explanation. The more committed empire supporters on the Right had never entirely accepted the abandonment of British responsibilities, even when significant amounts of British prestige, associated with world-power status, were not at risk. Even in 1960 there were diehards who could not easily contemplate Africans being given greater political responsibility for white men and who were still prepared to offer determined

Kenneth David Kaunda (b. 1924)

Kaunda was born in Lubwe, in Northern Rhodesia (now Zambia). He was the son of a missionary and of a teacher and completed his education at a missionary school and then at Munali Training School where he graduated as a teacher. He became headmaster at a school in Lubwe in 1944 and taught at other schools in Tanganyika and Muhlina in the years 1947 to 1948. In 1950, Kaunda's political career began when he became the secretary of the African National Congress (ANC) in Lubwe. He later became secretary-general of the ANC in 1953 and he also became editor of the *Congress News*, the ANC's journal. However, also in 1953, he was arrested for the first time and was later, in 1955, imprisoned for owning banned political literature. He was imprisoned for 2 months. In 1958 Kaunda left the ANC to form the Zambia African National Congress, but was arrested in 1959 and the party was also banned at that time. Upon his release in 1960, Kaunda was elected president of the United National Independence Party (UNIP), which formed a coalition government with the ANC in the year 1962. Kaunda was the minister for local government. In 1964, UNIP again won a convincing electoral victory and Kaunda took up the position of prime minister, and was later appointed the first president of independent Zambia. He remained in this position until suffering electoral defeat in 1991. In the 1970s, Kaunda was made chairman of the Organization of African Unity (1970–1) and also of the Non-Aligned Nations Conference (1970–4). In the 1980s he also helped negotiate the independence of Namibia, which was finally achieved in 1990.

resistance. That this was overcome is easy to ascribe to the growing effectiveness of mass-based African parties and to the momentum for decolonization, as what one country had obtained could not easily be withheld from another. The implications, for example, of the French territories being offered independence had implications for British Africa. If one country in East Africa was given an African majority, how could this be withheld from another? Yet reactions to the events of 1959 onwards and the demands of African leaders were also influenced by other concerns which contributed to the speed of the process. The process occurred as European trade grew in importance and trade between the developed countries in the North rose much more than that between the North and the Commonwealth countries in Africa and the Southern hemisphere. Britain's application to join the EEC in 1961 may have reflected a sea change in global focus. Far more important, however, was the influence of the Cold War and the fear of chaos and conflict that it induced and magnified. The Cold War had increasingly become an ideological battle for hearts and minds outside Europe by the second half of the 1950s. The focus was on Africa at the end of the decade where the Congo had revealed only too well how the problems inherent in European rule could develop into international crises. Fear encouraged the process by making the rapid transfer of power desirable if it avoided the type of situation that had developed in Algeria and the Congo. The British colonial empire's rapid demise in Africa did not come about because of foresight, strategy, or even as a careful readjustment to African demands. Its rapid termination offered the best prospect of preventing significant local difficulties becoming unmanageable and threatening Britain and the West with Cold War disasters that could have far more serious implications than the abandonment of colonies.

NOTES

1. Stanley Karnow, *Vietnam: A History* (Guild Publishing, London, 1983), 213.
2. Gerard J. de Groot, *A Noble Cause? America and the Vietnam War* (Pearson, Harlow, 2000), 68.
3. Robert K. Brigham, *Guerrilla Diplomacy: the NLF's Foreign Relations and the Vietnam War* (Cornell University Press, Ithaca, 1998), 18.
4. William J. Rust *et al.*, *Kennedy in Vietnam* (Da Capo, New York, 1985), 181.

5. Gary R. Hess, 'Kennedy's Vietnam options and decisions', in David L. Anderson (ed.), *Shadow on the White House: Presidents and the Vietnam War*, 1945–75 (University of Kansas Press, Lawrence, 1993), 82–3.

6. Lawrence J. Bassett and Stephen E. Pelz. 'The Failed Search for Victory: Vietnam and the Politics of War', in Thomas G. Paterson (ed.), *Kennedy's Quest for Victory: American Foreign Policy, 1961–3* (Oxford University Press, New York, 1989), 252.

7. We are indebted to Ryo Ikeda for this information.

8. M. Kahler, *Decolonisation in Britain and France* (Princeton University Press, Princeton, 1984), 355.

9. On the relationship between the two, see Tony Chafer, *The End of Empire in French West Africa: France's Successful Decolonization?* (Berg, Oxford 2002), 1–21.

10. J. Marseille, *Empire Colonial et Capitalisme Français* (Albin Michel, Paris, 1984), 367–73.

11. John D. Hargreaves, *Decolonization in Africa* (Longman, Harlow, 2nd edn., 1996), 186–90.

12. For a good account see R. D. Mahoney, *JFK: Ordeal in Africa* (Oxford University Press, New York, 1983).

13. Fernando Andresen Guimarães, *The Origins of the Angolan Civil War* (St Martin's Press, New York, 1998), 49–52.

14. J. Marcum, *The Angolan Revolution: The Anatomy of an Explosion 1950–1962* (M.I.T Press, London, 1969), 130–54.

15. Guimarães, op. cit., 60.

16. See Brian Lapping, *The End of Empire* (Granada, London, 1985) and the debate with Robert Holland in 'Did Suez Hasten The End of Empire?', *Contemporary Record*, 1 (1987–8), 39.

17. See especially, *British Documents on the End of Empire*, BDEEP, Series B, 4, pt I, *Egypt and the Defence of the Middle East 1945–1956*, John Kent (ed.), Introduction (Stationery Office, London, 1998).

18. In the event the Saudis were temporarily to support Nasser in opposing the British because of the dispute with the latter over Buraimi.

19. BDEEP, Series A, 4, pt. I. Ronald Hyam and Wm Roger Louis (eds), Introduction, xxxvi–xxxvii.

20. John Darwin, *Britain and Decolonisation: The Retreat from Empire in the Post-War World* (Macmillan Education, Basingstoke, 1988) 181–3.

21. BDEEP, Hyam and Louis, op. cit., xlv.

22. Ibid., lii–liii.

23. Ibid., liii–lvi; John D. Hargreaves, 217–18.

CHRONOLOGY: DECOLONIZATION, 1953–1994

1953

September	Central African Federation established.

1954

January	Nigerian Constitutional Conference takes place in Lagos.
June	Elections held in the Gold Coast.
July	Tanganyika African National Union is founded.
1 November	Algerian war begins.

1956

1 January	Independence of Sudan.
29 February	Gaston Defferre introduces *loi-cadre* for Black Africa.
July	Elections take place in the Gold Coast.

1957

6 March	Ghana becomes independent.
May–June	Second London conference on the Nigerian Constitution.

1958

8 February	France bombs Sakhiet in Tunisia.
February	Fall of Todd (S. Rhodesia, prime minister).
April	Accra Conference of African states begins.
13 May	Coup in Algiers.
2 October	Independence of Guinea.

1959

26 February	Emergency in Southern Rhodesia.
3 March	Emergency in Nyasaland.
July	Devlin report is completed.
14 October	British election: Macleod becomes colonial secretary.

1960

1 January	Cameroon becomes independent.
January	Lancaster House conference on the Kenyan Constitution takes place.
February	Macmillan in Cape Town.
	Monckton Commission in Salisbury.
March	Sharpeville shootings.
27 April	Independence gained by Togo.
26 June–1 July	The two Somalilands unite and become independent.
30 June	Belgian Congo becomes independent.
August	Ten new independent African states are formed after the break-up of the Mali Federation.
September	Monckton report on Central African Federation.
1 October	Independence of Nigeria.
November	Independence of Mauritania.
December	Review conference on the Federation meets.

1961

February	Patrice Lumumba is murdered.
March	South Africa leaves the Commonwealth.
13 March	The Union of the Peoples of Angola (UPA) supports attacks in North Angola.
April	Sierra Leone becomes independent.
20–26 April	Generals stage an unsuccessful coup in Algiers.
9 December	Independence of Tanganyika.

1962

19 March	Ceasefire declared in Algiers.
June	Front for the Liberation of Mozambique (FRELIMO) established in Dar-es-Salaam.
3 July	Independence of Algiers.
December	Rhodesia Front wins election in Southern Rhodesia. Britain accepts Nyasaland's right to secede.

1963

29 March	Britain accepts the dissolution of the Federation.
10 December	Independence of Zanzibar.
12 December	Kenya gains independence.
31 December	Central African Federation dissolves.

1964

26 April	Tanganyika and Zanzibar unite as Tanzania.

1965

18 February   Gambia becomes independent.

1967

May   Civil war in Nigeria begins.

1969

September   King Idris of Libya is overthrown by Qaddafi.

1970

January   Nigerian civil war comes to an end.

1972

December   Guerrilla warfare begins in Rhodesia.

1974

10 September   Independence in Guinea-Bissau.

1975

25 January   Mozambique becomes independent.
July   Sau Tomé & Principe, Cape Verde and Comoros become independent.
November   Angola gains independence and civil war begins.

1979

21 December   Lancaster House Agreement is reached on Zimbabwe.

1980

4 March   Robert Mugabe wins the elections in Zimbabwe.

1986

12 June   State of Emergency throughout South Africa.

1988

8 August   Ceasefire declared in Namibia.

1994

24 April   Nelson Mandela wins the first democratic elections in South Africa.

Part III

The Cold War of Peaceful Coexistence and the Rise of Multipolarity

1963–1971

INTRODUCTION

The international system that existed in 1963 was in many ways unrecognizable from that which was in place after 1945 or even 1953. The failed attempts to agree on the principles or the power political arrangements that should govern it had produced a Cold War and the possibility of armed conflict between two rival if unequal blocs culminating in the 1962 Cuban missile crisis. The Cold War had undergone a number of changes and it can be argued that in one fundamental way the Western aims by 1963, largely defined by the United States, had fundamentally altered. In addition, the creation of many new independent states in Asia, and particularly Africa, had by 1963 changed the global domination of the rival blocs. This was one factor in the emergence of a more multipolar world, which required a more complex approach to the maintenance and pursuit of interests by the end of the 1960s even for the United States. Another key factor was the split in the communist bloc with differences emerging by 1957 that grew and intensified, despite continued attempts at co-operation over the next 7 years. In addition, East–West relations and the nature of the Cold War's links to the preparations for hot war were dramatically affected by the development and spread of nuclear technology in the post-1953 thermo-nuclear age. And finally in economic terms, the success of the Bretton Woods system and the unrivalled dominance of the dollar were called into question as the 1970s began.

Many of these developments were clearly not the result of sudden changes in, or the disintegration of, the post-1945 global system but they were very much an indication of the long-term systemic shifts which were taking place. The 1960s saw signs of a world in which power relationships were more complex, states were more numerous, international institutions more important, East–West rivalry more tied up with regional issues, and the nature of the opposing blocs called into question. If the late 1950s had marked a move away from the attempts to destroy the power and influence of the other side, after 1962 the 1960s witnessed the further acceptance of peaceful coexistence. Anders Stephanson has seen this distinction as significant enough to suggest that the Cold War, as seen by the participants as a struggle for survival and continued existence of either the communist or capitalist worlds, was now over.[1] The confrontation engendered by the Cuban missile crisis made both sides acutely aware of the dangers of Cold War competition leading to hot war. Therefore the question of how the existing system, with its ideological competition and desire for global influence that accompanied it, could now best be manipulated assumed new importance.

From the Soviet perspective the lessons learned by 1963 were centred on the lack of traditional military and economic power and the failure to build sufficient strength before embarking on the kind of challenges that Khrushchev was disposed to mount. Always more concerned with the stark realities of power, the Soviet leadership that replaced Khrushchev saw the need to avoid any future humiliation similar to the Cuban crisis. In order to do this it was believed vital to increase all round Soviet strength to equal that of the United States. Before the crisis it had been Kennedy who launched a significant arms build-up but after it the Soviets led the way as the Americans got bogged down in Vietnam. This kind of American military expenditure did not reap dividends in strategic terms nor did it produce domestic or political benefits.

The Vietnam Issues

The Vietnam experience has been seen as a deep scar on American society and the US role in the world, even though the suffering and devastation was essentially borne by the Vietnamese. Its causes and consequences still remain controversial despite the vast literature on the subject. The fact that American involvement came from what was primarily a struggle against an anti-colonial movement with deep roots that came to be largely controlled by a communist leadership was one source of the inadequate US understanding of the struggle. At least the extent and nature of the South Vietnamese support for the communist-led resistance movement was not perceived accurately by American leaders preoccupied with communism as the explanation for anti-Western revolts. The nature of the revolt in South Vietnam has been interpreted both then and now as either essentially an indigenous movement or one provoked by exogenous forces sent from the North under the auspices of the communist government in Hanoi. In reality it was a combination of all these factors even though their timing and causation remains impossible to determine precisely. There is little doubt that the revolt was southern in origin. However, the issue is complicated by the number of insurgents who were originally natives of the North. The repression that followed limited the scope of the uprising in the South and its extension was undoubtedly connected to greater support from the North and the involvement of North Vietnamese regular armed forces. This in turn was part of a wider campaign to promote revolution which eventually received more effective support, if not instigation, from the North, communist China, and the Soviet Union.

What was the causal relationship, if any, between greater US involvement and the stages of these escalations between 1958–9 and 1963–4 remains a matter of controversy. For those who were opposed to the war Lyndon Johnson is often seen as the villain who led America to greater disasters and inevitable defeat by increasing the scale and costs of the conflict. Kennedy, on the other hand, refused to send in combat troops, and in the months before his death may have thought about scaling down the number of US military 'advisers' to the South Vietnamese government with a view to American withdrawal. The sending of ground troops in 1965 was accompanied by a bombing campaign to increase the costs to the North and eventually lead Hanoi to desist from aiding the South. Here was an example of the misguided American assumptions about the nature of a conflict with an essentially poor, predominantly rural state.

Along with the critics of the extent of American involvement are the charges levelled against Johnson that he fought the war with one hand tied behind his back. There is certainly substance to the charge of fighting a limited war but the idea that the war was ultimately winnable if only more resources had been used is far less convincing. In the first place, if American ground forces had been used to invade the North then the likelihood of direct Chinese intervention would have greatly increased. The possibility of another Korean conflict between the US and China would have constituted a major escalation and could have led to World War. At best it was likely to have brought American forces face to face with hundreds of thousands, if not millions, of Chinese, as in the Korean War from which they had escaped only in 1953. Even without that Johnson was reluctant to commit more than 500,000 US troops because of the political implications arising from such extra numbers which would require the call-up of reservists.

Internationally Vietnam was seen as part of the now accepted need to prevent the spread of communism anywhere. Key to this was deemed to be US credibility as a staunch ally, which had become much more important than at the time the Truman Doctrine claimed the US would support those resisting communism anywhere. If the Soviet Union, as the alleged orchestrator of international communism, rather than being weakened or destroyed, was now accepted as a permanent great power player on the international stage, it was far more vital to prevent any increase in its communist allies. In that sense the growth of the blocs, measured in terms of political allegiance, was now much more of a global issue. This increased competition for ideological loyalty had been created by the emergence of so many independent countries in the years up to the early 1960s. As this process was being completed, US troops were landing in Vietnam and Indo-China and became the most important element in this Cold War battle.

The debate on why the US lost in Vietnam relates not just to the extent of the military commitment, but to the tactics employed, the nature of the governmental processes by which information was obtained and acted on, the role of the press, the weaknesses of the South Vietnamese government and army, and to the fundamental fact that in order to triumph the insurgents did not have to win any battles but merely stay in the war. Both General de Gaulle and Ho Chi Minh were confident that the Americans would lose with Ho emphasizing that however long it took, the communist forces seeking to unite the country would stay and fight longer than the Americans who would give up before they did. In other words for the North and the insurgents in the South victory would only require continuing the fight.

There were other reasons for the difficulties Johnson got into in Vietnam. Some relate to domestic politics, some to the international situation, and some to the local situation. Undoubtedly one turning point which illustrates the political importance of military campaigns was the impact of the Tet offensive in 1968. This political and psychological victory for the North made a massive dent in Johnson's credibility even though American forces then inflicted a heavy military defeat on the North

Vietnamese. The role of the media may also have played a significant role in the political problems faced by Johnson as it was able to report events on television screens and in newspapers as they happened and without restriction. Vietnam was to be the last war where that kind of freedom to cover possible defeat was allowed. At home the protests were mounting when Richard Nixon became president in 1969 and it was becoming impossible for the US to stay in the war but almost as difficult to get out.

Nixon, however, claimed to have a 'secret plan' of how to do this. Never short of ideas on how to win elections Nixon claimed to have realized the way to escape from Vietnam through the achievement of 'peace with honour', but unfortunately this realization and secret plan existed neither in reality nor in Nixon's mind. Eventually the best that he could produce was the old idea of the 'Vietnamization' of the war, the failure of which had got America involved in the first place. To put pressure on the North Nixon tried extending the war outside Vietnam, negotiation, and the increased use of airpower. The North would be persuaded to accept peace by the increased use of air power as American troops left, and by the offer of simultaneous withdrawal from Vietnam. Nixon even offered to accept a ceasefire in place and thus allow Northern forces to remain in the south. Yet Hanoi had always refused to accept a ceasefire on anything other than the basis of US withdrawal and when US forces were now much weaker it had much less reason to do so. Why should it agree 'honourably' with what the Americans were going to do anyway? Hence the secret bombing and subsequent invasion of Cambodia. Yet bombing had never worked in the past and American intervention in Cambodia may have helped prepare the way for the triumph of Pol Pot's murderous communist regime there. The extension of the Vietnam War was in several ways having similar destructive effects in both Laos and Cambodia. The domino theory had predicted that the fall of Vietnam would lead to communist regimes seizing power in other parts of Indo-China and beyond. Events were now appearing to indicate that American action, as much as inaction, was helping the process by widening divisions and encouraging extremism. Peace with honour was further away than ever by 1971.

Problems in the Communist World

Central to the problems of preserving a global system based simply on competition between two opposing groups was the rift between the two communist powers. Assuming significance during Mao's November 1957 visit to Moscow when the Chinese leader indicated his reluctance to follow the Soviet ideological and policy lines, it become public by June 1960, assumed the proportions of an unbridgeable gulf by 1963, and came near to large-scale military conflict by 1969.[2] The reasons for this split which astonished many Western observers have been linked to a great variety of causes (see Chapter 7, C for its origins) but the power political implications of the final split were clearly significant (see Chapter 9, B). Power politics here is used to mean the growing competition between the Soviet Union and China not merely over leadership of the communist bloc and the relationship of this to ideology, but to their relative importance in international and regional affairs. The decade saw the growth and extension of each power's relations with states outside the communist bloc, notably India and Pakistan, which culminated in the Chinese–American links that began in 1971. Connected to this were the growing ideological divisions over the meaning of Marxist-Leninism for internal and external policy. In the latter case this essentially boiled down to a commitment to peaceful coexistence or revolutionary conflict in response to what was deemed the imperialism of the capitalist world. And then there was the question of the personalities of Khrushchev and Mao and the extent to which they contributed to each state's concerns over the general status of the two powers.

Whatever the factors behind the Sino–Soviet split, the fact that the relationship did not deteriorate uniformly, but was subject to a number of improvements on the way to the final 1963 split, owes much to the domestic constraints faced by the leaders, particularly in China. Similarly while cooperation was disrupted it was not totally ended prior to 1963. When Mao, who was determined to emphasize Chinese independence, felt in need of assistance as during the problems of the Great Leap Forward or the food shortages in 1961, attempts to improve relations were made. Khrushchev, facing his own domestic problems, even attempted to salvage the relationship after the Cuban missile crisis when insults and open ideological disputes had begun. The fact was that in both China and the Soviet Union there were those who either did not approve of peaceful coexistence or rejected the idea of inevitable conflict with the West and revolutionary wars of national liberation requiring great power military involvement. In that sense the divisions in the communist bloc, while essentially part of a power political conflict, cannot be understood without reference to the importance of ideology and domestic politics. Realist theorists, however, will always exclude these key parts of the equation from any analytical model of intrabloc competition.

The Failure of a More 'European' Europe

The Soviet Union also had continuing problems maintaining unity within its European satellite empire. Having moved in the 1950s under Khrushchev towards experimenting with less strict controls and then suffered a number of challenges to Soviet authority, Brezhnev was unlikely to tolerate further attempts at reform. The main challenge in the 1960s came from Czechoslovakia under Alexander Dubček. By then both sides had learned lessons from the Hungarian reforms and their suppression by Soviet troops. Dubček tried to ease Soviet fears by keeping the reformers within the Communist Party and emphasizing his commitment to the Warsaw Pact and to Soviet foreign policy in general. The Russians were more alert to the threat and planned military intervention well in advance while warning Dubček of that danger. They were fearful of any disorders spreading outside Czechoslovakia and of the military situation being exploited by NATO. And in terms of the ideological challenge to Soviet-style communism they had more reason to be concerned than in 1956. The Sino–Soviet split involved a Chinese challenge to Soviet ideology, which they presented as deviating from the true path of Marxist-Leninism. It was therefore no surprise that the Czech efforts to liberalize the strict ideological line required by Moscow led the latter to embark on another round of forcible repression in Eastern Europe. It also led, as part of the drive to preserve Soviet domination of the communist countries in Europe, to Brezhnev coming up with a justification based on the need to preserve the unity of the Soviet bloc. Known as the Brezhnev Doctrine (see boxed section), its commitment to prevent the spread of capitalism was in part the reverse image of the Western determination to prevent the spread of communism. It was also a sign to the Chinese and any others wishing to break free from Moscow that revealed again the connection between ideology and power politics in Soviet foreign policy. For Brezhnev it was necessary to emphasize the limited sovereignty that resulted from the importance of maintaining socialism in Europe and justify it in ideological terms. Yet the Doctrine was effectively geared to the maintenance of the Soviet satellite empire and Moscow's credibility in the global Cold War. By preventing the spread of capitalism and democracy in any form which would undermine the primacy of Soviet interpretations of Marxist-Leninsm, Soviet prestige and influence would continue.

Consequently, those leaders in Eastern Europe who achieved some small degree of independence from Moscow were those who, paradoxically, became closely attuned to the Kremlin's version of socialism and avoided any form of Western politics and economics. Ceauşescu's strategy in Romania was to try and carve out a more independent foreign policy from within the Warsaw Pact and Albania's was to move closer to the other leading communist power. Similar challenges were mounted in the Western bloc which was starting to run into economic difficulties as economic benefits were also becoming a less effective form of glue in the Eastern bloc. The Western bloc was to prove far more stable, having only one leading power, and because capitalism in Europe proved far more successful and adaptable than Soviet communism, despite the war in Vietnam creating difficulties for the global capitalist economy.

In the West there were changes within the bloc that have subsequently been seen as producing a massive shift in the nature of the state system through European integration. The further steps towards the economic integration of Western Europe and the creation of a powerful economic bloc not only caused interest and concern on both sides of the Atlantic but was challenged by the French leader Charles de Gaulle. De Gaulle embarked on a major effort to refashion the Alliance in order to enhance the role of Europe in general and France in particular through the modification of US dominance. This, it has been argued[3], was not simply the French assertion of a new leadership role in a Europe more independent of the US, but part of an attempt to weaken the two opposing blocs in order to build better relations with the East and create a more 'European' Europe. A more independent Western Europe was largely ruled out by the West German refusal to abandon the commitment to an 'Atlantic' Europe and, albeit temporarily, by the 1968 Soviet invasion of Czechoslovakia which revealed the lack of progress in the East.

The Politics of Nuclear Strategy

The attempts to change the nature of relationships within the Western bloc were very much related to the role and development of thermonuclear weapons. Meanwhile the Soviet rearmament effort had, arguably, for the first time produced a truly bipolar world as their nuclear forces had caught up with (some would later argue overtaken) the US. Their ability to project power over greater distances, as with the creation of an ocean-going navy, had also been developed by the end of the period. Yet the growing realization in the 1950s that the use of thermonuclear weapons on a major scale would make war unwinnable had come to mean that such weapons were in essence unusable. However, the weapons themselves symbolized power and consequently there was a strong case for making them seem usable. Opponents of such weapons argued that the effort to devise situations and strategies of use was simply trying to rationalize the irrational. Supporters claimed that nuclear weapons, when linked with conventional weapons in a clearly defined military strategy, would enhance deterrence. By making the use of nuclear weapons, in a limited and more flexible way short of global war, seem rational, an all-out exchange would become less likely as the deterrent became more credible. Hence the NATO development of 'flexible response' within the parameters of mutually assured destruction. The idea was that limited escalation would produce responses short of all-out war and encourage the opponent at some stage to abandon the conflict for fear of further punishment through escalation. Unfortunately in the Vietnam War it was proved to be incorrect as regards the use of conventional bombs.

There were a number of other problems in that the US Strategic Air Command did not accept either the idea of limited war or of flexible response. General Tommy Power, the head of the Strategic Air Command, said after listening to an explanation of the new concept 'Why do you want us to restrain ourselves? . . . The whole idea is to kill the bastards'[4] To many the only sensible way to use nuclear weapons was to use them all first in order to limit the retaliation that would inevitably come, but as the numbers of nuclear warheads expanded this was increasingly difficult to do. Moreover, the development of nuclear weapons was still influenced by interservice rivalry with none of the services prepared to leave the deterrent solely to another, so that by the 1960s the US was developing deterrents for all three services to deploy.

Whatever the strategic doctrine or military rationale, the political importance of nuclear weapons remained and was at the heart of the trans-Atlantic debate over the power relationships within the Western Alliance. Should not the Europeans have a say in the exercise of such powerful weapons? At issue was the continued, delicate question of Germans being in control of nuclear weapons, the nature of American leadership, and the problematic question of 'independent' nuclear weapons when an integrated flexible response was deemed necessary. From one predominantly American perspective the idea of a multilateral nuclear force (MLF) provided a solution to all three problems. The Germans could be treated as a more equal partner by being involved in a nuclear force, even if the weapons were supplied by the Americans, and might therefore never ask for national control over any nuclear weapons placed on their soil. NATO would be united in contributing to an alliance force and the appearance of American dominance would be reduced. Both these aspects could contribute to the strengthening of the alliance. At the same time, for those in the US who were worried about European independence the possibility existed of ensuring that the US effectively controlled these weapons. It was not just their targeting and supply but the importance of ensuring any use was in accordance with American wishes and strategy. As flexible response was being discussed this assumed more importance and was another way of attempting to counter the loss of American control stemming from the creation by 1964 of a French independent deterrent.[5] The last thing that the US wanted was a European power provoking a major nuclear exchange independently of the Americans. The British and the French were always opposed to the MLF concept. They believed it would damage their nuclear status and prove unwieldy to implement even if there was agreement as to how it was to be constructed, and after many talks the idea proved impossible to implement.

A Less Divided Europe?

The different views about the nature of the Western Alliance were eased with the departure of General de Gaulle in 1969. By then the German leader, Willy Brandt, had taken up the mantle of creating a new, less confrontational Europe of opposing blocs through his Ostpolitik. Brandt was building on the initiatives of Kurt Kiesinger in a quest to establish more economic links with the Eastern bloc, lessen the hostility between the two parts of Germany, and find some formula to reduce the possibility of armed conflict. There had been a number of contacts between Western leaders and the Soviets in the 1960s, in addition to de Gaulle, and there was a growing realization on both sides of the Iron Curtain of the benefits these could bring. There was the need to reduce the risk of military conflict, to resolve the German issue, to establish a more independent role within both blocs, and to benefit from economic contacts. All these were especially important for West Germans, but the Soviets too were attracted by the idea of obtaining technology and other economic advantages from the West and by implementing their long-standing idea of a European security system. Such a development would enable them to reduce the threat from Germany while removing the influence of the US from Europe and possibly create divisions within the Western camp. None of this meant that the Cold War was being superseded and the ideological requirements of either side changing. As in the past the new moves towards détente were in many ways part of a strategy in the West to gain a Cold War advantage and win the ideological battle. By opening up new contacts the attractions of a more successful economic system, as manifested in the more plentiful array of consumer goods, could prove attractive in the East if links could be established that would make this more evident.

For Brandt it was also a way of ending the division of Germany, and by establishing diplomatic relations with Eastern European countries he added to the impact of the ending of the Hallstein Doctrine whereby West Germany broke off relations with those countries that recognized the GDR in the East. In 1970 Brandt signed a treaty with Moscow renouncing force and increasing economic links, but also recognizing the inviolability of European boundaries. Ostpolitik had definite limitations as far as the erosion of the blocs and the *de facto* post-war outcomes were concerned. The four-power agreement which recognized the status quo in Berlin in 1971 was another indication of how new policies were not designed to make a clear break with the old concepts of a divided Europe. Political agreements on these lines would take a long time to have more than a limited effect and détente leading to the end of the Cold War was not something that was envisaged. The agreement in 1971 to hold a European Security Conference seemed only another sign of the desire to avoid hot war while the ideological battle continued apace.

Cold War in the Less Developed World

In the Western hemisphere the nature of the Cold War was particularly affected by the impact of the Cuban missile crisis and the earlier advent to power of Fidel Castro. It was the latter event that had galvanized Kennedy but it was his successor that was forced to deal with the consequences of his policy's increasing failure. If anything, by the mid-1960s it was clear that poverty and inequality were increasing in Latin America. Without structural change, such as land reform, the injection of capital was only likely to exacerbate the problems created by the structural inequality. If large landowners were given incentives to expand GDP by producing more cash crops, it required the removal of more land from food production and the creation of more landless labourers. What was then created was not a new middle class attracted to democracy but more landless labourers willing to support revolutionary movements. As such discontent grew, it became more likely that liberal reformists would appear a much riskier option than military dictators.

   The cycle of instability and the concern about left-wing regimes was what produced numerous twentieth-century American interventions, including that by Johnson in the Dominican Republic (see Chapter 11, A). As in the 1950s the fear was not what the communists might do (there were no strong communist organizations outside Cuba) but how they might be created and encouraged. The fact that a government or leader might pave the way for communists was what still concerned American policy-makers. There were the old implications for Cold War credibility and American economic interests which were more worrisome since Castro and his supporters were trying to produce exactly the result the US feared. This was the aspect of the Cuban threat which increasingly obsessed Washington. Security was, in concrete terms, nothing more than the threat of an odd gunboat unless of course, as the missile crisis had shown, the Soviets were given the opportunity to install weapons. Only by allowing communists to take power or to dominate the equivalent of Popular Front (broad-based left-wing) governments could this be prevented, although the political benefits of suppressing communism were much more of a consideration. In

Latin America the concern about the instability from which radicalism grew was, like a pendulum, swinging back towards support for dictators while Johnson and Nixon were in the White House. Eisenhower had seen dictators creating opposition which led to their overthrow and the risk of radicalism. Reform was therefore needed but as the failure of the Alliance for Progress became evident, Johnson and Nixon saw attempts to promote change leading to instability and the need for dictators to ruthlessly suppress any radical discontent.

Colonial and post-Colonial Conflicts in Asia

The British clash with Indonesia in 1963, known as the 'Konfrontasi' or Confrontation, was part colonial and part post-colonial in that it involved areas still subject to colonial rule and a number of independent states. The British became concerned to maintain their position in South-East Asia during the final years of their direct rule with a view to a future position of influence and the retention of great power status. By now the strains on an overstretched military position which symbolized this status, and which was generally referred to by policy-makers as 'responsibilities' or 'commitments', were increasingly severe. The centre of the dilemma in the early 1960s was Singapore, and Macmillan approved a scheme whereby the island colony would be incorporated into the pro-Western newly independent Malayan Federation thereby avoiding the danger of radical Chinese influence and saving Britain much of the expense of operating the naval facilities at Singapore. Unfortunately, like most attempts to avoid facing up to the hard choices involved in the loss of relative power and decline, the scheme went disastrously wrong; and it failed to postpone the inevitable which came, as in the Middle East (see Chapter 11, B), at much greater cost.

The scheme involved not just the creation of a new federal state, Malaysia, through the incorporation of Singapore, but also the incorporation of the North Borneo territories to ensure that the Chinese did not become a majority in the new federation. This alienated the Indonesians who had designs on North Borneo and they preceded to embark on a propaganda campaign and armed border raids short of full-scale war. In one sense this relieved Britain of the problem of providing token forces to support the Americans in Vietnam as the British could claim they were making a contribution to the Western cause in Asia. In another sense it imposed an increasingly heavy defence burden which was exactly what Malaysia had been designed to reduce. It was only with the collapse of the anti-Western Sukarno regime in Jakarta that the Confrontation ended, but with it went the American financial underwriting of the UK economy as the British were no longer making the desired military commitment in Asia or Europe. By January 1969 the British were therefore forced to accept the military withdrawal from East of Suez in order to cut defence costs. This was the first time in the post-war years that a significant 'responsibility' or commitment had been voluntarily abandoned.

In the subcontinent the post-colonial problem of the disputed territory of Kashmir continued to cause difficulties between the independent states of India and Pakistan and culminated in a war in 1965. The failure fully to understand the complexities of new regional rivalries in the context of the Cold War brought with it significant regional instability. And its effect on the relations between neutral India and Pakistan was responsible for the initial American tilt to Pakistan that was repeated in the Indo-Pakistani war over the creation of Bangladesh. On both occasions this led to undesirable consequences with the short-term danger of direct US military involvement in the latter case and increasing tensions in the 1950s. More importantly none of America's goals were achieved. China and Pakistan drew closer together which helped the Chinese in their brief war with India in 1962. By the time of the Indo–Pakistani war in 1965 it was no longer realistic to see regional crises as simply manifestations of a bipolar conflict. New states that had emerged did not always fit into such a framework as they had more important internal or regional considerations.

Both these aspects characterized the clash between India and Pakistan in 1971 which grew out of the break-up of East and West Pakistan and the creation of an independent Bangladesh out of the eastern section. As refugees fled from the East into India to escape from West Pakistan forces another Indo–Pakistani clash ensued. On this occasion the US came down on the side of Pakistan for reasons unconnected to the local conflict (see boxed section). The importance of the new link to China and the need to challenge the Soviet backing of India at the UN led Nixon and Kissinger to send US naval forces to the Bay of Bengal. Now even the Chinese, as a potential 'friend', had to see the US response as that of a credible Cold War partner when the Soviets were formalizing their links to India with a friendship treaty. The US navy was too late to avert a Pakistani defeat without full-scale war, but it made the Americans more determined to prevent a Pakistani defeat over Kashmir. War had been risked not over a local or even a regional goal but because of a threat to a particular global strategy. Astute observers would have reasoned that while instability in the less developed world continued, increasing Cold War tensions and conflict would be more likely to prevail than any concept of détente modelled on the extension of European developments. Moreover, in the 1960s both superpowers were slow to realize that less developed world conflicts could not be fitted into bloc conflicts despite US acknowledgement of the emergence of a more multipolar world.

The Origins of the Third Arab–Israeli War and Conflict in a Divided Middle East

The Middle East remained an extremely unstable region, dominated by the Arab–Israeli conflict. It was to produce a number of military conflicts in the 1960s stemming, as elsewhere, from the legacies of Western rule and the problems of colonial territories on the verge of independence. Inter-Arab rivalries developed to the extent of being referred to as an Arab Cold War[6] and continued to take several forms: the clash between conservative monarchists (as in Saudi Arabia), and radical republicans (as in Egypt); the rivalry over leadership of the Arab world, as between Iraq and Egypt; the battle between secular and religious ideologies, and the links to the respective superpower rivals. On top of this was the Arab–Israeli conflict and the fact that in this period there emerged for the first time a Palestinian organization prepared to stand up for a purely Palestinian rather that Arab cause. From all this underlying instability there developed the third war between Israel and the Arab states in 1967, a major inter-Arab war in the Yemen beginning in 1962, the British military campaign in Aden from 1963, and the Jordanian crushing and expulsion of Palestinians in 1970 which involved the Syrians and had the potential to spark a much bigger regional conflict.

In 1964 the completion of the Israeli scheme conveying water from the River Jordan to the Negev was accompanied by a rival Arab scheme in Syria to supersede it by diverting the river, which in turn produced Israeli attacks that effectively prevented its implementation. Disputes between Israel and Syria also centred on rights to use the waters of the Sea of Galilee, land use in the demilitarised zone (DMZ), and Syrian support from Palestinian guerrilla groups, the largest of which was *Al Fatah* led by Yasser Arafat. Arafat had ceased working with the Palestinian Liberation Organization, the umbrella organization set up in 1964 to provide a uniquely Palestinian voice, at the end of that year because of its ties with Egypt, which, like Jordan, was opposed to guerrilla attacks on Israel. These groups operated mainly from Jordan and were designed to drag Israel into a war with the Arab states but they contributed little to the 1967 conflict as compared to the growing hostility between Egypt and Syria.

In February 1966 a more radical Ba'athist group led by General Jadid seized power in Damascus and took a more aggressive, hard line stance against Israel. Lacking domestic support, the way to encourage this was seen to lie in a harsher response to Israeli actions. As Israeli–Syrian tension rose Cairo and Damascus came closer together and a major air and land battle near the Sea of Galilee in August 1966 ultimately led to the signing of a defence pact between Egypt and Syria in November. More immediately it produced Syrian threats to attack targets in Israel and suspicion and insecurity were obviously heightened within Israel. In November 1966 after the signing of the defence pact an Israeli Defence Force invasion produced attacks on three Jordanian towns which killed fifteen Arab Legion soldiers and involved con-siderable damage to life and property. These reprisals for guerrilla attacks or border disputes had been taking place for over a decade but rarely on such a large scale and were accompanied by UN condemnation of Israel. All these clashes produced accusations and counter-accusations of responsibility, as did the last act before the events in May 1967 from which the immediate causes of the war sprang. Again this occurred between Israel and Syria. In April 1967 six Syrian MIGS were shot down following disputes over land cultivation in the DMZ which had produced exchanges on the ground.

The events in May which preceded the June Israeli attack on its Arab neighbours are sources of such conflicting interpretations that these will be given in terms of pro-Arab and pro-Israeli claims of what each side intended and why (see Chapter 11, D boxed section). The central issues are whether the withdrawal of the UN peacekeeping force in Sinai, the subsequent Egyptian blockade of the Straits of Tiran, the statement by General Rabin that Israel would occupy Damascus, the security position on the Golan

Heights and in the old city of Jerusalem in particular, tell us about the plans of the two sides and whether they constitute legitimate grounds for an Israeli pre-emptive strike or not. If not, were the Arab fears of possible Israeli aggression justified? Finally, regarding the two superpowers, what can explain the Soviet warning that Israeli troops were massing on the Syrian border and what was the American spy ship USS *Liberty* doing and why did the Israelis sink it?

The war destroyed the Soviet-supplied Egyptian air force, led to the continuing and generally accepted illegal occupation of the West Bank, and the illegal annexation of East Jerusalem. It was probably the most significant act in the history of the Arab–Israeli conflict and the settlement (land for peace) suggested by the UN (resolution 242) remains the basis of the individual settlement made with Egypt and of the Saudi peace plan today. The reasons given by the Israelis for rejecting it then no longer exist today, indicating that land has become more important than peace whatever it was in the past. There was certainly no peace in the wake of the 1967 war. In 1969 a war of attrition began across the Suez Canal, and in 1970 Israel launched massive raids against Cairo. The following year came the second of the American attempts to bring about a settlement in the form of the Rogers Plan but land for peace could not come about while Israel refused to make the first move by giving up land and the Arabs refused to recognize the right of the state of Israel to exist in peace.

Further problems and human suffering were produced by King Hussein of Jordan's decision forcibly to expel Palestinians from Jordan in September 1970. By then the Palestinians had become a major challenge to Hussein's regime. These radical refugees, supportive of PLO resistance rather than Hussein's desire to avoid confrontation with Israel, unlike in other Arab countries, were granted full citizenship rights. Especially after the 1967 war and consequent loss of Jordanian territory, the social and demographic make-up of the country was rapidly changing and Palestinians in the East bank began to outnumber the original Transjordan population. Moreover, the Palestinians in the refugee camps, who were excluded from the political process, turned more to the PLO which was not only openly challenging Hussein but creating a state within a state with its own police and radio station. The Popular Front for the Liberation of Palestine (PFLP) called for the overthrow of the state, unlike *Al-Fatah* and Arafat with their policy of non-intervention. Things only changed when Hussein accepted the Rogers Plan in July 1970 and its call for negotiations on the basis of Resolution 242 that accepted Israel's right to exist. Things came to a head in September 1970 when the PFLP twice attempted to assassinate the King and carried out five aircraft hijackings. A showdown was unavoidable and both sides made preparations for the bloody conflict which led to the rout and expulsion of the Palestinians in what became known as Black September. Only Syria moved to give the Palestinians military support but was warned off by Moscow and a serious crisis was avoided even if the problems in the Middle East had increased.

The Legacy of Colonial Rule in Sub-Saharan Africa

Serious problems leading to civil war also occurred in Nigeria which was experiencing the legacy of British rule. In many African colonies the preparations for the transfer of power had been totally inadequate in terms of what the British Colonial Office intended (see Chapter 8, D). The difficulties of staying proved harder to face than the problems of leaving and this was true in the vast territory of Nigeria. African leaders tended to bury the problems they faced under a mound of optimism which saw the newly gained political kingdom as conquering the old economic difficulties and inadequate social and political structures. Some experimented with African socialism while others preferred to use more conventional Western methods of development but all faced corruption and poverty. Many of the vast array of African societies lacked any sense of civic consciousness and their loyalties lay with the extended family and ethnic group rather than with the African state. Impartial civil servants dedicated to government service were hard to find and even harder to educate. For many, independence came at the wrong time with the developing problems of the global economy, and the rising expectations at the start of the 1960s could not be sustained. The fight for day-to-day survival affected people and governments alike. Many regimes faced military coups and the idea of a one-party state became accepted by many as more suitable to African conditions and the suppression of political conflicts based on ethnic loyalties. Some saw visions of an African future built on cooperation and unity, but despite the foundation of the Organization of African States in 1963 its practical achievements were small and non-existent. African states were more likely to break apart than to come together in effective regional bodies and this was certainly the case even in Nigeria.

The British had been worried about Nigeria's future before its independence in 1960. Their policy of divide and rule was followed late in the day by one of unite and decolonize, but the basis of this unity was hard to detect. The British looked to a federal constitution to link local power in the three main regions to a central government in Lagos. But apart from the regional split between the three biggest of Nigeria's thousands of ethnic groups, the more heavily populated and Muslim north was far less developed than the eastern and western regions in the south. In 1966 the failure to reconcile Nigerians to a central political authority led to a military coup of predominantly Ibo officers from the eastern region and the end of the democratic advantage enjoyed by the more populous north. A second coup followed which brought General Gowan to power who belonged to one of the smaller ethnic groups but who failed to prevent a massacre of Ibos in the north.

The civil war which followed in 1967 was prolonged by the indirect involvement of France, the USSR, and Britain. The suffering it produced before its end in 1970 was a hint of what was to come in Africa. Paradoxically while even small states had produced empires on the continent the empires could not easily reproduce states. The divisions within them were exacerbated by internal conflicts accompanied by a need to preserve the artificially created boundaries out of respect for the successful liberation of the state. African wars of the 1960s were to become features of the international system in later years. If the challenges to the control of the powerful in Europe offered the prospect of greater independence and hopes for the future, the attainment of independence by Africans appeared to be bringing despair and disillusionment. By the start of the 1970s there were signs that neither democracy, socialism, or capitalism would do anything to prevent poverty, war, and suffering with or without the Cold War.

NOTES

1. Anders Stephanson's commentary in 'Symposium: The Origins of the Cold War', *Diplomatic History*, 2 (1993).
2. Odd Arne Westad (ed.), *Brothers in Arms: The Rise and Fall of the Sino-Soviet Alliance, 1945–1963* (Stanford University Press, Stanford, 1998), 20–9.
3. F. Bozo, *Two Strategies for Europe: de Gaulle, the United States and the Atlantic Alliance* (Rowman & Littlefield, Lanham, 2001), xi–xiii.
4. Fred Kaplan, *The Wizards of Armageddon* (Simon & Schuster, New York, 1984), 246.
5. The British 'independent' deterrent was not regarded by many on both sides of the Atlantic as truly independent and this view was also privately expressed by officials in Britain. The key thing was to ensure that the deterrent appeared to be independent.
6. See Malcolm Kerr, *The Arab Cold War: Gamal 'Abd Al-Nasir and his Rivals, 1958–1970* (London, Oxford University Press, 3rd edn., 1971).

PART III CHRONOLOGY: THE RISE OF MULTIPOLARITY, 1963–1971

1963

20 January	Indonesia begins opposition campaign to creation of 'Malaysia'.
5 August	Test Ban Treaty signed in Moscow.
16 September	Formal launch of Malaysia leads Sukarno of Indonesia to intensify 'confrontation' with it.
1 November	Overthrow of President Diem of South Vietnam following months of instability.
22 November	President Kennedy assassinated in Texas.

1964

February–March	Fighting between Greek–Cypriot and Turkish–Cypriot communities, leads to deployment of UN peacekeeping force.
2–4 August	Gulf of Tonkin incident: supposed attacks on US ships by North Vietnam.
14 October	Khruschev replaced by Brezhnev and Kosygin.
16 October	First Chinese atom bomb exploded.
3 November	Johnson wins US election.

1965

24 February	US begins 'Rolling Thunder' bombing of North Vietnam.
8 March	Marines are first US ground troops deployed in Vietnam War.
25 April	Attempt to overthrow Cabral government in Dominican Republic.
28–29 April	Johnson sends Marines to forestall leftist drift in Dominican Republic.
August	Indo–Pakistani tension mounts in disputed Kashmir.
22 September	Cease-fire in Indo–Pakistani War.
30 September	Coup in Indonesia followed by army crackdown on Communist party.

1966

January	Violent overthrow of Abubakar's government in Nigeria.
10 March	De Gaulle quits NATO military structure.
March	General Suharto effectively becomes Indonesian leader.
20 June–1 July	De Gaulle visits USSR.
July	Warsaw Pact calls for Pan-European security system.
August	Indonesia ends 'Confrontation' with Malaysia.
September	Violence in Northern Nigeria, directed against Ibos from the Eastern Region.

1967

7 April	Israelis shoot down several Syrian aircraft in latest border tension.
5–10 June	Six day Arab–Israeli war.
23–25 June	Glassboro' meeting of Johnson and Kosygin.
5 July	Civil war begins between Nigerian government and secessionist 'Biafra'.
22 November	UN resolution 242, on Middle East, passed.
14 December	NATO adopts Harmel Report, opening way for talks with Warsaw Pact.

1968

23 January	North Korea seizes USS *Pueblo*: not released until December.
30 January	Start of 'Tet' offensive in Vietnam.
31 March	Johnson starts partial 'bombing halt' in Vietnam and leaves US presidential race.
April	Czechoslovakian Communist Party, under Dubček, begins to liberalize.
1 July	Non-Proliferation Treaty signed.
Late August	USSR leads invasion of Czechoslovakia to end liberalization.
5 November	Nixon wins US Presidency.

1969

2 March	Major Soviet–Chinese border clash on Damyansky island.
25 July	Nixon's 'Guam Doctrine' on Vietnam: will hand fighting over to South Vietnamese.
17 November	SALT talks open between US and USSR.

1970

January	Nigerian forces overrun what remains of 'Biafra'; major international aid programme to relieve famine there.
18 March	Prince Sihanouk of Cambodia overthrown by Lon Nol.
April–June	US and South Vietnamese launch incursion into Cambodia.
7 August	Cease-fire agreed in Arab–Israeli 'war of attrition', which followed the 1967 war.
12 August	Soviet–West German Treaty signed.
September	Civil war in Jordan between royal government and Palestinians.

1971

February/March	South Vietnamese incursion into Laos.
15 July	Forthcoming visit of Nixon to China announced.
15 August	US introduces trade restrictions and ends convertibility of dollars into gold.
3 September	Four-power agreement on Berlin signed.
20 October	Brandt of West Germany wins Nobel Peace Prize for Ostpolitik.
25 October	UN votes for Communist Chinese membership.
November	Rising Indo–Pakistani tension over East Pakistan.
10 December	NATO agrees to Warsaw Pact proposal for a European Security Conference.
16 December	Cease-fire in Indo–Pakistani War over 'Bangladeshi' independence.

9 The Eastern and Western Blocs in the 1960s

A. US–Soviet Relations from the Missile Crisis to Détente, 1963–1971

Khrushchev, Kennedy, and the Test Ban Treaty

In the wake of the Cuban missile crisis (see Chapter 7, D) the Soviet leader, Nikita Khrushchev, felt far less confident than he had been a year before about dealing with American power. Apart from the Cuban setback, Soviet interests had not advanced much in the Congo or Laos; the building of the Berlin Wall had staunched the haemorrhage of the East German population to the West, but essentially left the German problem as deadlocked as ever; and Khrushchev was beset, within the communist bloc, by continuing criticism from China. Within the USSR itself hasty, ill-considered reforms of industry and agriculture had done nothing to push forward

his self-declared aim of matching US economic strength within 20 years. Kennedy in contrast could be more confident at the end of 1962. The Bay of Pigs humiliation had been expunged, the Democrats fared well in the November Congressional elections, and America's nuclear superiority had just been demonstrated clearly to the world. But Arthur Schlesinger, the President's in-house historian, believed that Kennedy's 'feelings underwent a qualitative change after Cuba: a world in which nations threatened each other with nuclear weapons now seemed . . . an intolerable . . . world.'[1] Indeed, both superpower leaders seemed to be thinking the same way about the need for nuclear arms control after the recent crisis, for on 19 December Khrushchev wrote to Kennedy urging progress on the Test Ban Treaty, which had been discussed for almost 5 years without result. The need to reduce the possibility of hot war between the world's two great rivals was now more pressing.

Nuclear arms control became a more pressing issue after 1962 leading to at least three significant agreements within a decade: the Test Ban Treaty of 1963, the Non-Proliferation Treaty of 1968, and the first Strategic Arms Limitation Treaty of 1972. Indeed, the nuclear issue provided a constructive and consistent focus for US–Soviet discussions which had been absent since 1947. However, the image of Kennedy and Khrushchev turning easily to a policy of détente after the psychological shock of seeming close to hot war is a simplistic one. Their relationship became less volatile and more rational, but they remained firm ideological opponents and there was no early rush into signing the Test Ban Treaty (TBT). Indeed, if anything, the early months of 1963 saw a retreat from the position of December. Khrushchev's letter had hinted at a major breakthrough, largely because he appeared ready, for the first time, to accept a long-standing American demand that a TBT be verified through on-site inspections. Previously the Soviets had often condemned any inspections on their soil as unnecessary, an infringement of sovereignty, and likely to be exploited by the West for espionage purposes. Yet the Americans had always insisted that, if there were to be a ban on *underground* nuclear tests, it could only be properly enforced through inspections. (Atmospheric and underwater tests were easily detectable, but underground ones could be disguised, if small enough, or confused with other seismic activity.) Khrushchev was offering to allow only two or three inspections per year however, and the Americans felt this quite inadequate, believing seven to be the bare minimum they would accept. When Kennedy explained this to him, Khrushchev felt let down and by February 1963 the TBT talks had stalled.

By now such failures to achieve results in arms talks were becoming a pattern. The environmental danger posed by atmospheric tests had been an international concern since at least 1954, when a Japanese fishing boat had been caught in the fallout from a Pacific test. Various anti-nuclear groups had sprung up, especially in Western Europe, notably Germany's 'Campaign against Nuclear Death' and Britain's 'Campaign for Nuclear Disarmament'. In March 1958, Khrushchev had evidently spotted the propaganda value of the issue and began a unilateral moratorium on all tests. The US matched this 7 months later and talks on a test ban then began between the superpowers and the third nuclear power, Britain, in Geneva under UN auspices. The moratorium had held until August 1961, when the Soviets began a new series of tests, but the Geneva talks made little progress, partly because of the verification problem. When the Kennedy administration, too, revived its test programme the situation for a TBT seemed bleak, yet there were strong reasons to revive it in late 1962: not only to ease East–West tensions after the missile crisis, and to satisfy world opinion, but also to begin a policy of non-proliferation. The prospect of a large number of countries obtaining nuclear weapons, increasing the dangers of a nuclear war, was a concern to both superpowers and a TBT might help to deter states from developing them. The deadlock on a treaty in early 1963 was partly due to Khrushchev's weakened domestic position following his failure to appease the hardliners by securing Soviet gains from the missile crisis. For a time he was in danger of being replaced; however, in April his main critic, deputy premier, Frol Kozlov, suddenly died.

In mid-1963, following Kozlov's death, a series of events suggested a marked improvement in US–Soviet relations. On 9 June, at the American University in Washington, Kennedy gave a major address in which he denied any desire for a 'Pax Americana' and urged a genuine peace with the USSR, based on mutual understanding, with a revival of TBT talks. A full translation of the speech was, unusually, printed by the Soviet daily *Izvestia*. Eleven days later the superpowers signed the 'hot line' agreement, establishing a teletype link between the Pentagon (later moved to the White House) and the Kremlin, to allow direct, rapid communication in times of crisis. On 2 July Khrushchev, in a speech in Berlin, welcomed these recent moves and made a definitive offer of a TBT, which was then negotiated in Moscow between 15 and 25 July, with a US team headed by the veteran envoy Averell Harriman, and a British team under Lord Hailsham. The TBT was formally signed by the three foreign ministers on 5 August and, despite some fear of Soviet 'cheating', it was ratified by the US Senate on 24 September. Finally, on 9 October, the first US sale of grain to the

USSR was announced. It was this series of positive developments which created the impression of a new dawn for East–West relations, which, in retrospect, some of Kennedy's staff saw as being brutally ended with his assassination in Dallas, Texas on 22 November. 'The breathing spell had become a pause, the pause was becoming a détente and no one could foresee what further changes lay ahead.'[2] Indeed, it was probably because of the improvement in relations that suspicion of Soviet involvement in the assassination was quickly discounted.

The extent of détente in 1963 is easy to exaggerate however. As Michael Beschloss writes, Kennedy's pro-peace speech at the American University, 'though deeply felt, was as much the product of political calculation as any address (he) ever gave', designed to revive progress on the TBT, win public support and placate Khrushchev after their New Year wrangle over verification.[3] As to the 'hot line' agreement, it was a useful, practical step but it had taken a series of misunderstandings and near-nuclear war over Cuba to bring it about—and it was only to be used at the most critical moments. Even the TBT, significant as it was as a first step in nuclear arms control and welcome as it was in ending radiation releases from atmospheric tests, had two vital flaws. First, because of the continuing disagreements over verification, it was not a comprehensive ban on tests. It ended them in the atmosphere and underwater, where verification was easy, but not underground. Second, and even more harmful from the non-proliferation point of view, the treaty was not signed by the latest nuclear power, France, nor by the likely next nuclear power, China. The grain deal was an indication that superpower relations might be becoming more 'normal', but other problems persisted, not least over Berlin. Kennedy had visited the city in June 1963, making his celebrated remark 'Ich bin ein Berliner', which only highlighted Western determination to remain there; in October, Soviet harassment of traffic into the city was revived and lasted several weeks. October also saw Khrushchev take offence at NATO discussions on a 'Multilateral Nuclear Force' (see Chapter 9, D), in which West Germany might share control of nuclear weapons. And the last noteworthy event in bilateral relations before Kennedy's death was the expulsion of an American professor from the USSR on suspicion of espionage. Kennedy and Khrushchev may have succeeded in reducing tensions after Cuba, therefore, making more agreements in mid-1963 than the two countries had since 1947, but ideological differences, security suspicions, and periodic irritations went on. The Cold War still assumed importance even if there was less chance of it leading to a global catastrophe.

In the Shadow of Vietnam, 1964–1968

Signs of détente did not end with Kennedy's assassination. Soviet pressure on Berlin eased once more; in April 1964 Khrushchev and the new American President, Lyndon Johnson, agreed to reduce their production of fissionable uranium in a further attempt to ease public fears of the nuclear danger; and on 1 June 1964 a consular agreement was signed which freed travel between the superpowers. But the pattern of relations was similar to Kennedy's last months, with plenty of signs of suspicion and difference. Johnson refused to be drawn into an early summit with Khrushchev, well aware of what had happened to Kennedy at Vienna in 1961; the Soviets remained agitated by the prospect of West Germany gaining access to nuclear weapons via a Multilateral Force (MLF); and, partly thanks to the FBI's fear of internal security problems in the US, the consular agreement was not ratified by the Senate until March 1967. In the second half of 1964 both countries were preoccupied by domestic events. Johnson was elected President by a landslide in November but, less than three weeks earlier, on 14 October, Khrushchev was thrown out of office following a Kremlin coup. His unpredictability, the failure of his agricultural reforms, and foreign policy setbacks (such as Cuba's alienation)—plus his intention to replace some Politburo members—led to his ousting as Communist Party leader by Leonid Brezhnev. Brezhnev (see boxed section) proved a far more cautious, unadventurous leader and one prepared to share power with a team of ministers. In the international field he relied heavily on his foreign minister, Andrei Gromyko, as well as the prime minister, Alexei Kosygin. In fact, whilst Brezhnev, as party leader, took charge of relations with other communist states, it was Kosygin who often handled

Alexei Kosygin (1904–1980)

Raised in St Petersburg (Leningrad), Kosygin trained as a textile engineer while also developing a political career and, as Mayor of Leningrad at the outbreak of the Second World War, was a key figure in its resistance to siege by the Germans. He rose slowly in the Soviet leadership under Stalin and Khrushchev, becoming deputy prime minister in 1960. Like Brezhnev, with whom he allied to overthrow Khrushchev, Kosygin was a competent, reliable administrator, hard-working, sensible, and straightforward, but also cautious and uninspiring. After 1964 Kosygin was determined to safeguard his position as premier by controlling foreign policy with non-communist states. It was he, not Brezhnev, who met President Lyndon Johnson at Glassboro' in June 1967. He also made numerous other foreign trips, speaking at the United Nations and holding discussions with British premier, Harold Wilson, in February 1967 in a bid to broker a Vietnam settlement. Yet for all his self-reliance, knowledge, and toughness, Kosygin was never a real threat to Brezhnev's predominance in the post-Khrushchev leadership, and it was Brezhnev who took the leading role in developing détente with the United States after 1971. Although Kosygin continued to serve as premier until a few months before his death, he had a far lower profile in the 1970s than he had in the 1960s, and was increasingly plagued by ill-health.

relations with non-communist states, at least until the early 1970s. Compared to Khrushchev's years this later period saw few head-to-head arguments between Moscow and Washington.

Anatoly Dobrynin, the long-serving Soviet ambassador to Washington, has written that in the 1960s, despite the less frantic atmosphere 'peripheral issues kept interfering with the development of Soviet-American relations, creating tensions and putting off the settlement of really important problems.'[4] The most important, and persistent, 'peripheral issue' was the Vietnam War which, in 1965, saw the deployment of US combat forces, as well as large-scale bombing of North Vietnam. The Soviets had little interest in letting the war intensify, given the dangers it presented to international stability. Nonetheless, they had little choice but to back their fellow Marxists in the North, especially given China's attempt to outbid Moscow for the leadership of the communist world by supporting Hanoi strongly (see Chapter 10, B and C). The fact that the USSR supplied North Vietnam with arms influenced Congress to block Johnson's attempts to improve links with the Eastern bloc through a 1966 trade bill. The MLF was less important as a bone of contention after Johnson ceased to promote it in late 1964, but West Germany did not accept its demise until 1966. Other peripheral issues included the Middle East where, in early June 1967, the Six Day War saw both superpowers back opposing sides. The war overshadowed the only meeting Johnson had with a high-ranking Soviet leader, the so-called 'mini-summit' with Kosygin at Glassboro', New Jersey, on 23–4 June. The atmosphere was friendly enough, with Johnson accepting an invitation to visit the USSR for a full summit with Brezhnev, but on all the substantive points the two seemed to differ. Thus Kosygin criticized Israeli expansion against its Arab neighbours, urged America's withdrawal from Vietnam, and was unwilling to discuss the USSR's deployment of a new weapons system, the 'Galosh', a type of anti-ballistic missile (ABM).

Despite such differences—and the first ever use of the 'hot line' during the Six Day War—pressures were growing for a relaxation of Cold War tensions in Europe (see Chapter 9, E) and there was continuing progress, in the wake of the TBT, on nuclear arms control. On 27 January 1967, after nine months of talks, the US, USSR, and numerous other countries signed an Outer Space Treaty, demilitarizing the moon and other celestial bodies. The smooth negotiation of this treaty reflected the fact that the militarization of space was a remote possibility, but in 1968 talks began on a more immediately useful agreement to demilitarize the seabed. Most important of all, with the danger of German nuclear weapons receding, progress was possible on a Non-Proliferation Treaty (NPT) designed, as the TBT had partly been, to prevent ever more countries obtaining nuclear weapons. The US tabled a draft NPT as early as August 1965, but the German problem and the technical nature of the talks meant it was not signed until 1 July 1968 (see boxed section). It had one of the same fundamental flaws as the TBT, in that many of the countries who were most likely to develop nuclear weapons, such as Israel and India, refused to sign it. But it also promised

Non-Proliferation Treaty, 1 July 1968

Negotiated over several years and designed to stop the spread of nuclear weapons beyond those countries who already possessed them, the Non-Proliferation Treaty was signed by most UN members but with crucial omissions— such as India, South Africa, Israel, and Brazil—who were the very countries most likely to develop such weapons. Two other non-signatories were France and China, who already had nuclear weapons and might supply advice to others. The signature was accompanied by a US–Soviet announcement that they would be negotiating limits on their own strategic nuclear arsenals, thus meeting the criticism that it was unfair of them to prevent a spread of nuclear arms while they were building up ever-larger arsenals.

The key provisions of the Treaty were as follows:

- Under Article 1 each nuclear power that signed undertook 'not to transfer . . . nuclear weapons . . . or control over such weapons . . . directly, or indirectly and not in any way to assist . . . any non-nuclear

weapon State to manufacture or otherwise acquire nuclear weapons . . .'
- Under Article 2 each non-nuclear power that signed undertook not to receive, manufacture, 'or otherwise acquire' nuclear weapons.
- Article 3 provided for safeguards against proliferation, with a verification system under the auspices of the International Atomic Energy Agency to be carried out in non-nuclear-weapon states.
- The peaceful use of atomic energy was to continue and a system was outlined which would allow non-nuclear-weapon states to gain benefits from the peaceful applications of nuclear explosions.
- Article 6 committed all signatories 'to pursue negotiations . . . relating to cessation of the nuclear arms race . . . and to nuclear disarmament . . .'. It was this provision which satisfied non-nuclear powers that the existing nuclear powers would limit and reduce the size of their arsenals; and it led on to the next phase of nuclear discussions, the Strategic Arms Limitation talks.

to lead to further progress on arms control: 'By its very nature . . . the Non-Proliferation Treaty discriminates against non-nuclear countries,' conceded the US Secretary of State Dean Rusk, 'and non-nuclear countries understandably sought a quid pro quo.'[5] The quid quo pro which the superpowers offered was that they would seek to control their own nuclear capabilities through Strategic Arms Limitation talks (SALT).

The US had first approached the USSR about the possibility of controlling long-range nuclear weapons in December 1966, partly because the Soviet deployment of the 'Galosh' ABM had put Johnson under pressure to develop a similar system. ABMs were a defensive system, designed to shoot down offensive nuclear missiles. Yet, despite their 'defensive' nature they threatened to accelerate the arms race, partly because they were a new development which both sides were now likely to deploy, and partly because both sides would also be tempted to deploy a greater number of offensive missiles in order to overcome the other side's ABM system. At first the Soviets had shown little urgency about strategic arms talks which were in any case surrounded by problems. In particular, whilst the

Americans would have been happy to 'freeze' the size of nuclear arsenals, thus preserving their current superiority, Moscow wanted to create a more genuine balance of security, reducing the US lead. True, the NPT negotiations added urgency to the issue, hence the decision to accompany the signature on 1 July with an announcement that SALT talks would begin; and a month later the Soviets suggested that, in order to get SALT off to a strong start, Johnson and Brezhnev should hold a summit. But this idea was immediately scotched by another of those 'peripheral issues' which plagued the superpower relationship in the mid-1960s: within days the Soviets had led an invasion of Czechoslovakia (see Chapter 9, C), forcing the SALT talks to be put on hold. Lyndon Johnson—who, for all his anti-communism in Vietnam, could never be described as rigidly anti-Soviet—became the only Cold War president never to meet his Soviet opposite number.

Détente Deferred, 1969–1971

Richard Nixon's administration began with the bold assertion about superpower relations, in his inaugural address, that 'after a period of confrontation we are entering an era of negotiations' and, notwithstanding his reputation as an anticommunist, his Presidency eventually became identified with a policy of East–West détente. Yet in the early period the Nixon years were characterized not by rapid strides in superpower relations but by caution and uneven progress. This was caused in part by the very same factor which made the US more eager to relax Cold War tensions: its vulnerability on the world stage because of the Vietnam imbroglio. By the end of the Johnson presidency, Vietnam had become 'unwinnable' for the US, costly in lives, money, and national morale; it had even called into question the country's ability to implement its policy of defeating communism wherever it threatened to expand (see Chapter 10, D). Meanwhile, the USSR under Brezhnev and Kosygin had avoided foreign adventures and concentrated on achieving nuclear parity with America, so as to prevent another humiliation like the Cuban missile crisis. In 1969 the Soviets had roughly equalled the number of US inter-continental ballistic missiles (ICBMs) and, though they were still behind in submarine-launched ballistic missiles, they had reached a situation known as 'Mutual Assured Destruction'. Often referred to under the apt acronym, MAD, this meant that, even if one superpower launched a sudden nuclear attack on the other (a 'first strike'), the second superpower would retain enough weapons to launch a devastating counter-attack (or 'second strike'). In 1962 only the Americans had had such a second-strike capability, but now that the Soviets had matched it there was a 'balance of deterrence', making it impossible for Washington to meaningfully threaten nuclear war without risking massive destruction as it had done under Eisenhower.

The 'unwinnable' war in Vietnam, the costs of meeting the communist challenge, and the arrival of MAD posed a difficult challenge to Nixon and his most important foreign policy aide, the national security adviser, Henry Kissinger. On the one hand, the situation led to a retrenchment of US policy as defined in the Nixon Doctrine (see Chapter 10, D) with its implication that countries threatened by communism must in future look primarily to defend themselves, albeit with some American support. On the other hand, the Nixon White House reacted firmly, some would say irrationally, when it felt US interests were being threatened: 'an important element in Nixon's diplomacy was to keep the other side off its guard by showing readiness to employ force in an unpredictable manner.'[6] Thus, in April 1969, when the North Koreans shot down an American EC-121 reconnaissance aircraft the White House's preferred reply was a retaliatory military attack, an option that the military and CIA successfully opposed. In 1970, far from retreating precipitately from Vietnam, Nixon launched an incursion into neighbouring Cambodia, and in December 1971, when India went to war with America's ally Pakistan (see Chapter 11, C), Nixon despatched a fleet to the Bay of Bengal and, for the first time during his presidency, used the 'hot line' to Moscow. Determined to limit Soviet power, and especially to prevent the USSR stirring up difficulties in the less developed world, Nixon and Kissinger were careful to develop détente slowly and carefully. Thus, although the State Department would have liked to open SALT talks as soon as possible, Nixon delayed them until November 1969, a step which led the Kremlin too to become more cautious about strategic arms control.

On coming into office Nixon and Kissinger *were* interested in reaching agreements with the USSR, but not in order to achieve a mere improvement in the international atmosphere or to please popular opinion. For them agreements like SALT or greater trade links, which both of them believed Moscow desired, were to be used as part of a strategy to ensure Soviet good behaviour in the world. In essence this meant gaining acceptance of the status quo and ensuring that US interests were not threatened. The superpowers should show 'restraint' in their actions, not seeking unilateral advantages over each other; meetings between them should address 'concrete' problems; and, most importantly, there should be a 'linkage' between the different elements in their mutual relations. As Kissinger explained it, 'We proceeded from the premiss that to separate issues into distinct compartments would encourage the Soviet leaders to believe that they could use cooperation in one area as a safety valve while striving for unilateral advantages elsewhere. This was unacceptable.'[7] The White House demonstrated how it would meet such unacceptable behaviour in what Kissinger called 'the autumn of crises' in 1970. The election of a Marxist, Salvador Allende, as President of Chile on 4 September led to a (failed) US bid to prevent his inauguration; in mid-September, the outbreak of civil war in Jordan, in which Syria briefly intervened, led Nixon to toy with the idea of a counter-intervention by Israel (see Chapter 11, D); and the discovery, by a U-2 spy plane, of work on a submarine base at Cienfuegos in Cuba led to strong diplomatic protestations. Cuba was a particularly delicate issue for America, and Nixon could not afford to appear weaker than Kennedy had been in 1962. The Cienfuegos crisis ended in early October, with an assurance from Soviet ambassador Dobrynin that no submarine base would be built, and a formal American confirmation of Kennedy's promise not to invade the island.

Taken together these crises showed that however much the world had shifted from a bipolar balance to a complex multipolarity, the White House still interpreted events largely in a 'zero-sum' manner, in which any gain for the USSR was a loss for the US. The Soviets might have achieved nuclear parity but America still had to be the greatest nuclear power and Kissinger wanted to limit communist advances through active diplomacy (closely controlled from the White House) and the use of 'linkage'. The Soviets, for their part, never accepted linkage but rather developed the old logic of 'peaceful coexistence'. They saw anti-imperialist unrest in the Third World as historically inevitable, and there to be exploited, whilst SALT and freer East–West trade were desirable in themselves, not as part of some linkage strategy. Nonetheless, in May 1971, at the Communist Party Congress, Brezhnev—as well as securing his own primacy in the leadership—was able to commit the USSR to a policy of relaxing tension. This would restrain the financially draining arms race, secure greater access to Western technology (which would invigorate economic growth), lessen the dangers of nuclear war, and make possible agreements on such issues as Berlin. A few months later, however, Brezhnev was given another reason to improve superpower relations when, in July, it was suddenly revealed that Nixon was to visit Beijing the following year. America's 'Opening to China' which came after years of deteriorating Sino–Soviet relations, gave Nixon another means by which to pressure Moscow for concessions and led Brezhnev to try to outbid China for American cooperation. As a result America, so crippled by the Vietnam War a few years before, now found itself courted by both major communist powers. On 12 October 1971 it was announced that, in addition, to visiting Beijing, Nixon would also be travelling to Moscow, in May 1972, when it was planned to complete the long-awaited SALT treaty.

CHRONOLOGY: EAST–WEST RELATIONS, 1963–1971

1963

March	Chinese question validity of Soviet border.
10 June	Kennedy's speech at the American University, in Washington, favouring relaxation of the Cold War.
20 June	'Hot line' agreement signed.
26 June	Kennedy's 'Ich bin ein Berliner' speech at the Berlin Wall.
5 August	Nuclear Test Ban Treaty signed.

1964

12 January	First US–Soviet grain deal made.
20 January	France recognizes Beijing government.
16 October	First Chinese atomic bomb tested.
October	Khrushchev's departure

1965

20 January	Warsaw Pact calls for a European Security Conference to include East and West bloc.
7 February	US aircraft bomb North Vietnam while Soviet premier Kosygin is in Hanoi.
April	Launch of Cultural Revolution by Mao Zedong.

1966

February	Anti-dissident campaign in USSR begins with trials of Andrei Sinyavsky and Yuli Daniel.
10 March	De Gaulle pulls out of NATO's military command structure.
7 April	Ceauşescu declares Romania's independence within the Eastern bloc.
June–July	De Gaulle in the Soviet Union.

1967

January–February	Soviet embassy in Beijing surrounded by demonstrators.
27 January	Outer Space Treaty signed, demilitarizing the moon and other bodies.
31 January	Romania becomes only Eastern bloc country, apart from USSR, to recognize West Germany.
5–10 June	Six Day War in Middle East.
17 June	China tests a hydrogen bomb.

23–25 June	Glassboro' conference of Johnson and Kosygin.
18 September	US announces deployment of an anti-ballistic missile system.
14 December	NATO Council accepts both Harmel Report and idea of 'flexible response'.
	US announces decision to test a multiple independent re-entry vehicle.

1968

5 January	Alexander Dubček becomes leader of Czechoslovakian Communist Party.
31 January	'Tet' offensive begins in Vietnam.
May	Student unrest in Paris.
June	Student unrest in Yugoslavia.
1 July	Non-Proliferation Treaty signed.
20 August	Five Warsaw Pact states, led by USSR, invade Czechoslovakia to end Dubček's reforms.
12 November	Brezhnev Doctrine speech.

1969

20 January	Nixon's inaugural hopes for an 'era of negotiations' between East and West.
2 March	Soviet–Chinese border clashes on Ussuri River begin.
2–3 August	Nixon visits Romania.
17 November	Strategic Arms Limitation talks open in Helsinki.

1970

10 March	US announces it will deploy a multiple independent re-entry vehicle.
19 March	First ever meeting of West and East German prime ministers.
22 June	Warsaw Pact makes latest call for a European Security Conference.
12 August	Soviet–West German treaty signed.
25 September	US warns USSR not to build a submarine base at Cienfuegos, Cuba.
7 December	Polish–West German treaty signed.
December	Unrest in Poland leads to fall of Gomulka.

1971

10 June	US ends trade embargo against China.
15 July	It is announced that Nixon will visit Beijing in February.
3 September	Four-power agreement on Berlin.
12 October	It is announced that Nixon will visit Moscow in May.
10 December	NATO agrees to a European Security Conference.
12 December	'Hot line' used for first time under Nixon, due to Indo–Pakistan War.

B. The Superpowers and the Emergence of an Independent China

Khrushchev's last years, 1963–1964

One of the most significant signs after 1962 that the world was moving from a balance of power focused on the superpowers, to a more complicated 'multipolar' system, was the final breach between Communist China and the USSR. Paradoxically, as the Soviets began to attain military parity with the US, the significance of bipolar equality was being reduced, not least through the Sino–Soviet split. Western governments generally treated the Communist bloc as a monolithic one, but by 1963 the differences between Beijing and Moscow were deep and wide-ranging. It took almost a decade for policy-makers in Washington to realize what was happening but its significance was immense. The US now had two ideological enemies with different approaches to international order. Moscow was prepared to advocate peaceful coexistence in private and public but Beijing was determined on the spread of revolution, which was deemed to involve the use of force, and arguing for the inevitable clash with the capitalist world.

From work based on Soviet archives it is now clear that 1963 marked the effective completion of what became known as the 'Sino–Soviet split'. Prior to that year Sino–Soviet relations had experienced a number of ups and downs as disagreements occurred and attempts to improve the deteriorating relations were made (see Chapter 7, C). The last of these was made by Khrushchev in July 1963, probably because his weak domestic position after the Cuban missile crisis, which would indicate how domestic and international weakness tended still to promote the continuation of Sino–Soviet cooperation by the respective leaders. In December 1962 the Soviets provided ground-to-air missiles and in January 1963 they agreed to continue with helping to develop a Chinese airforce. However, the events of the last quarter of 1962 seemed to convince Mao that a more determined revolutionary approach to the global struggle was correct. In addition, his domestic

political strength stemming from his June 1962 attack on the Chinese advocates of peaceful co-existence combined with the success of the October/November Chinese attack on Indian forces in the disputed border areas to increase his confidence about going alone. The July 1963 meeting between Suslov and Deng Xiaoping was abandoned without a date for any future meetings being fixed.[8] In that sense the Sino–Soviet split was formalized in the same manner as the split between the wartime allies in 1947. Mao was now more than ever convinced that the future development of the Chinese Revolution and the triumph of what he referred to as the east wind over the west wind would come from a revolutionary international struggle not from peaceful coexistence.

The breakdown was followed by a Chinese attempt to forge a completely independent policy, not only at home but also in its foreign and defence policies, whilst continuing to act as a loyal defender of Marxist-Leninism. Indeed, one problem for the Kremlin was that Mao posed as being truer to the Communist past, and more committed to the anti-imperialist struggle than Khrushchev. This presented difficulties both within the Eastern bloc and for the USSR's wider international policy. Not only did China help protect Albania, and its Stalinist dictator Enver Hoxha, from Soviet pressure to conform with the post-Stalinist order, but Mao also encouraged Romania's attempts to distance itself from the USSR (see Chapter 9, C). In reply the Soviets accused Mao of abandoning true Leninism, and the Sino–Soviet dispute took on features of a religious schism, with each side claiming to be the only 'true believers'. Indeed, so deep did the ideological divide become that their ideological attacks on each other differed 'little from those applied against Western capitalism.'[9] The Chinese ridiculed Khrushchev's foreign policy, especially his performance during the Cuban missile crisis and, in 1963, condemned the Test Ban Treaty as a selfish attempt by the superpowers to preserve their privileged nuclear status, denying equality to others. The Chinese were already developing their own atomic bomb, having been refused assistance from the Soviets—another cause of contention between the two. Such a weapon was successfully tested on 16 October 1964, only two days after the overthrow of Khrushchev, and did more than anything else to establish China's credentials as the world's third greatest power which, with the largest population on earth and vast, untapped economic potential, might one day match its Soviet neighbour. China's independent self-assertion even stretched to pressure on Moscow to restore land that had been taken by the Tsars in the 'unequal treaties' of the nineteenth century. This issue had first been raised in 1957, about the same time that China questioned the Indian border, and it had been pressed again in 1960. In February 1964 the Soviets and Chinese actually opened border discussions but they were suspended in October because of the extent of differences between the two sides.

Whilst challenging the Soviets in Eastern Europe, the Chinese tried to establish their own following in the less developed world. They had been invited to the first Afro–Asian Conference at Bandung in 1955, where anti-imperialism and non-alignment were seen as the basis on which an Afro–Asian identity might be constructed. Zhou en Lai had accepted the five principles of coexistence as a means of getting greater international acceptance and an important Asian role. However the increasing radicalism of Mao and the presence of the Soviet Union at the second Afro-Asian conference in Cairo 1957–8 did not make any form of unity easy, let alone behind communist China. The Chinese were not invited to the first conference of non-aligned states in December 1961. After the split in 1963–4 Zhou Enlai made a three-month tour of twelve (mainly African) Third World countries, plus Albania, but, remarkable as this was in scale, its meagre results only confirmed the limits of China's attraction as an ally. It lacked the potential of either America or the USSR to provide large-scale economic aid or modern military equipment and, except for Albania, those who wished to pursue an anti-Western policy saw the Soviet Union as a far more attractive sponsor. Only a few countries, notably Nyerere's Tanzania, showed much interest in identifying with China. The Egyptian leader, Nasser, was not even present in Cairo

when Zhou arrived; the Tunisian President, Bourguiba, was openly critical of China's 1962 attack on India (others Zhou met were just as critical in private); and planned visits to certain destinations were hastily cancelled. China's explosion of an atomic bomb drew more international condemnation, its subsequent call for an international conference to ban nuclear weapons being seen as an unconvincing attempt to enhance its reputation.

Yet for China there was no going back to the Soviet fold even with Khrushchev ousted. Zhou was sent to Moscow immediately afterwards, to celebrate the October Revolution at the Kremlin's own invitation, but relations were frosty with neither side ready to back down on points of contention. It was clear that the Sino–Soviet split went deeper than mere personality clashes. Nonetheless, this did not prevent one Politburo member suggesting to Zhou that, with Khrushchev ousted, it might also be appropriate for the Chinese to overthrow Mao! Zhou made no secret of this proposal on his return to Beijing and it became one more nail in the coffin of the Sino–Soviet alliance. One Western commentator even described relations between Moscow and Peking as 'the New Cold War' and talked of 'nothing less than a complex, perhaps cataclysmic, process of fission within the Communist movement.'[10]

Foreign Policy and the 'Cultural Revolution', 1965–1969

In 1965 China continued its efforts to play a role in the non-aligned movement, distancing itself from both the US and USSR, but the strength of the non-aligned movement was declining. After the 1964 conference in Belgrade a series of meetings took place over the next quarter of a century but in the 1960s they attracted little world attention. In South-East Asia, where Mao particularly hoped to export his own brand of communism, the Chinese again met with little succes. In Indonesia, the Communist Party were all but wiped out by the army late in the year (see Chapter 11, B); but in Vietnam the Chinese found a cause which allowed them to resist US 'imperialism', compete with the Soviets for influence, and demonstrate the continuing applicability of Maoist guerrilla tactics (see Chapter 10, C). It was the fear that, at home, Maoism was losing its vigour which led in May 1966 to the launch of the 'Cultural Revolution'. Supposedly intended to wipe out all remaining bourgeois influences in society, the Revolution was spearheaded by youthful 'Red Guards', armed with Mao's 'Little Red Book'. Their enthusiasm, ruthlessness, and immaturity led them not only to terrorize ordinary Chinese, but also to target moderates in the communist leadership for condemnation and to launch investigations of officials at all levels. The main victim was Mao's deputy, Liu Shoaqi, who was purged from the party in 1966. The future leader Deng Xiaoping found himself out of favour and Zhou Enlai barely held onto office. By the end of 1967 national government was effectively breaking down.

The Cultural Revolution wreaked havoc with the country's foreign policy. In May 1967 Red Guards invaded the foreign ministry, destroying many of its records. Numerous ambassadors were recalled from abroad, including all from those African countries that Zhou had tried to court so assiduously a few years before. The foreign minister, Chen Yi, disappeared from public view for months, so that external observers even doubted whether the post was filled any longer. As part of a new, revolutionary foreign policy, the Red Guards urged Chinese minorities in South-East Asia to overthrow their governments, stirred up anti-British feeling over the colony of Hong Kong (the British embassy was attacked in August 1967) and, in January–February 1967, besieged the Soviet embassy. Despite this, the mid-1960s were not without their successes for China. Its strong support for Hanoi was rewarded by America's increasing discomfort in the Vietnam War. In 1967 a showpiece aid deal was agreed with Tanzania and Zambia, to build a 1,200-mile railway line between the two. And, in June 1967, China exploded its first hydrogen bomb, pointedly refusing to contemplate non-proliferation, while also developing long-range rockets to carry nuclear warheads. Given the near-anarchy created by the Red Guards, however, the superpowers reacted to China's growing nuclear capacity with great concern. The Johnson administration, in contrast to its successor, did nothing to exploit the Sino–Soviet split but instead treated China as a pariah: 'throughout Asia,

China became the focus of (Secretary of State) Rusk's campaign against Communism. Russian ambitions had been checked in the early 1940s. Now Mao assumed the role of aggressor.'[11] For its part, the Kremlin developed the Galosh ABM system chiefly as a means to defend Moscow from an attack by the embryonic Chinese nuclear forces.

Throughout the period of the Cultural Revolution Sino–Soviet relations worsened. The two Communist Parties broke off relations in 1966, all Soviet economic advice to China ended, and there were already intermittent small-scale border incidents, especially over disputed islands in the Amur and Ussuri rivers. The worst clash to date came in January 1968, when four Chinese were killed. Meanwhile, the USSR gradually increased its forces on its 4,500-mile eastern border, from 12 divisions in 1961, to 17 in 1964 and 27 by 1969, with medium-range ballistic weapons in support. The tension intensified further in late 1968 because of the invasion of Czechoslovakia and Brezhnev's subsequent assertion that the USSR had the right to intervene in states where socialism was under threat (see Chapter 9, C). For the Chinese, this rekindled fears that Moscow was determined to dictate policy to all other communist countries and it put back Mao's hopes that Eastern Europe might be able to loosen the Soviet grip. He condemned the invasion of Czechoslovakia and even seems to have feared war with the USSR as the year ended, a fear which may have been behind the relaxation of the Cultural Revolution at this point. However, in line with their uncompromising foreign policy the Chinese were determined to stand up to the Soviets and in March 1969 the Sino–Soviet relationship reached another critical point. On 2 March, after several weeks of mounting border tension, large-scale fighting occurred on Zhen Bao island (known as Damyansky island to the Russians and situated near the confluence of the Amur and Ussuri rivers) when Chinese troops ambushed a Soviet patrol, killing more than 20. It was an event which tellingly underlined the depths of Sino–Soviet division and helped bring about an unexpected rapprochement between China and the USA. But that was far from being Mao's original intention. True, he did publicly speak of preparing for war and he may have hoped to exploit the border tension as a way of mobilizing the

Chinese people behind him, now that the Cultural Revolution was drawing to an end. But privately he was keen to avoid the crisis running out of control. Chinese evidence suggests that 'although Beijing's policy-makers ... had prepared to ... teach the Soviets a bitter lesson, they had not intended to enter a major military conflict with Moscow.'[12]

The Beginnings of 'Triangular Diplomacy'

The Kremlin was stunned by the events of 2 March 1969 and, already convinced of Chinese irrationality, feared that the crisis could run out of control, or even that Mao would deliberately launch war. Determined not to appear weak, the Soviets employed heavy artillery in another clash on Zhen Ba island on 15 March but again found the Chinese well prepared. Moscow followed this up on 21 March with an offer to talk. There was in fact a division in the Soviet government between hardliners, led by defence minister Grechko, who was ready to consider war, and moderates like premier Kosygin, who favoured negotiation. But the Chinese refused even to reply to Kosygin's offer of talks for several weeks and there was a further series of border incidents in April-May, with clashes now spreading to the Kazakhstan border. Incidents continued for 6 months, with a particularly bitter exchange on the Kazakhstan border on 13 August, when the Soviets wiped out a 30-man Chinese patrol. Neither side seemed ready to back down and in China too, now, there was a genuine fear of war as events moved far beyond what Mao originally intended. Later that month he mobilized China's border defences. But then tension receded, with neither side prepared to initiate a full-scale conflict. In total over a hundred Soviets were killed, probably with similar Chinese losses, during the clashes of 1969. Zhou Enlai and Kosygin finally met on 11 September in Beijing, in the aftermath of Ho Chi Minh's funeral and both appeared to strike a deal, on the basis of respecting the status quo for the present. But when official talks opened on 20 October they made no progress and each side continued to condemn the other on ideological grounds. So great was the Soviet fear of China that Marshal Grechko supported the idea of a

pre-emptive strike against Chinese nuclear facilities. Brezhnev, backed by most of the Politburo, preferred a continued build-up of conventional forces linked to a diplomatic campaign to isolate China, but in mid-August the Soviets were inept enough to sound out the US on its likely reaction to a pre-emptive strike—an approach which confirmed the growing belief in Washington that Sino–Soviet differences could be exploited in America's favour.

When Richard Nixon entered the White House in January 1969 relations with the USSR were much better than those with China. Beijing was still blamed for the drawn-out war in Korea in the 1950s, it was behind the communists in Vietnam, its Maoist ideology was a world apart from liberal democracy and its revolutionary diplomacy made it, apparently, impossible to deal with on a rational basis. Like the USSR, the US was building an ABM system, which Nixon named 'Safeguard', that was seen as primarily useful against a Chinese nuclear attack. Yet the new president, for all his anti-communist past, had written in a 1967 article, in *Foreign Affairs*, that 'we simply cannot afford to leave China forever outside the family of nations'[13] and by June 1969 the White House believed that it might be possible to use improved Sino–American relations as a pressure point on the USSR, easing the danger that it would exploit the crisis in American policy caused by Vietnam. An improved Sino–American relationship also appealed to Mao and Zhou, who now believed China to be far more threatened by the USSR than it was by the US. As a communist power bordering on China, the Soviet Union was seen by Mao as a potential menace to Chinese domestic stability, whereas America, thanks to Vietnam, seemed to be losing the battle for influence in East and South-East Asia. On 11 July 1969 a study of the international situation by a high-level group neatly summed up the fear that 'The Soviet revisionists have made China their main enemy, imposing a more serious threat to our security than the US imperialists.'[14] The timing of this report supports the view that it was the summer 'war scare that—both in a strategic and a psychological sense—created the necessary conditions for the [Chinese] leaders to reconsider the ... policy of confrontation with the United States.'[15]

Yet suspicion between China and the US ran deep, they had no diplomatic relations, and both approached their rapprochement with caution. Such caution was reinforced on the American side by the desire to avoid a precipitate move, which could worsen Washington's international problems rather than ease them. 'If we moved too slowly', wrote Kissinger, 'we might feed Chinese suspicions of Soviet–American collusion ... As for the Soviets, we considered the Chinese option useful to induce restraint; but we had to take care not to pursue it so impetuously as to provoke a Soviet pre-emptive attack on China.'[16]

Nixon first signalled his readiness to improve relations by relaxing trade and travel with China in July 1969. Diplomatic contacts proved possible via third parties, such as the Romanian and Pakistani governments, and via meetings between US and Chinese diplomats in Warsaw. The American incursion into Cambodia in spring 1970 set back relations and within both governments there were divisions about the wisdom of a rapprochement, but in April 1971 the possibility was publicly acknowledged when the Chinese invited an American table-tennis team to Beijing. This 'ping-pong diplomacy' was followed by another relaxation of US trade with China and by intensive discussions on an idea the Chinese had raised some months before of Nixon sending an emissary to Beijing. The emissary selected was the national security adviser, Henry Kissinger, who travelled to Peking on 9 July, via Pakistan. A cover story, that he had fallen ill whilst visiting Pakistan, held throughout two days of talks with Zhou Enlai and it was on 15 July that the world learnt, not only that Kissinger had made his journey but that Nixon too would be visiting Beijing in early 1972.

C. Unity and Division in Eastern Europe: The 'Prague Spring'

Eastern Europe in the 1960s

Although the Kremlin had used armed force to restore communist control in Hungary in 1956 (see Chapter 6, A), this did not restore the full unity of the Eastern bloc under Soviet domination. Certainly, East European leaders were reluctant in future to experiment with any radical reforms that might undermine the one-party state. Even Khrushchev himself backed off from his 'deStalinization' progress, which had helped spark problems in Poland and Hungary; only around 1961 did he revive his attacks on Stalinism and tolerate a limited amount of intellectual diversity in the USSR. But, inspired in part by Mao's China, East European leaders were suspicious of Khrushchev and keen to establish a degree of equality for themselves within the bloc, so that they did not slavishly have to mirror every major turn in Soviet policy. Certain leaders, such as East Germany's Walter Ulbricht and Bulgaria's Todor Zhivkov, were quite happy to retain elements of Stalinism and it was hard-line communists, rather than would-be reformers, who were often most successful at distancing themselves from Moscow's authority in the 1960s. At the extreme, Enver Hoxha, the thoroughly Stalinist dictator of Albania was able to assert his full independence in 1960, openly criticizing Khrushchev and relying on Chinese aid to compensate for the economic embargo which the Soviets tried to impose. In December 1961 Moscow severed relations with Albania, though it remained a nominal member of the Warsaw Pact until 1968. In 1966 Hoxha, emulating Mao, even launched his own 'cultural revolution' but Chinese aid was paltry and Albania remained the poorest country in Europe. It was geographically cut off from the rest of the Soviet bloc, bordering only on Greece (a NATO member) and Yugoslavia, which maintained its own independent form of communism under Tito. The Kremlin therefore showed no interest in terminating Hoxha's independence by force while it showed no sign of tilting towards the capitalist West.

Other countries in Eastern Europe, larger than Albania and geographically closer to the USSR, found it more difficult to pursue their own course, but a wide degree of autonomy was achieved, in particular by Romania. The key element here was, once again, that Romania's leaders followed a ruthless, authoritarian form of rule internally, while gradually asserting an independent foreign policy. This allowed them to pose as defenders of *national* interests and, they believed, brought them domestic popularity. Under George Gheorghieu-Dej Romania's Latin—as opposed to Slavic—identity was fostered; the withdrawal of the Red Army was secured in 1958; reliance on trade with the USSR was reduced; Khrushchev was criticized for risking war over Cuba in 1962; and all attempts by Khrushchev to integrate the East European economies were opposed. In 1961–3 the Soviet leader, partly in response to the EEC's success in Western Europe, tried to encourage integration via Comecon, the organization for economic cooperation set up by Stalin in 1949, but hitherto insignificant. However Gheorghieu-Dej feared that such a policy would leave Romania as an agricultural state, while industrial production was concentrated in East Germany and Czechoslovakia. He preferred the Stalinist practice of industrializing across the Eastern bloc and his dogged campaign proved successful. All that came from Khrushchev's schemes was the establishment of a Comecon bank, for settling mutual debts, in 1964. There were some joint projects between Comecon members and another attempt at broad cooperation was made in the 'Complex Programme' of 1970–1, when an investment bank was founded. But supranationalism on the lines of the EEC proved impossible. Comecon's cohesion was harmed by the admission of developing countries like Mongolia (1962) and Cuba (1972), and its members tended to follow competitive rather than cooperative policies, not least in their creation of similar, heavy industrial economies.

Gheorghieu-Dej's successor in 1965 was Nicolae Ceauşescu, who largely built on existing policies while denigrating his predecessor's memory and concentrating power in his own hands. Internal repression was accompanied by an ever more assertive foreign policy. He broke Eastern bloc unity by recognizing West Germany in 1967; he stood aside from the invasion of Czechoslovakia in 1968 (discussed below); he ended active involvement in the Warsaw Pact military command; and in 1970 he

Nicolae Ceauşescu (1918–1989)

Ceauşescu came from a poor, peasant family in Romania and joined the Communist Party whilst still a teenager before the Second World War. The Soviet invasion of Romania in 1944 and subsequent communist domination of political life, allowed such an early member of the ruling Party to rise in the political elite. Under Gheorge Gheorgieu-Dej, the Stalinist leader of the 1950s, Ceauşescu became second-in-command and later modelled himself on Dej's practice of enforcing a rigid, Soviet-style system within Romania (complete with secret police and central planning) while pursuing an independent line in foreign policy. Dej particularly opposed the attempts by Khrushchev to impose an integrated economic policy on the Eastern bloc.

In March 1965 Ceauşescu was the natural successor to Dej as Communist Party leader. He retained membership of the Warsaw Pact while refusing to intervene in Czechoslovakia in 1968, maintaining links to China, and welcoming a visit from America's President Nixon in 1969.

Ceauşescu also kept up an oppressive form of internal rule, backed by the *Securitae* secret police force, and attacks on non-Latin minority groups, while developing trading links with the West and winning various accolades from Western countries (including, for example, an honorary knighthood from Britain). Ceauşescu became increasingly dictatorial and self-obsessed, appointing his wife, Elena, and other family members to key positions. At first his independent line in the Eastern bloc seemed to make him immune from the anti-communist sentiment which swept Eastern Europe in the autumn of 1989 but December saw mounting dissatisfaction among the Hungarian minority in the country. Ironically, Ceauşescu was re-elected communist leader just as popular demonstrations against his rule became widespread in the capital. He and Elena tried to escape from Bucharest but were captured and, at Christmas, executed, many of their former supporters having switched allegiance to the opposition.

even raised border claims against the USSR. None of this was welcome to the Kremlin, which excluded Ceauşescu from a new series of bilateral Eastern bloc treaties and from certain Warsaw Pact discussions. Yet Ceauşescu remained a member of the Pact and his policies were interpreted, not as some maverick bid for complete independence of the Soviets, but as an eastern equivalent of Charles de Gaulle's policy. De Gaulle, too, distanced himself from his superpower ally (America), adopted a semi-detached approach to his military allies (in NATO) and tried to maximise national independence by maintaining links with both power blocs (see Chapter 9, D). It was not surprising that de Gaulle and Ceauşescu co-operated together in advocating a loosening of alliance structures, a lowering of Cold War tensions and—the essential corollary—greater freedom from superpower domination for the countries of Eastern and Western Europe.

The only Warsaw Pact member which experimented much with decentralization in the 1960s was Hungary where the events of 1956 had not ended the belief that the oppression of Stalinism should be relaxed. Janos Kadar waited until 1961 before releasing some political prisoners and relaxing censorship, emulating Khrushchev's moves in the USSR at that time. In 1963 some private enterprise was also reintroduced in Hungary, with the ability of farmers and artisans to earn extra income. The atmosphere was less conducive to reform after Khrushchev's fall: in 1965 Brezhnev tightened up central control of the economy (after an ill-fated attempt at regional planning under Khrushchev) and cracked down on dissidents (beginning with the arrest of the writers Yuli Daniel and Andrei Sinyavsky in September). But Kadar's reforms continued in 1967 with provision for a choice of candidates in elections—though all had to be from the Communist Party—and, more importantly, in 1968 with the introduction of the 'New Economic Mechanism'; this localized planning and introduced competitive elements into industrial production, although all industry remained in state ownership and the government continued to set long-term economic targets. The purpose of such reforms was to try to raise the sluggish economic growth which Eastern bloc countries encountered in the 1960s, when the inefficiencies of the Stalinist model of industrialization became clear: labour-intensive, responsive to government predictions rather than market demand, and overseen by a cumbersome planning machine, the communist economies were wasteful of resources, geared to heavy industrial production rather than consumer goods and shoddy in workmanship. This was one reason why, in the late 1960s, many Eastern bloc leaders were interested in technology transfers from the West as a way to boost growth, hence the popularity of détente (see Chapter 9, E). Yet such was the continued commitment to the Soviet version of Marxism and the fear of internal problems if the events of 1956 were repeated, that Kadar's reforms were viewed with suspicion throughout the bloc. This suspicion was only intensified by events in Czechoslovakia in 1968, when another attempt to introduce liberalization led to fears that communism could collapse there, and prompted a Soviet-led invasion.

Czechoslovakia's 'Prague Spring'

Under the leadership of Antonin Novotny after 1953, Czechoslovakia was one of the most orthodox and stable countries in the Eastern bloc and one where communism was maintained without the presence of Soviet troops (who had withdrawn in late 1945). But the harshness of the regime, the rigid planning system, and the stagnation of economic growth in the early 1960s created doubts within the Communist Party about Novotny's leadership. A relaxation of censorship, the rehabilitation of some former anti-Stalinists and, in the mid-1960s improved growth rates failed to satisfy his critics, led by a Slovak politician, Alexander Dubček. In January 1968 Dubček replaced Novotny as party leader, though the latter retained the presidency until March. In those few months Czechoslovakia turned from being a conventional communist state to being of deep concern to the Kremlin, which had originally hoped to work with Dubček even if it was not completely happy with the abrupt replacement of Novotny. Dubček was in fact a loyal Marxist-Leninist, but he and his fellow reformers hoped to improve the Czechoslovak system by breaking with the Stalinist past, decentralizing decision-making, introducing market elements into the economy, and allowing non-communist organizations to form. Their first step to achieving this new situation was to allow freer discussion of reform in Czechoslovakian society through a marked relaxation of censorship. This move, however, led to the publication of anti-communist views, spearheaded by *Literary Pages*, first issued on 29 February 1968, by a group that included the poet Vaclav Havel and which wanted to form a legal opposition Party. Such a radical response provoked immediate divisions among Dubček's communist supporters, who began to argue about the scale, pace, and areas of reform.

On 6–7 March, at an Eastern bloc summit in Dresden, Brezhnev and other leaders expressed concern at Dubček's reform programme, pointing out the dangers of losing control of events. Yet, over the following few months open opposition to the regime, including frequent popular demonstrations, continued and on 4–5 May Dubček was berated by Brezhnev again, this time at a bilateral meeting in Moscow. It was in the wake of this meeting that Dubček decided to call a party congress, to be held in mid-September, where he would put his authority behind a moderate reform programme, purging both Stalinists and radicals. But the Soviet military had already (in April) begun to plan for possible armed intervention in Czechoslovakia and on 8 May there was a meeting between Brezhnev, East German, Polish, Bulgarian, and Hungarian leaders, at which Brezhnev criticized Dubček as weak, inexperienced, and unreliable. Among the 'Group of Five', only Kadar tried to defend the Czechoslovakian leader, while Ulbricht (of East Germany) and Zhivkov (for Bulgaria) urged action to restore order, if necessary by force. Within the Kremlin, too, there were divisions, with Kosygin, who visited Prague in mid-May, ready to deal with Dubček, but others increasingly concerned at events. The second group included the Ukrainian Communist leader, Petro Shelast, who feared unrest spreading over the Czechoslovakian border into the Ukraine; the KGB, under Yuri Andropov, who also feared for Soviet internal security and believed NATO could exploit the Czechoslovakian situation; and the military, led by Marshal Ustinov, who had been keen for some time to station nuclear forces on Czechoslovakian soil and feared a breach in Warsaw Pact defences.

For the moment Brezhnev was unsure about intervention but, significantly, a group of conservatives in Prague led by the Slovakian communist, Vasil Bilak, also wanted to end the Dubček regime and secretly began to provide Moscow with information.

Military manoeuvres to intimidate the Czechoslovakians were begun by the Warsaw Pact in late May but Dubček was not easily frightened, refusing to meet with Soviet leaders in June and for most of July. 'In many ways Dubček was naïve in his dealings with Russians,' admits one of his biographers; 'Nevertheless throughout the summer, he played an extremely delicate . . . political game' based on the belief that the Soviets would not intervene.[17] He believed his reforms were too popular in Czechoslovakia, and the Soviets too divided on how to respond to him, for military action to be an easy option. He also tried to minimize the justification for external intervention by following an orthodox foreign policy: 'the Dubček government seized every opportunity to emphasize its loyalty to the Warsaw Pact.'[18] But on 27 June the non-communists published a manifesto urging the people to mobilize behind reform and in July even Kadar gave up on supporting Dubček, who further harmed his standing in Moscow by turning to Yugoslavia and Romania for diplomatic support. Another meeting of the 'Group of Five', in Warsaw in mid-July, demanded that the Czechoslovakians restore order. And at the end of the month, when Dubček finally met Soviet leaders, Kosygin bluntly warned that military intervention was possible. On 3 August they met again in Bratislava but still seemed far apart. Over the following weeks, as Brezhnev and other Eastern bloc leaders urged Dubček to end dissent within Czechoslovakia, plans were finalized for armed intervention, a course which the Politburo finally approved in mid-August. The invasion, launched on 20–21 August under the codename 'Operation Danube', was meant to be accompanied by a domestic coup against Dubček, led by Bilak and other conservatives. As one American diplomat speculated, 'That is perhaps why the invader came with the claim of having been invited to rescue the country.'[19] However, the domestic side of the operation was botched, because Dubček managed to retain both popular sympathy and majority support at a key meeting of the ruling

Presidium. Instead the Soviets were forced to arrest Dubček and other leaders, taking them to Moscow for several days of talks, during which they were forced to agree to the country's 'normalization' as a loyal member of the Soviet bloc. Bilak's embarrassing failure allowed Dubček to remain party leader for the time being, though a moderate figure, Gustav Husak, soon emerged as an alternative.

'Operation Danube' brought half a million troops into Czechoslovakia from the 'Group of Five' by the end of August, a force large enough to prevent any armed response and ensuring a low casualty rate of about 100 Czechoslovakians. The Red Army stayed in the country until 1991. The occupation *was* opposed, however, by a widespread passive resistance campaign which harmed economic output and undermined the Soviet claim to be acting in the interests of the Czechoslovakian masses. Dubček remained in office until April 1969 and began the 'normalization' process by restoring censorship, centralizing control under the party once more, and ending all public signs of factionalism within the government. On 19 January 1969 a student, Jan Palach, burnt himself to death in Prague, as a protest against the return of totalitarianism but organized, large-scale opposition proved impossible. One significant feature of the Prague Spring was that the Communist Party itself had not only remained strong, but was joined by many would-be reformers. 'Throughout this period the Communist Party remained the primary organized political force, exercising control over . . . government and most of the mass associations.'[20] Dubček's successor, Husak, purged it of reformers and, by 1970, had ended all signs of dissent. The problems of stability in the Soviet bloc were highlighted in December of that year, however, in Poland where price increases led to widespread rioting by workers and the sudden downfall of party chief Wladislaw Gomulka. The new Polish leader, Edvard Gierak, succeeded in restoring order but only by reversing the price increases.

The international price that the USSR had to pay for intervention was similarly short-lived. Even among communist states there were critics and the gravest cost of Operation Danube may well have been its impact on Chinese policy (see Chapter 9, B). Tito of Yugoslavia was concerned enough by events to draw away from the USSR and, in 1969, restore diplomatic relations with China, after they had been broken for 11 years. Ceauşescu's fears of Soviet domination also deepened and in 1971 he became the first Warsaw Pact leader in more than a decade to visit China. The invasion also had a predictably

Brezhnev Doctrine, 12 November 1968

Several weeks after the Soviet-led invasion of Czechoslovakia the Soviet communist leader, Leonid Brezhnev, attended the Fifth Congress of the Polish Communist Party and, on 12 November made a speech that included what became known in the West as the 'Brezhnev Doctrine'. The speech interpreted recent events as part of the continuing struggle between the communist and imperialist-capitalist systems, in which anti-communist elements had tried to subvert Czechoslovakia and detach it from the Eastern bloc. Brezhnev defended armed intervention as follows: 'when . . . forces hostile to socialism seek to revert the development of any socialist country towards the restoration of capitalism . . . this is no longer a problem of that country's people but . . . the concern of all socialist countries.'

Thus, action was necessary in Czechoslovakia to safeguard the unity and borders of what he called the 'Socialist Commonwealth', and he insisted that this did not infringe the country's sovereignty; rather, 'fraternal solidarity' had priority over national sovereignty in such a crisis. There was already a precedent for such action in Hungary in 1956 and Brezhnev was clear that the idea of 'limited sovereignty' would hold good in future, where the unity of the Soviet bloc was threatened. The doctrine was evidently interpreted according to circumstances: Yugoslavia and China had already broken free of Soviet domination; Albania left the Warsaw Pact in 1968; and Romania developed a form of independence from the USSR whilst remaining a Warsaw Pact member. But the invasion of Afghanistan in 1979 could partially be justified on the grounds of 'limited sovereignty' and the doctrine was only abandoned under Gorbachev in the late 1980s, when Afghanistan and Eastern Europe broke free of Soviet control.

detrimental impact on Soviet relations with the Western powers, who roundly condemned it. There was a double impact on détente: first because the US was reluctant to improve relations after such an event, hence Johnson's cancellation of his planned summit with Brezhnev (see Chapter 9, A); and second, because the Soviets themselves were unwilling to pursue détente while their alliance bloc appeared so divided, hence a hiatus in Warsaw Pact calls for a European Security Conference.

Nevertheless, as over Hungary in 1956, there was nothing practical that the Western powers could do to help Czechoslovakia short of risking war. Their actions against the USSR were therefore little more than gestures of disapproval and they quickly returned to their earlier efforts to promote détente

with the Eastern bloc (see Chapter 9, E). As a guidance telegram to British diplomats in late October 1968 argued, such a policy was not designed to make life easy for the Soviets, far from it. 'We recognize that in the longer term contact with Eastern Europe is the principal means by which we can hope to encourage liberal forces in these countries.'[21] In the long term the beneficial impact of détente—linked to the detrimental impact of continuing Soviet domination—would destroy communism in Eastern Europe. However, in the immediate term, it has been argued that 'NATO's policy not only failed to prevent the Soviet invasion, but may even have encouraged it . . . by giving Soviet leaders a high degree of confidence that they could move into Czechoslovakia with a free hand.'[22]

D. **Unity and Division in the Western Bloc**

NATO in Travail

The years 1963–71 were a troubled period for NATO. They were marked at first by arguments over how to share the use of nuclear weapons for European defence, in the middle period by Charles de Gaulle's decision to withdraw France from the alliance's military-institutional structure, and in the later period by the Nixon administration's relative neglect of Europe's concerns, as it focused its attention on Vietnam, superpower relations, and the opening to China. Between February and August 1964, there was a grave danger that two NATO members, Turkey and Greece, might go to war over Cyprus, when fighting between the Greek-Cypriot and Turkish-Cypriot communities broke out. This was triggered by the attempts of the former to alter the constitutional balance agreed upon only four years before, when independence was won from Britain. In March a UN peacekeeping force was deployed on the island but the most dangerous moment came in early August when Turkish aircraft bombed Greek Cypriot positions. (After this there was an uneasy decade of stability on the island, though some further inter-communal violence occurred in 1967.) The mid-

1960s were overshadowed by growing concern in the alliance over America's mounting involvement in Vietnam, which made Washington less able to focus on Atlantic concerns and triggered grave unease among West European populations about US prosecution of the war. Previously, not least under Kennedy, America's moral reputation among Europeans stood high, but Vietnam called its liberal credentials into question and even close allies, like the German and British governments, had to be wary of arousing public discontent by supporting Johnson, or later Nixon, on Vietnam. Relations between America, Britain, and Germany were in any case disrupted in 1965–7, by arguments over the financial costs the first two faced for basing their military forces on German soil; and this developed into broader disagreements over 'burden-sharing' in the alliance. Finally, there were also divisions within the Atlantic alliance over the pace of détente (discussed more fully in Chapter 9, E below).

The nuclear-sharing question had already had a detrimental impact on Kennedy's vision of an 'Atlantic partnership'. But in December 1962 at the Nassau conference, where the president agreed to supply Polaris missiles to Britain (see Chapter 6, B), the US reaffirmed its support for a Multilateral Nuclear Force (MLF) in NATO, to be manned and financed by several alliance countries. The MLF, which originated in ideas for nuclear-sharing under the Eisenhower administration, was intended to overcome criticism of America's monopoly control of the Western deterrent and also to forestall West German ambitions to develop nuclear weapons. However, the fact that Germany would share in running the MLF, whilst it pleased Germans themselves, provoked criticism both within the Western alliance and from the Eastern bloc. The USSR wanted to see the MLF abandoned before negotiating the Non-Proliferation Treaty. De Gaulle never liked the MLF, partly because it was linked to US ambitions to end the independent status of the French and British nuclear deterrents. For the same reason the British were always lukewarm about it and in late 1964 the incoming Labour government of Harold Wilson proposed an alternative scheme, the Atlantic Nuclear Force, which would maximize British independence. This threw negotiations back into limbo and it was just before meeting Wilson for the first time that, in December 1964, Lyndon Johnson effectively abandoned the MLF idea. A formal renunciation of it was impossible at this time, given Germany's continued commitment to it; but during 1965 the US Defense Secretary, Robert McNamara, pressed an alternative, far less ambitious scheme for improved nuclear consultations in NATO. This led, in 1966, to a Nuclear Defence Affairs Committee being set up to discuss nuclear policy-making in the alliance. 'The attempt to establish . . . nuclear sharing on the basis . . . of allied ownership and control of nuclear weapons was effectively abandoned in favour of a consultative approach to . . . nuclear policy.'[23] It was an approach that left Washington largely unimpeded in its control of the West's nuclear arsenal. Under the new Committee was a seven-member Nuclear Planning Group, including the US, Britain, and Germany, which first met in April 1967 and which helped the Americans educate their allies about problems associated with nuclear weapons, whilst giving the European allies a share in planning for their use. In the light of this development, Germany effectively accepted the collapse of MLF. Bonn did this partly in order to

preserve NATO, which at that point faced a grave internal crisis.

De Gaulle's announcement on 10 March 1966 that France was leaving the organizational side of the alliance came as a blow to NATO's confidence, even if an expected one. Given his desire to maximize French independence, his criticism of American 'domination' of Europe and the fact that he had long since (in 1959) pulled French ships out of NATO's Mediterranean command, his withdrawal had long been predicted. He probably timed his action in 1966 because of his successful re-election as president four months before. He never actually ended France's commitment to the 1949 North Atlantic Treaty, which bound it to aid fellow members if they were attacked, but for a few years it was feared that he would do so and this cast a pall of uncertainty over Western cooperation. Neither did he categorically state that NATO could not use French soil in the event of war; and French troops actually remained in Germany, under a bilateral agreement, as part of the front line against the Warsaw Pact. But France's semi-detached role raised the danger that it might pursue a defence policy that was out of step with other Western powers. Indeed, one feature of French policy was the claim that, with the advent of Soviet nuclear parity, an American President might not be willing to go to war in Europe's defence; in this case France, free of US control and with its own nuclear deterrent, could be a more reliable opponent of the Soviets. France's withdrawal did cause administrative inconvenience, too, in that NATO headquarters had to be moved from Paris within a year. A new site was selected, just outside Brussels. Lyndon Johnson's response to de Gaulle's action was remarkably accepting: 'when a man asks you to leave his home, you don't argue, you just get your hat and go.'[24]. But one reason for the president's low-key response was the need to avoid even deeper rifts in the Atlantic alliance, while America was so embroiled in Vietnam.

The danger of a disintegration of NATO in 1966 seemed real, not only because of uncertainty about de Gaulle's next move, but also because of growing differences between America, Britain, and Germany—the trio now very much at the centre of alliance relationships—over so-called 'offset costs'. In 1965 the US had 392,000 personnel committed to NATO, with the bulk of them (262,000) serving in Germany,

Charles de Gaulle (1890–1970)

Born into an intensely nationalist family, de Gaulle became a professional soldier and was one of the few French generals to appreciate the potential of armoured warfare in the 1930s. After the fall of France in 1940, when he briefly served as under-secretary of defence, he refused to accept defeat and instead founded the 'Free French' movement in London. He had 'a certain idea of France', an almost spiritual concept which saw greatness as part of the nation's inner being: since the collaborationist regime of Marshal Pétain was a denial of such greatness then he, de Gaulle, would stand up for true French interests and restore the country's status. In 1944 he became head of the French government, through force of will and the support of resistance groups. However, in January 1946 he suddenly resigned, having fallen out with other political leaders who were unwilling to see him establish a strong presidential form of government. De Gaulle believed they would soon be forced to recall him, but the Fourth Republic survived for 12 years. In 1947 he launched the right-wing 'Rally of the French People' but it failed to win the 1952 election and de Gaulle retired to his home at Colombey-deux-Eglises.

He was recalled to power in May 1958, when the Fourth Republic, dogged by unstable governments, entered a terminal crisis over the colonial war in Algeria. By 1962 de Gaulle had ended the war and meanwhile established the Fifth Republic, based on the strong, elected Presidency that he had wanted in 1946. Able to appoint his own prime minister, and backed by a Gaullist political party, he took a particular interest in foreign and defence policies. In order to assert French greatness on the world stage he developed the nuclear 'force de frappe'; tried to limit the centralizing policies of the European Community, whilst also vetoing British membership and retaining France's leading role in the organization; distanced the country from what he saw as US domination, particularly by quitting NATO's organizational side in 1966 and, as a corollary, also asserted his independence by developing links to Eastern bloc states. Internal unrest shook his confidence in 1968 however and, with the franc on the brink of devaluation, he resigned in 1969. He died suddenly the following year, leaving behind a much more stable form of government in France than before, as well as an independent line in foreign policy which his successors found it prudent to continue.

whilst Britain had 51,000 troops there. In the late 1950s and early 1960s, when the German economy was still recovering from the War and there were periodic crises over Berlin, these deployments aroused little controversy in America and Britain. But by the mid-1960s, the West German economy was one of the strongest in the world, the main Cold War crises were all outside Europe and no one believed war in Europe to be imminent, whilst the US and Britain both faced balance of payment difficulties. The German government agreed in principle to try to 'offset' the Anglo-American costs by buying expensive military equipment from them, but such purchases fell well short of what Britain, in particular, believed to be fair. A British balance of payments crisis in mid-1966 led the country to talk of reducing its NATO commitment and Johnson, fearing an 'unravelling' of the whole alliance in the wake of de Gaulle's departure, put pressure on both his allies to begin three-way talks with America on the problem. As with French withdrawal, this issue ultimately showed the resilience of NATO, however,

because in May 1967 a trilateral agreement was reached which increased German military 'offset' purchases from America and Britain, minimized British costs, and allowed the US to reduce its commitments, whilst maintaining its readiness to act in Europe, through a policy of 'dual-basing'—effectively, the rotation of units between bases in Germany and America. The agreements were not welcome to all members of the alliance. 'In particular, the Belgian ambassador, André de Staercke, was critical that the trilateral agreements confronted NATO . . . with faits accomplis.'[25] But another cause of Western division had been successfully overcome.

The common interest of the US and Western Europe in defending the continent from communism was still the proclaimed *raison d'être* of the alliance, and its continuing vitality was confirmed by the December 1967 Atlantic Council meeting which took two important decisions. First, it accepted that NATO should have a role in developing détente with the Eastern bloc, a subject discussed more fully below. Second, it accepted a new defensive strategy, known as 'flexible response' which had been discussed for several years and which reflected the fact that the USSR could now match the US in nuclear weapons. It has been pointed out that a 'crucial factor' in getting agreement on this policy was 'de Gaulle's decision to withdraw France from the military functions of the alliance': before 1966 he had opposed attempts to define a new alliance strategy and had questioned the validity of America's nuclear guarantee.[26] 'Flexible response' accepted that it was no longer possible to threaten all-out nuclear war in the event of a Warsaw Pact attack. Instead there would be a graduated escalation of conflict, beginning with a conventional effort and working through different levels of nuclear response, before there was a strategic nuclear exchange. In order to make 'flexible response' credible, however, and prevent an early use of nuclear weapons, the US military believed a larger number of conventional forces was required, and (despite improvements in force levels in the early 1960s) these simply could not be found. America itself, thanks largely to Vietnam, had reduced its NATO commitment to about 300,000 in 1968, while West European countries were reluctant to spend more money on defence. It was partly because of this that the Atlantic Council, meeting in Reykjavik in June 1968, proposed talks with the Warsaw Pact on mutual, balanced force reductions (MBFR). But, since the Warsaw Pact had a clear conventional superiority, they were not eager to respond.

The result was that, increasingly, NATO was plagued by arguments over 'burden-sharing'. The US, especially, pressed the case that, with West European economies having recovered from the War, its own share of NATO defences in Europe should be reduced. By 1971, US troop levels in NATO were reduced to 282,000 but in the Senate a group led by Senator Mike Mansfield demanded more swingeing cuts. In May 1971 he introduced an amendment in Congress that would have halved the US presence. However, for the American government, this would have again risked a collapse of the alliance, and it would have weakened the West in dealing with the Soviets. President Nixon campaigned strongly against Mansfield and the amendment was defeated by 61 to 36. Once again, a potential disaster had, in the end, been overcome

and if anything this latest crisis confirmed the Nixon administration's belief that NATO could be treated as a secondary concern, not because it was without significance but because, in the last analysis, the US and Western Europe needed each other too much to drift apart.

The EEC from Veto to Enlargement

In January 1963 de Gaulle vetoed Britain's first application to join the EEC that had been launched 18 months before. The application had always been surrounded by conditions on Britain's part, it had not been pressed vigorously, and it divided both the British Commonwealth and the main political parties. One historian has written that 'had it been handled differently, Britain's . . . application should have reached a successful conclusion long before de Gaulle was . . . strong enough to intervene.'[27] However, the signs were that the negotiations would have succeeded except for de Gaulle's action, which he had probably intended for some time, though in the event it was prompted by Britain's decision to buy Polaris missiles from America. He argued that this proved Britain's commitment to the 'special relationship' with Washington in preference to Europe. Others saw the veto as proof of the General's desire to predominate in the EEC. He was able to accompany the veto with a Franco–German Treaty, which cemented his own 'special relationship' with chancellor Konrad Adenauer and which forced the other four Community members to accept the veto. Adenauer's readiness to back de Gaulle, even when the latter criticized the Atlantic alliance, upset other German politicians however and, during a debate in May, the Bundestag reasserted both the importance of the alliance and the desirability of British entry to the EEC. In October the ageing Adenauer resigned, to be succeeded by his more Atlanticist deputy, Ludwig Erhard, and relations between de Gaulle and his European partners continued to worsen thereafter. In 1964 the French leader was upset by Erhard's interest in the US-proposed Multilateral Nuclear Force for NATO and by the failure to make progress on a Common Agricultural Policy (CAP) for the EEC, from which France especially would gain. In 1965 he became increasingly concerned too by the centralizing tendencies of the EEC, which might undermine French independence. There were proposals to give the EEC its own budgetary resources and to increase the power of the European Parliament and Commission. Furthermore, under the Treaty of Rome, the EEC was due to begin making decisions by majority votes in 1966.

In July 1965, to try to prevent further centralization, de Gaulle launched the 'empty chair' crisis, a French boycott of EEC bodies. This secured him an apparently significant concession in January 1966 when, in the so-called 'Luxembourg compromise', it was agreed that any EC member could veto decisions which harmed essential national interests. But it was not clear how this would operate in practice and the fact is that de Gaulle had been driven to negotiate (and to end the 'empty chair' policy) by his continuing desire for the CAP and by setbacks for the Gaullists in the December 1965 French election. The compromise has been described as 'more of a statement of disagreement' than a long-term settlement.[28] As with NATO, where de Gaulle's anti-Americanism led him to withdraw from the military structure while his anti-communism led him to remain an alliance signatory, so with the EEC he was determined to maximize French independence yet simultaneously recognized that supranational cooperation could bring benefits like the CAP. In 1967 de Gaulle's position was still strong enough to allow him to veto a second, short-lived British attempt at EEC entry and he certainly succeeded in slowing up progress on Community integration. The only major step forward in the later 1960s was the institutional merger in 1968 between the EEC and two other supranational bodies, the European Coal and Steel Community and the atomic energy community, EURATOM. But in May 1968 de Gaulle's position was shaken by domestic unrest in Paris and other cities, which harmed the economy and called into question the General's authority. Faced with the prospect of having to devalue the franc, de Gaulle chose to resign in April 1969, freeing the EEC to make swifter progress.

De Gaulle's successor, Georges Pompidou, was a Gaullist former prime minister but he had good reasons to alter the General's European policy. In particular, Pompidou was fearful of increased German power and its readiness, under Willy Brandt

after September 1969, to pursue an independent foreign policy, at least regarding Eastern Europe. The strengthening of EEC institutions seemed the best way to limit German ambitions and this policy might also benefit from British entry. 'Britain's membership would be a counterweight to growing German influence in the EEC.'[29] Pompidou also wanted, finally, to achieve a fully operational CAP and he had reason to court popular support at home by pursuing a more 'pro-European policy'. At a summit meeting of Community leaders in The Hague in December 1969, it was therefore possible to agree both on the completion of the CAP and on enlargement talks with Britain, Denmark, Ireland, and Norway. These talks got underway in June 1970 and, in contrast to previous attempts, the British kept their entry conditions at a minimal level. There were still problems over monetary and trade issues, as well as the size of Britain's financial contribution, the last made worse by the costs of CAP. But a summit between Pompidou and Britain's premier, Edward Heath, provided a breakthrough. Although Norway voted against membership in a referendum, the other three signed a Treaty of Accession in January 1972, to take effect a year later. This 'northern enlargement' was only one of the advances made by the EEC at the time. The decision to finance the CAP by giving the Community its own financial resources (in the form of income from tariffs and expenditure tax) strengthened the Commission's independence. In October 1970 the 'Werner Report' proposed greater monetary cooperation in the EEC, with a centralized 'economic and monetary union' in the long term. And the following month EEC foreign ministers began to meet together to discuss common foreign policy issues, a practice known as European Political Cooperation and which marked a development going beyond the original Treaty of Rome.

Yet this new surge of European integration also contributed to growing trans-Atlantic difficulties. Until the 1960s the US had backed integration as a way to create a united, economically robust, and politically liberal Western Europe which could resist Soviet communist encroachments. Formally, Washington was still committed to this aim, but there was also wariness about European success. Pressures for 'burden sharing' in NATO have already been discussed; and strong EEC economic growth, linked to protectionist trade practices, provoked US fears of unfair commercial competition. In May 1967, after five years of talks, the 'Kennedy Round' of tariff reductions, carried out under the auspices of GATT, had reached a critical phase due to trans-Atlantic differences: the EEC was resentful of the American use of import quotas to restrict trade; while the US was critical both of the nascent CAP, which harmed US agricultural sales in Europe, and of preferential EEC commercial relations with former French colonies. These differences did not prevent the 'Kennedy Round' being completed the following month, but they were a warning of further arguments over trade to come. Under Nixon, the American secretary of the treasury, John Connolly, was especially keen to press 'burden-sharing' and fair trade on the Europeans (and Japan), especially as the US dollar was in a weak position by 1970—not helped by devaluations of sterling (1967) and the franc (1969). Neither were bilateral relations with major West European allies smooth at this time. France was a well-established thorn in the side of attempts to reinvigorate Atlantic cooperation. But in 1970–1, partly in order to end the threat of a veto of his campaign to join the EEC British premier Heath—though a loyal enough NATO ally—played down his reliance on the US and refused to use the term 'special relationship'. After 1969 there were growing suspicions, too, between the US and West Germany, although these focused principally on issues of détente, which will now be discussed.

The Western Economies in the 1960s

In the 1960s the economic growth of the previous decade was generally sustained but at a decreasing rate. Lower growth was accompanied by the spectre of inflation and associated with social unrest, but the dramatic Paris riots of May 1968 stemmed from alienation. In Italy, a post-war success story (where the 'economic miracle' brought average growth rates of 7 per cent in 1958–63), there was a spate of strikes, inflation of 8 per cent and a sudden return to a trade deficit in 1962–3. This led to an experiment with left-leaning coalitions under Aldo Moro in the mid-

1960s, but 1969 nonetheless saw the 'hot autumn' of strikes and demonstrations. There was a similar move to the Left elsewhere: in Britain there was a substantial victory for the Labour Party in 1966, and the same year the social democrats entered the German government for the first time in a generation. Even a strong economy like Germany saw inflation rise from 2 per cent in 1969 to nearly 5 per cent in 1971. In the US, fuelled by spending on Vietnam, inflation was already nearly 5 per cent when Lyndon Johnson left office and it continued to rise under Nixon, to almost 9 per cent in 1974. The one continuing success story among the advanced economies was Japan, where growth rates between 1950 and 1973 averaged over 9 per cent, turning it into the world's second largest manufacturer, after the US. Japanese growth, which was twice the average of Western economies was helped by high savings rates and relatively low wages.

Particular challenges were created for the West in this period by balance of payments difficulties, which had a detrimental effect on monetary stability. The British pound, long undermined by the country's poor economic performance compared to its main industrial competitors, was devalued in 1967, after a financial crisis triggered by the latest Arab–Israeli war; and the French franc, weakened by the troubles of 1968, was devalued in 1969. By then the key question was whether the US dollar, the backbone of the Bretton Woods monetary system, would also have to be devalued. America had faced increasing balance of payments problems since the late 1950s as the European and Japanese economies became increasingly strong competitors, and the inflation associated with (but not solely caused by) the Vietnam War added to the problems. Throughout the 1960s the US had urged 'burden-sharing' on its allies in order to cut its overseas defence expenditure and under Nixon, at first, the treasury secretary, John Connelly, concentrated on criticisms of 'unfair' trading practices by Japan and Western Europe. There were also hopes that the Bretton Woods system of stable exchange rates might be shored up through the revaluation of the two strengthening currencies, the Japanese yen and the German mark. And by 1971 the International Monetary Fund had been provided with $30 billion worth of funds, from the leading Western economies, to try to help those facing payments problems. But in August 1971 Nixon finally introduced a package of measures to limit imports and restrict wage/price increases, as well as ending the convertibility of dollars into gold. This 'Nixon Shock' heralded the end of Bretton Woods and the beginning of a decade of economic stagnation in the West.

The problems of the developed economies in the 1960s should not be exaggerated however. Eastern and Western blocs' living standards continued to rise; consumer goods production was increasing (with about 23 million cars produced in 1971 for example—five times the 1950 figure); and welfare services were improving. A situation of full employment was maintained, even if unemployment was beginning to rise by 1970 (reaching 6 per cent in the US). A slowing of growth rates from the heady days of the late 1950s and early 1960s was probably inevitable, as the post-war reconstruction period ended and industrial states 'caught up' with the years of depression and war which arguably stretched all the way back to 1914. The rising social discontent in France, Italy, and elsewhere was caused less by fear of poverty than a desire to maintain the wage increases and improved working conditions that higher growth rates and full employment had allowed. The 'high growth rate was coming to an end as the technological catching up phase tapered off, so that a gap began to open ... between the declining productivity increases and the continued high annual wage increases'.[30] In many ways the Western economies, at least, were as wealthy as ever. The US might have lost its clear predominance in the world economy, which had been so evident in 1945, but in 1971 it still had a third of world manu-facturing production and its industrial efficiency (measured by output per worker) was still twice that of Japan and Germany.

The Western economies were also becoming more closely integrated in terms of trade and investment. In Europe the EEC proved a remarkable success, creating a free trade area by 1969. (Attempts to integrate East European economies, via COMECON, proved far less successful.) However, there were also important links between the US, Europe, and Japan. About two-thirds of the trade of industrialized countries was with other industrialized countries. By the mid-1960s America had over $50 billion invested abroad and its businesses controlled about 8,000 subsidiaries in the EEC and Britain alone. Since about 1958 when US investors realized they could escape restrictions on earnings from interest at home, by investing in Europe, the scale of trans-atlantic integration in investment had increased. By 1971 the so-called 'Eurodollar' market was worth over $100 billion. Meanwhile, in the trade field, the 'Kennedy Round' of trade reductions, negotiated by GATT between 1963 and 1967, cut tariffs by an average of 25 per cent; and it did so across a wide range of produce rather than (as in previous efforts) by concentrating on particular items. The fact that it concentrated on manufactured goods made it most beneficial to the developed Western countries however, and it was they who generally gained most from the continuing growth of global commerce in the 1960s. By 1971 world trade, which had actually outpaced economic growth, was five times its 1948 level, but it was concentrated in manufactures rather than primary products, the price of which remained low—to the detriment of producers in the less developed world.

E. **The Rise of European Détente**

Motives for European Détente

Down to 1972, as the US and USSR moved fitfully towards improved bilateral relations, more rapid and certain progress was made with détente in Europe.

Indeed, it has been stated that détente 'emerged first in Europe. The groundwork was laid by President de Gaulle ... and then, on a more lasting basis, by the West German Ostpolitik.'[1] In fact European détente can be said to have had an even longer pedigree.

Attlee had considered the idea of détente and Winston Churchill had first urged an East–West summit to discuss Cold War tensions in 1950 and three years later, following the death of Stalin, had pressed strongly for greater diplomatic contacts, increased trade, and a system of border guarantees in Europe. In November 1954, France's prime minister, Pierre Mendés-France, had used his address to the UN General Assembly to urge East–West talks and the mid-1950s had seen at least one major step forward in Europe, the 1955 Austrian State Treaty (see Chapter 5, B). There were good reasons why British and French leaders should go further than the US in their eagerness for détente. The West European great powers had a different diplomatic tradition to the US, less ideological in its emphasis, readier to accept the current state of power, politics and, especially in Britain's case, keen to ensure that commerce flowed freely across borders whatever differences might exist between governments. The Cold War had certainly forced the British and French, as well as the Germans and Italians, to alter their approach. No longer able to shape world affairs, in the late 1940s and early 1950s, they had tied themselves closely to America, followed determinedly anti-communist policies (despite the grave divide this opened in French and Italian society) and agreed to restrict East–West trade severely through the COCOM organization.

Nonetheless, there were also powerful forces at work which tended to foster a pro-détente approach even when the Cold War was at its height. For both Western and Eastern Europeans inevitable concern developed from their being so close to the dividing line between the two camps, organized as these were into military alliances backed by the nuclear arsenals of the superpowers. In the event of war much of Europe would be obliterated. This was one powerful reason for European leaders to pose as potential mediators in a US–Soviet settlement. Furthermore, a lowering of tensions was the surest way to make the European countries less reliant on their superpower protectors, and to improve the freedom of diplomatic manoeuvre they had between the US and USSR. On both sides of the Iron Curtain, European leaders had an interest in treating each other as independent equals, rather than as pawns of Moscow and Washington. In the 1960s it was not surprising that

détente was keenly advocated by France's President de Gaulle and Romania's Nicolae Ceauşescu, both of whom had a highly developed sense of the need to reduce superpower domination in order to maximize national independence. There were always limits to how far European détente could go, however, especially if the superpowers were not in favour of it. De Gaulle, who in any case concentrated until 1962 on ending the colonial war in Algeria rather than developing détente or challenging US predominance, was always a firm anti-communist; just as Ceauşescu always maintained a political system in Romania that was amongst the most oppressive in the Eastern bloc.

It is arguable that for many, on both sides of the Curtain, the division of Europe brought one great benefit: it kept Germany divided and weak. For East Europeans, their deep-seated fear of Germany provided a powerful motive for remaining closely allied to the USSR, especially while there was a danger of Bonn securing access to nuclear weapons. Even in the West, however, France, Britain, and others were happy to see the old enemy split into two, unassertive in its foreign policy, yet providing resources that strengthened Western defence. Integrating West German resources into the Western bloc was also a means of containing the danger of a revived Germany. It is also important to appreciate that both sides in Europe had reasons to pursue détente which had more to do with continuing an ideological struggle than with ending it. Indeed, détente can be seen as fighting the Cold War by means other than the diplomatic deadlock, commercial freeze, and nuclear threats which, it could be argued in retrospect, had merely cemented the unity of both blocs until about 1962. It was also a safer option than offensive covert measures that were increasingly seen as too big a risk. For the Soviets, prime motives for relaxing tensions in the 1960s 'included a desire to ... exploit divisions in the Western camp, obtain Western capital and technology to spur the lagging Soviet economy, and ... cover themselves in the West against the risks of ... conflict with China in the East.'[2] To these may be added the hope of 'decoupling' the US from Western Europe defence through the pursuit of an all-European security system. In the West, whilst some leftists were ready to tolerate the continued existence of communism, most advocates of détente in government saw it as a way of undermining the Eastern bloc by peaceful means: by respecting the European status quo in the short term, the West would use trade, talks, and other contacts to break down barriers and suspicions with the East, proving the superiority of Western economic goods, infiltrating liberal ideas across the Iron Curtain, and so diluting the cohesion of the Soviet bloc. The logic was admirably set out in a British policy paper of March 1960 which stated that 'We were working for a reduction of tension in Europe. If this was successful it might create pressures inside the Communist camp which could, in due course, loosen the Russian grip on Eastern Europe. It was not a policy of appeasement but a means of carrying the offensive into the Communist camp.'[3] Such a policy may have begun to have success in the 1960s, hoping to 'dilute the Soviet challenge: as the Soviet people became . . . aware of the realities of the world outside, their expectations and interests came into tacit collision . . .' with the centralized economic planning system at home. But this took time to have effect and 'meanwhile the imperial outreach of the Soviet Union continued', as seen in Czechoslovakia in 1968.[4]

Progress on Pan-European Contacts, 1966–1971

The years 1966 and 1967 saw substantial progress in European détente, aided by the improvement in superpower relations since the Cuban missile crisis, the steady approach to foreign policy of Brezhnev's Kremlin, and West European concern over America's Vietnam policy. Early in 1966 the State Department remained sceptical about the prospects for détente in general, suspicious of Soviet motives, and determined only to negotiate from strength. However, pressure for détente was growing on the European front from a number of directions. One was the behaviour of de Gaulle who, since 1962, had not only blocked deeper integration and enlargement of the EEC, and increasingly criticized US policy in Vietnam and Europe, but had, in January 1964, opened diplomatic relations with communist China, despite the depth of US–Chinese enmity. The

same month he signed an agreement on economic, cultural, and scientific exchanges with the USSR. In March 1966, of course, he quit NATO's institutional structure and, in June 1966, visited the USSR. Already, in February 1965, de Gaulle had spoken of restoring the broad unity of Europe 'from the Atlantic to the Urals' and his meetings in Moscow, coming so soon after the exit from NATO, were designed both to underline French independence of America and to demonstrate the possibility of pan-European links. He did not believe the Soviets intended to launch war on the West, so that there seemed little risk in such a policy. Instead, French power would be maximized in a system of more independent European states, no longer dominated by Moscow and Washington. Yet, as with his EEC and trans-Atlantic policies, de Gaulle's approach to détente lacked coherence. His determination to break the superpower domination of world affairs meant that some of his actions, including recognition of China as well as his growing friendship with Ceauşescu, upset the Soviets. The idea that France alone could achieve much in drawing down the Iron Curtain was absurd, especially since de Gaulle always made clear that, in a major East–West crisis he would side with the other democracies. French trade with the Eastern bloc barely increased in the 1960s and the USSR itself, in its actions over the following years, showed itself less interested in a deal with France than with a broader European security agreement or, more especially, a deal that would neutralize any threat from Germany.

De Gaulle was not the only West European leader to visit Moscow in 1966. The British Prime Minister, Harold Wilson, had been there in February mainly to develop trade and technological exchanges. Commercial motives were also at the centre of increasing Italian interest in détente, with the Soviet President, Nicolae Podgorny, visiting Rome in January 1967. Such events did not arouse the same popular interest as de Gaulle's behaviour, largely because Britain and Italy were perceived as loyal Atlanticists. However, to the Johnson administration, it was increasingly clear that many West European governments, backed by their parliaments and popular opinion, were keen to develop East–West links. (One of the few exceptions in 1966 was West Germany, but that was soon to change.) What was more, in the immediate aftermath of de Gaulle's visit, the Warsaw Pact met in Bucharest and renewed its pressure, first begun in 1954 (see Chapter 5, A and B) but not pressed much by Khrushchev, for a pan-European security system. As in 1954, the proposal was not put in a way that attracted serious Western interest: America and Canada were to be excluded from the new system—and thus 'decoupled' from West European defence—and NATO was to be wound up; the existing status quo in Europe was to be recognized, thus condoning Soviet domination of the East; and trade was to be freed from Western security controls. Yet, in December 1966 the North Atlantic Council responded to the increasing pressures for détente by asking a committee chaired by the Belgian Prime Minister, Pierre Harmel, to study the Alliance's options regarding détente. A year later, with France now outside the organization, the Council (at the same time as adopting 'flexible response') accepted the Harmel Report. 'Its lifeblood was the statement . . . that the Alliance had two functions: military security and a policy of détente, and that these were not contradictory but complementary.'[5] On the one hand, détente should only be pursued in so far as it preserved Western security. On the other, military deadlock at the heart of Europe

could only end if political issues were addressed and henceforth NATO should provide a multilateral context for Western talks with the Warsaw Pact (see boxed section).

The Harmel Report potentially opened the way to East–West talks on an unprecedented range of political, military, and economic issues. But actually little happened in the short term. The Soviets showed no enthusiasm for the Report, partly because it failed to welcome the idea of a pan-European security system, partly because it adhered to a policy of Western military strength, hoping to retain the US presence in Europe while seeking a favourable deal with the East. In June 1968 NATO followed it up with calls for pan-European talks on Mutual Balanced Force Reductions (MBFR), but these held little interest for the Soviets, who would be expected to surrender their conventional superiority in Europe. A few months later, of course, the invasion of Czechoslovakia proved a setback for détente and made NATO cautious when, in April 1969, the Warsaw Pact renewed its call for a pan-European security system. In December of that year, in Brussels, the Atlantic Council made it clear that any talks with the Warsaw Pact on European security must proceed on the basis of sovereign states, free

The Harmel Report

Actually entitled 'The Future Tasks of the Alliance', the Harmel Report was published as an annex to the communiqué of the North Atlantic Council meeting of December 1967, at which it was accepted as policy. The report had been requested a year earlier, after growing pressures to look afresh at NATO's role in a world that had changed much since the Atlantic Pact was signed in 1949. The Sino–Soviet split, Moscow's interest in 'peaceful coexistence', Western Europe's post-war economic growth, and the process of decolonization were some of the main developments noted in the report itself, which was written by a six-man committee, drawn from several members and chaired by the Belgian prime minister, Pierre Harmel. The report saw a continuing security role for NATO, given the continuing existence of the Warsaw Pact and the fact that, at the heart of Europe, the German problem remained unresolved. However, the key development which Harmel and his colleagues

wished to see was a new emphasis on NATO's 'second function, to pursue the search for . . . a more stable relationship in which the underlying political issues can be solved' between East and West. 'The way to peace and stability in Europe', it was stated, 'rests in particular on the use of the Alliance constructively in the interest of détente.' The tone of the report was cautious, emphasizing the need to maintain Allied unity and predicting that détente would take time to evolve. It declared that the 'relaxation of tensions is not the final goal but is part of a long-term process to promote better relations and to foster a European settlement. The ultimate political purpose . . . is to achieve a just and lasting peaceful order in Europe accompanied by appropriate security guarantees.' The report pointed the way to multilateral negotiations between NATO and the Warsaw Pact on European security which began a few years later.

to shape their own destinies, unthreatened by the use of force—conditions which had not been respected in Czechoslovakia. NATO ministers also made clear their desire to see increased cultural, personal, and information exchanges across the Iron Curtain, underlining the danger of what the Soviets called 'cultural subversion' from the West. Despite this the Warsaw Pact made a key concession at its June 1970 meeting, agreeing that the US and Canada could take part in a European security conference and, in 1971, as on superpower détente and the Sino–American rapprochement, there was a real sense of forward momentum in European détente. In May 1971 Brezhnev agreed that MBFR talks might be useful. The timing of this move was important because it came as the Nixon administration was under pressure, from the Mansfield Amendment, to cut troop levels in Europe unilaterally. Brezhnev's announcement allowed Nixon to argue that multi-lateral talks, rather than unilateral cuts, were the best way to secure troop reductions. In December, the Atlantic Council reciprocated by agreeing in principle to a European security conference. This sense of progress was greatly helped, however, by parallel advances on the issue which remained at the centre of European security, the future course of German policy.

The Emergence of Ostpolitik, 1966–1971

Between 1948 and 1961 the German problem, and more specifically the position of Berlin, had been the main East–West flashpoint in Europe. The Western powers had refused to recognize East Germany's existence and the Eastern bloc had condemned West Germany's economic and military resuscitation. However, the building of the Berlin Wall in 1961, while it sparked a crisis in the short term, was followed by a recognition on both sides that the division of Berlin and Germany would continue for years to come. Increasingly, newly independent states in the less developed world gave diplomatic recognition to East Germany, undermining West Germany's Hallstein Doctrine (under which it had no relations with governments who recognized East Germany). 'Instead of isolating the GDR from the

rest of the world, [West Germany] faced the prospect of being isolated itself.'[6] Furthermore, 'in the 1960s, a majority of West Germans started to identify with the Federal Republic, based on the success story of the "economic miracle" and the country's political stability.'[7] After December 1966 the West German 'Grand Coalition' government of Kurt Kiesinger tentatively began a new policy, Ostpolitik, designed to improve relations with the Soviet bloc by abandoning the Hallstein Doctrine, opening up trade, and offering agreements which included the mutual renunciation of force. This 'eastern policy' became identified with the social democratic foreign minister, Willy Brandt, who, as Mayor of Berlin had already negotiated an agreement in 1963 for Christmas visits to be made between the two halves of the city. He believed that the division of Germany could only be broken down through a gradual relaxation of tension, rather than the confrontational policies favoured by the Adenauer governments of 1949–63. The Soviets, still concerned about West Germany's nuclear ambitions, were initially sceptical, and the East German government insisted on Western diplomatic recognition as a condition of any agreements with West Germany. Yet Brandt was able to establish diplomatic relations with two of the more independent states in the Eastern bloc, Romania in 1967 and Yugoslavia in 1968. In a speech in Nuremberg in 1968 he also made a significant concession by offering to compromise on the issue of Germany's borders, opening the way to territorial deals with Poland, Czechoslovakia, and the USSR. But that same year, in an article in *Foreign Affairs*, he was careful to 'reject any German foreign policy that lessens the solidarity of [NATO] or limits the decisive participation of the United States in safe-guarding freedom in Europe'.[8]

In October 1969 Brandt became West German chancellor and, within 2 months, signed the Non-Proliferation Treaty, ending Warsaw Pact fears of a German nuclear arsenal. Christian Democrats, who had hitherto dominated government in the Bonn Republic but were now excluded from it, had their doubts about Ostpolitik, and in the White House, Henry Kissinger feared that Brandt's enthusiasm might open NATO to 'selective détente', whereby the Soviets would 'ease tensions with some allies while

Willy Brandt (1913–1992)

A German social democrat and firm opponent of Naziism, Brandt went to live in Norway during the Hitler years but returned soon afterwards and, in 1949, became a member of the first West German parliament. He was one of a revisionist group who, in the 1950s, worked to make the Social Democratic Party (SPD) more electable by toning down its Marxist elements and shifting its foreign policy away from a readiness to deal with the USSR, to support for such Western organizations as NATO and the European Community. Brandt rose to world prominence as Mayor of West Berlin after 1957, in which position he saw out the crisis of 1958–9, when Khrushchev threatened to drive the Western powers out, and the raising of the Berlin Wall in 1961. His firmness under pressure, together with his liberal views and experience of running the West Berlin government, made him an obvious candidate for the SPD to put forward as chancellor. However, it was in the joint position of vice-chancellor and foreign minister that he first entered national government in December 1966, as part of a 'Grand Coalition' with the Christian Democrats, West Germany's largest party.

The 'Grand Coalition;' was intended by Brandt and his colleagues to provide the SPD with experience of government, having been excluded from it since 1930. As foreign minister, Brandt was able to lay the foundations for his later Ostpolitik, by improving relations with the Eastern bloc countries, who the Christian Democrats had previously been unwilling to recognize. Such successes helped make Brandt himself chancellor in October 1969, after which he pursued Ostpolitik with vigour, making treaties with the USSR, Poland, and Czechoslovakia which resolved problems going back to the War. More remarkably he secured better access between the two Berlins and, controversially at home, proved ready to deal with East Germany under the formula of 'two states in one nation', which kept up the image of a single entity. The high point of his Premiership was the November 1972 election, which gave the SPD 46 per cent of the vote—outstripping the Christian Democrats for the only time in West German history. But in May 1974 he felt forced to resign, an East German spy having been discovered working on his staff. Brandt remained SPD Party chairman for some years and maintained his international profile with the 1980 Brandt Report, drawn up by an international group that he led, which vainly pressed the case for tackling the world's North–South divide between rich and poor.

maintaining an intransigent position towards us'.[9] Such fears proved exaggerated. Within a year, on 12 August 1970, Brandt signed the Moscow Treaty with the USSR which became the basis for later Ostpolitik agreements. It involved the renunciation of the use of force, increased financial-commercial ties and—the point which caused most controversy in Germany—a recognition of the inviolability of existing European borders, including those between East and West Germany and between Poland and Germany. Brandt did not give up the ambition of eventual German reunification, he did not recognize the East German government, and he insisted that, before the Moscow Treaty could be ratified, there must be an agreement on Berlin that recognized West Berlin's links to West Germany. This breakthrough agreement, which helped remove fears of German revanchism in the East, was followed by the Warsaw Treaty of 7 December with Poland, which confirmed the German–Polish border. In a symbolic gesture of reconciliation, which was

criticized in some circles in Germany, Brandt knelt at the memorial to the Jewish ghetto in Warsaw.

Talks over Berlin proved more difficult, partly because the Stalinist East German leader Walter Ulbricht was reluctant to deal with Bonn, and partly because, where Berlin was concerned, agreement was needed from the four occupation powers. West Germany, the US, USSR, Britain, and France began to discuss Berlin in March 1970 and Brandt was determined to get an agreement here before ratifying the Moscow and Warsaw Treaties. His aim was to win concessions from the USSR on Berlin in return for his acceptance of Germany's post-1945 borders. Ulbricht's doubts led to slow progress at first. He had earlier tried to forestall East European recognition of the Bonn government and to have Berlin recognized as separate from West Germany. But in May 1971 he was replaced by Erich Honecker who, though an orthodox enough communist, was ready to accept that times had changed. The Berlin agreement of 3 September 1971, between the four occupying powers, essentially recognized the existing status quo but was nonetheless significant. It guaranteed Western access to the city (reducing the risk of another blockade such as that of 1948–9) and gave both sides concessions on the question of political links between Berlin and Bonn. The Soviets recognized the legitimacy of such links but Brandt agreed to reduce West Germany's political role in Berlin and gave up on hopes of fully integrating the city into West Germany. This was a dramatic advance on the situation of a decade before, when the Berlin Wall had been erected. The new agreement helped pave the way both to wider détente in Europe and to a fuller settlement between the West and East German governments (see Chapter 13, D).

NOTES

1. Arthur M. Schlesinger, *A Thousand Days: John F. Kennedy in the White House* (Andre Deutsch, London, 1965), 762.

2. Theodore C. Sorensen, *Kennedy* (Hodder & Stoughton, London, 1965), 745.

3. Michael R. Beschloss, *The Crisis Years: Kennedy and Khrushchev, 1960–63* (Harper Collins, New York, 1991), 600.

4. Anatoly Dobrynin, *In Confidence* (Random House, New York, 1995), 122.

5. Dean Rusk, *As I Saw It* (Norton, New York, 1990), 343.

6. Peter G. Boyle, *American-Soviet Relations* (Routledge, London, 1993), 165.

7. Henry Kissinger, *The White House Years* (Weidenfeld & Nicolson, London, 1979), 129.

8. Odd Arne Westad (ed.), *Brothers in Arms: The Rise and Fall of the Sino-Soviet Alliance 1945–1963* (Stanford University Press, Stanford, 1998), 27–8.

9. Alfred D. Low, *The Sino-Soviet Dispute* (Associated University Presses, London, 1976), 343.

10. Edward Crankshaw, *The New Cold War* (Penguin, London, 1963), 153.

11. Thomas W. Zeiler, *Dean Rusk* (Scholarly Resources, Wilmington, 2000), 100–1.

12. Yang-Kuisong, 'The Sino-Soviet Border Clash of 1969', *Cold War History*, 1 (August 2000), 48.

13. Richard Nixon, 'Asia after Vietnam', *Foreign Affairs*, 1 (October 1967), 111–25.

14. Chen Jian and David Wilson, 'New Evidence on the Sino-American Opening', *Cold War International History Project Bulletin*, 11 (Winter 1998), 166–7.

15. Yang-Kuisong, 'The Sino-Soviet Border Clash', 49.

16. Henry Kissinger, *The White House Years* (Little, Brown, New York, 1979), 177–8.

17. William Shawcross, *Dubček* (Hogarth Press, London, 1990), 138–9.

18. Philip Windsor and Adam Roberts, *Czechoslovakia, 1968* (Columbia University Press, New York, 1969), 19.

19. Kenneth K. Skoug, *Czechoslovakia's Lost Fight for Freedom* (Praeger, Westport, 1999), 141.

20. H. Gordon Skilling, *Czechoslovakia's Interrupted Revolution* (Princeton University Press, Princeton, 1976), 498.

21. *Documents on British Policy Overseas, Series III, vol. 1: Britain and the Soviet Union, 1968–72* (Stationery Office, London, 1997), 85.

22. James G. McGinn, 'The Politics of Collective Inaction: NATO's Response to the Prague Spring', *Journal of Cold War Studies*, 1/3 (Autumn, 1999), 136.

23. Paul Buteaux, *The Politics of Nuclear Consultation in NATO* (Cambridge University Press, Cambridge, 1983), 60.

24. Lyndon B. Johnson Library, oral history interview with John Leddy.

25. Helga Haftendorn, *NATO and the Nuclear Revolution, 1966–7* (Clarendon Press, Oxford, 1996), 290

26. David Schwartz, *NATO's Nuclear Dilemmas* (Brookings, Washington, 1983), 187.

27. Piers Ludlow, 'A Mismanaged Application', in Anne Deighton and Alan Milward (eds), *Widening, Deepening, Acceleration: the EEC, 1957–63* (Bruylant, Brussels, 1999), 273.

28. Peter Stirk, *A History of European Integration since 1914* (Pinter, London, 1996), 175.

29. Martin Dedman, *The Origins and Development of the European Union, 1945–95* (Routledge, London, 1996), 119.

30. Sidney Pollard, *The International Economy since 1945* (Routledge, London, 1997), 108.

31. S. R. Ashton, *In Search of Détente* (Macmillan, London, 1989), 105.

32. A. W. De Porte, *Europe between the Superpowers* (Yale University Press, New Haven, 1986), 176.

33. Public Record Office, Kew, CAB 134/1929, FP(20) 1st, 23 March 1960.

34. Vladislav Zubok, 'Unwrapping the Enigma: the Soviet challenge in the 1960s', in Diane Kunz, (ed.), *The Diplomacy of the Crucial Decade* (Columbia University Press, New York, 1994), 173–4.

35. Helga Haftendorn, *NATO and the Nuclear Revolution, 1966–7* (Clarendon Press, Oxford, 1996), 374.

36. Josef Korbel, *Détente in Europe* (Princeton University Press, Princeton, 1972), 147.

37. Gottfried Niedhart, 'Ostpolitik', in Caroline Fink *et al*. (eds.), *1968: the World Transformed* (Cambridge University Press, Cambridge, 1998), 190.

38. Willy Brandt, 'German Policy towards the East', *Foreign Affairs*, 3 (April 1968), 477.

39. Henry Kissinger, *The White House Years* (Little, Brown & Co., Boston, 1979), 410.

10 The Vietnam War

A. The Escalation of US Involvement, 1963–1965

Continuing Instability in South Vietnam

Lyndon Johnson inherited the Vietnam conflict in difficult circumstances. He had not been elected President in his own right and so, perhaps, believed that he should carry on with Kennedy's policies. It was unclear what exactly Kennedy would have done in Vietnam, but Johnson retained his predecessor's foreign policy team (see boxed section) and did not question the basic principle of America's foreign policy, which called for communism to be resisted, wherever and whenever it threatened. It would have been difficult for anyone, even a newly elected President, to go against the consensus in Washington that opposed the spread of communism; and, as Senate Democrat leader in the Eisenhower years, Johnson had always backed that consensus. With thousands of US military advisers in South Vietnam already, any precipitate retreat would amount to a public admission of defeat, and even Kennedy had only talked of making any such withdrawal *after*

securing his re-election in November 1964. Johnson's preference, given his determined, self-confident personality and his disdain for anything that smacked of appeasement, would probably have been keen to pursue the war with greater vigour, ending Kennedy's ambiguity and trying to force a decisive victory. But in 1963–4 he too had to focus on the upcoming Presidential election, which he desperately wanted to win. The election, he decided, was safest fought without any particular emphasis on the difficult struggle in South-East Asia.

As if Kennedy's death and the approaching US election were not challenges enough, Johnson also had to deal with a South Vietnamese political situation which, in the wake of Diem's assassination, was wracked by instability, tempting the communists to believe that the war could soon be decided in their favour. In December 1963 the war in the South intensified with improvements in the Ho Chi Minh trail allowing a greater supply effort from the North. Johnson has often been criticized as a leader unfamiliar with foreign policy issues. According to an early assessment of his Presidency he 'entered the White House not only little concerned with the outer world but leery of it.'[1] His anti-communism was of a crude sort, he showed little understanding of Third World problems, and though he had visited South Vietnam as Vice-President, his attitude towards the Vietnamese was condescending and racist. Yet he had been canny enough to oppose the overthrow of Diem and it was not his fault that he had to pick up the pieces in the wake of it. The coup in Saigon might have got rid of an increasingly embarrassing and unpopular figure, but it did not necessarily guarantee a more popular replacement, nor mean that South Vietnam's internal problems were removed. True, Buddhist discontent lessened for a while, only reviving on a serious scale in March 1966. But the government remained corrupt, dominated by Catholics and unwilling to carry out reforms, such as land redistribution, which might have won peasant sympathy.

The fact was that the war was also a political struggle like the fight against colonialism and foreign interference from which it emerged. For many non-political Vietnamese the French defeat at the hands of the Japanese destroyed their legitimacy and neither Bao Dai, Diem, or their successors could regain it. They were perceived, like the Americans, as aliens who in addition were corrupt and inefficient supporters of oppressive landlords who were opposed to the kind of reforms that would appeal to the peasant masses. Ultimately, however, the Americans were precluded from embracing the kind of reform programme that would build the support of the rural masses. Whatever the flaws in the conception and administration of the strategic hamlets programme or Operation Phoenix, the ultimate need was radical land reform and redistribution. Whether referred to or not as 'communist' such concepts were beyond the pale for any American approach to private property. No amount of welfare, education, and development could compensate for that in the eyes of most Vietnamese peasants struggling with rents and inadequate land. The Americans could not promote land reform any more than they could build snowmen in Saigon.

The military too, despite ever more US advice and supplies, continued to perform badly against the Viet Cong. As under Diem, army officers were promoted for political loyalty rather than ability and they refused to take risks with their units, for fear either of sustaining heavy losses if defeated, or of arousing the suspicion of superiors if successful. Wealthy Vietnamese often bribed their way out of military service, while the poor simply deserted. On paper in 1964 the ARVN numbered half-a-million men, but the desertion rate that year was about 50,000 and few of the rest saw serious action against the Viet Cong. Indeed, some ARVN units made tacit 'peace' agreements with the communists at local level. That same year Johnson increased the number of US advisers in the country by 7,000, a reflection of the growing belief that only an increased American effort could offset South Vietnamese failings.

Just as the Truman–Eisenhower reliance on the French to defeat the communists had ended in disappointment in 1954, and just as the Eisenhower–Kennedy faith in Diem had evaporated in 1963, so in 1964 Americans came to doubt whether any potential South Vietnamese leader could stem the Viet Cong tide. As a result, many of the President's advisers came to believe that the US must effectively fight the war with its own armed forces. Diem's immediate successor, General 'Big' Minh, was the head of an unelected military junta which quickly became factionalized. Worse than that in American eyes, Minh showed signs of wanting to negotiate with the NLF, perhaps striking a deal that would neutralize Vietnam in the Cold War. Neither was General Minh alone in believing that Saigon's best option was to seek a settlement with its enemies: Diem's brother, Nhu, had had similar ideas. In late January 1964 the Americans encouraged Minh's replacement by the vain, volatile General Nguyen Khanh, who dominated the South Vietnamese leadership for the following year, despite a bewildering series of changes in the government, as attempts were made to replace him or to force him to share power. Khanh somehow survived despite his failure either to control the army factions, to win genuine popularity, or to prosecute the war with vigour. Indeed, he too showed signs of wanting to talk with the NLF before finally being expelled from office in February 1965. After that there were several more months of instability before, in June 1965, the junta fell under the domination of a flamboyant new Prime Minister, Air Vice-Marshal Nguyen Cao Ky, who survived in office for 2 years before losing a power struggle with his deputy, General Nguyen von Thieu, who was more trusted by Washington. Through all these changes of government, it was increasingly clear, in fact, that American requirements decided who held power in Saigon. Despite US claims to be protecting South Vietnamese 'independence', it was the US which effectively ensured that its allies abandoned all thought of neutralism and focused on opposing the Viet Cong, in a war where Americans took on a greater burden of fighting, in the air and on the ground.

The Gulf of Tonkin Resolution

In March 1964, the US Defense Secretary, Robert McNamara, visited South Vietnam, saw the growing frustration of the US military at South Vietnamese ineffectiveness, and reported to Johnson that increased American action was necessary to save the country from communism. The Joint Chiefs of Staff favoured a much tougher approach to the war, including large-scale use of bombing (in Laos as well as Vietnam) and covert operations against the North. The use of air power against North Vietnam, which was seen as lying behind the Viet Cong campaign in the South, was especially attractive to American planners. They had clear superiority in the air, could hope to destroy communist fuel, weapons, and communications through air attack, and an air campaign risked far less casualties than one on land. It was an obvious area in which the US might bring to bear its technological advantages over the communists. However, whilst Johnson allowed preparations for air strikes to be laid (with reconnaissance flights over possible targets) from May onwards, he was reluctant to bomb the North in an election year and possibly still hoped that a strengthening of Southern resolve might make such action unnecessary. During the election Johnson wanted to focus the electorate on his plans for a major social reform programme, the 'Great Society', which he dreamed would be more important than Roosevelt's 'New Deal'. Regarding Vietnam he undertook simply to assist in opposing communism and even suggested that substantial numbers of American troops would

never be sent to fight in Asia again. He left it to his Republican opponent, the extreme right-winger, Barry Goldwater, to alienate voters with a rabidly anti-communist, warmongering campaign. The reward was a landslide victory in the November election, which gave Johnson greater confidence about defining his own Vietnam policy in future.

Three months before the election his ability to fight the Vietnam war as he pleased was strengthened by a brief clash with the North. On 2 August North Vietnamese torpedo boats attacked an American vessel, the USS *Maddox*, operating in the Gulf of Tonkin where US covert operations, intelligence gathering, and support of commando raids on North Vietnam had been taking place. Two days later American ships reported a further attack (but one that probably had not taken place). The sense of outrage in Washington, at what was seen as an unprovoked assault, was such that, on 7 August, a motion was introduced in the Senate allowing Johnson to take 'all necessary measures to repel any armed attack against the armed forces of the United States and to prevent further aggression.' Democrats were keen to support the President ahead of the upcoming election, Republicans did not want to appear less 'patriotic' than the Democrats, and so the 'Gulf of Tonkin' resolution was duly passed, with little real discussion, by 88 votes to 2. Not repealed until 1970, it effectively gave Johnson a carte blanche to deal with the Vietnam conflict as he pleased. But at first it was not clear how he would exploit it. In the wake of the Gulf of Tonkin incident, US aircraft attacked the North for the first time, but only in limited, retaliatory raids, not the all-out bombing campaign which US military leaders favoured. With the Presidential election only days away, Johnson even reacted mildly to a communist attack on Bienhoa airbase, in which several Americans were killed. And, once elected, Johnson would have preferred to focus on the 'Great Society' programme which itself demanded large sums of money that a war in Vietnam could only compromise. Yet the US commander in South Vietnam after June 1964, General William C. Westmoreland, had no doubt that, to avoid a communist victory, the US must take over the war from the unreliable ARVN and pursue a war of attrition using American units. The Viet Cong were now reckoned to have about 200,000 fighters; in the wake of the Gulf of Tonkin episode infiltration from the North began to increase; and the attack on Bienhoa had shown that they were prepared to target US forces directly. Until August 1964 Hanoi had doubted whether Johnson would expend large-scale resources for the sake of the crumbling South, but now it was prepared for the possibility of a direct struggle with the Americans.

1965: Johnson's Decision to Escalate

In early 1965 American policy on Vietnam reached what McNamara called 'the fork in the road' and two fateful decisions were made: first, to begin a long-term bombing campaign against the North; and second, to deploy US ground troops to fight in the South. Both options had been pressed by the military for several months, but McNamara himself later criticized the way in which America slipped into war: 'Why did we escalate rather than withdraw? Why did we fail to see the implications of our actions?'[2] In fact there was some questioning of escalation in Washington. Indeed, there is evidence that, despite the criticism often levelled at him for being bent on war, Johnson 'reached widely for advisory . . . encounters'[3] and that, there were several Democratic Party senior figures who warned of the likely public backlash to escalation. There was also a leading figure in the administration, Under-Secretary of State George Ball, who preferred negotiation with Hanoi and stated about military escalation, in a memorandum of October 1964, that 'Once on the tiger's back we cannot be sure of picking the place to dismount.'[4] But Ball and the others were heavily outnumbered by those of the President's team urging greater US involvement to save South Vietnam. In the wake of the November election, Johnson had set up a working group on how to proceed in Vietnam which did not even view withdrawal as an option, because defeat at the hands of the communists seemed unthinkable. Instead three courses were considered. The first, continuing with current policies, seemed no better than withdrawal given the South's poor performance in the war. The second, a rapid build-up against Hanoi, would mean a costly commitment of US resources at

an early date, with the risk of provoking a violent Chinese response, which might lead to another Korean War—a war which had ended in a costly stalemate. The preferred option, therefore, was the third, a gradual application of pressure against the North to strangle its support for the Viet Cong. Such pressure would take the form of bombing but, since this might not break the North's resolve and might even provoke it to greater efforts, some of the Working Group also wanted to deploy US combat troops on the ground.

Johnson himself recognized the possible limitations of a bombing campaign and was troubled by the prospect of war but, faced by the continuing political instability in Saigon, he was increasingly prepared to accept the third option. Then, on 6 February 1965 a Viet Cong attack on Pleiku killed eight Americans, leading Johnson to approve retaliatory air attacks on the North, as he had after the Gulf of Tonkin episode. The Pleiku attack had probably been timed to coincide with a visit by the Soviet premier, Andrei Kosygin, to Hanoi; and the harsh US response, while Kosygin was still there, helped ensure Soviet sympathy for the North, an early demonstration that, if anything, bombing played into communist hands. Certainly the very need to bomb the North implied that the communists were winning the struggle in the South. Nonetheless, Johnson's advisers believed that a permanent bombing campaign would blunt the North's war effort, as well as giving a boost to Southern morale. Another Viet Cong attack on 10 February, this time in Saigon, killed over twenty Americans and was answered by further retaliatory air attacks. More importantly, Johnson was now convinced that a permanent campaign, codenamed Operation Rolling Thunder, should begin. Delayed at first by poor weather, it went ahead on 2 March. The Joint Chiefs would have preferred a massive bombing campaign, to include Hanoi and the major North Vietnamese port, Haiphong, rather than the gradual build-up of pressure (initially limited in its target areas) favoured by Washington. Even so Rolling Thunder, which went on until 1968 and eventually did strike targets around Hanoi and Haiphong, involved the use of B-52 aircraft which could each carry 30 tons of bombs, capable of levelling 1.5 square miles at a time.

The military could also be satisfied that, on 8 March, the first US ground troops arrived in South Vietnam, when 3,500 marines landed at Da Nang, already the location of a large American airbase. Some of Johnson's advisers were less certain about this step than they were about bombing, because of the risk of greater American casualties in an unconventional war for which they were not prepared. As with Rolling Thunder however, the ground war unfolded in a gradual way for Americans: the marines were initially deployed only to defend airbases, then in April they were allowed to extend operations to a radius of 50 miles and their numbers were increased, with the first regular army units arriving in May. Indeed, the gradual nature of escalation, both in the air and on the ground, was partly designed to prevent a war frenzy, or alternatively a major outcry against the war, at home. With a friendly Congress and an overwhelming election victory behind him, Johnson believed he could carry opinion with him in executing a limited war, and he still hoped to focus on his dream of a 'Great Society' rather than conflict overseas. Only in retrospect would it become clear that, with the launch of Rolling Thunder and the arrival of the marines, America was fatally committed to a quagmire war from which there was no easy escape. Yet, even at the time 'informed observers knew that a key moment had come and a line had been crossed'[5] and it did not take long for the policy of escalation to run into problems, in Vietnam, at home in America, and internationally.

B. **America versus North Vietnam, 1965–1967**

The Course of the War

In the wake of the first American troop commitments it became easier for General Westmoreland to win support for offensive 'search and destroy' missions against the communists. The alternative approach of concentrating on the defence and pacification of heavily populated areas on the coast and in towns, the so-called 'enclave strategy', was favoured by the marines, but did not promise rapid results. The pattern of escalation continued along the lines of early 1964: the area of bombing over the North was gradually extended, with oil depots around Hanoi and Haiphong hit in June 1966 and the US air force eventually risking raids close to the Chinese border; the numbers of troops was also raised gradually, without any formal, dramatic announcement to the American people. Thus on 27 July 1965, after an intensive debate among his advisers, Johnson announced that he was sending an additional 50,000 men to South Vietnam but kept quiet the fact that he had privately agreed to send 50,000 more than that (taking the total in Vietnam to 175,000). He also doubled the quota of draftees into the US armed forces to 35,000 but, in another example of his reluctance to risk controversy, refused to call up trained reserves because, while this might have produced a substantial, trained force more rapidly, it would also have meant forcing older men to fight. The President also gave the impression that US troops were merely supporting the ARVN, he made no stirring patriotic appeal, and he refused all calls to estimate the cost or duration of the conflict.

In early full-scale battles Westmoreland's conventional warfare approach seemed successful. At Chu Loi in August US marines killed about 600 Viet Cong for the loss of only 50 to themselves, an attrition rate which it seemed must ultimately force the communists to back down. Then, in October–November, in the Ia Drang valley of the Central Highlands, the regular North Vietnamese Army (NVA) lost over 1,500 compared to 300 American dead. The American use of helicopters, airlifted artillery, and B-52 bombers in the battle underlined their technological superiority. After this bloody encounter, however, the communists simply changed tactics, refusing to engage in large-scale clashes, harassing US forces when they were at company strength or less—and then only at close

Lyndon Johnson and his Foreign Policy Advisers

When the assassination of John F. Kennedy brought Johnson (1908–73) to the Presidency, the latter had only limited experience in the foreign policy field. Since his early political life, in his home state of Texas, the new President had been far more interested in social reform programmes, being an ardent supporter of Franklin Roosevelt's 'New Deal'. Entering the House of Representatives in 1937 and the Senate in 1948, Johnson was an energetic, driven figure who, as Democratic leader in the Senate from 1953 to 1961, proved able to manipulate and dominate the other ambitious politicians around him. He also strongly backed the bipartisan consensus in favour of an anti-communist policy. Even a serious heart attack in 1955 could not force him out of political life and, as a well-known Southern politician, he was an obvious choice to strengthen the Kennedy ticket in the 1960 election. As Vice-President, Johnson visited South Vietnam, without gaining much of an understanding of local realities, and he chaired the National Security Council but he had little enthusiasm for the latter body, considering it prone to 'leaks'. As President he preferred to rely on so-called 'Tuesday luncheons': select meetings in the White House with those he trusted.

Whilst never personally close to Kennedy, Johnson kept his predecessor's appointees in key positions in the foreign policy making machine. Indeed, the Secretary of State, Dean Rusk (1908–94), served in this role throughout the Kennedy and Johnson administrations. Partly educated at Oxford University on a Rhodes Scholarship, Rusk had originally begun his career as a professor of international relations but, after war service, had worked in the State Department and by 1952 was well enough networked to become President of the Rockefeller Foundation. He had been one of several candidates recommended to Kennedy as Secretary of State and, partly because of his age (most of Kennedy's aides were in their forties) had not been personally close to the President. However, these very facts, combined with his southern background, may have helped Rusk work with Johnson. Philosophical and deferential, Rusk was happy to let the Defense Department play the leading role on Vietnam policy but, as a convinced anti-communist, supported the escalation of the war, whose prosecution he continued to defend when in retirement.

Ironically, this could not be said of the Secretary of Defense for most of the 1960s, Robert McNamara (b. 1916). From California, educated at Berkeley and at Harvard Business School, McNamara's force of character and quick-mindedness helped him rise through the Ford Motor Company to be its President in 1960, before joining the Kennedy administration at the age of 44. In many ways McNamara was also the ideal character to get on with Johnson, who valued his loyalty and energy. However, McNamara's interest in statistics, technology, and managerial techniques, while they helped him make the Defense Department's planning and budget systems more efficient, proved inappropriate for fighting the Vietnam War, where he was slow to understand the psychology and determination of the communists. By 1967 he was increasingly concerned about the way the conflict was going and in August admitted to a Senate enquiry that the US bombing of the North had achieved little. Three months later it was announced that he was moving to head the World Bank. In 1995 he published *In Retrospect*, critical of the escalation of the Vietnam War which he had helped to direct 30 years before.

One novel feature of policy-making under Kennedy was the rise in significance of the National Security Adviser (NSA), as a Presidential appointee (not subject to Congressional approval), based in the White House itself. Such a position had existed under Eisenhower, but mainly in the role of supporting the work of the National Security Council. Under Kennedy the NSA, McGeorge Bundy (1919–96), became an important influence on Presidential decision-making. Bundy came from a privileged Boston background, educated at Yale and Harvard, later teaching government at the latter. A self-controlled, laconic figure, he too shared a tough, anti-communist outlook and was retained by Johnson until February 1966, when disagreements over Vietnam, added to differences of personality, led him to return to academic life. His successor was his former deputy, Walt Rostow (b. 1916), from Russian immigrant stock, but another product of Yale and an academic background. A convinced 'hawk' on Vietnam, energetic, and self-confident, Rostow advocated a firm military policy in Vietnam, including large-scale bombing of the North and, like Rusk, continued to defend the war after returning to private life in 1969.

range (so that B-52s and artillery were harder to use)—and melting away in the face of 'search and destroy' missions, only to return to old haunts when the Americans had moved on. As one military historian notes, 'ironically, one of the safest places for a US soldier to be in Vietnam was in one of Westmoreland's big battles, since they provided the best opportunity to minimize contact with the enemy.'[6] Visiting Vietnam in late November, McNamara reported that the North seemed to be matching the US escalation and that over half-a-million men might be needed there in the next few years with no firm promise of victory. Communist numbers in South Vietnam in 1966 probably numbered about 50,000 NVA, 225,000 active Viet Cong (both guerrillas and regular troops) and a further 150,000 'local defence' forces, the last a kind of part-time militia.

The military conduct of the war can be criticized on a number of grounds. The reliance on the effectiveness of the South Vietnamese army, which was often devoid of the will to fight and the technical competence to do so, was never likely to bear fruit either at the beginning or the end of the conflict. Moreover, the tactics and strategy employed by the Americans were often counterproductive. In one general sense the political need to win support in the countryside was undermined by the military actions. Ignorant of the customs of South Vietnamese peasants and their attachment to the local village, the Americans effectively destroyed the peasant way of life. They forced villagers away from their homes in the strategic hamlets programme and then deprived more than 3 million of them of any homes at all by accidental and deliberate bombing, by the creation of fire zones, and by search and destroy missions.[5] If villagers were not political or supporting the insurgents before losing their homes, and sometimes their wives and children, they were certainly likely to become so and actively to oppose the Saigon government and their American backers afterwards.

Moreover, the communist Viet Cong would be difficult to distinguish from those not involved in the fighting and for much of the war would often engage American forces and then melt into the jungle. Efforts to search and destroy them measured in terms of a 'body count' were seen by the commander of US forces in Vietnam as the key to victory

through the crushing of the Viet Cong. The body count of Americans, large as it was, tended to be very substantially lower than North Vietnamese losses and in that sense a 'success' of the search and destroy missions. It could therefore be argued, and certainly was at the time, that the Americans were winning the war. But by making the issue manpower losses this played to the insurgents' strengths as they could find replacements much easier than the Americans and were immune to the kind of political consequences that body bags arriving at US airports inevitably produced. It also encouraged the kind of indiscriminate destruction of towns and village, along with many of their inhabitants, that the fear of an elusive enemy often produced. As one US army officer said about the almost complete destruction of the city of Ben Tre, occupied by the Viet Cong in 1968 and subjected to indiscriminate US air and naval bombardment: 'It became necessary to destroy the town in order to save it'.[6]

In 1966 the US military predicament became clearer. While the NVA remained the key threat in the Central Highlands, the far more densely populated Mekong Delta was largely the preserve of the Viet Cong. Tackling these two enemies meant that the US could not even make secure South Vietnam's short, northern border—ironically called the Demilitarized Zone—which the NVA crossed with impunity. Large-scale bombing neither destroyed the North's ability to wage war nor prevented sufficient arms and equipment coming down the Ho Chi Minh trail to maintain the war in the South, which it is estimated required only ten tons of supplies per day (many weapons being captured from the ARVN). US troops, the bulk of them young draftees, found it a difficult, demoralizing war to fight, far from home, in a hot climate, with no obvious 'front line' and under constant danger from surprise attacks, landmines, and booby traps. Communist tactics after the battle of Ia Drang valley, proved very frustrating: only one in a hundred 'search and destroy' missions made contact with the enemy. And technological advantages provided no magic breakthrough but instead alienated the South Vietnamese people. The use of defoliants, in 'Operation Ranch Hand', caused environmental havoc to a fifth of the country in an attempt to remove the vegetation used by the communists as cover; the use of bombs and other explosives, together with the creation of 'free fire zones' (removing peasants from whole regions, so that the US and ARVN could concentrate on communist fighters who remained) helped render over 4 million South Vietnamese homeless by 1968; and American attempts to measure communist deaths proved unreliable, partly because many peasants remained inside 'free fire zones' and, if they were killed, there was no way to tell them from guerrillas.

Nonetheless, in January 1967 Westmoreland was confident that, with estimated communist deaths running at twelve times the American figure, the war of attrition was working, even if he could not prove that Viet Cong numbers were in decline. That month he launched Operation Cedar Falls, in the Viet Cong controlled 'Iron Triangle' north of Saigon. Bombs and artillery were followed up by the bulldozing of whole villages. Yet by summer the Viet Cong were back in control of the area. Despite the evidence of such failing tactics, there was only a belated attempt to improve pacification techniques, the so called Phoenix Programme, designed to win 'hearts and minds' and wipe out the Viet Cong by covert means, in mid-1967. The Thieu-Ky team remained the Americans' preferred government in Saigon despite periodic Buddhist unrest (especially in spring 1966) and despite winning only 35 per cent of the vote in elections in September 1967. The government was now seen to be completely dependent on Washington and little respected by most of its own people. Civilian leaders in Washington were increasingly frustrated with the military failure to break communist resolve; military leaders, for their part, were resentful at the political constraints put on their operations by the nature of 'limited war', with Johnson's gradual escalation of pressure against the North and the reluctance to bomb areas near the Chinese border. A school of thought has always claimed that, if the US had been tougher earlier, the war could have been won. For example, the wider air war might have been launched at an early date. As it was, by the time Rolling Thunder was extended, anti-aircraft defences had been improved over the North, so that US aircraft losses were high. One critical American analysis argues that 'instead of seeing it was possible to fight and win a limited war in Asia . . . we allowed our fears to become a kind of

self-deterrent and surrendered the initiative to our enemies.'[9] However, even at its most intense, and with all the North's large facilities and factories destroyed, bombing showed no sign of forcing Hanoi to back down. The rural economy survived and the North was never dependent on sophisticated technology. As to the war on the ground, 'looking at numbers . . . deployed, . . . their straining at the margins of the existing logistics infrastructure . . ., it is possible to argue that the . . . build-up . . . was as decisive as it could have been.'[10] An invasion of the North was considered but swiftly dismissed as it would almost certainly have brought China into the war, making the costs incalculable—and certainly not guaranteeing victory.

By 1967 Johnson was obsessed by Vietnam, monitoring daily operations in the White House Situation Room, and despairing of mounting divisions among his advisers. The continued problem of how to be sure of the situation on the ground and how to decide between conflicting advice was now opening up more serious divisions within the administration. As early as mid-1966 McNamara doubted the value of continued escalation and in 1967 went public with such criticisms. The President was also troubled that, despite his earlier attempts to underplay the significance of the war and concentrate on domestic reform, public opposition was becoming ever more vocal and the 'Great Society' programme stalling. March 1965 had seen the first university 'teach-in' against the war, reflecting doubts among the younger generation. In August 1965 a National Coordinating Committee was set up as an umbrella organization for the political, religious, and humanitarian groups opposed to the war and in October 1967 the largest anti-war demonstration of all took place, when 100,000 marched on the Pentagon. By then draft resistance was widespread. Meanwhile, in Congress, doubters led by Senator William Fulbright had forced special hearings on the war as early as February 1966. Yet in 1967 few in Congress were ready to advocate unilateral withdrawal, most media reports still accepted official versions of events in Vietnam, and two-thirds of American people still supported 'saving' Vietnam from communism, even if more than half were unhappy with the war's progress. Domestic opposition was, therefore, far from crippling the war effort, which Westmoreland in December 1967 believed was at a critical phase. Convinced that the communists had reached the 'crossover point', beyond which they were unable to compensate for their losses, he saw increased clashes with the NVA along the Laos border as evidence that a decisive struggle was imminent.

The Vain Search for Peace

From the start of direct American involvement, in early 1965, Johnson tried to disarm critics at home and abroad by posing as an advocate of peace talks. His first offer to negotiate came in a speech at Johns Hopkins University in April that year (see boxed section) and in mid-May he initiated the first 'bombing halt', a suspension of the Rolling Thunder campaign, designed to give the North a chance to talk. A longer 'bombing halt' was called between Christmas and the end of January 1966. Meanwhile, numerous potential intermediaries came forward, trying to broker a peace deal between Washington and Hanoi. There were various peace initiatives by the UN Secretary-General U Thant; the British government, co-chair (along with the USSR) of the Geneva conference, made three bids to establish a dialogue with North Vietnam in 1965; and there were efforts by, among others India, Canada,

Sweden, Norway, and Romania. In October 1966 the US, and other countries fighting alongside it in Vietnam, met in Manila and made an offer to withdraw if the North did likewise and this was followed by a Polish attempt, codenamed 'Marigold', to bring Hanoi and Washington directly into contact. Then, in February 1967, came the 'Sunflower' initiative, arguably the most promising peace bid before 1968: another bombing halt was accompanied by talks between the British premier, Harold Wilson, and Soviet premier, Andrei Kosygin, in London. Still there was no breakthrough however.

In his memoirs Johnson inserted a 10-page list of the various negotiation attempts and insisted 'I did everything I could to make one fact clear: that the United States sought only a peaceful settlement to the turmoil that . . . raged in Vietnam'. He had no doubt that the reason all efforts failed was that the North Vietnamese were 'never . . . ready . . . to negotiate seriously the terms of a fair peace settlement'.[11] Yet, in a seminal account of the war, the journalist Stanley Karnow, stated that during the 'Marigold initiative it was Johnson who had not been ready to talk—unless, of course, the enemy submitted to his terms'; whilst the 'Sunflower' initiative collapsed when Johnson toughened the US negotiating terms while the talks were underway. Such failures showed that neither belligerent was ready 'to shift the conference table before they had improved their

---

Two Approaches to Peace: the Johns Hopkins University Speech and North Vietnam's 'Four Points', 7 and 8 April 1965

President Johnson accompanied the escalation of the Vietnam War in the first half of 1965 with an address at Johns Hopkins University in Baltimore, in which he hoped to show a more positive side to US policy. The main points of the speech were:

- the US would resist Chinese Communist expansion which threatened all Asia,
- America would also 'help South Vietnam defend its independence',
- but he was ready to enter 'unconditional discussions' on a peaceful settlement in Vietnam,
- and he offered a one billion dollar aid package to provide food, health, and education to help Vietnam develop after peace was achieved.

The following day the North Vietnamese Prime Minister, Pham Van Dong, replied with a four-point programme:

- the US bombing campaign against the North should stop,
- US forces should withdraw from South Vietnam,
- South Vietnam's political future should be decided 'in accordance with the programme of the National Liberation Front',
- and Vietnam should then be reunited peacefully.

Taken together these statements showed the two sides to be far apart. America wanted an independent South Vietnam and an end to what it saw as Communist 'aggression'. Hanoi wanted Vietnam's reunification and an end to what it saw as American interference in Vietnamese affairs.

battlefield postures'.[12] In fact Washington and Hanoi consistently talked past each other when it came to negotiating terms. Reflecting the view that the North was guilty of aggression, Johnson was only prepared to wind down the US war effort after Hanoi ended its infiltration of troops and supplies into the South; and he was determined that Saigon's independence be preserved. To Hanoi, however, South Vietnam was an American puppet state; the Viet Cong was fighting a legitimate struggle against a corrupt regime and in favour of the reunification which Vietnam should have won after the Geneva conference; and the Rolling Thunder campaign was itself an act of aggression.

There were differences on the communist side as the war escalated in 1965. In the Hanoi government 'worried that American bombing threatened socialist construction in the North, some members wondered aloud if the southern insurgency was worth the high price', whilst Viet Cong leaders feared that the government would indeed 'put the long-term interests of the North before Southern liberation'.[13] In May, Johnson's first 'bombing halt' provoked considerable debate in Hanoi, with the NLF opposed to any negotiations ahead of a US withdrawal, but some northerners were ready to open a diplomatic dialogue with Washington. There was, in fact, an attempt to establish a link to the US government through Paris over the next few months. However, Johnson's continuing escalation of the war (especially with his increased troop commitments in July), and evidence that the US call for talks was insincere, gave ammunition to Le Duan and other hardliners. By August the Paris channel had closed and in early 1966 Hanoi's line was firmly behind a military victory. Ho Chi Minh showed little interest in peace feelers before 1968 and Johnson's own much-trumpeted offers to negotiate were designed more as publicity exercises than genuine attempts to talk. The difference between the belligerents was highlighted in a further exchange of public statements in late 1967. On 29 September, in a speech at San Antonio, Johnson offered to halt the bombing in return for a firm promise of discussions and an end to further infiltration; but in December Hanoi replied that Rolling Thunder must end before discussions began. By then each side was preparing for a military showdown.

International Factors

Another way in which Johnson tried to maintain domestic support for the war was to suggest that the defence of South Vietnam was a general Western interest, and his peace offers were designed in part to secure international sympathy. Washington especially hoped that the members of the South-East Asian Treaty Organization, or SEATO, founded in 1954 would join in defending Saigon. In fact some members of the organization who felt particularly threatened by the spread of communism in Asia did take part: Australia and New Zealand sent troops in June 1965, followed by the Philippines in 1966 and Thailand in 1967. However, these contingents were too small to have any impact on the war and they were actually outnumbered by the 45,000 men contributed by a non-SEATO country, South Korea. The terms of SEATO did not oblige its members automatically to go to war in the event of communist expansion and some of them were distinctly unsympathetic to the US. In the mid-1960s America's relations with Pakistan were troubled, partly because Pakistan had improved its relations with Communist China following the Sino–Indian war of 1962. France, under the anglophobe de Gaulle, and in the wake of its own departure from Vietnam, was critical of the US war effort: in August 1966 de Gaulle, on a visit to Cambodia, called on Johnson to withdraw. Even the British, usually America's closest Western ally, and one with political and commercial interests in Hong Kong and Malaysia, resisted pressure to commit troops to Vietnam. Britain, like other Western European countries, was troubled by the war which, as in America, became the focus of leftist criticism and youth protest. Even Laos and Cambodia, two South-East Asian states that SEATO claimed to protect, did nothing to help the US effort to defeat communism in the region. In Laos, the revived struggle between the Pathet Lao and the royal government, together with the country's position on the Ho Chi Minh trail, led the US to drop three million tons of bombs on it between 1964 and 1973. In Cambodia, also on the trail, the government of Prince Sihanouk subtly tried to maintain a neutralist policy. On the one hand, he broke diplomatic relations with the US in 1965 and allowed the communists to receive supplies through the chief port, Sihanoukville. On the other, he tried to limit communist numbers within Cambodia and, in 1968 tolerated US 'hot pursuit' of the Viet Cong over the border.

North Vietnam may have fought its war on the front line alone, but it had significant diplomatic, economic, and military assistance from the Eastern bloc, and indeed was able to exploit rivalry between the USSR and China to maximize the scale of this. The Chinese had been unenthusiastic about Hanoi's decision in 1959–60 to expand the guerrilla war in South Vietnam, believing it better to concentrate in the North on economic consolidation at that stage. But the Chinese provided a range of supplies, from ammunition, rifles, and artillery to radio sets, lorries, and uniforms, as well as agricultural produce, increasing deliveries as US involvement escalated. Mao's support for Hanoi was based both on a desire to counter American 'imperialism' and an eagerness to outbid the Soviets for North Vietnamese support. Ho Chi Minh was reluctant to take sides in the Sino–Soviet split but by 1964 felt he had little choice other than to rely most on China, since Moscow seemed more interested in improving East–West relations. In 1964 China strengthened its armed forces on the Vietnam border, and Johnson was probably correct in his belief that, if US military action went too far, Mao was prepared to defend North Vietnam. The Chinese were already intolerant of America's meddling near their borders (in Korea and Taiwan), were entering a new policy phase at home—the Cultural Revolution—and were keen to support Wars of National Liberation in the less developed world. Ho Chi Minh visited Beijing in April 1965 and over 300,000 Chinese troops were sent to North Vietnam over the following years, many of them engineers, helping to run installations, man anti-aircraft batteries, build airfields and roads, and thereby freeing North Vietnamese troops to fight in the South. Mao and his colleagues 'were genuinely concerned about the American threat from Vietnam . . . and adopted significant measures in war preparations at home'—so that Johnson was right to fear Chinese direct intervention in the war if he invaded the North.[14] Even with their indirect involvement, over a thousand Chinese troops were killed in Vietnam, before they left in 1970. By then

the Chinese were critical both of Hanoi's decision to launch the Tet offensive and its subsequent readiness to open peace negotiations with Washington. Mao was also offended by growing Soviet influence in Hanoi, whilst the North Vietnamese had always been wary of the danger of Chinese domination, a fear based on long historical experience.

The Soviet Union and its East European satellites did send military advisers and supplies to North Vietnam before 1965, but on a more limited scale than China and, until he lost power, Khrushchev was reluctant to antagonize the US by backing Hanoi too strongly. In November 1964, however, his successors decided that they must try to match Chinese influence, partly because Moscow saw itself as the leader of the communist world, partly it seems in order to act as a moderating influence on Ho and prevent the war spreading. Andrei Kosygin's visit to Hanoi in February, coinciding as it did with US airraids, confirmed the USSR in its determination to aid the North Vietnamese. Diplomatic and propaganda support for them was intensified and Moscow, at least in 1964–6, refused to become involved in any peace attempts. By 1968 Soviet aid to the North, in the form of arms, aircraft machinery, medicine, and raw materials, amounted to half of all aid to the country and outstripped Chinese assistance, thus reversing the situation of 1964. But this did not necessarily outweigh China's predominance, which was partially based on common values: 'The North Vietnamese leadership shared with its Chinese counterpart many ideological views, including the assessment of the world communist movement and the international situation.'[15] Also, the number of Soviet advisers, at about a thousand (mainly in the air defence field) was much fewer than the Chinese. In 1968 the Soviets were able to outmanoeuvre China on the issue of negotiations, and helped bring Hanoi and Washington to the negotiating table. The North's preference, however, was to avoid becoming reliant on one ally, and to continue securing aid from both Moscow and Beijing which, together with East European support was valued at about a billion dollars in 1968. Little wonder that Johnson's successor, Richard Nixon, saw improved relations with the USSR and China as one possible way to pressure the North into a settlement.

US Force Levels in Vietnam

The 1954 Geneva settlement limited the number of American military personnel in Vietnam to 342 (the number actually present on 21 July) but by the end of the Eisenhower administration, in December 1960, 685 US military advisers were there. The US Military Assistance Command was created on 6 February 1962 when over 3,000 advisers were present, rising to about 11,000 in December 1962 and almost 17,000 in November 1963 when President Kennedy was assassinated. In December 1964, a year into the Johnson Presidency, there were 23,000 US personnel in Vietnam.

The first US combat troops arrived on 8 March 1965.

Subsequent figures for US personnel, at the end of each year were:

1965—185,000
1966—360,000
1967—480,000
1968—540,000
1969—475,000
1970—320,000
1971—160,000

By April 1972 only 6,000 out of 70,000 US personnel were on combat duty in Vietnam. In December only 24,000 Americans remained and the last left on 29 March 1973.

CHRONOLOGY: VIETNAM— ESCALATING AMERICAN INVOLVEMENT, 1959–1965

1959

May	North Vietnamese ruling party agrees to support armed struggle in South Vietnam.
8 July	Two US military advisers killed in an attack by Viet Cong on Bienhoa.

1960

11 November	Failed attempt at a coup against Diem by army elements.
2 December	North Vietnam sponsors the creation of the National Liberation Front (NLF), a shadow government for South Vietnam.

1961

28 January	Kennedy's incoming National Security Council decides to boost aid to South Vietnam.
16 May–23 July	Geneva conference reaches compromise settlement on political future of Laos: neutralist coalition formed.
3 November	After leading a US military mission to Vietnam, General Maxwell Taylor recommends sending a limited number of US combat troops, but Kennedy rejects this idea.

1962

6 February	US forms Military Assistance Command, Vietnam (MACV), reflecting the rise in US advisers to Vietnam to over 3000.
27 February	Failed attempt by airforce elements to kill Diem and his brother Nhu.
March	Launch of the 'strategic hamlets' programme to isolate South Vietnamese peasants from the Viet Cong.

1963

2 January	Battle of Ap Bac, effectively a defeat for the South Vietnamese army.
8 May	Serious Buddhist unrest against Diem; troops shoot nine demonstrators in Hue.
11 June	A Buddhist Priest, Thic Quang Duc, burns himself to death in Saigon, in protest at Diem's regime.

21 August	Government troops attack on Buddhist pagodas.
1 November	Diem and Nhu assassinated after an army coup; new government formed under General Duang Van ('Big') Minh.
22 November	Kennedy assassinated; succeeded by Lyndon Johnson.

1964

16 January	Johnson approves covert operations in North Vietnam itself.
3 January	'Big' Minh replaced by General Nguyen Khanh.
June	US begins bombing communist 'Pathet Lao' bases in Laos in 'Operation Barrel Roll'.
2 August	US destroyer, *Maddox*, attacked by North Vietnamese torpedo boats in Gulf of Tonkin.
4 August	Claims of more attacks on US ships.
5 August	US aircraft launch limited raids on North Vietnam.
7 August	Gulf of Tonkin resolution: Congress gives Johnson a blank cheque to deal with Vietnam situation.
3 November	Johnson wins Presidential election.
24 December	Viet Cong attack on US base in Saigon.

1965

5 February	Soviet premier Kosygin visits Hanoi, underlining support for the North.
7 February	Viet Cong attacks a US base at Pleiku, killing eight.
8 February	US retaliatory air raids launched on North Vietnam, while Kosygin is still in Hanoi.
10 February	Twenty-three Americans killed in a Viet Cong attack on Qui Nhon; leads to more retaliatory air raids.
17 February	After months of internal unrest, General Khanh is overthrown for good and goes into exile.
24 February	Start of 'Operation Rolling Thunder': long-term bombing campaign by US of North Vietnam.
8 March	US marines land at Da Nang: first commitment of US ground troops.

C. 'Tet' and its Implications, 1968

The 'Tet' Offensive

At the start of 1968 with half a million US troops in Vietnam and a Presidential election beginning, Westmoreland's confidence that the war was going well had some basis. The Thieu regime seemed stable even if it was not popular; urban centres were securely under government control and heavy losses were being inflicted on the Viet Cong and the North Vietnamese army (NVA). Westmoreland remained wedded to his belief that large-unit conventional warfare, rather than a drawn-out, 'pacification' effort, would wear down the communists and he saw an NVA build up around Khe Sanh (near the Demilitarized Zone) as an opportunity to score a decisive victory. Suspecting that the NVA were planning the long-awaited conventional invasion of the South, he concentrated 50,000 troops around Khe Sanh. But, in line with a plan drawn up by General Giap six months before, Khe Sanh was a lure, designed to draw Westmoreland's attention while the Viet Cong guerrilla army prepared for a general offensive inside the South. The communist aim was to attack urban centres, undermining Thieu and demoralizing the Americans, perhaps even sparking a popular uprising that would sweep the NLF to power. The offensive went forward at the Vietnamese new year, Tet, on 30–31 January, when half the ARVN was on leave and a ceasefire was supposed to be in place. In a damning indictment of US and South Vietnamese intelligence, the communists achieved complete surprise, helped by the fact that, for the first time in the war, they concentrated their attacks on major towns and cities. Targets were hit all over the country and in Saigon even the American embassy compound was partially occupied for several hours.

The Tet offensive went on for weeks before dying down, with the former imperial capital, Hué, not being cleared of Viet Cong until 24 February. The dead in Hué numbered 500 Americans or ARVN, 5,000 Communists, and 10,000 civilians, many of the last executed by the Viet Cong for working with

the Thieu regime. Nationally too the 'kill ratio' between the communists and their opponents was now about 10:1, an attrition rate that still pleased Westmoreland, who could reasonably claim a military victory. He may have misjudged the significance of Khe Sanh, from which the NVA retreated once Tet was over, but the Viet Cong attack on urban centres proved disastrous for them. In the towns the guerrilla army made a more obvious target than in the countryside, unable to melt so easily away, and losses to their front line forces were probably around 35,000, a large proportion of their number. Significantly, in future, the NVA would bear a greater share than the decimated Viet Cong of the fighting in the South. Significant too was the fact that there had been no popular uprising against Thieu and that the ARVN did not crumble in the face of widespread initial setbacks. A second round of communist attacks on towns in early May inevitably proved less dramatic and a third round, 'Tet Three', in August, confirmed that the Viet Cong were far away from a decisive military victory. Indeed, one historian describes Tet as 'a colossal blunder which prolonged the war, causing unnecessary suffering on both sides'.[16]

Yet, if Tet proved a setback for the communists on the ground, in retrospect it is remembered primarily as an American defeat, the turning point in a war which was now recognized to be 'unwinnable' for Washington. As one communist General later admitted 'In all honesty, we didn't achieve our main objective which was to spur uprisings throughout the South . . . As for making an impact in the United States, it had not been our intention—but it turned out to be a fortunate result.'[17] Indeed it did. The fact that the Viet Cong could launch such an audacious countrywide assault, seizing control of so many cities, and catching Westmoreland by surprise, after his recent assurances that victory was only a matter of time, came as a profound psychological shock to many Americans. The public and the press increasingly lost faith in official pronouncements on the war. Johnson's chances of winning re-election in November were almost immediately called into question when he only narrowly won the New Hampshire primary over an 'anti-war' opponent, Eugene McCarthy. Furthermore, claims that Tet was a defeat were simply not believed with any confidence. America's international problems were underlined by the seizure, a week before Tet, of a US navy ship, the *Pueblo*, by North Korea (the vessel was only released at the end of the year after a humiliating apology from Washington for its intelligence-gathering mission). Regarding Vietnam, Westmoreland now believed that he needed a further 206,000 troops, plus an intensified bombing campaign throughout Indo-China, in order to achieve victory. Yet he could not say how long victory would take to win and the new Defense Secretary, Clark Clifford, feared that the request would simply lead to higher costs and casualties. Few Americans advocated withdrawal, some even hawkishly advocated all-out war on the North, but the Defense Department now preferred to 'de-Americanize' the conflict, handing fighting back to the ARVN. A group of 'wise men', called together to give the President advice at this critical point, and comprising such foreign policy luminaries as Dean Acheson and George Ball, also recommended disengagement as the best course. And on 31 March Johnson made a national address which not only limited US bombing of the North to areas below the 19th parallel, but also offered peace negotiations and withdrew his candidacy from the upcoming election. Johnson preferred to let a new President tackle the Vietnam challenge. But his withdrawal from the race was the clearest indication to the world that America no longer expected an outright victory in Vietnam.

The War after Tet

Whilst each side could claim a victory of sorts after Tet, it was the case that 'the position of each was also significantly weakened and neither emerged with sufficient leverage to force a settlement.'[18] Some of Johnson's aides, such as his National Security Adviser, Walt Rostow, still believed it possible to put military pressure on Hanoi but, with the administration increasingly divided against itself, defining US military strategy was as difficult as ever. Johnson

had been careful only *partially* to limit the bombing campaign in his 31 March speech but he called a complete bombing halt on 31 October, partly to help the election chances of his Vice-President, Hubert Humphrey. Troop figures continued to drift up, but by the time of the election it was widely accepted that they had reached their peak. However, with a greater emphasis on 'pacification' within South Vietnam and helped by Viet Cong losses during Tet, the US and ARVN forces were actually able to extend the area of government control. Despite Johnson's 31 March speech, US bombing in the South was as intense as ever.

The weakening of the Viet Cong, together with America's partial bombing halt, induced Hanoi to adopt a new tactic of 'fighting while talking', which mirrored what Johnson himself was now attempting. The North accepted the idea of talks on 3 April and the two sides opened peace negotiations in Paris on 13 May, with the veteran ambassador Averell Harriman leading the US delegation and Xuan Thuy the North. However, much of the discussion was then spent in trying to design a table at which both the South Vietnamese and NLF representatives could sit. The South Vietnamese, fearing that their independence could only be compromised by discussions, were reluctant to talk at all and certainly did not want to recognize the NLF. Even if this problem had been resolved earlier, it is doubtful whether the peace talks would have got far by the end of the year. For one thing, the two sides were still diametrically opposed on likely peace terms, with the US hoping for a withdrawal of their forces after a North Vietnamese withdrawal from South Vietnam and Thieu's survival in power, neither of which was acceptable to Hanoi. Another problem was that the North's 'fighting while talking' tactic, probably meant that they had no intention of serious negotiations before the Viet Cong's 'Tet Three' offensive was over.

While the war in the South settled back into deadlock and the Paris peace negotiations made laborious progress, the clearest signs that events had decisively swung in the communists' favour were to be found in the United States. Anti-war protests grew, the media became highly sceptical about official statements on the conflict, and only about a third of Americans felt progress was being made in Vietnam.

This still meant that there was a sizeable group in favour of fighting on, and the war actually remained quite popular among, for example, young, white males. But the very danger of a polarized society helped influence Johnson's decision to pull out of the election race. As he told an aide, the President felt he could have won the election, but the result 'would be too close for me to be able to govern. The nation would be polarized.'[19] Instead of allowing a popular alternative to step into power and reunite the country, however, the election soon became a nightmare, underlining the violence, racism, and political division in American society. On 4 April the Black civil rights leader, Martin Luther King, was assassinated in Memphis; on 5 June Robert Kennedy, brother of the late President, was shot dead, immediately after winning the Democrat Primary in California; and on 28 August the Democratic Party convention in Chicago became the scene of rioting as the police tried to break up a demonstration. The nightmare only ended in November when the Republican Richard Nixon narrowly beat Humphrey to the Presidency, with a third, populist candidate, Henry Wallace, winning 13.5 per cent of votes on a hard-line, pro-war ticket. The result only confirmed the confusion in America over Vietnam, and suggested that a majority favoured persevering with the struggle even if they doubted it could be won.

Communist Resistance in Crisis: the Cost of the War for the US by 1968

Deepened political divisions associated with the war in Vietnam were not the only problem for America. By the end of the Johnson Presidency the burdens of conflict affected the US economy, its social cohesion, international standing, and self-confidence. Taken together these costs also called into question the whole policy of resisting communism, predicated as it was on America's ability to meet the communist challenge wherever it threatened. The most obvious costs were linked directly to the war itself: by the end of 1968 about 30,500 Americans had been killed (over 14,000 that year alone) and 536,000 were

serving in South Vietnam; America had dropped well over a million tons of bombs on the South and about 650,000 tons on North Vietnam, without destroying the communists' ability to wage war, but with the loss of about 500 aircraft, whose crews often became prisoners of war; and the financial price tag of the war was now running at about $20 billion per year (eventually totalling $150 billion over the whole period of direct US involvement from 1965 to 1973). Anti-war demonstrators also protested against non-American casualties in the war. In 1968 alone the US military reckoned it had killed about 180,000 Viet Cong and North Vietnamese, whilst 28,000 ARVN and almost 1,000 other allied troops had been killed. Civilian casualties were less easy to calculate but also ran into tens of thousands in the year of Tet. The casualty figures on the communist side were substantial but this in itself underlined a vital point: 'they were fighting a war to the death . . . the United States commitment fell far short of that' and this simple fact lay at the heart of the war's 'unwinnability' by 1968.[20]

The cost of the war to the Americans in economic terms was also clear by 1968, even if it was not the only reason for a worsening position. Inflationary pressures already existed in the shape of high consumer demand, low business investment, and social spending. Interest rate rises helped keep inflation to less than 3 per cent, even in early 1967, but by late 1968 it was nearly 5 per cent and defence spending was undoubtedly a factor in causing this. Defence took up 7.9 per cent of GDP in 1966, 9 per cent in 1967, and 9.7 per cent in 1968. As well as paying for their own forces, Americans were maintaining a South Vietnamese army of 850,000 in 1968. In certain other respects the shape of the US economy was surprisingly good: unemployment was only 3.5 per cent when Johnson left office, the balance of payments was in surplus, and the tax burden, at about 28 per cent, was about 5 per cent less than the advanced European economies. However, a reluctance to increase taxes to pay for the Vietnam War was one of the factors which contributed to inflation. Johnson himself fought off such increases for as long as he could, before asking Congress to approve a 6 per cent tax surcharge in January 1967, later raised to 10 per cent. Congress was reluctant to grant this, however, without corresponding cuts in government expenditure, so as to drive down demand in the economy, and a long tussle between the White House and Capitol Hill on these points was not resolved until June 1968, after Johnson agreed to wipe $6 billion off the budget. Meanwhile these problems also affected confidence in the US abroad, especially after the devaluation of the British pound in November 1967, which sparked off months of monetary upheaval. Pressure on the dollar, linked to an outflow of gold from America, led to a critical situation in March 1968, the same month that Johnson shifted policy in Vietnam and chose to pull out of the Presidential race.

The destruction of Johnson's own career was another cost of the Vietnam imbroglio. The man who had won a landslide victory in 1964 found his approval rating at below 50 per cent in mid-1966 and below 40 per cent a year later. But the war also affected Johnson and the Presidency in two other significant respects. First, the need to restrain, then cut, domestic government expenditure to pay for Vietnam inevitably affected the Great Society programme. Numerous measures had been carried through, from medicine and urban renewal programmes to vocational training and environmental protection, but they were now underfunded. As to Johnson's hopes of tackling racial problems, they evaporated in the unrest that followed the assassination of Martin Luther King. Again, Vietnam did not create problems but, as with inflation, it added to existing social pressures and prevented them being tackled properly. Second, Vietnam called into question Presidential domination of the foreign policy process, the so-called 'Imperial Presidency', as well as bipartisan support for countering the communist threat. After 1968 Congress was far more questioning about foreign policy, repealing the Gulf of Tonkin resolution in 1970 and eventually, in the 1973 War Powers Act, limiting the President's freedom to commit troops abroad.

Finally, linked to the foreign policy theme, Vietnam called into question America's international reputation, weakened its position in the Cold War and provoked a crisis in its whole approach to world affairs. The country's moral standing, as a defender of democracy and freedom, was compromised by its use of carpet bombing, napalm, and defoliation, all in the defence of a corrupt, unelected regime. Allies, in Western Europe in particular, were critical of the US obsession with South-East Asia and the USSR was able to achieve effective nuclear parity with its superpower rival by 1968. This last development had been predicted for some time but it now came at the worst possible point, when America's ability to contain communism was being called into question.

Historical Debate: 'LBJ's War'?

Perhaps the most discussed aspect about the escalation of US involvement in Vietnam in the mid-1960s is whether it was due to the personality and decisions of Lyndon Johnson, or to structural factors in America's approach to world affairs which made escalation inescapable. The conflict became known as 'LBJ's War' and student demonstrators at the time had little doubt where responsibility lay, chanting

> 'Hey, hey, L.B.J.,
> How many kids did you kill today?'

However, some historians have been sympathetic to Johnson's predicament. Thus Gary Hess in *Vietnam and the United States* (Twayne, New York, 1990, 88), writes that having 'seen themselves in the previous two decades as the guardians of democracy in Greece, Berlin, Korea and elsewhere, Americans in 1965 saw the burdens of world leadership thrusting a new challenge' in Vietnam, which there was little alternative to confronting. More tellingly, Michael Hunt, in *Lyndon Johnson's War* (Hill & Wong, New York, 1996, 107) insists that the war reflected 'a firm Cold War consensus amounting almost to a religion ... It was the product of a string of ... Presidential decisions, of which Johnson's happened to be the last.' Structural factors working in favour of escalation included:

- America's liberal-democratic political culture and universalist ideology with
- its antipathy to communism (confirmed in the Gulf of Tonkin resolution) which demanded that the communist threat be met worldwide and saw any retreat as a defeat;
- even more specific, the commitment of previous Presidents, since 1950, to 'save' Vietnam from communist domination, partly through fear of a 'domino effect' in South-East Asia if Vietnam fell;

- Johnson's particular inheritance, as the heir to John F. Kennedy, who had increased the number of US advisers in South Vietnam from less than 1,000 to more than 16,000;
- growing fear of the People's Republic of China, which was seen as a more revolutionary, fundamentalist communist menace than the USSR in Asia;
- the need to stand by any ally, for the sake of demonstrating America's reliability to friends and enemies alike which was essential for the maintenance of Cold War credibility;
- the self-confidence, born of America's wealth, military might, and technological prowess, which suggested that it could meet any threat successfully—a confidence shared by almost all Johnson's advisers.

Despite these weighty influences however, the fact is that other Presidents since 1947 had tolerated communist advances where it seemed too costly to reverse them. Truman was blamed in 1949 for 'losing' China to communism; Eisenhower had accepted the creation of a communist regime in North Vietnam in 1954; and Kennedy had agreed, in 1962, not to overthrow Castro's government in Cuba by military force. In contrast to these cases, Johnson took a number of decisions which drew the US into a large-scale commitment in Vietnam that might have been avoided. As Larry Berman argues, in another work entitled *Lyndon Johnson's War* (Norton, New York, 1989, 203), the President 'chose to Americanize the war . . . to accept General Westmoreland's attrition strategy . . . to paint optimistic scenarios for the American public . . . to hide the anticipated enemy build-up prior to Tet.' Among the criticisms levelled at Johnson are that:

- he was a domineering, arrogant individual who either failed to listen to alternative views—or else he heard and ignored them when they were put to him (by Under-Secretary of State George Ball for example) because he could not bear to retreat;
- he was unskilled in foreign and military affairs, showed little understanding of the Vietnamese and vastly underestimated the determination of Hanoi to achieve the reunification of Vietnam;
- he suggested in the 1964 election that he would not escalate the war, yet within months had both begun the 'Rolling Thunder' bombing campaign *and* sent ground troops to Vietnam;
- he continued deliberately to mislead the US public by avoiding a full explanation of the escalation, and as a result he forfeited public trust;
- he backed a corrupt, unrepresentative government in Saigon, without any serious attempt to induce it to reform; instead he relied on a destructive military campaign to maintain South Vietnam;
- he presided over an inefficient bureaucratic machine (typified by 'Tuesday luncheons' of key advisers in the White House) which never properly defined US political aims in the war.

Therefore, whatever pressing general factors led Johnson to believe that South Vietnam must be preserved, the responsibility for fighting a 'limited war', relying on an attrition strategy and without a proper explanation to the American people, must lie with him. As Frederick Logevall writes in his detailed study of the years 1963–5, *Choosing War: the Lost Chance for Peace and the Escalation of War in Vietnam* (University of California Press, Berkeley, 1999, 394), while the responsibility for the outcome of the policy process rested with all those who participated in it, it rested chiefly with the President.'

CHRONOLOGY: THE QUAGMIRE: AMERICA'S 'UNWINNABLE' WAR IN VIETNAM, 1965–1971

1965

7 April	Johnson lays out terms for Vietnam peace settlement in speech at Johns Hopkins University.
8 April	North Vietnam puts forward its own peace terms.
11 June	Nguyen Cao Ky, an airforce officer, becomes South Vietnamese Prime Minister.
2 July	Johnson decides on large increase in US troop numbers to 125,000.
Mid-October	First anti-war demonstrations in America.
24 December	US initiates a 'bombing halt' over Christmas period, partly in an attempt to encourage peace talks.

1966

March	A new wave of Buddhist unrest begins in South Vietnam.
29 June	US extends bombing to areas near Hanoi and Haiphong: widely condemned.
13 October	Johnson rejects idea of a new 'bombing halt' as possible first step to negotiations.

1967

February	Soviet Premier Kosygin, in London, fails to broker deal with British Premier Harold Wilson on an end to US bombing and start of peace talks.
19–21 March	In a conference on Guam with South Vietnamese leaders, Johnson decides to maintain military pressure on North Vietnam.
3 September	Nyugen van Thieu, an army general, becomes South Vietnam's President, with Ky Vice-President.
29 September	San Antonio speech: Johnson says he will end bombing if peace looks achievable.

1968

30–31 January	Launch of 'Tet' offensive: communist attacks on numerous cities and military installations.
25 February	Ancient capital of Hué retaken from communists.
22 March	General Westmoreland relieved as commander of US forces in Vietnam, confirming that Johnson will not escalate the war further.
31 March	Johnson announces partial bombing halt and withdraws from Presidential election race.

| 13 May | Peace talks open between US and North Vietnam in Paris but make no progress. |
| 1 November | Complete bombing halt by US on North Vietnam. |

1969

20 January	Inauguration of Richard Nixon.
18 March	US begins secret bombing of communist bases in Cambodia.
8 June	Nixon announces withdrawal of 25,000 men from Vietnam: beginning of slow process of withdrawal.
25 July	On Guam, Nixon launches 'Vietnamization': handing ground-fighting over to the South Vietnamese.
4 August	Several rounds of secret talks begin between US and North Vietnamese representatives in Paris.

1970

18 March	Pro-American general, Lon Nol, overthrows Prince Sihanouk of Cambodia.
20 April	Nixon announces latest reductions in US force levels in Vietnam: another 150,000 to leave.
30 April–29 June	US and South Vietnamese forces attack communist 'sanctuaries' in Cambodia.
2 May	Large-scale US bombing of North Vietnam, suspended under Johnson, restarted by Nixon.
4 May	Four anti-war protestors shot at Kent State University.

1971

| 8 February–24 March | South Vietnamese attacks on Ho Chi Minh trail in Laos. |
| 3 October | South Vietnamese Presidential election, in which Thieu is the only candidate. |

D. Nixon's War in Vietnam, 1969–1971

The Continuing Failure of Peace Talks

Inevitably, the Vietnam War was the most serious challenge facing Richard Nixon when he entered the White House. During the election campaign he had claimed to have a 'secret plan' to resolve the conflict but once in power no such plan was unveiled. It may be that he hoped to emulate Eisenhower (to whom he had been Vice-President), who had ended the Korean War in 1953 after threatening to use atomic weapons. Certainly Nixon tried to demonstrate toughness to the communists. When they launched an offensive in February 1969, indicating that there would be no let up in their own campaign, the President decided to launch a clandestine bombing campaign against the Ho Chi Minh trail in supposedly neutral Cambodia. Neither the North Vietnamese nor the Cambodians made any public complaint about this, helping to keep the raids secret for months: the former were flouting Cambodian neutrality themselves; the latter were happy to see communist numbers on their borders reduced. The bombing showed a President ready to widen the conflict and resort to extreme tactics, but did nothing to weaken Hanoi's resolve to replace Thieu and turn the Americans out of South Vietnam. Like Johnson before him, Nixon found there was no easy way to force the communists to the peace table on anything less than their terms, which for America signified defeat. Even most Democrats hoped for peace terms based on a mutual withdrawal by both sides, linked to a negotiated political settlement within South Vietnam among the warring local groups. Secretary of State William Rogers, all too aware of domestic opposition to the war, favoured a similar compromise and the President took the view that 'I would have to end the war as quickly as was honourably possible.'[21] But when, in May, Nixon offered an 'eight-point programme' which embodied a mutual *simultaneous* withdrawal (in contrast to Johnson's demand that the North withdraw first), the communists saw no need to respond. In July

Nixon's National Security Adviser, Henry Kissinger, did secretly meet North Vietnam's Xuan Thuy in Paris, but the best they could do was to agree to meet again.

Twelve rounds of secret talks took place down to September 1971 between Kissinger and either Xuan Thuy or Le Duc Tho. Regarding a peace deal, Nixon made one major concession in a speech in October 1970: urged on by US critics of the war, he offered the North a 'ceasefire in place'. The significance of this was that it would allow a ceasefire to occur before negotiations on a North Vietnamese withdrawal from South Vietnam took place. Nixon still hoped for a mutual withdrawal and he wanted the South Vietnamese to decide their own form of government; he was not offering to overthrow Thieu. But clearly the 'ceasefire in place' could seriously undermine the government in Saigon, since the North Vietnamese army might hold onto areas of the South after a ceasefire, when there would be intense international and popular pressure on the Americans to leave regardless of the North's behaviour. Furthermore, in another concession, Kissinger assured Xuan Thuy that any US military withdrawal would be total. But a series of long, sometimes hopeful talks in Paris in 1971 ended in ultimate disappointment, with the North still keen to put an end to Thieu. He was 're-elected' President of South Vietnam, in October 1971 but, since he was the only candidate in the election, the event was ridiculed by the North.

Nor did domestic events in the US help Nixon. Congressional criticism and popular demonstrations against the war (often numbering tens of thousands in 1969–70) went on; the November 1970 Congressional elections proved a setback for Republicans, making Nixon even more desperate to end the war before seeking re-election in 1972; and in June 1972 the White House was embarrassed by the leak of a substantial volume of official documents on Vietnam, the so-called 'Pentagon Papers'. Some critics even urged a simple, unilateral withdrawal from Vietnam. Such a course would have meant the blatant betrayal of an ally, harming American credibility worldwide, and it is easy to see why an arch anti-communist like Nixon dismissed it. As he told his Cabinet in September 1969, he did not want to be 'the first American President to lose a war'.[22] Yet at the other extreme, the choice of escalation of the war, perhaps an invasion of North Vietnam or even the local use of atomic weapons, was denied him because of public opposition, international criticism, and the danger of Chinese entry into the conflict, which might then prove even more bloody and protracted. If the costs of hanging on in Vietnam were great, the cost of radical options like withdrawal or escalation could be greater.

The Guam Doctrine and Vietnamization

Despite domestic criticism, the failure to progress in the peace talks and the absence of a realistic, quick route out of Vietnam, the Nixon administration did develop a strategy of sorts for fighting the Vietnam War, holding out the hope of a negotiated settlement in future whilst reducing the current cost of the war to America in lives and money. The strategy lacked coherence and it was essentially forced on the White House by circumstances, but it was given respectability by being linked to a new approach to foreign policy in general, and it did succeed in reducing the vocalness of domestic opposition to the war.

The new strategy centred on 'Vietnamization', a policy particularly identified with the Defense Secretary, Melvyn Laird, but which had its origins in the Johnson administration's hopes of 'De-Americanizing' the war and in the earlier hopes of President Kennedy to avoid the sending of combat troops. Under Johnson, after March 1965, the US had increasingly taken on the primary role in South Vietnam of fighting the communists and the war had thereby become 'Americanized'. By 1968 this was seen as a mistake and the aim of 'Vietnamization' was to reverse the process, putting the onus of fighting back on the South Vietnamese themselves whilst decreasing US troop levels: 'reducing losses to American forces became the goal of US commanders. In so far as US troops did enter the field they accompanied the . . . [ARVN], offering instruction in rooting out guerrillas.'[23] The attractions of the policy were clear. A reduction in the US presence would please domestic opinion but resistance to the communists would go on. Yet there were also obvious flaws in 'Vietnamization'. It would take time to train, equip and galvanize the South Vietnamese to fight for themselves, if indeed they ever would have the skill and morale to do so. Meanwhile, US troops could only be withdrawn gradually. Also, such withdrawals might simply encourage the communists to hold out for a complete victory. Certainly Kissinger believed that Vietnamization, along with domestic opposition and the weakness of the Thieu regime undermined his attempts to negotiate peace in Paris. If the North would not agree to a settlement when there were over 500,000 American troops in Vietnam, why should they agree when there were less than 100,000? 'Troop cuts poulticed public sores at home', he later wrote, 'but they were evaporating Hanoi's need to bargain about our disengagement.'[24]

Despite these problems, Nixon and Thieu met at Midway and agreed to begin the US troop withdrawals. Shortly afterwards on 25 July 1969 Nixon gave an important, yet apparently unplanned explanation to journalists of the new approach to international challenges, which his administration would pursue. This so-called 'Guam Doctrine' was related directly to 'Vietnamization', stating that in cases of non-nuclear aggression 'we shall furnish military and economic assistance . . . but we shall look to the nation directly threatened to assume the primary responsibility of providing manpower for its defence.' These points dovetailed with the general policy of US retrenchment abroad after 1968, sometimes called the 'Nixon Doctrine' (see boxed section) and contrasted with the crusading tone of earlier Presidents. In September 1969 Nixon announced more troop withdrawals, despite a lack of concessions from Hanoi, and further steps in 1970 took the total number of withdrawals above 150,000. But at the same time Nixon maintained US air support for South Vietnam, with regular bombing raids by B-52s. His strategy was not simply one of relying on a defensive posture, but of continuing to put military pressure on the North, a point further emphasized by the controversial invasion of Cambodia in spring 1970.

The Cambodia and Laos Operations

The Vietnam War always had a major impact on neighbouring states and Nixon's bombing of Cambodia in 1969 had already shown how the war, though often described as limited and local, could spread. In early 1970 trouble in Laos intensified once more. The 1962 agreement to respect the country's neutrality had long been undermined by both sides, with the North Vietnamese using Laos as part of the Ho Chi Minh trail and the CIA possessing links to various anti-communist elements in Laos. February 1970 saw a communist offensive in Laos and further use of American B-52s to help the royal government to stop it. Then, in March, the neutralist Prince Sihanouk of Cambodia was overthrown by his Prime Minister, an army general named Lon Nol, known as a firm anti-communist. Sihanouk had long tried to play off the Americans and communists against each other, keeping contact with all sides, tolerating the use of Cambodian territory to supply the Viet Cong yet not complaining about the US secret bombing of 1969. There were immediate suspicions that America had helped Lon Nol's coup but it did not necessarily help them. He too was now faced by communist threats, including Pol Pot's Khmer Rouge movement, an extremely violent, Maoist Party, hitherto lacking much popularity.

Despite Lon Nol's appeals for help, the Americans lacked resources to fight a long campaign in Cambodia and were, of course, set on a policy of de-escalation in South-East Asia. Another round of US troop withdrawals was publicized on 20 April. Nonetheless, only 10 days later, in a move that confused and surprised the US public, Nixon announced a cross-border attack into Cambodia. Nixon's initial aim had been to use a mainly South Vietnamese force to attack North Vietnamese sanctuaries in one border region of Cambodia, known as Parrot's Beak, but he soon decided to attack another area, Fishhook, in a joint US–South Vietnamese operation. It marked the last large-scale use of US ground forces in offensive operations during the war. Incursions were limited to 30 kilometres into Cambodia, the operation ended on 30 June and it captured large amounts of communist supplies. But it proved costly in several ways. North Vietnamese troops simply retreated and avoided heavy losses; diplomatic efforts to improve relations with China were set back because Beijing opposed the operations (see Chapter 9, B); whilst, in America, Congressional opposition was revived and the Cooper–Church amendment was passed which effectively prevented US ground forces launching any more operations outside South Vietnam. There was also another bout of anti-war demonstrations and in one protest, on 4 May, four students were shot dead by National Guardsmen at Kent State University. The President boasted about the falling number of American casualties in the war after the Cambodian operation and this fact certainly helped reduce the number of anti-war protests in 1971–2. But US losses were only falling as a natural result of Vietnamization: casualties among the South Vietnamese army were increasing. Meanwhile, in Cambodia, a fully fledged civil war began with the Khmer Rouge, North Vietnam, and Prince Sihanouk forming an alliance to overthrow Lon Nol. 'Pol Pot could not have asked for a better recruiter than Nixon.'[25]

The mixed results of the Cambodia operation did not deter plans for another, similar bid to disrupt communist supply lines in early February 1971. This time the South Vietnamese army alone, though with US air support, launched an ambitious assault on the Ho Chi Minh trail, in Laos. At first the operation seemed quite successful but the North Vietnamese responded by sending their best troops against the South Vietnamese and even used tanks. By mid-March the South's forces were in retreat and question marks were raised about the success of Vietnamization. Thieu's army had fared badly without American troops alongside it. The 'offensive designed to prove that Vietnamization was working had turned into a rout … The images of ARVN troops hanging onto helicopter skids', as they tried to escape from Laos, had a 'devastating' effect on US popular opinion.[26] By December 1971 there were only 140,000 Americans in Vietnam, with few of those on combat duty, but Hanoi showed little interest in entering meaningful peace talks at this stage. One year away from the next Presidential election Nixon seemed no nearer to a Vietnam settlement than he had been in January 1969.

The Nixon Doctrine

The 'unwinnable' war in Vietnam called into question the whole US approach to the Cold War. Since the 1947 Truman Doctrine (see Chapter 1, E), America had been publicly committed to a policy of 'containment', ostensibly seeking to resist communist advances wherever they threatened. But the 1968 Tet offensive showed that a decisive defeat of the communists in Vietnam was impossible. This left the incoming Nixon administration in 1969 with a fundamental dilemma. Neither 'containment' nor roll back seemed to be working in Vietnam so what should they present as America's Cold War strategy in a multipolar world?

In contrast to earlier Presidential doctrines, the 'Nixon Doctrine' was not stated in one single document, but was refined through several. In tone it certainly represented a departure from the Truman Doctrine: retrenchment and a concentration on US interests, replaced the crusading, globalistic declarations of the earlier document. It was on the island of Guam, on 25 July 1969, that Nixon first broadly outlined the ways in which America might avoid further Vietnams. These 'off the record' remarks were clarified in an address to the nation on 3 November, the essential points of which were:

- America would adhere to its treaty commitments,
- it would 'provide a shield if a nuclear power threatens the freedom of a nation allied with us, or . . . whose survival we consider vital to our security . . .',
- in the event of non-nuclear threats the US would provide military and economic aid 'as appropriate. But we shall look to the nation directly threatened to assume the primary responsibility of providing the manpower for its defence.'

But whilst the tone might be less forthright than Truman, the Nixon Doctrine was deliberately vague on details: it was not clear when nuclear weapons might be used and even the use of US ground troops was not categorically ruled out. It was also, still, global in its implications given that the US had allies in many regions, who might have to be defended, even if they were now treated more as partners than clients. America's Cold War policy might be less self-confident in the wake of Tet but, under Nixon, it still proclaimed ineffectively the containment of communist expansionism—but the reality with or without honour, was rather different in Vietnam.

NOTES

1. Eric F. Goldman, *The Tragedy of Lyndon Johnson* (MacDonald, London, 1969), 378.

2. Robert S. McNamara, *In Retrospect* (Times Books, New York, 1995), 169.

3. David M. Barrett, *Uncertain Warriors: Lyndon Johnson and his Vietnam Advisers* (University Press of Kansas, Lawrence, 1993), 193. Barrett goes on to argue (194) that Johnson and his advisers were 'rational, well-intentioned' but blinded by their commitment to the containment of communism.

4. Quoted in Marilyn B. Young, *The Vietnam Wars, 1945–90* (HarperCollins, New York, 1991), 127.

5. Frederick Logevall, *Choosing War* (University of California Press, Berkeley, 1999), 375.

6. Spencer C. Tucker, *Vietnam* (UCL Press, London, 1999), 131.

7. James S. Olson and Randy Roberts, *Where the Domino Fell: America and Vietnam, 1945–1995* (St Martins Press, New York, 2nd edn., 1996), 163–4.

8. Ibid.

9. Harry G. Summers, *On Strategy: Critical Analysis of the Vietnam War* (Dell, New York, 1982), 93.

10. John Prados, *The Hidden History of the Vietnam War* (Ivan R. Dee, Chicago, 1995), 110.

11. Lyndon B. Johnson, *The Vantage Point* (Weidenfeld & Nicolson, London, 1971), 249–50.

12. Stanley Karnow, *Vietnam: a History* (Guild Publishing, London, 1983), 494, 496.

13. Robert K. Brigham, *Guerrilla Diplomacy* (Cornell University Press, Ithaca, 1998), 41.

14. Qian Qichen, *China and the Vietnam Wars, 1950–75* (University of North Carolina Press, Chapel Hill, 2000), 155.

15. Ilya V. Gaiduk, 'The Soviet Union and Vietnam', in Peter Lowe (ed.), *The Vietnam War* (Macmillan, London, 1998), 145.

16. Gerard J. de Groot, *A Noble Cause? America and the Vietnam War* (Pearson, Harlow, 2000), 182.

17. Stanley Karnow, op. cit., 545.

18. George C. Herring, *America's Longest War* (Temple University Press, Philadelphia, 1986), 220.

19. Quoted in de Groot, op. cit., 176.

20. James S. Olson, op. cit., 284.

21. Richard Nixon, *RN: the Memoirs of Richard Nixon* (BCA, London, 1978), 349.

22. Melvin Small, *The Presidency of Richard Nixon* (University Press of Kansas, Lawrence, 1999), 74.

23. Robert D. Schulzinger, *Henry Kissinger* (Columbia University Press, New York, 1989), 34–5.

24. Henry Kissinger, *The White House Years* (Little, Brown & Co., Boston, 1979), 475.

25. Gerard de Groot, op. cit., 223.

26. Stephen Ambrose, *Nixon, II: 1962–72* (Simon & Schuster, New York, 1989), 420.

11 Other Regional Conflicts

A. Latin America: US Intervention in the Dominican Republic

The United States and Latin America after the Missile Crisis

Lyndon Johnson's decision in the spring of 1965 to escalate the war in Vietnam may have been encouraged by events on the other side of the world, in the Caribbean, where armed intervention by US marines put a rapid end to the supposed menace of communism in the Dominican Republic. This action showed the US concern, after the Bay of Pigs episode and the Cuban missile crisis (Chapter 7, D), to prevent a second Castro-like regime coming to power in Central or South America. Arguably it also reflected a change of priorities from the Eisenhower and Kennedy periods, when there were high hopes of the American government stimulating Latin American economic development. Under Kennedy's 'Alliance for Progress' (see Chapter 6, C) Washington even appeared ready to undermine right-wing dictator-

ships in order to bring reformist, liberal governments into office. This had been seen not least in the downfall of the Trujillo regime in the Dominican Republic in 1961. The events in Cuba that had helped produce the Alliance for Progress as an alternative to Castro's left-wing ideas on development, made the Western hemisphere an important ideological battleground. Marxist revolutionaries, moderate reformists, and right-wing dictators were fighting it out on America's doorstep with the key Cold War requirement for the US remaining the defeat of the former.

On assuming the Presidency, Johnson committed himself to fulfil the Alliance for Progress, just as he was committed to Kennedy's policies elsewhere, and in his early months, at least, he did devote some energy to the task. But the programme had serious internal contradictions. On the one hand, the US wanted to treat the Latin Americans as equals, who were supposed to contribute to the programme a rough equivalent of the $20 billion promised by Kennedy over 10 years, much as Europeans had done in the Marshall Plan of 1948–52. But, on the other hand, the Latin Americans lacked the wealth, transport infrastructure, and educated population which the West Europeans had been able to offer, and neither was the US genuinely ready to treat them as equals. In Congress, the idea of providing unconditional aid was unpopular. Another difficulty was that, whilst the Kennedy administration hoped that the Alliance for Progress would lead to more liberal and stable political regimes, Latin America tended to remain dominated by the military or other forms of dictatorship. Among the main South American countries for example, after 1964, Brazil, Paraguay, Argentina, Peru, and Bolivia were all under military domination; Colombia's post-1958 democracy was permanently unstable; and only Ecuador, Venezuela (helped by its oil wealth) and, above all, Chile, seemed stable constitutional systems. Kennedy's Presidency coincided with six military coups in Latin America. Military rule did not always equate with pro-American sympathies, as shown by the regime of General Juan Velasco, in Peru, between 1968 and 1975; but generally it did. Whatever hopes Kennedy may have had, attempts to replace dictatorships with liberal government always ran the danger of instability and rising radicalism, as in Cuba or the Dominican Republic.

The scale of the developmental challenge facing the Alliance for Progress was formidable and additional problems included bureaucratic inertia in the member countries, the indifference of US business, and Johnson's growing preoccupation with the Vietnam War. The Latin Americans complained that the US effectively discriminated against them in its trade policies, through tariffs and export subsidies. 'Already by 1964 the dollar injections failed to compensate the Latin American countries for the loss of income as a result of deteriorating terms of trade.'[1] But the US was frustrated because, whilst claiming equality with America, the Latin Americans seemed to want to rely on US handouts. Whatever the roots of economic underperformance, during the 1960s Latin American growth rates averaged less than 2 per cent and its share of the US market fell, from about a quarter to about a sixth. Johnson increasingly paid little attention to the region, tended simply to react

to events, and where there was a choice to be made put the need for stability above the need for democracy and development. And this was the case *before* the escalation of the Vietnam War.

In January 1964, in an early hint of a liberal approach, Johnson reacted to anti-US riots in Panama by expressing a readiness to discuss the restoration of Panamanian sovereignty over the American-controlled Panama Canal zone. But negotiations on this soon stalled. On 18 March 1964, Johnson's lead policy-maker on the region, Under-Secretary of State Thomas Mann, announced the 'Mann Doctrine', effectively stating that the US was interested mainly in the stability and dependability of Latin American regimes, whether democratic or dictatorial: if they were capitalist in their pursuit of growth, safeguarded US investments, desisted from meddling in their neighbour's internal affairs, and were anti-communist—then Washington would work with them. 'Mann and Johnson thus dropped two of the Alliance's original goals, democratization and structural change, to concentrate on economic development and anti-Communism.'[2] The idea that development would create the conditions for the emergence of a middle class wedded to American political values was now effectively dead. Later that month, the Johnson administration condoned, even encouraged, a military coup against the Brazilian President, Julio Goulart, who favoured land reform, introduced elements of economic planning, and had developed links to the USSR. The US quickly approved economic assistance to the new government of General Castello Branco, who began two decades of military rule in Brazil. There was little questioning of this action in Washington, where 'the administration frequently referred to the military's seizure of power as an anti-communist revolution. No one . . . questioned this odd defence of democracy through the overthrowing of the constitutional president.'[3] Also, in 1963–4, the British were pressured not to allow their colony of British Guyana (on the northern coast of South America) to become independent under Chaddi Jagan, the leader of the immigrant Indian community, who was suspected of leftist sympathies. Ironically, under this US pressure, the British altered the electoral system to ensure the victory of Jagan's rival, Forbes Burnham, who after independence in 1966, moved rapidly towards a radical programme. The one consistent point about Johnson's policy was its determination to prevent a second Cuba and in this it can be said to have been successful, albeit at the cost of strangling economic and political reform.

The Dominican Crisis of 1965

In common with many Central American and Caribbean states, the Dominican Republic, on the island of Hispaniola, found itself dominated by America in the twentieth century. Washington first despatched troops there in 1905 to ensure the repayment of foreign debts and for 12 years after 1916 the country was occupied by US marines, who helped lay the foundations for the rule of Rafael Trujillo, a right-wing strongman perfectly suited to American needs in the region. Trujillo and his family controlled both the military and the key agricultural crop, sugar. In the early 1950s they seemed to embody the US interest in putting stability and anti-communism above democracy or social reform, and after Castro came to power in 1959 the significance of the Dominican Republic to American Cold War interests greatly increased: the Republic was less than 200 miles from Cuba, and even closer to US-controlled Puerto Rico. However, this very fact meant that the Eisenhower administration, particularly after 1958, was cautious about endorsing Trujillo's dictatorship any longer. The Dominican Republic, with its large proportion of landless labourers working the plantations of a wealthy minority, seemed a potential hotbed of discontent, just as Cuba had been under the rule of Batista. In 1960 Eisenhower decided it was better to work for Trujillo's replacement, easing the oppression in the Dominican Republic, rather than risking an up-surge of revolutionary discontent. The CIA established links to Trujillo's opponents; diplomatic relations were severed with him in mid-1960 (after his agents were implicated in the assassination of the Venezuelan President); and eventually plans were even laid to assassinate him.

Trujillo eventually was assassinated on 30 May 1961, but by then John Kennedy was President and the US was not directly involved in the act, even if it was no secret that America welcomed the end of

the dictatorship. Over the following months the US pressed the Dominican Republic to hold free elections, provided both economic aid and counter-insurgency advice to the interim government, and made it clear (through naval operations off the coast) that it had the ability to intervene militarily if necessary. Such a display of force helped prevent the Trujillo family from launching a counter-coup and ensured that free elections were eventually held in December 1962. These brought the victory of Juan Bosch, leader of the Dominican Revolutionary Party, who won 60 per cent of votes with promises of land reform, and was inaugurated President in February 1963. A journalist, who had been in exile since the 1930s and lacked government experience, he seemed on the surface to fit the democratic, freedom-loving image which Kennedy wanted. But once in power Bosch showed little of the strength or ability needed to attempt the enormously difficult task of transforming the Dominican Republic into a stable democracy. He alienated landowners and the military with his social reforms, he criticized US 'imperial' domination and, worse still in American eyes, he seemed ready to tolerate the existence of communist organizations. In response the US refused him significant economic aid and, in September 1963, condoned his overthrow in a military coup, which led to the Presidency being handed to a businessman, Donald Reid Cabral. He was prepared to work closely with the Americans and to plan for elections in late 1965 but was heavily reliant on the military and never won much popularity. Fears that he might cancel the forthcoming elections helped lead to a counter-coup, on 24 April 1965, by supporters of Bosch, who was living in exile in Puerto Rico.

The Johnson administration refused to help the unelected Cabral, who resigned on 25 April, but the Americans had no liking for Bosch either and, given previous events in Cuba, they were also deeply concerned at the danger of the Dominican Republic slipping into communism. Over the following days Johnson concluded he should intervene militarily in the Dominican Republic, even though there was little evidence of any real communist menace. With Cabral out of the way, a power struggle immediately developed between the pro-Bosch group and elements in the military who wanted to set up another military junta. General Elias Wessin, who had led the 1963 coup against Bosch, launched air attacks on the pro-Bosch elements and tried to install such a junta under Colonel Pedro Benoit. But on 28 April the balance in the capital was still uncertain and Benoit appealed to the US ambassador, John Martin, for help. In backing this request to Washington, on 28 April, Martin, who had already rejected an appeal from the pro-Bosch group for assistance, effectively came down in favour of military rule, at least in the short term, rather than the return of an elected President. Martin claimed both to see a communist menace in the Dominican Republic and argued that the lives of US citizens there were in danger due to the continuing violence.

On 29 April 4,000 US marines landed in the Republic and by early May the number had mushroomed to 23,000, which was roughly half the level of US deployments in South Vietnam at that time. At first this sudden, large-scale intervention was justified by the need to protect American citizens and restore order, but soon emphasis was being put on the potential communist menace, with the State Department naming fifty-eight communists supposedly at work within the Dominican Republic. On closer analysis this list turned out to contain exiles, certain individuals in prison, and some double-counting, yet US public opinion welcomed the intervention and felt that Johnson had little choice other than to act against a potential second Cuba. The ease of military victory, combined with such popular support, can only have encouraged the President to hope that firm action in Vietnam would be rewarded. He and his advisers knew that the 25 April coup had actually been launched by political moderates (they even called themselves 'constitutionalists') seeking to restore an elected leader, but it was the *potential* for communists to exploit this situation, combined with dislike of the leftist Bosch, which led Johnson to act. 'The US government's preoccupation with avoiding a "second Cuba" had structured the way American officials looked at the Dominican Republic ... Dominican communists were seen as potential agents of extra-continental power, not as weak and fragmented groups of dissidents.'[4] In early May, Johnson followed the invasion up with a statement

that America would not allow another Castro-style government in the Americas; a statement which became known as the 'Johnson Doctrine' (see boxed section). 'Hence, what began as a civil war ended as an international crisis linked to the US military intervention in Vietnam, US policy against Cuba and, later, to the declared US intention of saving democracy in the Dominican Republic.'[5]

After the invasion Johnson acted to achieve three things: first, to calm international concern over his action, especially among Latin American states; second, to see that a stable, preferably elected government emerged in the Dominican Republic; and finally to ensure that the government was not led by Bosch. In this he was quite successful. On 6 May he persuaded a meeting of the OAS—an organization he held in such contempt that he accused it of being unable to 'pour piss out of a boot if the instructions were written on the heel'[6]—to set up a peacekeeping force, under US control, in the Republic. Several OAS members, including Mexico, refused to take part, seeing America's military action as heavy-handed bullying. But the OAS, despite these divisions, secured a formal ceasefire in the capital and in September installed a moderate interim premier, Hector Garcia Godoy, who was acceptable to pro-Bosch elements. At an OAS conference in November, certain members were fully behind an anti-communist policy. The Brazilian government, brought to power by the recent coup there, was even prepared to create a permanent OAS force, ready to intervene against any potential new Cuba. Only Colombia openly condemned US action in the Dominican Republic. Elections were finally held there in May 1966 and won by Joaquin Balaguer, a former Trujillo supporter. Despite continuing violence on the streets, foreign troops withdrew a few months later and Balaguer was able to maintain a fairly stable regime thereafter, although about 4,000 Dominicans were killed in Right–Left conflict over the next decade. US intervention could be defended in retrospect as doing no long-term harm to the Dominican Republic, in that Balaguer was finally defeated by a leftist candidate, Antonio Guzman, in elections in 1978. But it took revived violence and US pressure to force Balaguer to accept the election results, and in many ways Dominican politics were unchanged: in 1986

Balaguer was elected President again, with Bosch in third place.

The Dominican intervention showed, more so than any other event in the 1960s, that the US stood ready, as it had earlier in the century, to use its vast economic and military might to defend its own ideological and economic interests; and that it was ready to intervene or back military coups in Latin America to protect conservative elements and forestall radicalism. For Latin American states, more interested in long-term problems like development and trade, and anxious to achieve more equality with their northern neighbour, the intervention confirmed both their relative powerlessness and the limited significance of the Alliance for Progress which had seemed, at the opening of the decade, to promise a new course in US–Latin American relations. 'The problem', as one academic writes, 'was that in dealing with crises of stability, the administration could focus only on the threat of Communist advantage and allowed democracy and development to slip from view'.[7] Arguably, in the remainder of the Johnson Presidency, Latin America itself slipped completely from the view of the White House, despite the nominal survival of the Alliance for Progress through periodic conferences (even a summit in 1967) and such institutions as the Inter-American Development Bank. Under

> ### The Johnson Doctrine, 2 May 1965
>
> The key element in the Johnson Doctrine was the unequivocal statement that 'the American nations . . . will not permit the establishment of another communist government in the Western Hemisphere'. The statement came in a weekend evening television and radio address by the President, in the wake of US intervention in the Dominican Republic, in which he argued that the recent instability there was in danger of being exploited by communist conspirators, trained by Castro's Cuba. He portrayed the decision to intervene as a testing one, which showed that America would defend itself and its allies.
>
> The idea that the US would act to prevent a second Castroist regime being set up in the Americas was nothing new, but Johnson's forceful action meant that his successors had to measure their performance against this commitment.

Johnson's successor, Richard Nixon, things were just as bad. Preoccupied with superpower diplomacy and unable to retreat from the Johnson Doctrine, Nixon was initially affronted by Latin American demands for fairer trade and equality at the May 1969 Vina del Mar conference, then concerned by the challenge of an elected Marxist President, Salvador Allende, in Chile (see Chapter 13, E).

B. South-East Asia: The Malaysia–Indonesia 'Confrontation' of 1963–1966

Origins of the 'Konfrontasi'

The Vietnam War was not the only conflict in South-East Asia in the 1960s. Indeed, it was partly because of the potential instability of the region as a whole, that the US government feared the so-called 'domino effect' which argued that, if South Vietnam were 'lost', then communism could expand in neighbouring areas. In Laos, of course, a vicious struggle went on throughout the Vietnam War, with the US using air power in particular to counter the danger

of a victory by the communist Pathet Lao; whilst in Cambodia, South Vietnam's other neighbour, war between the government and the communist Khmer Rouge only accelerated after 1969. On the western border of these two countries, the kingdom of Thailand, under military rule, provided bases for the American airforce after 1964, whilst being menaced on the Laotian border by communist insurgents. Burma, also under military rule after 1962, was less sympathetic than Thailand to the US escalation in Vietnam. Historically suspicious of China and threatened by ethnic divisions, Burma, under General Ne Win, followed a policy of international isolation combined with internal centralization, trying to destroy all domestic opposition, whether from communists or democratic political parties. In the south of the region too, there were threats to stability. In Indonesia the regime of Ahmed Sukarno, who had led the country to independence from the Netherlands, relied on an uneasy alliance between the well-organized PKI—the Indonesian Communist Party which was especially strong on Java, the most heavily populated island—and the army, whose generals were suspicious of communism and well-disposed to Washington. In the mid-1960s Borneo, Malaya, and the Philippines became involved in a dispute, focusing on the island of Borneo, which threatened to spill over into war between Indonesia and Malaysia.

The dispute was triggered by the transformation of Malaya, Singapore, and the North Borneo territories of Sarawak and Sabah into the federation of 'Malaysia'. The idea of a federation involving Malaya had been explored by the British since the 1940s and by 1960 it appealed to them for a number of reasons. Malaysia would solve the problem of the island-city of Singapore, where leftist and pro-independence feeling was growing among its majority Chinese population. An independent left-wing government might well end the British presence at their most vital naval base east of Suez. Moreover, while Singapore was British the cost of the base would fall on the cash-strapped London government. If Singapore was incorporated into Malaysia, both problems would be solved: the pro-Western Malayan leader, Tunku Abdul Rahman, would allow Britain to retain a presence in the base but much of the cost would be borne by the Federation. Meanwhile, the more conservative Malays would counter any Chinese radicalism in Singapore. For this to be achieved though Malays had to be in the majority and that required the incorporation of the North Borneo territories. The creation of Malaysia also offered Britain the chance to counter criticism of its colonialism in Asia and to reduce its force levels east of Suez. Finally by maintaining the Singapore base, which was essential to Britain's world role, this would help London influence American policy.

In 1961 local opinion also moved determinedly in favour of a Federation. The Singaporean premier, Lee Kuan Yew, leader of the People's Action Party (PAP), saw membership of Malaysia as a way to satisfy popular demands for independence from Britain while providing the island with a secure economic future. He adhered to this course even when left-wingers in the PAP opposed him and, in the summer of 1961, split to form their own party. Tunku Abdul Rahman saw a Federation as a way not only to please the British (on whom Malaya still depended for defence), but also as way to increase territory and influence, whilst preserving the position of the ethnic Malays in the expanded state. If the Borneo territories were included in the Federation, then Malays would make up 40 per cent of the population, almost as many as the Chinese (who formed 43 per cent). Without Borneo, the Chinese would have a clear majority. Although there was no love lost between the Tunku and Lee Kuan Yew, both of whom had ambitions of dominating the Federation, in August 1961 the two leaders agreed in principle on the Malaysia idea and in 1962 it was confirmed that such a Federation would be established, with effect from 31 August 1963. A few weeks later Singapore approved the decision in a referendum. One difficulty in all this was that the Borneo territories had not been given much preparation for independence and, whilst a British-created Commission reported in 1962 that the territories were happy to join Malaysia, doubts were expressed about the accuracy of this judgement. A second problem was that both Indonesia and the Philippines had claims on the British territories in Borneo and now decided to press them. 'Setting up Malaysia, though ... a concept long in the minds of the British, could also be seen as a major restructuring of the political map of South-East Asia that affected other states in the area. Over this issue the British were insensitive.'[8] The Philippines claimed, in June 1962, to be the legal inheritor of the nineteenth-century Sultan who had ruled North Borneo. But, given the country's close links to the West (with SEATO membership and US military bases), the Philippines was unlikely to press such a claim forcibly. More worrying was the mounting criticism of Malaysia from Indonesia in 1962, spearheaded by the PKI and coming after years of anti-Western gestures from Sukarno.

Until December 1961, when the communists condemned the Malaysian proposal as a neocolonialist venture and forced Sukarno to face up to the issue, Indonesia had expressed no opposition to the Federation, although its dislike of Britain's military presence in Malaya and Singapore was well known. Before that, Sukarno's anti-Western policies had focused on the aim of taking the colony of West Irian (the western part of New Guinea) from the Dutch, whose nationals he had expelled from Indonesia in late 1957. The US and Britain, concerned by such radicalism and the danger of a complete PKI takeover in Indonesia, had supported a short-lived uprising among disaffected elements in Indonesia, centred on Sumatra. When this failed, Washington and London tried a new tactic of minimizing their support for the Dutch, whilst offering arms and aid as a way to moderate Sukarno, keep links to the army, and limit PKI influence. But this did not prevent Sukarno from establishing closer ties to the USSR (which provided aid and arms to Indonesia on a large scale) and, in 1960, intensifying his demands for West Irian. His apparent success in playing off the two superpowers against each other was highlighted by the fact that, whereas Khrushchev visited Indonesia in 1960, Sukarno was nonetheless invited to meet Kennedy in the US in 1961. Kennedy was far keener on a policy of conciliation than Eisenhower had been. And Sukarno's successes continued when, on 15 August 1962, after several months of talks and under US pressure to concede, the Dutch agreed to hand West Irian to UN control. Nine months later the Indonesians took it over. Freed from this problem the triumphant Sukarno, instead of becoming more pro-Western, as Kennedy had hoped, was able to focus on Malaysia. In particular he questioned whether the Borneo territories wanted to join the Federation; the alternative was that they should merge with Indonesia. In December 1962 he covertly supported an uprising in one of the territories, Brunei. This was put down by British troops within a few weeks but the widespread popular support for it, and the fact that Brunei's Sultan now decided to remain outside Malaysia, encouraged Sukarno to believe that the Federation was unpopular in northern Borneo and could be forestalled.

The 'Konfrontasi'

On 20 January 1963 Indonesia formally rejected the Malaysia proposal and launched what it called a 'confrontation'. At first it was not clear what form this would take, but the British favoured a robust response and looked to their main allies in the region—America, Australia, and New Zealand—for support. These three were not so keen to antagonize Sukarno however. If he had launched an invasion of Malaysia, they would certainly have opposed it, but the 'confrontation' at first mainly took the form of a propaganda campaign, followed in April by localized armed clashes on the Malaysia–Indonesia border. This sometimes involved guerrilla incursions across the border, but fell short of outright war and was accompanied by signs that Sukarno was also ready to talk to the Tunku about a diplomatic settlement. The US, especially, believed it unwise to antagonize the Indonesian leader who, on the one hand, seemed highly popular with his own people because of his outspoken attacks on the West and, on the other hand, despite age and ill-health, was at least able to keep the PKI in check. Indonesia, with about 100 million people, had the third highest population in Asia and the sixth highest in the world. It had substantial oil, rubber, and mineral resources. Its fate was too important for America to alienate it, perhaps driving it into Soviet or Chinese arms, without good reason and the creation of Malaysia was not high in Kennedy's list of priorities: it was a British-led concept in which the US had little involvement. Singaporeans too 'began to resent the strains . . . which merger in Malaysia involved. Indonesian confrontation brought physical violence and damaged trade.'[9] By June 1963 even the Tunku seemed ready to compromise when he met Sukarno and the Philippines President, Diasdado Macapagal, in Manila. Here it was not only agreed that the UN Secretary-General should investigate the true state of opinion in northern Borneo, but also that talks should begin on a possible federation between their three countries, the so-called 'Maphilindo' project.

Such diplomatic efforts to settle the region's divisions did not last. The UN Secretary-General, U Thant, soon concluded that North Borneo and Sarawak were indeed happy to join Malaysia (Brunei received self-government under its Sultan and only became fully independent from Britain in 1984). Meanwhile, despite their continued bickering, the Tunku and Lee Kuan Yew persevered with talks on the federation. Although they set its creation back until mid-September, the Indonesians with some justification believed they had intended to proceed with it even if U Thant's report had been negative. Once it was created the Indonesians reacted with predictable violence. The British embassy in Jakarta was burnt down by a mob on 18 September, diplomatic relations with Malaysia were broken, and the confrontation was intensified, which led Australia and New Zealand to provide more assistance to the British. Again Britain showed surprising firmness in its response, given that it had limited defence resources and an increasingly weak economy. About 80,000 troops were deployed to protect Malaysia, counter-incursions were launched into Indonesia, covert operations were mounted to support Indonesian separatists, and a diplomatic effort was launched to persuade America that Sukarno was a menace. Lyndon Johnson, the US President after 22 November 1963, at first persisted with a policy of providing economic and even military aid to Indonesia and was concerned, with the mounting problems in Vietnam, not to spark off a second conflict in South-East Asia. However, Johnson and the American Congress were irritated by the unpredictable, neutralist Sukarno and US aid was gradually reduced, being focused on the Indonesian military, partly in order to strengthen them for any struggle with the PKI. Sukarno refused to answer US calls for a ceasefire in 1964 and instead there were increased border incidents later that year.

As 1965 progressed there seemed no hope of a settlement but all the main parties were in difficulty. The British government (which, of course, had originally seen the Malaysia proposal as a way to *reduce* overseas expenditure) was increasingly keen to hold down defence costs, but could not run down its presence 'East of Suez' until the confrontation ended. Then, in August 1965 Chinese–Malay tensions (reflected in the enmity between Lee and the Tunku) led to Singapore suddenly declaring itself independent, thus removing a key component from Malaysia. Far from opposing the move, the Tunku encouraged it, mainly because Malays became the

dominant ethnic group in Malaysia once Chinese-dominated Singapore was lost. Despite grave concern in London at the time, the separation did not lead to defeat in the confrontation. Instead, despite some continuing Malay–Chinese ethnic tension, culminating in considerable violence during 1969, Malaysia continued to hold together and it was Indonesia which backed away from the confrontation, largely because the Johnson administration decided that Sukarno should be removed.

From Washington's viewpoint, Sukarno seemed increasingly dangerous and irrational in 1965, and quite unsusceptible to American influence. Not only did he improve relations with communist China and continue to buy Soviet arms, he also walked out of the United Nations (in protest at the admission of Malaysia), criticized Johnson's escalating involvement in Vietnam, and spoke ominously about a 'Year of Living Dangerously'. Furthermore, 'by 1965 it seemed that the PKI was riding high . . . A situation in which Sukarno had . . . manipulated Army and PKI alike and had been . . . the apex of the triangle . . . seemed to have given way to a situation in which the PKI's corner of the triangle was rising . . . and the army's . . . slipping down.'[10] The CIA was already close to opponents of Sukarno in the army but reluctant to topple him, largely because there was no obvious alternative leader. Then, on 30 September 1965, in a confusing episode, which may have been sparked by false rumours of Sukarno's death, pro-communist elements in the army murdered several leading generals. Anti-communists, led by General Suharto, quickly struck back and predictably won US support. The Americans were determined to prevent any PKI takeover but reluctant to intervene directly in the country, so that aid for Suharto and the army was an ideal solution. The CIA provided covert assistance and helped identify PKI members. In the ruthless purge that now took place, up to 500,000 were killed, including the PKI leader, K. N. Aidit, and many people who were not communists at all. By March 1966 the PKI was effectively destroyed and, although Sukarno retained the Presidency, Suharto was now the real power in Indonesia, able to open diplomatic feelers to Malaysia, using Thailand as a go-between. There was a great irony in this dramatic turn of events from the US perspective. Whilst becoming embroiled in Vietnam, and just when Sukarno seemed completely beyond control, what one historian has called 'a wholly unexpected . . . windfall' came to Johnson's aid. 'However favourable to Washington the outcome proved, neither the coup attempt itself nor the army's prompt response to it were influenced to any significant degree by the United States.'[11]

The confrontation with Malaysia was finally called off by Indonesia in August 1966 and a year later both countries, together with the Philippines and others, joined together to form the Association of South-East Asian Nations, ASEAN, which helped foster stability and economic growth in the region (see Chapter 22, E). Sukarno resigned as President in 1967 and died 3 years later, by which time Suharto was secure in power, helped by substantial American aid. Meanwhile another pro-American strongman, Ferdinand Marcos, had come to power in the Philippines in 1966, and had also improved relations

with Malaysia. Thus, whatever the problems faced by the US in Vietnam in the late 1960s, the rest of South-East Asia was, from a Western perspective, stable and secure. The end of the confrontation also allowed Britain to run down its military presence in the region. Indeed, a monetary crisis and the devaluation of sterling, in late 1967, led to an announcement of a complete British withdrawal from its east of Suez bases (principally Singapore), to be completed by the end of 1971. Despite some concern from Singapore and Malaysia over their future security, the withdrawal was carried out without major incident. The countries of the region were able to stabilize themselves internally, and develop new forms of cooperation along anti-communist, free-market lines, despite the withdrawal of one Western power, Britain, from the region and the problems faced by another, the US, in Vietnam.

C. South Asia: The Indo–Pakistan Wars of 1965 and 1971

The War of 1965

In South Asia, as in the Malaysia–Indonesia confrontation, the roots of conflict could be said to be lie in the colonial inheritance. The separation of India and Pakistan in 1947, after independence from British rule (see Chapter 3, A), had left deep animosity as well as a collection of border and property claims. The worst cause of tension between the two countries was Kashmir, which was 80 per cent Muslim by population but whose ruler had opted to join India. War in 1948 had ended with the creation of an uneasy ceasefire line across Kashmir: the UN planned in 1949 to hold a plebiscite there, but it was never held. The Pakistani government claimed that, in a plebiscite, the Kashmiris would vote to join their fellow-Muslims in Pakistan; but the Indian government was reluctant to settle the dispute in this way, mainly because India was a multireligious, non-secular state, even if Hindu-dominated.

The Indian leader, Jawaharlal Nehru, pursued a non-aligned policy and seeking to exploit relations with both blocs made his country the largest recipient of Soviet aid outside the Eastern bloc itself. It was largely Moscow's diplomatic support which kept the UN from pressuring India about a plebiscite in Kashmir. 'Nehru's intransigence regarding Kashmir, his courtship of China and his . . . Indian–Soviet friendship—chilled Indian–US relations . . .' and prevented these two democracies from working together.[12] In contrast Pakistan, although its democracy proved unstable and it fell under the military rule of Ayub Khan in 1958, initially aligned itself with the West. It was a member of both the Baghdad Pact and SEATO and hoped to gain some military advantages through aid and arms supplies from the Americans. In return it provided the US with base facilities, including an intelligence-gathering facility at Peshawar but never received the kind of benefits it expected which would enable it to gain the upper hand in the Kashmir dispute.

Pakistani disillusionment continued to grow in the 1960s. First, in May 1960, the U-2 incident (see Chapter 5, B) led Ayub Khan to fear that he had become over-reliant on America—the U-2 spy plane, which so enraged Khrushchev, had flown from a Pakistan airbase—and so he began to improve relations with both the USSR and China. Second, the arrival of John F. Kennedy as President in January 1961 led the US to court India as a large, democratic state in Asia which might potentially limit Chinese power. Kennedy's forthright approach offended Ayub Khan without having any impact on Nehru's dedication to non-alignment. Then, in December 1961, India's invasion of the Portuguese enclave of Goa, though it could be defended as an anti-colonial step (and thereby won considerable sympathy in the less developed world), undermined Nehru's reputation as an enlightened, non-violent leader. It both offended Kennedy and aroused Pakistani fears of Indian aggression. Finally, the short-lived war between India and China in 1962 upset everyone's calculations and cemented links between Pakistan and China, revealing the failure of US efforts to benefit from integrating Pakistan into the Western system of alliances. What had developed was an increasingly unstable situation which it was difficult for Washington to influence. The US, seeing a renewed chance to turn India into an ally against China, now provided Nehru, for the first time, with *military* aid. The Indians, stunned by the surprise invasion, became far less self-confident in their foreign policy, while the Pakistani armed forces were more hopeful about defeating India in a war. And Ayub Khan, despite his links to the West, was keen to draw closer to China as a possible ally against India. The Sino–Indian War also made it more difficult to resolve the Kashmir problem because the Indians now saw Kashmir, which bordered on China, as having a strategic significance should a second war with China occur. It was partly for this reason that US-sponsored attempts to get an Indo–Pakistani deal on Kashmir, in 1963 and 1964, made no progress.

In early 1965 India still adhered to its non-aligned policy, although Pakistan remained a member of SEATO as well as CENTO formed in 1959 after the collapse of the Baghdad Pact. The Indian Prime Minister was now Lal Shastri, Nehru having died the previous May. India felt beleaguered abroad, with Chinese relations as bad as ever and the US pressing for negotiations on Kashmir which were likely to result, if they resulted in anything, in a Kashmiri vote to join Pakistan. Pakistan, on the other hand, had settled its own border disputes with China in 1963 and Ayub Khan was now able to visit Beijing. This upset the Johnson administration in Washington which was, as ever, preoccupied by Cold War considerations and deeply antagonistic to China. Ayub Khan's obsession was increasingly with Kashmir; he was frustrated at the lack of diplomatic progress upon it, suspicious of continued American military aid for India, and even threatened to leave SEATO. In April 1965, largely in frustration at Ayub's closeness to China, Johnson abruptly cancelled a visit to Pakistan. Then, because he could hardly meet Shastri without doubling the offence to Ayub, the US President cancelled a planned visit to India as well. This, however, further underlined the bankruptcy of US attempts to fit Indo–Pakistan affairs into a Cold War mould, and severely reduced American influence in both countries during the critical events that followed. In April 1965 limited border clashes had already begun in the Rann of Kutch, a marshy area far removed from Kashmir and, since it was under water for half the year, not worth a serious struggle. The British, as leaders of the Commonwealth, of which India and Pakistan were both members, were agreed as arbitrators of the dispute in June (and a border deal was eventually reached in 1968). But the Rann of Kutch episode, however limited in itself, led both sides to mass forces in Kashmir and encouraged the Pakistanis in particular to feel highly confident about an armed clash.

From April 1965 onwards tension in Kashmir was mounting, as the Pakistanis supported irregular forces in sabotage raids across the ceasefire line. The arrest by the Indians in May, of the local Muslim leader, Sheikh Abdullah, had inflamed passions further. Then, at the end of August, full-scale war began, with both sides accusing the other of initiating it. Both had been involved in increasingly frequent clashes through August but the first full-scale attacks seem to have been made by Pakistan. In early September it appeared to be the Pakistanis who were having the best of the conflict, with a drive into Indian-ruled territory in southern Kashmir. In fact this soon stalled and Ayub seems to have planned to run the war down. However, around 6 September the Indians struck back with an offensive towards Lahore, followed up by an attack much further south, on Gadra (not far from the Rann of Kutch), taking the Pakistanis by surprise: 'the most surprised person was Ayub' who had 'assumed that . . . the Indians would relax' once the violence died down in Kashmir.[13] By the middle of the month the war was deadlocked, but with Pakistan's confidence blunted and the Indians happy to have recovered from early setbacks. Except for the odd diplomatic foray over the Sino–Indian border, China was quiescent during the war, and the US and Britain had suspended military supplies to both sides once the war began, with India complaining that Pakistan had used military equipment from both these Western countries for aggressive purposes. This deadlock harmed Pakistan most, since India continued to receive Soviet supplies. In reply, Pakistan argued that (in contrast to its own actions in disputed Kashmir) India had launched an attack across an internationally recognized border, an argument that seems to have won some sympathy in Britain, which issued a statement critical of India's conduct. For this reason the British were not seen as a potential arbitrator in the conflict, as they had been in the case of the Rann of Kutch. Instead, when a UN-sponsored ceasefire took effect on 22 September, it was the USSR which took the lead in trying to broker an Indo–Pakistani settlement. American policy seemed in disarray: 'Indians were outraged at the equation, implicit in the embargo of American weaponry to both sides, of their actions with those of Pakistan . . . In Pakistan . . . Ayub . . . lost no opportunity to . . . blame . . . Pakistan's frustrations on Washington. . .'[14] The Soviets hoped not only to maintain their links to India, but also, now, to draw Pakistan away from the US, and Premier Andrei Kosygin brokered a settlement between Ayub and Shastri, at a conference in Tashkent in January 1966. However, this did little other than restore the status quo and Indo–Pakistani diplomatic relations. The vexed question of Kashmir was unresolved, Soviet influence made no great advance, but if America could be pleased with the re-establishment of peace its influence was no longer decisive. Pakistan was still nominally tied to the West but on good terms with the Chinese who, while not able to exploit South Asian differences with any

significant consequences, remained an important regional actor whom the West had to consider. And the danger of close Indo–Soviet relations remained. Regional alliances in the context of the Cold War had proved to be more destabilizing than a source of Western strength and influence. The lesson that the conflict between two blocs could no longer be the defining priority of international relations was there to be learned.

The War of 1971

Lal Shastri collapsed and died at the end of the Tashkent conference, to be succeeded by Nehru's daughter, Indira Gandhi. She maintained her father's non-aligned policy, accepting the revival of US military aid in 1967 while criticizing Johnson over Vietnam. In Pakistan Ayub was succeeded by another general, Yahya Khan, in 1969, a year after terminating the US lease on its Peshawar base. Pakistan's rulers were happy to see America recommence its military aid programme in 1970 but they were also determined to hang onto their Chinese alliance. This had harmed Pakistan's standing in Washington's eyes while Lyndon Johnson was in office, but the situation changed after Richard Nixon became President. Nixon never got on personally with Indira Gandhi. Furthermore, in great secrecy, he and his National Security Adviser, Henry Kissinger, came to rely on Pakistan as a line of contact for their 'Opening to China' (see Chapter 12, A). It was from Pakistan that Kissinger made his all-important visit to China in July 1971. By then tension in South Asia was rising once more, not this time over Kashmir, but about a very different problem, the growing rift between the two halves of Pakistan, West and East.

In 1947 Pakistan had been formed from Eastern Bengal and the so-called 'North-West Frontier' which were about a thousand miles apart. The East had the bulk of the population but was poorer and, because it was low-lying and subject to heavy monsoons, prone to natural disasters, especially floods and cyclones. It was West Pakistan which included the capital city, Islamabad, which dominated the armed forces and which had its own language, Urdu, accepted as the official one. This caused deep resentment in East Pakistan and was compounded by the fact that 'Pakistani' foreign policy often seemed designed to defend specifically Western interests, based on the West's proximity to the USSR and China, and on its close interest in the Kashmir problem: the East was almost surrounded by Indian territory and virtually indefensible from an attack by her. In 1970, after more than a decade of military rule, Yahya Khan was planning a return to parliamentary government, expecting that this would preserve national cohesion. However, severe cyclones in November killed about 200,000 in Bengal and helped create a situation whereby, in elections the following month, most East Pakistanis voted for the Awami League of Mujibur Rahmann, known simply as Mujib, whose aim was to secure an autonomous 'Bangladesh'. Meanwhile, West Pakistan overwhelmingly voted in favour of Ali Bhutto's Pakistan People's Party, which favoured a more centralized government. This outcome threatened to tear the country in two, especially since it was the Awami League (thanks to the East's larger population) which won a parliamentary majority, leading Bhutto to boycott the National Assembly in March 1971. This 'created an explosive situation and a point of no return.'[15] As a result Yahya Khan decided to suspend the meeting of parliament, to introduce martial law in East Pakistan— backed by 40,000 troops—and to imprison Mujib without charge.

Far from solving Pakistan's problems, Yahya's insensitive policy simply worsened them. Instead of wanting mere autonomy, Mujib now demanded full independence; up to ten million East Pakistanis fled abroad to neighbouring India, putting the latter's food and aid resources under great strain; and Indira Gandhi was under increasing pressure to help 'Bangladesh' militarily. In April 1971 Indian-trained 'Mukti Bahini' resistance fighters began an armed campaign against the Pakistani army in East Pakistan. Western opinion tended to side with the Bangladeshis, who were seen as being subjected to military oppression after a recent natural disaster. A large-scale international aid programme to East Pakistan was already underway. The Indians also continued to have Eastern bloc support. Indeed, on 9 August the USSR moved to consolidate its ties to India when Andrei Gromyko signed a 24-year friendship treaty in New Delhi. This mainly involved tech-

nical assistance but also provided for consultations should one of them be attacked. Nixon and Kissinger were surprised by this step even though it could be read as a reaction to Chinese sympathy for Pakistan. In contrast to most Western opinion the White House was convinced that it must back West Pakistan, while encouraging Yahya to show moderation (see boxed section). The concessions Yahya made, however, such as opening talks with Awami moderates and, in September, reintroducing a civilian administration in the East, proved too little, too late. Meanwhile, 'Indira Gandhi's goals became more precise . . . to win recognition for Bangladesh nationalism . . . [and] to make it clear that the continuing threats to Indian security posed by the crisis in Pakistan gave New Delhi the right to resolve the situation by any means it deemed effective.'[16] The Bangladeshis were now determined on independence and, in November 1971, border incidents intensified, with a massing of forces on the Indo–Pakistani border in both East and West.

As in 1965, both sides blamed each other for the outbreak of war, with the Indians accused of launching an invasion of East Pakistan in late November, and the Pakistanis accused of beginning large-scale hostilities with an attack in Kashmir and Western India in early December. Whoever was most to blame, it was always clear that India had the upper hand in the East. The Soviets, who continued to supply India with arms, vetoed a potentially embarrassing UN resolution in favour of a mutual withdrawal on 4 December. India recognized Bangladeshi independence two days later and by 10 December it was clear that Pakistan's forces in the East were overwhelmed. As in 1965, Chinese support for Pakistan was mainly verbal, evidently accepting that Bangladesh was a lost cause. Indeed, it was the US which did most to press India to end the war. In the so-called 'tilt' towards Pakistan, and despite public criticism in America, the White House now made fully apparent its support for Yahya Khan. A US naval task force was despatched towards the Bay of Bengal and, on 12 December, for the first time in the Nixon administration, the 'hot line' to Moscow was used in order to press for a ceasefire. Nixon and Kissinger particularly wished to demonstrate to China that they could be relied upon in a crisis; and they were determined that India should not follow up its victory in the East, by defeating Pakistan in Kashmir as well, potentially putting the country's existence under threat. On 16–17 December a cease-fire finally took hold on the borders of both West and East Pakistan. This ended fears of a full-scale war over Kashmir, for which neither side was properly prepared, given their concentration on the war in the East. 70,000 Pakistani troops were prisoners of war and diplomatic efforts now focused on their release, while the Bangladeshi state won international recognition, even if Chinese opposition kept it out of the UN until 1974.

Bangladesh was not able to establish a stable democracy, despite the high hopes of 1971. It remained an extremely poor country, reliant on overseas aid, and prone to natural disasters. Mujibur became its first President but was killed during a military coup in 1975 after which long periods of military rule were interspersed with attempts to return to democratic government. In Pakistan, the 1971 defeat undermined the position of the military and led Yahya Khan to hand power to the popular Ali Bhutto, but the latter was overthrown (and later executed) by General Zia ul-Haq in 1977 and military rule returned for many years. After Zia's death in an air crash in 1988, there was an uneasy return to civilian government for several years, with the premiership twice falling to Bhutto's daughter,

Benazir. Yet the army was always a force in the background and again seized power in 1999. Only India survived as a democracy, despite considerable internal religious–ethnic divisions, the rise of Hindu militancy, and the assassinations of both Indira Gandhi (by her Sikh bodyguards in 1984) and her son, Rajiv, who had also become Prime Minister (in 1991 by a Tamil group who supported a separate Tamil state in nearby Sri Lanka and resented his interference in the dispute). Meanwhile, despite periodic attempts at a rapprochement, Indo–Pakistani tension continued, focused on Kashmir. There were border clashes in 1985–6 and later, from 1989 onwards, India faced intermittent unrest within Kashmir from Muslim groups. The Indian government blamed both this, and also Sikh discontent, on Pakistani trouble-making, but other Islamic states also became critical of Indian policy. In mid-1999, there were Pakistan-backed incursions into Indian-controlled Kashmir, accompanied by further internal unrest. By that time the danger of a major upheaval was worsened by the fact that, in 1998, both countries had tested nuclear weapons in quick succession. Although it had not sparked outright war for a generation, the Kashmir problem remained one of the world's potentially most destructive flashpoints, with both antagonists convinced of their own rectitude.

D. **The Middle East: The Arab–Israeli Six Day War**

The Middle East in the mid-1960s

When the White House decided to oppose India in the 1971 war, one of its arguments was that force should not be rewarded for fear of triggering instability elsewhere. And one of the key areas in the less developed world in which Henry Kissinger feared violent upheaval was the Middle East where, just as the Indo–Pakistani War broke out in 1971, tension finally seemed to be settling down in the aftermath of the conflict in Jordan and the dramatic Israeli advances during the so-called Six Day War. That conflict itself had broken out quite suddenly and

taken the world by surprise despite the serious underlying tensions between Israel and Syria. In the early 1960s Arab–Israeli enmities had been overshadowed by conflicts in the Arab world and there was limited superpower concern over the region. Israel, which had proved its military superiority in the wars of 1948 and 1956 (see Chapters 3, C and 8, C), was the dominant regional power. Despite intermittent Palestinian guerrilla attacks and border clashes with Syria, a nuclear weapons programme was well under way and the state seemed relatively secure. Palestinian attacks were little more than an irritant until after the 1967 war. The Arabs, on the

The 'Tilt': Why did the White House favour Pakistan in the 1971 War?

In the spring of 1971, tension in East Pakistan grew, the majority of US public opinion was sympathetic to the Bangladeshis, and the State Department favoured a policy of pressuring the Pakistani government into concessions, by reducing economic and military aid. There seemed several strong arguments in favour of an anti-Pakistani, pro-Indian stance by America:

- India was, in terms of population, the world's largest democracy whereas Pakistan had been ruled for years as a military dictatorship;
- the Pakistani ruler, Yahya Khan, had ignored the results of the December 1970 election, which had given victory to the East Pakistani Awami League of Mujibur Rahmann. Mujib had even been arrested;
- the Pakistani army had begun an oppressive military occupation of East Pakistan;
- the East was still recovering from the devastating humanitarian impact of cyclones and flooding in late 1970;
- millions of East Pakistanis fled from military rule into neighbouring India, which had to carry the burden of housing and feeding the refugees.

Despite these pro-democratic, anti-militarist, and humanitarian considerations President Nixon and his National Security Adviser, Henry Kissinger had arguments of *realpolitik* for 'tilting' towards Pakistan:

- given the history of Indo–Pakistani conflict, India's motives were not pure: in threatening war and in backing Bangladeshi resistance fighters (the Mukti Bahini), India's aim was certainly to divide East and West Pakistan, perhaps even to destroy Pakistan itself—which America could not allow;
- it still seemed possible, for much of 1971, that Pakistan could reach an internal solution to its problems and, on a visit in July, Kissinger pressed Yahya Khan to be moderate;
- Pakistan had been a Western ally since the 1950s and it would harm US credibility if it let down an ally in time of difficulties, even if the government was dictatorial (many US allies were);
- India, on the other hand, had long followed a neutralist policy and, at certain points leant towards the USSR: in August 1972, the Indians and Soviets signed a friendship treaty, and the USSR supplied India with armaments;
- because of their continuing problems in Vietnam and the danger of Soviet links with developing countries, the US wanted to avoid conflict in the less developed world wherever possible: instability would spread if the use of force increased as a way to resolve disputes;
- most important of all perhaps, Pakistan had a 'geopolitical' significance because of Nixon's 'Opening to China': in July 1971 Kissinger secretly visited China via Pakistan; Pakistan was a friend of China, which might assist it in a war, whereas China and India had fought a war only 9 years before.

Therefore in December 1971, when war broke out, the White House saw it not as a localized problem but as a menace to its new link to China, a test of US resolve in the face of a Soviet-backed challenge, even as raising the danger of a Sino–Soviet war. As Kissinger later wrote in his first volume of memoirs, *The White House Years* (1979, 913–14), 'The assault on Pakistan was a most dangerous precedent . . . Had we acquiesced . . . we would have sent a wrong signal to Moscow and unnerved all our allies, China, and the forces for restraint in other volatile areas of the world.' The result was the use of the 'hot line' to Moscow, the despatch of a carrier force to the area, and warnings to India not to destroy West Pakistan.

Critics have continued to see the White House line as misguided and unnecessary, exaggerating the dangers in South Asia;

- the war was essentially a regional problem, centred on Bangladeshi problems;
- it was Pakistan which opened the war on the Western front and India did not seek to destroy West Pakistan;
- the Soviet–Indian friendship treaty was about technical links and consultation, not a military alliance, and India was neutralist not a member of the Eastern bloc;
- China did not seriously threaten to become involved and it accepted the outcome of the war;
- White House policy was unpopular with the US people, failed to prevent war breaking out and ended up backing a certain loser.

Thus, William Bundy in *A Tangled Web: the Making of Foreign Policy in the Nixon Presidency* (New York, 1998) writes, on 291, that 'No national interest remotely warranted the risks . . . Nixon ran, not to mention the domestic controversy that would . . . have ensued if there had been a direct confrontation with the Soviet.'

other hand, appeared increasingly divided. The union of Egypt and Syria into the United Arab Republic had broken down, after less than 4 years, in September 1961. Iraq had fallen under radical leadership in 1958 but the government faced challenges from the Iraqi communists and supporters of Nasser's brand of Arab nationalism. In 1963, the secular, leftist-but-nationalist Ba'ath Party took power there; but deep-seated Iraqi–Egyptian rivalry for Arab leadership prevented the two countries from working together. The final split between the Syrian and Iraqi sections of the party did not occur until 1966 but different factions in both countries meant that the Ba'ath provided no basis for the creation of Iraqi–Syrian unity. Arab radicals of all factions despised the conservative regimes in Jordan and Saudi Arabia although they failed to undermine them: Jordan survived an attempt by Nasserites to overthrow King Hussein in early 1963; and internal differences among the Saudi royal family were resolved in 1964 when Feisal became King. The worst problem seemed to be in Yemen where a civil war had broken out in 1962 that embodied this conservative–radical split.

When John F. Kennedy became President the US did try to improve relations with Nasser as a step to building links with radical elements in the Arab world and thereby reducing the opportunities for the Soviets to gain more influence in the Middle East. Central to the approach to Nasser through aid and assistance was the agreement to put the Palestinian issue 'on ice'. However, America's links to Israel, Jordan, and Saudi Arabia put strict limits on such a policy which was eventually undone by the war in the Yemen (see below). Moreover, in the 1960s both superpowers increasingly armed their respective clients in the Arab–Israeli conflict. In 1962 Kennedy had agreed to supply anti-aircraft missiles to Israel, in the mistaken hope that a more effective defence would no longer require them to develop nuclear weapons. The key turning point came in 1965 with Johnson's decision to supply the Israelis with advanced offensive weapons for the first time. With the Soviets supplying Egypt and Syria well before the 1967 war, 'the Middle East had already been . . . integrated into the existing bipolar world order',[17] raising the danger that any local conflict would assume much wider significance.

By the mid-1960s tensions in the region had grown considerably. Most serious was the civil war in Yemen which broke out in September 1962, after radicals under Colonel Abdullah Sallal overthrew the traditionalist government of the Imam, Mohammed Al-Baar. Egypt backed the former, Saudi Arabia the latter and considerable external forces were involved in the civil war. When Egyptian planes attacked the Saudis in 1963 Kennedy was forced to choose between the conservative or radical elements in the Arab world. Despite an attempt by Nasser and Feisal to compose their differences in 1965, neither side would give way and the East–West split was largely replicated in the Middle East. The Western position was weakened in 1966 when Britain announced that, within two years, it would be pulling out of the neighbouring South Arabian Federation, which included the wealthy trading port of Aden. The British were being pressed to withdraw by nationalist groups in Aden, who carried out a terrorist campaign supported by Nasser and Sallal. Indeed, despite the fact that he had already been committed to a costly, deadlocked war for five years without result, Nasser's hopes of achieving victory once the British left, led him to commit 70,000 troops to the Yemen conflict by 1967.

Other disputes in the region had a definite Arab–Israeli significance, especially the Jordan waters dispute, a long-standing argument over how to exploit the River Jordan. It had flared up again because an Israeli plan to divert water, for industrial and irrigation purposes was completed in 1964. In January that year Arab leaders gathered together in Cairo, at Nasser's invitation, agreed on their own plan which would bypass the Israeli construction, and now that the loss of water was deemed to threaten the existence of the Arab nation, they declared that they would together plan the forces that would ultimately lead to the destruction of the state of Israel. Work on the scheme in Syria then led in 1965 and 1966 to Israeli attacks to prevent its completion. This was one of the major points of dispute between the two countries along with guerrilla attacks within Israel. The others concerned territory in the Demilitarized Zone (DMZ) and particularly the use of the Sea of Galilee which was entirely in Israel but whose northern shore belonged to Syria.

The first Arab summit in 1964 was also important for promoting the creation of a political body to head the Palestinians, some of whom were still living within Israel, but many of whom were scattered in refugee camps, particularly in the Egyptian-controlled Gaza Strip and the Jordanian-controlled West Bank of the River Jordan. The Palestinian Liberation Organization (PLO) was an Egyptian-backed umbrella organization, born from a meeting of 422 delegates in 1964 which resolved to liberate the Palestinian homeland and destroy the Jewish state which had occupied it. Initially led by Ahmed Shuqqairi the PLO, with its disparate groups, soon suffered from internal conflict, often linked to criticism of its ties with Egypt. Radical Palestinian groups engaged in guerrilla attacks, such as the Heroes of the Return and the Palestine Liberation Front, resented the determination of the Egyptian and Jordanian governments to prevent such raids taking place from their territory. After the Six Day War their leaders came together under the PLO umbrella and with the Vengeance Youth formed the Popular Front for the Liberation of Palestine which was led by George Habash. At the end of 1964, another group, led by Yasser Arafat, which had contacts with the Palestine Liberation Front, left the PLO and began commando raids against Israel. Known as *Al Fatah* and formed in the late 1950s, it established a militia *al-Asifa* (the Storm) whose members received training in Syria. Many of these raids and those of other radical groups were launched from Jordan and their realistic aim was to provoke conflict between Israel and other Arab governments. They were certainly followed by tough Israeli reprisals, culminating in November 1966 when the IDF attacked the West Bank towns of Samu, Jimba, and Khirbet Karkay south of Hebron causing 72 casualties, 18 fatal (three civilian), and destroying 140 houses, a clinic, and a school. Although the reactions to this may be seen as the start of the road to war, the real problem was not the raids of Palestinian fighters and the Israeli Defence Forces in Israel and Jordan but the deterioration in Israeli–Syrian relations. Raids and retaliations became more frequent with disputes about the initial responsibility, and the situation worsened with the seizure of power in February 1966 by a more radical Ba'ath group. As the Israeli Foreign Minister, Abba Eban,

later wrote: 'I regarded this Syrian terrorism as an early stage of malignancy. It could not be left alone.'[18]

The Six Day War

By 1966 the conflict between Israel and its Arab neighbours more and more reflected the superpower rivalry for influence in the Middle East. Syria and Egypt were stockpiling large amounts of arms from the USSR, encouraged by the US government's firm support for Israel. Khrushchev had visited Cairo in 1964, making Nasser a 'Hero of the Soviet Union', and his successors maintained their support. In the US Kennedy's shift to Saudi Arabia in the conflict with Egypt over the Yemen was followed by the Johnson administration severing all aid to Egypt in 1966, giving up on Kennedy's attempts to improve US–Arab relations.

In August 1966 Syrian and Israeli air and ground forces fought a fierce battle in the Sea of Galilee area which led to Syrian threats to strike targets within Israel. It also contributed to the new regime drawing closer to Egypt and signing a defence pact in November 1966 that was followed by the Israeli attack on Jordan. In turn *Al Fatah* raids into Israel were stepped up and the escalating cycle of violence continued into the following year. On 7 April 1967 there was a major border incident in which the Israeli airforce attacked Syrian positions on the Golan Heights, shooting down several Soviet-supplied MIGs. Moreover, in May the Israelis were now (12 May) threatening to attack Syria and strike at Damascus. While such statements were not supported by any evidence of troop build-ups, and a UN investigation found no evidence to substantiate these fears, the following day Nasser received information from Soviet intelligence that around 12 Israeli brigades were concentrating on the Syrian border. The events in May mark the time when interpretations became diametrically opposed (see boxed section for two radically different explanations).

The Syrians were blamed by Israeli leaders for the mounting number of terrorist raids on the country. But at least one Jewish historian has argued that 'Israel's strategy of escalation on the Syrian front was probably the single most important factor in dragging the Middle East to war ... despite the

The Pro-Arab and Pro-Israeli Explanations of the Six Day War

The Israeli Version

The Israelis point to the first Arab summit in January 1964 and say this confirmed and strengthened the terrorists who were launching attacks on Israel. The first formal statement of the Arab states' intention to bring about the destruction of Israel was made in a joint statement at the summit and was confirmed by the first Palestinian National Council in early 1964. The guerrilla attacks on Israel, conducted from Syria, emphasized the insecurity of Israeli farmers around the Sea of Galilee. Moreover, with the more radical Ba'athist government in Damascus from February 1966 the support and training given to Palestinian groups operating from Jordan increased. In August 1966 after a fierce skirmish when Israeli forces were attacked around the Sea of Galilee growing Arab hostility led to Syrian threats to strike targets within Israel. Israel was under siege and its retaliatory raids were failing to provide a deterrent. Its insecurity was heightened in November 1966 with the Egyptian–Syrian mutual defence pact. In April 1967 when the Syrians began shelling Israeli settlements the Israeli airforce was called into action and clashed with its Syrian counterpart. It began to look as if Israel was about to face a major military challenge. On 13 May the Soviets falsely claimed that Israeli troops were amassing on the Syrian frontier. When Nasser insisted on the withdrawal of UN peacekeeping forces from Sinai on 16 May the fears of a major attack appeared to be confirmed. Nasser was keen to respond to the Soviet information designed to lead to Cairo joining with Damascus in a combined assault on Israel. His determination to crush the Israelis was further demonstrated by his blockade of the Straits of Tiran on 23 May after the UN forces had left which made an Israeli response unavoidable. Hence the surprise attack on Egyptian and Syrian airfields.

The Arab Version

After 1965, having received offensive arms, the Israelis were determined both to crush Arab resistance to the illegal occupation of Palestine and to ensure that further expansion of the state of Israel took place. With these goals in mind they sought the right moment to seize an opportunity to justify an attack on their Arab neighbours. Their military superiority would be total if an air strike was made in a surprise assault on Arab airfields which would enable them to exploit the absence of 70,000 Egyptian troops in the Yemen.

In 1964 the Israelis were enabled to justify attacks on their neighbours in retaliation against Palestinian freedom fighters which were far in excess of retaliatory raids and enabled Israeli Defence Forces to undertake operations in preparation for the more serious conflict that was being planned. The Israelis also began to attempt provocative settlements in the Demilitarized Zone with Syria and these conflicts with Syria became more serious in 1966 as air and ground forces on both sides became involved in these border clashes. In particular, the Israelis tried to prevent Syrians accessing the waters of Lake Galilee from its northern shore and attacked Arab workers trying to complete works that would regain the vital water of the River Jordan now being used for Israeli irrigation projects. Significant military battles were fought in August 1966 and April 1967. On the latter occasion 6 Syrian MIGs were shot down by Israeli fighters. It was barely a month after that when General Rabin announced that it was about time Israeli forces marched on Damascus. When the Soviets confirmed that Israeli troops were amassing on the Syrian border on 12 May, Nasser believed the danger to Syria was so acute that something had to be done to try and deter more Israeli aggression. In an effort to deter the Israelis by aiding the Syrians, which he could barely afford to do with his commitments in the Yemen, Nasser asked for the UN forces to be partially withdrawn thus exposing part of Israel to attack from Egypt. When the UN insisted that all of its forces or none would have to be withdrawn Nasser reluctantly agreed to the former and then decided to try and regain the Arab position in the Straits of Tiran by closing them to Israel on 23 May. Had the Israelis also been keen to avoid war they would have accepted the troops on the Israeli side of the border. The Arab world now tried to mobilize to deter an Israeli attack on Syria but more hawks came into the government in Tel Aviv. The Arab efforts were therefore in vain and the Israelis launched an unprovoked attack on 5 June. The fact that the aim was to gain territory at the expense of the Arabs was revealed by the ground attack on Syria which was more necessary to take land than to achieve a military victory and which was concealed from the US by the sinking of the spy ship USS *Liberty*.

conventional wisdom ... that singles out Syrian aggression as the principal cause.'[19] But the Syrian government, unstable and nervous, continued to fear an attack. Nasser, anxious to be seen to back Syria and reluctant to lose face, mobilized his army on 14 May; and the Soviets, keen not to lose their allies, seemed prepared to support them. One major feature of superpower involvement in the Middle East during the Cold War was 'the difficulty that the superpowers encountered in controlling the behaviour of their clients. The local powers invariably had their own agenda and they employed various tactics ... to mobilize their superpower ally behind this.'[20] In 1967, the USSR and US ended up backing their local clients even though there was little desire, in either Moscow or Washington, for an East–West confrontation.

Whenever concerns about Israel grew in the Arab world, Nasser had to consider his reputation as the leading Arab nationalist and the very fact that he had failed to triumph in the Yemen, increased the pressure in May 1967 for him to be seen supporting Syria. Nasser had two armoured divisions and 300 front-line aircraft, which was what the Israelis feared and he was generally better equipped than in 1956.

On the other hand, there was no logical reason for him to go to war when he had 70,000 men committed to the Yemen quagmire. Yet given the military balance there was a distinct advantage to be had by the side that struck first.

In the second half of May it was events on the Egyptian–Israeli border which drew attention away from the Israel–Syria clashes. On the 16 May Nasser declared a state of emergency and asked the UN to withdraw the force which it had installed in Sinai after the 1956 war. King Hussein had previously accused Nasser of hiding behind the UN forces separating Israel and Egypt at the same time as he was calling for active opposition to Israel and criticizing Nasser for failing to respond to Israeli attacks on Jordan. Secretary-General U Thant was criticized for agreeing to the withdrawal and pulling UN troops out over the next week. They might, it was argued, have deterred a war if they had remained or if they had been positioned in Israel. But he felt he had no choice: opinion in the UN was divided on the Arab–Israeli issue, the troops were on Egyptian sovereign territory (Israel had refused to have them on its side of the border), and Nasser could easily have used force to remove them. The reality was that

Sithu U Thant (1909–1974)

Originally trained as a schoolmaster, U Thant worked for the Burmese government, after the country won independence from Britain in 1948. In 1952 he was a member of Burma's delegation to the United Nations and, in 1957, became the country's permanent ambassador to the organization. When Dag Hammarskjöld was killed in an air crash in September 1961, whilst trying to end the Katangan secession in the Congo, U Thant was chosen as successor. Initially appointed only to serve out the remainder of Hammarskjöld's term of office, U Thant went on to serve as Secretary-General from 3 November 1961 to 31 December 1971, longer than any other twentieth-century incumbent. He was the first representative from the developing world to hold the position and brought to it a self-disciplined and calm, yet realistic approach to international affairs, showing good judgement in a number of difficult situations.

Although the Cold War inevitably restricted the UN's ability to shape world affairs, U Thant was deeply involved in several crises during his Secretary-Generalship. In the Congo he worked to maintain the country's unity, secured the final withdrawal of the former-colonial power,

Belgium, and provided economic aid which prevented a humanitarian disaster so that, when UN forces left in June 1964, the Congo operation could be counted one of their great successes. Meanwhile, during the Cuban missile crisis, he also played a positive, but low-key role in trying to hold down tension. He despatched a peacekeeping force to Cyprus in the summer of 1964, after fighting between the Greek and Turkish communities, and he helped secure a ceasefire in the Indo–Pakistani War of 1965, flying to the crisis zone in person. But he could do no more than anyone else to bring peace to Vietnam, despite a number of initiatives, and he was heavily criticized in the West in May 1967 for pulling out the UN peacekeeping force in the Sinai desert. Whilst the critics argued that he thereby removed a barrier to conflict, supporters argued that he effectively had no choice, given that UN forces were on Egyptian soil. Whatever the justification for U Thant's action he lost standing with the US and Britain, both Security Council members, and played a subsidiary role in world affairs until the end of his term.

Disputed Middle-East Waterways

The armistice in the first Arab–Israeli War of 1948–9 did not lead to an Egyptian lifting of the blockade of Israeli ships in the Suez Canal. The Egyptians argued that a state of belligerency still existed because no peace settlement had been signed. Therefore while ships of foreign powers not carrying contraband were allowed to go through the Canal on their way to and from Israel, Israeli ships were prevented from so doing. The Israelis argued that the armistice meant that the Egyptians were not entitled under international law to exercise belligerent rights. The Egyptians used Oppenheim's *International Law* to support their case that truces and the subsequent cessation of hostilities could not be comparable to peace and that its regulation of shipping when a state of belligerency existed was confirmed under the Suez Canal Convention. The Israeli argument was exactly the opposite and the British, who had an interest in stopping Egyptian interference with shipping, contemplated taking the case to the International Court of Justice. The Foreign Office legal department examined the case and argued the Egyptians would win. However, a UN resolution was passed in 1951 condemning Egyptian actions in the Canal, denying their claim to exercise belligerent rights and calling on them to cease their interference with shipping.

The Straits of Tiran issue was rather different. The Egyptians argued that all states in the Middle East, including Israel, claimed their territorial waters extended 6 miles from shore. Therefore the Straits of Tiran (and part of the Gulf of Aquaba) were wholly within their territorial waters. The Israelis argued that they were an international waterway and outside Egypt's lawful control. This argument was not compatible with the position of the Suez Canal which was accepted by the British. They accepted that the Suez Canal was an international waterway wholly within the sovereign territory of the state of Egypt but which had to be operated as an international waterway because of the existence of an international convention governing its use that had survived from the period when Egypt was under Ottoman rule. No such convention existed for the Gulf of Aquaba. The Egyptians also argued that the reason Israel's claim that the Straits were an international waterway was invalid was because their occupation of the port of Eilat was illegal. The Jewish state, they claimed, had occupied the port after signing an armistice agreement with Egypt and in violation of several Security Council resolutions. Legal opinion on these matters differs.

Source: Based on Mark Tessler, *A History of the Israeli–Palestinian Conflict* (1994), 330–5.

neither side was now prepared to have an effective peacekeeping force in place. The UN withdrawal gave Egypt control of the Straits of Tiran, on which Israel relied for access to the Red Sea (Egypt would not allow Israeli ships through the Suez Canal) and around 23 May, Nasser closed the Straits of Tiran to Israeli shipping, provoking international concern. In 1957, in order to secure Israel's withdrawal from Sinai following the recent war, America had promised to support Israel's right to send its own ships through the Straits in future. Now the Americans, who had insufficient forces near the Red Sea, told the Israelis to take no action while they attempted to form an international naval force to fulfil the undertaking, but the scheme came to nothing. If anything the closure of the Straits of Tiran, restoring the 1956 *status quo ante* the Israeli attack on Egypt, marked the crucial watershed between war and peace (boxed section on the waterways issue).

President de Gaulle did join the chorus of appeals for restraint from the Arabs and Israelis, but the USSR rejected his idea for a four-power conference. On 27 May the Israeli government, a coalition led by the distinctly unwarlike Levi Eshkol, voted 9–9 over whether to launch a pre-emptive strike. On 30 May, a dramatic turn of events stemming from Hussein's visit to Cairo produced a reconciliation between him and Nasser which even placed the Jordanian army under Egyptian command in the event of war.[21] This step, made out of fear, produced a classic illustration of the security dilemma in that it produced more fear in the adversary they were afraid of.

Israeli contacts with the US government suddenly indicated a shift away from urging restraint to diplomatic backing for Israel at the UN and intervention if the Soviets became involved. They coincided with the formation of a national government including the former terrorist and future Prime Minister Menachem Begin with Moshe Dayan as Defence

Minister. With the military determined to launch an attack approved by the new Cabinet on 5 June the Israelis struck. The key to the ensuing, rapid victory was the surprise destruction of the Arab airforces while they were largely still on the ground, which left the Israelis with a marked advantage in reconnaissance, aerial support of ground attacks, and the dropping of paratroops. The USSR must shoulder some of the blame for Arab failures because of their misleading intelligence, and failure to appreciate the consequences of attaching so much importance to assisting the regime in Syria.[22] By the morning of 8 June, on the Egyptian front, Israeli forces had reached the Suez Canal while paratroop and naval forces had captured Sharm el-Sheikh at the bottom of the Straits of Tiran: all the Sinai peninsula was soon in Israeli hands. Meanwhile, 8 June also saw Israeli forces reach the River Jordan, having overrun the whole of the West Bank including the Eastern half of Jerusalem. The victory was completed with an assault, on 9 June, on the Golan Heights, from which the Syrians withdrew the following afternoon. It was an assault surrounded with controversy. The Defence Minister initially opposed the attack and then changed his mind apparently because of intelligence that Nasser was urging a ceasefire to protect Syrian forces; these events coincided with the Israeli sinking of the American spy ship USS *Liberty* and with accusations that the real reason for going to war with Syria was to obtain land for Israeli settlers. The Security Council had called for a ceasefire on 6 June and it was accepted by Egypt, Jordan, and Syria on 9 June. Yet the Israeli assault continued with the USSR threatening to review its relations with Tel Aviv and threatening intervention.[23] As the US Sixth Fleet approached the Washington–Moscow 'hot line' was used for the first time in a crisis. A ceasefire was then agreed which left the Arab armed forces humiliated and the Israelis with new, more defensible military borders that were still short of the original Zionist ideas on the boundaries of a Jewish state. Nasser immediately offered to resign but popular acclamation kept him in power. It was 'the most spectacular military victory in Israel's history',[24] greater even than those of 1948 and 1956. The consequences of the war remain central to the future conflict and its resolution in that the Palestinian issue and the extension

of Israeli settlement began to emerge as the crux of the dispute.

Aftermath: the 'War of Attrition'

In the immediate wake of their success, some observers hoped it would be possible to make a trade of 'land for peace' quite quickly: Israel would return all or most of the conquered territories in return for Arab recognition of its right to existence and to do so in peace. The closure of the Suez Canal, now the front line between Israel and Egypt, increased international pressures to find a solution. In July 1967 a joint Soviet–American UN proposal proved unacceptable to both sides. An Arab summit the following month agreed neither to recognize nor negotiate with Israel, many Arab states broke off diplomatic relations with America, and there was a short-lived Arab oil boycott of Western pro-Israeli states (a precedent for more dramatic action the next time war occurred). In November a 'land for peace' deal did form the essence of a UN Resolution, number 242, which became the basis of all future attempts to achieve an Arab–Israeli settlement (see boxed section). And there were some clandestine Israeli–Jordanian contacts, late in the year, to explore the possibilities of this. But peace proved impossible to achieve. Israel, believing it had acted in self-defence and backed by the US, was reluctant to abandon its conquests without the Arabs *first* guaranteeing the right of Israel to exit. Moreover it, did not wish to give up certain territories, not least East Jerusalem, which held great religious significance for both Muslims and Jews. For their part, the Arabs, backed by the USSR, held Israel guilty of launching an unprovoked attack and continued to refuse to recognize a Jewish state, on what they took to be Arab soil. Thanks to the war about 250,000 Palestinians fled from the West Bank into Jordan, worsening the problem of refugees from lands that the Arabs considered to be 'occupied' by an enemy and increasing the PLO's moral standing in the Arab world. There was even a far-reaching attempt to settle differences within the Arab camp between radicals and conservatives, in that oil-rich Saudi Arabia and Kuwait agreed to provide financial aid to Egypt and Syria in return for Nasser's withdrawal

UN Security Council Resolution 242 of 22 November 1967

Following long discussions about the Arab–Israeli conflict, the Security Council adopted a British-drafted resolution, the full text of which is given below. Resolution 242 was based around the idea of a 'land for peace' arrangement but was carefully worded to try to please all sides. Thus the Israelis were asked to withdraw 'from territories occupied in the recent conflict' but not from *all* the territories—creating a fundamental ambiguity about what a 'land for peace' deal might include.

'The Security Council

EXPRESSING its continuing concern with the grave situation in the Middle East.

EMPHASIZING the inadmissibility of the acquisition of territory by war and the need to work for a just and lasting peace in which every State in the area can live in security.

EMPHASIZING further that all Member States in their acceptance of the Charter of the United Nations have undertaken a commitment to act in accordance with Article 2 of the Charter.

1. AFFIRMS that the fulfilment of Charter principles requires the establishment of a just and lasting peace in the Middle East which should include the application of both the following principles:

   (i) Withdrawal of Israeli armed forces from territories occupied in the recent conflict;

   (ii) Termination of all claims or states of belligerency and respect for and acknowledgement of the sovereignty, territorial integrity and political independence of every State in the area and their right to live in peace within secure and recognized boundaries free from threats or acts of force;

2. AFFIRMS further the necessity

   (a) For guaranteeing freedom of navigation through international waterways in the area;

   (b) For achieving a just settlement of the refugee problem;

   (c) For guaranteeing the territorial inviolability and political independence of every State in the area, through measures including the establishment of demilitarized zones;

1. REQUESTS the Secretary-General to designate a Special Representative to proceed to the Middle East to establish and maintain contacts with the States concerned in order to promote agreement and assist efforts to achieve a peaceful and accepted settlement in accordance with the provisions and principles in this resolution;

2. REQUESTS the Secretary-General to report to the Security Council on the

3. progress of the efforts of the Special Representatives as soon as possible.'

from the Yemen conflict which, by 1970, was effectively resolved in the Saudis' favour. International opinion also became more sympathetic to the Arabs in the late 1960s: 'Israel fought the Six Day War in a favourable climate of world opinion. Its extension of Israeli sovereignty to Arab Jerusalem, and the picture of poor Arab refugees crossing from the West Bank into Jordan . . . soon dispelled this.'[25]

Rather than a peace settlement on the basis of Resolution 242, the next few years in Arab–Israeli relations were characterized by a 'war of attrition', between Egypt and Israel in particular. Arguably, it began in October 1967 with the Egyptian sinking of an Israeli ship, the *Eilat*. It came to include raids, often by Palestinian paramilitary groups, from Jordan, Syria, and Lebanon. In 1968 the Palestinians also began a series of aircraft hijackings which advertised their cause to the world. In 1968 *Al Fatah*,

the largest of the Palestinian groups and boosted by the famous Battle of Karameh (Honour) in which they inflicted significant casualties on the IDF effectively challenged the PLO leadership and transformed the organization into a political front uniting the guerrilla groups bar the PFLP. The following year they won control of the PLO executive committee and the process of unification under *Fatah* leadership was completed by 1970.[26]

Across the Suez Canal the war of attrition initially took the form of limited-scale, punitive raids in the form of shelling, bombing, and commando operations, by one side on the other. Once the war was formally declared by Nasser in March 1969 it assumed new dimensions. In December 1969 the American Secretary of State, William Rogers, launched the 'Rogers Plan', designed to achieve a ceasefire as a prelude to 'land for peace' talks. Almost immediately the Israelis rejected the plan and began actively to oppose it. In January 1970 the Israelis tried to use their air superiority to intimidate Egypt by inflicting unacceptable losses on the Egyptian hinterland but Nasser simply secured better air defences from the Soviets, worsening Israel's aircraft losses. In June Roger launched plan B which was designed to secure a ceasefire, to get acceptance of 242, and start negotiations. In August 1970 a cease-fire was finally agreed in the war of attrition on the basis of Rogers B and for a brief moment peace talks seemed possible, spearheaded by the UN's special envoy Gunnar Jarring. However, once the Egyptians breached the standstill agreement in the ceasefire the Israelis withdrew from the talks. US President, Richard Nixon, let his Secretary of State take responsibility for an initiative that was always likely to fail. Indeed, he even contributed to it by making clear that the Israelis would not be pressured to accept the terms of the original Plan involving a settlement of the refugee problem as well as Israeli withdrawal. Moreover, in September the Arab position was harmed by a civil war in Jordan.

The Jordan Crisis of 1970

Although Jordan had joined in the 1967 war against Israel, the ruler, King Hussein, was a conservative in the Arab camp who retained close links to America and Britain. After the Six Day War, however, Jordan, which already had a substantial Palestinian population, had become the main base of the Palestinian Liberation Organization (PLO), which favoured a more determined, anti-Israeli policy and hoped for Hussein's overthrow as a step to radicalizing the Jordanian government. On 1 September 1970 the latest of several assassination attempts on Hussein sparked off several days of fighting between the PLO and the King's army. This had just begun to die down when, between 6 and 9 September, an extremist group, the Popular Front for the Liberation of Palestine, hijacked four civilian airliners, flew three of them to Amman (Jordan's capital), and took hundreds of passengers—from an assortment of, mainly Western, nationalities—hostage. The hijackings ended without the widely feared bloodbath: the hijackers won the release of several Palestinian

prisoners from Western Europe, the aircraft were blown up and, by the end of the month, all the hostages were released. But the hijack crisis led to a security crackdown on Palestinians living in Israel, to a US naval force being sent to the Lebanese coast, and to a decision by Hussein to force a showdown with the PLO in Jordan.

On 16 September Hussein formed a military government in Amman and the following day civil war broke out with the Palestinians. The royal army had the better of the fighting but on 19–20 September another critical point was reached when neighbouring Syria, sympathetic to the PLO, sent tanks over the border to attack the Jordanians. Hussein was in such difficulties that he told the US and British governments that airstrikes were needed to halt the Syrian advance. The US, reluctant to intervene itself, then encouraged Israel to plan air-raids in support of Hussein. This desperate solution—which in any case had little appeal to Hussein—proved unnecessary however. Jordanian resistance stiffened; the USSR, fearful of a mounting crisis, urged Syria to back down; and on 23 September Syrian tanks were withdrawn, leaving the PLO to be defeated. For Palestinian radicals the month became known as 'Black September'. Instead of overthrowing Hussein, he was now as safely in power as ever, and in 1971 the PLO was forced to switch its headquarters to nearby Lebanon. The Jordanian civil war had only served to highlight Arab divisions and weaknesses, with Syria forced into retreat and the humiliating prospect being raised of Israeli military assistance to an Arab government. To make matters worse, September 1970 ended with the sudden death, on the 28th, of Egypt's President, Gamal Abdul Nasser.

His successor, Anwar Sadat, at first seemed committed to existing policies, whilst the radical cause was strengthened by the coming to power in Syria of a ruthless, determined radical leader, Hafez al Asad. In April 1971 an attempt to revitalize the Rogers Plan came to nothing. The two sides, armed by the superpowers, seemed as far apart as ever and Arab–Israeli tensions would continue to menace world peace. The Arabs were now in a desperate position after yet more humiliation and division as a result of the Six Day War and there seemed little prospect of persuading the protagonists to make a determined effort at peace.

E. **Sub-Saharan Africa: The Nigerian Civil War**

Africa in the 1960s

The bulk of the British empire in Africa had been given independence by 1964, as had all the French and Belgian possessions. In the mid-1960s the break-up of British rule continued apace with the independence of Zambia and Malawi (1964), Gambia (1965), Botswana and Lesotho (1966), and finally Swaziland (1968). Ironically the last European countries to give up their colonies had also been the earliest empire-builders: Spain granted independence to Equatorial Guinea in 1968 but held on in the Spanish Sahara until the mid-1970s; most determined of all, Portugal retained its three African colonies (Angola, Mozambique, and Portuguese Guinea) until 1975. One unusual case was Southern Rhodesia, which had been 'self-governing' and free from Colonial Office control since 1923 under the domination of white settlers and which, in November 1965, declared independence from Britain unilaterally rather than accept majority rule. By then there were about 220,000 Europeans in the country (easily outnumbered by 2.5 million Africans) and led after 1964 by Ian Smith, they were inspired by South Africa's example to believe that white rule could be maintained. 'Rhodesia', as the country was now called, faced strong international condemnation and was subjected to UN economic sanctions after December 1966 but, aided by South Africa and Portugal, Smith maintained his independence until a British-brokered settlement in 1979. Legal independence was only finally won in April 1980, as 'Zimbabwe'.

In the 1960s several challenges faced the newly independent sub-Saharan states. They needed to stabilize their political and administrative systems, develop their economic potential, and find a voice on the world stage. None of this was easy, given that colonial rulers had often given little preparation for independence, had on occasion undermined traditional structures, and relied on methods of 'divide and rule'. Most African states were heavily reliant on a few agricultural products, suffered from widespread illiteracy, poor transport systems,

rapid population growth, and little investment or industry. Efforts to overcome this by Britain and especially France had made litle impact because of the scale of the problems. As these were reduced with independence some states initially managed to find a degree of stability, though generally through the domination of one strong leader, such as Léopold Senghor, who survived as Senegalese President from 1960 to 1981, or Julius Nyerere, who was Tanzania's leader from 1961 to 1985. Both experimented with socialist central planning and like most of Black Africa presided over corruption, poverty, and growing foreign debt. In other countries there were economic problems and profound instability as their new leaders succumbed to military coups. Kwame Nkrumah, who had led Ghana to independence in 1957, was overthrown in 1966 by the army; Milton Obote of Uganda was deposed by the army commander, Idi Amin, in 1971. Although liberal ideals had taken some root in Africa, stability and economic development were often seen as better secured through dictatorial rule. Army officers, being educated as well as armed, frequently saw themselves as potential national saviours.

On the international plane, thirty-two states formed the Organization of African Unity (OAU) at Addis Ababa in 1963, with the aim of ending colonialism and fostering African cooperation, though only within established borders. Although colonial boundaries often made little sense in terms of local geographical and ethnic realities, calling them into question risked provoking instability and bloodshed throughout the continent. Over the following years the OAU mediated solutions to disputes and helped secure a joint African policy on certain issues, not least the condemnation of apartheid. In the United Nations the OAU often found a common interest with the Eastern bloc in attacking apartheid and capitalism. The USSR was seen as a model for rapid, planned development by many African leaders, yet it failed to establish any lasting alliance with even one of them in the 1960s. One of its rivals for influence now was China which tried to enter

African politics in a dramatic way in 1963–4, when Prime Minister Zhou En-lai visited several capitals, setting up a close relationship with Nyerere. But China could offer little economic aid, and it was a lack of financial resources which also harmed Soviet policy. Ironically, both were easily outspent by the former colonial powers. The French, helped by European Community funds, were able to retain a close relationship with almost all their former colonies whilst, among ex-British colonies even Nkrumah, a leading Pan-Africanist, kept Ghana in the Commonwealth until his overthrow. Indeed, so limited was the Soviet and Chinese threat in Africa that, under Johnson at least, the US showed little interest in the continent. One area where the USSR and US had competed for influence in the early 1960s was the Congo (see Chapter 8, B), but by 1965 the situation there had stabilized, under the pro-American dictator General Joseph Mobutu. The Congo conflict was an example of the danger of fragmentation within African states, made more dangerous by ethnic division, economic inequalities and external intervention. Similar factors came into play a few years later in Nigeria.

Roots of the Biafran Secession

When Nigeria gained its independence in October 1960, it seemed in a more promising position than many African states. It was only the second British colony on the continent (after Ghana) to become independent; it was one of the largest African countries in geographical area and, at almost 55 million, the largest sub-Saharan state in terms of population; and, with oil and gas resources discovered in the Niger river delta in the 1960s, it was potentially wealthy. It also had a federal Constitution, which sought to balance regional interests, and was led by a coalition government under Sir Abubakar Balewa, who had led a pre-independence administration since 1957. But, however coherent and well ruled it looked on the surface, Nigeria was a colonial creation with deep internal divisions on ethnic, religious, social, and economic lines. South-west Nigeria, including the capital, Lagos, was populated by the Yoruba; the south-east mainly by the Ibos; the north by the Hausa. The British had

divided Nigeria into North and South for administrative purposes as early as 1899, and not without reason. The North was principally a dry grassland region, populated by Muslims with a long history of their own political structures, and it included slightly over half the population. The South was characterized by jungle and, especially around the Niger delta, swamplands; in the past its people had been mainly animist, but many had embraced Christianity after the British arrived. The South had been divided into Eastern and Western regions in 1939 and by the 1950s three main political parties existed which largely reflected the threefold administrative and ethnic divisions of the country, a division which always threatened to tear Nigeria apart.

Abubakar's three-party coalition at the time of independence was made up of his own Northern People's Congress, another (smaller) northern party, and the Nigerian Democratic Party of Nmandi Azikiwe, the 'father of Nigerian independence', who had long hoped to become a truly national leader but whose following was mainly among the Ibos in the south-east. The Eastern and Western regions were both resentful of an electoral system which gave the North 174 seats in the 320 seat Federal House, and there were bitter disputes over the census figures on which this system was based, but the coalition suggested that a deep political divide in the country was not inevitable. True, the Western leader, Obafemi Awolowo, leader of the Action Group Party, condemned Abubakar's administration and chose to lead the opposition in parliament. The Action Group was soon divided over the wisdom of excluding itself from office, however, and in 1962 Awolowo was imprisoned. His deputy, Samuel Akinfola, then became the chief figure in Western Nigeria and was more ready to work with Abubakar. Fresh elections in late 1964, and Western regional elections in 1965, provoked more problems, with complaints of rigged results, popular disturbances, and growing ethnic tension especially between the Ibos in the south-east and the Yorubas in the south-west. Abubakar's government survived uneasily and he bickered with Azikiwe, who had assumed the Presidency in 1963 when Nigeria declared itself a republic. There was, then, a 'cumulative progression towards . . . internal collapse,'[27] yet none of these events really prepared

Nigerians for the bloodbath which occurred in January 1966 when Abubakar, Akinfola, and other leading politicians were assassinated in a sudden military coup.

The coup was led by mainly-Ibo, middle-ranking officers following disturbances in Northern Nigeria in which Ibos had been attacked. Army officers were among those targetted by the plotters, reflecting differences within the army. The coup brought General Johnson Ironsi, an Ibo, into power. He was not a coup leader, indeed he may have been intended as a victim of it; rather he was one of several senior officers who stepped forward to end the bloodshed. He soon alienated Northerners however, by promoting Ibos to key positions and seeking political reforms that would limit Northern predominance, forming a more centralized state, and in July 1966 he was overthrown and murdered in a second coup. The new leader was General Yakubu Gowan who, although a Northerner, was from a minority group (the Ngas), a Christian by religion, and hoped to hold the country together through constitutional changes to the federal system, perhaps including the subdivision of the three main regions into smaller units, which would weaken Northern power. In September 1966, however, there was further violence in the Northern region in which several thousand Ibos were massacred and tens of thousands became refugees. After this constitutional talks ground to a halt and the ambitious Military Governor of the Eastern region, Colonel Emeka Ojukwu, who was contemptuous of Gowan, began to plan an independent state, arguing that this was the only way for Ibos to find security. 'The events of September had given most Ibos a strong attachment to the idea of secession.'[28] Talks designed to prevent a secession failed, non-Ibos in the Eastern region were attacked, and on 27 May 1967 Ojukwu proclaimed its independence, calling it 'Biafra'. He was confident that the Ibos were united behind him, that he had an efficient, if small, army, and that he could finance his new state because of the oil and gas reserves that were concentrated in Biafra. The Federal government, in contrast, seemed divided into Northern and Western factions, and was initially reluctant to use force. Belatedly, Gowan had announced a scheme to divide Nigeria into twelve smaller regions, but (since this would have reduced the predominance of the Ibos in the Eastern Region) it may even have precipitated a final breach. On 5 July full-scale war broke out between the Federal government and the secessionist region.

Civil War and External Intervention

Biafra's best chance of winning the war came in its early months when Ojukwu's army struck westwards in a series of rapid advances, which came within 150 miles of the Federal capital, Lagos. The offensive surprised Gowan, who had expected Biafra to adopt a defensive strategy, but he refused to negotiate and the crisis soon passed. In August the Biafran advance had stalled and by early 1968 they were on the defensive. Arguably Ojukwu's one chance of victory had already passed and by mid-1968 it seemed only a matter of time before he must admit defeat. Not only had Federal forces driven the Biafrans out of Western Nigeria, they had also advanced from Northern Nigeria and seized the Biafran capital, Enugu, as early as October 1967; even more seriously, they had landed on the southern coast and, helped by non-Ibos in the region, had cut off Biafran access to the sea, as well as seizing control of oil-producing areas. Port Harcourt, the Biafrans' chief harbour, fell in May 1968. Ojukwu was reduced to holding a land-locked enclave between the Niger and Cross rivers, amounting to less than a quarter of Eastern Nigeria, and was effectively blockaded. The Federal government had been able to exploit its larger population to expand its army rapidly and, whilst Federal generals showed no particular offensive flair, sheer numbers helped them overcome the Biafrans who showed more stubbornness than military ability.

The reason the Nigerian civil war lasted beyond 1968 had much to do with the impact of external factors. Initially it seemed that, in terms of foreign support, the Federals had as clear an edge as they had in population numbers. The OAU tried to mediate between the two sides on several occasions in 1967–9, as did individual leaders like Haile Selassie of Ethiopia, but the OAU confirmed its established policy of only settling the civil war on the basis of maintaining Nigeria's existing borders. Some African states actively supported the

Federals, with Egypt being particularly important for loaning pilots. The United Nations did not become involved in the dispute because it treated it as an 'internal' issue. Three permanent members of the Security Council strongly supported the Gowan government however, and significantly they bridged the East–West divide (a reminder that not all international disputes necessarily reflected Cold War divisions). The USSR backed Gowan with aid and arms not only because he cooperated with pro-Soviet politicians in Lagos and was viewed as 'progressive' in his policies, but also because the Soviets were keen to work with OAU members in general and did not want to be seen breaking up an African state. Britain supported the Federals because, as the ex-colonial power it was committed to Nigeria's existence, it was already the country's largest arms supplier, and it wanted to limit Moscow's hold over Gowan. The United States also decided that Nigeria's survival as a single entity was best for African stability, but it had enough problems elsewhere in the world without concerning itself too much with Biafra and it let Britain take the leading role in arming and advising the Federals. 'From beginning to end the State Department . . . took the view that the conflict fell within the British sphere of influence.'[29]

Despite such considerable backing for Gowan, it was Ojukwu who realized that his survival increasingly depended on his ability to win allies and sympathy outside Nigeria. From the start he had support from three right-wing governments, whose interests in southern Africa pointed them to dividing Black Africans wherever possible: South Africa, Rhodesia, and Portugal (still with its colonies in Black Africa) all provided Biafra with financial support to buy arms. However, it was de Gaulle's France which surprisingly emerged as Ojukwu's saviour in 1968–9. It broke its own arms embargo to provide Biafra with modern armaments channelled secretly via two former French colonies, the Ivory Coast and Gabon, both of whom also recognized Biafra diplomatically, thereby breaching OAU solidarity. 'De Gaulle's anglophobia, and his determination to initiate foreign policies . . . independent of Washington and London, naturally predisposed him to the Biafrans.'[30] But there was more behind his policy than this. The French had long wanted to

weaken Nigeria and outbid the British for support in the region, and in a sense de Gaulle could not lose by meddling in the civil war: if Biafra won, then France would have an oil-rich, grateful ally; but if the Federal government won, it had already shown itself anxious to strike a trade deal with the European Community, on which French views would be decisive. French arms supplies not only allowed Ojukwu to halt the Federal advance by the end of 1968, they also allowed a Biafran counter-offensive to be launched towards Port Harcourt in early 1969. Another vital factor after late 1968, which won Biafra sympathy from liberal opinion throughout the Western world, was Ojukwu's ability to exaggerate Biafran suffering through a remarkable propaganda campaign. By accusing the Nigerian airforce of indiscriminate bombing, arguing that the Federals prevented humanitarian aid supplies and claiming that, by late 1969, over a million Biafrans were starving, Ojukwu created an image of a Federal government bent on 'genocide' through mass starvation, and he won considerable public support even in countries like Britain and America, whose governments were, of course, backing Gowan. Foreign concern 'resulted primarily from humanitarian rather than from political or ideological concerns. Barely a year after Biafra's secession . . . the war ranked as the most important foreign issue in public opinion surveys throughout Western Europe, and it was . . . second only to Vietnam among . . . Americans.[31] Even some other OAU states, Tanzania and Zambia, decided to recognize Biafra because of their concerns about a humanitarian disaster. By then Ojukwu could claim an unholy alliance of supporters from right-wing authoritarians to radical leftists.

Ojukwu's propaganda claims had some basis. Bombings of civilians and starvation certainly occurred and there was a long-running problem over relief supplies to Biafra. But there was no 'genocide' against Ibos. Red Cross estimates later put the total deaths for both sides in the war at 50,000, well below Ojukwu's claims and by 1975 the Nigerian population was estimated at 69 million, suggesting a healthy growth rate since independence. Aid relief was disrupted due to arguments between the two sides for which both were responsible: the Federals were ready to allow humanitarian supplies to Biafra, but only during daytime and along

Federal-controlled routes, so that no arms could be smuggled through at the same time; but Ojukwu wanted night-time flights, outside Federal control, partly because he *was* smuggling arms, partly because he did not want Biafrans to see that Gowan was allowing aid, and partly because he feared the Federals would use airflights as cover for an attack. The same distrust pervaded attempts to secure a ceasefire: the Biafrans wanted any ceasefire to be a respite, allowing them time to prepare for a revived struggle; the Federals were determined on a lasting agreement which ended the secession.

Eventually, Gowan decided he must overrun the remaining Biafran enclave. In late December 1969 Federal forces launched an offensive which split the enclave in two, then in January 1970 they drove across both halves, as Ojukwu fled into exile. In this final stage it has been argued that, for Biafra, 'the most important factor which undermined the will to resist was the waning fear of genocide.' Despite Ojukwo's claims there was simply no evidence that genocide was the Federals' aim.[32] Gowan made a point of following a policy of reconciliation after victory, allowing food aid into Biafra and further exposing Ojukwu's claims of genocide as lies. The Federal victory was complete, with no need for political compromises, a fact which helped ensure that there were no further attempts at secession. It also, along with earlier events in the Congo, helped other African states defend the legitimacy of their own borders, despite internal ethnic divisions. For Nigeria, however, problems such as inequality of wealth, an inept, corrupt administration, and political instability—focused on the army—continued. In 1975 it did become, thanks to its population size and oil wealth, the key player in the Economic Community of West African States (ECOWAS), an organization designed to foster trade and development in the region. But that same year Gowan was overthrown in a coup. Attempts to return to civilian rule, in the early 1980s and the mid-1990s, proved short-lived.

NOTES

1. Frank Niess, *A Hemisphere to Itself* (Zed Books, London, 1990), 176.

2. Walter LaFeber, *Inevitable Revolutions: the US in Central America* (Norton, New York, 2nd edn., 1993), 159.

3. David F. Schmitz, *Thank God They're on our Side: the US and Right-Wing Dictatorships* (University of North Carolina Press, Chapel Hill, 1999), 276–7.

4. Abraham Lowenthal, *The Dominican Intervention* (Johns Hopkins University Press, Baltimore, 1995), 153.

5. Frank Moya Pons, 'The Dominican Republic since 1930', in Leslie Bethell (ed.), *The Cambridge History of Latin America, VII* (Cambridge University Press, Cambridge, 1990), 527.

6. *New York Times*, 9 May 1965, quoted by Walter LaFeber, op. cit., 158.

7. Joseph S. Tulchin, 'US Relations with Latin America', in Warren Cohen and Nancy Tucker (eds), *Lyndon Johnson Confronts the World* (Cambridge University Press, New York, 1994), 233–4.

8. Nicholas Tarling, *The Fall of Imperial Britain in South-East Asia* (Oxford University Press, New York, 1993), 201.

9. C. M. Turnbull, *A History of Singapore* (Oxford University Press, Kuala Lumpur, 1977), 290.

10. J. D. Legge, *Indonesia* (Prentice-Hall, Sydney, 1980), 162–3.

11. Robert J. McMahon, *The Limits of Empire: the US and South-East Asia since World War II* (Columbia University Press, New York, 1999), 123.

12. Stanley Wolpert, *Nehru* (Oxford University Press, Oxford, 1996), 466.

13. Altaf Gauhar, *Ayub Khan* (Oxford University Press, Karachi, 1996), 223.

14. H. W. Brands, *The Wages of Globalism* (Oxford University Press, New York, 1995), 139.

15. G. W. Choudhury, *The Last Days of United Pakistan* (Hurst, London, 1974), 231.

16. Surjit Mansingh, *India's Search for Power* (Sage, New Delhi, 1984), 223.

17. Bassam Tabi, *Conflict and War in the Middle East* (Macmillan, London, 1998), 68.

18. Abba Eban, *Personal Witness* (Putnam, New York, 1992), 353.

19. Avi Shlaim, *The Iron Wall: Israel and the Arab World* (Allen Lane, London, 2000), 235.

20. Yezid Sayigh and Avi Shlaim (eds), *The Cold War and the Middle East* (Clarendon Press, Oxford, 1997), 281. Edgar O'Ballance, *The Third Arab–Israeli War* (Faber, London, 1972), 278.

21. Mark Tessler, *A History of the Israeli–Palestinian Conflict* (Indiana University Press, Bloomington, 1994), 387–97.

22. Avi Shlaim, op. cit., 237.

23. Avi Shlaim, op. cit., 248–9.

24. Ibid., 241.

25. Ritchie Ovendale, *The Origins of the Arab–Israeli Wars* (Longman, London, 1992), 208.

26. Tessler, op. cit., 425–9.

27. A. H. M. Kirk-Greene, *Crisis and Conflict in Nigeria: I, 1966–7* (Oxford University Press, Oxford, 1971), 23.

28. Elizabeth Isichei, *A History of Nigeria* (Longman, London, 1983), 473.

29. Suzanne Cronje, *The World and Nigeria: the Diplomatic History of the Biafran War* (Sidgwick & Jackson, London, 1972), 322.

30. Ibid., 323.

31. John J. Stremlan, *The International Politics of the Nigerian Civil War* (Princeton University Press, Princeton, 1977), xi–xii.

32. John de St Jorre, *The Nigerian Civil War* (Hodder & Stoughton, London, 1972), 408.

Part IV

The Détente Era
1972–1980

INTRODUCTION

The 'era of negotiations', which Richard Nixon had proclaimed in 1969, finally emerged 3 years later with his visits to Beijing and Moscow, the signature of a major nuclear arms agreement (SALT I), promises of increased US–Soviet trade and, even, an attempt to regulate superpower behaviour during crises. Between 1972 and 1975 the Soviet leader, Leonid Brezhnev, met Nixon and his successor, Gerald Ford, on five occasions and there were advances, too, in Europe with a continent-wide agreement on security, signed at Helsinki in 1975. Yet, even in 1973 there was a severe super-power confrontation—the worst since Cuba eleven years before—over the Middle East and throughout the decade East–West relations were troubled by a series of regional problems in the less developed world, from Angola and the Horn of Africa to South-East Asia and Afghanistan. The attempt to stabilise East–West relations, which had begun in the 1960s with the Test Ban Treaty and the hot-line agreement, broke down into acrimony by 1979, and in 1980, following the Soviet invasion of Afghanistan, there was a return to Cold War confrontation.

The Origins and Nature of Détente

The 1970s were the Era of Détente, but there was, and is, great debate over what exactly détente signified. This debate also affects any explanation of the apparent rise and fall of détente and of its relation to the changing international system with the increasing signs of multipolarity emerging at the end of the 1960s. There was, in the early 1970s at least, an undoubted attempt to reach a broad range of agreements (from arms and borders to commerce and scientific research) and to establish more formal modes of behaviour (where previously such modes of behaviour had been tentative and unwritten). Not only was the propaganda war between the two sides relaxed and high-level meetings held, but also limits were put on nuclear arsenals, the division of Europe was mutually recognized, and a plethora of personal contacts built up. Yet, in contrast to the relaxation of tension in the late 1980s, the 1970s did not end in the disintegration of one bloc. Throughout the decade both sides remained ideologically far apart, conventional arms reductions by NATO and the Warsaw Pact were impossible to achieve, and the superpowers continued their dangerous rivalry for influence in Asia and Africa. Why these processes occurred can be interpreted in a number of ways as attempts to end the expensive military confrontation, or to manage the emergent multipolar balance of global power, or as attempts to preserve or destroy American hegemony.

One reason why the US and USSR may have felt able to pursue détente was that they believed they could safely enter agreements whilst balancing the power of the other. The Americans were still far superior to the Soviets in terms of industrial power, trade, and technology, even though the Soviets were out-producing them in some basic items such as coal and steel. The Soviets were now also in front of the Americans regarding numbers of missile launchers, but the US had many more nuclear warheads and a larger navy. While the Vietnam War sapped national confidence, inflation, economic decline relative to major trading rivals in Europe and Japan and, in 1973–4, the Watergate scandal also hinted at American weakness. Yet NATO held together even though it was troubled by France's continued distance from the alliance, arguments over arms expenditure and political turmoil in some member states, especially Portugal and Italy.

In Eastern Europe, Nicolae Ceauşescu's Romania continued to steer an independent course, but the Warsaw Pact held together under Soviet domination and experienced no major upheavals. Even Ceauşescu did not defect from Moscow in the way Tito and Mao had earlier. The Soviets were aware of their inferiority in warhead numbers but given the belief in Mutual Assured Destruction (MAD) that hardly seemed to matter. Moreover, their nuclear arsenal continued to be upgraded, with ever-larger intercontinental missiles and more accurate SS-20s in Europe that gave the impression of increasing military strength and nuclear parity. Under Marshal Andrei Grechko (Defence Minister in 1967–76), conventional armed forces also greatly expanded but there were problems with unreliable equipment, low morale, and alcoholism among conscripts. A 'blue water' navy and improved air transport gave the Soviets the ability to act in the less developed world at a time when, thanks to Vietnam, the US were more restrained. The USSR had truly become a global power yet was facing not only the Western challenge but dealing with the hostility of the Chinese that could be exploited by the US to the disadvantage of Moscow . In short, both superpowers had problems and strengths which could be balanced or exploited by a process of détente.

Détente and the International System

This mixture of fear and ambition had long been a feature of both sides' approach to the Cold War, but what may be seen as new was the more complicated relations that Washington and Moscow had to conduct with the rest of the world. On the other hand, perhaps little had changed. A multipolar world may have emerged in the 1960s, and China might be an important 'third power' in international affairs, but the strategic balance in the world may still be seen as bipolar and US–Soviet rivalry continued to impact on all parts of the globe. China's anti-Soviet policy was of great concern to the Kremlin, but China's nuclear arsenal was puny, it faced political turmoil in the mid-1970s, and it did not achieve a normalization of relations with America until the end of the decade. It could therefore be that détente was simply another phase of the old bipolar relationship. Yet multipolarity, Chinese power, relative US economic decline vis-à-vis the European Economic Community, differences within the Western military bloc, and instability in the less developed world could be seen as new challenges to an old order. It was either the same old bipolar Cold War world, with a repeat of the attempts in the mid-1950s to reduce the dangers of nuclear weapons, or a new and uncertain world for both superpowers to confront afresh in the light of new problems.

The Origins of Détente and the New Problems and Challenges of the 1970s

Interpretations of détente emerging from the same bipolar Cold War world can easily explain détente as the replacement of confrontation with a more trusting relationship that could lead, in Western eyes, to greater economic contacts and the adoption of liberal values on a universal scale. The Soviets, for their part, with Brezhnev politically secure at home and the country militarily stronger abroad, may have felt able to act with greater boldness and confidence vis-à-vis Washington. On the other hand, it is arguable that they were now preparing to move to winning the Cold War in ideological terms while, as in the past, reducing the risk of hot war through détente. They could then also address some of the problems in the domestic economy and society through cooperation with the West.

If the idea of radical international change and new challenges to the superpowers is accepted, then détente can be interpreted as driven by those very uncertainties that were forcing the adversaries together in an attempt to manage the changed international environment. Each sought to do so while preserving or developing their primary roles as important actors in world politics. As each became more aware of their respective strengths and weaknesses the incentives grew to work together to exploit the new situation. For the Soviets the fear of China may have been paramount, or the need for Western technology, or the desire to support wars of national liberation for ideological reasons while avoiding nuclear war.

While both may have had a similar interest in détente their precise reasons for pursuing it differed. For the Americans it offered the immediate and important possibility of Soviet cooperation in extracting them from Vietnam. As the declining hegemon, or the hegemon under threat, the Americans also had every reason to look beyond the old-style Cold War confrontation to the more long-term control of Soviet behaviour via cooperation. There were power political and economic reasons for wooing the Soviets into an acceptance of the global status quo which would preserve American dominance. In this scenario the opening to China was seen by Henry Kissinger, Nixon's National Security Adviser, as heralding the possibility of a return to old-fashioned power politics. Ironically this was the world in which Kissinger appeared to envisage American actions taking place free from bipolar Cold War considerations. Yet when the Soviets and others acted forcefully he continued to see the old Cold War bipolarity as the prime explanation for local conflicts. In many ways this mix of old goals and new circumstances characterized the world of the early to mid-1970s which was experiencing dramatic developments in the nature of superpower relations and the importance of economic power.

The Economics of Détente and the Collapse of the Post-War Economic System

Economics was perhaps the area where the United States and the Soviet Union were most under challenge. The Vietnam war and the oil price increase associated with the 1973 Arab–Israel war created severe domestic differences in the United States and much of the Western world. The strain on the American economy caused by the Vietnam War was serious when the 1970s began with the US balance of payments massively in the red and the dollar—and hence the Bretton Woods system—on the verge of collapse. Towards the end of his first term Nixon made an extraordinary speech revealing American concerns, particularly about the new economic forces at work, even before the oil shocks. He referred to the 'five great economic superpowers' (the US, Russia, Japan, Western Europe, and China), 'four of whom challenge us on every front'. 'Because economic power will be the key to other kinds of power . . . in the last third of this century', and since domestic and foreign policies were so interlinked, Americans had to discipline themselves or face the 'decadence' that had brought ruin to Greece and Rome.[1]

What they did face was first the end of Bretton Woods system of fixed (but flexible) exchange rates with the end of the dollar's convertibility against gold on which it was based in 1971. And then in the wake of the US supplying Israel with arms during the 1973 War a temporary embargo of OPEC oil exports from the Middle East and a dramatic increase in the price of oil. OPEC (Organization of Oil Exporting Countries) had been fighting since the 1960s to secure higher prices and better returns for its thirteen members seven of whom were Arab countries. The massive price rises hit the poorest countries hardest, produced enormous inflationary pressures, led Western banks, flooded with oil revenues, to be over eager in lending to less developed countries, and posed large questions about the problems of the international economy.

Already in the 1960s difficulties were being experienced by newly independent countries in successfully developing their economies along standard Western lines. Diversification was proving difficult and the returns on the production of primary products, especially tropical ones, were falling. The terms of trade were moving against primary producers (it now took the sale of more produce to purchase the same quantities of manufactures goods). As the Bretton Woods system passed into history, in the developed world a set of ideas based around Ricardian concepts and the value and importance of market forces began to gain credence. The problems were thus blamed on government intervention which had brought social reform after 1945 and shifted the balance between workers and owners of capital in favour of the former. Now it was claimed that the unbridled pursuit of wealth through the seizing of market opportunities would bring greater benefits to everyone. Even if the wealthy benefited more initially, this wealth would trickle down as the market rewarded all who were able to compete within it. If only the heavy hand of the state, often deemed to be deeply corrupt as well as incompetent, could be removed and even the kind of controls involved in fixed exchange rates terminated, then the world economy could recover. National governments merely had to act in accordance with enabling market forces to operate. Marx may have seen men as born free but everywhere in chains, but the neoliberals saw market forces in the same light.

At the same time other ideas challenged both the diagnosis of the world's economic problems and the cure. Particularly in the less developed world, problems were blamed on the workings of capitalism where any surplus/profit is not divided solely amongst the producers of that surplus. The profit/surplus allocated to shareholders as owners of capital was seen as maximizing their gains at the expense of those directly involved in the production process. Likewise in the international context foreign investment and the operations of multinational companies were seen as essentially transferring resources away from those poorer countries and their producers. The latter, whether workers or peasants, lacked the ability to influence world market prices unlike consumers and purchasers in the developed world who could control or influence such prices. In other words there were forces acting in the international economy system which, if not checked by state action (assuming any such action could be effective), would prevent development taking place in the less well-off countries. Variously attributing this to the legacy of colonialism, the competitive disadvantage from entering late into manufacturing, or to the extension of the global division of labour, dependency theorists and world system theorists saw the structure of the international economy as accentuating the divisions between the rich and the poor.

Neither interpretation of the problem is entirely accurate. Some countries outside Europe and North America did develop but other countries got poorer, and the issue is whether or not this can be explained primarily with reference to the specific circumstances of the particular country. The fact that the issue became more noticeable in the 1970s was connected to the growing shift in the balance of world trade as well as the general world economic problems. Whereas trade involving manufactures formed 17 per cent of world trade in the late 1940s by the start of the 1970s it constituted 58 per cent and the increasing strength of the developed world was behind the calls for a New International Economic Order. The concern with the less developed world culminated in the high-profile Brandt report in 1980 but then became buried by the growing dominance of neo-liberalism in the 1980s.

The communist bloc was certainly not free from the troubles afflicting the capitalist world. As the march of technology quickened and sophisticated consumer goods were in growing demand, the Soviet economy was finding it difficult to adapt or innovate. In the 1990s it was revealed to have stagnated around 1975 and to have been about one-sixth the size of America's. Increasingly inefficient and unresponsive to consumer needs, the weakness of the Soviet economy meant that Moscow could not match America's generosity with financial aid and technological assistance to the less developed world even if it could provide education, arms, and raw materials to its allies. Surprisingly the USSR was the world's largest oil producer in the 1970s with much of it shipped to Eastern Europe. But this only illustrated the drain on the Soviet economy for ideological reasons and the political need to maintain the unity of the Eastern bloc under Soviet leadership.

Different Expectations of Détente

These problems and those faced by the Americans as a consequence of the Vietnam War gave both sides a similar economic rationale for détente, not least because of the cost benefits of arms reductions. Despite this the fundamental problem for détente was that both sides interpreted it and its desired outcomes very differently. In particular the expectations of détente's effect on the other side were also radically different. For the Soviets, it can be suggested that the overriding goal was the continuation of the quest to achieve more recognition of their claim to equality with the US. Formal agreements such as SALT I, indicating that there was some form of parity between the two countries' arms levels, might certainly produce this. Involvement in the resolution of regional conflicts, as in the Middle East, would also provide recognition of a dual peacemaking role for both adversaries. It would involve a new and more prominent international role for the Soviets but one reflecting their commitment to a peaceful world and the reduced hostility towards the Americans. The USSR and Warsaw Pact would balance the US and NATO in Europe and in the arms race, while events continued to unfold elsewhere in Moscow's favour. Brezhnev, who became closely identified with détente as he secured his political predominance in Moscow during 1971, was allegedly determined to put superpower relations on a stable, equal, peaceful basis while maintaining strong armed forces, weakening domestic opposition, and preserving support for Soviet leadership of international communism.

A less charitable interpretation is that the Soviets saw détente in realist terms as another means of obtaining power and influence at the expense of the Americans either by gaining an advantage in arms control or in the creation of communist satellites in the less developed world. The Soviets allegedly sought to win the ideological battle by aiding wars of national liberation and therefore they remained firmly committed to victory in the Cold War. Thus in line with the precepts of 'peaceful coexistence' East–West competition would continue in ideological terms. This could be done because the USSR was still an attractive ally for less developed states. Even if few of them were conventionally Marxist-Leninist, they did wish to assert their independence of the West and to find an alternative economic model to capitalism. However economically inefficient, corrupt and stagnant the Soviet system had become, and however divided the communist world, Marxist doctrine continued to influence Soviet foreign policy. A belief in class struggle, an urge to help fellow Marxists where possible, and a confidence in the historic inevitability of communist triumph still guided the Kremlin.

We now know that there were considerable differences in the Kremlin about détente. Marshal Grechko and Brezhnev argued over the resources to be devoted to the military and several Politburo members doubted the wisdom of relying on

Western trade and technology. Moreover, the wisdom of supporting national liberation movements seeking revolutionary change was questioned. Brezhnev took a lot of convincing that the risks and dangers of the policy were worth it, but Andropov was committed to maintaining this ideological component of Soviet foreign policy and eventually won the argument. Another indication that ideology was still a major influence on how foreign policy was formulated in the Kremlin.[2]

For the Americans led by Nixon and Kissinger, who became identified with the 'new' policy, détente and ideological competition were seen in precisely the opposite terms. Détente was clearly expected to stop the Soviets from supporting revolutionary movements, and lead them to behave as a 'normal', non-revolutionary state. Those who interpret American policy in a favourable light believe Nixon and Kissinger were also determined that, in contrast to the mid-1950s, détente should involve more than an improved international atmosphere. Concrete agreements, of benefit to both sides, would help commit the Soviets to cooperation and the world would be a safer place through the establishment of arms control. Making the Soviets reasonable was based on the expectation that the Soviets would accept the American definition of 'reasonableness' in return for the US offer of aid and technology transfers. If it was made clear that Moscow could only expect to gain from détente under the principle of 'linkage', which Kissinger defined as the formal acceptance of greater equality of status for the Kremlin in return for the USSR restraining itself in the less developed world, progress would be made. Improved Sino–American relations could be used as an additional lever against the Soviets, forcing them to respect the international order.

A more critical analysis of American aims would define them in terms of ambition and the maintenance of American hegemony, which perhaps were precursors of the future policy of post-Cold War administrations. Détente was the way of getting the Soviets and the Chinese to cooperate in the preservation of a world order run primarily for the advantage of the United States and which was now under threat. The key aim was to manipulate these relations to maximize benefits for the Americans, much in the same way, critics argued, as Kissinger approached the SALT negotiations. The aim here, allegedly, was not the preservation of peace and stability but the maintenance of the American nuclear superiority by exploiting the development of MIRV (Multiple Independent Re-entry Vehicle) missiles. The Soviets lacked the ability to produce missiles with multiple warheads (although they would soon develop it) which on re-entering the atmosphere would separate from the missile itself and independently guide themselves to a variety of different targets.

Similarly, bad relations between the Soviets and Chinese could be exploited to induce Moscow at least to accept the American conception of linkage, which would increasingly come to demand more and more from the Soviets in line with American wishes. Ultimately under President Carter the very basis of Soviet domestic policy would be undermined as human rights became more of an issue in the continuation of American aid. In the less developed world the aim of stopping Soviet support for revolution was, allegedly, to maintain influence for the benefit of Western world. Not so much for economic benefits, but the ideological superiority that enhanced the status and influence of the US and the leading capitalist powers who claimed to support freedom and democracy. For the Americans too, détente can be interpreted as simply another way of winning the Cold War. Moreover, the whole idea that the Soviets should cease supporting left-wing groups seeking to change the domestic status quo in Angola and Ethiopia smacked of hypocrisy. Whatever the nature and extent of Soviet interference in parts of Africa and Asia, it cannot be denied that American interference in Angola, Chile, or Indo-China was equal to, if not more consequential for the internal situations in other countries than any Soviet involvement. The conflicting views as to what détente should mean for the less developed world may well have been the most important factor in influencing its demise.

The Achievements of Détente?

Perhaps the main question is whether the world became a safer and more stable place during and after the détente process. The SALT treaties were important steps in arms control although they did not formalize nuclear parity and American nuclear superiority was retained even if the Soviets had significantly closed the gap. The bad atmosphere created by propaganda and disinformation campaigns was significantly reduced. Increased trade, with the American provision of grain to the Soviet Union leading the way, began the opening of the Eastern bloc through economic contacts.

The Kremlin believed that East–West agreements, like SALT and Helsinki, were valuable in themselves, that both sides gained from arms control and European stability, and that America should support these policies without insisting on 'linkage'. In the less developed world it was quite acceptable for ideological rivalry to continue. For Marxists it was inevitable that wars of national liberation would occur and that the balance of power should gradually shift against the Imperialists. From the Soviet perspective détente was successful in that it allowed communism to advance without risking general war. The important point was that regional crises should not raise the danger of nuclear war or threaten Soviet security. In that sense détente for Moscow was a success. The Kremlin believed that by maintaining the Eastern bloc, securing nuclear parity, and winning allies in the less developed world, they had actually 'forced' Washington into détente. They were determined in fact to be formally recognized by America as an equal in world affairs. Such recognition would help win more allies abroad, demonstrate that the communist model of development could match capitalism, and ought also to give the USSR a voice in resolving the world's regional problems. In that sense from the Soviet perspective détente was a failure. Moreover, ultimately the greater access to consumer goods, the emphasis on human rights, and the commitment to cooperation may have paved the way for the changes in the Eastern bloc which brought the collapse of communism and the end of the Cold War.

From the American perspective détente showed that the Kremlin was not ready to accept US restraints on its behaviour and that it did not respect the principles of linkage. Success would have been making Moscow behave in an acceptable fashion compatible with American perceptions of world order and US influence. The establishment of a code of conduct in the 'basic principles' agreement devised at the 1972 Moscow summit was undoubtedly a success but it remained vague even if the Helsinki agreement reflected an agreement on American-type values. After that, from 1975 much of the burden of maintaining détente fell on the SALT II negotiations which, along with concerns that détente was undermining American power, ran into domestic opposition in the United States which heightened a sense of failure.

Perhaps the fact that the Americans expected more from changed Soviet behaviour was crucial in terms of détente's ultimate success or failure. Whereas the Soviets saw détente as allowing their goals to be realized without America changing its behaviour, the Americans required that cooperation embody a change in Soviet behaviour both at home and abroad. With Moscow seeing the capitalists as still seeking communism's destruction, the preservation of the USSR itself remained Moscow's priority. If the Americans were committed to better relations, then for Moscow all that was required was the acceptance of their support for wars of national liberation

Overall in the short term it is difficult to detect any major benefits produced by détente. The prospect of the world becoming a less threatening place was to be followed by the increased hostility of the late 1970s and early 1980s. Robert Keohane in his book *After Hegemony* sees the 1970s as the end of American hegemony and the emergence of new forms of cooperation in the Western world. By focusing not so much on détente and the Cold War as on the new challenges of cooperation facing the Western world Keohane sees the hand of progress and the benefits of cooperation being realized. Particularly in economic terms cooperation in a multipolar world might be more problematic because this new world signified the end of American hegemony. Yet the passing of US-dominated institutions such as those created at Bretton Woods, through which hegemony had been exercised, meant new opportunities in the 1970s. New institutions, now defined less as concrete organizations but as regimes or abstract sets of expectations and common practices could be the beginning of a new international order. In an age where cooperation began to replace confrontation arguably they formed the background to a process which ended with the Soviet leadership desiring to adopt some of the ideas and practices of the Western world. Before that however there was to be the collapse of détente and the reversion to an old form of confrontation.

Crisis in the Less Developed World

The opportunities for greater cooperation that arguably were there in the developed world following the collapse of US hegemony and the rethinking it provoked were certainly not present in the less developed world. The apparent successes of British and French decolonization were being undermined by political and economic problems facing much of the developed world. Stability through pro-Western regimes was not to be so easily achieved. Rivalry between and within new states was accompanied by wars, weak governments, military coups, and instability. Moreover, because this instability was associated with revolutionary or left-wing movements it was at the heart of détente and its failure. One can see these challenges emerging in a period of domestic uncertainty for the leading Western powers following the collapse of Bretton Woods and the oil price rises. They faced internal unrest and the emergence of new lifestyles and cultures which however superficial and peripheral to mainstream society posed questions about the values of liberal, capitalist democracy. The international economic order was also under scrutiny and experiencing the previously unknown and largely unsuspected problems of 'stagflation'. It was a picture in which the central themes were the challenges within the Western world *and* the growing problems with the less developed world which the Americans, rattled by their looming defeat in Vietnam, hoped to alleviate through détente.

Between 1962 and 1974 in Cold War terms the West had clearly triumphed in the battle for the hearts and minds of newly independent peoples. Only in South Yemen was there a case of a revolutionary seizure of power, but between 1974 and 1980 left-wing or revolutionary movements came to power in fourteen countries if Angola, where the MPLA was the strongest but not the dominant force, is counted. Ethiopia, Cambodia, South Vietnam, Laos, Guinea-Bissau, Mozambique, Cape Verde, Sao Tome, Angola, Afghanistan, Iran, Grenada, Nicaragua and Zimbabwe all gained anti-Western regimes.[3]

There are many different explanations for this, all connected to particular problems or dynamics within radically different geographical and cultural regions. The fact that the Soviet Union now had the capacity to airlift troops and equipment made the situation more dangerous in that defeat for pro-Western groups seemed more possible. It was also more plausible to see a coordinated plan behind Soviet support for these left-wing movements in the form of creating satellites which would spread Soviet ideology and influence through proxy wars. Thus Vietnam invaded Cambodia after the victory of the North and Cuba intervened in several African countries. For those like Brzezinski who interpreted these events as both Soviet-inspired and motivated by ideas of geopolitical expansion, Afghanistan and the Soviet invasion were the last act in a power political game to which the US had to respond and win. There were of course other explanations for these events and for the Soviet involvement. The Soviet Union may be seen as a reluctant participant in such costly conflicts but having, for ideological reasons, to provide some support for revolutionary movements. This alleged half-hearted commitment may have been strengthened by the need to make sure Beijing did not emerge as the sole supporter of revolution or opponent of imperialism. It seems unlikely that the Soviet Union had ambitious plans to create satellites through proxy wars not least because Cuba, whose troops did intervene in Africa, was by no means the puppet of Moscow and acted for its own reasons rather than at the Kremlin's behest. One key question is whether the Soviets were the instigators of revolution, as part of a geopolitical plan or ideological commitment, or merely taking the opportunity to embarrass the West in the Cold War. Conservatives like Brezhnev were reluctant to take risks especially if they might lead to war but in true Marxist-Leninist fashion always committed to the ultimate triumph of the alleged victims of capitalism. The interesting thing is the relative weight of ideology and power politics in the Kremlin's motivation. It is easy to say that the concern with protecting the interests of the Soviet state had always been paramount but there were clear connections between the two. Protecting the ideas associated, correctly or not, with the Russian Revolution could be seen as requiring a powerful Soviet state. And the Cold War was seen by both sides as part of a global struggle for influence where the triumph of revolutionary movements in the less developed world were seen as affecting the global balance of power. In that respect the peoples of the less developed world can again be seen as central to détente's failure and to the Cold War itself.

The Collapse of Détente

At a general level it was almost inevitable that the different interpretations of what détente was to involve would lead each side to believe the other was taking unfair advantage. In a sense the failure of the process indicates that one or both sides were being disingenuous. The fact that they attached more importance to the specific advantages they expected détente to bring for them than to the general advantages to be gained from a relaxing of international tension is significant. The collapse may have been brought about by a series of specific crises, by the Soviet invasion of Afghanistan or by the general fear that expectations would not be met and instead of advantages détente would bring disadvantages instead.

By the second half of the 1970s, especially in America, the value of détente was much questioned. There was talk in 1980 of a 'decade of neglect' in which the US had made needless concessions to Moscow and allowed the Soviets to make major advances in the nuclear arms race. It seemed to some, notably the American Right, and particularly the Committee on the Present Danger, formed in 1976, that the Cold War had continued, albeit less intensely, and that the Soviets were still determined to further Marxist-Leninism and undermine the US. Détente, they argued, was just a cover for Soviet expansion. It had not helped the US extricate itself from Vietnam (in reality the Soviets were in no position to force Hanoi to abandon the struggle). America was allegedly abandoning its commitment to resist the evils of communism and neglecting its military responsibilities to the extent that American power was now becoming inferior to that of the Soviets. In the second half of the 1970s domestic pressures in the US were increasingly important in opposing 'détente'. In the USSR where the opening of economic links to the West had not revived the Soviet economy, which if anything had got worse as growth rates continued to decline, and where allowing Jewish emigrants to leave had merely produced further pressures to deal with human rights issues, domestic opposition was also in evidence.

The problems which undermined détente were a classic mix of domestic and international forces which came together in mid-1978. Soviet support for left-wing movements in Vietnam, Angola, and Ethiopia had angered the Americans even though they too were active in conflicts in the less developed world. They had undermined the Marxist President Salvador Allende in Chile, for example. The US, like the USSR, continued to see the less developed world as an arena of superpower competition. Thus the 'Nixon Doctrine' may have marked a rhetorical shift to a less globalistic, less adventurist foreign policy but it actually sought to continue old anti-Soviet policies, by placing more of the burden of resisting communism onto America's allies. The Kremlin actually believed that it acted with restraint in conflicts in the less developed world and it was confused by the growing popular criticism of détente in the US. Soviet exclusion from any part of the less developed world seemed, even in a peacekeeping role seemed to be the prime US aim.

American support for human rights and Soviet dissidents had angered the Kremlin, especially after Jimmy Carter became President in 1976. Carter had an idea of making human rights a major concern of US foreign policy and initially combined this with a focus on the North–South divide. Carter was also interested in the 'trilateral' relationship between America, Western Europe, and Japan. He had been the only southern representative on the Trilateral Commission, a group of private individuals concerned with the economic problems of the Western world and how these might be resolved through cooperation. But by 1978 East–West issues had assumed centre stage perhaps more as a result of domestic differences within the Carter administration than of concerns over particular international developments. Of 'the many foreign policy debates within the Carter administration that over policy toward the Soviet Union was the most prolonged and intense.'[4]

This was the old problem of the relationship between the Cold War and regional or local conflicts. The Soviets believed the Americans were simply being unrealistic if they did not expect the anti-imperialist forces to gain the upper hand in Africa and Asia. And the Americans were no more realistic. Kissinger was never able to reconcile his emotive anti-communism with his intellectual *realpolitik* in assessing whether regional conflicts had to be analysed in terms of their effect on the Cold War or as things caused by the Cold War. Under Carter the problem was that Brzezinski, his National Security Adviser, was a hard line anti-communist whereas Cyrus Vance, his Secretary of State, was more of a pragmatist willing to compromise, able to see that the communists were not behind everything that produced instability in the world, and aware that friendly contacts could well be used to undermine the Soviet system.

Brzezinski and Vance engaged in a battle to win the President's support but by 1978 the former had essentially triumphed and Vance resigned in 1980. The second oil-price rise shock of 1979 created renewed economic pressures in the Western world in the wake of the Iranian revolution and the holding of American hostages in Tehran. A sense of America lacking the will to act assertively and of becoming a victim of circumstance accompanied the fatal blow to détente which came with the Soviet invasion of Afghanistan. Carter's response was to increase the US military build-up which had begun *before* the invasion and to announce the 'Carter Doctrine' which pledged the US to intervene, unilaterally if necessary, to prevent Soviet control of the Persian Gulf.

In the early 1980s Carter was castigated in retrospect for having failed to stand up to the Soviets when their ambitions had (supposedly) been plain for all to see. But there were a number of problems with such arguments. For one thing, Carter did stand up for American interests. He modernized the armed forces, improved relations with China, and pressed for improved human rights in the Communist bloc before taking a tough response to the invasion of Afghanistan. Also, Soviet advances were not as great as Americans supposed: Angola and Ethiopia became pro-Soviet but they were poor, politically divided countries; the invasion of Afghanistan soon turned into a disaster; defence expenditure and assistance to allies put pressures on an already-inefficient Soviet economy. The Soviets disliked the attempt to 'interfere' in Soviet domestic affairs through Carter's emphasis on human rights and in the later 1970s Moscow blamed the US for undermining good relations.

There were always problems in managing détente and the policy was undermined by a wide range of factors. Disagreements over the very meaning of their new relationship were compounded by inevitable misperceptions and misunderstandings. The occasion for the final collapse of détente was the Soviet invasion of Afghanistan, but it was in decline long before that and its problems cannot be blamed only on one side. As with the origins of the Cold War, ideological and power political issues, a lack of mutual understanding and developments beyond superpower control led to the breakdown of trust and cooperation between them. Each side took decisions which troubled the other and by 1980 it was clear that the détente era had not altered the basic structure of the Cold War even within a changed international system. The US and USSR with less control of an ever more complex world, were still seen as its predominant powers, unable to escape profound differences of belief and interest. The next phase in the Cold War with the revival of a blunt American anti-communism was to change that.

NOTES

1. *Public Papers of the Presidents . . . Richard Nixon . . . 1971* (Washington, DC, 1972), 806–12. Cited in W. LaFeber, *America, Russia and the Cold War, 1945–2000* (McGraw-Hill, New York, 9th edn., 2002), 279.

2. We are indebted to Arne Westad for this information based on his research in Moscow for a forthcoming book, *Global Intervention: Cold War in the Third World 2004*.

3. F. Halliday, *The Making of the Second Cold War* (Verso, London, 2nd edn., 1986), 81–104.

4. Z. Brzezinski, *Power of Principle* (Farar Straus Giroux, New York, 1983), 146.

PART IV CHRONOLOGY: THE DÉTENTE ERA, 1972–1980

1972

21–28 February	Nixon's visit to China includes meetings with Mao Zedong.
30 March	North Vietnam launches offensive in Vietnam.
15–16 April	Breakthrough on SALT in 'tundra talks' between US and Soviets in Finland.
17–19 May	West German Bundestag ratifies 'Ostpolitik' treaties with USSR and Poland (signed in 1970).
22–26 May	Nixon–Brezhnev summit in Moscow.
17 June	Watergate break-in: Democratic Party HQ in Washington entered by a group linked to Nixon.
18 July	President Sadat of Egypt expels thousands of Soviet advisers.
1 August	US–North Vietnamese peace talks reopen.
3 September	US–Soviet–British–French agreement on future of Berlin.
18 October	US–Soviet trade deal finalized.
7 November	Nixon defeats George McGovern in landslide election win.
18–30 December	'Christmas bombing' campaign by US against North Vietnam.
21 December	'Basic Treaty' on bilateral relations between East and West Germany.

1973

1 January	Britain, Ireland and Denmark join the EEC, in its first enlargement.
27 January	In Paris a Vietnam peace settlement is signed.
22 February	US and China agree to open 'liaison offices' in the other's capital.
23 April	Kissinger, speaking in New York, proposes a 'New Atlantic Charter'.
30 April	Watergate crisis begins to intensity, with resignations of key White House staff.
18–24 June	Nixon–Brezhnev summit in Washington.
3 July	Thirty-five countries begin talks on European security in Helsinki.
15 August	US ends all military involvement in Cambodia.
12 September	President Allende of Chile toppled in a military coup.
6–29 October	Middle East War.
18 October	Arab oil producers raise prices and introduce oil embargo against US.
30 October	'Mutual Balanced Force Reduction' talks open in Vienna between NATO and Warsaw Pact.
7 November	US Congress passes War Powers Act.
11 December	West German–Czechoslovakian Treaty signed.

1974

1 January	New price rises, introduced by Organization of Petroleum Exporting Countries, take effect.
25 April	Portuguese dictatorship overthrown by the military, leading to Leftist-dominated governments.
18 May	India explodes its first atomic bomb.
27 June–3 July	Nixon–Brezhnev summit in USSR.
16 July	Coup against President Makarios of Cyprus.
20 July–16 August	Turkish military intervention in Cyprus.
8 August	Nixon resigns over Watergate scandal.
12 September	Emperor Haile Selassie overthrown by Marxist army officers.
23–24 November	Ford–Brezhnev summit in Vladivostok.

1975

14 January	US–Soviet trade deal collapses over Jackson–Vanik amendment.
Late March	Major communist advances in South Vietnam.
16 April	Fall of Phnom Penh, capital of Cambodia, to Khmer Rouge
25 April	Communists fare badly in Portuguese elections.
30 April	Fall of Saigon to communists.
12 May	Cambodians seize US ship, the *Mayaguez*.
15 May	US attacks on Cambodia; crew of *Mayaguez* released.
10 June	Rockefeller Commission (sitting since January) reports that the CIA had spied on US citizens.
30 July–1 August	Helsinki summit of US, Canada and European states; signs Helsinki Accords.
23 August	Vientiane, capital of Laos, falls to communist Pathet Lao.
11 November	Angolan independence from Portugal; rival governments established by three independence movements.
1–5 December	Ford–Mao summit in Beijing.

1976

11 February	Organization of African Unity accepts pro-Soviet MPLA as government of Angola.
15 March	Egypt ends its 1971 treaty with USSR.
13 April	Kissinger opposes a communist role in Italian government
21 June	Christian Democrats only narrowly ahead of communists in Italian elections.
9 September	Death of Mao Zedong.
2 November	Democrat Jimmy Carter wins US Presidential election.

1977

17 February	Carter letter to dissident scientist, Andrei Sakharov, backs human rights in USSR.
27 February	USSR rejects Carter's hopes of a major change of direction in SALT II talks.
30 June	Carter cancels B-1 bomber.

5 July	Ali Bhutto, President of Pakistan, overthrown by military under General Zia ul-Haq.
July	Fighting breaks out between Ethiopia and Somalia over disputed Ogaden.
7 September	Treaties signed to transfer Panama Canal from US to Panamanian sovereignty.
4 October	'Follow up' conference to Helsinki, on European security, opens in Belgrade (closes 9 March 1979).
18 October	Vaclav Havel and other 'Charter 77' members are sentenced to imprisonment in Prague.
13 November	Somalia ends its 1974 friendship treaty with USSR; Soviets and Cubans are supporting Ethiopia in Ogaden War.
19–21 November	President Sadat of Egypt visits Israel and addresses its parliament.
31 December	Cambodia breaks diplomatic relations with Vietnam due to border clashes.

1978

Late March	Somali forces withdraw from Ogaden.
5 April	West Germany's Chancellor, Helmut Schmidt, agrees to deployment of controversial neutron bomb in Europe.
7 April	Carter suspends production of neutron bomb.
28 April	President Daud of Afghanistan overthrown by communists led by Mohammed Taraki.
18 May	Soviet dissident Yuri Orlov imprisoned.
7 June	Carter warns Soviets they must choose between confrontation and détente.
12 August	Sino–Japanese friendship treaty signed.
6–17 September	Camp David Summit on Middle East peace, between Carter, Sadat and Begin.
3 November	Vietnam and USSR sign a Friendship Treaty.
6 November	Martial law declared in Iran after mounting unrest.
5 December	Soviet–Afghan friendship treaty.
25 December	Vietnamese invasion of Cambodia.

1979

1 January	Normalization of Sino–American relations.
7 January	Vietnam replaces Pol Pot's Cambodian government.
16 January	Shah of Iran goes into exile.
28 January–5 February	China's Deng Xiaoping visits USA.
1 February	Ayatollah Khomeini returns to Iran.
17 February–15 March	Chinese invasion of North Vietnam, followed by withdrawal.
26 March	Egyptian–Israeli peace treaty signed in Washington.
15 April	New round of oil price increases led by Iran.
28 May	Greece becomes tenth member of EEC.
7 June	Carter decides to build 'MX' missile.
15–18 June	Vienna Summit of Carter and Brezhnev; SALT II treaty signed.
17 July	President Somoza of Nicaragua overthrown by Sandinistas.
31 August	US complains over Soviet troop presence in Cuba.
10 September	Soviets say their troops have been in Cuba since 1962.

16 September	President Taraki of Afghanistan overthrown by Hafizullah Amin.
22 October	Shah of Iran arrives in US for medical treatment.
4 November	Occupation of American Embassy in Tehran.
10 December	NATO agrees to deploy intermediate range Cruise and Pershing missiles in Europe.
25 December	Soviet troops invade Afghanistan; replace President Amin with Babrak Karmal.

1980

4 January	Carter suspends ratification of SALT II.
23 January	'Carter Doctrine' speech on defence of Persian Gulf.
29 January	Meeting of Islamic states condemns Soviet invasion of Afghanistan.
4 March	Robert Mugabe wins first free elections in Zimbabwe.
25 April	Failed US attempt to rescue the Tehran hostages.
4 May	Death of President Tito of Yugoslavia.
14 August	In Poland, Gdansk shipworkers demand right to form a free trades union.
5 September	Polish communist leader Edward Gierek resigns.
22 September	Launch of 'Solidarity' union by Gdansk shipworkers; legalized on 10 November.
22 September	Iraqis launch invasion of Iran.
4 November	Republican Ronald Reagan wins US Presidential election.

12 An Era of Negotiations, 1972–1973

A. 'Triangular Diplomacy' and the East Asian Balance

Sino–American Rapprochement

The most dramatic change in international diplomacy in the early 1970s was the rapprochement between Beijing and Washington. After two decades of enmity it had been announced on 15 July 1971 that Richard Nixon was to visit China. The 'Opening to China' fitted the Nixon–Kissinger hope of maintaining a favourable position vis-à-vis the Soviets despite America's problems in Vietnam. The Sino–Soviet border clashes of 10 years earlier had exposed the bitterness of relations between the two leading communist states and if Washington could improve relations with both it might hope to play a pivotal role between them. The policy required careful execution since the White House did not want to seem to 'threaten' the Soviets by moving towards the Chinese too quickly. Thus, on 16 July 1971, Kissinger publicly stated that the moves towards rapprochement with China were not 'in any way

directed against any other countries, and especially not against the Soviet Union'.[1] The aim was not to take sides in the Sino–Soviet rivalry, but to obtain the advantages of cooperation with both. Most obviously, Moscow and Beijing might be prepared to put pressure on Hanoi to agree to a Vietnam peace settlement. Also, once America left Vietnam, as it seemed certain it would in the aftermath of the Tet offensive, it was important that China and the USSR should be dissuaded from an adventurist policy in East Asia. The potential of the Opening to allow a retrenchment of American commitment whilst avoiding a drift into neo-isolation, was emphasized by the implications for the country's military planning. Previously planners has to cope with a so-called 'two-and-a-half war strategy': any global conflict was likely to involve a regional war and all-out confrontation with the USSR and China. But if a rapprochement with China were successful, resources could be concentrated on fighting the USSR, in a 'one-and-a-half war strategy'. This meant a much reduced burden on the Pentagon's military planners who could now, for example, focus the US nuclear arsenal at the USSR alone. (It is rather ironic, in light of this, that the Reagan administration later characterized the 1970s as a 'decade of neglect' in US defence policy.) At a time when Western economies were in the doldrums, with low growth and high inflation, the Opening also promised investment and trade opportunities.

For China's leaders Mao Zedong and premier Zhou Enlai it made strategic sense to move closer to Washington in order to counter Soviet power, which now seemed more threatening to them than the US. 'For Mao, the decision to make common cause with China's old enemy, the United States, against the new enemy . . . in Moscow was a repetition of the Communists' strategy during the Second World War, when they joined forces with Chiang Kai-shek's nationalists against Japan.'[2] China had become increasingly independent of Soviet influence since 1956, had mixed attempts to preserve cooperation with fighting a vitriolic ideological battle with Moscow throughout the late 1950s and early 1960s and came close to armed conflict with its mighty

Mao Zedong (1893–1976) and Zhou Enlai (1898–1976)

Mao and Zhou were the dominant figures in the Chinese Communist regime, for the first quarter century of its existence, Mao as party leader and inspiration for China's brand of agrarian socialism, Zhou as Premier (1949–76) and for a time Foreign Minister (1949–58). They were also both founder members of the Chinese Party, though they came from rather different backgrounds. Mao, born into a peasant family in Hunan province, had trained as a teacher, then worked as a library assistant. Zhou was from a wealthier background, in Jiangsu province, and had been partly educated in Japan and France. But both had taken part in anti-government agitation before 1920 and by 1927 they were emerging as key figures. Zhou helped the capture of Shanghai that year in alliance with Chiang Kai-shek's Nationalist forces; Mao was already developing ideas for a peasant-based revolution, in contrast to the traditional Marxist emphasis on factory workers.

When Chiang Kai-shek turned against the Communists in 1927, Zhou at first favoured urban uprisings against the Nationalists but the failure of these led the party to turn more to Mao's ideas for winning peasant support, through promises of land reform and lower taxes. In 1934–5 Mao led the 'Long March' to Shensi province in the north of China, breaking free of Chiang Kai-shek's increasing stranglehold. But there were then attempts to form an alliance with Chiang in order to fight the Japanese, negotiations in which Zhou played a leading role. Zhou was also at the forefront of attempts to strike a deal with the Nationalists in 1946, before the full-scale civil war broke out that carried the Communists to power three years later.

Once in power Mao not only redistributed land to the peasants, but also emulated the Stalinist model of rapid industrialization and Personality Cult. He hoped to harness China's huge population to Socialist doctrine, building a strong, united, egalitarian society and he was not afraid to fight the United States in Korea (1950–3). Increasingly after 1956 Mao fell out, too, with the new Soviet leader Khrushchev. Zhou was less enthusiastic about this course, but played a leading role in building up China's position as a friend of anti-imperialism and the non-aligned movement, notably at the 1955 Bandung conference. Mao and Zhou also had their differences on domestic policy. Mao, more doctrinaire and determined to resist bureaucratization, inspired increasingly disruptive attempts to create a socialist society, including the intellectual fervour of the 'hundred flowers' movement (1958–9), the ill-fated attempt at a 'great leap forward' in industrialization and, after 1966, the institutionalized intolerance of the 'Cultural Revolution'. Zhou, more pragmatic, and accepting of bureaucratic necessities, was especially out of sympathy with the Cultural Revolution and found himself eclipsed for a time by Lin Biao, the Defence Minister.

But Mao and Zhou were brought together by 1971 thanks to their mutual fear of Soviet power, made stark by border clashes, and US difficulties in Vietnam. With Mao increasingly frail, it was Zhou who played the leading diplomatic role in the rapprochement with America. He was also able to restore the fortunes of old allies like Deng Xiaoping, who had suffered in the Cultural Revolution. Any hopes that Zhou might succeed Mao were dashed, however, by the former's sudden deterioration of health. He died a few months before Mao, whose fourth wife, Jiang Qing, then gained in influence. Her radical 'Gang of Four' was defeated by Deng, and other former allies of Zhou, in a power struggle following Mao's demise.

neighbour in 1969. The Americans, on the other hand, seemed increasingly troubled, both politically and economically. In East Asia, the most vital region for China, the US had acknowledged the Vietnam War to be unwinnable whereas the Soviets were expanding their Pacific Fleet and moving more army divisions to the Chinese border, even hinting at nuclear war with China. Despite its own nuclear arsenal, its entry into the space race and its attempts to win influence in the less developed world, China could not actually be considered a global power. In 1972 it only had a few hundred nuclear weapons, mostly based on aircraft, its navy was paltry, and its economy technologically backward. Indeed, its limited ability to provoke trouble in Africa and elsewhere may have helped induce the Americans to seek a rapprochement. But with the US and USSR now more evenly balanced, especially in nuclear terms, China could play a significant role as the third power in a system of 'triangular diplomacy' and, with its huge army, it was of clear importance in East Asian politics.

Not all Chinese leaders supported Mao's view that the USSR had become a more serious threat than the US. The Defence Minister, Lin Biao, designated Mao's successor in April 1969, was the main opponent of a rapprochement with America. In common with other military figures, he doubted the wisdom of offending the USSR and it has even been argued that his 'overweening political ambitions in late 1970 stimulated' Mao and Zhou 'to become more serious about a rapprochement with the United States'.[3] But he was overruled in August 1970 and he failed at the same time in a bid to be named Chinese President. In April 1971, his close ally, Chen Boda, was purged from the leadership. Lin then apparently planned to assassinate Mao but was himself killed in September 1971 in an air crash, trying to flee to Moscow after the failed coup attempt. The following month the advantages of the new approach were seen when Beijing achieved a long-standing aim, taking over China's United Nations seat. Since 1949 America had stood in the way of this step. China also won diplomatic recognition from an ever-growing number of states in the early 1970s. Yet the rapprochement with America never quite went the way Mao hoped. He wanted Beijing and Washington to move close together and confront the USSR, in direct contrast to the hopes of Nixon and Kissinger, of reducing tensions with both the major Communist powers while the US recovered from the Vietnam trauma. 'China was disconcerted by the continued links between the United States and Taiwan and by America's refusal to establish full diplomatic relations. America's efforts in developing US–Soviet cooperation ... aroused even greater dissatisfaction.'[4]

Reactions to the 'Opening' in Moscow and Tokyo

The Sino–American rapprochement nonetheless provoked concern in the USSR, which in October 1969 had warned the US not to exploit the growing divide in Sino–Soviet relations. When the rapprochement became public the Soviets foresaw many potential problems for themselves. First, it was clear that Mao now had even less need to seek an accommodation with Moscow: talks on border dispute began in late 1969 but ended without agreement 3 years later, and renewed border clashes occurred in December 1972. Meanwhile, the number of Soviet units on the Chinese border continued to grow, from twenty-seven divisions in 1969 to forty-five in 1973. This, in turn, highlighted a second problem. Whereas for the Americans the 'Opening to China' eased the challenge facing war-planners, for the Soviets it raised the spectre of a two-front conflict, against NATO in Europe and China in Asia. Thus, whereas for the US the strain on their strategic forces was easing (further helped by a reduced involvement in Vietnam after 1969), the Soviets' strategic challenges were increasing. In East Asia, which given America's retreat from Vietnam increasingly seemed an arena dominated by Sino–Soviet rivalry, Moscow was also concerned about the situation of its allies, Mongolia and North Vietnam, which bordered on China. North Vietnam, which was encouraged by China during 1972 to make peace with America, drew closer to the USSR in the early 1970s. This was in marked contrast to the situation a decade before when Mao had encouraged Hanoi in its attempts to overthrow South Vietnam and the Soviets had been cautious. Differences between Hanoi and Beijing did not become fully apparent, however, until 1974, when China occupied part of the Paracel Islands, ownership of which was disputed by the two countries. At a global level there was also concern in Moscow that China could influence America to abandon détente. The Soviets, who considered themselves much more important than China in the global balance, were dismayed that Nixon did not keep them informed of his China policy. In June 1973 Leonid Brezhnev frankly admitted to Nixon that what worried Moscow most was the prospect of Sino–American military links. But it was precisely such doubts and fears, as well as Brezhnev's desire for a SALT deal, which allowed America to open up relations with Beijing whilst pursuing an unprecedented improvement in negotiations with Moscow. However much they disliked the rapprochement, the Soviets could not afford to drive America and China even closer together.

America's alliances in East Asia—with Japan, South Korea, Thailand, and the Philippines—all continued in the long-term but, in the aftermath of the announcement of Nixon's visit, there were doubts in all these countries about America's intentions. The Japanese, still heavily reliant on the US for security and already concerned over events in Vietnam, were especially hurt because the July 1971 'Nixon Shock' came without any prior warning. Indeed, relations between America and its key East Asian ally became quite poor at this time. The White House was trying to reduce Japanese textile exports to America and August 1971 saw a second 'Nixon shock' when the President announced several measures which were likely to harm Japanese trade. Significantly Japan adopted 'a more active and independent foreign policy despite still sheltering under the American security umbrella' after 1971.[5] Japan was however the prime example of how an initial sense of concern over the changed power relationship in 1971 gave way to new opportunities. Despite historic rivalry, radically different ideologies and territorial disputes over various island groups, China and Japan had strong reasons to cooperate. The Chinese saw Japan as vital in containing the USSR; the Japanese had a vested interest in stability in East Asia after Vietnam and wanted access to Chinese markets. The replacement of the pro-Taiwanese Prime Minister, Eisaku Sato, by Kakuei Tanaka paved the way to the normalization of diplomatic relations in September

1972, and Japan soon became China's biggest trading partner. 1972 also saw a boost to Japanese–American relations with the restoration of Okinawa to Japanese sovereignty (under a deal negotiated by Sato in 1969). In contrast Japanese–Soviet relations were worsening. It still proved impossible to reach a peace treaty between them and Moscow became quite threatening in the mid-1970s with naval manoeuvres near the Japanese coast.

The Beijing Summit and the Position of Taiwan

The Opening to China was an example of the possible advantages of the secret diplomacy practised by Nixon and Kissinger who left the State Department almost completely uninformed about their China policy in 1969–71. Those years saw cautious steps on both sides towards a rapprochement, with numerous setbacks along the way, not least because of the American incursion into Cambodia in 1970. Pakistan, Romania, and France acted as intermediaries at times and some direct Sino–American contacts took place via their embassies in Warsaw. The positive 'diplomatic signals' became clearer in April 1971 when America greatly liberalized trade with China (the first steps in this direction having been made in July 1969) and the Chinese welcomed an American table tennis team. A secret visit by Kissinger to Beijing, via Pakistan, in July 1971 provided an opportunity for discussions with Zhou Enlai on the global balance, Vietnam, and the position of Taiwan. The last issue was difficult because of America's protection of the Nationalist regime on the island. But the announcement of Nixon's visit, followed by Taiwan's departure from the UN (neither Beijing nor Taipei would accept a 'two China' presence there), showed that the issue could not forestall the rapprochement. The Nixon–Kissinger commitment to the Opening was further emphasized by their actions during the December 1971 Indo–Pakistani War (see Chapter 11, C): with Pakistan a conduit to China the White House felt it essential to support her, whatever the rights and wrongs of the local situation. Nixon's visit to China went ahead on schedule on 21–8 February 1972 and included a meeting with Mao, although most of the negotiating was conducted on the Chinese side by Zhou. It was a well-managed media event, which boosted Nixon's hopes of re-election later in the year, especially when it was followed after 3 months by another summit in Moscow (see Chapter 12, B). Even if, to Chinese satisfaction, Nixon had visited Beijing before Moscow, the concrete results of the event were few. As one account pointed out, the summit may have represented 'a magnificent victory for the Chinese nation' on one level, but since the Americans were still fighting in Vietnam, 'it would be hard to describe it as a socialist foreign policy'.[6] There was no major US–Chinese agreement signed and, as seen above, there was no change in America's alliance system in East Asia—although it might be argued that the purposes of these alliances had changed in that they were no longer anti-Chinese. Washington even

continued to recognize Taiwan as the official Chinese government. Indeed, the Shanghai Communiqué, issued at the end of the visit, was remarkable for its statement of differing Chinese and American attitudes to Taiwan which Beijing still hoped to reabsorb. But Nixon underlined the real purpose of the visit when he told the Chinese, 'We have great differences today. What brings us together is that we have common interests which transcend those differences.'[7] In particular both countries wished to contain Soviet power, a point the Shanghai Communiqué underlined by stating their mutual opposition to any state which sought hegemony in the Asia-Pacific region. There was no formal Sino–American alliance, then, but the two countries would pursue 'parallelism', avoiding clashes with each other while resisting any gains for Soviet communism.

The Shanghai Communiqué, 28 February 1972

Communiqués are usually bland, factual documents designed to provide a basic amount of material to the public about an official meeting. But the 'Shanghai Communiqué', issued on the last day of Nixon's path-breaking visit to China, is remarkably long, extraordinarily honest in its admission of Sino–American differences but also revealing about how these differences could be handled as the two countries came closer together. It was important, too, because no formal agreements or treaties were signed during the visit and so it became the main statement of the motives for Sino–American rapprochement. The idea of stating their different views on key subjects like Taiwan was highly unusual, but had been agreed the previous October, when Kissinger visited Beijing. He and the Deputy Chinese Foreign Minister, Ch'iao Kuan-hua, spent hours working on the draft but the precise wording on Taiwan was not agreed until the early hours of 28 February.

Apart from giving the factual details of Nixon's visit, the communiqué included:

- A statement of each country's view on the international situation. While professing a desire for 'a just and secure peace', the US side stated the need for a negotiated settlement in Vietnam on the basis of self-determination for the South; it also stated its support for South Korea and for close friendship with Japan. The Chinese side stated its support for national liberation movements, including those in Indo China; it hoped for the peaceful reunification of Korea and opposed any revival of Japanese militarism.

- A statement of each country's view on the Taiwan problem: the Chinese side insisted that the Beijing government was 'the sole legal government of China', that 'Taiwan is a province of China', and that all US forces should leave Taiwan; the US side acknowledged that 'there is but one China and that Taiwan is a part of China', affirmed 'the ultimate objective of the withdrawal of all US forces', and said there must be 'a peaceful settlement of the Taiwan question by the Chinese themselves'.

- A statement that the US and China would 'conduct their relations on the principles of respect for the sovereignty and territorial integrity of all states, non-aggression against other states, non-interference in the internal affairs of other states, equality and mutual benefit, and peaceful coexistence.'

- More specifically they stated their desire: to 'progress toward the normalization of relations' between them; 'to reduce the risk of international military conflict'; and to oppose efforts by any country (including themselves) to establish hegemony in East Asia. The last statement that was seen as being directed against the USSR, although that country was not specifically mentioned in the communiqué.

- A statement of support for increased personal contacts and trade between the two countries, as well as continued diplomatic contacts.

B. The Moscow Summit and SALT I

The first Nixon–Brezhnev summit, announced in October 1971 and held in Moscow the following May, symbolized the great strides in détente between the spring of 1971 and summer 1973. En route to Moscow an exuberant Kissinger declared 'This has to be one of the great diplomatic coups of all times.'[8] It witnessed various agreements, including attempts to avert future superpower crises and promises of scientific cooperation, and the centrepiece was the Strategic Arms Limitation Talks (SALT) agreement on nuclear arms control. SALT, following the 1963 Test Ban Treaty and Non-Proliferation Treaty of 1968, confirmed the superpowers' desire to restrict the impact and spread of nuclear weapons, to maintain a supposedly secure balance based around 'Mutual Assured Destruction' (MAD), and to keep defence costs under control. Arms agreements seemed an obvious area in which to demonstrate the relaxation of tension between them and build trust. Yet neither side rushed into a SALT treaty or a summit (see chapter 9, A). The Soviets had been sceptical about strategic arms talks until 1968 and Nixon did not agree to open conversations on the subject until November 1969. By early 1970 Nixon, anxious to boost his domestic popularity and win Soviet support for a Vietnam settlement, wanted to hold a summit conference, but only in mid-1971, as Brezhnev tightened his grip on the Kremlin, were the Soviets won over, leading to the October announcement that such a meeting would take place. Various

---

Brezhnev's Statement to the 24th Congress of the Soviet Communist Party, 30 March 1971

Although he had replaced Khrushchev as General Secretary of the Communist Party of the Soviet Union (CPSU) in 1964, it was only at the 24th Party Congress in Moscow in 1971 that Brezhnev emerged as the dominant personality in the Kremlin. Until then he had seemed part of a collective leadership in which the Prime Minister, Andrei Kosygin, had handled many foreign policy issues. The Party Congress was also significant, however, for Brezhnev's statement of support for the process of détente, which was then at an important juncture. The possibility of an American–Soviet summit meeting—the first since 1961—had been discussed but a date had not yet been set and the Kremlin sometimes seemed doubtful about the proposal. In Europe, Brandt had begun to open contacts with the East through his Ostpolitik, but negotiations between the four occupation powers on the future of Berlin were making only fitful progress.

Brezhnev's statement on détente came as part of his lengthy 'Report of the CPSU Central Committee' to the Congress. The report also dealt with economic, socio-political, and intra-party issues, but following a brief introduction, foreign policy was placed first in the list of main subjects. Much of the section on foreign policy (which ran to about thirty printed pages) concerned the Soviet bloc's desire for peace, the success of its 'fraternal' cooperation with allies, and its continuing 'anti-imperialist' struggle. Brezhnev praised the survival of communism in East Germany, backed 'the struggle of the peoples . . . of Indochina against the imperialist interventionists', attacked 'the slanderous inventions concerning the policy of our Party . . . which are being spread from Peking', and defended the 1968 invasion of Czechoslovakia.

However, the Report also spoke of 'a substantial shift in our relations' with West Germany, urged a settlement of the Berlin problem, and hoped to see an all-European conference on security. It backed non-proliferation and SALT talks, noted that relations with the capitalist world had recently become 'active and diverse', and declared that 'An improvement of Soviet–American relations would be in the interests of the Soviet and American peoples, the interests of stronger peace.' Then again, Brezhnev reminded his audience of 'US aggressive actions in various parts of the world' and said that relations could only improve on the basis of 'a real desire to settle outstanding issues'. It still took until August 1971 before the date for a summit with Nixon was set and until September to achieve a four-power agreement on Berlin.

crises, from the Jordanian civil war of 1970 to the 1971 Indo–Pakistani War, could have wrecked the summit plans, as could a badly managed 'Opening to China' by the US (see Chapter 12, A). Even at the last moment, the US feared that the summit would be cancelled owing to a new bout of violence in Vietnam, where the launch of a major Communist offensive on 30 March was followed by America's mining of Haiphong harbour. Some in the Kremlin were indeed offended by this latest example of US 'imperialism' but Brezhnev argued that détente was of great long-term importance, that (thanks to Vietnam) the Soviet Union was in a strong position to deal with Washington and that the summit itself promised major gains—not only SALT, but also a recognition of the USSR's equality of status as a super-power by America, something of enormous signifi-cance to the USSR's self-esteem and its standing in the world. The conference also helped ensure the ratification of the various 'Ostpolitik' treaties with West Germany (see Chapter 12, C) and blunted China's sense of triumph after the Beijing summit.

The SALT Negotiations

The SALT treaty was the result of a number of developments including the development of rough nuclear parity, popular enthusiasm for arms control, and concern, both in the Kremlin and the US Con-gress, over the costs of nuclear arms which were becoming ever more technologically advanced. Two developments in particular in the 1960s had threatened to upset the nuclear balance: the anti-ballistic missile (ABM) and the multiple independent re-entry vehicle (MIRV). The first threatened to pro-voke a new spiral in the arms race, because if either side developed an effective ABM it might also be tempted to launch a 'first strike' on its opponent; and the other side was likely to counter such a threat by building additional offensive missiles to over-come the ABMS. In March 1969, Nixon renamed the ABM shield 'Safeguard' and planned to use it to pro-tect offensive missile sites in the American mid-West but it was only approved by Congress in August by one vote. These events gave both sides reason to seek an ABM treaty. The USSR wished to pre-empt US advances in the field, whilst the Nixon administra-tion recognized that a treaty might be preferable to defeat at the hands of Congress.

The second development, MIRV, was a means of improving US strike capacity without increasing the number of inter-continental ballistic missiles (ICBMs) or submarine-launched ballistic missiles (SLBMs). The number of ICBMs and SLBMs was actually frozen by the Johnson administration in 1968, at 1054 and 656 missiles respectively, but the purpose of this was to concentrate on improving such weapons rather than halting the arms race. MIRV testing had been announced in December 1967. Independently targettable warheads which could hit separate targets man miles apart allowed a marked increase in nuclear warheads but was cheaper than building new missiles. The Soviets—who concentrated in the 1960s on building ever-larger, but less advanced missiles, like the giant SS-9—were well behind in this area and finally agreed to SALT negotiations in June 1968. The invasion of Czechoslovakia in August prevented talks beginning but they remained a popular idea in the US State Department. The Nixon administration was determined not to rush into détente but it did soon accept the aim of 'sufficiency' in nuclear arms. As one arms control expert explained it: the 'nation only needed to maintain a force capable of inflicting a destructive level of damage on the USSR.'[9] It was hard to define precisely yet made arms talks easier because it implied that the US need not match the Soviets in all categories of nuclear weapon. However, the administration's decision to proceed with the testing and, in 1970, deployment of MIRVs was arguably a fatal error, for once the US successfully tested such a system the Soviets were bound to wish to do the same, so as not to risk falling behind in the arms race in future. This made it virtually impossible to negotiate a limit on MIRVs. MIRV was 'a less convincing bargaining chip than the Safeguard ABM . . . because neither side [was] serious about limiting MIRVs' once one side had decided to develop them.[10] In that sense SALT I was dead in the water before it was actually launched.

The SALT talks took place over several sessions from November 1969, oscillating between Helsinki and Vienna. The challenges were enormous. Each side's nuclear arsenal had a different make-up, with the US possessing a 'triad' of land-, sea-, and aircraft-based systems, whilst the Soviets mainly had land-based weapons, though their submarine capacity was growing. It was difficult to decide what actually represented 'equality' between them and the possibility of one side stealing a march was always present even without MIRVs. This problem was compounded by the existence of British and French nuclear arsenals on the Western side and the existence of American 'forward-based systems' (FBS) in Europe, which could strike Soviet territory but which the Americans were unwilling to include in strategic talks because of their limited range. The two sides also set out with opposite aims: the Soviets were keen to achieve an ABM treaty, and to offset US technological advances by preserving their own ability to expand their ICBM arsenal; the US was anxious to preserve its technological lead while restricting the growth of Soviet ICBM numbers. Soviet opposition to onsite verification of an arms deal was not, however, the barrier to agreement it had been in the past, because the CIA believed it possessed other means, such as satellite surveillance, to police any agreement. Some confusion was caused on the US side by the existence of an official negotiating team, from the Arms Control and Disarmament Agency, headed by Gerard Smith, and an unofficial, so-called 'backchannel', set up in 1969 between Kissinger, and Soviet ambassador, Anatoly Dobrynin. The 'backchannel' allowed the White House to control the tempo of the talks and brought the breakthrough agreement of May 1971, which finally excluded forward-based systems from the talks and confirmed there would be a freeze on ICBM—steps which pleased the US—but which also promised the USSR an ABM deal. This skeleton arrangement still left a lot of details undecided and it gravely upset Smith that Kissinger had struck a deal behind the back of the official negotiators: 'The delegation's trust in Washington authorities was never restored.'[11] Nonetheless, once the Moscow summit was announced the pace of negotiation increased. The April 1972 'Tundra Talks' in Lapland, which effectively finalized the ABM treaty, were followed by a visit from Kissinger to Moscow, where a high ceiling on Soviet SLBM numbers was agreed. A few final points were hammered out at the summit itself, at the cost of some ambiguity (not least over what constituted a

'heavy' missile, one of the categories of weapon SALT sought to control).

The Moscow Summit and its Limitations

The Moscow conference of 22–26 May 1972 proved to be one of the most successful East–West summits of the Cold War partly because it was carefully stage-managed and well-prepared in advance. Yet, given the last-minute threat posed by the Communists' spring offensive in Vietnam, it has been said that, 'The importance of the conference . . . lay in the fact that it was held at all.'[12] For this confirmed that the new relationship with Washington was more important to Brezhnev than solidarity with his fellow Marxist-Leninists in Hanoi. Ten documents were signed but they had largely been negotiated beforehand. Apart from SALT (see boxed section) these included greater cooperation on health and the environment, a joint Apollo-Soyuz space mission (which went ahead in mid-July 1975), improvements in the 'hot-line', an agreement to avoid accidents at sea, and steps to reduce the risk of accidental nuclear war. A Joint Commercial Commission was established which negotiated a trade deal between the two countries 5 months later, involving a settlement of war debts, a US commitment to give the Soviets 'most favoured nation' status (that is equal to that of other major trading partners), and the opening of trade offices in each other's capital. For the Soviets, another important document was the 'Basic Principles Agreement' (based on an October 1971 arrangement between Brezhnev and France's Georges Pompidou), which laid down twelve principles for the conduct of superpower relations. These included the acceptance of peaceful coexistence and mutual equality, restraint during crises, avoiding confrontation, and refraining from the use of force.

Moscow was intended to be the first of a series of summits and further Nixon-Brezhnev meetings did occur, in America from 16 to 24 June 1973 (when the venue moved between Washington, Camp David, and San Clemente, California) and again in Moscow from 27 June to 3 July 1974. The 1973 conference saw more minor agreements, on cultural exchanges, agriculture, and transport, some discussion of a SALT II treaty and, most importantly, an Agreement on the Prevention of Nuclear War. The last developed the Basic Principles Agreement and was again urged most by the Soviets, who had long wanted the US, with its nuclear superiority, to promise it would not be the first side to use nuclear weapons in war. The Agreement was much diluted by the Americans however and promised no more than that the super-powers would consult together if nuclear war ever threatened to involve one of them. By June 1973 the Nixon administration was already overshadowed by the Watergate scandal, and this was even more the case with the 1974 summit which did, however, see an important ABM deal, cutting the number of missiles on each side to one hundred.

Moscow and the SALT treaty were celebrated by both sides in 1972, understandably so. Brezhnev used them to solidify his control of the Kremlin, removing opponents from the Politburo in 1973. He pointed to the Basic Principles Agreement as evidence that the US both accepted the USSR as an equal and was ready to embrace the long-standing Soviet concept of peaceful coexistence. Nixon and Kissinger, in an election year, were bound to hail Moscow as qualitatively different from previous summits—with concrete agreements, not just an improvement in the international atmosphere—and to praise SALT as a breakthrough in East–West relations. Alongside the Beijing summit, and signs of a Vietnam settlement, the Moscow summit made 1972 seem a world away from 1968, the previous election year. In fact, however, the positive side of the meeting was oversold, helping breed dissatisfaction in future. Both sides were still determined to maintain strong defences and to treat the other as an ideological enemy. The Soviets still supported National Liberation movements in the less developed world and maintained the Brezhnev Doctrine; America had no intention of abandoning its NATO allies or its new relationship with China and flaws were soon clear in some of the main agreements. However important the Basic Principles were to Brezhnev, the Americans never saw them as more than a broad 'code of conduct', one against which Soviet as well as US behaviour could be measured. It was unclear what the Principles would mean in practice and little thought was given to their enforcement. As to the commercial agreement, it did lead to a major trade expansion in 1972–3, alongside large US credits to the USSR. But this was soured in American eyes by the so-called 'Great Grain Robbery' when the Soviets, faced by a harvest failure, were sold large amounts of grain, pushing up US prices and costing American taxpayers large subsidies.

The most significant flaws, however, lay in SALT I, the greatest symbol of US-Soviet trust and equality. Criticism must be tempered by the fact that SALT was an interim measure, designed to lead to a SALT II deal within 5 years. Certainly the ABM treaty was a precise arrangement, strictly limiting a whole category of weapons. But in a sense the ABM treaty was of limited importance because the technical problems and financial costs made ABMs difficult to build anyway. The Soviets never believed they could out-match the US here and the Nixon administration, aware of Congressional and public opposition, seems to have used Soviet fears of 'Safeguard' simply as a 'bargaining chip' to get a better deal on offensive missiles. Whilst confirming, or paying lip-service, MAD, the offensive missile agreement itself had many shortcomings. It controlled missile numbers, but the 'ceilings' were set at a high level and there was no control on the number of MIRVs, so that the quantity of warheads continued to increase. In 1972 the US still had a marked advantage in warhead numbers: the 1,054 American ICBMs actually had 1,474 warheads on them thanks to MIRVing, and there were over 3,000 warheads on the 656 SLBMs; in contrast the Soviets, without MIRVs and with only about 1,500 ICBMs and 500 SLBMs, were still well below the SALT ceilings. The Soviets could eventually use the opportunity to expand warhead numbers which SALT I presented once they obtained MIRV technology. One especially critical account argued that there 'were no Soviet concessions during the Moscow summit . . . The only major concessions were made by Henry Kissinger.' It pointed out that the decision to allow the USSR more SLBMs was particularly puzzling. The US had long held superiority in SLBM numbers so why had they not simply been frozen?[13] Another account felt that the Soviets could hardly have refused a deal because Kissinger 'made the terms palatable to the Soviets by permitting them to fulfil their planned programmes'—including the expansion of SLBM numbers.[14] It was

---

The SALT I Agreements, May 1972: main points

Two arms control agreement were signed.

1. The Anti-Ballistic Missile (ABM) Treaty:

- restricted the US and USSR to two ABM missile fields each, one to protect their capital, one to protect an ICBM field;
- placed a limit of one hundred on the number of missiles in each of the fields (that is, two hundred missiles in total for each superpower);
- banned certain new ABM developments, including multiple warheads and space-based systems; limited the location of early-warning systems; was to be monitored by an Oversight Commission;

- was of indefinite duration, but either side could withdraw after six months notice.

2. The 'Interim Agreement on Offensive Missiles':

- subjected strategic offensive weapon launchers to the following, unequal 'ceilings':
  Intercontinental Ballistic Missiles (land-based): 1,054 for the US and 1,618 for the USSR;
  Submarine-launched Ballistic Missiles: 656 for the US and 740 for the USSR;
  Strategic bombers: 455 for the US and 140 for the USSR;
- had a duration of 5 years, during which time a SALT II agreement was to be negotiated.

---

certainly possible to defend the summit if one took a long-term perspective. 'For all the flaws ... Nixon had achieved a symbolic breakthrough, namely that the two sides could set limits on their destructive capability.'[15] And the flaws could be dealt with in subsequent negotiations. However, many Congressional critics in the US soon decided there was cause for concern, because the Soviets *were* allowed to deploy more offensive missiles than America under

the Treaty, they had much larger missiles, and they began to MIRV them in 1975 (after successfully testing a MIRV 2 years beforehand—much earlier than the US expected). The belief that the 1972 agreement would ultimately give the USSR the advantage in nuclear arms numbers, despite the short-term US advantage in warheads, provoked grave doubts in the US about a second SALT agreement and made its negotiation all the more difficult.

C. The Vietnam Settlement, 1972–1973

Vietnam in Early 1972

Despite the gloom surrounding its policy in Vietnam in late 1971 (see Chapter 10, E), the situation from America's viewpoint was not hopeless. The incoherent strategy pursued by Nixon in Vietnam had some favourable results. US troop levels were about to fall below 100,000. This arguably weakened America's hand in negotiations but, since no new conscripts were being sent to Vietnam, anti-war protests at home had subsided. The incursion into Laos showed the South Vietnamese army probably could not launch successful offensive operations; but, when put on the defensive, they might fare better, especially since the Americans still provided them

with large-scale air support. The 'Nixon Doctrine' reassured President Thieu that, while his forces must now bear the brunt of ground fighting, the US would not abandon its allies and Nixon himself had several times demonstrated his readiness to match tough rhetoric with strong action. 'Pacification' policies, used to undermine Viet Cong support in the South, had become more sophisticated and, in some cases, more successful. Furthermore American relations with both the USSR and China were improving, raising the possibility that those countries might press Hanoi to make peace. In fact, despite détente, the USSR seems to have done little to help the Americans escape from the Vietnam embroglio, and any of its efforts were unlikely to have borne fruit. 'The Soviet Union was a reluctant player in the diplomatic settlement in Vietnam ... despite the efforts of the Nixon administration and its policy of linkage', the logic of which was that Moscow should seek to reduce conflicts in the less developed world in return for cooperation with Washington.[16] The Chinese were rather more helpful however. In November 1971, during a meeting in Beijing, Mao Zedong told North Vietnam's Prime Minister, Pham Van Dong, that compromise was now the best course. The Chinese did not necessarily want Thieu to survive in the long-term but, arguably, if the North could negotiate America's military withdrawal from Vietnam, Thieu's days would be numbered anyway; there was no need for Hanoi to continue pressing for a communist-influenced coalition government in South Vietnam as the price of peace with America. 'He was arguing for Nixon,' one North Vietnamese diplomat complained, 'Mao was telling us to maintain the status quo.'[17]

In order to undermine his domestic critics, in January 1972 Nixon published the fact that Kissinger had held twelve rounds of secret peace talks with North Vietnamese representatives, and that the US position had been more conciliatory than that stated in public. Coming at the start of an election year, after Congressmen had attacked his failure to negotiate realistically, this was an astute move which caught Hanoi by surprise. The Beijing summit in February was another success for Nixon and an unwelcome event for North Vietnam, and of course the Soviets too were preparing a meeting with Nixon. Even if the Soviets did not, in actual fact, put pressure on the North to make a settlement of the war, the Hanoi politburo may have feared that both its major patrons were now ready to give relations with America a higher priority than Vietnamese interests. Thus it has been speculated that it was to try to undermine the budding US–Chinese and US–Soviet links, 'that the politburo decided finally on the spring offensive' of 1972.[18] Then again, it was predictable for other reasons that North Vietnam would launch a major attack on the South during 1972. The 'Tet' offensive of early 1968 had shown the rewards that such an attack could bring during an American election year, sapping morale and destroying a President's re-election bid, even if

Communist losses were formidable. Indeed, it was because the Viet Cong had lost so many fighters in 1968 that the North Vietnamese army were to shoulder most of the 1972 operations. The North perhaps hoped that Nixon would wish to settle the war before the election if possible and that military success would ensure that this was done on Communist terms. 'At its maximum, the leadership hoped, the offensive might actually cause the collapse of the Saigon government; at the very least it promised a victory ... which would undermine the policy of Vietnamization.'[19] The downside was that North Vietnamese forces would be fighting a more conventional war to which the Americans were more suited.

The Spring Offensive

The spring offensive began on 30 March, being partly designed to upset the forthcoming Moscow summit, perhaps even force its cancellation. And, despite the widespread expectation of an offensive, its timing and execution came as a surprise to Saigon and Washington. Its timing was surprising because, just before the first attacks, Hanoi had been discussing another round of peace talks with the Americans. Its execution was a surprise because the North Vietnamese Defence Minister, General Vo Nguyen Giap, not only launched his primary assault across the narrow, well-defended Demilitarized Zone between the North and South; but also he used three-quarters of all the North's available forces to launch a series of conventional attacks, led by artillery bombardments and tanks, on Thieu's million-strong army. Not only were whole South Vietnamese divisions shattered in a four-pronged North Vietnamese attack but on 1 May the Communists seized control of a major city, Quang Tri, and they threatened to capture the ancient royal capital of Hue. If it fell, it would prove a dire psychological blow to Saigon; even if it did not, there was always the danger that the National Liberation Front would set up a provisional government in Quang Tri.

The North's offensive threw the White House into panic for a time. 'Nixon was impaled on the horns of a dilemma. If he did not support the South Vietnamese with heavy bombing ... a US ally might well be defeated. But if he did escalate the war . . . he would face the probable cancellation of the Moscow summit by the Soviets.'[20] Hanoi was mistaken, however, if it believed that Nixon wanted peace at any price before the election. In fact, in line with his previous penchant for toughness, he quickly decided to use all available US aircraft to blunt Giap's assault, then agreed to use B-52s to bomb targets in North Vietnam. It was the first time since 1968 that American heavy bombers had attacked the North and, from 15 April, the targets included the major cities of Hanoi and Haiphong. In the past such attacks would have drawn a harsh response from Beijing and Moscow but on this occasion, in another worrying sign for Hanoi, there were few complaints. Although Soviet vessels were struck by US bombs in Haiphong harbour, plans for the Moscow summit continued. A secret meeting between Kissinger and North Vietnam's Le Duc Tho on 1 May confirmed that the North still wanted Thieu's removal as the price of peace, but this diplomatic impasse simply made the Americans more determined to deny Giap a military breakthrough. On 8 May Nixon announced a blockade of North Vietnam, with the mining of Haiphong and other harbours. This was a dramatic step but it did not stop the Moscow summit going ahead. By late May Giap had committed all his reserves to the spring offensive but the South Vietnamese held onto Hue and, in June, were able to counter-attack, retaking Quang Tri. The offensive had failed in its main purposes: the South Vietnamese army survived; the Moscow and Beijing summits made it likely Nixon would be re-elected even if there were no peace in Vietnam; and the Soviets, far from abandoning détente, now sent President Nikolai Podgorny to Hanoi with the latest American peace offer.

The Peace Accords

Despite Giap's failure, North Vietnam was hardly in a weak position when Le Duc Tho and Kissinger revived their peace talks in mid-July 1972. The USSR and China might favour compromise, but they were not going to break with Hanoi over it; the North Vietnamese army and Viet Cong still controlled large tracts of South Vietnam; despite the US blockade,

war supplies continued to reach the North; and Nixon was still committed to withdrawal. In August all US army combat missions in Vietnam ceased and only 30,000 American troops remained, none of them draftees. Furthermore the Americans continued to offer concessions in the Paris talks. Most important, Kissinger had implicitly told the Soviets that, if a 'ceasefire in place' could be agreed the US would not demand the subsequent withdrawal of North Vietnamese units from the South. All that America wanted was that Thieu should remain in power after the ceasefire, to take part in a political settlement negotiated by the various South Vietnamese political groups. By late September, rather than insisting on a coalition government which excluded Thieu, the North was prepared to accept that his regime might continue for a time. In a series of meetings between 8 and 11 October the outline of a peace settlement was hammered out, which Hanoi hoped could become a signed accord by the end of the month. They now wanted an agreement before Nixon's hand was strengthened by a successful re-election.

The proposed settlement gave something to both sides. The Americans would have their prisoners of war returned (an essential point for domestic opinion) and the Thieu regime would survive. The North Vietnamese won a 'ceasefire in place', a promise that all US forces would withdraw, and an imprecise political arrangement that might, through a process of reconciliation and elections, reunite Vietnam. But by late October the settlement was already breaking down, largely thanks to President Thieu. Despite the vital importance of any settlement to South Vietnam, he had been kept only partially informed of the US–North Vietnamese contacts and was furious about the draft agreement when Kissinger brought it to Saigon on 19 October. He particularly disliked the idea that, under a ceasefire in place, the North Vietnamese could hold onto areas they occupied in South Vietnam, and he was unimpressed by Kissinger's reassurance that the South had a 'fighting chance' of survival once the Americans left. Despite Kissinger's celebrated remark on 26 October, that 'we believe that peace is at hand', hope of signing the accords by the end of the month evaporated.[21] As expected Nixon won a landslide re-election on 7 November. He then tried to win

Thieu over to a settlement, partly through diplomatic pressure and partly by a massive supply of arms to South Vietnam, so as to leave it in the best military position after a ceasefire. He also secretly undertook to restart US aid to Saigon if Hanoi breached the ceasefire on a large scale. But this strengthening of Thieu's armed forces simply led the North to ask for changes in the draft accords and by the middle of December negotiations had stalled.

The stall in the Paris negotiations was followed by the so-called 'Christmas Bombing' of Hanoi, Haiphong and other targets in North Vietnam, one of the most controversial of all Nixon's actions. 'It was the most devastating bombing campaign of the entire war.'[22] Having been told 'peace was at hand', public opinion was shocked by the round-the-clock raids of B-52s near heavily populated areas (although, thanks to the North's civil defence preparations, actual casualties were limited to a few thousand). The raids did bring Hanoi back to the negotiating table. Le Duc Tho and Kissinger met again on 8 January 1973 and initialled a peace agreement on the 23rd. Yet the 'bombing did not produce a settlement markedly different . . . from the October agreement.', again raising the question of why the Christmas Bombing was necessary.[23] Several factors seem to have influenced Nixon. One, certainly, was a desire to resolve the Vietnam War before his second term began and while an acceptable agreement seemed possible. Bellicose action also fitted in with his established behaviour and showed that, even at the end of its disastrous Vietnam involvement, America was capable of firm action. Significantly, such bellicosity also helped reassure Thieu of American resolve and gave credibility to Nixon's promises that Washington would not tolerate a major Communist breach of any settlement. 'The bombs . . . were not just aimed at targets a few thousand feet away; their real target in a sense was Saigon.'[24] But also, the President knew that he might not be in such a strong position for long. His landslide re-election was a remarkable achievement. But at the same time a new Congress had been elected which was ill-disposed to him and was expected to introduce a War Powers Act to limit the President's independence in foreign affairs. Ideally, therefore, Nixon needed to resolve the Vietnam War before Congress met in late January.

The ceasefire in place in Vietnam went into force on 27 January, preceded by a 'land-grabbing' exercise by Hanoi and Saigon. Within 60 days of that all American forces were to be withdrawn and all prisoners-of-war were to be released. The conditions for US withdrawal were clear enough, but many other parts of the Accords were flawed. Rumours persisted for decades afterwards that Hanoi held more prisoners than the 591 Americans actually set free, and this soured relations between the two countries. Neither North Vietnam nor America was supposed to resupply either side in the South with troops or weapons, but there was a provision for 'replacement' of materials which allowed for breaches in the conditions. An international commission, with representatives from the Eastern and Western blocs, was supposed to police the ceasefire but was never effective. As to the process of 'national reconciliation' which was supposed to take place in the South, it was a dead letter. And though the accords talked of elections being held they did not set a date. Also the ceasefire only applied to Vietnam, not to Cambodia or Laos, where the civil wars continued.

The Nixon administration defended the Paris accords as an honourable settlement. 'I believed . . . that the agreement could have worked,' insisted Kissinger, 'it reflected a true equilibrium of the forces on the ground' and he blamed subsequent unforeseen developments for its collapse.[25] South Vietnam had not fallen to communism and, with American supplies and secret promises of support if the settlement broke down, Thieu might yet survive for many years. Some take the view that, 'Almost certainly, no better terms could have been secured.'[26] But critics pointed to the flaws in the settlement, the failure to achieve a political solution in South Vietnam, and the weakness of Thieu's regime given the North Vietnamese army's continuing presence in the South. Nixon, it was argued, had simply won a 'decent interval' between US withdrawal and Thieu's inevitable fall. 'As it turned out, the main thing Nixon and Kissinger achieved was a "decent interval" . . . between America's withdrawal and the defeat of the government it had committed itself to defend.'[27] Except that, as it turned out in retrospect, the 'interval' was a rather indecent two years. America in January 1973 might be at peace but in

Richard Nixon (1913–1994) and Henry Kissinger (b. 1923)

The two men who dominated US foreign policy-making between 1969 and 1974 came from very different backgrounds. Nixon was born into a poor, pioneering, Quaker family in California. Educated as a lawyer, he learnt the art of debating at college, made political contacts and, after wartime naval service, stood successfully for Congress in 1946. By 1950, when he entered the Senate, he had made his name as a strong anti-communist, notably in the Alger Hiss spy case. Nixon's anti-communism helped him become Eisenhower's running mate in the 1952 election, followed by 8 years as Vice-President. But his underhand tactics, and accusations that he had misappropriated funds in one election, earned him the nickname 'Tricky Dicky' and in 1960 he narrowly lost the Presidential race to John Kennedy. Another setback in 1962, when he failed to become Governor of California, seemed to spell the end of his political career. However, his ambition and persistency, linked to upheaval brought by the Vietnam War, helped him re-emerge as the successful Republican candidate in the 1968 election.

In contrast, Kissinger was born into a middle-class, Jewish family in Germany and only came to America as a teenager in 1938, fleeing oppression by the Nazis. He became a naturalized American in 1943, by which time he was living in a close German immigrant community in New York, with ambitions of becoming an accountant. Wartime service in Army Intelligence widened his ambitions and gave him a taste of responsibility: in 1945–6 he was administrator of a district of occupied Germany. In 1947, when he returned to the US, he enrolled at Harvard, specialized in international relations and went on to write a Ph.D., on the 'Congress System' in Europe after the Napoleonic Wars. Becoming an academic, he eventually won full professor status in 1960, but by then he had won a name for himself writing *Nuclear Weapons and Foreign Policy* and, as Director of the Harvard International Seminar, he had made many political contacts. He worked for a time in both the Kennedy and Johnson administrations (specializing in the later period on Vietnam) but, unusually for academics, was himself a Republican. On the liberal wing of the party, Kissinger acted as foreign policy adviser to Nelson Rockefeller, a candidate for Republican Presidential nominee in both the 1964 and 1968 elections.

Kissinger was asked to become Nixon's National Security Adviser, despite criticizing the latter ahead of the election. On the surface the right-wing professional politician and liberal-leaning immigrant, academic looked an unlikely team. But Nixon was tempted by the idea of having a respected intellectual on his White House staff, while Kissinger relished the opportunity to play a leading policy role. They never became close friends but they did establish a fruitful working relationship, underpinned by shared outlooks on such problems as China and Vietnam. Both had risen from unpromising backgrounds, neither was a traditional 'establishment' figure, and both had a fascination with the study of history. They were also firmly anti-Communist, determined to be 'tough' in prosecuting foreign policy and ready to use secret diplomacy, concentrated in the White House, to achieve their aims. Indeed, under Nixon's first administration, the Secretary of State, William Rogers, had only a limited policy-making role. Inevitably, as President, it was Nixon who long had the upper hand in the relationship with Kissinger; and who also pressed first for some of their more innovative policies, not least the 'Opening to China'. It was Kissinger, however, who provided an intellectual underpinning for 'Nixingerism', controlled much of the advice the President received on foreign policy, and carried out many diplomatic initiatives personally, not least the Vietnam peace talks.

In September 1973 Kissinger combined the position of National Security Adviser with that of Secretary of State, a commanding position, further reinforced by Nixon's embroilment in the Watergate scandal, which brought the Presidency to an end in August 1974. Kissinger continued in his dual-post under Gerald Ford—himself no expert on foreign policy—until November 1975, and even then was replaced as National Security Adviser by a close ally, his former deputy, Brent Scowcroft. But during the 1976 Presidential election it was evident that Kissinger's public reputation had fallen since its height in 1972–3. The breakdown of the Vietnam peace settlement and disappointment with détente harmed the administration in the run-up to the election and the Democratic candidate, Jimmy Carter, pressed an idealistic, human rights-based foreign policy, very different to the amoral, realpolitik of 'Nixingerism'. Over the following decades Kissinger was able to play an occasional front role in policy-making again, notably as head of a Commission on policy towards Latin America in 1983–4. But his former boss, Nixon, though he wrote several books on foreign policy, remained tainted by Watergate and never took a part in government after his resignation.

Vietnam neither side respected the ceasefire, and in Cambodia the US airforce continued to aid the Lon Nol regime until mid-August, when Congress insisted such assistance must end. Attempts to improve relations with Hanoi by offering billions of dollars in 'reconstruction aid' backfired at home, where it was condemned as a 'reparations' payment.

Reparations, of course, are usually paid by defeated powers. Yet, even so, at the time the settlement seemed to crown eighteen months of remarkable achievement by the Nixon–Kissinger duo, building on the China 'Opening' and the Moscow summit, and reversing the sense of helplessness in foreign affairs that had beset America only 4 years before.

NOTES

1. Quoted in Marvin Kalb and Bernard Kalb, *Kissinger* (Hutchinson, London, 1974), 256.

2. Philip Short, *The Dragon and the Bear: Inside China and Russia Today* (Hodder & Stoughton, London, 1982), 480.

3. Dick Wilson, *Chou: The story of Zhou Enlai* (Hutchinson, London, 1984), 272.

4. Roy Medvedev, *China and the Superpowers* (Blackwell, Oxford, 1986), 105.

5. Michael Yahuda, *The International Politics of the Asia-Pacific* (Routledge, London, 1996), 241.

6. John Gittings, 'The Statesman', in Dick Wilson (ed.), *Mao Tse-tung in the Scales of History* (Cambridge University Press, Cambridge, 1978), 264.

7. Quoted in Richard Nixon, *RN: the Memoirs of Richard Nixon* (Sidgewick & Jackson, London, 1978), 565.

8. Quoted in Nixon, *op. cit.*, 609.

9. Gerard Smith, *Double Talk* (University Press of America, Lanham, 1980), 23–4.

10. John Newhouse, *Cold Dawn: the Story of SALT* (Pergamon-Brassey's International Defense Publishers, London, 1989), 30–1.

11. Smith, *op. cit.*, 235.

12. Newhouse, *op. cit.*, 272.

13. Seymour Hersh, *The Price of Power* (Summit, New York, 1983), 535.

14. Raymond Garthoff, *Détente and Confrontation* (Brookings Inst., Washington, 1985), 163.

15. Stephen Ambrose, *Nixon, II: The Triumph of a Politician* (Simon & Schuster, London, 1989), 548.

16. Ilya Gaiduk, *The Soviet Union and the Vietnam War* (I.R. Dee, Chicago, 1996), 222.

17. Quoted in Hersh, *op. cit.*, 442.

18. Jeffrey Kimball, *Nixon's Vietnam War* (University Press of Kansas, Lawrence, 1998), 284.

19. Marilyn Young, *The Vietnam Wars* (HarperCollins, New York, 1991), 269.

20. Jonathan Aitken, *Nixon: a Life* (Weidenfeld & Nicolson, Washington, 1993), 436.

21. Henry Kissinger, *The White House Years* (Weidenfeld & Nicolson, London, 1979), 1399.

22. Gary Hess, *Vietnam and the United States* (Twayne's Publishers, Boston, 1990), 133.

23. George Herring, *America's Longest War* (McGraw Hill, New York, 1986), 255.

24. Walter Isaacson, *Kissinger* (Faber & Faber, New York, 1992), 470.

25. Kissinger, *op. cit.*, 1470.

26. William Bundy, *A Tangled Web* (Hill & Wang, New York, 1998), 368.

27. Isaacson, *op. cit.*, 485.

CHRONOLOGY: THE ROAD TO A VIETNAM SETTLEMENT, 1972–1973

1972

25 January	Nixon reveals that secret US–North Vietnamese peace talks have been held regularly since 1969.
30 March	North launches its 'Spring Offensive' against South Vietnam.
15 April	US bombers strike targets around Hanoi and Haiphong for first time under Nixon.
4 May	North Vietnamese take Quang Tri city.
8 May	US begins to mine Haiphong harbour.
1 August	Peace talks reopen between Kissinger and Le Duc Tho in Paris.
15 September	South Vietnamese retake Quang Tri.
8 October	In Paris talks, North Vietnamese effectively concede President Thieu can remain in power after a ceasefire.
12 October	Kissinger and Le Duc Tho agree on outline of a settlement.
18–23 October	In talks with Kissinger, Thieu rejects much of the settlement arranged in Paris.
26 October	Hanoi publishes the draft agreement; Kissinger tells a press conference 'peace is at hand'.
7 November	Nixon re-elected by a landslide.
20 November– 13 December	Further talks between Kissinger and Le Duc Tho in Paris fail to agree on a final settlement.
18 December	US begins 'Christmas Bombing' of North Vietnam, using B-52s, including attacks on Hanoi and Haiphong.
28 December	Hanoi agrees to resume peace talks on basis of previous proposals.
29 December	End of 'Christmas Bombing' campaign.

1973

2–13 January	Final round of Paris talks reaches agreement on settlement.
5 January	Nixon assures Thieu that the US 'will respond with full force should the settlement be violated by North Vietnam'.
21 January	Thieu reluctantly accepts the settlement.
27 January	Peace agreement signed in Paris.
12 February	First American POWs released by North Vietnam.
29 March	Last US servicemen leave Vietnam.

13 'Stagflation' and the Trials of Détente, 1973–1976

A. The October 1973 Middle East War

Sadat and the Origins of the War

In the aftermath of Israel's victories in the 1967 Six Day War (Chapter 11, D) a situation of 'no peace, no war' prevailed in the Middle East. Israel, having captured control of the Sinai peninsula, the West Bank of the Jordan, and the Golan Heights was in a strategically strong position against its Arab neighbours, especially when backed by American military supplies and diplomatic support. Attempts in 1970–1 by the United Nations' envoy, Gunnar Jarring, and the American Secretary of State, William Rogers, to make progress on a peace settlement came to nothing. The Israelis saw little reason to negotiate away their recent gains, especially when the Arabs refused to recognize Israel's right even to exist. The

Arabs, in a position of weakness, could wield little influence over the Israelis or the superpowers.

In September 1970 the sudden death of Nasser, brought another military figure, Anwar Sadat, to power in Egypt, the most populous and powerful Arab state. His early forays in the international arena suggested confusion rather than any intelligent plan to regain the lost territories. Keen to maintain Egyptian leadership of the Arabs and consolidate his domestic support he publicly threatened to make both 1971 and 1972 a 'year of decisions' in the Middle East, but failed to force a showdown with Israel. In May 1971 he signed a 15-year Friendship Treaty with the USSR, which already had over 12,000 men in Eygpt (some of them operating surface-to-air missile sites and piloting warplanes) and which now increased its military supplies. But at the same time he purged a pro-Soviet group in the Cairo government and the following year, on 23 July 1972, expelled almost all the Soviet advisers, leaving only those manning the missile sites. For 3 months afterwards the Soviets suspended arms supplies to Egypt. Sadat also secretly opened contacts with the White House in 1972 but the Americans, bemused by his erratic policy and eager to maintain the Israeli-dominated status quo, did not exploit his desire to talk.

It eventually became clear however that Sadat's behaviour had more logic to it than it appeared. Indeed, he was capable of outmanoeuvring both superpowers. Basically he was determined to strike an independent course. He believed the Soviets to be cautious, self-seeking allies who would not give Egypt the military help they needed to overcome the defeat of 1967. They armed Egypt, but treated her as a pawn in superpower diplomacy and they would not willingly back a military reconquest of Sinai. Their influence over Egyptian politics and the military had to be cut back, hence the expulsions of July 1972. 'As a result of the 1967 war the balance at local level had tilted strongly in favour of the Israelis, so the only option to Egypt was to lift the conflict onto the higher, international level, where the balance was more equal.'[1] Sadat's attempts to deal with the Americans reflected his appreciation that only they could induce the Israelis to make concessions. But it was increasingly clear that he must do something dramatic to force the superpowers—and world opinion—to end the diplomatic stalemate in the Middle East. He was particularly offended by the Soviets' pursuit of détente with the Americans in 1971–2, without consulting Egypt or their other allies. Significantly the Middle East was barely mentioned at Nixon and Brezhnev's Moscow summit. In 1972 Sadat determined to force the Middle East onto the international agenda by launching an attack, in league with Syria's Hafez el-Assad, on Israel. 'I began to prepare for the battle,' he later wrote, 'although I knew that the entire world . . . had interpreted my expulsion of the Soviet military experts as an indication that I wasn't going to fight.'[2] In doing so he proved the point, seen often before in the Cold War, that whilst the East–West struggle might dominate world affairs, there were limits to the influence of the superpowers. America and the Soviet Union could sometimes be put at the mercy of their allies and clients, who dragged them into unwanted confrontation. In October 1973 the Egyptian–Syrian attack provoked the most serious US–Soviet tension since the Cuban missile crisis, challenged the May 1972 'Basic Principles' agreement between them and called the whole détente process into question.

Regional Conflict and Superpower Confrontation

The Middle East War began on 6 October with an Egyptian advance over the Suez Canal. As one Israeli leader later admitted, a 5 October meeting of the General Staff was told that 'the probability of war breaking out was regarded as "the lowest of the low".'[3] Until the last moment, the Israeli and US intelligence services had not expected such an attack, and for good reason. Not only had Sadat prepared for war twice before without result, but it was obvious that, given Israel's military superiority, Egypt and Syria must lose any conflict. What the Israelis and Americans failed to consider was that Sadat and Assad would launch a war they knew they would almost certainly lose. Victory was not the point of their action. The aim, rather, was to force Israel and the world to see that there must be negotiations about the lost territories. The Americans complained that the Soviets should have warned them of the attack, in the spirit of the Basic Principles. But the USSR itself was only told by the Syrians of the forthcoming campaign a few days before. True, the Soviets had, for months, been building up the Egyptian armed forces but Moscow had also denied the Egyptians the latest MIG-23s, encouraged the Arabs to seek peace, and had warned the Americans repeatedly that a dangerous situation was brewing in the region. Immediately before the Arab attack the Soviets very publicly evacuated their civilians from Egypt and Syria, but again the US and Israeli intelligence services failed to draw the correct conclusion. The Soviets could hardly give a categorical warning to America without seeming to betray their Arab allies and losing future influence with them. Israel only finally guessed what was

Anwar al-Sadat (1918–1981)

Raised as part of a large family, living in the Nile delta, Sadat trained as a soldier in the late 1930s, soon joining Gamal Abdul Nasser in a group of officers who resisted British rule in Egypt. For a time Sadat was an admirer of Hitler, being twice imprisoned during the Second World War for his links to the Germans. After the War Sadat became involved in politics and as a Free Officer he actively worked for the overthrow of the monarchy in 1952 and became a member of the Revolutionary Command Council in 1953. Under Nasser, who emerged as Egypt's leader in 1954, Sadat rose to be Vice-President, fully sharing Nasser's vision of a secularized, modern state, non-aligned and anti-imperialist in its foreign policy, with socialist development policies at home. Sadat succeeded Nasser following the latter's sudden death in 1970, freed the country from heavy reliance on the USSR, and restored Egypt's military pride, through early advances in the 1973 war with Israel. Thereafter he established close relations with the US and opened peace talks with Israel. He hoped these policies would both ease the defence burden on the Egyptian economy and restore control over Sinai, which in turn would help economic development and reduce social discontent. In 1979 he signed a peace treaty with Israel that won back the Sinai. But the deal offended other Arab states without bringing the hoped-for economic improvements. Faced by dissatisfaction among Muslims, he took steps to make the sharia the basis of Egyptian law, but he was assassinated by an extremist group within the army in October 1981, while attending a parade to celebrate the 1973 offensive against Israel.

Chronology: The 1973 Middle East War

1973

6 October	On the Jewish holy day of Yom Kippur, Egyptian forces cross the Suez Canal into Sinai, while Syrian forces advance on the Golan Heights.
9–10 October	While urging the Arabs to accept a ceasefire, the USSR begins large-scale arms supplies to Egypt and Syria.
10 October	US Vice-President, Spiro Agnew, is forced to resign over corruption allegations.
11 October	Israeli forces counter-attack into Syria.
13 October	Large-scale US airlift of arms supplies to Israel gets underway.
16 October	Israeli forces begin counter-attack across the Suez Canal; Soviet premier Kosygin, in Cairo, urges Sadat to accept a ceasefire.
17 October	Arab oil producers, meeting in Kuwait, announce cuts in production; some producers also increase oil prices.
18 October	Brezhnev appeals to Nixon to help achieve a ceasefire.
20 October	Kissinger flies to Moscow to discuss a ceasefire. Arab oil producers begin a boycott of supplies to US; speculation mounts in US that Nixon is to be impeached over the Watergate scandal.
22 October	US and USSR jointly sponsor a ceasefire resolution at the UN; but the ceasefire soon breaks down on the Sinai front.
24 October	As Israeli forces threaten to surround the Egyptian Third Army, Sadat urges both superpowers to send forces to the area; Moscow supports the proposal.
25–6 October	US forces put on a high level of alert worldwide.
27 October	Israeli and Egyptian representatives agree to meet to work out a ceasefire.
29 October	The war ends.

happening a few hours before the attack and was further hampered in its response by the fact it was the Jewish festival of Yom Kippur, a national holiday. The Arabs initially advanced on both fronts, expunging some of the memory of their dismal 1967 performance. 'The operation had been well planned, and was executed by the Arab soldiers with tenacity, courage and skill.'[4] In contrast to the Six Day War not only did Egypt and Syria have the element of surprise but they neutralized the Israeli airforce with surface-to-air missiles. The Arabs also discovered, at this time, the potency of oil supplies as a weapon against America and the West (see Chapter 13, B). Washington was initially too sanguine about an Israeli victory, starting an airlift of supplies on 9 October but at first using only aircraft of the Israeli airline, El Al. A full-scale US airlift only began on 13 October, 3 days after the Soviets had started a similar programme. But even the Soviets seem to have had little faith in Arab aims and, to Sadat's annoyance, did their utmost to urge a ceasefire in the first week. In the second week of the war the tide moved in Israel's favour and on 15–16 October a counter-offensive carried them back over the central part of the Suez Canal. They then struck south, threatening to surround the Egyptian Third Army which was still on the Sinai side. Meanwhile in Syria, the Israelis reversed their initial retreats in the Golan Heights and advanced towards Damascus. On 16–19 October the Soviet Premier, Andrei Kosygin, visited Cairo and persuaded Sadat to agree to a ceasefire, a move followed by US–Soviet attempts to secure such a step, with the new American Secretary of State, Henry Kissinger, visiting Moscow from the 20th to the 22nd. Now, however, it was the Israelis who upset the attempts at superpower cooperation. A ceasefire was agreed on 23 October but, unpopular with Israel's generals, it quickly broke down. With Egypt's Third Army now in dire peril, the war entered its most dangerous stage.

Increasingly desperate to save the Arabs from the humiliation and preserve their own influence in the Middle East the Soviets threatened, in a message from Brezhnev to Nixon on 24 October, to intervene militarily to end the war. This step was intended to force the Americans to put pressure on Israel rather than as a serious proposition. But it caused consternation in Washington. Sadat was prepared for both superpowers to send peacekeeping forces to the region, but the US had no desire to legitimatize a Soviet military presence there. Kissinger 'felt it was important to get the Israelis to obey the ceasefire, but he considered it even more important to keep Soviet forces out of the area.'[5] With Nixon increasingly beset by the Watergate scandal, it was Kissinger who played the leading role in Washington, eager both to minimize Moscow's influence in the Middle East and become the chief mediator in the conflict, winning Arab confidence whilst preserving the Israeli alliance. Following Brezhnev's warning, American strategic forces were placed on a high level of alert, Moscow was warned on the 25th not to intervene in the conflict, and pressure was successfully put on Israel to agree to end their advance. Since the Third Army was now entirely surrounded the Israeli generals could afford to be moderate, meeting the Egyptians on 27 October to discuss implementation of the ceasefire. The following day, Kissinger's success in making America the mediator in the conflict was confirmed when Egypt's Foreign Minister, Ismail Fahmy, visited Washington. 'His management of the October War', it has been said, 'occasioned for Henry Kissinger perhaps the greatest personal successes of his career.'[6] Largely left in control of US decision-making, he had used arms supplies to underscore Israeli dependence on Washington yet was also courted by the Arabs as the pivotal player in post-war diplomacy.

'Shuttle Diplomacy'

The 1973 war was followed by months of talks, centred around Kissinger's 'shuttle diplomacy' in which he visited the capitals of the Middle East several times, consolidating the ceasefire, making step-by-step progress on a wider political settlement, and sidelining Soviet influence. Israel had won the war but in a very different way to 1967, with its weaknesses exposed: it was a small country, unable to fight a long war, reliant on US support, and vulnerable to surprise attack. More divided among themselves than in the past, many Israelis now believed it sensible to bargain away the lands won in 1967 in return for security and peace. As Kissinger himself put it, 'Israel was exhausted no matter what the military maps showed. Its people were yearning for peace as only can those who have never known it.'[7] For his part Sadat was already disposed to deal with the Americans and distance himself from the Soviets. At the first meeting between Sadat and Kissinger, on 6 November, 'the fate of the Soviet Union in the Middle East was sealed.'[8] In order to win the return of Sinai (with its oil wells), ease the

The End of the Imperial Presidency? Watergate, War Powers, and the Church Committee

In November 1972 Nixon was re-elected by a landslide over his Democratic opponent, George McGovern. But during the campaign a clandestine group known as the 'Plumbers' (employed to 'plug leaks' of government information) had been caught breaking into Democratic Party offices in the Watergate hotel in Washington. They were immediately shown to have links to the White House but the Senate only began to investigate the matter in May 1973. Nixon was never proven to have advanced knowledge of the Watergate break-in but the following 15 months saw a series of embarrassing revelations that dominated US political life and indicated that he had mounted a 'cover up'. On 30 April, even before the Senate hearings began, key White House officials were forced to resign and in June a former White House legal adviser, John Dean, gave damning testimony against the President, who was ordered, in August, to produce tapes he had made of his conversations. The sense of corruption was increased by the resignation of Vice-President Spiro Agnew in October after tax-evasion charges. Nixon's attempts to impede the Watergate investigation led the House of Representatives to vote for impeachment. Hearings about this began in May 1974 and formal proceedings on 27 July. On 8 August the President resigned after admitting to withholding evidence.

The long-running scandal made it more difficult for Nixon to concentrate on foreign policy and Secretary of State Kissinger complained that this harmed the effectiveness of US policy abroad. It tarnished American democracy in the eyes of world opinion and may have harmed détente: the Soviets, who worked well with Nixon, did not welcome his political demise. However, the impact of the scandal should not be exaggerated. Domestically, American resolve was already weakened by a series of assassinations (John and Robert Kennedy, Martin Luther King), racial tension, social distress, and economic problems. Abroad, the Vietnam War had had a profound effect on US confidence and Congress was determined to place limits on the 'Imperial Presidency' passing the War Powers Act on 7 November 1973. Under the Act the President, when committing forces overseas, must seek Congressional support for a combat operation after 60 days and Congress may terminate an operation after 90 days. Even without Watergate, US foreign policy would have been constrained in Nixon's second term by economic difficulties and memories of Vietnam. Yet American peace was not crippled. In the Middle East in particular Kissinger was able to use 'shuttle diplomacy' to put Washington at the centre of events, sidelining Soviet influence.

Despite Nixon's resignation public concern remained high about secrecy in the US government. Press reports about the CIA's involvement, both in attempts to overthrow foreign leaders (notably Chile's Salvador Allende) and in surveillance of the anti-Vietnam War movement, led to Senator Frank Church being appointed to lead a Senate Committee on Intelligence activities in 1975. Large numbers of embarrassing revelations about the CIA followed and the Agency was forced in future to pay more attention to Congressional wishes. Previously it had very much been part of the Imperial Presidency, working largely at the President's behest.

burden of defence spending on the economy, and reopen the lucrative Suez Canal, the Egyptian leader was ready to offer Israel its long-desired promise of recognition. In doing so he was also prepared to compromise the interests of the Palestinians, for whom the Arabs had hitherto tried to secure a homeland. This divided him from Assad, who remained opposed to recognizing Israel, worked closely with the Soviets, and kept open the option of future military action—even if, without Egyptian participation, an Arab attack on Israel was unlikely.

Kissinger's 'shuttle diplomacy' succeeded in November 1973 in confirming the ceasefire in Sinai, securing supplies for Egypt's beleaguered Third Army, and arranging a release of prisoners-of-war. As yet, however, there was no proper military disengagement. 'Although nominally aiming at a general peace . . . Kissinger concentrated on a series of small local disengagement agreements.'[9] On 21–22 December an ambitious conference was held in Geneva between Israel and some of the Arab states, under joint US–Soviet chairmanship, to discuss a comprehensive regional settlement but it only confirmed the difficulties of achieving such an aim. The Israelis refused to recognize the Palestinian Liberation Organization (PLO) as the representative of the Palestinian people; Syria attended with reluctance and showed no enthusiasm for a deal. Yet this political setback did not prevent progress on military disengagement. On the Syrian front a separation of forces was concluded in May 1974 and the more complicated, mutual withdrawal of Egyptian and Israeli forces took place over several stages in 1974–5. These steps were accompanied by the re-establishment of US–Egyptian diplomatic relations in February 1974, by a triumphant visit from Nixon to the Middle East in June and by grants of US economic aid to Egypt and Jordan. The Israeli agreement to pull back from Suez allowed the Canal to be reopened in September 1975, following 8 years of closure, Egypt agreeing that Israeli goods could be transported through it. Sadat's shift in diplomatic loyalties was confirmed by his cancellation, in March 1976, of his friendship treaty with Moscow. But the Soviets were not yet powerless in the Middle East. 'The Soviet reaction to the absence of significant success in its Middle East policy was an increasingly anti-American, pro-radical line in the region.'[10] They maintained links not only with Syria, but also with radical regimes in Iraq and Libya, and in August 1974 they gave diplomatic recognition to the PLO. This, alongside the united Arab insistence (confirmed by the October 1974 Rabat conference) that the PLO was the only legitimate voice of the Palestinians, and the invitation the following month to the PLO leader, Yasser Arafat, to address the UN, added to Israel's continuing sense of insecurity and made it even more difficult to contemplate a comprehensive regional settlement. In 1975 a majority of states in the UN General Assembly even voted to condemn Zionism as a form of racism.

Whatever the problems, 'shuttle diplomacy' had helped secure de facto peace in the area; and however insecure the Israelis might feel, their American ally was confirmed as the principal factor in Middle East diplomacy. 'In September 1973, no one would have dared to prophesy that within two years America would be restored to more influence in the Arab world than it had had since 1948.'[11] Yet this had only been achieved at great cost to US–Soviet relations. In the 1973 war, the first real test of détente, the American public believed it had been treated badly by the Soviets. They had armed the Arabs, failed to warn Washington of the impending conflict, and even threatened military intervention. The fact that Moscow had shown restraint during most of the war and that the superpowers ultimately achieved a ceasefire, was forgotten, largely because of the frightening events of 24–25 October, when the Americans had exaggerated the Soviet menace partly to induce Israel to end the war. Thereafter it was the Soviets who felt that America was exploiting the situation, seizing the diplomatic initiative in the Middle East and refusing to treat the USSR as an equal in the peace process. A recognition of equality was one of the most important prizes Brezhnev wanted to win from détente. Then again, the Soviets did not become disillusioned with détente because of these events, nor did they do much to maintain good relations with Sadat. Even with their radical allies in the Middle East the Kremlin demonstrated restraint: Soviet arms supply policy was designed 'not to allow the Arab countries a configuration of their armed forces such that they would be tempted to go for an all-out offensive war.'[12] There would be no repeat of 1973. The October war was a serious blow to détente, but not its death knell.

Instability in Lebanon, 1973–1975

The ending of the latest round of hostilities in the Arab–Israeli conflict did not produce the same kind of problems that the 1967 war had in terms of its regional impact on the radicalization of Palestinian resistance to Israel. Nor did it produce moves to a regional settlement, but it did presage the later peace between Israel and Egypt. The Sinai II interim agreement between Israel and Egypt also had the unfortunate consequence of deepening divisions between Syria and Egypt. That had implications for the position of Lebanon which was rapidly to descend into civil war, although for many other internal reasons apart from the regional factors which were to influence the continued instability of the country.

The conflict has been interpreted in a number of ways—from an Arab–Christian civil war to an element in East–West competition—many of which misread or oversimplify the situation. One, retrospective study notes 'the Lebanese conflict is indeed complex. No more so, however, than the war in Yugoslavia ... In any event it did not result from some mysterious thunderbolt out of a tranquil sky, but from internal and external historical processes whose protagonists, Lebanese, regional, and international are identifiable.'[13] The key issue is perhaps whether the civil war, which began in 1975, was really a product of internal divisions or a reflection of the divisions in the Middle East from which the Lebanon could not escape. In many respects its territory became a battlefield on which most of them were directly fought out.

Lebanon is a small, mountainous country with close historical links to its larger neighbour, Syria. But the ethnic and religious mix of Lebanon was extremely complex. In mid-century slightly more than half its population was Christian, divided into Orthodox, Catholics, and the predominant, wealthy Maronites. The Muslims included not only Shi'ites and Sunnis, but also the Druze, believers in a mystical offshoot from the Shi'a branch of Islam and a fiercely independent sect with strong family ties. For many years these groups had existed in a Lebanon economically dominated by their seaport capital, Beirut—an important trading and banking centre. However, the maintenance of the Lebanese state was threatened on a number of fronts: the ethno-religious Constitution imposed by the French that increasingly failed to represent the population balance; the failure to link the poorer mountainous regions economically with the more prosperous coastal plain; and the interference of the Palestinians, Syrians, and Israelis. These problems for the state reinforced the tendency of people to give their loyalty to localities and ethno-religious groups rather than to the government. The Maronites had a majority in parliament and always took the Presidency, while representatives of the Sunnis, Shi'ites' and Druze held other key appointments. Thus the Sunnis took the premiership and the Shi'as the speakership of parliament. Indeed, where 'Lebanon parted company with the Arab state system was in its non-authoritarian state and open society', but it has been argued that this very openness 'left it open to being torn apart and subject to outside intervention'.[14]

After the American armed intervention in 1958 (Chapter 8, B) the regime's stability was restored by the new President, General Shihab, who secured the support of both the Maronite right-wing (the Phalange) and the Druze. However, the balance was then undermined by three key developments. First, the Arab defeat in the 1967 war which both deflated Arab nationalism and led to a radicalization of certain groups, most importantly the Palestinians. Second, the emergence of new political forces, notably the impact of Palestinians in Beirut, the establishment of a Maronite coalition, and the creation of Kamal Jumblatt's Lebanese Nationalist Movement. These more formalized divisions again served to weaken Lebanon's cohesion and challenge central authority. Palestinians had been arriving in Lebanon in increasing numbers especially after 1967 and the Palestinian Liberation Organization (PLO) set up its headquarters in Beirut in 1970. Soon there were about 400,000 Palestinian refugees living in Lebanon and their presence further shifted the population balance in favour of Arabs and Muslims. Some also created problems by using bases in the south to launch attacks on Israel, which struck back in kind by bombing Beirut and crossing into Lebanese territory for the first time in 1972. 'Thus the war that it did not take part in [1973] ... had more dramatic consequences for Lebanon than for any other Arab country. In 1970 it became, and until 1982 would remain, the chosen terrain for the Palestinians' struggle to recover their lost homeland.'[15]

In 1973 President Suleiman Frangieh announced that he would never allow the Palestinians to create 'a state within a state' in Lebanon and there were violent clashes between the PLO and the government army. The PLO was confirmed by the Arab League, at its Rabat summit in 1974, as the true representative of the Palestinian people and its self-confidence began to grow as the weakness of the Lebanese state became more evident. The Maronites began to believe that the army would become increasingly hamstrung by the Muslim elements and began to prepare themselves to act more decisively against the PLO. In April–May 1975, an obscure argument over Muslim–Christian fishing rights led to clashes, and when the bodyguards of Bashir Gemayal were murdered revenge was taken on the Palestinians who would play little part in the next phase of the conflict. But the civil war was underway, the government had collapsed, and battles were raging between militias of the various Lebanese factions. It 'was not just a military confrontation between two hostile groups, but a conflict of communities, ideologies, power politics, parochial interests and values.'[16] Within the region the Israeli government was adamantly refusing to speak to the PLO despite their growing recognition as the sole and legitimate representatives of the Palestinian people, the corollary being that King Hussein of Jordan could no longer represent them in any peace process. Yet in one sense there were signs of moderation emanating from the Palestinian

National Council and its call for a political solution by stages rather than an armed struggle. However, Rabin, the new Israeli Prime Minister in 1974, believed that while taking risks for peace was justified, peace should be approached cautiously and moves towards it should be made slowly. Moreover, he described the coming years as 'seven lean years' because of Arab oil power and superpower rivalries which would hopefully be followed by 'seven fat years'. In the meantime he had growing instability and conflict on Israel's northern border to contend with.[17]

B. The Era of 'Stagflation'

Challenges to the Bretton Woods system

Beyond the Middle East, the most significant result of the October war was the sudden, steep increase in oil prices which helped produce a global situation of stagnant growth rates and high inflation (hence the term 'stagflation'). But, the economic doldrums of the mid-1970s also had longer-term origins and in one vital aspect—the end of currency stability in the Western world—the turning point had been reached 2 years before. At the end of the Second World War, from the time of the Bretton Woods Conference, the Western powers had tried to create the conditions for a stable, expanding international economy in which trade was maximized and unemployment minimized. The International Monetary Fund (IMF) provided help for those with balance of payments problems, the World Bank gave funds to developing countries and monetary stability was provided by a system of fixed exchange rates, in which countries valued their currency against the dollar, which itself was pegged against the value of gold (see Chapter 2, A). In the 1950s and well into the 1960s this system seemed successful. Western economies experienced consistently high growth rates, especially in Germany, Japan,

and Italy; the volume of world trade expanded; service industries (like transport, banking, insurance, and tourism) increased markedly and typically, in 1970, provided about a third of jobs; and there was a particular demand for new consumer goods, from radios and vacuum cleaners to refrigerators and televisions.

However, by the late 1960s, growth rates were becoming less impressive, partly because post-war population growth had tailed off. The US economy was especially troubled, having had a worsening trade balance since the late 1950s and facing the burden of the Vietnam War. The US found itself increasingly in a poorer financial and commercial position vis-à-vis Europe and Japan, the regions it had put on the road to recovery after 1945. While it invested capital overseas and used up its gold reserves, they increased their reserves substantially. The most formidable new industrial competitor was Japan which overtook the British economy in size in 1962 and that of Germany in 1967. By 1972 Japan had a $4 billion trading surplus, much of it with the US, which accounted for about one-third of Japanese imports and exports. Between 1952 and 1970 the Japanese economy grew five times over, its people ready to deny themselves high wages and consumer goods in order to generate national wealth and full employment.

Such changes in world trading patterns caused resentment in the United States. There was pressure on Japan from the late 1960s to expand its armed forces and its aid to the less developed world, so as to reduce the relative burden of these on the US. In the 1968 election, Richard Nixon promised Americans that he would reduce the imports of cheap Japanese textiles, something he achieved in an agreement of October 1971. Japan and NATO countries were also pressed to make 'offset purchases' of American military hardware, to help cover the cost of US forces based on their soil. Since these armed forces spent substantial sums locally, they effectively added to America's balance of payments problems as well as its defence budget, which by 1969 stood at $4.85 billion. There was considerable pressure from Senator Mike Mansfield and others in Congress to halve US force levels in Europe in the early 1970s. Nixon successfully resisted this, but the atmosphere in the Western alliance was poisoned. America's allies resented the implication that they were not cooperating fully or contributing enough to Western defence when the US still controlled nuclear weapons in Europe. True, NATO countries spent an average of 5 per cent of national income on defence, while America spent 9 per cent, but much of the US defence budget was devoted to the Vietnam War: in 1964–5, before the war began in earnest, defence spending had been less than $3 billion.

From Fixed to Floating Exchange Rates

One casualty of the increasingly volatile commercial and financial situation, and particularly of America's relative decline compared to Western Europe and Japan, was the system of fixed exchange rates. The US was no longer prepared to prop up the global monetary system when its own position was being damaged by the effort involved. By 1970 America's inflation had reached 6 per cent (having been barely noticeable a decade before), interest rates had to be raised and unemployment rose above 5 per cent. Nixon, hoping for re-election in two years time wanted to improve the country's economic competitiveness by lowering the value of the dollar. As

gold and foreign currency reserves continued to deteriorate a devaluation of the dollar was widely expected and instability already affected other currencies. In November 1967 Britain, which had held the value of sterling constant against the dollar for 18 years, was forced to devalue largely because of chronic balance of payments problems; in August 1969, a year after severe domestic unrest, france devalued the franc by 11 per cent; and in May 1971—in a sign of things to come—the Germans, who were under pressure to revalue because of their strong trading position, decided to 'float' the Deutschmark, allowing its value to be influenced by the market, rather than being fixed at a certain value against the dollar.

Nixon finally launched a 'New Economic Policy' on 15 August 1971. To the rest of the world it became known as the 'Nixon shock'. It included wage and price controls intended to limit inflation, a temporary 10 per cent surcharge on imports to help trade figures, and the end of the dollar's convertibility into gold. The last measure effectively implied 'that the Bretton Woods system was no longer viable'[18] and led more countries to 'float' their currencies over the following months including, in August, Japan. There were grave doubts, however, about whether a system of floating exchanged rates could work. If currencies altered in value against each other on a daily basis, it was feared that trade would suffer. Exporters who set a price one day might find it an uncommercial one when it came to the delivery date. The French government, which had worked to undermine the position of the dollar in the 1960s, had long urged a return to the Gold Standard, which had operated earlier in the century, but the proposal was too obviously designed to benefit France itself, which had been amassing gold for years. The US still had the world's largest economy and about one-third of its gold reserves.

There were discussions among the leading industrial nations about creating a new system of fixed exchange rates, following a devaluation of the dollar and a revaluation of the Japanese yen. Such a currency realignment was achieved to some extent in the Smithsonian Agreement of December 1971, but the pressure on currencies continued in 1972. In June the pound sterling was forced to float due to industrial unrest and inflationary pressures in

Britain. In March 1973, at a meeting in Paris, the G-10 group of industrial powers effectively abandoned all attempts to save fixed exchange rates, although a group of West European countries, led by West Germany, tried to 'peg' their currencies within a certain value of each other through the so-called 'Snake'. Over summer 1973 the world discovered that the new system operated quite well. Dire warnings of a return to the 1930s, with a collapse of world trade and rocketing unemployment, were not fulfilled. But already there were signs of another economic crisis, over oil. So-called 'managed floating' now 'became the exchange rate policy of almost all industrial countries. . . . It did not prevent some very severe disturbances but it continued to provide a moderately orderly framework and . . . a fair degree of responsiveness to market forces.'[19]

The Impact of OPEC

Western economic growth in the 1950s and 1960s relied in part on the supply of cheap fuel for industry and transport. Even when the Organization of Petroleum Exporting Countries (OPEC) was founded in September 1960 to protect producers' rights an oil glut in the mid-1960s limited its potential power and preserved cheap access to oil for the developed world. Then the situation began to change. 'Around 1970 a shortage of oil developed, US production began to decline rapidly, estimates of reserves ceased to increase more rapidly than production and there was a sudden consciousness that oil was finite.'[20] Western economies were now heavily dependent on oil imports, making little effort at energy conservation. In 1968 the Arabs formed their own group within OPEC and in September 1969 Colonel Muammar Gadaffi came to power in Libya, taking a strong line in support of higher prices. In 1971 OPEC agreed to press for higher prices from the producers and a bigger share in profits; and in 1972 the Arab oil producers already talked about limiting oil production as a way to push up prices.

Although Western countries were already concerned about future oil supplies and prices before October 1973, it was the Middle East War which revolutionized relations between the oil producers

and their suppliers. On 16 October OPEC unilaterally increased oil prices by two-thirds. Four days later the Arab oil producers, controlling about a third of world oil reserves, launched a complete embargo of supplies to those countries who had aided Israel, including America, Holland, Portugal, and South Africa. (Japan and most West European countries had been careful not to offend the Arabs.) To American annoyance, West Germany would not allow the Israelis to be resupplied from bases on its soil; Spain would not let its airspace be used; and Britain cut off arms supplies to all Middle East countries, a step which harmed Israel in particular. There were limits to what the oil producers could do without completely alienating their customers and some Western countries were more vulnerable to pressure than others. Thus America only imported about 5 per cent of its oil from the Middle East, while Holland was almost entirely dependent on Arab supplies. Certain oil producers, especially Saudi Arabia and (non-Arab) Iran were close allies of America. Nonetheless, the oil embargo against the US remained in force until March 1974 and by then oil prices had risen by about four times the level of the previous year. The impact on the Western economies was startling. Measures to reduce oil consumption and develop alternative energy sources were hard to achieve and could not prevent substantial balance of trade problems, an alarming fall in industrial activity, and a new twist to inflation. Certain countries Japan, for example, coped well with the challenge. 'On the eve of the war Japan was the world's second largest consumer of petroleum and . . . was dependent on outside sources for 99.7 per cent of its oil', four-fifths of which came from the Middle East.[21] But, after slipping into a trade deficit in 1973, although its growth rates were cut, it generally maintained an export surplus, began to invest large sums abroad and, most significantly, turned from energy-demanding industries to high-technology products such as radios, televisions, and computers. Others suffered markedly. In Italy inflation reached 19 per cent in 1974 and in Britain in 1974–5 it peaked at over 20 per cent. Developing countries too were badly hit, although the Eastern bloc was shielded by high Soviet oil output. The oil companies saw profits increase. Oil producers, unsurprisingly, saw their trade surpluses leap, winning money for economic development and arms purchases. Saudi Arabia, the largest OPEC oil producer, experienced a tenfold increase in its national wealth by 1977.

Between 1974 and 1978 oil prices held steady and there was a slow recovery of economic stability in the West. In 1974 the American-led bid to create an International Energy Authority, to facilitate joint action by the Western powers, had little effect. But in 1975–6, at French instigation, the leading economies (America, Japan, Germany, France, Britain, Italy, and Canada) had more success in founding the G-7 annual summits. This showed that, whatever their differences during the 1973 war, Western Europe, America, and Japan were capable of concerted 'trilateral' action. However, attempts to tackle the problems of less developed world states—other than the oil producers—proved less successful. The energy crisis deepened concern about the 'North–South' divide in the world and in 1974 developing countries called for the creation of a New International Economic Order.

The quest for a New International Economic Order was accompanied by a general move by Western banks to increase loans to developing countries. Indeed, in 1976 nearly $10 billion was lent in this way, a fivefold increase on the 1972 level. This shift from government-led aid to private assistance with development was another by-product of the oil crisis. Western governments were keen to restrict their expenditure in the mid-1970s and there were limits to the money banks could make from loans to the troubled Western economies. But the OPEC countries invested much of their new found financial wealth, known as 'petrodollars', in the Western banking system, 'which in turn had to find borrowers and offered low rates of interest.'[22] The need for banks to maximize profits by returns on the available capital seemed to offer developing

The Proposed New International Economic Order

The idea of a New International Economic Order originated in the work of Raoul Prebisch, who in 1964 as the Secretary-General of the United Nations Conference on Trade and Development (UNCTAD) wrote a report entitled 'Towards a New Trade Policy for Development'. The timing of the resolution put forward by a group of less developed countries (LDCs) and adopted by the UN General Assembly in December 1974 was influenced both by the success of OPEC and the failure of import substitution as a development strategy. It called for the formation of LDC producer associations, some stable linkage between produce prices and the prices of manufactured goods to stop the deterioration in the terms of trade experienced by LDCs, the right to nationalize foreign enterprises, and the drawing up of regulations to be applied to the activities of multinational corporations (MNCs). It was not based on the idea of the overthrow of the international capitalist system but on the reform of that system. Reform would give LDCs more control over their natural resources, better terms of trade, reductions in the cost of obtaining Western technology, greater access to Western markets, and more control in the decision-making of international economic institutions. By the mid-1980s the attempt to establish a New International Economic Order had clearly failed. The failure can be attributed to the LDCs receiving no backing from the powerful OPEC countries, the increasing difficulties inherent in high oil prices and growing debts, and most of all to the refusal of the Western countries to make concessions that would lead to higher domestic food prices for their voters.

World Oil Production in the 1970s: Top Twelve Producers as a Percentage of World Output

1970	1980
1 USA 21%	USSR 19%
2 USSR 16%	Saudi Arabia 15%
3 Saudi Arabia 8%	USA 13%
4 Venezuela 8%	Iran 5%
5 Iran 7%	Iraq 5%
6 Libya 7%	Kuwait 4%
7 Kuwait 6%	Venezuela 4%
8 United Arab Emirates 4%	Nigeria 4%
9 Iraq 3%	China 4%
10 Canada 3%	Libya 3%
11 Nigeria 2%	Indonesia 3%
12 Indonesia 2%	Britain 2%
(Others 13%)	(Others 19%)

countries the cheap loans they needed in order to boost their own growth. Only in the early 1980s did the potential problem of lending vast sums to poor countries in the less developed world become apparent (see Chapter 18, D). For the Western powers, the 1970s ended on a pessimistic note when oil prices began to mushroom again, thanks to the fall of the Shah of Iran in December 1978. The decade's apparently never-ending economic malaise undermined Western morale and led Americans to ask whether they were in long-term decline. This in turn helped give the impression of a world where Soviet communism and Western capitalism were equally strong, when in actual fact US wealth and industrial capacity far outstripped that of the Soviet Union.

C. Political Problems in Europe

An Era of Doubt in the West

The economic difficulties of the late 1960s and 1970s helped create a climate of self-doubt in the Western alliance, and Western Europe in particular saw industrial, social, and political divisions greater than any since the slump of the 1930s. At the same time the continued division of Europe, the fear of nuclear war and, thanks to Vietnam, moral doubts about US leadership led to a greater Western tolerance of communist policy in Eastern Europe and a readiness to embrace détente. Also, a new post-war generation had grown up which, never having experienced the slump or war, questioned the values of their parents. At the turn of the decade, both in the US and Western Europe, a counter-culture had emerged, largely amongst middle-class youth which condemned materialism and consumerism, inequalities of wealth-and the power of elite groups. This counter-culture, with its rejection of liberal capitalism and its refusal to adopt traditional social values in the West, presented a political threat when, most notably in France in 1968, protests were supported by manual workers. In 1969 Italy suffered a 'hot autumn' of strikes which rumbled on for years as workers sought to increase wages and win better working conditions.

The emergence of urban guerrilla movements, such as West Germany's middle class Baader–Meinhof gang, became an international problem in the early 1970s. The working-class Italian Red Brigades presented yet another violent challenge to liberal, capitalist society. The leftward trend in governments and society in Europe was not universal, but it indicated that the 'never had it so good' society of the late 1950s and early 1960s was failing to maintain consensus. It may have helped détente and certainly encouraged the desire to avoid violence and radical ideas—in Britain trades unions were able to win a 'social contract' with the Labour government in 1974—but economic changes heralded a new era made worse by the 1973 oil crisis. Inflation and high government borrowing (in an attempt to maintain social spending despite the slackening of growth) afflicted some countries, notably Italy and Britain, where in 1976 the International Monetary Fund demanded government spending cuts as the price of a substantial loan. Unemployment rose above a million and 1979 saw a further bout of strikes in the so-called 'winter of discontent'. In Italy meanwhile unemployment hit 7.5 per cent, inflation was stubbornly high, and the communists seemed on the brink of overtaking the pro-American Christian Democrats as the leading party. Not all countries suffered so badly. West Germany managed, through deflation and a focus on exports, to hold inflation down to about 5 per cent in the mid-1970s, when it touched 20 per cent in Britain and Italy. But the social, economic, and political divisions had an inevitable impact on the international scene. An American attempt to reinvigorate NATO, with the so-called 'Year of Europe' in 1973, came to little. The European Community (EC) found that economic difficulties and British membership were hampering attempts at further integration. And there were particular problems in the shape of Italian communism, a revolution in Portugal in April 1974, and a revival of the Cyprus problem. The years of détente were years of disruption and change in many aspects of Cold War society, but the problems of the liberal, social reform consensus and its international economic order in place since 1945 did not lead to radical, domestic change or the end of international tension. Instead they produced the kind of conservatism with a hard, more ruthless edge that would eventually characterize the international policies of much of the Western world in the early 1980s.

NATO and the 'Year of Europe'

Although it had survived France's withdrawal from the military command structure in 1966, by the 1970s the cohesion of the Atlantic alliance was again being called into question. European members had recovered economically from the Second Word War and were now major trading rivals of the US. As Vietnam grew more costly, Americans came to resent the perceived reluctance of West Europeans to pay more for their own defence. It was not that the alliance was about to disintegrate. Indeed, one reason why Nixon and Kissinger did not focus much attention on reforming NATO before 1973 was that the underlying reasons for the 'Atlantic Partnership' continued: Europe gained a sense of security and political confidence behind which it could build material prosperity; America secured liberal-capitalist allies on the front line of the ideological struggle with Moscow. West Germany, Britain, and others had fully demonstrated their loyalty to the alliance in 1966.

But NATO's problems were real and growing. The USSR's achievement of near strategic nuclear parity led Europeans to doubt whether a US President would really defend them in war, and such distrust was only accentuated by the 'burden-sharing' debate. Whilst supporting the principle of détente, Europeans resented their lack of influence over the SALT process and even feared the creation of a US–Soviet condominium, which would shape

Europe according to superpower interests. Nixon's August 1971 economic measures, affecting trade and monetary policy, added to the growing sense of distrust. For its part, having fostered European unity in earlier decades, the US government under Nixon continued to fear the European Community as a rival trading bloc, with a population roughly equal to America's once Britain, Denmark, and Ireland became members in January 1973. There were also bilateral problems to take into account. Apart from Franco–American differences, which continued under de Gaulle's successors, Pompidou (1969–74) and Giscard d'Estaing (1974–81), the US was also suspicious of West Germany's Ostpolitik under Willy Brandt (Chapter 9, E) and there was no personal warmth between Nixon and Britain's pro-European premier Edward Heath (1970–4).

The 'Year of Europe' was launched by Kissinger in a speech on 23 April 1973, in which he tried to underline the mutual benefits of the Atlantic alliance whilst proposing solutions to various problems. Unfortunately, the speech itself generated suspicion. Its timing suggested that Kissinger had decided to deal with European problems only because he had time on his hands after resolving more important problems, like Vietnam. The idea that America could choose when to launch a 'Year of Europe' was distasteful to West European countries, who saw themselves as America's equals in the alliance. 'Pompidou remarked that for France every year was a year of Europe.'[23] Kissinger's promise to support European unity, to continue the American military presence, and to safeguard European interests in the détente process were all very well. But his complaints about EC protectionism and the lack of burden-sharing were obviously designed for a US audience. The climax of the speech was the call for a 'New Atlantic Charter' to embrace Japan as well as NATO. But, especially for the French (who recalled the original Atlantic Charter of 1941 as an Anglo-American propaganda document) a New Charter could be no more than a new justification of US domination. Thus Kissinger discovered that dealing 'with several sensitive allies, each with its own interests and public opinion to consider, was not remotely the same as dealing with a handful of leaders controlling totalitarian governments', such as produced his earlier diplomatic successes.[24] Then again, with the Watergate crisis, the oil crisis, and an upcoming (if unforeseen) war in the Middle East, 'he could hardly have picked a worse twelve months' for his initiative.[25]

Within months the 'Year of Europe' was a virtual dead letter. Instead, the October Middle East War (Chapter 13, A) became the occasion for a deep transatlantic rift. The French were pro-Arab from the outset; most NATO members refused to let their soil be used for America's supply of arms to Israel; and Europeans were gravely offended, in the last phase of the war, when US forces were put on a high level of alert without consultations in NATO. Europeans feared that Washington could have dragged them into a nuclear war in which they had no direct interest, whilst Americans publicly criticized the Europeans for following an anti-Israeli policy, influenced by the selfish desire to safeguard oil supplies from the Middle East. Kissinger's April 1973 speech did result, in June 1974, in NATO's Ottawa declaration which restated the purposes of the alliance. However, it fell far short of a new Atlantic Charter, excluded Japan and had little public impact. Kissinger himself described it as 'drained of ... moral and psychological significance by a year of bickering'.[26] 1974 instead became a year of political turmoil in the West, as Heath, Pompidou, Brandt, and Nixon were all replaced in turn. Heath narrowly lost an election called against the background of a coalminers' strike, Pompidou succumbed to cancer, Brandt was toppled by a spy scandal, and Nixon destroyed by Watergate.

The Eastern Bloc in the 1970s

In the aftermath of the Czechoslovakian crisis (see Chapter 9, C) the Communist regimes of Eastern Europe returned to their attempts to make the Soviet economic and political model more effective. 'The Eastern European regimes were politically stable, secure beneath the Soviet umbrella ... and the economies appeared to have staved off the "oil shock" from which the rest of the world had suffered.'[27] Whilst retaining central planning, there were efforts to simplify its cumbersome bureaucracy

and poor quality goods. Hungary in particular, after 1968, experimented with a 'New Economic Mechanism' which, while preserving the essential elements of Soviet planning, sought to decentralize economic decisions, introduce an element of competition, and make factories work more profitably. As a result Hungary was treated favourably by the West, joining GATT in 1973 and the IMF in 1982. But even in Hungary the reformers faced a fightback by 'recentralizers', whilst other East European leaders viewed the Hungarian experiment with suspicion. 'With the exception ... of Hungary, economic reform ... remained a timid, faltering enterprise.'[28] East Germany, Bulgaria, and Czechoslovakia, the last under its new leader, Gustav Husak, were the most loyal to the USSR. In East Germany, Erich Honecker even tightened up central planning in 1971, after a period of decentralization. Indeed, the 1970s saw a continuing trend towards a diversification of practice in the bloc, with each country trying to emulate the Soviet model, but in its own way. In Romania, for example, Nicolae Ceauşescu maintained central planning and signed a new friendship treaty with Moscow in 1970, but continued to steer as independent a line as possible in foreign policy, preserving relations with China despite the Sino–Soviet split and, like Hungary, joining GATT in 1971. Attempts to integrate the bloc more closely together, in emulation of the European Community, came to nothing. Under the 'Complex Programme' of 1970–1, COMECON developed joint projects and an investment bank, but these achieved very little and the extension of the organization to Cuba (1972) and Vietnam (1978) merely underlined its fundamental lack of cohesion.

One important way in which Eastern European Communists tried to overcome inefficient management, poor production levels, and a lack of competitiveness on world markets was to rely on technological inputs from the West. Indeed, the desire for freer access to Western technology was a strong motivation for them to pursue détente in the 1970s. Eastern bloc leaders, like their colleagues in the Third World, also exploited the readiness of Western banks (at a time of 'stagflation' at home) to lend substantial sums for investment. Paradoxically, the West was supposed to compensate for the inefficiencies of communism. Unfortunately, however, the top-heavy, centralized planning systems were unable to adopt Western technology effectively and, with little success in boosting their export trade (though some, like Bulgaria, developed a tourist industry), their economies became massively indebted to Western banks. They also began to 'import' inflation from the West and as early as 1975 Hungary, which imported large amounts of Western goods, had to introduce an austerity programme to hold down prices. Furthermore, the decade of détente carried with it a political cost. Western trade and tourism, and agreements such as those made at Helsinki, opened the East to disruptive influences (Chapter 12, C). 'Increasingly the political legitimacy of the regimes of eastern Europe ... came to rest on their socio-economic accomplishments ... But as the economies began to deteriorate ... even this source of legitimacy disappeared.'[29] Communist leaders were never ready to legitimize themselves by holding democratic elections, but their people were now more aware of Western economic success and political freedoms, whilst the Helsinki process put a new emphasis on the importance of human rights. There was also some interest in the 'Eurocommunist' ideas of the French and Italian communist parties, which suggested that national self-determination and Marxist-Leninism could be combined. The result was movements like Czechoslovakia's Charter 77, in which over 200 leading figures joined together to demand respect for human rights. This and similar, smaller groups elsewhere were extinguished by the secret police, but such a response only highlighted the lack of political freedom: 'the party's political monopoly ... left society with no effective role in the system, except as passive objects of policy.'[30] Communist rule continued to rely on a mixture of ruthless security forces, apathy, control of the media, subsidized housing, some slow improvements in living standards, and the genuine support of certain sections of the population such as managers, bureaucrats, and those workers in inefficient industries who would otherwise be unemployed.

Western critics of détente argued that the process of East–West contacts itself shored up communist regimes and helped them escape serious unrest in the 1970s. But the crises in Hungary (1956) (see Chapter 6, A) and Czechoslovakia (1968) had shown that, short of provoking nuclear war, the West was powerless to help those who rose up against Soviet domination, and the logic espoused by many exponents of détente was to wean the East Europeans away from communism through contacts which would increase awareness of the economic benefits available in the West. Nixon was, of course, both a convinced anti-communist and an architect of détente, who used visits to Romania (1969) and Poland (1972) to demonstrate that East Europeans could develop their own links to the West. The extension by Washington of 'most-favoured nation' trade status to Romania (1975) and Hungary (1978) delivered a similar message, and the April 1976 'Sonnenfeldt Doctrine', named after a State Department official, set out the logic of encouraging greater autonomy in the communist bloc (though, once more, critics saw it, like Helsinki, as legitimizing Soviet domination). The West's potential to disrupt the communist system was not, however, revealed until 1979–80, when the process of détente ended and the Cold War returned. By 1979 US, West European, and Japanese banks were owed nearly $70 billion by the Eastern bloc states, compared to $10 billion in 1971. Any idea that they could survive in isolation from the capitalist world had disappeared and the Soviets, whose own economy had become stagnant, were faced with a growing threat to their economic predominance in the Warsaw Pact. Indeed, by absorbing huge amounts of financial aid and subsidized raw materials, such as oil, the Eastern bloc had already become a serious liability to the Soviet economy. The return to the Cold War forced the East Europeans to reduce investments and consumption once more, having actually made only marginal economic improvements in the mid-1970s. 'Economic failure, common throughout the region, was openly acknowledged ... in Poland and Hungary, where high levels of foreign debt could [not] be concealed.'[31] And détente had brought sufficient gains for East Europeans to regret its passing. Especially in East Germany, usually extremely loyal to Moscow, the process of Ostpolitik, accompanied by growing commercial and financial links to West Germany, had been popular. At the end of the 1970s Europeans on both sides of the East–West divide were reluctant to resurrect the Iron Curtain and served to constrain both superpowers as tensions between Moscow and Washington increased.

The Community of the Nine

The 'northern enlargement' of the EC to Britain, Ireland, and Denmark in January 1973 created a market of about 250 million people and accounted for about 20 per cent of world trade. The expansion was accompanied by great expectations of new political and economic cooperation among the members, encouraged by their October 1972 summit meeting in Paris which planned a full 'European Union' by 1980, including monetary union and joint action in new areas like social welfare, regional development, and the environment. However, the following decade was largely one of disappointment and slow progress for the Community, mainly because the years of 'stagflation' sapped its vitality. Indeed, even an optimistic account of the EEC argues that, 'Apart from the Community's enlargement the two decades from the mid-1960s to the mid-1980s can be seen as a long period of stagnation.'[32]

Economic and Monetary Union, the subject of the 1970 Werner Report (which might have led to a single currency) was a direct victim of 'stagflation'. The instability of the world's commercial and financial system, with high inflation and the move towards floating exchange rates, damaged any prospects of European currency stability. The different experiences of countries like Germany and Italy in this period also made economic coordination between them more difficult. In April 1972 the nine EC members formed the 'snake' to try to preserve monetary stability by valuing their currencies within a certain percentage of the dollar. But Britain was almost immediately forced out, others followed, and within a few years the 'snake' was limited to a small number of countries, dominated by Germany. In 1973 a Monetary Cooperation Fund was established to help weak currencies but had little success and only in 1978–9 was it possible to create a more stable European Monetary System, the main element of which was an Exchange Rate Mechanism (ERM). The ERM was a much improved 'snake', valuing member currencies within a certain percentage of a central rate. It too suffered instability, leading to several renegotiations of the central rate, before providing greater stability after 1983. By then healthy growth rates had returned to Europe, global trade was expanding, and a stable ERM proved a valuable weapon against inflation.

One country which did not join the ERM was Britain, the principal new member of 1973, when it was led by a convinced pro-European in Heath. He lost office in February 1974 of course and, for the next 10 years, Britain seemed ill-fitted to the Community. Faced by higher food prices (due to the Community's common agricultural policy), inflation, and low growth the British people could see little benefit from membership. The new Labour government was itself divided over the wisdom of membership and, having criticized the terms under which Heath had entered, decided to renegotiate them, winning slightly improved financial arrangements. These were then put to a referendum in 1975 and approved, but the substantial 'yes' vote did not reflect any deep popular enthusiasm for the EC. Labour rejected all idea of sharing Britain's newly discovered oil reserves with the Community, delayed the introduction of direct elections to the European parliament, and stood aside from the ERM. When the Conservatives, under Margaret Thatcher, returned to office in 1979 they too avoided ERM membership, were critical of the common agricultural policy, and began a campaign to reduce Britain's net financial contribution, which now amounted to £1 billion. Arguments over the 'British Budgetary Question' dominated EC discussions until a compromise was reached in 1984.

There were some successes for the EC in this period. In 1979 a Treaty of Accession was agreed with Greece, which became the tenth member in 1981, and the first direct elections to the European parliament were eventually held in June 1979. But the parliament itself had only limited powers and could not fulfil the role of a strong, popular institution, able to control national policies. Instead, a more important development was the inauguration in

1975 of regular summit meetings, which emphasized the power of national governments in shaping the Community. Other attempts to restructure the EC, such as the 1976 Tindemans Report or the 1981 Genscher–Colombo Plan had limited results and, though a regional development fund was created in 1975, it was poorly resourced. Dramatic progress with European integration only revived in the mid-1980s.

Discord in Southern Europe

A series of crises in Southern Europe in the mid-1970s threatened to divide NATO. A possible communist-led government in Italy, a military coup in Portugal, and a Greek–Turkish crisis over Cyprus made the years 1974–6 ones of great uncertainty in the region although by 1979 the sense of crisis was overcome and in fact liberal democracy advanced, replacing right-wing regimes in Portugal, Greece, and Spain.

Communist parties in Western Europe all tried to widen their appeal in the wake of the 1968 Czechoslovakian crisis by distancing themselves from Moscow, accepting the existing political system, and even tolerating the existence of NATO. In 1976 the French communists abandoned their commitment to a 'dictatorship of the proletariat', but their loyalty to Moscow continued to cost them votes and it was the Italian communists who proved more successful in pursuing a 'Eurocommunist' line. In 1973 their general secretary, Enrico Berlinguer, expressed a readiness to work with other parties in order to contain the extreme Right, preserve social reforms, and demonstrate that communists could be trusted in office. He hoped that a deal with the Christian Democrats could help 'unblock the political system', paving the way for a communist role in government, as well as 'preventing . . . economic difficulties from causing a dangerous drift toward an authoritarian right-wing regime'.[33] Given Italy's dire problems with strikes, inflation, and terrorism some moderate Christian Democrats, including premier Aldo Moro (1974–6), believed that cooperation with the communists, in a 'historic compromise', made sense. It could preserve Italian unity through a difficult period. In a sense the Christian Democrats 'had

little choice. Their regime was collapsing around them, amid economic crisis, financial scandal [and] incipient terrorism' from the Red Brigades.[34] Although Moro was assassinated in 1976, his successor Giulio Andreotti relied on communist support in parliament, even agreeing a common programme with them in 1977. Such cooperation was helped by the communists' acceptance, in 1975, of NATO membership and by the closely fought 1976 election when they won 34.5 per cent of the vote to the Christian Democrats 40 per cent. The Italian Right and the Americans, however, were deeply concerned by such developments. In April 1976 Kissinger warned that the communists must not be brought into the Italian government and, in fact, a formal coalition was avoided by the Christian Democrats. In 1979 the communists ended their parliamentary support for the government and in the ensuing election their share of the vote fell to 30 per cent.

The dangers for NATO in Portugal in the mid-1970s appeared far worse. The country had been ruled by a right-wing dictatorship since 1932, first under Dr Antonio Salazar and then, after 1968, under Marcel Caetano. The existence of such an authoritarian regime in a founder member of NATO called the alliance's democratic credentials into question. All opposition to Salazar was crushed, little was done to tackle illiteracy and poverty, and protectionist economic policies were followed which limited economic growth and industrialization. Equally important however, Portugal tried to hold onto its empire in the face of colonial wars in Angola, Mozambique, and Portuguese Guinea, which proved increasingly 'unwinnable'. On 24–25 April 1974 the regime was suddenly overthrown, by left-wing army officers who were determined to resolve the colonial wars (Chapter 13, D) and modernize the country. This 'Carnation Revolution' went off surprisingly peacefully but was followed by 2 years of political turmoil. Although a respected, conservative army general, Antonio de Spinola, was appointed President many army officers had absorbed Marxist ideology and were determined to pursue radical policies. A civilian cabinet was formed but its members lacked administrative experience and were faced by impossible demands for land reform, greater social spending, and nationalization, at a time (in the aftermath of the Middle East War) of inflation and fuel shortages. In July a new Cabinet was formed under a left-wing colonel, Vasco Goncalves, who allied with the communists, and in September a power struggle led to Spinola's resignation, leaving the far Left in the ascendant. Potentially this could have led to a major international crisis: 'as seen from Washington, Portugal could become a focus of Marxist contagion in southern Europe at a time when Generalissimo Francisco Franco, the Spanish dictator, was nearing death, and the power of the Communist Party was growing in Italy.'[35] Apart from some financial assistance to the communists however, the USSR did not try to exploit the situation, apparently accepting that Portugal, as a NATO member with an Atlantic coastline, was firmly in the US sphere of influence. Kissinger publicly expressed concern over the threat of Portugal's loss to the alliance and a new, strong-minded US ambassador, Frank Carlucci, was appointed to Lisbon. Significantly, the Portuguese people themselves showed their desire for liberal politics in a general election in April 1975, when the communists won only 17 per cent of the vote, an event which seriously undermined their claim to a major political role. Mario Soares' Socialists won 38 per cent and the centrist Popular Democrats 26 per cent. By the time a constitution was published in April 1976 stability had been restored and Portugal was allowed to return to NATO's Nuclear Planning Group, having been suspended since the 1974 coup. At this same time instability was avoided in neighbouring Spain, despite the death in November 1975 of Franco. His successors, King Juan Carlos and premier Adolfo Suarez, moved quickly to legalize opposition groups and elect a constitutional Assembly, which published a liberal constitution in October 1978. Spain too was then set on a course towards stable democracy.

In Cyprus the delicate 1960 Constitutional settlement (see Part II) had soon been called into question. As early as 1963 an attempt by President Makarios to reform it in the Greek Cypriots' favour led to Greek–Turkish intercommunal violence and a threat by the Turkish government to intervene. In 1967, when a group of colonels seized power in Athens, there was another bout of intercommunal violence, but it was only in 1974, with their regime unpopular at home, that the colonels decided to stir up trouble over Cyprus. On 15 July, dissatisfied with Makarios' policies, the colonels instigated a coup against him, but the operation was botched, the President escaped and Cyprus rapidly slipped into violence. On 20 July a Turkish force landed in the north of the island, insisting on the right to defend the Turkish-Cypriot community. Powerless to prevent such a disastrous development, the Athens junta collapsed and a former Prime Minister, Constantine Karamanlis, returned to power, restoring Greece's pre-1967 constitution. Meanwhile, in Cyprus the situation grew worse. The failure to reach a compromise at talks in Geneva led the Turks to renew their attacks in the north, partitioning the island with 37 per cent now under Turkish-Cypriot control. (They made up about 18 per cent of the island's population.) In protest over NATO's failure to halt the Turks, Karamanlis pulled Greece out of the alliance's military command until 1980 and the US Congress, sympathetic to Greece, suspended military aid to Turkey in 1975 for 3 years. Karamanlis and the Turkish Premier Bulent Ecevit met to discuss their differences in 1978, ending the immediate crisis, but the Turkish army remained in Cyprus and the Turkish-Cypriots set up their own 'Turkish Republic of North Cyprus' in 1983. There were numerous rounds of talks over the following years to consider a possible settlement, but it proved impossible to satisfy both the Greek-Cypriot desire for reunification under majority rule with the Turkish-Cypriot desire for security against Greek domination under such a system. Turkey and Greece remained members of NATO, which had survived yet another dangerous moment, but there was periodic tension between them especially over claims to islands in the Aegean Sea.

D. **European Détente at its High Point**

The Road to Helsinki

Despite the economic and political problems that beset Western Europe in the mid-1970s, these years saw better East–West relations across the Iron Curtain. Superpower détente had begun to turn sour just as European détente reached its height in the Helsinki conference of 1975. Yet European détente proved more stable and long-lasting than the superpower version over the decade as a whole with firmer, widely based domestic support. European détente was an established tradition, stretching back through France's President de Gaulle in the 1960s to Britain's Premier Churchill in the 1950s, both of whom were prepared to visit Moscow in order to reduce tension. Western European countries had a less ideologically driven foreign policy than the US and, being close to the dividing line between East and West, were more concerned about the likely results of a nuclear exchange between NATO and the Warsaw Pact; they also recognized that a lowering of tensions would bring rewards, not least in the commercial field. Although some West European Leftists may have been ready to condone the practices of communism, Churchill and other advocates of détente saw it as a way of undermining communism by peaceful means: by respecting the present status quo in Europe, the West could use trade and contacts to break down barriers and suspicions with the East, eventually diluting the Soviet bloc; Cold War strategies, it could be argued in contrast, simply helped cement the Eastern bloc. In the Eastern bloc too, of course, there was a continued tendency towards greater independence of Moscow, not least from Yugoslavia and Romania. On both sides of the Iron Curtain, European countries had an interest in treating each other as equals, easing superpower domination and expanding trade (see Chapter 9, E.).

While pursuing détente both sides were clearly trying to defend their own interests. The Western powers hoped to reduce Soviet conventional superiority while opening the communist system to liberal ideology and commerce; the Eastern powers to 'decouple' the US from European security while giving international legitimacy to the Soviet-led satellite bloc. NATO was well aware that the Soviets could exploit détente to 'drive wedges' between members of the Western alliance, but the Czechoslovakian crisis had confirmed that the Soviet position in Eastern Europe could not easily be broken down. It now seemed even more unwise to try and liberate Eastern Europe by force given Soviet nuclear strength. The USSR was aware of the dangers that increased Western cultural and economic contacts might bring to the communist world but, faced by the Chinese menace in Asia, the Kremlin was anxious to stabilize Europe's borders and to gain some Western acknowledgement of its predominance in the East. Before meaningful talks could begin, there had to be compromises and the key steps came in May 1971, when Leonid Brezhnev agreed to Mutual Balanced Force Reduction (MBFR) talks on the military side; and in December 1971, when NATO accepted that a European Security Conference should meet. At their Moscow summit in May 1972 Brezhnev and Nixon agreed that both these developments should go ahead. Preparatory conversations on MBFR began in Vienna in January 1973 and formal talks began 9 months later, but they proved highly complex and, lacking political commitment on the Soviet side, made no progress until they were replaced by talks on 'Conventional Forces in Europe' in the late 1980s (Chapter 20, D). Preparatory conversations on a European Security Conference began in Helsinki in November 1972 and the first round of Foreign Ministers' talks started in July 1973. Thirty-five states took part including all Warsaw Pact and NATO members, together with neutral and non-aligned nations, Albania being the only European country not present. Ahead of the meetings the Soviets vainly tried to reduce the Eastern bloc's need for Western economic assistance by initiating a new ten-year COMECON plan. At the same time the Americans were keen to demonstrate their lack of respect for the Brezhnev Doctrine, with visits by Nixon to Poland and his Secretary of State, William Rogers, to several East European states. Such behaviour emphasized that, whatever the improved atmosphere in Europe, ideological differences were deep and two well-armed alliances continued to face each other.

Continued Success for Ostpolitik

Across the European divide, however, relations seemed more relaxed because of a continuing improvement in relations between West Germany and its Eastern neighbours, thanks to Chancellor Willy Brandt's Ostpolitik. In 1970 he had signed treaties with the USSR and Poland, accepting Germany's eastern borders and renouncing the use of force (see Chapter 9, E). These Moscow and Warsaw 'Eastern Treaties' were ratified on 17 May 1972 with the Christian Democrats abstaining. The Christian Democrats, who had dominated German government for two decades before 1969, had never reconciled themselves to a policy that seemed, in effect, to recognize Germany's division into two halves. To them, and to some of the centrist Free Democrats, Ostpolitik 'appeared to be an unconstitutional acceptance of the permanent division of Germany, given the explicit commitment in the Basic Law [Germany's Constitution] to work towards German reunification.'[36] However, the popularity of Ostpolitik was confirmed in the November 1972 elections, which gave the Social Democrats the best result they ever achieved in West German polls. Recognition of Brandt's achievement was also seen in the award of the 1972 Nobel Peace Prize and it has been argued that, given the advances in superpower détente, 'had the German government not been willing to take its initiatives in Ostpolitik at this time, the Federal Republic would have appeared as a recalcitrant Cold War relic, and its vital interests could have been bartered away by others.'[37] In May 1973 Brandt followed up the Soviet and Polish arrangements with a German–Czechoslovakian Treaty that invalidated the 1938 Munich Treaty and confirmed Czechoslovakian control of the Sudetenland, thus resolving German relations with another of its neighbours. But by then the focus of Ostpolitik had moved to the more controversial and difficult question of a deal with East Germany.

The September 1971 Berlin agreement, between the four occupation powers (the US, USSR, Britain, and France) had marked a first step towards an improved atmosphere between West and East Germany, who still did not recognize each other's existence. Brandt's concept of 'two Germanies in one nation' was meant to allow Germany's division into separate states to be accepted in the short term, while reassuring the German people that the hopes of eventual reunification had not been abandoned. Indeed, for Brandt the hope was that a relaxation of tension would lead to the eventual withering away of the division of Germany: the Ostpolitik treaties 'did not affect our claim to self-determination and national unity.'; rather, 'we had to accept the status quo territorially in order to dislodge it politically' (a logic that was applicable to European détente more generally).[38] In December 1971 and May 1972 agreements were signed on improved communications between the two Germanies, whilst ratification of the Eastern Treaties paved the way to negotiations on a 'Basic Treaty' on East–West German relations. Significantly, this was signed on 22 December 1972, in the immediate wake of Brandt's election triumph. The Treaty embodied the ideal of 'two Germanies in one nation' by extending the diplomatic recognition that the West had hitherto always denied to the East. It allowed both countries to enter the United Nations in 1974 with the approval of both superpowers and, although it implied a short-term acceptance of Germany's division, it was ratified more easily than the Eastern Treaties. Personal contacts between East and West Germany (where some families, not least in Berlin, had been separated for years) were especially welcomed at a popular level. West Germany also gained from greater trade with the Eastern bloc. More widely, countries from each side of the Iron Curtain were now able to establish diplomatic relations with both Germanies and the chances of another international crisis like the Berlin Blockade were much reduced. The division of Germany was now an accepted fact of European life. Predictably, many interpreted the Basic Treaty as 'an admission by Bonn that Germany's division was, if not permanent, at least an existing reality' but the West German government reiterated that 'Reunification is required under constitutional law ... The treaty is no treaty of partition.'[39] Ironically the success proved short-lived for Brandt. He resigned as Chancellor in April 1974 after an East German spy was exposed in his private office. But the policy of Ostpolitik was maintained by his successor, Helmut Schmidt.

The Helsinki Conference and its 'Final Act'

The multilateral summit of European states, plus the US and Canada, at Helsinki between 30 July and 1 August 1975, marked both the culmination of the talks on European security and the high point of European détente. In some ways it could be seen as representing the comprehensive post-Second World War 'peace settlement' that the Cold War had hitherto prevented. On the other hand, it did little more than accept existing territorial realities and bred new controversies of its own. Both sides could feel that they had made significant gains from the 'Final Act' of the conference, which included a range of agreements divided across three 'baskets'. The first of these concerned security issues. This section stated the principles of respect for sovereignty and non-interference in the domestic affairs of others, as well as respect for human rights. Some elements could be taken to be critical of Soviet domination of Eastern Europe, but the Kremlin also later exploited the principle of non-interference to oppose Western criticism of the domestic policy of communist states. Most importantly this 'basket' declared European borders to be inviolable. This was not the same as unchangeable (as the Warsaw Pact had wanted), but it did mean that any border changes had to be made by peaceful means. The Eastern bloc treated this as de facto acceptance of the post-war territorial settlement and for this reason it was criticized by some in America and Western Europe as condoning Soviet domination in the East. 'After all, Moscow had obtained what it had fought for since the 1950s: the recognition of post-war borders ... and thus the legitimatization of its East European sphere of influence.'[40] But again, it needs to be borne in mind that on the territorial issue, Helsinki 'essentially did little more than confirm ... what the West had already accepted.'[41] No one in their right mind

believed that European borders could be forcibly changed anyway, whereas the possibility of peaceful change remained open, allowing the dramatic redrawing of the map that would come in 1989–91. The problem was that too many 'western commentators critical of the Final Act ... uncritically [repeated] Soviet claims about ratification of the post-war territorial and political status quo' and failed to emphasize that 'the Western negotiators managed to secure language that sanctioned the possibility of peaceful change in Europe.'[42] The Western powers effectively separated territorial realities and the military balance from issues of political legitimacy, and intended that the legitimacy of the Soviet system should be undermined by the greater East–West contacts fostered by baskets 2 and 3.

'Basket 2', arguably the least important, covered economic, commercial, cultural, scientific, environmental, and other forms of cooperation. Trade between Eastern and Western Europe saw especially strong growth in the 1970s, much more than that between the superpowers, and the US became concerned at the scale of West European reliance on trade with the East. But this could hardly be attributed to the Helsinki agreements in themselves, even if the Final Act did seem to endorse the process. In any case, in the long term, as Churchill and others had always expected, it was the Eastern bloc that became vulnerable to 'ideological subversion' because of its everyday contacts with the liberal democracies, not least because of the Communist regimes' cravings for Western loans and imports. Of greater importance on this front was 'Basket 3', which dealt with respect for human rights, exchanges of visits, and the free flow of information and ideas, something the West had been pressing for since the 1955 Geneva summit. The Soviets agreed to this in order to make gains on territorial security and trade in the other baskets, but the West hoped that the stress on individual freedom and human rights would encourage political evolution in the communist bloc, undermining the Brezhnev Doctrine. The Final Act gave encouragement to Eastern European anti-communists who soon began to establish 'monitoring groups' to test how far they could now push the authorities to acknowledge human rights.

Helsinki was followed by other meetings of the

Conference on Security and Cooperation in Europe (CSCE), beginning with the Belgrade meeting in October 1977. Inevitably, both sides emphasized different aspects of the agreements—the West human rights, the East territorial stability—and criticism soon deepened in America among Democrats and the Republican Right. Later academic accounts

Leonid Brezhnev (1906–1982)

Born in the industrial town of Dneprodzerzinsk, in the Ukraine, Brezhnev, himself the son of a steelworker, trained as a steel engineer before moving into full-time political work. At first he concentrated on administrative work in the Ukraine and focused on its industrial reconstruction after the war. But under Khrushchev, he successfully managed the Communist Party in Kazakhstan, joined the Politburo and, in 1960, rose to be Soviet President. It was partly through fear of being removed from the Politburo that he led the overthrow of Khrushchev in 1964. By then Brezhnev was the consummate Kremlin insider: a competent, experienced bureaucrat, orthodox in his opinions, with a strong sense of duty, who had risen to high level despite his natural caution. His very lack of individualism or charisma made him attractive in the wake of Khrushchev's adventurism and, fulfilling the expectations of his supporters, in the 1960s he neither ran risks abroad nor espoused reformism at home. At first, in the position of General Secretary of the Communist Party, he shared power with the Premier, Alexei Kosygin, and others. But he was always the most influential figure in the leadership and by 1971 Kosygin was very much in his shadow. At home he tried to improve living standards while cracking down harshly on all signs of dissidence. Abroad, he came to support a policy of relaxing tension with the West in the 1970s while becoming ever more estranged from Communist China. After 1975 Brezhnev was increasingly troubled by personal ill-health, stalling industrial output, and heavy defence spending. His final years were overshadowed by the demise of détente, economic stagnation, and an ill-fated decision, in 1979, to invade Afghanistan.

could be similarly dismissive, arguing that Helsinki 'scarcely justified the high hopes placed in it' and that Soviet indifference to human rights in its aftermath 'encouraged the view that totalitarian states were not capable of reform from within'.[43] With the crushing of Yuri Orlov's 'Helsinki Monitoring Group' by the KGB in May 1976 the Soviets certainly exposed the limited impact of 'Basket Three' in the short term and, during the ensuing Presidential election in America, there was severe criticism of President Gerald Ford for having signed the Helsinki Accords. One critic was the Democratic Senator, Henry Jackson, who argued that the president had 'sold out' to the Soviets. This led the State Department's Helmut Sonnenfeldt to counter that, in fact, the US was supporting the 'aspirations in eastern Europe for a more autonomous existence within the context of a strong Soviet geopolitical influence'.[44] But the logic of the 'Sonnenfeldt Doctrine' proved difficult to defend in 1976 and Jimmy Carter was able to exploit the issue against Ford in their head-to-head television debates. In Western Europe the increased personal contacts, trade, and tourism brought by détente gave Helsinki somewhat greater popularity and, in the wake of the collapse of communism in 1989, it was easier to see that the 'Helsinki process' might have had a very important role in generating self-doubt within the Eastern bloc. High-quality Western imports, the realization that the West was not a relentless military threat, the recognition of the importance of individual rights—all these slowly served the purposes of 'ideological subversion' and called into question the value of the planned economy, high military expenditure, and the totalitarian state. The late 1980s would reveal that at least some of the totalitarian states of Eastern Europe were 'capable of reform from within'. Thereafter it was possible to claim that 'the Helsinki process—particularly its human rights aspect—played a significant role in bringing about the dismantling of Communist rule in . . . Europe by undermining the legitimacy of these regimes.'[45]

E. Crises in the Less Developed World

Détente and the Less Developed World

As seen above, the October 1973 Middle East War led to questioning in America of the value of détente, only eighteen months after the Moscow summit. The War also reflected the inability of the superpowers to control their 'clients' in developing countries and showed that, however much the US might wish to stabilize the less developed world, conflicts there would go on. Indeed, from 1973 to 1979 there was a series of crises in the less developed world—the October War, the fall of South Vietnam (1975), the civil war in Angola (1975–6), the Ogaden conflict (1977–8), and the Soviet invasion of Afghanistan—which did much to destroy superpower détente. To a growing number of Americans the common element in these crises was the Soviet determination to advance the cause of Marxist-Leninism worldwide, something which Nixon and Kissinger had hoped détente would prevent. By the time Kissinger left office in 1976 disaffection with détente in America was considerable. Having defined a policy of 'linkage', under which the Kremlin could only expect the gains of cooperation (trade and arms control) in return for restraint in regional conflicts, it was increasingly difficult to justify the continuation of détente if Soviet support for 'wars of national liberation' went on.

The Soviets however had a different view of these problems. To them it seemed ridiculous to expect changes in the less developed world to cease. Its Marxist beliefs, however diluted by the 1970s, did lead Moscow to see wars of national liberation as 'inevitable'; and Brezhnev had always made clear that, in the Soviet interpretation of détente, superpower rivalry in the less developed world would continue. Besides, although Western interests generally seemed to be on the defensive in Africa and Asia in the 1970s, the Americans had their successes. In the Middle East, the US edged Russia out of the post-1973 peace process; in South-East Asia, the fall of Vietnam was not followed by the loss of Thailand, Malaysia, and Indonesia as had once been feared; and in East Asia America could always 'play the China card' against the Soviets (as occurred in 1978–9). Neither did Americans show restraint in the less developed world when their interests were at stake and they felt powerful enough to act. Unsurprisingly, given past policy in the Western hemisphere, they were especially determined to prevent pro-Soviet influence spreading in Latin America.

Chile and Allende

The violent overthrow of Salvador Allende, the Marxist President of Chile, on 11 September 1973 has often been blamed on the US. In fact, despite numerous other revelations about America's Chilean policy and the activities there of the Central Intelligence Agency (CIA), 'there is no evidence of direct involvement in, or provocation of, the 1973 coup by the US government.'[46] Ultimately the Chilean military, under Augusto Pinochet, were responsible for the coup. Kissinger insisted that 'Allende was brought down by his own incompetence and inflexibility. What happened, happened for Chilean reasons, not as a result of the acts of the United States.'[47] However, the US government and multinational companies who were affected by Allende's nationalization policies, did much to undermine his position before the military acted and it was no secret that Washington would welcome his fall. Thus, it can be argued that 'even if Nixon and Kissinger were not working toward a coup, they were eager to have Allende discredited in order to bring about his defeat in the 1976 elections.'[48] And, 'through the CIA's covert operations in Chile, the application of vast economic pressures, and military assistance to the Chilean armed forces, the United States government did without question help to create a situation in which the anti-Allende coup became possible.'[49]

The CIA had first used covert propaganda and funding of his opponents to prevent Allende coming to power at the head of a 'Popular Front' coalition in 1964. The victor on that occasion was Eduardo Frei Montalva, a Christian Democrat whose attempts at moderate reform could not prevent rising inflation and rural poverty. At the next election in 1970, despite CIA attempts to prevent it, Allende narrowly won a three-cornered race and was duly installed as President. This created a dilemma for the US: Allende had been legally elected in a country which, in contrast to the rest of Latin America, had retained a stable liberal democracy since 1938; but this was the first time a Marxist had been freely elected as the President of a country, he was a friend of Fidel Castro and, despite the narrow election victory, began a radical programme of land reform and nationalization. This had a profound effect on society: 'All aspects of life became politicized, and politics became polarized—it was impossible not to be either for or against the government.'[50] The CIA continued to fund both his opponents and adverse press reports on Allende, whilst the US government successfully managed to cut off most external financial aid to Chile. This, alongside rising inflation and upheaval in the valuable copper market, caused severe economic problems, leading to strikes and a growing number of anti-Allende demonstrations. Allende's policies also alienated important groups in Chilean politics, including the Church, landowners, and of course the military, who eventually toppled him even though they had never taken a leading role in Chilean politics in the past.

The fall of Allende demonstrated that even success in a democratic election would not make Marxists acceptable to Washington. Press revelations about CIA involvement led to an embarrassing Congressional investigation into the Agency's activities in the late 1970s. And Pinochet's brutal regime was an embarrassment to the US through the 1980s. Successfully confirmed in office in a 1980 referendum, Pinochet failed a similar test in 1989 and resigned, though he remained an important force in the background. Under his elected successor, the centrist Patricio Aylwin, Chile experienced good growth rates, comparable to other parts of the 'Pacific Rim' in the early 1990s and a stable liberal democracy seemed to have returned.

The Fall of South Vietnam and Cambodia

The January 1973 peace settlement (Chapter 12, C) in Vietnam removed American forces from the country but never brought real 'peace' to the South, where the communists and the Thieu regime continued to struggle for power. In 1973–4 over 50,000 South Vietnamese troops and twice as many communists, as well as thousands of civilians, died in the continued fighting. Thieu refused to recognize the existence of the opposition National Liberation Front or to accept the losses of territory which the 1973 settlement implied. But his regime was dogged by high inflation, widespread corruption, and large-scale desertions (about 200,000 in 1973–4) from its army. With one million men and with American equipment, the army looked strong on paper but its morale and leadership remained poor. About one-third of South Vietnam's 17 million people were reduced to refugee status by 1975, many had moved from the countryside to overcrowded towns, and agriculture had been so devastated that the country had to import its staple food, rice. Meanwhile, with the fall of Nixon and the determination of Congress to avoid further involvement and expenditure in South-East Asia, there was increasingly little chance that America would fulfil Nixon's promises of helping Thieu if the communists reneged on the 1973 settlement. Hence Kissinger's later claim that any hope of enforcing the 1973 settlement or of saving Cambodia 'was torpedoed by the United States Congress and our domestic turmoil' over Watergate.[51] Others however, reject such logic; 'given the public's antipathy toward Vietnam . . . it is doubtful if the United States could have regenerated a commitment to rescue Thieu's government. The Vietnamese Communists . . . were determined eventually to gain power in Saigon. And Thieu, inept and corrupt, was unable to stop them.'[52]

The North Vietnamese continued to probe the South's military weak points in 1973–4 but only in December 1974 did Hanoi decide to abandon the Paris agreements completely and seek Thieu's overthrow. 'A string of local victories gave those in favour of a bolder strategy an edge at a politburo meeting in December 1974, and a two year plan was drawn up' for conquering the South.[53] The Politburo was surprised by the easy advances in the Central Highlands in January 1975 and astonished by how quickly a further offensive, in March, broke the Thieu regime. Thieu himself made the disastrous decision to withdraw his forces from much of the country to the Saigon-Mekong delta area, where more than half the South's population was concentrated. Asked to conduct such a long and dangerous retreat, his demoralized army was soon routed. On 21 April, under US pressure and still refusing to contemplate a coalition government with the communists, he resigned, blaming Washington for the collapse. His successor, Duang Van ('Big') Minh, called a ceasefire 9 days later and the way was clear for the communists to create a united, centralized Vietnam. Economic planning was introduced, land redistributed, Southern officials 're-educated' or executed, and Saigon renamed Ho Chi Minh city (after the nationalist leader who had died in 1969). Despite some attempts to establish diplomatic links in 1977–8, the Americans showed little desire to help Vietnam recover from three decades of destruction. Whilst complaining that the Vietnamese were not doing enough to find the few American troops still posted as 'missing in action', Washington froze Vietnamese assets, cut off all aid to the country (as well as to Laos and Cambodia), and reneged on earlier promises of financial assistance.

Meanwhile, in Cambodia there had never been the shadow of a peace agreement in 1973, although Congressional action meant that US military support for the Lon Nol government ceased in mid-August. The extremist Khmer Rouge were suspicious of Hanoi after its settlement with the Americans, rejected the idea of forming a coalition government with the royalist leader, Prince Sihanouk, and exploited rural poverty and US bombing to win local support. By January 1975 only the capital, Phnom Penh, remained in Lon Nol's hands and it fell to the Khmer Rouge on 17 April, just days before the fall of Saigon. The American government demonstrated the following month that it was not quite powerless in the region: when the Khmer Rouge seized a US merchant ship President Ford despatched the marines on a rescue mission which, though unnecessary (the ship was released as the mission began) proved popular at home. The new Cambo-

dian regime, under Pol Pot, proceeded to empty Phnom Penh and conducted a campaign of genocide against upper- and middle-class groups in a ruthless attempt to turn the country into a Maoist rural utopia. By the end of 1978 about 2 million people had died in Pol Pot's 'killing fields' or of starvation and disease.

The image of communist success in South-East Asia was completed in December 1975 by the triumph of the Pathet Lao in Laos, a country which had been subjected to even more American bombing than Cambodia. (Laos had been bombed since 1964, Cambodia only since 1969.) But the old American fear that the fall of one 'domino' would lead to another proved baseless. Propped up by the US, the royalist government in Thailand survived and within a few years the regions' communists were at each other's throats, with Vietnam invading Cambodia in 1978 and China striking against Vietnam in 1979 (Chapter 14). The number of deaths in the post-war Indochina wars by then ran into several millions, the exact total incalculable.

Angola: the End of Portugal's Empire

The April 1974 'Carnation Revolution' in Portugal which toppled the Salazar dictatorship was a military coup which led to the decision to grant independence to the colonies. The empire had been central to Salazar's vision of Portuguese greatness; it provided food and raw materials, and by 1968 half a million Portuguese had settled in the two main colonies, Angola (the wealthiest) and Mozambique. The divisions between the two main anti-colonial movements in the north of Angola, which were associated with the outbreak of what may be seen as a spontaneous rebellion in March 1961 (see Chapter 8, B) had widened in the 1960s. The difference was that after Lyndon Johnson became President, the dominance of the National Front for the Liberation of Angola (FNLA), led by Holden Roberto, was completely undermined and the leading movement in the struggle to represent Angolan nationalism became the Popular Movement for the Liberation of Angola (MPLA). The latter movement had succeeded after 1964 partly by developing links with the Soviet Union and Cuba after which it assumed a more Marxist position and partly by winning support from the Congo (Brazzaville) leader Massemba-Debat. This enabled Agostinho Neto, the MPLA leader from December 1962 after his escape from a Portuguese jail, to rebuild the organization from a headquarters in Brazzaville. Meanwhile the FLNA suffered from the replacement of Cyrille Adoula, the close associate of Holden Roberto, as Prime Minister of the Congo, later Zaire, in 1964. The FLNA leader was only saved by the coup in the following year which brought General Joseph Mobutu to power in Leopoldville.

The importance of external influences on the development of anti-colonial movements in Angola had always been evident and may have contributed to the failure of any genuine nationalist movement (representing peoples from most of Angola) to emerge before independence in 1975. On the other hand, internal divisions were also evident, although it is important that these should not simply be seen in terms of the ethnic groups associated, but never exclusively so, with the main political parties. Angola had many minor parties and the political fragmentation was made worse in 1966 by the formation of another major grouping, the National Union for the Total Liberation of Angola (UNITA), under Jonas Savimbi, who defected from the FLNA in 1964. The founding of UNITA gave a voice to the southern peoples of rural Angola who were generally regarded as less advanced than those in the North. Now there were three groups largely based on the Mbundu, Ovimbundu, and Bakongo people. In addition the MPLA, in contrast to UNITA and the FLNA, was a *mestico*- (mixed race) dominated party with its strength in Luanda. This injected an urban and a racial element into what was to become a civil war as the other two main parties were essentially Black African led. Partly as a result of these divisions 'the nationalists posed no critical threat to the Portuguese presence in Angola during the armed struggle.'[54] But then neither could the Portuguese regain complete control over the country which they had been trying to do since 1961. There were also the ideological differences between the increasingly Marxist MPLA and the more pro-Western groupings, although the Chinese injected the Sino–Soviet split

into the Angolan issue by establishing links to the FNLA in the 1970s. From the time a FNLA delegation met with Deng Xaioping in December 1973 China supplied military training and arms until October 1975. Clearly once the government in Lisbon collapsed in 1974 and independence became inevitable, the Cold War then became an even more important channel for outside intervention. The question of who should inherit Portuguese power became urgent and greater internal conflict over the succession was linked to larger-scale external interference.

The American response to these events was confused. In contrast to the Kennedy administration, which saw the Cold War in Africa being won through links with pro-Western Africans who would need help in achieving independence, Kissinger saw things differently. He made in fact precisely the same mistake as the British advocates of multiracialism (see Chapter 8, D) and saw the Portuguese as able to resist radical African challenges. After the coup and collapse of Portuguese rule Kissinger had to come to terms with the failure of his assessment but refused to try for an Angolan coalition government with left-wing elements or to consider working with those successful but radical movements in other parts of Portuguese Africa. Firing those who suggested such options, Kissinger opted to work with General Mobutu in the Congo to help the FLNA, together with the Chinese, in their bid to inherit power.

In Mozambique there was a single independence movement, FRELIMO, formed from three exiled organizations in 1962 with the encouragement of Tanzania's Julius Nyerere; it launched a military campaign in late 1964 but failed to make serious inroads against the Portuguese until 1972. A far more successful campaign was conducted in a much smaller colony, Portuguese Guinea, where Amilcar Cabral had founded the PAIGC in 1956, launched a guerrilla campaign in January 1963, and soon controlled much of the countryside. For a time after 1968 a new Portuguese commander, Antonio de Spinola, managed to keep Cabral under control and the latter was assassinated (apparently by his own side) in 1973. But that same year the PAIGC secured deliveries of surface-to-air missiles from Eastern Europe and began to threaten Portugal's hold on the cities. The financial cost of the three guerrilla wars to Portugal was not huge (it devoted about 7 per cent of national income to defence) and army deaths (at about 5,000 in 1961–74) were also limited; but the conflicts sapped national confidence and seemed 'unwinnable'.

The 1974 revolution in Portugal was not solely produced by the colonial wars in Africa but its timing was influenced by the problems they brought. In the first place the increase in the numbers of conscripts and the resultant drop in morale brought about by the general stalemate produced growing dissatisfaction. In a sense the Caetano government was strengthening the forces which would eventually destroy the regime. And the April 1974 catalyst was giving conscripted officers the same route to promotion and higher pay as volunteer personnel. The end of the Caetano dictatorship catapulted General Spinola to power, who was initially in favour of some grandiose overseas Portuguese federation. It was those on the Left, including the leader of the Socialist Party Mario Soares, who supported independence and their talks with FRELIMO and the PAIGC forced Spinola to concede independence on 27 July 1974[55].

On 10 September Portuguese Guinea, already recognized by many states, formally won its independence as Guinea Bissau, and on 21 September, after some violence from White settlers, a transitional government took power in poverty-stricken Mozambique where FRELIMO's Samora Machel became President in June 1975. In Angola the situation was more problematic. 'When Caetano's regime collapsed, the whole colonial administration fell with it. Soldiers . . . would no longer risk their lives defending a defunct ideology. . . . Officials were simply no longer obeyed.'[56] With the collapse of Portuguese authority in Angola international involvement now became more important as it was unclear to which of the factions power would be transferred. Indeed, when the Portuguese flag was finally lowered on 11 November 1975 the High Commissioner handed power to no one group but to the Angolan people as a whole.

The initial idea had been to get the three main parties working together as a coalition in the form of a transitional government before the formal transfer of power in November 1975. But there was continued fighting for much of the period after July 1974 despite UNITA agreeing to a ceasefire with

Lisbon in June 1974 and the MPLA and FNLA following suit in October. Talks between all the parties then led to the 15 January 1975 Alvor Accord, under which a government was to be formed, but the external supply of aid and arms was soon to transform three relatively small and lightly armed forces into major combatants. As early as July 1974 the CIA had begun making payments to the FNLA which, along with Chinese weapons, considerably boosted the effectiveness of Roberto's organization and allowed it to consolidate its position in Northern Angola. In January 1975 the US agreed through a subcommittee of the National Security Council to fund the FLNA to the tune of another $300,000. More dramatic was the subsequent Soviet and Cuban support for the MPLA which followed.[57]

At that time the FNLA with an army of 10–20,000 easily outnumbered the MPLA (8,000) and UNITA (6,000). Moreover in 1973–4 the MPLA was again bitterly divided as it had been in 1963. The 'Eastern Revolt' led by Daniel Chipenda led to significant fighting and, with the MPLA weak and Neto's leadership under threat, to the virtual ending of Soviet assistance in 1972 and 1973. Chipenda eventually defected to the FLNA and Soviet aid was completely cut off one month before the coup in Lisbon. The resumption of Soviet aid has been dated to between March and October 1974 and was to play a major role in the revival of the MPLA's fortunes in 1975, particularly after March of that year when the MPLA began to receive major Soviet arms shipments. Two months later the first Cuban military advisers began to arrive in Angola.[58]

One important question concerning this vital Soviet and Cuban support was whether the Cubans were acting as proxies of Moscow at the Kremlin's instigation or not. The evidence now suggests that the Cubans had their own reasons for intervening independently in Angola even though cooperation with the Soviets was soon established. Cubans had intervened in Algeria and Guinea and, according to one source, in Syria during the 1973 Arab–Israeli War, out of a commitment to international revolutionary solidarity. Castro and the Cubans had their own links with the MPLA and were almost certainly asked for help by Neto. 'Castro initiated Cuban armed support for the MPLA without Moscow's . . . knowledge.'[59] Kissinger's claim that Cuban intervention was, like many other problems, part of a Soviet geopolitical threat is almost certainly a misperception. As in Vietnam, there is a long-running debate over which side (in this case the Americans, the Cubans, the Soviets, or the South Africans) intervened in response to whom and who was responsible for the escalation. It is probably the case that once independence was conceded by Portugal, the Soviets, Americans, and Cubans had all decided independently to intervene in some form or other irrespective of the actions of the others. It was only the scale of the intervention which may have been influenced by the activities of rival powers.

The Soviets with their commitment to wars of national liberation had, some claim, not only to undermine the Americans but to outbid China for African support. 'The real object of Moscow's rivalry in Angola was less Washington than Beijing.'[60] This line is taken by a number of analysts and it becomes plausible if large amounts of Soviet aid are taken to be in response to the arrival of Chinese advisers in Angola in May 1975 (the same month the Cubans are alleged to have been deployed). On the other hand, if the arrival of significant Soviet aid is taken as March 1975, in response perhaps to discovering the US funding of the FLNA, the line that the US was always Moscow's main opponent in the less developed world becomes more credible, especially when it is remembered that Chinese assistance began in December 1973 without provoking a response from Moscow.

The Soviets may have had contact with the MPLA under its original leader Mario Andrade in the early 1960s but had not provided significant military aid before 1975. The total sums, from 1964 when aid began to 1975 when it was vastly increased, are estimated to have been between $55 million and $63 million. One explanation for this relatively paltry sum may have been the caution of the Soviets, for as long as they were involved in supporting insurgents against a NATO member there was a greater prospect of provoking major conflict than when involved in a civil war. As it was Soviet aid in 1975 allowed the MPLA to recover and then to expel the FNLA and UNITA from the capital Luanda on 9 July.

The July expulsion was almost certainly assisted by Cuban military advisers who had arrived in May (this is disputed, see above) although whether these advisers were involved in combat missions as some of Kennedy's military advisers were in Vietnam is another issue. They could at least give training in the Soviet weaponry. The Cuban intervention coincided with Kissinger overruling those in the State Department who saw African problems rather than Soviet geopolitical ambitions at the root of the conflict. As the Assistant Secretary of African Affairs in the State Department resigned in protest against the prospect of a covert war in Angola, President Ford approved Kissinger's request for $32 million of aid (which actually turned out to be over $60 million) and $16 million of military equipment.[61] Following the MPLA victory and the prospect of it inheriting power, the FLNA was being assisted by Mobutu in Zaire, the Chinese, and the US (covertly). Then in August UNITA formally entered the fray in support of Roberto and was secretly supplied by the Americans the following month. It only remained for the South Africans to throw in their forces in an attempt to destroy the MPLA, preferably before power was to be formally transferred in November.

In the face of the threat to the success of what Castro and the Soviets saw as a genuine national liberation movement the Cuban presence was increased. Some have argued that it was in response to the South African threat that led to Cuban advisers arriving in August or September and troops being deployed in October after the South Africans invaded on a significant scale. Logistically, however, this is unlikely. At the very least there must have been plans in place to send in more troops if necessary and, as Guimares has claimed, there were probably 1,500 Cuban troops in Angola just prior to the South African attack. Moreover, it is unlikely that the initial triumph in Luanda was purely down to the MPLA. It is however true that the South Africans were launching raids in the summer and had a significant presence in Angola in September before the assault the following month.

In late September and early October a lot of supplies and equipment arrived from Cuba by boat and they were soon needed. The South African invasion force, including Chipenda's eastern rebels, UNITA soldiers, a small Portuguese force and about 2,000 men of the South African Defence force, was rapidly closing on Luanda from the south. They may well have been able to take the capital but stopped

100 miles south perhaps because of the political consequences of having the forces of colonialism and apartheid capture an African capital.[62] It has been suggested that the Americans insisted that this be prevented and that it would be much better for FLNA forces to take the city from the north and be in charge when independence was formally achieved.

Faced with the prospect of defeat, the MPLA turned again to the Cubans who one week before independence despatched a battalion of crack troops to assist in the defence of Luanda. The result was that the FLNA failed to take control of the city or the enclave of Cabinda and eventually suffered a disastrous collapse despite the presence of Zaire troops. The US successfully pressed Caribbean countries not to allow Cuban transfer flights which meant the Soviets then provided Cuba with long-range IL-62 aircraft. In November Operation Carlota began a sizeable development of the Cuban presence after independence was conceded with the MPLA still in charge in Luanda. In January 1976 the Soviets began to airlift Cuban troops themselves and by the end of the year it is estimated that there were nearly 10,000 in Angola rising to 14,000 in February. By then the groups seeking to prevent the MPLA governing Angola faced further problems. In December 1975 the American press unearthed the fact that the government was engaged in a covert assistance programme for groups within Angola. Almost immediately, with concerns about another Vietnam very much present, the Senate passed the Clark amendment cutting off funds for covert operations in Angola. In February the MPLA government in Luanda was recognized by the OAU and in April it became a member of the United Nations. Many Americans were left doubting the wisdom of backing the FNLA in the first place, in a far-off country where few direct US interests existed.

The American-backed FNLA failure in Angola in the face of Cuban and Soviet intervention has come to be seen as a key turning point in the collapse of détente. Yet Kissinger claims he never raised the issue with the Soviets until October 1975. His argument was that up until then it was only a question of the strength of the MPLA being raised to equal that of the FLNA rather than to supersede it. Effectively this meant that the US thought its supporters could win if it channelled vast amounts of aid to them; the consequences for détente emerged when it began to appear they might not. The troubles in Angola, which were part of a continuing and very bloody conflict that was to last for decades, were clearly exacerbated, if not caused, by the involvement of external forces. Whatever Kissinger may have claimed about their implications for détente they revealed more than anything that the battle for the hearts and minds of newly independent people was even more intense. The Cuban and—as it was perceived—Soviet 'victory' in Angola did add to the questions surrounding détente and indicated that both powers were prepared to put their Cold War interests above that of cooperation. The continuing civil war thus remained an important and tragic issue in superpower relations.

NOTES

1. Mohammed Heikal, *Sphinx and Commissar* (Collins, London, 1978), 243.

2. Anwar el-Sadat, *In Search of Identity* (Collins, London, 1978), 232.

3. Chaim Herzog, *The War of Atonement* (Weidenfeld & Nicolson, London, 1975), 51.

4. Ritchie Ovendale, *The Origins of the Arab-Israeli Wars* (Longman, London, 3rd edn., 1999), 220.

5. Walter Isaacson, *Kissinger* (Faber & Faber, Boston, 1992), 529.

6. Gil Carl Alroy, *The Kissinger Experience: American Policy in the Middle East* (Horizon Press, New York, 1975), 85.

7. Henry Kissinger, *Years of Upheaval* (Weidenfeld & Nicolson, London, 1982), 560.

8. Heikal, op. cit., 263.

9. M. E. Yapp, *The Near East since the First World War* (Longman, Harlow, 1996), 423.

10. Galia Golan, *Yom Kippur and After* (Cambridge University Press, Cambridge, 1977), 250.

11. Coral Bell, *The Diplomacy of Détente* (St Martin's Press, London, 1977), 96.

12. Amnon Sella, *Soviet Political and Military Conduct in the Middle East* (Macmillan, Basingstoke, 1981), 122–3.

13. Elizabeth Picard, *Lebanon: a Shattered Country* (Holmes & Meier, New York, 1996), x–xi.

14. Farid el Khazen, *The Breakdown of the State in Lebanon* (Harvard University Press, Cambridge, 2000), 388.

15. Picard, op. cit., 81.

16. El Khazen, op. cit.

17. Avi Shlaim *The Iron Wall* (Penguin, London, 2002), 327.

18. Derek Urwin, *A Political History of Western Europe since 1945* (Longman, Harlow, 1997), 216.

19. William Ashworth, *A Short History of the International Economy since 1850* (Longman, London, 1987), 299–300.

20. Yapp, op. cit., 422.

21. Paul Bailey, *Postwar Japan* (Blackwell, Oxford, 1996), 132–3.

22. David Fieldhouse, *The West and the Third World* (Blackwell, Oxford, 1999), 229.

23. Frank Castigliola, *France and the United States* (Macmillan, New York, 1992), 174.

24. William Bundy, *A Tangled Web* (Hill & Wang, New York, 1998), 415.

25. Robert Schulzinger, *Henry Kissinger* (Columbia University Press, New York, 1989), 212.

26. Kissinger, op. cit., 193.

27. Geoffrey and Nigel Swain, *Eastern Europe since 1945* (St Martin's Press, New York, 2nd edn., 1998), 146.

28. Z. A. B. Zeman, *The Making and Breaking of Communist Europe* (Blackwell, Oxford, 2nd edn., 1991), 268.

29. David Mason, *Revolution and Transition in East-Central Europe* (Westview Press, Boulder, 2nd edn., 1996), 34.

30. George Schopflin, *Politics in Eastern Europe* (Blackwell, Oxford, 1993), 158.

31. Swain and Swain, op. cit., 147.

32. John Pinder, *The Building of the European Union* (Oxford University Press, New York, 1998), 16.

33. Patrick McCarthy, *The Crisis of the Italian State* (Macmillan, Basingstoke, 1995), 106.

34. Martin Clark, *Modern Italy* (Longman, London, 1996), 387–8.

35. Tad Szulc, *The Illusion of Peace* (Viking Press, New York, 1978), 764.

36. Mary Fulbrook, *Germany 1918–90* (Blackwell, Oxford, 1991), 209.

37. Anthony Nichols, *The Bonn Republic* (Longman, London, 1997), 235.

38. Willy Brandt, *People and Politics* (Collins, London, 1978), 498.

39. Dennis Bark and David Gress, *Democracy and its Discontents* (Oxford, 1993), 221.

40. Klaus Larres, 'International Security and Relations', in Mary Fulbrook (ed.), *Europe since 1945* (Oxford University Press, Oxford, 2001), 220.

41. Urwin, op. cit., 208.

42. John van Oudenaren, *Détente in Europe* (Duke University Press, Durham, 1991), 327.

43. Philip Thody, *Europe since 1945* (Routledge, New York, 2000), 54.

44. Both quoted in Richard Stevenson, *The Rise and Fall of Détente* (Macmillan, Basingstoke, 1985), 173.

45. Clive Church and Gisela Hendriks, *Continuity and Change in Contemporary Europe* (Elgar, Aldershot, 1995), 137.

46. Paul Sigmund, *The Overthrow of Allende* (University of Pittsburgh Press, Pittsburgh, 1977), 286.

47. Kissinger, op. cit., 374.

48. Edy Kaufman, *Crisis in Allende's Chile* (Praeger, New York, 1988), 11.

49. Szulc, op. cit., 720.

50. Leslie Bethell, *Chile since Independence* (Cambridge University Press, Cambridge, 1993), 158.

51. Kissinger, op. cit., 369.

52. Stanley Karnow, *Vietnam* (Viking Press, New York, 1985), 656–7.

53. Marilyn Young, *The Vietnam Wars* (HarperCollins, New York, 1991), 292.

54. Norrie MacQueen, *The Decolonization of Portuguese Africa* (Longman, London, 1997), 35.

55. Fernando Andresen Guimaraes, *The Origins of the Angolan Civil War* (Macmillan, Basingstoke, 1998), 89–92.

56. Malyn Newitt, *Portugal in Africa* (Hurst, London, 1981), 245.

57. Soviet caution reflected the caution of Leonid Brezhnev who was pressured by Andropov to provide more support for revolutionary movements for essentially ideological reasons. We are indebted to Arne Westad for this information obtained from his research in Soviet archives details of which can be found in his forthcoming book, *Global Intervention: The Cold War in the Third World 2004*.

58. Guimaraes, op. cit., 98, 103.

59. Odd Arne Westad, 'Moscow and the Angolan Crisis', *Cold War International History Project Bulletin*, nos. 8–9 (Winter, 1996–7), 21.

60. McQueen, op. cit., 194.

61. Guimaraes, op. cit., 166, 176, 186, 190; Raymond L. Gartoff *Détente and Confrontation* (Brookings Institution, Washington, 1985), 508–11.

62. J. Marcum, *The Angolan Revolution*, vol. 2, *Exile Politics and Guerrilla Warfare 1962–1976* (M.I.T. Press, Cambridge, 1981), 269–71.

14 Détente in Decline, 1977–1979

A. Détente and the Carter Presidency

Questioning of Détente in America by 1976

In March 1976, as he set out on the Presidential campaign, Gerald Ford decided that 'détente' had become so unpopular that the word should not even be used by his election team. In 1972 the Peking and Moscow summits had been oversold to help Nixon's re-election and since then numerous events had bred scepticism about détente in the US. It suffered in part from being identified with Nixon, who was discredited by the Watergate scandal. But his downfall also removed the one leading right-wing politician who was both trusted in the Kremlin and able to reassure American conservatives that national interests were not compromised by talks with the Soviets. After 1973 conservatives increasingly questioned détente, felt that SALT I (with its

larger number of Soviet missiles) benefited the USSR most, and were particularly disturbed by an apparent pattern of Communist adventurism abroad, in the 1973 Middle East War, Angola, and Vietnam. Kissinger's argument that the Soviets could be co-opted into an orderly, 'normal' pattern of behaviour through a process of détente was questioned by those who believed they saw a determined Soviet strategy to advance in the less developed world whilst dividing NATO (by supporting communists in Italy and Portugal) and seeking nuclear superiority. Moscow, it was argued, was still bent on spreading Marxism and détente was no more than a cynical change of Soviet tactics. Richard Pipes, one of the most consistent academic critics of détente, considered that the Soviets had abandoned confrontation 'in favour of less risky, flanking movements carried out, preferably by proxy forces, by way of the less developed world', that they hoped to divide the West by relaxing tension, and that they pursued 'at the same time, a major rearmament programme for possible World War III by projecting a peaceful image to weaken the Western defence effort.'[1]

Liberals in the Democratic Party, who had supported the Cold War consensus until Vietnam but then became increasingly critical of the Imperial Presidency, were also doubtful about détente and the amoral outlook of foreign policy under Nixon and Kissinger. After Vietnam it was perhaps inevitable that the crusading, idealistic element in US policy—which had helped lead to the Vietnam War in the first place—would reassert itself. Whereas, on the Republic Right, such idealism took the form of patriotic anti-Communism, in the Democratic Party it tended towards liberal anti-totalitarianism. Both groups criticized the 1975 Helsinki agreements for their failure adequately to protect human rights in the Eastern bloc and for condoning Soviet domination of the region. They also criticized the USSR's failure to allow sufficient Jews to emigrate. The Democratic Senator, Henry Jackson, a 'Presidential hopeful', began a campaign in 1972 which linked both criticisms of SALT and the emigration issue. In December 1974 Ford was forced to accept the Jackson–Vanik amendment which made an expansion of US–Soviet trade (under their 1972 commercial agreement) conditional on greater Jewish emigration. On 7 January Kissinger warned Ford that this would severely damage America's ability to influence Moscow through 'linkage': 'The Soviets have to keep détente going for political reasons, but our hold on them is gone. These economic projects would have gotten our hooks into them for years.'[2] Sure enough, Jackson–Vanik immediately backfired. On 10 January, the Soviets, unwilling to accept such 'interference' in their internal affairs, simply scrapped the trade deal. Then they cut back the number of emigrants: in 1973 about 35,000 Jews had been allowed to leave the USSR, a massive increase on the few hundred who left in 1968, but in 1975 the number fell to only 13,000. (It revived again after 1977.) Yet whatever its direct outcome Jackson's campaign succeeded in highlighting the strength of opposition across the political spectrum, to détente. On the Republican Right, Reagan 'saw the issue as tailor-made for his campaign against the Washington establishment. Using Henry Kissinger as a foil,

he could attack the Ford administration without attacking Ford.'[3] Hence the President's decision to distance himself from the policy. Even then, détente cost the President dear because, in the closing stages of the election campaign, his careless remarks about the Helsinki agreements and Soviet domination of Eastern Europe were used by Jimmy Carter to outscore him in their 'head-to-head' television debates.

The Soviet Union and the Interpretation of Détente

Disappointment with détente was not one-sided. Moscow argued that the Americans were undermining it with their own actions in the less developed world (notably the campaign against Chile's Salvador Allende), their refusal to give the USSR a full role in Middle East peacemaking, and their attempts (at least from Congress, with Jackson–Vanik) to interfere in Soviet domestic politics. Once the Watergate scandal broke the Soviets also felt US politics to be beyond comprehension. In 1974–5, with Nixon's resignation and Kissinger's unfriendly strategy in the Middle East, expectations in the Kremlin about détente were lowered. Defence Minister Marshall Grechko (1967–76) was fearful that military agreements with the US might compromise the strength of Soviet armed forces, even if he continued to recognize the political benefits of a decrease in tensions. But in contrast to America, real faith in détente did survive in Moscow. Soviet politics were, of course, much less volatile than America's. With no public opinion to measure and no free press, the Kremlin was better able than the White House to control the policy-making machine. Brezhnev, though in physical decline (he suffered strokes in 1975 and 1978), kept the Politburo favourable to détente, despite the increasing doubts of some members. Even though the SALT II talks stalled in 1975–6 and the US–Soviet trade deal was scrapped, there were no major foreign policy humiliations—such as America suffered in Vietnam—to cause a questioning of Brezhnev's policy. Any failures were compensated for by the success of Soviet allies in Angola and Vietnam, and by advances in European détente. Besides, the USSR always had a more flexible view of détente than the US, arguing that it should include elements of cooperation, such as nuclear arms control, but also allow for competition in the less developed world. Thus, at the 25th Soviet Communist Party Congress in February-March 1976 Brehznev spoke in favour both of détente and of wars of national liberation. As Anatoly Dobrynin put it, 'members of the Politburo lived in the certainty that a historical process was under way: the collapse of the old colonial empires and the general weakening of the capitalist system. . . . For ideological reasons we should support this process whenever possible, but this did not mean that we deliberately were trying to undermine . . . American interests . . .'[4]

One central problem with the détente process of course was that each superpower did have different interests in pursuing it, different interpretations of how it should work, and different expectations about where it should lead. Neither side had ever intended to give up its ideology, dismantle its alliances, or abandon the processes of power politics. But, 'while both superpowers were engaged in a process of adjustment, they were adjusting to different vulnerabilities and responding to different concerns.'[5] Thus, whereas the Soviets expected to win equality of status with the US, to retain their hold on Eastern Europe, and to secure agreements on trade and SALT, whilst continuing to support wars on national liberation, Americans had other expectations. Faced by relative American decline, economic problems, and the costs of Vietnam, Nixon and Kissinger hoped to use 'linkage' to secure Soviet good behaviour and an acceptance of the existing world order especially in the less developed world, in return for SALT and trade deals.

But in a pluralist Western system, it was harder for US leaders to keep NATO or the American body politic united behind détente and 'linkage' proved difficult to manage in practice. Soviet advances in the less developed world, mounting problems in NATO, and Congressional opposition made it more important for Kissinger to demonstrate a tough approach to the Soviets where he could, in the Middle East or the SALT II talks for example; but this in turn harmed trust between the superpowers. To many Americans it was quite clear that, through its interference in Africa and South-East Asia, the USSR

had violated détente but 'while it is possible to take issue with the premises . . . of Soviet policy . . . it is harder to argue that they sought to delude the West about their understanding of . . . détente, or to speak of Soviet violation of détente.'[6] because, again, their view of détente was, quite simply, not the same as America's. The problems of Soviet adventurism in the less developed world, America's political volatility, and defining a fair nuclear balance became even more intense when Jimmy Carter became President.

Policy-making under Carter

Although he avoided major military involvement abroad, Carter's foreign policy has often been criticized as incoherent, misguided, and at the mercy of events. One blunt judgement, from a major study of US foreign policy, is that he 'confused friends and enemies alike, provoking contempt at home and abroad'.[7] He came to power as a Washington outsider who exploited popular dissatisfaction with the Nixon–Ford era, tried to appear during the 1976 election as 'all things to all men', and promised more than he could deliver. He seemed a decent, hard-working, well-intentioned, certainly intelligent and well-informed leader, inspired both by liberal idealism and evangelical Christianity. But he lacked an overall programme (equivalent for example to Johnson's 'Great Society'), became obsessed by policy details, and was unable to master Congress, making effective government very difficult. He was not even very popular in the Democratic Party and in 1980 the Republicans successfully tarred him with the image of retreat and decline. To be fair to him, he faced problems which would have tried any President. Inflation, the energy crisis, the Vietnam syndrome, a shift in popular support away from costly Federal spending programmes, and Congressional limits on Presidential powers abroad, were all bad enough. But Carter was also elected in the bicentenary year of American independence, when expectations of a new era of achievement were high. He certainly tried to rise to the occasion in his acceptance speech at the 1976 Democratic Convention, describing America as 'a pioneer in shaping more just and decent relations among people' and stating that this required 'nothing less than a sustained architectural effort to shape an international framework of peace within which our own ideals gradually can become a global reality.'[8] Three years after the War Powers Act, two years after Nixon's resignation, and one year after the fall of Saigon, Carter believed the US still had the capacity to shape the world in its own image. But what followed failed to live up to such ambitious rhetoric.

Carter's policy-making machine has received particular criticism, not least because of the tension between his Secretary of State, Cyrus Vance, and National Security Adviser, Zbigniew Brzezinski, who particularly differed over détente. Vance, an Establishment figure who had served as Under-Secretary of Defence in 1964–7, was known for his pragmatism, caution, persistence, and common sense. He shared Carter's desire to improve relations with less developed world states. But he was not the President's first choice for the State Department and gradually lost influence to Brzezinski, who had sat with Carter before 1977 on the 'Trilateral Commission', a group formed to improve relations between America, Western Europe, and Japan—the three pillars of the Western alliance who had seemed to drift apart in the Kissinger years. Given to outspoken statements and to toughness in crises, Brzezinski believed the Soviets must be resisted in the less developed world and was ready to work with Peking against Moscow. Vance in contrast was keen to proceed with SALT II, reluctant to cooperate with China, and sceptical about the USSR's ability to shape conflicts in the less developed world. In Afghanistan after 1979 he was eventually proven correct in his belief that the Soviets could no more manipulate poor, predominantly rural societies than America had been able to do in Vietnam.

Carter himself sometimes seemed to view the Brzezinski–Vance relationship as one of creative tension, an improvement on the Nixon–Kissinger era when one adviser had tried to monopolize policy. But the division among his aides often seemed to run out of control and did not help Carter escape his own frequent indecision. Rather than giving consistent direction to policy he was a workaholic who often became preoccupied with the complexities of a particular issue, refused to delegate

work despite the enormous pressures on his own timetable, and appeared to pursue several different tracks at once. Then again, it has been argued that, in trying (in contrast to his successor, Ronald Reagan) to come to terms with a complicated world, he was 'championing a post-Cold War foreign policy before the Cold War was over'.[9] His previous experience of office may have been limited to the Governorship of Georgia, and in domestic politics he may have been too much in the hands of old friends from the 'Georgia Mafia', but he had many years naval service behind him, his role in the Trilateral Commission reflected a deep interest in international affairs, and he surrounded himself with able, experienced figures in the foreign and defence fields, not just Brzezinski and Vance, but also Defence Secretary Harold Brown and the arms control expert Paul Warnke.

Confident that the US was far stronger than the USSR if it came to war but recognizing that the 'Vietnam Syndrome' virtually ruled out the limited use of military force, Carter and his team at first believed it sensible to restrain military spending and concentrate on such issues in East–West relations as arms control, trade, and human rights. Aware too that there was now a 'multipolar' world, beyond the domination of the superpowers, they were anxious to address the North–South divide, to improve relations with NATO and Japan, and to retreat from America's past support for right-wing dictators in the less developed world. In 1977 there were even attempts to normalize relations with Vietnam and Cuba. Carter became the first President openly to condemn apartheid in South Africa whilst, in July 1979, he accepted the overthrow of the long-standing US ally, Anastasio Somoza of Nicaragua, by the left-wing Sandinista movement. Carter's readiness to devote personal attention to entrenched, complex problems was certainly rewarded in two important cases, the Camp David breakthrough in Egyptian–Israeli relations and the Panama Canal treaties (see Chapter 14, B). Yet the administration's attempt to break free of America's long obsession with the Soviet Communist menace, always carried tensions within it. Carter's policy may actually have made some sense, but it was poorly articulated and executed. Carter himself, though determined to maintain détente on the arms control front, was a strong liberal and Christian, who had triumphed over Ford in 1976 by attacking Soviet domination of Eastern Europe and who talked of an 'absolute' commitment to human rights in his inaugural address. His belief that détente could safely be combined with an attack on the Soviet's human rights record proved naïve. As early as February 1977 Brezhnev, as confused as anyone about what the new President stood for, and perhaps insulted by his attempts to downgrade the importance of East–West relations, complained about a letter he wrote to the leading dissident scientist, Andrei Sakharov. Despite positive statements from both Brezhnev and Carter about bilateral relations in January 1977, it was soon clear that there would be trouble between them.

By highlighting Soviet internal repression and increasing expenditure on such propaganda outlets as Radio Liberty and Radio Free Europe, Carter hoped both to restore a moral tone to foreign policy after the Nixon years and to satisfy the anti-détente lobby in the US, who had already expressed support for dissidents like Sakharov and the writer Alexander Solzhenitsyn (expelled from the USSR in February 1974). Brzezinski 'saw in human rights an opportunity to put the Soviet Union ideologically on the defensive.'[10] Concern over human rights in East–West relations was, of course, nothing new and the suppression of Yuri Orlov's 'monitoring group', set up after the 1975 Helsinki Conference, caused outrage in the West. In 1976 Congress passed an Arms Control Export Act, which implied that arms exports should be denied to regimes that consistently violated human rights.

But Nixon had been little interested in the human rights issue and under Ford the so-called 'Sonnenfeldt Doctrine' had argued that the best way to change the Soviet system was to encourage gradual evolution to a less oppressive regime via cultural, scientific, and media contacts. Nor did Carter's more ideologically driven campaign have any immediate success. Instead, like the Jackson–Vanik amendment,

it only angered the Soviets, who abhorred any meddling in their internal affairs. In 1978 harsh sentences were imposed on Yuri Orlov and others, some of whom were accused of working for the CIA. Only in the long-term, building on the Helsinki agreements, did the emphasis on human rights do much to undermine the Soviet political system.

Repression in the USSR encouraged American critics of détente, whose leaders launched the 'Committee on the Present Danger' in November 1976. The Committee argued, in contrast to Carter and some of his advisers, that the USSR was an increasing threat to US interests, that the Soviets might soon overtake America in terms of military power, and that there must be a return to confrontational resistance. By appealing to familiar ideas in post-war foreign policy, claiming to be bipartisan, and exploiting Soviet actions in the less developed world, the Committee won increasing sympathy in the press and among the public. Such fear of the Soviets was echoed by Brzezinski and in 1978–9 Carter did concentrate more on East–West relations. But too often he was depicted as lagging behind the Committee in his appreciation of the Soviet menace. Carter's human rights emphasis, indeed, proved a poor focus for foreign policy. It appealed to the idealism of Americans perhaps but the President himself knew that he lived in an imperfect world where foreign policy could not be executed according to a rigid morality. It was obvious, whatever transpired in Nicaragua in 1979, that America was reliant on any number of distasteful but pro-American and anti-Communist regimes from the Shah's Iran to Ferdinand Marcos's Philippines. It was also very difficult to criticize the authoritarianism of Communist China when Brzezenski was determined to 'play the China Card' against Moscow. As a result, the human rights policy was 'often ambiguous, sometimes proved divisive and held only a tenuous relationship to many of Carter's more pragmatic policies'.[11]

Carter, Vance, and Brzezinski

Whereas foreign policy under Nixon had been dominated by the President and Kissinger, under Carter there was a broader group of policy-makers, including the Defence Secretary, Harold Brown, and ambassador to the UN, Andrew Young, but with the key characters being the Secretary of State, Cyrus Vance, and National Security Adviser, Zbigniew Brzezinski. Jimmy Carter himself had only limited experience of foreign affairs before entering the White House. Born James Earl Carter, in Plains, Georgia in 1925, he had served in the navy during the War, going on to become an officer, and serving in submarines between 1948 and 1953. He then took over the family peanut business and, in the 1960s, became active in Georgia politics. But nationally he was a virtual unknown quantity when he entered the race for the Presidency. A 'born again' Christian, politically liberal yet from America's 'deep south'—which hadn't provided a President for more than century—he won the Democratic nomination surprisingly easily, before beating the incumbent Gerald Ford. Carter laid great emphasis on human rights in his foreign policy and had some major successes, notably over Panama and Egyptian–Israeli relations. But he suffered setbacks over Iran and the revival of the Cold War in 1979–80, as well as over the economy, where unemployment was rising. In the 1980 election he was challenged by Edward Kennedy from within his own party, then beaten by Ronald Reagan. In contrast to many Presidents, however, Carter continued to play an active international role after his defeat, championing human rights and taking part in peacemaking efforts under Bill Clinton, eventually winning the Nobel Prize.

One of the criticisms levelled at Carter was that he failed to prevent growing tension between Vance and Brzezinski. Both shared Carter's belief in an active US diplomacy in the wake of the Vietnam failure, continued engagement with détente, and an emphasis on human rights. But Brzezinski was more determinedly anti-Soviet, increasingly sceptical about détente, and ready to intimidate Moscow

through the 'normalization' of relations with China. Like his rival Kissinger, Zbigniew Brzezinski was an academic writer on international affairs, who was not American by birth. Born in Warsaw in 1928, the son of a Polish diplomat, he had been educated in Canada after the War, before studying for his Ph.D. at Harvard in 1950–3 and taking American citizenship in 1958. He headed the prestigious Institute on Communist Affairs at Columbia University in the 1960s and acted as an adviser to both the Kennedy and Johnson administrations. He met Carter on the Trilateral Commission, set up in 1973 to improve US relations with Western Europe and Japan, Brzezinski being its Director.

Cyrus Vance was somewhat older than either Carter or Brzezinski, being born in West Virginia in 1917; and he had a more traditionally 'establishment' background, educated at Yale Law School, and working for a New York law firm (1946–61) following wartime naval service. After 1957 he served as counsel to the Senate Armed Services Committee and in 1961 he was brought into government by Kennedy, serving as Secretary of the Army. Under Johnson in 1964–7 Vance was Deputy Secretary of Defence, in which position he was involved in various diplomatic discussions. In 1968, having become a critic of the Vietnam War, he was part of the US team in the Paris peace talks that were opened with Hanoi. Vance thus brought considerable experience in diplomatic and defence matters to the Carter team and had a primary negotiating role over Panama, the Middle East, and SALT. By 1980, however, it was definitely Brzezinski's tough anti-Communism that held the upper hand in Washington. Brzezinski also backed the ill-fated attempt to rescue US hostages in Iran that April, which Vance opposed, choosing the issue to resign over. In the 1980s Brzezinski returned to academic life and Vance to law practice. But the latter, like Carter, did re-emerge as an international figure in the 1990s, notably trying to settle the Bosnian problem in 1992–3.

B. The Egyptian–Israeli Peace Process

The Lebanese Civil War

The Civil War in 1975 was characterized by a series of exchanges between Muslim and Christian militias, while after June Arafat decided to try and keep the

PLO out of the conflict. By the end of the year, fighting and religious killings were seriously affecting Beirut and the Christians were expelling Muslims from quarters under their control. Kamal Jumblatt, leader of the Lebanese National Movement (LNM), now sought to seize control of the Lebanon and establish a secular state as the Christian Maronite position was weakening.[12] Demographic factors meant that the Maronites were declining as a percentage of the population and the Shi'ites in particular increasing, raising the issue of the constitutional order. The fighting in Beirut was sucking the PLO back into the conflict and arousing the concerns of the Israelis and Syrians who were both fearful of a Jumblatt-PLO victory. Syria had long had a keen interest in developments within the Lebanon, not least because the country contained the main opposition elements to its government. In 1975 the Syrian president Hafiz al-Asad, who came from the minority Alawi sect, had close connections with leading Maronite families, but the collapse of the Lebanese state presented him with new problems. The Syrians first sought to re-establish the old constitutional arrangements in modified form which would have ended the Christian parliamentary majority in return for the Muslims no longer holding the majority of important offices. The Constitutional Document, largely influenced by the Syrians, was rejected in February 1976 by the Muslims largely because they were in a strong position on the ground. Consequently Asad 'was filled with horror at the prospect of a radical, adventurist Lebanon on his flank, provoking Israel and alarming the West.'[13] Moreover, if the Druze and the PLO triumphed the Maronites would be pushed firmly into the arms of the Israelis which Asad hoped to avoid by military intervention in June 1976 on the side of the Maronites.

Usually seen as a radical Arab leader, Asad was keen to pacify the situation on his borders, to gain some influence over Druze and PLO activities and prevent a war with Israel breaking out. The Israelis for their part established direct contact with the Christian militias in 1976 but were hampered by divisions over the extent to which they should involve themselves on the side of the Maronites. By the summer of 1976 the Israelis were promising arms and training to the Maronite forces in the North and providing assistance to the smaller militias in the South where their influence on the Lebanese side of the border was increasing as a result. On 15 October Syria proclaimed a ceasefire and the following day an Arab mini-summit considered the

situation in the Lebanon and agreed that the Syrian forces would be transformed into an Arab Deterrent Force. The first phase of the Lebanese Civil War was effectively over.

It had produced much loss of life and rather than solving Lebanon's problems had largely made them worse. The army had broken up and the population had regrouped geographically to reflect the confessional divisions between different areas more firmly. The political position of the PLO was now much stronger, if its military position was weaker. 'It was now politically established and secure, recognized, and taken seriously in the world of international diplomacy, and in possession of a platform that many judged to be pragmatic [an independent Palestine state] and a basis for serious negotiation.'[14] Initially, however, the Syrians were keen to use their forces against the PLO to restore order, although they did not want a strong Lebanese state. But the Israelis were too suspicious of this and insisted on what became known as the red line in Southern Lebanon established on the basis that the Syrians would not despatch forces south of the line from Sidon to the Lebanese–Syrian border. The only problem was that PLO activists, rather than face the Syrian army, moved themselves to the very area that they could do most harm to Israel. A haven for terrorists had been facilitated by the Israelis who were bound sooner or later to try and destroy it. The quest for security was actually bringing greater danger.

In 1977 a bad situation became worse. The Likud, a more extreme party determined to maintain the sacred land of Israel, was elected for the first time. And as Egypt's President Sadat launched his peace initiative with Israel the consequence for the Lebanon was to push the PLO and the Syrians back together again. The LNM began to fall apart and Kamal Jumblatt was assassinated in March 1977. The conflict was now beginning to focus on the PLO and the Israelis. The latter began to create and finance an ally in the South, Major Saa'd Hadad, a Greek Orthodox army officer, to weld the Christian militias together. In March 1978 there was a short-lived Israeli invasion of southern Lebanon authorized by the new, right-wing Likud government of Menachem Begin. It was widely condemned and led to the establishment of a small UN 'Interim Force' (UNIFIL), but the situation in South Lebanon was getting worse. The PLO was no longer the only opponent of Israel there. Militant Shi'ites were not always part of the PLO and from 1978 many of them looked to AMAL, the armed wing of the Shi'ite Movement for the Dispossessed, established in the year of the Israeli invasion and funded by the Syrians. The Israelis continued to support Haddad, and the 1978 invasion witnessed the first of many massacres by Christian militia supervised by Israeli forces. In the North traditional Maronite leaders, such as former President Camille Chamoun, lost influence to hard-line Phalangists, led by Bashir Gemayel. The Israeli intervention was weakening the position of the Syrians but their influence was being replaced by other more radical forces which made divisions and conflict more likely yet an Egyptian–Israeli peace agreement was about to be made.

Chronology: Civil War in Lebanon, 1975–1979

1975

26 February	'Fishermen's Dispute' begins in Sidon: army clashes with Shi'a fishermen who are protesting against grants of fishing rights to Maronites.
13 April	Clashes begin between (Christian) Maronite Phalangists and Palestinian Liberation Organization in Beirut, following 2 years of increasing tension.
25 May	First attempt at a ceasefire quickly breaks down into new bloodletting.
29 June	First high-profile kidnapping of a Westerner in Beirut: American Colonel Ernest Morgan seized by a Palestinian group.
24 October	Start of the 'Battle of the Hotels' for control of part of north-west Beirut; most of Beirut now divided between Muslims (West Beirut) and Maronite (East) along the 'Green Line'.
6 December	'Black Sunday': Phalangists kill about 150 Muslims in Beirut.
7 December	Muslim militia kidnap and kill about 150 Christians in revenge for 'Black Sunday'.

1976

February	Syrian attempt to get settlement and agreement on revised Constitution.
March	Lebanese Army splits between Christians and Muslims.
9 April	Large-scale intervention by Syrian regular troops begins, focused on the Bekaa Valley.
21 April	Israel warns Syrian not to deploy troops near Lebanon's southern border.
16 June	US ambassador, Francis Meloy, assassinated.
12 August	Christian militias overrun Palestinian refugee camp of Tel Zaatar after 8 months siege.
18 October	Riyadh peace agreement initiates yet another ceasefire on 21 October (there had now been more than 50), says combatants should withdraw to their April 1975 positions, and sets up an 'Arab Deterrent Force' (in practice dominated by Syria).

1977

February–April	Sporadic Christian–Palestinian clashes.
16 March	Druze leader Kamal Jumblatt assassinated. The Druze attack Christian communities in response.
17 May	First major fighting in the South between Palestinians and Shi'ite Muslim ('Amal') militias.
17 May	Right-wing Begin government comes to power in Israel, concerned at Palestinian presence in Southern Lebanon.

1978

11 March	Palestinian commando raid into Israel kills over 30 Israelis.
14–21 March	Israelis launch 'Operation Litani', setting up a 10-kilometre deep 'security zone' in southern Lebanon and establish links to local Maronite militia under Said Haddad.
22 March	UN 'Interim Force in Southern Lebanon' (UNIFIL) begins deployment.
May	First major fratricidal clashes between Christian militia, who differ over cooperation with Syria.

The Origins of the Egyptian–Israeli Agreement and the Problems of a General Settlement

The Israeli–Egyptian peace settlement, signed in Washington in March 1979—six months after a breakthrough summit at Camp David—was Carter's greatest foreign policy success as President and evidence that he was no luckless mediocrity. At the time it was signed, Brzezinski wrote of the 'electricity in the air, a sense of joy . . . for Carter, it was a spectacular and historic triumph'.[15] The complexities of Middle East politics fascinated a President who had a deep interest in the Bible, an idealistic commitment to peace, a desire to master details, and a reluctance to admit defeat. America also had a clear national interest in settling the Arab–Israeli dispute, partly to ease the pressure on oil prices and partly to avoid another regional war which might involve the superpowers. Both Secretary of State Vance and National Security Adviser Brzezinski agreed on the need for action and shared Carter's open-mindedness about how a general settlement should be achieved.

The basic formula for an Arab–Israeli agreement was provided by United Nations Resolution 242, passed after the 1967 War (Chapter 11, D), which broadly promised the Arabs the return of land conquered by Israel in return for a guarantee of Israel's right to exist. But, since the Israelis were reluctant to surrender their 1967 conquests, and since the Arab states refused even to recognize Israel's existence, no progress had yet been possible on the Resolution. An added problem was how to represent Palestinian Arab interests and resolve the future of Palestinian refugees. After the 1973 Middle East War a political conference had met in Geneva only briefly and, under Nixon and Ford, US policy focused on achieving a military disengagement of the two sides rather than a general settlement. US links to Israel remained close, and there was a strong Zionist lobby in America, yet Kissinger had also built a trusting relationship with several Arab leaders, not least Egypt's Anwar Sadat, who was ready to exclude the Soviet Union from peace-making attempts (Chapter 13, A). Despite such successes, however, 'Kissinger's step-by-step diplomacy avoided the central issues

of the Arab–Israeli conflict', not least the Palestinian problem and the territorial issues left by the 1967 War.[16]

In early 1977 Brzezinski began to study possible ways to achieve a general settlement in stages, while Vance visited Israel and Arab capitals in order both to explore their views and reinforce US diplomatic links in the region. Vance found most countries ready to compromise and he thought it might be possible to reconvene the Geneva conference at an early date. But when the Israeli Premier Yitzhak Rabin, visited Washington in March, Carter managed to upset both the Arabs and Israelis. By speaking indelicately of Israel's need for defensible borders he suggested that the 1967 frontiers would not be fully restored, but by talking of the need for a Palestinian 'homeland' he provoked controversy in Israel ahead of its May general election. Carter's first meeting with Sadat, in April, was rather more successful. The Egyptian President was keen to see America involve itself closely in the Arab–Israeli dispute; indeed, this was one main reason why he had developed links to the US and had broken with the USSR. 'Developing the dialogue with Washington could translate into pressure on Israel to return territory, relieve Sadat of having to deal directly with Israel, and obtain financial and military assistance from the United States.'[17] He wanted Sinai to be returned to Egypt and was ready to be flexible on the issue of recognizing Israel. He also quickly developed a trust of Carter, describing him as 'true to himself and true to others. It is because he is so honest . . . that is why I have no difficulty in dealing with him.'[18] By mid-May Carter had also seen King Hussein of Jordan and President Assad of Syria and believed rapid action on a general settlement was possible, despite some obvious difficulties. He hoped that the Israelis might concede a Palestinian homeland, however controversial, if the Arabs normalized their relations with Israel after accepting its right to exist. But the Israeli election in May produced a shock. Rabin and the Labour Party, which had dominated Israeli politics since 1948, were replaced by a self-righteous former terrorist, Menachem Begin, and his hard-line Likud coalition. Likud was committed to retaining the West Bank and Gaza. 'In early encounters with Carter . . . Begin brought maps with which to illustrate his standard lecture on Judea and Samaria', as he called the West bank. 'History and religion were at the heart of his claim to these territories, not just security.'[19] All of which was going to make a settlement extremely difficult, or so it seemed.

The Americans were still keen to begin a peace conference in Geneva in 1977, but they recognized that it was impossible to dictate a settlement—even a balanced one—to the local powers and it was soon decided to invite Begin to Washington to explore ideas with him. He came in July and, whilst ready to talk to the Arabs and consider a withdrawal from Sinai, he wanted to retain territory on the West Bank and objected to anything that suggested that an Arab Palestinian state could be created in Gaza and the West Bank. Despite these unpromising views, some Americans hoped Begin might make concessions once the Geneva conference convened, and Vance made another tour of Arab capitals in August to pave the way for such a meeting. This was followed by a series of visits by Middle Eastern Foreign Ministers to Washington in September, but these only highlighted the scale of differences between the various countries. There was no agreement about how to represent the Palestinians at Geneva as Israel would not recognize the Arab-backed Palestinian Liberation Organization. Israel, Sadat, and many Americans, including Brzezinski, disliked the idea of Soviet co-chairmanship of the Geneva conference. Since this had been agreed back in 1973, it was hard to refuse, but when the decision was announced on 1 October it was much criticized in the US. Syria and Jordan were deeply suspicious that Sadat would break ranks and vainly tried to force him into a single Arab delegation at the conference. And Begin seemed unlikely to offer concessions anywhere other than Sinai. Carter became increasingly indecisive and the road to Geneva appeared blocked.

Sadat's Peace Initiative

It was Sadat who broke the growing deadlock by abandoning hopes of a successful Geneva conference and adopting a radical alternative. On 9 November he dramatically announced his readiness to address the Israeli parliament and 10 days later stood before it, saying 'that we accept to live with you in permanent peace based on justice', with self-determination for the Palestinians, secure borders for Israel, and the return of the 1967 conquests.[20] In private discussions he still hoped Israel would make concessions on the Palestinians on the West Bank and Gaza, but agreed with Begin that the Geneva conference, if it ever met, would merely be ceremonial and both men were ready to press on with bilateral Egyptian–Israeli talks. But Sadat was over-optimistic in believing that his peace gesture would win Israeli concessions on the Palestinian front, the US was sceptical about relying on an Egyptian–Israeli deal, and other Arab countries were furious about the Egyptian President's initiative. Even the Egyptian press questioned the wisdom of the Jerusalem visit and Sadat's Foreign Minister resigned over it. When Begin returned Sadat's visit and met the latter in Ismailia on 25 December it was clear that the most Israel would do for Palestinians would be to offer a severely limited form of self-government. But another mission by Vance to the Middle East showed that Syria and Jordan would only tolerate Sadat's strategy if it won real political rights for Palestinians and led on to a general settlement.

In early January 1978 Carter, reduced to a spectator after Sadat's 9 November initiative, made his own limited tour of the Middle East and, though still sceptical of the value of an Egyptian–Israeli deal, decided to become more directly involved in the bilateral peace process. Sadat welcomed America's involvement, again because he believed this would increase the pressure on Begin to compromise. Sadat 'felt that the American role was essential, especially after his unproductive meeting with Begin in Ismailia . . . what Sadat now sought was an American proposal to break the deadlock' in the direct Egyptian–Israeli talks.[21] By the middle of the month the Egyptian–Israeli talks had stalled, but a visit by Sadat to Washington in February showed that the Egyptian leader was ready to make more concessions in the face of Israel's continuing hard line. He was now prepared to make a bilateral deal, as Begin wanted, on the Sinai front in return for some general principles being agreed on a wider settlement, including the Palestinian problem. Nonetheless, several months of further argument, and strong American pressure on Israel, failed to find an acceptable formula for a bilateral deal. The US, Egyptian, and Israeli Foreign Ministers met at Leeds Castle in England in mid-July but Israel was unwilling to concede the Egyptian desire for a statement of intent on withdrawal from all the occupied territories. It was the failure of this conference that led Carter, on 20 July, to decide that a summit should be held between himself, Sadat, and Begin. The American President was sorely in need of a foreign policy success, Begin's position had been tough throughout the talks, and Sadat—who had made concessions, but often impulsively and with no clear sense of direction—was increasingly frustrated by the lack of progress.

Camp David and the Peace Treaty

Carter, Sadat, and Begin met at Camp David for 12 days, beginning on 5 September 1978. The Americans believed that such a long summit, in a secluded location, would allow both Israel and Egypt to clarify their positions and explore a solution, with Carter acting as a mediator. Both Sadat and Begin arrived in a determined mood and for a time the talks were deadlocked, but on 17 September two 'accords' were signed. The first concerned an Egyptian–Israel peace treaty, to be completed in 3 months, and its formula was unsurprising: in return for normal diplomatic relations (and therefore recognition of its right to exist) Israel would withdraw from the Sinai Peninsula within 3 years. The second was a much vaguer document on the West Bank, which revealed further retreats on Sadat's part. Israel made no promises about Palestinian independence, the special status of Jerusalem, or even on limiting Jewish settlements in the area, and the document was understood to be totally separate from the peace treaty—so that the treaty could proceed regardless of what happened to the West Bank and Gaza. There was little in the Camp David agreements for Arab states other than Egypt,

---

The Egyptian–Israeli Peace Treaty of 26 March 1979

The Treaty of Peace was signed by Egypt's President, Anwar Sadat, and Israeli Premier Menachem Begin in Washington, with President Carter as witness. In the preamble it referred to three other important documents that he preceded it: UN Resolution 242, which had first set out the 'land for peace' formula in the wake of the 1967 Six Day War; Resolution 338, which had called for 'negotiations . . . aimed at establishing a just and durable peace in the Middle East' following the October 1973 War; and the 'Framework for Peace' agreement reached by Sadat, Begin, and Carter at Camp David in September 1978, a document which had hoped for a wider Arab–Israeli settlement. The preamble put forward the hope that a narrow Egyptian–Israeli deal would prove 'an important step in the search for a comprehensive peace in the area' and it invited 'other Arab parties to this dispute to join the peace process.'

One important reason why other Arab countries did not, in the immediate term, take up this invitation, was that the peace treaty did nothing concrete for the Palestinian cause. The best Sadat could achieve here was a letter, signed alongside the treaty, in which Begin undertook to open talks in the near future, with the objective of establishing a 'self-governing authority in the West Bank and Gaza.', in line with the Camp David framework. The peace treaty included nine articles, but the essence of the agreement was contained in the first two paragraphs of Article 1:

The state of war between the parties will be terminated and peace will be established between them upon the exchange of instruments of ratification of this treaty.

Israel will withdraw all its armed forces and civilians from the Sinai, behind the international boundary between Egypt and mandated Palestine . . . and Egypt will resume the exercise of its full sovereignty over the Sinai.

The Israeli withdrawal was to be achieved in stages and, in another letter separate from the treaty, Sadat undertook to exchange ambassadors with Israel within a month after Israel had completed its withdrawal to an interim line. Each country recognized the other's sovereignty, territorial integrity, and right to live in peace. Special security arrangements were made for their mutual border and Israeli ships were guaranteed access through both the Suez Canal and Strait of Tiran—tension over which had helped spark the 1967 War.

therefore, and Sadat was now increasingly ostracized in the Arab world. There was in fact, from the outset, a deep divide between Egypt and Israel over what Camp David symbolized. 'Whereas the Egyptians saw [it] as the model for similar understandings with Jordan and Syria . . . Begin saw it as the precise opposite . . . the withdrawal from Sinai would be the end of the story.'[22] He was always determined to hold onto the West Bank.

The Camp David breakthrough was widely seen as being due to Carter's perseverance, skills as a mediator, and (in contrast to his March 1977 behaviour) realism about what might be achieved. But there were difficulties in carrying the agreements out in detail and it proved impossible to draw up an Egyptian–Israeli peace treaty by December, as originally hoped. Whilst pressing for a treaty to be completed quickly, with promises of an early exchange of ambassadors, Begin not only refused to move on the issue of Palestinian rights but also extended Jewish settlements on the West Bank. It even seemed at times that the Camp David deal might unravel. However, the fall of the pro-American Shah of Iran in January 1979 (Chapter 15, B) provoked concern in Washington, Cairo, and Tel Aviv and led to the so-called 'Camp David II' conference, of Foreign Ministers in late February, where both Egypt and Israel were ready to comprom-ise. A personal visit by Carter to the two countries was followed, on 26 March, by the signature of an Egyptian–Israeli peace treaty in Washington. 'Des-pite six months of negotiation, recrimination, and threats of total breakdown, the final treaty contained no important departures from the Camp David framework.'[23] The Israeli withdrawal from Sinai could now proceed, Sadat promised to exchange ambassadors within a month, and America gave both sides military aid, totalling $4.5 billion, to cement the deal.

The peace treaty caused controversy on both sides. The Israelis had secured peace and normal diplomatic relations with their most powerful Arab neighbour, but withdrawal from the Sinai involved the abandonment of oil wells and Jewish settle-ments there, which upset domestic opinion. There was also some concern in Israel over America's closer military relationship with Egypt and Carter's periodic sympathy for Palestinian rights. In August 1979 a meeting between America's UN ambassador, Andrew Young, and the PLO leader, Yasser Arafat, provoked outrage in Israel. 'The Israelis assumed that . . . Young's meeting signalled a major change in US policy.'[24] Young, who in fact had not con-sulted the State Department before the interview, was forced to resign. For Sadat, the Sinai was won back but, despite American hopes, even moderate Arabs refused to follow him on the path to peace. The Arab League expelled him, he became heavily reliant on American money, and he had won almost nothing for Palestinians. Furthermore, at home a 'perceptual gap developed within the Egyp-tian public between what Sadat said was possible and what actually materialized.'[25] Instead Begin, narrowly re-elected in 1981, increased Jewish settlements in the occupied territories, which in turn simply increased Arab loathing of Sadat. On 6 October 1981 he was assassinated by a radical Mus-lim group in the army, to be succeeded by Hosni Mubarak who, while maintaining peace with Israel, slowly rebuilt relations with the Arab world. As to Carter, he took much of the credit for the peace treaty and continued to exclude the USSR from the peace process, but it was far removed from the gen-eral Middle Eastern settlement for which he had originally hoped, and even before it was achieved the focus of concern in the Middle East had moved to Iran, where he faced his worst foreign policy humiliation.

The Panama Canal Treaties

Alongside the Camp David settlement, the other great success for Carter's personal approach to complex challenges in 1977–8 was the Panama Canal deal, but it was a settlement that was much criticized by Republicans as evidence of the President's weakening of the US global position. The canal, linking the Atlantic and Pacific Oceans, had been completed in 1912 under the terms of a 1903 treaty which, the Panamanian government later argued, was extracted under duress. The US operated the Canal itself and held sovereign rights in a 10-mile wide strip on each side. The Canal was of value not only as a trade route but also for the US navy. In the 1960s local feeling against the American presence mounted and in 1964 several Americans and Panamanians were killed during riots, but popular and Congressional opposition in the US helped deter attempts by Johnson and Nixon to renegotiate the 1903 treaty. Despite the problems President Carter was determined to resolve the issue, seeing it as a question of justice. More practically, the US military believed the Canal could only be operated safely with Panamanian approval.

Talks with the government of General Omar Torrijos began as soon as Carter was inaugurated, and two treaties were signed on 7 September 1977. One provided for the joint operation of the Canal until the end of the century when Panama would take full control; meanwhile America would be the senior partner and retain its forces there. The other treaty permanently neutralized the Canal but gave the US the right to defend it from external attack, while Panama handled internal security. In America, the necessary approval of the treaties by the Senate took 7 months to achieve, but opinion polls became well-disposed to the deal and Carter went to Panama in June 1978 to sign a formal transfer agreement. Even then it took until September 1979 before Congress reluctantly approved detailed laws on the new Canal regime. For Americans the treaties provided a long-term guarantee of the Canal's security, a step to improved relations with Panama, and a retreat from their Imperial position in Latin America. Panama won sovereignty over its own soil, an opportunity for income and self-respect.

CHRONOLOGY: THE ROAD TO AN ISRAELI–EGYPTIAN PEACE TREATY, 1977–1979

1977

9 March	President Carter, in office since January, says there should be a genuine peace in the Middle East including recognition of Palestinian rights and secure borders for Israel.
16 March	Carter talks of a Palestinian 'homeland', upsetting Israeli opinion.
4–5 April	Carter and Sadat meet for the first time, in Washington.
17 May	Successes for right-wing Likud coalition in Israeli elections.
21 June	Menachem Begin appointed Israeli Premier.
19–20 July	Carter and Begin meet for the first time, in Washington.
24 September	Carter writes to Begin complaining about Israeli military activity against the Palestinian Liberation Organization in Lebanon.
1 October	US and USSR jointly call for a comprehensive peace settlement in the Middle East.
21 October	Carter writes to Sadat urging him to help break the impasse in Middle East peace efforts.
9 November	Sadat publicly states his readiness to visit Jerusalem and speak to the Israeli parliament (Knesset).
19 November	Sadat speaks with Begin in Jerusalem.
20 November	Sadat's speech to the Knesset, urging a peace settlement.
25–26 December	Further Sadat–Begin talks in Ismailiya, Egypt.

1978

11 March	PLO attack on an Israeli bus kills more than thirty.
13 March	Israel launches 'Operation Litani', an invasion of Lebanon to drive PLO from the Israeli border.
March–June	Various proposals put forward for a solution to the Palestinian issue.
17–19 July	Talks at Leeds Castle, England, between the US, Israeli, and Egyptian Foreign Ministers fail to provide a breakthrough.
6–8 August	US Secretary of State Vance visits Begin and Sadat to invite them to a summit with Carter.
5–17 September	Camp David summit of Carter, Begin, and Sadat agrees a framework for peace.
5 November	Arab leaders (other than Sadat) meet in Baghdad, attack the Camp David accords, and try to dissuade Egypt from proceeding.

1979

15 January	Shah of Iran overthrown.
7–13 March	Carter goes to Middle East to finalise an Israeli–Egyptian peace treaty.
26 March	Peace treaty signed by Begin and Sadat in Washington.

C. **The Ogaden War**

Marxist Advances in the Horn of Africa

Hopes that superpower détente might revive after the trials of the mid-1970s were dashed in 1977–8 largely because of events in the Horn of Africa, where a war between Somalia and Ethiopia was again portrayed in the US as evidence of Soviet adventurism in the less developed world. Echoing events in Angola a few years before, the Ogaden War was another African conflict with complex local roots in which Cuban forces intervened decisively, this time on the Ethiopian side. Rather than being seen as a triumph for the Soviet cause, however, later evidence suggests that the conflict wrong-footed Moscow, whose ambitions in the Horn were strictly limited.

In the 1960s and early 1970s it was Somalia which seemed closest to the communist camp while Ethiopia, under Emperor Haile Selassie had made a defence agreement with the US as early as 1953. The Horn of Africa was poor and sparsely populated but it assumed some importance because of its proximity to the Middle East. Somalia, formed in 1960 from the former colonies of Italian and British Somaliland, controlled the strategically placed port of Berbera, positioned where the Red Sea opened into the Indian Ocean. In 1969 Siad Barre became the Somali President, declared a Socialist Republic, and increasingly aligned his foreign policy with Moscow. A Somali–Soviet friendship treaty was signed in 1974 and military aid began to flow 2 years later. Meanwhile, in neighbouring Ethiopia, the ageing Haile Selassie was overthrown in a military coup in September 1974, his traditionalist regime replaced by a Marxist-influenced, authoritarian government controlled by the 'Dergue', a council of military officers. After a long and confusing power struggle, in which many original revolutionary leaders were killed, Colonel Mengistu Haile Mariam ruthlessly eliminated his opponents and seized the leadership of Ethiopia on 3 February 1977. Until then the 'Dergue' had seen China or Yugoslavia, rather than the USSR, as possible models and allies, but an Ethiopian delegation visited Moscow in July 1976 and the Soviets were probably forewarned of Mengistu's coup.

After February 1977, Ethiopia moved quickly towards Moscow. The ruthless, intelligent Mengistu distanced himself from China, ended the defence arrangements with the US (which had decided to cut military aid to Ethiopia), and welcomed Cuba's Fidel Castro to Addis Ababa. Although Mengistu had shown no pronounced Marxist commitment in the past, Castro was personally impressed by him and it seemed that the Eastern bloc now had complete control of the Horn of Africa. The Soviets were disturbed by Mengistu's capacity for violence, Ethiopia's economic turmoil, and the lack (until 1984) of a local communist party but hoped to keep both Mengistu and Siad Barre jointly committed to a Marxist future. 'Both Mengistu and Siad Barre were stubborn and ambitious leaders who confronted the Kremlin with difficult choices, which it tried to avoid for as long as possible.'[26] After their success in the Angolan civil war, the USSR and Cuba increasingly saw Africa as a continent where they could limit both American and Chinese influence. Dobrynin writes that 'having suffered no major international complications because of its interference in Angola, Moscow had no scruples about escalating its activities in other countries' in Africa. But he adds that, from 'the long-term geopolitical point of view, the developments in ... Africa were unmistakably of local importance, and ... Moscow regarded them as such.'[27] The Soviets also hoped to counter the US success in dominating the Middle East process, a success that was confirmed in 1977–8 by Carter's leading role in the Camp David peace process. 'Cuba's policy in Africa was guided by Cuban national interest and ideology'[28] rather than the dictates of Moscow. In March 1977 Castro even had hopes of sponsoring a confederation between Ethiopia, Somalia, and South Yemen (the last a radical Marxist regime on the opposite side of the Red Sea). Within months, however, such hopes were dashed: Ethiopia and Somalia were at war.

The Ogaden War

In the Horn of Africa, as in other regional conflicts throughout the Cold War, the designs of a superpower fell foul of deep-seated local enmities, and commitments to client states simply embroiled one superpower in a conflict in which it had no vital interests. Barre had never given up Somali claims to the Ogaden desert region of southern Ethiopia, where a secessionist, pro-Somali movement (the Western Somali Liberation Front) was active throughout the 1970s. This was not the only separatist movement with which the Ethiopians had to deal: in the north-east, along the Red Sea coast, the Eritrean People's Liberation Front, which had the backing of some Arab countries, had been active since 1961, pressing for an independent state. But the Ethiopians, whether under Haile Selassie or the Dergue, were determined to maintain a united country.

Both Mengistu and Barre were stubborn nationalists, but it was the latter who, in spring 1977, rejected Castro's proposal for an Ethiopian–Somali confederation. As the year went on he also became increasingly concerned about Soviet–Cuban links to Addis Ababa. In May the Soviets began arms supplies to Ethiopia and the Cubans sent a military mission there. In response, Barre took some aid from China and began to sound out America about assistance. For a time this threw US policy into confusion: in July 1977 America, Britain, and France agreed in principle to supply arms, but as conflict escalated in the Horn of Africa the Western powers felt it inappropriate to fuel the tension, and in September the State Department publicly said there would be no arms deliveries. 'American interest in detaching Somalia from the Soviet Union was now more than counterbalanced by reluctance to support a blatant invasion of one country by another.'[29] Barre, whose military actions in the Ogaden at this time may have been encouraged by the hope of US arms, felt betrayed. Between July and September his forces had overrun most of the Ogaden.

Yet if American policy was confused, Soviet actions seemed hopelessly contradictory as their policy of maintaining Somali–Ethiopian unity fell apart. At first it was not clear which side they would support. Having provided Somalia with weapons and advisers, Moscow must have been aware of planning for the Ogaden invasion and they did not sever arms supplies to Barre until August. Vain attempts to reach a local settlement also seem to have persisted until then and Mengistu himself criticized the USSR for having built up Somali military power during Ethiopia's years of turmoil. Eventually however the Soviets came down on Ethiopia's side and began to provide her with massive arms supplies in late 1977, as the Somali offensive in the Ogaden stalled. Somalia might be militarily better prepared for war but Ethiopia was wealthier, larger in both area and population, and more centrally placed in North-Eastern Africa. Then again, only in August did the Kremlin finally decide to back Ethiopia. It was argued near the time that the 'inadequacy of other explanations for Soviet intervention forces one back to the residual explanation, opportunism: that the Russians will be happy to extend their influence . . . where it appears they can do so without appreciable risk.'[30] It is not an interpretation that has stood the test of time. Evidence from the former Eastern bloc suggests, not the expansionism of a Marxist automaton, but a 'relatively benign Soviet Union confronted with a situation it neither anticipated nor desired'.[31] In propaganda terms, however, it was easier to defend a country which was the victim of aggression and Moscow believed Mengistu to be more trustworthy and less devious than Barre. The Cubans too were much better disposed to Mengistu (who had earlier so impressed Castro) than Barre (who was now blamed for dividing the Marxist camp). Between November 1977—when Barre tore up his friendship treaty with Moscow—and February 1978 about 15,000 Cuban troops and 1,500 Soviet advisers were sent to Ethiopia and by the end of March they had helped liberate all the Ogaden. The operation was carried out as quickly as possible, to reduce the risk of any outside interference, and the Ethiopian–Cuban forces were careful to call a halt once they reached the Somali border, for fear of upsetting African opinion (and being labelled as aggressors) if they crossed it. Although most Arab states backed the Somalis, most African countries tolerated the Cuban intervention in the Ogaden because local borders were respected. The lack of an invasion of Somalia also made it more difficult for the Americans to condemn Soviet and Cuban activities. But that did not stop the conflict having a detrimental impact on superpower relations and appearing to divide Carter's advisers. On 1 March Brzezinski stated that Soviet behaviour could lead to problems with SALT II, but the following day Vance insisted, 'There is no linkage between the SALT negotiations and the situation in Ethiopia.'[32]

An 'Arc of Crisis'?

Although guerrilla activity rumbled on for years in the Ogaden, by March 1978 the Soviets and Cubans seemed to have turned the confusion and embarrassment of the previous summer into a decisive triumph. Mengistu's regime survived until 1991, by which time the Cold War had ended. Yet in some ways the confusion went on: whereas the Soviets also now helped Mengistu in his attempts to crush Eritrean separatism, the Cubans saw the Eritreans as pursuing a 'justified national liberation' struggle, a struggle which eventually resulted in success in May 1993. (It should also be noted that the USSR's ally Syria helped its fellow Arabs in Eritrea, whereas America's ally Israel had long been well-disposed to non-Arab Ethiopia.) These differences also underline the fact that Castro was no mere Soviet proxy in Africa. As in Angola, the Cubans proved reliable and successful allies for Moscow, but they acted on their own motives, anti-American and pro-revolutionary, and were proud of their own standing in the less developed world, a standing confirmed when Havana hosted the sixth summit of non-aligned countries in September 1979. To many in the US, however, the crude message of the Ogaden War was of a Soviet success, brought by violence and, thanks to Cuban help, without the need for direct Soviet involvement. The Angolan and Ogaden contests may have differed markedly—the first a civil war fought as colonial rule ended, the second an attempt by one country to take advantage of its troubled neighbour in a long-running border dispute—but Cuban armed intervention made them seem part of the same struggle for influence in the less developed world.

In fact there was evidence of mutual superpower restraint during the war. The US had refused to arm the Somalis, the Soviets and Cubans had refused to violate Somali territory. There had even been an offer to the US from Moscow in January 1978 of joint mediation in the conflict but Washington had rejected this as likely to legitimatize the Soviet–Cuban intervention. For American critics of Soviet policy, like Brzezinski, the Ogaden War was not the only problem. Rather, it followed earlier episodes, like Angola and the fall of Vietnam, and it was only the most important part of an 'arc of crisis'—a term first used by Brzezinski in December 1978—stretching from Africa, through the Middle East to Central Asia. 'An Arc of Crisis', he said, 'stretches along the shores of the Indian Ocean, with fragile social and political structures in a region of vital importance to us threatened with fragmentation. The resulting political chaos could well be filled by elements hostile to our values.'[33] Throughout this vast area, it was argued, there was evidence of Soviet trouble-making. In pro-Western Zaire, separatists in the Shaba region (formerly Katanga) had support from the Angolan government and, in May 1978, the US condemned Soviet and Cuban activities there, despite a lack of evidence that they were directly involved. In the late 1970s a rebellion in Oman had the backing of pro-Soviet South Yemen. In South Yemen itself in June 1978 an extremist coup coincided with the assassination of the President of North Yemen, at that time aligned with America's ally, Saudi Arabia. Unrest in Iran, political instability in Turkey, and growing Soviet influence in Afghanistan, added to the sense of Western concern.

In fact all these conflicts had complicated local origins and it was simplistic to see all of them as part of an East–West rivalry: 'the events of the Arc of Crisis cannot be reduced to a simple picture of Soviet trouble-making. ... A straightforward adversary policy is not justified by the facts.'[34] It was easy to misread volatile local situations: the North Yemen government, for example, gladly accepted Saudi aid against South Yemen in 1978–9, but then decided to enter an arms deal with the Soviets, partly to prevent Saudi domination. The US and other Western powers were active enough themselves in many conflicts: France and Belgium helped prop up Zaire, whilst pro-American Iran aided Oman. In fact both superpowers used allies to advance their influence in the less developed world, both were often forced to back these allies in unpleasant struggles, and both tended to simplify local situations, blaming the other super-power for creating problems. But, in surveying the rivalry of the mid-1970s, Americans believed that they had made the main retreats in Angola, South-East Asia, and the Ogaden. The fact that the Kremlin, even while espousing détente, posed as a defender of national liberation struggles, seemed to confirm the image of a one-sided Communist advance and, at the same time, the Soviets were developing the military capacity to act far afield, with airlifts of Cuban troops and an expanded, 'blue water' navy. The fact that the USSR had lost an ally (Somalia) in the Ogaden War was soon forgotten by Brzezinski who was anxious to punish Moscow for its supposed adventurism. But for the moment his anti-Soviet tendencies were tempered by others in the adminis-

tration. In early 1978 Cyrus Vance, who pointed out that the Somalis were the aggressors in the Ogaden and that the Soviets had limited aims, joined Defence Secretary Harold Brown in resisting Brzezinski's pressure for a demonstration of US naval power in the region. The Secretary of State also rejected Brzezinski's claim that the SALT II talks had been 'buried in the sands of the Ogaden'.[35] For Vance, of course, these two issues should not be linked: SALT remained valuable to the US in its own right. 'If the United States accepted the essentially competitive nature of the US–USSR relationship and . . . wanted a SALT agreement, it could not make the latter conditional on Soviet withdrawal from less developed world involvements.'[36] Brzezinski had better success however when he set out to face the Soviets with a US–Chinese combination in the wake of the Ogaden War.

D. Sino–US 'Normalization' and the Sino–Vietnamese War

'Playing the China Card'

The Soviet Union had always feared, in the early 1970s, that China would exploit its rapprochement with America to tempt the latter away from détente. And, after Nixon's triumphant meeting with Mao in 1972, the US continued to demonstrate its new friendship with China: in December 1975, for example, Mao and Ford met in Beijing. But Nixon and Ford were keen to maintain good relations with both major Communist powers. The aim of the 'Opening to China' had been to provide a counter-weight to Soviet power, not to threaten the USSR. The Chinese were disappointed with the successes of détente in 1972–5, fearing that the Soviets would now concentrate their military forces in Asia. Yet Beijing continued its policy of improving relations, not only with America, but also with other pro-Western states in East Asia like Japan and Malaysia. The fall of Vietnam removed an old problem in Sino–American relations and intensified Sino–Soviet competition for influence in the region since the

Vietnamese, historically fearful of Chinese domin-ation, now looked to Moscow as a protector. True, the whole course of Chinese policy was thrown into doubt in 1976, with the deaths first of Zhou Enlai in January, then of Mao himself on 9 September. The option of returning to a radical Maoist path was, however, removed with the arrest of Mao's widow and other members of the so-called 'Gang of Four'. A power struggle then began between the Communist Party chairman, Hua Guofeng, and Deng Xiaoping. Previously number three in the party hierarchy (after Mao and Zhou), Deng had been ousted by the Gang of Four in April 1976 but was rehabilitated in July 1977 and established his predominance in government over the following year. He was suspi-cious of the Soviets and keen to modernize China through the decentralization of decision-making, production of consumer goods, and trade with the West.

Despite the political turmoil in China and the problems created by American friendship with Taiwan, the Carter administration was ready from its outset to consider 'normalizing' relations with Peking by exchanging formal diplomatic recognition. This was not just an important symbolic step, it would also show the USSR that Sino–American relations were continuing to improve and, significantly, it would involve the US in severing formal diplomatic relations with Taiwan (since the Communists and Taiwanese both claimed to be the only legitimate Chinese government). When Cyrus Vance visited Beijing in August 1977, however, the problems with such a course were exposed. Whilst Vance was eager to maintain the policy of 'balance', talking to China and Russia, the Chinese were critical of the SALT II negotiations and wanted a tougher anti-Soviet policy. Also, as Vance told Carter, 'I do not believe that we should feel so compelled to establish diplomatic relations with Beijing that we jeopardize the well-being and security of the people of Taiwan.'[37] Events in the Ogaden (Chapter 14, C) however made the US more anxious to deter Soviet intervention in the less developed world and Brzezinski became a strong advocate of 'playing the China card', in the global struggle for influence which he believed was intensifying between Washington and Moscow. 'I had . . . become quite preoccupied with Moscow's misuse of détente . . . especially through the Cuban military presence in Ethiopia', he later wrote. 'I believed that a strategic response was necessary.'[38] In May 1978 he made his own visit to Beijing, discussed the strategic threat posed by the USSR, made tough anti-Soviet statements, and even revealed some secrets to the Chinese about American security policies. The contrast between his visit and the earlier journey by the more cautious Vance could not have been greater. The Chinese warmly welcomed Brzezinski; the Soviets were deeply suspicious and continued to strengthen their defences, now deploying Backfire bombers in Asia. There was also renewed Sino–Soviet border tension and Chinese relations with other Eastern bloc states, especially Vietnam, became very poor. On the Chinese side, plans 'for normalization . . . moved parallel to stepped-up preparations for military action on China's northern and southern borders' and Beijing's 'need to build a counterweight to Moscow forced a softening of its bargaining position vis-à-vis Washington.'[39] In particular, China proved ready to tolerate US arms sales to Taiwan

beyond normalization. (In July 1978 in a noteworthy side effect to improved relations with America, China cut off its aid to Albania, which was bitterly critical of the US and now followed Stalinist policies in complete isolation.)

Sino–American normalization was finally agreed on 16 December 1978 and took effect on New Year's Day, 1979 with embassies being officially opened in each capital on 1 March. The Soviets expressed concern at this process on several occasions but, as with the 'Opening to China' in 1971–2, tried not to make their distress too obvious. To Chinese annoyance, the SALT II talks continued but there was no doubt that, in contrast to the early 1970s, the improvement in Sino–American relations in 1978–9 was accompanied by a deterioration in Soviet-American détente. Whereas Nixon and Kissinger had been able to use Sino–Soviet antagonism to play off each Communist power against the other, Carter and Brzezinski effectively adopted a one-sided policy that deepened US–Soviet divisions. 'The timing of Sino–American normalization was clearly a triumph for Brzezinski. He strengthened containment while outmaneuvring . . . Vance and his preferred sequence requiring that SALT take precedence.'[40] Certainly, closer links brought benefits to both America and China. In January-February 1979 Deng made a lengthy visit to Washington, discussing trade and investment, and in April the Chinese even allowed the US to use their soil for electronic intelligence gathering about Soviet nuclear missiles. An agreement in July (effective in January 1980) granted China 'most favoured nation' trading status in America. But at the same time the dangers of the new relationship were apparent, especially in East Asia where the US was drawn into increasingly tolerating bellicose Chinese activity.

The East Asian Impact of Normalization

The improvement in Sino–American relations was accompanied by a similar process between two historic rivals, China and Japan. Talks on a Soviet–Japanese peace treaty (to settle problems left by the Second World War) came to nothing in the mid-1970s, largely because of Moscow's threatening tone and its rejection of Japanese territorial claims to certain islands which had been seized by the Soviets in 1945. The Soviets had probably expected that tough diplomacy would deter Japan from moving closer to China and Tokyo certainly hoped at first to avoid joining China and America in an overtly anti-Soviet combination. But the Soviet tactics backfired, causing grave offence in Japan which, on 12 August 1978, signed a friendship treaty with Beijing. An expected boost in Japanese investment was not forthcoming, largely because of bureaucratic and infrastructure problems in China, yet within 'the next five years, the relationship flourished until China became Japan's number two trading partner—just behind the United States.'[41] The 'growing friendship and economic partnership between the two giant Asian powers fuelled Moscow's anxiety about encirclement' and led the Soviets to strengthen their links to Vietnam.[42]

The 'normalization' process had a direct impact on two other US allies in the region, South Korea and of course Taiwan. Although South Korea had relied on the US for protection since 1950 and had sent 50,000 troops to fight in the Vietnam War, Carter had controversially promised, during the 1976 election, to withdraw US forces from the country. He retreated from this pledge once in office—Korea, like Taiwan, had strong supporters in Congress—but force levels were reduced and this helped improve relations with China. Taiwan was, unsurprisingly, an even more difficult issue, another country under American protection but which Beijing claimed as part of its own territory. Even here however the drive for improved Sino–American relations allowed problems to be overcome, through a compromise which was painful to all sides. The Americans abrogated their defence treaty with Taiwan on 31 December 1979, withdrew US forces from the island, and ended their *de jure* diplomatic recognition of the Taipei government; but diplomatic contacts were effectively maintained via an 'American Institute' in the capital, American arms were sold to the country in April 1979, and Congress forced a Taiwan Relations Act on Carter, which stated that America would forcibly resist any invasion of the island by China. The Act reflected 'a suspicion that China had not given up its option on the use of force to regain Taiwan.'[43] The Chinese did

not give up their claim to Taiwan, but did adopt a less threatening tone towards it and said they would seek reunification by peaceful means.

When Deng visited Washington in early 1979 he made it publicly clear that China had been willing to compromise on Taiwan and other issues in order to form an anti-Soviet front. Although the SALT II talks were continuing and Carter was unwilling to join in any anti-Soviet tirades, Deng was critical of Moscow throughout and even threatened to attack her ally, Vietnam. His 'meeting with members of Congress who encouraged China to teach Vietnam a lesson, his visits to US defence industry corporations, and his generally masterful public relations campaign all suggested enhanced US-[Chinese] security co-operation vis-à-vis the Soviet Union and Vietnam.'[44] Relations between China and Vietnam had been worsening since the fall of Saigon in 1975. With the removal of American influence, old Sino–Vietnamese rivalry reasserted itself, fuelled by Vietnam's reliance on the USSR for military and economic aid. Instead of an expansion of Communist influence outside Indo-China, as the US had earlier feared, the various Communist regimes in the area began to fall out. In particular China backed Pol Pot's Khmer Rouge government in Cambodia (then called Kampuchea), which was both Maoist and anti-Vietnamese. Despite a visit by Pol Pot to Hanoi in September 1977, Vietnamese–Cambodian border tensions mounted, with China arming the Khmer Rouge and Russia the Vietnamese. By 1978 Sino–Vietnamese border tension was also apparent and both those countries laid claim to the Spratly and Paracel islands in the China Sea. The Vietnamese initiated a campaign of discrimination against their million-strong Chinese minority, about a quarter of whom fled across the border. Neither side showed any sign of compromise. While China improved its relations with America and Japan, the USSR allowed the Vietnamese into COMECON in June 1978 and signed a 25-year friendship treaty with them on 3 November. The treaty included a commitment to 'consult' each other if either was attacked and it probably confirmed the Chinese determination to proceed with the normalization of American relations the following month. Already, in July, China had severed all its remaining aid programmes to Vietnam.

The Vietnamese Invasion of Cambodia and Sino–Vietnamese War

On 25 December 1978, months of border incidents culminated in a full-scale Vietnamese invasion of Cambodia. Ideological differences had developed between the Vietnamese and Pol Pot which were exacerbated by the latter's alliance with China. The capital, Phnom Penh, was taken on 7 January and a pro-Vietnamese regime established under the Presidency of former Khmer Rouge guerrilla, Heng Samring. The gruesome story of Pol Pot's policy of genocide in Cambodia was now fully revealed. His regime had killed about two million people (out of seven million) over the previous 3½ years. But China, America, and other pro-Western countries continued to recognize Pol Pot's government, which launched a guerrilla war from bases on the Thai border. The Vietnamese invasion was treated in the West not as a 'humanitarian intervention' but as an act of aggression which could not be condoned, however distasteful the Khmer Rouge were. The civil war in Cambodia ran on through the 1980s. American aid helped Thailand cope with the refugee crisis on its border; Japan and most non-communist countries in South-East Asia condemned Hanoi; and China accused Vietnam of seeking to dominate all Indo-China.

Following Deng's return from his American visit the Chinese themselves invaded Vietnam on 17 February 1979. Their 300,000 troops destroyed four provincial capitals and devastated large areas, but did not fare well against Vietnam's experienced armed forces and withdrew within a month. They did however warn, in June, that there would be a second invasion if Vietnam should threaten Thailand. And they had certainly demonstrated their opposition to Vietnam's occupation of Cambodia. The US knew in

---

Pol Pot (1925–1998)

In his early life Pol Pot, remembered as the murderer of two million of his countrymen, had been intended for the Buddhist priesthood. Born into a peasant family, with the name Saloth Sar, he was educated in a Buddhist monastery before joining the Indo-Chinese Communist Party in 1946. He spent four years at a technical school in France before becoming a teacher in 1953. Ten years later he went into hiding, with the pseudonym Pol Pot, and became leader of the Khmer Rouge, an extreme Maoist movement, with hopes of overthrowing the Cambodian government through guerrilla warfare and establishing an agrarianized, egalitarian society. The movement had little success until 1970, when the combination of American bombing (linked to the war in neighbouring Vietnam) and a military coup by the pro-American general Lon Nol, gave the Khmer Rouge both a nationalist cause to fight and a useful political ally in the former ruler, Prince Sihanouk, who himself had Chinese backing.

In 1975, Cambodia was the first of the three Indo-Chinese governments to succumb to communism. The capital, Phnom Penh, was entered by Pol Pot's followers in April and immediately emptied of its inhabitants. In fact, all urban centres were abandoned, land collectivized, and middle-class groups systematically destroyed, as the Khmer Rouge pursued their agrarian dream. Pol Pot became Prime Minister, of what was now called the Khmer Republic, but was overthrown only 3 years later by his former allies, the North Vietnamese, who resented his links to China and were concerned at his extremism. Only then was the full extent of the Cambodian 'killing fields' revealed: political murder, starvation, and disease had claimed countless lives.

Pol Pot escaped, however, leading a guerrilla campaign against the North Vietnamese puppet regime in Phnom Penh. He again allied with Sihanouk and the Chinese; and, because of their determination to resist North Vietnamese expansionism, Thailand, America, and other Western countries continued to recognize the Khmer Rouge as the legitimate government. An embarrassment to his allies, Pol Pot was said to have resigned—or been removed from—his position of leadership in 1985 but it is clear that he remained an influence behind the scenes. In 1993 he broke with Sihanouk over moves towards an internal settlement in Cambodia, but the Khmer Rouge began to fall apart in the years following this move, an increasingly isolated and despised force. Pol Pot died in 1998, soon after being imprisoned by some of his own followers.

advance of the Chinese attack but did not consult the Soviets about it, preferring to urge them to show restraint. There was no 'joint planning' of Sino–American policy at this time, but the term 'parallelism' began to be used about the fact that they often moved in unison and it has been said that by his timing of the war 'Deng made it appear that the United States was a silent partner in the invasion, an attack on a Soviet ally'.[45] Such 'parallelism' only convinced the Soviets, however, that détente was becoming less valuable and, although the USSR and

Vietnam found themselves virtually isolated in East Asian politics, they refused to be cowed. Vietnam now decided to allow the Soviets the use of air and naval facilities, while the Soviets decided that they must assert their strength in Afghanistan, where a Marxist government was coming under increasing strain. 'The rapid pace of rapprochement between the United States and China, based as it was to a large extent on an anti-Soviet posture, was evidently one of a number of reasons why the Soviet Union decided to send its troops into Afghanistan.'[46]

E. **The SALT II Treaty**

By early 1979, following the Ogaden War and Sino–American normalization, the SALT process was the only real evidence that superpower détente remained alive. But, rather than giving the process a new hope, the signature of a SALT II treaty in June 1979 was surrounded by doubt. Two years overdue and the product of many compromises, the treaty was immediately called into question in the US Senate and its ratification was eventually suspended.

The Vladivostok Framework

Whatever its success as an arms restraint measure and evidence of improved superpower relations, the SALT I treaty (Chapter 12, B) on offensive missiles had only ever been an 'interim agreement', to be succeeded by a new arrangement within 5 years. It also had obvious omissions which a future treaty would have to tackle, not least the Multi-Independent Re-entry Vehicle (MIRV), which allowed missiles to be armed with several, individually targeted warheads. The SALT I talks had shown the problems of achieving a balanced US–Soviet agreement. The Soviets were concerned that it did not cover American 'forward-based systems' (FBS) in Western Europe which could hit the USSR; Americans were concerned that (in order to compensate for Soviet technological deficiencies) SALT I left the USSR with more land-based and submarine-launched missiles, many of them much larger than

US missiles. From the start Senator Henry Jackson, the leading critic of détente, pressed hard for SALT II to be based on equal numbers (or 'ceilings') of missiles on each side, to prevent the possibility of the Soviets gaining nuclear predominance. Technology was advancing all the time and the USSR's success in MIRVing its missiles after 1973 added weight to Jackson's arguments. Within the Nixon administration the Defence Department took a tough approach to the SALT II talks especially, between July 1973 and November 1975, under James Schlesinger. He was identified with the doctrine of 'extended deterrence', announced in January 1974, a vitally important step in nuclear strategy which shifted US war-planning from a reliance on massive missile strikes to a readiness to fight a 'limited nuclear' war. This might mean the targeting of Soviet missile silos and command centres in order to cripple their war-making ability without the need for nuclear Armageddon. Sometimes called the 'Schlesinger doctrine', it theoretically gave US planning greater flexibility but it also introduced the danger that US planners might believe they could successfully fight a nuclear war, thus making it more likely. New weapons planned by America included the Poseidon SLBM, a powerful MIRVed replacement for Polaris to be launched from Trident submarines.

Although the SALT II talks formally began in November 1972, progress was slow and not helped by Nixon's decision, partly influenced by Jackson's criticisms, to replace the whole US negotiating team in January 1973. After the President's position was undermined by the Watergate scandal, insufficient time was given by the Americans to SALT II and the talks became bogged down for months on the issue of 'equal ceilings'. To the Soviets, still technologically behind America even if they had now developed MIRVs, it made no sense to concede equal numbers of missiles. 'Unequal ceilings' had been a main Soviet gain in SALT I, not to be surrendered lightly, especially given the existence, not only of FBS but also of the British, French, and Chinese deterrents, all targeted on the USSR. Kissinger may have been ready to concede unequal ceilings again in SALT II, hoping to use that treaty to consolidate the US lead in MIRVed weapons, but Schlesinger totally opposed such a deal being made and, once President Ford was in office, the Kremlin realized it must retreat. In their summit at Vladivostok on 23–4 November 1974, Ford and Brezhnev agreed a framework SALT II deal. Despite the doubts of the Soviet military, Brezhnev conceded an equal ceiling of 2,400 missiles or bombers on each side, 1,320 of which could be MIRVed. The USSR also agreed to exclude FBS.

Kissinger claimed that the Vladivostok deal left SALT 90 per cent complete and he hoped a treaty might be signed in 1975. He also insisted that the deal protected US interests: 'Brezhnev had settled for the equal numbers across the board that the Pentagon had been urging . . . we had made no significant concession.'[47] But the remaining 10 per cent of the treaty included highly technical details and the negotiations continued to be dogged by weapons advances and, more importantly, US domestic politics. Senator Jackson 'ignored the point that his demand for equality had been met and instead began to castigate the administration for what had been left out of the treaty.'[48] One key problem was, whether, or how, to control a new American innovation, the low-flying (and hard to detect) 'cruise' missile. Another, vital to Jackson, was the new Soviet 'Backfire' bomber, which could fly to the US but only one way and with refuelling—and which the Kremlin therefore treated as a non-strategic weapon. Jackson also pressed the case for limiting the size of Soviet missiles, arguing that 'heavy' launchers would be able to carry more multiple warheads than US missiles. Schlesinger was removed from the Defense

Department in November 1975, during the so-called 'Halloween Massacre', but Kissinger was still unable to secure a SALT II deal when he visited Moscow 2 months later. Thereafter the Ford Presidency was absorbed in the 1976 Presidential election.

Delays under Carter

Although Carter was keen to pursue arms control and his Secretary of State, Vance, saw SALT II as central to détente, the new administration almost immediately put the arms talks in jeopardy. Eager to distance himself from his Republican predecessors and keen to reduce nuclear weapons numbers as far as possible, Carter made a well-intentioned but naïve attempt, in February 1977, to abandon the Vladivostok formula and press for much lower ceilings. If this strategy had worked, 'the administration would have answered the arms control critics of both the Right and Left. They would be taking a strong response to the Soviet threat while making a commitment for both superpowers to accept meaningful reductions in their strategic forces.'[49] But Brezhnev, who had recently made a speech at Tula supporting both détente and SALT, felt betrayed by Carter's move. The Soviets had spent years negotiating the Vladivostock formula and had no wish to restart the SALT II talks from scratch. When Vance visited Moscow in March, Gromyko told him, 'we are wholly opposed to tampering with the Vladivostok accords. They took too much effort from both our sides to achieve.'[50] The Soviets said that, on the positive side, they were ready to extend talks on military détente (working groups were established on such issues as anti-satellite weapons and a comprehensive test ban), but they rejected the new US negotiating position on SALT II outright. In April, when the US began to talk about a possible summit, the Kremlin made clear that it only wanted such a meeting if a SALT II treaty was on the table. The series of annual summits initiated by Nixon and Brezhnev could not be revived and it took several months before the SALT II talks were put back on track. Only in September, when Andrei Gromyko visited Washington, did the Carter administration accept the Vladivostock formula in return for a promise of further arms cuts in a SALT III treaty.

Meanwhile, like Nixon and Ford before him, Carter faced growing domestic criticism of SALT. His nominee as head of the US negotiating team, Paul Warnke, was only narrowly approved by Congress in March; in June the President's cancellation of the expensive B-1 bomber project was criticized as a blunder (because the cancellation could have been used as a 'bargaining chip' to obtain an equivalent Soviet concession); and the elite Committee on the Present Danger began to warn that, if the Soviets continued to MIRV their heavy missiles, a 'window of vulnerability' would open up in the 1980s, when the US would find itself running second in the nuclear stakes. Actually claims of a 'window of vulnerability' were as empty as claims, 20 years before, that a 'missile gap' was opening up between America and Russia. In focusing on the deployment of more accurate and MIRVed SS-18s and SS-19s by the USSR, the Committee on the Present Danger overlooked the modernization of US systems, with the development of cruise missiles and the deployment, in May 1977, of a new Minuteman ICBM. And in pointing up Soviet talk of 'nuclear war fighting', American critics overlooked that, in the Schlesinger Doctrine (which Carter maintained and developed), the US was doing the same. In August 1977 Carter approved a Presidential Directive, PD-18, which 'represented a fairly major step toward prescribing a war-waging capability' even if 'for the purpose of reinforcing deterrence by providing a resort if deterrence should fail.'[51]

Until 1976 at least the CIA was not overconcerned by Moscow's improving nuclear capability and in 1977 the tone of their intelligence reports may only have changed due to the prevailing political atmosphere in Washington. Later evidence showed that Soviet defence spending levelled off in 1976, never having been as great as the CIA estimated. In contrast, Carter was strengthening US defence by expanding conventional spending, modernizing America's nuclear arsenal, and beginning experiments with laser particle-beam weapons. Brezhnev's insistence that he wanted a fair SALT II treaty, solidifying nuclear parity not superiority, seems to have been honest enough. Having been the inferior power in the past, the Soviets were quite content with nuclear parity and feared being outrun in any new technological race with America. In 1977

America's submarine-launched missiles remained largely immune to a Soviet 'counterforce' attack (even if land-based weapons were vulnerable) and, besides, the US had about 8,500 nuclear warheads compared to the USSR's 4,000.[52] US critics of SALT were sometimes sincere, sometimes scaremongering, but what most seems to have concerned them was the issue of prestige. America's old superiority had gone, approximate nuclear parity had apparently made the Soviets bolder in conflicts in the less developed world, and there was a growing pessimism about American prospects, which exaggerated both the scale of the country's 'decline' and the advances of the other side. In 1978, however, thanks to the Ogaden War, there was growing pressure within the Carter administration to 'link' progress on SALT II to Soviet behaviour in the less developed world, just as Nixon and Kissinger had tried to do around 1970. Brzezinski, though a consistent supporter of the SALT process, did not feel that the talks could be insulated from other areas of superpower relations. Vance, in contrast, was more ready to accept that détente included elements of competition as well as cooperation, and still argued that a SALT II treaty was valuable in itself: 'we should face the fact of competition with the Soviets, and we should not link Soviet behaviour in the less developed world to issues in which we had so fundamental an interest as SALT.'[53] In late 1978 he especially believed that SALT must be maintained in order to counteract the negative effect on Moscow of Sino–US normalization.

Carter found it difficult to choose between Vance and Brzezinski on the issue of 'linkage'. On 17 March 1978 he made a speech which pleased his critics by expressing concern over the Soviet arms build-up, promised to maintain strong US defences, and stated that any SALT deal must preserve the nuclear balance. On 7 June, at Annapolis, he warned that the Soviets must choose between 'confrontation or cooperation'. Yet he never categorically linked SALT II to events in the less developed world and he continued to insist that he was loyal to détente. The Soviets studied such declarations with concern. *Pravda* pointed out that the President was being contradictory and the Politburo, noting Carter's continuing attacks on their human rights record, 'had the impression that Carter was leaning toward a policy of confrontation rather than détente'.[54] But in the second half of 1978, at least until the formal normalization of Sino–US relations in December, there were few specific problems in US–Soviet relations, allowing Vance and Gromyko to make steady progress on SALT II.

The Treaty and its Non-Ratification

Continuing his paradoxical approach to superpower relations, Carter saw no need for normalization to interfere with SALT II and there was even talk of granting 'Most Favoured Nation' trade status to both China and the USSR. Anxious not to cement the Sino–American relationship, the Soviets too decided to persevere with détente and a final treaty text was announced on 9 May. Less than one month later however, in another example of his schizophrenia, Carter announced a further significant modernization of the US nuclear arsenal, the development of the Missile Experimental, popularly known as 'MX'. This was a 'heavy', MIRVed missile, designed to match the SS-18s and 19s and allow the US to attack Soviet missile silos. Two hundred were to be built and, in an extremely ambitious building project, announced in September, they were to be protected by being placed on underground railway tracks, with twenty-three possible silos from which each missile might emerge. Ironically, while satisfying some critics, MX was soon questioned on grounds of cost and necessity: it would be the largest US public construction project ever and at the same time the 'Trident II' submarine was being developed, also armed with MIRVed missiles but less vulnerable to Soviet attack.

SALT II was eventually signed at the only Carter–Brezhnev summit, in Vienna on 15–18 June 1979. By accepting 'equal ceilings' and controlling MIRVs, it marked a major departure from SALT I (see boxed section). But in contrast to the 1972 Moscow summit, there were no other major US–Soviet agreements. Instead Carter again criticized the USSR on human rights, Brezhnev (who was clearly unwell) attacked US links to China and both sides differed on the causes of conflicts in the less developed world. The Soviets ratified the treaty quickly but, in America it was already in serious trouble. 'In retrospect it is

---

The SALT II Agreement, June 1979: key points

- There was to be an equal 'ceiling' of 2,400 strategic nuclear weapon launchers or heavy bombers in the arsenal of both superpowers (reducing to 2,250 by 1985);
- up to 1,320 of these launchers could either be Multi-Independent Re-entry Vehicles (MIRVs) or Air-launched Cruise Missiles (ALCMs);
- up to 1,200 launchers could be MIRVs;
- up to 820 of these MIRVs could be on Inter-Continental Ballistic Missiles;
- the USSR could only deploy 308 'heavy' missiles;
- limits placed on the number of warheads on a MIRVed missile;
- limited the deployment of new types of missile;
- to last until 1985.

In addition the following related points were agreed at the June 1979 Vienna summit:

- An interim protocol to SALT II, to last until 1981, placed limits on Air-Launched Cruise Missiles (ALCMs) and Ground-Launched Cruise Missiles (GLCMs) with a range over 600 kilometres;
- the USSR gave a written guarantee that its 'Backfire' bomber would not be used as a strategic weapon;
- SALT II should be followed by a SALT III treaty, including reductions in weapons numbers and possible controls on intermediate-range weapons in Europe;
- in the Vienna communiqué the US and USSR undertook not to seek military superiority over each other.

---

clear that the Carter administration did not do an adequate job preparing the ground . . . to ensure sufficient public and congressional support for the SALT II treaty.' Now, 'for the first time he had a public document to defend' whereas his opponents had 'one to attack'.[55] Many in the Senate were absolutely convinced that the strategic balance was moving in Moscow's favour and that SALT was useless for halting this trend. The treaty was criticized for failing properly to control the size of Soviet missiles or the 'Backfire' bomber, and for having inadequate verification arrangements. A brief crisis over Cuba in late August and early September underlined the fragility of superpower relations. The Carter administration, keen to appear tough in its dealings with Moscow, claimed to have 'discovered' the existence of a 2,800-strong Soviet army brigade in Cuba and there were immediate demands from Congress and the US press that it be withdrawn. It soon emerged that the brigade had been there since 1962. Even so, to Cuban annoyance, the Soviets were anxious that the issue should not upset the prospects for SALT II and agreed to downgrade the brigade to a 'training unit'.

Carter's toughness on Cuba helped him avoid amendments to SALT II in the Senate in late 1979 and in November the Senate Foreign Relations Committee actually recommended, by 9 votes to 6, that it be passed. But the danger of amendments soon re-emerged and ratification was suspended following the Soviet invasion of Afghanistan (Chapter 15, C). In 1980 both superpowers agreed that they would adhere to the treaty's terms but in 1986 President Reagan said he would no longer respect these, claiming the Soviets were breaching the limits on launcher numbers and new missiles.

NOTES

1. Richard Pipes, *US-Soviet Relations in the Era of Détente* (Westview Press, Boulder, 1981), xii.

2. Henry Kissinger, *Years of Renewal* (Simon & Schuster, New York, 1999), 307.

3. John Robert Greene, *The Presidency of Gerald R. Ford* (University of Kansas Press, Lawrence, 1995), 164.

4. Anatoly Dobrynin, *In Confidence* (Random House, New York, 1995), 408.

5. Mike Bowker and Phil Williams, *Superpower Détente: a Reappraisal* (Sage, London, 1988), 257.

6. Raymond Garthoff, *Détente and Confrontation* (Brookings Institute, Washington, rev. edn., 1994), 57.

7. William Cohen, *The Cambridge History of US Foreign Relations, IV* (Cambridge University Press, Cambridge, 1993), 208.

8. Jimmy Carter, *Why not the Best?* (Bantam Books, Eastbourne, 1977), 190.

9. David Brinkley, 'The Rising Stock of Jimmy Carter', *Diplomatic History*, 4 (1996), 522.

10. Zbigniew Brzezinski, *Power and Principle: Memoirs of the National Security Adviser 1977–81* (Weidenfeld & Nicolson, London, 1983), 149.

11. David Skidmore, 'Carter and the failure of foreign policy reform', *Political Science Quarterly*, 4 (1993), 714.

12. Helena Cobban, *The Making of Modern Lebanon* (Hutchinson Education, London, 1985), chs. 2 and 3.

13. Patrick Seale, *Asad of Syria* (Tauris, London, 1988), 281.

14. Mark Tessler, *A History of the Israeli–Palestinian Conflict* (Indiana University Press, Bloomington, 1994), 499.

15. Brzezinski, op. cit., 288.

16. Ishaq Ghanayem and Alden Voth, *The Kissinger Legacy* (Praeger, New York, 1984), 174.

17. Kenneth Stein, *Heroic Diplomacy* (Routledge, New York, 1999), 9.

18. Anwar el-Sadat, *In Search of Identity* (Collins, London, 1978), 302.

19. William Quandt, *Camp David* (Brookings Institution, Washington, DC, 1986), 65.

20. Quoted in David Hirst and Irene Beeson, *Sadat* (Faber, London, 1981), 269.

21. Quandt, op. cit., 166–7.

22. Ezer Weizman, *The Battle for Peace* (Bantam, New York, 1981), 190–1.

23. Seth Tillman, *The US in the Middle East* (Indiana University Press, Bloomington, 1982), 32.

24. Steven Spiegel, *The Other Arab–Israeli Conflict* (University of Chicago Press, Chicago, 1985), 375.

25. Stein, op. cit., 258.

26. Paul B. Henze, 'Moscow, Mengistu and the Horn', *Cold War International History Project (CWIHP) Bulletin*, nos. 8–9 (Winter 1996–7), 45.

27. Dobrynin, op. cit., 403–4.

28. Piero Gleijeses, 'Havana's Policy in Africa', *CWIHP Bulletin*, 8–9 (Winter, 1996–7), 12.

29. Garthoff, op. cit., 702.

30. Christopher Clapham, 'The Soviet Experience in the Horn of Africa', in E. J. Feuchtwanger and Peter Nailor (eds), *The Soviet Union and the Third World* (Macmillan, London, 1981), 218.

31. Henze, op. cit., 46.

32. Brzezinski, op. cit., 185.

33. *Time Magazine*, 15 January 1979.

34. Fred Halliday, *Threat from the East?* (Penguin, Harmondsworth, rev. ed., 1982), 129.

35. Brzezinski, op. cit., 189.

36. David McClellan, *Cyrus Vance* (Rowman & Allanheld, Totowa, 1985), 52.

37. Cyrus Vance, *Hard Choices* (Simon & Schuster, New York, 1983), 76.

38. Brzezinski, op. cit., 203–4.

39. Richard Thornton, *China: a Political History* (Westview Press, Boulder, 1982), 404.

40. Richard Thornton, *The Carter Years* (Paragon House, New York, 1991), 124–5.

41. Walter Lafeber, *The Clash: US-Japanese Relations* (W. W Norton & Co., New York, 1997), 369.

42. Christina Holmes, 'The Soviet Union and China', in Gerald Segal (ed.), *The Soviet Union in East Asia* (Heinemann, London, 1983), 25.

43. Rosemary Foot, *The Practice of Power* (Clarendon Press, Oxford, 1997), 228.

44. Robert Ross, *Negotiating Co-operation* (Stanford University Press, Stanford, 1995), 141.

45. Walter Lafeber, *America, Russia and the Cold War* (McGraw-Hill, New York, 1992), 293.

46. Roy Medvedev, *China and the Superpowers* (Blackwell, Oxford, 1986), 124.

47. Kissinger, op. cit., 342.

48. Greene, op. cit., 125.

49. Robert Strong, *Working in the World* (Louisiana State University Press, Baton Rouge, 2000), 38.

50. Andrei Gromyko, *Memories* (Hutchinson, London, 1987), 287.

51. Garthoff, op. cit., 868.

52. It should always be remembered that there are significant problems related to any figures purporting to reveal relative weapons' strengths. Warheads may include bombs released from aircraft or they may not. Independent institutes' figures may deviate from government figures by a factor of three. Weapons can also refer to intercontinental, intermediate, medium, short-range, theatre, or battlefield weapons and numbers may reflect which categories have been included or excluded. The problem became notoriously difficult in terms of the argument over Euromissiles. It should also be noted that independent institutes generally try to factor in effectiveness by assessing the number of missiles likely to reach their targets (survivability and accuracy) and those capable of destroying hardened underground silos.

53. Vance, op. cit., 102.

54. Dobrynin, op. cit., 411.

55. Garthoff, op. cit., 906; Strobe Talbott, *Endgame: the Story of SALT II* (Harper & Row, New York, 1979), 16.

15 The Return to Confrontation, 1979–1980

A. NATO's 'Dual Track' Decision

The Nuclear Balance in Europe

However slow the progress of the SALT II talks, strategic weapons were at least subject to some efforts at control. Short-range and intermediate-range nuclear weapons, in contrast, continued to grow in number and sophistication, particularly in Europe, where NATO and Warsaw Pact forces still prepared for war against each other, whatever the advances in détente. And the failure to control theatre nuclear weapons led to a new twist in the European arms race at the end of the 1970s which helped to undermine recent improvements in East–West relations.

In the late 1950s and early 1960s the Kremlin had built up an arsenal of about 600 intermediate-range SS-4 and SS-5 missiles in Europe but in the late 1960s, as the US deployed submarine-launched ballistic missiles (SLBMs) and nuclear-armed F-111 aircraft in the theatre, the Soviets had ceased their expansion. The deployment of the SS-20 missile in 1976–7 therefore seemed a 'new' departure and provoked concern in the West. The SS-20 marked a major advance on the older weapons systems it was to replace (SS-4s and SS-5s), being both solid fuelled (and therefore mobile, able to be launched quickly, and less vulnerable to attack) and MIRVed (with several independently targeted warheads on each launcher). SS-20s were also deployed against the Chinese in Asia and were intended not only as a counter to US 'forward-based systems' in Europe, but also as a match for the Chinese, British, and French nuclear arsenals. The Soviets described the SS-20s as a 'modernization' of their weaponry. The SS-4 for example was a missile similar to the Thors which the West had decommissioned in the 1960s and it was only accurate within a radius of 2.4 kilometres compared to Polaris which was likely to be accurate to 900 metres and Pershing I with an accuracy of 450 metres but with a range of only 750 kilometres. But to some in the West they marked an attempt by the Kremlin to win theatre nuclear superiority.

American critics of the SALT II negotiations saw the SS-20s, the Warsaw Pact's continuing conventional superiority in Europe and the existence of a large Warsaw Pact chemical weapons capability as evidence that the Soviets wished to outmatch the US in more and more areas. At a time of apparent global nuclear balance a combination of conventional and nuclear superiority in Europe might, it was argued, allow the Soviets to intimidate West European countries, inducing them to leave NATO. In extreme circumstances, it had been feared since the 1960s (when the Soviets acquired the ability to inflict enormous damage on the US after absorbing a first strike) that the Kremlin might launch an attack on Western Europe, confident that the US would not risk a strategic nuclear exchange. Now it seemed that the Warsaw Pact's theatre nuclear weapons were also superior to the West's. The situation threatened to break the so-called 'chain of deterrence' (building from battlefield to intercontinetal nuclear weapons) on which NATO's defence plans relied and it might also be intended to 'decouple' the US from European defence. Whatever the Soviet's main aim, it was soon clear that they had miscalculated the response. 'If the objective of the SS-20 deployment was to decouple Western Europe from the United States, it was ... counter-productive; if the deployment was based ... on military rationale, it was short-sighted, failing as it did to consider possible Western reactions.'[1]

The Carter administration was concerned about NATO defences on coming to office in January 1977, but mainly because of the conventional weapons situation. Carter immediately pressed his European allies to increase their defence budgets by 3 per cent per annum and this target was accepted at a summit meeting in May 1978. The move served as a boost to NATO morale and as a warning to Moscow, although not all West European governments met the target. At the same time in 1977–8 American troop levels in Europe were increased by over 30,000, more US nuclear bombers were based in Britain, and more SLBMs assigned to NATO use. Carter also began to plan for a conventionally armed 'rapid deployment force', able to act worldwide in a military crisis. His policy was therefore far from weak. He was determined to strengthen US capabilities to achieve a balanced SALT II deal and to attack the Kremlin on

the human rights front. But, even though America was developing intermediate-range Cruise and Pershing missiles, he was not yet convinced that nuclear weapons deployed in Europe needed to be updated and this opened him up to criticism in Europe and America. Even those European leaders like West Germany's Helmut Schmidt, who welcomed détente and a SALT II treaty, were determined to preserve a secure military balance in Europe. They did not wish to see the superpowers negotiate a freeze on their strategic nuclear arsenals whilst there was uncertainty about a stable European balance. American conservatives on the Committee on the Present Danger shared such concerns, warning that the Soviets could also use the 'new Backfire' bomber in the European theatre and pointing out that, whilst SALT II would do nothing to limit SS-20s, it would limit America's deployment of Cruise missiles. This was one reason why the eventual SALT II ceilings on Cruise were limited to longer-range versions of the missile.

Confidence in Carter was further damaged in 1977–8 by the neutron bomb episode. The neutron bomb, or enhanced radiation weapon, had been developed by the US for 'battlefield' use, and was capable of killing enemy personnel without destroying buildings or other structures. It seemed the perfect weapon to use against Red Army tank divisions in Europe without causing large-scale and long-lasting physical destruction. The NATO Commander, Alexander Haig, was a strong supporter of it. After June 1977, when word of its production was leaked, however, the Soviets launched a propaganda campaign against it as a 'capitalist' weapon, designed to kill people while preserving property. It provoked moral concern in Europe too, especially among left-wing groups, including the ruling parties in Britain and West Germany. In January 1978 the US announced that it would be deployed in 1980 unless the USSR ceased deployment of its SS-20s, but European governments were increasingly divided on the decision. The Dutch Defence Minister resigned over it in March. The situation improved on 5 April when, controversially, Helmut Schmidt agreed to accept the weapon but only 2 days later Carter decided to postpone production (which was only revived in 1981 by his successor, Ronald Reagan). Schmidt felt snubbed, European governments lost faith in Carter and his American critics renewed their attacks on his indecision. Meanwhile, however, while still not convinced of the need for it, the US administration did agree to study the modernization of theatre nuclear weapons.

The Cruise–Pershing Decision

In January 1979 Carter and Schmidt met with France's President Giscard d'Estaing and Britain's James Callaghan on the island of Guadeloupe. All the leaders were keen to maintain a stable nuclear balance in Europe. Thanks to the SS-20 deployment, Western European 'political elites had become increasingly sceptical of Soviet motives.'[2] Carter was anxious to silence his critics in Europe and at home, improving the chances of Congressional ratification of the SALT II treaty. But Schmidt was also determined to provide some concession to left-wingers in his Social Democratic Party and to the unilateral disarmament movement, which was reviving in numbers throughout Europe, after being in decline since the 1960s. The summit therefore agreed on a 'dual track' approach to theatre nuclear forces. First, a NATO study was set up to decide on the types and numbers of new weapons to be deployed in order to maintain the 'chain of deterrence' (rather than trying to match the number of SS-20s, which would have demanded a large number of warheads). Second, NATO would propose arms control talks on theatre nuclear weapons with the USSR. At the same time a propaganda effort was launched to convince European people that new systems were needed. The NATO study was completed in time for the Atlantic Council meeting of mid-December 1979 when it was agreed to deploy 464 ground-launched Cruise missiles and 108 Pershing IIs, each with a single warhead, by 1983. NATO, like the Soviets argued that this was simply a modernization, but , as with the SS-20s, there were important qualitative differences between the old and the new weapons. The stockpile of US nuclear weapons in Europe would actually be cut by 1,000 to 6,000 when including battlefield and short-range weapons. And there was the offer of arms control talks on theatre systems to be negotiated by the superpowers in parallel with a planned SALT III treaty. European leaders saw superpower arms control as going hand in hand with controls on intermediate-range nuclear forces and 'SALT II played a part in European willingness to accept intermediate-range forces.'[3] It was argued that the proposed deployments were simply a response to the SS-20s and that deterrence and détente would be built together. A NATO communiqué stated that the 'dual track' decision would 'promote stability and détente in Europe in consonance with . . . the Harmel Report.'[4]

Unfortunately the 'dual track' decision was made only 2 weeks before the Soviet intervention in Afghanistan, which put an end to détente and made meaningful US–Soviet talks impossible in the short-term (see Chapter 15, C and D). But even without Afghanistan, the NATO decisions provoked problems, both within the Western alliance and for détente. While Britain, West Germany, and Italy agreed to accept the new missiles on their soil, Belgium and Holland put off a decision, and Denmark and Norway refused to accept them. It was partly because of the deployment that nuclear disarmament movements in Western Europe continued to expand in membership over the following years. The Soviets certainly did not see the NATO decision as making a limited 'modernization' of Western forces. Cruise missiles were difficult to detect, either on the ground or when fired, and the Pershing II, though limited in range, had a performance equivalent to a counterforce 'first strike' weapon. It was fast, accurate, and could hit targets deep within the USSR, whereas no SS-20 could hit the US. From the Soviet point of view the deployment of Pershing IIs appeared as first-strike weapons which could be used to try and win a nuclear war in Europe. Also, the commitment of NATO to arms control talks seemed insincere. Schmidt might genuinely want a deal but NATO military officials apparently supported the 'dual track' approach mainly as a way to minimize popular opposition to the deployment decision. There were even doubts about whether control over intermediate-range weapons was technically feasible because their small size and mobility made verification of an agreement so difficult.

Apart from a visit by Schmidt to Moscow in June 1979, little attempt was made by the Western powers to explore Soviet reaction to the upcoming 'dual track' decision and in October Brezhnev began a public campaign against it with a vaguely worded and threatening speech, warning NATO not to deploy new missiles if it wanted to secure arms control. After the December Atlantic Council meeting the Kremlin bluntly rejected the idea of talks. It persisted in this approach for 6 months as, in the wake of Afghanistan, superpower relations passed through one of their worst phases. Tentative conversations finally opened in Geneva in October 1980 but made only slow progress. The arguments over theatre weapons had simply confirmed that each side in the Cold War could only see security issues from its own perspective. What one saw as a modernization of its forces the other saw as a new menace to the nuclear balance. Decisions were taken by each with little regard to the other side's reaction, helping to generate exaggerated fears about what 'real' intentions lay behind the other's move. In contrast to the advances détente made in the commercial and cultural spheres, therefore, military détente in Europe in the 1970s made little progress at all.

B. The Iranian Revolution

In the mid-1970s Iran seemed a stable pro-American state set on a course of industrialization and Westernization. Despite the existence of a Marxist Party, the Tudeh, and ethnic unrest from the country's Kurds, Arabs, and Azeris, the government's hold on the country appeared strong. The monarch or 'Shah', Mohammed Reza Pahlavi, had substantial modern armed forces and a ruthless, well-trained secret police, SAVAK. The Americans had built up the Shah's regime as a pro-Western bulwark in the region, with the close involvement of the CIA in the 1950s and early 1960s. As its growing oil wealth led to greater financial independence in the late 1960s, Iran developed a key regional role: 'with the British withdrawal [from east of Suez in 1968] looming . . . the US preoccupation with Vietnam, the continuing tide of Arab radicalism, and the fragility of Persian Gulf Arab states, Iran was the only regional country available to fill the vacuum.'[5] Massive arms sales to Iran formed part of the Nixon Doctrine to move the burdens of regional security problems from America to local powers, and Nixon first discussed Iran's role, as a US surrogate in the Middle East, when the Shah visited Washington in October 1969. Iran, being non-Arab, was prepared to supply oil from its massive reserves to America's other major ally in the Middle East, Israel. Nixon visited the country in 1972 and Jimmy Carter followed on New Year's Eve 1977, when he was effusive in his praise for the Shah and called Iran an 'island of stability in one of the more troubled areas of the world'.

Within months of Carter's visit the Shah was facing widespread unrest and in little more than a year his government was replaced by what, to Westerners, seemed a frightening, alien regime based on Islamic law. This 'Iranian Revolution' sparked off years of instability in the Persian Gulf–Central Asian region, undermined US power in the area, and brought Islamic fundamentalism into play as a new force in world affairs. After decades in which religion had seemed in worldwide retreat before materialism, humanism, and secularism the Islamic world was rocked by a new theological fervour. One of the victims was the Carter Presidency which, ironically, had triumphed in the unpromising Camp David peace process only to see attention quickly shift in the Middle East to the Persian Gulf region, where American policy was taken aback by events despite many warning signs that all was not well.

The Regime of Mohammed Reza Pahlavi

On returning to power in 1953, with the help of MI6 and the CIA, Mohammed Reza Pahlavi followed his father in taking a determinedly anti-leftist line while trying to modernize Iran, using its oil wealth to finance changes and risking aristocratic opposition by adopting land reform. Although at times he allowed civilian cabinets to function, he sacked any Prime Minister who displeased him and at times relied on military rule (1953–7) or the suspension of the parliament, the Majlis (1961–3). Abroad he joined the pro-Western Baghdad Pact in 1955 but also tried to maintain good relations with the USSR and, in contrast to Turkey, would not allow US nuclear weapons on Iranian soil.

In 1973–5 the Shah was at the height of his success. To avoid being drawn itself into a security commitment in the Persian Gulf, the American government was happy to build Iran up as a 'regional superpower'. Larger than its neighbours, untroubled by the Arab–Israeli feud, and a proven ally of the West, the country seemed an ideal partner. Washington helped train SAVAK until the early 1960s and then willingly provided military hardware. In return Iranian troops helped suppress a left-wing, Libyan-backed insurgency against the pro-Western ruler of Oman. The oil price rises which accompanied the 1973 Middle East War allowed the Shah both to finance military expansion and to press on with his hopes of creating a fully developed, industrialized Iran by 1990. The country's oil revenues leapt by eight times in 1973–5 and, between 1973 and 1978 defence spending grew about six times over. But such rapid expansion also brought high inflation and a move by millions of poor peasants into Tehran and other cities where the infrastructure could not cope with them. Iran's transport, housing, sewage, health, and educational systems were quite inadequate. About half the people were illiterate. The ill-advised dash to create industries, the wasteful concentration on defence expenditure, financial corruption, and autocratic rule made an unattractive mix for Western investors. 1975 saw a withdrawal of capital, a balance of payments deficit, and a sudden depression. The economic boom had come to a precipitous end.

The Iranian Revolution

The Shah was a hard-working but uninspiring leader, isolated from most of his people and attracting little loyalty beyond the army, SAVAK, and the affluent, educated upper class that profited from his policies. Although he created a political party to mobilize popular support, his regime relied on arbitrary, personal rule, a ruthless secret police, and an absurd propaganda campaign to convince people that his reign marked a return to ancient Persian Imperial might. There was no free press or freedom of assembly, the Majlis having been reduced to a rubber stamp. As economic conditions worsened after 1975 a diverse body of opposition grew up, ranging from the Tudeh and other left-wing groups, through middle-class liberals anxious to win political rights, to traditionalists who resented the rapid social changes in the country. The last group included Islamic religious leaders who disliked both the Shah's long-running attempts to control them and such modern trends as women's equality. Conservatives and Islamists disliked the Shah's reform programmes altogether; liberals and leftists disliked the direction it took. In 1975 there was widespread upheaval in the universities and the regime was criticized for its human rights record in the West. The Shah was initially disturbed when Jimmy Carter, with his emphasis on respect for human rights, entered the White House. But 'the Shah appears to have been desirous of placating the United States. He instituted a number of reforms in this area early in 1977.' It has even been argued that the president's human rights policy 'was a major, if inadvertent, factor' in leading to the revolution, because the Shah's rule relied in part on 'the belief of the Iranian people . . . that the US government was determined to maintain the royal dictatorship in power.'[6] Greater freedom of expression was allowed, a law was passed to end detention without trial, and an amnesty was announced for some political prisoners. But by the end of the year, upset that internal criticism of his regime simply became more vocal, the Shah launched another crackdown on his opponents. The US government avoided any condemnation of this, however, partly because Carter wanted the Shah's support for the Camp David peace process.

Serious disturbances in the universities revived in October 1977, with militant Islamic students in the forefront. The fundamentalist's leader was the Ayatollah Ruhollah Khomeini, who had left Iran in 1964 in the face of the Shah's attempts to suppress clerical independence. Khomeini, based in Iraq, then in France, had a deep personal hatred of the Shah and supported violent action as part of a determined campaign to destroy the current regime. In January 1978 government criticism of Khomeini led to large-scale riots in the holy city of Qom and sporadic violence continued for months, accompanied by left-wing terrorist activity and interspersed with periods of calm. Western observers long believed that the Shah could survive the troubles, and saw the Leftists as more dangerous opponents than the Traditionalists. Washington had no desire to see a pro-Soviet Iran. But Iran's liberals and Communists lacked a leader of the stature and ruthlessness of Khomeini. In August 1978 he called for the Shah's overthrow and even non-Islamic groups were willing to cooperate in the now-intensified campaign of opposition. The millions of uneducated poor living in the shanty-towns around Tehran were ready to demonstrate even in the face of the Shah's powerful military machine as discontent with the conditions under the Shah combined with traditional opposition to Westernization.

On 8 September a declaration of martial law in the capital was followed by the deaths of hundreds of demonstrators at the hands of troops. Marches, clashes, and widespread strikes continued in late September and into October. The oil industry was virtually closed down. The Shah made some attempt to satisfy traditionalist opinion by, for example, closing the country's casinos and launching an anti-corruption drive. He also eased censorship in mid-October. But it was too late. The US was anxious to see him retain power, seeing no acceptable alternative, but American support did him no good: such sophisticated equipment as the AWACS early-warning system, which Carter had provided, was no use against internal opposition; and the Islamic clergy saw America as representing the Godless materialism which they believed had created Iran's current problems. Furthermore, the policy machine in Washington 'was slow in seeing the seriousness of the crisis. Many of the Middle East experts were tied up with the . . . Camp David peace negotiations' and 'there was still strong resistance to any suggestion that the Shah might be slipping out of power', because his regime had appeared so stable for so long.[7] Carter himself has been criticized for being 'consistently baffled and frustrated by the . . . unpredictable nature of events.' in Iran and for

ignoring those who did warn of danger.[8] In early December religious festivals led to a new upsurge of violence and a general strike was called. The Shah now tried to hand power to a civilian cabinet, whilst retaining personal control of the army which, since mid-November, had effectively become the government. But it took until 31 December before a well-known, moderate politician, Shahpour Bakhtiar, agreed to serve as Prime Minister and he only took office on the understanding that the Shah would leave the country. Demoralized, though determined to retain some dignity, the Shah finally went into exile on 16 January 1979. Bakhtiar then hoped to restore order, but his attempts to deal with the Shah were condemned by Khomeini, and the army was unable to end the strikes and demonstrations.

On 1 February Khomeini returned to Tehran and created his own government. Bakhtiar, his attempts to form a coalition virtually ignored by other politicians, resigned on the 11th, and the Shah's armed forces disintegrated over the following days. Fears of a left-wing takeover or a descent into complete anarchy ended as Khomeini became the leader of a theocratic, Islamic Republic. Considerable turmoil and bloodshed went on as Khomeini's followers took their revenge on those of the Shah, then turned against the liberal and leftist groups who had helped overthrow him. Khomeini retired to Qom, only occasionally making his views publicly known during religious ceremonies, but he retained ultimate religious and political power until his death in 1989. A Prime Minister, Mehdi Bazargan, was appointed to head the civilian government but Islamic reform was kept on course by a Revolutionary Council and local revolutionary committees, defended by a new military force, the Revolutionary Guards. As under the Shah, the government controlled the press, the right of assembly, and freedom of expression. It also continued to make money from oil exports, the value of which increased by nearly half in the first 6 months of 1979, mainly because of the instability in Iran. But in contrast to the old modernizing and Westernizing policies, the new order marked a return to religious observance, traditional dress codes, and financial honesty. The events of 1978–9 were compared by some to the French and Russian Revolutions, inspiring a new emphasis on Islamic values elsewhere and provoking great concern in Eastern and Western bloc capitals, not least Washington.

The Hostages Crisis

The Western powers were closely identified, in the eyes of the Shah's opponents, with his corrupt, arbitrary regime and in late 1978 foreign businesses had been attacked by demonstrators. In December the US embassy was attacked by a mob, leading Washington to reduce the staff from over a thousand to less than a hundred. The Americans made some attempt to establish links to Khomeini's supporters, notably with a meeting between Cyrus Vance and the Iranian Foreign Minister, Ibrahim Yazdi, in September 1979. But President Carter also felt continuing loyalty to the Shah and, in late October 1979, after the latter became ill with cancer, decided to let him into the US for treatment on humanitarian grounds. Despite the danger signs, the Americans were surprised when on 4 November 1979, following 2 weeks of demonstrations outside, an Iranian mob seized control of the embassy and took fifty-three Americans hostage. Initial hopes that they would soon be released soon dissipated. It became obvious that the Iranian government was happy to see the embassy occupied, partly as a way of maintaining enthusiasm for the revolution. Indeed, the occupation may have been planned well in advance, the Shah's entry to America merely providing the excuse for it to go forward, hence the argument that, 'Given the forces at work in Iran at the time, it is difficult to see what the United States could have done differently ... that would have prevented the breach.'[9] By Christmas Carter and the American people were obsessed by the problem and the President, though faced by an election campaign in 1980, decided that while the crisis lasted he must remain in Washington. As he later admitted, 'The safety and well-being of the American hostages became a constant concern for me, no matter what other duties I was performing as President.'[10] He did not begin campaigning in the country until April by which time the humiliation of the siege and America's apparent powerlessness had gravely harmed his chances of a second term. A rescue

plan was considered, Iranian assets in the US were frozen, and purchases of Iranian oil were suspended but Carter was reluctant to move beyond limited, economic sanctions for fear of endangering the hostages' lives. One possible solution, returning the Shah to Tehran to stand trial, as the Iranians demanded, was too distasteful to contemplate.

Although the Iranian militants threatened to put the hostages on trial, the Americans were actually treated well enough. Several black and female prisoners were quickly released and in February 1980 there were signs that Iran wanted a settlement. A President, Adbulhassan Bani-Sadr, had now been elected who seemed anxious to control the militants and who the US believed to be a 'moderate' who it should encourage. There seemed good reasons why the Iranians should want to talk. Appalled by the seizure of an embassy and anxious to prevent the Americans from taking more extreme action, the West European and Japanese governments had joined Washington in taking economic sanctions against Iran. And tension was growing between Iran and its Arab neighbour, Iraq, which made it more urgent for Tehran to secure its oil revenues and overseas assets in case it needed to fight a war. Secret talks between Tehran and Washington led to a proposal for a UN-sponsored commission to investigate their differences, but the scheme floundered in the face of Iran's unpredictable politics. When a UN team arrived, Khomeini made a speech condemning US policy and the Revolutionary Council would not grant the team access to the hostages.

In the face of such confusion and failure, and despite the opposition of Cyrus Vance, the Secretary of State, Carter decided on 11 April to launch an armed rescue attempt. Vance 'was convinced that the decision ... carried great risks for the hostages and for our national interests' and said he would resign if the President did not call it off.[11] Carter refused. The attempt, strongly backed by Zbigniew Brzezinski, went ahead on 24 April but was never likely to be easy. The hostages were held in the middle of a populous city, hundreds of miles from any American base. Hopes of a surprise rescue by helicopters were dashed when insufficient aircraft made it through dust storms to a remote airfield inside Iran; and as the mission was aborted a crash between aircraft on the ground killed eight

Ruhollah Khomeini (1902–1989)

For the first 60 years Khomeini showed little active interest in politics. Born into a deeply religious family in the town of Khomein, as Ruhollah Hendi, he became a religious writer and scholar, rising to become an 'Ayatollah', a leading Shi'ite Muslim cleric. However, in 1962, the death of the leader of the Iranian Shi'ites, Ayatollah Boroujerdi, freed Khomeini to take a leading role in attacking the regime of the Shah. Khomeini resented the secularization of Iran, its links to America and Israel, and such reforms as votes for women. Exiled in 1963, he settled in neighbouring Iraq and made himself the best-known opponent of the Shah. In 1978 he was forced out of Iraq by Saddam Hussein and moved to Paris, but within months mounting discontent in Iran forced the Shah out of office. In February 1979 Khomeini was able to return triumphantly to Tehran, was popularly acclaimed as leader of the Iranian

Revolution, and, by the end of the year, had become Supreme Leader of an Islamic Revolution. He ruthlessly disposed of his opponents, and set up a theocratic state, putting the Shi'ite clergy in charge of all areas of life. Abroad, he hoped to spread the ideals of the Iranian revolution, he opposed both the US and USSR, and he was a reminder, as the Cold War decayed, that Communism and liberal-capitalism were not the only ideological and political systems that could command loyalties. But the term 'fundamentalist', which the West used to describe his regime, was not one he ever used himself. From 1980 his energies became focused on the war with Iraq. Despite the costs of the conflict, he described his acceptance of peace in 1988 as 'more deadly than power' and died soon afterwards.

Americans. Carter had to admit publicly to another failure and Vance resigned. Western allies were upset not to have been consulted about the American action in advance. The Iranians were elated and, despite the death of the Shah on 27 July, held onto the hostages (now dispersed around Tehran to prevent another rescue bid) until the US election was over. There were later claims that Carter's opponents, in Ronald Reagan's campaign team, had established links to Tehran and prevented an early hostage release: a 1992 Congressional investigation found these claims 'not proven' but did criticize the

behaviour of the Reagan camp. Carter paid the price for his failure in Iran as it probably contributed to the scale of his electoral defeat, but in its closing phases he handled the hostage crisis well. Following Algerian mediation all were released in return for an unfreezing of Iranian assets, just as Carter left the Presidency. His worst mistakes had arguably been prior to 1979, when he misinterpreted events in Iran, backed the Shah, and failed to establish links to the opposition. The danger of regional instability was meanwhile increased by events in neighbouring Afghanistan.

C. **Soviet Intervention in Afghanistan**

Debate over Soviet Motivation

Détente was clearly under threat well before 1979. Just as the Americans were increasingly disturbed by Soviet activity in the less developed world, especially because of events in Angola and the Ogaden War, so the Soviets—whilst keen to preserve détente if possible—were alienated by US activities in Latin America, Africa, and the Middle East and by criticism of their human rights policy, Carter's attempts to

recast the SALT II treaty, and Brzezinski's 'playing the China card'. However, it was events in Afghanistan at Christmas 1979 which finally spelt the end of détente and the dawn of a new Cold War. On 25 December, in a well-executed operation and without any explanation to Washington, ground troops of the Red Army crossed into Afghanistan while airborne troops landed in the capital, Kabul. Although Afghanistan was supposedly a non-aligned state, the Soviets claimed to have been invited in by its government. Yet two days later the Presidential palace was stormed and the Afghan leader, Hafizullah Amin, was killed, being replaced by a pro-Soviet alternative, Babrak Karmal. Within weeks the Red Army presence numbered over 80,000. The US government, which had issued various warnings against a Soviet intervention over the previous months was outraged. So was much of world opinion.

The return to a Cold War atmosphere in 1980 was largely because the Americans and others feared the Soviet action to be a well-considered act of expansion, perhaps aimed at exploiting the current turmoil in Iran and extending Soviet influence towards the Indian ocean and the oil-rich Persian Gulf. Zbigniew Brzezinski saw it as being the result of a US failure to demonstrate sufficient resolve on earlier occasions, noting in his diary that, 'Had we been tougher sooner, had we drawn the line more clearly . . . maybe the Soviets would not have engaged in this act of miscalculation.'[12]

However, Russian evidence on the intervention reveals a doubtful, divided leadership reluctantly acting to prop up communism in a neighbouring state which they believed to lie in their sphere of interest. Rather like Hungary in 1956 or Czechoslovakia in 1968, the Kremlin wished to replace a leader whose policies had become a menace to Soviet interests and who threatened to undermine local communist control. They had no wider expansionist ambitions, hoped to withdraw their troops quickly, and even naïvely hoped that the West would quickly accept their action, allowing détente to revive. 'Moscow did not envisage the long and costly guerrilla war which followed, nor did it see the Afghan adventure as a stepping stone to the Indian Ocean and the oil of the Gulf States.'[13] The Politburo may have seen the Afghan intervention as an application of the Brezhnev Doctrine, used to justify the invasion of Czechoslovakia by insisting on the USSR's right to preserve communist regimes when they came under threat. They also saw the threat to their position in Afghanistan as a 'special' case in the less developed world, different for example from the coups against nominally Marxist regimes in Africa since the 1960s that the Soviets had taken little action to prevent. Afghanistan was a neighbouring state, with numerous Soviet military

advisers on its soil already and an area of Russian activity since the mid-nineteenth century, when the 'Great Game' had been played with the British Empire for influence in Central Asia. It would be easy to see the Soviet invasion as linked to broader international developments. After all, it was launched only days after NATO's 'dual-track' decision. However, the precise reasons for Soviet intervention can only be understood against the background of Afghan internal politics in the 1970s. The internal situation, 'too often omitted in evaluations of Soviet policy . . . acted as the main stimulus, if not complete explanation' for their actions.[14]

Marxist Rule in Afghanistan

Afghanistan, a poor, mountainous country, with a diversity of ethnic groups, had been recognized as fully independent by the British in 1919, after 40 years in which London controlled its external affairs. Two years later the Afghans made a friendship treaty with the USSR but did not, during the inter-war period, fall into the Soviet sphere. In 1955 the government of Prince Mohammed Daud Khan, a cousin of the King, took Afghanistan into the non-aligned movement. Daud, Prime Minister for a decade after 1953, accepted development aid from both Moscow and Washington. He returned to power in 1973 as President of a new republic, after overthrowing King Zahir, and continued to pursue a non-aligned role, resisting Soviet attempts to draw him closer to them. Increasingly indeed Daud fell out with the Afghan communists, who had formed the People's Democratic Party of Afghanistan (PDPA) in 1965, only to split into two broad factions soon afterwards. The Khalq faction, whose leading figure was Nur Mohammed Taraki and which also included Hafizullah Amin, drew most of its support from rural areas and was opposed to working with Daud. But the Parcham, led by Babrak Karmal, which drew its support from Kabul and other urban centres was more moderate, being ready to work with Daud and other groups to secure reform. By 1978 however Prince Daud seemed bent on creating a one party state with himself as life President. His attempt to exclude the Parcham from power led them to draw closer to the Khalq, whilst his decision to arrest the PDPA leaders in April 1978 led to a successful coup against him. The coup which was apparently carried out by a Communist group in the Afghan army without major Soviet involvement brought the establishment of a 'Democratic Republic'. But it was significant that this was a coup by a narrow group, not a revolution backed by the Afghan masses. Afghanistan was now 'under the control of a small Communist movement . . . totally unprepared for the power that unexpectedly . . . fell into its hands. Its misuse of that power with a combination of idealistic reformism and brutal authoritarianism started the country on a downward spiral.'[15]

The new government continued to claim to be non-aligned and initially played down the Marxist elements in its policies, but it was dogged by the long-established Khalq–Parcham rivalry, was inexperienced in government, and had little real popular support. Experienced administrators were sacked if they were not prepared to be loyal to the tenets of Marxism. By September 1978 the Khalq were predominant and rapidly pushed on with a reform programme that was partly inspired by Marxist doctrine, partly by a simple desire to modernize. 'Never before in Afghan history had there been such a ruthless attempt to push through so many basic reforms and fundamental changes in so short a period of time.'[16] The programme included land reform and educational improvements but many elements, such as improved women's rights, offended Islamic opinion and disturbed the country's traditional social fabric. The use of a repressive secret police also alienated people and, despite the claim to non-alignment, the regime's reliance on the USSR offended the fiercely independent Afghan tribes. A Soviet–Afghan friendship treaty was signed on 5 December 1978 and the number of Soviet advisers in the country rapidly grew from 350 to 4,000. Such pro-Soviet leanings were emphasized in February 1979 when the American ambassador, Adolph Dubs, was kidnapped, only to be killed when the Afghans made a botched attempt to free him. This led the US, perhaps ill-advisedly, to give up its attempts to retain influence in Kabul: economic aid was slashed and members of the Peace Corps removed.

The Kremlin was always doubtful about the wisdom of pressing Marxist reforms on Afghanistan but pleased that, 'for the first time [it] had achieved ideological congruence and de facto alliance with its strategically situated neighbour.'[17] Neither was Moscow overconcerned about the domestic situation in Afghanistan until March 1979. By then a series of local uprisings had occurred against PDPA and Afghan refugees began to stream across the long-contested south-eastern border with Pakistan. The Pakistani leader, General Zia ul-Haq, was sympathetic to the pro-Islamic, anti-communist feelings of the exiles and ready to give shelter and aid to groups which formed in opposition to the PDPA. The Afghan government's conscript army was reluctant to put down the uprisings and increasingly the Kabul government's authority was called into question. March 1979 was significant for the Soviets because it saw the worst uprising so far, in Herat, where some of the Afghan army mutinied and a team of Soviet advisers was massacred. This led to an intense debate in the Politburo and requests from the PDPA for Red Army combat troops to prop up the regime. For the moment the Kremlin resisted such a course, preferring to increase the number of military advisers and the scale of arms supplies. There was reluctance to intervene directly in support of an unpopular government. In a sense Brezhnev and his ministers were in a similar position to that faced by the Americans in South Vietnam in the early 1960s: they felt a moral obligation to a friendly government to which they had provided large-scale assistance already, and which seemed likely to fall from power, with great uncertainty about what might follow; but they had no categorical treaty commitment to assist it, they were well aware of its failings, and they had little desire to see their own forces locked into a prolonged campaign against local insurgents.

The Decision to Intervene

In the last three months of 1979 the Kremlin's reluctance to intervene was overcome largely because of violence and instability within the PDPA. The intervention has been described as 'an avoidable tragedy . . . in which the final script was ordained by perceptions, personalities and ideology far more than "interests" and "strategies".' The Kremlin had gradually increased its commitment to the PDPA in 1978–9 despite clear problems in Afghanistan. There was an ideological confidence in Moscow that 'mass' support for Marxism would come in due course and this was accompanied by a belief that the USSR needed to secure its position because of the instability in Iran, which lay on Afghanistan's western border. The Soviets recognized the Iranian Revolution as a setback for Washington, but it did not necessarily help the Iranian Communists. It could lead to an increasing sense of pan-Islamic feeling among the USSR's Muslim peoples and there were also fears that it would lead to some American riposte in the region. Within the Kremlin decision-making was, as usual, confined to a narrow group, but this group was itself divided over policy options. Kosygin and the Chief of General Staff, Marshal Nikoloi Ogarkov, doubted the wisdom of intervention but the Defence Minister, Dimitri Ustinov, was keen to act. Brezhnev, old, suffering arteriosclerosis, and always cautious, was undecided on the course to follow but events in September-October tipped him in favour of intervention.[18]

In September the Afghan President, Taraki, visited Moscow. Uprisings against the PDPA were now regular and widespread, a third of a million Afghans had fled to Pakistan and the Soviets considered the wisdom of drawing non-Communists into the Kabul government as a step to moderating its policies and so ending the rebellions. Taraki came with a proposal that the Khalq's leading hardliner, the megalomaniac Amin, should be replaced before steps were taken to improve the government's popularity. The Soviets, keen to limit the power of the Khalq, agreed. 'It appears that the Soviets—quite correctly—placed the main blame for Kabul's unpopular policies on Amin.'[19] But when Taraki returned to Kabul he was arrested by Amin who made himself President. There were armed clashes in the capital between the PDPA factions and in October Taraki was executed. Brezhnev evidently felt personally responsible for Taraki's death and betrayed by Amin, whose behaviour seemed increasingly unstable. True, Amin tried to tone down the reform programme but he also began to hold secret talks with US officials, leading the Soviets to fear his possible defection from the communist cause. Amin

had once lived in America and he also showed a desire to improve relations with pro-Western Pakistan.

Ustinov began to plan actively for armed intervention, and to infiltrate special forces into Afghanistan in September. He soon won allies in the Foreign Minister, Gromyko and KGB chief, Yuri Andropov. (This trio indeed increasingly dominated policy-making in the years of Brezhnev's physical decline.) Gromyko was fearful of new US–Chinese links and aware that SALT II might not win Senate approval, so that the need to retain US friendship was not high on the list of Soviet priorities. Later claims by Western analysts, that the Kremlin was encouraged to act by Carter's supposed weakness of will, were apparently groundless. Andropov was evidently convinced of Amin's unreliability in November, when the latter demanded that the Soviet ambassador be replaced. Initially Andropov believed the KGB could remove Amin without the large-scale use of the Red Army, but an attempt to assassinate him in mid-December failed and there may have been one or more other efforts. The Politburo finally decided on military intervention, in Kosygin's absence, on 12 December, but hoped the action would have a limited duration, requiring 75,000 troops at most. The action was designed to replace Amin with a more acceptable leader, deter meddling by Pakistan or Iran in Afghan politics, broaden the government, bolster the Afghan army, and end the uprisings. In a sense it marked the continuation of established Soviet aims through new means. Increasingly Brezhnev and most of his ministers were convinced that military action was needed if the PDPA government were not to collapse. Ironically, when the Red Army arrived in force on Christmas Day Amin welcomed them, believing they had come to prop up his regime. Two days later he was dead and the Soviet argument that they had been 'invited' into Afghanistan by its government, in fulfilment of the friendship treaty, seemed ridiculous. A major international crisis had begun and, for the Soviets, years of war. 'If the Soviet leadership had moved against Amin to exploit the hatred the Afghan people felt for his autocratic rule, then it had failed to realize that after the night of 27 December, this hatred would be transferred to the Soviet Union.'[20]

Andrei Gromyko (1909–1989)

Gromyko, who came from Stare Gromyki, in Belarussia and joined the Communist Party in 1931, was educated as an economist, but entered the Soviet foreign ministry in1939 just before the Second World War and specialized in relations with America. The fact that the US and USSR soon became wartime allies, made Gromyko's expertise in this area invaluable and in 1943 he was catapulted into the position of ambassador to Washington. His caution, loyalty, and hard work were matched by a mastery of negotiating detail and an ability to draft perceptive reports, which made him an ideal diplomat. Under Joseph Stalin, in the post-war years, he served as representative to the United Nations between 1946 and 1948 (a post calling for careful public diplomacy), then more briefly, as ambassador to London (1952–3). With Stalin's fall he was recalled to Moscow, to act as deputy Foreign Minister under Molotov (1953–6) and Dimitri Shepilov (1956–7). In 1957, these two both became involved in the

'anti-party plot', a vain attempt to oust Khrushchev. In its wake Gromyko became Soviet Foreign Minister and though he only joined the Politburo in 1973, he held onto his post until 1985, when he was abruptly succeeded by Mikhail Gorbachev's ally, Edvard Shevardnadze. Gromyko, who had helped install Gorbachev into power, was moved to the relatively powerless post of Soviet President. Then, in 1988, when the Presidency was invested with greater powers, Gromyko was unceremoniously replaced by Gorbachev himself. Gromyko, who loyally executed Soviet foreign policy through the twists and turns of three decades—through the crises of the early 1960s, the rise of détente and the 'second Cold War'—and who was best known for his ability to 'stonewall' in discussions with his Western counterparts, ended his life as the embodiment of an ageing, decrepit leadership at a time when East–West relations were rapidly being normalized.

D. The Revival of Cold War

International Reaction to Afghanistan

Global reaction to the invasion of Afghanistan was far worse than the Kremlin feared. 'Because it involved Soviet troops rather than Cuban or Warsaw Past forces, the attention of the world was focused directly on Soviet expansionist goals'[21]—or what were assumed by some to be expansionist goals. The death of Hafizullah Amin made the Soviet action seem like blatant aggression against a neighbour, rather than an attempt to prop up a fellow communist regime. Western nations, China, and local countries like Pakistan and Iran, feared a general expansion of Soviet influence in the region, perhaps a drive towards the Persian Gulf, rather than the limited military operation which the Soviets actually planned. On 14 January 1980 the United Nations General Assembly voted by 104 to 18 to condemn the invasion and even friends of the USSR, such as India, were critical. Afghanistan had, even if only nominally, been a non-aligned state and the Soviets

could not cite the Brehznev Doctrine as justification for their action because it was only meant to apply to the maintenance of communism within the Eastern bloc (as in Czechoslovakia in 1968). Afghanistan was also an Islamic country and, in the wake of the Iranian Revolution, pan-Islamic feeling was increasing. On 29 January thirty-six Islamic states met in Islamabad, Pakistan to issue their own condemnation of the Kremlin. Some of these states quickly gave aid to the Mujaheddin opponents of the Soviets. Egypt and Saudi Arabia provided financial aid, Iran and Pakistan gave refuge to millions of refugees, and Pakistan allowed Mujaheddin guerrillas to operate from its soil. For Pakistan indeed there was a marked change in its standing with the West. General Zia ul-Haq, who had seized power in July 1977, had been widely criticized for the execution of his predecessor, Ali Bhutto, in early 1979. Concern over human rights had led the Carter administration to cut economic aid in April and US–Pakistan relations worsened in November, when a pro-Iranian mob burned the American embassy in Islamabad. But common concern over Soviet expansion led America and Pakistan to become close partners in 1980 in aiding the Mujaheddin. The Chinese were predictably delighted by the end of Soviet–American détente and 'all Chinese doubts about the direction of US Soviet policy fell away after the invasion of Afghanistan.'[22]

Having launched their invasion hastily, the Soviets had clearly also bungled their propaganda campaign in defence of it. Claims that the Western powers and China had been destabilizing Afghanistan were simply not credible. Outside Eastern Europe only a handful of states, such as Vietnam, supported Moscow's action. North Korea, Yugoslavia, and Romania now restored links to China, raising the old Soviet fear that Beijing could divide the Eastern bloc. Western European Communists also found it an embarrassing episode and it was one reason why the French Communist Party lost electoral support at this time. Even in the USSR itself there were critics of the invasion, such as the dissident scientist, Andrei Sakharov, who was punished by being sent into internal exile. The Soviets were also mistaken if they believed their difficulties over Afghanistan would soon cease. Even the experienced ambassador, Dobrynin, expressed surprise at the lasting strength of America's reaction, asking why it was 'so disproportionately strong when compared, for example, to the Warsaw Pact's invasion of Czechoslovakia'; and he wrote in his memoirs that it was not only the Soviet invasion but also 'the sharp response of the United States [that] proved a final turning point in Soviet–American relations', from which détente did not recover.[23] Neither could the Kremlin confine the adverse response to the US. Instead, as they became bogged down, fighting a guerrilla war, they were regularly criticized by Western, non-aligned and Islamic groups, many of which, for several years, refused to attend the annual celebration of the 1917 Revolution in Red Square. Furthermore, the summer 1980 Olympic Games held in Moscow, were boycotted by America, China, West Germany, Japan, and more than fifty other states. Then again, about eighty countries, including NATO members like Britain and France, did send teams to the Games and the intensity of international condemnation eased after several months. NATO states, for example, issued

condemnations of Soviet behaviour during a CSCE Conference in Madrid in late 1980 but most West European states wished to maintain the personal, financial, and commercial links with Eastern Europe which had built up through the decade of détente. For them Afghanistan was a remote concern and they considered some Soviet misbehaviour on the international stage to be inevitable. Once it became clear that the Soviets had no intention of launching an offensive against the Persian Gulf, it seemed better to concentrate on verbal criticism rather than to introduce sanctions, which would also damage Western interests. France's President Giscard d'Estaing and West Germany's Helmut Schmidt were both resentful of the lack of American consultation over its response to the Afghan crisis. Schmidt still hoped to maintain both détente and Germany's close alliance with Washington.

Carter's Cold War

In the weeks before Christmas 1979 American politics had been dominated by the Iran hostages crisis which, of course, ran on through 1980. During his last year in office, whatever his perceived weakness on Iran, Carter pursued a wide-ranging policy of toughness towards the USSR. Indeed, although Ronald Reagan became, in the eyes of the world, the personification of the New Cold War of the early 1980s, it was Carter who first adopted a confrontational stance, introducing economic sanctions, reducing high-level diplomatic contacts, and expanding America's nuclear arsenal. Indeed, if anything, Carter overstated the extent of the Soviet menace in Afghanistan, perhaps in order to win domestic support. Yet the message was not received in the way he intended. His admission in the *New York Times* on 1 January 1980 that recent events had made 'a dramatic change in my own opinion of what the Soviets' ultimate goals are' seemed naïve in one sense: it sounded like an admission that his critics in the Committee of the Present Danger had been correct all along, and that he had been too gullible and trusting of Moscow. The statement 'lent credence to the image of his naïvete', helped lead 'to a decline in his credibility and, ultimately, contributed to the election of Ronald Reagan'.[24] But the statement also reflected his own sense of betrayal by Brezhnev. Already, on 28 December, Carter had used the 'hot line' to warn the Kremlin that the Afghan situation posed a threat to world peace and this was followed up by what appeared to be firm action. On 4 January the President announced a series of measures including financial assistance to Pakistan, a suspension of cultural exchanges, trade restrictions, and a grain embargo. Carter also suspended ratification of the SALT II treaty, which had been of such symbolic importance to the détente process. But the impact of the suspension was blunted by two points. First, SALT II had been in such trouble in Congress that it would probably not have been ratified anyway. Second, the State Department made clear the following day that the US would respect the terms of SALT II despite its non-ratification. The Soviets agreed to do the same and the two sides were actually able to hold exploratory talks in Geneva, on a SALT III treaty, before the end of the year. Indeed, there is a case that, in response to Afghanistan, Carter actually took 'no decisive action. That was because there was none to take that would not penalize the United States as much as the Soviet Union.'[25]

It has been argued, with some justification, that the invasion of Afghanistan 'did not validate the argument of people who argued that Soviet strategy [was] expansionist worldwide. It did no more than justify Vance's position that Soviet behaviour was . . . determined by security and status as a superpower.'[26] Yet, at the time, there was a genuine fear in Washington that the invasion of Afghanistan heralded Soviet expansionism, whether or not as a result of détente. There had been examples of Soviet activism in the less developed world throughout the 1970s, and the deployment of Cuban troops in both Angola and Ethiopia had been detrimental to détente. Events in Afghanistan could be read as part of a continuing pattern of Soviet behaviour, designed to win influence in the less developed world whilst pursuing détente with America. But the use of the Red Army itself outside the Eastern bloc, for the first time since the Second World War, seemed novel and sinister. Also, the US specifically feared a 'pattern of Soviet expansion aimed at destabilizing core Western interests in the Gulf' because of the Iranian crisis, which had coincidentally 'heightened American sensitivity to

events in the area.'[27] Before the Soviet invasion few Americans knew anything about Afghanistan. Apart from Iran there were plenty of other pressing issues, such as the SALT II ratification and relations with China, and among leading figures only Zbigniew Brzezinski had been concerned by earlier Soviet interference in Afghanistan's internal affairs. (Brzezinski was one of those who were not shocked by the invasion.) The surprise, speed, and ruthlessness of the Red Army's action helped generate real fear. There was little attempt to understand the real Soviet motives for their action, which in any case would have been difficult given the Kremlin's own confusion and its public dishonesty. Cyrus Vance, the strongest defender of détente in Washington, fully accepted, during National Security Council discussions in January, that a firm stand must be taken. Already deeply 'affected by his experience of the Soviet record on human rights, the president jumped clearly in the direction of Brzezinski', taking the view that the 'Soviet regime was not only morally bankrupt it was expansionist as well.'[28] On 23 January, Carter therefore turned his State of the Union address into a declaration of America's determination to oppose further Soviet adventurism, especially in the oil-rich Gulf. It has been described as 'an epitaph for détente, highlighting as it did the American reversion to traditional notions of containment.'[29] (see boxed section).

In February the US demanded that the Soviets must withdraw from Afghanistan, restoring it to non-aligned status if détente were to be restored. Alongside aid to the Mujaheddin, which was provided in secret from January onwards, this was part of a policy of making the war costly for the Soviets, keeping them 'on trial' in the court of world opinion while deterring them from further aggressive action. The demand proved unwise because, as months passed, it became clear that the USSR had no intention of abandoning Afghanistan and the Americans came to appreciate that their own direct interest in Afghanistan was minimal, compared to the need to deal with Moscow on international issues. 'The Carter administration . . . seem not to have learned . . . [that] it is self-defeating to term not acceptable a situation that cannot be changed.'[30] But, under Carter, any return to détente was unthinkable. Vance did suggest discussing

Afghanistan with the Soviets but Brzezinski defeated the attempt: one important result of Afghanistan in Washington was that Brzezinski's warnings about the USSR's mendacity seemed proven correct and his standing improved. Another example of the Carter administration's toughness were the measures taken at this time to improve America's 'war fighting' capacity, building on the 1974 Schlesinger Doctrine (see Chapter 14, E). The basic idea was to strengthen America's ability to survive a nuclear attack, in particular by safeguarding command and communication centres, while developing the ability to hit such targets in the USSR. It was argued that, if America could cripple the Soviet government while preserving its own decision-making intact, it might be possible to win a nuclear war. Thus Presidential Directive (PD) number 57, of March 1980, concerned the mobilization of the US economy to fight a nuclear war; PD-58, of June, was directed at protecting key decision-makers in war; and most famously PD-59, of 25 July–parts of which were deliberately leaked to the press—concentrated on selective targeting of Soviet command centres and weapons sites, in various war scenarios. These frightening decisions, which became the basis of US nuclear doctrine throughout the Presidencies of Reagan and George Bush, did not necessarily mean the US was planning war: Brzezinski and the Defence Secretary, Harold Brown, believed they were responding to the USSR's own 'war fighting' plans. But they helped fuel growing public concern, especially in Western Europe, over the dangers of a nuclear exchange, fears which had not been so intense since the early 1960s and which highlighted the change of atmosphere brought by Afghanistan.

In the short term at least, US policy did nothing to force the Soviets out of Afghanistan even though some measures, especially the grain embargo, caused real harm. The Kremlin was dismayed by the US reaction to its invasion and did not properly under-stand it. Some Soviet leaders saw it as evidence that the Americans had been looking for an excuse to destroy détente all along and pointed to previous US actions, such as the slow ratification of SALT II and support for China's attack on Vietnam as evidence of this. Moscow never appreciated the adverse impact of its involvement in the less developed world and repeatedly stated its willingness to talk. Brehznev and the Politburo had evidently always hoped that, after the initial shock of the invasion, détente would revive. There were particular attempts to sustain it in Europe with a small reduction in the Red Army there—though critics argued this was simply to compensate for the deployment in Afghanistan. But the Soviets also gave a firm response to the Carter administration's revival of confrontation. The US was accused of breaching the Helsinki accords when it reduced its commercial, scientific, and cultural contacts with the Soviet bloc and the USSR now shifted import orders from America to Western Europe and Japan. Among a wide-ranging series of actions, Western broadcasts to the Eastern bloc were jammed once more, Jewish emigration was cut in 1980 below 100,000, and Soviet armed forces established new bases, notably at Cam Ranh Bay in Vietnam. The Kremlin also maintained its opposition to NATO's 'dual-track' decision on nuclear weapons in Europe. The resignation of Vance in April was seen, in the Kremlin, as another nail in the coffin of détente and thereafter the sense of crisis in East–West relations continued, though without ever really threatening a serious crisis. The death in May of Yugoslavia's leader, Tito, growing domestic unrest in Poland, and the outbreak of war between Iran and Iraq in September all added to international unease and, as Carter's chances of re-election evaporated, there seemed no hope of a return to détente, especially given the anti-communist, strong-arm rhetoric of his Republican opponent, Ronald Reagan.

The 'Carter Doctrine', 23 January 1980

The Soviet invasion of Afghanistan at Christmas 1979 created a major challenge for the administration of Jimmy Carter, who already had to face the embarrassing seizure of hostages in nearby Tehran. Carter's prime public response to the situation was delivered during the President's annual 'State of the Union' address to a joint session of Congress. The speech began with the assertion that 'it has never been more clear that the state of our Union depends on the state of the world', and it was international relations that took up most of the address. Carter was 'determined that the United States will remain the strongest of all nations' but he identified three factors that had created a new set of challenges: the steady growth and increased projection of Soviet military power beyond its own borders; the overwhelming dependence of the Western democracies on oil supplies from the Middle East; and 'the press of social . . . religious . . . economic and political change in . . . the developing world, exemplified by the revolution in Iran.' The Iranian occupation of the US embassy in 1979 had created one difficult problem, but the Soviet invasion of Afghanistan had added to America's difficulties enormously. After reviewing US policy during the Cold War, Carter accused the Kremlin of 'a radical and aggressive new step', which had to be resisted. He listed measures he had taken in response to the Soviet invasion of Afghanistan, including trade limits and an Olympic boycott, then he set out the strategic significance of the Persian Gulf area, which the USSR now seemed to menace: the Red Army was within 300 miles of the Straits of Hormuz, through which much of the West's oil was shipped. The heart of what became known as the Carter Doctrine was the statement that:

An attempt by any outside force to gain control of the Persian Gulf region will be regarded as an assault on the vital interests of the United States . . . and . . . will be repelled by any means necessary, including military force.

The statement was less 'globalistic' and less crusading in tone than the 1947 Truman Doctrine, but it could be compared to the 1957 Eisenhower Doctrine (on the Middle East) or the 1965 Johnson Doctrine (on Latin America) in its determination to prevent communist expansion in a particular region. And it was backed up by military preparations. Since 1977 in fact the Carter administration had planned to establish a 'Rapid Deployment Force' for use in emergencies beyond the US and Europe but the proposal made only slow progress. Now, as part of a substantial increase (5 per cent above inflation) in the defence budget a force of 100,000 men was created. The US also took steps to secure new bases in the Middle East region including the use of naval facilities and an airstrip at Berbera in Somalia (a recent victim, of course, of Cuban–Soviet policy) in return for military and economic aid. US arms supplies to Egypt, Saudi Arabia, and other countries were increased. Carter also made efforts to reduce America's dependence on oil imports.

NOTES

1. Mike Bowker and Phil Williams, *Superpower Détente: a Reappraisal* (Sage, London, 1988), 220.

2. Odd Arne Westad (ed), *The Fall of Détente* (Oslo University Press, Oslo, 1997), 11.

3. David McClellan, *Cyrus Vance* (Rowman and Allanheld, Totowa, 1985), 144.

4. Quoted in Raymond Garthoff, *Détente and Confrontation* (The Brookings Institution, Washington, 1995), 954.

5. Shireen Hunter, *Iran and the World* (Indiana University Press, Bloomington, 1990), 52.

6. Yonah Alexander and Allan Nanes, *The United States and Iran* (University Publications of America, Frederick, 1980), 435; Richard Cottam, *Iran and the United States: a Cold War Case* (University of Pittsburgh Press, Pittsburgh, 1988), 187.

7. Barry Rubin, *Paved with Good Intentions: the American Experience and Iran* (Oxford University Press, New York, 1990), 207–8.

8. James Bill, *The Eagle and the Lion* (Yale University Press, New Haven, 1988), 257.

9. Hunter, op. cit., 55.

10. Jimmy Carter, *Keeping Faith* (Collins, London, 1982), 459.

11. Cyrus Vance, *Hard Choices: Critical Years in American Foreign Policy* (Simon & Schuster, New York, 1983), 410.

12. Zbigniew Brzezinski, *Power and Principle: Memoirs of the National Security Adviser, 1977–81* (Farrar-Strauss-Giroux, New York, 1985), 432.

13. Martin Walker, *The Waking Giant* (Joseph, London, 1986), 105.

14. Fred Halliday, 'Soviet foreign policy-making and the Afghanistan War', *Review of International Studies*, 4 (October, 1999), 678.

15. Henry Bradsher, *Afghanistan and the Soviet Union* (Duke University Press, Durham, 1983), 74.

16. Sen Gupta, *Afghanistan* (Pinter, London, 1986), 55.

17. Alvin Rubinstein, *Soviet Policy toward Turkey, Iran and Afghanistan* (Praeger, New York, 1982), 162.

18. Odd Arne Wested 'New Russian Evidence on the Soviet Intervention in Afghanistan', *Cold War International History Project Bulletin*, 8–9 (Winter 1996–7), quote from 129.

19. Thomas Hammond, *Red Flag over Afghanistan* (Westview Press, Boulder, 1984), 80.

20. Raja Anwar, *The Tragedy of Afghanistan* (Verso Books, London, 1989), 192.

21. William Watson, *The Collapse of Communism in the Soviet Union* (Greenwood Press, Westport, 1998), 33.

22. Robert Ross, *Negotiating Co-operation: the US and China, 1969–89* (Stanford University Press, Stanford, 1995), 171.

23. Alexander Dobrynin, *In Confidence* (Random House, New York, 1995), 444.

24. Richard Stevenson, *The Rise and Fall of Détente* (Macmillan Press, London, 1995), 204–5.

25. Richard Thornton, *The Carter Years* (Paragon House, New York, 1991), 467.

26. McClellan, op. cit., 156.

27. Westad, op. cit., 24.

28. John Dumbrell, *The Carter Presidency* (Manchester University Press, Manchester, 1995), 129.

29. Bowker and Williams, op. cit., 235.

30. Garthoff, op. cit., 1066.

Part V

From Confrontation to Communist Collapse

1981–1989

INTRODUCTION

The 1980s saw a remarkable change in international relations. The decade began in an atmosphere of revived Cold War confrontation with the Western economies in depression, an uncertain leadership in America, and a number of apparent communist advances in the less developed world. They ended with the collapse of Soviet Communism in Eastern Europe, a resurgent US, a new approach to numerous long-running problems in the less developed world, and a relationship between Washington and Moscow which came close to friendship. In so doing these changes produced a number of fundamental changes in the mainstream political and economic values that dominated the developed world. The economic and political order desired by the Right in the wake of the 1970s collapse of the consensus established by the Second World War was strengthened by the subsequent defeat of Socialism. After victory in the Cold War the 1980s were to end with Western expectations of a completely new international order for the 1990s. Questions remain as to the extent of these changes and why they happened. Moreover, the links between the end of the Cold War and the events of the late 1970s, in particular, are worth examining to assess the continuities between the Cold War and post-Cold War worlds.

Reagan and Confrontation

In the West the Reagan Presidency that was deliberately promoted, if not manufactured, by the forces of the Right, such as the Committee on the Present Danger, marked for some the death of American liberalism. This death has been associated with the end of the Cold War by H. W. Brands who claims that liberalism, a term increasingly used in a derisory way, was maintained by the Cold War. It may thus be possible to argue that the forces of conservatism, which were weakening liberalism within the US, triumphed because of the winning the Cold War. For Brands the Cold War consensus which held liberal America together in the form of government intervention such as the Great Society programme of helping less well-off Americans was an unusual but Cold War feature of American history. Brands argues that the Cold War consensus within America was effectively broken by the Vietnam War and buried with the collapse of the Soviet Union.[1] By then what was emerging was a distrust of government, the emergence of radical conservatism, born-again right-wing Christian fundamentalism, and the glorification of the individual liberated from society. In foreign policy terms the question is how far the collapse of the Soviet Union was a result of global changes and how far the resurgence of the radical Right in the West produced or reinforced it.

Reagan's reference to the Soviet Union as the 'evil empire' was one feature of the renewed Soviet–American confrontation and antagonism in the early 1980s. Whether this was primarily influenced by the domestic climate or by international concerns is again a moot point but the two are clearly linked even if the causal connection appears difficult to find. Arguments based on the collapse of a Cold War consensus have to explain this 'second' Cold War. Another issue is whether a division of the Cold War into two phases reflects all the changes that took place in the Cold War international system. If, for example, one sees the Cold War as a power political struggle spiced with a large dose of ideology, did it really ever end? If the ideological battle was won by the Right, is the power political battle centred on US attempts to shape the international system still taking place? If one regards the two rivals as seeking to maintain advantages in managing or changing the existing Cold War system, what are the implications of the Cold War's end? If part of the goal of managing the international system is to preserve the socio-economic status quo for the elites that benefit from it, the Cold War may have reflected different ways of attempting to do this as the global distribution of power was transformed. Unless one accepts a simplistic belief in the idea of consistent Western 'containment' of the largely ill-defined ambitions of the other side, the idea of two Cold Wars sandwiched between a period of precarious détente seems increasingly problematic.

The early years of the Reagan administration produced concern in Western Europe about the president's anti-Communist rhetoric. Indications that his administration was prepared to fight a limited nuclear war in Europe with an expectation that victory could be achieved in such a scenario was especially worrying for many Europeans. The collapse of détente seemed to presage the Cold War becoming hot as defence expenditure continued to rise. Reagan, astonished to discover that none of this could actually protect ordinary Americans, became convinced that what became known as the Strategic Defence Initiative (SDI) or Star Wars could provide protection by intercepting nuclear missiles before they reached their targets. This was unlikely to be feasible, but if it was, it threatened the whole concept of deterrence by rendering the Soviet nuclear arsenal obsolete. The only way out would be the building of yet more missiles to overwhelm the anti-missile defences, thereby contributing to another arms race.

In the Soviet Union the early 1980s saw a procession of geriatric leaders who blamed the US for the breakdown of détente and who continued policies which maintained the atmosphere of confrontation. The Soviet intervention in Afghanistan became a full-scale guerrilla war, Poland was placed under martial law for a time, and it was the Soviets who, in late 1983, walked out of nuclear arms talks with the US. In pursuing this uncompromising policy, however, the Kremlin was matched by the Reagan White House. Reagan, a critic of détente and a life-long anti-communist, was more than ready to fight the Cold War which he inherited from the much maligned Jimmy Carter. The expansion of American defence spending, which Carter had initiated, went on at an even greater pace, and in the less developed world he was determined to challenge the communists' supposed advances. In response to Soviet support for 'wars of national liberation', Reagan advocated support for 'freedom fighters' who took up arms against Marxist regimes. In particular he supported the Mujaheddin in Afghanistan and the so-called 'Contras', who were seeking the overthrow of the leftist Sandinista regime in Nicaragua. Still fearful of another Vietnam-style imbroglio, yet denying that the Vietnam War had been a mistake, the President also proved ready to use military force in limited operations, such as the invasion of Grenada (1987) and the intervention in Lebanon (1982–4).

The most common reason provided for a fundamental change in Cold War attitudes centres on the influence of Mikhail Gorbachev who was elected as Soviet leader in March 1985. Six months before superpower relations were frozen in mutual suspicion, nuclear arms talks were in suspension and each side accused the other of planning for war. Yet, only eight months after becoming General Secretary, Gorbachev was in Geneva, holding a surprisingly successful summit with President Reagan, the first such summit meeting since June 1979. Gorbachev went on to press for substantial cuts in nuclear arsenals, to pull the Red Army out of Afghanistan, to reduce the USSR's conventional forces without a *quid pro quo* from the West, and, ultimately, to accept that the Soviet sphere of influence in Eastern Europe could not be upheld by force.

The End of the Cold War

Gorbachev undoubtedly provided a different approach to East–West relations as part of a reformist agenda albeit aimed at the maintenance of communism in the Soviet Union. After 1985 it also become clear that Reagan was willing to change from confrontation to dialogue. That shift is difficult to explain but could also be credited to Gorbachev, and one heavily criticized feature of US policy in the late 1980s was that it seemed to react to Soviet behaviour rather than being proactive and taking initiatives. Yet there were other reasons for Reagan to be more positive himself in 1985 and for contributing to the success of better US–Soviet relations. He had just secured a second term, with a convincing win over the Democrats' Walter Mondale in November 1984, and rather like Eisenhower, the last President to serve two full terms in office, wanted to make his reputation as a peacemaker. Also, those close to him in his first term knew that, if the Soviets changed their policies, Reagan was ready to talk

How Many Cold Wars were there?

It was suggested in Part I that the origins of the Cold War were related to the introduction of ideology into a power political dispute. Key elements of this dispute were the creation of regimes in Eastern Europe which would be answerable to Moscow and thereby remove some of the threats and problems on the borders of the Soviet Union; the preservation of regimes in the Middle East which would be subject to British influence; and the estab-

lishment of American military dominance in Japan and the Western Pacific. These features of this prologue, as it might be called, to the Cold War were power political disagreements about the way vital interests and new areas of influence would be reconciled as part of a new global order. The first Cold War might be said to have begun in 1946–7 as propaganda, ideological conflict and fears over the preservation of the respective social and political orders became evident with the West defining this as containing Soviet power. By 1948 a new Cold War began as the US sought to weaken and undermine communist control over Eastern Europe and the Soviet Union. Both leading powers seemed to believe that ultimately only one system would survive with many in the US arguing Soviet Communism would have to be destroyed if the nature of the Soviet state were to change and the Cold War end. The communists under Stalin believed that the contradictions of capitalism would ultimately destroy it if communism in Eastern Europe and the Soviet Union could survive under the auspices of a powerful state.

The third Cold War arguably began after Stalin's death when the contradictions of capitalism appeared less credible in the short term, the murderous nature of Stalin's regime less acceptable, and the idea of peaceful coexistence more desirable. By 1956 this had changed the Soviet approach and the Americans were questioning the prospect of destroying the Soviet satellite empire without resorting to hot war. The third Cold War was characterized by fears of a major hot war involving thermonuclear weapons, but a greater determination to fight the Cold War as the importance of the former colonial territories assumed greater importance. It took the Cuban missile crisis to convince both sides that Cold War competition could lead the two rivals to the brink of hot war outside Europe.

The fourth Cold War in the 1960s can perhaps be seen as the time of relative Soviet gains in military terms and Moscow's attempt to close the gap with the US whose capabilities previously surpassed those of the Soviet Union. The Americans were caught up in a struggle in South-East Asia which had only partially developed as a battle between communist and non-communist forces but which the US defined in those terms and tried and failed to resolve as part of the Cold War struggle. The relative strength of the two superpowers during the Cold War, highlighted by Soviet gains in this period, is another subject for debate and affects the description of the Cold War world as bipoplar and between equals. Again a more sophisticated analysis might reveal some subtle chronological differences and inequalities in a world generally deemed to be bipolar after 1945.

The fifth Cold War between the late 1960s and 1970s could be defined by the attempts at détente and the realization that the world was more complex than a struggle between the US and the Soviet Union. The results of decolonization, with the emergence of newly independent states and conflicts in and over the less developed world and in the oil-rich Middle East were only partially linked to global rivalries. The emergence of China as a significant force accompanied this and led to ideas of a multipolar world appearing. The fifth Cold War with its emphasis on détente can be defined as an attempt to manage this new, more multi-polar world in order to secure the same kind of advantages as were sought in the Cold War. Credibility and status as superpowers and the adoption of particular ideologies with their contrasting ways of life formed part of détente/Cold War and the attempt to preserve or change the global status quo in ideological and power political terms.

The failure of both sides to achieve what they wanted from détente may have led to the sixth Cold War from 1979 to 1985. It was characterized by a more proactive American policy with its renewed emphasis on confrontation and armaments and a determination to avoid any possibility of the Soviets appearing as effective challengers to American power. Why this sixth Cold War ended so suddenly and unexpectedly is a vital question which depends to some extent on what the two powers were trying to achieve through the years of what might be termed the final Cold War.

to them. His suspicion of the Kremlin ran deep but was not based on a sophisticated, broad grasp of international realities. He was ready to put forward some dramatic proposals to reduce tension, notably the 'zero option' (to remove all INF weapons) of November 1981; and he genuinely saw his Stars Wars anti-ballistic missile programme as the morally correct course.

The events that produced the end of the Cold War would not have unfolded in the precise way they did without Gorbachev's particular policies, but it is unhistorical to credit one individual with such a profound revolution in world affairs. There are a number of developments which may have had an important bearing on the end of the Cold War irrespective of the influence of individuals. Before 1985 the USSR had agreed that nuclear arms talks must recommence and there were signs of reformist tendencies under Andropov. For a few years afterwards there was intense debate in Western capitals about how far Gorbachev represented a real change in Soviet policy. Only in 1987–8, with the signature of a treaty abolishing intermediate-range nuclear forces (INF) and the settlement of the Afghan problem, was his true radicalism revealed. And even then there were arguments in the US over how best to respond, partly because of a reluctance to believe the Cold War was ending.

Exactly when it was over has been the subject of intense academic debate, similar to that surrounding the question of when the Cold War began and how it developed over time. Unlike interstate hot wars of course, there was no declaration by the protagonists as to when they were, or were not, engaged in Cold War, and how one chooses to date its end depends on what is seen as its key feature: a lack of regular, high-level diplomatic contact between Moscow and Washington, the existence of an ideologically based propaganda contest over rival economic and political systems, military competition with preparations for hot war, the existence of two sets of alliances, and involvement by proxy in wars and conflicts might all be taken as important general features. More specific (and therefore easier to measure) would be the division of Europe by the Iron Curtain or the severing of Berlin between Soviet and Western sectors. Some might date the end of the Cold War as early as the INF treaty in 1987, some as late as the disintegration of the USSR in 1991, but a more plausible choice is the 12 months following December 1988. That month Gorbachev effectively ended the ideological war between capitalism and communism by denying, in a speech to the UN, that Marxism had a monopoly of the truth. This was when a majority of the American public came to believe the Cold War was over. But only in May 1989 did George Bush, now President, announce the end of the policies designed to prevent the spread of communism which had served as a general guide to US decision-makers since 1945. And the greatest symbol of the division of Germany and Europe, the Berlin Wall, was not breached until November 1989.

Reagan's Victory?

Right-wingers in the US and realists thinkers in international relations have always argued that as the Cold War ended with a victory for the West—it was thanks to Reagan rather than Gorbachev. This was not because the President had finally embraced the détente he once despised, but because his tough policies of the early 1980s, the arms spending, and the support for 'freedom fighters', were seen as having put such strains on the Communist system in the USSR that it faced disintegration unless it attempted radical change. Thus, to the thesis which argued that Gorbachev had taken the initiative in ending confrontation, was opposed an alternative view that the Soviet leader only adopted 'new thinking' because he had to do so, and that this was thanks to Reagan.

A radically different view puts the emphasis not on Gorbachev moving away from confrontation but on a crucial change in Reagan's thinking. The opposite interpretation focuses on Reagan's conversion to a more cooperative and less confrontational position. The conversion was inspired by Reagan's concern for the vulnerability of Americans to nuclear war and his fears that confrontation might well bring it about almost by accident. The shooting down of KAL 007 and exercise Able Archer, a large-scale military exercise that produced a situation comparable to the command and communications procedures that would be used in a nuclear strike against the Eastern bloc were other factors. When monitoring Able Archer through listening devices the Soviets became alarmed not least because NATO had always refused to agree to a no-first-use policy on nuclear weapons. Statements made by leading Soviet figures expressed the need for great vigilance and in private pointed to the possibility of an imminent attack and if Soviet military doctrine had been followed a nuclear strike would have been launched. It was on the day that the exercise ended, 11 November 1983, that Reagan made his first public call for the abolition of nuclear weapons. The turning point in this argument about Reagan's contribution was the President's January 1984 speech calling for ways to reduce the fear of uncertainty and the possibility of misinterpretation over a surprise attack while insisting that the US posed no threat to the Soviet Union. This line of seeking co-operation as opposed to condemnation was possibly the key moment leading to superpower rapprochement.[2]

Yet any intention to achieve this by confrontation or compromise hardly fits with the ideas of Reagan, Bush and other conservative establishment figures. If Reagan was pressurising the Soviets with a view to ending the Cold War, as had been hoped for in its early years, nobody realized it at the time. And Bush was slow to accept it after it had happened. Not only was he at pains to insist that the Cold War was not over in 1988 but he seemed to long to return to the confrontational deterrence which seemed to him to characterize the early 1960s. Yet Gorbachev's UN speech on 7 December 1988 had referred to the rights of the individual, to freedom, self-determination, and threats to the environment. When the Soviet leader embarked on unilateral disarmament in 1989, officials in the Bush administration accused him of trying to split the Western alliance and the US began to modernize short-range NATO nuclear weapons in Germany. As Germans protested because the Soviets were removing their weapons the Bush administration, members of Congress, and the media were outraged. The same Cold War message came from Washington as many times before. Failure to install the weapons would weaken resolve and damage the Western alliance. Answering why the Cold War ended has also to involve answering why no one predicted it and why some took so long to realize it had ended. Ultimately this can only be explained by the enormous impact of the perceptions of actions of others previously defined and ingrained in human consciousness. Actions which differ markedly from expectations and which are used to justify a way of life or the essence of a foreign policy are initially ignored and events interpreted in order to fit preconceived ideas.

Explaining Gorbachev's Actions

Whatever the role of preconceptions it is certainly essential, in explaining why the Cold War ended, to ask why Gorbachev chose the course he did. Why did he not continue the hard-line policies of his predecessors, insisting on the end of the Star Wars project before agreeing to nuclear arms control? Why did he not require an internal settlement in Afghanistan before pulling out the Red Army? But it is not necessary to accept that he decided on reform at home and dialogue abroad in reaction to Reagan's toughness, or even that international considerations were of prime importance to the 'new thinking'. Instead it can be argued that Gorbachev was forced to make changes because of long-running problems within the Soviet Union itself, which would have reached critical proportions in the 1980s with or without Reagan's policies. In that interpretation the end of the Cold War was produced by Gorbachev acting in accordance with the constraints he was subject to as opposed to new ideas (ideational change) leading to new policies and changes in the international system.

The problems of the Soviet economy can be linked to defence expenditure and the war in Afghanistan but the real problem was more fundamental and went back at least to the policies of industrialization favoured by Joseph Stalin. Central planning, a concentration on heavy industrial production, and the ruthless exploitation of agriculture all helped create a system which was incapable of meeting the demand for modern consumer goods. Bureaucratic controls and a lack of competition led to inefficiency and waste made worse by production targets which were met on paper but never in reality. Nor did the Soviet system provide people with satisfactory housing or health care, even if it did control prices and guarantee employment. By the mid-1970s Soviet economic growth was stagnant, defence spending was destructively high, and any idealism about Marxist-Leninism was being sapped by corruption, careerism, and cynicism.

Yet Gorbachev's predecessors never responded to economic difficulties in the way he did. Even if the problems had got worse, the attempt to solve them by the methods Gorbachev employed still requires explanation. He may have been attempting to imitate the comparative success of Western economies believing rightly or wrongly that this was produced by market economics and political freedoms. If introduced to some extent in the Soviet Union, they could provide a panacea for the Soviet economy. In this scenario it was necessary to end the Cold War in order to get the military to accept the results of Gorbachev's unilateral disarmament that would save the money to implement economic reform. Khrushchev had reduced Soviet forces to cut defence expenditure with no significant impact on the Cold War but the two could be seen as two sides of the same coin. It might even be suggested that the Soviet leader thought ending the Cold War could best be done by talking the same language as the West. If so, Gorbachev failed to realize what impact this would have on the communist political and economic system which was based on Soviet control. More importantly, he forgot that the Cold War was a battle over which system would prevail not just an expression of military and power political rivalries which if negotiated away would produce a more acceptable form of interstate relations.

Other arguments point to the way in which *glasnost* unleashed uncontrollable forces in the conditions of the 1980s. Even if more freedoms had not been granted it would have been difficult to prevent access to greater knowledge about the benefits available to most people in the developed capitalist world. With access to computers and the internet and opportunities for travel opening up in Eastern Europe repression would have involved the same vicious circle of high defence expenditure, economic inefficiency, and the struggle for reform. And the Soviet people had long been disillusioned with the careerism and corruption of communist officials and cynical in their response to government propaganda. The average person increasingly believed little or nothing the government told them. They became more sceptical of the values of Marxist-Leninism and of the idea of containing the threat that the imperialist enemy allegedly posed to them. The situation was therefore ripe for pressure from below to play an important role in forcing the process of change and taking it further than Gorbachev had envisaged.

Realists deny the influence of internal forces on the making of foreign policy and cannot explain the end of the Cold War by pointing to ideational change in Soviet and American leaders. They are forced to explain events by pointing to the systemic effects of Reagan's confrontational policies, and their emphasis on military strength, which the Soviet Union could not match. Gorbachev's achievements, if any, were to realize that the system of state-controlled socialism was on the way out and then to promote the changes that resulted in Western-style reforms and the collapse of the communist system wherever it was in place in Europe. The Soviet Union was thus destroyed by the introduction of market economics and political democracy and the failure to match the economic and military strength of the West. It was Reagan, pursuing in realist terms the traditional quest for greater military power, who brought this about and the world could look forward to a decade of peace and prosperity.

Again, like everyone else, realist theorists did not predict this outcome and at least part of the reason lies in the Western failure to accurately understand the nature of the Cold War or to conceptualize it in ways in which peaceful change was seen as distinctly possible. The orthodox interpretation of the Cold War, based on a fundamentally expansionist Soviet Union deterred from pursuing its ambitious goals by Western containment, is one obvious conceptualization which, like realist ideas, prevents any prediction of developments leading to the Cold War's end. Described by John Lewis Gaddis in terms of its creation of a long peace, the alleged goal of Western policy was the prevention of war by vigilance and deterrence. The encouragement of change would not occur naturally with both sides locked into a process centred on

Soviet expansion for a mixture of imperial and ideological reasons. The only thing that has to be explained is why war did not come about. The fact that the Soviets might have had no greater inclination to expand than the US is not considered and therefore the end of the Cold War is hard to conceive.[3]

The Less Developed World

The ideas as to why Gorbachev, the surprise hero in the West, acted as he did against all expectations and whether he was a prisoner of domestic or international events remain to be resolved. But Reagan deserves some credit for at least enabling the ending of the Cold War to be facilitated. Like Gorbachev he may not have realized the full significance of what he was beginning, but from the American point of view relations with the Soviet Union were something of a triumph. Carter's refocusing on East–West relations rather than North–South ones were ultimately rewarded under Reagan even if the price was paid in less developed world countries. The less developed world mattered to Reagan not because of the challenge of the lack of development, but because of its significance to Cold War rivalries, especially in such countries as Nicaragua, El Salvador, and Afghanistan. The Iran–Iraq war (the longest-running conventional war since 1945) was treated as a mere sideshow and Latin America, along with Africa, was left sunk in debt, with little attention paid to the poverty in which billions lived. Here the moves towards reconciliation between Reagan and Gorbachev did not prevent the continuation of the struggle between advocates of revolution and supporters of the status quo.

In the early 1980s Reagan took the advice of those who continued to put their trust in authoritarian dictators in the less developed world who were seen as more suitable than totalitarian ideologues. Murder and the lack of political freedom continued to exist and for longer than some of the pro-American dictators, such as Marcos in the Philippines and Duvalier in Haiti, whose excesses helped modify US policy as poverty-stricken people resisted. In other countries such as El Salvador and Nicaragua resistance to American-backed groups continued. By the end of the decade 40,000 people had died as the US government, by fair and largely foul means, sought to overthrow the Sandinistas in Nicaragua. In El Salvador a 10-year war had claimed the lives of around 70,000 people most of whom were killed by right-wing death squads. Cold War conceptions continued in place at the end of the decade in parts of the non-European world. It was an open question as to whether this indicated a reluctance to take on board the post-Cold War world or whether the US was determined to pursue American interests by whatever means.

The losers were some of the people of the less developed world who found the new liberal economic consensus on developmental progress merely brought them greater poverty. The debt trap was consuming an extremely large percentage of some of the poorer countries' GDP, but the remedy was now deemed to be more engagement with the world economy. The model countries were those in Asia who by the end of the decade had managed to achieve thriving industrial economies dominated by the export trade. There initial progress had, however, been made with the aid of government controls to foster successful industrial development and those countries too poor to make the transition to industry now found themselves doubly penalized by the developed world. The IMF's structural adjustment programmes were based on controls which maintained low government expenditure and where welfare provision existed it suffered serious cut-backs. Yet access to developed markets in agricultural produce remained difficult for producers in the less developed world because of the kind of protectionist policies maintained, for example, by the European Community. The 1980s saw the start of a process whereby the poorest countries, mostly in Africa, were more and more marginalized in the global economy as they struggled with mountainous debts that the West had to reschedule or face the problems of defaulters.

In the developed world the end of the Cold War brought a sense of righteousness which ignored the problems facing many victims of capitalism in the less developed world. The sense of having been right all along was manifest even if it would take a while for this to be reflected in academic analyses of the benefits of capitalist democracy and orthodox interpretations of the Cold War. Socialism was deemed dead and the Soviet Union defeated. Triumphalism was largely buried by a sense of complacent satisfaction, but problems remained in the world and would eventually emerge to challenge the self-righteousness and rosy expectations that prevailed at the start of the 1990s. In a sense they would show that, notwithstanding the indisputable superiority of the Western world in producing consumer goods and maintaining political freedoms, there were many problems, often ignored, which had little to do with the Cold War and the alleged ambitions of the Soviet Union.

Retrospect

In retrospect, the new Cold War of the early 1980s can be seen as the last phase in which the USSR tried to equal US might, not by addressing weaknesses at home, but by posing as a military giant. Or it can be seen as the start of a new attempt by the American Right to dominate the exercise of global power in order to ensure that American interests prevailed. As the report of the British Foreign Office wartime enquiry into the attitudes of leading Americans put it with reference to some US organizations and groups in 1944, their attitude was 'America first the rest of the world nowhere'. The Soviet Union emerges as an empire in economic decline and unable to maintain its levels of defence expenditure and its controls over everyday life. In the early 1980s it was still able to uphold its allies in Eastern Europe, Cuba, and Vietnam while backing Marxists in civil wars in Afghanistan, Nicaragua, and Angola. However, even when Reagan came into office he was warned by the CIA of the poor state of the Soviet economy, a situation which continued to worsen. Around 1982 the USSR's oil production began to fall off and it was increasingly realized that the central planners could not provide raw materials to industry 'free' of charge. It also became clear that Eastern Europe, whatever its military value had been as a defensive wall, was an economic liability that could no longer act as a barrier to ideas and culture. The post-Cold War was to emerge with a resurgent America on the rise and its main rival no longer ale to provide a challenge.

To remedy this Gorbachev initiated the policies of 'openness' and 'reconstruction'—*glasnost* and *perestroika*—which were intended to revitalize Soviet Communism but which actually unleashed the forces of nationalism, self-determination, and consumer culture that destroyed the Soviet Union. This process might not have occurred so quickly had the US not emerged from the doldrums of the 1970s with a new agenda. Moreover, after 1982, the success of Western capitalism contrasted starkly with the fortunes of the USSR and Eastern Europe much more so than in the previous decade. Rapid technological change was beginning to revolutionize the nature of communication, the media's impact was more encompassing, more money was spent on better Western propaganda, and more economic benefits were available as access to consumer goods was for the most part made instantaneous because of easier credit facilities. These were the things unavailable in the Soviet Union where knowledge of Western culture and lifestyles began to cross the Iron Curtain on an extensive basis as Gorbachev entered the Kremlin.

The surprising thing was that many commentators continued to discuss not Soviet decline, but that of the US. When Gorbachev came to power he was apparently able to seize the initiative in East–West relations for a time, but the US easily remained the predominant superpower, even if its relative strength, compared to the late 1940s, had fallen off. The shape of international relations after 1985 was set, not by the Kremlin, but by the fundamental weaknesses of the state over which it presided. By December 1989 it was clear that the new order that was emerging would have America as the only superpower. And if at the time there was insufficient understanding of the complex history of the Cold War (a battle to get nuclear superiority as defined primarily by the Committee on the Present Danger), it becomes easier to appreciate why no one predicted it would end at all let alone so dramatically.

NOTES

1. H.W. Brands *The Strange Death of American Liberalism* (Yale University Press, New Haven, 2001), Chapters 5 and 6.

2. Beth A. Fischer, *The Reagan Reversal* (University of Missouri Press, Colombia, 1997), 102–43.

3. On the predictive failures of Western theorists see the introduction by Richard Ned Lebow and Thomas Risse-Kappento their edited work, *International Relations Theory and the End of the Cold War* (Columbia University Press, New York, 1995).

PART V CHRONOLOGY: FROM CONFRONTATION TO COMMUNIST COLLAPSE, 1981–1989

1981

11 January	Martial law declared in El Salvador.
20 January	Iran releases US Embassy hostages, held since November 1978.
9 February	General Jaruzelski becomes Prime Minister of Poland (and, on 18 October, Communist Party leader).
24 April	President Reagan ends anti-Soviet grain embargo, introduced by his predecessor after invasion of Afghanistan.
17 June	First American arms deal with Communist China.
23 September	US and USSR agree to open talks on intermediate nuclear forces (INF).
6 October	President Sadat of Egypt assassinated.
18 November	Reagan proposes the 'zero option', the complete destruction of INF weapons.
13 December	Jaruzelski declares martial law in Poland.

1982

2 April–14 June	The Falklands War: Argentinian forces invade the islands, which are reconquered by the British.
9 May	Reagan's Eureka College speech proposes Strategic Arms Reduction Talks (START), which will reduce nuclear arsenals.
24 May	In the Iran–Iraq War, Iranian forces recapture the key city of Khorramshahr.
6 June	Israeli invasion of Lebanon launched, to drive out the Palestinian Liberation Organisation (PLO).
29 June	START talks open in Geneva between the Superpowers.
14 July	In the Iran–Iraq War, Iranians cross the Iraqi border for the first time.
21 August	PLO begins to pull out of Beirut; moves headquarters to Tunis.
10 November	Death of Soviet leader, Leonid Brezhnev; succeeded next day by Yuri Andropov.

1983

9 March	Reagan describes USSR as an 'evil Empire'.
23 March	Reagan speech launches the 'Strategic Defense Initiative' (SDI) for space-based anti-nuclear systems.
21 July	Jaruzelski ends martial law in Poland.
1 September	A South Korean Airlines' Boeing 747, flight KAL 007 shot down by Soviets.
9 October	Several South Korean government ministers assassinated by North Koreans on a visit to Rangoon, Burma.
23 October	Over 300 US and French troops, part of a multinational peacekeeping force, killed in bombings in Beirut.

25 October	Invasion of Grenada by US Marines.
15 November	Deployment of Cruise–Pershing missiles begins in Western Europe, despite widespread protests.
23 November	Soviets walk out of INF talks due to Cruise deployments; START talks suspended on 8 December.

1984

9 February	Death of Andropov; succeeded on 13th by Konstantin Chernenko.
26 April–2 May	Reagan visits China.
8 May	USSR says it will boycott forthcoming Los Angeles Olympics.
28 September	Reagan meets Soviet foreign minister, Andrei Gromyko, for the first time.
22 November	Reagan re-elected President.

1985

4 February	New Zealand refuses to let nuclear-capable US ships into its ports; leads to virtual breakdown of ANZUS Pact (US suspends obligations to New Zealand in August 1986).
11 March	Mikhail Gorbachev succeeds Chernenko as leader of the Soviet Union.
12 March	INF and START talks reopen.
7 April	Gorbachev suspends new deployments of nuclear missiles and urges NATO to do the same.
26 April	Warsaw Pact renewed for twenty years.
1 May	US launches trade embargo against Nicaragua.
6 August	Gorbachev initiates a moratorium on nuclear tests (lasts until April 1986).
19–21 November	First summit meeting between Gorbachev and Reagan, in Geneva.

1986

15 January	Gorbachev accepts 'zero option' for destruction of INF systems.
25 February	In the Philippines, Ferdinand Marcos, after an election defeat, finally surrenders the Presidency to Corazon Aquino.
15 April	US air forces strike targets in Libya.
26 April	Chernobyl nuclear reactor melts down, near Kiev, USSR.
28 July	Gorbachev's Vladivostok speech urges improved relations with China.
23 August	Gennady Zakharov, a Soviet embassy official, is arrested for spying in US; on 30 August Soviets arrest Nicholas Daniloff, an American journalist.
30 September	Release of Zakharov and Daniloff.
11–12 October	Gorbachev and Reagan summit in Reykjavik breaks down over SDI.
3 November	The 'Irangate' scandal breaks: a Lebanese newspaper reveals that a high level US official visited Iran in May.

1987

| 10 April | Gorbachev's Prague speech advocates a 'common European home'. |
| 20 July | UN passes Resolution 598 on an Iran–Iraq cease-fire and return to border as it was in 1980. |

7 August	'Arias Plan', for peace in Nicaragua, put forward by Central American governments.
29 November	In Poland, the Communist government holds a referendum on economic reform but fails to get 50 per cent support.
7–10 December	Third Gorbachev–Reagan summit, in Washington. INF treaty signed on 8th.

1988

8 February	Gorbachev announces Red Army will evacuate Afghanistan in March 1989 if a peace settlement is made.
3 March	US Congress effectively cuts financial support to Contras in Nicaragua.
23 March	Cease-fire in Nicaragua between the Contras and the government.
14 April	Geneva peace agreement on a settlement in Afghanistan.
29 May–2 June	Gorbachev–Reagan summit in Moscow.
30 June	Vietnam begins withdrawing its troops from neighbouring Kampuchea (Cambodia).
20 July	Ayatollah Khomeini reluctantly agrees to end the war with Iraq.
31 August	Lech Walesa meets a Polish government minister to discuss mounting internal unrest.
8 November	George Bush wins Presidential election.
22 December	UN agreements on independence of Namibia and Cuban withdrawal from Angola.

1989

11 January	Non-communist parties legalized in Hungary.
15 February	Last Red Army troops leave Afghanistan.
6 March	Talks on reducing 'Conventional Forces in Europe' open between Eastern and Western representatives in Vienna.
26 March and 9 April	First elections for a 'Soviet Congress of People's Deputies'.
5 April	In Poland, the government agrees to recognize Solidarity and elect an assembly.
25 April	Soviets begin to pull troops out of Hungary.
7 May	In Panama, President Noriega annuls recent election results.
12 May	Bush's Texas A&M University speech effectively ends the policy of containment.
15–18 May	Gorbachev–Deng Xiaoping summit held in Beijing. First Sino–Soviet summit for thirty years.
21 May	Egypt rejoins the Arab League after ten years.
4 June	Chinese Red Army forcibly ends the occupation of Tienenmen Square, Beijing, by over 100,000 demonstrators (who had been there since 22 April).
4 and 18 June	Solidarity scores major successes in Polish elections.
23 August	Demonstrations in Estonia, Latvia and Lithuania, in favour of independence from USSR.
26 September	Last Vietnamese troops leave Cambodia.
9–10 November	Opening of the Berlin Wall.
2–3 December	First Bush–Gorbachev summit in Malta.
20 December	US forces invade Panama, to overthrow Noriega.
29 December	Czechoslovakia chooses the dissident Vaclav Havel as its President.

16 The 'Second' Cold War, 1981–1985

A. US–Soviet Relations and the New Cold War

Reagan's International Outlook and 'Reaganomics'

Ronald Reagan, a former movie actor and Governor of California, had been a firm anti-communist since his post-war days as President of the Screen Actors' Guild, when he had denounced leftist influences in Hollywood. He had already been a critic of détente and SALT when seeking the Republican Presidential nomination in 1976; in 1980 he triumphed over Carter and the divided Democratic camp by attacking the incumbent as a weak, indecisive figure whose economic policies had failed and who had lowered America's international reputation. Above all Reagan promised a disheartened electorate strong leadership and he came to power on the back of a general rightwards shift in the political mood. He dismissed détente as 'a one-way street that the Soviet Union has used to pursue its aims.'[1] Many former Demo-

crats (the so-called 'neo-conservatives'), dissatisfied with the SALT process and concerned by Soviet advances in the less developed world, had turned to the Right since 1976. In order to build a consensus behind its policies the new administration promised 'to restore the domestic economy, reward the anti-Communist friends of the United States abroad, halt the spread of Soviet influence and combat terrorism . . . without . . . risking another Vietnam-type conflict.'[2] In contrast to Carter, who was prepared to tackle complex issues like Middle Eastern peace, Reagan had little desire to master details whatever views he had, concentrated on a presentational role in government, and pursued a simple foreign policy. Neither intellectual nor particularly devious, he rejected détente as a communist trick, was initially determined to resist the spread of Soviet influence wherever it threatened, and, going beyond that, wanted to carry the New Cold War into the Soviet camp. In a sense this was nothing new. Even under

Truman, when the original idea of 'containment', appeared, American policy had soon developed a strong element of 'liberation', hoping to undermine the Eastern bloc through the use of covert action, economic pressures, and propaganda. Where Reagan differed from Truman was in his clear, public acknowledgement of the 'offensive' elements in the US arsenal. He wanted to force changes in Soviet policy by starving them of trade and technology in vital areas, by outspending them on defence, and by backing their opponents in less developed countries. The indigenous problems of the poorer regions of the world, the need to tackle poverty and local conflicts, were ignored as all foreign policy was interpreted on the light of Soviet–American confrontation. Under the 'Reagan Doctrine', the US promised support for so-called 'freedom fighters' in Afghanistan, Angola, and Central America. This strong-handed approach, underpinned by the President's public relations talents, went down well with the US public, which sensed that 'history had taken a U-turn. The United States . . . was reasserting its international hegemony [while the] Soviet Union was mired in a deeply unpopular war in Afghanistan.' Yet the appearance was deceptive. In fact the current perception merely reversed 'a short period of [false] images of American weakness and Soviet strength'.[3] 'The Reagan administration . . . brought a new sense of dynamism and assertiveness to the Soviet–American relationship.' perhaps, but the 'major changes . . . were in rhetoric rather than substance, and . . . it did little more than carry out the policies which had been formulated by Carter in . . . 1980.'[4]

In retrospect even Andrei Gromyko shared the impression that a major change occurred in January 1981: 'On the coming to power of the Reagan administration, tension in Soviet–US relations increased . . . The new US government did everything it could to undo the work of its predecessors.'[5] Yet, at first, Reagan's outlook did not necessarily imply a more dangerous US–Soviet confrontation than in Carter's last year. Moscow had seen Carter, with his human rights crusade, as a difficult figure and had never shared the fantasies of the Committee of the Present Danger that the US was in cataclysmic decline, with the Soviets about to overhaul it in the nuclear arms race. American defence spending was

already rising and, in talking of nuclear war-fighting doctrines, Reagan was largely building on Carter's Presidential Directive 59 (itself built on the 1974 Schlesinger Doctrine). Indeed, at the start of the new Presidency, an astonished Alexander Haig, the incoming Secretary of State, was told by Soviet ambassador Dobrynin that he 'failed to see any basic difference from the arrogant moralizing of the departed Carter administration'.[6] Some Soviet experts may have hoped that Reagan would prove as positive to deal with as Nixon, his Republican predecessor, who had also come to power as an outspoken anti-Communist. And behind the blunt exterior, there were important nuances in Reagan's outlook: despite the fears of Western liberals, he did *not* want confrontation to lead to war; whilst advocating US strength he was also ready to negotiate with the Soviets—if they respected US wishes; and he was capable of recognizing that the Cold War sometimes damaged American interests. Thus in April 1981, three months after entering the White House he both wrote to Brezhnev expressing a desire for peace and lifted the grain embargo on the USSR, which Carter had begun after the invasion of Afghanistan but which hit the profits of mid-West farmers. 'Perhaps', he wrote, 'this decision will contribute to creating the circumstances which will lead to the meaningful . . . dialogue which will assist us in our joint obligation to find lasting peace.'[7] He also quickly abandoned his earlier view that the Chinese Communists were as bad as the Soviets, and visited Beijing in 1984.

Closely linked to his determination to fight the Cold War worldwide was Reagan's campaign to reduce inflation and bring growth to the US after the poor economic performance of the 1970s. During his first few years in office, in fact, the state of the economy had precedence over foreign policy on the administration's agenda. Again, Reagan had no sophisticated ideology to guide him. Once a Democrat himself, he once admired Franklin Roosevelt, the father of the New Deal, which many Republicans saw as the root of 'wasteful' social spending and a bloated federal government. Reagan, however, became closely associated with the ideas of a particular school of neo-liberal economists and along with Margaret Thatcher was able to attempt to apply them.

Of those economists who in the 1970s had begun to challenge the post-war consensus of full employment and government intervention to counter other features of free-market capitalism which were seen as damaging to the social fabric, Milton Friedman, Friedrich Hayek, and the followers of the deceased Leo Strauss now came into their own under Reagan's presidency. It is important to emphasize that the ideas and theories they held were nothing new and had developed in the wake of the Second World War in opposition to the Keynesian consensus. They did however appear new to many who had become disillusioned with the failure of Bretton Woods in the 1970s and then with the troubles of the later years of the decade that emphasized social strife and continued inflation. In the 1980s they took over from Keynesian ideas as the dominant force in Western economics in a changed political and economic climate. Reagan had emerged as a leader with an instinctive sympathy with their views and was prepared to assume a leadership role in popularizing them. Yet the ideas themselves had appeared, in Hayek's case, as early as 1944 with his book *The Road to Serfdom* and its attack on any idea of state intervention. These advocates of the economics of the free market were united in the 1960s with philosophical libertarians and religious nationalists under the auspices of Leo Strauss at the University of Chicago. Strauss who saw connections between the interventionism of the Weimar Republic and the evils of the Nazis (the ultimate tragedy of market interference) was the precursor of the Christian religious Right that was to become a powerful force in the US by the beginning of the 1990s. Individuals had to be responsible for their actions to become virtuous citizens while the market, based on individual self-interest, and self-regulating when free from state intervention, would rule society.

The work of another member of the Chicago school, Milton Friedman, seemed particularly relevant to the end of a decade characterized by stagflation because he offered a simple explanation of inflation. Friedman claimed that the inflationary pressures which had grown so much in the 1970s were caused directly by the growth in the money supply produced by the state that had a monopoly of producing money. If the state allowed too much money to circulate by setting interest rates too low or

by high levels of public expenditure, then not only would the economy not respond to the market but inflation would result. The answer was to make sure the state did not print money and then inflation would come down along with the money supply. In the event such ideas were to be proved wrong, most notably in Britain, where the money supply increased but inflation came down nevertheless. Yet at the time they were extremely influential.

The fact that these ideas became attractive to leaders such as Ronald Reagan and Margaret Thatcher was helped by important right-wing think tanks in the US such as the American Enterprise Institute, the Hoover Institution, and the Heritage Foundation. This in turn was linked to the dissatisfaction with détente and the lack of American confidence associated with the sense of perceived national decline and loss of US global dominance. Economic problems perceived by many on the American Right required an approach which would liberate business from the constraints deemed to be at the root of American problems. As always it was believed that the removal of such constraints and the solving of US problems would be beneficial for the rest of the world as well as the United States. Those who see the attempt to implement what became known later as the Washington Consensus as part of a new post-Cold War international order should not forget its origins. These lay in the efforts to solve the perceived problems of the US economy in line with the ideas of the conservative American Right not from a global commitment to any universal values of mainstream liberal capitalism.

The Washington Consensus representing tax cuts, especially for the rich, balanced budgets, deregulation, anti-trades union legislation, and tight money controls was central to Reagan's ideology and to some extent key aspects of his policies. It became associated with key international financial institutions, still largely controlled by the US, and then with the idea of globalization and the spread of the post-Cold War ideas following the failure of the Bretton Woods Western system and the collapse of the Soviet Union. As a key influence on the impact of a revived American Right in reaction to the problems of the 1970s, Reagan certainly believed that reductions in marginal taxes and limits on state spending (as well as on economic aid to the less developed world) would encourage free enterprise. At first his policy of high interest rates (necessary because of the effect of tax cuts and rising defence expenditure), though it drove down inflation, also deepened the depression inherited from Carter: unemployment reached 11 per cent in 1981 and the economy, stagnant in 1980, actually contracted by 2 per cent in 1982. But growth revived in 1983, peaking at 7 per cent in 1984 and averaging almost 4 per cent per annum in Reagan's second term. Such sustained expansion, linked to a fall in inflation below 2 per cent in 1986, boosted national confidence through a consumer boom but produced a remarkably high budget deficit and a serious imbalance within the US economy.

'Reaganomics' worked no real economic miracle for America and 1980s growth rates in countries such as Britain have been exaggerated by unfair comparisons with the late 1970s. Over the long term, on both sides of the Atlantic, the decade as a whole was no more successful in producing growth than past decades with which it was broadly comparable. In the US the 40 per cent increase in defence spending in 1981–6 kept interest rates high in the long term, pushed up the value of the dollar, and, partly as a result, the trade deficit mushroomed, up from $25 billion in 1980 to over $140 billion in 1984. What was significant was the stagnation of blue-collar wages in the developed world as, particularly in America and Britain, successful enterprises were measured more and more by the value of the dividends paid to shareholders. And of course there was the reversal of the post-war trend in the developed world for the gap between the rich and the poor to narrow, with staggering increases in the incomes of the very rich. In the US the 1980s saw the incomes of the top 1 per cent double while the bottom 20 per cent suffered a 10 per cent decline.[8] Nevertheless it appeared that 'Reaganomics' and the arguments of the free deregulated marketeers with their tax cuts and cuts in social spending had won the day even if Reagan because of his defence expenditure actually imposed high levels of expenditure on the public purse. In a sense the apparent victory was not an economic one but a cultural one embodied in an increasingly expansive and powerful global media, largely in the hands of the Right.

However, in the 1980s even the market could not refashion American dominance of the world economy alone. The trade deficit with Japan was particularly worrying, growing from $16 billion in 1981 to $46 billion in 1985, despite Japan's agreement to restrain sales of cars and other products. Reagan's tax cuts tended to foster spending on imported consumer goods, while his simultaneous insistence on an expanded defence budget pushed up the national debt, from less than $1 billion in 1981 to more than $2.5 trillion in 1989. In 1985 America became a debtor nation for the first time since 1914, a statistic which could support a view that the country was still in decline relative to the other industrial powers, despite Reagan's promises to reverse the trend. By the end of the Presidency, America was the world's largest debtor, a statistic that caused problems for his successors in the White House. The conservative coalition was beginning to seem less secure when George Bush became President. The importance of right-wing Christian fundamentalism was increasing as the forces of the centre Right became more concerned about extremism.

It was the Japanese who exploited the opportunities offered by the economic situation most, buying up about a third of the expanded US deficit in Reagan's first term and becoming the world's largest creditor nation—but at the price of increasing American fear of Japan's burgeoning economic power. Japan, which imported all its oil but was a highly efficient producer of cars and electrical goods, continued to devote its wealth to investment rather than consumption. The Japanese trade surplus was partly offset decade by the nationalist Nakasone Yasuhiro's willingness to expand defence spending above the previous limit of one per cent of GDP. In particular Yasuhiro proved ready to answer US calls for an expanded Japanese naval presence in the Pacific. There was also an attempt to rectify the trade imbalance by letting the yen rise in value against the dollar: in the eighteen months following the September 1985 Plaza agreement, between Finance Ministers, the dollar fell by about a half against the yen (market interference to benefit the US economy). Yet Japanese manufacturers simply compensated for the change by reducing their profit levels and in 1988 Japan's surplus with America rose to $60 billion. The Japanese also continued to expand their investments in America, focusing on property purchases in the late 1980s, and their banks became some of the largest in the world.

By the end of the 1980s many Americans were still concerned with the idea of decline, as seen in the popularity of Paul Kennedy's 1988 book, *The Rise and Fall of the Great Powers*, with its theme of military 'overstretch' draining the economic resources of even the mightiest states. The US was deemed to be making the sacrifices to fighting the military battle against the real enemy of free enterprise while others gained the economic benefits of free-riding. Kennedy's theme was picked up by other works, who found striking statistics to prove their case. Thus, in 1950 the US had made nearly half the world's steel, but by 1990 only about a tenth, and it had been overtaken by both Japan and the European Community. As a result, one study argued, America 'found itself increasingly struggling to project power other than its military component.'[9]

The consequences of the changes in both the short and long term remain matters of debate. By 1985 the US economy *had* left the age of 'stagflation' behind and helped pull other Western economies out of depression. Yet whether this marked a sound long-term future for the world economy and whether it signified the failure of state planning under Communism or Social Democracy, or whether it was a success for the world or even the have been difficult questions to answer. The decline of the US and its recovery in economic terms may both have been more imaginary than real especially given the problems that appeared to blight the economic success of some Asian countries in the 1990s. The US remained in a strong position although its domination of the world economy was much reduced from the 1950s. The rise of Japan was of some concern especially now that one-fifth of American national wealth relied on foreign trade. But talk of 'American decline' was premature. The fact was that, under Reagan, the US retained its ability to pay for both strong defences and internal stability. It easily outmatched the Soviets in both economic and military power and easily remained the world's largest economy.

In the 1980s West European countries could not match America's or Japan's performance despite their high sales in the US and were now seen as a greater threat to American economic power. In Britain the Thatcher government cut taxes on the wealthy and placed tight controls on public spending while maintaining an overvalued pound which hit British manufacturing industry; unemployment of over 3 million was seen as the necessary cost to get inflation down below 5 per cent in 1983 and to secure several years of growth at over 2 per cent which in the late 1980s contributed to the economy overheating. In Germany after 1982, Helmut Kohl was rather less ideological in his approach but maintained the country's good record on growth, prior to the problems of reunification, while tolerating a higher level of unemployment than in the past. In Italy between 1984 and 1989 there was talk of another 'economic miracle' as growth averaged 3 per cent.

For much of the less developed world the picture was a lot more worrying and in some places verging on the catastrophic. In the US, Western Europe, and Japan the 1980s economic expansion was accompanied not only by a desire to reduce government spending at home but also to restrict development aid abroad. America in the era of Reaganomics and revitalized anti-communism wanted to see the less developed world countries embrace the free market, abandon state planning, and restrict government spending programmes. The threat to the provision of infrastructure, education, and health, all of which might help capitalism thrive, was seen as less damaging than state controls and high public expenditure. It is true that during Reagan's first term the US foreign aid budget expanded, but most of the increase was in the form of military assistance (which topped $7 billion in 1984, up from $3 billion in 1980) and even this fell off in the second term. Western countries now preferred the developing world to rely on private investment rather than foreign aid, and the US particularly pressed for the reduction of all forms of protectionism in order to boost global trade. Such aid as there was became conditional on the recipients accepting the need for 'structural adjustment'. The developing nations were thus required to emulate the free-enterprise policies now being embraced by the developed world and they had few weapons with which to fight back in the face of such pressure.

Moreover, they were increasingly hampered by the debt burden which was a legacy of the oil price rise and the ease with which Western banks lent money to poorer countries whose terms of trade declined and whose available income was more and more taken up with debt repayment. It was again easy to point to corruption as a feature of many of the poorer, particularly African nations but whether this was more a cause than an effect of their economic plight remains a controversial point, as did the benefits of aid to such regimes who were increasingly urged to subject themselves to the rigours of market discipline and extreme austerity for the ordinary masses. The last great call for a state-led transfer of resources from the North to the South (at $50 billion a year) was the 1980 Brandt Report, written by an international group under the former German Chancellor, Willy Brandt. The report argued that North and South had a vested interest in cooperation and that the alternative to tackling the problem was the creation of an ever more divided, insecure world. But these warnings caused little concern in Northern capitals where Brandt's interventionist, social democratic outlook was already giving way to the free-enterprise doctrines of the New Right. In any case, the 1980s showed that the poverty-stricken South presented little menace to the North and therefore the poor could be quietly ignored, except when the publicity given to them by the well-known and the famous (Bob Geldoff's use of musicians and records to raise money to help the starving) temporarily caught the attention of the Western public.

By the end of his second term Reagan had helped create the impression that the US had beaten the USSR in the economic stakes. For, as the CIA told Reagan, the USSR in the early 1980s—far from being an all-powerful menace—was locked into a situation of stagnant growth, inefficient central planning, and corruption. The burdens of its own high defence spending and the need to prop up the equally inefficient economies of Eastern Europe, whilst also aiding 'wars of national liberation' in Angola and Central America, and fighting the war in Afghanistan, exacerbated Soviet economic problems. As the failings of the Soviet model became

clearer, at least in the view of Reagan's supporters, Moscow was forced into radical reforms which ultimately destroyed the regime. The 1990s would see the US as the world's only economic and military superpower.

Years of Fear, 1981–1983

It was said by one leading academic observer of the international scene in 1985 that, during the first Reagan term, 'all was actually quiet, save on the rhetorical front, in the central confrontation between the superpowers.'[10] Nonetheless, whatever the limits to his bellicosity, Reagan's first few years in office saw popular fears that the superpowers might go to war and there was some justification for this. In order to give US armed forces global mobility and also to put strains on the Soviet economy, Reagan expanded the already high levels of defence spending (especially on strategic nuclear weapons and the navy), whilst adopting a sceptical approach to arms control. His Defence Secretary, Caspar Weinberger, believed that US military strength was 'the only thing that could persuade the Soviets that they could not take actions such as they had taken in the 1970s in Angola and Afghanistan . . ., Nicaragua, Ethiopia and elsewhere.'[11] The President reinvigorated the CIA, not least to tackle 'wars of national liberation' and support anti-communist 'freedom fighters' (its new Director, Bill Casey, proving a keen advocate of covert operations), as well as launching a new psychological warfare campaign against communism and trying to tighten up on trade links with the Eastern bloc. Finally, Reagan engaged in the most extreme anti-communist rhetoric since Kennedy. In his most famous declaration of all, on 8 March 1983, at Orlando in Florida, Reagan denounced the USSR as an 'evil Empire' and predicted the end of communism. Fifteen days later he followed this up with the announcement of the Star Wars programme (more fully discussed in Chapter 16, C) designed to counter a Soviet nuclear strike and therefore seen as a threat to the concept of mutually-assured destruction, whose logic of deterrence was seen by some as vital to superpower peace. This followed a series of what the Soviets saw as provocative decisions by Reagan: his March 1981 announcement of further aid to the Mujaheddin resistance in Afghanistan (see Chapter 16, D); his decision, 3 months later, to sell the first US arms to Communist China; his accusation in October 1981 that the Soviets planned to fight and win a nuclear war; his aid to the Contra rebels fighting the leftist Nicaraguan government (see Chapter 18, B) and his support for the Solidarity trades union in Poland (see Chapter 16, B). Unwilling, like Eisenhower, to talk to the Soviets until they showed a readiness to make concessions, he refused even to see their high-level emissaries. The President did not meet Ambassador Anatoly Dobrynin until February 1983 and a first meeting with Foreign Minister, Andrei Gromyko, only came in September 1984, when 'The conversation was edgy and . . . there was the inevitable confrontation' over Soviet aims in the world.[12]

For its part the Kremlin was predictably unwilling to concede that it was guilty of any wrongdoing in world affairs. In Afghanistan, of course, as also in Eastern Europe, it saw itself as struggling to preserve Socialism and stability, with no intention of offensive action beyond its own sphere. In Nicaragua and elsewhere in Central America it still saw 'wars on national liberation' as an inevitable reaction to capitalist oppression. Where the military balance was concerned, Moscow insisted it was committed to nuclear parity and to the fulfilment of SALT II—claims which were probably correct, since the Soviets always recognized that they would lose a technological race with America, hence their enormous fear of the Star Wars programme. Ideas explored by the Soviet military for nuclear war-fighting simply mirrored those being discussed in the US and Reagan himself caused consternation in Western Europe in November 1981 when he talked of localizing a nuclear exchange on the continent. At first the Soviet Politburo 'decided to follow a course for détente in the hope that Reagan little by little would become more reasonable', but within months they felt they were dealing with 'a deeply disturbing figure . . . Once they reluctantly came to the conclusion détente could not be recovered . . . the inclination grew inside the Kremlin not to pacify him but to fight back.'[13] Moscow's interpretation of US policy—and intervening in less developed world conflicts, undermining the nuclear balance, seeking to divide the Eastern bloc—was, ironically, a mirror

image of Washington's view of Soviet designs. As so often in the Cold War, it was genuinely difficult to divorce reality from propaganda. Thus, when the Soviets tried to convince Europeans that Reagan was running the risk of war, the Americans dismissed the accusation as a Kremlin ploy to divide the West. But Brezhnev's statement on 3 February 1982 that (a year into the Reagan Presidency) the international situation was at its worst since 1945, probably reflected genuine fear.

The situation was not helped by the instability and uncertainty of policy-making in Moscow. Even compared to the septuagenarian Reagan, the Soviet leadership seemed decrepit. Brezhnev, born in 1906, in power since 1964 and increasingly unwell since the mid-1970s, seemed the personal embodiment of the stagnation, corruption, and lack of idealism over which he presided. Even the KGB connived in scurrilous attacks on him before his death, which came in November. He was succeeded by the KGB chief, Yuri Andropov, 8 years younger, who seemed intelligent and decisive, who had served abroad and was reputed to have some liking for US culture, and who had strong support from Gromyko and Defence Minister Ustinov. But any hopes that Andropov would bring greater openness and imagination to superpower relations quickly faded. A loyal Communist and strict disciplinarian, who hoped to root out the crime and corruption of the Brezhnev era, his initial vigour was soon sapped by kidney failure. His mind remained clear but from February 1983 he relied on a dialysis machine. Suspicious of Reagan, Andropov nonetheless agreed that an attempt must be made to work with him and even exchanged some private messages with the White House over the summer, in which both sides professed a readiness to talk and a desire for peace. But on 1 September one of the few crises of the new Cold War suddenly occurred, when a South Korean airliner, code named KAL 007, was shot down by a Soviet warplane (see boxed section). Such an isolated incident was never likely to lead to war, but it soured East–West relations once more. Most Western countries denied landing rights to the Soviet airline, Aeroflot, as a sanction. On 28 September Andropov declared it was impossible to deal with the 'militarist' Reagan administration.

The KAL 007 Incident

KAL 007 was a regular Korean Air Lines flight from Anchorage, Alaska to Seoul, South Korea which was shot down by a Soviet jet fighter over the Sea of Japan on 1 September 1983. The Boeing 747 had 269 people on board, including 61 Americans, one of them a Congressman, the right-wing Larry McDonald of Georgia. The airliner was flying well off course and had been inside Soviet airspace over Kamchatka, as well as the island of Sakhalin, before two missiles were fired at it. Evidence from the USSR suggests that the Soviets mistook it for an American RC-135 spy plane (another of these was operating near Kamchatka at the time) and that they brought it down in haste, as it left their airspace, having taken a considerable amount of time to intercept it. There has been intense speculation about why the Boeing, with its experienced crew, could have been so far off course and why so little wreckage was recovered, with some conspiracy theories claiming that it was on a spying mission or that, rather than being brought down, it landed in Kamchatka. Others simply put the flight path down to pilot error, which some deemed impossible without resetting the plane's automatic navigation equipment, and the lack of wreckage down to the disintegration of the aircraft due to the force of impact.

At the time the incident was exploited by the Reagan administration to embarrass the Soviets, with claims being made that they knew it was a civilian airliner. American intercepts of Soviet military messages were released to try to prove this was the case. In retaliation the US and many other Western powers suspended landing rights for the Soviet national airline, Aeroflot, for some weeks. The response from Moscow was unapologetic and defensive, highlighting the regime's incompetence when it came to managing public opinion. The incident was, however, a short-lived, isolated act by the USSR which never threatened serious results and, a month later, global attention was focused on US actions in the Caribbean, with the invasion of Grenada.

Early Signs of a Thaw, 1983–1985

The US President too could seem blinkered in outlook and ready to risk nuclear war. In August 1984 he was heard joking about the subject. Easy-going in his approach to work, Reagan found it difficult to master complex issues and also found it difficult to deal with the idea that as President he should exercise a decisive influence on government. He often expected his staff to make policy and simply to tell him what required explaining to the people. His administration's decision-making process was therefore chaotic leading his first Secretary of State, Alexander Haig, to resign after less than 18 months, complaining 'there was no description of duty, no rules, no expression of the essential authority of the President to guide his subordinates.'[14] Reagan also surrounded himself with equally strong anti-communists like the Defense Secretary, Casper Weinberger, the National Security Adviser (1982–3), William Clark, and the ambassador to the UN, Jeanne Kirkpatrick. The last was ready to assist virtually any anti-communist regime, however dictatorial and distasteful, on the grounds that they might one day evolve into democracies; whereas communists were beyond the pale and could never change into liberal states. But Haig's successor at the State Department, George Shultz, brought a calmer, more patient approach to foreign policy. In their first conversation, Dobrynin found 'Shultz was at ease and did not use the sharp expressions characteristic of Haig. He conducted the conversation in a more businesslike manner.'[15] Shultz favoured a more positive policy, emphasizing Reagan's desire for peace and displaying a greater readiness than his colleagues to seek negotiations with Moscow. In a meeting on 25 March, Reagan listened to an outline of Shultz's approach and declared 'If Andropov is willing to do business then so am I.'[16] Two months later the Secretary of State argued before the Senate Foreign Relations Committee that it was possible to have a 'constructive dialogue' with Moscow on arms control, regional problems, even human rights, alongside a policy of firmness. This caused some confusion in the press and was very different from the 'linkages' approach of the 1970s, but it was little different to the old formula of 'negotiation from strength'. Shultz took the key element in his statement to be the declaration that 'strength and realism can deter war, but only direct dialogue and negotiation can open the path toward lasting peace.'[17] True, it proved difficult to execute. A new, $10 billion grain deal with the Soviets in July 1983 was followed by talk in Washington of a Reagan–Andropov summit, but then came the KAL 007 crisis, which left even Shultz livid at Soviet insensitivity, followed by the US invasion of Grenada (see Chapter 18, 3), where the troubled left-wing regime had close links to Castro's Cuba. In November the deployment of new, intermediate-range, US nuclear missiles (INF) in Western Europe led the Soviets to break off talks on nuclear arms control which had been underway in a desultory fashion for 2 years (see Chapter 16, C). And, at the same time, NATO carried out 'Exercise Able Archer', the largest ever 'war game'—so grand in scale that, as the spy Oleg Gordievsky reported to his British handlers, many Soviet experts feared it was a cover for an actual attack on the USSR. Elements of the Red defence forces were even placed on war standby. When provided with intelligence information of such Soviet fears, Reagan acknowledged 'it's something to think about' and the experience may have fuelled his desire to reduce nuclear arsenals.[18]

Yet, whatever the sense of tension in the closing months of 1983, there were signs that relations were about to improve. Shultz had never believed that a real change in superpower relations would be possible until the long-awaited INF deployment was completed. Once it was, Reagan could be persuaded that the West was in an excellent situation to pursue negotiation from strength. The President also recognized that a less bellicose policy could help him win a second term in the 1984 election and there was

concern in Washington at the evidence—some of it from the Soviet spy, Oleg Gordievsky, who had defected to Britain—that Moscow really did expect an American attack. The death of Andropov in February 1984 brought another ageing and ill leader to the General Secretaryship: Konstantin Chernenko, a Brezhnev loyalist with no overseas experience, seemed if anything a step backwards. But Chernenko, who had fully supported détente in the 1970s, left foreign policy in the hands of the experienced Gromyko and was ready to enter into a new exchange of messages with Reagan. The Eastern bloc's decision to boycott the 1984 Los Angeles Olympics was not a serious setback because it was a predictable act of revenge for the US boycott of Moscow 4 years before. No great breakthroughs were likely in a Presidential election year but the first Reagan–Gromyko meeting, on 28 September, was one of the most hopeful signs in superpower relations since 1979 and led to growing expectations of a new round of nuclear arms talks. Enraged as they were by America's INF deployment, the Soviets really needed such negotiations if they were to prevent Washington pulling ahead in the arms race. Reagan's landslide re-election was followed by two rounds of Shultz–Gromyko meetings, in November and January, which led to an agreement to resume negotiations in Geneva on both INF and strategic weapons. In retrospect it was easy to forget that, although these talks began on 12 March, one day after Mikhail Gorbachev became the Soviet leader, they had actually been planned under the unfortunate, colourless Chernenko.

Ronald Reagan and his Key Advisers

For the first 50 years of his life, Ronald Reagan seemed an unlikely prospect for the Presidency. Born in 1911 in Tampico, Illinois and educated at the little-known Eureka College, his first job was as a sports announcer on the radio before he entered film work. A well-known 'B-movie' actor, he made over fifty films between his debut in 1937 and his entry into full-time politics in 1964. His political interests first became obvious in 1947 when he became president of the Screen Actors' Guild, taking a leading role over the next few years in rooting out left-wing influences in Hollywood. In 1962 he switched from the Democrats to the Republicans, becoming a leading supporter of the

extreme right-winger Barry Goldwater in the 1964 Presidential election. Goldwater was crushingly defeated by Lyndon Johnson but the ever-resilient and confident Reagan went on to be elected Governor of California in 1966. His policies of tax cuts and restrictions on spending proved popular and he was re-elected Governor in 1970. Following unsuccessful bids for the Republican nomination in the 1968, 1972, and 1976 Presidential elections, Reagan finally triumphed over the luckless Jimmy Carter in 1980, particularly by exploiting the state of the economy.

As President, Reagan's domestic policies echoed those he had followed in California, with tax reductions and limits on social spending. But his external policies included massive defence expenditure, which resulted in a growing budget deficit. In his first term he pursued a determinedly anti-Soviet line, condemning the Kremlin's 'evil Empire' and providing aid to anti-communist 'freedom fighters' (under the 'Reagan Doctrine'). In his second term he seemed to reach the early stages of senility and his administration was discredited by the 'Irangate' scandal. But he also had remarkable successes to claim in foreign policy, as a process of conciliation began with Gorbachev's USSR. By 1988 Reagan could even claim that the Cold War was reaching its end and that this military expenditure had helped to break the back of the Soviet economy, although others argued that deep-seated problems had existed in the Eastern bloc even before Reagan came into office and that it was Gorbachev's policies that did most to end the Cold War.

His first Secretary of State, Alexander Haig (b. 1924), a former army general, White House chief of staff during the Watergate scandal, and then Supreme Allied Commander in Europe, found it particularly difficult to adjust to the uncertainty of the Reagan White House. Haig's successor, George Shultz (b. 1920), however, adapted well to Reagan's work methods and survived until the end of the Presidency. A former professor of industrial relations, Shultz had served under Nixon in several positions, most significantly Secretary of the Treasury (1972–4). Known as the 'Buddha' for his cautious, thoughtful approach to policy-making, he was ready to support such tough actions as the 1982 deployment of a US force in Lebanon

and the 1983 invasion of Grenada, but seemed more at home building up fruitful relations with the Soviets after 1985.

Shultz frequently differed with the equally long-lasting Secretary of Defense, Caspar Weinberger (b. 1917), a lawyer and business leader who had also served in the Nixon Cabinet, but who had been Reagan's financial director in California in the late 1960s. More outspoken than Shultz, Weinberger was always personally close to Reagan, supervised military expansion with enthusiasm, and supported a strong policy against the Soviets. He finally retired in November 1987, being succeeded for the administration's last year by Frank Carlucci. The primacy of Shultz and Weinberger was helped by Reagan's failure to appoint any National Security Adviser (NSA) who survived in the post for long. Reagan's first NSA, Richard Allen, survived less than a year because he was surrounded by allegations of financial misconduct. William Clark survived for longer but his lack of foreign policy experience drew ridicule and he was moved in October 1983 to be Secretary of the Interior. Robert McFarlane was then NSA until December 1985 but his influence was blunted by a feud with the White House Chief of Staff, Donald Regan. Admiral John Poindexter was forced to resign in December 1986, after only a year, because of involvement in the 'Irangate' scandal; Frank Carlucci then took up the post until November 1987; and that left only one year to serve for Reagan's last NSA, General Colin Powell, who later went on to be Chairman of the Joint Chiefs of Staff (1989–93) and, in 2001, Secretary of State.

B. **The Polish Crisis of 1980–1982**

The Emergence of Solidarity

The confrontation between the two blocs which reappeared in earnest as Ronald Reagan became President also featured difficulties within the Eastern bloc and indicated Moscow's initial determination to continue suppressing reform or dissent.

In Poland low growth, uncompetitive exports, and a desire to pave the way for economic reform, led the regime of Wladislaw Gomulka, with its 'nationalist' brand of communism, in December 1970 to recommend price increases. This sparked the already

hard-pressed shipworkers of the Baltic ports to riot and they attacked Communist Party offices and set up their own 'workers councils'. The shooting of strikers at Gdynia further inflamed the situation and led the Communist Party—as in 1956 (see Chapter 6, A)—to decide on a change of leader, partly to prevent any Soviet action. Edvard Gierek, a competent administrator, replaced Gomulka, withdrew the price increases and promised to consult about reforms in future. The situation then eased, until another round of strikes in 1976, but the lesson was not forgotten: by organizing themselves, industrial workers (supposedly the backbone of any Marxist revolution) had forced a reversal of policy and even a change of government.

At the end of the 1970s, Poland, a predominantly agricultural country, had run up debts to the West of nearly $20 billion. It even faced the humiliation of being a net food importer and its independent peasantry, unique in the Eastern bloc, were able to demand higher prices for their produce, so that the government was forced to hold down consumer costs by using substantial subsidies. In 1978 the election of a Pole as Pope John Paul II stirred up nationalist sentiment and underlined the importance of Roman Catholicism in the supposedly atheist regime, a Papal visit in 1979 drawing huge crowds. The 'appropriation of national symbols . . . by the Church left the state in an unusually weak position . . . a competition that the party-state simply could not win', at least in the long term.[19]

The USSR had always feared serious trouble in Poland, a large state, strategically placed between itself and Germany, with a strong anti-Russian tradition in the eastern part of the country. And John Paul II's success helped inspire a KGB propaganda campaign, in Eastern Europe and the West, against Catholicism. It was against this economic and political background, and faced by negative growth rates, that in 1980 Gierek reluctantly came to the same conclusion as Gomulka a decade before: if the Polish economy were ever to be reformed price subsidies had to be removed. This also coincided with a growing sense of foreboding in Eastern Europe because of the death in May, of Yugoslavia's veteran leader, Marshal Tito. Washington had warned Moscow not to exploit the uncertainty in Yugoslavia and the Soviets were careful not to do so. Serious unrest in Yugoslavia was avoided but in Poland, on 3 May, a group of workers was arrested for trying to set up unofficial 'workers committees' to press for reform. It was a sign of what was to come.

In early July 1980, in a striking parallel to events in 1970, the introduction of meat price increases sparked off a new round of unrest, focused on the Baltic ports. On 14 August, the dismissal of a worker, led to a strike being called in the Gdansk shipyard, where Lech Walesa soon emerged as a leading figure, and the strikes then began to spread, with the workers demanding free trades unions as well as better pay. At this point the strikers 'made no claim to be attacking the mainsprings of the party's power. The lessons of 1968 had been learned.'[20] With the country paralysed and widespread food shortages, the government on 31 August again caved into workers' demands, granting wage increases, a review of sentences on political prisoners, the broadcasting of religious services, and promising a free trades union, Solidarity. This agreement, 'although radical and a challenge to the system . . . fell within the accepted parameters of the Brezhnev doctrine' because it recognized 'the leading role of the party and . . . the established system of international alliances.'[21] But, in contrast to 1970 and 1976, these concessions were not followed by a return to calm. Instead ten million Poles rushed to join Solidarity which became an important political force in its own right, a workers' organization independent of the communist regime. Only when the government formally recognized Solidarity, in November, did the strike wave recede. By then Gierek had handed power (in September) to Stanislaw Kania, Solidarity was demanding liberal political reforms, and the Communist Party seemed to be disintegrating. As the Reagan administration entered office, many expected Soviet military intervention in Poland to restore communism on the lines of 1956 and 1968.

International Dimensions of the Crisis

'Martial law in Poland opened the 1980s with yet another demonstration of the limits to change in Eastern Europe.'[22] Once serious trouble broke out, the Soviets jammed Western broadcasts to the country, the Politburo set up a special commission to monitor the situation, and, as the CIA correctly deduced, contingency plans were made for a possible armed intervention with the aid of other 'fraternal' countries, namely East Germany and Czechoslovakia. Military manouevres began on the Polish border with the purpose of intimidating Solidarity. Solidarity, like the Roman Catholic Church, was seen as a 'counter-revolutionary' force in Moscow, an affront to the Brezhnev doctrine, exploiting Poland's economic malaise and national pride to threaten the communist system here and throughout the Soviet bloc, even inside the USSR itself. In October Gromyko told the Politburo that the loss of Poland was unacceptable, in November the East German government urged intervention, and on 3 December, in one of his last significant acts as President, Jimmy Carter sent a hot-line message to the Kremlin warning it to avoid military action. At a Warsaw Pact meeting 2 days later even Ceauşescu expressed concern about developments in Poland, but Kania requested more time to deal with the situation and Brezhnev decided to delay plans for an armed intervention. He realized that such a step would not only harm East–West relations, but could prove very costly in money and lives if the Poles resisted and a long-term occupation were needed. There was an alternative way to restore order and that was by *internal* action, as with Gomulka in 1956, but this time using the Polish armed forces. The Polish police and army remained loyal to Communism and even Kremlin hardliners like Ustinov (Defence) and Andropov (KGB) believed internal action was preferable to the use of Soviet forces. To pave the way for this, on 10 February 1981, General Wojtech Jaruzelski, the former Defence Minister, was made Prime Minister. Eight months later he replaced Kania as General Secretary, further highlighting the fact that it was the military that now maintained communism in Poland. Indeed 'Party leadership was barely evident in any real sense' and the regime was 'sustained by the influence of politically active generals'.[23]

After several strike-free weeks Solidarity was surprised and concerned by Jaruzelski's appointment to the Premiership. An outbreak of violence in March led to widespread expectation of martial law being introduced, but instead peace was restored—and a planned general strike avoided—when the government promised to punish those guilty of police brutality. While the Kremlin increasingly saw little alternative to martial law, Jaruzelski alternatively spoke of reconciliation and condemned Solidarity for provoking instability. In November 1981, he even tried to make peace with Walesa face-to-face. But the latter's demand for democracy and a share in power was difficult to meet and, having decided that direct Soviet intervention was all but impossible, Brezhnev demanded that Jaruzelski himself must act

forcefully. It has been argued that Jaruzelski had been 'expecting Soviet troops to be sent' and that he suffered a 'lack of confidence that the martial law operation would succeed'. What would have happened if he had refused to act, or if he had acted and failed, is not clear because the Soviets were so reluctant to become embroiled in a Polish war that they refused even to guarantee him military aid if he ran up against strong opposition. But he later insisted, 'nobody can say that I lacked in decisiveness or self-control'; and it is certainly true that on 12–13 December he acted successfully.[24] Using the excuse that Solidarity had again considered a general strike Jaruzelski took the union by surprise, introduced martial law, and arrested 200,000 Solidarity supporters, ruling Poland through a Military Council for National Reconciliation. Independent trades unions were banned, Solidarity was forced underground, and the Polish population was so fearful that substantial price increases were peacefully accepted.

The introduction of martial law in Poland 'achieved its immediate aims with tolerable success' even if the attempt to resolve the country's internal problems by force 'could only be transitional'.[25] The Soviets had avoided the grave risks of intervention and trouble was avoided elsewhere in the Eastern bloc. Indeed, in the rest of Eastern Europe there was remarkable political stability, despite the deep economic problems. Jaruzelski defended his action on the grounds that it avoided Soviet intervention and bloodshed, and that it did not prevent political change in Poland. Imprisoned Solidarity members were gradually released including, in November 1982, Walesa. The following month martial law was suspended. The international costs were limited. The US and other Western powers condemned Jaruzelski's action and the Reagan administration was keen to restrict trade with the Eastern bloc. This was not only due to Polish events but also because, in contrast to the détente era, some Washington officials wished to end Soviet access to Western technology and put the USSR's economy under pressure. In December 1981, after months of argument, Reagan prohibited American firms from cooperating with a planned Siberian pipeline project, which would bring Soviet natural gas to Western Europe. The ban affected European firms

Lech Walesa (b. 1943)

Walesa was brought up in a poor peasant family in eastern Poland, with a strong Catholic faith and an early aversion to Communist rule. Trained as a mechanic, he began to work as an electrician in the Gdansk shipyards, following a period of military service, and was first identified as a leader of protests during the strike wave of 1970 that ended Wladyslaw Gomulka's domination of Polish government. Sacked in 1976, he nonetheless tried to organize independent trades unions to press for workers' rights and, in August 1980, became a major figure in the strikes in the Lenin shipyard. As the Polish government seemed uncertain how to respond, Walesa was catapulted onto the international stage, becoming the leading figure in the Solidarity union and making several foreign visits. In 1981–2, as Communist authority was re-established by General Jaruzelski, Walesa was interred but his reputation as an opponent of oppression was confirmed by the award of the 1983 Nobel Peace Prize. He re-emerged to lead Solidarity in further discontent in 1987–8, saw trades unions legalized in 1989, and did much to break the Communist monopoly on power. In December 1990 he was the obvious choice to be elected the first President of a post-Communist Poland. However, economic problems tarnished his image and he lost the next elections in 1995.

manufacturing pipeline components under US licence. But this simply provoked a serious dispute in the Western alliance, especially after Reagan tried to apply the prohibition to US subsidiaries in Europe. Even Britain's Margaret Thatcher objected to such domineering behaviour by her ally and Reagan was forced to reverse his policy later in the year. One reason why he backed down was the need to reunite NATO ahead of its next challenge, the long-awaited introduction of new US INF weapons into Europe.

C. Nuclear Arms Control and the 'Year of the Missile'

Posturing and Propaganda in 1981

The Reagan administration inherited a complicated situation where nuclear arms talks were concerned. Although the SALT II treaty (Chapter 14, E) had not been ratified by Congress, both superpowers had undertaken to abide by its terms and Carter had entered exploratory talks with the Soviets on a SALT III agreement. At the same time NATO was committed to its 1979 'dual-track' decision (Chapter 15, A) to seek talks on the reduction of intermediate-range nuclear forces (INF) whilst planning the deployment of US Cruise and Pershing II missiles in Europe, timetabling this for 1983. The last decision probably made it inevitable that meaningful talks on nuclear arms control were impossible before 1984 at the earliest. Many of the positions adopted by the superpowers on the subject before that were mere posturing, because the Kremlin could hope that the Cruise–Pershing decision would not be carried out: if it were not, then there was no need to limit Soviet forces through an intermediate-range nuclear arms treaty. In particular Moscow hoped that anti-nuclear movements in Western Europe would persuade their governments not to make new missile deployments. Popular revulsion had already helped to defer production of the 'neutron bomb' in the late 1970s, and after 1979 nuclear disarmament groups grew in strength in West Germany, Britain, Holland, and elsewhere, fuelled by the new Cold War and by the fears raised over Reagan's anti-Communist rhetoric. Exploratory talks on INF weapons in October–November 1980 had suggested the two sides were far apart, with NATO only anxious to control land-based weapons but the Soviets keen to limit sea and air-based systems (which could more readily be deployed outside Europe) as well. These positions reflected the differing concerns of the two sides in a situation where SS-20s were already being deployed, whereas the Cruise and Pershing II missiles had yet to arrive in Europe but NATO had British sea-launched missiles and the Soviets faced a threat from the French deterrent. For the Soviets the increased fire-power stemming from the SS-20 replacing SS-4s and SS-5s equalized a European balance from which strategic US weapons were excluded. The West was keen to remove the threat from the land-based, mobile, and multi-warhead SS-20s if possible without having to face the financial cost and unpopularity of a Cruise–Pershing deployment; but the Soviets, with a superiority in land-based INF deployments, were keener to control Cruise missiles because these were a flexible weapon (either land-, sea-, or air-based) that could escape radar detection once launched.

Reagan's earliest moves on the nuclear front were hardly calculated to reassure his European critics. In May 1981 he restated the fact that America was under no legal obligation to fulfil SALT II, in August he announced the stockpiling of neutron bombs (though only in the US), and in October his new armaments programme included a strategic bomber project, which Carter had earlier cancelled. Reagan's policy was, in part, predicated on the argument that the USSR might soon stride ahead in the nuclear arms race, despite the fact that, when he arrived in office, America actually outmatched the Soviets' total of 6,000 warheads by over 50 per cent: only 2 years later did the CIA admit that, since 1976, it had greatly overestimated Soviet military spending; and only in April 1983 did a commission under Brent Scowcroft report that US nuclear defences were quite adequate, ending fears of a 'window of vulnerability'. But the Reagan–Weinberger policy was also 'designed to give priority to autarkic reliance on American military power . . . rather than the pursuit of . . . arms control' and it was accompanied by claims of a 'decade of neglect' of US defences in the 1970s.[26] In September 1981 Gromyko and Secretary of State Haig agreed to begin INF talks in Geneva within 2 months but the posturing of both sides ahead of this date was clear. The Soviets, for example, notably in a speech by Gromyko to the UN on 22 September, pressed NATO to agree to a universal renunciation of the 'first use' of nuclear weapons in a conflict. This was a clever propaganda move which the Soviets knew the Western powers would reject: NATO was inferior to the Warsaw Pact in

conventional weapons and had always planned to use nuclear arms in a response to any offensive from the East. But on 20 October, Brezhnev repeated the call for a 'no first-use' commitment. For his part Reagan attempted to steal the propaganda limelight on 18 November with a proposal for the complete destruction of INF weapons on both sides. This was the first time that the so-called 'zero option'— an idea that emerged from the German Social Democratic Party—had been officially adopted and it sounded a bold, imaginative initiative. But the Americans knew that the Soviets would never easily surrender their INF arsenal, the only nuclear area where they had a clear advantage over the West (if British and French weapons were excluded), especially ahead of the 1983 Cruise–Pershing deployment. Reagan had made his proposal knowing it would not be accepted, hence the argument that, while the zero option 'shored up political support in NATO countries for . . . deployment, the principal purpose of the administration, it also killed the prospect for serious negotiation.'[27] Only in the late 1980s did the 'zero option' become a serious proposal when, to American surprise, the Kremlin came round to the idea. Yet there is some evidence that, while being tough in negotiations, Reagan also had a hankering after controlling the arms race. Thus Casper Weinberger insisted that Reagan, 'contrary to virtually all the popular myths about him . . . had been very unhappy about the need to rely on nuclear weapons.'[28] Also, even if Reagan's proposal was no more than a propaganda, or time-buying, exercise, the Kremlin response was equally unconstructive. 'The Soviet negotiating position was designed to avoid . . . reductions in the SS-20s, while at the same time preventing NATO from acquiring a "unilateral advantage" with the Pershing IIs and Tomahawks.'[29] They now proposed a freeze on INF deployments (thus freezing their own SS-20 deployment) and wanted to count in the 'zero option' all nuclear systems 'intended for use' in Europe (a difficult concept to define, but including jet aircraft and the British and French deterrents). The US was never likely to negotiate on this basis, but it meant that the British and French systems, excluded from SALT, would also be excluded from disarmament talks pertaining to nuclear weapons in Europe.

INF and START, 1981–1983

The INF talks got underway on schedule on 30 November 1981, and there were soon fears that the Americans would link them to the Polish crisis, a possibility which, however, Haig ruled out in late January. Shortly afterwards the US rejected a proposal by Brezhnev to reduce INF numbers in Europe by two-thirds because the Soviets could deploy such systems in Asia: the mobile SS-20 could easily be redeployed to Europe in a crisis and the US had always been determined to restrict *total* INF figures, whether in Europe or beyond. Then in March Brezhnev tried another ploy to impress the West European peace movements and dissuade Washington from deploying the Cruises and Pershings. Of the 350 SS-20s deployed so far, about 240 were in Europe, but now he announced that no more would be sent to that theatre. Instead the future build-up would take place against China. Again, however, the ability of the Soviets to redeploy the SS-20s *in future*, ensured a US rejection of the proposal. Exactly how far either side was genuinely interested in arms control is unclear. Nonetheless, it is significant that, in mid-1982, when the two chief arms control negotiators from each side (America's Paul Nitze and the USSR's Yuri Kvitsinsky) drew up a dramatic scheme for INF limits, it was quickly rejected. Their July 'walk in the woods' deal would basically have limited each superpower to only seventy-five INF weapons in Europe, but the US Department of Defence argued that this would still leave Moscow at an advantage because the mobile SS-20s were more powerful than slow-moving Cruise missiles and the US would have to cancel deployment of the Pershing II. Haig's successor Shultz was anxious to show the West Europeans that America took the INF talks seriously, but the failure of the 'walk in the woods' seemed to support Soviet claims that the opposite was true (though there was no guarantee that Moscow would have accepted the proposal either). Another offer to reduce SS-20 deployments by the newly appointed Andropov in December came to nothing and in 1983 both sides waited on the outcome of the Cruise–Pershing deployment.

Meanwhile there had also been some movement on the strategic weapons front where Reagan, despite his hard-line persona, had a real interest in reaching

agreement. In May 1982, in a speech at Eureka College, he proposed that in future these should be 'Strategic Arms Reduction Talks' (START), an acronym designed to sound more positive than SALT. 'I decided that if we were to participate with the Russians in arms control talks, our goal should be to *reduce* nuclear weapons, not just limit their rate of increase, which is what past nuclear arms control agreements had done.'[30] Shortly afterwards he reiterated that America would adhere to the SALT II limits as long as the USSR did, and he successfully pressed for the START talks to begin in June in Geneva. But the US found it extremely difficult to agree on a detailed negotiating position and the talks immediately fell victim to the same mutual distrust, posturing, and slow progress which marred the INF discussions. In October, shortly before his death, Brezhnev accused Reagan of wanting nuclear war and in December the Kremlin condemned the US President for his decision to proceed with the deployment of the 'heavy', strategic MX missile, originally planned under Carter. In 1983 the accusations and counter-accusations continued with the US focusing attention on the Soviet decision to build a radar station at Krasnoyarsk, in Siberia, well away from the periphery of the USSR and therefore in contravention of the 1972 ABM treaty. Planned since 1979, there can be no doubt that this was a deliberate breach of the treaty, even if the Soviets saw it as a minor one.

The most celebrated step on the strategic arms front in 1983 was Reagan's 23 March announcement of the Strategic Defence Initiative (SDI), or Star Wars programme. Even Shultz, who only saw the announcement a day or two before, admitted 'I had been surprised by the idea' and acknowledged 'the vision came from Ronald Reagan'.[31] SDI was designed to create a defensive shield against incoming nuclear missiles, perhaps with space-based laser or particle-beam weapons. In one sense it was nothing new, since experiments on such weapons had already been carried out under Carter. In any case, many Western experts believed that the initiative would be expensive and fruitless; many dismissed the idea of space-based laser defences as pure science fiction, a fantastic product of the President's Hollywood past. The truth was probably more complex. Reagan did honestly believe it was morally right to seek protection from a nuclear attack, in which he feared that up to half the American population would be killed, and he even spoke of sharing a successful SDI system with the Kremlin. But he was certainly naïve in not realizing that the initiative would revitalize Soviet fears of US technological prowess and undermine deterrence. In 1975 the US had scrapped its previous ABM programme and the threat of 'Mutually Assured Destruction' by second-strike forces remained. But a successful SDI—which, however unlikely, had now to be considered—could render the existing Soviet nuclear arsenal redundant, forcing them to invest in a costly, similar programme or vastly to expand their nuclear arsenal, in order to try and nullify the proposed US system by force of numbers. SDI could only add to the growing belief in Moscow that Reagan was determined to humiliate or defeat the USSR, possibly in a nuclear war. Hence a Soviet general's warning to the Warsaw Pact in April that war was a real possibility. The Soviets criticized the initiative as a breach of the 1972 ABM treaty (which had forbidden development of new ABM systems) far worse than the Krasnoyarsk radar.

The 'Year of the Missile' and a Year without Talks

Whatever the ructions provoked by SDI, 1983 became the 'year of the missile' because of the INF debate, not because of strategic weapons developments. 'The most prominent struggle between Washington and Moscow in 1983 was over influence in Europe, specifically the battle over deployment of the new US intermediate-range missiles.'[32] As the deadline for the Cruise–Pershing deployment approached the Soviets shifted their propaganda campaign from one of offering concessions to one of making threats. In April 1983 Gromyko rejected a fresh offer from Reagan to cancel the US deployment, if the Soviets scrapped all their INF weapons, and warned that the arrival of the Cruise and Pershing IIs would lead them to walk out of the INF and START talks. The prospect of escalating international tension gave further impetus to the West European peace movements who, in late October, launched a series of large-scale demonstrations.

Nevertheless, on 14–15 November the INF deployments went ahead in Britain and a week later the West German parliament, too, agreed to accept them. The first Pershing IIs arrived on 23 November, described by Shultz as 'D-Day': he feared that 'demonstrations could break the will of Allied governments' and 'undermine our resolve to stand up to the Soviets in future'. Indeed, overcoming the demonstrators had arguably become Washington's main concern, one far removed from 1979, when it had been hoped that deployment would 'reinforce deterrence . . . reassure the allies, and . . . enhance allied unity . . . All of these aims were, to some degree, casualties' by 1983.[33] So too was the hope that the threat of deployment would induce the Soviets to negotiate an INF treaty, for now the Soviets carried out their threat to leave the Geneva talks. They walked out of the INF sessions on 23 November and the START talks were adjourned on 8 December without setting a date for future meetings. The following week the Vienna-based talks on conventional arms restriction, the Mutual Balanced Force Reduction (MBFR) talks, underway since the early 1970s, were also adjourned without the promise of further contacts. 'For the first time in nearly 15 years, the Americans and the Soviets were no longer negotiating in any forum.'[34]

With the Soviets' simultaneous fear that NATO's 'Operation Able Archer' might be the cover for an actual attack, the situation for European security at the end of 1983 seemed bleak indeed. Furthermore, Moscow insisted in December on proceeding with new INF deployments of its own. This move upset the usually loyal Erich Honecker of East Germany, whose country became, along with Czechoslovakia, the base for the additional SS-20s. He nonetheless agreed to cancel a planned visit to West Germany but another usually loyal ally, Todor Zhirkov of Bulgaria, underlined his own fear of the rising European tension by proceeding with a similar visit. Meanwhile NATO, with its deployments completed after so much doubt and tension, felt more confident about entering new INF talks from a position of strength. This situation, along with the forthcoming Presidential election, gave Reagan a strong incentive to avoid further confrontation. 1984 in fact proved oddly quiescent in superpower relations: with the

Margaret Thatcher (b. 1925)

The British Conservative Prime Minister was born in the provincial town of Grantham, the daughter of a grocer, but was educated at Oxford as a research chemist, married a wealthy businessman, and entered the House of Commons in 1959. She served as Education Minister in the 1970–4 government and was little known abroad when, in 1975, she challenged the incumbent Edward Heath for the party leadership. Her readiness to step forward as a representative of the Right won her wide respect and she eventually secured the leadership race against several better-known figures. In May 1979, helped by considerable social discontent, which undermined the Labour government, she won the Premiership. She was re-elected Prime Minister twice, in 1983 and 1987, and served in the position for the longest continuous period since 1812.

At home 'Thatcherism' pursued similar policies to those of the Reagan administration: taxes were cut, social spending restrained, private enterprise rewarded, and state intervention in the economy reduced. Abroad she made her name as a firm anti-Communist, America's most loyal ally in the 'New Cold War' of the early 1980s. But she was offended when Reagan invaded Grenada in 1983 because Britain had not been fully consulted on the invasion of this member of the Commonwealth. And in 1985 she quickly embraced Gorbachev as 'someone we can do business with'. On other issues she showed herself a strong defender of British national interests, opposing the extension of greater powers to the European Community (EC) and sending a force to reconquer the Falkland Islands, when they were occupied by Argentina in 1982. However, in 1989–90, after 10 years in power she seemed to many Conservative parliamentarians to be an electoral liability: she insisted on pursuing an unpopular reform of local taxation, she was opposed to German reunification, and she seemed increasingly unable to influence the course of EC debates. One of her last acts in office was to back a firm reaction to Saddam Hussein's invasion of Kuwait. After leaving office she continued to criticize the deepening of European integration.

Red Army bogged down in Afghanistan, the Polish crisis over, and other crises (the KAL 007 incident and invasion of Grenada) proving short-lived, there was no possible spark for an East–West conflagration. The Soviet refusal to talk to the West increasingly appeared an empty gesture, especially since Reagan seemed set to return to office for another 4 years. The MBFR talks were actually revived in March 1984, though the INF and START talks did not recommence for another year.

D. The War in Afghanistan to 1985

From Intervention to Embroilment

When the Soviets invaded Afghanistan at Christmas 1979 they hoped that their intervention might be of a limited scale and duration. They were well aware of the dangers of being dragged into a guerrillra war in difficult terrain, in defence of an unpopular government, and in the face of a determined enemy. But if a new, united government could be stabilized quickly under Babrak Karmal, and if the Afghan security forces remained loyal, then an early reduction in the Red Army presence might be possible. Despite the fears of Soviet designs on the Persian Gulf in America and elsewhere, Moscow had no ambitions to advance beyond Afghanistan and believed that Washington simply manipulated the crisis in order to reignite the Cold War. For the first few months, after the shock of the invasion, there was limited active opposition in Afghanistan itself to what had occurred. 'The Soviet invasion met with no armed resistance in the first month because its target was not the countryside, which was in a state of rebellion, but the . . . government itself.'[35] But unrest grew as winter progressed, with demonstrations in Kabul itself in February. Foreign intervention, accompanied as it was by the murder of the former leader, Hafizullah Amin, simply made the Marxist government in Kabul even more unpopular and, despite conscription, the Afghan army was reduced by desertion from 150,000 in early 1979 to no more than 35,000 men a year later, too few to maintain order. Soon, despite their original fears, the Red Army found itself having to take over the prosecution of the war. 'Conceived as a quick and decisive military operation, which would be followed by a rapid withdrawal of Soviet forces, the intervention in Afghanistan became the USSR's Vietnam.'[36] When the KGB chief, Andropov, visited Kabul in January 1980 it was clear that the Red Army would have to stay for some time. Andropov and Gromyko did study a possible political solution to the conflict, to pave the way for a Soviet withdrawal, but it was difficult to agree on what peace terms to offer to Afghan opposition groups. Global condemnation probably made it harder to consider retreat. The Soviets also hoped to negotiate from a position of strength, which simply did not exist at first. Besides, their opponents, the Mujaheddin, were both religiously inspired and divided among themselves, making negotiations doubly difficult. Indeed, when peace talks began in Geneva with a UN mediator, they were between the Soviet-backed Kabul regime and Pakistan, the Islamic state on whose territory the Mujaheddin leaderships were based. The talks did not begin until June 1982 and by the time of their fourth session, in August 1984, they had only just entered the 'proximity' stage—with the intermediary, Diego Cordovez, moving between the two delegations, who refused to meet face-to-face.

With the Afghan army so weak, the Soviets began to mount combat operations of their own against the Mujaheddin in February 1980, and the Red Army contingent of 50,000 men was soon increased to 80,000. Yet their 'presence spread and intensified the conflict from essentially a civil war among Afghans into primarily a national war of resistance to foreign invaders and their local puppets.'[37] Their generals did have contingency plans for a quick withdrawal and several realized that a political solution, based on a coalition government, was preferable to a long war that probably could not be won. However, the intervention soon assumed an air of permanency. Specialist counter-insurgency units were formed but the Soviets at first relied heavily on 'sweep offensives' with tanks and ground troops to root out their opponents. 'Soviet armed forces had very little

experience of dealing with insurgency . . . [They] had been trained for global war, not small war.'[38] Also, Soviet ideology was completely unprepared for war against a 'mass movement': the masses, after all, were supposed to be loyal to Marxism. But conventional methods proved ill-suited to a war against lightly armed guerrillas, in mountainous regions of extreme temperatures, who could find shelter and supplies in a neighbouring country, Pakistan. In late 1981 and during 1982 the Red Army turned more therefore to the use of lightly armed troops, with helicopters to improve mobility. It is unclear what impact political instability in Moscow had on the war. With Brezhnev in physical decline and then two rapid changes of leader, there was presumably a lack of commitment to a vigorous prosecution of the Afghan campaign. In 1984–5 Chernenko, though ill himself, evidently had hopes of winning the war quickly, rather than seeing it drag on. He launched six large-scale offensives, accompanied by heavy aerial bombing and raids on refugee camps in order to break enemy morale, albeit at the cost of greater Soviet casualties. In 1983 when the war seemed to be deadlocked, the wisdom of pursuing it was increasingly questioned in Moscow and Andropov seemed genuinely interested in negotiations, partly to allow him to tackle the USSR's domestic problems. A peace policy received no support from Reagan however, in the year of the 'evil Empire' speech, and it was opposed by Gromyko, Ustinov and the Chief of Staff, Nikolai Ogarkov. With the Mujaheddin fighting on in 1985, the conflict seemed as intractable as ever.

Despite their internal wranglings and faulty tactics it cannot be said that the Soviets were on the brink of defeat. Whatever the talk of a 'Soviet Vietnam' (see boxed section) they were careful not to escalate on the scale of the Americans in the earlier conflict. At its largest, in 1985, the Red Army presence only reached 108,000 and during the worst year for casualties, in 1984, it suffered only about 2,000 deaths in combat. Despite the continued division within the Afghan Communists (between the elitist, urban *Parcham* faction and the more extreme, rural *Khalq*), the Kabul government was not a complete liability. It was able to exploit differences among its opponents, to hold onto urban areas (where about 2 million of the 13 million Afghans lived), and to contribute to the war, not least through the expansion of the secret police, the KHAD. The Soviets were determined that any peace settlement should leave the communists in power (though possibly in a coalition government) and they were helped by the fact that the Kabul regime was a UN member, with widespread international recognition, whose opponents were rebels. The Soviets were also helped by the divided nature of the Mujaheddin, whose factions sometimes fought each other. There was no Afghan 'nationalism' in such a divided country. The Mujaheddin were willing to unite against communism and foreign intervention, but Afghanistan was made up of various ethnic groups (about 40 per cent were Pathans but there were also Turkomans, Tajiks, and others), who had a history of internal feuding and banditry, some of which reflected religious divisions between the majority Sunnis and minority Shi'as, some of which involved tribal warlords. One observer noted that 'warring factions have portioned out Afghanistan into separate ares of influence sharing nothing in common but hatred and lack of trust.'[39] Only in early 1986 did seven factions unite to form a single government-in-exile, but even the US felt it unwise to recognize it given the volatility of Mujaheddin politics. The guerrilla groups were resilient but ill-disciplined; experienced fighters but poorly armed. They were amateurish, lacking a united strategy, and without the heavy weapons, which might have threatened the Soviet hold on Afghanistan's towns and cities. The disparate nature of the opposition was 'in one sense a strength however: if the Soviets should succeed in destroying a few groups, many would be left. Like a bear attacked by a swarm of bees, the Soviet army [was] being hit from all directions.'[40]

External Involvement in the War

One advantage that the Mujaheddin had was the scale of external assistance. In the face of the early Soviet offensives, between two and three million refugees fled Afghanistan, crossing the mountains to Iran and Pakistan. By 1985 their numbers had grown to about five million and Pakistan especially proved a protector, providing not only a refuge, but also

guerrilla bases, arms, training, and military advice. 'The American-led support of the Mujaheddin was a multinational effort. Pakistan was the key, as the base for the rebels and as the conduit' for outside aid.[41] Some Pakistani troops were even sent into Afghanistan, though only as observers. Pakistan's leader, General Zia ul-Haq, used the Soviet threat in 1979–80—when some expected a Red Army advance across the Pakistani border or through Iran to the Gulf—to unite Pakistan under his dictatorial role. He also used his position as a 'front-line' state opposing the communist advance to improve relations with the West, having been criticized in 1979 for the execution of the former Prime Minister, Ali Bhutto. And Zia especially made Pakistan a close ally of the United States. Already, after the fall of the Shah, Pakistan, a US ally for most of the time since 1954, had agreed to host electronic monitoring stations for the Americans, replacing those lost in Iran. The relationship had its opponents on both sides. Some in the State Department questioned the wisdom of relying on an oppressive regime which was trying to become a nuclear power, a development which would increase tensions with its neighbour, India. And the Pakistani Foreign Minister, Agha Shahi, resigned in February 1982 because he doubted the wisdom both of enraging the Soviet Union and relying on the Americans, whom he felt to be volatile and unreliable. Nevertheless, Zia and the army were convinced of the advantages of getting close to Washington and such thinking was encouraged by the White House, under both Carter and Reagan. Just as aid from the US, China, and Arab states was dependent on Pakistani goodwill, so Pakistan enjoyed 'prestige as a frontline state and substantial aid from Western states'.[42]

Zia was careful, however, not to provoke discontent in Afghanistan to the point that he actually risked Soviet invasion. He tried to control the Mujaheddin groups in exile, even breaking up an attempt by non-fundamentalist, Pathan factions to form a coalition in 1980 because he believed was not in Pakistan's interest. Traditionally the Pakistanis were suspicious of the Pathan predominance in Afghanistan and Zia preferred to back the fundamentalists, who were strong among the minority ethnic groups, and who were ready to create a new kind of Afghan state, a centralized theocracy with ties to the wider Islamic world, including Pakistan. Of course, the fundamentalists were opposed to Western influences, as well as to communism, but this did not prevent Zia from steering American aid towards them. Zia was determined not to be treated as a US satellite. He wanted greater US assistance for Pakistan itself, as well as for the Mujaheddin, and he rejected an early offer of aid from Washington because it was not substantial enough. In June 1981 such tactics paid off with a $3 billion package of economic and military aid over five years, including F-16 aircraft. As seen above, when peace talks began in 1982, it was Pakistan, a UN-recognized government, which negotiated, effectively, for the Mujaheddin. But again, Zia pursued his own interests too, refusing to deal with the Kabul regime, face-to-face, determined to remove Karmal, who was seen as a Soviet stooge, and equally determined at first to exclude the Afghan Communists from power entirely, rather than accept a coalition government with them.

Pakistan was not the only Islamic state to aid the Mujaheddin. Iran, Egypt, and Saudi Arabia were among the others providing assistance, the last with massive financial aid. Up to 2.5 million refugees were accommodated in Iran. The USSR's rival, China, another neighbouring state, also gave arms to the rebel groups. It was the Egyptians and Chinese who helped the CIA early in the war by sending some of their own Soviet-made weapons to the Mujaheddin. Once these arrived in Afghanistan it was difficult for the Soviets to prove their source: the Mujaheddin could easily claim they had captured them from the Red Army. Given that the Kabul government was a legally recognized regime, it would have been embarrassing to Washington to have US-made weapons being used in these early stages because it could have seemed that America was equally responsible for the war.

It was the US, however, which remained the backbone of the external effort to arm the Mujaheddin and pin the Red Army down in an unwinnable war. In early 1980 Carter's National Security Adviser, Zbigniew Brzezinski, was especially keen to put the Soviets 'on trial' before the court of world opinion and he opposed suggestions from the Secretary of State, Cyrus Vance, that talks might be opened with Moscow on Afghanistan and wider security concerns in the region. US aid was markedly increased in October 1980, despite the reluctance of the CIA Director, Stansfield Turner. Such American behaviour made it less likely that the Soviets would talk peace: they had no desire in 1980 to be put 'on trial' or to admit defeat. Indeed, US policy did not seem so much to be aimed at ending aggression and pacifying Afghanistan, as at causing maximum cost to the Kremlin. This continued under Reagan for whom, of course, anti-Sovietism was the prime motive behind his foreign policy. The new CIA director, William Casey, had none of Turner's qualms about aiding rebels and became the leading 'hawk' in Washington. He argued that, if the Soviets were tied down in Afghanistan, they were less likely to cause trouble elsewhere and he saw the 1982 opening of peace talks as a Kremlin ploy. Others were more cautious, ready to aid the Mujaheddin but reluctant to escalate the conflict. In 1981–3 Casey was unable to increase US aid to the Mujaheddin much beyond that planned under Carter (which was already considerable enough). There *were* substantial increases in 1984, but the continuation of the war and its intensification under Chernenko, still led some in Congress to claim that the CIA was not doing enough. The result was a further increase in US aid in 1985 to $250 million, including anti-aircraft weapons, which might counter the Red Army's use of helicopters and thus reduce its mobility. The CIA also encouraged the Pakistani intelligence services to stir up fundamentalist discontent in the USSR's Central Asian republics, where most of the population was Muslim. In March 1985, as Mikhail Gorbachev came into power, the Afghan war raged as intensively as ever. That same month President Reagan, whose inaugural speech in January had confirmed his support for less developed world 'freedom fighters', decided that the aim should no longer simply be to make the war costly for Moscow but to drive the Soviets out of Afghanistan.

Afghanistan and Vietnam: a Comparison

The Soviet War in Afghanistan was often compared at the time to the American war in Vietnam, and there were good reasons for talking of a 'Soviet Vietnam':

- both superpowers intervened to prop up a friendly regime in the face of ideological enemies;
- both Washington and Moscow were prepared to replace local leaders who failed to attract sufficient local support: Diem in South Vietnam in 1963 and Amin in Afghanistan in 1979;
- both found that the replacement of these leaders simply bred additional problems: Diem's overthrow was followed by years of political instability; Amin's undermined Soviet claims to have been 'invited' to intervene;
- both superpowers began with a limited intervention which gradually escalated to the point where withdrawal proved difficult and painful, putting national credibility at stake;
- both tried to use predominantly conventional tactics against a determined guerrilla enemy (the Viet Cong ideologically inspired, the Mujaheddin religiously inspired) in difficult terrain;
- both effectively took over the prosecution of the war from the country they were supposed to be defending, because its own armed forces proved inadequate; and both later concluded that this had been a mistake and so handed fighting back to their clients (the processes of 'Vietnamization' and 'Afghanization');
- both found that the cost of the war, in lives and money, drained national morale and had an important domestic political impact. The 'Vietnam syndrome' still affects US military activity. Some argue that the Afghan commitment did much to destroy Soviet Communism;
- both found it impossible to prevent neighbouring states providing succour and supplies to their enemies (China for North Vietnam, Pakistan for the Mujaheddin), whilst the other superpower also provided arms;
- both ultimately failed in their aims, created huge economic and refugee problems in the countries they 'assisted' and left behind insecure regimes which lost power after a few years.

There are however important limits to such comparisons and, at the very least, the Soviets can be said to have learnt from the earlier American experience:

- whereas US deployments in Vietnam topped half a million, the height of the Red Army involvement in Afghanistan was only about 108,000 and casualties were correspondingly less. Neither can the financial costs of the war cannot be said to have destroyed Soviet Communism;
- the Americans intervened in a country several thousand miles away, whereas Afghanistan bordered on the USSR, where it was easier to argue that Soviet interests were directly threatened;
- the Karmal regime in Kabul was more stable than those which succeeded Diem in Saigon; and the Mujaheddin were far less united than the Viet Cong and North Vietnamese;
- the US extended the war with bombings and major incursions into Laos and Cambodia, but the Soviets launched no major attacks on Afghanistan's neighbours, Pakistan and Iran;
- under Gorbachev the USSR was ultimately ready to begin a timetable for withdrawal without the promise of a long-term settlement, whereas the Nixon administration had effectively rejected such a course in Vietnam after 1969;
- Vietnam was reunited under a single government in 1975 and, though poverty-stricken, was then politically stable, whereas Afghanistan has been unstable since the collapse of the Communist government.

NOTES

1. Quoted in Raymond Garthoff, *The Great Transition* (Brookings Institution, Washington, DC, 1994), 8.

2. Richard A. Melanson, *American Foreign Policy since the Vietnam War* (Armonk, New York, 2nd edn., 1996), 142.

3. Odd Arne Westad, *The Fall of Détente: Soviet–American Relations during the Carter Years* (Scandinavian University Press, Oslo, 1997), 1 and 14.

4. Mike Bowker and Phil Williams, *Superpower Détente: a Reappraisal* (Sage, London, 1988), 250.

5. Andrei Gromyko, *Memories* (Hutchinson, London, 1988), 296.

6. Alexander Dobrynin, *In Confidence: Moscow's Ambassador to America's Six Cold War Presidents (1962–1986)* (Random House, New York, 1995), 484.

7. Ronald Reagan, *An American Life* (Hutchinson, London, 1990), 273.

8. Will Hutton *The World We're In* (Little, Brown, London, 2002), 106–10 citing Paul Krugman, *Peddling Prosperity* (Norton, New York, 1994) 135.

9. Thomas G. Patterson, *On Every Front: The Making and Unmaking of the Cold War* (W.W. Norton, New York, 1992 edn.), 199.

10. Coral Bell, quoted in Melanson, op. cit., 149.

11. Casper Weinberger, *Fighting for Peace: Seven Critical Years at the Pentagon* (Joseph, London, 1990), 25.

12. Gromyko, op. cit., 305.

13. Dobrynin, op. cit., 495.

14. Alexander Haig, *Caveat: Realism, Reagan and Foreign Policy* (Macmillan, New York, 1984), 355.

15. Dobrynin, op. cit., 508.

16. George Shultz, *Turmoil and Triumph* (Macmillan, New York, 1993), 270–1.

17. Ibid., 277.

18. Don Oberdorfer, *How the Cold War Came to an End: the US and the Soviet Union, 1983–90* (Jonathan Cape, London, 1992), 66–7.

19. George Schoplin, *Politics in Eastern Europe* (Blackwell, Oxford, 1993), 217.

20. Michael Waller, *The End of Communist Power Monopoly* (Manchester University Press, Manchester, 1993), 130.

21. Geoffrey and Nigel Swain, *Eastern Europe since 1945* (St Martin's Press, New York, 2nd edn., 1998), 168–9.

22. David Mason, *Revolution and Transition in East-Central Europe* (Westview Press, Boulder, 2nd edn., 1996), 41.

23. Paul Lewis, *Political Authority and Party Secretaries in Poland* (Cambridge University Press, Cambridge, 1989), 198.

24. For the debate see Mark Kramer, 'Jaruzelski, the Soviet Union and the Imposition of Martial Law in Poland', and Jaruzelski's 'Commentary', in *Cold War International History Project Bulletin*, 11 (Winter, 1998), quotes from 9 and 32.

25. Robin Edmonds, *Soviet Foreign Policy: the Brezhnev Years* (Oxford University Press, Oxford, 1983), 202.

26. Garthoff, op. cit., 505.

27. Ibid., 510.

28. Weinberger, op. cit., 240; see also Haig, op. cit., 222.

29. Strobe Talbott, *Deadly Gambits* (Picador, London, 1984), 87.

30. Reagan, op. cit., 549.

31. Shultz, op. cit., 261.

32. Oberdorfer, op. cit., 34.

33. Shultz, op. cit., 373. Garthoff, op. cit., 553.

34. Talbott, op. cit., 4.

35. Olivier Roy, *Islam and Resistance in Afghanistan* (Cambridge University Press, Cambridge, 1986), 118.

36. Geoffrey Roberts, *The Soviet Union in World Politics* (Routledge, New York, 1999), 81.

37. Henry Bradsher, *Afghanistan and the Soviet Union* (Duke University Press, Durham, 1983), 205.

38. Caroline Kennedy-Pipe, *Russia and the World* (Arnold, London, 1998), 165.

39. Raja Anwar, *The Tragedy of Afghanistan* (Verso, London, 1988), 238.

40. Thomas Hammond, *Red Flag over Afghanistan* (Westview, Boulder, 1984), 157.

41. Garthoff, op. cit., 713.

42. Anthony Hyman, *Afghanistan under Soviet Domination* (Macmillan, London, 3rd edn., 1992), 218.

17 Middle East Conflicts in the 1980s

A. Lebanon and the Israeli Invasion

The Israeli Invasion and the Multinational Force, 1982–1985

The Camp David settlement did not bring peace to the Middle East and merely confirmed that providing an Egyptian–Israeli settlement would not resolve the conflict between Israel and the Arab states, let alone with the Palestinians, nor bring stability and peace to the region. Sadat and Begin had achieved peace between Egypt and Israel and had met Israeli concerns with recognition and an acceptance of their right to live in peace. Egypt, for its part, had abandoned the myth of Arab unity between the competing states of the region and pursued national interests. Yet there were other conflicts being played out in the region, not least those arising from the Lebanese Civil War (see Chapter 14, B), which were adding to the fundamental failure to deal with the Palestinian question. In fact it could be argued that Camp David produced more regional

instability and increased the level of conflict between Israel and the Palestinians. The Israelis could rightly point out that their statehood had only been accepted by Egypt while the Palestinians could equally well point out that the problem of the refugees expelled from the homes and the right to a state in which to live in peace had equally not been addressed. The ideas of Ben Gurion about how a strong Israeli state could achieve peace with its Arab neighbours no longer seemed relevant. And Palestinian militants, expelled from one country after another were still able to inflict damage on Israel from within the troubled and chaotic state of Lebanon.

In June 1981 Israeli–Palestinian tensions began to rise and were to culminate in the next Middle Eastern military conflict the following year—the Israeli invasion of the Lebanon. The bombing of the Iraqi nuclear reactor at Osirak near Baghdad was followed later in the month by another Likud election victory and the appointment of Ariel

Sharon as Minister of Defence. Prime Minister Begin now relied on several right-wing parties for his majority and the new coalition spelt out its determination to interpret the Camp David agreement in line with its own requirements. The statement on Palestinian autonomy meant a guarantee that the Palestinians would never attain sovereignty over an independent state. At the end of the transition period Israel would make additional sovereignty claims including the Gaza strip. In the meantime settlement in the land of Israel was defined as a right and as essential for the nation's security. Tension continued to grow as the right-wing Likud government moved closer to full armed confrontation with the Palestinians in Lebanon. The installation of Syrian surface-to-air missiles in the Bekaa Valley and raids and shelling across the Lebanon–Israel border led to the 'Two Week War' in July 1981 which was only ended with the mediation of a US envoy, Philip Habib. 'America had now become involved in Lebanon and Reagan was staking a considerable amount of prestige on Washington's "honest broker" role.'[1] Likud attention now turned to Lebanon where the PLO had shown considerable constraint since the ceasefire agreement of July 1981. Immediately after the Golan annexation the Israeli Cabinet discussed two plans for the invasion of Lebanon. One called for the ejection of the PLO from South Lebanon, the other for a drive to the Beirut–Damascus highway, the surrounding of Beirut after a seaborne landing, and the destruction of the PLO infrastructure throughout Lebanon in cooperation with the Phalange.[2] The attempted assassination, on 3 June 1982, of Israel's ambassador to London, Shlomo Argov, was used as the excuse to launch a full-scale invasion of Lebanon on the 6th. 'It was Israel's determination to clean out PLO strongholds in Southern Lebanon, rather than recent aggression by Arafat's guerrillas, that provided the impetus for the invasion.'[3] The well-planned attack brought Israeli forces to Beirut in only three days, brushing aside both PLO and Syrian attempts at resistance. The driving force behind these operations was Ariel Sharon who had grandiose plans for their ultimate objective. Once the PLO military position in Lebanon was destroyed and its political organization weakened Sharon planned to work with his Maronite allies to establish a new political order in

Lebanon. But this was only the first stage of the planned redrawing of the Middle East's political map. The next stage was the absorption of the West Bank into Greater Israel leading those Palestinians fleeing from Lebanon and the West Bank to cross into Jordan where they would ultimately bring down King Hussein and establish a Palestinian state on the East Bank of the Jordan.[4] The dilemma of having to give up the West Bank or absorb large numbers of Palestinians into Israel would be ended.

However, the renewed danger of an Israeli–Syrian war brought Philip Habib back to the Middle East where, in early July 1982, he secured an outline agreement on a settlement of the crisis: the Israelis would begin a ceasefire without entering central Beirut, the PLO would leave the city, and a Multinational Force (MNF) would be deployed to ensure a peaceful PLO exit. Alexander Haig, at the end of his time as US Secretary of State, even hoped to seize the chance 'to move all foreign forces . . . out of Lebanon and return the country to the Lebanese'.[5] It proved an over-ambitious hope, quickly undermined by renewed fighting in Beirut, arguments over where the PLO might be sent, and public debate in the US about an American role in the MNF. Then again, after weeks of further tension a peace deal was secured and, on 21 August, the PLO exit began. Over the following days, 11,000 PLO personnel and fighters left by sea. Arafat himself went on 30 August, soon establishing a new headquarters in Tunis, far enough away from Israel for Begin to feel that the main aim of the invasion had been achieved. The PLO fighters were scattered around the Arab world: after the civil wars in Jordan and Lebanon, no Arab country wished to play host to them en masse. Begin now hoped to secure a peace treaty with Lebanon to ensure that it was never again used as a base by radical Muslim opponents of Israel.

However, the Israeli success soon turned sour. On 23 August, the Christian Phalangist leader, Bashir Gemayel, was elected Lebanon's President, apparently further emphasizing Israeli success: the Phalangists, never happy about accepting Syrian protection, now looked to Israel as the saviour of the Maronite cause and some Israeli leaders saw Gemayel as their potential puppet. But barely three weeks later, on 14 September, Bashir, and dozens of his supporters, were killed by a huge bomb. Despite American and UN condemnation the Israeli army then marched into central Beirut supposedly to maintain order, but they effectively let the Phalangists take revenge on their enemies. The PLO may have left Beirut but thousands of unarmed Palestinian refugees were left behind, huddled into the camps of Sabra and Shatila, and these the Phalangists proceeded to slaughter over a two-day period. When word leaked out there was an international outcry. 'The Israelis had watched their allies massacre innocents and had done nothing to prevent the atrocity.'[6] The Begin government denied a direct hand in the massacres. Nevertheless, Israel's standing in Western countries suffered a major blow. 'Morally, and in terms of its influence on world opinion, the siege and bombardment of Beirut were a turning point' in this respect.[7] Even in Israel itself there were calls for the Prime Minister to resign but an investigation into the massacres, published in February 1983, claimed only one Cabinet victim, the Defence Minister, Ariel Sharon, and he would eventually return as Israeli Prime Minister.

Meanwhile, on 21 September 1982 the Israelis had begun to withdraw from Beirut and the same day Bashir Gemayel's brother, Amin, was elected President in his place. The Americans produced a peace plan known as the Reagan Plan which proposed Palestinian self-government in association with Jordan. Both a Palestinian state and Israeli West Bank settlements were ruled out. In May 1983 Amin made a peace treaty with the Israelis which was designed, in part, to bring about a joint Israeli–Syrian withdrawal. But Asad, who in 1982 had survived both the Lebanese crisis and an attempt to overthrow him at home, refused to pull his army out. The Israelis, faced by a war which was unpopular at home and a drain on their economy, were thus forced into a gradual, unilateral withdrawal back to Southern Lebanon, which ended in June 1985. By then it was evident that the 1982 invasion had only had mixed results at best. Arafat had gone but the cost to Israeli finances and reputation was considerable and much was unchanged: the Lebanese government was as powerless as ever, Syrian influence remained strong, and Israel continued to sustain a Phalangist regime in the South, where Palestinian activity had revived. Furthermore, in the wake of the Israeli invasion,

Iran had sent over one thousand Revolutionary Guards to Lebanon, where they supported the 'Hezbollah' (Party of God) that had sprung up in reaction to the Israeli invasion. Their 'goal was to launch a war against Israeli occupation, which would eventually grow to embrace the task of ridding Lebanon ... of western ... influence.'[8] Moreover the aim of Sharon and those seeking to reduce pressure on the Israelis to give up the West Bank had not been achieved and the Palestinian problem had grown.

To the costs of the invasion had also to be added the experience of the MNF, which had originally begun to arrive in Beirut in August 1982, spearheaded by a French contingent though the Americans were the driving force behind it and it also included Italian troops. The French, of course, had been the colonial power in Lebanon, the Italians had a strong interest in stabilizing the Mediterranean, and the Reagan administration believed it must contribute to pacifying the Lebanon, partly because the Israeli and Lebanese governments both wanted this. Reagan acted despite the doubts of the Department of Defence under Caspar Weinberger, who believed, in light of the Vietnam experience, that 'we should not commit American troops to any situation unless the objectives were so important for American interests that we had to fight, and that if those conditions were met, then we had to commit ... enough forces to win.'[9] Israel preferred a US-led force to another UN operation, given the ineffectiveness of the latter in the past; the US were anxious that other countries should serve alongside them so that it appeared a genuinely international effort. At first the MNF was only supposed to cover the PLO withdrawal, but the massacres at Sabra and Shatila led it to be immediately reconstituted, with the Americans, French, and Italians soon being joined by a small British contingent. Instead of contributing much to the long-term stability of Lebanon however, the MNF was soon the focus of Shi'ite attacks. On 18 April 1983 dozens were killed in a bomb attack by the pro-Iranian 'Islamic Jihad' group on the US embassy in Beirut; and on 23 October 241 US marines and 58 French troops were killed in separate attacks, following the bombardment by US naval vessels of Muslim positions. Radical anti-Western groups were now becoming part of the increasingly problematic Middle Eastern scene. With an election year forthcoming and faced by a potentially intractable conflict if the MNF remained, Reagan led the way in withdrawing. On 7 February 1984 he announced the 'redeployment' of US forces. By the end of March they had been 'redeployed' entirely out of the region.

The Search for a Settlement, 1985–1992

In the wake of the withdrawal of Western forces and the Israeli retreat into south Lebanon the lack of a government and army left the militias struggling for power. In the new situation the Syrians and their 30,000 strong army, having fallen out with the Phalangists, at first supported the Druze (now led by Kamal Jumblatt's son, Walid) and the Shi'ite Amal militias (led by Nabih Berri). But later, notably in early 1987 and 1989–90, the Syrians tried to reach an internal settlement. Among the Shi'ites, pro-Iranian feeling remained important, notably in the shape of Hezbollah which became active in South Lebanon and was eager, like the Palestinians, to launch attacks on Israel. Amal and Hezbollah fought each other for influence in the Shi'ite community, just as Maronite factions continued to vie with each other for Christian support. Between 1984 and 1987 Hezbollah and other Shi'ite groups also took ninety Westerners hostage including the CIA station chief, William Buckley. The assassination by Maronites of the Sunni Prime Minister, Rashid Karawi, in 1987, was followed in 1988 by the formation of two separate governments, a Muslim one under Selim al-Hoss and a Christian one under General Michel Aoun, who had the unlikely ambition of expelling the Syrians and re-establishing Maronite predominance.

By 1989, however, many Lebanese groups realized that hopes of ultimate victory promised only an endless round of violence, and the country was physically, economically, and psychologically shattered. In October the remaining members of the last parliament, first elected back in 1972, met in Saudi Arabia to discuss a settlement. The Saudis had long been the strongest supporters of Asad's efforts to pacify the situation and had argued against Jordanian and Iraqi attempts to oppose Syrian intervention—attempts, driven by fears of a 'Greater Syria', which had even led the Iraqis to deny Syria oil exports. The latest attempt at peacemaking led to an agreement to restore stability with a renewed Muslim–Christian political balance, but at first it seemed likely to collapse. The newly elected Maronite President, René Mouwad, was soon assassinated and General Aoun resisted attempts to sack him from command of what remained of the Lebanese army. But yet another President, Elias Hrawi, took Mouawad's place and in late 1990 the Syrian army overwhelmed Aoun. The civil war then effectively ended, but South Lebanon remained in turmoil, with the Israeli-backed Phalangists, the Palestinians, and Hezbollah all active there and the UN force in the area virtually powerless. (The Israelis did not withdraw their forces from the South until 2000.) But 'the Republic of Lebanon ... had survived. Partition had been narrowly avoided. Asad had ... managed to disarm the major Lebanese armed militias, previously thought to be an impossible task.'[10] Beirut was restored to stability and a massive rebuilding programme begun, with parliamentary elections being held in 1992. At around the same time the Gulf War (see Chapter 21, B) brought the US and Syria closer together, and the new Iranian government, following Khomeini's death in 1989, was ready to see Hezbollah release its remaining Western hostages.

CHRONOLOGY:
THE ISRAELI INVASION OF
THE LEBANON, 1981–1990

1979

18 April	Haddad declares pro-Israeli 'Lebanese Free State' in South Lebanon and clashes with UNIFIL.
May	Several Israeli raids into South Lebanon.

1981

April–June	Syrian armed forces besiege Christian Phalangists in Zahle and force their withdrawal from the town.

1982

6 June	Israel launches a massive 90,000-strong invasion of Southern Lebanon to force Palestinians from border areas.
8–9 June	Major clashes between Israeli and Syrian air forces.
11 June	Israeli forces reach outskirts of Beirut and soon begin siege of Palestinian positions.
14 June	Iran sends 'Hezbollah' fighters to Lebanon. Under Sheikh Fadlallah they form a Lebanese Hezbollah movement.
18 August	Palestinian Liberation Organization (PLO) agrees to evacuate Beirut; Yasser Arafat leaves on the 30th.
14 September	Christian President-elect Bashir Gemayel killed with sixty others in a bomb explosion.
16–17 September	Christian militias massacre about 800 Palestinian refugees in Shatila and Sabra camps of West Beirut, an area under Israeli control.
21 September	Bashir's brother, Amin Gemayel, elected President.
Late September	Multinational force created by US, France, and Italy (later Britain too) and deployed in Beirut.

1983

18 April	Suicide bomber kills over 60 in the US embassy compound, Beirut.
4 September	Israeli forces begin to withdraw from Beirut to South Lebanon.
23 October	Hezbollah suicide bomb attacks on US and French forces kill over 300 troops.

1984

17 February	US begins withdrawal of its contingent from Beirut.

1985

January–June	Israelis withdraw from Sidon, Tyre, and Bekaa valley areas, retaining a security zone on the border.
20 May	Amal militia launches attacks on Palestinians in Beirut, aiming to drive PLO from Lebanon completely. Further Amal–PLO clashes in 1986–7.

1987

22 February	Syrian army begins to take control of West Beirut, clashing with Hezbollah.
2 June	Assassination of premier Rashid Karami, succeeded by Selim Hoss.

1988

17 February	Conflict breaks out between Amal and Hezbollah, rivals for influence in the Shi'ite community.
23 September	Christian General Michel Aoun sets up a government in Beirut, but Muslims continue to recognize the Hoss administration.

1989

14 March	General Aoun launches 'war of national liberation' against Syria.
23 September	A widespread ceasefire takes effect.
22 October	A meeting of Lebanese deputies (originally elected in 1972) in Taif, Saudi Arabia, agrees on a redistribution of political power between Muslims and Christians and disbandment of militias. Rejected by Aoun.
2 November	The deputies elect Rene Moawad, a Maronite, as President.
22 November	Moawad assassinated; succeeded by Elias Hrawi.

1990

12–13 October	Syrian forces overrun areas controlled by Aoun, who seeks refuge in the French embassy.
24 October	Lebanese army begins to resume control of Beirut; militias withdrawn by mid-December.

1991

March–May	Disarmament and disbandment of militias.
22 May	Hrawi signs a 'Treaty of Brotherhood' with Syria; condemned by Israel as giving Syria control of Lebanon.
1–11 July	Lebanese army takes over PLO-controlled areas in Southern Lebanon.
26 August	National Assembly grants an amnesty for crimes committed in the civil war, with a few specific exceptions.

B. The Arab–Israeli Dispute and the Palestinian Question

The Failure to find a Settlement

While Lebanon slipped into anarchy, for much of the 1980s the wider Arab–Israeli conflict rumbled on without any sign of a long-term resolution. There was no follow-up to the Camp David agreement (Chapter 14, A) and this has been blamed in part on the failings of Carter's successor: 'Reagan's dis-engaged style as president, his lack of curiosity, and his passivity on the Middle East were impediments to creative US peace diplomacy.'[11] Obsessed by the Soviet threat here as elsewhere, Reagan's first instinct on becoming President was to hope—as Dulles had in the 1950s—that the Arabs and Israelis might be persuaded to settle their differences under the umbrella of a common opposition to Communism. Egypt, Saudi Arabia, and Jordan seemed likely candi-dates for such cooperation, and, after the fall of the Shah, the Carter administration had already started the practice of joint exercises with friendly govern-ments in the region. One early decision by the new administration was to sell state-of-the-art, early-warning aircraft (AWACS) to the Saudis so that they could contribute to the defence of the Middle East against the Soviets and their clients. The Saudis seemed a particularly good replacement for Iran as an American ally and were well placed to act against socialist governments in South Yemen and across the Red Sea in Ethiopia. Furthermore, Carter had previously deployed AWACS in Saudi Arabia, even if he had not actually sold them to the Saudi govern-ment. The AWACS deal became an early indication of how difficult it was to reduce Arab and Israeli hostility when the Israelis, backed by the powerful Zionist lobby in Congress, tried to sabotage the arrangement. 'The Reagan administration, like its predecessor, laboured in vain to escape the dilemma of competing "special relationships". Neither Israel nor Saudi Arabia ... could be convinced of the advantages ... of joining together ... against the Soviet Union.'[12] It took considerable efforts from the White House, supported by the business and

trades union lobbies, to drive the sale through, with reassurances to Israel about the uses to which the aircraft could be put. This was not the only early setback in Israeli–American relations under Reagan. Washington was concerned not only by the July 1981 bombing raids on the PLO headquarters in Beirut, but also by an Israeli air attack the previous month on an Iraqi nuclear reactor at Osirak. Indeed, for a time, the US held back on promised financial aid and aircraft sales to Israel.

Such signs of animosity, however, quickly faded as Reagan recognized that Israel was likely to prove his most loyal and powerful ally in his Middle Eastern against the Soviet Union. In November 1981 the two countries signed an agreement to oppose Soviet influence in the region and, across the Reagan Presidency as a whole, the US supplied Israel with $23 billion in aid. The assassination of Anwar Sadat in October 1981 probably reinforced this pro-Israeli trend, because while Sadat's successor, Hosni Mubarrak, maintained pacific relations with Israel, these were never warm and he took none of the diplomatic risks associated with Sadat. Instead, after securing Israel's final withdrawal from the Sinai in 1982, Mubarrak concentrated on restoring Egypt's relations in the Arab world. Most of the Arab states had, of course, broken diplomatic relations with Egypt after the 1979 peace treaty with Israel, even though it was the most populous and military powerful Arab nation. In 1984 Mubarrak took Egypt back into the Islamic Conference and five years later (following a decision by the November 1988 Amman summit) he rejoined the Arab League. This was a reward in part for his reaction to the Israeli invasion of Lebanon where he had, at first, broken off talks (agreed in the 1979 treaty) on the Palestinian issue, and then, after the Sabra and Shatila massacres, recalled his ambassador to Tel Aviv. Mubarrak also gave considerable assistance to his fellow Arab leader, Saddam Hussein, to help prosecute the latter's war against Iran. Indeed, the surprising thing is that Israeli–Egyptian relations did not break down completely in this period. But this could have destroyed Cairo's close relationship with Washington, carefully built up under Sadat, and for their part the Israelis acted with some restraint. Thus in 1989, after arbitration, Israel conceded certain changes to its border with Egypt. Other Arab states continued to be offended by Israel's actions and refused to contemplate a peace treaty that would recognize its right to exist. Outside Lebanon the Begin government declared Jerusalem the country's capital in 1980, despite its religious importance to Muslims. Until the 1967 Middle East War, East Jerusalem had been under Jordanian rule but under the UN partition plan Jerusalem was deemed sufficiently important to be excluded from the area to be divided between Israelis and Palestinians. In 1981 Begin embarked on more Israeli expansion after signing a strategic cooperation agreement with the Reagan government in November. Furthermore, Israel annexed the Golan Heights in December 1981. In so doing Begin was in breach of international law, the May 1974 Israeli–Syrian disengagement agreement, UN Resolution 242, and the Camp David Accords. The Americans responded by temporarily suspending the strategic cooperation agreement. Such was the enormity of the act that some historians have speculated as to whether it was designed to stop the post-Camp David momentum for a comprehensive peace. The annexation 'put great strain on Israel's relations with Egypt . . . Syria reacted angrily.'[13] But it also confirmed Begin's credentials as a right-wing nationalist, pleasing his supporters at home.[14]

Meanwhile, Israel also continued to hold onto the West Bank and Gaza, where 1.5 million Palestinians lived and to which a similar number of refugees living in neighbouring Arab states hoped, one day, to return. Before they were broken off in 1982, the Israeli–Egyptian conversations on the Palestinian question achieved nothing, not even an arrangement for limited autonomy. Sadat's earlier claims that the 1979 deal would lead over time to a wider settlement increasingly sounded hollow. Israeli policy in Lebanon, its continued refusal to recognize the PLO as the representative of the Palestinian people, and the extension of Jewish settlements in the West Bank all contributed to the lack of progress on the Palestinian question. Rather than settling the issue, Begin's Likud coalition, narrowly re-elected in

1981 (and more dependent thereafter on the support of small, extremist religious groups in parliament), seemed determined to cripple the PLO and treat the West Bank as part of the 'Land of Israel'—as, according to the Old Testament of the Bible, it was.

The Israeli invasion of Lebanon led to another period of strain in US–Israeli relations and saw Reagan's only major attempt to resolve the Arab–Israeli conflict. The 'Reagan Plan', launched in a speech on 1 September 1982, followed Philip Habib's success in extracting the PLO from Beirut and was quite a bold step for any American President, since it tried to set out the specifics of a Palestinian settlement: there would be a freeze on Israeli settlements and a five-year period of Palestinian autonomy to show that such a situation was no threat to Israel's existence; the long-term future of the West Bank, Gaza, and Jerusalem would be decided by negotiation (but the US favoured a form of Palestinian autonomy in cooperation with Jordan in the West Bank and Gaza). Though the Israelis and some Arab governments had been consulted in advance however, the Reagan Plan satisfied neither side. The Begin government feared it offered the Palestinians too much and would weaken Israeli security just at the point they had driven Arafat out of Beirut. King Hussein of Jordan showed some interest but, in September 1982 at the Arab League summit in Fez, he backed the consensus that there must be a fully independent Palestinian state with Jerusalem as its capital.

Significantly, 'although the Reagan Plan fell short of what the PLO could accept, Arafat and . . . the mainstream leadership did not reject it outright' but wished to discover whether 'limited self-government could lead in time to full self-determination',[15] an approach that would be revived a decade later, with better results. But over the following years the US strengthened relations with Israel once more, while neglecting the difficult Palestinian problems that the Reagan Plan had tried to address. Even the discovery of an Israeli spy, Jonathan Pollard, at the heart of the Pentagon in 1985, only upset these improved relations momentarily. With the Israeli retreat from most of Lebanon attention was given again to a settlement based on Jordan and an association with the Palestinians that provided some form of autonomy for the latter and could replace Israeli authority in the West Bank and Gaza. Since 1984 there had been a coalition government in Tel Aviv with Shimon Peres, the Labour leader, in favour of moves towards peace whereas the Likud leader, Yitzak Shamir, who alternated as Prime Minister with Peres, was instinctively averse to it. His famous and oft-repeated statement about Palestinian hostility to Israel's existence claimed that 'the Arabs are the same Arabs and the sea is the same sea'. Moreover, Shamir, like Begin a former terrorist, was committed to the retention of all of the 'Land of Israel'.[16]

The issues in the talks between Hussein and Shimon Peres were the role of the PLO in any moves to autonomy for the Palestinians and the process of reaching an international agreement on a comprehensive Arab–Israeli settlement. By 1986 an agreement between Israel and Jordan had been worked out on how negotiations would proceed, but the Palestinian role in the proposed international conference remained to be determined. Hussein had agreed with Arafat on their involvement but the Israelis remained adamant that they would not negotiate with the PLO. Only three months earlier Israeli F16s had attacked the PLO HQ in Tunis killing 56 Palestinians and 15 Tunisians in response to an extremist Palestinian group, the Palestine Liberation Front, hijacking a cruise liner, the *Achille Lauro*, killing one American passenger. On the other side the PLO declared that they would recognize Israel's right to exist through recognition of Resolution 242 if the Americans guaranteed their participation at the international conference and recognize the Palestinians' right to self-determination. The first part was acceptable to Washington but not the second and Hussein failed to persuade Arafat of the importance of achieving a diplomatic breakthrough on that basis. The result of all these efforts was nothing but a split between Hussein and the PLO.

1987 and 1988 were, however, two crucial years in the Israeli–Palestinian conflict. For decades neither violence nor diplomacy had succeeded in making significant progress towards a settlement based on the rights of each side to live together in peace. Almost inevitably the longer the stalemate persisted the more scope there would be provided for extremism, if it did not already predominate. Moreover, conditions for Palestinian refugees were stead-ily worsening and any solution to the problem of the occupied territories in the West Bank and Gaza would have to confront more and more Israeli settlements, even though the construction of new settlements had slowed after 1984 the number of settlers was increasing. Under Begin, between 1977 and 1983 about 25,000 Jewish settlers moved into the area, a figure that excludes the thousands more who settled in East Jerusalem. Previously there had only been 10,000 Jews in the West Bank; by 1992 there were about 100,000.

The Start of the Intifada

After two decades of international failure to make any progress on, the Palestinian question, it was the Arab population of the West Bank and Gaza who finally took matters into their own hands—though without at first producing new movement on the issue. On 9 December 1987 a traffic accident led to an outbreak of violence in Gaza. Previously, despite the presence of Israeli troops, the expansion of Jewish settlements, lack of economic development, and severe limits on their political rights, there had been only sporadic violence from the Palestinian people under Israeli rule. Despite the poverty of the densely populated Gaza strip, the Israelis had always claimed that their rule was benign and that, despite PLO propaganda, most Palestinians were happy under Israeli rule. But, to the surprise of everyone, even the PLO, 9 December proved the beginning of a lengthy and widespread Intifada, or uprising, against Israeli rule. Demonstrations and marches were accompanied by stone-throwing at troops, who often overreacted, firing on the crowds and killing protestors. None of this helped Israel's international standing. As more and more Palestinians joined in the movement, Israeli rule was increasingly seen, even by US opinion, as oppressive. 'Palestinians, through the Intifada, [rejected] anything that represented Israeli rule . . .; they were no longer willing to pay taxes without representation, to fund the military occupation of land which they perceived as their own.'[17] The PLO could hardly be said to have planned the uprising and the benefits it may have gained came by chance rather than design. If world attention was now focused on Israel and the occupied territories, the PLO was losing its grip on the resistance to Israel. In November 1988 Arafat declared Palestine's independence and in 1989 established a government-in-exile to which many countries gave diplomatic recognition. Crucially he restricted the boundaries of a Palestinian state to the West Bank and Gaza, and he acknowledged Israel's right to exist. It has been argued that the 'success of the Intifada gave Arafat and his followers the confidence they needed to moderate their political programme' and so put Israel on the diplomatic defensive.'[18] At all events the long-held Israeli claim to security and the threat of the Arab drive to the sea no longer formed a barrier to a settlement. The Israeli–Palestinian dispute had with hindsight reached a watershed.

It was the Intifada which finally induced the Reagan administration to renew its interest in the Palestinian–Israeli dispute. In March 1988 George Schultz, the US Secretary of State, was set to revive the peace process with the idea of Israeli talks with a Jordanian-PLO delegation on a transitional arrangement, followed by a long-term settlement, of the Palestinian issue. This again fell foul of Israeli opposition however, with Yitzhak Shamir, now Prime Minister for the whole term of the new Labour-Likud coalition government, unwilling to deal with the PLO or concede Palestinian autonomy. It was also difficult for the US to run risks for the sake of a settlement during a Presidential election year. But as the Intifada continued, the PLO was increasingly acknowledged as the only genuine representative of the Palestinian people and various indirect, secret links were established between the organization and Washington. Then, just before the Reagan administration came to an end, there was a significant advance. The President himself had always said he would only talk directly to the PLO if it renounced violence, and there had been no official talks between Arafat and the US since 1975, when Henry Kissinger had insisted that the PLO should recognize Israel. But, in addressing the UN on 13 December 1988, Arafat effectively renounced terrorism, at which point Shultz conceded that direct talks were possible once more. They began, in Tunis, on 16 December and continued into the Bush administration in 1989. In retrospect this heralded a period in which US–Israeli relations would be much

less warm. The general lack of progress on talks on a settlement (see Chapter 22, C) could now be ascribed on the one hand to Israeli desires for settlement rather than their need for security. On the other hand the nature and extent of hard-line opponents of Israel was exceeding the capacity of the PLO to control.

If the talks failed now that violence had been renounced and Israel's right to exist accepted, the Palestinian advocates of an agreement would have no more cards to play. With the benefit of hindsight one can argue that from this moment the longer a settlement was delayed it would be the more difficult to reach. As the arguments in 1986 over who should represent whom were raging at the highest levels, at the grass roots ominous developments were taking place some under the cover of the Intifada. Islamic Jihad emerged in 1986 and its influence was evident in the encouragement of participation in the Intifada the following year. One significant aspect of the Intifada was the creation of the Unified National Leadership of the Uprising (UNLU) which was composed of the most radical factions within the PLO and those outside its umbrella. The leaders of UNLU were no longer members of the bourgeoisie who had previously characterized Palestinian political life but were drawn from groups who had no connection with traditional Palestinian elites. Younger and more determined, many had a firm commitment to radical social change but remained within the PLO while increasingly denouncing the leadership in Tunis. There was cooperation between UNLU and Islamic Jihad but the crucial difference was that the latter totally rejected the idea of a two-state solution and demanded the liberation of Palestine.

However, in January 1988 another Muslim extremist group emerged advocating, like Islamic Jihad, a more direct and confrontational challenge to Israel. The Islamic Resistance Movement (Hamas) had links with the Muslim Brotherhood, but it was more militant, had no connection with the merchants and notables in the Brotherhood, and merged religious faith and Palestinian nationalism into a potent and violent political cocktail. And it helped extend the Intifada into a full-blown rebellion while rejecting any peace conferences because it claimed the only solution lay in Jihad or holy war. James Baker, who had been Reagan's Chief of Staff during the ill-fated Lebanon intervention, felt 'there

Yasser Arafat (b. 1929)

Despite his high international profile, Arafat's origins are shrouded in mystery. His precise name at the time of his birth, and even his place of birth itself, are disputed. Palestinian sources variously say that he was born in Jerusalem or the Gaza Strip, but it has also been claimed that he was born in Cairo. His father was evidently a merchant, who travelled between Palestine and Egypt, and Yasser was partly raised in Jerusalem, becoming an active opponent of Jewish attempts to set up the state of Israel. In 1948, with Israel established, he went to study civil engineering at the University of Cairo, but he also became a leading figure among Palestinian students in Egypt and in 1956, the year of the Suez crisis, founded the radical Al Fatah movement.

From 1965 onwards Fatah launched small-scale attacks on Israeli territory, aiming to return Palestine to Arab control. The 1967 'Six Day War' made Arafat's violent resistance more popular among Arab leaders and in 1969 he became Chairman of the Palestinian Liberation Organization (PLO), originally founded under more moderate leadership a few years before. Initially based in Amman,

Jordan, he was forced to move from there in 1970 after armed clashes with the Royalist government, setting up new headquarters in Beirut, Lebanon. He was able to address the United Nations in 1974 but Israel condemned him as a terrorist and drove him from Beirut by force in 1982, after which he moved to Tunis.

In 1988 Arafat surprised the world by renouncing terrorism and offering to recognize Israel's right to exist, but he also declared an independent Palestinian state. Clandestine contacts with the Israeli government, backed by the popular uprising (Intifada) among Palestinian Arabs, helped bring the 1993 Oslo Accords on the establishment of a Palestinian authority in the Gaza Strip and limited areas of the West Bank. For this achievement, Arafat shared the 1994 Nobel Peace Prize with two Israeli politicians, Premier Yitzhak Rabin and Foreign Minister Shimon Peres. In January 1996 Arafat was overwhelmingly elected President of the Palestinian National Authority but over the following years, his followers were increasingly discontented because of the failure to achieve real independence and his authoritarian style.

was no real evidence to believe the climate was ripe for generating any momentum' and 'frankly saw the Arab–Israeli dispute as a pitfall to be avoided rather than an opportunity to be exploited.'[19]

C. **The Iran–Iraq War of 1980–1988**

Origins of the Conflict

The outbreak of war between the oil-rich states of Iran and Iraq in September 1980 was closely linked to the events surrounding the fall of the Shah the year before (see Chapter 15, B). In the 1970s, following the departure of British forces from the Persian Gulf, the Shah had been built up by the US as a regional strongman. Pro-western and non-Arab, and leading a large, oil-rich country, he seemed the ideal candidate for the role, and his actions included helping the Sultan of Oman put down a rebellion (underway between 1965 and 1977) in Oman's Dhofar province. But during this time the Shah also took the chance to press Iranian nationalist demands

in the Gulf, seizing certain islands in the Straits of Hormuz (at the southern end of the Gulf) in 1971. In particular, he pursued a hard line against Iraq, with which there was a border dispute focused on the Shatt al-Arab waterway. In 1974–5 he encouraged a revolt by Iraq's oppressed Kurdish minority, then forced Baghdad to agree, during talks in Algiers, to a new definition of their border, down the middle of the Shatt al-Arab. There was little sympathy in the West for Iraq in all this because, since the Ba'ath coup in July 1968 and the emergence of Saddam Hussein, Iraq had opposed Resolution 242 and signed an agreement with the Soviets on oilfield development the same year. Partly in reaction to pressure from the Shah Baghdad, having already broken off diplomatic relations with Tehran in 1971, then nationalized the Iraq Petroleum Company and signed a friendship treaty with the Soviets the following year. It was to use its enormous oil wealth to purchase military equipment from the Eastern bloc and also bought high-technology equipment from France and began to develop a nuclear capability—which the Israelis blunted in 1981 with their bombing raid on the Iraqi facility.

The fall of the Shah and the establishment of a theocratic regime in Iran after February 1979 revolutionized the situation in the Gulf. By the end of the year Washington and Tehran were locked in bitter argument over the seizure of the US embassy staff as hostages and on 30 October the Iraqi leader, Saddam Hussein, grasped the opportunity to challenge the 1975 Algiers agreement. Saddam, a ruthless figure even in the merciless world of Iraqi politics, had only recently made himself chairman of the country's Revolutionary Command Council, and then, in 1979, President. Like most other Arab leaders—the only exceptions being Syria and Libya—he was deeply concerned about Ayatollah Khomeini's Islamic Revolution, with its propaganda in favour of a united Islamic world under Iranian leadership, which threatened to stir up religious fervour among Iraq's Shi'ites—a majority of the population—and challenge the position of the secular, radical, and Sunni-dominated regime. Because of the threat he posed, Khomeini had been expelled from Iraq in 1978, having lived in exile there since 1965, and there was no love lost between him and the Iraqi leadership. In April 1980 he condemned Saddam as an 'enemy of Islam' and relations between the two continued to deteriorate. 'Baghdad was to argue later that by encouraging Islamic and Kurdish dissidents to overthrow the Ba'athist regime, Tehran's revolutionary leaders had effectively revoked the 1975 treaty which barred each country from provoking subversion in the other.'[20] But territorial wrangles also continued. On 4 September, following months of border tension, Iranian artillery shelled Iraqi positions and, on the 17th Saddam denounced the 1975 border treaty. With strong ideological fears of the neighbouring regime and a desire for revenge for the Shah's earlier humiliation of Iraq, Saddam seized the chance, five days later, to invade Iran. The Iraqis thereafter argued that the war had been started by Iraq on the 4th but the Iranians always dated it from the Iraqi invasion on the 22nd.

Deadlocked War and the World Response, 1980–1986

In launching his invasion, Saddam clearly hoped that the removal of US support from Iran (including the supply of American military equipment, on which the Iranian armed forces relied) and the upheaval caused by the Islamic Revolution would make the war a short, victorious one. His own forces were well prepared and Iraq was now the world's second largest oil exporter. At first all this seemed a reasonable analysis and within two days, on 24 September, his forces had seized the city of Khorramshahr. Soon the Iraqis occupied much of south-western Iran, an Arab-populated region and a centre of oil production, though they were never able to seize control of their main target, and the central city for the Iranian oil industry, Abadan. The UN called for a ceasefire but neither side wished to talk: Iran would not negotiate from a position of weakness and in any case Khomeini treated the conflict as a holy war; Saddam wanted to press home his advantage and faced little real pressure from the international community to make peace. As he expected, most Arab states verbally backed him for reasons of 'racial and religious solidarity', even if 'explicit support for Iraq [was] not . . . forthcoming, mainly because Saddam treated it as "his" war and had done nothing to consult his fellow Arabs before launching it.[21] The US, at the time the war broke out, had relations with neither Tehran nor Baghdad, but was happy at first to see the Iranians on the defensive. The Soviets were not entirely happy with Saddam, who had tried to destroy the Iraqi Communist Party, and they did not want to appear too anti-Iranian for fear of stirring up discontent among their own Muslims in Central Asia. Despite US fears of Kremlin involvement, the Soviets actually cut off arms to both sides in the war, joined the calls for a ceasefire and maintained diplomatic contacts with both Baghdad and Tehran. But, preoccupied with Afghanistan and committed to the 1972 Friendship Treaty, they too were not initially unhappy with the situation. Iraq was now one of their few allies in the Middle East, whereas one of the features of the Iranian revolution was its condemnation of Marxism.

A change in American policy might have been expected in early 1981 when the hostages' crisis ended and Reagan came into office. But lingering resentment over Iran's recent behaviour and Khomeini's continuing support for radical Islamic groups beyond Iran, continued to drive Washington and Tehran apart despite their shared anti-communism. Given its Cold War obsessions, the Reagan administration found the situation very confusing because, whatever the ill-feeling towards Iran, Iraq was both pro-Soviet and an opponent of the Camp David peace process. Cold War rhetoric could not explain, still less resolve, the Iran–Iraq conflict. The US supported Khomeini's opponents yet had no desire to see the Soviets exploit an Iraqi triumph, especially following Moscow's intervention in nearby Afghanistan. The result was that America, while showing a preference for Iraq (largely because of a fear of Islamic radicalism spreading throughout the Middle East), wanted neither side to win, hoped to keep the conflict localized and tried to restrict arms sales to both sides. Therefore for both superpowers in 1980–2 the Iran–Iraq War, however intensely it raged, became something of a sideshow in the new Cold War. Neither had much to gain from it and so 'for seven years America and the Soviet Union did no more than dabble, seeking rather . . . to contain the war than to bring it to an end, much less exploit global advantage.'[22]

In 1981 the war became deadlocked in south-western Iran, as the Iraqi offensive ground to a halt. Iran had not proved the weakened victim that Saddam originally hoped. Larger than Iraq in size and population, Iran retained sufficient industrial output to produce an adequate supply of arms and its Revolutionary Guards were better motivated than the Iraqi army, helping to offset the latter's advantages in equipment. By 1982 the war seemed to move in Iran's favour. Khorramshahr was retaken in April and, three months later, the Revolutionary Guards drove the Iraqis back across the border. Saddam's offer, in June, of a ceasefire was ignored: it simply underlined how anxious he had become. Instead, Khomeini demanded Saddam's replacement

and the payment of reparations by the Iraqis. The following four years saw only a slow advance by the Iranians, however, as they tried to threaten the strategic city port of Basra and periodically bombarded Baghdad itself. It seemed that both sides would exhaust each other, as the struggle became the longest conventional conflict of the twentieth century, with long periods of trench warfare reminiscent of the First World War and substantial losses on both sides, but especially among the Revolutionary Guards. Saddam was consistently ready to end the war but, given his enemy's religious inspiration, decided he could only bring about a settlement by intensifying the conflict. In particular, aware that he could never win a conventional war on land, he came to rely on the superiority of his airforce and on the use of unconventional weapons such as poison gas. He also hoped for growing international pressure on Tehran to make peace.

Iran's expulsion of the Iraqi invaders in 1982 provoked growing concern in Western countries, who continued in public to support UN peace efforts and an arms embargo but increasingly, and secretly, tried to arm Iraq. Arab states, such as Saudi Arabia and Kuwait, neither of them great friends of Iraq in the past, but both autocratic monarchies who felt threatened by the forces behind the Iranian Revolution, also gave aid to Iraq. Meanwhile the policies of Reagan administration were still very confused. Washington's essential aims remained that of avoiding outright victory for either side, whilst also preventing both the growth of Soviet influence in the region and the advance of Iranian fundamentalism. There were serious differences, however, over how to achieve these. The State and Defense Departments preferred to build up Iraqi power to contain Iran; in 1983–4 they launched 'Operation Staunch', which effectively directed arms to Iraq while denying them to Iran; and in November 1984 supported the re-establishment of diplomatic relations with Baghdad, for the first time since 1967. But the CIA and key National Security Council staff felt that Iran's anti-communism might be exploited, and that a more moderate leadership could be encouraged in Tehran if American policy were more friendly. Such a policy might also help secure the release of Western hostages held by Shi'ite groups in Lebanon. In contrast a pro-Iraq policy might, it was feared, drive the Iranians towards Moscow: after all, Tehran had taken economic aid from the Eastern bloc during the 1979–80 hostage crisis. It was thinking such as this which led to a highly secret attempt to ship arms to Iran and a visit by Reagan's then National Security Adviser, Robert McFarlane, to Tehran in May 1986. The policy was not, it seems, foredoomed to failure: Iranian leaders had one 'pressing motive' to improve relations and that was 'to obtain US arms . . . The Iraqi bombing of Iranian cities and economic installations was becoming increasingly effective, bringing tremendous psychological pressures to bear.'[23] But the revelation of the McFarlane visit by a Lebanese newspaper later in the year began the 'Contragate', or 'Contragate' scandal (discussed more fully in Chapter 18, B). Apart from the controversy this stirred in America, the revelation also caused great confusion among US allies in the Middle East, not least Saudi Arabia and Kuwait, who had believed Washington was pursuing a pro-Iraqi policy.

The 'Tanker War' and a Settlement, 1986–1988

In 1986 the Iranians seized control of the strategic Fao peninsula and over the following two years the war was at its worst, with the Iranians besieging Basra and the Iraqis making greater use of poison gas attacks. In 1987–8, in the so-called 'war of the cities', bombs and missile attacks were directed by both sides on urban centres. At the same time there were increasing attacks by the two sides on shipping in the Persian Gulf. These attacks became known as the 'tanker war' and, as Saddam seems to have intended, they both pushed up the price of oil (helping Iraq finance its war effort) and led to increased international efforts to resolve the conflict (which he now had little hope of winning). Saddam had first attacked the Iranian oil terminal at Kharg Island in August 1982 and by 1986 he was able to target all Iran's ports on the Gulf. This was a very worrying development for Tehran which had to export all its oil—vital for foreign earnings—via tankers down the Gulf: Iraq in contrast could export oil westwards through pipelines. In response, rather than submit, Iran decided to intimidate Iraq's Gulf allies,

especially Kuwait, by laying mines, threatening to close the 24-mile wide Straits of Hormuz, attacking ships of all countries which were bound for Kuwait, and, in October 1986, launching a missile strike on the major Kuwaiti oil terminal. They also broke off diplomatic relations with Kuwait and Saudi Arabia, who lacked the naval power to defend themselves.

Faced by such pressure the Kuwaiti government approached both the Soviet and US governments to try to secure protection. By now Mikhail Gorbachev was in power in Moscow and simultaneously the 'Contragate' revelations made the Kuwaitis and Saudis suspicious of US intentions. Even so, Washington was taken aback by Gorbachev's offer in February 1987 to lease some Soviet-flagged tankers to Kuwait. Suspicious of his motives and anxious to reconfirm its trustworthiness, the US itself now agreed to reflag and escort Kuwaiti tankers in the Gulf. By the end of the year a mixed armada of US, Soviet, and West European minesweepers was active in the area. Ironically it was an *Iraqi* attack on an American warship, the USS *Stark*, in May 1987, killing 37 servicemen, which finally convinced the US people of the need to protect Gulf shipping. It has been said that, by 'agreeing that the Kuwaiti tanker fleet could sail under the American flag, the United States effectively joined, on the Iraqi side, the . . . tanker war in the Gulf.'[24] So anti-Iranian did Western policy now become that the US and West Europeans were willing to condone Iraqi attacks on any ships bound for Iran and even to overlook Saddam's use of poison gas. By early 1988 nearly fifty US vessels and twenty from Western Europe were on patrol. Yet attacks on neutral ships and the laying of mines by Iran actually increased, as did the dangers of a US–Iranian conflict. In April 1988 a clash between their forces led the Americans to sink half the Iranians' navy (admittedly small: it had only twelve ships in total). Then, three months later, on 3 July, a US warship, the USS *Vincennes* shot down an Iranian airliner, mistaking it for a military target. All 290 passengers and crew died. The incident shook Washington, which offered to pay compensation. It may also have influenced Tehran to end the war.

In the mid-1980s the Western powers had tried to blame Iran entirely for lengthening the war and framed UN resolutions in a way which Iraq found easier to accept. But in July 1987, with relations between the superpowers beginning to improve, the US and USSR had both supported Resolution 598 calling for an immediate ceasefire and a withdrawal to the 1980 border, which could be seen as a neutral basis for a settlement. At first the Iranians refused to respond to the proposal, either positively or negatively. But the hopelessness of securing a decisive victory was by now quite obvious. In early 1988 there was a new round of Iranian offensives but Saddam again responded, this time with gas and missile attacks which included rocket attacks on Tehran itself. One gas attack was directed at the

Kurdish village of Halabja, on Iraqi territory but a centre of resistance to Saddam's rule; it killed about 5,000 civilians, embarrassed Saddam's supporters, and led some to press peace on him more seriously. Such evidence of the Iraqi President's inhumanity reinforced the Western view that the best way for the war to end was as a stalemate. But meanwhile the Halabja incident may have helped demoralize the Iranians, who 'feared the use of chemicals against their cities. It became obvious to them that the cries of human rights organizations . . . mattered little in the face of American determination to help

---

The Revival of the United Nations?

The late 1980s and early 1990s saw a revival of fortunes for the United Nations, a new respect for the organization as a peacemaking body, and a return to the original hopes, of 1945–6, that the Security Council might prove a forum for the great powers to work together. Certainly Mikhail Gorbachev treated it more seriously than previous Soviet leaders. The successes of the UN included:

- The April 1988 Geneva Agreement between Afghanistan and Pakistan, guaranteed by the US and USSR, which paved the way for a Soviet withdrawal from Afghanistan. The agreement followed a series of talks since 1982, chaired by the UN's Diego Cordovez.
- The end of the Iran–Iraq War in July 1988 on the basis of Resolution 598 of twelve months earlier. The Resolution included a ceasefire, a return to the pre-war status quo, and an international commission to decide who was responsible for the war.
- The signature of agreements at the UN on 22 December 1988 on problems in southern Africa, following a series of talks since the previous January. The settlement provided for the independence of Namibia (previously the South African-administered mandate of South-West Africa) and for the withdrawal of Cuban troops from neighbouring Angola, where they had been since 1975.
- The liberation of Kuwait by a US-led force in early 1991, which might have gone less smoothly but for the UN's immediate condemnation of the original Iraqi invasion (Resolution 660 of 2 August 1990) and the agreement of the Security Council on subsequent steps (though China abstained on

Resolution 678, authorizing members 'to use all necessary means' to remove Iraq).

- The restoration of Cambodian independence, after more than a decade of Vietnamese occupation, in the Paris agreements of 23 October 1991. These followed years of UN mediation attempts and put various responsibilities on the organization including supervising the ceasefire, organizing elections, and repatriating refugees.

Such successes led to high hopes of a major UN role in world politics in the 1990s. But:

- on closer inspection some of the settlements were seriously flawed. Resolution 598 produced no long-term settlement and Afghanistan continued to suffer internal turmoil;
- many long-running international problems (Cyprus, Palestine, the division of Korea) continued without sign of imminent resolution;
- a number of conflicts in the 1990s (Somalia, Bosnia, Rwanda) harmed the UN's reputation and confirmed that it was at the mercy of the wishes of its members; a useful vehicle for talks when governments wanted this but with limited influence if they were unprepared to keep the peace;
- the UN Secretary-General, Xavier Perez de Cuellar, admitted in his memoirs, *Pilgrimage for Peace* (Macmillan, London, 1997, 15–16), that the successes of 1988–91 were largely dependent on the newfound cooperation of the US and USSR: 'It would have been self-defeating hubris to assume that the United Nations . . . could independently bring peace in any one of these cases.'

Saddam.'[25] The concern of Khomeini's advisers intensified still further when, in May 1988, a new Iraqi offensive threatened to cross Iran's borders once more. Khomeini himself declared that peace was 'worse than taking poison' but on 20 July 1988 he accepted Resolution 598. Neither side had gained any territory as a result of almost eight years of war. Both were economically shattered and faced the expensive challenge of reconstruction—the outcome that the US had hoped for when the war began.

It was partly in order to obtain the resources needed for such reconstruction that Saddam, in August 1990, invaded Kuwait, provoking another major conflict (see Chapter 21, B). He initially tried to portray himself as the victor of the Iran–Iraq war, on the grounds that Iran had suffered far more casualties, but such claims were undermined by his decision, on 15 August 1990, to reaffirm the 1975 Algiers agreement on the Shatt al-Arab border: he was forced to do this, in order to concentrate on the Kuwait war. As to Iran–Iraq relations they remained poor thereafter. There was no full exchange of prisoners and both countries continued to give assistance to the other's political opponents. The result was rather better for the US and the West, who had long favoured a stalemate and were happy to see both Iran and Iraq weakened and divided against each other. The only international actor to gain much was the United Nations, which could claim to have provided the diplomatic machinery for a settlement between two bitter enemies (see boxed section).

D. Libya and 'International Terrorism'

Despite the Vietnam syndrome, the Reagan administration was clearly not beyond limited military operations in the Middle East where these seemed to be in the US interest. The role of the US marines in the Lebanon Multinational Force in 1982–4 and the naval commitment in the Gulf in 1987–8 were obvious examples of this. But a much sharper, and no less dramatic intervention, took place in April 1986 when US aircraft bombed Libya. The reasons for this action lay in a growing exasperation with the behaviour of Libya's ruler, Colonel Gadaffi, Muammar especially his backing for what Washington condemned as 'international terrorism'.

Gadaffi's External Policy and Intervention in Chad

Libya was a former Italian colony, a poor, sparsely populated, largely desert kingdom. Its economic fortunes were much improved by the discovery of oil in 1959, though at first this was principally of benefit to Western oil companies, the main impact in Libya being an increase in levels of corruption. On 1 September 1969 King Idris was overthrown whilst on a visit abroad, and replaced by a Revolutionary Command Council headed by Gadaffi. A militant pan-Arab who espoused what he termed 'Koranic Socialism', Gadaffi closed both American and British military bases, forced Italian settlers out of the country, and became an irrepressible advocate of federations with other Arab countries. He came to power while Nasser still dominated Egyptian politics and just as another radical leader, General Gaafar Nimeiry, had come to power in the Sudan and there was talk of a union between these three north-east African states and Syria in 1970. Gadaffi believed that 'if Arab countries stopped feuding and pooled their money . . . and military might, they would create a power bloc that could rival the superpowers and destroy the state of Israel.'[26] But Anwar Sadat's policies soon stirred up differences among the group. Gadaffi was also at the forefront of efforts by oil-producing countries to control prices more effectively, which finally won success in 1973. Oil wealth allowed the charismatic but volatile Gadaffi to improve Libya's housing, education, and health care, as the country's per capita income mushroomed. But he also tightened his grip on power by maintaining a repressive regime and liquidating any opposition.

At first Gadaffi's regime was also marked by its firm

anti-communism: there were even rumours that the US had helped him into power in order to modernize the country. But by March 1973, when Libyan aircraft fired on US airplanes over the Gulf of Sidra, relations between the two countries were very poor, while Libyan–Soviet links strengthened, so that 'in the years 1979–83 Libya was the only major African recipient of Soviet arms.'[27] In 1973 Gadaffi broke off diplomatic relations with Egypt, after the failure of talks on a federation. He was already known to provide support for organizations like the PLO and IRA. A dedicated opponent of post-1973 Middle East peace attempts, Gadaffi was said to have plotted the assassination of Henry Kissinger and in 1974 secured a major arms deal with Moscow. Libya's power was still restricted by its development needs, its small population, and the limited size of its armed forces but in the mid-1970s it began to gain a reputation as a radical, violent force in world politics. Relations with Gadaffi's former allies in Egypt and Sudan were particularly difficult. He was accused of trying to overthrow General Nimeiry in 1975–6; and in 1976 the Americans assured Sadat that they would protect him from Soviet intervention if he went to war with Libya. Gadaffi was predictably aghast at the Camp David peace process and there was almost war between Libya and Egypt in 1978. He was one of the few enthusiastic supporters of Syria's intervention in Lebanon, he aided those trying to overthrow the Sultan of Oman, and after 1969 he was a firm supporter of Uganda's dictator, Idi Amin, until the latter's overthrow ten years later, following a Tanzanian invasion. Amin too was a military figure who expelled foreign immigrants (in his case 95,000 Asians) and backed the Palestinian cause.

In 1980 Gadaffi's impact on African politics reached new heights. In January he backed an attempt to overthrow the neighbouring Tunisian government with which he had earlier (1984) considered forging a union. Later in the year he was variously credited with helping rebel groups in Niger, Upper Volta, and Guinea-Bissau, and several African nations broke off relations with him. One study described him as 'perhaps the leading exponent of the tactic of the proxy military coup'.[28] His only serious, long-term foreign adventure however was in Chad, a neighbouring state, dry and sparsely populated, beset by divisions and poverty.

Libya had a claim to Chad's northern, Ouzou, region and, for some years before Gadaffi seized power, had sponsored a liberation movement there. In maintaining this policy, Gadaffi 'identified himself with what he [saw] as the struggle of all Chadian Muslims . . . against an alien and oppressive minority of Christians and animists, supported by France and . . . the United States.'[29] But it has also been argued that his ambitions went far beyond Chad itself: he 'saw the country as a . . . bridgehead into Black Africa where he aimed to spread his revolutionary Islam-based ideology.'[30] His pro-Arab, pan-Islamic, and anti-Western views led him to simplify Chad's complex ethnic and religious make-up. The Chadian government had briefly broken off diplomatic relations with Gadaffi in 1971–2, before accepting his occupation of the Ouzou strip. During the 1970s Gadaffi aided the opponents of the pro-French government in Chad (France being the former colonial power) and, in 1980, used a brief military incursion to help install a friendly government, under Goukouni Ouddei. Then, in 1981, the Libyan leader announced a union between the two countries, proposals for unions with fellow Arab states having being one of the persistent, if unsuccessful elements of his foreign policy.

At this point 'Libya seemed to have replaced [the] French military presence at the geographical heart of the continent'[31] but it also stirred up suspicion among neighbouring states, leading to the deployment of an OAU peacekeeping force in December 1981. Thereafter, Gadaffi clung onto Ouzou. But, despite large expenditure (financed from Libya's vast oil reserves), he was unable to protect his clients during the civil strife that persisted in Chad. Instead the French soon helped to restore a former President, Hassan Habre, who in 1986–7 even restored control of the Ouzou strip, a 1984 deal on mutual Libyan–French withdrawal having proved abortive. Between 1973 and 1987 it is estimated that the Libyans lost 3,500 dead in Chad which became the place where Gadaffi's 'adventurism exacted its heaviest toll and the disproportion between performance and ambition was most cruelly revealed'.[32] Habre was in turn overthrown by the Libyan-backed Idris Debi in 1990 but Gadaffi was unable to restore the commanding position he had held in Chad in 1980–1.

Reagan and Gadaffi

Meanwhile, by 1980, relations with the US had grown even worse. In December 1979, pronouncing its sympathy for Iran in the hostages dispute, a mob attacked the American embassy in Tripoli. The following May President Carter, without fully breaking relations, expelled most Libyan diplomats from their so-called 'People's Bureau' in Washington. The Reagan administration despised Gadaffi from the start, as a paymaster of terrorists and because he was seen as a Soviet stooge. In May 1981 the Washington 'People's Bureau' was closed down altogether and the US set out to isolate Libya diplomatically. Attention soon focused on the Gulf of Sidra, which Libya claimed to be entirely its own territorial waters, a claim the US denied. On 20 August 1981 two Libyan aircraft were shot down after firing on US airplanes over the Gulf. Seven months later America introduced economic sanctions against Libya (but was unable to persuade its NATO allies to follow suit). Rather than being cowed by this Gadaffi, seen as a hero by Arab radicals, increased his support for anti-Western terrorist groups and was again rumoured to be planning the assassination of US political figures. Terrorist attacks were nothing new and Libya was not the only government accused of supporting them. Syria and Iran were both blamed for bombings in Lebanon. Iran was also responsible for a December 1983 attack on the American embassy in Kuwait and, exactly a year later, for the hijacking of a Kuwaiti airliner which led to two Americans being killed. Indeed, the CIA recognized Iran as the worst culprit in the scale of its backing for such actions. But it was also the hardest to attack in terms of its geographical position, it seemed likely to react strongly to any US countermeasures, there were persistent fears of driving it towards the Soviets, and, by the mid-1980s, the Reagan administration had hopes of moderating Iranian policy through clandestine contacts. Libya, in contrast, was already close to Moscow, geographically well placed for an attack and—given the way it alienated its neighbours—relatively easy to isolate. And Gadaffi continued to draw attention to himself: in mid-March 1984 there was a Libyan bombing raid on the Sudanese capital, Khartoum, and a month later a British policewoman was shot dead outside the Libyan 'People's Bureau' in London.

In 1985 international terrorism reached a new intensity, much of it linked to the Palestinian cause but with attacks sponsored by Iran, Syria, and Libya. The 'Islamic Jihad' group launched bomb attacks in Madrid and Riyadh in the spring; Frankfurt airport was bombed in June; October saw the seizure of the *Achille Lauro* cruise ship; in November sixty people died when an Egyptian aircraft was hijacked and on 27 December simultaneous attacks at Rome and Vienna airports killed twenty people. In response Reagan was determined to act and the CIA shifted its operations from simply predicting and analysing terrorist attacks, to meeting and punishing them. There was some concern that retribution against Libya might lead Gadaffi to seize American hostages: despite economic sanctions about 1,000 US citizens were working for oil companies there. But contingency plans for a strike on Libya were laid and, in July 1985, consideration was even given to a joint US–Egyptian invasion. In early January 1986 Reagan publicly accused Libya of aggression against the US and announced new economic sanctions, including severe travel restrictions and a freeze on Libyan assets. But, once again, America's NATO allies—who took 90 per cent of Libya's oil—refused to join in these steps, expressing doubts about the effectiveness of sanctions and fears that Gadaffi would become more of a problem if he were hounded. In January the US navy also renewed its manoeuvres in the Gulf of Sidra, another provocative move which won little NATO support. The Americans judged the Gulf to be an ideal place to challenge Gadaffi because it was easy for them to operate there and, though it was not tested, they believed they had a strong case in international law. 'No real effort was made, however, to disguise the fact that the operation was a warning signal about Libyan-inspired terrorism, rather than about maritime navigation rights.'[33] A few months later Gadaffi rose to the bait. On 24 March the Libyans fired on US aircraft and the Americans retaliated by sinking two patrol boats.

US–Libyan tension finally reached a crisis in April 1986. On the 5th a bomb attack by Palestinians in West Berlin killed two American servicemen and injured many others. Intercepted messages from the 'People's Bureau' in East Berlin linked the attack to Libya and a consensus was reached in Washington in favour of a retaliatory strike. On 14 April aircraft from bases in Britain and carriers in the Mediterranean bombed Gadaffi's home and other targets, including barracks and airfields, in the Tripoli and Benghazi regions. There were also CIA attempts to stir up internal dissent in the country. The Secretary of State, George Shultz, had already publicly justified the action by insisting, 'There is substantial legal authority for the view that a state which supports terrorist ... attacks against another state ... is responsible for such attacks. Such conduct can amount to ... armed aggression ... under international law' and he later warned Gadaffi 'You've had it, pal.'[34] But others doubted that America was justified in invoking the right of self-defence under Article 51 and the scale of the raids seemed out of all proportion to the West Berlin bombing. Furthermore, Gadaffi—despite the apparent hope of killing him in the attack—remained securely in power, becoming a hero in radical Arab eyes. Indeed, one reading is that he 'defied his critics and bounced back on the world stage . . . He had challenged one of the world's superpowers and survived.'[35] In 1989 in another clash with the US in the Gulf of Sidra two Libyan aircraft were shot down; and Libyans were later implicated in the December 1989 bombing of a Pan-Am airliner over Scotland. The American action was not only criticized by the Eastern bloc and the non-aligned world, but also by moderate Arab countries like Egypt and Saudi Arabia, and by NATO governments. In contrast to the British, both Italy and Greece refused to allow their airbases to be used for the raids; France and Spain had refused to allow the American aircraft to overfly their territory. The attack seemed an act of frustration against a relatively easy target, and a reflection of America's inability to shape Middle East politics constructively. Then again, it boosted Reagan's popularity at home and seems to have led to a lessening of terrorist sponsorship by a shaken Gadaffi.

NOTES

1. Robert Fisk, *Pity the Nation: Lebanon at War* (Deutsch, London, 1990), 193.

2. Shlaim, *Iron Wall: Israel and the Arab World* (Allen Lane, London, 2000), 396–7.

3. Tessler, *A History of the Israeli–Palestinian Conflict* (Indiana University Press, Bloomington,1994), 571.

4. Shlaim, op. cit., 396.

5. Alexander Haig, *Caveat: Realism, Reagan and Foreign Policy* (Macmillan, New York, 1984), 342 and see 351.

6. Fisk, op. cit., 383.

7. Sasson Sofer, *Begin: an Anatomy of Leadership* (Blackwell, Oxford, 1988), 214.

8. Hala Jaber, *Hezbollah: Born with a Vengeance* (Columbia University Press, New York, 1997), 20–1.

9. Caspar Weinberger, *Fighting for Peace: Seven Critical Years at the Pentagon* (Joseph, London, 1990), 111.

10. Edgar O'Ballance, *Civil War in Lebanon, 1975–92* (Macmillan, London, 1998), 216–17.

11. William Quandt, *Peace Process; American Diplomacy and the Arab–Israeli Conflict* (Brookings Institution, Washington, DC, 1993), 378.

12. Seth Tillman, *The US in the Middle East* (Indiana University Press, Bloomington, 1982), 122.

13. Avi Shlaim, *The Iron Wall: Israel and the Arab World* (Allen Lane, London, 2000), 394, citing Ilan Peleg *Begin's Foreign Policy 1977–1983: Israel's Move to the Right* (Greenwood Press, New York, 1987), 190–5.

14. Shlaim, op. cit., 394.

15. Alan Hart, *Arafat* (Sidgwick & Henry, London, 1984), 460.

16. Shlaim, op. cit., 426.

17. Beverley Milton-Edwards, *Contemporary Politics in the Middle East* (Blackwell, Polity Press, Cambridge, 2000), 102–3.

18. Shlaim, op. cit., 466.

19. James A. Baker, *The Politics of Diplomacy* (G. P. Putnam's Sons, New York, 1995), 115.

20. John Bulloch and Harvey Morris, *The Gulf War: its Origins, History and Consequences* (Methuen, London, 1989), 38.

21. G. H. Hansen, 'The Attitudes of the Arab Governments', in M. S. El-Azhary (ed.), *The Iran–Iraq War: An Historical, Economic and Political Analysis* (Croom Helm, London, 1984), 81–2.

22. Bulloch and Morris, op. cit., xvii.

23. Shireen Hunter, *Iran and the World: Continuity in a Revolutionary Decade* (Indiana University Press, Bloomington, 1990), 66.

24. Andrew and Patrick Cockburn, *Out of the Ashes: The Resurrection of Saddam Hussein* (HarperCollins, London, 1999), 81.

25. Said Aburish, *Saddam Hussein, the Politics of Revenge* (Bloomsbury, London, 2000), 250.

26. David Blundy and Andrew Lycett, *Qadaffi and the Libyan Revolution* (Weidenfeld & Nicolson, London, revised edn., 1988), 30.

27. Peter Lyon, 'The End of the Cold War in Africa', in Oliver Furley (ed.), *Conflict in Africa* (British Academic Press, London, 1995), 176.

28. Colin Legum *et al.*, *Africa in the 1980s* (McGraw-Hill, New York, 1979), 42.

29. John Wright, *Libya, Chad and the Central Sahara* (Hurst, London, 1989), 139.

30. Arthur Gavshon, *Crisis in Africa* (Penguin Books, Harmondsworth, 1981), 173.

31. Wright, op. cit., 132.

32. Rene Lamarchand, 'Libyan Adventurism', in John Harbeson and Donald Rothschild (eds.), *Africa in World Politics* (Westview Press, Boulder, 1991), 152.

33. Coral Bell, *The Reagan Paradox* (Elgar, Aldershot, 1989), 86.

34. George Shultz, *Turmoil and Triumph* (Macmillan, New York, 1993), 678 and 688.

35. Blundy and Lycett, op. cit., 26.

18 Instability in Latin America

A. The Reagan Doctrine and El Salvador

Reagan's Policy towards Latin America

In the early 1970s, when the Nixon administration was obsessed by Vietnam and détente, Latin America had not figured prominently in Washington's world-view. Apart from Chile, where the left-wing regime of Salvador Allende was toppled in 1973, the region seemed relatively stable, despite widespread poverty, illiteracy, and repressive government. Under the Nixon Doctrine the US had relied on local governments to maintain authority and, although Cuba still existed as a Soviet ally in the Western hemisphere, communism was virtually non-existent and Castro was unable to promote revolution successfully. America's domination of the Latin American economies was in decline but still considerable; in the mid-1950s it absorbed about half their exports, twenty years later it took around a third. In the 1970s the Latin American countries joined with other developing economies, in the G-77 group, to press for a 'new International Economic Order' that would redistribute wealth globally, but the US Trade Act of January 1975 put up greater barriers to Latin American exports. Economic changes in mid-decade had a profound impact on local societies. The oil crisis of 1973–4, followed as it was by trade deficits, depression, and high inflation, helped promote revolutionary ideas among the landless peasants and urban poor of many Latin American countries. (One of the few to benefit from this period, thanks to its oil wealth, was Venezuela). In particular the poverty-stricken 'banana republics' of Central America became prone to unrest and this situation persisted through the next world economic depression in 1979–82.

Under Jimmy Carter, with his interest in promoting human rights, a more active and enlightened US policy towards Latin America might have been expected but in this region, as elsewhere, Carter's aims were inconsistent, as the moral cause of human rights clashed with local realities and other American interests. He did manage to cut military aid to Latin America by about a quarter in 1976–9 and one study found that, in 'several Latin American countries, the 1970s ended with a considerable increase in the level of respect for human rights related to the physical integrity of the person', with a reduction in torture and detention without trial.[1] But by the end of this period the Cold War with Moscow was reviving, leftist guerrillas were active in most Central American states, and 'the military governments affected by the arms restrictions lashed out at what they viewed as a new form of US intervention in their internal affairs.'[2] Rather than have Carter cut their military aid completely, several states—Argentina, Brazil, El Salvador, Guatemala, and Uruguay—declared that they no longer wanted US arms, and began to make purchases elsewhere. The military dictatorships of Argentina and Brazil, whose violent oppression caused Carter special concern, simply decided to pursue their own line regardless, jointly backing a military coup in Bolivia in 1980, developing links to right-wing regimes on other continents (such as South Africa), and encouraging other Latin American states to break free of US tutelage.

Any hopes that Carter could induce such regimes to democratize gradually, therefore proved naïve. And any hope that America could use its wealth to launch a new effort at economic development in Latin America, given the failure of Kennedy's 'Alliance for Progress', was an illusion: American public opinion was shifting to the Right as most people looked for state spending to be reduced. Carter's policy finally proved ineffective in July 1979, when he did little to prevent a leftist movement, the Sandinistas, toppling the long-standing Somoza dictatorship in Nicaragua (fully discussed in Chapter 18, B). In Carter's eyes Somoza could be compared to other dictators, like Batista of Cuba, ousted in 1958, or Trujillo of the Dominican Republic, murdered in 1961, whose economically bankrupt, police states had simply become an embarrassment to their foreign supporters. 'Administration spokesmen emphasized that here was an opportunity for the United States to demonstrate that it could respond positively to revolutionary change in the developing world.'[3] However, in 1980,

with the new Cold War underway, it was easy for Republicans to accuse Carter of having made one more, grave error. In Nicaragua, a leftist regime, now allied to Fidel Castro, had been allowed into power and it might spread revolution to neighbouring Central American states, notably El Salvador. This was seen by some as an advance for Soviet interests in America's 'own back yard' and attributed to Washington's declining power, which Ronald Reagan was determined to reverse. Then again, as in US–Soviet relations, a 'change of policy . . . had been effected well before . . . Reagan entered the White House.' In Central America in 1980, Carter sought to 'erect a cordon sanitaire around Nicaragua, the Americans once again began to dispense generous military aid to the neighbouring countries [and] military advisers were sent to El Salvador.'[4]

In contrast to the Nixon period a decade before, the Reagan years saw Latin America, or more specifically Central America, assume a primary importance in US foreign policy. 'For Reagan, Central America was the focal point of his tough new foreign policy . . . where Washington would draw the line against the spread of communism in the less developed world.'[5] Here was a testing ground for the Reagan Doctrine, with its promise of support for any 'freedom fighters' who were struggling to liberate their countries from communism. It was especially important too, after Carter's apparent retreats, to reassert US strength in an area long seen as its own sphere of influence and to reassure the region's right-wing governments that they could rely on Washington's leadership. 'We had already lost Cuba to Communism,' Reagan later wrote. 'I was determined the Free World was not going to lose Central America or more of the Caribbean.'[6] As elsewhere, therefore, the main thrust of Reagan's policy was remarkably simple: previous ideas of support for human rights, encouraging democratization, and providing economic development aid were pushed aside more firmly than under Nixon by a determined anti-communism although, in January 1984, a commission under Henry Kissinger reported that economic aid should be a vital component of policy in Central America, *alongside* covert operations and assistance to anti-communists. The new policy *did* have an intellectual justification, provided by the ambassador to the UN, a former social science academic, Jeanne Kirkpatrick. In an article entitled 'Dictatorships and Double Standards', published in 1979, she argued that, although 'authoritarian' regimes might suppress freedom, they *were* pro-US, open to capitalism, protective of traditional values, and might be reformed over time; 'totalitarian' regimes on the other hand, such as those in the Communist bloc, were anti-US, inimical to capitalism and (or so she argued) incapable of reform. In 1980 the recent examples of what had occurred in Iran and Nicaragua seemed to provide ample evidence in Kirkpatrick's favour and against Carter. In each case, she argued, 'the American effort to impose liberalization and democratization on a government confronted with violent internal opposition not only failed, but actually assisted the coming to power of new regimes in which ordinary people enjoy fewer freedoms . . . regimes, moreover, hostile to American interests.'[7] Reagan believed that the Kirkpatrick thesis 'provided . . . intellectual foundation for the argument he had been making . . . about the Carter policies . . . weakening US . . . influence . . . under the banner of advancing human rights.'[8]

Criticized at the time as being based on a poor grasp of history, it did not take many years for the flaws in the Kirkpatrick thesis to become apparent. Under Reagan, as in previous decades the 'authoritarian' regimes which the US supported, actually proved extremely unwilling to reform, they hardly provided the ideal, stable conditions for capitalism to thrive, and they frequently clashed with such traditional institutions as the Roman Catholic Church. Their violence and oppression remained an embarrassment to America and, in one case, foreign adventurism by the Argentinian dictatorship of General Leopoldo Galtieri, provoked a major crisis: on 2 April the Argentineans occupied the sparsely populated, British-ruled Falklands Islands in the South Atlantic to enforce a territorial claim; though the British had shown little interest in the islands in the recent past, the government of Margaret Thatcher would not tolerate such an affront to national dignity and sent a naval force to retake them (see boxed section). Ironically, given Kirkpatrick's lack of support for British action, it was the Argentinian defeat which led to a return to democracy in 1983, after years of dictatorship, during which around 6,000 opponents of the mili-

tary had 'disappeared'. As the 1980s proceeded two points became even more obvious. One, of course, was that 'totalitarian' states in the Eastern bloc, *were* capable of political and economic reform, as witnessed by the dramatic changes under Gorbachev after 1985: 'the final judgement on Kirkpatrick's theory occurred in Eastern Europe . . . when totalitarian regimes . . . were replaced by elected governments.'[9] The other was that there could be genuinely democratic uprisings against dictators, most obviously, not in Latin America but in the ex-US colony of the Philippines in early 1986. Here the corrupt but overconfident Ferdinand Marcos, President since 1966, agreed to hold elections only to be defeated by Carazon Aquino, the wife of a former opposition leader who Marcos had murdered. Marcos tried to falsify the results but was faced by massive demonstrations and this 'people power' convinced Washington that he must be told to leave. Yet in the later 1980s the 'Kirkpatrick Formula'—that rightist dictatorships were capable of reform—did seem to find justification in one area, when several of Latin America's dictatorships held elections: Brazil, Uruguay, and Peru in 1985, Guatemala in 1986, Chile and Paraguay in 1989.

El Salvador

Whatever the lessons of events in the Philippines, in Central America the US government stuck doggedly to a policy of upholding right-wing governments, however vicious and unpopular, against left-wing guerrillas, supposedly backed by the Eastern bloc. 'American charges of Soviet and Cuban responsibility for revolution in Central America were . . . more convenient than acknowledging failures of reactionary regimes to provide for needed peaceful change.'[10] It was particularly important, in Reagan's view, both to prevent the Nicaraguan revolution from spreading beyond its own borders and to try to undermine the Sandinista regime. There were guerrilla movements in South America, notably the Maoist 'Tupac Amaru' who began to make advances in the Peruvian countryside in 1980. But US efforts concentrated on helping several Central American states resist the supposed attempt of Cuba and Nicaragua to export revolution. Those deemed most under threat included Honduras, Guatemala, and El Salvador. (Mexico, the largest Central American state, escaped serious internal dissent in this period; only in January 1994 did the Zaptista National Liberation Army become active in Chiapos province among the poor peasantry.) Honduras, the poorest country of the region, was heavily dependent economically on the US and seen by Washington as relatively secure. Guatemala, dominated by the military and wealthy landowners since 1954, was more troubled, having suffered an earthquake in 1976 which added to its economic problems; however, the government was ruthless in eliminating its opponents, not only leftists, who had begun a guerrilla campaign in 1962, but even Christian Democrats. By the time the leftist insurgency in Guatemala ended in December 1996 it was estimated that 200,000 had been killed, mostly by the army, making the process of national reconciliation very difficult. Carter had been so alienated by such repression that he cut off military aid to Guatemala, but Reagan used the country, like Honduras, as a base for covert operations against Nicaragua. Costa Rica was the only proper democracy in Latin America in 1980 but, paradoxically, something of a problem for Washington, because the Costa Rican government followed an independent line abroad, providing some economic aid to the Sandinistas and, especially after 1986 working for the reconciliation of the opposing forces in Nicaragua, rather than the destruction of the Sandinista regime.

'The most urgent visible crisis during the initial years of the Reagan period, however, was over El Salvador.'[11] Indeed, it was the need to prevent a leftist overthrow of the government in El Salvador which initially gave Reagan the justification to boost aid to those fighting the Nicaraguan Sandinistas. El Salvador, a major coffee exporter with a population of five million, was another country dominated by a landowning oligarchy, firmly supported by the military. About a third of the rural population owned no land; illiteracy, homelessness, and malnutrition were widespread. In 1969 the country won the short-lived 'Soccer War' (so-called because it was sparked by a football match) with neighbouring Honduras, but the triumph was financially costly and it also helped kill off lingering hopes for a Central American common market, a free trade

zone, first proposed in the 1960 Managua Treaty. Support then increased in urban areas for the Christian Democratic Party, founded in 1960 with the support of the Roman Catholic Church and led by José Napoleon Duarte. But when Duarte appeared likely to win the 1972 elections, the government cancelled them, drove Duarte into exile, and ruthlessly extinguished the ensuing signs of discontent. This experience meant that the regime's opponents then turned to non-democratic means to gain power. In 1977 General Humberto Romero was elected President amid violence and blatant corruption. Despite the opposition of the Catholic Church, the US decided it must supply him with more economic aid. One important feature of El Salvadorian politics was the degree to which the Church criticized repression and spoke out in favour of the poor. The opposition of an influential national, traditional institution was of grave concern to the military, who murdered several priests in the 1970s. Such actions were difficult to justify in terms of anti-communism.

In mid-1979, concerned at the fall of Somoza in Nicaragua and evidence that Cuba was training El Salvador's leftist insurgents, the Carter administration decided to press for a change of government. On 15 October General Romero was duly overthrown by fellow officers, who established a junta with several civilian members and promised reform, and in January 1980 the Christian Democrats were brought into government. 'If the admittedly weak regime could be sustained by the United States in the short run, US officials believed, its programme of social reform would eventually attract support, rebuilding a political centre where none now existed.'[12] But the junta soon became divided, the landowners opposed even limited land reform, and there were no talks with the insurgents. Even when Duarte, with US encouragement, was installed as President, the violence continued. Events in Nicaragua also had a significant impact on El Salvador: 'The Sandinista victory ... not only encouraged the Left, it had also galvanized the Right.'[13] The urban and rural poor were no longer impressed by Duarte's liberal credentials, whilst the army and police increasingly took decisions into their own hands, murdering their opponents. In March 1980 they even killed the country's religious leader, the outspoken Archbishop Oscar Romero, in his own cathedral. This, alongside the murder of three American nuns, caused an outcry in the US and led Carter to threaten a cut in aid. Leftist terrorism and army massacres seemed to be turning El Salvador towards anarchy, with about 10,000 dying through violence during 1980. Landowners, financiers, and military leaders began to move their money out of the country (thus provoking an investment collapse) and to connive in the activities of right-wing death squads. The most notorious of these was the 'White Warriors' led by a US-trained, ex-intelligence officer, Major Roberto d'Aubuisson. But in the face of the onslaught and ever-greater poverty, the leftists, hitherto very divided, became more united and determined. In October 1980 they formed a national liberation front (FMLN) and, though there were only a few thousand guerrillas, they took control of much of the countryside. A secret attempt by Duarte to talk to some of his opponents in November 1980 was ruined when the military discovered it and murdered the leftist delegates—making them reluctant to risk talks again.

Under Carter in 1980 the US was already providing El Salvador with considerable aid and even military advisers, and this trend inevitably continued under Reagan, urged on by Secretary of State Alexander Haig, who feared the country would be the next Latin American 'domino' to fall to the Soviets and Cubans. It was also an excellent opportunity to prove that, notwithstanding Vietnam, 'national liberation' movements could be defeated. Haig had no doubt of Soviet and Cuban involvement and 'believed that our policy should ... through the application of a full range of economic, political, and security measures, convince them to put an end to Havana's bloody activities.'[14] But there were several problems with this approach. First, despite the publication of a State Department paper on the subject in February 1981, it was very difficult to prove that the Soviets and Cubans were involved on any meaningful scale in El Salvador: the local support for the guerrillas was genuine and only a few Soviet arms were sent—arguably as a riposte to CIA activities in Afghanistan. The White Paper claimed to provide 'definite evidence of the clandestine military support given by the Soviet Union, Cuba and their allies to Marxist-Leninist guerrillas now

fighting to overthrow the established government of El Salvador.'[15] But a number of press reports 'shredded the White paper's claim.'[16] Second, despite $200 million in military aid from the US in 1981–4, as well as schooling in counter-insurgency techniques, the Salvadorian army was unable to secure a decisive victory, or even to calm the situation. The US also had an embarrassing time trying to maintain Duarte. In March 1982, in elections which the leftists boycotted, he was defeated by the National Republic Alliance (ARENA), led by d'Aubuisson, who proved that there was a considerable body of genuine support for his extreme right-wing views, even among the smaller landowners. Washington poured over a million dollars into the Christian Democratic coffers ahead of the next election in May 1984, but Duarte won only narrowly and he was still unable to overcome the problems of poverty and corruption, or to control the activities of the death squads.

By 1989 ARENA was back in power, with their candidate Alfredo Cristiani, triumphing in that year's Presidential election. By then about 70,000 had been killed in ten years of trouble but the 50,000 strong army was no nearer to defeating the guerrillas, who probably numbered considerably less than 10,000. Outrages continued on both sides, the latest being the murder of six Jesuit priests by the army. US economic and military assistance had continued to flow into the country ($600 million in 1988 alone) but many Salvadorians turned against the American presence: 1986 saw widespread anti-US protests. With the Cold War over, a settlement achieved (in 1990) in Nicaragua and with both sides in El Salvador exhausted, a ceasefire was finally agreed in September 1991. A peace agreement was signed under UN auspices three months later, with both sides now ready to compromise. Cristiani 'pursued peace doggedly, despite resistance from the Right. The FMLN had given up its demands for powersharing ... settling for changes in the armed forces.'[17] The death of d'Aubuisson, from cancer, in 1992 probably helped cement a settlement in which the leftists had a share in policing the country and a purge was carried out of those army officers who had participated in the death squads. But elections in 1994 confirmed that it was the Right, in the form of ARENA, which held the balance of popular support.

The Reagan Doctrine

As with the Nixon Doctrine, the Reagan Doctrine was not included in a single statement but rather was explained by the President, and by other members of his administration, on several occasions. However, an important, early summary came in the February 1985 'State of the Union' address, where Reagan told Congress:

We must not break faith with those who are risking their lives, on every continent from Afghanistan to Nicaragua, to defy Soviet aggression . . . support for freedom fighters is self-defence.

In subsequent speeches the Secretary of State, George Shultz, made clear that the Doctrine was meant to reverse the idea that the Soviets could expand their influence through 'wars of national liberation' and that the West was incapable of reversing the process. The Doctrine pleased the Republican Right. It seemed to go beyond the narrow defence of American interests that had characterized the Nixon Doctrine; and it marked a revival of 'rollback' and 'liberation' ideas that had been advocated in Eisenhower's early years.

In actual fact, to the disappointment of some right-wingers, and despite the potential 'globalistic' nature of Reagan's rhetoric, the focus of US assistance was mainly on the Mujaheddin of Afghanistan and the Contras of Nicaragua (though there was diplomatic support for the opponents of pro-Soviet regimes in Angola, Mozambique, and Cambodia). Furthermore, Reagan had been helping these two causes since early in his first term, so that the Doctrine did not mark a new departure so much as a justification of existing practice. Opponents pointed out that some of those who received aid were hardly models of liberal-democratic ambition. In Cambodia in particular the US was backing an alliance of forces that included the mass murderer, Pol Pot. In Nicaragua, some argued, it was the US rather than the USSR which was trying to curtail the country's independence. Yet despite the fears of his critics, Reagan avoided a serious, direct clash with the Soviets, partly because the Doctrine largely employed clandestine assistance to low-intensity conflicts. And over the following years the Soviets did retreat from less developed world involvement in Afghanistan which the Reagan Doctrine targeted.

B. Nicaragua and the 'Contragate' Scandal

The Fall of Somoza

In Nicaragua, in contrast to El Salvador, the Reagan administration's aim was to topple a government rather than to maintain it. But the enemy, the radical Left, was the same and the conflict proved just as long-lasting and destructive. There was a long history of US involvement in Nicaraguan politics stretching back to the 1890s and it had been under virtual American occupation for two decades before 1933. Thereafter, it was dominated by the Somoza family, corrupt and oppressive but also trusted anti-Communists who helped the CIA-backed operation to overthrow Guatemala's Jacobo Arbenz in 1954 (see Chapter 6, C) and whose dictatorship was the region's most stable and lasting. In 1967 Anastasio Debayle Somoza succeeded to the Nicaraguan leadership and, through the economic troubles of the 1970s, came increasingly to rely on the National Guard to maintain him in power. As in El Salvador, land ownership was concentrated in a few hands and there was a large number of landless labourers. An earthquake (in 1972) devastated large areas and wealth was monopolized by the Somozas and their supporters, who also cornered much of the foreign aid that flowed in after the earthquake. Opposition was led by the Sandinistan National Liberation Front (FSLN), who were named after Augusto Sandina, an inter-war hero who had resisted American domination, before being murdered by Anastasio Somoza. The FSLN had been founded in 1961 and, while its main support came from rural areas, it launched attacks on urban centres after 1966. With a fragmented leadership, it had had limited success in fighting Somoza until the earthquake. Now things were different. The uprising was soon widespread and in January 1978 they began a mass uprising. A few months later, in their most daring operation so far, the Sandinistas seized control of the National Congress, releasing its members in return for concessions. But Somoza was unwilling to strike any lasting deal with the Left and, in late 1978, turned to ruthless suppression, murdering thousands and escalating the violence. In early 1979 Somoza's hold on power still seemed reasonably secure but events in Nicaragua were already of international concern, with some nearby governments sympathetic to the rebels. Costa Rica allowed the Sandinistas to establish a government-in-exile in 1978, and in May 1979, as a major rebel offensive was launched, Mexico decided to withdraw diplomatic recognition from Somoza, thus risking American displeasure.

Arguably the US shared the blame for the rising violence in Nicaragua. Carter's human rights policy had probably encouraged Somoza's opponents to seek reform in 1977 and it was partly to please the new President that the dictator himself had eased repression for a time, a move which simply made the opposition more vocal. Somoza himself even complained that Carter's pressure on human rights 'was his vehicle for the destruction of me.'[18] Yet on the other hand, a strong 'Somoza Lobby' in Congress ensured that America continued to provide arms for the National Guard into 1979. By then Carter was caught in a difficult situation. 'On the one hand the Carter administration wanted to remain true to its human rights policy . . . but on the other hand the Sandinistas were leftists who would . . . take Nicaragua . . . toward Marxism.'[19] Ideally, he would have liked to find some moderate alternative (such as Duarte's Christian Democrats in El Salvador) to both Somoza and the Sandinistas. The latter, relying as they did on Cuban arms and training, were not a welcome replacement for the dictatorship in American eyes, yet Somoza's extreme oppression made it impossible for Carter to maintain him by force. In June 1979, when the CIA warned that the regime was in grave danger, the White House decided that nothing could be done to save him and instead continued to hope that a 'moderate', non-Sandinista replacement could be found who might pursue a gradual reform programme. A plan was devised whereby Somoza would resign in return

for a Sandinista ceasefire; the National Guard would remain intact to maintain order and this would buy time for a non-revolutionary government to be formed. 'The White House was especially eager to ensure the survival of the National Guard who . . . could provide a counterweight to the Cuban-trained Sandinista army in a post-Somoza Nicaragua.'[20] But such hopes were fanciful. It has been argued that if America had been 'willing to demand Somoza's resignation nine months earlier, a constitutional solution might have been feasible' but by late June 'even the most conservative Nicaraguan opposition groups had already endorsed the Sandinistas' provisional government.'[21] Somoza's regime was on the brink of collapse, a 'moderate' alternative did not exist, and the National Guard, which had killed up to 40,000 people in recent years, was hated. A scheme to send a peacekeeping force from the Organization of American States was vetoed by Costa Rica, Mexico, and others. Even the US public turned against Somoza on 20 June when National Guardsmen murdered a US journalist in front of film cameras.

Somoza was finally forced to leave the capital, Managua, on 17 July 1979, going into exile in Paraguay, a military dictatorship, where he was assassinated the following year. The National Guard disintegrated after his departure, though many of them too fled abroad, hoping to carry on their opposition to the new government, which the Sandinistas formed on 19 July. In some ways their government, though radical, was not as extreme as the US feared. There were arrests and the use of censorship but violence quickly died down, justice was largely maintained (even in the case of judgements on former National Guardsmen) and, despite an ambitious programme of nationalization, many private businesses continued to flourish, not only those whose owners had turned against the corruption and arbitrary rule of the Somozas, but also some which were American-owned. The new government declared itself to be non-aligned and, in order to ensure the continuation of such moderation, Carter agreed to provide $20 million in economic aid. Congress agreed to provide further aid in 1980, but this was partly because of the desire of 'North American, European and Japanese banks to avoid a Nicaraguan default on the country's $1.5 billion debt',[22] and by then US–Sandinista relations were very poor. For, even if Nicaragua claimed to be non-aligned, in effect it was close to the communist bloc, buying East European arms and accepting several thousand Cuban advisers. The Sandinistas refused to condemn the Soviet invasion of Afghanistan and in May 1980 some of the more moderate members, including Violetta Chamarro, quit the government. The CIA was fearful that Nicaragua, backed by Cuba and the USSR, would aid leftist insurgents elsewhere, most obviously in El Salvador. And President Carter, accused by his opponents of having 'lost' Nicaragua to communism, began to approve limited covert operations against the Sandinistas.

Reagan and the 'Contras', 1981–1986

In 1979–80 Carter effectively carried out a dual-edged policy towards the Sandinistas, establishing links to their opponents yet also using financial assistance to draw them away from Cuba. Under Reagan there was a simpler policy of trying to destroy the Sandinistas who were depicted as Soviet stooges, totalitarian and militaristic. The limited scale of Soviet aid and the fact that US companies could still operate in Nicaragua were ignored. Instead the country, like El Salvador, became a focus of American efforts to turn the communist tide in the less developed world and reverse the supposed defeats for the Western cause under Carter. Nicaragua eventually overtook El Salvador as the focus of US activity in the region, although in 1980 it was seen as a subsidiary issue, important mainly because it was a conduit for arms supplies to the El Salvadorean guerrillas. Alongside Afghanistan, Nicaragua also became the main focus of Reagan's ambition to support 'freedom fighters' in the liberation of their country from communist domination. To Washington, 'the Sandinistas were Marxist-Leninists. If they stayed in power, they would guide Nicaragua ... toward a one-party ... dictatorship, alliance with the Soviet Union and subversion of their neighbours.'[23] By late 1981 the National Security Adviser, Robert McFarlane, was coordinating a wide range of activities to undermine the Sandinistas without provoking outright war or

too much international outrage. These included diplomatic, psychological, economic, and military steps. On the diplomatic front the Secretary of State, Alexander Haig, encouraged by Mexico, did make a secret attempt in November 1981 to persuade the Cubans to end their support for radical movements. But this failed: the Cubans argued that problems in Latin America were internally generated and that they were bound to help their fellow leftists. The US thereafter relied on isolating the Sandinistas diplomatically, especially in Latin America, and trying to prevent them receiving foreign aid and conducting trade. In 1982, the US also used its influence to have the World Bank end its loans to Nicaragua. Securing the support of dictatorships like Honduras and Guatemala for such a policy was easy, but backing from others was more difficult to secure: in 1981 Mexico, keen to limit US domination of the region, provided Nicaragua with $200 million in aid. Reagan confirmed in April 1981, that all US aid to Nicaragua would end, pressure was put on companies to end ties, and eventually, in 1985, a full trade embargo was introduced. 'By the end of 1985, the United States ... had effectively foreclosed any possibility of the Sandinistas obtaining loans from any of the major international lending agencies.'[24] On the psychological front the State Department formed a new department, the Office of Public Diplomacy, to direct the propaganda effort against the Sandinistas. But this Office was put under the direction of a CIA official and it was the CIA which soon gained the leading role in trying to destroy the Sandinistas. The Agency's Director, Bill Casey, became quite obsessed with the idea of Nicaragua as the main base for Soviet-Cuban activity in Central America.

Despite the above measures it became clear that the 'most effective weapons in Washington's arsenal were political and military, namely the financing of right-wing opposition parties in Nicaragua and the ... training of Nicaraguan exiles ... into a guerrilla force.'[25] By 1982 the 'purpose of US activity was no longer just interdiction of arms shipments to neighbouring El Salvador. It became, first and foremost, an attempt to topple the Sandinista government.'[26] Although Ronald Reagan was one of the few leading Americans still to defend the Vietnam War, he recognized that the time had passed when

US marines could be despatched to enforce order in the Central American states. Not only popular opinion, but also expert advice from the Department of Defence, was opposed to any action that risked 'another Vietnam'. So, given Reagan's determination nonetheless to put *military* pressure on the Sandinistas, the administration had to support a force of Nicaraguan-born 'freedom fighters' who would carry out a campaign of sabotage, assassination, economic disruption, and general harassment in their own country designed to demoralize the Sandinistas and drain their treasury. In fact the CIA had virtually to *create* such a force because, despite Reagan's confidence that the Nicaraguan people were living under an unpopular oppressor, there was little active opposition to the government. The 'Contras', as the opposition became called, were often former members of the National Guard but from April 1982 the CIA also funded a former Sandinista leader, Eden Pastora, who had gone into exile in Costa Rica. Since their existence soon became publicly known, the cover story was invented that they were operating only on the Nicaragua–El Salvador border, to try to stop the Sandinistas arming their fellow leftists in El Salvador; 'the Reagan administration vehemently insisted during 1982 and 1983 that it was not trying to overthrow the Sandinistas, despite mounting evidence to the contrary.'[27] In December 1981 only about 500 Contras were supported, with an initial fund of $19 million, and Argentina helped in their training. But by 1984 there were up to 12,000 of them, mainly operating from bases in Honduras which became a virtual 'American Fortress' and the vital channel for financial aid to the Contras. They were engaged not only in murdering Sandinista officials and attacking military installations, but also in more general, poorly directed acts of terrorism, bombing workplaces, and ravaging villages. Such activities did nothing to win popular support; neither did their lack of an attractive political programme. According to McFarlane, the Contras became 'one of President Reagan's personal causes. In his eyes [they] were modern-day minutemen ... whose struggle on behalf of liberty ... deserved America's wholehearted ... support.'[28] But in mid-1983, as it seemed increasingly unlikely that there would be an outright Contra victory, the President decided to supplement

Contra pressure by intensifying naval exercises near the Nicaraguan coast: one feature of US policy was to keep the Sandinistas fearful of a full-scale invasion, forcing them to spend money on defence and creating a siege mentality. In September 1983 the CIA organized raids on Managua airport—which embarrassingly occurred just as two US Senators were flying in. In 1984 there were some diplomatic talks with the Sandinistas, but these were largely to make Reagan appear moderate in election year and at the same time Nicaraguan harbours were mined: incredibly, Congress, which had earlier objected to a naval blockade, was told but failed to grasp the significance of the step. In 1985 CIA-directed sabotage efforts focused on Managua itself.

The US-Contra campaign had a terrible impact on Nicaragua. By 1986 about 7,000 had been killed there and an estimated $2.5 billion lost in physical destruction and reduced trade. Spending on infrastructure and reform programmes had to be cut, people were regularly drilled to prepare for a US invasion. 'Defence soaked up 40 per cent of the nation's budget by 1984 to pay for the now 75,000 active-duty army. Social programmes suffered. Polio, once eliminated by vaccination programmes, reappeared.'[29] About 350,000 had become refugees. Ironically, the US trade embargo 'pushed the Sandinistas into greater dependence on Cuba and the Soviet Union'.[30] The latter provided $250 million in aid in 1984. Yet the Contras failed to take control of any areas of the country and the campaign was not without cost to the Reagan administration. There were internal divisions between those who favoured a tough military policy (Casey, Kirkpatrick and, at Defense, Weinberger) and those who wanted a less violent, more diplomatic line (Haig and his successor, Shultz); there were also members of the CIA who disliked Casey's methods and, remembering the Congressional investigations of the 1970s, wanted to work in line with public opinion. The public were increasingly concerned about the anti-Sandinista campaign, with only about a third of people approving Reagan's policy; and the press outcry in 1984 over the mining of Nicaraguan harbours almost led the Democratic-dominated Congress to sever support to the Contras completely. In December 1982 the first Boland amendment (named after Congressman Edward Boland) had already tried to stop money being spent to 'overthrow' the Managua government but Reagan skirted this by claiming the Contras were ready to talk to the Sandinistas. In October 1984, in the midst of the US Presidential election campaign, the Boland II amendment cut all *lethal* aid to the Contras. 'Any attempt to get money from Congress for the Contras in the near future would be fruitless', Shultz recognized, complaining that 'As a result there was no chance that the Sandinistas would negotiate seriously.'[31] In fact the administration was not able to restore aid until October 1986 when $100 million was provided.

American policy was also widely condemned abroad, being seen as no more than an attempt by one country to overthrow another government by force. In 1983 a number of Latin American states— Mexico, Panama, Colombia, and Venezuela—met on Contadora island and discussed a peace plan: both sides should respect human rights, Contra subversion should end, the US should withdraw its advisers from El Salvador, and the Sandinistas should both end their support for the Salvadorian leftists and hold free elections. To Reagan's embarrassment the OAS and most Central American States backed this scheme and Nicaragua began to fulfil the Contadora Principles, holding an election in November 1984. But the President was determined to proceed with his military policy, refused to pull US advisers out of El Salvador and actually bribed anti-Sandinista politicians to boycott the Nicaraguan elections. There was still a 75 per cent turnout, with several parties running, and the Sandinista leader, Daniel Ortega, only won the Presidency with about 60 per cent of the vote. But since the Contras did not stand, Reagan could discount the result. In 1986 he also decided to ignore a judgment by the International Court that the US was guilty of supporting terrorism in Nicaragua (this in the same year that America punished Libya for its support of terrorism by bombing it). In late 1986, with lethal aid to the Contras restored, Reagan hoped that they might be able to launch a decisive campaign against Managua. But it was then that his administration paid its highest price for the Nicaraguan involvement, with the breaking of the so-called 'Contragate' scandal.

'Contragate' and a Nicaraguan Settlement

The 'Contragate' (or 'Irangate') scandal, which at one point threatened to topple Reagan as Watergate had toppled Nixon, and which overshadowed the remainder of the Presidency, sprang directly from the administration's attempts to circumvent the Boland II amendment. If Congress would not provide sufficient aid to the Contras, then it might be possible to secure it from private donations and foreign sources. The National Security Council had actually approved such efforts in January 1984 but it was the Boland amendment nine months later which convinced Casey and the National Security Adviser, Robert McFarlane, to pursue the idea with determination. One of McFarlane's staff, Oliver North, helped obtain money from donors within the US and finance was also secured from Saudi Arabia, Taiwan, Brunei, and other strongly anti-communist governments, with about $37 million being raised in total, without the knowledge of Congress. In 1985 these activities became linked to secret US efforts to deal with Iran (Chapter 17, C). A complicated scheme was concocted whereby after November 1985 arms were secretly delivered (via Israel at first) to Iran (then fighting the war with Iraq) and the money earned was diverted to the Contras. It was also hoped that the Iranians would help secure the release of Western hostages in Lebanon. But in October 1986 the process began to unravel when a cargo aircraft was shot down in Nicaragua. One crewman survived and admitted he was a CIA operative supplying arms to the Contras. Then, on 3 November, a Lebanese journalist reported that McFarlane had visited Tehran six months before and US press interest in the question became intense. Finally, on 25 November, Attorney-General Edwin Meese revealed the diversion of $4 million in arms earnings from Iran to the Contras.

Like Watergate, Contragate highlighted the fact that dishonesty, secrecy, and outright illegality were to be found at the top of the American body politic. 'Unelected and unaccountable military officers . . . worked with key State Department personnel to defy US laws.'[32] Some in government believed that they alone interpreted the national interest and that

Congress and the public could be ignored. Reagan, who pleaded ignorance about the operation, avoided impeachment and insisted that, while he 'wanted the Contras maintained', it was 'only later . . . that I learned that some NSC staff had gone farther.'[33] The ensuing investigations focused on Oliver North, McFarlane, and the latter's successor, John Poindexter, though it was clear that many others knew about the Iran–Contra link. North, who (like Poindexter) was found guilty of law-breaking only to have the conviction lost on a technicality, became a hero for the American Right. But the scandal seemed a fatal blow to the Contras, who in any case were suffering casualties at the rate of 400 per month. Congress was now unwilling to give them any money despite requests from Reagan, and on 23 March 1988, the Contras were forced to agree to a ceasefire. In return, and partly due to pressure from Gorbachev, the Sandinistas offered an amnesty, a chance for their opponents to reintegrate into national life and a promise of new elections in 1991. Pressure for such a deal had been building among other Central American states, especially thanks to the efforts of Costa Rica's President, Oscar Arias, who in January 1987 launched a revised version of the Contadora Principles, including a ceasefire, amnesty, and elections. In effect, the Arias Plan 'furnished both the Sandinistas and the Reagan administration with one of their major desires: an end to support for the Contras, and pressure on the internal democratization process.'[34] A meeting of Central American leaders, including Ortega, at Esquipulas in Guatemala, accepted the 'Arias Plan' in August 1987. Arias went on to win the Nobel Peace Prize and the Sandinistas began to liberalize their regime, with a freer press and the release of political prisoners. The truth was that, whatever the troubles Reagan and the Contras faced, the Sandinistas were saddled with problems exacerbated by US subversion: high inflation, unemployment, falling wage levels, and financial weakness, especially as Gorbachev's increasingly troubled USSR now cut back on its aid programme—and ended all military assistance in 1988.

Although Reagan believed, to the end of his Presidency, that the Sandinistas could be removed by force, his successor and former Vice-President, George Bush, all too aware of Congressional sensibilities, pursued a more pragmatic approach. 'To show his independence of Reagan and stress the non-ideological nature of his administration, he replaced confrontation with compromise.'[35] Furthermore, Bush did not give Central America the significance that Reagan had. The 'main priority was to get Central America off the foreign policy agenda so he could concentrate on important matters such as US–Soviet relations.'[36] The US economic stranglehold on Nicaragua clearly was having a profound effect on the country and Ortega's desire to be moderate was confirmed by his February 1989 offer to bring the election date forward to 1990. James Baker masterminded a policy that 'emphasized the promotion of democracy by diplomatic rather than military means', using trade and aid as pressure points on the Sandinistas, while urging the USSR and Cuba to stop aiding them.[37] He believed that the Arias Plan, with its 'call for democratic reforms, elections, and an end to regional subversion was politically unassailable', especially since 'it was an arrangement negotiated by the parties themselves, not something forced upon them' by America. This fitted in with Baker's wider approach to 'rolling back Soviet beachheads', which placed an emphasis on using 'elections as a tool to dislodge them', exploiting 'Gorbachev's own emphasis on *glasnost.*'[38] There were still causes for concern: in July 1988 the US embassy in Managua, kept open throughout the Contra campaign, had been closed by the Sandinistas because of its links to their opponents; Nicaragua continued to help the leftists in El Salvador; and Cuba had boosted its arms supplies to the Sandinistas to make up for the Soviet withdrawal. But, unable to get more for the Contras from Congress than a limited amount of non-lethal assistance, Bush and Baker decided they must rely on Ortega's opponents winning the elections. In 1989 the US and USSR both undertook to respect the outcome of these. Bush then focused his efforts on building and supporting the National Opposition Union (UNO), a movement so broad-based that it included both conservatives and Communists, and which was led by the ex-Sandinista Cabinet minister, Violetta Chamorro. Despite the scale of US support there was still some surprise when the Sandinistas, with 41 per cent of the vote, lost the February 1990 election to the UNO coalition. Nicaraguan electors seemed keen to escape US opposition and the trade boycott, and to begin the task of reconstruction. Bush ended the trade embargo and provided $230 million in aid, but was aware that the Sandinistas remained a potent political force, with the largest number of seats in parliament and an influential role in the trades unions and armed forces. His successful gamble on the elections had paid off and, with the resolution too of the El Salvador-Panama problems (on Panama see Chapter 18, C), US policy in Central America was in a better state that at any time since 1978. The settlement also helped heal the domestic wounds of the Iran–Contra scandal. 'By pursuing a policy of pragmatic accommodation and giving just enough to both supporters and foes of the Contras it had successfully resolved one of the most . . . divisive conflicts in US politics of the previous decade.'[39]

C. Two American Invasions: Grenada and Panama

In El Salvador and Nicaragua the US lent economic, diplomatic, and covert support to those who opposed Marxism but avoided the open use of American armed forces. In two cases in the 1980s, however, Washington was prepared to use an actual invasion to remove governments. Grenada, in 1983, and Panama, six years later, were in many ways very different problems. In the first case, the Reagan administration acted swiftly to overthrow a regime on a small Caribbean island, which was seen as increasingly pro-Castro. In the second, the Bush administration resorted to armed force only after trying for several years to overthrow a volatile, oppressive dictator in a strategically important Central American state. Both invasions, however, were highly successful in terms of fulfilling the main US aims, even if the first in particular stirred international controversy, and both showed that the US was capable of taking military action despite the 'Vietnam Syndrome'. The Syndrome made the Department of Defence reluctant to deploy conventional forces except in a narrow range of circumstances. Indeed, in October 1984 Casper Weinberger laid out several preconditions for any military action, including: the deployment of forces only in the defence of vital national interests, the assurance of popular and Congressional support, clear aims, continuous reassessments, and the ability to pull out of any commitment which went wrong. But to Secretary of State Shultz such conditions were too restrictive, undermining the effectiveness of US diplomacy, which 'could work . . . most effectively when force—or the threat of force—was a credible part of the equation.'[40] Reagan, too, was sometimes keen to use force in order to blunt any potential Soviet advance. In Lebanon (Chapter 17, A) the Defense Department's caution seemed justified and the US was driven to withdraw rather than become embroiled in a complicated civil conflict. But in Grenada and Panama the US began to recover its faith in its ability to deploy force successfully in limited operations.

Grenada, October 1983

Grenada, with a population of about 85,000, had been given its independence from Britain in 1974, under the leadership of Eric Gairy, a man obsessed with the paranormal, the occult, and UFOs, who soon proved oppressive and unpopular. On 13 March 1979 he was overthrown in a coup by the Marxist-influenced 'New Jewel Movement' led by Maurice Bishop, who set up a 'Peoples Revolutionary Government' and, whilst avoiding any extreme radicalism at home, soon started to import arms from the USSR and Cuba. In mid-1979 the Carter administration, concerned about the Latin American implications of Moscow's build-up of Cuban military power, had secretly made an approach to Castro: in a marked departure from the usual policy of isolating and harassing him, the US was ready to end its trade embargo on Cuba if it ended its interventionist policy in Angola, Ethiopia, and elsewhere. But Castro made no response. At the same time Carter also hoped to use covert operations to undermine the New Jewel Movement in Grenada but, given the widespread suspicion of the CIA in America in the late 1970s, this proved difficult. Objections from the Senate's Intelligence Committee forced the CIA to end is operations in Grenada. So, in late 1979, Bishop continued to develop his pro-Cuban policy and Castro took advantage of the opportunity to extend his influence. In September Cuban troops arrived in Grenada on a training mission and in December began to construct an airport with a long runway, which the US feared could become a staging post for Cuban intervention elsewhere—though its prime purpose at first was to help boost the island's tourist industry by allowing jet airliners to land.

On coming into office in January 1981, the Reagan administration ended all development aid to Grenada, including some which had gone to build the new airport. But real trouble between Washington and Grenada only blew up, quite suddenly, over two-and-a-half years later. The leaders of the New Jewel Movement had long had divisions between them and on 13 October 1983 Premier Bishop was arrested by his deputy, Bernard Coard, and six days later executed—following an attempt by supporters to free him. A 'Revolutionary Military Council' was then formed. Several days of violence followed, which was of concern both to neighbouring Caribbean countries and to the US, the latter because nearly 500 American students were studying at a medical school on the island. Preparations for an invasion were made hastily. An appeal from the Organization of Eastern Caribbean States (possibly orchestrated by the US) helped give the impression that Washington was reacting to local concerns and on 22 October Grenada was suspended by another body, the Caribbean Community (CARICOM). Legitimacy was also given to the US action by the island's Governor, Sir Paul Scoon, who requested US aid. But, despite local fears and the vulnerability of American citizens, Reagan's decision on 24 October to approve armed intervention was undoubtedly primarily shaped by his anti-communism and his desire to teach Castro a lesson. On 25 October 2,000 American troops landed on Grenada; 4,000 more followed over the next few days. They lost only 19 dead but killed several dozen Grenadians and Cubans, many of them around the airport. The

discovery of several Soviet advisers on the island was an unexpected bonus, which helped Reagan prove to the satisfaction of the US public that Grenada had fast been becoming a 'Soviet colony' and a centre for communist activity in the Caribbean. Others were less happy about such ruthless action. Apart from the predictable complaints of the Eastern bloc, the United Nations General Assembly and the Organization of American States were both concerned about yet another example of the US tendency to bludgeon Caribbean and Latin American countries into line, colonial-style, with little justification in international law. 'The action also conveyed the message that the United States opposed far-reaching economic and social reform in its own backyard.'[41] More unusually, Reagan's ally in London, Margaret Thatcher, was dismayed by the invasion, without proper consultation, of a Commonwealth country of which Queen Elizabeth II was Head of State. It should also be noted that the operation was less smooth than it appeared. As Colin Powell later conceded, 'it took most of a week to subdue all resistance' and the 'invasion was hardly a model of service cooperation'.[42] The protests, however, were soon forgotten, as Grenada held elections (in 1984) and US economic aid was provided. US troops left in December 1983. For Reagan the invasion had been a low, risk yet quick, triumphant, and high-profile operation which boosted his popularity a year ahead of the next Presidential election and helped to offset the ill effects, in public relations terms, of the Lebanon imbroglio. He could claim both to have restored order and democracy in one country and to have deterred the communists from acting against others. Whatever the lack of interservice cooperation the 'Pentagon's post-Vietnam skittishness about using military force in the less developed world receded a bit.'[43] The invasion, which the Soviets were powerless to oppose, also helped confirm 1983 as one of deep Cold War tensions.

Panama: the Noriega Regime

In contrast to Grenada, the invasion of Panama came at a time of much improved US–Soviet relations and, although the invasion was on a much grander scale, it did not stir up the same degree of international controversy. American intervention in Panamanian politics was well established. Even so, a large-scale invasion towards the end of the century was a remarkable and unexpected event, which the US government itself went to some lengths to avoid.

The last democratically elected Panamanian government had been overthrown in 1968 by General Omar Torrijos, who established a military dictatorship and made himself popular by pressing for the US to hand over the Panama Canal to Panamanian sovereignty. In 1978 Jimmy Carter agreed to do this at the end of the century (see Chapter 14, A) but in the interim the US continued to have an interest in Panamanian stability and in maintaining their military base on the Canal. Arguably the Canal was of limited strategic importance, with aircraft carriers too large to use it and nuclear submarines having to surface to pass through, but some US military leaders argued that, in the event of global war, it could prove vital once more. Indeed, one 1977 study warned that 'if the United States government were to relinquish control of canal operations, then it should be prepared for that day ... when Washington would be forced to make a ... landing ... to regain control.'[44] Partly to please Carter, Torrijos claimed to be moving towards elections but was killed in an air crash in 1981. There *were* Presidential elections in 1984, won by Nicolas Barletta. But in effect the army continued to hold power, tolerated by the Reagan administration, which of course, was determined to avoid a repetition of events in Nicaragua and El Salvador—especially given the strategic significance of the Panama Canal. The Panamanians proved a valuable channel for arms to the Contras and also gave diplomatic support to the US in its struggle with the Sandinistas. Particularly loyal to the Americans was General Manuel Noriega, Commander of the National Guard in 1983, who made himself dictator in 1986. Like El Salvador's right-wing leader d'Aubuisson, Noriega had partly been trained in counter-insurgency techniques at the US 'School of the Americas'; and he had close links to the CIA. Yet it did not take long for him to become an embarrassment to Washington, being involved in drug-trafficking, developing links to Castro and murdering opponents. As elsewhere the Americans

tried to simplify a problem by personalizing it: Noriega was only one man and Panama had been unstable for years but by mid-1987 his removal became a prime aim of Congress (despite its dislike of Reagan's meddling in Nicaragua). 'Noriega had supplanted Iran's Ayatollah Khomeini and Libya's Gadaffi at the top of American international demonology.'[45] On 26 June only two Senators voted against a motion calling for democracy to return to Panama.

The problem was that, unpopular as Noriega appeared to be in his own country, any US attempt to replace him was not guaranteed success and it could stimulate Panamanian nationalist feeling in an anti-American direction, perhaps threatening the security of the canal zone. The US hoped that popular opposition might force him out of office, as it had done Ferdinand Marcos in the Philippines; various plans were put forward for a transition to democracy and America sent diplomatic messages to the dictator suggesting he should go, with Reagan ready to barter Noriega's freedom from arrest for the end of his regime. US financial aid to the country was suspended in 1987 and other economic sanctions were introduced in March 1988, including the end of private bank loans. In Panama, as a result, there were bankruptcies and petrol shortages. In addition the US sent covert aid to Noriega's opponents and encouraged the idea of a coup, but it was a Florida court—not the government in Washington—which, in February 1988, ignored the evidence of the Drug Enforcement Agency (which argued that he had helped break up drug rings) and indicted Noriega for drug-trafficking. The US government regretted the court's decision because, by threatening the dictator with up to 145 years in prison, it made him unlikely to strike a deal to secure his peaceful departure. 'The final break had come, but the indictment was unsuccessful to the extent that Noriega could not be brought into a US court without resorting to force in Panama.'[46] In fact Noriega felt no need to resign, doubting that Americans would use force to remove him, despite the economic and psychological warfare techniques they employed. He secured foreign assistance from non-US sources and internal discontent remained at a manageable level, even when he annulled the result of the May 1989 elections, in which Washington had financed his opponents. With apparent American support, two coups were launched against Noriega, on 16 March 1988 and 3 October 1989, but both were failures.

'Operation Just Cause'

Whatever Noriega's resilience in the late 1980s, and however unpopular he became, the Organization of American States (with its opposition to US colonialism) and the American military (ever fearful of 'another Vietnam') long resisted his armed overthrow. But as the 1990s approached, the US 'could not tolerate a drug-dealing dictator who, if left alone, would become responsible for the defence and operation of the Panama Canal.'[47] And, in view of the lack of alternatives, after January 1989, the new administration of President George Bush began to consider military action. This was actively planned from October 1989 and on 15 December the Panamanian National Assembly declared a 'state of war' with Washington. The following day several American troops, one of whom was shot dead, were harassed by Panamanian troops and the day after that Bush approved 'Operation Just Cause', the invasion of Panama with the purpose of replacing Noriega—despite the danger that, if US policy did not alter, he might simply give way to another oppressive, unreliable dictator. The Operation went ahead, unexpected by the Panamanians, on 19 December with 25,000 American troops, half of them coming from the canal zone and half shipped in from beyond. The campaign also marked the first use of 'Stealth' aircraft, which could escape radar detection and which, at the end of the Cold War, underlined America's technological superiority over all other states.

The Americans lost only twenty-three dead in 'Operation Just Cause', a codename chosen (like later ones) for its propaganda value. In contrast to Grenada, the operation was based on extensive contingency planning and implemented very effectively. US forces seized key points throughout Panama, attacked military installations which remained loyal to Noriega and quickly set up a government under those politicians who had been successful in the May 1989 elections, led by Guillermo Endarma. Physical destruction was limited in the well-planned campaign and, despite several days of resistance by pro-Noriega forces, the Canal was reopened to shipping on 21 December. Noriega himself initially escaped, taking sanctuary in the Papal nuncio's residence, but he surrendered on 4 January 1990 to the Americans, after they used loud rock music, which he hated, in an unusual demonstration of 'psychological warfare' exercise, to drive him out. For him trial in Florida was preferable to a form of music he could not tolerate. (In 1992, claiming to be a 'political' prisoner, he was sentenced to forty years in prison.) Rather than opposing the Operation, some Panamanians demonstrated in America's favour, only complaining that the dictator had not been removed earlier. Later they also complained about the low level of American economic assistance to help them recover. It was not the first time that Panamanians had relied on the US to resolve their problems, refusing to risk death themselves in overthrowing an oppressor. The American public also praised Bush's action, giving him 85 per cent approval ratings. There were few ready, anywhere in fact, to defend Noriega. James Baker even wrote that, in Operation Just Cause, the US 'was simply enforcing the will of the Panamanians by restoring the legitimately elected government to authority.'[48] Moscow, of course, was currently preoccupied with events in Eastern Europe—on which, indeed, most world attention was focused. But this did not mean that 'Just Cause' lacked disturbing elements. The operation was the largest-scale US military action since the Vietnam War, though soon overshadowed by the liberation of Kuwait in the Persian Gulf. It showed that Washington was ready to overthrow Latin American regimes that it disliked even after the Soviet threat was removed and in a sense confirmed American contempt for, and desire for hegemony over, states in the region. 'One of the most striking facts about the whole episode was the extent to which questions about international law or Panamanian sovereignty were a non-issue in US policy-making circles.'[49] At another level, rather than demonstrating strength, it suggested limits to US power—the blunt weapon of intervention had only been used after covert action, economic warfare, and diplomatic pressure failed—and confusion in Washington's outlook—the Republicans had

The 1982 Falklands War

The Falklands, known as the Malvinas in Spanish, are a group of islands about 300 miles from the South American coast, in the South Atlantic. The British were the first to land on them, in 1690, but the first settlement was built by the French in the 1760s and the islands subsequently sold to Spain. On winning its independence, Argentina inherited the Spanish claim to the islands but a British expedition expelled the Argentineans in 1833. Argentina revived its claim to the group in the twentieth century and took the issue to the UN in 1964, leading to years of fruitless talks with Britain over the status of the islands. Argentina tried to portray the British position as a 'colonial' one; Britain based its continued possession on the fact that almost all the local population, of about 2,000, favoured British rule. The Falklands were also the administrative centre of other British possessions in the South Atlantic, including the island of South Georgia.

In mid-March 1982, after many earlier small-scale incursions, an Argentinean force landed on South Georgia and on 2 April a more substantial force arrived in the Falkland Islands proper, attacking the capital, Port Stanley. Argentina was at that time ruled by a military junta, headed by General Leopoldo Galtieri, which was facing rising discontent due to political oppression and the effect of high inflation. The junta had hastily planned the invasion as a way to win popularity by exploiting nationalist feeling ahead of the 150th anniversary of the loss of the 'Malvinas'. They expected little resistance from the British government of Margaret Thatcher, which was then engaged in reducing defence expenditure and had just announced the withdrawal of its only naval vessel in the area, HMS *Endurance*. Soon, despite a UN call for Argentina to withdraw, the junta had deployed 10,000 troops on the islands, under General Mario Menendez.

Thatcher proved unwilling to accept this affront to British prestige however, and a naval force was quickly put together to launch a re-invasion of the islands, 8,000 miles to the South. South Georgia was retaken as early as 25 April. The European Community backed Britain with economic sanctions against Argentina, but most Latin American states strongly supported Galtieri's action and the United States at first tried to play a mediatory role, reluctant to alienate either Britain or the Latin American states. Only on 30 April did President Reagan finally back Britain publicly, though the US military were already providing some assistance to Britain. Any chance of a peaceful settlement ended with the sinking of the Argentinean warship *General Belgrano*, on 2 May, with the loss of about 400 lives. An intermittent naval and air war then began, followed on 21 May by the first British landings on the Falklands. After defeating the Argentineans at Goose Green on 28 May, the British advanced against Port Stanley, which Menendez finally surrendered on 14 June. About 240 British servicemen died in the struggle for the islands, compared to over 650 Argentineans and, whereas the war helped Thatcher to secure re-election in 1983, the Galtieri junta soon collapsed, bringing a return to democracy in Argentina.

criticized Carter for allowing the fall of Somoza in Nicaragua, yet were as active as they could be in toppling Noriega, despite his anti-communism. It also showed the President acting without the need to consult Congress, in a way reminiscent of pre-Nixon days: 'On this occasion, as on others, President Bush effectively treated the War Powers Resolution of 1973 with contempt.'[50] As to the local impact, the OAS condemned the Operation as an imperialist venture, and in May 1994 Panamanian voters opted to replace the US-installed Endarma with one of Noriega's deputies, Ernesto Peres Balladores. As in El Salvador the extreme Right proved that it had some genuine popular appeal.

D. **The 'Lost Decade': Latin America's 'Debt Crisis'**

Another major reason why the South seemed powerless to alter the global economic order in the 1980s was that most of its countries were heavily in debt to Western banks. In the 1970s it was not the case that developing countries relied on government-led aid from the North. The banks expected that the money would lead to rising exports and growth, so that repayments would not be a problem;

developing countries were attracted by the fact that, because of high inflation, the *real* interest payments on loans (that is the cost of the actual interest rates minus the rate of inflation) was historically low at that time. By 1980 over $300 billion in loans had been made to the less developed world and more continued to be run up during the depression of 1979–82. Indeed, in this period the 'greatest source of international demand, the countries of the OECD, started to reduce the volume of imports. . . . . Poorer countries . . . found rather more unfavourable export conditions. . . . Within a few years the threat that some large debtors would be unable to meet their foreign obligations had begun to loom.'[51] Latin America had particularly large debtors, notably Brazil and Argentina. On average, Latin American borrowing grew eight times over in 1970–82. Many Latin American and African states needed to borrow more money to cover the rising costs of oil imports. However, this meant that the loans simply helped to maintain current levels of imports and did not help to generate the expected increases in growth and exports. Only a few Latin American countries, Mexico and Venezuela, had substantial oil production of their own. Although the 'phenomenon of easy access to bank loans was common to all developing regions, in Latin America the inflow of foreign capital was more marked, and as a result it had a greater impact on . . . national development.'[52]

The problems with this system soon became apparent. A stronger dollar and falling global inflation meant that real interest rates rose, adding to the costs of loans so much that the borrowers could barely cover the interest charged. Not just the price of oil, but the price of raw materials generally was falling, so that the less developed world found it even more difficult to make money from exports. It was soon obvious too that, despite the massive injection of money from Western banks, no economic miracle had occurred in Latin America. Some investments were eaten up by the corruption of ruling oligarchies. In many areas the problems of poverty, famine, and urban sprawl were worsened by rapid population increase and the failure to provide basic social services. 'In 1980 the region's economic growth fell below its population growth. Unemployment shot upwards as trade collapsed.'[53] The IMF, responsible for preventing monetary

instability and heavily influenced by the Reagan administration, urged less developed world governments to reduce their public expenditure by cutting food subsidies and social spending, which made poverty even worse. Partly because of inadequate investment, what small indigenous Latin American industries there were remained uncompetitive in world markets; the 'banana republics' of Central America were still dependent on one or two crops and vulnerable to any shift in demand. The Falklands War helped call into question the wisdom of lending to military dictatorships like Argentina and, in any case, by the second half of the 1980s the Western banks could make a safer profit in the now-expanding economies of America, Europe, and Japan.

That the gathering crisis would be focused on Latin America became obvious in August 1982 when the US had to lead a $9 billion rescue package for Mexico, which despite its oil, was almost bankrupt and had to default on its debt payments. 'When Mexico suspended, the banks quickly cut back their lending to all debtors and that threw all of them into crisis. . . . [The] debtors had to conserve foreign exchange by reducing their imports. That required them to slash domestic investment.'[54] (True, in March 1981 a European country, Poland, had earlier introduced a moratorium on loan repayments, but it was a highly exceptional case.) In 1982–4 several more Latin American governments announced that they had to reschedule their debts. Latin America as a whole became 'mired in the greatest depression in the continent's history.'[55] Though their confidence was shaken, the banks themselves survived this situation because they had sufficient profits from elsewhere to ride out the crisis; also debts *were* rescheduled—or else Western governments stepped in to help—so that the banks were still receiving money from their loans; and the banks themselves loaned new money simply to cover old debts. But, with no new money from the banks for economic development, real incomes fell throughout Latin America in 1980–5. The Latin American governments demanded lower world interest rates and complained that the IMF was acting in an 'imperialist' fashion, working to a Western agenda. In September 1985 they even got a dramatic joint effort by the IMF, the World Bank, and the commercial banks to finance about $30 billion in debts over the next two years, in the 'Baker Plan' (named after the then US Treasury Secretary). In return for restructuring old debts the Latin Americans were, in effect, forced to work with the Western governments and the banks: when one country, Peru, tried to act alone in limiting its debt payments in 1985 it found that the US and the IMF suspended all further aid to it. The Baker Plan proved no more than a palliative, as seen by the fact that it was followed in 1987 by a 'Baker B Plan'. In 1989 another US Treasury Secretary, Nicholas Brady, gave his name to a further rescue plan, designed to reduce debt, cover loan repayments, and restructure Latin American economies in a more market-oriented way. The price for readjustment, in line with the dominant ideology, was paid primarily by the poor who suffered most from reductions in government spending. The Brady Plan had more success in stabilizing the situation but in 1991 it still cost the Latin Americans $50 billion simply to service their foreign debts and this took resources away from both capital investment and income. The total debt was nearly $500 billion (up from $375 billion in 1985) with Mexico and Brazil continuing to run huge liabilities. In February 1995 the IMF reluctantly agreed to another enormous $18 billion package to bail out the Mexican economy.

The 1980s were looked back on as 'the lost decade' for Latin America, in which the liquidity crisis damaged industrial expansion, social services provision, and attempts to improve the import–export balance. Instead, austerity packages were introduced,

imports of high-technology goods had to be cut, export performance was poor, and there was a permanent risk of social discontent. A World Bank study in 1989 suggested that poverty had risen worldwide since the largely ignored Brandt Report, with nearly one-third of people living in this situation. At the same time the Western world increased the barriers for immigrants from the developing world: in America there was particular concern with the scale of illegal immigration via Mexico. Ironically the debt crisis could be blamed in part on the very free enterprise system which America, Britain, and others now espoused, given that it was the short-term and unregulated profit-seeking of the banks in the late 1970s which helped create the original problems. Arguably, 'Latin America has never been a major beneficiary of US economic aid. On the contrary, it has been an area from which American companies have drawn huge profits.' For example, in the decade 1966–76, Esso invested less than £2 million in Brazil for a return of £40 million.[56] Yet the late 1980s *did* see growing democratization in Latin America, with the end of several military dictatorships, alongside a distinct liberalization of economic policies. The end of the Cold War made it even less easy for the developing South to resist the economic and ideological domination of the North. The capitalist world now argued more confidently that, if only the South emulated the capitalism and liberalization of the North it too could eventually share in the wealth and personal freedom that the Americans, Japanese, and Europeans enjoyed.

NOTES

1. Lars Schoultz, *Human Rights and US Policy towards Latin America* (Princeton University Press, Princeton, 1981), 346.

2. Michael Kryzanek, *US–Latin American Relations* (Praeger, New York, 1990), 76.

3. John Dumbrell, *The Carter Presidency: A Re-evaluation* (Manchester University Press, Manchester, 1995), 159.

4. Frank Niess, *A Hemisphere to Itself: US-Latin American relations* (Zed Books, London, 1990), 191–2.

5. William LeoGrande, *Our Own Backyard: the US in Central America, 1977–92* (University of North Carolina Press, Chapel Hill, 1998), 578.

6. Ronald Reagan, *An American Life* (Hutchinson, London, 1990), 239.

7. Quoted in Peter Smith, *Talons of the Eagle* (Oxford University Press, New York, 1996), 160.

8. Allan Gerson, *The Kirkpatrick Mission* (Free Press, New York, 1991), xv.

9. Walter LaFeber, *Inevitable Revolutions: the US in Latin America* (W.W. Norton, New York, 1993 edn.), 277–8.

10. Raymond Garthoff, *Détente and Confrontation: American–Soviet Relations from Nixon to Reagan* (Brookings Institution, Washington, DC, 1995), 1140.

11. Coral Bell, *The Reagan Paradox* (Elgar, Aldershot, 1989), 113.

12. LeoGrande, op. cit., 43.

13. Richard Thornton, *The Carter Years* (Paragon House, New York, 1991), 511.

14. Alexander Haig, *Caveat* (Macmillan, New York, 1984), 122.

15. Quoted in Smith, op. cit., 181.

16. LaFeber, op. cit., 279.

17. LeoGrande, op. cit., 577.

18. Quoted in Robert A, Strong, *Working in the World: Jimmy Carter and the making of American foreign policy* (Louisiana State University Press, Baton Rouge, 2000), 90.

19. Kryzanek, op. cit., 78.

20. Dumbrell, op. cit., 157.

21. LeoGrande, op. cit., 26.

22. LaFeber, op. cit., 241.

23. LeoGrande, op. cit., 108.

24. Benjamin Keen and Keith Haynes, *A History of Latin America* (Houghton Mifflin, Boston, 2000), 570.

25. Niess, op. cit., 197.

26. Smith, op. cit., 183.

27. LeoGrande, op. cit., 301.

28. Robert McFarlane and Zofia Smardz, *Special Trust* (Cadell & Davies Natl Book Network, New York, 1994), 67.

29. LaFeber, op. cit., 307.

30. Thomas Skidmore and Peter Smith, *Modern Latin America* (Oxford University Press, Oxford, 1997), 343–4.

31. George Shultz, *Turmoil and Triumph* (Macmillan, New York, 1993), 426.

32. Lafeber, op. cit., 338.

33. Reagan, op. cit., 485.

34. David Ryan, *US-Sandinista Diplomatic Relations* (Macmillan, London, 1995), 135.

35. Raymond Moore, 'Foreign Policy', in Dilys Hill and Phil Williams, (ed.), *The Bush Presidency: Triumphs and Adversities* (Macmillan, London, 1994), 165.

36. LeoGrande, op. cit., 578.

37. David Mervin, *George Bush and the Guardianship Presidency* (Macmillan, Basingstoke, 1996), 165.

38. James A. Baker, *The Politics of Diplomacy* (G. P Putnam's Sons, New York, 1995), 53 and 46.

39. Steven Hurst, *The Foreign Policy of the Bush Administration* (Cassell, New York, 1999), 23.

40. Shultz, op. cit., 650.

41. Benjamin Keen and Keith Haynes, *A History of Latin America* (Houghton Mifflin, Boston, 2000), 565.

42. Colin Powell, *My American Journey* (Ballantine Books, New York, 1995), 281.

43. LeoGrande, op. cit., 348.

44. Paul B. Ryan, *The Panama Canal Controversy* (Stanford University Press, Stanford, 1977), 155–6; but for a counter case see Walter LaFeber, *The Panama Canal: The Crisis in Historical Perspective* (Oxford University Press, New York, 1978), 222–3.

45. Larry Berman and Bruce Jentleson, 'Bush and the Post-Cold War World', in Colin Campbell and Bert Rockman (eds.), *The Bush Presidency* (Chatham House Publishers, Chatham, 1991), 109–10.

46. William Drohin, 'The Development of US-Panamanian relations', in Bruce Watson and Peter Tsouras eds.), *Operation Just Cause* (Westview Press, Boulder, 1991), 25.

47. Michael Hathaway, 'The role of drugs in the US-Panamanian relationship', in Watson and Tsouras (eds.), op. cit., 42.

48. Baker, op. cit., 193–4.

49. Hurst, op. cit., 55.

50. David Mervin, *George Bush and the Guardianship Presidency* (Macmillan, Basingstoke, 1996), 168–9.

51. William Ashworth, *A Short History of the International Economy since 1850* (Longman, London, 1987), 307.

52. Ricardo French-Davis, 'The Latin American Economies, 1950–90', in Leslie Bethell, (ed.), *The Cambridge History of Latin America* (Cambridge University Press, Cambridge, 1994), 239–40.

53. LaFeber, op. cit., 285.

54. Robert Solomon, *The Transformation of the World Economy* (Macmillan, London, 2nd edn., 1999), 167.

55. Keen and Haynes, op. cit., 571.

56. Peter and Susan Calvert, *Latin America in the Twentieth Century* (Macmillan, London, 2nd edn., 1993), 189.

19 The Decline of the Cold War, 1985–1989

A. The Impact of Gorbachev, 1985–1987

Gorbachev's 'New Diplomacy'

When Mikhail Gorbachev became General Secretary of the Soviet Communist Party on 11 March 1985 he was, at 54 years of age, much younger than his two predecessors, Andropov and Chernenko, and seemed destined to remain in power for some time. He was also twenty years younger than Reagan and soon proved able to match the US leader in the public relations field. Gorbachev's election as leader was no foregone conclusion: he had, after all, lost to Chernenko in 1984; there was, in the person of Moscow Party boss Victor Grishin, a hard-line alternative candidate; and much relied on good fortune, including the death of the conservative Defence Minister, Marshal Ustinov, in December 1984, and the unexpectedly firm support of the chair of the meeting, Andrei Gromyko, who used his casting vote in favour of Gorbachev. Thus, 'Gorbachev had won, but only by the slenderest and most artificial of

margins.'[1] Then again, he was at the forefront of a body of opinion that had grown up within the USSR in the 1970s which was determined to break from the stagnation of the Brezhnev era, address the country's economic and political problems—the corruption and alcoholism, the careerism and cynicism in the Communist Party, the inadequate social provision, the inefficient industry—and adopt a more imaginative, less doctrinal foreign policy. 'Soviet economic growth in real terms had come to a complete halt,' while 'the West . . . was conducting a . . . technologically sophisticated arms build-up', so the new leadership wanted to become competitive, in both military and economic terms.'[2] Like many other leading economists, diplomats, and scientists, Gorbachev had lived most of his life in the post-Stalin era, was well educated and had travelled abroad. He was a long-serving and loyal communist but also imaginative, ready to debate and explore new ideas, confident too about pursuing new policies in a way no Soviet leader had been since Khrushchev.

Nonetheless, when the Politburo chose Gorbachev it did not expect him to pursue the radical course that he did. Gorbachev was expected to ease the stifling atmosphere of the Chernenko period, when would-be reformers had been dismissed from office, and he was expected to attack corruption, but he could easily have done this by his mentor Andropov's preferred method of tightening up the police state and introducing greater discipline into all walks of life. Why Gorbachev adopted the particular policies he did is not yet fully understood and interpreting his decisions is not helped by his enigmatic character, which made it difficult even for close colleagues to comprehend him. His early reforms were in fact quite cautious: in 1985–6 he '*talked* about technological innovation, about greater openness ... about encouraging personal initiative ... but made very little progress towards these goals.'[3] At first he was probably genuinely uncertain about the direction to take at home and did show signs of using greater discipline: officials were executed for accepting bribes. He was also probably unaware of the exact scale of the USSR's economic inefficiencies. One of the features of the Brezhnev era had been the way figures on industrial output were massaged to suggest growth, when actually, under the central planning system, factories produced low-quality goods for which there was frequently no demand. It was a system which kept everyone employed, but it did not lead to competitiveness in world markets, and it was wasteful of raw materials (including Soviet oil reserves, which began to decrease in volume in the early 1980s). Two elements that Gorbachev did introduce quickly, however, were *glasnost*, a greater 'openness' about the problems of Soviet society, and *perestroika*, a determination to 'restructure' that society so that it became more disciplined and efficient. His aim was not to end communism but to make it work better and in 1985–6 his economic reforms involved little more than organizational changes and better incentives for workers. Political innovations were more far-reaching, with the replacement of many leading officials at the February 1986 Congress, the freeing of many dissidents, and suggestions of an increased respect for human rights. There were many

hard-line opponents of these reforms and a reversal of policy was always possible, but in 1987 the pace of reform began to quicken and, arguably, to run out of control. It began, in June 1987, with the limited use of multi-candidate elections at local level, a reform that suggested alternatives to communist rule were now possible and that nationalist groups might challenge the unity of the USSR itself. Gorbachev then began to chart what has been called a 'path of well-meaning destruction', making him 'the Soviet Union's gravedigger'.[4]

In foreign policy Gorbachev's first two years in power also saw mixed messages about his intentions, leading to uncertainties abroad, especially in the US, about whether a substantial change in East–West relations was possible. At Chernenko's funeral Gorbachev called for an end to confrontation and progress on nuclear arms control, but even Chernenko had been a supporter of Brezhnev's détente policy and had presided over moves to restart arms control talks. Gorbachev inherited an ambitious defence programme, initially intensified the war in Afghanistan, and in 1985–7 continued to provide aid to Cuba, Vietnam, Nicaragua, and other less developed world allies (discussed in Chapter 19, C), all of which made Washington very suspicious. Britain's Margaret Thatcher met Gorbachev in December 1984 and declared, 'We can do business together.'[5] Her confidence that East–West relations could be improved had an important impact on both Washington and Moscow. After all, she was nothing if not a tough negotiator and an anti-communist, trusted by Reagan who, in his second term, was anxious to make his reputation as a peacemaker. At Chernenko's funeral, where Vice-President Bush represented America, Gorbachev was given an invitation from Reagan to visit the US for a summit. But many of Reagan's advisers were cautious about trusting the new Soviet leader and some were still determined to undermine Soviet power through a policy of relentless competition, especially in the nuclear arms area. Gorbachev's early claims about wanting to improve the international atmosphere were good public relations, but on the surface little more. Thus, on 7 April 1985 he announced a temporary freeze on deployments of Intermediate Nuclear Forces (INF) in Europe and offered to make this permanent if the US froze its deployments. He also suggested a freeze on strategic and space-based systems. But this was never likely to impress the US since the Soviets already had a superiority in INF systems in Europe and were trying, not only to maintain this, but also to forestall Reagan's 'Strategic Defense Initiative' (SDI) for a space-based nuclear shield. In his first letter to Reagan, Gorbachev emphasized the need to avoid nuclear war but wrote in terms reminiscent of 'peaceful coexistence': 'Each social system has the right to life, and it should prove its advantages not by ... military means, but on the path of peaceful competition with the other system.'[6] Meanwhile, the USSR continued to devote a large proportion of its limited national resources to defence spending and deployed new types of nuclear missiles. Neither was the situation helped in Gorbachev's early months by the Red Army shooting, in late March 1985, of a US major, Arthur Nicolson, in East Germany or by the defection of a KGB officer, Oleg Gordievsky, to London in July.

After the collapse of the USSR, documents became available which showed that, behind the scenes, Gorbachev's early policy shifts were not mere presentational devices. He *did* wish to reduce arms spending, press on with nuclear arms control, and adopt a more flexible, less ideological foreign policy, the so-called 'new diplomacy'. He believed that 'a less confrontational stance towards the outside world would provide greater security than endless rearming.'[7] Even before he realized the full depths of his country's economic malaise, he hoped to end the confrontation with the West and reduce the danger of nuclear war. He also wanted to improve relations with China. It has been noted that, conceptually, changing foreign policy 'was much easier for Gorbachev than domestic change. It consisted of moving towards Western positions and hence it was easy to decide what the Soviet Union had to do.'[8] As time progressed, however, strong links developed between the new diplomacy and domestic reform. Gorbachev and his Foreign Minister, Eduard Shevardnadze (who surprisingly replaced the veteran Gromyko when the latter became Soviet President in July 1985) realized that calm abroad would better help them restructure society at home. 'From the outset, it was clear ... that the old methods of confrontation ... were no longer suitable,' wrote Shevardnadze. 'By remaining stuck in the old

positions, we would not stop the arms race, which was bleeding our already anemic country.'[9] Also an extension of links with the West, including greater trade, would encourage industrial competitiveness and bring injections of advanced technology. Yet there was always a danger in this: 'It also followed that if capitalism was no longer threatening, then Soviet society was no longer divided into ... those who supported the Soviet system and "bourgeois subversives".'[10] Gorbachev and his aides were ready to concede that Soviet actions, not least in Afghanistan and the nuclear arms field, *had* contributed to worsening relations with the West and China; they knew that the USSR could not compete with the US in such areas as development aid and defence technology, and they doubted whether China and West Germany really posed a menace to Soviet security. Their new diplomacy was, as with domestic reform, uncertainly developed and was definitely not intended to lead to the USSR's demise. But it *was* intended to end the Cold War, to guarantee Soviet security via cooperation not confrontation, and to adapt to the realities of a multipolar, interdependent world.

Uncertain Steps to Engagement

Shevardnadze's succession to the foreign ministry brought a more human, if less experienced, figure to the forefront of Soviet policy abroad and one who rejected the logic of Khrushchev's 'peaceful co-existence' because it 'cannot remove the cornerstone of confrontation: the original premise that the victory of one socio-political system over the other is inevitable.'[11] His appointment was soon followed, in August, by the announcement of a moratorium on nuclear tests, which Gorbachev introduced despite the doubts of his military advisers. It had already been agreed in May 1985, after a wrangle over the venue, that a Gorbachev–Reagan summit should be held in November, in Geneva, and the run-up saw more, dramatic moves on the nuclear arms front by Moscow. On 27 September Shevardnadze, on his first US visit, proposed the halving of the superpowers' nuclear arsenals, an idea publicly repeated by Gorbachev a week later. But the Soviets were always careful to make such a step conditional on Reagan's abandonment of SDI, which the President refused to do. In August Gorbachev had insisted that SDI be controlled, declaring that without this, 'it will not be possible to reach an agreement on the . . . reduction of nuclear weapons either. The interrelationship between defensive and offensive arms is so obvious as to require no proof.'[12] Many US experts doubted the Star Wars project would come to much and there was some public frustration that it seemed to stand in the way of a major step towards the reduction of nuclear tension. But on 6 October Reagan's National Security Adviser, Robert McFarlane, announced that the US now considered SDI legal under the 1972 Anti-Ballistic Missile (ABM) treaty—a 'broad' interpretation which Moscow and even some of the US administration disputed. The arguments over SDI overshadowed the Geneva summit of 19–21 November, which saw no substantial progress. Reagan's offer to share Star Wars technology with Moscow if it worked was dismissed as naïve. But the meeting was surprisingly friendly in atmosphere; it was the first such conference since Carter and Brezhnev met in Vienna six years before, and the two agreed to meet again. Gorbachev noted that 'our dialogue was very constructive and intensive, sometimes even emotional.' Soviet Ambassador Dobrynin felt this was a turning point because he sensed that 'changes appeared in the thinking of Reagan about the Soviet Union. He began to depart from unconditional confrontation and display some sense of realism toward negotiation.' However, Reagan merely felt that 'after almost five years I'd finally met a Soviet leader I could talk to.'[13]

By early 1986 the US government was deeply divided over whether Gorbachev's policy changes were substantial or merely rhetorical and what, if anything, was his international strategy. The CIA believed that he would have to make concessions on arms control in due course (as well as to embrace radical reform at home), because of his country's poor economic state. Gorbachev certainly proved able to retain the initiative in world affairs, offering in a letter to Reagan of mid-January 1986 to eliminate all INF systems in Europe, followed by all other nuclear weapons by the end of the century. This effectively matched Reagan's 1981 offer of a 'zero option' on IMF. The price, however, was still the

end of SDI, an insistence which only convinced Washington that the Soviets were terrified by the Star Wars project. Opinion about the Soviet leader was already beginning to fracture in Washington however. Caspar Weinberger, Reagan's Defence Secretary, believed that 'Gorbachev is clearly adept at public relations in international politics. There is a great danger . . . that his approach will obscure the fundamental and unchanging nature of the Soviet system.' It was a view shared by CIA Director, Bill Casey, who still considered the USSR a serious military threat. But as early as May 1986 Secretary of State Shultz felt otherwise, telling a high-level meeting, 'My conclusion is radically different . . . The Soviets have lost the ideological battle. Their idea is receding; ours is moving forward.'[14] On 6 March, during the Communist Party Congress, Gorbachev had argued forcefully that nuclear defence was illogical and that the superpowers must agree to solve their differences on the basis of 'equal security'. This was another important statement because it suggested that, rather than the old doctrine of 'peaceful coexistence', Gorbachev now espoused genuine interaction with the West and China, no longer emphasizing competition but rather wanting to work with others to build security. Nonetheless, despite these positive signs, East–West relations worsened rather than improved over the following months. The date for another summit was pushed back because Gorbachev refused to meet Reagan if no concessions on SDI were on the table and hoped that the latter would be more likely to make concessions later in the year, as the Congressional elections approached. In March the US demanded that the USSR's delegation to the UN be drastically reduced because so many officials were suspected of espionage; in April Shevardnadze cancelled a visit to Washington because of the American bombing raids on Libya; and in May the US accused the Soviets of being in breach of the SALT II treaty so that it too need no longer adhere to the limits. (The US actually breached the treaty in November.) The worst crisis, however, arose in late August when the Americans arrested a KGB agent, Gennadi Zakharov, and the Soviets responded by seizing a US journalist, Nicholas Daniloff, who had unwittingly been used in CIA operations: the two were effectively 'swapped' in September, after which each superpower expelled numerous officials from the other.

Throughout these difficult months there were, nonetheless, more positive signs. On 18 April Gorbachev proposed deep cuts in *conventional* arms in Europe and on 25 July the US put forward a plan to eliminate all ballistic missiles—but, since this did not offer anything on SDI and since it would freeze US advantage in aircraft and short-range nuclear weapons, Gorbachev rejected it. The Soviet leader did, however, make progress on relations with China. In the early 1980s Brezhnev had tried to reopen links to Beijing, at a time when Reagan was neglectful of Sino–US relations, but the Chinese were still concerned by the Soviet arms build-up, the Afghanistan War, and the Vietnamese presence in Cambodia. There were good reasons to expect an improvement in Sino–Soviet relations however. Despite Reagan's visit to Beijing in 1984, the Chinese *were* disturbed by his anti-communism, the new US assertiveness in the world, and Washington's sympathy for Taiwan. On 28 July 1986, during a speech in Vladivostock, Gorbachev signalled a major shift of policy. He not only expressed a wish for improved relations with China but also offered to reduce troop levels in Afghanistan and, on the Chinese border, Mongolia. This led to talks on the disputed Sino–Soviet border beginning in February 1987.

Superpower relations finally seemed to emerge from the doldrums on 30 September 1986 when Reagan unexpectedly announced that an 'interim' summit was to be held on 11–12 October in the Icelandic capital, Reykjavik. This was intended by the US as a brief, working meeting to prepare for a more substantial conference. Gorbachev had initiated the idea, hopeful that a personal meeting with Reagan could break the current deadlock in US–Soviet arms talks and Reagan hastily agreed in order to impress the public before the Congressional elections. But the Americans were again wrong-footed by Gorbachev, who arrived in Reykjavik with some unexpectedly far-reaching proposals. Now he was not only ready to halve the superpowers' nuclear arsenals and to make an INF treaty, but to extend the ABM treaty for ten years (the US preferred five) and to make new concessions on the verification of these agreements. Previously the Soviet's refusal to allow 'on site' verification had always been a serious impediment to arms control. Once again, however, Gorbachev expected concessions on SDI and once again Reagan was not prepared to bargain. The earlier US offer to ban ballistic missiles was met by Gorbachev's demand that all categories of nuclear weapon should be destroyed. Despite an extension, the conference, hastily called and held in cramped conditions, ended in failure and recrimination, with the press generally blaming Reagan's SDI obsession for the breakdown. The President was typically unapologetic: when Gorbachev remarked, as they left the conference, 'I don't know what else I could have done,' Reagan replied, 'You could have said yes.' But Gorbachev was determined to exploit his opponent's hard line, telling the Politburo, 'we have to score propaganda points, continue our offensive of enlightenment intended for the . . . public.'[15] Nor did relations improve over the following months. At the New Year there was no exchange of messages between the White House and the Kremlin as there had been the year before. And in early February 1987 there was uproar in the US and European media when it was reported that Reagan was about to agree to SDI's deployment.

In retrospect Reykjavik was not the disaster it seemed, for it evidently convinced Gorbachev that it was pointless to continue calling for the end of SDI. In fact the US Ambassador to Moscow, Jack Matlock, believed that the summit had 'produced breakthroughs that cleared the way for subsequent treaties'; and even that it was 'just as well that no final agreement was reached at that time', because the eventual INF treaty was superior to anything that would have emerged from Reykjavik.[16] By now Gorbachev was irretrievably set upon his course of decentralization and openness at home, alongside a freeze on defence spending and further steps to reduce tension abroad. His key initiative, on 28 February 1987, was to 'decouple' the INF talks from other issues and declare his readiness to sign an INF treaty regardless of what happened to Star Wars. This concession was publicly welcomed by Reagan on 6 March, but did not necessarily mean that the American was now in a dominant position: in November the Republicans had lost their majority in the Senate and, soon after, the administration was rocked by the Iran–Contragate revelations.

Gorbachev and Shevardnadze

The two men who dominated the foreign policy of the USSR in its closing years, were both identified as leading would-be reformers before 1985; loyal and long-serving members of the Communist Party of the Soviet Union (CPSU), but also firm opponents of inefficiency and corruption. Shevardnadze was born in Mamati, Georgia in 1928, joined the CPSU in 1948, and rose in the party hierarchy to become the First Secretary in Georgia by 1972. Gorbachev was slightly younger, being born in 1931 in Privnolye, in the Stravropol region of Southern Russia, joining the CPSU in 1952 and becoming head of agriculture in Stavropol region in the 1960s. But it was Gorbachev who came to national prominence first, being elected to the Central Committee of the USSR in 1971 and joining the Politburo in 1980. Shevardnadze only joined the Central Committee in 1976.

Between 1978 and 1985 Gorbachev was the Central Committee's Secretary for Agriculture in which position he was critical of the inefficiencies of central planning and a close ally of Yuri Andropov who, as Soviet leader in 1982–4, launched an anti-corruption drive. Gorbachev failed to succeed Andropov in 1984, but did not have to wait long for another opportunity. In March 1985 he became General Secretary of the CPSU and rapidly began to promote other reformers. No appointment caused greater surprise than that of Shevardnadze to the Foreign Ministry, in succession to the veteran diplomat, Andrei Gromyko. But Shevardnadze had impressed Gorbachev in earlier encounters as a determined yet open-minded figure and, despite the Georgian's lack of experience overseas, they worked together closely over the following years to reduce Soviet involvement in conflicts in the less developed world and improve relations with the West. At home, Shevardnadze was a firm supporter of Gorbachev's policies of *glasnost* ('openness') and *perestroika* ('reconstruction').

In 1990, with the Eastern bloc breaking up, Gorbachev won the 1990 Nobel Peace Prize. But, criticized at home for the 'loss' of Eastern Europe and concerned that the USSR might be heading back towards dictatorship, Shevardnadze resigned as Foreign Minister in December of that year. Gorbachev, who by then had become Executive President of the USSR, with an elected assembly, seemed increasingly uncertain about the pace of reform. In August 1991, an attempted coup by hard-line communists seemed to justify Shevardnadze's earlier fears. The coup, though defeated, effectively broke Gorbachev's hold on power and precipitated the disintegration of the USSR itself. Shevardnadze returned for a brief time as Foreign Minister in November–December 1991, but then focused his energies on the politics of Georgia, which now became independent. He was Georgia's head of state from 1992 onwards, being elected President by popular vote in 1995 and re-elected in 2000. He survived two assassination attempts and civil war in the process. Gorbachev, in contrast, had very little political success in post-Soviet Russia. His attempt to run for the Presidency in 1996 resulted in a paltry vote of less than one per cent and many Russians blamed him for their economic and political difficulties, even if he continued to be lauded in the West as a far-sighted reformer, who had done most to end the Cold War.

Also one of those leading figures who had doubted Gorbachev's sincerity, CIA Director Bill Casey, was forced to resign through illness on 30 January. The scene was set for the early conclusion of a major superpower arms deal and a general improvement in East–West relations which, within eighteen months, led some to conclude that the Cold War was over.

B. Is The Cold War Over? 1987–1989

Gorbachev's Reforms Gather Pace

In 1987–8, although Western public opinion was very favourable to Gorbachev, there were still fears in Western capitals that the USSR could revert to its old ways. It was still a centralized communist state and, under any 'realist' interpretation of international relations, it was unthinkable that Gorbachev would set out to retreat from positions of strength, weaken his country, and ultimately bring about his own fall. Such, indeed, was not his intention. But, domestically and internationally, as he pressed on with new initiatives more vigorously after 1987, he began to lose control of events. His reforms at this time went far beyond his early, cautious experiments and have been called 'perestroika mark 2'. They 'soon led him into uncharted territories, awakening suspicion . . . among some of those who had helped him come to power.'[17] At home he finally introduced a major economic reform in early 1988 with the 'self-financing' system under which state enterprises were to become more profitable and efficient, making their own business plans, and facing closure if they did not succeed. Politically, following a special party conference in mid-1988, an element of choice was introduced into elections, held in March 1989, for a 'Congress of People's Deputies', which in turn elected the Supreme Soviet. Neither of these reforms marked the abandonment of the command economy or the primary role of the Communist Party in Soviet life, but they were fiercely resisted in some quarters. The economic reforms in particular were modest and easy for opponents to undermine, yet provoked enough confusion for major shortages of certain goods to appear. Politically the conservatives forced the removal of a leading reformer, Boris Yeltsin, from the Politburo in late 1987 but he was able to exploit the new openness to win election to the Supreme Soviet in 1989, where he continued to advocate a rapid move to market economics and pluralist politics. Others in the USSR wanted to divide the country up. The Union was actually composed of fifteen republics, in many of which nationalist feeling and dislike of Russian domination was strong. The danger, unthinkable since the 1920s civil war, that the USSR could break into several states, became very real by 1989. As early as December 1986 there had been nationalist violence in the Central Asian republic of Kazakhstan. The democratization process 'resulted not in a cleansing and strengthening of the Communist Party', as Gorbachev had hoped, 'but rather in a widespread defection from the Party's ranks', with anti-communist and nationalist movements emerging.[18] Whilst trying to reform communism, therefore, Gorbachev failed to foresee that *glasnost* and *perestroika* might simply provoke confusion, uncertainty, and opposition from various quarters from those who felt that changes went too far and those who wanted them to go much further.

In foreign policy too Gorbachev hoped for managed change rather than a revolution. His desire for economic reform was closely linked to his wish to match the West and continue to play a leading role in world affairs. But in the short term he needed to reduce the strains on the economy and pursue détente with the West. Also he remained genuinely eager to promote peace and to remove the danger of nuclear war. In his book, *Perestroika*, he wrote that nuclear weapons placed 'an objective limit to class confrontation in the international arena' and argued that 'the backbone of the new way of thinking is the recognition of the priority of . . . humankind's survival.'[19] This implied that the expansion of communism worldwide was no longer a priority. When, in August-September 1987, there was a clash in the Politburo between Shevardnadze and the ideology chief, Yegar Ligachev, it was Ligachev, the proponent of class-based international relations, who was sacked. Shevardnadze's less ideological, non-confrontational, and non-militarist approach was now predominant. Gorbachev's and Shevardnadze's aims were to be achieved, however, by means which seemed to mark a retreat abroad and ultimately called into question the USSR's readiness to hold onto its long-standing sphere of influence in Eastern Europe. Gorbachev continued to restrain defence spending and used an embarrassing episode in May 1987—when a young German aviator, Matthias Rust, flew a small airplane through Soviet air defences and into Red Square—to purge the armed forces of his opponents, including the Defence Minister, Sergei Sokolov. Furthermore, on 30 May, the Warsaw Pact announced a new, defensive military doctrine, saying it would not start a war or be the first side to use nuclear weapons.

In the less developed world the years 1987–9 saw important steps towards resolving the conflicts in Afghanistan, Angola, and Nicaragua, the most dramatic step being the Red Army's withdrawal from Afghanistan by mid-February 1989 (see Chapter 19, C). These moves in the less developed world were made without abandoning Moscow's clients: the communist government in Kabul eventually outlasted the USSR, the Angolan MPLA survived to win the country's first free elections in 1992, and though the Nicaraguan Sandinistas lost elections in 1990, they remained a leading force in the country's politics. But the general trend did suggest that, in order to pacify the West, Gorbachev was ready to goad his allies into compromise. And in Eastern Europe in 1989, when he was faced with the most serious crisis of all for Soviet power, he chose to abandon the Brezhnev Doctrine rather than rekindle the Cold War by using repression (Chapter 19, D). He hoped, perhaps, to replace the old division of Europe, between NATO and the Warsaw Pact, with a new united 'Common European Home', an idea first mooted in a speech in Paris in February 1986 and developed in Prague in April 1987. But, as with his domestic reforms, Gorbachev was not precise about what this meant and he tended, in practice, simply to press for the Conference on Security and Cooperation in Europe (CSCE) to be given a more significant role. By the end of 1989, though Washington deliberately avoided any overt triumphalism, it seemed that the Soviets had very definitely 'lost' the Cold War. They were out of Afghanistan, their days in Eastern Europe were approaching an end, and even the cohesion of the USSR itself was in doubt. It was inevitable that, popular as he was in the West, Gorbachev was blamed by his own people for his country's dwindling power.

Reagan, Gorbachev, and INF

In mid-April 1987 the US Secretary of State, George Shultz, the leading figure in Washington to believe that an arms deal was both possible and desirable, flew to Moscow to discuss the issue and propose a summit. Here Gorbachev continued his policy of offering concessions by saying the USSR would scrap its short-range SS-12 and SS-23 missiles, of which the West had no equivalent. Shultz was restrained by the doubts of others about the wisdom of a deal, but in May-June the Warsaw Pact and NATO alliances both approved an INF treaty in principle, and in August the German Chancellor, Helmut Kohl, agreed to dismantle his country's Pershing 1A missiles (with US-controlled warheads) as part of a deal. Gorbachev periodically raised SDI as a problem, and at one point

threatened not to attend a summit without an SDI deal, but he also continued to make concessions, not least on his original desire to retain a substantial number of INF weapons on the border with China. The danger that SDI would produce a major technological breakthrough was reduced in late 1987 anyway, partly because of Congressional restrictions on its funding and partly because one of its key advocates, Weinberger, resigned in early November. The INF treaty, which virtually eliminated all nuclear weapons of an intermediate range, was signed during the Washington summit of 7–10 December, which also saw talks on regional problems, notably Afghanistan and Nicaragua, and led to expressions of hopes for a strategic arms reduction (START) treaty, despite the continuation of SDI. The INF treaty was especially important for reducing tensions in Europe, though there were some fears in NATO that it harmed the logic of escalated deterrence and flexible response. The Soviet leadership interpreted it as 'a major victory for the new thinking' but Weinberger described it as 'a monument to President Reagan's determination to regain our military strength', which had forced the Kremlin to strike a deal.[20]

The Intermediate Nuclear Forces Treaty

Signed in Washington on 8 December 1987, by Mikhail Gorbachev and Ronald Reagan, the treaty:

- eliminated all INF systems, mostly in Europe but also in Asia, these being missiles whose range was between 500 and 5,500 kilometres;
- included onsite verification and was to be carried out within three years;
- meant that the Soviets gave up about 1,750 nuclear missiles (some with multiple warheads) to the Americans' 850 (all single warhead);
- represented a real cut in nuclear arsenals and was therefore a true *disarmament* measure, in contrast to the SALT I and II treaties which had merely established 'ceilings' on nuclear weapons and were thus *arms control* agreements; and
- ended almost a whole category of weapons, but only actually reduced total nuclear warhead numbers controlled by the superpowers by less than 7 per cent.

Nineteen eighty-eight was a difficult year for Gorbachev at home, as ethnic problems, conservative opposition, and shortages began to mount, but internationally it was one of great success, with US–Soviet relations almost approaching warmth. In the less developed world there was a ceasefire in Nicaragua (23 March), an Afghan settlement was agreed (14 April), and accords were signed on Angola (22 December), while the Vietnamese began to withdraw from Cambodia. The steps in Afghanistan and Cambodia paved the way for a further improvement in Sino–Soviet relations, as did Gorbachev's readiness to eliminate INF weapons. Indeed, ironically, by the time Gorbachev visited Beijing for a summit meeting in May 1989, the Chinese were most concerned, not by the USSR's military power but by the danger which *perestroika* represented to communism everywhere. Diplomatic relations between the two were restored and Gorbachev undertook to reduce the Red Army on the border by 120,000 but the Soviet domestic reform programme had helped inspire dissidents in Beijing who occupied Tiananmen Square during the summit. Meanwhile, the US and USSR had proceeded to ratify the INF treaty and another summit was arranged for Moscow, between 29 May and 2 June, to exchange the instruments of ratification. It was not possible to complete a START treaty before the conference because of the complexities involved. But the atmosphere at this, the fourth Gorbachev–Reagan meeting in three years, was the best yet and it had an important impact on Soviet domestic politics as Ambassador Matlock understood: 'Gorbachev needed Reagan's endorsement and Reagan's visit to prove that his policy was bearing fruit. A successful summit would give him momentum for the Party conference, which, he hoped, would endorse a more radical course for reform.'[21]

Such a frequency of high-level contact had only been seen in the détente era of 1972–5 and, although Reagan himself would never use the much aligned term 'détente', he did walk through Red Square on 31 May and, when asked by a reporter about his 'evil Empire' speech, replied, 'I was talking about another time, another era.'[22] It was this remark which led Reagan's Vice-President and would-be successor, George Bush, to insist the following day that 'The Cold War's not over.' Five months later Bush was

elected President and the key question was how he would deal with the Soviet leader when the Cold War, if perhaps 'not over', was clearly fading. This point was underlined by a remarkable speech from Gorbachev to the UN on 7 December, the first time a Soviet leader had addressed the organization since Khrushchev's embarrassing visit in 1960. Gorbachev's speech ranged from reflections on the way world affairs should now operate, including an appreciation of interdependence and a belief that freedom should be respected, to a specific proposal for conventional arms reductions, including a shrinking of the Red Army by half a million. It also included an important declaration that Marxist-Leninism was not an absolute truth, so that ideological conflict between East and West was no longer necessary. But later that day when Gorbachev met both Reagan and his successor-elect, Bush said very little. The Soviet leader was then forced to return home early because of a devastating earthquake in Armenia, and so was unable to fulfil his hope of winning Bush over to a hopeful, positive relationship. Shultz, about to leave the State Department, was not without fear for the future: 'President Reagan and I were handing over real momentum. I hoped it would not be squandered.'[23]

Bush and Gorbachev in 1989

George Bush had been born into a political family and had considerable first-hand experience of national security policy, not only as Vice-President (1981–9), but also as ambassador to the UN (1971–2), envoy to China (1974–5), and Director of the CIA (1976–7). Cautious and pragmatic, he had doubted the wisdom both of Reagan's early anti-Sovietism and his later enthusiasm for embracing Gorbachev. As he had made clear in 1988, the new President doubted whether the Cold War had ended and preferred to keep the USSR under pressure while hoping that it would continue to change. 'The initial attitude of the incoming Bush administration towards the ongoing changes in the USSR was one of hope tempered by scepticism,' with Bush later saying 'I was probably less suspicious of Gorbachev than were others in my incoming team.'[24] His inaugural speech promised to maintain good relations with

Moscow. In January he gathered around him a group of old friends in key positions including James Baker, who had been Reagan's Chief of Staff in 1981–5 as Secretary of State, and Brent Scowcroft, back as National Security Adviser, a post he had last held under Gerald Ford. They kept their disagreements to themselves and appeared a coherent team, determined to improve on the hasty, ill-coordinated decision-making of the Reagan period. But to the press and public this did not necessarily seem an improvement. Rather than an active, welcoming response to Gorbachev, Bush set out on a three-month review of international issues, which was meant to clarify problems and allow for well-informed decisions, but which seemed simply to be wasting time. The 'impetus in Soviet–American relations was ... lost as.... Bush took time to reappraise his policy options.'[25] Baker did not make his first visit to Moscow until May and Scowcroft's first public statement claimed that Gorbachev was 'interested in making trouble within the Western alliance,' adding 'I think the Cold War is not over.' Scowcroft felt, for example, that in the less developed world, the 'few positive regional changes which had occurred ... [stemmed] more from Soviet failures than from a general change of attitude about regional superpower competition.'[26] The review did not, as it transpired, produce any great change where US–Soviet relations were concerned. It concluded that Gorbachev *had* altered Soviet foreign policy and that he was the best leader to work with, but the future was uncertain and there were grave doubts about whether Gorbachev could stabilize and improve the Soviet economy.

Bush's policy review also meant that no progress was possible on the START treaty. Meanwhile Gorbachev was upset that the 'Americans were apparently still influenced by obsolete stereotypes'[27] and he continued to win in the public relations stakes. He announced a major reduction of the Red Army in Mongolia in March and, in May, told Baker that there would be a large unilateral cut in Soviet theatre nuclear weapons in Europe. On 6 March 1989 NATO and the Warsaw Pact opened negotiations in Vienna on conventional arms reductions: these negotiations, which replaced the former Mutual Balanced Force Reduction talks, underway with little success since the early 1970s. They were

renamed the 'Conventional Forces in Europe' (CFE) talks and it was clear that they would become part of a public relations battle, as Gorbachev would no doubt want to outbid Washington with concessions. Bush was determined to match his Soviet colleague on the CFE front however, and by late May both sides were actually quite close in their proposals. Bush, with some trouble, persuaded a NATO summit on 29 May to offer a 10 per cent reduction in US forces, matched by cuts in other categories of weapons, all to be achieved by 1992. Meanwhile, in mid-April, the President had also begun a series of speeches in the US, to follow up the recent policy review. The most important of these, for superpower relations, was at the Texas A and M University on 12 May where he revived Eisenhower's 'Open Skies' proposal (to allow flights over each other's territory (see Chapter 5, B), offered to expand trade and

---

Gorbachev's United Nations Speech of 7 December 1988

Gorbachev made numerous speeches on foreign policy in the late 1980s but one of the most significant was his first address to the UN in New York, just as the Reagan administration was coming to an end. The speech began with a reference to the significance of the Russian Revolution and it denied that the USSR was abandoning its communist philosophy, but Gorbachev stated that there was emerging 'before us a different world, for which it is necessary to take different roads towards the future'. The world was becoming more 'integrated', ideological differences were becoming less vital than 'the interests of all mankind' and 'force and the threat of force can no longer be ... instruments of foreign policy.' Thus, the speech marked a recognition of globalization and what the Soviet leader called the 'de-ideologication' of international relations. It also talked of the need to respect human rights and the freedom of all countries, hinting at the liberalization of the Soviet bloc that was to come the following year. On specifics, however, the speech was most noteworthy for announcing large-scale cuts in the Soviet Union's conventional armaments, amounting to a reduction of half a million personnel, with major withdrawals from Eastern Europe. To this was linked the aim of a halving of strategic nuclear weapons via the START talks.

seemed to accept the waning of the Cold War by stating that America could move 'beyond containment', to a new policy, 'one that recognizes the full scope of change . . . around the world and in the Soviet Union itself . . . Ultimately, our objective is to welcome the Soviet Union back into the world order.'[28] Thus, despite 'the initial stumble of the policy review . . . by the end of 1989 the Bush administration had begun to develop a fairly coherent policy . . . based on the idea of "testing" Gorbachev and pushing him to translate his rhetorical commitment into concrete policies.'[29] As James Baker put it, 'Gorbachev was making powerful promises—and our job was to hold him to his word. The boldness . . . of Gorbachev's pronouncements made him vulnerable to being hoisted on his own petard.'[30]

The first Bush–Gorbachev summit was not discussed until July 1989, by which time there were already serious signs of difficulty for the Soviet-led system in Eastern Europe, which the US President toured that same month (Chapter 19, D). Bush wanted a conference, not to push the START treaty, which was still the subject of debate in Washington, but simply to re-establish relations on a private, informal basis. Some very friendly meetings between Baker and Shevardnadze in Washington and Wyoming in September gave encouragement to the idea. It was here that the Soviets finally gave up linking START to the scrapping of SDI. They also agreed to dismantle the Krasnoyarsk radar, the building of which had breached the ABM treaty. Gorbachev agreed in October to a summit and the date was brought forward to 2–3 December partly because of the gathering pace of events in Eastern Europe. By now Bush 'was convinced that he . . . should support *perestroika*.'[31] But it was hardly the most successful of superpower meetings. The venue, Malta, was as badly chosen as Reykjavik in 1986; storms in Valetta harbour made it difficult to travel

---

Bush's Texas A&M University Speech

Delivered on 12 May 1989, during a commencement ceremony at College Station, this was Bush's most important policy speech on the USSR and the Cold War. It followed a comprehensive review of US foreign policy during the early months of his Presidency and was part of a series of statements on the subject that had begun in mid-April, with a speech in Michigan giving support to reform in Eastern Europe. In the 12 May speech Bush declared that 'We are approaching the conclusion of a historic post-war struggle between . . . tyranny and . . . freedom.' He announced that 'Containment worked' and in effect declared that it had ended: the American policy would now aim at 'integration of the Soviet Union into the community of nations', as the USSR became a more democratic and open society.

The speech pointed out that the USSR was still a formidable military power and that the success of *perestroika* was not absolutely certain, and Bush called on the Kremlin to reduce its conventional forces, allow self-determination in Eastern Europe, contribute to settling disputes in the less developed world, and respect human rights. The President also revived Eisenhower's 'Open Skies' proposal of 1955, to allow peaceful overflights of each other's territory, so as to survey military activities. Finally, Bush raised the prospect of granting 'Most Favoured Nation' trading status to the USSR, if it relaxed its emigration policy and ended discrimination against US companies.

---

between the US and Soviet ships which carried the two leaders. There were no substantive agreements, because none had been planned. But there was discussion of arms issues, trade, and regional problems, and another meeting was planned for June. By the time that was held, however, the political revolution in Europe was complete and few could doubt that, whatever the earlier doubts of Bush and Scowcroft, the Cold War had indeed ended.

C. Ending the Cold War in the Less Developed World: Afghanistan, Angola, Cambodia

One of the key features of international relations in the later 1980s, which stood in stark contrast to events of a decade before, was the retreat of the Soviets and their allies, Cuba and Vietnam, from the active policy they had adopted in the less developed world. In March 1983 Shultz had written to Reagan that a 'litmus test of Soviet seriousness in response to our concerns would be whether they are moving seriously toward a real pull-back from one of the positions gained in the 1970s.'[32] The Reagan Doctrine had been targeted at reversing the supposed Communist advances in Afghanistan and Cambodia, Angola and Nicaragua. Under Gorbachev the USSR was no longer willing or able to finance such commitments and the 'new diplomacy' called for tensions to be lowered with the West on a global scale. As early as October 1985 he told the Politburo, 'we should firmly adopt a course leading to our earliest withdrawal from Afghanistan' due to the economic and political costs of the war there.[33] By the end of 1989 the Red Army had left Afghanistan and the Angolan and Cambodian problem seemed less acute. But this process of retreat was neither swift nor simple. Until 1987, when Reagan considered 'we were at last seeing real deeds from Moscow',[34] important elements in the US government doubted whether Gorbachev was in fact ready to resolve Afghanistan and other less developed world problems; the US response to his moves has been described as 'reactive, cautiously encouraging, but wary';[35] and in all the places where a retreat occurred, the Soviets were able to secure some concessions to help their local clients.

Gorbachev and Afghanistan

Within six months of coming to power Gorbachev looked at the option of withdrawing from Afghanistan and by the end of 1985 he had decided in principle to pursue this policy, hence his critical line on the war at the February 1986 Communist Party

Congress. Here, as elsewhere, Gorbachev gave a new direction to policy after years of uncertain leadership. It has been noted that 'One result of Gorbachev's reforms was to marginalize the issue and importance of less developed world revolutions. . . . The 1986 party programme barely mentioned the less developed world.'[36] He had actually questioned the wisdom of the conflict under Brezhnev, when the high costs of the invasion were already apparent. It was a public relations disaster, upsetting not only the Western powers, but also China and the Non-aligned Movement. As an 'unwinnable' war it demoralized an army whose conscripts already experienced low pay, poor training, and alcoholism: as with the US army in Vietnam, the Red Army's 'Afgantsy' troops—about 750,000 served some time in the war—generally came from poorer, less influential families and they soon felt both betrayed by their leaders and ostracized from society. Economically too the war, while (at 2 per cent of the budget) affordable, was an unwelcome burden on an already tottering economy. At home the war became a symbol of communist failure and the need for reform. But Gorbachev did not want a withdrawal to appear as a defeat for the USSR. He needed to put the Kabul government in a strong position for talks with its adversaries on an internal settlement and he also had to consider the views of those Soviet hardliners, including Gromyko and the Defence Ministry, who wanted to fight on. It was for these reasons that at first, in 1985–6, Gorbachev allowed some of the most destructive Red Army offensives of the war, with the use of special troops and aggressive new tactics, including the widespread laying of mines and the greater deployment of helicopter gunships, all of which caused high civilian casualties.

It was because of this intensification of the war that the CIA feared Gorbachev was determined to fight on and the US increased its aid to the Mujaheddin, up from $250 million in 1985 to $630 million in 1987, with similar amounts being provided by Saudi

Arabia. One decision, taken by Reagan in early 1986, was to supply the Mujaheddin with advanced shoulder-held, anti-aircraft missiles, called 'Stingers'. Supported by Shultz, he did this despite their obvious US origin and Defense Department fears that the Soviets might capture, and copy, them. 'Unless we hurt the Soviets in Afghanistan,' Shultz believed, 'they would have no interest in dealing with us to end the war there.'[37] The Stingers made it more dangerous to transport Soviet troops and supplies by air and proved a particular headache to Red Army commanders, but the idea that the missiles had a major impact on withdrawal is a myth: by the time the Stingers started to be used (after an essential period of training), round about September 1986, Gorbachev was already preparing for withdrawal. In May he had Babrak Karmal replaced with the more flexible Mohammed Najibullah who, though he was a former head of the KHAD secret police, recognized the communists could not win the war and was ready to attempt a 'national reconciliation' with their opponents. To this end he offered a ceasefire, invited opponents to enter government, and in 1987 promulgated a new Constitution. There was now an 'Afghanistanization' of the war, with the Red Army lessening its involvement and handing areas over to the Afghan military or local militia. But the 'regime's wooing of the Afghan opposition had . . . only patchy results, in spite of war weariness and the toll of destruction.'[38] Meanwhile there had been progress on the Geneva peace talks, which had been underway since 1982. In June 1985 both superpowers agreed to support the peace process, though the actual negotiations were in the hands of the Afghan and Pakistani governments. In December 1985, following the first Gorbachev–Reagan summit, the US agreed that it would guarantee a settlement so long as there was a timetable for Soviet withdrawal. And in May 1986, as Najibullah came to power, the seventh and last round of proximity talks between Afghanistan and Pakistan opened in Geneva.

Despite the apparent progress in 1986, it was only on 8 February 1988 that Gorbachev publicly stated his hope that Soviet troops would be out of Afghanistan in thirteen months time and, even then, the moderate Soviet Foreign Minister, Shevardnadze, doubted the wisdom of such a declara-

tion. For all sides the peace process was surrounded by uncertainty. Hardliners within Kabul and among the Mujaheddin did not want to talk at all, and the Afghan and Pakistani delegations in Geneva only met face-to-face on the day a peace agreement was signed on 14 April 1988 (see boxed section). Even Najibullah, who was told by Gorbachev in December 1986 about the planned withdrawal, hoped that the Red Army would actually stay to protect him. In Washington, the Reagan administration became divided between those who were ready to negotiate a settlement (and, until early 1988, even they had grave doubts about whether it could be achieved) and those who saw Afghanistan as a way to 'bleed' the USSR, forcing Gorbachev into ever more radical changes at home. The latter group doubted the wisdom of supporting a settlement and were determined to oust the communists from power in Kabul. A vital issue was whether, if peace was achieved, the US would end its assistance to the Mujaheddin: the danger that the US would continue such assistance was of concern to Gorbachev, provoking fears that he would not go ahead with a settlement; but the US

The Geneva Accords on Afghanistan, 14 April 1988

The principal agreement was between the Afghan and Pakistani governments who agreed:

1. They would respect each other's independence and integrity.
2. They would refrain from using force against the other.
3. They would not let their territory be used to violate the territory of the other or to encourage rebellion there.
4. There would be a voluntary repatriation of refugees.
5. There should be an internal settlement in Afghanistan between the Kabul government and other elements.
6. The Red Army would withdraw from Afghanistan within nine months.

In addition the USSR and US guaranteed the settlement but the US, in a verbal statement, reserved the right to resupply the Mujaheddin if the USSR continued to aid the Kabul government.

Defense Secretary, Caspar Weinberger, was determined to resupply the Mujaheddin until the communists were ousted. In January 1988 Reagan said that America would only end aid to the Mujaheddin *if* the USSR ended aid to the Kabul government. The latter was a step Gorbachev would not take because the Kabul government—a legally recognized government fighting against rebels—would be placed in an impossibly weak position. If the USSR were not to appear a 'defeated' power, it was essential that Najibullah should survive. Shevardnadze acknowledged to Shultz that Najibullah might fall anyway, 'but nature must take its course after we leave and not be pushed by us beforehand.'[39] Yet, in defiance of the views of Shevardnadze and the KGB chief, Vladimir Kryuchkov, Gorbachev *did* rule out the idea that the Red Army could return to Afghanistan if the Geneva settlement unravelled.

The Geneva agreement was only a partial settlement, which, to the benefit of the Soviets, kept Najibullah in power and eased the danger of Pakistani interference in Afghanistan, but which, on the negative side from Moscow's viewpoint, did nothing to end the civil war and committed the Red Army to withdrawal. It 'marked a major new stage in the Afghan struggle ... Rather than guaranteeing peace ... the agreement promised instability and indefinite warfare for the Afghan people.'[40] The fulfilment of the withdrawal promise, despite America's refusal to abandon the Mujaheddin, was one of Gorbachev's most remarkable decisions as Soviet leader. The last Soviet troops crossed the border at Friendship Bridge on 15 February 1989, having suffered 14,500 combat deaths in Afghanistan, 20,000 dead from other causes, and about 50,000 wounded. Just prior to this, anticipating a triumphant Mujaheddin advance on the capital, Western diplomats quit Kabul. But, to the annoyance of American right-wingers, the Najibullah regime did not collapse and it was the Mujaheddin who suffered setbacks in 1988–9 notably the death of their chief supporter, Pakistan's General Zia, in an air crash (July 1988) and the failure of their siege of Jalalabad (March 1989). Determined never to become directly involved in Afghanistan again Gorbachev rejected pleas from the Kabul government to help them with air support

during the siege, but he did resupply them with arms, just as the US and Pakistan resupplied the still-divided Mujaheddin. The Geneva agreement thus failed to prevent continued external interference in Afghanistan. Despite UN efforts and some desultory talks it also failed to lead to an internal settlement. There was rather more success in resettling refugees: about four million, out of six million, returned in 1988–90.

Some progress was finally possible in September 1991 when the US and USSR agreed to cut off arms supplies to their clients, a policy which Pakistan, Iran, and Saudi Arabia also supported for a time. But the agreement only became effective in January 1992, by which time the Soviet Union had ceased to exist and the Mujaheddin were closing on Kabul. In April 1991 they had taken Khost, proving that the government could no longer protect its urban strongholds and, backed by the US, they continued to demand Najibullah's resignation. He finally offered to go in March 1992, on condition that a broad-based interim government was formed (as the UN had been working for), but in mid-April the Mujaheddin seized Kabul anyway, establishing an Islamic state amid chaos, violence, and continued tribal divisions which made stable government impossible. Najibullah took refuge in the UN compound in Kabul where he remained until September 1996 when a more united Islamic movement, the Taliban seized the city and executed him. The Taliban had been backed since 1994 by Pakistan, which was increasingly frustrated by the failure of the Mujaheddin to work together. For a time it seemed that the Taliban would unite the whole country but they met resistance in the north from one of Najibullah's former generals, Abdul Dostom, a champion of the Uzbeki minority, who defeated them in May 1997 at Mazari-al-Sharif. In 1997–8 the US revived its efforts to end external interference in Afghanistan and form a coalition government. The Taliban's 'fundamentalism', their support for certain terrorist groups abroad, notably Osama bin Laden's Al Qaeda network, and Afghan drug production—all these continued to make the country of concern to Washington. Meanwhile, the civil war dragged on in a country which had already lost over a million dead since the communist coup of 1978, with the Taliban being resisted by an increasingly beleaguered

'Northern Alliance'. Eventually, in September 2001, following Al Qaeda links to attacks on New York and Washington, in which around 4,000 died, America would find itself launching a war against Afghanistan.

Angola and Namibia

The situation in Angola differed from Afghanistan in that the Marxist government had armed support, not from the USSR, but from Cuba and about 40,000 of its troops. Also, in the 1980s the Angolan problem could not be tackled in isolation because, after 1981, the US and South Africa insisted on tying it to the neighbouring Namibian question. Namibia was the former German colony of South-West Africa which, after the Second World War, was never made a trust territory and this led to controversy over whether its status as a League of Nations mandate under South African administration remained in force or not. In 1966, strong anti-apartheid feeling in the UN had led the General Assembly to terminate the mandate, thus theoretically placing South-West Africa under UN control. But in reality the South Africans continued to occupy it and it was from there, after 1975, that they aided Jonas Savimbi's UNITA movement which was fighting a guerrilla war against the Angolan government (see Chapter 13, E). After earlier hoping to annex South-West Africa the South Africans accepted by 1975 that it ought to become independent, but they refused to deal with Sam Nujoma's South-West African People's Organization (SWAPO), which the UN accepted as the voice of the Namibian people. By 1978 UN-sponsored talks had led to a plan for a ceasefire between the South Africans and the SWAPO guerrillas (who operated from Angola), followed by elections and independence. But the South African government, under P. W. Botha, was unwilling to proceed while the communist threat existed in Angola and while SWAPO seemed at one with the Cubans and the Angolan government. Botha won predictable support in 1981 from the equally anti-communist Ronald Reagan and from then onwards the previously separate Angolan and Namibian questions tended to become linked in talks.

UN attempts to make progress on southern Africa failed in the early 1980s. In 1983–4, with UNITA in retreat and the US more active in exploring a settlement, the South Africans agreed to pull their own units out of Angola if SWAPO and Cuba did not exploit this: the Cubans should pull out of southern Angola and Angola should end its support for SWAPO attacks on Namibia. But this hopeful move failed to bring a settlement. The Reagan administration stepped in to support UNITA, the Cubans increased their troop numbers in Angola, and the Angolan government backed off from peace talks. At the same time the South Africans offended SWAPO by setting up a puppet 'transitional government' in Namibia. For their part, the South Africans were offended when Reagan, under pressure from Congress on the apartheid issue, introduced economic sanctions against them, which undermined any US attempts to explore peace. Also important, however (and further evidence of the confused nature of American policy), was the UN Congress's August 1985 decision to repeal the decade-old Clark Amendment, which had previously prevented Reagan from providing aid to UNITA. Among the lethal aid given by the CIA in 1986, using Zaire as a conduit, were Stinger anti-aircraft missiles, the weapons which had had an important military impact in Afghanistan. They now enabled UNITA to defeat a government offensive in southern Angola and helped convince the Angolan government, of Eduardo dos Santos, to talk to the US. US–Angolan talks began in 1987 and were joined by Cuba in January 1988. By then, of course, Gorbachev was anxious to reduce Cold War tensions and pressed the Cubans, whose presence in Angola he effectively bankrolled, to talk. In fact Gorbachev's decision to pursue a settlement in 1987 was probably *more* significant than the military pressure now being exerted by UNITA and South Africa. In any case, in March 1988 the Cubans and Angolans scored an important victory, forcing UNITA to raise its siege of Cuita Cuanavale. Both the South Africans and the Angolan government were now keen to talk, not least to help their domestic economies. 'The warring parties mobilized ever greater resources. . . . Yet they seemed to achieve less and less. . . . In 1987–88, the . . . moment of maximum risk became converted into a magic moment of opportunity.'[41] As to the

US, Shultz's strategy, geared as it was to dealing with a perceived 'Cold War' problem, was clear and simple: 'we tied Namibian independence to Cuban withdrawal from Angola.'[42]

The result was that, in May 1988, the US Assistant Secretary of State for African Affairs, Chester Crocker, along with the USSR's Anatoly Adamishin, helped broker a deal in talks in London whereby the Cubans would leave Angola in return for a South African withdrawal from Namibia. By the end of August all South Africa's troops were probably out of Angola, the Cubans agreed in principle to complete their withdrawal from Angola within three years, and a date for independence was set for 1990, following elections. A formal agreement on these lines was signed by South Africa, Cuba, and Angola at the UN on 22 December 1988, with Shultz and Shevardnadze attending to underline the superpowers' interest in a settlement. Both sides had gained from such a settlement: South Africa had secured the Cubans' departure from Angola but Angola had the assurance that South African forces would leave Namibia. In Namibia, at least, the settlement operated reasonably smoothly. There was a crisis in April 1989 when as a South Africa–SWAPO ceasefire took effect and just before the Namibian elections, with only a small UN peacekeeping force deployed there, SWAPO fighters crossed over the Angolan border en masse; but a tough South African response and the threat of independence being suspended led SWAPO to reinstall the ceasefire. SWAPO's move was difficult to explain, since they won the elections with 57 per cent of the vote. Independence for Namibia went ahead in March 1990. But an internal settlement proved more difficult to achieve in Angola. It has been argued that the incoming Bush administration, with its doubts as to whether the Cold War had ended, 'showed little interest in seizing the opportunity' for an Angolan peace, increased its aid to UNITA, and thereby 'ensured that Savimbi felt no need to go to the negotiating table'.[43] But James Baker has argued that he fully understood that 'by 1989 neither of the superpowers had overriding reasons for being involved in this conflict' and that the real cause of difficulty was the Angolan government's launch of a new offensive in December 1989.[44] Either way, by late 1989 civil war was raging once more. A UNITA-

government ceasefire in May 1991 was secured through the mediation of the former colonial power, Portugal. It was linked to a promise of elections and seemed likely to hold, partly because both sides had effectively lost key external supporters: the USSR was deeply troubled and South Africa was in the process of dismantling apartheid. But when the Marxist MPLA won the September 1992 elections, Savimbi refused to accept the result and UNITA relaunched the civil war, seizing the oil-producing centre of Sayo four months later. By now, with the USSR gone, the US was committed to peace in Angola and, in May 1993, decided to give diplomatic recognition to the government, having withheld this since 1975. In November 1994 the chances of a permanent settlement seemed to improve further when government forces seized the UNITA headquarters at Huambo, and Savimbi's lieutenants pressed him to agree to another settlement. But an agreement on the formation of a government of national unity was only reached in March 1996 and it soon proved stillborn. In early 1999 the civil war renewed in intensity but it finally ended after Savimbi was killed in 2002.

Cambodia

In Cambodia, or Kampuchea as it was then called, the Vietnamese continued to uphold the government of the Hun Sen with about 250,000 troops throughout the early 1980s, boycotting UN-sponsored peace talks and trying to extinguish Pol Pot's Khmer Rouge who, despite their genocidal policies in 1975–9, were still recognized as the legal government of Cambodia by China and the Western powers. About 300,000 Cambodian refugees had fled to Thailand, another government which backed the Khmer Rouge, seeing them as a barrier to Vietnamese expansion. By the mid-1980s various intermediaries were at work trying to bring peace between the four factions in Cambodian politics, that is the Hun Sen regime, the Khmer Rouge, Prince Sihanouk (the former monarch), and another group led by Son Sann, who had joined with Sihanouk in 1982 to form a 'Coalition Government of Democratic Cambodia'. In 1984 the Vietnamese said that they would be ready to leave Cambodia (as the UN had demanded since 1979), but only on condition, first, that the Khmer Rouge were eliminated as a political force and, second, that China's borders with Vietnam and Laos were guaranteed. These conditions were not acceptable to China. But 1987–8 of course saw key changes in Soviet policy towards Afghanistan, Angola, and Nicaragua, with a greater willingness so settle these issues and there was evidently pressure on Vietnam from Moscow to discuss withdrawal. Hanoi also found the occupation of Cambodia very costly and some Vietnamese troops began to leave in 1987. More withdrawals were announced in May 1988.

By July 1988, when the four Cambodian factions met in Jakarta, the general shape of a likely settlement was clear: the Vietnamese would announce their intention to leave completely, the internal factions would agree a ceasefire, a provisional government would be formed under Sihanouk, the factions would disarm, elections would be held, a UN peacekeeping force would be deployed, and refugees would return. But it took years to flesh out the details of this settlement. The key first move came in April 1989, when the Vietnamese, under Soviet pressure, announced that they would withdraw all their troops by September—a promise which helped ensure an improvement in Sino–Soviet relations at this time. In the middle of this withdrawal, in July, France (the former colonial power) and Indonesia, began to co-chair an eighteen nation peace conference in Paris. Here, the joint agreement of the five permanent members of the Security Council— something which would have seemed impossible four years before—was of vital importance. A framework document was completed by August 1990, in April 1991 all the internal factions agreed a ceasefire, and on 23 October 1991 agreements were signed which confirmed the ceasefire, the disarmament of the factions, the formation of a joint interim government, the election of a constituent assembly, the repatriation of refugees, and foreign aid programmes, all to be carried out under UN supervision.

The settlement marked yet another boost to the UN in the years 1987–91 and the responsibilities given to the organization showed the respect in which it was now held. The Western powers would have liked to see the removal of the Hun Sen regime but it proved remarkably resilient, with a substantial army, and seemed the only barrier to the return of the murderous Pol Pot. Then again, as one study of Bush's policies noted, there had been 'Western victories' in Afghanistan, Angola, and Nicaragua; and of the four countries targeted by the Reagan Doctrine, 'only Cambodia remain[ed] under . . . a Communist government, and that conflict has been relegated to obscurity.'[45]

As with the Geneva Accords on Afghanistan and the Angola–Namibia settlement, the Cambodia agreements did not mark a complete victory for one side or the other. Hun Sen indeed proved better able to cooperate with Sihanouk (restored to this throne in September 1993) than did the Khmer Rouge, who—rather like Savimbi in Angola—refused to respect the results of the 1993 elections. For a time a vicious civil war erupted once more, but by now there was little support for the Khmer Rouge and it was soon in steep decline. In mid-1997 Pol Pot was arrested by his own followers and sentenced to life imprisonment, after trying to eliminate some key deputies. The following year he died. There was a crisis in the new government, too, in 1997, after Hun Sen fell out with the royalist Prime Minister, Prince Ranariddh, forcing him into a short-lived exile. But Sihanouk, now King of Cambodia, remained in his position and Ranariddh was able to return in 1998. By then too relations had been normalized between the US and Vietnam and had greatly improved between the communists of Vietnam and Laos, on the one side, and the Association of South-East Asian States (previously seen as a pro-Western, capitalist organization) on the other. In South-East Asia, as in Central Asia and southern Africa, the decline of the Cold War had thus had a profound effect. The most astonishing effects of all, however, were in Eastern Europe.

D. The Demise of Soviet Communism in Eastern Europe

Eastern Europe and Perestroika

The resolution of the conflicts in Afghanistan, Angola, Nicaragua, and Cambodia could be seen as reversing the pattern of success for Soviet-backed left-wing forces in the less developed world that had done much to bring about the new Cold War of the early 1980s. But the disintegration of the Soviet puppet governments of Eastern Europe in late 1989 removed a problem in East–West relations that had existed since the onset of the Cold War. Indeed, just as Stalin's imposition of communist control in areas of Eastern Europe occupied during the Second World War was central to original Cold War tensions, so Gorbachev's readiness to accept its removal was the most vivid evidence that the Cold War had ended. Yet, when Gorbachev became General Secretary the USSR's domination of Eastern Europe seemed as secure as ever, with the Warsaw Pact being renewed for twenty years on 26 April 1985, and the end, when it came, came quickly. Experienced diplomats and academic experts alike failed to predict the coming collapse even a few months beforehand, most adhering to the long-standing belief that any fundamental change in the communist system could only be effected gradually. As one leading analyst later admitted, 'I knew in the last months of 1988, that the communist regimes in Eastern Europe would have to change. But their swift collapse a year . . . later was impossible to predict.'[46] Bush's call in Mainz on 31 May 1989 for the Berlin Wall to come down—which merely echoed a similar plea by Reagan from June 1987—was timely in retrospect but not made with the expectation that it would fall within six months. Brent Scowcroft later candidly admitted, 'it would be gratifying to say that our Eastern European policy . . . had been among the catalysts of the changes' that came in 1989, 'It was not.'[47] Even Gorbachev's statement, in Strasbourg on 6 July, that force should never be used again in Eastern Europe, did not convince Western observers that the Red Army would avoid armed intervention

to uphold Marxist-Leninism. Memories of Hungary in 1956 and Czechoslovakia in 1968 still carried great force. Yet by 25 October Gorbachev's press aide, Gennadi Gerasimov, had replaced the Brezhnev Doctrine of 'fraternal intervention' with the 'Sinatra Doctrine', whereby individual East European states 'did it their way'.[48] On 4 December 1989 a Warsaw Pact meeting condemned the 1968 invasion of Czechoslovakia and the following day Gorbachev declared in *Pravda* that the Cold War had ended.

It is important to underline the point that it was only those communist states founded under Soviet domination which disappeared in Eastern Europe in late 1989. Two Marxist governments survived in the region who had long since distanced themselves from Moscow and where communists had come to power in 1945 largely through their own exertions: in Yugoslavia, where Tito had shaped a particular brand of communism until his death in 1980, and in Albania, where the Stalinist Enver Hoxha had been succeeded by his loyal lieutenant, Ramiz Alia, in 1985. These communist systems would disintegrate over the following years. Also, even in the Soviet sphere, many representatives of the old regime survived, generally by turning themselves into 'socialist' parties (under various names). Sometimes they returned spectacularly to power, as in Poland in November 1995 when an ex-communist, Alexander Kwasniewski, was elected President. They may have been resented in the past, but that was partly because they symbolized domination by a foreign power: after the upheavals of the early 1990s they often came to symbolize stability and experience in office. In Bulgaria and Romania especially some communists were astute enough to turn against the existing system in 1989 before genuine liberals gathered strength. Thus one of Ceauşescu's ministers, Ion Iliescu, was able to be elected and survive as President until November 1996.

The reasons why communism was weak in Eastern Europe in terms of popular support are not difficult to fathom. As in the USSR itself the system had never been legitimized through free elections; central economic planning in Eastern Europe had failed to deliver the same levels of wealth, health, education, and social provision which most people enjoyed in the West; and any idealism which once inspired the communists themselves had been dissipated by corruption and careerism. Unlike the USSR, communism in Eastern Europe had few local roots in the first place (except, arguably, among the heavy industrial towns of Czechoslovakia). It was imposed by Red Army bayonets and once it was clear that those bayonets would not be reintroduced it rapidly unravelled. A more interesting question therefore is why Gorbachev allowed the system to disintegrate by refusing to resort to armed force. But here, as elsewhere, the Soviet leader's exact motivations are difficult to comprehend. Indeed, where Eastern Europe was concerned (and in contrast to Afghanistan for example) Gorbachev refused to turn his attention to the region's problems. Even before 1985 he was apparently a critic of Soviet domination of Eastern Europe, at least in its dictatorial form, and by 1989 he recognized that it placed a serious strain on Soviet resources, as well as embarrassing Moscow in its dealings with the West. During the critical year of 1981 Poland had cost Moscow $3 billion in support. 'Gorbachev regarded the Warsaw Pact as expendable because the strategic dividends that the USSR received from control of these countries were not worth the cost of the subsidies they received from the USSR in the era of *perestroika*.'[49] The USSR not only had to police and defend the region, it also provided cheap oil supplies and favourable trade deals. That Gorbachev had an interest in breaking down the barriers between East and West Europe was reflected in his talk about a 'Common European Home' in 1987, echoing as it did de Gaulle's ideas two decades before when European détente got underway in earnest (even if Gorbachev's ideas on European unity were never precisely explained).

But to the arguments that communism in Eastern Europe collapsed because it had no roots, or because the Soviet leader felt it a liability, must be added two other considerations: in the late 1980s Eastern Europe saw both an intensification of its economic problems and a risky attempt at far-reaching reform of the communist system, a policy similar in fact to that which Gorbachev pursued in the USSR. Since

the dawn of Soviet domination of the region in the 1940s, successive Soviet General Secretaries had tried to mould it in their own image: Stalinization had been followed by Khrushchev's reforms and these in turn by Brezhnev's tolerance of divisions over economic practices, and of large financial loans from the West, so long as the political system remained communist controlled. It was unsurprising then that Gorbachev should expect East European leaders to mirror his own policies of *glasnost* and *perestroika*, but by now the countries of the area were quite diverse in their economic and political practices, reluctant to shift their own attitudes to suit Moscow. Gorbachev's policies simply provoked uncertainty and division. Would-be reformers were encouraged but, as in the USSR, they had their own agendas, geared to local considerations, and soon came to question the communist system itself. Communist leaders often tried to resist change but feared that Moscow would no longer back them and had no idea how to escape their economic and political sclerosis. In his memoirs Gorbachev argued that Soviet intervention in the affairs of its 'satellites' had no place in his new thinking about world politics: 'Such procedures were against the principles of equality, independence ... and full responsibility of the leadership of each country before its own people, all of which had been formally proclaimed even in Communist Party documents.'[50] Finally, when the gathering crisis entered its decisive phase in the autumn of 1989, Gorbachev decided that he could not put at risk his improved relations with the West by turning to repression. 'If he sanctioned the use of force in Eastern Europe, it could terminate hopes of ending the Cold War.'[51] And if the Cold War was really ending there was no need to maintain a defensive glacis in Eastern Europe. Once the protection of the Red Army was effectively removed, most local communist leaders lost their nerve and then tried to come to terms with the new reality. 'The system expired and the empire fell apart because they had been drained of both legitimacy and power.'[52] Yet, while he won the Nobel Peace Prize in 1990, the results of events in Eastern Europe for the Soviet leader were mixed. 'The collapse of the Berlin Wall ... strengthened Gorbachev's standing in the West, but it did nothing to help him at home.' where hardliners blamed him for weakening the Soviet position in the world while reformers clamoured for greater change.[53]

The Soviet System Unravels

Ironically, liberalization in Eastern Europe took off with the greatest vigour in the same two countries which had been most affected by Khrushchev's 'destalinization' process, Poland and Hungary. Poland had, of course, been the scene of intense anti-communist dissent in the early 1980s, centred on the Solidarity trades union (see Chapter 16). General Jaruzelski had restored order there by the use of martial law, but the Communist Party machine never recovered and Solidarity continued its activities underground. The country was, furthermore, heavily indebted to the West and its continued economic underperformance forced it, repeatedly, to reschedule repayments on its loans. Although he had successfully cowed the opposition, or at least dissuaded it from open revolt, Jaruzelski decided in 1987 to emulate Gorbachev and embrace reform. He not only advocated decentralized decision-making in industry but also multi-candidate (though not multi-party) elections and in November actually held a referendum on his proposals. This provided the ideal occasion for Solidarity to organize once more. Less than half the electorate backed the government in the referendum and, in spring and summer 1988, there were widespread strikes. In February 1989, after months of uncertainty, the government entered round-table discussions with the ever-influential Roman Catholic Church and, more controversially the Solidarity leader, Lech Walesa. This led to the dramatic decision in April to relegalize the free trades union and call elections for June, in which Solidarity did very well. 'The open, honest elections . . . proved to be a fiasco for the Communists—a humiliating, definitive repudiation by the Polish people.'[54] Although many seats were 'reserved' for Communists, by September Jaruzelski had been forced to appoint a non-communist Prime Minister though, in Tadeusz Mazowiecki, a nervous and ineffective one. It was a key moment for all Eastern Europe, because it meant that the Warsaw Pact now included a non-communist government,

the leading position of the Communist Party having ended. Yet Gorbachev accepted this with equanimity and from then on the pace of change in Poland was remarkable, with moves to a convertible currency, a market economy, and in December 1990 free Presidential elections, won by Walesa. Poland remained reliant on Western financial aid and its people were so disheartened by the lack of economic progress that—as under Jaruzelski—less than half voted in the next general election in October 1991, but they had pointed the way for others to follow.

Events in Hungary moved hardly less quickly and had, if anything, a greater international impact. There were already signs of radical economic reform here in the early 1980s, before Gorbachev came to power, with reduced central planning, scope for private ownership of farms and small businesses, the closure of some particularly inefficient factories, and even the beginnings of a stock market. Yet this did not prevent growing indebtedness, inflation, and a growing 'underground' economy. There was also an experiment with political liberalization: a 1983 law allowed multi-candidate elections and in 1985 a number of independents entered parliament—though they had to swear loyalty to the existing system. By 1987, Gorbachev had made it clear that he would accept further changes and the veteran communist leader, Janos Kadar, spoke of involving people more in decision-making. Opposition groups were soon openly tolerated and, as in 1956, the Communist Party itself became a centre of reform demands. The party replaced Kadar with Karoly Grosz in October 1988. In January 1989 it was Hungary that became the first Eastern European state to promise free multi-party elections and to legalize organizations outside communist control. In June Imre Nagy, the hero of 1956, was reburied and over a quarter of a million Hungarians attended the funeral. By October, as in Poland, events were moving at a pace which was difficult to believe: elections had been set for March 1990, the communists had become the Socialist Party and Hungary ceased to be styled a 'People's Republic'. But Gorbachev signalled his approval of such developments by promising, in April 1989, to withdraw the Red Army from the country.

The liberalization of Hungary, which eventually led to a non-communist coalition being formed in

April 1990, was doubly important because it was accompanied by the opening, in May 1989, of the country's borders. This allowed thousands of East Germans to move into Hungary as the first step towards entering West Germany (via Austria). Until then the regime of Erich Honecker had been one of the most conservative in the communist bloc, resisting Gorbachev's reforms as irrelevant. East Germany was also the wealthiest communist state, in terms of income per head of population, but it had one decisive defect: its per capita income was less than half that of its neighbour, West Germany. 'The proximate cause of the ... collapse of the GDR ... was the Hungarian decision to allow German "tourists" ... to emigrate over the borders with Austria. But there was an economic ... frustration in the GDR which manifested itself ... in the desire for foreign travel.'[55] In September more than 10,000 people fled East Germany for the West. The gathering crisis provoked some concern in the US, where it was feared there could be a 'drawing of the line' by Gorbachev. 'Moscow had shown consistently during the Cold War that it would not tolerate a revived German threat,' noted James Baker. 'This ... made any change in East Germany potentially far more dangerous in terms of Soviet reactions than in any other country in eastern Europe.'[56] However, in early October, when visiting the country, Gorbachev— instead of urging a crackdown—accused Honecker of failing to respond to popular opinion. Opposition groups had already begun to form, mass demonstrations were being called in major cities, and faced by Soviet opposition to repression the government belatedly began to reform. Honecker resigned in mid-October and his successors, on 9 November, decided to allow freedom of travel. For the rest of the world this decision led to the clearest indication yet of the collapse of Soviet domination in Eastern Europe, because it immediately led to the opening of the Berlin Wall, which had been the greatest symbol of communist repression since 1961. The opening was followed by serious consideration of German reunification (see Chapter 20, A).

In the wake of Honecker's departure, two other orthodox communist governments in the region also gave up hope, though in radically different ways. In Bulgaria, always very loyal to Moscow, there was a 'palace coup' against Todor Zhivkov, who had dominated the government since the mid-1960s. The new leader, Petar Mladenov, evidently had Gorbachev's support, promised reform and easily won elections in June 1990 as head of the renamed 'Socialist Party'—though he was forced to resign soon after by revelations of how closely he had been associated in the repression of the Turkish minority and others in Zhivkov's last years. Bulgaria, like Hungary and Poland, has been described as a 'negotiated revolution' in 1989, because of communist power being surrendered with little struggle, in contrast to the 'last ditch' examples elsewhere.[57] In Czechoslovakia meanwhile another veteran leader, Gustav Husak had initially tried to repress opposition in early 1989, only to face criticism from Gorbachev. Rather than a palace coup, the whole Politburo was forced to resign on 24 November after days of mass demonstrations. But this did not prevent a general strike on 27 November, leading to the end of the communist monopoly of power two days later. Here there is 'thought to have been a KGB-approved attempt to provoke a minor crisis and install a reform communist regime', such as Gorbachev could cooperate with; but the pro-Gorbachev forces lost control of events.[58] The new party leader, Karel Urbanek, lasted barely a fortnight before giving way to a non-communist government. By the end of the year Alexander Dubček, the reformist leader of 1968, had become the speaker of parliament, and the best-known Czechoslovakian dissident, Vaclav Havel, had been made President.

The unravelling of the Soviet position took place without any superpower crisis. The CIA Director, Robert Gate, considered this was partly thanks to Bush's restrained response: 'He did not gloat. He did not make grandiose pronouncements. He did not declare victory.'[59] Remarkably, too, the only serious loss of life in these epochal developments occurred in Romania, a country which for three decades had tried to distance itself from Soviet control, under Nicolae Ceauşescu, who posed as a defender of the country's distinct, Latin heritage. He had managed to repay the country's debt in the 1980s, but only at the cost of low growth, food shortages, and a dearth of consumer goods. He had also put down all political discontent, but only by vastly expanding the Securitate secret police and victimizing the

Hungarian minority. It was this minority in fact which initiated unrest against Ceauşescu in mid-December, only weeks after he had been unanimously re-elected communist leader. Foreign allies, such as the Americans and British, who had previously lauded his resistance to Moscow, now clamoured for his removal, as did Gorbachev, whilst his colleagues among the Communist Party, as well as the army, decided to abandon him. Instead of being swept away like the leaders of Czechoslovakia and East Germany, some hoped for a transfer of power on the Bulgarian model. But, as the Securitate tried to repress the opposition, leading to bloodshed, 'Ceauşescu's overthrow could only be accomplished by force: the absence of a coherent opposition . . .

the social and economic decay and the atrophy of . . . leadership . . . guaranteed this outcome.'[60] The army captured and (on Christmas Day, 1989) executed Ceauşescu, while his lieutenants formed a National Salvation Front. One leading ex-communist, Ion Iliescu, became President and at first violently repressed any opposition. However, when they won elections in May 1990, the National Salvation Front, despite their communist pedigree, emulated other East European governments by dismantling the centralized economy, embracing private enterprise, and accepting the costs of this in the form of inflation and unemployment, problems familiar to the West but novel in the former communist world.

NOTES

1. Mark Galeotti, *Gorbachev and his Revolution* (Macmillan, Basingstoke, 1997), 49.

2. John Dunlop, *The Rise of Russia and the Fall of the Soviet Empire* (Princeton University Press, Princeton, 1993), 4–5.

3. Geoffrey Hosking, *The Awakening of the Soviet Union* (Heinemann, London, 1990), 140.

4. Rachel Walker, *Six Years that Shook the World* (Manchester University Press, Manchester, 1993), vi.

5. Quoted in Martin McCauley, *Gorbachev* (Longman, London, 1998), 44.

6. Reproduced in Ronald Reagan, *An American Life* (Hutchinson, London, 1990), 613.

7. Hosking, op. cit., 157.

8. Martin McCauley, *Gorbachev* (Longman, London, 1998), 77.

9. Eduard Shevardnadze, *The Future belongs to Freedom* (Sinclair-Stevenson, London, 1991), xi.

10. Walker, op. cit., 216.

11. Shevardnadze, op. cit., 48.

12. Quoted in Don Oberdorfer, *The Turn: How the Cold War Came to an End: the United States and the Soviet Union 1983–1990* (Jonathan Cape, London, 1992), 128.

13. Mikhail Gorbachev, *Memoirs* (Doubleday, London, 1996), 405; Alexander Dobrynin, *In Confidence* (Random House, New York, 1995), 564; Reagan, op. cit., 641.

14. Caspar Weinberger, *Fighting for Peace* (Joseph, London, 1990), 233; George Shultz, *Turmoil and Triumph* (Maxwell Macmillan International, New York, 1993), 712.

15. Oberdorfer, op. cit., 205; McCauley, op. cit., 82.

16. Jack Matlock, *Autopsy on an Empire* (Random House, New York, 1995), 97.

17. Hosking, op. cit., 141.

18. Dunlop, op. cit., 9–10.

19. Mikhail Gorbachev, *Perestroika* (Collins, London, 1986), 146.

20. Andrei Gromyko, *Memories* (Hutchinson, London, 1990), 343; Weinberger, op. cit., 246.

21. Matlock, op. cit., 123.

22. Quoted in Oberdorfer, op. cit., 299.

23. Shultz, op. cit., 1138.

24. Steven Hurst, *The Foreign Policy of the Bush Administration* (Cassell, London, 1999), 23; George Bush and Brent Scowcroft, *A World Transformed* (Random House, New York, 1998), 9.

25. McCauley, op. cit., 139.

26. Michael Beschloss and Strobe Talbott, *At the Highest Levels* (Little, Brown, Boston, 1993), 18; Bush and Scowcroft, op. cit., 135.

27. Gorbachev, op. cit., 501.

28. *Public papers of the Presidents of the United States, George Bush, 1989, Book 1* (Washington, 1990), 541.

29. Steven Hurst, *The Foreign Policy of the Bush Administration* (Cassell, London, 1999), 28–9.

30. Baker, op. cit., 69.

31. Matlock, op. cit., 271.

32. Shultz, op. cit., 266.

33. Dobrynin, op. cit., 442.

34. Reagan, op. cit., 687.

35. Raymond Garthoff, *The Great Transition: American-Soviet Relations and the End of the Cold War* (Brookings Institution, Washington, DC, 1994), 748.

36. Caroline Kennedy-Pipe, *Russia and the World* (Arnold, London, 1998), 196.

37. Shultz, op. cit., 692.

38. Anthony Hyman, *Afghanistan under Soviet Domination* (Macmillan, London, 3rd edn., 1992), 229.

39. Shultz, op. cit., 1086.

40. Hyman, op. cit., 256.

41. Chester Crocker, *High Noon in Southern Africa: Making Peace in a Rough Neighborhood* (W.W. Norton, New York, 1992), 464.

42. Shultz, op. cit., 1112.

43. Hurst, op. cit., 138.

44. James A. Baker, *The Politics of Diplomacy* (G. P. Putnam's Sons, New York, 1995), 599.

45. David Franklin and Robert Shepherd, 'Is Prudence a Policy?' in Ryan Barilleux and Mary Stuckey (eds), *Leadership and the Bush Presidency* (Praeger, Westport, 1992), 167.

46. Z. A. B. Zeman, *The Making and Breaking of Communist Europe* (Blackwell, Oxford, 1991), 312.

47. Bush and Scowcroft, op. cit., 180.

48. He actually said 'had it my way': see Michael Waller, *The End of Communist Power Monopoly* (Manchester University Press, Manchester, 1993), 196–7.

49. William Watson, *The Collapse of Communism in the Soviet Union* (Greenwood Press, Westport, 1998), 13.

50. Gorbachev, op. cit., 486.

51. McCauley, op. cit., 135.

52. G. R. Urban, *End of Empire: the Demise of the Soviet Union* (American University Press, Washington, DC, 1993), xxxii.

53. Archie Brown, *The Gorbachev Factor* (Oxford University Press, Oxford, 1996), 239.

54. Joseph Rothschild and Nancy Wingfield, *Return to Diversity: a Political History of East Central Europe Since World War II* (Oxford University Press, Oxford, 3rd edn., 2000), 230.

55. Geoffrey and Nigel Swain, *Eastern Europe since 1945* (St Martin's Press, London, 2nd edn., 1998), 183.

56. Baker, op. cit., 161.

57. Michael Waller, *The End of Communist Power Monopoly* (Manchester University Press, Manchester, 1993), 220–6.

58. Swain and Swain, op. cit., 187.

59. Robert Gates, *From the Shadows* (Touchstone, New York, 1996), 449.

60. Jonathan Eyal, 'Why Romania could not avoid bloodshed', in Gwyn Prins (ed), *Spring in Winter: the 1989 revolutions* (Manchester University Press, Manchester, 1990), 157.

CHRONOLOGY: THE END OF SOVIET DOMINATION OF EASTERN EUROPE IN 1989

1989

31 May	President Bush, speaking in Mainz, says the Berlin Wall must be opened.
4 June	Successes for Solidarity in Polish elections.
16 June	Hundreds of thousands turn out for reburial of Imre Nagy in Hungary.
6 July	In Strasbourg, Gorbachev says violence should never be used between European states again, even within alliances.
9–12 July	Bush visits Poland and Hungary.
19 July	General Jaruzelski only narrowly elected Polish President.
24 August	Jaruzelski asks a non-communist, Tadeuz Mazowiecki, to form a government.
10 September	Hungary allows East German 'tourists', who had been arriving since May, to cross into Austria. Triggers exodus of East Germans to West Germany.
6–7 October	Fortieth anniversary of East Germany. Gorbachev visits and criticizes failure to liberalize.
17 October	Hungary announces multi-party elections for 1990.
18 October	East German communist leader, Erich Honecker, gives way to Egon Krenz.
23 October	Hungary no longer a 'People's Republic'.
25 October	Soviets agree statement with Yugoslavia effectively renouncing Brezhnev Doctrine.
9–10 November	Berlin Wall is breached after East German government allows freedom of travel.
10 November	Petar Mladenov overthrows Todor Zhivkov of Bulgaria in palace coup.
17 November	Anti-government demonstrations begin in earnest in Czechoslovakia.
19 November	Civic Forum opposition launched in Czechoslovakia.
24 November	Resignation of Czechoslovakian Politburo.
27 November	General strike in Czechoslovakia.
10 December	Non-communist coalition formed under Marian Calfa in Czechoslovakia.
15 December	Unrest begins in Transylvania, Romania.
21 December	Riots in Bucharest, capital of Romania.
24–25 December	Nicolae Ceauşescu of Romania captured and executed; Ion Iliescu becomes President.

Part VI

The Post-Cold War World

1990–2000

INTRODUCTION

The events of 1989 in Eastern Europe were not accompanied by an explosion of triumphalism in the West. From the point of view of the US and West European governments this was deliberate, in that no one wished to humiliate the Soviet leadership for fear of undermining the position of Mikhail Gorbachev, who had seemed so essential to achieving the peaceful revolution in world affairs since March 1985. In order to move forward to a new era it was important for the West to be seen as magnanimous and as the embodiment of a new conflict-free liberal international order. If international cooperation and broad-based government was now to be the norm, with less heed paid to the needs of individual states, it was important to attempt to integrate the Soviet Union into the new post-Cold War world. Moreover the growing liberal perceptions of international problems, that no longer appeared to centre on power political competition, required a more universal commitment to common (Western) values.

For a time, there was a belief, not least among certain US policy-makers, that the international environment was now guaranteed to evolve according to a Western agenda. The birth of democratic regimes in Eastern Europe, the continued reform of the USSR, and moves towards German reunification all pointed to a general realization of long-established Western aims in Europe. In a sense the Cold War goals and what the US had tried to achieve by subversion had all been realized in a way which indicated not just the superior attractions of Western commercialism and standards of living but the superiority of Western ideas. State Department official, Francis Fukuyama, even boldly postulated 'the end of history'. He did not mean by this that there would no longer be an unfolding of events, or a cessation of international tension and conflict. But he did believe that the ideological struggles of the twentieth century had come to an end.

Bush and the New World Order

The term 'New World Order' actually began to be used in the summer of 1990 when Saddam Hussein's Iraq invaded the neighbouring oil-rich state of Kuwait, sparking the first major international crisis of the post-Cold War world. Significantly, the Bush administration did not rush to embrace the term and its exact meaning was never closely defined in any official US statement. But the President had, in a sense, pointed to certain features of a new world order in speeches he made during 1989, notably at the Texas A and M University in May when he accepted that the Cold War had ended and that the USSR was now a 'normal' part of global society. Bush therefore built on

Reagan's success with arms control, by joining Moscow in pursuing the START process with greater vigour. This was one of the many factors in world politics from previous decades which continued after the Cold War ended, so that Bush's caution in modifying policy made sense: NATO and the European Community remained in existence and the problems of the less developed world were, if anything more acute.

In political terms the war to liberate Kuwait suggested the possibility of new elements in the picture: a renewed respect for, and greater unity within, the United Nations (where it was possible for the Security Council to approve the use of force against Saddam); an acceptance that the US held particular leadership responsibilities; and a readiness to respond forcefully to those who used aggression to challenge the new order. The routing of the Iraqis in February 1991 seemed to prove that such order could be successfully enforced and future aggressors deterred from emulating Saddam. In a sense the agenda that America pursued in the wake of the Cold War was similar to that pursued at the end of the Second World War, when the Roosevelt administration had hoped to build future foreign policy around the United Nations, Great Power cooperation, and expanded world trade. The US would lead the world away from the old balance of power approach to international security and foster a 'universalist' alternative, with a reinvigorated United Nations and a new World Trade Organization. At the same time as at the end of the Second World War it was possible to detect more ominous possibilities. In 1945 the US devoted a large amount of bureaucratic time to planning the precise nature of the post-war political and economic order it wanted to implement to best serve US interests. Even to the extent of considering how the US might ensure that leaders agreeable to US interests might come to power in other countries.[1] Consequently a lot would depend on whether the now undisputed hegemony would act in accordance with internationalist principles or with American interests, assuming the two did not involve the same thing. Many in the West at the start of the 1990s were too easily attracted by the idea that the world would be policed by the US, ignoring the fact that the US might not be willing to bear the cost and the possibility that the exercise of US hegemony might not be universally welcomed.

In Europe the fact that the Soviets accepted the incorporation of a united Germany into NATO further brought home the scale of the communist defeat. Europe was to be remade in the mould political liberalism linked to market economics. At a global level poverty and exploitation would not only lead to their victims considering communism and socialism as impractical solutions but also the 'revolutionary' factors in Soviet foreign policy would no longer be a concern. The origins and end of the Cold War were global not European phenomena. Moscow's retreat from the Third World and the ideological 'victory' of the West promised a world in which both Western values and security interests were secure. 'Wars of National Liberation' would now be things of the past and in India and Africa, as in Eastern Europe, because there was nothing meaningful in ideological or practical terms to liberate them from the values of Western capitalism.

The implications of all this were not sufficiently considered at the start of the 1990s.

Just as the Cold War had often led those in the West to give insufficient weight to the regional or territorial problems so it had led them to ignore the practical problems of capitalism and to focus too much on its advantages, at least for those members of the developed world. It was now difficult for governments not to retreat from a reliance on economic planning, to embrace privatization, reduce state expenditure, and encourage free enterprise—as if these would automatically produce prosperity now that markets were seen as all powerful and any form of state control was anathema. In many ways the collapse of communism and the embrace of free-market economics was seen as the way to enable the countries of the Soviet satellite empire to recover from the impact of stagnation induced by state controls, as if the only problems for the economies of Eastern Europe were government controls and as if Stalinism was the same as the kind of mixed but planned economy desired by social democratic governments in the West particularly after the Second World War.

The problems of bringing the Eastern economies close to being able to provide similar living standards of the West were similar to bringing the war-torn economies of Europe up to the standard of living enjoyed in the US in 1945. Only fifty years later there were two problems. First, the idealistic panacea of free-market economics had not been in vogue in 1945 and secondly there was massive aid from the US made available to reconstruct Western Europe through the Marshall Plan which, while many governments would have liked to provide it in the early 1990s, important political constraints prevented them from doing so. Consequently there was no Marshall Plan for the reconstruction of the former Soviet Union or its satellites and the con-sequences have been at best mixed. The arrival of organized crime, significant unemployment, and greater inequality have created a degree of dissatisfaction to at least open the door for communist electoral successes. The attraction in other words of greater political freedom and more consumer goods had been acquired at a price. Arguably this has also been paid in part by Western Europe with the enormous resources West Germany had to provide for the East leading to a slowdown in overall German growth rates and the disinclination to use fiscal measures. As the German economy slowed so did the rest of Europe and with inbuilt deflation, because of the reluctance to raise taxes or contemplate deficit spending. In a sense there were incen-tives for cooperation created when the Soviet threat was believed to exist, because taxpayers and national governments were more willing to consider making sacrifices for a greater cause than short-term self-interest. The future direction of Western Europe was uncertain in the early 1990s as there was the possibility of the American connection being lost and the momentum for further integration was seemingly in the balance, partly because of the political need to incorporate the countries of the former Eastern bloc but at considerable economic cost.

US commentators hoped that capitalism would bring greater wealth and demo-cracy would bring peace to Europe with fascism, communism, and state controls assigned to the dustbin of history. Different forms of dictatorship might survive for a time but they could not provide a long-term alternative to Western values, and it was arguable that the incidence of armed conflict would now be reduced, while 'general war' had become unthinkable. But, while it was broadly true that democracies did not go to war against democracies, it was also the case that democratic states were more unstable and warlike than dictatorships.[2] And there was the all too obvious fact that in parts of Eastern Europe there were groups whose past suppression by the Soviets was not an unmitigated disaster from the point of view of peace and stability. Once the harsh communist controls were lifted there was the possibility that groups previously associated with fascist or other extreme right nationalists might come to power in former communist countries. The dangers of this combined with the evidence that democratic states were war-prone seemed nearest to realization in the former Yugoslavia. The moves under Tito towards decentralization encouraged the rapid speed up of that process and the reduction of centralized Serbian power which rapidly led to calls for independence from Belgrade. Led by the Croatians and then the Slovenes the march towards independence gathered pace and by the beginning of the 1990s had become a serious problem, focused on minority ethnic groups in those areas where secession had taken place or in Bosnia, where the complexities of the racial and religious mix made a simple political solution linked to territorial division problematic.

More significantly events in Yugoslavia raised the question of nationalism and the relationship of society to the state. The idea that nationalism was a movement from below which grew out of identity and consciousness of larger communities was seriously challenged by the actions of Milošović in Serbia and Tudjman in Croatia. The possibility that nationalism could be imposed from above by states and the elites that controlled them in order to build political support was a concept which now had to be taken more seriously. The repeated reference to past Balkan conflicts appeared to divide communities that had lived together for hundreds of years and myths associated with identity, as laid down by elites, seemed potent even in a continent which had prided itself on the suppression of twentieth-century nationalism which was seen as a negative and destructive force. The wakening of the state might not lead, as in Western Europe, to greater cooperation and prosperity on a transnational basis but to violence and ethnic hatred in which politicians could use nationalist myths and old experiences for political advantage.

By the mid-1990s the feeling of satisfaction in the West had been dimmed and, instead of world order, many found it difficult to discern any pattern or system to international relations. Those who could discern a pattern were liable to be radically more pessimistic, and less 'universal' in their vision, than Fukuyama had been. Most celebrated of all, Samuel Huntington foresaw a coming 'clash of civilizations' in which groups of states would ally on the basis of cultural links, of religion or ethnicity perhaps, and would compete with other such groups for resources. This helped stir up fears for a time of a clash between the West and Islam, though this was as undesirable as it was unlikely (not least because Islam was itself a world of diversity and included some key American allies). The sense of confusion was not just generated by the lack of a central theme in world politics such as the Cold War provided or by the bloody upheavals in the Balkans and Rwanda, but by concerns over the possible negative effects of what became known as globalization and by doubts over the commitment of the new US administration to a just global order.

Clinton and World Order

After January 1993 the Clinton administration maintained some of the elements of the 'new world order' approach even though Clinton initially seemed to have little personal interest in foreign or defence policy. In particular, America continued to seek the extension of liberal democracy and free enterprise ideals, whilst those who chose to oppose these were condemned as 'rogue states' and ostracized. This was seen most starkly in the Clinton administration's 'En-en' policy, which justified the continuing 'engagement' of the US in world affairs in order to pursue the 'enlargement' of areas under liberal, free enterprise regimes. Clinton recognized that, while the US was unique in its military strength, it could not contemplate isolationism because it needed to preserve access to global markets for its own economic good. The 'rogue states' that did not embrace liberalism included not just diehard Marxist-Leninists like Fidel Castro and Kim Il-Sung, but also countries like Iran, Iraq, and Libya who were accused of backing international terrorism.

Even before Clinton came to office, however, there were signs that the American public were less interested in foreign affairs now that the Soviet menace had been removed. Clinton defeated Bush in the 1992 election by exploiting the slogan 'It's the economy, stupid' against a President who focused on world politics while US living standards were stagnant. As to the New World Order and the 'end of history' idea, they were soon challenged by the start of vicious local conflicts in Bosnia, Somalia, and later Rwanda. These conflicts—especially Somalia, where a disastrous US intervention occurred—led some Americans to believe they should distance themselves from global affairs. There was no return to pre-war isolationism: it was recognized that US security could be threatened from outside, not least through the medium of international terrorism, which now touched America itself. Clinton repeatedly pointed out US reliance on exports, and the American people could still be motivated to act abroad in certain circumstances, not least by humanitarian concerns. But it proved impossible to develop coherent, consistent, determined US policies after the Cold War, especially when Congress battled with the White House for the control of policy. And Clinton himself soon began to see the economic difficulties of undertaking open-ended intervention, as in Somalia, on behalf of the world community, however humanitarian or altruistic such interventions might be. Any sustained, idealistic vision was potentially dangerous and military involvement had to be limited and given defined objectives. Clinton, in the wake of Somalia, laid down clear conditions relating to aims and an exit strategy for any future intervention on humanitarian grounds. Clinton was perhaps beginning the US move towards a more assertive, unilateral role in world affairs in which US interests would triumph over the idea of contributing to a new world order.

Yet his foreign policy could claim some notable successes by the time he left the White House in January 2001 and he definitely had not shirked difficult decisions, including military commitments. The administration had supported the move to majority rule in South Africa (Chapter 22, A), as well as the breakthrough Israeli–Palestinian agreement (Chapter 22, C). It had maintained good relations with Russia while consolidating Bush's arms control agreements (Chapter 21, C), had restored the elected President of Haiti (Chapter 21, C), overseen a thaw in relations between North and South Korea, and taken an active role in moves towards a settlement of the 'troubles' in Northern Ireland, where there had been sectarian violence since 1968. The peace moves in Ireland stalled in early 1996 but revived in the summer of 1997 and reached a deal on creating a new Assembly, representative of all groups in the province, in April 1998. Even more remarkably, the Clinton administration had stepped in to achieve a Bosnian settlement (Chapter 20, C). The strategic vision may have been difficult to see but, while 'Clinton got off to a rocky start, he eventually developed into an able practitioner of Band-Aid diplomacy', helping heal various wounds.[3] Furthermore the closing months of 2000 saw the first foreign ministers-level talks with Iran for twenty years (at the UN in September) and Clinton's own visit to Vietnam, the first by a President since the war there. The only real disaster had come in Somalia but the original decision to intervene there had been Bush's.

Indeed, despite the criticisms levelled at him by Republicans, Clinton was not lacking in ideas for a central direction for US foreign policy, even if these were developments of certain aspects of Bush's New World Order. His first National Security Adviser, Anthony Lake, a former head of the State Department's Policy Planning Staff under Jimmy Carter, recognized the need to explain foreign policy not in terms of the balance of power but of 'enlarging' the regions of world living under liberal democracy, the corollary of which was that opponents of the liberal order—such as Cuba, Iran, and Iraq—were to be isolated and condemned as 'rogue states'. It was in September 1993 that Lake said 'the successor to a doctrine of containment, must be the strategy of enlargement—enlargement of the world's free community: we must counter the aggression—and support the liberalization—of states hostile to democracy.'[4] At first it was hoped that the US would act in line with its allies and the UN, but in his second term Clinton seemed more ready to act unilaterally (as in Haiti) and accepted the limitations of the UN (as in Bosnia). Apart from dealing, on the whole successfully, with regional problems, the Clinton administration also continued to devote considerable energy to arms control and non-proliferation (see Chapter 21, C) and tackled those 'new' security problems that had become important under Bush.

New World Order or Disorder in the Early 1990s?

The Cold War world has generally been seen as a battle with weapons of mass destruction both threatening and keeping the peace. Power politics and ideology combined to heighten tensions which if they escalated into war would risk the future of the planet. In the West, fighting the Cold War justified in the name of a way of life emphasizing political and economic freedom and the importance of the individual. The end of the Cold War was expected to end the conflict between two contrasting ways of life, the confrontation of opposing blocs, and the emphasis on a bipolar world of competition. The post-Cold War world was anticipated in very different terms. Power politics and state-centric bipolarity would be superseded by a multipolar world in which cooperative institutions of a governmental and non-governmental nature and organized more and more on interstate lines would play key roles in a new international order. At the same time the idea that America should take the lead in establishing a 'new world order' in 1990–1 became quite widely accepted, being reinforced by the continued difficulties of Gorbachev's USSR, which eventually disintegrated in December 1991, leaving what has commonly been perceived as a 'unipolar' world. By then the Warsaw Pact and COMECON, which had held the Eastern bloc together, militarily and economically, had also been wound down and a line had been drawn behind which old problems would disappear.

Such was the liberal desire to welcome this new order that the end of the 1980s and start of the 1990s have been seen as the start of a completely separate era in which the study of contemporary history and international relations must be restarted afresh because of such a cataclysmic change in the nature of the international order. It is simply not viable to separate the Cold War world entirely from the 1990s and to assume that it needs to be analysed in new ways. There have been continuities as well as changes and old problems like poverty in the less developed world, how to achieve deeper integration in Europe or how to control nuclear weapons, have not disappeared. Yet the ideas of the liberal internationalists—in themselves far from new—seemed to have more scope for implementation now that international cooperation was not constrained by the Cold War paralysis of the United Nations. And the acceptance of liberal capitalism was deemed to open new opportunities for a more prosperous world with less resources wasted on armaments, and market forces being developed through international institutions and organizations working for the benefits of a global community. A globalized community was increasingly seen as interdependent especially in economic terms. Conflict, so it was believed, would thus be less likely and greater prosperity would result from the acceptance of Western norms and political and economic values. The idea that such values were limited to the West and had no relevance to many members of the post-Cold War world, was initially not much in evidence.

Nor was the possibility readily entertained that the loss of state power might have implications for stability and order. Values such as self-determination could be a double-edged sword. Eastern Europeans might embrace them but there were many ethnic groups whose acceptance of controls and order had been the involuntary result of communist power. Now that it had evaporated it was only natural that there would be competition and conflict over which group should inherit it, especially where racial or religious differences were present. In Europe this was actually less of a problem than in areas like Nicaragua, Ethiopia, Afghanistan, Angola, Mozambique, or Vietnam. Capitalism, with or without colonialism, had done little for such areas in the past, and it began to look in the 1990s that there would be no easy solution provided by neo-liberal free-market economics. Yet liberalism and capitalism, led by America, held the field and appeared to offer the only viable model to which states would aspire. Those that did not, or did so without success, were increasingly marginalized. States may have helped increase inequality and exacerbate the problems of corruption, but the IMF structural adjustment programmes were seen by some as making a bad situation worse. In these circumstances, the struggle to gain advantage by seizing political power became more of an option and violence between groups competing for power became commonplace—hence the growing problems in Somalia and Ruanda to name but two of the hardest hit countries. And even Europe was not immune from such conflicts in the 1990s.

There was also a sense that the very concept of security was changing as governments concerned themselves less with the military balance and territorial disputes, and more with such issues as trade, the environment, terrorism, and narcotics, challenges which were at once national and transnational. The communications revolution and growing economic interdependency appeared to challenge national sovereignty, leaving states at the mercy of global trends. Yet persuading the world's governments to tackle the pressing challenges of the 1990s in a cooperative way proved very difficult

The UN, though it appeared better able to act now that the US–Soviet feud had ended, had always been at the mercy of its individual members, lacking strong, central institutions and primarily concerned with preventing recourse to war. It proved effective in supporting the war against Iraq in 1990–1, but largely because of the determination of the Americans and others to see the conflict through. In Bosnia, Somalia, and Rwanda the story was very different. In the trade field GATT was transformed into the World Trade Organization in 1994 but in some ways the world also became more fractured in commercial terms as, with US encouragement, a series of free trade areas was created. Partly inspired by the success of the European Community, but lacking that body's supranational elements, free trade schemes were pursued in North America, the Western Hemisphere, and the Asia-Pacific. This was not the only way in which America's free enterprise approach, linked as it was by a desire to protect US interests, fostered certain trends in the global economy. Freed from the need to prevent Soviet advances in Asia, Africa, and Latin America, Washington also cut back even further on foreign aid programmes and demanded that the developing countries adopt liberal trade policies, privatization, and reduced government expenditure. Foreign aid declined consistently from a peak of $25 billion in 1985. By 1992 it had fallen by a third: US assistance to Africa was only about a dollar per person per year. Yet the free-enterprise approach worked no economic miracle. In 1997 Third World debt totalled about $2,200 billion (a 50 per cent rise on the 1990 figure). One-third of the world's population lived on fewer than $400 per year.

The environmental challenges were faced at international gatherings in the l990s, beginning with the vast Rio Summit of 1992, but the results, particularly in terms of cutting 'greenhouse' gases, fell short of what expert advice demanded. The major conflict centred on the differences between the United States and the less developed world. The latter was reluctant to constrain its development without compensation, given that the industrialized nations of the Northern hemisphere had been able to industrialize without the environmental constraints that less developed nations were now being required to adopt. The split in the Western world was characterized in terms of the 'modernists' versus the 'eco-radicals'.[5] The 'modernists' foresaw environmental problems being overcome by technological advances that will avoid the destruction of the environment, while the eco-radicals see the problems as insurmountable. Population growth and the needs of an increasingly consumer-orientated global society, they claim, will ultimately exhaust the planet's natural resources unless the lifestyles prevalent in the developed world, and sought in many parts of the less developed world, are radically changed. Sustainable development that will enable greater harmony to exist between man and nature must become a goal. Yet the problems of how best to create any form of development in many areas of the world lacking significant industrialization remains unsolved. Those that did manage to achieve breakthroughs into modern industrial economies as in South Korea, Singapore, and Taiwan did so by state controls and going against the neo-liberal consensus. As soil erosion afflicts so many poorer countries and the production of agricultural surpluses becomes ever more difficult the impact of new technology may be reduced significantly.

Globalization

Comprehending the post-Cold War world was made more difficult by the fact that globalization (which called into question the value of the nation state for the management of political, economic, and social life) moved to the fore just as ethnicity and nationalism seemed to find a new potency in areas like the former USSR, the former Yugoslavia, and Central Africa. Globalization is perhaps best defined as a 'significant shift in the spatial reach of social action and organisation.'[6] The obvious changes in technology and communication have reduced the distances between large areas of the globe. Consequently the state has shrunk in comparison to the region and greater interregional flows of people, goods, and ideas have taken place. The market has been at the heart of this as old structures are replaced by new networks of power, and advocates of globalization's importance focus on the changes to the prevailing modes of socio-economic organization, the loss of power as embodied and exercised by the state, and the growing insignificance of the territorial state as the basis of inter-national relations. This organizational base is thus being replaced by new social, economic, and political links and the role of the individual assumes new importance as the boundaries within which human activity was formerly contained disappear. Globalization for its advocates spells real change in the 'scale of modern social organization'[7]

Others dispute the value of a term a such as globalization on the grounds that the nineteenth-century changes which brought in railways, the steamship, and the telegraph were more significant for reducing distance and bringing different parts of the globe closer together. To be able to travel from New York to Chicago in hours rather than days, for example, may have had a more dramatic impact on societal relations than even air travel. In addition there remain parts of the earth where developments in technology such as the use of the internet and improved travel and communications have had little impact. Therefore the global element of globalization is inaccurate with regard to place, if not time, critics of the concept argue. Hence the claims that Westernization is a more apt description of the changes at the end of the twentieth century than globalization. The end of the Cold War simply ensured that the values and lifestyles of the victors would be diffused throughout the globe much more effectively.[8] Thus globalization is seen as an ideological construct to carry forward neo-liberal ideas and explain the benefits of international capitalism in the post-Cold War world.

If this is the case, it follows that in the areas of media and communications there has been an expansion in the availability of information but a reduction in its breadth and variety. The dominance of global media conglomerates with narrowly based owner-ship have developed an approach that claims to represent a consensus of a particular Western type. Consequently, knowledge may not have broadened but narrowed while being transmitted more widely in a way that justifies a particular view of society and international affairs. An appreciation of global diversity should not be assumed to accompany globalization. At the same time it becomes possible to escape from reality more easily than to understand it. The lives of characters in soap operas and partici-pants in game shows help to prevent the questioning of the neo-liberal consensus whether or not history is assumed to have ended.

In economic terms the idea of a globalized economy had taken root since the mid-1980s not least because the volume of international production (companies based in one state producing goods in another state) had overtaken the volume of inter-national trade. Multinational enterprises, cross-border banking services, information technology, and cultural diffusion were all part of a process that broke down national differences and trade barriers. They could be seen as the further development of liberal theories emphasizing the value of an interdependent world and the erosion of national forces with the increasing transnational focus of trade and finance.

Future Directions: Disorder, Chaos, and Insecurity or Order, Cooperation, and the Reduction of Conflict

Whatever the sense of disorder in the 1990s the fact was that the post-Cold War world did have elements of stability and hope. For one thing, there was clearly only one superpower that at least aspired to uphold values other than state interest. Russia, though it could potentially cause problems for the US, in areas like the former Yugoslavia and the Middle East, was militarily and economically weak, a shadow of the old Soviet power. There were also signs, in certain regions, that the hopes of 1989–91 for a more peaceful, stable world were not mere illusions. Particular encouragement came from the end of apartheid in South Africa, the beginnings of an Israeli–Palestinian dialogue, and moves towards a settlement of Northern Ireland's intercommunal strife. Globalization offers new opportunities for greater knowledge, experience, and understanding. Yet such changes can be interpreted in both positive and negative ways and can be seen as bringing advantages and disadvantages.

America's technological prowess, its economic wealth, and its military reach had never been greater and it *was* able to secure some of its aims in world affairs. This may not be such an unmitigated benefit as is often assumed in the West. The crucial issues relate to the extent and nature of American hegemony that provided the means to achieve this. The more dominant the United States and the more generally beneficial its vision of world order based on American values, the more ordered and secure the world will become in comparison with the Cold War period. Yet if this hegemony is threatened by counterforces, as in the Cold War, when arguably an unsuccessful Soviet challenge occurred to the exercise of the American hegemony that was in place in 1945, then instability might increase. In addition the US might decide to act unilaterally, to exploit its power in a selfish and arrogant ways that will preserve America's significant economic and military advantages. The sources of opposition to the exercise of American power may become more diverse than state-sponsored communism and less easy to contain through the exercise of state power. This may change the US approach to foreign affairs and further divorce American society from a marriage to internationalism if the human and material costs become too high.

The diverse nature of many intrastate conflicts and the loss of state control over some aspects of warfare, along with the problems of fighting so-called Low Intensity Conflicts, may yet impose a heavy price on the US and its allies. With such conflicts more difficult to control, especially in less developed parts of the world, it becomes more important to ensure that means are found to reduce their impact and occurrence. Access to advanced weapons and to the nuclear technology of the former Soviet Union add to the fears of increasing insecurity. Without the repression or discipline of the Cold War, the new world order may not be an unmitigated blessing. Suicide bombs, the increasing commitment to mass killing by international terrorists, the importance of intrastate conflicts, and violent disputes over political power at local levels may create yet more chaos in the future. Such problems do not have to be so apocalyptic or simplistic as Huntington's clash of civilizations, but responses to a globalized world where a sense of community based on shared experiences is replaced by new sources of identity and resentment at the lack of economic and political power while democracy becomes global. As old sources of identity are lost and new ones invented they invariably give rise to greater economic and political expectations. A sense of national identity can be invented and imposed by ruthless leaders out to seize political power in ways far more dangerous than those of the corrupt elites who may have exploited a concept of nationalism and economic and political weakness to wrest power from their European rulers.

In some ways the new types of conflict and instability can be related to the consequences both of globalization and liberalism. For many liberals, even those not of the 'neo' persuasion, the end of a world order based on state power was welcomed. Interdependence was seen as strengthening the bonds of the global community and wars would become even more disastrous irrespective of the role of nuclear weapons. Regional groups would erode nationalism as people would develop transnational links in economic and political terms. Foreign policy-makers would focus less on narrow national interests as they were continually required to work closely with their counterparts in regional or global organizations. A broader understanding of global problems would follow from such links as the world became a more closely intercon-nected and cooperative place. Regimes would develop as norms and customs became more widespread and worked for the general good. The influence of Non-Governmental Organizations (NGOs) would add knowledge and experience to international discourse and work for the benefit of humanity rather than for particular interests. International society would become more firmly established as power political rivalries, ostensibly part of the Cold War, would no longer trouble world peace. Americans would strive to bring a sense of unity and purpose to foreign affairs in a new world order and display a readiness to make sacrifices. Firm US action was self-evidently successful in the first part of the decade in the 1994 invasion of Haiti and the 1995 Dayton Accords, which settled the Bosnian conflict and might therefore form a key element in the twenty-first century.

Somalia, however, told a different story and could be seen as a precursor for the increasing collapse of so-called 'failed states', other examples being Sierra Leone and Liberia. The phenomenon of failed states could be linked to the neo-liberal global economy based on the Washington consensus of balanced budgets, low government expenditure, and conformity to the iron law of the market. The process of state collapse could be seen as the further extension and enforcement of Western domin-ation as expressed in the interests of multinational capital and could constitute the latest manifestation of Western imperialism. The world's poorest countries continue to get poorer in both relative and absolute terms and in many parts of Africa death rates are rising and being helped by the impact of incurable diseases such as Aids. Terms of trade show little sign of moving in ways which will benefit producers in poorer countries to the detriment of consumers in the richer ones, and the signs of greater economic inequality can be seen as ominous global developments.

On the other hand, many are convinced that, by encouraging free trade agree-ments and ensuring that the IMF and World Bank support its free enterprise model of economic development with technological and scientific advances, prosperity will become more widespread. The Western world as a whole continues to hold together and to see its ideals develop. In some ways, in fact, the world is a more hopeful place for the Western powers than had seemed likely when the Cold War ended. Then there had been predictions of trade wars between America and Japan and America and the European Community, but they have not yet actually broken out, despite some undoubted points of tension. Capitalism and democracy survived and were strengthened in much of Eastern Europe, despite predictions of poverty, anarchy, and a return to dictatorships there. And liberal political ideals also seemed to gain new life in Latin America where, among others, the Pinochet dictatorship in Chile came to an end in 1991.

One can look back on the Cold War as a period of certainty, in which the Western and Eastern blocs knew who their enemies were, with the tension between them creating a (supposedly) stable balance, and in which leaders in the less developed world had been able to play off Moscow and Washington in order to gain development aid. Much of the Cold War was a battle about ideas and rival social and economic orders, but, sometimes conveniently forgotten were the elements of instability in the Cold War years. The power rivalries in Asia and Africa, which treated developing nations as pawns in a greater game, turning Korea, Indochina, and Angola at various points into war zones. And there was frequent confusion in US and Western policy (Vietnam being only the worst example), oppression in the Eastern bloc, and the ever-present danger of nuclear Armageddon. The post-Cold War world may seem disorderly, unfamiliar, and frightening, but so too, to take just one example, had the mid-1970s when the Middle East war threatened to drag in the superpowers and the ensuing oil price rises had thrown the international economy into the doldrums. Prospects looked somewhat less rosy when in 1997–8 a new economic crisis, sparked by problems in East Asia, struck, which seemed to presage a worldwide depression and widespread political upheaval, including Russia, and there was a major crisis in South Asia when India and Pakistan, still at loggerheads over Kashmir, both tested nuclear bombs. But even the fears justified by these events proved short-lived. Compared with earlier decades of the twentieth century and the later problems sparked by Al Qaeda's attacks on the US in September 2001, the 1990s may even be looked back on as a period of relative calm, when no major war threatened, international crises were kept localized and liberal ideals advanced in all continents.

NOTES

1. Minutes of the Advisory Committee on Postwar Foreign Policy, 12 February 1942, Notter files, box 54. We are indebted to Chris O'Sullivan for this reference.
2. Edward D. Mansfield and Jack Snyder 'Democratisation and the Danger of War', *International Security*, 1 (1995).
3. Stephen Ambrose, *Rise to Globalism* (Penguin Books, New York, 8th edn., 1997), 426.
4. Quoted in Spanier and Hook, *American Foreign Policy*, 321.
5. This is the idea of Robert Jackson and Georg Sorenson in *Introduction to International Relations Theories and Approaches* (Oxford University Press, Oxford, 2nd edn., 2003), p. 271.
6. D. Held and Anthony McGrew 'The Great Globalisation Debate' in D. Held and Anthony McGrew (eds), *The Global Transformations Reader* (Polity Press, Cambridge, 2000), p. 3.
7. Ibid., 6–8.
8. See D. Reynolds, *One World Divisible a Global History since 1945* (Allen Lane, Penguin Press, London, 2000), p. 3.

CHRONOLOGY: THE POST-COLD WAR WORLD, 1990–2000

1990

10 February	In Moscow, Gorbachev and Kohl agree to principle of German reunification.
26 February	Nicaraguan elections won by 'Uno' coalition of Violetta Chamorra, defeating the Sandinistas.
2 March	Nationalists win elections in Lithuania, the first free elections ever in the USSR; Lithuania declares independence on 11 March.
11 March	President Augusto Pinochet of Chile hands over to a civilian successor, Patricio Aylwin.
18 March	Christian Democratic 'Alliance for Germany' triumphs in East German elections.
30 May–4 June	Bush and Gorbachev meet in Washington.
29 June	Lithuania suspends its declaration of independence, following an economic blockade (since 17 April) by Moscow.
1 July	Economic and monetary union takes effect between the two Germanies.
5–6 July	London summit of NATO leaders redefines the alliance's role in the post-Cold War world.
2 August	Iraqi invasion of Kuwait takes place.
9 September	Bush and Gorbachev meet in Helsinki.
12 September	US, USSR, Britain, France, and the two Germanies sign Moscow Treaty on a reunified Germany, which takes effect on 3 October.
19 November	Treaty on Conventional Forces in Europe signed in Paris.
2 December	Helmut Kohl elected the first Chancellor of a reunified Germany.

1991

2 January	Lithuania revives its claim to independence.
13 January	Thirteen die in clashes with the Red Army in the Lithuanian capital.
17 January	US-led alliance begins airstrikes in Iraq.
24–28 February	Allied forces liberate Kuwait.
15–19 May	Jiang Zemin becomes first general Secretary of Chinese Communists to visit Moscow since 1957.
21 May	Collapse of the Marxist regime of Colonel Mengistu in Somalia, which slips into anarchy.
12 June	A popular vote in the Russian Federation (the largest republic in the USSR) elects Boris Yeltsin President.
13 June	End of communist domination of Albania, as a coalition government is formed.
23 June	Ceasefire agreed in Cambodia between Hun Sen government and Prince Sihanouk.
25–26 June	Yugoslav army attacks Croatia and Slovenia when they declare their independence.
1 July	Warsaw Pact is wound up.

29 July–1 August	Bush and Gorbachev finalize and sign START I treaty in Moscow.
18–21 August	A coup of hardliners against Gorbachev is opposed in Moscow by Yeltsin and rapidly collapses.
9–11 December	Maastricht summit of European Community leaders signs a Treaty on European Union and plans a single currency.
25 December	Gorbachev resigns as President of the USSR, which breaks up into its fifteen constituent republics.

1992

1 March	Bosnia-Herzegovina votes for independence from Yugoslavia.
27 March	Bosnian Serbs set up a separate government in Bosnia and fighting begins.
16 April	Fall of Marxist regime of Mohamed Najibullah in Afghanistan.
30 May	UN Security Council agrees first sanctions against Serbia over Bosnian conflict.
14 August	UN Human Rights Commission condemns Serb policy of 'ethnic cleansing' in Bosnia.
4 October	Treaty ends conflict between Mozambique government and RENAMO guerrillas.
9 October	UN Security Council introduces a 'no-fly' zone over Bosnia.
20 November	Macedonia declares its independence from Yugoslavia.
4 December	American forces land in Somalia to guarantee food supplies.
8 December	Serb siege of Sarajevo begins.

1993

1 January	'Velvet divorce' separates Czech Republic and Slovakia.
3 January	Bush and Yeltsin sign START II treaty in Geneva.
15 January	Chemical Weapons Treaty signed by numerous UN members, banning manufacture of such weapons.
12 April	NATO starts to enforce Bosnia 'no-fly' zone.
13 September	Palestinian leader Yasser Arafat and Israeli Premier Yitzhak Rabin sign a peace declaration in Washington.
24 September	Sihanouk returns as King of Cambodia.
3–4 October	Hundreds killed in clashes in Somalia between US forces and militia of General Aidid.
4 October	Russian forces storm the Congress of Peoples Deputies in Moscow.
7 November	US President Clinton threatens force against North Korea if it obtains nuclear weapons.
17 December	US begin to withdraw forces from Somalia.

1994

11 January	NATO launches 'Partnership for Peace' programme with ex-Eastern bloc States.
14 January	Ukraine agrees to destroy its nuclear arsenal (the third largest in the world).
28 February	In NATO's first military action, Yugoslav aircraft are shot down over Bosnia.
29 April	African National Congress under Nelson Mandela wins first free elections in South Africa.

17 June	North Korea agrees to end its nuclear programme.
19 September	US forces land unopposed in Haiti to restore its elected President Aristide.
5–6 December	Summit of Conference on Security and Cooperation in Europe agrees to turn itself into a permanent Organization.

1995

1 January	Austria, Finland, and Sweden join the European Union.
15 January	After a month of fighting, Russian forces capture Grozny, capital of Chechnya, from rebels.
11 July	UN 'safe-haven' of Srbrenica is overrun by Serbs in Bosnia and many Muslims massacred; more 'safe-areas' are then attacked.
30 August	NATO launches 'Operation Deliberate Force', with air attacks on Serbs in Bosnia.
31 October– 21 November	Bosnian peace agreement brokered in Dayton, Ohio.

1996

12 March	Clinton approves Helms-Burton Act, raising possibility of sanctions against any country trading with Cuba.
23 March	First free elections for a Taiwanese President; bitterly criticized by China.
30 June	Communists lose power after elections in Mongolia.
3 July	Yeltsin re-elected Russian President after run-off against Communist Gennadi Zyuganov.
6 August	Chechen rebels seize control of Grozny.
29 August	Russia agrees to withdrawal from Chechnya.
27 September	Taleban movement seizes control of Afghan capital, Kabul.

1997

17 April	Communist China and Taiwan open direct sea link for first time.
16–17 May	President Mobutu of Zaire overthrown by Laurent Kabila after seven months of civil war.
27 May	NATO–Russian Founding Act signed.
1 July	Hong Kong returns to Chinese sovereignty from British rule.
4 December	Most UN members sign a treaty to ban anti-personnel mines; but not America, Russia, or China.
9 December	Geneva talks open between US, China, and the two Koreas to try to secure lasting Korean settlement.
14 December	President Khatami of Iran offers 'dialogue' with America.

1998

4–24 February	Crisis in Gulf as US and British mass forces because of Iraq's refusal to allow arms inspectors to continue their work.
11–30 May	Series of nuclear tests by India, then by Pakistan.
21 May	Reorganization of President Suharto of Indonesia after five months of unrest.

7 August	Bomb attacks on US embassies in Kenya and Tanzania kill over two hundred; US launches retaliatory strikes on Sudan and Afghanistan on the 20th.
17 August	Economic crisis in Russia deepens, with value of rouble cut by a third.
September	Intensive fighting breaks out in Kosovo between Yugoslavian forces and local Albanians, after sporadic violence since March.
27 September	Following election defeat, Helmut Kohl loses power in Germany after sixteen years.
15–23 October	Clinton brokers Israeli–Palestinian peace deal at Wye Plantation, Maryland, ending 18-month stalemate in peace process.
25–30 November	Jiang Zemin becomes first Chinese Head of State to make an official visit to Japan.

1999

1 January	Introduction of the 'euro' as a single currency between most European Union members.
7 January	Trial of Clinton opens in Washington on charges of impeachment over the Monica Lewinsky affair.
12 February	US Senate throws out the impeachment charges against Clinton.
6–23 February	Rambouillet talks on Kosovo situation fail to secure a settlement.
12 March	The Czech Republic, Hungary, and Poland join NATO.
24 March	NATO begins air strikes against Yugoslavia.
7 May	US aircraft mistakenly bomb Chinese embassy in Belgrade.
10 June	NATO suspends its bombing campaign as Serb forces withdraw from Kosovo.
12 June	NATO ground forces begin deployment in Kosovo.
30 August	Referendum in Indonesian-controlled East Timor votes for independence, sparking weeks of violence.
4 September	Israel and Palestinian leaders sign the Sharm el-Sheikh agreement, supposedly paving the way for a 'final' settlement in a year.
30 September	Following a month of tension, Russian ground forces invade Chechnya.
19 December	Portuguese-ruled Macao is handed over to Chinese sovereignty, ending the last colonial possession in mainland Asia.
31 December	Panamanian sovereignty over Panama Canal takes effect.
	Sudden resignation of Yeltsin as President of Russia; Vladimir Putin becomes acting President.

2000

6 February	Putin announces the fall of Grozny, the Chechen capital, to Russian troops.
26 March	Putin is elected Russian President in his own right.
14 April	Russian parliament ratifies the START II treaty (signed in 1993); also ratifies the Comprehensive Test Ban treaty on 21 April.
17 April	US and Russia open exploratory talks on a START III treaty in Geneva.
24 May	US Congress approves equal trading status for China.
	Israel withdraws its last troops from its 'security zone' in southern Lebanon.
13–15 June	Presidents Kim Dae Jung of South Korea and Kim Jong Il of South Korea meet in Pyongyang.

17–19 July	Russian–Chinese (Putin–Jiang) summit in China condemns US plans for a 'National Missile Defence' system based on Star Wars research.
24 September	Vojizlav Kostunica wins Yugoslavia Presidential election, but Slobodan Milošović refuses to concede.
28 September	A visit by the right-wing Israel politician, Ariel Sharon, to the Dome at the Rock in Jerusalem sparks serious Palestinian unrest; becomes the 'second Intifada'.
6 October	After several days of unrest, Milošović finally stands down as Yugoslav President.
7 November	Closely fought US Presidential election; Republican George W. Bush not declared the winner until 13 December.
16–19 November	Bill Clinton becomes the first US president to visit a united Vietnam.

20 Europe and the Former Soviet Union

A. German Reunification

The collapse of communism brought about the greatest changes in the map of Europe since 1919, with the political disintegration of three Eurasian countries: the then USSR (Chapter 20, B) with localized outbreaks of violence; Yugoslavia (Chapter 20, C) with several years of bloody civil war; and Czechoslovakia (Chapter 20, C) where the Czechs and Slovaks peacefully agreed to go their own way as of January 1993, in the so-called 'velvet divorce'. Elsewhere it led to profound political changes, notably in Italy where the Christian Democratic Party, which had dominated government since 1947, lost its principal *raison d'être* and fell apart, leading to a new constellation of parties. But in one vital case communism's demise brought reunification to a divided nation. The return of a single Germany was in many ways a natural result of Soviet retreat: the division of the country in 1945–9 was largely a result of the Cold War. The Western

powers had always insisted that West Germany was the only legitimate German government, a point reiterated by Bush in a speech in Mainz as recently as May 1989. The West German Basic Law provided for easy accession by the Eastern provinces and in 1989–90 a clear majority of the German people wished to assert their national self-determination and have unity restored. In West Germany nationalist opinion clamoured for this, with little attention to the potential financial cost of absorbing the East; in the East the very desire to share in the West's wealth did much to undermine the Marxist state. Nevertheless, the process of reunification, though achieved in the space of a year, was far from simple. Given Germany's strategic position, industrial might and historic importance many European nations—not just the USSR, Poland, and Czechoslovakia but also Britain, France, and other European Community members—were concerned about its return as a united power. Neither the Kohl administration in Bonn nor its main ally, America, wished to alienate Gorbachev in the process, since this might risk a resurgence of Soviet militarism and imperial ambition. And many details of reunification, both inter-German and international, called for delicate judgement.

Reunification becomes Possible

The euphoria that accompanied the breaching of the Berlin Wall on 9 November 1989 was followed by confusion as to what would happen next. Reunification was immediately discussed in both West and East Germany but some East Germans hoped to reform their own state, while the Social Democrats and Greens in the West were fearful of a return to extreme nationalism and expansionism in a resurgent, single country. Even Kohl had his doubts about how to proceed at first, but events on the ground demanded a response: polls soon showed that 70 per cent of West Germans favoured reunification and the East German state was obviously collapsing, its people threatening to move *en masse* to the West, now that the border was breached. It did not seem that international opinion would put up great resistance to reunification at this point. The US soon became enthusiastic, whilst Soviet policy appeared hopelessly confused. Bush believed West Germany was deeply committed to the Western alliance and that reunification 'would end the division of Europe on Western terms'.[1] On 28 November, reasonably certain that Washington was ready to exploit the fluidity in Europe to reshape the continent in Western interests, Kohl put forward a 'Ten Point Plan' for reunification. Vague on some key details, including the time frame, the plan proposed building cooperation with East Germany, transforming it into a liberal, capitalist regime and creating joint institutions, which would lead on to a single federation, while acting in line with the European Community and the 1975 Helsinki Accords. At this time, however, both France's President, Francois Mitterrand, and Britain's Premier, Margaret Thatcher, became concerned about the potential predominance of German power in Europe in future. Mitterrand even talked to Gorbachev,

in Moscow on 6 December, about how to halt the reunification process, which was troubling the Kremlin too. But Bush continued to support Kohl strongly, Gorbachev was divided in his own mind over what to do, and a Mitterrand–Thatcher axis failed to emerge. Whereas the former was determined on a course of containing the new Germany in stronger European Community (EC) institutions, the latter had no enthusiasm for European integration. An EC summit in Strasbourg in late December effectively accepted that reunification was likely. As to Gorbachev, his confusion was apparent at the Malta summit in early December, where he publicly called the division of Germany 'the decision of history' while privately telling Bush that he agreed with self-determination in principle and simply did not want 'to force issues'.[2]

Events within East Germany continued to force the pace. On 3 December the communist leader of only six weeks, Egon Krenz, resigned with all the Politburo, leaving Premier Hans Modrow as the predominant leader, but one who was quite unable to control the situation. Hopes of reforming the existing system soon evaporated. The planned economy was in tatters, the currency worthless; opposition groups had been allowed to form and in mid-January the Stasi secret police was disbanded. It was still felt, even in West Germany, that the full achievement of reunification could take several years, but the question now was how and when it would occur, not whether it would. A key point would be the first free East German elections, which Modrow conceded to the opposition groups in December. The original date set for these was May, but on 28 January that target was brought forward to 18 March. Modrow also agreed on 28 January to form a coalition government immediately. So it was that the communist cause in Germany evaporated, the Soviets were kept permanently off balance by their lack of means to control the situation, and Kohl pressed on determinedly towards the aim of reunification, the wisdom of which he never doubted. The German Chancellor was worried, however, that Gorbachev might successfully press for four-power talks, in which the former occupiers (the US, USSR, Britain, and France) would dictate a settlement, perhaps even reviving such questions as reparations. Modrow fed such fears by resuscitating the old Soviet aim of a reunited but neutralized Germany, detached from NATO. As to Bush, he recognized that 'if we were to see progress on reunification, it would be our role to work with Moscow as an equal on the issue', so as to minimize Gorbachev's domestic problems.[3] But, on 30 January, Gorbachev publicly conceded that reunification was possible and, as elsewhere in Eastern Europe, it was quite plain that he was ready to compromise on previous Soviet position in order to preserve peace and establish a stable, new balance of power. It has been argued that three factors in particular led to the USSR's 'dramatic retreat' on Germany in 1990: 'the internal collapse' of East Germany; the Soviet Union's own economic problems; and the 'active policies of the West', with whom Gorbachev was desperate to build cooperation.[4] The West Germans did seem ready to offer some concessions to placate him: on 31 January their Foreign Minister, Hans Dietrich Genscher, proposed that alongside reunification Germany would remain in NATO but that former areas of East Germany would not be utilized by NATO armed forces. There was deep concern among some Soviet leaders about the situation. Even the liberal Alexander Yakovlev declared that 'the security of our borders must be firmly guaranteed. We must avoid the emergence of any kind of a new threat from the well-known direction.' But Foreign Minister Shevardnadze saw little alternative to moving towards agreement with the West: the 'alternative was to use our half-million troops in east German to block unification. We can imagine what that would have entailed.'[5]

A Settlement takes Shape

In early February 1990 the machinery by which the German question would be settled took shape. First, on 6 February Kohl said there could be talks on economic and monetary union with East Germany, a step which would prevent the East's economic collapse but which would also effectively destroy its socio-economic system by absorbing it into the capitalist world. The likely political absorption of the East, via the adoption of the West German Basic Law, was already clear enough. Economic reunification was a difficult challenge, but the simplest method,

and the way eventually adopted despite its potential cost to the West, was to exchange the Deutschmark for the Eastern mark at the ratio of one-to-one. The second important organizational step was the US proposal, put to the Soviets by Secretary of State Baker on 8 February after consultation with the other two Western powers, for the so-called 'two-plus-four' talks, through which the two Germanys would settle many (principally domestic) problems while the four ex-occupation powers would tackle the international dimensions of reunification. Baker saw this as 'a process that could steer the two Germanies to unification while also giving Gorbachev a place at the table, so he could explain to hardliners that Moscow was still in the game.'[6] The 'two-plus-four' approach, effectively a compromise between the German desire to dominate events and the Soviet–British-French wish to have a say, was confirmed by the breakthrough summit of NATO and Warsaw Pact nations in Ottawa on 13–14 February. Meanwhile, on 10 February, Kohl had travelled to Moscow and offered economic aid to the USSR in return for Bonn's predominant role in setting the future pace of reunification. On 24–5 February he was at Camp David, agreeing that a reunited Germany should stay in NATO, with its forces on its soil, although East Germany might have a 'special' status, free of NATO units for a time. It was the first time a German Chancellor had been invited to the Presidential retreat at Camp David. For the Bush administration 'the key to future security and the development of East–West relations became German reunification, with Germany remaining in NATO, and Soviet acquiescence'—with all three of these having to be achieved together.[7]

The idea that East Germany could drive a hard bargain with the West on social and political concessions faded quickly after this, as did any Soviet hope of controlling the timetable of reunification. Modrow's government was already desperate for the West's financial support when, on 18 March, the East German elections resulted in a 48 per cent vote for the Christian Democrats and their allies. The Socialists won only 22 per cent and the Communists, who had ruled the country for forty years, a mere 16 per cent. The election results were seen as a vote for reunification and specifically East German political movements did very badly. A new, Christian Democrat-dominated coalition was formed in mid-April, under Lothar de Mazière, who soon agreed that his country should be, in effect, swallowed up by the West. The only serious problem during these weeks was created by Kohl himself who, worryingly, questioned the validity of the German–Polish border. His reason for doing this, he said, was that he did not want to commit the government of a reunited Germany on the issue, but he inevitably stirred fears in Poland and elsewhere of a resurgence of German expansionism. This fear was only expunged in late June when the West and East German parliaments each confirmed the Polish border, with a chastened Kohl telling the Bundestag 'Either we confirm the existing border or we gamble away the chance of German unity.'[8] (A border treaty between Germany and Poland was signed in June 1991.)

West Germany and the US hoped from the start that the 'two-plus-four' talks would achieve German reunification within NATO, but without offending the USSR or risking European stability. The USSR still hoped that the talks would adopt a broad approach and might be used both to delay the pace of progress and prevent German membership of NATO. But the US took a narrower view of the talks: Washington did not, for example, want them to embrace general European security or arms control issues, although they should discuss issues relating to Allied rights and German sovereignty. The US also wanted East Germany to be brought fully within NATO in future, even if it had some special status. Certainly the US, supported by France and Britain, had no interest in a 'neutralized' East Germany. Scowcroft recognized that a 'Germany outside NATO would "gut" the alliance' and that, without Germany, the US 'military presence in NATO would be difficult if not impossible to maintain.'[9] As to the West Germans, they hoped for a rapid move to reunification, the withdrawal of the Red Army from the East, and the restoration of full sovereignty—including the right to remain in NATO. The 'two-plus-four' talks began, among officials, on 14 March but progressed slowly at first. A month later the USSR still hoped to avoid German membership of NATO, even if German reunification was inevitable. Some in the USSR felt that a compromise could be reached on the basis of German membership of both NATO *and* the Warsaw

Pact, even though the latter organization had a doubtful future.

The first ministerial-level 'two-plus-four' talks took place on 5 May, by which time the US, Britain, and France had smoothed out their original differences on reunification. Mitterrand was happy with Kohl's continuing commitment to European integration, while Thatcher understood that reunification was unavoidable. The Soviets initially took a tough approach, hoping to 'decouple' the internal and external aspects of reunification, the main demand from Moscow still being that Germany should be neutralized. But increasingly it became evident that Kohl could hope to buy off the USSR with financial aid and a few concessions, including limits on the size of the German army. In mid-May, when he first began to hope that all-German elections might be held before the end of the year, he also secretly offered financial aid to Gorbachev in order to cover the costs of the Red Army's withdrawal from East Germany. From now until July, there were frequent, bilateral Soviet–German contacts to smooth the way to a deal. Furthermore, on 31 May the Washington summit between Bush and Gorbachev saw reassurances being giving to the latter that German reunification would not be exploited to the USSR's detriment. By now Gorbachev well knew that the 'question was not how to prevent the unification, but what the pace and conditions of this process should be.'[10] Even so, it was hard for the Soviets to accept the condition that Germany should remain in NATO. Before the summit, Kohl had encouraged the US to make concessions to the increasingly troubled Soviet leader, who was now facing both dire economic problems and severe unrest in Lithuania. Bush was able to give 'nine assurances' including reductions in the size of Germany's armed forces, recognition of Germany's established borders, German economic support for Moscow, and a more significant role for the all-European organization, the Conference on Security Cooperation in Europe (CSCE), which Moscow hoped would play a leading role in continental security following the Cold War. After this meeting Gorbachev seemed to accept that Germany could choose its own international future, including NATO membership, even if he still hoped that it might also enter the Warsaw Pact.

Germany Reunified

On 1 July East and West Germany achieved the domestically popular aim of economic and monetary union. The danger of an East German economic collapse and mass emigration to the West was thereby removed, even if the financial cost to West Germans would prove immense. The rest of the month was dominated by efforts to solve the international dimensions of the German problem and progress was now very rapid. The Soviet Foreign Minister, Shevardnadze, set the tone by telling the Communist Party Congress in Moscow of his own support for reunification; and it seems that Gorbachev was only waiting to get through the Congress in order to resolve the German problem for good, also accepting that NATO would include the reunited country. In return for this positive approach he could expect further rewards. On 5 July a NATO summit in London took measures to make the organization appear less threatening to the USSR (see Chapter 20, D). Not only would the German army be reduced, but also the aims of the organization were altered to put greater emphasis on cooperation with Moscow and the role of the CSCE in developing pan-European security. On the economic front, the G-7 meeting in Houston on 9–12 July began a new study of Soviet needs, intending that an aid package should come later. This cautious policy reflected US and British doubts about the wisdom of pouring large sums into the ailing Soviet economy and it was much less than Kohl had wanted. But on 15–16 July the German Chancellor had his own bilateral talks with Gorbachev and promised large-scale technical and financial assistance to the USSR.

The German aid package was part of a more general deal between the two leaders that included several other significant aspects. Kohl confirmed the reduction of the Bundeswehr to 370,000, again undertook to pay for the staged withdrawal of the Red Army from East Germany (to be achieved by 1994), accepted the existing borders of Germany, and agreed to sign a friendship treaty with Moscow. He also said that, after 1994, only German troops (albeit under NATO command) would be based in the former East Germany and that no nuclear weapons would be based there. For his part Gorbachev accepted the full restoration of German sovereignty, its membership of NATO, and the end of the USSR's occupation rights. There was some surprise, even in Western capitals, at the suddenness and scope of this agreement, which to some extent sidestepped the two-plus-four process. In effect Kohl had exchanged financial and security guarantees in order to get the Red Army out of East Germany as soon as possible. It helped create the impression that this was no 'dictated peace. ... No other examples come to mind where ... the occupation and indemnity were imposed by the vanquished on the victor.'[11]

The next three months saw a series of treaties to confirm the new German settlement, with several tracks moving in parallel. On the West–East German front there was an agreement on 3 August to hold all-German elections by the end of the year and a Reunification Treaty was signed on 31 August, coming legally into force on 3 October, when the Eastern provinces effectively joined the Bonn Republic. On the German–Soviet front a friendship treaty was signed on 13 September, and between Germany and Poland there was a border treaty signed on 14 October. The two-plus-four negotiations ended on 12 September in Moscow, with a treaty recognizing Germany's borders, ending German territorial claims against others, restoring German sovereignty, and placing certain military limits on Germany, including confirmation of a promise, first made to the Western alliance in 1954, that it would not manufacture atomic, bacteriological, or chemical weapons. The treaty also embodied the special military status of the former East Germany, as agreed by Kohl and Gorbachev in mid-July. Four-power rights in Berlin and Germany were ended by an agreement of 1 October. This settlement was clearly better for the West than for Gorbachev, even if some Western nations were still concerned about the possible resurgence of an expansionist Germany. The USSR had had to retreat from its original hopes of delaying reunification and neutralizing Germany. Then again, the concessions on economic aid, the reform of NATO, and the strengthening of the CSCE showed that it was far from being a complete Soviet defeat. Washington, which had consistently backed and encouraged Kohl, could feel rather more satisfied, perhaps, than Paris or London, who were still concerned about their status in Europe compared to

Helmut Kohl b. 1930

Kohl, who was born in the town of Ludwigshafen in the Rhineland, was just beginning military training when the Second World War ended and the Nazi regime collapsed. A Roman Catholic, who had seen at first hand the destruction that political extremism could bring about, he joined the new Christian Democratic Party (CDU) when only 16 and, like its leader Konrad Adenauer, became a firm believer in European unity. Educated at Frankfurt University and later obtaining a doctorate from Helidelberg, Kohl at first worked in industry before becoming a full-time politician in 1969. Already the chairman of the CDU in the Rhineland-Palatinate, he was elected that year to be Minister-President of West Germany's most wealthy and populous province. Four years later he was elected chair of the national CDU and ran for the Chancellorship for the first time in 1976. Much criticized as a lacklustre, undynamic figure, he nonetheless engineered the parliamentary overthrow of the Chancellor, Helmut Schmidt, in 1982, thus ending thirteen years of Social Democratic government. Re-elected West German Chancellor in 1987, Kohl showed great diplomatic skill in securing Germany's peaceful reunification in 1989–90 and then served two further terms as Chancellor, despite the economic problems that reunification brought. In 1998 the Social Democrats finally defeated him and soon after Kohl was beset by accusations of financial improprieties whilst in power. In January 2000 he resigned as the CDU's honorary chairman, his reputation tarnished.

that of Germany. Clearly, it was Kohl who gained most, winning the first all-German elections since 1932, with 46 per cent of the vote going to his Christian Democrats on 2 December 1990. The Social Democrats came second with 33 per cent and the ex-communists fourth with 10 per cent, a shade behind the liberal Free Democrats. Kohl, hitherto an uninspiring Chancellor, 'was saved from an unfavourable historical verdict by having the German question thrust upon him, and by seizing the opportunity with considerable astuteness and strength.'[12] Apart from his gaffe on the Polish border, he had resolved a highly complex problem with remarkable speed. But the economic price of such swift reunification had yet to be paid. The 1990s, which began with so much hope for Germany, became blighted by unemployment, which eventually rose to more than four million, as spending was restrained and interest rates increased to cope with the costs of modernizing the former East. In 1998 Kohl, the Chancellor for sixteen years, was roundly defeated at the polls, and he was later accused of financial corruption during his long years in office.

B. The Break-Up of the USSR and the Wars of Succession

Gorbachev and the End of Soviet Power

By early 1990, after only five years as Soviet leader, Mikhail Gorbachev had transformed the country's political landscape and its foreign policy. To Western observers he seemed an enlightened, intelligent leader who had recognized the failings of communism, adopted liberal values, and greatly reduced international tension, putting an end to the Cold War. But to many of his own people he had abandoned the certainties of the Brezhnev era for the uncertainties of free enterprise, with its bankruptcies, price rises, and unemployment; his political changes had encouraged regional independence in the republics, and so threatened the USSR's cohesion; and, by losing the country's grip of Eastern

Europe, he had seriously compromised its security, wasting all that had been gained in the Second World War. In fact, the late 1980s revealed a great paradox: whilst no one individual could control the pace of change in the Soviet Union, it was equally difficult to see that things would have happened in the way they did without Gorbachev. His 'less-than-great personality shaped the end of the Cold War' because, even if he could not control events, 'many of the most extraordinary aspects of this remarkable' period could '*only* be understood by according primary importance to the Gorbachev *personality* factor.'[13] Gorbachev had decided reform was essential, thanks to the corrupt and inefficient politico-economic system he inherited, and he was optimistic that the Soviet people could handle radical changes. But if anything the pace of his reforms had been slow, undermined, especially on the economic side, by the conservatism of the Communist Party, and by his own uncertainty over precisely how to proceed. The growth of regionalism had largely been unexpected, as had the rate of decline in manufacturing output, and the two became linked, for the failure of reform to bring material benefits merely hardened support for secession.

Abroad Gorbachev had taken a line no former Soviet leader had dared, engaging with the West and ending the USSR's reliance on force. But here too his optimism proved ill-founded, he failed to see difficulties, and he ended up reacting to events rather than controlling them. He expected a gradual, mutual, and agreed reduction of tension, which would preserve Soviet security in a new international environment. But he was fundamentally weakened in 1985–9 by the USSR's poor economic and financial situation, at a time when the Western powers appeared politically stable and economically resurgent. Also, at first, many Western leaders saw his policies as a reaction to economic failure and did not accept, until 1989, that he was really ready to cooperate. In 1985–7, while the USSR compromised its position in Afghanistan, southern Africa, and South-East Asia, the developing world was ever more indebted to the West, and America—despite being wracked by doubts about its own 'decline'—was actually in an ever stronger position. In 1989–90, while the Red Army prepared to leave Eastern

Europe, NATO retained its unity and Germany was reunited on terms largely dictated by Washington and Bonn. Yet, none of this was as catastrophic as what was to follow in 1990–1.

If Gorbachev failed to carry through his programme for more democratic institutions and free enterprise elements in the economy, then there seemed only two real alternatives by 1990. Either, as the CIA increasingly feared, the communist machine would strike back in an attempt to return to totalitarianism; or—and this seemed equally difficult to come to terms with—the USSR would dissolve and its fifteen republics would become independent, with their own constitutions and economic policies. Despite becoming Executive President in March 1990, Gorbachev seemed at a loss how to deal with the unexpected, yet potent challenge of regionalism. In January 1991 he sought to prevent an immediate break-up of the USSR by promising a Law on Nationalities, including the right to secede, but he worked on this only slowly and, in March, he sent the Red Army into Lithuania when it precipitately declared itself independent under its recently elected President, Vytautas Landsbergis. Lithuania, along with Latvia and Estonia, was one of the three Baltic States, forcibly absorbed into the USSR by Stalin in 1940. They led the way among the constituent republics in pressing for autonomy. Estonia had actually issued a declaration of sovereignty (short of independence) in November 1988, followed by Latvia and Lithuania eight months later, after which Lithuania had declared the 1940 annexation illegal. In August 1989 a million people had joined hands across the Baltic States in a symbolic gesture of freedom. Gorbachev's action in March 1990 suggested he might resist the USSR's break-up by force, provoking concern in the West and immediately putting at risk a proposed US–Soviet trade deal—a sign that the Cold War might not yet be over. Soviet troops disarmed the Lithuanian National Guard and arrested young Lithuanians who resisted conscription into the Red Army. Then, however, Gorbachev turned to an economic blockade, forcing Landsbergis to suspend independence in June, while the promised Law on Nationalities, now referred to as the 'Union Treaty', was completed. Once again, Gorbachev decided that force was not the answer: 'the chosen alternative was a war of nerves . . . to induce Lithuania to step back ... and to show the secessionist forces in the ... republics that pulling out of the USSR would not be painless.'[14]

The relaxation of tension allowed a highly successful summit, between Gorbachev and America's George Bush, to be held in Washington in May–June (see Chapter 21, C). Meanwhile, in May, Gorbachev's old rival and former minister, Boris Yeltsin, was elected as President by the assembly of the USSR's largest constituent republic, the Russian Federation. He not only resigned from the Communist Party, but also set out to create an alternative power centre to the Kremlin, asserting the Russian Federation's right to sovereignty on 12 June. Within weeks Moldova, Ukraine, and Belorussia had followed suit, all of them now with mass popular movements pressing for autonomy. 'From then on', Gorbachev later recalled, 'no major issue could be resolved outside the context of the relationship between the Union and the republics' and he admitted that he had simply 'underestimated the phenomenon of the election of Yeltsin in Moscow'.[15] Although Bush himself continued to hope for Gorbachev's survival, the CIA warned that 'like Moses, having brought his people out of bondage, it is increasingly evident that Gorbachev cannot lead them over into the Promised Land.'[16] Yeltsin increasingly seemed the man of the future.

By December 1990 the situation was ever more confused. With the beleaguered and uncertain Gorbachev promoting traditional communists back into the Politburo and taking new powers for himself, the reformist Foreign Minister, Edvard Shevardnadze, resigned, fearing of a return to dictatorship. In January 1991 another reformist, Premier Nikolai Ryzhkov, was replaced by Valentin Pavlov, who accused the West of trying to destabilize the country by pressing it to adopt capitalism without providing adequate financial support. But then, just as the conservatives seemed back in the ascendant and with the Union Treaty still not completed, Landsbergis ended his suspension of Lithuanian independence, provoking another crisis over the regionalization issue. As the Red Army tried to seize key buildings in the Lithuanian capital, thirteen people were killed and five more died in clashes in neighbouring Latvia, where there was considerable sympathy for the Lithuanian case. 'If the forces

of the centre can do this to the Balts,' a worried Yeltsin told the US ambassador, 'they can do it to us.'[17] Though preoccupied by the Gulf War against Iraq (see Chapter 21, B) and anxious not to be seen advocating the USSR's disintegration, the US government expressed concern and a planned Gorbachev–Bush summit was postponed. Yeltsin also lent his rhetorical support to the Baltic States and Gorbachev again drew back from repression. On 7 March he finally published the draft Union Treaty, which allowed the republics a wide degree of autonomy. A majority of Soviet votes approved this in a referendum ten days later, but this did not end Gorbachev's problems because six republics boycotted the poll. On 3 March Latvia and Estonia had followed Lithuania by declaring independence. Soon afterwards the Caucasian republic of Georgia joined them. Furthermore, in July, Yeltsin reinforced his position by being popularly elected Russian President. The whole Soviet Union was now faced by permanent food shortages and widespread strikes, with little hope of large-scale Western aid: in late July the G-7 London summit had reluctantly decided that Gorbachev's economic reforms were too modest to deserve extra financial support.

The decisive crisis for the USSR came in mid-August 1991 when hardline communists, many of them recently promoted by Gorbachev, launched a coup, hoping to forestall the signature of the Union Treaty. They imprisoned Gorbachev but were a group of little-known bureaucrats, lacking in confidence and unable to muster support. They could not command the loyalty of such essential centre of power as the armed forces or even of the capital, Moscow, where Yeltsin held out against them. Within days the coup collapsed and Gorbachev was freed. The coup failure was quickly followed by the abolition of the KGB and the suspension of the Communist Party itself. Yet the person who gained most from these events was not Gorbachev, who had been powerless throughout the coup, but Yeltsin, who was widely credited with defeating it. He now worked with other leaders of the constituent republics to destroy the USSR. He felt, perhaps, that he had little choice: after the August coup 'we had a complete vacuum at the political centre. The centre—in the person of Gorbachev—was totally demoralized. The emerging national states had lost their faith in him.' But Gorbachev remembered things differently, believing that the 'Soviet Union really was a strong and solid multinational state. Its dissolution was by no means inevitable.' He claimed that Yeltsin and his entourage 'sacrificed the Union for the sake of realizing their ardent desire to reign in the Kremlin.'[18] Some republics opted for complete independence, but on 21 December eleven formed a loose confederation, named the 'Commonwealth of Independent States'. When Gorbachev resigned as Executive President on 25 December the USSR ceased to exist. The attempt to democratize the country had only succeeded in dividing it against itself, giving power to ethnic majorities in the republics that wanted to be free of Russian control. Other than in Lithuania and parts of the Caucasus, this process had been achieved with remarkably little violence and, partly thanks to a lack of triumphalism in the West, no major international crisis. Apart from the Russian Federation it left a series of new countries not only in Eastern Europe (the Baltic States, Ukraine, Belarus, Moldova) and the Caucasus (Georgia, Armenia, Azerbaijan), but also in Central Asia (Kazakhstan, Kyrgyzstan, Tajikistan, Uzbekistan, Turkmenistan). But all of these inherited social and economic problems from the former USSR and many also faced internal political divisions and foreign challenges which brought instability for many years afterwards.

Russian Policy and the Wars of Succession

The conflicts in the former Soviet republics took various forms, from ethnic tensions and ideological disputes that resulted in civil wars, to border disputes between the newly independent states. There were numerous minor disputes of short duration and some potentially serious border claims (as between Russia and Kazakhstan, or Tajikistan and Uzbekistan), which failed to become critical. But some conflicts such as the attempt by ethnic Russians to establish an independent 'Transdniester Republic' in Moldova (1990–4) or the Tajikistan civil war (1992–7, fought between ex-communists and Islamic groups) lasted several years. And at least three were very intense, creating long-term instability in an especially complex region, the

Caucasus: the Armenian–Azerbaijani war—over the disputed region of Ngorno-Karabakh (1992–3, with renewed tension late in 1999), the ethnic Abkhazi revolt against Georgian rule (1992–3), and the Chechen bid to secede from the Russian Federation (post-1994). Most of these had their origins in much earlier periods. Ngorno-Karabakh, for example, though mostly populated by (Christian) Armenians, had been put under (Muslim) Azerbaijani administration in 1923, under Lenin. Violence had first broken out in the enclave in February 1988, with Armenia backing a secessionist movement opposed to Azerbaijani rule and leaders in both states exploiting the issue to win popular support. When war broke out between the two, now-independent republics in 1992 the Armenians, whose territory virtually surrounded the enclave, had a clear strategic advantage and soon captured all the urban centres, but Azerbaijan refused to accept its loss and the danger of a renewed conflict persisted.

Despite the break-up of the USSR, Yeltsin's Russia was frequently active in trying both to limit these conflicts, to make Russian borders secure, to protect the rights of ethnic Russians in the successor states, and to assert Moscow's continuing influence in most of the republics it previously ruled, areas which were now referred to as the 'near abroad'. In both Georgia in December 1993, and Tajikistan in June 1997, Russia played a leading role in brokering a peace settlement; and these settlements were both policed by forces from the Commonwealth of Independent States (CIS). There had been hopes in Moscow in early 1992, that the CIS might prove a vehicle for Russian predominance, even taking over the armed forces of the former USSR. This proved too ambitious and in March 1992 Yeltsin confirmed that Russia would create its own defence forces. Cooperation between Russia and the other republics tended to take the form of free trade agreements and friendship treaties, rather than political and defence cooperation, but was particularly close with the two Slav republics of Belarus and Ukraine—the original proponents, with Yeltsin, of the CIS in 1991. For much of 1992 Russia and the Ukraine had been divided over the disposal of the Soviet Black Sea Fleet, before deciding to share it equally, and there was tension too over the treatment by the Ukraine of ethnic Russians in the Crimea (which had been part of Russia until 1954). But relations gradually improved. Both Ukraine and Belarus elected pro-Russian Presidents in 1994; and in May 1997 there was both a ten-year Russo–Ukraine cooperation agreement and a Russo–Belarus 'Charter of Union'. The latter was potentially far-reaching, but it was vague on detail and there was no timetable for its achievement. As to the CIS, it remained in being, held regular summits, and in its first five years of existence drew up about 800 agreements between its members. But many of these agreements were not signed by all the states and, after a few years, it was beginning to look insignificant, a focus for technical rather than substantive cooperation.

Russia was by far the largest of the former Soviet republics and Yeltsin's attempts to 'lead' the others and to protect ethnic Russians were designed to satisfy his nationalist and communist critics, who, though divided between themselves, tried to outbid the pro-reform lobby for popular support and posed as defenders of 'national' interests over the supposedly pro-Western policy of Yeltsin. In the December 1993 Russian parliamentary elections there was a worrying success for an extreme nationalist party led by Vladimir Zhirinovsky, which won 23 per cent of votes; two years later the communists emerged in first place in elections, with 22 per cent of the vote. Nationalists and communists might be divided on domestic and economic policy, and they were far from having an overall majority but, abroad, they both advocated cooperation with fellow Slavs (including Serbia), the assertion of Russian power in such former areas of influence as the Caucasus and Central Asia, and resistance to any sign of Western domination. A strong foreign policy was made difficult by the country's continuing economic weakness, by the poor quality and low morale of its armed forces, and by political divisions in Moscow, even among Yeltsin's supporters, over the pace and direction of reform. The political division reached its greatest crisis point in September-October 1993 when Yeltsin, criticized for months by the Congress of People's deputies, tried to dissolve it, only to have the deputies barricade themselves inside the parliament building and try to seize control of the state television headquarters. Earlier, in April, he had silenced his opponents by winning a popular referendum on his leadership and market-based economic policies. But now he turned to brute strength, using tanks to bombard the parliament and force the deputies to surrender. Over a hundred people were killed in the operation and those who were arrested afterwards included a former Vice-President, Alexander Rutskoi. 'From one perspective this was the end of the Soviet Empire', in that Yeltsin's old Communist opponents had been signally defeated; but the bombardment also seemed reminiscent of Stalinist tactics and 'made an unpleasant and lasting impression in Russia and the West'.[19] Such firmness, and a lack of widely acceptable alternative leaders, helped Yeltsin win the mid-1996 Presidential elections, but he was also, by then, troubled by ill-health and did not serve out his second term in full (see Chapter 21, C).

In Georgia, Yeltsin was pitted for a time against another reformer from the Gorbachev era, the ex-Foreign Minister, Edvard Shevardnadze. Shevardnadze was elected head of state at his home republic on 11 October 1992 after months of internal political uncertainty. By then there was already a powerful secessionist movement in Abkhazia and a bid, too, from the Muslim-populated region of South Ossetia, for independence from Georgia. The Abkhazis are an ancient Black Sea people. They number only about 100,000 and are in a minority even in Abkhazia itself but, as elsewhere in the disintegrating USSR, they had been encouraged to work for increased national rights in 1988–9, had asserted the sovereignty of their own republic in August 1990, and even talked of joining the Russian Federation to escape Georgian domination, a move which generated some sympathy for the Abkhazis in Russia. Georgia was weakened in the face of this challenge by its own divisions: in early 1992 its then-President, Zviad Gamsakhurdia, had been overthrown and he subsequently tried to use Abkhazia as a base for revival. On 7 July the Abkhazis declared independence, Georgian armed forces were sent to quell the rebellion, but Russia tried to bring about a ceasefire. In mid-1993, as the war continued, Yeltsin was blamed for helping the Abkhazis besiege Sukhumi, which Shevardnadze personally went to defend. When it fell, Shevardnadze faced personal humiliation, was forced to turn to Russia for help (agreeing a friendship treaty with them in February 1994 and joining the CIS), and had to accept a settlement in April 1994 which virtually gave Abkhazia independence. About 10,000 had died in the conflict, but many Georgians remained determined to reconquer Abkhazia and there were periodic outbreaks of violence, as in May 1998 when Abkhazi forces entered the neutral zone between the two sides, following attacks by Georgian partisans.

Chechnya

If Yeltsin managed to exploit Georgia's difficulties in order to assert Russian power, he had far less success a few years later within his own borders, in another area of the Caucasus, Chechnya. The Russian Federation, though it had been constituted as a single, united republic of the USSR, was itself a vast Eurasian country, with numerous ethnic and religious minorities and various types of regional government within it. Over twenty million people in the Federation lived under their own republican governments (twenty-one in number); others were part of autonomous 'Okrugs' (ten in number). The Russian republics all had a substantial non-Russian population, and many of the ethnic groups, such as the Tatars of Tatarstan, had a long history of resistance to rule from Moscow. In some of the autonomous areas, communists clung to power and undermined Yeltsin's reform programme; in others constitutions were drawn up in the 1990s that violated the federal constitution by maximizing local autonomy. Chechnya became the principal test case of whether, in the wake of the USSR's demise, Russia itself would break up and the outcome, for Yeltsin, was not hopeful.

Chechnya, as the republic of Chechen-Ingush became known, had a mixed population of 58 per cent Chechens, 23 per cent Russians, and 13 per cent Ingush, the last a Muslim people who tended to ally with the ethnic Russians to prevent local Chechen domination. The Chechens themselves were Sufi Muslims, who had resisted Tsarist conquest in the 1850s and subjected to mass deportation under Stalin in the early 1940s. The republic first declared its independence of Russia on 1 November 1991 under its newly elected President, a former Soviet air-force officer, Dzhokar Dudayev, who had previously been reckoned an ally of Yeltsin. Turkey, Iran, and other Muslim states gave diplomatic recognition to Chechnya and, at first, the Russian parliament resisted Yeltsin's attempts to crush the secession, fearful that a military success for him in the Caucasus would strengthen his hand in dealing with opponents nearer home. Also, at least until 1994, there 'was simply . . . no pressing need for the Russian state to take action; there were few signs that the "Chechen infection" of radical nationalism . . . was spreading to other Russian autonomous republics.'[20] Moscow instead had to rely on an economic blockade and military manoeuvres on the border to intimidate Dudayev, whose increasingly authoritarian, personal rule stirred up civil war in early 1994, leaving the republic even more lawless. Thereafter, Russian policy became tougher, partly influenced by a need to meet the challenge from nationalists. For a time Yeltsin hoped that Dudayev would be overthrown or assassinated by his domestic opponents. But in August 1994 the Chechens began to prepare for a Russian invasion, which seemed increasingly likely and for which the Russian army was clearly preparing. The invasion finally came on 11 December 1994, when three divisions marched on the capital, Grozny.

Few expected that the Chechens—poor, divided, and ill-armed as they seemed—could resist the Russians for long. However, the invasion soon turned into embarrassment for Moscow. The army reached Grozny in five days, leading about 200,000 refugees to flee the city, yet despite repeated claims of victory from Yeltsin, the Presidential palace was not taken until 15 January 1995 and the city was not declared clear of Chechen fighters until 8 February. Many Russians backed the invasion on patriotic grounds, keen to prevent a break-up of the Federation, but they also questioned the destructive scale of the operation and Yeltsin's approval rating dropped to 20 per cent. 'Buried in Grozny was Yeltsin's magic ability to read Russia's mind.'[21] The morale of the army was low and Russian generals bickered among themselves. After Afghanistan and the collapse of the USSR, the armed forces lacked the will to prosecute a war. Some soldiers were ready to sell their arms, even their tanks, to the enemy. Typically in guerrilla warfare, all Chechnya's urban centres fell into Russian hands in the spring of 1995 but the Chechens, though numbering only a few thousand fighters, held on in the countryside and hit back in a series of surprise operations: in May they again infiltrated Grozny; in June they seized hundreds of hostages in Budennovsk, on Russian soil, and only released them in return for a safe passage home; and in October, despite several preceding weeks of peace talks, they tried to assassinate the Russian commander, Lt. Gen. Anatoli Romanov. In January 1996 there were more successes for the guerrillas, with another hostage seizure at Kizylar and the capture of hostages on a Black Sea ferry. Yeltsin himself became involved in peace talks in March but would not concede Chechen demands for a Russian withdrawal and independence. Dudayev was killed by a rocket attack in April 1996 but his successor, Aslan Maskhadov, maintained the independence demand and on 6 August the Russian military was embarrassed once more, as Chechen guerrillas again occupied the centre of Grozny.

Faced by what seemed an 'unwinnable' war, and one which had already cost about 50,000 lives, Yeltsin sent his national security adviser, General Alexander Lebed to Grozny, with executive powers, to negotiate a settlement. Lebed was a tough soldier-turned-politician, an ex-paratrooper, and veteran of Afghanistan, who had come third in the recent Russian Presidential elections—though only with some help from the Yeltsin camp, which had used him to split the opposition vote. The General's solution to the Chechen problem was hardly calculated to please Russian nationalists but it was founded on his knowledge of the scale of the problems facing the Russian armed forces, and its manner confirmed his reputation for decisiveness. He quickly agreed to a ceasefire and, on 31 August, reached a settlement with Maskhadov based on a Russian military withdrawal, with a deferral of the independence issue until 2000–21. Until then the exact fate of Chechnya was uncertain and not everything looked negative for Moscow. After the bloodshed there other republics were reluctant to assert their own independence of Moscow just yet, so that a temporary settlement was not disastrous from Yeltsin's point of view. Also, there was some hope of working with Maskhadov who 'promised the restoration of internal . . . stability, and the reconstruction of the economy in cooperation with Russia.'[22] But the state of the Russian army was clearly terrible: the Defence

Ministry admitted, in early 1997, that it was on the verge of disintegration. Furthermore, Maskhadov, who was popularly elected President of Chechnya in February 1997, seemed in a position to assert the republic's full independence in a few years time, with Russian control largely nominal. Although Yeltsin sacked Lebed in October 1996, after accusing him of planning a mutiny, and thereby removed a potentially strong rival, there was always a danger that other opponents could exploit the failure to win a decisive victory over the Chechens. Neither would the Chechen problem disappear, given that a final decision on its future had merely been delayed.

By the summer of 1999 the situation appeared as difficult as ever. On 5 March Russia's Deputy Minister of the Interior, Gennadi Shipigun, had been kidnapped in Grozny. He was later murdered. In August and September there was a series of bomb attacks in Russia by Chechen terrorists determined to secure their independence and dozens of Russians were killed. Just as worrying for Moscow, Chechen guerrillas, under the warlord Shamil Basayev, had begun to operate in the neighbouring region of Dagestan, again raising the prospect that the Russian federation could disintegrate. Meanwhile the Chechen government seemed quite unable to establish order. But Yeltsin was increasingly unwell, the economy was in tatters, and a series of prime ministers had come and gone in rapid succession, none of which suggested that a reassertion of Russian control in Chechnya was likely (see Chapter 21, C). The latest Prime Minister to be appointed soon determined to show otherwise however. Vladimir Putin, formerly a spy chief and head of Yeltsin's Security Council, believed that the regime might not survive the loss of Chechnya and that action had to be taken soon, both to preserve the federation and to prevent communists or extreme nationalists taking power if Yeltsin should die. Putin bluntly stated on 8 September, 'Russia is defending itself. We have been attacked. And therefore we must throw off the guilt syndrome.'[23] Despite doubts about the fighting fitness of the armed forces, the Russians began large-scale air attacks on Chechen rebel forces on 23 September and launched a ground invasion of Chechnya one week later. By the end of October the Russians had secured their position in the north of the region and had reached the outskirts of Grozny, which was then virtually razed to the ground, before being entered on 6 February. The ruthless campaign, which strongly contrasted with the confusion and ineptitude of 1994–6, created over 100,000 refugees and was widely criticized outside Russia because of reports of atrocities by its army. But at home it established Putin's reputation as a firm leader after years of weakness, it helped him secure the succession to Yeltsin when the latter resigned at the New Year, and it ensured a clear victory in the March 2000

Presidential election—held only weeks after Grozny's fall. Sporadic violence continued, but Putin was unapologetic about the methods used, describing the rebels as 'terrorists', successfully controlling much of the news that came out of Chechnya, and resisting external involvement on the grounds that Chechnya was a domestic matter. In contrast to Lebed, Putin had been able to exploit the issue to secure himself in power and he had done so by removing the possibility of Chechnya's independence that had earlier been conceded.

C. Yugoslavia's Break-Up and the Bosnian War

The Break-Up of Yugoslavia

Although two East European Communist states, Yugoslavia and Albania, had long been independent of Moscow's control radical political changes occurred there in the wake of the collapse of the Soviet system. In Albania the dictator Ramiz Alia, facing daily demonstrations in the capital, Tirana, was forced to concede free elections in late 1990. These were held in March 1991 and, though the communists did surprisingly well in rural areas, emerging in first place overall, there was continued unrest. A coalition government was formed three months later. Further elections, held in March 1992, were won by the Democratic Party, but they had only limited success in tackling the economic troubles of Europe's poorest country: in early 1997 a financial crisis, brought on by the collapse of so-called 'pyramid selling' schemes, led to martial law, the fall of the government, and in April the deployment of an Italian-lead peacekeeping force within the country. But, meanwhile, in Yugoslavia the end of the old order had proved far more divisive and violent. Indeed, the Yugoslav state, founded in 1918 through the union of several South Slav peoples, broke up amid the worst bloodshed seen on the continent since the Second World War, with the upheaval spreading to Albania at the end of the 1990s.

Although Yugoslavia seemed quite stable and

united under both the inter-war monarchy (despite its pro-Serb policy) and between 1945 and 1980 under Marshal Tito (also repressive, but with the non-Serbs better treated), there were always deep ethnic tensions underlying the political order. 'To say that there [was] no Yugoslav nationalism is a euphemism. In 1919 the grouping of southern Slavs was brought about . . . by a will to escape' from German and Hungarian domination.[24] But the southern Slavs fell into several distinct ethnic groups and the Second World War had shown how quickly they could fall into vicious intercommunal conflict: particularly merciless at that time was the anti-Serb campaign of the Croatian 'Ustashas', which claimed around 400,000 victims. The Croats who, along with the Slovenes, populated northern Yugoslavia, had long been wealthier and better educated than the Serbs and the various other groups—Bosnians, Montenegrins, Albanians, and Macedonians—who lived to the south. There were also important religious divisions, the Serbs being Eastern Orthodox, while the Croats and Slovenes were Roman Catholic, and the Albanians and Bosnians included many Muslims. Indeed under Tito, the Bosnian Muslims gained recognition as an ethnic group—not merely a religious group (as they had previously been seen)—in their own right. Tito tried to balance Yugoslavia's constituent republics against each other and, following serious unrest in Croatia, tried to strengthen their powers under the 1974

Constitution. But he could not prevent a growing sense of division before his death in 1980 and, indeed, this constitutional reform probably only encouraged hopes of greater autonomy from the centre. It 'became apparent that the effective power resting at the level of the republics was so strong that the parts were able to dictate the rules to the whole.'[25] Economic problems helped clinch the divide. The northern republics resented having to subsidize the poorer south; the Croats still felt that the Serbs, with control of the federal capital, Belgrade, and leading positions in the armed forces, were politically predominant; and the Serbs disliked Tito's attempts to curb their power, notably his decision to grant autonomy to the province of Kosovo which, though predominantly Albanian by population, had been part of Serbia for centuries.

Tito's successors, a collective group, at first not dominated by any one leader, inherited both inter-republican tension and economic problems of indebtedness to the West, a trade deficit, and poor growth. His attempt to marry central planning with central free-market elements had only succeeded in combining the inefficiencies of the first with the unpleasant side effects of the second, such as inflation and unemployment. In 1983 the IMF had to step in to reschedule the country's debt and, in looking for a radical solution to their problems, the collective leadership, all members of which represented one Yugoslav republic or another, began to look both at greater free enterprise and at a regional solution to their problems. In 1987 this tendency took a new turn when Serbia's communists elected a crafty, outspoken nationalist, Slobodan Milošović, to lead them. In parallel with developments in the USSR, but with far bloodier results, 'What began as rivalry among the republics, communist parties turned into full-blown ethnic politics by the late 1980s.'[26] Milošović not only set out to reduce the autonomy of Kosovo, he also provoked fear in Croatia and Slovenia that, unless resisted, there would be a return to a Serb-dominated system in Yugoslavia. By 1990 there was strong support in Croatia and Slovenia for independence and virtual economic warfare had broken out between them and Serbia, with a severing of commercial links. A clear sign of Yugoslavia's political disintegration was the holding of free elections on different dates in the various republics, with the communists holding onto power firmly only in Serbia and Montenegro. These two, indeed, continued to function together as a federal republic in the 1990s, still calling itself Yugoslavia, while the other republics (not only Croatia and Slovenia, but also Bosnia-Herzegovina and Macedonia) sought independence. Everywhere leaders exploited fears that had been dormant in the early post-war decades but 'the politicians could not have succeeded if there had been no embers to fan.'[27]

After vain attempts to negotiate a loose confederation, Croatia and Slovenia finally declared independence from Yugoslavia on 25 June 1991. A key influence on their decision was Serbia's refusal to accept a Croat as Yugoslav President in May, despite the fact that this should have occurred under the Constitution (which provided for the Federal Presidency to 'rotate' between the republics). Milošović would not at first concede independence and the Serb-dominated Yugoslav Federal army invaded both republics. In a matter of weeks he gave up on the attempt to suppress Slovenian independence, mainly because the Slovenes had prepared their defences well and captured several army units. But in Croatia fighting went on for many months, partly because of the existence there of a large Serbian minority, which made up a tenth of the population and hoped for the formation a 'Greater Serbia', drawing together all of Yugoslavia's ethnic Serbs under the rule of Belgrade. The Croats had elected their own extreme nationalist President, Franjo Tudjman, in May 1990 and were never likely to withdraw their declaration of independence. Faced by such determined resistance, Milošović's aims soon became more modest, involving support for the local autonomy of Croatia's Serbs, notably those living in Eastern Slovenia (on the border with Serbia itself) and Krajina (to the south-west, on the border with Bosnia). In September 1991 the UN introduced an arms embargo on all the former Yugoslavia in an attempt to arrest the drift to war. By the New Year both Serbia and Croatia had agreed to the deployment of a UN 'Protection Force' to police the uneasy balance which had settled between their forces on the ground and which put almost a third of the country under Serb control. The force was formally established on 7 April 1992 but could not prevent several months of renewed fighting in early 1993. Meanwhile, on 15 January 1992, following six months of urging by Germany, the European Community (EC) recognized Croatian and Slovenian independence, despite doubts both about their political stability and their respect for the human rights of minority groups. Recognition, though intended to stabilize the situation by forcing Milošović to come to terms with the end of the old Yugoslavia, proved a fateful decision because it gave international encouragement to the country's rapid break-up without sufficient attention being paid, either to the problems that might follow or to the EC's ability to deal with them. In mid-1990 a majority of EC members had preferred to hold Yugoslavia together, but by October they had come to see its break-up as inevitable and, though they preferred to see this come in an orderly way, had increasingly fallen out with Serbia. The US had followed a similar, reactive pattern, failing to heed warnings from its ambassador in Belgrade that the country was being torn apart by the demagoguery of Milošović and Tudjman. True, the EC did not recognize Macedonia's independence, but that was largely because one Community member, Greece, objected to the use of the name 'Macedonia', claiming that this should be reserved for the northern Greek province of the same name and fearing territorial claims by the former Yugoslav republic. Also, the EC did not at first recognize the independence of Bosnia-Herzegovina, but that was mainly because a referendum on the republic's independence had not yet been held. One was held on 29 February-1 March, followed by a formal declaration of independence on 3 March and recognition by both the EC and America on 6–7 April. The last date also marked the start of the Bosnian War.

War in Bosnia-Herzegovina

It had long been clear that the republic of Bosnia-Herzegovina presented a particularly difficult challenge for those bent on destroying Yugoslavia, because of its complex ethnic mix. About 45 per cent of the population were Muslims who, under President Alija Izetbegovic, elected in November 1990, had increasingly wanted to emulate Croatia

and Slovenia by seeking independence. The November elections were significant for being won by recently created nationalist parties, representing the Muslims, Serbs, and Croats. These parties 'were, in their anti-Communism and their championing of the market economy, very close in terms of programmes', and even formed a joint Cabinet, but they soon found it impossible to continue working together.[28] The Muslims had no wish to live under Serbian domination in a rump Yugoslav state and Izetbegovic consistently argued that the partition of his republic—a course which Milošović and Tudjman discussed in early 1991—made no sense because the republic's ethnic groups were mixed together, so that the drawing of borders between them was a daunting problem. Yet about a third of the population were Serbs, many of who wished to remain tied to Serbia-proper, hence Milošović's interest in dividing Bosnia-Herzegovina and expanding his own republic's borders at its expense. Bosnia's ethnic Serbs began, in 1991, to set up their own autonomous regions as well as, in October, their own parliament. They boycotted Izetbegovic's referendum on Bosnian independence, held their own vote in favour of Yugoslav unity, and on 27 March 1992 declared their independence as the Bosnian Serb Republic. The other important ethnic group were the Croats, who made up about 18 per cent of the population. Many of these wished to be tied to Croatia-proper and, like the Serbs, they too began, in late 1991, to set up their own autonomous communes. Tudjman, who remained as keen on the partition of Bosnia-Herzegovina as Milošović (and with the same motive, of expanding his own area of control), backed the creation in December of a Bosnian Croat state, named Herzeg-Bosnia, under the leadership of Mate Boban.

In early 1992, therefore, Bosnia was on the brink not only of an ethnically based civil war but also of a war in which two other neighbouring republics, Serbia and Croatia, were closely involved. Despite their own animosity over the break-up of Yugoslavia, Milošović and Tudjman found a common cause, at some points, in advocating partition as preferable to Izetbegovic's dream of a unitary state. In mid-March the EC, in an attempt to forestall bloodshed, devised a plan whereby Bosnia would remain a legal entity but be divided into three autonomous units on ethnic lines. It was the first of many similar schemes and it failed to prevent the outbreak of full-scale war in early April. From the start, little mercy was shown by any side. Although Muslims, Serbs, and Croats had lived together reasonably peacefully in the past (the Second World War being the exception rather than the rule), they soon took to driving each other from their homes, setting up internment camps, and massacring opponents. It was the Serb irregulars however, backed by Milošović's Federal Army and airforce, which proved most successful in grabbing territory and most ruthless in the policy of mass killing that they called 'ethnic cleansing'. They quickly seized about half of Bosnia and besieged the capital Sarajevo, whose population of 350,000 was threatened with starvation. At first the Muslims and Bosnian Croats united against the Serb onslaught, which appeared to threaten the survival of them both; but by October there were serious clashes between them, focused on western Bosnia, with its substantial Croat population. By the end of 1992 millions of Bosnians had either been killed, interned, or become refugees, some of them fleeing to neighbouring states.

That such a vicious conflict could break out at the heart of Europe, after half a century of relative stability, put pressure on the EC in particular to find a solution to the problem. The US was anxious to limit its own overseas commitments and still fearful of 'another Vietnam', so that Secretary of State Baker publicly declared 'we don't have a dog in this fight.'[29] Washington was keen to see the EC play a leading role in Bosnia and the Community's creation of a Common Foreign and Security Policy (CFSP) under the February 1992 Maastricht Treaty (see Chapter 20, C), led to real hopes of concerted action by the wealthy, well-armed West Europeans. Indeed, when the war began, the Luxembourg Foreign Minister, Jacques Poos, then chairing the EC Council of Ministers, stated that 'If one problem can be solved by the Europeans it is the Yugoslav problem . . . It is not up to anyone else.'[30] The UN, with recent successes at peacemaking in Angola, Cambodia, and the Gulf War, was also pressed to act. In April-June it agreed to extend its activities in Bosnia, sent a thousand troops to protect food supplies to Sarajevo, and introduced far-reaching sanctions against Serbia, which soon caused shortages and encouraged hopes

that Milošović would compromise on Bosnian independence, as he had already compromised over Croatia and Slovenia.

In August the Security Council agreed to extend the UN's military presence in Bosnia, while the Human Rights Commission condemned the 'ethnic cleansing' policy. But such international efforts proved limited in their impact. The UN only gave protection to humanitarian aid supplies, it did not try forcibly to prevent the fighting, and at least one of its policies could be said to benefit the Serbs: by forbidding arms supplies to all sides the UN, though it sought to be even-handed, made it difficult for the Muslims to secure advanced weapons whereas Milošović helped supply the Bosnian Serbs with tanks, heavy artillery, and aircraft. 'Serb military superiority was an established fact. If the embargo was not lifted . . . the Bosnian government stood no chance of military success.'[31] The US began to criticize the arms embargo, but Britain and France argued that its removal would intensify the conflict and, perhaps, lead Russia to supply the Serbs, thus dragging the major powers in, on different sides. Izetbegovic called for outside intervention to save Bosnia, and he secured some military aid from certain Islamic states, but the EC proved especially reluctant to be drawn into an intractable, ethnic conflict where a full-scale military intervention could prove long-lasting and costly, both in lives and money. The US too showed that there were limits to what it would do to maintain world order when there was no clear American interest at stake and the conflict was so complex. President Bush, who had recently claimed to have ended the 'Vietnam syndrome' through victory in the Gulf War, now said that he did 'not want to see the United States bogged down in any way into some guerrilla war. We lived through that once.'[32]

The US was readier than the EC to condemn Serbia, and Britain and France were particularly loath to escalate tension or even 'take sides', because they had troops on the ground in the UN 'protection force' which would bear the brunt of any fighting. They preferred instead to try to limit the conflict to Bosnia and to avoid intervention from outside the old Yugoslavia, while relying on economic pressures to control Serbia. EC governments made some dramatic gestures, notably with the visit to Sarajevo by France's President Mitterrand in June 1992; and the EC's peace envoy, Lord Carrington, made various attempts to broker a ceasefire. But the August 1992 London Conference (which drew together not only the EC, but also the US, Russia, the former Yugoslav republics, and others, including some Muslim states), showed that, while outsiders were prepared to discuss the principles of peace in Bosnia they would do little concrete to achieve it. After this Carrington gave way to another former British Foreign Secretary, Lord Owen who, along with the UN special envoy, the former US Secretary of State Cyrus Vance, chaired a permanent peace conference, set up in Geneva. In January 1993 this produced the Vance–Owen plan, another bid to end the conflict on the basis of an ethnically divided Bosnia within a single, decentralized state. For a time it seemed to win international support but it also, ironically, helped to intensify the scramble for territory between Muslims, Serbs, and Croats, and by May had run into the sand in its original form.

In May the new Clinton administration talked of forcing a settlement with air strikes and a lifting of the arms embargo ('lift and strike'). It feared that the Vance–Owen plan effectively rewarded Serb aggression, by giving the Bosnian Serbs autonomous control over a large area of the republic. Air strikes would have been the least costly method of US involvement, avoiding a commitment of ground troops, but whether Clinton (who had already raised the proposal in his election campaign) could have pushed the idea through against military doubts and public opposition in Washington was never tested. Britain and France, with Russian approval, predictably rejected 'lift and strike', a decision that led Clinton to back off from military involvement and rely on the UN to defend Muslims. The Bosnian Serbs formally rejected the Vance–Owen plan and chose to fight on, controlling about 70 per cent of Bosnia by mid-1993. Another attempt by Milošović and Tudjman to partition the republic into three autonomous states was made soon afterwards but understandably rejected by the Muslims in August.

By early 1994 the war seemed endless, with Sarajevo still under siege and the Serbs predominant. But a Bosnian Serb mortar attack on a Sarajevo market place in early February provoked international outrage and led NATO to begin the enforcement of a 'no-fly zone' over Bosnia, thus neutralizing the Serbian air force. Such a 'no-fly zone' had first been declared by the UN in late 1992 but relied on the Western powers to be put into effect. NATO was also ready, now, to use its air power to protect UNPROFOR troops and to force the withdrawal of Serb artillery units from around Sarajevo. Perhaps more valuable to the Muslims was the agreement by the Bosnian Croats—concerned by the scale of Serb advances—to form a single federation, with a single parliament and bureaucracy, following considerable diplomatic pressure on Tudjman from the US. This did not quite end local Muslim–Croat clashes but broadly it meant that from now on they would fight against the Serbs together. NATO and US action provoked concern in Russia, which had never recognized Bosnian independence and, encouraged by pan-Slavic feeling, posed as the defender of Serbia. But President Yeltsin was assuaged in April 1994 by the formation of a 'Contact Group' between Russia and the major Western powers (including America, Britain, France, and later Germany), which from now on played a major role in peace attempts. 'For Moscow, the group offered a way to confirm Russia's continuing international standing as a major power.'[33] In summer the Group launched a plan for a twofold partition of Bosnia, between the Bosnian Serbs and the Muslim-Croat Federation. This succeeded in dividing Milošović, who sensed a reasonable chance for agreement and supported the plan, from the Bosnian Serb leader, Radovan Karadzic, who wanted even more concessions and rejected it. The UN even agreed to ease sanctions on Serbia because of Milošović's stance, but this did not prevent an intensified period of conflict later in the year, which was only brought to an end by the onset of winter and a ceasefire brokered by the former US President Jimmy Carter. 'Indeed, even had the great powers set out to manufacture a state of permanent turmoil in the Balkans, it is unlikely they could have created a greater quagmire.'[34]

Achieving the Dayton Accords

Despite its unpromising beginning, 1995 proved the decisive year of the war, partly because of a military revival by the Muslims and Croats, partly because of mutual exhaustion, but also because of America's growing readiness to play an active role, backed by real force, in place of the ineffective EC and UN. In May the UN suffered the humiliation of having hundreds of its soldiers held hostage by the Bosnian Serbs in retaliation for NATO air strikes; they were only released after several weeks thanks to Milošović's help. Then, in July, the UN was powerless to prevent the Bosnian Serb commander, Radko Mladić, from overrunning Srebrenica, a Muslim enclave that had previously been designated a 'safe area' under UN protection. In the worst outrage of the war, Mladić's forces slaughtered about 8,000 of the male inhabitants, before overrunning another 'safe area', Zepa. It was these very events, however, which provoked such a strong response both locally and internationally that determined action was finally possible to thwart Serb ambitions. In early August the armed forces of Croatia, seeking to ease the pressure on their Bosnian allies, suddenly attacked the autonomous Croatian Serb region of Krajina, which was completely conquered in less than a week. In the US, Congress renewed its pressure to allow the Muslims arms and the government now backed tougher NATO action. The National Security Adviser, Anthony Lake, did much to press an active policy and the President was keen to resolve matters before the 1996 Presidential campaign: 'Clinton's political fortunes could not be held hostage to events in the Balkans.'[35] He sent a special envoy, Richard Holbrooke, to try to achieve a diplomatic settlement. Holbrooke, a tough and experienced negotiator, recognized that the offensive in Krajina could mark a turning-point: 'we could not expect the Serbs to be conciliatory at the negotiating table as long as they had experienced nothing but success on the battlefield.'[36] With the Croats and Muslims now making major advances on the ground, NATO aircraft used airstrikes in August-September to force the Bosnian Serbs back from Sarajevo, and in mid-October Holbrooke secured a ceasefire by all sides, to be followed by peace talks. Suddenly 'the conditions were ripe for peace. Milošović might get . . . sanctions lifted. The Bosnian Serbs could head off further losses on the ground. The Croatians could consolidate their new territorial gains.' Ironically, it was the hard-pressed Muslims who were most sceptical about negotiation, though

tempted by the prospect of getting firm Western backing for any settlement.[37]

The peace talks were held in Dayton, Ohio, further highlighting America's close involvement in a settlement, in contrast to the early years of the Clinton administration. The negotiations took the form of proximity talks, with US officials as the mediators between the Presidents of Bosnia, Croatia, and Serbia: there was no place for the Bosnian Serb leader, Karadzic, who was effectively forced to accept the settlement by pressure from Belgrade. Milošović, having been powerless to save Krajina, could see no point in fighting a war where the Bosnian Serbs were in retreat and the UN could revive sanctions against Serbia. Nor could he rely on strong Russian backing: Yeltsin had been critical of NATO airstrikes but, keen to assert Russia's standing in the world and desperate for Western financial aid, he also approved of the Dayton talks, being hopeful of taking part in a peacekeeping force. On 21 November 1995 the Dayton peace accords were finalized. Remarkably similar to earlier plans, the accords created a de-centralized Bosnian government, with 51 per cent of the country in the Bosnian-Serb Federation, the rest under the Bosnian Serbs. This, of course, was far less an area of control than the Serbs might have hoped for a year earlier and it reflected the defeat of their attempt, in the spring of 1995, at complete victory. The settlement, which involved military withdrawals by all sides, a return of refugees to their homes and free elections, was to be policed by a 60,000-strong NATO-led, 'Implementation Force' (IFOR). This would include not only 20,000 US troops but also, to Yeltsin's satisfaction, 2,000 Russian troops, who would be independent of NATO command.

Initially the force was to remain in Bosnia only for a fixed period, but in late 1997 President Clinton, encouraged by European states, extended its mandate indefinitely. In its first few years it did not experience any large-scale challenges, but the Muslims, Croats, and Serbs within Bosnia were far from agreeing joint policies (or even a 'national' flag) for their country, and the renewal of war was a permanent danger. In the first three-way elections for the rotating Presidency, in September 1996, the communities voted on strongly ethnic lines and, while the Muslims confirmed support for

Izetbegović, the Bosnian Serbs chose a suspected war criminal, Momcilo Krajisnik, as their leader. The Implementation Force did periodically capture some of those accused of genocide, who were sent to face a war crimes tribunal in the Hague, which held its first trial in May–November 1996. But many of those who had led the way in ethnic cleansing, such as Karadzic and Mladić, though indicted, remained free.

The conflict had been successfully contained with the former Yugoslavia, and brought to an uneasy settlement, but it had exposed the limits to the powers of both the UN and the EC's common security policy, and had further highlighted the continent's continuing reliance on the US as a guarantee of stability. Washington was praised for the Dayton achievement but its very success in 1995 reinforced arguments that, if it had become active much earlier, perhaps backing the Vance–Owen Plan more forcefully, many thousands of lives might have been saved. Owen himself certainly believed this, arguing that, by failing to support the plan in 1993, the Clinton administration 'had decided that the price of putting US troops on the ground in order to reverse ethnic cleansing was too high ...' and that the cost was two more years of carnage.[38] It is also arguable that, in the short term, 'the Dayton settlement had the general effect of strengthening Milošović's rule in Serbia', because he now seemed to be accepted as a negotiating partner by the West.[39] This was a background factor in the outbreak of violence in another Balkan troublespot, Kosovo, in 1998–9, which however was followed by the fall of Milošović and, later, his own appearance before the Hague tribunal.

The 1999 Kosovo Crisis

In the wake of the 1995 Dayton Accords on the future of Bosnia, several potential causes of tension still existed in the former Yugoslavia. The Dayton Accords themselves might have broken down; there was potential discontent among Serbia's Hungarian minority, mainly living in the Vojvodina region; and there was also the possibility of Montenegro, the only Yugoslav republic remaining in federation with Serbia, declaring independence. Some problems

actually eased in the late 1990s: in 1998 the Serbs pulled out of Eastern Slavonia, their last enclave on Croatian territory. But serious trouble arose in the Serbian region of Kosovo. With a population of two million that was ethnically 90 per cent Albanian, Kosovo had lost its status as an autonomous province of Yugoslavia in 1989. Serbian national identity was closely wrapped up in possession of Kosovo, not least because of the battle of Kosovo where a Serb army was defeated by the Turks in 1389. Until the seventeenth century it had been at the heart of Serbian territory but there had then been an exodus of Serbs as they fled from Ottoman rule. In 1990 the Serbs also closed the local Kosovan assembly and during the 1990s Kosovo became a place where about 20,000 Serbs were resettled from elsewhere in the Balkans, especially from Krajina after it was conquered by Croats in 1995. But only in the first months of 1998 did Slobodan Milošović initiate a harshly oppressive policy in the region, which was condemned on 31 March by the UN Security Council. In May 1998 there was some hope of a negotiated settlement, thanks to a US-sponsored meeting between Milošović and the ethnic Albanian politician, Ibrahim Rugova. But some Kosovan Albanians already feared that Rugova was proving too moderate. A small Kosovan Liberation Army (KLA) had already been formed and had begun to target Serb officials.

Serious fighting erupted in Kosovo around September 1998, with Serb atrocities against the ethnic Albanians, creating tens of thousands of refugees. It was in late September, with no desire to repeat the Bosnian experience and under mounting pressure from the public, that NATO began contingency plans for airstrikes against the Serbs, a step which may have induced Milošović to attempt compromise. On 13 October, after days of talks with the US envoy, Richard Holbrooke, a ceasefire was agreed and an OSCE monitoring mission for Kosovo was then set up. There was renewed violence in December, however, and international concern intensified with the discovery, in mid-January, of a massacre of Albanians in the village of Racak. NATO began a naval build-up in the Adriatic and Milošović was again urged to talk by the 'contract group' (already set up to deal with Bosnia) of America, Russia, Britain, France, Germany, and Italy.

The British and French Foreign Ministers chaired 'proximity talks' between Serbian and KLA representatives in Rambouillet, France in February and a second round in mid-March. The Albanians were ready to accept a deal on autonomy for three years, followed by talks on a permanent settlement but they would not accept Serb demands that the KLA be disarmed. The Serbs, determined to maintain their sovereign rights over Kosovo, refused demands for a NATO peacekeeping force to be deployed and for a referendum on Kosovan independence to be held in due course. One key problem was that Kosovo was constitutionally a part of Serbia and if it were broken off by force it would set an unwelcome precedent for conflicts elsewhere. Borders throughout the Balkans would be thrown into doubt. Indeed, during the whole 1999 crisis, NATO never questioned that Kosovo was part of Serbia. Paradoxically, however, NATO did feel it morally right to intervene in Kosovo by force to protect the Albanians, even though intervention in a 'civil' conflict was unjustified under international law. With the KLA limited in strength and a ground invasion by NATO forces likely to be costly in lives and money, it was decided to put pressure on Milošović by the use of air attacks. These were to be carried out by NATO, rather than a UN force, because UN action could have been impeded by Russia.

The failure of the Rambouillet talks was followed by a rapid escalation of violence. As Serb forces began large-scale attacks on the Albanians the OSCE mission was withdrawn. Last-minute talks between Holbrooke and Milošović on 22–23 March failed to achieve anything. On 24 March NATO began a series of bombing attacks, 'Operation Allied Force', against Serb military targets, communications systems, and fuel depots in Kosovo and in Serbia proper. Economic sanctions against Serbia were also strengthened, with an EU oil embargo enforced on 26 April. Yet rather than backing down, Milošović intensified the efforts at 'ethnic cleansing' and even tried to depopulate Kosovo by driving the ethnic Albanians out. There were about half a million refugees by the end of April, most of them fleeing into the neighbouring country of Albania, itself poor and unprepared for such an influx. Over 100,000 fled south to Macedonia, which had its own Albanian minority. NATO found its expectations of a swift victory unfulfilled. The alliance's air campaign was blunted by poor weather, the Serb military's deployment of 'dummy' targets, and increasing concern over civilian deaths. Another problem for NATO was the potential support for Serbia from its fellow Slavs in Eastern Europe, not least Russia, as well as from other countries who were concerned about American-led military action, such as China. On 12 April, to raise the spectre of pan-Slavism, the Yugoslav parliament voted in favour of a union with Russia and Belarus, whilst Sino–American relations were thrown into the crisis by the accidental bombing of the Chinese embassy in Belgrade by US jets on 7 May. Yugoslavia also tried to take NATO to the International Court over the legality of the bombing campaign. There was evidence of growing opposition to the campaign in some NATO countries, not least Italy, but the bombing was intensified in late May by attacks on Serbia's power and water supplies, and on 27 May Milošović was himself indicted for war crimes by the UN. In early June Milošović showed signs of wanting a settlement and began to pull his army out of Kosovo, which led NATO to suspend its air campaign on 10 June.

The crisis, which cost perhaps 10,000 lives, was widely seen in the West as having been resolved thanks to firm military action, with Serbia the defeated party. This impression was strengthened by the deployment of a NATO-controlled peacekeeping force, KFOR, and by the withdrawal of the last Serbian armed forces on 20 June. By early July most ethnic Albanians had returned to a devastated Kosovo. But the eventual settlement was something of a compromise, with Kosovo remaining part of Serbia, no promise of a referendum on its future, and an undertaking by KFOR to protect Kosovan Serbs as well as Albanians. In addition to the military activity there had also been considerable diplomatic endeavours to bring peace, notably contact between the Russians and the Finnish President, who acted as a mediator with NATO. The Russians even deployed their own element in KFOR, initially beating British and French troops to the key town of Pristina, before accepting overall NATO command on 18 June. (That Russian soldiers could serve in a NATO-led force was itself a remarkable development, ten years after the end of the Cold War.) But Milošović held onto power for barely a year afterwards. He had survived mass demonstrations against him in Serbia in the winter of 1996–7 but in early October 2000 his regime collapsed in the face of renewed demonstrations, following his refusal to accept defeat in a general election that had been held the previous month. His successor, Vojislav Kostunica, surrendered Milošović to the UN for trial in April 2001, improving Serbia's relations with the West in the process. At the same time, the KLA ceased to be valuable to the West as allies and instead, as the new millennium began, were threatening to stir up unrest among ethnic Albanians in Macedonia. Despite the bitter experiences Bosnia and Kosovo, the Balkans remained a potential source of conflict, with Macedonia the most likely flashpoint.

D. **NATO and European Security**

NATO outlives the Cold War

One of the most remarkable features of international relations in the wake of the Cold War was the survival of the North Atlantic Treaty Organization (NATO). NATO had been created in 1949 as a means of strengthening Western Europe's resistance to Soviet influence (Chapter 4, B). Its military role soon became linked to the unclear forces which would compensate for the West's numerical inferiority in conventional forces. In 1967, following the Harmel Report, it had taken on a second role as a participant in East–West détente. But by 1992 the military threat from the Eastern bloc had disappeared and relations with Moscow had moved beyond détente to normality. NATO therefore seemed to lack a *raison d'être*, and it seemed possible that the US and Western Europe would drift apart, divided by trade rivalry and differences in socio-political outlook. Yet the organization not only outlived the Cold War, it thrived in the new atmosphere, playing a more effective role in the Bosnian War (see previous subsection) than did either the UN or the European Community, and by the end of the century it was expanding its membership to former communist states. Declared by its own leaders in July 1990 to be 'the most successful defensive alliance in history', its resilience underlined the fact that, whatever the compromises on European security that Gorbachev and Yeltsin hoped to secure, the Western powers did most to shape the post-Cold War world. This was not only true of the process of German reunification, which, albeit under limitations, brought the former East Germany into NATO in 1994 (see Chapter 20, A); it was also seen in the end of the USSR's conventional superiority in Europe, the winding up (on 1 July 1991) of the Warsaw Pact and the fact that Moscow's preferred security organization, the Conference on Security and Cooperation in Europe (CSCE), was given only a subsidiary role in peacemaking.

In 1989, before the collapse of the Soviet position in Eastern Europe, large-scale cuts in conventional armaments on the continent had already been proposed, by both alliance blocs. In March 1989 the 'Conventional Forces in Europe' (CFE) talks opened in Vienna and, in May, the Warsaw Pact accepted a NATO proposal for common ceilings on various categories of weapon. Around the same time the Bush administration in Washington decided that it must match Gorbachev's long-established propensity to offer arms cuts, by proposing swingeing reductions in conventional forces. The National Security Adviser, Brent Scowcroft, even considered a mutual withdrawal of US and Soviet troops from Europe. By the end of the year, however, it was clear that NATO could expect more than an end to Soviet conventional superiority on the basis of equal ceilings and mutual concessions. Events in Eastern Europe included the beginnings of the Red Army's withdrawal from Czechoslovakia and Hungary and, whilst they remained for the moment in Poland and East Germany, it was clear that the West was now in a commanding negotiating position. It was in order to realize its Cold War 'victory', not least in Germany, while keeping Moscow cooperative, that the US developed a policy known as the 'New Atlanticism'. In a speech on 4 May Bush promised that the next NATO summit would give the alliance a greater political role and US officials put great effort into preparing this. A US-led NATO would be maintained, greater integration would be encouraged in the European Community (EC), and a reunited Germany would be treated as Washington's most important ally in both structures; NATO's role would be altered to allow it to deal with regional conflicts; and, to please the USSR, the role of the CSCE would also be expanded. Reliance on nuclear weapons would also be reduced, James Baker believing that 'a shift in nuclear strategy would do more than anything else to show the Soviets that the world had been transformed.'[40]

The 'New Atlanticism' created something of a crisis within the Western alliance, where Britain and France were concerned about Germany's increased standing. Thatcher especially was sceptical about reducing the role of nuclear weapons in European defence. Talks on the West's future defence doctrine led to a compromise at NATO's London summit of July 1990. Nuclear arms would still exist and might even be modernized, but they were to be fewer in number and treated as weapons of 'last resort': with the USSR's declining strength on the conventional side, NATO need no longer consider the 'first use' of such systems. There were also changes to conventional weapons doctrine, with a less 'forward' defence strategy and the creation of more multinational units. On the political side, NATO welcomed the strengthening of the CSCE and also established closer military contacts with its former enemies by allowing Warsaw Pact members to set up liaison offices in Brussels. The London summit thus proved one of the most important in NATO history, maintaining the alliance's existence, altering its military doctrine, and opening the way to greater cooperation with the East. This was followed by the creation of a North Atlantic Cooperation Council in 1991, as an institutional link to the East Europeans.

Meanwhile, on 19–21 November 1990, a CSCE summit had been held in Paris, which was heralded by France's President Mitterrand as marking 'the end of the Cold War'. The most important document signed was the CFE treaty, which confirmed the end of Soviet armoured superiority and placed equal limits on types of military hardware. These limits were placed both on individual countries and alliance blocs as a whole: thus the maximum number of tanks any county could have was 13,300, but there were only 20,000 in total for either NATO or the Warsaw Pact. Then again, within months the end of the Warsaw Pact left the USSR in a much weakened position than envisaged at Paris: 'Moscow, which had controlled up to two-thirds of the conventional arms in Europe, would now control . . . only about a third.'[41] The Paris conference also included a declaration of democratic rights and individual freedom, emphasizing the ideological triumph of Western values, though there was no machinery to enforce this. And there was, for the first time, the creation of a formal institutional structure for the CSCE, with annual meetings of Foreign Ministers, two-yearly summits, and a 'conflict prevention centre', based in Vienna. But the last were modest steps, of uncertain significance, and over the following years it became clear that the West would only treat the CSCE with the minimum seriousness necessary to placate Moscow. The CFE treaty proved 'far from a panacea for the problems of European security' because in the 1990s crucial questions came to 'have less to do with force levels . . . than with broad political and security arrangements.'[42] In July 1992 another conference, known as 'Helsinki II', agreed to turn the CSCE into a permanent body, to establish a parliamentary assembly, and set up a forum to discuss arms control and disarmament. The Russians still hoped that it might become the most significant security institution in Europe, outmatching NATO. After all, by including the US and Canada, the CSCE stretched in an easterly direction 'from Vancouver to Vladivostok' and there were doubts that NATO could outlive the Cold War. But the Organization of Security and Cooperation in Europe (OSCE), with a Permanent Council in Vienna, was not launched until the December 1994 Budapest summit. Among other diplomatic tasks, it took on a role in peacekeeping (most notably on the disputed Armenian–Azerbaijani border in 1992–4), in conflict resolution (with little success in the case of the former Yugoslavia or Chechnya), and in democratization (it supervised elections in Bosnia and Albania in 1996 and in Chechnya in 1997). It set up an Office for Democratic Institutions and Human Rights, and it appointed a Commissioner for national minorities. But its potential as a pan-European body was undermined by the desire of

East European states to join NATO, and by the fact that, with 54 members by 1995, it was too large and unwieldy to take rapid or effective action on international problems, especially since it had to work on the basis of unanimity, lacked a military force of its own, and could not make decisions binding on its members. The US and Britain were reluctant to rely upon the OSCE, but even its key defender, Russia, was keen to prevent it meddling in Chechnya, which Moscow defined as a 'domestic' issue.

NATO Enlargement and the 'Partnership for Peace'

As it entered the post-Cold War era, NATO had both to satisfy its own members about its continued utility and to meet the demands of the former Warsaw Pact states—and even of some former Soviet republics—for entry to the organization. There were difficult challenges, which alternately threatened the Atlantic alliance with internal division and a revival of tension with Moscow. The threat from within came in the form of the Western European Union (WEU). Originally formed in the mid-1950s, but of little real significant for almost 30 years, the WEU was revived by Mitterrand in 1984 as a potential defence aim of the EC, most of whose members were members of it. In 1990–1 the EC discussed the creation of a Common Foreign and Security Policy (CFSP), as included in the February 1992 Maastricht Treaty, and raised US concerns of a growing US–EC divide on defence matters as East–West tension receded. The US 'did not want to . . . kill off all further movement towards greater Western European defence cooperation', especially if this could remove some burdens from the back of the US, 'but nor did it want to let that movement be in directions it regarded as threatening to NATO.'[43] In November 1991 Bush even publicly warned that the EC must not try to push America out of its European security role, focused on NATO. Ideas for a Franco–German military grouping led to fears of 'a new European defence force wholly dependent of NATO . . . Such an arrangement could presage a future clash of interests.' even within Europe, where

the British and others would resent Franco–German predominance.[44] But by 1993 the incoming Clinton administration could afford to be more relaxed. The WEU and CFSP had remained separate entities, most West European states had no wish to compromise the US security guarantee, and CFSP had failed to prevent war in Bosnia, so that there seemed little chance of a coherent EC policy developing in the field of defence. Indeed, with the mounting difficulties in the Balkans and a desire to concentrate on its own domestic economic problems, Washington was actually eager to see the West Europeans take on a greater defence burden. A compromise position was effectively reached whereby the WEU was seen as reinforcing NATO and the US tolerated a strengthening of WEU activities, allowing the West Europeans to contemplate military operations independent of the US. Thus in 1994 France and Germany created the so-called 'Eurocorps' (first discussed in 1992) but committed it for use by NATO first of all. Also, in 1996 there was an agreement on 'Combined Joint Task Forces', under which the WEU might carry out operations of its own beyond the NATO area whilst using the NATO infrastructure. One result of this was that France, after thirty years of separation, became part of the alliance's military structure once more. Yet it was an exaggeration to claim that NATO's European members were somehow equal with Washington now, or that the West Europeans could really act without US approval. For only America had the long-range air transport facilities necessary for the Joint Task Forces to work and in technological terms US weaponry was becoming ever more advanced relative to its European allies.

If Washington had to temper its continuing military and political superiority in order to cooperate with West European governments, it was just as essential that it tread carefully in the East. Following the collapse of the Warsaw Pact, some of its former members looked to NATO members to provide them with military advice, armaments, and ultimately a security guarantee. Russia, however, was suspicious of Western attempts to enlarge their alliance eastwards and there was particular concern that the Baltic states, on the Russian border, were among those hoping to join NATO. The Atlantic Alliance had, therefore, to steer a delicate course between alienating Russia and disappointing the newly independent Eastern Europeans. 'The West must seek to move closer to Russia ... while keeping NATO as a non-provocative insurance policy in case things go wrong', one study recommended.[45] The Bush administration was extremely cautious about upsetting Moscow and, for most of its first year in office, the Clinton administration seemed more focused on the Asia-Pacific region. Thus the lines of a considered policy were only set in January 1994 when NATO's Brussels summit initiated the 'Partnership for Peace', itself rather tentative and disappointing to the Eastern Europeans. Under this programme, ex-Warsaw Pact members, ex-Soviet republics, and neutral countries could enter into military cooperation agreements with NATO short of full membership. Enlargement might come in due course—and that possibility still disturbed Moscow—but for the moment what was on offer were military consultations, joint exercises and the like, rather than any security guarantee. Despite disappointment with this in the East, countries subsequently signed up for the Partnership, beginning with Hungary in April. By June it seemed that Russia would also join. But, when the Russian Foreign Minister, Andrei Kozyrev, visited Brussels in December he surprised his hosts by refusing to sign. Increasingly criticized by communists and nationalists at home for failing to protect Russian interests, he was determined to show that he was ready to risk a crisis with the West.

Kozyrev's resistance did not last long. As in other spheres, Russia was too weak, economically and politically, to stem the Western advance. On 31 May the Foreign Minister was back in Brussels to sign a Partnership agreement. Yet the fear of a NATO–Russian crisis, which might also complicate attempts to resolve the Bosnian War, continued to hold back the process of actual NATO enlargement. There was a vigorous debate in Western capitals about the wisdom of admitting former communist states to alliance membership, with Germany tending to be more favourable than France or Britain. Germany was keen to stabilize the new democracies in the East and argued that NATO need not be seen as a threat to Russia. But critics countered that neither was Russia a threat to Eastern Europe any longer, so that NATO enlargement was unnecessary. At best such enlargement would draw a collection of militarily weak and financially dependent states into the alliance; at worst it could provoke a new Cold War. In Washington the debate finally favoured the East Europeans and in 1996 the outgoing US Secretary of State, Warren Christopher, said that NATO enlargement could not be put off forever. Boris Yeltsin was facing a re-election campaign in June-July and, rather put his Presidency at risk by helping the communist opposition, Washington decided not to press the issue. But, in his second term, Clinton 'decided to adopt the enlargement of NATO as the emblem of his foreign policy.'[46]

Once the election was over the US concentrated, not on dealing with the East Europeans, but on negotiating an agreement with Russia that would set out the principles for her future relations with NATO. This gave Yeltsin the sense that he was being consulted as an equal, but the result of the talks, which included a Clinton–Yeltsin summit, was an agreement which confirmed that enlargement would take place without providing much succour to Moscow. The NATO–Russian 'Founding Act' of May 1997 created a permanent joint command to discuss security problems (including nuclear safety, peace-keeping operations, and counter-terrorism) but there was to be no Russian veto on NATO activities. It also included a statement that NATO had 'no intention' of deploying 'substantial' numbers of troops in any new member states, but the wording of this undertaking was much weaker than Moscow wanted. Statements that Russia and NATO did 'not consider each other adversaries', and would seek cooperation rather than confrontation, were backed up by Yeltsin with an announcement that Russia would no longer target NATO countries with nuclear missiles. Yet at the signature he also made clear that he was not happy about enlargement. Two months later a NATO summit in Madrid formally invited Poland, Hungary, and the Czech Republic to join with effect from April 1999, and others might follow later. In 1998 President Clinton confirmed that these might include former Soviet republics. The three new members took part in their first NATO gathering in Washington in March 1999, celebrating the fiftieth anniversary of the alliance. It was an occasion that confirmed that a Western agenda had dominated the

---

The 'Open Skies' Treaty, 24 March 1992

The proposal for an 'Open Skies' treaty had first been put forward by President Eisenhower at the 1955 Geneva summit (see Chapter 5, B), with a view to allowing the US and USSR to over-fly each other's territory in order to ascertain that no threatening military preparations were underway. The Soviet Union rejected the idea on the grounds that it infringed sovereignty but it was reinvigorated in 1989 by President Bush, as the Cold War ended. Negotiations began under the auspices of the Conference on Security and Cooperation in Europe in February 1990 and a treaty resulted two years later, signed by NATO states and former members of the Warsaw Pact.

It was an extremely long and complicated document, including as it did a system of quotas for flights by each member country over other states. Signatories were obliged to accept flights in a number proportionate to their geographical area. The treaty, which was of unlimited duration and covered most of the Northern hemisphere, also set out detailed arrangements for notification of flights and specific limits on the type of surveillance equipment that could be used. An 'Open Skies Consultative Commission' was set up in Vienna to supervise it. Since the major powers already had access to spy satellites, it was believed that the smaller countries would gain most from the treaty but the process of ratification proved very drawn out. By 2000, Russia and Belarus had still to approve the treaty, although some limited overflights had already begun between other signatories.

---

post-Cold War security debate in Europe. The contrast with the situation ten years earlier was stark and underlined the diverging fortunes of Washington and Moscow: 'Former members of the Warsaw Pact have not simply defected from that alliance, but have joined what was once its opposition.'[47]

E. From European Community to European Union

The Single Market and Maastricht

The decade following the 'northern enlargement' of the European Community (EC) to Britain, Denmark, and Ireland in 1973 had been marked by disappointments for the organization. 'There were few new initiatives and no further successful integration.'[48] Stagflation had done much to destroy hopes of monetary union, though the 1979 Exchange Rate Mechanism (ERM) helped create some currency stability, especially in the mid-1980s. The years 1979–84 were dominated by arguments over Britain's budget contribution (see Chapter 13, C) and only after that was resolved did the fortunes of the Community begin to revive. In 1986 Spain and Portugal joined to complete the 'southern enlargement' of the EC: Greece had been a member since 1981. This not only increased the size of the EEC to twelve states, but also forced greater spending on social and regional policies, through 'structural funds', to help the poorer Mediterranean states compete in the common market. It also encouraged consideration of institutional reform in order to strengthen the cohesion of the enlarged Community. At the same time Western Europe's economies were growing strongly, making it easier to contemplate a new drive towards deeper integration, and there was widespread concern in Europe about the need to match US and Japanese competition, especially in the production of high-technology goods. In 1984–5 France's President, François Mitterrand, and West Germany's Chancellor, Helmut Kohl, both convinced 'pro-Europeans', worked together to support the establishment of an Intergovernmental Conference (IGC) on Community reform. The other original EC members—Italy, Belgium, Holland, and Luxembourg—strongly supported this, as did Spain, Portugal, and Ireland, three countries who gained significantly from the structural funds. But Britain, Denmark, and Greece were fearful of a loss of national power in the process.

The result of the 1985 IGC was the 'Single European Act'. This was something of a disappointment to keen 'federalist' states like Italy and Belgium. In many ways it simply codified changes that had happened in the Community since its creation in 1957, such as the process by which, since 1974, the leaders had met in biannual summits. But it did include a number of institutional changes which made it easier in future to press on with integration, including greater powers for the European Parliament, and more importantly the expanded use of 'qualified majority voting' (rather than unanimity between all the member governments) in the Council of Ministers. It extended the scope of the EC, to such areas as technological cooperation and the environment, and it included a commitment to Economic and Monetary Union (EMU), which would prove highly significant in future. Most important at the time, however, the Act included the undertaking to create, by January 1993, a genuine 'single market' not only in goods but also in services, capital, and people. 'The key motive behind the Single European Act was to resume the dynamic benefits of one large single market for European industry and commerce', following the growing protectionism of the 1970s.[49] It was mainly the last aspect which convinced the British government to support the reform programme, despite doubts about institutional reform and despite the fact that the process of creating the single market would strengthen the main supranational element in the Community, its executive body, the Commission. To the British, under Margaret Thatcher, the institutional changes seemed modest, whereas the single market promised to create a thriving European market, with a minimum of bureaucratic controls and maximum free enterprise, such as 'Thatcherite' policies aimed to achieve in Britain. An important factor was that, in order to force the british along 'various items on the agenda of integration—completion of the common market ... and the rather ambitious proposals for institutional reform—had been refined ... in a single package', so that all had to be accepted together.[50]

Over the following years, three developments in the EC ran alongside each other. One was the preparation for the 'single market', which was achieved on schedule in 1993, but without quite the dramatic effect that had been hoped, since by then the economic boom of the 1980s had ended. The second was the creation in mid-1988 of a committee under the Commission President, France's Jacques Delors, to study EMU. Britain and Denmark had little liking for this, believing that it could lead on to a full economic union and a major loss of national sovereignty. But the French were keen because EMU would fulfil their old aim of a European currency zone, in which German monetary power would be contained in a wider whole. EMU could also be seen as building on the single market, removing the cost of currency transactions from intra-EC trade and boosting growth. In April 1989 the Delors Plan was published, aiming to bring about a single currency in stages. Delors was in a strong position after successfully achieving the Single European Act and EMU was clearly his next aim. In October 1990 he openly declared 'we need a single currency before the year 2000.'[51] The third important development was also linked to the single market programme and backed by Delors. It was the proposal for a 'Social Charter', published in June 1989, which would guarantee minimum social welfare standards for the people of the Community and so protect them from the potential adverse impact of the free-enterprise Europe that the single market aimed to create.

Events at the end of 1989, with the collapse of Soviet Communism in the East, increased both Mitterrand's and Kohl's desire to strengthen EC institutions, primarily as a way to ensure that a reunited Germany remained committed to a European future, rather than the nationalism and militarism of the past. Indeed Kohl (like Adenauer in the 1950s) made it the central plank of his policy to tie Germany to its Western neighbours. In December 1989 EC leaders both expressed their support for German reunification and agreed that another IGC should meet to look at carrying the Delors Plan into effect. Later it was agreed to set up two IGCs, the second to study a further round of institutional reforms. There was also, already at this time, talk of an 'eastern enlargement' of the Community to former communist states, though in the short term it was more realistic to think of bringing in countries like Austria, Finland, and Sweden who had been neutral during the Cold War but who, with East–West tension in decline, could contemplate joining the EC.

The IGCs opened in late 1990 and the results of their work came before the European summit meeting at Maastricht, in Holland, in December 1991. Here changes were agreed which were embodied in a Treaty on European Union, signed at Maastricht in February 1992. 'The essence of the deal in Maastricht—like so much in the history of the EC—was a Franco–German bargain'[52] The treaty had some similarities to the Single European Act, in that it further strengthened the European parliament, as Germany wanted, and expanded the use of qualified majority votes. But it also included the creation of a single European currency (the key French aim) by 1999 at the latest, it made the people of the EC citizens of a 'European Union', and it adopted the social charter. In all this it seemed a great advance for advocates of integration but there were problems. First, the British government, now under John Major, secured 'opt outs' from both EMU and the social protocol, believing Britain would be more competitive without these. Second, the supranational element in the Community was now only one 'pillar' among three. Other 'pillars' were created in the areas of a common foreign and security policy (CFSP) and of justice and home affairs (JHA), but here the greater coordination of European policy would be achieved by intergovernmental cooperation, on the basis of unanimity between the member states. The limits to supranationalism were further emphasized by the principle of 'subsidiarity', also part of the treaty, under which decisions were supposed to be taken at the lowest possible level, so that local, regional, and national governments retained wide responsibilities.

The Road to a Single Currency

Despite its complexities, the Maastricht Treaty proved to be a seminal point for the Community, the most important reform since the Treaty of Rome itself. Maastricht could not come into operation, however, until it had been ratified by all the members and this proved a difficult process, which for a time threatened to tear the Community apart. In all countries there was debate over what the treaty really signified. Did it, as the British government claimed, mark the limits of integration, with the principle of subsidiarity a brake on the powers of the Commission once the single market was achieved? Or did it, as others argued, represent an important step forward, with strengthened central decision-making and the promise of a leap towards full economic union (with, perhaps, a common tax and spending system) thanks to EMU? In Denmark, one of the most 'sceptical' states where deeper integration was concerned, this debate was especially important because ratification was dependent on a referendum. Denmark, unlike Britain, had won no 'opt out' on the EMU, and on 2 June 1992 its people voted narrowly against the treaty.

The Danish referendum result threw the Community into turmoil, for two reasons. First, most obviously, it was not clear how to save the carefully framed Maastricht agreements, which required ratification by every member. An Irish referendum in mid-June in favour of the treaty could not prevent critics becoming more vocal elsewhere. In Britain, 'Eurosceptics' were euphoric and the government suspended the ratification process. Mitterrand tried to restore faith in the process of integration by calling a referendum in France, which he initially seemed likely to win easily; but by the time it was held, in September, it had become a vote of confidence in the President's leadership and he came within a whisker of losing. Meanwhile, the second problem created by the Danish 'no' vote, was currency instability. By threatening Maastricht the Danes also questioned the likelihood of the single currency ever being achieved and deepened problems in the money markets, which were already troubled by the impact of low growth, rising unemployment, and, importantly, the economic costs of German reunification. By September the ERM was in crisis and several currencies were forced to leave it, including Britain (a member since 1992) and Italy (a founder member). Now, not only was the future of Maastricht in doubt, so was that of a well-established body, the ERM.

The specific problem of Danish doubts was resolved in a second referendum in May 1993, which the 'yes' camp won because the government had now negotiated an ERM 'opt out'. The Maastricht Treaty came fully into operation on 1 November, and at that point the EC became the European Union (EU). But by then there was little popular enthusiasm for integration even in France (where the 1992 referendum had shown the potential strength of the Eurosceptical lobby) or Germany (where there was real concern over the loss of the Deutschmark, which had become the greatest symbol of national economic virility since 1949). With Europe back in the economic doldrums the ERM was still unstable and, in early August 1993, became virtually meaningless when its remaining members decided to widen their possible fluctuations of exchange rates to a massive 15 per cent. Over the following years it seemed that a single currency, the most significant promise of the Maastricht Treaty, might not come about or that, if it did, there would be few members. In order to join, countries had to achieve certain 'convergence' targets involving public debt, inflation, and budget deficits, and it seemed that even France and Germany might fail to meet these. Even as it became a 'Union', the EC seemed to be diversifying in ever more confusing ways. Britain and Denmark had their EMU opt outs. Seven countries, including France and Germany, joined together in the Schengen agreement (effective in 1995) to end passport controls on their shared borders, but the other members stood aside. Most countries were members of the Western European Union, which some saw as a potential defence wing for the EU, but Ireland was stubbornly neutral. Thanks to such diversity the British government now advocated a 'multi-speed' Europe in which, instead of seeking integration of a common pace, members would pick-and-choose the areas in which they cooperated. In 1996–7 a review of the Maastricht Treaty was carried out by another IGC but the results, codified in the Amsterdam Treaty, were very modest. In retrospect Maastricht represented 'the high-water mark of the elite-driven reform agenda of the 1980's relaunch … provoking a popular backlash which subsequently strained the reform process.'[53]

Yet, however difficult the mid-1990s proved, the EU did continue to advance and in January 1995, it was joined by Austria, Sweden, and Finland. This was soured somewhat in February 2000, when the ultra-right-wing Freedom Party entered Austria's coalition government, leading to seven months of sanctions by the EU. But agreement had already been reached, in the early 1990s, that there should be a further enlargement in future to certain East European countries, including Poland, the Czech Republic, and Hungary. Talks on the eastern enlargement got underway in 1998 and, like the proposed expansion of NATO, showed that some key Western organizations, which had been created during the Cold War, could continue to thrive after it. In 1993–4 greater spending on 'structural funds' was agreed to help the poorer members with infrastructure projects in such areas as transport. There were further measures to create uniform practices across the EU, as in the field of health and safety at work and in 1997, when the Conservatives were voted out of office in Britain, the new Labour government signed up to the social protocol of the Maastricht Treaty. The most important, positive sign of all, however, was that, despite their economic difficulties, the single currency idea remained intact and that most members remained committed to it. The 1997 target date may have been missed but in the spring of 1998 it was decided that, of those who wished to proceed, only Greece failed to meet the convergence criteria. The rest—minus Britain, Denmark, and Sweden, none of whom wished to be part of the 'first wave' of members—created the 'euro' in January 1999 as an accounting currency. Actual euro notes and coins began to circulate in January 2002. The EU therefore fulfilled the ambitious hopes of Maastricht in the end, but there were those who warned that EMU had become a political aim rather than an economically sound proposition. Only the new century would show whether the euro provided a new boost for trade and integration or whether, by locking some states into a position of poverty, it became a divisive element in the Union.

NOTES

1. Steven Hurst, *The Foreign Policy of the Bush Administration* (Cassell, New York, 1999), 64.

2. Philip Zelikow and Condoleezza Rice, *Germany Unified and Europe Transformed* (Harvard University Press, Cambridge, 1995), 128–30.

3. George Bush and Brent Scowcroft, *A World Transformed* (Vintage Books, New York, 1998), 203–4.

4. Timothy Garton Ash, *In Europe's Name* (Random House, New York, 1993), 349–50.

5. Don Oberdorfer, *How the Cold War Came to an End: The US and the Soviet Union 1983–90* (Jonathan Cape, New York, 1992), 391; Edvard Shevardnadze, *The Future belongs to Freedom* (Sinclair-Stevenson, London, 1991), 134.

6. James Baker, *The Politics of Diplomacy* (G. P. Putnam's Sons, New York, 1995), 198.

7. Raymond Garthoff, *The Great Transition: American-Soviet Relations and the End of the Cold War* (Brookings Institution, Washington, DC, 1994), 412.

8. Quoted in Stephen Szabo, *The Diplomacy of German Unification* (St Martin's Press, New York, 1992), 75.

9. Bush and Scowcroft, op. cit., 196–7.

10. Mikhail Gorbachev, *Memoirs* (Doubleday, London, 1996), 532.

11. Ian Clark, *The Post-Cold War Order: The Spoils of Peace* (Oxford University Press, Oxford, 2001), 92.

12. Mary Fulbrook, *Interpretations of the Two Germanies* (Macmillan, Basingstoke, 2nd edn., 2000), 84.

13. Vladimir Zubok, 'Gorbachev and the End of the Cold War', *Cold War History*, 2 (2002), 62.

14. Oberdorfer, op. cit., 402.

15. Gorbachev, *Memoirs*, op. cit., 372 and 346.

16. Robert M. Gates, *From the Shadows* (Touchstone, New York, 1997), 496.

17. Michael Beschloss and Strobe Talbott, *At the Highest Levels* (Little, Brown, Boston, 1993), 304.

18. Boris Yeltsin, *The View from the Kremlin* (HarperCollins, London, 1994), 105–6; Mikhail Gorbachev, *On My Country and the World* (Columbia University Press, New York, 2000), 83–4; Gorbachev, op. cit., 658.

19. G. D. G. Murrell, *Russia's Transition to Democracy* (Portland, Brighton, 1996), 184.

20. Anatol Lieven, *Chechnya: Tombstone of Russian Power* (Yale University Press, New Haven, 1998), 101.

21. Leon Aron, *Yeltsin, a Revolutionary Life* (HarperCollins, London, 2000), 570.

22. Lieven, op. cit., 145.

23. Quoted in Boris Yeltsin, *Midnight Diaries* (Public Affairs Press, 2000), 335.

24. Michael Foucher, 'Western Europe and the Balkans' in F. W. Carter and H. T. Norris, (eds.), *The Changing Shape of the Balkans* (University College London Press, London, 1996), 124–5.

25. 'Introduction' to D. A. Dyker and I. Vejvoda (eds.), *Yugoslavia and After: A Study in Fragmentation, Despair and Rebirth* (Addison-Wesley Longman, New York, 1996), 19.

26. John Lampe, *Yugoslavia as History* (Cambridge University Press, Cambridge, 1996), 325.

27. Tim Judah, *The Serbs: History, Myth and the Destruction of Yugoslavia* (Yale University Press, New Haven, 1997), 309.

28. Xavier Bougarel, 'Bosnia and Hercegovina', in Dyker and Vejvoda, op. cit., 98.

29. Quoted in R. A. Melanson, *American Foreign Policy since the Vietnam War* (M E Sharpe, Armonk, 1996), 256.

30. Quoted in Mark Almond, *Europe's Backyard War* (Heinemann, London, 1994), 32.

31. John Hulsman, *A Paradigm for the New World Order* (Macmillan, Basingstoke, 1997), 129.

32. Quoted in Hurst, op. cit., 217.

33. Ivo Daalder, *Getting to Dayton* (Brookings Institution, Washington, DC, 2000), 28.

34. Christopher Bennett, *Yugoslavia's Bloody Collapse* (Hurst, London, 1995), 236.

35. Daalder, op. cit., 166.

36. Richard Holbrooke, *To End a War* (Modern Library, New York, 1998), 73.

37. William Hyland, *Clinton's World: Remaking American Foreign Policy* (Praeger, Westport, 1999), 41.

38. David Owen, *Balkan Odyssey* (Victor Gollancz, London, 1996), 196.

39. Noel Malcolm, *Kosovo: A Short History* (Macmillan, London, 1998), 353.

40. Baker, op. cit., 258.

41. Garthoff, op. cit., 535.

42. Phil Williams, 'CFE and the future of NATO', in J. Philip Rogers (ed.), *The Future of European Security* (Macmillan, Basingstoke, 1993), 144.

43. Hurst, op. cit., 211.

44. Peter Duignan and L. H. Gann, *The US and the New Europe* (Hoover Institutuion, PaloAlto, 1994), 257.

45. Trevor Taylor, *European Security and the Former Soviet Union* (Royal Institute of International Affairs, London, 1994), 137.

46. Hyland, op cit., 43.

47. Ian Clark, *The Post-Cold War Order: The Spoils of Peace* (Oxford University Press, Oxford, 2nd edn., 2001), 92.

48. Martin Dedman, *The Origins and Development of the European Union* (Routledge, London, 1996), 123.

49. Dedman, op. cit., 126.

50. Paul Taylor, 'The New Dynamics of EC Integration in the 1980s', in Juliet Lodge (ed.), *The European Community and the Challenge of the Future* (Pinter, London, 1989), 8.

51. Quoted in Desmond Dinan, *Ever Closer Union?* (Macmillan, Basingstoke, 1994), 418.

52. Charles Grant, *Delors: Inside the House that Jacques Built* (Brealey Publishing, London, 1994), 206.

53. Philip Lynch, Nanette Neuwahl, and Wyn Rees (eds.), *Reforming the European Union: from Maastricht to Amsterdam* (2000), 235.

21 US Predominance and the Search for a Post-Cold War Order

A. US Foreign Policy in the 1990s: the Search for Direction

The Bush Administration

George Bush had come to power in January 1989 with an uncertain political programme, either at home or abroad, but with considerable experience in foreign policy-making behind him. In the 1970s he had served as ambassador to the UN, envoy to China and Director of the CIA, whilst in the 1980s, as Vice-President under Reagan, he had held special responsibilities in the international field. As President he very much concentrated on world affairs and drew an experienced, loyal team around him of old colleagues like the Secretary of State, James Baker, and National Security Adviser, Brent Scowcroft. Criticized at first for failing to define

his policies promptly, and with some Republicans doubting the depth of his conservativism, he nonetheless had a series of foreign successes before the end of 1991 and was prepared to take tough, military action when he felt it justified. By then he had overthrown General Noriega of Panama, successfully managed the collapse of communism in Eastern Europe, encouraged the peaceful replacement of the Sandinista regime in Nicaragua, backed Helmut Kohl in achieving the reunification of Germany, triumphantly dealt with Saddam Hussein's invasion of Kuwait, made progress on Arab–Israeli talks, and saw the disintegration of the Soviet Union. His cautious, pragmatic, orderly approach carried both advantages and disadvantages. On the one hand he escaped any major disasters abroad and avoided antagonizing the USSR or rekindling the Cold War; but, on the other hand, he seemed undynamic and at the mercy of events—he could hardly, for example, claim credit for the demise of communism in Eastern Europe and the USSR—and he failed to give the world a sense of the overall direction of US foreign policy once the Cold War ended. He did not appreciate early enough that, with the Cold War apparently 'won', the American people had become preoccupied with domestic concerns, notably the poor shape of the economy. Here at least Bush was a victim of his predecessor's policies: the high defence spending and tax reductions of 'Reaganomics' may, in some eyes, have resuscitated free enterprise and helped 'defeat' the Soviets, but they also left behind a massive budget deficit, which climbed to $230 billion in 1990. It was possible to reduce defence spending from the late 1980s onward but this did not come quickly enough to work any economic miracle and in 1991–2 there was a depression. Furthermore, the President failed to demonstrate how his concentration on foreign policy benefited the US and 'by late 1991 the public began to feel that Bush's international activities were actually hurting his ability to handle the economy.'[1] In 1992 his much younger Democratic opponent, Bill Clinton, exploited concerns over lack of investment in the economy to achieve a victory in the Presidential election that had seemed highly unlikely twelve months before. Bush also alienated the public by appearing to renege on his initial promise of 'no new taxes'. And, even in the foreign policy field there were criticisms, especially because 'Bush and his team were frequently intensely secretive, unaccountable and contemptuous of Congress.'[2]

For a time in 1990–1 it appeared that Bush might seek to build policy around the concept of a 'New World Order'. It was clear, even before the Kuwait crisis, that trying to secure old Cold War aims was no longer adequate. But what was now required remained far from clear. The USSR, even before it collapsed and even if it retained a huge nuclear arsenal, had ceased to be the ideological and security threat that it had been as recently as 1985. With the important exception of China—a country that continued to present its own special problems for Washington—very few Marxist-Leninist regimes had

failed to collapse or come to terms with US predominance by 1992. Neither was the advance of democratic institutions only a product of Communist retreat. In Chile the Pinochet dictatorship came to an agreed end in March 1990 while in South Africa apartheid was being wound down. Yet, whatever the scale of hopeful changes, Bush believed the US must remain engaged in world affairs to ensure peaceful developments and remove new threats, and Saddam Hussein's invasion of Kuwait seemed to justify this. The decision to place the punishment of aggression at the centre of the 'New World Order' concept 'accurately reflected the administration's conservative understanding of world politics, its preference for stability to reform, and its identification of stability with the status quo', notwithstanding all the changes going on around it.[3] But the New World Order was never defined very precisely by Bush. When he explained it to Congress on 11 September 1990 he spoke of 'a world where the rule of law supplants the rule of the jungle, a world in which nations recognize the shared responsibilities for freedom and justice', but this left much to be interpreted.[4] It has been said that 'many of the broader objectives sought by the United States since 1989 actually bear a strong resemblance to those it pursued before the end of the Cold War', including a rejection of isolationism, support for democracy, and a tendency to see the new order as coterminous with American national interests.[5] This had been equally true of the Truman Doctrine, though that had understandably emphasized anti-communism as well.

One sympathetic study of Bush's foreign policy has argued, however, that 'the New World Order was about much more than resistance to aggression: it did, in fact, represent a relatively coherent and plausible strategy for US foreign policy in the post-Cold War era'; in addition to 'order' it set out broad aims of peace, democracy, and free trade, which Bush hoped to achieve in cooperation with other countries and which had the sympathy of most Americans.[6] Another study accepts that a global, non-discriminatory trade system and a new 'system of collectivised security' were two vital aims of Bush, and adds, regarding the third, that 'liberalism was consciously . . . deployed at the end of the Cold War as an instrument for consolidating its . . . beneficial outcomes.' Liberalism became a vehicle for encouraging capitalism and democratic rights in former communist societies, for justifying 'humanitarian intervention' where states became anarchic and for ostracizing those regimes that did not want to be part of the new order. In all areas, however, the US was actually highly selective in the way it interpreted Bush's principles.[7] A major problem was that such objectives, like free trade, peaceful cooperation, and the fostering of liberal democracy, were more difficult to translate into precise strategic priorities when there was no single major power that presented a threat to them. US policy during the Cold War had hardly been flawless—Vietnam was testament to that—but it had an overriding strategic direction, boosted Presidential power, and at times (albeit less consistently after Vietnam) fostered bipartisanship in foreign affairs. Certainly, Bush wished to achieve some specific aims, such as strategic arms control agreements, the strengthening of the United Nations, and the punishment of Saddam Hussein's attack on Kuwait. But arms control agreements seemed less urgent after the Cold War; the powers of the UN were limited, as seen in its failure to deal with the conflict in Bosnia; and Saddam's Iraq, whatever its threat to the Middle East, was hardly a substitute for the Soviet Union as a rival to the US for global hegemony. There was also the old question of whether the US possessed the will and the resources to shape the world it wanted, especially when there was 'a more fragmented, and more politicized foreign policy process' than during the Cold War, with Congress very assertive and the press more active in whipping up public opinion.[8]

The very ease of the military victory over Iraq, added to the end of the USSR, led Americans to feel that they were safe from outside attack, with no major enemy to worry about, a view that would persist until the terrorist bombings of New York and Washington on 11 September 2001, which were reminiscent of the shock caused by Pearl Harbor. Such feelings were reinforced by the belief, which predated the end of the Cold War, that America's allies in Europe and Japan should bear more of the burden of their own defence. As to the UN, despite Bush's encouraging rhetoric, it was hardly a popular institution in the US, being seen as financially wasteful, dominated by a Third World agenda, and likely to draw America into problems that were none of its concern. The determination of the US to avoid any part in the Bosnian War in 1992 drew many of these elements together. Most Americans felt they had no security stake in the conflict, they wanted to leave its resolution to the European Community, and were baffled by the extreme hatreds of such ethnic conflict. Yet an important, paradoxical development in the outlook of the American public was that, while power-political motives for action had become less important, idealistic ones loomed larger, leading to the greater popularity of 'humanitarian intervention'. The desire to foster liberal values, linked to the lack of a major enemy, led the American media to demand action in Somalia in 1992, where the risks of involvement seemed few and the opportunity to end human suffering clear. This was despite the fact that the US, in the wake of Reagan, was unenthusiastic about huge-scale development aid to the Third World. The emotional and hasty decision to intervene in Somalia was arguably one of Bush's few foreign policy errors, but one taken in order to satisfy public and media opinion and done with the approval of President-elect Clinton, who soon inherited the problem.

New Agendas: the Narcotics Trade and Environmentalism

Apart from the 'New World Order', before the 'war on terrorism' was declared by George Bush Jnr. in 2001, there were several candidates for the issue that might provide a focus for American foreign policy after the Cold War. One was that Washington should treat so-called 'Islamic fundamentalism' as its chief ideological enemy following the Communist retreat, and certainly the policies of Iran, the country most associated with 'fundamentalism' in US eyes, remained a key concern under Bush. But there was no major US–Iranian crisis and fundamentalism was an amorphous factor in world politics (even if a potent bogey in America). Furthermore, any attempt to treat 'fundamentalists' as enemies ran the risk of creating an unnecessary religious conflict between Christians and Muslims, when numerous Muslims states—Egypt and Jordan, Pakistan and Morocco—

were US allies. A more promising focus for popular hatred was the drugs trade, which Bush in September 1989 described as the 'gravest domestic threat' to America. The issue was far from new: the US government had been trying to tackle the international commerce in narcotics since before the First World War. But, again, the end of the Cold War meant that the problem loomed larger. Already, under Reagan, the US has decided that it was easier to tackle the *supply* of drugs from traffickers and growers abroad rather than the *demand* from addicts at home. There was particular concern, from the mid-1980s, about cocaine production in the Andean nations of South America, where economic problems made the profits of the drugs trade tempting. Colombia was seen as the worst problem and here the US Drug Enforcement Agency, as well as some American military advisers, worked with the government to intercept shipments, seize the financial assets of known traffickers, and eradicate crops of coca leaf. For a time Colombia also allowed the extradition of traffickers to the US. Yet many Colombian officials themselves became implicated in the trade and the scale of the local 'drugs war' soon threatened the country's political and social fabric, as well as taking the focus away from measures to relieve poverty. A Presidential candidate was assassinated by the Medellin drugs cartel, headed by Pedro Escobar, in 1989; and in 1990 the government decided on a more moderate line which, among other things, meant that Escobar gave himself up, being imprisoned for only a year. By 1992 Bush was spending $10 billion per year on drug control but cocaine use in America continued to grow apace.

If the war on drugs failed to provide a successful centrepiece for foreign policy-making, another growing international concern—the state of the environment—was even more problematic. Like the concern over narcotics, fears for the environment were far from new in 1990. The UN had held its first environmental conference in Stockholm in 1972 and there had already been several attempts to secure international cooperation in the area, such as the 1983 London Convention to prevent the dumping of toxic and nuclear waste at sea. There were obvious problems with persuading all the world's countries to agree and pay for environmental protection measures, but the dangers of

doing nothing were just as clear. As well as periodic environmental disasters, such as the meltdown of the Chernobyl nuclear reactor in the USSR in April 1986 and the massive oil spill from the tanker *Exxon Valdez* in Alaska in March 1989, there was growing scientific evidence of two types of damage to the earth's atmosphere. One was the erosion of the ozone layer (protecting the planet from ultraviolet radiation) due to the production of chlorofluorocarbons, or CFC's, a process which was likely to lead to increasing problems with skin cancer and which had first been recognized in the mid-1980s with the discovery of an ozone 'hole' over Antarctica. The other was 'global warming', or the 'greenhouse effect', which it was claimed was occurring because of a mixture of the burning of fossil fuels and deforestation, and which was likely to lead to a rise in sea levels, threatening low-lying areas around the world. 'The environmental system, in particular the earth's climate, used to be regarded as relatively resilient . . . in the face of human insults. But now it is widely believed to be . . . unpredictable.' In the early 1990s the environment became an important area in which traditional interpretations of 'security' were challenged because, the 'threat is not seen . . . as being posed by weapons systems . . . and by one state against another, but by a range of environmental problems . . . that are threats to everyone.'[9] There was actually action taken at a conference in Montreal in 1987 to protect the ozone layer by reducing certain chemical substances that were harmful to it. One sign of the potential divisions that could arise between countries over the environment however, was that whereas the developed countries wished to see an end to the destruction of tropical rainforests (especially the Amazon), the developing countries focused on the pollution coming from industry in the developed states. About a third of the world's CFC emissions, for example, were produced by the US. Other concerns included the production of 'acid rain' by industry, the growth of the world's population (it was 5.5 billion in 1990 and likely to double by 2070), the overworking of land in the Third World, and the gradual exhaustion of non-renewable raw materials. In 1987 the UN's Brundtland Commission had called for policies of 'sustainable development' but it was not clear how to achieve this.

One of the key international events of Bush's last year in office was the 'Earth Summit' in Rio de Janeiro. The largest conference ever held to that date, though it was surpassed as a gathering of world leaders by the September 2000 UN Millennium summit, it involved both governments and various international bodies. It led to a number of agreements, most importantly the Biodiversity Treaty, to protect plants and animals from extinction, and the Climate Change Convention, which established the principle of emission targets for 'greenhouse' gases in developed countries and obliged governments to report gas emissions. But the summit was just as noteworthy for the divisions it revealed between those present. Oil producers were reluctant to accept measures that limited oil use; small island states were preoccupied with the dangers of rising sea levels thanks to global warming; the Pope was opposed to population control; and the agreements reached represented a 'lowest common denominator approach' in which US leadership was scrupulously lacking. Washington not only refused to sign the Biodiversity Treaty, it only reluctantly accepted the Climate Change Convention (its doubts being mainly due to the omission of developing countries from it). The Convention was, in any case, hardly radical. It allowed emissions to rise globally by 3 per cent by 1997. For America it was clear that environmentalism was a complex area, in which national interests were to be protected and agreements should be negotiated grudgingly.

Indeed, environmental problems and narcotics simply served to highlight how confusing the world was, now that old, Cold War reference points had been stripped away, and this very fact made the US public less ready to seek involvement abroad. Yet there was one area where, despite the complexities of 'globalization', Americans could not wish themselves off the world scene. In finance and commerce the world was ever more independent, with huge cross-border investments, a reliance on trade for ever larger proportions of national income and the possibility, thanks to the 'communications revolution', of moving large sums of money worldwide in an instant. The US itself relied on external trade for about one-fifth of its GNP and its share of world output in 1992 was about a quarter (a big reduction on the 40 per cent of 1950 but still formidable). It

was partly to safeguard this position that Bush pursued a North American Free Trade Area. This proposal, signed in late 1992, only came to fruition under Clinton, for whom freer trade eventually provided something of the long-sought, central reference point in post-Cold War foreign policy.

The Clinton Administration and 'Enlargement'

Clinton beat Bush in the 1992 election mainly by concentrating on domestic economic concerns. The former Arkansas governor, accused of 'draft dodging' at the time of the Vietnam War, certainly did not share his predecessor's great experience in the field of national security. Clinton's priorities on entering office were ambitious but almost all focused on the domestic sphere: to reduce debt while using government policy to stimulate growth; to carry through welfare, health, and education reforms; and to deal with environmental threats. But, he had made clear the need to protect US markets abroad, he had criticized Washington's alliances with dictatorial regimes, and he urged an active policy, not excluding military force, to back global democratization. Furthermore, as the Somali situation became desperate (Chapter 21, E) and the Bosnian war continued, it was soon clear that the new President could not ignore events overseas. Along with his Secretary of State, Warren Christopher, he was accused of lacking any direction abroad and Republicans liked to portray this as part of a general weakness in the President's make-up. One early academic study of his foreign policy was damning in its judgement: 'In 1993, Clinton was the leader of an unrivalled superpower; six years later he was a badly crippled lame duck. . . . A magnificent opportunity to shape the international system had been missed.'[10] While he became mired in financial and sexual scandal at home, and was even impeached, a series of crises abroad, from Somalia and Rwanda to Bosnia and Kosovo, called into question the notion of a democratic world order. But Bush, for all his experience, had already shown how difficult it was to provide a sense of cohesion and direction to foreign policy after the Cold War and probably no one could have done so. The US was, apparently, 'secure' in terms of facing no imminent military threat from abroad. Talk of America's declining power vis-à-vis other states, a strong feature of political debate in the mid-1980s, no longer seemed relevant. Its economy was twice as large as Japan's, the world's second largest; its nuclear power and technological prowess were amply demonstrated by such developments as the Trident missile and Stealth bomber; and in the eyes of some it was to be feared as a potential hegemon, dictating its own values and policies to the rest of the world. This was especially the case in the economic sphere where it insisted that developing countries adopt free-market policies that were interpreted by the countries themselves as a recipe for Western exploitation. On the other hand, some countries, as with Britain and Germany in NATO, still welcomed US leadership and it could not escape its predominant position in the UN.

By 1993 it was evident that American power could not be turned into any consistent bid for hegemony. The world was too complex to interpret events reliably; the US people were too reluctant and emotional to act abroad with consistency; and Congress was too determined to assert itself against the White House, especially after the November 1994 elections when the Republicans won control at both Houses for the first time since 1954. This was largely because of problems with Clinton's domestic policies but it had an impact on foreign policy because Republicans generally 'sought a more modest role for the United States since the Soviet threat had disappeared. . . . In their view American policy should be based on tangible self-interests rather than ambiguous global concerns.'[11] Also, the policy-making machine through which American power was exercised—from the military and the intelligence services, to development aid and embassy staffs—suffered from spending cuts, because they appeared less necessary in the wake of the Cold War. In the case of the CIA things were made worse by the exposure of two of its officials as Russian spies: Aldrich Ames in February 1994 and Harold Nicolson in November 1996. By the end of Clinton's first term of office, important decisions in American foreign policy sometimes seemed at the mercy of certain interest groups, minorities, or state governments (the last were entitled to introduce their own economic sanctions against foreign

countries). Most notable was Clinton's decision to concede to pressure from Jesse Helms, right-wing chairman of the Senate Foreign Relations Committee, for sanctions against those foreign countries trading with Cuba. Such a step was of doubtful international legality and it provoked bitter condemnation abroad, even if it satisfied the Cuban community in Florida.

Yet Clinton's foreign policy could nonetheless claim some notable successes by the time he left the White House in January 2001 and he definitely had not shirked difficult decisions, including military commitments. The administration had supported the move to majority rule in South Africa (see Chapter 22, A), as well as the breakthrough Israeli–Palestinian agreement (see Chapter 22, C). It had maintained good relations with Russia while consolidating Bush's arms control agreements (see Chapter 21, C), had restored the elected President of Haiti (see Chapter 21, E), oversaw a thaw in relations between North and South Korea, and took an active role in moves towards a settlement of the 'troubles' in Northern Ireland, where there had been sectarian violence since 1968. The peace moves in Ireland stalled in early 1996 but revived in the summer of 1997 and reached a deal on creating a new Assembly, representative of all groups in the province, in April 1998. Even more remarkably, the Clinton administration had stepped in to achieve a Bosnian settlement (see Chapter 20, C). The strategic vision may have been difficult to see but, while 'Clinton got off to a rocky start, he eventually developed into an able practitioner of Band-Aid diplomacy', helping heal various wounds.[12] Furthermore, the closing months of 2000 saw the first Foreign Ministers-level talks with Iran for twenty years (at the UN in September) and Clinton's own visit to Vietnam, the first by a President since the war there. The only real disaster had come in Somalia but, of course, the original decision to intervene had been Bush's. Also, at home the economy was much improved, with consistent growth, falling unemployment, and a move towards a balanced federal budget (finally achieved in 1998). It was largely thanks to the fulfilment of his economic promises that Clinton was re-elected in November 1996, defeating the lacklustre Bob Dole.

Despite the criticisms levelled at him by Republicans, Clinton was not lacking in ideas for a central direction for US foreign policy, even if these were developments of certain aspects of Bush's New World Order. His first National Security Adviser, Anthony Lake, a former head of the State Department's Policy Planning Staff under Jimmy Carter, recognized the need to explain foreign policy not in terms of the balance of power but of 'enlarging' the regions of world living under liberal democracy, the corollary of which was that opponents of the liberal order—such as Cuba, Iran, and Iraq—were to be isolated and condemned as 'rogue states'. It was in September 1993 that Lake said 'the successor to a doctrine of containment, must be the strategy of enlargement—enlargement of the world's free community: we must counter the aggression—and support the liberalization—of states hostile to democracy.'[13] At first it was hoped that the US would act in line with its allies and the UN, but in his second term Clinton seemed more ready to act unilaterally (as in Haiti) and accepted the limitations of the UN (as in Bosnia). Apart from dealing, on the whole successfully, with regional problems, the Clinton administration also continued to devote considerable energy to arms control and non-proliferation (see Chapter 21, C) and tackled those 'new' security problems that had become important under Bush. Where the narcotics trade was concerned, the Drug Enforcement Agency had a major success in Colombia in 1995, by breaking up the Cali drug cartel, but lasting success proved as elusive as under Bush. The drugs traffic simply splintered among smaller groups and was, if anything, more difficult to control. Colombia, its independence undermined, was increasingly resentful of US policy, and in Washington sympathy grew for the argument that the drugs problem should be tackled by focusing on users in America itself, and not offloaded on the rest of the hemisphere. However, the Clinton administration continued to pour money into Colombia. In 2000 a new $1.5 billion aid package was agreed, mainly in the form of military assistance to tackle the drugs trade. By then much of the trade was under the control of leftist guerrillas, who had been fighting against the government since the 1970s and whose popularity among the rural poor was, if anything, boosted by their opposition to American intervention.

On the environmental front, there was a series of meetings culminating in the ten-day Kyoto Conference of December 1997. But despite talking a great deal about its enthusiasm for environmentalism, not least through Vice-President Al Gore, the Clinton administration proved no more imaginative and responsive on this front than had Bush. Nor was the environmental cause helped by the Republicans' electoral successes in 1994. As the world's largest carbon emitter, the US was reluctant to accept radical cuts in 'greenhouse' gases by an early date. Agreement was eventually reached on a complex system of targets, aimed at reducing emissions by 5 per cent by 2012, but developing countries were not covered (it would have caused them difficult economic problems if they had been) and there was no agreement about how to punish those who exceeded their targets. There was also concern that the agreement allowed countries to 'trade' emission targets, so that if one did better than the target, another could do worse. Doubts were immediately raised about America's ability—and willingness—to meet the targets, though pressure to do so was particularly strong from its allies in Europe. In November 2000 a UN World Conference on Climate Change, made up of one hundred and eighty states, broke down largely because the US and the European Union could not agree on ways to cut greenhouse gas emissions. There was, however, a Biosafety Protocol agreed that year, which allowed countries to protect themselves from 'genetically modified' products.

Interdependence and Free Trade Areas

One essential point, of which Clinton was always aware, and which built on Bush's policies, was that the future health of the US economy was heavily dependent on the state of the world economy, so that, whatever some Americans might wish, the country could not retreat from global involvement: foreign and domestic policies could not be divorced. Since the mid-1980s it had been recognized that the global economy was becoming more 'interdependent' as multinational companies, cross-border services, especially in the banking and insurance sector, and information technology broke down interstate boundaries. Companies with high export earnings were particularly likely to back free-trade zones. 'What engaged Clinton most . . . was the economy, and he and his advisers . . . appreciated the intimate relationship between the domestic and the international economy.'[14] The result was a series of initiatives designed to safeguard America's competitiveness in the market, which among other things made the Department of Commerce (under Commerce Secretary, Ron Brown, until his death in an air crash in 1995) a key factor in US foreign policy-making. The general theme was a reduction of trade barriers. There was some activity on a global level in 1994. The World Trade Organization (WTO) was created as a successor to GATT in setting rules for commercial exchange, resolving trade disputes, and carrying our trade talks. Meanwhile, GATT's latest comprehensive look at the reduction of trade barriers, the so-called Uruguay Round, had been completed and promised to cut tariffs by 38 per cent between 1995 and 1999. But the US could not guarantee that the WTO would achieve a more open global commercial system in future—it failed, for example, to agree in 2000 to negotiate a new round of reductions in trade barriers—and other moves by Clinton involved arrangements with regional economic groups. There was always a danger that such a policy might fragment the world economy, but such groups were forming anyway.

With the end of the Cold War, the significance of America's trade relations with Western Europe and, more especially, Japan became more significant relative to their political ones, placing emphasis on competitive rather than cooperative elements in relationships among the developed countries. Japan exported twice as much to, as it imported from, the US but continuing pressure on Tokyo to rectify the situation had little effect and America's trade deficit proved difficult to reduce. Nonetheless, while being ruthless in protecting US interests, Clinton decided that the best route to preserve and expand trade opportunities was through multilateral action. In this he built on the policies of his predecessor: Bush too had backed free trade in general but had also tried to build up specific trade links, especially to Latin America, in order to counter European and Japanese competition. Where the European Union

(EU) was concerned, there had been growing concern from American farmers over the Common Agricultural Policy as a discriminatory trade measure but, despite continuing arguments, Clinton felt the EU to be too important to European stability to risk a fullyfledged trade war. Instead, a series of annual US–European summits was inaugurated in 1994; and in 1995 a 'New Transatlantic Agenda' was agreed, which aimed to boost the volume of transatlantic trade by, for example, establishing common safety regulations. Other measures to maintain healthy trade included the renewal of China's 'Most Favoured Nation' status (despite political differences and US complaints about Chinese trade practices) and Clinton's September 1994 announcement that the 1972 Jackson–Vanik Amendment (which had linked a trade deal with the USSR to its policy on Jewish emigration) need no longer hinder Russo-American commerce. The Clinton administration also tried to identify 'big emerging markets' in the developing world, trying to foster greater trade with them.

The most interesting developments in US trade policy in the 1990s concerned North America and the Asia-Pacific. Although it was Clinton who focused most on commercial issues, it was Bush who signed the North American Free Trade Area (NAFTA) agreement, with Canada and Mexico, just before losing the 1992 election. This built on a US–Canadian trade treaty of 1988 and moves to liberalize the Mexican economy after the debt problem of the mid-1980s. Mexico had pressed strongly for such a deal since mid-1990 and the Bush administration took up the idea despite Canadian doubts. Other states in the Western hemisphere were also showing an interest in free trade areas as a way to develop trade, if not to protect themselves from US competition and two other groupings slightly predated NAFTA: the Common Market of the South (MERCUSOR), dominated by Brazil and also including Argentina, Paraguay, and Uruguay, included two-thirds of South Americans; whilst twelve Caribbean islands formed another common market (CARICOM). Two other groups already existed in the Central American Common Market (Costa Rica, El Salvador, Guatemala, Honduras, and Nicaragua) and the Andean Group (Bolivia, Colombia, Ecuador, Peru, and Venezuela). NAFTA created a single trading zone of over 350 million people (rivalling the EU but without the latter's political integration), facilitated US investment in Mexico (a cheap source of labour), and was also intended to stabilize Mexican politics by boosting its economic performance. Mexico was responsible for half of Latin America's exports to the US and relied on America for two-thirds of its export sales. Bush had also had hopes of developing it into a Western hemisphere free trade area and this proposal too came to fruition under Clinton. Following two summits of American countries, in Miami in December 1994 and Santiago in April 1998, from which Cuba was the only absentee, thirty-eight countries agreed to negotiate a 'Free Trade Area of the Americas' (FTAA) within ten years.

Yet, from the outset NAFTA was dogged by controversy. The free trade area, to be created by 2009, did not include the free movement of labour, for example, because of Congressional fears of large-scale Hispanic immigration from Mexico. Even then, it had a difficult path through Congress, where there were criticisms of Mexico's environmental record and the danger of cheap goods flooding into the US from its southern neighbour, putting US firms out of business. The public and labour organizations were also divided over the wisdom of the initiative. Once it came into effect on 1 January 1994, NAFTA fell foul of events in Mexico. That very day an uprising began among the Chiapas Indians, led by the 'Zapatista' resistance movement; and later in the year the troubled Mexican economy, already heavily in debt, required a large—$20 billion—reserve package from the IMF to stay afloat. By 2000 an uneasy peace had been reached with the Zapatistas but Mexico was still barely able to cover its short-term debts. Meanwhile the FAA had also developed problems. Although Central and South American states recognized their reliance on US finance and markets, the MERCUSOR states in particular feared American domination and were keen to develop their own links to the EU and other trading blocs. Brazil, especially, demanded concessions from the US before signing up to the FTAA. Partly because of such difficulties, Clinton also focused on the Pacific.

The process of Asia-Pacific Economic Cooperation (APEC) also predated the Clinton administration, being launched, largely thanks to Australian and Japanese encouragement, in 1989. Until then, the expanding markets of the 'Pacific Rim' had lacked any regional forum for discussion. APEC was a modest body, principally an annual meeting of government representatives with consultative powers only, largely because South-East Asia nations were keen to safeguard the primacy of their own cooperation through ASEAN (see Chapter 22, E). A permanent Secretariat was only established in September 1992; based in Singapore, it studied ways to harmonize trade controls and improve mutual access to markets. But the organization had a wide membership: the inaugural conference in Canberra in November 1989 was attended by America, Japan, Australia, New Zealand, Canada, South Korea, and all the ASEAN members, and subsequently, it was joined by China, Taiwan, and Hong Kong (1991), Mexico and Papua New Guinea (1993), and Chile (1994). On coming into office Clinton, who believed the Pacific Rim would prove an important area for economic growth in future, decided to make APEC more significant. At first he even seemed likely to concentrate on Asian-Pacific matters to the detriment of transatlantic ones. At Seattle in November 1993 he presented his version of APEC as a vehicle to liberalize trade and open greater US–Asian commercial links. A year later, at Boyar, Indonesia, a resolution was passed in favour of a free trade area among APEC's industrialized states by 2010, drawing in the developing countries by 2020. Serious planning for the reduction of trade barriers began after another meeting at Subic in the Philippines in 1996.

But as with NAFTA, the story of APEC was a troubled one, with modest advances dogged by mutual suspicion. Whilst the US criticized some APEC members over human rights and the pirating of intellectual property, the developing Asian nations accused America of dictating its own moral and political values to them, and of placing selfish aims, such as trade liberalization and the protection of patent rights, above successful development policies. In the US itself, furthermore, Clinton's interest in free trade projects was greeted by most Americans with indifference and in 1997 he was forced to give up on an attempt to have Congress grant him the power to negotiate 'fast track' trade deals. The tendency to set up trade groupings on a regional basis—NAFTA and APEC added to older

George Bush and his Foreign Policy Team, 1989–1993

George H. W. Bush Snr., had enormous experience of foreign policy before becoming President. Born in 1924, his father was a New York banker who served as Senator for Connecticut (1952–63). After wartime service as an airforce pilot, the President-to-be studied law at Yale but then distanced himself from his privileged, East Coast background by going to work in the oil industry in Texas. He made a fortune from an offshore drilling company which he founded before going into politics. He became a Republican Congressman in 1966 and served under Nixon and Ford as ambassador to the UN (1971–2), envoy to China (1974–5), and Director of the CIA (1976–7). In 1980 he ran for the Republican Presidential nomination, which was won by Ronald Reagan. Reagan, however, chose Bush as his running mate and he served as Vice-President for two terms (1981–9), before being elected President in his own right. In 1991, with the end of the Cold War, and following the successes of the Gulf War and Panama, Bush was very popular, but he nonetheless lost the 1992 election due to America's economic problems. The disappointment of being a one-term President was offset by the election of his son, George Bush, Jnr., to the White House in 2000.

As President, Bush Snr. gathered a close-knit group around him on foreign policy matters. His Secretary of State was James A. Baker (b. 1930), educated at Princeton and the University of Texas, who served in the marines (1952–4), and practised law before becoming Secretary of Commerce under Ford in 1975. Baker ran Bush's presidential bid in 1980, then served as White House Chief of Staff (1981–5). He returned to the Chief of Staff position in August 1992, in a vain attempt to reinvigorate Bush's election campaign. As Secretary of State he was criticized by some for arrogance, but paradoxically was also seen as mediator par excellence, helping to bring an end to the Cold War by building up a good working relationship with Moscow.

The National Security Adviser, Brent Scowcroft (b. 1925) had also served in the Ford administration in the same position (1975–7). A US airforce officer and West Point graduate, Scowcroft had gained a doctorate from Columbia University in 1967 and has spent much of his military career in teaching and in planning, before serving as Deputy National Security Adviser to Henry Kissinger in 1973–5. In contrast to Kissinger, Scowcroft did not take a leading public role in policy-making but acted more as a coordinator of national security work.

Richard Cheney, the Defense Secretary for almost all the Bush Presidency, the youngest of all the foreign policy team, was born in 1941. Educated at Yale and the University of Wyoming, he worked for Republican Congressman Don Rumsfeld, who became Ford's Chief of Staff in the White House in 1974. When Rumsfeld moved to become Secretary of Defense in 1975, he recommended that Cheney succeed him. Cheney then became the youngest person to serve in the position and was thus in a high position in the Ford administration at the same time as Bush (CIA director), Baker (Commerce), and Scowcroft (National Security Adviser). After the Ford Presidency, Cheney entered a political career of his own, being elected Congressman for Wyoming. As Secretary of Defense under Bush, his most important task was the organization of Operation Desert Storm. In 2000 his links to the Bush family helped him to become Vice-President to George Bush Jnr.

Another leading member of the 1989–93 administration was Colin Powell, the Chairman of the Joint Chiefs of Staff throughout the period. The son of Jamaican immigrants, Powell (b. 1937) had become a professional soldier, fought in Vietnam, and rose to command a brigade in the prestigious 101st Airborne Division. In contrast to the rest of the Bush team, he had no role in the Ford administration but was an adviser to the Defense Department under Reagan in 1983–6 and served as National Security Adviser in 1987–8. The youngest ever chairman of the Joint Chiefs, he was rumoured to have ambitions of becoming President in the long term. In 2000 he became the first black Secretary of State.

---

groups like the EU and ASEAN—also threatened to fragment the management of the world economy, hardening the perception of the post-Cold War world as an increasingly divided place. Then, in 1997–8, the financial crisis in East Asia (see Chapter 22, E) threatened a new world recession and particularly undermined the efforts of liberalization through APEC.

B. Enforcing Order: the Gulf War of 1990–1991

The Iraqi invasion of Kuwait on 2 August 1990 took the world by surprise and was rapidly seen as the first great 'test' of the international community's ability to maintain stability in the wake of the Cold War. Saddam Hussein's action threatened to create another oil crisis, driving up prices. It challenged the recent revival in status of the United Nations. And it raised questions about the readiness of the US and USSR to cooperate with one another, in a situation where Moscow had links to Iraq but Washington was determined to liberate Kuwait. When it became clear that the last aim could only be achieved through the use of military force the crisis also raised questions about the unity of the Western alliance, the ability of the US to maintain good relations with other Arab states, and America's determination to prosecute a war when memories of Vietnam were still vivid. The war proved of central importance to the Bush administration because it forced the US to try to define a post-Cold War foreign policy and proved, on the whole, a major success. But there were criticisms of American policy too: 'that it failed to deter Iraq's initial invasion of Kuwait; that it refused to accept a negotiated settlement.; that it resorted to force without determining whether . . . economic sanctions would achieve its goals; and that it ended the war too early, allowing Saddam Hussein to survive.'[15]

Saddam's Invasion and America's Reaction

With the end of the eight-year Iran–Iraq war in 1988 (Chapter 17, C), Saddam Hussein inevitably had to concentrate on rebuilding his country structurally and militarily. The last thing Iraq wanted, or so it seemed, was another major conflict. Yet the decision to invade Kuwait, a country that had aided Saddam during his war with Iran, was closely linked to Iraq's reconstruction needs. The country was about $80 billion in debt and could only realistically hope to pay this off by exporting oil. But oil prices had been drifting down since the early 1980s and attempts by the oil-exporting countries of OPEC to reverse this

trend by introducing quotas to limit production had little effect. To Saddam's annoyance, Kuwait was one country that broke the quota policy and so was blamed for pushing prices lower. For Iraq, the virtual halving of oil prices in the 1980s was a terrible blow and arguments with Kuwait on this issue alone had created enormous ill-feeling by 1990. Saddam wanted Kuwait and Saudi Arabia, both oil-rich yet sparsely populated states with none of Iraq's economic problems, to demonstrate Arab solidarity by cancelling their wartime loans to Baghdad and handing over some of their oil production quotas to him. In February 1990 a series of talks began involving Iraqi and Kuwait representatives, and in July Kuwait agreed that it would restrict its oil exports, an undertaking that would take effect in October. By then Kuwait had been invaded and, on 8 August, annexed by Iraq, which now controlled one-fifth of OPEC oil production.

The need to obtain greater oil reserves was the primary, but not the only, reason for Saddam's action. Iraq also had a territorial claim on Kuwait from the days of the Ottoman Empire and had already threatened to invade it in 1961, when British troops had been rushed to its defence. The small Sheikhdom, strategically placed at the top of the Persian Gulf, had been severed from the Ottoman Empire by Britain in 1899 and controlled as a protectorate from London. The Iraqis were therefore able to condemn it as a creation of British imperialism. But their own claim over it had severe flaws. Kuwait had had a separate existence under the Ottomans, being ruled by the Al-Sabah family since 1756; Iraq itself had been created by the British from several Ottoman provinces after The First World War; and Iraq had also recognized Kuwait's independence in 1963. There were, however, disputes over the exact line of the Iraq–Kuwait border and Saddam had pressed these, alongside the arguments over oil and loans, in the July 1990 talks. The demanding tone of the Iraqis in these negotiations and the fact that Saddam massed his army on the border provoked concern among Arab capitals and in the US. US–Iraqi relations had been strained since the end of the Iran–Iraq War reduced Washington's need of Saddam as an ally and in April 1990 he threatened to attack Israel. It was well known that, despite Iraq's other problems, Saddam had continued to maintain substantial armed forces, had a capability in chemical and biological warfare, and was trying to develop both long-range weapons and a nuclear reactor. He had Soviet-supplied Skud missiles, which could strike as far as Israel, and he had been secretly armed by the Western powers during the war with Iran. Yet few expected he would actually invade his small, vulnerable neighbour and the US ambassador to Baghdad, April Glaspie, told him that Washington had no firm position on the border disputes with Kuwait.

Once the invasion took place, the main question was how America would react and whether it could persuade its allies, the Arab world, and the USSR to support its action. In America there was little enthusiasm for war but plenty of reasons to contemplate it. Saddam had carried out a blatant act of aggression against a pro-Western state and, from his position in Kuwait, could now threaten a more important US ally and oil producer, Saudi Arabia. Whether an invasion of Saudi Arabia was likely did not matter: after Kuwait, Saddam seemed capable of anything and he had similar arguments with the Saudis, over oil and loans, as he had had with Kuwait. The US had helped build up the Saudis' military power since the early 1970s and they had become even more important to the defence of American interests in the Gulf since the fall of the Shah. If Saddam did overrun Saudi Arabia, he would have a huge proportion of the world's oil reserves and it would be very difficult to remove him. Liberating a small country like Kuwait would be an easier matter and President Bush soon decided that this must be done, ideally by diplomatic pressure backed by the threat of force, but if necessary by the use of such force. In the past the US had hoped that its local allies could maintain stability in the Gulf region or, in the 1980s, it had been able to rely on the deadlocked Iran–Iraq war to check the ambitions of both Baghdad and Tehran. But now direct US intervention seemed essential to deter an invasion of Saudi Arabia, punish Iraq, and restore Kuwaiti independence. In deciding to make a stand, Bush personally seemed impressed by a most simple argument: 'we could not let aggression stand.' He told his children, 'I look at today's crisis as "good" versus "evil". Yes, it is that clear.'[16] But some critics pointed out that the US had been less than eager to punish some past acts of aggression—not least Saddam's invasion of Iran in 1980, which had also been designed to give him greater oil resources and better access to the Gulf, and which was launched on the pretext of a border claim. Then again, perhaps the President felt betrayed by the invasion of Kuwait, for 'Bush had been a Saddam supporter, both under Reagan and after he became President.'[17] Another factor was that, with the Cold War over and Kuwait no democracy, Bush was forced to revert to 'World War II metaphors and referred to Kuwait as a victim of Nazi-like aggression',[18] when America's real motives for action had more to do with the fact that about half of America's energy needs were met by Middle East oil.

The Liberation of Kuwait

After invading Kuwait, Saddam portrayed himself as a hero to his fellow Arabs, hoping to win over allies in the region and make it difficult to remove him. He believed the Soviets would support him and doubted that the Western powers would have the necessary will and unity to fight. At first he seized dozens of Westerners in Kuwait as hostages and, though these were later released, he made it clear that he would extract a heavy price if attacked, perhaps launching Skud missiles against Israel. Eventually, when the allies struck he also set Kuwait's oil wells alight. But it was soon clear that, as in 1980, he had severely miscalculated the effects of military action, underestimating the resilience of his enemies and overestimating the strength of his position. He made a diplomatic settlement virtually impossible on 12 August when he made a withdrawal from Kuwait conditional on a US withdrawal from Saudi Arabia and an Israeli withdrawal from all the occupied territories. The Western powers were ready to fight, with Margaret Thatcher telling Bush on 21 August, 'this is no time to go wobbly.'[19] The Soviets did no more than try to postpone the US assault and few countries, even in the Arab world, offered Saddam much support. Indeed only the

Marxist government in Yemen, King Hussein of Jordan, and Yasser Arafat's Palestinian Liberation Organization defended him. Some Arabs, notably the Egyptians, who had a centuries-old rivalry with Iraq for the leadership of the Arab world, were keen to condemn the annexation of Kuwait and welcomed US action, as of course did the Saudis. The UN, partly thanks to US–Soviet agreement, was quick to condemn the invasion and call for Iraq to leave Kuwait. With such strong support it was unsurprising that Bush decided to rely on military force to deal with Saddam, rather than economic sanctions, which would take time to make effective and might not work. And America's 'Rapid Reaction Force', built up since the Carter Doctrine on Gulf security in 1980, and already used to joint operations with other powers, was deployed in Saudi Arabia at a remarkable rate. By the end of the year about 400,000 US troops were there, alongside more than 100,000 from other Western states, including Britain and France.

Washington succeeded in creating a broad coalition against Saddam while preserving its own domination of the decision-making process on the war and minimizing differences with Moscow. When the Iraqi invasion took place the US Secretary of State, James Baker, was actually in the Soviet Union for talks with Edvard Shevardnadze, and believed 'that we needed the Soviets more than anyone else'.[20] They immediately agreed to back a UN arms and trade embargo against Iraq. This included the end of oil exports from Iraq and Kuwait, thus cancelling one of the gains Saddam hoped to make from the invasion. Other OPEC countries, not least Saudi Arabia, raised their production levels to stabilize supplies and, though oil prices climbed steeply for a time, they soon fell back. Later, on 24 August, Shevardnadze supported another UN resolution, allowing military action to help enforce the sanctions policy; and on 8 September Bush and Gorbachev met in Helsinki, agreeing that force might be used to remove Saddam from Kuwait. This policy was not popular with everyone in the Soviet government and Gorbachev's special envoy, Yevgeny Primakov, travelled to Baghdad to press a diplomatic solution on Saddam. The Russian was only one of many emissaries to do so. But by late September it was clear to most observers that

Saddam would not withdraw and that all-out war was inevitable. The argument that America must act quickly if it was to preserve the anti-Saddam coalition was highlighted by Arab outrage at the killing of twenty-one Palestinians on Temple Mount in Jerusalem in early October. There were also doubts in Congress in November about the rising number of troops in the Gulf and some support for a policy of economic sanctions. But US propaganda exploited Saddam's human rights record and supposed nuclear ambitions to maintain domestic and international support for the war preparations.

The most important UN resolution on Kuwait was that of 29 November, which authorized the use of 'all means necessary' to free the country and which set a deadline of 15 January for Iraqi's withdrawal. It was the first time since the outbreak of the Korean War in 1950 that the UN Security Council had approved military sanctions against an aggressor and, although China abstained on the vote, it showed a remarkable and unprecedented sense of unity between the permanent members. A number of governments, apart from Kuwait and Saudi Arabia (who provided $15 billion each), helped pay for the war effort, including Germany and Japan (who provided about $20 billion between them). Eventually about three-quarters of American military costs were covered by its allies. There was still room for division: the French, whilst ready to liberate Kuwait, questioned the wisdom of restoring the authoritarian Al-Sabah family; Gorbachev subsequently tried to get the 15 January deadline pushed back; and efforts at a diplomatic solution continued, with last-minute trips to Baghdad by China's Foreign Minister, Qian Qichen and the UN Secretary-General, Perez de Cuellar. Talks were held in Geneva on 9 January between Baker and the Iraqi Foreign Minister, Tariq Aziz, but Saddam refused to withdraw from Kuwait. Bush then secured a Congressional vote in favour of war and on 16 January 1991 allied forces, led by the US, began air attacks on Iraq. The aim of this was to weaken Saddam's war machine and ensure a rapid victory for the allies when they eventually launched a land campaign. Although, in contrast to the Vietnam War, US media coverage of the conflict was closely controlled by the military, there was still a deep fear in the US of large casualties from the war and the Senate had only approved the use of force by a majority of 5. There were now 540,000 American troops in the Gulf, approximately the same figure who had been in Vietnam at the height of that conflict. The air war lasted for six weeks and, despite some civilian deaths and a failure to destroy Saddam's chemical weapons production, it succeeded in 'softening up' the Iraqi military, while also demonstrating the allies' easy domination in the air and US technological virtuosity, with its Cruise missiles and Stealth aircraft. Saddam did fire over eighty Skud missiles at Israel and Saudi Arabia, but they were randomly targeted and some were brought down by US 'Patriot' missiles.

Finally, on 24 February the allies, under the US General Norman Schwarzkopf, launched Operation 'Desert Storm' to liberate Kuwait. Saddam had earlier promised his people 'the mother of all battles' but it proved a one-sided contest. The Iraqis were bundled out of Kuwait almost as quickly as they arrived, with allied forces also striking into southern Iraq. About 100,000 Iraqis were killed for the loss of only about 150 allied troops, many of these accidentally killed by their own side. Within four days it was all over. On 27 February Saddam agreed to comply with UN resolutions on Kuwaiti independence and the US military, as well as Bush, could congratulate themselves on a successful campaign, with Kuwait restored to freedom and none of the feared mass casualties among American troops.

The War's Impact

In the wake of victory Bush declared that the US had 'kicked the Vietnam syndrome'.[21] But, while avoiding a repetition of Vietnam, the US arguably made new mistakes, allowing Saddam and most of his armed forces, including his elite troops, to survive. The Gulf War, as a conventional war against an undoubted aggressor, had little in common with Vietnam anyway and, as later seen in Somalia, it did not mean that America was now equipped to deal with civil conflicts. A closer parallel could be drawn with the Korean War in 1950, where the attempt to conquer the Communist North, after liberating the South, had turned to disaster. A whole-sale invasion of Iraq to depose Saddam could have tarnished the US claim to be liberating a victim of

aggression, it would have threatened the carefully constructed relationship with Moscow, it might have stirred up ill-feeling among other Arab countries, and, it might have led to a long-running, costly occupation of the country which the Iraqi people would have resisted, the US people would have come to oppose, and which would have gone beyond what UN resolutions allowed. An alternative leader might not actually prove better than Saddam, who for a time appeared cowed and humiliated. Nonetheless, the failure to remove Saddam carried its own costs. Allied forces had to remain in Kuwait and Saudi Arabia, and from time to time had to be strengthened because the Iraqi dictator again seemed threatening as happened in October 1994. Bush made plenty of remarks that suggested he wanted rid of the Iraqi leader. He evidently hoped Saddam might be toppled by a coup but all attempts to launch one ended in failure. Baker later admitted, 'we never really expected him to survive a defeat of that magnitude.'[22] But that is what Saddam did and he even became involved in an attempt to assassinate George Bush in 1993.

A particular problem was that, under the ceasefire agreement which ended the war, the UN was able to inspect Iraqi territory to check for chemical, bacteriological, and nuclear weapons, which were to be destroyed. This was confirmed by a UN resolution of 3 April 1991, which effectively dictated a settlement to Iraq and also included recognition of the existing Kuwait border, and a demilitarised zone between the two countries, the return of stolen Kuwaiti property from Iraq, and the fulfilment of Iraqi debt obligations to Kuwait. Meanwhile the trade embargo stayed in place. But periodically Saddam would refuse to work with the UN inspectors or to comply with UN sanctions. 'Years before he had determined to build himself weapons that would force his neighbours . . . to acknowledge his power. Now the victorious allies made him accept a group of officially sanctioned spies, charged with rooting out the weapons.'[23] But when he resisted the US was tough in its response. This happened in January 1993, when there were cruise missile attacks on Iraq; in October–November 1997, when Russian mediation defused the crisis; in January–February 1998 when the UN Secretary-General, Kofi Annan, persuaded the Iraqi leader to conform with UN inspections after a massive US and British force gathered in the Gulf; and again in December 1998, when US and British airstrikes took place over four days. Saddam also continued to offend the West by oppressing the Kurdish and Marsh Arab minorities in Iraq, a policy that led in April 1991 to the creation of 'no-fly' zones over the north and south of the country, enforced by allied aircraft. This attempt to provide some protection for the minorities had only a limited effect however and, like the weapons inspections, it became another long-term commitment that carried its own dangers of violent confrontation: in August 2000 there were US and British air strikes on Iraqi anti-aircraft defences, which were threatening allied aircraft in the 'no-fly' zones. Despite their supposed sympathy for the Kurds the Western powers were unwilling to contemplate a Kurdish state because this would offend Turkish and Iranian opinion: they too held land that was populated by Kurds and Turkey was a NATO ally.

The Gulf War, then, was undoubtedly a success for the US, but not untainted. Bush had asserted his country's leadership at the UN as the Cold War ended, had kept the USSR and China quiescent while punishing a Third World dictator, and had constructed a remarkable alliance, including European states, Japan (at least on the financial side), Israel, and Saudi Arabia. By adhering to the limited aim of liberating Kuwait the US and its allies had kept the moral high ground, given the military a clear objective, and ultimately allowed the clear nature of their victory to emerge more starkly. Kuwait might be devastated and its oil wells in flames, but it had been liberated nonetheless, and in only a few days. The US had projected its power on the other side of the world, fully justifying the concept of the Rapid Reaction Force and perhaps it did help, to some extent, to reverse the lack of faith in military power that had followed Vietnam. Yet Saddam remained in power, eventually outlasting most of the allied leaders—Bush, Thatcher, Mitterrand—who had fought against him. Sanctions on Iraq remained too, but with steadily lessening support in the UN, and the danger to Kuwait had not disappeared. The US carried more influence in the Persian Gulf but had to pay for this with a significant, continuing military presence. And, as events in Bosnia soon showed, Operation Desert Storm did not necessarily provide a model for resolving crises elsewhere. It was a unique war sparked by Saddam's miscalculation of the world's response. Other conflicts would look less clear-cut in moral terms and be less open to a conventional military solutions.

Saddam Hussein (b. 1937)

Saddam came from a poor peasant background in Tikrit, Iraq and entered radical politics as a teenager, joining the secular Ba'ath Party. In 1958 he was imprisoned for his activities and in 1959 was involved in an attempt to assassinate the Prime Minister, Abdul Kassem. Wounded by one of Kassem's guards, Saddam fled into exile in Nasser's Egypt, was sentenced to death in abstentia but used his time abroad to study law at Cairo University. He was able to return to Iraq in 1963, when the Ba'ath briefly held power, but was imprisoned again for his part in a coup attempt the following year. Escaping from prison in 1967 he took part in yet another coup, this time successful, in July 1968, after which he became Vice-President of the 'Revolutionary Command Council' led by General Ahmed Bakr. During the 1970s Saddam was particularly responsible for building up the regime's secret police force and in 1976 was promoted a general in the army.

Saddam effectively overthrew Bakr in 1979, though nominally the latter retired. Promoted not only to the Presidency, but also to the leadership of the Ba'ath Party and the rank of Field Marshal, Saddam exerted a strong grip on power. A veteran of coups, imprisonments and exile himself, he proved ruthless at wiping out opponents and potential rivals. He even shot one of his own ministers dead during the course of a cabinet meeting. Despite the costly deadlock of the 1980–88 war with neighbouring Iran, he retained the loyalty of the military and the secret police. Defeat by a US-lead coalition in the Gulf War of 1990–1 provoked some internal discontent and led to both isolation abroad and grave economic problems within Iraq. Yet Saddam clung onto power, only being ousted by a second invasion in 2003.

CHRONOLOGY:
THE GULF WAR 1990–1991

1990

25 July	April Glaspie, US Ambassador to Baghdad, tells Iraq that growing dispute with Kuwait is up to Arabs to resolve.
2 August	Kuwait invaded by Iraqis.
6 August	UN initiates economic sanctions against Iraq; and King Fahd of Saudi Arabia asks for US military assistance.
7 August	First American aircraft arrive in Saudi Arabia. British, French, and others follow.
8 August	Iraq formally annexes Kuwait.
9 August	UN Security Council condemns the annexation.
18 August– 11 October	Iraq detains, but eventually releases non-Kuwaiti nationals in Kuwait.
9 September	Bush and Gorbachev meet to discuss the Kuwaiti crisis in Helsinki.
29 November	UN Security Council resolution allows 'all means necessary' to expel Iraqis if they do not withdraw by 15 January.

1991

9 January	US Secretary of State, James Baker, and Iraqi Foreign Minister, Tariq Aziz, meet in Geneva but make no progress.
12 January	Congress approves use of US forces in offensive role.
15 January	UN deadline for the withdrawal of Iraqi forces expires.
17 January	Allied air attacks on Iraqi forces begin: operation 'Desert Storm'.
17–18 January	First SCUD missile attacks by Iraq on Israel; Saddam Hussein speaks of the 'mother of all battles'.
20 January	First SCUD missile attack on Saudi Arabia.
26 January	Over 70,000 march in anti-war protest in Washington.
30 January– 1 February	Iraqi land attack on Saudi Arabia is repulsed.
15 February	Iraqi offer to withdraw from Kuwait on conditions (including reparations payments by allies) is dismissed by Bush.
17–19 February	Iraqi Foreign Minister, Tariq Aziz, in Moscow, fails to reach an acceptable peace deal: Bush rejects Iraqi–Soviet ideas on 22 February.
24 February	Ground offensive by Allied forces begins, under General Norman Schwarzkopf; Iraqis set fire to Kuwaiti oil wells.
26–27 February	Kuwait City liberated.
28 February	Ceasefire takes effect unofficially.
6 April	Iraq accepts official ceasefire terms; takes effect 11 April.

C. Washington and Moscow in the 1990s

The Last Phase of US–Soviet Relations, 1990–1991

By the beginning of 1990 it was clear that the Cold War was over and George Bush, who had initially been reluctant to rush into a policy of US–Soviet friendship, became more anxious to support the position of Mikhail Gorbachev, seeing him as the only hope for a stable, reformist USSR. The collapse of its position in Eastern Europe had confirmed that the Soviet regime had indeed fundamentally changed, although doubts about Gorbachev's ability to carry reform through persisted. The US Secretary of State, James Baker, had decided, even before the Berlin Wall fell, that 'Any uncertainty about the fate of reform in the Soviet Union . . . is all the more reason, not less, for us to seize the present opportunity' and to 'lock in as much change as possible'.[24] In 1990–1 Bush continued to back this policy even when others began to see Gorbachev's position as increasingly hopeless and, for a time, the US government proved none-too-enthusiastic about the break-up of the Soviet Union—even though this could be seen as final confirmation of America's 'victory' in the Cold War. Yet at the same time Bush was criticized for failing to provide the extensive financial aid that might have allowed the last Soviet leader to cling onto power. There were, in fact, good reasons to believe that Gorbachev's economic policies simply would not work, and Congress itself might not have approved larger sums than were provided. But, as events continued to move at breakneck pace, the US President repeatedly seemed to be left behind by them, unable either to shore up Gorbachev's position or to contemplate a Soviet Union without him. Doubtful about Gorbachev's commitment to reform in the late 1980s and slow to develop a Soviet policy in 1989, Bush and his team continued to react to the revolutionary upheaval in the USSR in a pragmatic, cautious way that seemed inappropriate to critics. In contrast his successor, Bill Clinton, was far keener to embrace Gorbachev's *bête noire*, Boris Yeltsin, to encourage reform in Moscow and to give advice to the Russian government.

Whatever the criticisms levelled at Bush, the years 1990–1 saw remarkable achievements in relations between Washington and Moscow. This was the period of course in which the democratization of Eastern Europe was consolidated and German reunification achieved, and both these processes were achieved without humiliating Gorbachev or rekindling the Cold War (see Chapter 20, A). Bush himself wisely declared 'I'm not going to dance on the [Berlin] Wall', because he did not want to humiliate Gorbachev and risk a Soviet backlash.[25] Furthermore, economic and political reform did continue in the USSR and there were major steps in arms control. Signs of a repressive Soviet policy in the Baltic States provoked concern in the US, especially over Lithuania in the early months of 1991: at the end of January the US postponed a summit meeting that had been planned for the following month. But at the same time the two countries worked tolerably well together over the Gulf War (see Chapter 21, B), progress was being made in arms control negotiations, and a high point of the Bush–Gorbachev relationship came at the Washington summit of 31 May-1 June 1990. Beforehand, the Soviet leader, despite his great popularity in the West, seemed in grave trouble at home, where a new economic reform programme was announced amid much scepticism on 24 May and where, on 29 May, Boris Yeltsin strengthened his position as a potential alternative leader by winning a popular vote to confirm his position as President of the Russian Federation. This was also a key point in the process of German reunification, with the Soviets still reluctant to concede German membership of NATO.

The Washington summit confirmed, however, that Bush was anxious to prop up Gorbachev, just as the Soviet leader was ready to continue his retreat in the face of Western security demands. As well as agreements on cultural cooperation, educational exchanges, and nuclear tests, there was a grain deal, a long-awaited commercial agreement was signed, giving the USSR 'Most Favoured Nation' trading status, and conventional weapons reductions in Europe were discussed. Gorbachev conceded that a reunited Germany could be a NATO member and further progress was made on a Strategic Arms Reduction Treaty (START), despite the Bush team's initial doubts about the whole START process. Arguably most important, however, was an agreement by the two countries to destroy over three-quarters of their chemical weapons stocks. As a public relations exercise the summit was a great success, being followed up by more talks at Camp David, the Presidential country retreat, and a visit by Gorbachev to California, where he once again met Ronald Reagan. In contrast to his scepticism about Gorbachev in mid-1989, Bush now acknowledged 'We've come a long, long way from the depths of the Cold War', while Gorbachev 'was left with the impression of a growing understanding among Americans that the new Soviet Union . . . was consistent with the interests of the United States.'[26] Yet at home the Soviet leader's problems continued to mount, as food supplies faced serious disruption and Yeltsin's Russian Federation led the way in pressing for greater autonomy for the USSR's fifteen constituent republics. In October 1990 came the 'War of Laws', when the Russian and Ukrainian parliaments declared their legislation superior to Soviet law, only to have the Supreme Soviet insist that this could never be the case. Two months later Gorbachev proposed a period of executive rule, promoted hard-line communists back into top positions, and seemed ready to crack down forcefully on the separatist movements in the republics.

Yet again, however, Gorbachev backed off from any confrontation with the West and Bush avoided public criticism of the Soviet leader. By May 1991, with the situation in the Baltic States defused (see Chapter 20, B) and the West triumphant in the Gulf War, the State Department and CIA were primarily concerned with Gorbachev's weak domestic position. His promotion of hardliners, with no personal loyalty to him, had made him vulnerable to a palace coup, and the previous weeks had seen a series of strikes, which further damaged industrial output. The most difficult problem facing Bush was whether to provide large amounts of financial aid to bail his Soviet counterpart out of the gathering crisis. The problem was that, however radical Gorbachev

seemed in Soviet terms, Western experts were not convinced his economic reform programme would work. It tried to preserve too much central planning, was likely to be undermined by the unsympathetic Soviet bureaucracy, and had already absorbed a large amount of Western aid—much of it from Germany—with little effect. In late May Gorbachev sent his foreign policy adviser, Yevgeny Primakov, to convince Washington that the reform programme *was* a meaningful one, but the US was reluctant to pour more money into a losing concern. Gorbachev himself attended the G-7 summit in London on 21 July to plead for large-scale assistance but, despite some sympathy from Germany and France, could win little more than emergency humanitarian assistance. He consoled himself with the belief that he had 'achieved a fundamental political agreement about the integration of our country into the world economy', breaching another wall between East and West.[27]

A week later Gorbachev and Bush met in Moscow for another summit. Though they were to meet once again (on 30 October, in Madrid, where multilateral talks on a Middle East peace settlement took place) this was to be the last ever US–Soviet summit and it had one major arms control achievement to its credit. The START I treaty, under negotiation since the Reagan period, slashed strategic nuclear missile numbers on both sides by almost a third (see boxed section). By now the US government was more than ever concerned about the possible break-up of the USSR, perhaps leading to a series of wars among its successor states. So, on a visit to the Ukraine, Bush made a controversial speech saying that nationalist feeling must not become ethnic hatred (as was already the case in certain conflicts in the Caucasus) and warning that it was pointless to replace the old Soviet totalitarianism with a brand of nationalist despotism. The speech upset Ukrainian opinion, however, and within weeks Gorbachev's position was fatally undermined by the abortive August coup by hardliners, which Yeltsin did most to defeat. For a time, in the wake of the coup, US–Soviet relations seemed as fruitful as ever, with statements from both about their determination to reduce nuclear forces. But a State Department memorandum of 25 October bluntly warned that, 'The Soviet Union as we know it no longer exists . . . Our aim should be to make the crash as peaceful as possible.'[28] By the end of the year the US had to accept that, whatever the uncertainties this created, the USSR had ceased to exist.

The US and Yeltsin

Well before the USSR disintegrated, Bush had begun to establish links with the republican governments that became its successor states. Yeltsin and Bush had met in Washington on 20 June 1991, getting on better than expected, and in November–December the leaders of the USSR's republics were careful to keep Washington informed of their plans. Bush in fact was told of the intention of these leaders to dissolve the Soviet Union before the unfortunate Gorbachev. Bush was also keen to build on the success of the START treaty and to press on with nuclear arms reductions before any authoritarian regime returned to power in Moscow. Even START I would leave both sides with enormous destructive power and, now that the Cold War was definitely over, Congress was keen to make major defence savings. There were problems on both sides with the continuation of the START process however. For one thing, America was determined to confirm its technological superiority and maintained, for example, research on the Strategic Defence Initiative. For another, the break-up of the USSR, however welcome to the US in other ways, created three new nuclear powers: as well as Russia, there were strategic weapons bases in the Ukraine (for a time the world's third largest nuclear power), Belarus, and Kazakhstan. The destruction of those ex-Soviet nuclear warheads outside Russia became a priority for American and Russian arms control policy. Until this was achieved it was impossible to carry START I into effect.

Despite these problems, and despite his reluctance to embrace Yeltsin as an alternative to Gorbachev, Bush pressed on towards a START II treaty with remarkable speed. The President's urgency was increased by the evidence of Gorbachev's last months about just how uncertain Russian politics had become; and the treaty was pursued despite serious doubts in the Department of Defense about reducing the US nuclear arsenal. Bush was helped by Yeltsin's equal determination to cut back on nuclear arms, not only because of the cost of maintaining these but also because Russian security seemed to rely, not on preparations for war with America, but on a continued relaxation of tension. The two leaders held their first, US–Russian summit in February 1992, yet the START II treaty was signed only eleven months later. Not only was its negotiation far swifter than that of START I, but the new treaty also marked a more dramatic reduction of strategic nuclear arsenals by about two-thirds (see boxed section). In the interim in May 1992, the US and the relevant former Soviet republics had also signed a protocol to the START I agreement, aiming at the elimination of the Ukrainian, Belarussian, and Kazakh nuclear arsenals, which were of grave concern to the US. By the time he left office Bush could claim to have negotiated two massive reductions in nuclear arms, and these within eighteen months of each other.

The START treaties: Principal Features

START I
- signed in Moscow by Gorbachev and Bush on 31 July 1991;
- to be carried out over eight years with onsite inspections to verify its execution;
- each side to be restricted to 1,600 launchers (land-based and submarine-based intercontinental ballistic missiles, plus strategic bombers);
- each side to be restricted to 6,000 warheads of which up to 4,900 could be on ballistic missiles, 1,540 on 'heavy' missiles, and 1,100 on mobile, land-based missiles;
- the USSR to halve its number of 'heavy' missiles;
- a separate agreement limited the number of submarine-launched cruise missiles to 880 each.

START II
- signed in Moscow by Bush and Yeltsin on 3 January 1993;
- cut strategic nuclear arsenals by about two-thirds, compared to START I's one-third reduction;
- again provided for onsite verification;
- by 2003 all 'heavy' missiles and multi-warhead intercontinental ballistic missiles to be eliminated;
- by 2000 the total strategic nuclear systems on each side should be no more than 4,250 and by 2003 should not exceed 3,000;
- by 2003 the maximum number of submarine-launched ballistic missiles to be 1,750.

President-elect Clinton had criticized Bush earlier for backing Gorbachev for too long and not embracing Yeltsin soon enough, but the incoming President fully supported the START II signature and made arms control an important theme of his own relationship with Russia. In 1993 Belarus and Kazakhstan gave up their nuclear weapons; the Ukraine followed in January 1994, signing an agreement with the US and Russia after being promised assistance with its nuclear energy programme by Clinton. This paved the way for the fulfilment of both START treaties, although the ratification of START II by the Russian parliament proved a slow process because communists and nationalists were concerned not to reduce Russia's ability to defend itself. Meanwhile, the two governments were set on negotiating still more cuts in a START III treaty and the US provided technical assistance, both to close down unsafe nuclear reactors and to destroy nuclear weapons in the former Soviet Union. There was a serious danger of these falling into criminal or terrorist hands, or of a nuclear accident resulting from Russia's crumbling infrastructure and the poor state of its armed forces. The possibility of disaster was underlined in 1995, when the Russians momentarily mistook the launch of a Norwegian rocket (of which they had been forewarned) for a nuclear assault; and again in 2000, when a Russian nuclear submarine, the *Kursk*, sank in the Barents Sea. It was not just Russian nuclear weapons that were of concern to America. There was also a determination to prevent any proliferation of nuclear know-how from the former USSR to non-nuclear powers. Thus, pressure was put on Moscow not to provide Iran with help on a nuclear reactor, because this might lead on to a military programme by Saddam Hussein; and in 1995 America and Russia led the way in extending the nuclear Non-Proliferation Treaty (the NPT, originally signed in 1968) for an indefinite period. This was done despite the complaints of non-nuclear states that the nuclear powers were not doing enough to disarm themselves and that America condoned certain countries, notably Israel, which had developed a nuclear deterrent.

Certainly, as in so many other aspects of US policy after the Cold War, there was an element of hypocrisy in expecting other countries to adhere to the NPT while America—notwithstanding the START process—retained a large nuclear arsenal. There was an important alteration in US strategic planning under Clinton, away from a focus on war with Russia to the danger presented by 'rogue states', but the strategy continued to rely on the use of nuclear weapons. North Korea was successfully pressured, in 1994, into respecting the NPT (see Chapter 21, D) but the difficulties of enforcing such a policy were highlighted in May 1998 when India, and then Pakistan, successfully tested nuclear weapons, raising the spectre of a nuclear confrontation in South Asia, where both countries continued to bicker over the fate of Kashmir. Despite a summit meeting between India's Atal Vajpayee and Pakistan's Nawaz Sharif in January, there was an upsurge of violence in Kashmir in mid-1999, with India using airstrikes for the first time since the 1971 Indo–Pakistani War. Clinton tried to deal with the crisis over nuclear proliferation, first by introducing sanctions against the two states at the time of the tests, then, in March 2000, by a visit to the region. But his brief stop in Pakistan was overshadowed by the recent military coup that had brought president Parvaz Musharraf to power.

However, Clinton was not solely interested in the non-proliferation of *nuclear* arms. In fact, he was interested in preventing all weapons of mass destruction falling into the hands of 'rogue' states and chemical weapons were a particular concern. Here too he continued a policy begun under Bush, and supported by Moscow, of reducing the size of arsenals. In September 1991, at the Washington summit, Bush and Gorbachev had agreed to cut their chemical weapons stocks by over three-quarters. In mid-January 1993 there was also a UN-sponsored Chemical Weapons Ban treaty designed to prevent the development, production, and use of such arms. But, whilst it was ratified by sufficient states (eighty of them) to come into force in April 1997, it was not signed by some of those states most likely to practise chemical warfare, especially Iraq. Therefore, even joint US–Russian leadership of a particular development could not guarantee its acceptance. Third countries might no longer be able to play Washington and Moscow off against each other any longer, but that did not mean that a US–Russian condominium existed in the world. Each state continued to look to its own security, well aware that the great powers did the same, and neither did the great powers always set the best example. It was significant in December 1997, for example, that whereas most of the world's nations were prepared to sign a treaty banning anti-personnel mines, the US and Russia were among the minority who refused.

Clinton's readiness to focus on relations with Russia even though the Cold War had ended was due to more than a desire for arms control and non-proliferation. 'For an administration routinely accused of foreign policy incoherence ... its approach to Russia appeared quite consistent and even sophisticated.'[29] From the outset he sought a 'strategic alliance' with Yeltsin, whom he first met at Vancouver in April 1993, and this alliance included support for reform in Russia. Moscow might only command a shadow of its former, global power but its stability was vital to the wider stability of all Eurasia, a new kind of Cold War was always a danger, and Russia could have created severe difficulties for American policy on such issues as the Bosnian War (see Chapter 20, D) or the 'dual containment' of Iraq and Iran (see Chapter 21, D). There was still considerable popular suspicion of the US in Russia and even reformers were disappointed at the scale of American aid. It was a particularly delicate matter to extend NATO into Eastern Europe, given Russia's historical and strategic interest in the region (see Chapter 21, D). American Republicans were often critical of Clinton for failing to press on with NATO enlargement, thereby tying Eastern Europe to the West, and for failing to oppose Russian predomination in areas formerly ruled by the USSR. But for the President it was pointless to antagonize Russia when it no longer represented an immediate security menace, and when Yeltsin's likely successors were either extreme nationalists and pan-Slavists, such as Vladimir Zhirhovsky (who emerged as an important figure in the December 1993 elections) or the Communist Party, which still commanded a fifth of the national vote.

The danger of collapse in Yeltsin's position was especially apparent at the start of the Clinton Presidency: the months from March to October 1993 were ones of constant crisis in Russia, only finally brought to an end by Yeltsin's decision to bombard the parliament building to force opposition deputies

into line. Despite such extreme action, and despite his ill-health and drunkenness, the US still saw Yeltsin as the best hope for stability and democracy. Clinton's 'strong political and diplomatic support reached its peak during the failed 1993 coup ... where the US found itself ... endorsing the shelling of a parliament.'[30] On his visit to Moscow in January 1994—where both sides said they would no longer target each other with nuclear arms—Clinton described his Russian counterpart as an equal and a partner, and in March backed a large IMF loan to Russia. As to Yeltsin, he too felt a close partnership with Clinton: 'No other US president engaged in such intensive negotiations with the leaders of our country. ... Sometimes it seemed ... that we were establishing ... a new future for our planet.' Then again, even Yeltsin soon recognized that 'Russia and the United States viewed few conflicts in the world in the same way. We had different interests.'[31] And there was more to the sense of separation between Moscow and Washington than different interests on particular issues. In 1989, the two had been equals and, in 1990–3, they worked quite closely together to prevent a return of the Cold War; but after 1994 the US felt more confident about pursuing its own agenda. The 'relationship with the West became more testing' and US policy amounted to 'a very substantial marginalization of Russia' in world affairs.[32]

The year 1994–5 proved a difficult one in US–Russian relations, however, with a more assertive Russian role in Bosnia, Yeltsin's opposition to NATO's 'Partnership for Peace' with Eastern Europe, the start of the war in Chechnya, and the sale of two Russian nuclear reactors to Iran. But the Clinton policy, of a cautious approach to NATO enlargement while accepting Russian assertiveness in the former USSR, gradually brought results. In 1995–6 the Bosnian settlement, the prolongation of the NPT, and Russia's acceptance of the Partnership for Peace were accompanied by Yeltsin's—and Clinton's—successful re-election. Thereafter it was possible to begin the actual enlargement of NATO while rewarding Yeltsin with more financial aid, which was one main aim of his pragmatically pro-Western policy. A false note was the replacement of the Russian Foreign Minister, Andrei Kozyrev in January 1996 after long criticism in the parliament of his

Comprehensive Test Ban Treaty, 23 September 1996

A Comprehensive Test Ban Treaty (CTBT) was first proposed in the 1950s but only a limited treaty was achieved in 1963, which banned most nuclear tests, but not those carried out underground. Underground tests were viewed as difficult to verify and the existing nuclear powers remained keen to test weapons. A further, limited advance proved possible in 1974, when the US and USSR signed the Threshold Test Ban Treaty, which limited the yield of underground explosions to 150 kilotonnes, but talks on a comprehensive ban in the late 1970s came to nothing before Cold War tensions revived with the Soviet invasion of Afghanistan.

Interest in a CTBT revived in the late 1980s. In 1991, just before the collapse of the USSR, Gorbachev initiated a one-year moratorium on tests and sympathy grew for a reciprocal move in the US. The Clinton administration proved more enthusiastic than its predecessor about a ban and talks opened, under United Nations auspices, in Geneva in January 1994. Despite talk of allowing certain levels of test explosion to continue, a CTBT was finally approved by the UN on 10 September 1996. Sixteen days later it was signed by an initial forty-four countries. By 2001, 160 had signed. Although it ran to seventeen

articles, the key undertaking was in Article One, which prohibited any nuclear weapons test or nuclear explosion, and which also prevented signatories from helping other states to carry out such a test. An 'International Monitoring System' was created to provide verification that the CTBT was being followed.

The CTBT was intended to stop both the spread of nuclear weapons to non-nuclear states and improvements to existing weapons by nuclear states. However, the ratification process proved difficult. One important point was that the treaty listed forty-four key countries with nuclear capabilities, who had to ratify it before it could enter into force. But these included three countries— North Korea, India, and Pakistan—who had not even signed the CTBT by 2001. The Russian Federation did not ratify the treaty until June 2000 and an early attempt to ratify it by the US Senate failed in October 1999. Opponents argued that a test ban would harm the future effectiveness of the US nuclear deterrent, and that other countries would 'cheat' the verification system. President Clinton said that he would continue to seek the ratification of the treaty but this had still not been achieved by the time he left office.

---

pro-Western policies. Under Kozyrev's successor, Yevgeni Primakov, Russian policy was marked by a more nationalist tinge, notably in the attempts to prevent American attacks on Iraq when Saddam Hussein obstructed the work of UN weapons inspectors. But the continuing weakness of the Russian economy and the decrepit state of the armed forces—said by the Defence Minister in February 1997 to be on the verge of disintegration—pointed Yeltsin in the direction of cooperation with Moscow's former enemies. To this end he signed a trade deal with the European Union (July 1995), began a series of annual conferences with the German and French leaders (1997), and held a series of summit conferences with China's Jiang Zemin, crowned in November 1997 by the settlement of their generation-old border dispute.

Not all of Yeltsin's policies were to the taste of the US, then, but their general direction was, and serious crises between Moscow and Washington seemed a thing of the past. As to Clinton's policy, it may have been criticized by Republicans at home, and

its caution may have seemed similar to that of Bush. But it did allow the US to keep its former arch-enemy quiescent, while other difficult problems were addressed, such as freer trade and the challenge of 'rogue states', at a time when the American public were reluctant to play an active overseas role in any case. The pay-off for supporting Yeltsin was that Russia continued on a capitalist, democratic course. In contrast to earlier decades, if Clinton's policy did have a fault in his second term, it was that he was too supportive of the Moscow regime for its own good. In particular, by backing Yeltsin in his attempts to maintain the value of the rouble in 1997–8, the US and the IMF probably drove the Russian economy deeper into depression. The country's economic and social problems were immense and included unemployment, growing inequalities of wealth, limited savings, low industrial production, a large public deficit, and an inadequate tax system. It is easy to see why Yeltsin's economic reforms were more to American taste than Gorbachev's had been. Yeltsin had embraced a more radical line in 1992, abandoning

Boris Yeltsin

Born in the Sverdlovsk region, into a peasant family, in 1931, and trained as a construction engineer, Yeltsin joined the Communist Party in 1961 and rose to become the chief Party official in the city of Sverdlovsk by 1976, being recognized as one of the rising generation of reformers in the USSR. Promoted under Gorbachev in 1985 to be the Party boss in the capital, Moscow, he at first cooperated with the Soviet leader but then fell out with him, complaining about the slow pace of reform. Sacked from the Politburo in 1987, Yeltsin did what previous disgraced politicians in the USSR had been unable to do: he rebuilt his position by taking a high public profile and by securing a key appointment outside the communist hierarchy, as President of the most important Soviet republic, the Russian Federation, in May 1990. The following year he greatly strengthened his position by winning a popular election to confirm his Presidency. In contrast, Gorbachev was increasingly unpopular and could not risk a free vote on his leadership.

Yeltsin cemented his reputation as a democrat and strong-willed man of principle by resisting the August 1991 coup of communist hardliners. In the following months he worked for the destruction of the USSR, having already quit the Communist Party. Unpredictable,

alcoholic, and increasingly dogged by ill-health he nonetheless dominated Russian politics after December 1991. His radical reforms brought economic chaos, his democratic credentials were dented by his October 1993 attack on the Russian parliament, and his foreign policy was criticized as betraying Russian interests to the West. But the pace of reform was maintained, cooperation with the West brought the rewards of peace and financial support, and he was successfully re-elected President in July 1996, beating the communist candidate, Gennady Zyuganov in a run-off. In November he had complex heart by-pass surgery, form which his health never fully recovered, and he lost popularity thanks to continuing economic problems and the failure to deal effectively with Chechnya. In March 1998 he suddenly sacked his long-serving Prime Minister, Viktor Chernomyrdin, but did not find it easy to secure a successor: three more Premiers were sacked over the next eighteen months before Yeltsin appointed the more successful Vladimir Putin on 9 August 1999. Meanwhile, in the year since August 1998, the rouble had lost about three-quarters of its value on international markets. Ill-health forced him to hand power to Putin on 31 December 1999, but even the timing of this move caught the world by surprise.

---

central planning as quickly as he could, privatizing industry, and (at the cost of high inflation) ending price controls. But he was forced to rely on the same civil servants who had served the communist regime, and the beneficial effects of the free market were further undermined by the failure to tackle growing corruption. Yeltsin was also increasingly unwell. A heavy drinker and workaholic, he spent several weeks in 1995 in hospital with heart problems and in late 1997 needed major by-pass surgery.

The 1997–8 world economic crisis, which began in South-East Asia, exposed the fragility of the Russian economy and of the man who for all his flaws, Clinton backed as the best hope for capitalist reform and good US–Russian relations. In March 1998 Yeltsin, after another bout of heart trouble, decided on dramatic action, unexpectedly sacking Premier Viktor Chernomyidin and replacing him with a young, inexperienced and little-known reformer, Sergei Kiriyenko, who was only reluctantly confirmed by the Russian parliament. Two months later the

government introduced a tough package to stabilize the currency, reduce tax evasion, tackle inflation, and press on with privatization. This impressed the IMF, which in July 1998 agreed a massive $22.6 billion loan, but it only propped up the rouble for another month and did nothing for Yeltsin's popularity. His decisions seemed increasingly desperate as when, in late August, with widespread fears of a Russian economic collapse, he suddenly sacked Kiriyenko and brought back Chernomyrdin. A sense of stability was only restored in August 1999 when Vladimir Putin became the fifth Russian Prime Minister in seventeen months. Colourless but tough, efficient, and young (he was born in 1952), Putin's appointment led to renewed US concern about the future of Russian democracy because he was a former KGB officer and in 1998–9 head of the Russian intelligence service, the federal Security Bureau. He also renewed efforts to crush the separatist movement in Chechnya (see Chapter 20, B). Yet it was his success in the last operation that established his popularity and made him the natural successor to the increasingly decrepit Yeltsin, who gave one last surprise to the world with his sudden resignation on 31 December 1999. Putin, initially appointed Acting President, was elected into the position in his own right on 26 March 2000, with 52 per cent of the vote. He showed some readiness to stand up to Washington, not least in his criticism of the continued development of the Star Wars project, now nearing deploy-

ment as the 'National Missile Defence System.' Indeed, in a revival of an old, Cold War alliance, he joined with China in condemning this. Yet personal relations between Putin and Western leaders developed well and, as with Yeltsin before him, he was seen as far preferable to the communist and ultra-nationalist alternatives. If, in Chechnya, he satisfied Russian nationalist opinion, he also persisted with a parliamentary system and economic reform.

D. **The Clinton Administration and 'Rogue States'**

The Concept of 'Rogue States'

One important way in which the Clinton administration tried to mobilize US and world opinion against its enemies was to press the concept of 'rogue' or 'backlash states'. Whilst trying to 'enlarge' the area of the world that was part of the American-led liberal order, it was also necessary, in the eyes of Clinton and his National Security Adviser, Anthony Lake, to isolate those states whose ideologies or support for terrorism made it impossible to deal with them on a normal basis. Thus, in spring 1994, Lake wrote of:

[R]ecalcitrant and outlaw states that not only choose to remain outside the family but also assault its basic values . . . Ruled by cliques that control power through coercion, they . . . exhibit a chronic inability to engage constructively with the outside world. . . . As the sole superpower, the US has a special responsibility . . . to neutralize, contain and . . . perhaps eventually transform these backlash states into constructive members of the international community.[33]

In November 1997, when making its first major change in nuclear targeting policy since 1980, the US retained a deterrent capacity against Russia and China, but widened its potential targets to include 'rogue states', on the grounds that they had access to weapons of mass destruction.[34] Yet, as with roll-back during the Cold War, the concept of 'rogue states', though easy enough to explain in general terms, was difficult to execute in practice and surrounded by contradictions. The new doctrine was tolerant of

any number of oppressive regimes so long as they were friendly to the US. Cynics charged that it also targeted small, isolated countries—like Cuba or Libya—which were no real threat to American interests, whilst a large, strategically significant country like China was dealt with through the alternative approach of 'constructive engagement'. Notwithstanding its Communist ideology and questionable human rights record, Clinton decided that Beijing was too important as a trading partner, and too vital to East Asian security, to treat as an enemy (see Chapter 22, D). But it was not the case that US policy-makers victimized every small, Marxist state that had outlived the Cold War. The Marxist-led government of Angola, for example, was given recognition by Clinton in 1993 because it had shown a readiness to hold free elections even if the 'pro-Western' opposition leader, Jonas Savimbi, did not respect the result and the civil war there continued until he was killed in 2002. More remarkably, Vietnam's willingness to engage with the West, introduce free-market elements into the economy, and provide information on those US troops reported missing-in-action during the Vietnam War, led to American diplomatic recognition in 1995. This was followed by a US–Vietnamese trade deal in July 2000 as well as by visits from Madeleine Albright in September 1999, and from Clinton himself at the very end of his Presidency, so that his second term became a time of reconciliation with the most dogged of Cold War enemies. Cases where a continued adhesion to Communist doctrine led to US economic sanctions and attempted diplomatic isolation were actually limited to two, Cuba and North Korea.

The concept of 'rogue states' was useful to the Clinton administration because of the fact that, after the collapse of the Soviet Union, it was so difficult to mobilize the US people in favour of an activist foreign policy. Under Bush, American policy had initially seemed successful in bringing a peaceful end to the Cold War, securing German reunification, and dealing with Third World dictators, Noriega in Panama and Saddam Hussein in the Gulf War. Indeed, Noriega and Saddam had already shown the value of pointing up certain distasteful regimes as primary threats to the New World Order. After 1991 American foreign policy, its 'victory' over the USSR complete, seemed more aimless, not helped by the ill-fated intervention in Somalia (see Chapter 21, E) or the intractability of the Bosnian conflict. True, it was possible to focus on challenges like the international drugs trade, 'global warming', and the interdependency of world trade, and Clinton did try to tackle these. A commitment to free trade areas in the Western Hemisphere and Asia-Pacific was central to his world outlook. But narcotics, environmentalism, and trade were all complex issues; they were difficult to make progress upon and, especially in the case of the latter pair, they aroused controversy in the US about how best to tackle them. In contrast, it was quite easy to win support for attacks on those who were threatening their neighbours, developing chemical and nuclear weapons, or sponsoring international terrorism.

The last, of course, was an old problem, which had already led to US bombing raids in 1986 on Colonel Gadaffi's Libya (see Chapter 17, D). Libya was a leading candidate for the title 'rogue state' in the 1990s, not least because it refused to hand over two officials who were suspected of involvement in the 1988 bombing of an American Boeing 747 airliner over Lockerbie, Scotland, in which 270 people died. The US and Britain, backed by France—which blamed Gadaffi for the loss of a French airliner over West Africa in 1989—were able to secure UN sanctions against Libya in April 1992, and to maintain these despite the increasing doubts of the Organization of African Unity and the fact that Gadaffi ceased to be a high-profile sponsor of terrorism after 1986.

In May 1994 he also agreed to withdraw from the disputed Aozou strip, on the border with Chad, which his forces had occupied since the 1970s. He continued to offend Washington, by offering to finance Louis Farrakhan's 'Nation of Islam' movement in the US, for example, and (apparently) trying to build a chemical weapons plant. But relations eased when he agreed to hand over, for trial in Holland, two Libyans who were suspected of involvement in the Lockerbie bombing. The trial opened in May 2000 and one Libyan was subsequently found guilty.

Neither was Libya the only Arab-led, Muslim, North African state accused of supporting terrorism. So, in August 1993, was the Sudan where the Islamic National Front had come to power in 1989, adopting the Sharia (holy law) and prosecuting more vigorously the civil war, which had been underway since 1983 against the black, Christian south of the country. For a time Sudan also provided a safe haven for the anti-American Al Qaeda terrorist network and its leader, the Saudi dissident, Osama bin Laden. Neighbouring countries like Uganda and Ethiopia were keen to see the Sudanese government replaced, foreign aid to it was cut back severely, and in November 1997 the US introduced economic sanctions against it. But Al Qaeda was not cowed: on 7 August 1998 it launched simultaneous bomb attacks on the US embassies in Kenya and Tanzania, killing more than two hundred people. The US responded two weeks later with cruise missile attacks on suspected terrorist bases in both Sudan and Afghanistan, which had also given facilities to Al Qaeda. Bin Laden was then forced to leave the Sudan but his terrorist network remained intact. By 2000 there was widespread famine in southern Sudan and the next few years brought moves to end the war in the South.

One feature of the 'rogue states' concept, which was of concern to the US government itself, was that it could easily turn into an anti-Muslim policy. Apart from Libya and the Sudan, other key 'rogue states' were Iran and Iraq, and there were various reasons why Americans should have particular fears about what was termed 'Islamic fundamentalism'. As a doctrine it seemed alien to core US values and, with the evident bankruptcy of communism, could be seen as the primary ideological competitor to liberal democracy. In Iran, of course, it had emerged as a threat to US interests as early as 1979, with the fall of the Shah and the seizure of the American embassy in Tehran. It was easy to ignore the ideals of mercy and tolerance in Islam, the deep divisions within the Islamic world—between for example the theocracy of Iran, the secularized Iraqi state, or the Saudi monarchy—and the genuine reasons for Muslim resentment of Western injustice and Christian enmity stretching back centuries. Muslims were critical of European imperialism, the creation of Israel, and more recently US attempts to foist its own political values and economic system on their own, well-established way of life. But in the 1980s and 1990s there were many incidents of violence that Americans associated with Islamic radicalism, not only in Iran and the Sudan, but also in Algeria, the Lebanon, at least in the 1980s, and Afghanistan, which gave refuge to Osama bin Laden when he was forced to flee the Sudan and which was subjected to limited US sanctions after November 1999. In Algeria up to 100,000 people were killed during the 1990s, in a vicious civil war between the military-dominated government and the main opposition party, the Islamic Salvation Front. Furthermore the 'fundamentalists' seemed to be advancing in Central Asia, in Afghanistan, and the former Soviet republic of Tajikistan, and at times even seemed a threat to pro-Western governments in Egypt, Pakistan, and Turkey. Of the many terrorist incidents associated with Islamic groups, the most shocking was the bombing of the World Trade Center in New York in late February 1993, just after Clinton's election, though it was only a shadow of the attacks that would come in September 2001. But, as with Bush, the new administration could never entertain a crudely anti-Islamic policy, because too many of its friends and allies were Muslim states (Egypt, Saudi Arabia, and Indonesia to name just a few) and those like Turkey and Pakistan, who at times seemed likely to turn to fundamentalism, needed the firmest US support. As with the treatment of Marxist states, it was best to deal with those who would cooperate and isolate those who seemed the greatest threat.

Key Examples: Korea, Cuba, Iran, Iraq

Apart from Libya and the Sudan, the main 'rogue' states which the Clinton administration tried to isolate were the two Marxist regimes of Cuba and North Korea, and two Middle Eastern countries, Iran and Iraq. All, in fact, had been seen as opponents of US interests since before Clinton was elected. North Korea, indeed, had been an opponent since 1950. It still laid claim to South Korea and periodically tried to destabilize it, by stirring up border tension, infiltrating saboteurs, and carrying out assassinations. The worst incident was the murder of a seventeen-strong South Korean delegation to Burma in October 1983. But such intimidation failed to prevent South Korea's economy growing apace, while the North's stagnated, and the South was able to exploit the decline of the Cold War to host the Olympic Games (1988) and establish diplomatic relations with the North's former protectors, the USSR (1990) and China (1992). It seemed unlikely that the North would reopen the Korean War but it remained a centralized communist state, with substantial armed forces, under its 'Great Leader', Kim Il Sung. Attempts to turn the 1953 armistice agreement into a proper peace treaty had never advanced far and in 1991 it was feared that, in order to strengthen its position, the North might be building a nuclear weapon. If it succeeded, this would be of concern not only to South Korea, but to other pro-Western states in the region, like Japan, and to the South's key protector, America.

Initially, a crisis was avoided: the US was ready to withdraw any nuclear weapons it had based in the South, the North proved ready to fulfil the Non-Proliferation Treaty, and in December 1991 the South signed two agreements with the North to keep the peninsula nuclear-free. But, whilst the South now hoped for a gradual move to reunification, Kim Il Sung was determined to preserve its independent political development, and in March 1993 the nuclear agreements began to unravel, when the North started to block inspections on its soil by the International Atomic Energy Authority. By November the Clinton White House was threatening to use force if the North obtained a nuclear weapon.

In 1994 this dangerous crisis between the North and the US was only eased when, in July, Kim suddenly died, just as ex-President Jimmy Carter began to act a go-between for Clinton. In October the North agreed to wind down its nuclear programme in return for help with energy supplies, trade, and investment, as well as an assurance that it would not be subjected to nuclear threats by the US. The years following this breakthrough were not easy, partly because the North was slow to carry out its promises. In April 1996, now under Kim Il Sung's son, Kim Jong Il, the North said it would no longer recognize the demilitarized zone; in September another group of Northern infiltrators landed in the South from a submarine. But the North was growing ever weaker in economic terms, facing widespread famine after 1997, and the Chinese pressed it to talk to the South. In May 1997 the South agreed to provide food aid to the North and, at the end of the year, talks opened between these two, alongside America and China, in Geneva to try to frame a permanent settlement of the Korean problem. Progress was fitful but June 2000 saw a summit meeting between Kim Jong Il and South Korea's Kim Dae Jung, cross-border reunions began in August between families that had been divided for decades, and the two countries competed at the Olympics that summer under a joint flag. Strains following this confirmed that reunification was still a distant project, even if renewed war seemed unlikely.

There was no similar relaxation of tension between Washington and another old enemy, Fidel Castro of Cuba. Castro's position, like Kim Il Sung's, was weakened by the end of the Cold War. In 1991 the USSR was still providing Cuba with about $2 billion in aid and 10,000 troops but Gorbachev, even before his downfall, announced this would end (the troops left in 1993) and meanwhile, in the Nicaraguan elections of February 1990, Castro had lost his only ally in the Western hemisphere. 'Today we hear the breaking and crumbling of Castro's dictatorship', Bush announced.[35] Unable to trade on favourable terms with his former COMECON partners, the Cuban leader decided to maintain his dictatorship but now allowed some free-market elements and foreign investment in the economy. He also showed, over the following years, that he was not completely isolated: the Russians kept a small presence in Cuba of signals intelligence experts, eavesdropping on the US; in August 1992, as part of a process of courting Latin American sympathy, he signed the Ttatelolco Treaty (the 1967 pact between Latin American and Caribbean countries, banning nuclear weapons in the region); in 1995 he was able to address the UN; and in 1998 Cuba was visited by Pope John Paul II. Castro even proved able to embarrass the mighty US in August 1994 when he ended the long-standing ban on emigration from Cuba. Not only did this seem an important act of liberalization, it also meant that tens of thousands of people now clamoured to leave Cuba and enter the US. This proved Washington's claim that many Cubans were unhappy living under communism, but it also stirred up ill-feeling in America about high levels of Hispanic immigration. So great was the pressure that in September, Clinton was forced to strike a deal with Castro on emigration levels.

Whatever the signs of political change in Cuba, the US was determined to maintain its pressure on Castro. Cuba might be small and lacking strong friends, but its leader had provoked a deep, personalized loathing in the US since the Bay of Pigs in 1961. Cuba was seen as an oppressive, totalitarian regime, and it had a wealthy, influential body of opponents in the Cuban-American community of Florida. The 'Cuban–American National Foundation' led the campaign against Castro, insisting that the trade embargo be maintained. US hatred of Latin American radicalism ran deep and Cuba lay on its very doorstep. The 1962 settlement of the Cuban missile crisis meant that force was ruled out as a way to topple Castro but a trade embargo had been introduced that same year and in the 1990s was tightened up, as economic warfare became America's principal weapon against him. The 1992 Torricelli Act extended the embargo to overseas subsidiaries of US companies, and more controversially, the March 1996 Helms-Burton Act, allowed the prosecution of foreign-owned businesses that traded with Cuba. Clinton disliked the latter measure but 1996 was an election year, Florida was a key electoral battleground, the Republican-dominated Congress was firmly anti-Castro, and the Cubans had just (in February) shot down two aircraft carrying opponents of the regime off the island. It was questionable, however, whether America's toughness was not self-destructive. The European Union and Latin American states were offended by the Helms-Burton Act, claiming that it was illegal under the rules of the World Trade Organization. Arguably it simply helped Castro to pose as the defender of Cuban independence against US imperialism. A policy of 'engagement' (as followed by Clinton with China) would have been a swifter way of ending the Castro regime. As it was, the campaign against Cuba seemed a telling example of America's determination to interpret general principles, like free trade and respect for human rights, in its own interests. It was a case of post-Cold War foreign policy being decided by domestic political considerations. Then again, a visit to Cuba by the Russian President, Vladimir Putin, in December 2000 served as a reminder that there was still some sympathy for Castro from his former Cold War allies.

Castro, while he survived in power, was an easier challenge with which to deal than Iran and Iraq. These countries, given their proximity and capacity for military action had to be dealt with under a policy known as 'dual containment'. Saddam Hussein's decision to invade Kuwait in 1990 created a double dilemma for US policy: not only had he to be removed from Kuwait, but Iraq now became the second state in the Persian Gulf which threatened regional stability in the long-term (Iran having been such a threat since 1979). In the 1980s, of course, Iraq and Iran had effectively 'contained' each other by fighting a long and bitter war, and one helpful factor in the 1990s, from the US viewpoint, was that they remained deeply suspicious of one another. There was always the danger that a hard-line American policy might drive them together and make each of them even more militant. But Washington felt it must take that risk. Both countries were opposed to the Israeli–Palestinian peace process, both supported international terrorist groups, both were known to be developing weapons of mass destruction, and both were seen as potentially aggressive against their neighbours. Also 'Dual containment . . . built on policies that have long guided US Middle East policy . . . namely guaranteeing a continuing flow of oil . . . and keeping other powers from supplanting American dominance in the region.'[36] On several occasions after 1991, crises blew up over Saddam's threats to Kuwait and his refusal to allow UN inspections (see Chapter 21, B), whilst Iran's attempts to build a nuclear weapon, linked to its support for terrorism, led Clinton to introduce a complete trade and investment embargo against it in June 1995. Meanwhile, the US still retained $11 billion of Iranian assets frozen in 1979 and the CIA was in contact with various opposition groups.

If anything Iran, through its size and revolutionary fervour, seemed the more dangerous opponent, but there were indications that it might be possible to work with the regime. The death of the Ayatollah Khomeni in June 1989 had led to a strengthening of the political position of the President, as opposed to the supreme religious leadership, now held by Ayatollah Khameni. After 1989 the President was Ali Akbar Rafsanjani, who adopted free-market reforms and helped secure the release of Western hostages in Lebanon. More dramatically, Rafsanjani's successor, Mohammed Khatami, seemed ready in December 1997 to offer improved individual rights within Iran and spoke of opening a 'dialogue' with the US. Iran had also been able to improve its relations with France and Russia, while fellow Islamic states like Saudi Arabia wanted to see better US–Iranian understanding. There were other reasons for Clinton to respond positively to Khatami: dual containment was costly and had failed to change the regime in either Iran or Iraq; and it was tempting to exploit Iran as an opponent of Saddam Hussein, in order to try to stabilize the Persian Gulf through an alternative policy. But Clinton was careful in evolving a policy. Thus, in June 1998 the Secretary of State, Madelaine Albright, talked of breaking down barriers with Iran but, in return, wanted it to end its support for terrorism and its attempts to obtain weapons of mass destruction. Albright eventually met her Iranian opposite number in September 2000, but only on the neutral ground provided by the United Nations in New York and whilst relations showed signs of becoming more 'normal' they were still surrounded by mutual suspicion.

E. 'Humanitarian Intervention' in Somalia and Haiti

Dilemmas of Humanitarian Intervention

One way in which Western governments were pushed by their own media and public opinion to decide foreign policy priorities after the Cold War, was on the basis of respect for human rights. In particular, in conflicts like Bosnia (see Chapter 20, C) and Rwanda (see Chapter 22, B), there was considerable pressure to intervene on humanitarian grounds, to end inter-ethnic violence, and guarantee both food and medical aid with the use of 'peacekeeping' missions. With about 20 million refugees in the world by the mid-1990s, the breakdown of order in so-called 'failed states' like Somalia, Liberia, and Sierra Leone, and vicious civil conflicts in the Sudan, Algeria, and elsewhere, it seemed essential to consider humanitarian intervention as a way to realize the promises of stability and plenty which had been generated by talk of a New World Order. Furthermore, with the end of the Cold War, it seemed possible to intervene without raising the danger of superpower tension ensuing. The idea of humanitarian intervention was far from new and there had been plenty of examples of mass murder in the twentieth century, not least the Holocaust, to support the argument that the world community should try to prevent such events occurring. A classic definition of such intervention emerged as the 'use of force by a state, or states, to protect citizens of the target state from large-scale human rights violations'.[37] But the 1945 UN Charter had respected both human rights *and* the national sovereignty of member states, with the latter generally winning out over the former. Since all states had a vested interest in preserving the sanctity of national sovereignty there were few political leaders who were genuinely prepared to entertain the idea of intervention in another country's affairs purely on humanitarian grounds. In any case, who was to judge when human rights violations became 'large-scale' enough to justify intervention?

Humanitarian intervention was, in any case, a far more complex moral issue than the Western media liked to pretend, and ethical questions were always tied up with issues of international law, self-interest, and political expediency. It could be argued that oppressive states forfeited legitimacy, so that their national sovereignty need not be respected but, given the number of oppressive regimes in the world and the fact that many were political allies and trading partners of the West, or else too strong and stable to allow intervention, it was difficult to decide at what point intervention was both opportune and possible. 'Domestic' and 'foreign' policy matters could become hopelessly confused in this debate, with universal values and national sovereignty also in the melting pot. At what point did judicial executions (a feature of legal life even in the US) or intercommunal violence (a feature of society in many Western states) justify external interference? And who should make this decision? A majority vote in the UN General Assembly might be best for giving legitimacy to such a condemnation, and many states were ready to respect a decision to use force by the Security Council, but it was notoriously difficult to get the UN to act in unison and in practice it was left to individual states to decide on intervention, often for mixed motives. The Western definition of human rights was not necessarily shared in Asia or Africa; too often 'humanitarian' intervention seemed a disguise for what the non-aligned movement interpreted as 'imperialist' behaviour, 'to cover actions taken for other purposes', or even simply 'to justify continuing high military spending' after the Cold War;[38] and there was the basic dilemma of whether it could even be morally justifiable to use military force, with the inevitable civilian deaths that followed. Also, was intervention in the interests of those who carried it out? One critic accused Clinton of engaging in 'foreign policy as social work'.[39]

Many of these problems had in fact been seen during the Cold War when, despite the overwhelming tendency to treat any conflict as an extension of East–West rivalry, there had been various examples of 'humanitarian' action, or at least claims that states were motivated by humanitarian concern. The US had tried to use this argument to excuse its invasions of the Dominican Republic in 1965 and Grenada two decades later, but did not impress anyone. More seriously, the use of economic sanctions against South Africa and Rhodesia was defended as helping to put an end to racist oppression. Few objected to the overthrow of the dictator Idi Amin of Uganda by a Tanzanian-led invasion in 1979, or when the French toppled the equally oppressive 'Emperor' Bokassa of the Central African Republic the same year. But these were unusual examples of actions that were tolerated by both the Western and Soviet blocs, as well as the Non-Aligned Movement. South Africa and Rhodesia were guilty of a particular type of human rights abuse; other types went unchallenged by UN sanctions. Tanzania (backed by the West) had reasons of self-interest to overthrow a crazy dictator on their borders; there was no similar invasion to oust the equally cruel regime of Amin's eventual successor, Milton Obote. And the French only turned against Bokassa after building up his position in the first place. Elsewhere during the Cold War, even actions that self-evidently saved thousands of human lives, were likely to be condemned if they offended one of the superpowers. Thus the US was critical of India's support for Bangladeshi independence in 1971 (because this represented a defeat for America's ally, Pakistan) and condemned the Vietnamese invasion of Cambodia in 1978 (because, although it put an end to the murderous Pol Pot regime, it represented an advance for 'pro-Soviet' interests).

There were several examples of interventions after the Cold War that were influenced by humanitarian pressures, some involving UN approval and some not. They included: Iraq, where Allied forces acted in April 1991 to provide protection for the Kurds and Marsh Arabs; Bosnia, where the UN acted after 1992 only with the Bosnian government's consent and had a limited impact; Liberia, where the Nigerians dominated attempts by fellow West African states to end the post-1990 civil war; and Rwanda, where the UN endorsed French intervention only to find that the Paris government took sides among the

locals (see Chapter 20, B). However, there were two other examples of intervention, where the US took a leading role and where radically different outcomes showed both the perils and opportunities of humanitarian action. These were Somalia and Haiti, both of which fell into the category of so-called 'failed states'.

Somalia

Somalia, led since October 1969 by Siad Barré, had been of great significance to the breakdown of East–West détente in the late 1970s, thanks to the Ogaden War against Ethiopia (see Chapter 17, C). After suffering defeat in that conflict, various opposition groups became active against Barré and, as the Cold War wound down in the late 1980s, the fate of the Horn of Africa became less important to the superpowers. In the early 1990s both Somalia and Ethiopia suffered deep internal traumas. In Ethiopia's case this took the form of having to concede, after decades of war, the independence of Eritrea in 1992, but at least the central government survived and was even able to fare well in a border conflict with Eritrea in 1999–2000. In Somalia's case, in contrast, there was a decline into virtual anarchy. Along with the rest of Africa, Somalia, never a wealthy country, received little Western aid or investment and by 1990 there was widespread famine. But there were enough weapons left over from the Ogaden War to keep the political factions well armed. On 27 January 1991 Barré was forced to flee into exile, having lost control of the capital, Mogadishu, to the forces of the United Somali Congress. Despite its impressive title, this was only one of several opposition groups, most of which relied on the support of particular Somali clans, and it was unable to agree with the rest. In the North one group, the Somali National Movement, declared independence, basing its borders on those of the former colony of British Somaliland, which had been united with Italian Somaliland to form Somalia in 1960. By September 1991 the political divisions had grown worse, as the United Somali Congress split between the supporters of its Chairman, General Mohammed Aideed, and the President, Ali Mahdi. The UN tried to broker ceasefires and form a coalition government. In April 1992 it also set up the UN Operation in Somalia (UNOSOM) to help secure peace and humanitarian assistance. The force was deployed in August, but initially limited to about a thousand personnel.

Meanwhile, as images of starving Somalis filtered through to American television screens, there were calls for Bush to intervene on a large scale to protect food supplies. Since Aideed had earlier seemed to approve UNOSOM, there appeared little danger of US troops running into a Vietnam-style imbroglio. It was felt that American forces, fresh from their success in the Gulf War, could easily handle a famine relief mission in a poor country like Somalia. It would, however, be a marked departure from existing policy: in the wake of the Cold War, despite complaints from the Congressional Black Caucus and others, the US had run down aid to Africa. Aid to Somalia had been cut in July 1989. True, Bush had sent a force of marines to Liberia in West Africa in June 1990, but this was a limited operation to evacuate American citizens. 'That Bush, in so many ways a practitioner of Realpolitik, would have intervened in an area now devoid of strategic significance, appeared to expand considerably the meaning of his "New World Order".' Yet this is what happened. The intervention 'was justified purely on humanitarian grounds. There was no strategic, economic or narcotics interest that propelled the . . . US into action, nor foreign territory that had been invaded.'[40] Neither did the Somali authorities request external intervention.

In December 1992 the outgoing Bush administration, in full agreement with President-elect Clinton, launched 'Operation Restore Hope', with over 20,000 American troops despatched to Somalia under US, not UN, command. There was no opposition to their arrival but Somali politics remained anarchic and Aideed's attitude towards such a large-scale external intervention became more ambiguous. Coordination between the relief effort and the military command was poor and there was little attempt to consult the Somalis. In May 1993 the Americans still seemed likely to escape without loss, since they were due to be replaced by a substantial new 'UNOSOM II' presence. But, partly in order to make it safe for new UN deployments, in an example of 'mission creep', the US had moved beyond its narrow humanitarian

action, to try to disarm the local militias. This could only provoke concern among warlords like Aideed. It was then, in early June, that Aideed's followers massacred twenty-three Pakistani UN soldiers, leading the UN to order his arrest. On 17 June American forces had their first clash with Aideed's men and the date for withdrawal was pushed back, even though there was still no direct US economic and political interest in the conflict. Clinton later remarked that he did not want to 'pull out and have chaos, anarchy, starvation return'.[41] But the US mission had now become one of fighting Aideed. Eventually on 3–4 October the Americans launched a full-scale helicopter and troop attack on his headquarters in Mogadishu but they became trapped and shot their way out. Hundreds of Somalis were killed in the process but the US public were mainly concerned with the death of thirteen of their own men. Having clamoured for intervention in the first place, the public were suddenly unwilling to support the Somali operation. For Clinton Operation Restore Hope had become the most disastrous failure of his first year in office. Between December 1993 and March 1994 the US troops were withdrawn, though UN forces remained to guard the harbour and airport of Mogadishu for another year. By then Aideed's forces were in the ascendant in Somalia and they continued to expand their area of control without securing outright victory, until the General's death in August 1996. Ironically his successor was his son who, in 1992, had been a member of the US marines. Meanwhile, in May 1994, Clinton had issued a Presidential Directive to the effect that future military interventions would be to defend vital interests and with clear aims of success. It was a Directive, however, that would cripple America's response to the next humanitarian crisis in Africa, focused on Rwanda.

Haiti

Operation Restore Hope had unexpectedly turned from a humanitarian venture into a dangerous military embarrassment for the US, rekindling fears of 'another Vietnam'. But predicting the course of military action is never easy and in Haiti in 1994 the Clinton administration had almost the opposite experience to Somalia over another problem inherited from Bush: intervention was only decided with great reluctance yet, once underway, brought an easy victory—even if the internal politics of the country remained unsettled.

1994 was not the first time that the US had intervened in Haiti. The country had been under partial American occupation for two decades after 1915, but this had done nothing to help democratic ideals take hold. Instead, by the 1960s the Caribbean island was dominated by François ('Papa Doc') Duvalier and his son, and eventual successor, Jean Claude, known as 'Baby Doc'. Papa Doc had originally been elected leader in 1957, but soon became one of the most ruthless and eccentric of the Western hemisphere's dictators, appointing himself President-for-life in 1964 and using the paramilitary 'Tontons Macoutes' to terrorize the population. This did not dissuade US governments from maintaining the Duvaliers in power for the sake of anti-Communism and regional stability. But in 1986 the poverty and dissatisfaction of Haitians were such that there was widespread unrest and Baby Doc was forced to flee. Even so, thanks partly to the opposition of the police and army, it took until December 1990 before free elections were held and the winner, a Catholic ex-priest called Jean-Bertrand Aristide, proved a volatile leader. His reforms threatened the position of the landowners, the business community and the army, and in August 1991 he was overthrown in a military coup. The Americans, whilst critical of Aristide's performance, did not welcome his replacement. With the Cold War over and little to fear from Communism in the Caribbean, a repressive government in Haiti was an embarrassment. It was one case where the triumph of Western liberal values round 1989–91 seemed to go into reverse. The Organization of American States (OAS) opposed the military government from the outset and introduced a regional trade embargo against it. The UN followed suit and, with US approval that would have seemed unlikely in earlier decades, introduced economic sanctions culminating in an oil embargo in 1993. Furthermore, the Bush administration soon found itself facing tens of thousands of would-be immigrants from Haiti. Both Bush, and in early 1993 Clinton, felt they had little alternative to the forced repatriation of these refugees, but it was

an embarrassing policy for America to adopt. Black Americans in Congress took up the Haitian cause and one leading activist, Randall Robinson, went on hunger strike to force Clinton into action.

In July 1993 a UN-sponsored mediation effort led the Haitian military government, under General Raul Cédras, to agree to let Aristide resume power by the end of October, in return for an amnesty for his opponents. But when October came, partly encouraged by Clinton's current humiliation in Somalia, Cédras decided to renege on the agreement. A US warship was refused the right to dock in Haiti, Republicans questioned the need for military action, and Clinton felt powerless to respond. Yet, as the months passed, American public opinion became increasingly concerned about the plight of ordinary Haitians, which was not helped by the economic blockade and which still led many 'boat people' to risk escape to the US. In July 1994 a UN resolution approved 'all necessary means' to remove the military government and, as diplomatic pressure on Cédras mounted, the US openly prepared for an invasion. It was eventually time-tabled for mid-September, under the code word Operation Uphold Democracy, and apart from backing the democratic cause, was intended to remove the refugee problem. But even as it was being launched Cédras was induced to stand down. In an eleventh-hour mission to Haiti, ex-President Jimmy Carter persuaded the military to allow Aristide's return. As a result, Operation Uphold Democracy, which Clinton had taken so long to launch, went ahead on 19 September without opposition. Even one critical account concedes that in Haiti, 'the combination of power and diplomacy that the administration had talked about . . . worked rather well.'[42]

Up to 20,000 troops, from other countries in the region, as well as the US, arrived to restore Aristide, and in March 1995 the UN then took over control of the peacekeeping mission. US–UN relations were much better than they had been in Somalia and only one American was killed. Not everything went smoothly. There was sporadic violence between pro- and anti-Aristide factions and, whilst UN troops were withdrawn in November 1997, a police presence had to remain. Elections in April 1997 were marred by accusations of corruption. Years of low

Bill Clinton and his Secretaries of State

Clinton was born William Jefferson Blythe IV in Hope, Arkansas in 1946, but his father was killed in a car accident before he was born and he took a new surname when his mother married Rodger Clinton. When aged 16, Clinton met President Kennedy and determined to become a politician himself. He studied international relations at Georgetown University, Washington; won a Rhodes Scholarship to the University of Oxford; then trained in law at Yale, where he met his wife, Hilary Rodham. Clinton became Attorney-General of his home state in 1976, only three years after leaving Yale, and by 1978 was the youngest state Governor in America. His liberal views cost him the 1980 election, however, and he then became more circumspect in his approach. Returning to the Governorship in 1982, he held on to it for the next decade, slowly improving Arkansas's provision of schools and social welfare.

His bid for the Presidency in 1992 was helped by the fact that most other leading Democrats decided not to run, having decided that the Republican, George Bush, was in an impregnable position. Clinton exploited difficulties in the US economy to overcome Bush, then became the first Democratic President since Roosevelt to serve out two full terms. This was despite the failure of his health reforms, the loss of both the House and Senate to Republican control in 1994, and questions surrounding his finances (the 'Whitewater Affair') and private life (the Lewinsky Scandal, which even briefly led to his impeachment). His greatest success at home was to reduce the government deficit and preside over healthy economic growth. In his foreign policy he was often accused of lacking an overall direction yet he encouraged the peace process in the Middle East and Northern Ireland, took firm action over Haiti and Somalia, and could even claim a belated success in Bosnia.

Clinton's Secretary of State in his first term was Warren Christopher. Born in 1925 in South Dakota he had been educated in law at Stanford and throughout his career interspersed law practice with government service. He was Deputy Attorney-General of the United States in 1967–9, under Johnson, and Deputy Secretary of State in 1977–81, under Carter. In the latter post he had a key role in dealing with the Iran hostage crisis. As Secretary of State he again focused much of his time on Middle East issues and travelled over 750,000 miles, further than any of his predecessors.

In the second term (1997–2001), Clinton chose Madeleine Albright to succeed Christopher. Albright had been born Maria Jana Korbelova in Prague in 1937, the daughter of a Czechoslovakian diplomat. Her family lived in England during the Second World War, after fleeing the Nazis, but settled in Denver, Colorado in 1948. The multi-lingual and academically gifted Albright, received her Ph.D. from Columbia University in 1976 and specialized in international relations, particularly Eastern Europe, working at the School of Foreign Service at the University of Georgetown in the 1980s. But she was also developing a political career, working for Senator Edmund Muskie (1976–8) and then on the staff of the National Security Council under Carter (1978–81). In 1993 she joined the Clinton administration as ambassador to the United Nations. As the first female Secretary of State she proved outspoken and blunt but popular, taking a particularly firm approach when dealing with Serbia.

investment in Haiti meant there was widespread poverty, unemployment, and a lack of basic amenities or an adequate transport system, which in turn undermined social and political stability. In contrast to 1915, the Americans had come and gone quickly, taking care that the UN and OAS approved their action, but the fact was that Haiti still needed external intervention to preserve the hope of a democratic future. 'Indeed, the operation can be seen as a typical case of "regional power projection" by the US government, in its own area of influence', the key contrast with some earlier interventions in the region being that 'there was a strong will amongst the local population in support of the intervention' and a legitimate government being restored.[43]

NOTES

1. Richard A. Melanson, *American Foreign Policy since the Vietnam War* (M. E. Sharpe, Armonk, 1996), 210.

2. John Dumbrell, *American Foreign Policy, Carter to Clinton* (Macmillan, Basingstoke, 1997), 171.

3. Melanson, op. cit., 220.

4. Quoted in Dumbrell, op. cit., 168.

5. Michael Cox, *US Foreign Policy after the Cold War* (Pinter, London 1985), 5.

6. Steven Hurst, *The Foreign Policy of the Bush Administration* (Cassell, London, 1999), 134.

7. Ian Clark, *The Post-Cold War Order* (Oxford University Press, Oxford, 2001), 169, 202, and 217.

8. David Deese, *The New Politics of American Foreign Policy* (St Martin's Press, New York, 1994), xiv.

9. Thomas Homer-Dixon, 'Global Environmental Change and International Security', in David Dewitt et al. (eds.), *Building a New Global Order* (Oxford University Press, Oxford, 1993), 186; Roger Cary, 'The contemporary nature of security' in Trevor C. Salmon (ed), *Issues in International Relations* (Routledge, London, 1999), 59.

10. William Hyland, *Clinton's World: Remaking American Foreign Policy* (Praeger, Westport, 1999), 204.

11. John Spanier and Steve Hook, *American Foreign Policy since World War II* (CQ Press, Washington, 14th edn., 1998), 326.

12. Stephen Ambrose, *Rise to Globalism* (Penguin Books, New York, 8th edn., 1997), 426.

13. Quoted In Spanier and Hook, op. cit., 321.

14. Melanson, op. cit., 255.

15. Hurst, op. cit., 86.

16. George Bush and Brent Scowcroft, op. cit., 371, 435.

17. Said Aburish, *Saddam Hussein: The Politcs of Revenge* (Bloomsbury, London, 2000), 296.

18. Melanson, op. cit., 220.

19. Quoted in Michael Beschloss and Strobe Talbott, *At the Highest Levels* (Little, Brown, Boston, 1993), 254.

20. James Baker, *The Politics of Diplomacy* (G.P. Putnam's Sons, New York, 1995), 281.

21. Quoted in Robert McMahon, 'Contested memory: the Vietnam War and American society', *Diplomatic History*, 2 (2002), 170.

22. Baker, op. cit., 42.

23. Andrew and Patrick Cockburn, *Out of the Ashes: the Resurrection of Saddam Hussein* (HarperCollins, New York, 1999), 85.

24. Quoted in Hurst, op. cit., 46.

25. Quoted in Beschloss and Talbott, op. cit., 135.

26. Don Oberdorfer, *The Turn: How the Cold War came to an End: the United States and the Soviet Union 1983–1990* (Jonathan Cape, London, 1992), 428; Mikhail Gorbachev, *Memoirs* (Doubleday, London, 1996), 537.

27. Ibid., 617.

28. Baker, op. cit., 558.

29. Melanson, op. cit., 270.

30. John Hulsman, *A Paradigm for the New World Order* (Macmillan, Basingstoke, 1997), 115.

31. Boris Yeltsin, *Midnight Diaries* (Public Affairs Press, 2000), 135.

32. Clark, op. cit., 88, 150.

33. A. Lake 'Confronting the Backlash States', United States Information Service, 10 March 1994 (reprinted from *Foreign Affairs*, March-April 1994), 1–2.

35. Quoted in Thomas Paterson, *Contesting Castro* (Oxford University Press, New York, 1994), 263.

36. Charles Kegley and Eugene Wittkopf, *American Foreign Policy: Pattern and Process* (Macmillan, Basingstoke, 5th edn., 1996), 77.

37. Simon Duke, 'The state of human rights', *International Relations*, vol. XII, no. 2 (1994), 27.

38. Mark Curtis, *The Great Deception: Anglo-American Power and World Order* (Pluto Press, Sterling, 1998), 204–6.

39. The title of an article by Michael Mandelbaum in *Foreign Affairs*, 1 (1996).

40. Melanson, op. cit., 259; Karin von Hippel, *Democracy by Force* (Cambridge University Press, Cambridge 2000), 55–6.

41. Quoted in op. cit., 76.

42. Hyland, op. cit., 63–4.

43. Von Hippel, op. cit., 117.

22 Stability and Instability in the Developing World

A. Southern Africa: The End of Apartheid

South Africa's Growing Isolation

One of the signs, alongside the end of the Cold War, that old enmities were breaking down and a more liberal world order might be emerging, was the end of the system of apartheid in South Africa. This development did have some links to the end of the Cold War, but it also followed a long period in which White supremacy had been in decline in southern Africa, leaving the home of apartheid exposed to strong external pressures. South Africa had of course, been widely condemned by much of the international community, and especially the newly independent Black African states, since apartheid had been introduced by the Nationalist Party, which dominated the country's government after 1948. 'Apartheid stirred the international conscience as few other post-war issues had, in a sense making South Africa the world's favourite pariah.'[1] In the early 1960s South Africa had been forced out of the Commonwealth and various UN bodies, despite arguments that a state's *internal* policies were no reason to ostracize it in *external* relations. In 1963 the UN General Assembly had voted for a voluntary arms embargo against South Africa, which most nations respected, including the US (despite its own segregationist policies in the southern states). In 1964 South Africa was also excluded from the Olympics. But Pretoria did not retreat in the face of such pressure. It developed links to the other anti-Communist states that felt threatened by the current international system, not least Israel, and it exploited its position as a major exporter of diamonds, gold, and other minerals. Britain and the US were anxious both to preserve their investments in South Africa and appreciated its value as a firm anti-Communist state, the wealthiest, most powerful military force in sub-Saharan African, and the country which controlled the Cape of Good Hope, between the Atlantic and Indian Oceans. The importance of the last point was underlined in 1967–73 when, thanks to the Arab–Israeli War, the Suez Canal was closed to shipping and the Cape route was more extensively used.

In 1969 the Nixon administration decided it should try to work with South Africa in order to moderate and influence its policies, reasoning that an early collapse of apartheid was unlikely. A 1969 policy review argued that the 'whites are here to stay and the only way that constructive change can come about is through them. There is no hope for the blacks to gain the political rights they seek through violence, which will only lead to chaos and increased opportunities for the Communists.'[2] At that time South Africa's strategic position seemed very secure: it was occupying the South-West Africa, a UN mandate since 1919 which had not been made into a trusteeship for South Africa in 1945 like the mandates of other countries; its northern neighbours included both Ian Smith's White supremacist regime in Rhodesia and the Portuguese colony of Mozambique; and the Black southern African states (such as Botswana, Swaziland, and Lesotho) were very weak, military and economically. South Africa could be considered a 'regional superpower' and the logic of the Nixon Doctrine was that the US should rely on such strong, local powers to maintain stability. As the 1970s progressed, however, the logic of this position was called into question and the trend, at global and regional level, was for South Africa to be isolated. In 1974 its spokesman was not allowed to address the General Assembly; in 1977, following the police murder of the black activist, Steve Biko; a mandatory arms embargo was introduced; and at the same time remaining sports links with the outside world were cut. Of more immediate worry to Pretoria, were events in Angola and Mozambique in 1974–5, where Marxist governments came to power following the end of the Portuguese colonial empire (see Chapter 21, E), and in Rhodesia, where Ian smith's regime was increasingly beleaguered. Lacking South Africa's size and mineral resources, Rhodesia was badly affected by UN sanctions and after 1975 two guerrilla armies led by Black nationalist politicians, Robert Mugabe and Joshua Nkomo, became a serious menace, using

bases in Mozambique. Even Pretoria believed that Smith would have to compromise and the election of Jimmy Carter, with his assertion of human rights, increased the pressures on Rhodesia. An attempt by Smith to install his own favoured Black Prime Minister, Bishop Abel Muzorewa, failed to impress world opinion and in 1979 Britain—still the legal ruler of Rhodesia—brokered a settlement. Smith's 'Unilateral Declaration of Independence' was made void and in December a British governor returned, though only until March 1980, when Mugabe was elected Prime Minister. Rhodesia then became independent under the name of Zimbabwe. Mugabe and Nkomo fell out in 1982, leading to violence between the latter's Matabele people and the majority Shonas, but reasonable stability was maintained until the end of the century, when the oppressive nature of Mugabe's regime began to provoke increasing international concern.

Whilst the independence of Zimbabwe emphasized South Africa's lack of friends on its borders, Mugabe was no more a threat to South Africa's existence than were Botswana or the other former High Commission southern African territories. Zimbabwe needed to recover from the recent guerrilla war and was a poor, landlocked state, its external trade effectively controlled by South Africa. What happened to those who chose actively to oppose South Africa was revealed most starkly in Mozambique, where Ian Smith's intelligence service had already helped create an anti-government guerrilla movement, RENAMO (Mozambique National Resistance). In 1979–80 this was taken over by the South African intelligence service, BOSS, and began an ever more vicious campaign, terrorizing the countryside and helping reduce Mozambique to one of the poorest countries in Africa. Mozambique's crime was to act as a guerrilla base for the African National Congress, a long-standing Black South African political organization, which had decided in 1961 to use violent means to overthrow apartheid. By March 1984 Mozambique was in such turmoil that it offered, in the Nkotami Accord, to end ANC activities there if South Africa abandoned RENAMO. But Pretoria would not honour such a deal and it was only in October 1992, after the demise of apartheid, that an internal peace agreement was reached in Mozambique, which led to elections under UN supervision in November 1994 (won by the government party). At times, notably in May 1986, the South Africans also launched attacks on ANC facilities in Botswana, Zambia, and Zimbabwe; and there were attempts to 'destabilize' these states through support for dissident groups, though never on the scale of Mozambique.

Meanwhile, in the late 1970s and early 1980s, the internal politics of South Africa seemed beyond peaceful change. The ANC leader, Nelson Mandela, remained in prison and other Black nationalists were exiled or murdered. The apartheid laws were maintained and the best reform that Pretoria could offer was to form small, autonomous administrative units in poorer areas (starting with Transkei in 1976) and claim that these were independent Black African nations. Other governments refused to recognize them. A series of school riots in 1976, in the country's largest Black township, Soweto, showed the country was not quiescent in the face of continued discrimination, but the ANC guerrilla campaign had little impact on Pretoria. After 1978 a new President, P. W. Botha, initiated a few reforms, but of a limited nature, such as the legalisation of non-white trades unions and of mixed marriages. Any modest extension of political rights, as in 1984, was restricted to two non-Black minorities, the Indians and mixed-race 'Coloureds'. From 1981, with the replacement of the moralistic Carter by the fiercely anti-communist Reagan, South Africa's international position improved somewhat. Reagan, in defiance of the UN view, insisted that Pretoria's occupation of South-West Africa could not end until Cuban troops left Angola (see Chapter 19, C). The influential Assistant Secretary of State, Chester Crocker, advocated a policy of 'constructive engagement', in a *Foreign Affairs* article of 1981, arguing that the best way to change South African policy was gradually, through cooperation and persuasion, not sanctions and isolation. Crocker himself insisted that this was 'not a formula for a love-in with apartheid ... As a multiracial democracy, the United States cannot endorse a system that is racist in purpose or effect.' But some critics saw it differently: 'Crocker ... ruled out economic sanctions, thus removing from consideration the one policy tool ... viewed as the greatest threat by successive South African administrations.'[3] The

Thatcher government in Britain, still South Africa's most important trading and investment partner, also argued that UN sanctions had harmed poor blacks without bringing down apartheid.

From Botha to Mandela

In August 1984 a fresh outbreak of internal violence began to rock South Africa's Black townships. Eventually, on 25 July 1985, the government responded with a partial state of emergency. Young blacks, frustrated by a system that kept wealth and political power in the hands of whites, when they themselves faced poverty and unemployment, took part in months of riots and demonstrations. In the government crackdown that followed about 2,000 were killed and tens of thousand detained. Such violence, together with Botha's failure to embrace radical reform, led to the growing doubts in America about the policy of 'constructive engagement'. Congress at first forced Reagan to introduce limited sanctions in September 1985, then, in August 1986, passed a comprehensive Anti-Apartheid Act, with wide-ranging measures including a ban on new investments. Pressure for firmer sanctions also revived in the UN and the Commonwealth, backed by South Africa's Church leader, the Nobel Prize Winner, Archbishop Desmond Tutu. Thatcher resisted the change of policy and, together with Reagan, prevented the UN from adopting a mandatory embargo. But other Commonwealth and European Community states introduced their own extra sanctions. The state of emergency was suspended for a while, only to be reimposed in June 1986, but the situation for the government was not yet critical: over the years it had built up its industries and had stock-piled oil and other resources, so that it could cope with isolation; it was still the regional superpower with little to fear from the 'front-line' Black African states to the North; diamonds and gold exports were strong; and some states, notably Germany and Japan, boosted their trade with South Africa at this time. Furthermore, there were divisions among black South Africans, especially between the ANC and the Zulu political movement, 'Inkatha', led by Chief Mangosuthu Buthelezi. But there were serious problems of falling external investment in

South Africa, a worsening balance of payments and currency instability, and there was a growing belief among some of the White elite that radical reform was inescapable.

In 1989 two major events occurred inside South Africa. First, in a general election, the National Party lost votes both to right-wingers, who rejected all change, and left-wingers, who wanted reform. Second, Botha suffered a stroke and was succeeded by F. W. de Klerk who decided on a programme of change in preference to growing economic troubles and a potential bloodbath. At the same time, whilst disliking sanctions and still hoping for peaceful change, the Bush administration came to power in Washington with a more critical public line than Reagan on apartheid. The Angolan and Namibian disputes had now been settled (see Chapter 19, C). Despite widespread scepticism about de Klerk's intentions, Botha's successor not only spoke of a 'new' South Africa but also set out to create one. He was helped in this by the decline of communism in Europe and the Cuban withdrawal from Angola, which neutralized those—both inside and outside the country—who had always feared that reform would lead Marxist regime in Pretoria. De Klerk 'faced an entirely new set of political challenges within his own constituency base, as well as quite a different set ... of international challenges', so that some shift in policy was unsurprising. But the scale of what followed surprised everyone: 'It is almost unprecedented in history for a government, enjoying the loyalty ... of its security forces and bureaucracy, to begin a process which could imply the termination of its rule.'[4] In July 1989 de Klerk met Nelson Mandela, the greatest symbol of Black nationalism, for the first time and on 2 February 1990, after further meetings, released him from prison. In the interim the government moved from legalizing peaceful protests, to recognition of the ANC and other opposition groups, and then to the promise of constitutional talks. The state of emergency was lifted in stages after June 1990, coming to an end five months later. In August 1990 a deal was reached whereby the government issued an amnesty for political prisoners and let exiled opposition leaders return home while the ANC suspended its guerrilla campaign. Just as significant, in June 1991, the main laws that upheld apartheid

were repealed, notably the Group Areas Act which had segregated the races from one another.

In this process the two sides had different goals. De Klerk's policy was to 'change the system sufficiently to restore social peace and normalize South Africa's relations with the rest of the world, but avoid a complete transfer of power to blacks'; while the ANC was 'confident it would take over after the demise of the white regime'.[5] As events unfolded it was increasingly difficult to deny that de Klerk was seeking fundamental changes, and pressure grew to ease UN sanctions against South Africa. Britain led the way in this, relaxing some of its own sanctions in early 1990. The US was slower, ending all sanctions by mid-1991. At the same time, sports links to South Africa were reopened by international bodies. There was a continuing danger that the peace moves would be undermined by violence: indeed, especially in Natal, thousands of people died in the early 1990s in clashes between that ANC and Inkatha, with the latter receiving encouragement from the police and army, elements of which were opposed to de Klerk's policies. Also, sanctions were eased when blacks were still without the vote: constitutional talks, through the 'Convention for a Democratic South Africa', only began in December 1991 and white voters only approved reform in a (whites-only) referendum in March 1992. But the international community felt it must act to encourage de Klerk by ending sanctions and the policy was justified by events. Within South Africa the National Party, ANC, and other groups found it difficult to pull back from negotiations: 'despite the many differences between these parties on their ideal visions of a future state, there was among them ... a considerable convergence on a post-apartheid democracy.'[6] Though troubled in 1992, and even suspended for several months, the constitutional talks resulted in agreement in February 1993, which led to equal political rights for all, free elections, and guarantees that the National Party might retain a share in power for five years. The April 1994 elections, boycotted by Inkatha, were easily won by the ANC, which had effectively secured most from the negotiations with the National Party, at least on the political front. By then apartheid had disappeared as an international problem, the southern Africa region was at peace for the first time in a generation, and the new South

Nelson Mandela

The first black President of South Africa was born in 1918, the son of a chief of the Thembu tribe. Trained as a lawyer, with a BA degree from the University of South Africa, he gave up the position of Chief when he inherited it, preferring to pursue his political ambitions. Mandela joined the African National Congress (ANC), the main movement working for equal rights among the country's racial groups, in 1944. He was soon a leading figure among the radical, younger members of the party and became head of its youth league in 1951. Over the following years he took part in non-violent resistance to the growth of the 'apartheid' system, introduced by the white supremacist National Party, and seen most notoriously in the Group Areas Act. In 1952, despite being banned by the government from attending public meetings, Mandela became a vice-president at the ANC and in 1956–61, along with other Congress leaders, he successfully fought off government accusations of treason in a long-running court battle.

The Sharpeville massacre of 1960 led to a decision by the ANC to set up a paramilitary wing, the 'Spear of the Nation' in 1961, of which Nelson Mandela became head. But this shift to a readiness to use violent tactics made it easier for the government to resuscitate charges of treason against him. He was arrested in 1962 and sentenced to life imprisonment two years later. For the next eighteen years Mandela was incarcerated on Robben Island but in the process became the greatest symbol of resistance to apartheid. In the 1980s, as South Africa's international position became more isolated, there was mounting pressure to release him. Despite government fears of his radicalism, he entered secret talks with them in 1986 and, although it caused some controversy in the ANC, he even met the South African President, P. W. Botha, in 1989. In February 1990 Mandela was finally released from prison, in 1992 he was elected ANC president, and in 1993 he shared the Nobel Peace Prize with Botha's successor, F. W. de Klerk, following an international settlement of the country's problems. Old age meant that Mandela served only one term (1994–9) as President himself, being succeeded by his former deputy, Thabo Mbeki. In 1996 after nearly forty years of marriage, Mandela divorced his second wife, Winnie, who had become identified with radical violence and been implicated in murder. On his eightieth birthday he married Graca Machel, widow of a former President of neighbouring Mozambique.

African President, Mandela, was recognized as a statesman of global stature. For South Africa itself however, notwithstanding its natural resources and its power in the region, the challenges of national reconciliation, boosting black incomes and providing genuine equalities of opportunity were immense. There was a bold attempt to address the first problem by setting up a 'Truth and Reconcili-ation Committee', which held hearings down to 1998 to try to investigate outrages carried out by all sides in the apartheid era. As to economic problems, there was some disappointment at the government's failure to redistribute wealth and a feeling that it had adopted a conservative approach to high finance, but that did not prevent the ANC winning the June 1998 general election by another clear margin.

B. Central Africa: Rwanda and Zaire

Poverty and Instability below the Sahara

If the peaceful transition to majority rule in South Africa was one of the most hopeful changes in international politics in the 1990s, it could not mask the fact that the continent south of the Sahara contained the world's poorest regions. In the mid-1990s three-quarters of the countries designated by the World Bank as 'heavily indebted' were in sub-Saharan Africa, with total debts there of about $200 billion. Whereas Latin America's debts had fallen as a percentage of gross national product since the 'debt crisis' of the 1980s (see Chapter 17, D), Africa's had continued to rise until many countries had debts in excess of their GNP. Many ordinary Africans lacked a basic education, health care or even clean water but their governments and Western aid agencies had no solution to the situation. There was simply no agreement on the root cause of African problems. The former colonial powers were variously blamed for dividing the continent up with little regard to local factors, either geographical or ethnic, and for abandoning the newly independent countries around 1960 with little preparation in economic or political terms. Subsequently Western countries had shaped a global economy which let Africans run up huge debts but gave them paltry reward for their exports. In the 1980s the IMF and World Bank became 'the most significant external influences on the political life of many African countries', acting in a way that some criticized as 'tantamount to a new form of colonialism'.[7]

African countries themselves had often adopted a centralized political model, based around strong leaders and socialist-style economic planning, which sometimes broke down into dictatorship, military coups, and financial corruption. Given sub-Saharan Africa's ethnic differences, military regimes, and economic problems, it is surprising that there was not more *international* conflict. But beyond southern Africa, and after the civil wars in the Congo and Nigeria in the 1960s (see Chapters 8, C and 11, E), the number of conflicts in the area was remarkably few. The Tanzanian-led invasion of Uganda in 1979 proved a unique example of one Black African state helping to overthrow the dictator of another by armed force. And here, once Idi Amin was replaced, the Tanzanians quickly withdrew. There was some interference from the former colonial powers, especially the French who, also in 1979, helped overthrow the dictator of the Central African Republic, Jean Bokassa. By the mid-1990s, however, there were a number of civil conflicts in sub-Saharan Africa which threatened to draw in outside states and which led, by 1994, to 7.5 million refugees on the continent. All of them involved questions of the future of the state. Two were in West Africa where Nigeria, despite being ruled by an oppressive military dictatorship, played a leading role in peacemaking efforts: in Liberia a multinational force was sent by other West African countries after civil war broke out in 1990 between rebels of the regime of Samuel Doe

(who had launched a military coup in 1980); and in Sierra Leone there was a series of coups in the wake of the dictatorship of Siaka Stevens (1968–85), culminating in a Nigerian-led intervention in early 1998. On the latter occasion the Nigerians themselves became enmeshed in the violence and there were further interventions by both the UN and the former colonial power, Britain. Across the continent, in the southern Sudan, there was a long-running uprising, begun in 1983 by the Black, Christian population against the Arab, Islamic fundamentalist regime in Khartoum. Here the rebels had the backing of neighbouring Uganda but they faced an increasingly determined Sudanese army and by 1998 had to cope with a widespread famine. Only in 2002 was a ceasefire achieved, under US pressure. Small wonder that some experts considered that, of all Africa's problems, 'the crisis that is affecting the state is by far the most threatening for the future.'[8] The most bloody and dangerous conflicts of all arose in Central Africa, centred on the conflict between Tutsis and Hutus in Rwanda.

Civil War and Genocide in Rwanda and Burundi

Rwanda and its equally small neighbour, Burundi, had been given their independence by Belgium in 1962. Both were landlocked countries with a majority from the Hutu people but it was the minority Tutsis who had been favoured—at least until the 1950s when they began to take a lead in anti-colonialism—under Belgian rule, as part of an apparent process of divide and rule. Both countries had also suffered political upheaval but seemed to be moving towards greater stability and a decentralization of government in the summer of 1993. Burundi, after military coups in 1976 and 1983, had returned to civilian rule in 1992 and held its first free elections in June 1993. Rwanda had been dominated by a Hutu-led military regime under Juvenal Habyarimana since 1993 and faced rebellion from the Ugandan-based Tutsi-led Rwandan Popular Front (FPR) after mid-1990, but in 1992 agreed to a ceasefire. In August 1993, at Arusha in Tanzania, a peace was agreed which promised a Tutsi share in power, a transitional government and elections.

A small UN-approved international force was sent to monitor this. But within months both countries were in turmoil. Burundi's President was killed in a failed coup in October, to be succeeded by Cyprien Ntaryamina who was unable to a rising tide of inter-ethnic violence. In Rwanda fulfilment of the Arusha accords was repeatedly delayed and the military were in fact planning to massacre the Tutsis. Then, on 6 April 1994 the Presidents of both countries were killed in a rocket attack over Rwanda, while travelling together on an aircraft.

In Burundi, the violent death of the second President in six months, led to an intensification of the violence which already existed. Attempts were made to form a broad-based government in September 1994, but it proved unstable and by 1996 deaths were running at about 1,000 per month. In April of that year the US and the European Union suspended aid to Burundi because of the government's failure to protect the Hutus from Tutsi attacks. Then on 25 July the Tutsi military, under Major Pierre Buyoya, seized power, suspended parliament, and closed the country's borders. But, even after rebellion broke out in the north in September 1996, the level of violence in Burundi was far less than that in Rwanda And given what had happened to the latter, the international community was anxious to prevent the Burundi situation worsening. In Rwanda, the death of President Habyanimana had been followed by the massacre of thousands of opponents of the military government, both Hutu and Tutsis. The victims included the Prime Minister, several other ministers, and some Belgian peace monitors. The government, now under Theodore Sindikubgabo, blamed the Tutsis for downing Habyanimana's aircraft. But it was not clear what the Tutsis hoped to gain from the assassination of a President who had negotiated the Arusha agreement with them. The FPR, which refused to recognize the Sindikubgabo regime, blamed the air crash on Hutu militants in the military, who, from the speed of reaction to it, had clearly been planning the massacres for a long time. Even the elite Presidential Guard joined the rank-and-file and Hutu youths in butchering Tutsis.

The Tutsis had been subjected to periodic bouts of victimization in the past, but the new massacres soon took the form of a campaign of genocide.

Within weeks it was claimed that up to 200,000 had been killed and a later UN report suggested that 500,000 people died in Rwanda, a country of only 8 million, by the end of June. Nothing had been seen in Africa on this scale since the Nigerian civil war in the late 1960s (see Chapter 11, E). Many Tutsis also fled abroad to Tanzania but the FPR was determined to strike back with its efficient and well-armed military. Meanwhile, the reaction of the international community to the Rwandan tragedy was hesitant, confused, and ineffectual. It was probably have been impossible to prevent many of the deaths that occurred, because the violence took off so quickly. But the Organization of African Unity pointed out that the UN had been quick to send troops to Bosnia when ethnic conflict broke out among Europeans. Africa was treated differently. Here the UN felt it had little choice other than to *reduce* the peace monitors in Rwanda, mainly because the Belgians, having helped to evacuate foreign nationals, were determined to leave. The UN Secretary-General, Boutros Boutros-Ghali, was appalled that the 'international community did little or nothing as the killing in Rwanda continued', but he was already running seventeen peacekeeping operations around the world and was entirely dependent on the UN member states providing for the resources to intervene in central Africa.[9] Aid was provided to refugees and there were attempts to broker a ceasefire, but only France showed much desire to intervene in the Rwandan bloodbath. The US had taken little interest in Africa since the Cold War, apart from Somalia—but what had occurred there helped ensure that President Clinton was unlikely to intervene in a second African country (see Chapter 21, E). In June the Security Council approved 'Operation Turquoise', a supposed humanitarian intervention by 2,500 French troops to try to keep Hutus and Tutsis apart. But France was the worst possible choice for such a force, because the FPR blamed Paris for having backed the Habyanimana regime. The French had helped to arm the Rwandan military since 1975 and had greatly intensified this aid after the FPR opened the civil war in 1990, even sending several hundred troops. There were some rumours that they were involved in the fateful air crash of 6 April and certainly the Rwandan military hoped for a continuation of support from Paris. This was in line with

French policy elsewhere in French-speaking Africa: in 1990 the French had military advisers in twenty-six African countries. Without French backing, it could be argued, Hutu militants could never have hoped to begin their policy of genocide. Thus, 'although France was undoubtedly well placed to intervene from a technical point of view, politically and morally the situation was more ambiguous.'[10] Via Operation Turquoise the French government hoped to recover from accusations at home that it had helped bring about the Rwandan crisis and at the same time it wanted to demonstrate to other African allies its ability to act militarily on the continent, even though the prime aim of the operation was to provide humanitarian aid.

By the time the French arrived the FPR army was in control of most of Rwanda. Indeed, on 19 July they claimed victory over the Hutu military and set out to fulfil the Arusha accords, forming a coalition government which, while it was determined to track down those responsible for the recent genocide, included Hutus as well as Tutsis. There was a Hutu President, Pasteur Bisimurgu, and Prime Minister. But such signs of a desire for reconciliation did not convince many Hutus who, encouraged by their own military leaders, began to flee over the western border, into Zaire. For a time the French set up a 'safe zone' in part of Rwanda for the fleeing Hutus and, in an extraordinary twisting of their UN mandate, threatened to exclude the FPR from this by force. By late August however Operation Turquoise was brought to an end and the new Rwandan government could try to rebuild the country without direct external interference. There were cases of Hutus being killed but these were blamed on maverick elements, official policy being to put those individuals responsible for genocide on trial. In November the UN set up its own International Criminal Tribunal in Rwanda and in December, after an investigation into the massacres, agreed with the FPR claim that the genocide, far from being the side effect of a lurch into anarchy after Habyanimana's sudden death, had been the premeditated action of the French-backed Hutu militants. For Rwanda, however, the threat of violence had not ended because many Hutu militants were now based in camps in Rwanda, where a million Hutu refugees were housed.

Zaire: The Fall of Mobutu

The situation surrounding the Hutu refugee camps in eastern Zaire eventually created such instability in that country that it brought a change of regime. There were, once again, attempts by the UN to get the problem under control but, as in Rwanda in April 1994, it proved impossible to create a sizeable multinational force to police the refugee camps. The responsibility for this task therefore fell on the regime of Mobutu Sese Seko, the general who had seized power in Zaire, the former Belgian Congo, in 1965. Despite his dictatorial rule and his practice of taking national wealth into his own hands, Mobutu had been backed by the West as the only strong figure who could hold his sprawling country together. He protected the interests of Western companies and opposed the Marxist regime in Angola, on his south-western border but, in the wake of the Cold War, Mobutu's eccentricity and oppressiveness became increasingly embarrassing. The US, France, and Belgium were now less likely to give him firm backing. Despite Zaire's size and mineral resources, it was deeply in debt. Inflation was high, the economic infrastructure was in tatters, and Mobutu's repeated promises to democratize had come to nothing. Yet his personal wealth stood at $10 billion and he was increasingly too ill to hold power effectively. In 1990 he showed signs of wanting to consult public opinion and, in April, even announced the end of one-party rule, which led to an opposition group, the 'Sacred Union', being formed under Etienne Tshishekedi. In September 1991 Mobutu's hold on power was shaken by army mutinies over low pay and for a time Tshishekedi became Prime Minister. Mobutu soon took the reigns of power back into his own hands but another threat to his position existed in the form of regionalism within the sprawling Zairean state.

One aspect of Mobutu's policy since the 1980s had been his victimization of Zaire's own Tutsi minority. These were concentrated in the east of the country, in the very area to which a million Rwandan Hutus now fled. As with its support for France and Operation Turquoise, the UN's decision to let Mobutu police the situation in eastern Zaire was regrettable. It was, of course, impossible to deny a role to the Zaireans in keeping order within their own country, but an international force might have prevented what occurred in 1995–6 and—ironically—might have helped Mobutu's regime survive. Throughout 1995 and into 1996 the Hutu refugees remained in their Zairean camps, despite overcrowding and disease, believing that they would be slaughtered if they returned home to Rwanda. Hutu militants stirred these fears and used the camps as bases for a political and military revival of their cause. They not only planned to return to power in Rwanda but also, with the connivance of some of Mobutu's troops, attacked the Zairean Tutsis. The latter, however, could now rely on help from the Rwandan government—which also wanted to see the Hutu refugees return home and the militants rooted out. In September 1996 widespread fighting broke out in eastern Zaire while Mobutu was out of the country, receiving treatment for cancer in a Swiss hospital. While Hutu militants and Zairean troops attacked local Tutsis, the Rwandan government sent troops over the border to help a rebel force led by Laurent Kabila. He had been a would-be Marxist revolutionary back in the 1960s, had backed the secession of Shaba province at one time and now gathered behind him several groups opposed to Mobutu. Uganda, which also feared a spread of Hutu violence, supported the Rwandans, as did an old enemy of Mobutu, the Angolan government.

By the end of October 1996 the Zairean army, demoralized, underpaid, and ill-equipped, was retreating before Kabila. The UN again considered sending a substantial, multinational force to central Africa, this time to prevent a widely feared bloodbath in the Hutu refugee camps. But the speed of Kabila's advance easily outpaced the decision-making of the UN and the refugee problem soon began to resolve itself. Most Hutus in the camps decided that it was, at last, safer to return to Rwanda than to stay in a war-zone where the FRP govern-

ment, and its ally Kabila, were in the ascendant. Faced by this crisis Mobutu did not return home until mid-December but, after pausing to form a new cabinet, he was soon abroad again, residing in his French villa. In early 1997 Kabila's forces made a remarkable advance across Zaire as Mobutu's support crumbled and those with influence and wealth scrambled to come to terms with the new leader. Attempts by South Africa's Nelson Mandela to mediate a settlement came to nothing. Mobutu again returned home for a time but on 16 May fled to Morocco, where he died four months later. Zaire then became, under Kabila, the 'Congo' once more. Until the end Mobutu had hoped for support from his old allies abroad, but the Americans decided that Kabila—despite his Marxist past, his failure to democratize, and his slaying of opponents during his advance—was a preferable strong-man. As to his other main Western ally, France, it had already suffered a loss of face in Rwanda and could not hope to shore up such a corrupt regime in the wake of the events of 1994–7; indeed France was much less active trying to shape African politics. This did not prove an untarnished gain for the Rwandan government however. They had done much to bring about a change of regime in their giant neighbour but had not yet extinguished Hutu militancy. Late 1997 saw further inter-ethnic violence after Hutu rebels, still surviving in the Congo, attacked across the border. As to Kabila, he proved little more competent and democratic than Mobutu had done and soon fell out with the Rwandans and Ugandans, partly because he sought to restore good relations with his own Hutu minority. In August, in a virtual replay of events barely two years before, Rwanda and Uganda backed an anti-Kabila rebellion in eastern Congo. This time there was no irresistible advance on the capital but Kabila was not in office for long, being assassinated in January 2001.

CHRONOLOGY: THE ZAIREAN CIVIL WAR, 1996–1997

1996

23 October	President Mobutu of Zaire says Rwanda and Burundi are to blame for growing clashes between Tutsis and Zairean troops around refugee camps on Rwandan border, where there are perhaps over one million Rwandan Hutus.
24 October	Rebel forces under Laurent Kabila seize the town of Nyangezi, as hundreds of thousands of Hutu refugees flee from their camps.
28 October	Rebel forces take the town at Bukavu, saying their aim is to overthrow Mobutu.
30 October	Rwanda admits it is helping the rebels, who form a 'Democratic Alliance of Forces for the Liberation of Congo-Zaire' and clash with the Hutu militias.
3 November	The city of Goma captured by rebels, as the Zairean army in the border area disintegrates. International concern for the plight of refugees mounts.
9 November	UN defers a decision on French proposal for a multinational force to be sent to eastern Zaire.
Around 15 November	With Hutu militias being driven out of the area, many Hutu refugees begin to return to Rwanda; massive humanitarian problem now builds on the Rwandan border.
29 November	Agreement reached on a multinational force, led by Canada, for relief role.
Early December	Ugandan troops occupy areas of eastern Zaire, in support of the rebels.
Mid-December	Canada begins to wind down multinational force due to effective end of refugee problem in Zaire.
17 December	Mobutu returns to Zaire, after months of treatment for cancer in France, but he intermittently returns to France over following months.

1997

Early January	Fighting breaks out between different rebel factions.
Late January	Counter-attacks by Zairean army in eastern Zaire.
Early February	Rebel advances are made, possibly with Ugandan support.
18 February	UN Security Council Resolution 1097 calls for a ceasefire, withdrawal of any foreign troops from Zaire, and peace talks.
19 February	President Mandela of South Africa offers to mediate between Mobutu and Kabila.
1 March	Rebels take Kisangani; French forces help evacuate foreign nationals.
26 March	First direct meeting of rebel and government representatives at an OAU summit in Lome.
2 April	In contriving attempts to broaden his government, Mobutu appoints an opposition politician, Etienne Tshisekedi as Prime Minister.
5 April	Rebels take Mbujmayi; Lubumbashi falls on 9 April; rebels are accused of massacring civilians.
14–16 April	General strike against Mobutu in the capital Kinshasa.

29 April	Rebels take Kikwit.
4 May	Mobutu and Kabila meet face-to-face in talks chaired by Nelson Mandela but Kabila insists Mobutu must surrender power.
16 May	Mobutu finally flees Kinshasa for Morocco.
17 May	Kabila names himself Head of State and renames Zaire the 'Democratic Republic of the Congo'.

C. **The Middle East: Progress and Retreat on Palestine**

The Bush Presidency and the Washington Talks, 1989–1993

After the neglect of the Arab–Israeli dispute under Ronald Reagan (see Chapter 17, B), the Bush Presidency proved more determined in seeking a negotiated settlement, which would include security guarantees for Israel and progress on the main sticking point in previous talks, Palestinian rights. The US public was dismayed by Israel's killing of hundreds of Palestinian protestors in 1988 and, with the fading of the Cold War, it no longer seemed necessary to build Israel up as an anti-Soviet ally in the Middle East. Thus Bush, though personally well disposed to Israel, seemed to be in a position to pressure it to moderate its policies. Since December 1987 the Palestinian uprising, the Intifada, Yasser Arafat's Palestinian Liberation Organization (PLO) had exploited the situation by condemning Israel's human rights record and by pursuing a more sophisticated diplomatic and military strategy. Terrorist attacks by the Palestinian Liberation Front (PLF) were now concentrated on Israeli targets; a government-in-exile was created but it limited its territorial claim to the West Bank and Gaza, rather than the whole of Israel; and the PLO were prepared to recognize Israel's existence. By now, as one leading Palestinian intellectual put it, 'The central problem is the official Israeli refusal to recognize . . . the fact of Palestinian nationalism.'[11] Israel's attempt to undermine the PLO's popularity in the occupied territories by encouraging a rival organization, Hamas, turned to disaster. The fundamentalists of Hamas, set up in 1988 under Sheikh Ahmed Yassin, became tough and ruthless opponents. Ironically, in the 1990s, when Israel finally decided to deal with the PLO, Hamas were strong enough to threaten the peace process by a series of bomb attacks largely outside Arafat's control.

Israel's failure to contain the Intifada and its reliance on the Americans for $3 billion of military and economic aid each year, did not however make it eager to rush into a settlement. Enmities and suspicion in the region were deep-seated, the right-wing Likud Party continued to dominate the government in Tel Aviv and there was a strong Zionist lobby in Congress and outside which opposed Bush's attempts to use aid as a lever for concessions. Israelis remembered too many terrorist attacks in the past to deal with Arafat willingly. The Israeli Prime Minister, Yitzhak Shamir, was unwilling to make real concessions, himself believing that 'the only peace the PLO could produce in terms of Israel was the peace of the cemetery.'[12] Also, the contacts between Washington and the PLO, which had been taken up at the end of the Reagan Presidency, proved tenuous. In June 1990 the US side severed then, following a PLF terrorist attack on an Israeli beach, and at the same time the Intifada assumed a new vigour. Only in late 1991 were Bush and Baker able to make progress on the Middle East and this thanks to two major developments. First, the continued weakening of the USSR, linked as it was to Gorbachev's willingness to discuss an Arab–Israeli settlement, showed hardline Arab governments like Syria, that they could no longer rely on Soviet backing in a crisis, that the US was now the only superpower with which to deal, and that negotiations were probably inevitable. A side effect of the USSR's retreat from Marxist-Leninism however was the increased flow of Soviet Jews to Israel: more than 350,000 in 1990–1. This helped Israeli–Soviet relations but it also increased the pressure to expand Jewish settlements on the West Bank, which in turn offended the Arabs, who did not see why refugees from far away should be settled on Palestinian land when so many Palestinian refugees were unable to return to their homes in Israel. The issue of new settlements also proved a running sore in Israeli–US relations and was the main justification for Bush's efforts to restrict aid to Israel in 1990 and 1991.

The second major development in 1990–1 was the Gulf War (see Chapter 21, B) which led to improved relations between America and Israel—especially after US missiles were deployed on Israeli soil to protect it from Iraqi missile attacks—and between America and those Arab states, including Egypt and Syria, who were opposed to Saddam Hussein. The war had a mixed effect on the Israeli–Palestinian issue. On the one hand the Arabs were divided, a radical Arab leader, Saddam Hussein, was defeated and Arafat alienated the US through his ill-judged support for Iraq. On the other hand, in order to keep his Arab allies happy, Bush agreed to work for a resumption of the Geneva Conference of Middle East states, which had first met after the 1973 War. Victory over Saddam gave the US even greater influence in the region, as well as bolstering Bush's position at home, and US officials were determined to exploit this to end, for good, the dangers of an Arab–Israeli conflict. The killing of 21 Palestinians on Temple Mount in October 1991 had helped maintain some sympathy in the West for their plight. Therefore in March 1991, the US Secretary of State, James Baker, began a series of visits to the Middle East in order to arrange a conference. Among others, on 12 March, he talked to Palestinian leaders in the occupied areas. The result was the Madrid conference, which opened on 30 October 1991. As with Geneva in 1973 the meeting was co-chaired by the US and USSR, both Bush and Gorbachev being present, and attended by Israeli and Arab delegations. Even Syria attended and, while Israel still refused to accept PLO representatives, there was a Palestinian group within the Jordanian delegation, and this was in contact with Arafat. But, hopeful as this was, the talks saw as many mutual recriminations (especially between Israel and Syria) as attempts at agreement and broke up in less than a week.

Madrid showed that the US was more interested in bringing negotiations about than in pointing them in a particular direction. It made its general views on a settlement—Israeli security, Palestinian rights—clear enough but wanted the protagonists themselves to produce detailed ideas and had no wish to become involved in a long-term, complex process of mediation. Bush was also aware of his limited ability, because of the Jewish lobby, to press Israel for concessions, despite Arab hopes that he would do

this. But, disappointing as Madrid was, it did not end American attempts to maintain Arab–Israeli contacts. Far from it. For a time there seemed to be a 'reversal of the Palestinian and Israeli positions in relation to American policy in the Middle East', with one Israeli official describing his side as 'riddled with doubt, suspicion and even dread concerning what the future might bring'.[13] In December 1991, the US called more talks, this time in Washington, and these continued with several rounds throughout 1992. There were both bilateral talks and multilateral ones (not all held in Washington), on a wide range of issues from the main political problems to general subjects like regional transport, health, and culture. But the key subject was the make-up and powers of any Palestinian authority in the West Bank and Gaza. On this there were, predictably, wide differences and when the government of Yitzhak Shamir began to discuss a possible form of interim self-government for Palestinians, its coalition supporters became divided.

The departure of two extremist groups forced an election which was won on 23 June by a Labour-led coalition under Yitzhak Rabin. This was welcome news to Bush. Rabin was better disposed than Shamir to a peace agreement and restricted the pace of new Jewish settlements on the West Bank. The new Premier even talked of achieving peace within a year. His Foreign Minister, Shimon Peres, was influenced by the Bosnian crisis to 'believe in the need for political separation between Israelis and Palestinians' and now ready to place 'the future of Gaza in the hands of the people who lived there', even if he knew that the future of the West Bank would be more difficult to settle. Even more remarkably, in August 1992 he suggested 'that Israel should reconsider its position on negotiating with Arafat'.[14] But events in the second half of 1992 dampened such expectations. In America, Bush was preoccupied by his failing re-election campaign and in Israel the continuation of terrorist attacks, alongside the Intifada, made it difficult for Rabin to contemplate concessions. 1992 ended with Bush's election defeat in November, and the breakdown of the Washington talks in December. The Arabs walked out of the negotiations after Israel expelled over 400 suspected members of Hamas.

The 1993 Oslo Accords

The breakdown of the Washington talks and the election of Bill Clinton, a firm pro-Israeli, as US President hardly augured well for a Middle East settlement. But events were set in train in December 1992, in great secrecy and entirely without American involvement, which brought a surprise break-through more quickly than anyone hoped. The 'benign neglect shown during the first months of the Clinton administration ... created space for Norwegian mediation', which 'provided both sides with the possibility of exploring each other's position without recognition, commitment, or ... violating Israel's law under which meetings with the PLO were illegal.'[15] A highly secret contact was established between a narrow group of Israeli and Palestinian academics, using Norwegian social scientist, Tarje Larsen, as a go-between. An initial contact in London was followed by months of talks in Oslo, with the Norwegian government becoming involved. Rabin, once informed of the contact, was concerned that the PLO might leak word of the fact, so as to embarrass Israel. He would

have preferred to concentrate on the Washington talks, which were resumed in the spring, but these were too public to allow either side to discuss substantial concessions and Rabin was anxious to fulfil his promise of progress towards peace, ending the Intifada and securing Labour's re-election. For his part Arafat, far from wishing to embarrass Israel by leaking word of the talks, was anxious to challenge the popularity of Hamas in the occupied territories and show some results for the more realistic political strategy he had followed since 1988, so as to prevent moves being made to replace him. He also needed to recover, in the eyes of world opinion, from the costly mistake he had made in 1990–1 of backing Saddam Hussein's invasion of Kuwait.

During the Oslo talks the Israelis were keen to defer discussion on difficult problems like the status of East Jerusalem (claimed by Israel, but part of the West Bank until 1967), which were impossible to settle in the foreseeable future, and to concentrate instead on the possible autonomy of Gaza which was densely populated by Palestinians, though it did include some Jewish settlements. The Palestinians

---

The 'Declaration of Principles on Interim Self-Government', 13 September 1993

The Declaration, signed in Washington in the presence of president Clinton, by Palestinian leader Yasser Arafat and Israeli Premier Yitzhak Rabin, was the basis of all future Israeli–Palestinian peace efforts. It had actually been nego-tiated via secret contacts in Oslo and opened with a statement that the two sides:

agree that it is the time to put an end to decades of confrontation and conflict, recognize their mutual legitimate political rights ... and achieve a just, lasting and comprehensive peace settlement

Article One, set out the aim of their negotiations as being 'to establish a Palestinian Interim Self-Government Authority ... for the Palestine people in the West Bank and Gaza Strip, for a transitional period not exceeding five years, leading to a permanent settlement bases on Security Council Resolutions 242 and 338.' Article Three stated that elections for such an Authority would be held within nine months of the declaration entering into force.

Whilst Article Four made clear that the Authority should have jurisdiction over the Bank and Gaza Strip, Article Five stated that 'the five-year' transitional period 'will begin

upon the withdrawal from the Gaza Strip and Jericho area,' so that the initial area controlled by the Palestinians in the West Bank was quite limited. Other issues, including Palestinian refugees, Jewish settlements on the West bank, and the future of Jerusalem—none of them easy to resolve—were to be the subject of negotiations which would open 'not later than the beginning of the third year of the interim period'. In fact, once such talks began, they proved very slow and difficult.

Article Eight of the Declaration covered the difficult issue of security in Palestinian areas. The Palestinian Authority, or Council, was to 'establish a strong police force, whilst Israel will continue to carry the responsi-bility for defence against external threats, as well as the responsibility for overall security of Israelis.' The Declaration, which ran to seventeen articles in all, and had a number of annexes, also dealt with economic and development programmes, the details of Israeli withdrawal, and ways of resolving future disputes (mainly via a Joint Liaison Committee, set up under Article Ten).

were divided about this approach to the problem: some wanted much more substantial gains, others were happy to accept any land. But Arafat decided to ask for both Gaza and the key West Bank city of Jericho, reasoning that this would give the Palestinians an autonomous foothold in the West Bank which could later be expanded. Behind the territorial issues was another question, of whether the creation of a Palestinian political entity would lead to full sovereignty. Arafat hoped it would, but the Israelis were ambiguous because their aims were rather different. As their negotiator, Uri Savir, put it, 'The Palestinians needed to know that autonomy could lead to a state, while we needed to know it would bring security.'[16] The PLO representatives, led by Abu Alaa soon, confirmed their seriousness in the talks by agreeing to concessions on such issues as self-government in the Israeli settlements and the right of Israeli troops to remain in areas of the West Bank. For a time in July Arafat did toughen his demands, mainly it seems in an attempt to maximize the Israeli concessions, and with a breakdown looming Israel did make a highly important offer: after twenty-nine years of refusal, they were ready to recognize the PLO officially. On 30 August the talks were finally made public, provoking surprise everywhere, not least in the Washington talks where even the Palestinian team had not been told of the Oslo contact. Ordinary Israelis and Palestinians were both concerned about what had been conceded, but two-thirds of Israelis soon claimed to support the Accords and Arafat was, for a time, able to carry the Palestinians with him. Although he had nothing to do with the negotiations, President Clinton was keen to steal some of the limelight and on 13 September hosted a meeting at the White House where the Oslo 'Declaration of Principles' was signed and Arafat, previously condemned as a terrorist by the US and Israel, shook hands with a reluctant Rabin.

The Oslo agreement provided for a self-governing Palestinian Authority (most certainly not a proper government) under an elected council, which would exist for a transitional period of five years (from the date of Israel's initial withdrawal) during which time a permanent settlement, including the status of Jerusalem and Jewish settlements, would be negotiated. The West Bank and Gaza were to be treated as one unit and Israel retained an overall responsibility for the defence and security of these areas, but the Palestinians would be able to govern and police Gaza and Jericho. Even in the short-term much was unclear, including the exact dates for executing parts of the agreements and the pace of future Israeli withdrawals. It set various deadlines for future talks but was deliberately ambiguous on some important issues of territory and transfer of powers to the Palestinian Authority. Also, opposition had immediately gathered on both sides, from Likud in Israel and Hamas in the occupied territories. But there was no doubting the significance of the breakthrough. While world attention had focused on the Washington talks, which proceeded slowly and uncertainly, the Oslo negotiations had produced an agreement which, however modest it appeared in detail, marked an unprecedented psychological breakthrough in Israeli–Palestinian relations, with the potential to produce a full agreement within a decade. It was 'intended as just a stepping stone along the road to peace, graduality being the guiding principle.'[17] Furthermore, it was followed by Israeli talks with both Jordan and Syria. Jordan was anxious to settle the problem of the West Bank, which it had ruled between 1949 and 1967, and to settle the future of the Palestinians for good. Rabin and King Hussein of Jordan signed an agreement in Washington in July 1994, agreeing to end the state of war between them and recognize one another, and this was followed by a peace treaty on 26 October, with Clinton present at the signature. By February 1995 it was even possible to hold a summit in Cairo between Rabin, Arafat, Hussein, and President Mubarrak of Egypt, the first Arab country to make peace with Israel in 1979. An Israeli–Syrian deal proved elusive, however, despite strong US encouragement which led Clinton to visit President Asad in Damascus in January 1994. The Israeli military were also keen on a settlement with Syria, recognizing this would remove the danger of another Arab–Israeli war: some indeed would have preferred this to the Oslo deal with the PLO. But Asad's suspicion of Israel was such that, though talks were held, they proceeded only slowly with Syria determined to win back all of the land on the Golan Heights seized by Israel in 1967.

The Stalling of the Oslo Accords

The gravest disappointment in the years after September 1993 was not the elusive Israeli–Syrian peace but the failure to realize the full promise of the Oslo principles. From the start they were dogged by terrorist attacks, extremist opposition, and genuine disappointments between the Israelis and Palestinians. Arguments over border controls for example, meant that the original date of 13 December 1993 for the start of Israeli withdrawals was missed. Then, on 25 February 1994 an Israeli fanatic killed nearly fifty Palestinian worshippers at a mosque in Hebron, leading the PLO to break off talks for several weeks. But there was a basic problem with the Accords that perhaps always made a comprehensive settlement unlikely: 'The arch-enemies . . . entered into short-term cooperation in order to build a lasting foundation for . . . their long-term interests', but 'The parties' long-term objectives are still very much in conflict.'[18] Israelis hoped to end the Intifada and establish peace with their Arab neighbours, but to keep the Palestinians economically and politically subservient, with Arafat taking on the role of preventing Palestinian violence against Israel. Israel also hoped to maintain Jewish settlements in the West Bank and to retain all of Jerusalem. But Palestinians eventually hoped for a state in the whole of the West Bank and Gaza, free of Israeli domination, and with Arab refugees able to return to their ancestral homes inside Israel.

Given the scale of the differences of long-term vision, the surprising point is that, for a time, the peace process seemed to be advancing well. An agreement on Palestinian self-rule was finally signed by Rabin and Arafat in Cairo on 4 May, leading to Israel's military withdrawal from Gaza and Jericho in mid-month, the first meeting of the 'Palestinian National Authority' (PNA) on 26 June and Arafat's triumphant return to the Gaza strip on 1 July, after a quarter century of exile. Despite clashes in Gaza between the PLO and Hamas, and the ill-feeling created in late 1994 by new Jewish settlements in the West Bank, progress continued, albeit rather slowly. 'As Arafat lost more . . . of his support base, he grew less able to make concessions to Israel, making it that much more difficult for Rabin, himself harassed by . . . the Israeli Right, to

proceed with the process.'[19] On 28 September 1995 the so-called 'Oslo B' agreement was concluded. Fourteen months later than scheduled, this provided for full PNA control of only 4 per cent of the West Bank but partial control (where Israel retained a security presence in another 23 per cent). Significantly this included the most heavily populated areas with about two-thirds of West Bank Palestinians living in them. This agreement cleared the way for the first Palestinian elections in January 1996, predictably won by Arafat and his al-Fatah faction of the PLO.

By the time of Arafat's triumph, the peace process had suffered its worst setback so far. On 4 November 1995 Rabin, whose election had done so much to change Israeli policy, was assassinated by an opponent of the process. Though this further highlighted the fragmentation of Israeli society, it did not at first threaten the Oslo principles because Rabin was succeeded by another architect of dialogue with the PLO, Shimon Peres, who felt confident enough in February 1996 to call a general election. Within weeks, however, a series of three Hamas 'suicide bomb' attacks killed nearly sixty people and the opinion polls began to move against Peres, with some Israelis coming to believe that Oslo had merely encouraged Palestinian violence. The division between the 'pro' and 'anti' peace lobbies in Israel was such that on 29 May Peres lost the election to Likud's Benjamin Netanyahu by only 30,000 votes. Netanyahu's coalition government now included hard-line religious groups which made peace less likely. That the peace process was in serious trouble was obvious for, while 'Arafat has never deviated from his goal of establishing a Palestinian state . . . Netanyahu's policies preclude the creation of this.'[20] Netanyahu had criticized the Oslo agreement from the outset and, though he undertook to honour it, he minimized any concessions to Arafat, whom he at first refused even to meet. Relations with Syria became frozen. In January 1997 US mediation did help to secure the Hebron Accords, which showed limited compromise was still possible, the Accords promising further Israeli withdrawals in three stages, though Israeli settlers would remain in the Hebron area. But by March the new agreement had become deadlocked over the precise scale of the withdrawals, with the Israelis offering to pull back from only a few per cent of the West bank in the first phase, while the Palestinians hoped for much more.

In March, July, and September 1997 there were further Hamas suicide bombings, making it more difficult for Netanyahu to make concessions. Both 'Netanyahu and Arafat descended into mutual distrust . . . handicapped by extremist political con-stituencies', but with the Israelis easily continuing to hold the military advantage if it came to a showdown.[21] The Israelis condemned Arafat's failure to crack down on Hamas and increasingly tried to tackle the problems themselves. After all, one reason Israel had favoured the Oslo Accords was because it was hoped that Arafat would be able to control Palestinian attacks. But when in October 1997 two intelligence agents tries to assassinate a Hamas leader in Jordan, they were captured and had to be exchanged for numerous Palestinian prisoners, including Hamas's spiritual leader, Yassin. Netanyahu, increasingly criticized for indecision, continued to resist major withdrawals from the West Bank and instead supported new Jewish settlements there. January 1998 saw the resignation of his Foreign Minister, David Levy, in frustration over the stalled peace process and the US and European Union both increased their pressure on Israel to compromise. But at talks in London and Washington in May 1998, attended by Netanyahu, Arafat and the US Secretary of State, Madelaine Albright, agreement proved impossible even though the main point of difference between the two sides seemed very narrow: the PNA would accept an ini-tial Israeli withdrawal from 13 per cent of the West Bank but the most Netanyahu could accept was 9 per cent. There were much deeper differences on territory and political rights in the background: the Palestinians still hoped to rule 90 per cent of the West Bank in due course; Netanyahu was thinking of about half and this without sovereign rights. For months after that the Israeli Premier refused to attend talks in Washington and though, in October, he made the Wye Accords with Clinton, which offered 17 per cent of the West Bank to the Palestin-ians, these too proved stillborn. Further upheaval was added to the situation by the death on 6 Febru-ary 1999 of King Hussein of Jordan, long a source of stability in the region. He was succeeded by his son,

Abdullah. For a time Arafat even threatened to declare Palestinian statehood, a move that might have triggered full-scale war, but he agreed to defer such a step when Israeli elections were called for mid-May, raising the prospect of Netanyahu's removal.

Netanyahu did indeed lose the election but his opponent, Ehud Barak, leader of the Labour-dominated 'One Israel' movement, was without a clear majority and only able to form a government in July. Formerly the Commander-in-Chief of the Israeli armed forces, yet a firm supporter of the Oslo Accords, Barak seemed in a good position to pursue peace while reassuring Israelis that they were secure and at first he showed energy and determination, even having a friendly exchange of messages with Assad of Syria. On 4 September, at a conference in Sharm-el-Sheikh in Egypt, Barak and Arafat reactivated the Wye Accords, leading to the release of Palestinian prisoners and paving the way for a 'final' agreement. The high point of this new period of hope came in early November when the two leaders met Clinton in Oslo, quickly followed by the opening of 'final status' talks. But these talks failed to meet the February 2000 target date for a preliminary agreement and, although Barak agreed in May to pull Israeli troops out of southern Lebanon, the situation steadily worsened. In May unrest was renewed in the West Bank and Gaza; in June the death of Assad (succeeded by his son Bashar al-Assad) provided more instability; and in July Barak's fragile coalition fell apart over his plans for concessions to the Palestinians.

Following a new peace effort by Clinton, there was a final attempt to save the situation in August through fresh peace talks, but they became dead-locked on the vexed situation of East Jerusalem, one of the 'conquered territories' of the 1967 War but which the Israelis, partly for religious reasons, were reluctant to give up. Finally, in exasperation, ordinary Palestinians spontaneously began the so-called 'second Intifada'. Arafat had his autonomous 'Authority', he had been confirmed as Palestinian leader democratically, and he had won considerable international standing since his ill-judged support for Saddam Hussein. But he had full control of only a fraction of the West Bank, had failed to achieve the Oslo target of a permanent peace settlement by the end of the century, and he faced bitter condemnation from many Palestinians. As to the Israelis, they had secured peace with Jordan at least, but they not fulfilled their hopes of ending Palestinian violence. The second Intifada was actually sparked off on 28 September by a visit from the right-wing Israeli politician, Ariel Sharon, to the Dome of the Rock, one of Islam's holy places. Yet in early 2001 it was Sharon, a determined enemy of Arafat, who won a clear electoral victory over the luckless Barak, becoming Israel's Prime Minister. With the second Intifada showing no sign of abating, Israeli–Palestinian relations seemed to be moving ever further away from the hopes of Oslo.

D. **East Asia's Changing Balance**

The Decline of the Cold War in East Asia

Just as the Gorbachev era saw improved US–Soviet relations, lowered tensions in Europe and a retreat from Soviet intervention in Afghanistan and Angola, so in East Asia there was an improvement in Moscow's relations with China and Japan, reduced tension on the Sino–Soviet border, and a retreat of Soviet-backed Vietnamese intervention in Cambodia. Yet whereas in Eastern Europe, and ultimately in the USSR itself, Communism collapsed, in East Asia several Marxist regimes—most of those in the world now—remained in existence, including countries with which the US had fought bitter conflicts during the Cold War: China, North Korea, and Vietnam. The end of the Cold War led to some reduction in American force levels in the region, notably with the closure of the Philippines bases, though the US continued to use facilities in Japan. There was also a suspension of the Australian-New Zealand-US (ANZUS) Pact after August 1986 because at the New Zealand government's refusal to allow visit by nuclear-capable American warships. And, as elsewhere, the end of the Cold War raised questions about Washington's ability to remain involved in regional politics: without its previous anti-Soviet reference point, how could the US frame a coherent policy for an area as vast as East Asia? However, just as the US military presence seemed likely to follow the Soviets into retreat, so East Asia was growing in commercial and financial significance, partly because China's economy was now open to the West, and local capitalist governments were increasingly fearful of the rise of Chinese power. The retreat of Soviet power emphasized China's potential all the more.

In 1978–9, as the era of détente came to an end, China and the US had strengthened their relations in the face of the Vietnamese invasion of Cambodia and Soviet involvement in Afghanistan. But a decade later Sino–American relations had cooled whilst Sino–Soviet relations were improving. In the early 1980s the Chinese, under Deng Xiaoping had decided that, given Reagan's assertiveness and the USSR's troubled situation, it was better to steer a more independent line between the superpowers. But the Afghanistan and Cambodia problems, as well as the presence of substantial Soviet forces on the Chinese border, meant that China effectively remained closer to the US, with which there were few specific arguments, despite underlying ideological differences and American support for Taiwan. In January 1984 China's Premier, Zhao Ziyang, visited Washington and a few months later Reagan made a week-long visit to China. Another factor was that Deng wanted to concentrate on economic development, so that an anti-American policy made no sense: it would simply drain Chinese resources into defence and deter Western investment. It was the advent of Gorbachev which allowed the real change in Sino–Soviet relations and the East Asian balance of power. The Soviet Red Army's withdrawal from Afghanistan, moves to settle the Cambodian question, and the reduction of Soviet forces on the Chinese border, as well as the destruction of SS-20s under the 1987 INF treaty, meant that Gorbachev had addressed all Deng's concerns. In 1988 Gorbachev had even made clear that he would not back

Vietnam in its dispute with China over the Spratly Islands in the South China Sea and so encouraged Vietnam to improve its own relations with China. Indeed, it was to crown these advances with a normalization of relations, that the Soviet leader visited Beijing in May 1989, only to see his visit overshadowed by the student occupation of Tiananmen Square at the heart of the city. Depicted in the West as 'pro-democracy' demonstrators, the students and the young workers who joined them, in fact had a range of concerns and their action had been sparked by the death of a leading modernizer, the former party secretary, Hu Yaobang. 'While centring on corruption and undefined notions of democracy . . . the student demands for freedom were essentially a protest against bureaucratic controls . . . which circumscribed their education, job prospects, right to travel.'[22] But they challenged the predominance of the ruling Party and raised the danger that Chinese communism might accompany that in Eastern Europe into oblivion. Furthermore, the demonstrations began to spread to other major cities. On 4 June, once Gorbachev had departed, the demonstrations were ruthlessly crushed, with the loss of around a thousand lives, and the new party secretary, Zhao Ziyang, who had followed a more moderate policy, was sacked. His successor, Jiang Zemin, soon emerged as the likely predominant leader once Deng died.

Deng Xiaoping had eventually decided to back repression over conciliation and the price was a worsening in relations with America and Western Europe most of whom cut their investments in China (harming growth rates for a time), severed military cooperation, and were unready to meet Chinese leaders for some years. But Deng's policies had been based on a mixture of economic modernization and the preservation of communist rule since he emerged as the predominant Chinese leader in 1978. Thus, in 1979, he had established the first special economic zones for foreign investment and thereby opened his country to greater outside contacts, but there were only four such zones at first and most of industry remained under central control. In the 1980s private ownership was extended, a market economy was created in agriculture, and healthy growth rates were achieved, albeit at the cost of inflation and growing corruption among officials.

But the Western expectation that economic liberalization must be accompanied by greater political freedom proved false. The Chinese saw the one-party state as a guarantee of stability and effective rule over their huge population. Reform was focused on providing social welfare and rooting out corruption rather than improving human rights, and it was possible to be imprisoned without trial for several years. The events of 3–4 June 1989 were therefore predictable but, especially given the hopes raised by the decline of communism elsewhere, so was the Western reaction. James Baker noted that 'The collapse of the Soviet Union had weakened the domestic consensus for engaging the Chinese as a counterweight to the Soviets' and, from June 1989 to the end of the Bush administration in January 1993, Sino–American relations 'essentially treaded water'.[23]

Then again, however shocked Western opinion might be, Tiananmen Square did not prove a foreign policy disaster. In its immediate aftermath Deng, after criticizing the demonstrators, restated the need for economic growth. 'The second part of Deng's speech attracted little attention abroad. Yet it showed that an acute political mind was still at work.' He would not let Tiananmen throw the reform process into reverse and would pursue modernization and openness to external contacts while maintaining the one-party state.[24] Many of China's pro-Western neighbours were anxious to preserve the improved relations of the 1970s and 1980s not least Japan, which had massive trade and investment interests in China. In August 1991 the Japanese Premier, Toshiki Kaifu, became the first major Western leader to visit Beijing since Tiananmen Square. Even South Korea and Taiwan had been improving relations with China in the late 1980s. South Korea, which established diplomatic relations with the USSR in 1990, did the same with China in August 1992. More remarkably, while Taiwan could not think in terms of mutual recognition of Beijing—both claimed to be the sole representative of a single China—the two governments were now able to sit in international organizations together. This began when Beijing accepted Taiwan as a member of the Asian Development Bank, not as an independent state, but under the title 'Taipei, China'. By then there was considerable Taiwanese trade with the mainland and personal visits were allowed after 1987. The US government also recognized that Peking was too significant a force in world politics to ignore and, despite some Congressional pressure for a policy of sanctions to force change in China, the Bush administration, while banning military exports, kept non-military trade flowing and maintained secret contacts. In 1990 Bush, who had been the first US envoy to Communist China in the 1970s, also renewed China's 'Most Favoured Nation' trade status in the face of Congressional criticism. 'The administration's limited response was dictated by the belief that, if it was to exercise any leverage over Chinese actions, it had to remain "engaged".'[25] China's old enemy Vietnam also continued to improve relations, normalizing diplomatic relations with Beijing in November 1991. Indeed, since 1986, Vietnam had itself been pursuing a modernization programme, with greater private ownership and openness to foreign trade on lines similar to Deng's.

As with South Korea's friendlier policy to both the USSR and China, so Vietnam's move was part of a general reconciliation of old enmities, as the end of the Cold War altered everyone's security consideration in the region. In September 1990 the Vietnamese Foreign Minister, Nguyen Co Thach even met America's James Baker on the neutral ground of the UN in New York. A month later Thach was in Tokyo, showing that Hanoi could now talk to America's leading ally in the Far East. It was a similar story for the Soviets. In May 1991 Gorbachev welcomed Jiang Zemin to Moscow, the first visit by a Chinese Party Secretary since Mao in 1957. The two of them not only stated that 'a new page is being opened in relations' bilaterally but also stated their readiness 'to make efforts together with all states of the world to institute a new world order', suggesting that this was no anti-American alliance that was being forged.[26] The previous month the Soviet leader had himself visited Tokyo, an important sign of improved relations which Gorbachev had wanted since at least his Vladivostok speech of 1986. In the late 1980s, in contrast to other Western countries, Japan had refused to join in the rush to make loans to the USSR because of the continuing dispute over the 'Northern Territories', the four Kurile Islands seized by the Red Army in August 1945. The dispute

had prevented a peace treaty between the two countries being made after the Second World War but in 1989 a study group was set up on the issue. Gorbachev evidently had hopes of resolving it before his fall from power in December 1991. The break-up of the USSR came as a profound shock to the Chinese who, whatever their past differences with Moscow, found little joy in the collapse of the world's first communist state. Nonetheless, and notwithstanding the Tiananmen episode, the years 1985–91, could be seen to have benefited China more than most in East Asia. The Chinese Communist Party remained secure in power, Deng's modernization policies continued, and China faced no serious external security threat. China was 'more secure . . . than at any time under Communist rule, or indeed at any time in the several hundred years since the coming of Western imperialism to East Asia.'[27]

After the Cold War: China, America, and Japan

With the collapse of Soviet power, some events in East Asia could be seen in part as a consolidation of those trends evident before 1991. Chinese military and economic power was of concern to all other states in the region but, despite some critical moments, the prevailing policy was to work with Beijing in the hope of controlling its ambitions through cooperation. Moscow was still a player, though one much reduced in significance. Yeltsin kept up the good relations with China achieved by Gorbachev, making visits to Beijing in 1992 and 1996, but Russian nationalist feeling prevented progress with Japan on the Northern Territories dispute. So although Russia and China were able to end their thirty-year-old border dispute in 1997, and despite a visit by Yeltsin to Tokyo in 1998, a Russo–Japanese peace treaty remained unsigned. In Cambodia there was an internal settlement between the pro-Vietnamese regime of Hun Sen and his royalist opponents (see Chapter 19, C). Vietnam continued its emergence from isolation, most dramatically through improved relations with America. In April 1992 Bush eased the post-1975 economic embargo on Vietnam and in December, aware that other countries were taking advantage of the new investment and trade opportunities, allowed US companies to deal with the former enemy. The IMF and World Bank were able to resume their lending to Vietnam and in February 1994 President Clinton ended the economic embargo altogether. Most important of all, however, on 11 July 1995 US–Vietnamese diplomatic relations were opened and, at the very end of his Presidency, Clinton made a historic visit to Vietnam. The US continued to reduce its military forces in East Asia, while those of China continued to expand, but Washington remained a powerful force in the region and in 1993 East Asia was probably the primary focus for the new Clinton administration. Most important was Clinton's own commitment to commercial involvement in the region, best seen in his support for Asia-Pacific Economic Cooperation (APEC) (see Chapter 21, A).

For the US the three vital challenges in East Asia after the Cold War were: the protection of US trade and investment interests (worth about $350 billion in 1990); tackling the Japanese over their increasing trade surplus with America (up from $50 billion to $64 billion during the Bush Presidency), while maintaining then as a military ally; and dealing with China, still a communist state with a poor human rights record, but ever more important in East Asia in economic and political terms. Despite its defeat in Vietnam, the US had emerged from the Cold War in a strong position in the Far East. It had preserved Taiwan and South Korea while improving relations with China, had fostered liberalism in Japan, and saw modern capitalist economics emerge in much of South-East Asia. But there were numerous difficulties, too. The end of the Cold War made Japan's importance as a political ally seem less vital than its commercial rivalry and there was persistent US pressure on Tokyo, going back to the 1970s, to deal with the trade imbalance; pressure which was resisted. Japan did take some action to reduce impediments to US exports, but Congress remained disappointed and even Bush, who felt good relations with Tokyo should be preserved, made commercial issues central to his visit there in January 1992. Clinton too found it popular in America to tackle Japan on trade but by the mid-1990s the Japanese economy was in the doldrums and the long post-war

predominance of the Liberal Democrats was being replaced by political instability. As 'the American economy boomed and the Japanese economy weakened, the Clinton administration retreated from its confrontational trade policy.'[28] Among America's other allies, Taiwan and South Korea were democratizing but others, especially Thailand and Indonesia, were still authoritarian and, as seen in the latter in 1998, prone to internal discontent. Relations with Vietnam might be improving but those with another communist state, North Korea, became critical in 1994 (see Chapter 21, D). The Soviet menace might have ended, but the region's capitalist nations still saw America as a protector and the latent Chinese military threat meant that US forces could not be cut as much as originally hoped. Unlike the situation in Europe, America lacked a multilateral alliance like NATO to help manage its relations, and deal with security problems in East Asia. Clinton evidently hoped that APEC would increase in significance as a multilateral organization, but it was only a trading organization, lacking a military-political rationale.

Washington might have been able to reduce its costs further if Japan had been ready to take on a greater defence burden. But instead, as in Western Europe, Tokyo continued even after the Cold War to restrict its own forces and rely on America for strategic defence. For years this problem ran alongside that of trade in relations between the two countries. True, in the 1970s, partly because of trade tensions with Washington and the shock of Nixon's 'Opening to China', Japan had begun to play a fuller role in East Asian politics (see Chapter 12, A). But only in January 1983, at the depth of the New Cold War did Premier Nakasone Asuhiro tell Reagan that the country's self-defence forces would have more than one per cent of GDP spent on them. Even then, with Japan set to take over much of the air defence of the Western Pacific, it took until 1987 before the one per cent limit was broken and by 1990 it was back below it again. There was strong internal resistance to Nakasone's policy of greater international assertiveness in league with the US, most Japanese preferring both to avoid any resurgence of nationalism and to escape subservience to Washington. Rather than being translated into political and military power, Japan's position as the world's second largest economy bred a defensive-mindedness, not helped by the increased criticism it received from other Western powers. In 1989 the critics were answered on one point when Tokyo became the world's largest donor of development aid, but at the same time (as seen above) the Kurile Islands issue meant that Japan refused to give much financial help to Gorbachev's USSR. In 1990–1 Tokyo's refusal to send forces to expel Saddam Hussein from Kuwait—despite Japan's reliance on Middle East oil imports—provoked more criticism. The Japanese responded by providing $10 billion towards the costs of those who did fight, but this only further emphasized that the country was an economic giant unwilling to take any political risks. The 'impression of a free ride in the Gulf fed the Japan-bashers' in the US.[29]

After 1991 the political criticisms continued, the Japanese being attacked over the their failure to apologize to the Koreans, Chinese, and others over wartime atrocities, their restrictive immigration policy, and their failure to back Washington in the 1994 nuclear crisis with Korea—again despite the fact that Japan was one of those most at risk if North Korea did obtain nuclear weapons. In 1992 a new law allowed the self-defence forces to be deployed abroad, but only in UN peacekeeping operations and with a maximum of 2,000 personnel. Some troops were subsequently sent to police the Cambodian settlement, but this could be seen as a reflection of Japan's interest in good relations with South-East Asian states in general. South-East Asia was also one of the areas where Japan had become more diplomatically active since the 1970s (see below) and it was well aware that, after the experience of the Second World War, none of the states there really wanted to see a revival of Japanese military power. It was not that Tokyo was without international concerns or ambitions. Already part of the G-7 group of leading industrial states, it pressed after 1993 for a permanent seat on the UN Security Council. And, with the decline of Russia power and the rising Chinese profile, it was particularly concerned about the changing power balance in north-eastern Asia. The lowest point in relations with China after the Cold War came in 1995 because of a Chinese nuclear test. Yet, despite all the developments around them, the Japanese were reluctant to depart from the policy formula, first espoused by Premier Shigeru Yoshida

in the 1950s, of limited armed forces, the US alliance, and a concentration on economic expansion. There was an internal debate in the 1990s over how involved Japan should be in world affairs, how its defence role might change, and what the future shape of relations with America should be, but it reached no firm consensus before 1998 when the dawn of economic recession emerged as a new frightening challenge.

Japan's reluctance to become a forthright military-political force in East Asia made developments in Sino—American relations even more significant, yet it was difficult to trace a particular pattern in these periods of crisis alternating with calm. Chinese economic growth was strong once again after 1991, with strong exports, healthy foreign reserves, and lower inflation. There seemed to be significant contradictions within their modernization process: what remained of state-owned industry was inefficient and unprofitable, but the shift towards free competition led to income inequalities and unemployment. Nonetheless, the communist leadership survived the death of Deng Xiaoping in February 1997, serious discontent was confined to Xinjiang province (where the Muslim Uighurs, China's largest ethnic minority, sought autonomy), and the government was able to use the return of Hong Kong to whip up popular support (see boxed section). The Chinese were sometimes disturbingly assertive abroad, as in the 1995 crisis with Thailand over the ownership of Mischief Reef in the South China Sea. More seriously, in March 1996 Beijing fired ballistic missiles during intimidating military exercises off the Taiwanese coast, ahead of the islands first Presidential elections. The communists feared that the election winner, Lee Teng-hui, might declare Taiwan fully independent. By now Taiwan had diplomatic relations with over thirty countries and the US had revived large-scale arms sales to it in 1992, partly to match purchases from Russia. There was further tension during the next Taiwanese elections in March 2000. But generally, as over the Hong Kong negotiations with Britain, the Chinese relied on diplomacy rather than intimidation. Communist and Taiwanese officials had held their first bilateral meeting since the Civil War, in Singapore in April 1993. And in April 1997 a direct shipping link was opened between Taiwan and the mainland, also for the first time since 1949. Elsewhere, China helped achieve a Cambodian settlement and to defuse the 1994 North Korean crisis (by providing the North with economic aid), it improved relations with India and South-East Asian states, and it joined in regional bodies like APEC. In 1996 China and Vietnam also resolved their long-running border dispute.

Yet, whatever the positive elements in Chinese policy, relations with America were dogged by a number of problems. It was clear that the end of the Cold War had not allowed a US retreat from East Asia any more than one from Europe and 'China's economic dynamism, its growing military capability, its central role in the . . . resolution of regional tensions . . . underscored the long-term strategic significance of relations between China and the United States.'[30] One problem, as with US–Japanese relations, was trade rivalry. Although Bush and Clinton, under pressure from US business interests, annually renewed China's Most Favoured Nation status, the threat that it would not be renewed was ever present. China, like Japan, maintained a large trade surplus with the US and in 1993–5 there were particular arguments about China's pirating of US designs of patents. Although, in May 1994, Clinton said the US should 'delink' human rights and trade, America refused to support Chinese membership of the World Trade Organiza-

tion (WTO) for most of the decade. Congress remained concerned about China's human rights record, especially its treatment of ethnic Tibetans. Another US concern was China's arms export policy and the fear that it would help Pakistan or Iran to build an atomic bomb. In 1991 the Chinese undertook to curb arms sales and respect the Non-Proliferation Treaty but in August 1993 the US introduced certain economic sanctions because of Sino–Pakistani nuclear links. China's own nuclear tests also caused concern in America. Taiwan was another flashpoint, with Beijing upset that President Lee Teng-hui was allowed into the US on a 'private visit' in 1995 and the Americans deeply concerned by the March 1996 crisis. Jiang Zemin and Yeltsin also showed signs of working together against the US in the later 1990s, particularly criticizing the continuation of the Star Wars defence project. They not only ended their border dispute and expanded trade links but also, at a summit in Moscow in April 1997, rejected claims 'by any one country to the role of absolute leader'.[31]

Clinton's China policy appeared hopelessly confused both to his Congressional critics and the Chinese themselves. But, after a difficult first term he became more confident in pursuit of a policy of 'constructive engagement', even if some saw this a s freeing Beijing to abuse human rights and intimidate its neighbours. Like Bush, Clinton recognized that

Deng Xiaoping (1905–1997)

Born Deng Xixian, in the Sichuan province of China, Deng came from a landlord family and was partly educated in France before joining the communists in 1924. Becoming a firm supporter of Mao Zedong, he took part in the Long March of 1934 and was elected to the Central Committee in 1945. His rise through the communist bureaucracy took him to the General Secretaryship of the Central Committee in 1954 but during the Cultural Revolution of the later 1960s he was condemned as a 'capitalist roader,' losing all his official posts. He was rehabilitated thanks to the support of Zhou Enlai and by 1975 was Chinese Vice-Premier. Following the death of Mao Zedong and the defeat of the radical 'Gang of Four', Deng won a power struggle with Hua Guofeng to become China's paramount leader in 1978.

Deng maintained his primacy in Chinese politics for most

of his remaining life despite old age, the onset of Parkinson's disease, and an increasing lack of formal positions: he resigned as Vice-Premier in 1980 and quit his last official post in 1989. The key to his predominance was the loyalty of the armed forces and his promotion of trusted lieutenants, such as Zhao Ziyang, to key positions. Yet Deng was also ruthless enough to remove Zhao as Prime Minister in 1989 and crush the student demonstrations in Tiananmen Square that had seemed to threaten communist rule. As leader, Deng was particularly identified with a modernization programme that allowed greater freedom for peasant farmers and 'Special Economic Zones', where there was foreign, capitalist investment. He criticized some elements of Maoism while maintaining one-party control and, as the Soviet Union collapsed, he shifted from close relations to the United States to more circumspect ones.

enmity with China could prove costly to America in terms of lost trade and military outlays, without any promise of reforming Beijing's approach to human rights, copyright law, or the Taiwan problem. Engagement on the other hand, while criticized by Republicans, might lead to mutual concessions and induce some change in Chinese policies, as had earlier occurred in the USSR. The US also had no desire to harass China when Deng was increasingly old and unwell, because such harassment might merely encourage an anti-American policy from his successor. As it was, Deng's death in February 1997 was overcome quite smoothly and, in October–November 1997, Jiang Zemin, who had already met Clinton at APEC summits in 1993 and 1996, visited the US and the framework of a Sino–American understanding became clear. Washington wanted China to support non-proliferation, peace in East Asia, and a free-market approach to economic problems in the developing world. In return China wanted to be treated as an equal partner, to join the WTO, and to reduce US arms sales to Taiwan. A return visit by Clinton to Beijing in June 1998 showed that such an arrangement might work.

Clinton spoke out on human rights, even on Tibet and Tiananmen Square, but he also said that Taiwan should not have independence. He and Jiang signed a trade deal and both criticized the recent nuclear tests by India and Pakistan. Ironically, however, such a friendly meeting between the regions most powerful actors, provoked concern in other East Asian capitals: the summit might be reassuring, in the sense that it gave a promise of regional stability, but none of the smaller nations wished to be dictated to by a Sino–American agenda. Sino–American relations were soured in 1999 by the 'accidental' bombing of the Chinese embassy in Belgrade during the Kosovo crisis, but the Clinton administration was quick to offer compensation and November saw China achieving one of its greatest international ambitions, when agreement was reached on its entry to the WTO. There were inevitable worries that Clinton's departure would spell the end of 'constructive engagement', however, especially when the Republican George Bush Jnr., was elected in his place. Meanwhile, since mid-1998, the focus in East Asia had shifted to the region's economic difficulties.

Chronology: The Return of Hong Kong to China

1842   China ceded the island of Hong Kong to Great Britain, following the Opium War, with full sovereignty.

1898   Britain secures a 99-year lease on the 'New Territories' adjacent to Hong Kong island. The lease therefore expires in 1997.

1972   Aware that Hong Kong island would be non-viable once the New Territories were returned, Britain concedes that the whole colony will revert to China at some point.

1982   Deng Xiaoping and Britain's Margaret Thatcher agree to talks on Hong Kong to China, with 'one China, two systems': for seventy years it is to be a special administrative region, with indepen-

dent legal and legislative systems under its own government and guarantees of personal freedoms and private property.

1989   Chinese government's crushing of demonstrations in Tiananmen Square provokes concern over what might happen to Hong Kong after 1997.

1992   The new and final British governor, Chris Patten, begins a policy of greater democratization of Hong Kong, including more representative elections in September 1995.

1997   China takes back Hong Kong and its thriving financial and commercial enterprises. Only Macao remains as a European enclave in China: under a 1987 agreement with Portugal, it reverted to Chinese rule in December 1999.

E. ASEAN, the 'Tigers' and the Post-1997 Economic Crisis

The Rise of ASEAN, 1967–1989

ASEAN was founded at a meeting in Bangkok on 8 August 1967 between Indonesia (rich in oil and by far the largest member in terms of population), Malaysia, the Philippines, Thailand, and Singapore. All were now pro-Western, capitalist, anti-communist, developing states, keen to maintain regional stability in order to reduce the dangers of domestic upheaval and provide a healthy basis for economic development. The new organization was also designed to develop economic, social, and cultural interference in the region and to improve the diplomatic weight of its members: 'achieving peaceful accord would enable resources to be concentrated on fostering strong economies and social harmony', which would in turn prevent Communism having an appeal.[32] It started out therefore as a modest but practical structure which tried to control local problems, albeit at a slow pace: thus, while Malaysia and the Philippines re-established diplomatic relations in 1969, the latter only gave up its claim to Sabah in 1992. The main policy body was an annual meeting of Foreign Ministers. A security dimension to the Association was avoided, partly because some already had regional security commitments. Thailand and the Philippines were SEATO members until that organization was disbanded in June 1977; Malaysia and Singapore had military links to Britain and partly to avoid alienating the non-aligned movement by appearing to be a pro-Western military organization. This did not stop the Chinese bitterly denouncing ASEAN and supporting local communist parties against its member governments. On the commercial front, preferential tariffs were established between ASEAN members, but only on a voluntary basis at first, and on individual products.

Between 1967 and 1971 the region saw more instability. The Americans began to reduce their troop levels in Vietnam, the British decided to withdraw from their 'East of Suez' bases, and the USSR remained keen to maintain some influence in East Asia. ASEAN states were troubled both by America's 'Opening to China' and China's entry to the UN. Such feelings of insecurity led them in November to declare their region a 'Zone of Peace, Freedom and Neutrality', calling on all outsiders to respect this. After this regional developments began to move in their favour. Alongside its rapprochement with America, China ceased to condemn ASEAN and in return, in 1974–5, Malaysia, Thailand, and the Philippines all recognized Mao Zedong's government. ASEAN states saw that China could serve a purpose, helping to contain the USSR and its ally Vietnam, while offering commercial opportunities. Self-interest and realism overcame old suspicions. Japan too was keen to improve relations with South-East Asia, so as to expunge memories of the Second World War, ensure East Asian stability after America's Vietnam withdrawal, and expand its trade in the region. In August 1977 the Japanese Premier, Takeo Fukuda told a conference in Manila that his country was committed to building peace and prosperity in the region, to forge political, economic, and cultural ties, and to provide development aid to ASEAN. Japan soon began to hold regular dialogue with the Association, as did Australia and New Zealand.

Relations were more troubled with Vietnam, after its reunification in 1975, since Hanoi saw the organization as a continuation of the pro-American South-East Asian Treaty Organization (which was now disbanded). When the Vietnamese invaded Cambodia in 1978 and installed a puppet government there the Thais (bordering Cambodia) were particularly concerned and ASEAN refused to recognize the new regime. These events undermined hopes, which had been evident in 1977–8, that Vietnam might be tempted from its alliance with the USSR, that America might recognize Hanoi, and that communist states in South-East Asia might become associates of ASEAN, helping to stabilize the region. The same events did, however, foster improved relations between the ASEAN states and

China, which sought to placate them ahead of its 1979 War against Vietnam. In 1981 Chinese premier Zhao Ziyang was even able to speak of 'our friendship and cooperation with ASEAN countries'.[33] Vietnam and Laos only won observer status in the organization in July 1992, by which time an internal settlement at the Cambodian problem was well underway.

On the institutional side, ASEAN began to hold summit meetings after the 1976 Bali Conference, where common measures against insurgents were agreed, but these only took place at irregular intervals and annual ministerial meetings remained the most important forum for decision-making. Also in 1976, a Treaty of Amity and Cooperation was signed, establishing machinery to settle disputes between the member states though, as it transpired, it has never (to 1998) been used. There was particular success in the late 1970s in restoring internal stability—always a key aim of ASEAN—in Thailand, albeit under military domination. Despite the Communist advance in Vietnam, Laos, and Cambodia, Thailand saw a decline in Right–Left tension as the 1970s progressed and its security situation was helped by the growing tension between Vietnam and the Khmer Rouge of Cambodia. In the 1980s ASEAN also made greater progress with tariff reductions. From the 1960s to the 1980s there was a 'fundamental transformation' of the South-East Asian economies, 'dominated by a marked decline in the relative importance of agriculture and an increase in that of modern industry.' The transformation, typical of industrializing economies in the West a century earlier, was most pronounced in Indonesia where agriculture fell as a share of gross domestic product from 56 per cent in 1965 to 26 per cent in 1986, while industry rose from 13 per cent to 32 per cent.[34] The regimes of ASEAN were not free of internal upheaval, however, especially if they failed to deliver material rewards to their people, as seen with the fall of Ferdinand Marcos of the Philippines. Marcos, who had declared himself President-for-Life in 1972, tried to bolster his popularity in 1986 by holding an election. But most votes went to Corazon Aquiro, the widow of an opposition leader who Marcos's supporters had earlier murdered. The President first tried to deny the result then, as popular demonstrations mounted and the army defected, he was forced to flee. Order was thereafter slowly restored and, with the end of the Cold War and the November 1992 closure of US military bases (a vestige of imperial rule which had long irked the Philippine parliament), the government was even able to achieve a settlement at its long-lasting campaign against Communist insurgency.

ASEAN and the 'Tiger' Economies in the 1990s

For most of ASEAN in the late 1980s and early 1990s were years of strong economic expansion, with new industries, growing exports, and bullish stock markets. From 1989 to 1996 average growth rates across ASEAN topped 7 per cent, with particularly good rates in Indonesia, Malaysia, Thailand, and to a lesser extent the Philippines, the so-called 'ASEAN four'. This was part of a wider phenomenon in East Asia, where South Korea, Taiwan, and Hong Kong had average growth rates of more than 9 per cent in the 1980s. These three, together with Singapore, became known as the 'Asian tiger' economies because of their formidable expansion, sustained over many years. Explaining why some countries experience stronger economic growth than others is not easy, but the 'availability of fine-skilled, low-wage labour ... made all these countries ... attractive to advanced enterprises elsewhere, especially from places with overvalued currencies', including Japan.[35] Clearly in the case of ASEAN and the 'tigers' a commitment to democracy was not essential for them to outperform countries in Africa and Latin America at this time. But those with the healthiest growth rates 'all had strong governments with very considerable bureaucratic abilities', leading one expert to conclude that 'it is primarily the quality of government that enables a Third World country to move up the escalator to affluence.'[36] Yet it was also possible to point to aspects of government control, notably in restricting international compitition within the domestic market and very high levels of investment. Specific countries had particular strengths. For example, Malaysia, by pursuing export-led growth, was especially attractive to foreign investors and planned to become fully developed by 2020, whilst Singapore became a centre for oil-refining, banking, and shipping with one of the highest standards of living in the world. It was all a telling contrast to the uncertainties of 1966–8, and the difficulties created by the Vietnam War. Furthermore, ASEAN and the 'tigers' were a significant part of a broader development around the Pacific Ocean, from Chile in South America, through California, round to Japan and China, and down to Australia—a vast area known as 'Pacific Rim'—of strong growth rates and greater commercial ties that suggested that these countries could outperform the 'Atlantic' economies of Western Europe and the eastern United States in future. 'The rise of the Asia-Pacific economy is . . . the most striking event in the economic history of the late twentieth century', was one typical judgement of the period.[37]

By 1990 ASEAN 'was probably the most effective of Third World organizations.'[38] Furthermore, economic success helped attract new membership to the organization. Brunei, the small but wealthy Borneo sultanate, had joined in 1995. Having begun to liberalize its markets in 1986, and to seek foreign technology and investment, Vietnam fitted into the ASEAN framework, of free-enterprise economies with less-than-democratic politics, quite well. The one-party state was not seen as a problem and ASEAN leaders, such as Malaysia's assertive Dr Mohammed Mohathir, resisted Western pressure to define progress primarily in terms of the achievement of improved human rights: it was up to Asian countries to find their own ways forward. The only real departure with Vietnam's entry was that a communist country had joined an organization that had hitherto been partly defined by its anti-communism. The entry of three more states in 1997 emphasized these points. Burma, Cambodia, and Laos were all rural, underdeveloped states with decades of authoritarian rule and immense economic problems. Burma's membership drew particular criticism from Western states because of its military government's human rights record and its treatment of the opposition leader, Aung San Suu Kyi. Potential political problems with the new members were underscored when Cambodian membership had immediately to be suspended because the pro-Vietnamese Premier, Hun Sen, overthrew his royalist colleague, Prince Narodom

Ranariddh. The latter was only able to return in April 1998.

One other factor which the new members, but particularly Vietnam, had in common with the old was a fear of Chinese expansion, economic and political, in the region. Until the 1990s, notwithstanding their capitalist economic systems and links to the West, the ASEAN states had defined themselves in international terms as non-aligned. But a deep suspicion of Chinese power had always existed and this was, paradoxically, intensified by the end of the Cold War because, with the retreat of the Soviet Union and the decision of the US to reduce its military presence in East Asia, Chinese power seemed all the more threatening. The Philippines and Vietnam had territorial disputes with China in the South China Sea and the Chinese navy was growing. In 1992 therefore, and ironically just at the same time as US withdrawal from its Philippine bases, ASEAN actually declared that it saw America's military presence in the region as desirable. The organization also called for all territorial disputes to be settled peacefully. This assertive line gave way in July 1993 however to an attempt to draw China into dialogue through the creation of a 'Regional Forum', covering all East Asia. Apart from ASEAN and China, this included other states which had already set up a regular dialogue with the organization (such as America, Japan, Australia, New Zealand, and the European Community), as well as Russia. Meetings between these were held *after* the regular ASEAN conferences. In fact it was Japan which had originally suggested something like the Regional Forum in 1991, itself concerned by Soviet decline and China's rising power. Continuing concern about security was seen in ASEAN's 1995 decision to make itself a nuclear weapons-free zone.

China's economic power was no less threatening than its military might. The formidable growth of the Chinese economy under Deng Xiaoping both reinforced East Asian growth in general and threatened to turn the South-East Asia states into economic satellites of Beijing. Yet ASEAN had only limited success in building up a regional trading bloc, on the lines of the European Community, such as might help to match China. The majority of ASEAN members traded more with America and Japan than with each other and pursued separate development strategies. Many for example were trying to create their own automobile manufacturers and to create high-technology industries, and they were all trying to attract outside investment. The expansion to four new, agricultural members in the 1990s altered this picture of 'parallel' development somewhat but created its own major problem: how could countries like Vietnam and Burma hope to stand alongside 'tigers' like Malaysia if genuine integration were pursued? In 1992 ASEAN did agree to create a free trade area among its members but it would be limited to industrial goods and the target for achieving it was soon deferred for fifteen years. Then again, in 1993 and again in 1995, the target date was brought forward to 2003, then 2000. In 1997, now with the ten members and a combined population of nearly 500 million, ASEAN produced a development plan that included a developmental fund to help the poorer members and hopes of achieving free capital movement by 2020. The great question by then was whether ASEAN, stimulated by suspicion of China, could be as successful a body in the areas of regional security and economic integration, as it had been in fostering political stability and a common external outlook among its members.

1997–1998: Asia's Economies in Crisis

In the mid-1990s it seemed that 'the centre of gravity of the world economic system has begun to shift towards the Pacific.' This change was based in part on the performance of China and some historically advanced economies, especially in Japan and California, but its major feature was that a 'number of formerly peripheral countries in that region now challenge the core of the world's manufacturing system.'[39] Before 1997 ended, however, the prospects for ASEAN, now a generation old, had dimmed significantly. Since the summer stock market and currency values had been in decline and there were suddenly serious worries over the region's economic future because of income inequalities, over expansion of the property market, and rising public debt. Concern soon spread to Hong Kong, just restored to Chinese rule, and Japan, whose economy had been in the doldrums since the early 1990s but which now threatened to tumble into recession.

Taiwan and, more particularly, South Korea, were two more 'Asian tigers' in difficulty, and whilst falling currency values ought to have helped the East Asians export more, it was difficult to achieve this because they were all trying to expand in an unfavourable market. By early 1998 it was clear that the gathering crisis had worsened the economic problems of Yeltsin's Russia and that it might also blunt China's economic miracle. Given the interdependent nature of the world economy, such a widespread malaise in the Far East also threatened to damage the investment, trade, and production of America and Western Europe. The Asian crisis helped bring about a new downturn in oil prices, threatening the income of oil-producing states, and it came at a time when many South American countries were still heavily indebted (especially Brazil and Argentina), while an economic crisis was also gathering in South Africa.

Since the 1950s growth in the Japanese economy had helped the rest of East Asia to prosper, taking over a quarter of ASEAN's exports in the 1970s for example. But now the situation had changed. Japan had shared in the generally depressed state of the Western economies at the start of the 1990s, when the ASEAN states were expanding strongly. By 1995–6 Japanese growth had recovered to about 3 per cent per annum but there were good reasons for concern about the its long-term economic health, after three decades of remarkable success. A lack of liquidity at home, linked to low income from many investments in the US and Europe, led the Japanese to cut back savagely on their outward investment programmes. From $48 billion in 1990 it fell to only $7 billion in 1992. Japan maintained a healthy trade surplus, helped by a weakening of the yen, but its banking system was troubled by corruption and bad debts, not least to ASEAN, Taiwan and South Korea. After overexpanding, property prices were falling as was the stock market, and there was a growing threat from the cheap exports of the ASEAN states. The Liberal Democrats, who had dominated post-war politics, began to lose their popularity and turned in January 1996 to a more dynamic, decisive Prime Minister in Ryutaro Hashimoto, but the decision-making process was too slow and consensus-driven to allow for radical reform. There was an attempt to boost domestic demand through cutting back of the country's high taxes but the Japanese people were too wedded to the old recipe for success—hard work and high savings—to respond to this impetus and in 1996–7, for the first time in more than twenty years, the Japanese economy contracted. Yet, however sluggish Japan's performance, the depression which struck in 1998, would not have been so deep and sudden without the problems elsewhere in Asia, and especially within ASEAN.

The growth rates experienced by ASEAN in the early 1990s led to an excess of optimism and overexpansion resulting in high debts on current accounts, balance of payments problems, a bloated property sector, labour shortages, and a credit glut. The realization that the bubble would burst first affected the stock market in Thailand, one of the weaker ASEAN founders in July 1997, but soon spread to Indonesia, the Philippines, and Malaysia. Thailand and Indonesia quickly turned to the IMF for massive loans, but they could not escape a large currency devaluation and there were fears that the restructuring demanded by the IMF could prove harmful in future. The Fund tended to favour an 'Anglo-Saxon' model of economic recovery based on privatization, reductions in government spending, free capital movement, and the end of price controls. This had been the IMF's recipe for tackling Western problems in the 1960s and 1970s, and had been forced on South America in the 1980s debt crisis. But it was partly designed to tackle inflation (not a problem in ASEAN), it harmed growth and employment (thereby raising the danger of social discontent), and it tried to force developing states to accept a Western-dictated version of capitalism (which some criticized as reworking of imperialist approaches). Then again, given the depths of East Asia's problems, countries needing IMF aid had little choice but to accept the price of restructuring.

By late November 1997 the gathering crisis had spread to South Korea, the most formidable of the Asian 'tigers' and the eleventh largest economy in the world, which had to ask the IMF for a $20 billion loan—the largest so far. Despite its political instability, the influence of the military and a lack of social provision, South Korea was one of the most remarkable economic successes in East Asia. As in Japan, its people had been happy to work hard and

save assiduously, the reward being an increase in average income from fewer than $100 in 1960 to about $10,000 in 1995. But after borrowing in the years of plenty, many South Korean companies were indebted to several times their value and now they faced collapse, threatening their employees with falling salaries or unemployment. One result was serious unrest, with sporadic outbreaks of strikes and demonstrations. But the IMF, World Bank, and other countries responded to Korea's predicament in December by producing a $35 billion rescue package in total, with a $20 billion fallback. These sums quite dwarfed any previous economic salvage operation but South Korea's total debt was reckoned to be $150 billion. It was in the middle of these events that on 24 November 1997 one of Japan's largest banks, Yamaichi Securities, collapsed with $14 billion in liabilities, raising fears of a collapse of the world's second largest economy and a liquidation of Japan's still considerable foreign investments. The total bad debt liabilities of Japanese banks were estimated at $550 billion. In January 1998 the stock market also went into steep decline in Hong Kong, where there were also problems in the overextended banking and property sectors, and unemployment was soon increasing.

The East Asian economic crisis had an impact beyond East Asia, particularly in Russia, which came close to economic collapse in August 1998, as the value of the rouble fell (see Chapter 21, C). But in Western Europe and North America, despite years of poor performance in the financial markets and some trouble with rising oil prices after 1998, a depression was staved off. The main political cost was also borne by local leaders. In Japan, for example, premier Hashimoto was forced to resign on 13 July 1998 after humiliating results for the Liberal Democrats in elections to the Upper House. Far worse results, however, occurred in Indonesia. Indebted to a total of $120 billion and faced by the IMF's demands for economic restructuring, Indonesians were faced, like Koreans, by salary cuts, unemployment, and shortages, and they reacted even more violently. For weeks in early 1998 there were protest marches calling for an end to the regime of General Suharto, the dictator since 1966. Condemned for corruption and nepotism, and no longer able to rely on the army to crush the opposition he finally resigned on 21 May, but left power in the hands of a former associate, Bacharud-din Jusut Habibie. Unrest continued, with increased activity among separatist groups in the sprawling Indonesian archipelago, although Habibie did preside over the dismantling of Suharto's police state and also, in January 1999, announced the government's readiness to grant independence to East Timor. This former Portuguese colony had been invaded by Indonesia in 1975 but had fought for its independence ever since, at the cost of tens of thousands of lives. Unfortunately the prospect of a referendum on East Timor's future sparked a new upsurge of violence as the Indonesian army, which had lost about 20,000 men in two decades of fighting for the province, armed local militias who were opposed to independence. The referendum, eventually held on 30 August, saw 78 per cent vote in favour of independence but even that did not halt the massacres carried out by the anti-independence militias and the UN agreed to send an Australian-led peacekeeping force to East Timor in late September, which soon established a sense of order. Habibie bowed out in October 1999 and the Consultative Assembly elected as President an Islamic liberal, Abdur Rahman Wahid. But in less than two years as President, this old and ailing figure presided over a halving in value of the national currency, Christian–Muslim violence, and the increased demands for autonomy from outlying provinces.

NOTES

1. Dean Guldenhuys, 'International involvement in South Africa's political transformation,' in Walter Carlsnaes and Marie Muller (eds.), *Change and South Africa's External Relations* (International Thomson Publishers, Johannesburg, 1997), 47.

2. Quoted in Guy Arnold, *South Africa* (St Martin's Press, New York, 1992), 126.

3. Chester Crocker, *High Noon in Southern Africa: Making Peace in a Rough Neighbourhood* (W W Norton, New York, 1992), 77–8; Robert Scott Jaster, *The Defence of White Power* (Palgrave Macmillan, 1988), 111–12.

4. Lawrence Schlemmer, 'The Turn in the Road,' in Robin Lee and Lawrence Schlemmer (eds.), *Transition to Democracy: Policy Perspectives* (Oxford University Press, Cape Town, 1991), 14 and 20.

5. Marina Ottaway, *South Africa: the Struggle for a New Order* (Brookings Institute, Washington, 1993), 13–14.

6. Timothy Sisk, *Democratization in South Africa: The Elusive Social Contract* (Princeton University Press, Princeton, 1995), 199.

7. 'Introduction' to Phyllis Martin and Patrick O'Meara (eds.), *Africa* (Indiana University Press, Bloomington, 1995), 7.

8. Tiebile Drame, 'The Crisis of the State,' in Stephen Ellis (ed.), *Africa Now: People, Policies and Institutions* (J. Currey, London, 1996), 209.

9. Boutros Boutros-Ghali, *Unvanquished*: a US–UN Saga (Random House, New York 1999), 138 and 141.

10. Alain Destexhe, *Rwanda and Genocide in the Twentieth Century* (Pluto, London, 1995), 51.

11. Edward Said, *The Question of Palestine* (Routledge, London, 1980), 242.

12. Yitzhak Shamir, *Summing Up: An Autobiography* (Weidenfeld & Nicolson, London, 1994), 196.

13. Avi Shlaim, *The Iron Wall: Israel and the Arab World* (Allen Lane, London, 2000), 491; Eytan Bentsur, *Making Peace* (Praeger, Westport, 2001), 121.

14. Shimon Peres, *Battling for Peace* (Weidenfeld & Nicolson, London, 1995), 373 and 377–8.

15. Kirsten Schulze, *The Arab–Israeli Conflict* (Longman, New York, 1999), 85.

16. Quoted in David Makovsky, *Making Peace with the PLO* (Westview Press, Boulder, 1996), 47.

17. Andrew Buchanan, *Peace with Justice* (Macmillan, Basingstoke, 2000), 216.

18. Nils Butenschon, 'The Oslo agreement', in George Giacaman and Dag Lanning (eds.), *After Oslo* (Pluto Press, Chicago, 1998), 42.

19. Benny Morris, *Righteous Victims: a History of the Zionist–Arab Conflict* (Alfred A Knopf, New York, 1999), 626.

20. Said Aburish, *Arafat* (Bloomsbury, New York, 1999).

21. Buchanan, *op. cit.*, 367–8.

22. Alan Lawrance, *China under Communism* (Routledge, London, 1998), 120.

23. James Baker, *The Politics of Diplomacy* (G. P. Putnam's Sons, New York, 1995), 112–13.

24. Richard Evans, *Deng Xiaoping and the Making of Modern China* (Hamish Hamilton, London, 1993), 300.

25. Steven Hurst, *The Foreign Policy of the Bush Administration* (Cassell, New York, 1999), 40.

26. Quoted on Raymond Garthoff, *The Great Transition: American–Soviet relations and the End of the Cold War* (Brookings Institution, Washington, DC, 1994), 659.

27. Gerald Segal, 'Foreign Policy', in David Goodman and Gerald Segal (eds.), *China in the Nineties* (Clarendon Press, Oxford, 1991), 160.

28. William Hyland, *Clinton's World* (Praeger, Westport, 1999), 134.

29. Dennis Smith, *Japan since 1945: The Rise of an Economic Superpower* (Macmillan, Basingstoke, 1995), 159.

30. Michel Oksenberg, 'The Asian Strategic Context', in Robert Zoellick and Philip Zelikow (eds.), *America and the East Asian Crisis* (New York, 2000), 11.

31. Quoted in Lawrance, op. cit., 135.

32. C. M. Turnbull, 'Regionalism and Nationalism', in Nicholas Tarling (ed.), *The Cambridge History of South East Asia, v 2. The Nineteenth and Twentieth Centuries* (Cambridge University Press, Cambridge, 1992), 616.

33. Quoted in John Garver, *Foreign Relations of the People's Republic of China* (Prentice Hall, Englewood Cliffs, 1993), 170.

34. Ian Brown, *Economic Change in South-East Asia* (Oxford University Press, Oxford, 1997), 66–7.

35. David Landes, *The Wealth and Poverty of Nations: Why are Some so Rich and Some so Poor* (W.W. Norton, New York, 1998), 475.

36. D. K. Fieldhouse, *The West and the Third World: Trade, Colonialism, Dependence, and Development* (Blackwell, Oxford, 1999), 346–7.

37. Eric Jones, Lionel Frost, and Colin White, *Coming Full Circle: an Economic History of the Pacific Rim* (Westview Press, Boulder, 1993), ix.

38. Turnbull, op. cit., 641.

39. Peter Dicken, *Global Shift: Transforming the World Economy* (Guilford Press, New York, 3rd edn., 1998), 68.

Bibliography

The aim of this bibliography will be to enable wider reading to be done in a way which will cover interpretation and new material rather than provide an in-depth list of books providing basic information. There is no intention of making this a comprehensive bibliography. For those requiring more details and insights into particular topics covered here the documents in *Foreign Relations of the United States* and the *bulletins* and *working papers* of the Cold War International History Project are indispensable. Both provide access to primary sources.

General Section

D. Reynolds, *One World Divisible: a Global History since 1945* (Allen Lane, Penguin Press, London, 2000).

On theories of the Cold War:
Odd Arne Westad (ed.), *Reviewing the Cold War: Approaches, Interpretations, Theory* (Frank Cass, London, 2000).

Richard N. Lebow and Thomas Risse-Kappen (eds.), *International Relations Theory and the End of the Cold War* (Columbia University Press, New York, 1995).

Allen Hunter (ed.), *Rethinking the Cold War* (Temple University Press, Philadelphia, 1998).

On general Cold War surveys:
R. E. Powaski, *The Cold War: the United States and the Soviet Union, 1917–1991* (Oxford University Press, New York, 1998).

S. J. Ball, *The Cold War: an International History 1947–1999* (Arnold, London, 1998).

Walter LaFeber, *America, Russia and the Cold War, 1945–2000* (McGraw-Hill, New York, 9th edn., 2002).

On Vietnam:
Robert McMahon (ed.), *Major Problems in the History of the Vietnam War* (D. C. Heath, Lexington, 2nd edn., 1995).

James S. Olson and Randy Roberts, *Where the Domino Fell: America and Vietnam, 1945–95* (St Martin's Press, New York, 2nd edn., 1996).

Kevin Ruane, *War and Revolution in Vietnam, 1930–75* (University College London, London, 1998).

Armaments and Military Strategy:
M. Trachtenberg, *History and Strategy* (Princeton University Press, Princeton, 1991).

J. D. Boutwell (ed.), *The Nuclear Confrontation in Europe* (Croom Helm, London, 1983).

J. Haslam, *The Soviet Union and the Politics of Nuclear Weapons in Europe, 1969–1987* (Macmillan, Basingstoke, 1989).

D. Holloway, *The Soviet Union and the Arms Race* (Yale University Press, New Haven 1984).

D. Johnstone, *The Politics of Euro-Missiles* (Verso, London, 1984).

Robert Jervis, *The Illogic of American Nuclear Strategy* (Cornell University Press, Ithaca, 1984).

D. Ford, *The Button: the Pentagon's Strategic Command and Control System* (Simon & Schuster, London, 1985).

R. Jervis, 'The Military History of the Cold War' *Diplomatic History* (1990).

J. H. Mueller, 'The Essential Irrelevance of Nuclear Weapons: Stability in the Postwar World', *International Security* (1998).

J. Newhouse, *The Nuclear Age: From Hiroshima to Star Wars* (Michael Joseph, London, 1989).

M. Trachtenberg, 'Strategic Thought in America' *Political Science Quarterly* (1989).

On the Eastern bloc:
Geoffrey and Nigel Swain, *Eastern Europe since 1945* (Macmillan, Basingstoke, 2nd edn., 1995).

Z. A. B. Zeman, *The Making and Breaking of Communist Europe* (Basil Blackwell, Oxford, 2nd edn., 1991).

On European integration see:
Martin Dedman, *The Origins and Development of the European Union, 1945–95* (Routledge, London, 1996).

Desmond Dinan, *Ever Closer Union? An Introduction to European Integration* (Macmillan, Basingstoke, 1994).

John W. Young, *Britain and European Unity, 1945–99* (Macmillan, London, 2000).

On the Arab–Israeli Conflict:
Benny Morris, *Righteous Victims: a History of the Zionist-Arab conflict* (John Murray, London, 1999).

Avi Shlaim, *The Iron Wall: Israel and the Arab World* (Allen Lane, London, 2000).

Mark A. Tessler, *A History of the Israeli-Palestinian Conflict* (Indiana University Press, Bloomington, 1994).

On the Far East:
John Garner, *Foreign Relations of the People's Republic of China* (Englewood Cliffs, 1993).

On Latin America:
Benjamin Keen and Keith Haynes, *A History of Latin America* (Houghton Mifflin, Boston, 6th edn., 2000).

Leslie Bethell (ed.), *The Cambridge History of Latin America* (Cambridge University Press, Cambridge, 1994).

Peter Calvert, *The International Politics of Latin America* (Manchester University Press, Manchester, 1994).

Michael Kryzanek, *US-Latin American Relations* (Praeger, New York, 1990).

Walter LaFeber, *Inevitable Revolutions: the US in Latin America* (Norton, New York, 1993).

On international economic issues:
William Ashworth, *a Short History of the World Economy since 1850* (Longman, London, 1991).

D. K. Fieldhouse, *The West and the Third World* (Blackwell, Oxford, 1999).

James Foreman-Peck, *A History of the World Economy* (Harvester Wheatsheaf, London, 1995).

Eric Jones, Lionel Frost, and Colin White, *Coming Full Circle: an Economic History of the Pacific Rim* (Westview Press, Boulder, 1993).

On the end of Empire:
J. Darwin *Britain and Decolonisation* (Macmillan, Basingstoke, 1988).

R. F. Holland, *European Decolonization 1918–1981: an Introductory Survey* (Macmillan, Basingstoke, 1985).

John D. Hargreaves, *African Decolonisation* (Longman, London, 1996).

British Documents on the End of Empire, Series A, vol. 2: R. Hyam (ed.), *The Labour Government and the End of Empire* (Stationery Office, London, 1992).

British Documents on the End of Empire, Series B, vol. 1, R. Rathbone (ed.), *Ghana* (Stationery Office, London, 1992).

On the US and the less developed world:
Peter Hahn and Mary Ann Heiss (eds.), *Empire and Revolution: The United States and the Third World since 1945* (Ohio State University Press, Colombus, 2001).

Robert J. McMahon, *The Limits of Empire: the US and South-East Asia since World War II* (Columbia University Press, New York, 1999).

On US foreign policy:
Stephen Ambrose, *Rise to Globalism* (Penguin, London, 8th edn., 1998).

John Dumbrell, *American Foreign Policy: Carter to Clinton* (Macmillan, Basingstoke, 1997).

Richard A. Melanson, *American Foreign Policy since the Vietnam War* (M. E. Sharpe, Armonk, 2nd edn., 1996).

John Spanier and Steve Hook, *American Foreign Policy since World War II* (Congressional Quarterly, Washington, 1998).

On Soviet foreign policy:
Caroline Kennedy-Pipe, *Russia and the World, 1917–91* (Arnold, London, 1998).

Sven Holtsmark, Iver B. Neumann, and Odd Arne Westad (eds.), *The Soviet Union and Europe in the Cold War 1945–1989* (Macmillan, Basingstoke, 1994).

On American strategy for subversion and intelligence:
Richard J. Aldrich, *The Hidden Hand Britain America and Cold War Secret Intelligence* (John Murray, London, 2001) provides illuminating detail but fails to incorporate into a coherent new analysis.

On Japan and the American occupation and reconstruction:
M. Schaller, *The American Occupation of Japan: The Origins of the Cold War in Asia* (Oxford University Press, Oxford, 1985).

W. LaFeber, *The Clash: A History of US-Japan Relations* (W. W. Norton & Co., New York, 1997).

Part I, 1945–1953

There is a vast literature on the origins of the Cold War. Students who wish to read a general account of the origins of the Cold War from an orthodox or traditional post-revisionist perspective should sample one of the following texts:

J. L. Gaddis, *The United States and the Origins of the Cold War 1941–1947* (Columbia University Press, New York, 1972).

Randall B. Woods and H. Jones, *Dawning of the Cold War: The United States Quest for Order* (University of Georgia Press, Athens; London, 1991).

Those wishing to evaluate revisionist or non-orthodox post-revisionist works should look at:

M. P. Leffler, *A Preponderance of Power. National Security, the Truman Administration and the Origins of the Cold War* (Stanford University Press, Stanford, 1992).

T. McCormick, *America's Half Century: US Foreign Policy in the Cold War and After* (Johns Hopkins University Press, Baltimore, 2nd edn., 1995).

T. G. Paterson, *On Every Front: the Making and Unmaking of the Cold War* (W. W. Norton, New York, 1992).

On the issue of whether the Cold War was primarily about power or about ideology and culture:

H. Jones and R. B. Woods *et al*, 'The Origins of the Cold War: A Symposium' *Diplomatic History* (1993) and the commentaries by E. Rosenburg, A. Stephanson, and B. Berstein Michael Hunt, *Ideology and Foreign Policy* (Yale University Press, New Haven, 1987).

J. L. Gaddis, 'The Emerging Post-Revisionist Synthesis on the Origins of the Cold War' and 'Responses to John Lewis Gaddis, "The Emerging Post-Revisionist Synthesis on the Origins of the Cold War" ' *Diplomatic History*, 2 (1983).

For more theoretical works which incorporate some assessment of the empirical evidence:
Odd Arne Westad (ed.), *Reviewing the Cold War: Approaches, Interpretations, Theory* (Frank Cass, London, 2000).

Allen Hunter (ed.), *Rethinking the Cold War* (Temple University Press, Philadelphia, 1998).

Anders Stephanson, 'Fourteen Notes on the Very Concept of the Cold War' *http://h-net2.msu.edu/~diplo/stephanson.html*

Cold War writing in the West has often been confined to a set of assumptions such as an expansionist Soviet Union, the idea of containment, the influence of communism as a crusading ideology, and has assessed the Cold War in terms of who was most to blame. In terms of these standard parameters two books deserve particular mention for challenging them:
Scott Lucas, *Freedom's War: The US Crusade against the Soviet Union 1945–1956* (Manchester University Press, Manchester, 1999).

Gregory Mitrovich, *Undermining the Kremlin America's Strategy to Subvert the Soviet Bloc 1947–1956* (Cornell University Press, Ithaca, 2000).

On the tensions in the Grand Alliance that developed in 1945 and early 1946:
R. L. Messer, *The End of an Alliance* (University of North Carolina Press, Chapel Hill, 1982).

J. Kent, *British Imperial Strategy and the Origins of the Cold War 1944–1949* (Leicester University Press, Leicester; New York, 1993).

J. L. Gormly, *The Collapse of the Grand Alliance 1945–1948* (Louisiana State University Press, Baton Rouge, 1987).

On Cold War economic policy:
R. A. Pollard, *Economic Security and the Origins of the Cold War 1945–1950* (Columbia University Press, New York, 1985).

M. J. Hogan, *The Marshall Plan: America, Britain, and the Reconstruction of Western Europe, 1947–1952* (Cambridge University Press, Cambridge, 1987).

On post-war atomic issues:
G. Herken, *The Winning Weapon: the Atomic Bomb in the Cold War 1945–1950* (Knopf, New York, 1980).

D. Holloway, *Stalin and the Bomb: The Soviet Union and Atomic Energy 1939–1956* (Yale University Press, New Haven, 1994).

F. Kaplan, *The Wizards of Armageddon* (Simon & Schuster, New York, 1983).

On NATO and militarization:
J. Kent and J. W. Young, 'Britain the Third Force and the Origin of NATO: in Search of a New Perspective', in B. Heuser and R O'Neill (eds.), *Securing Peace in Europe* (Macmillan, London, 1992).

J. Kent and J. W. Young, 'The Western Union Concept and British Defence Planning 1947–48' in Aldrich (ed.), *British Intelligence Strategy and the Cold War* (Routledge, London, 1992).

T. P. Ireland, *Creating the Entangling Alliance* (Aldwych Press, London, 1981).

E. R. May (ed.), *American Cold War Strategy; Interpreting NSC-68* (Bedford Books of St Martin's Press, Boston, 1993).

On the crises in the Middle East and the Mediterranean:
J. Kent, *British Imperial Strategy and the Origins of the Cold War 1944–1949* (Leicester University Press, Leicester; New York, 1993).

E. Mark, 'The War Scare of 1946 and its Consequences', *Diplomatic History* 3 (1997).

L. L'Estrange Fawcett, *Ian and the Cold War: the Azerbaijan Crisis of 1946* (Cambridge University Press, Cambridge; New York, 1992).

B. Kuniholm, *The Origins of the Cold War in the Near East* (Princeton University Press, Princeton, 1980).

On the Soviet actions in Eastern Europe:
Caroline Kennedy-Pipe, *Russia and the World 1917–1991* (Arnold, London, 1998).

V. Zubok and C. Pleshakov, *Inside the Kremlin's Cold War from Stalin to Khrushchev* (Harvard University Press, Cambridge, 1996).

V. Mastny, *Russia's Road to the Cold War* (Columbia University Press, New York, 1979).

V. Mastny, *The Cold War and Soviet Insecurity the Stalin Years* (Oxford University Press, New York, 1996).

N. Naimark and L. Gibianskii (eds.), *The Establishment of Communist Regimes in Eastern Europe 1944–1949* (Westview, Oxford, 1997).

On Western Europe:
John W. Young, *France, the Cold War and the Western Alliance 1944–1949* (Leicester University Press, Leicester, 1990).

Alan Milward, *The European Rescue of the Nation-State* (Routledge, New York, 2nd edn., 1992).

Alan Milward, *The Reconstruction of Western Europe, 1945–1951* (Methuen, London, 1984).

On the German question:
C. Eisenber, *Drawing the Line: The American Decision to Divide Germany 1944–1949* (Cambridge University Press, New York, 1996).

S. Mawby, *Containing Germany: Britain and the Arming of the Federal Republic* (St Martin's Press, New York, 1997).

On Palestine and the Middle East:
Mark A. Tessler, *A History of the Israeli-Palestinian Conflict* (Indiana University Press, Bloomington, 1994).

Wm. Roger Louis, *The British Empire in the Middle East 1945–1951: Arab Nationalism, the United States, and Postwar Imperialism* (Clarendon, Oxford, 1984).

On the Iranian crisis:

J. A. Bill, *The Eagle and the Lion: the Tragedy of American-Iranian Relations* (Yale University Press, New Haven, 1989).

M. J. Gasiorowski, 'The 1953 Coup d'Etat in Iran', *Journal of Middle East Studies* (1987).

For the CIA:

R. Jeffreys-Jones, *The CIA and American Democracy* (Yale University Press, New Haven, 2nd edn., 1999).

V. Marchetti and J. D. Marks, *The CIA and the Cult of Intelligence* (Jonathan Cape, London, 1974).

J. Ranelagh, *The Agency: the Rise and Decline of the CIA* (Weidenfeld & Nicolson, London, 1986).

For Soviet intelligence and subversion see:

C. M. Andrew and O. Gordievsky, *KGB: the Inside Story* (Hodder & Stoughton, London, 1990).

C. M. Andrew and Vasily Mitrokhin, *The Mitrokhin Archive The KGB in Europe and the West* (Allen Lane, London, 1999).

J. T. Richelson, *Sword and Shield: Soviet Intelligence and Security Service Operations* (Ballinger, Cambridge, 1986).

On China and Korea and the nature of East Asian problems not defined in terms of a Soviet–American global confrontation:

O. A. Westad, 'Losses, Chances and Myths: the United States and the Creation of the Sino-Soviet Alliance, 1946–1950' *Diplomatic History*, 2 (1997).

Chen Jian, 'The Myth of America's Lost Chance in China', *Diplomatic History*, 2 (1997).

Shen Zhihua, 'Sino-Soviet Relations and the Origins of the Korean War: Stalin's Strategic Goals in the Far East' *Journal of Cold War Studies*, 2 (2000).

W. W. Stueck, *The Korean War: an International History* (Princeton University Press, Princeton, 1995).

Chen Jian, *China's Road to the Korean War* (Colombia University Press, New York, 1994).

S. N. Goncharov, J. W. Lewis, and Xue Litai, *Uncertain Partners. Stalin, Mao and the Korean War* (Stanford University Press, Stanford, 1993).

Part II, 1953–1963

On Eisenhower:

S. Ambrose, *Eisenhower, vol. 2, The President, 1952–1969* (Allen & Unwin, London, 1984).

For a favourable and revisionist view of his Cold War strategy:

Robert R. Bowie and Richard Immerman, *Waging Peace: How Eisenhower Shaped an Enduring Cold War Strategy* (Oxford University Press, Oxford, 1998).

R. Divine, *Eisenhower and the Cold War* (Oxford University Press, New York, 1981).

S. Dockrill, *Eisenhower's New Look National Security Policy* (Macmillan, London, 1996).

For critical views of his Cold War strategy and a more precise understanding of Cold War fighting:

Scott Lucas, *Freedom's War: The US Crusade against the Soviet Union 1945–1956* (Manchester University Press, Manchester, 1999).

Gregory Mitrovich, *Undermining the Kremlin: America's Strategy to Subvert the Soviet Bloc 1947–1956* (Cornell University Press, Ithaca, 2000).

John W. Young, *Winston Churchill's Last Campaign: Britain and the Cold War, 1951–5* (Clarendon Press, Oxford, 1996).

For Khrushchev:

V. Zubok and C. Pleshakov, *Inside the Kremlin's Cold War from Stalin to Khrushchev* (Harvard University Press, Cambridge, 1996).

W. J. Thompson, *Khrushchev: A Political Life* (Macmillan, Basingstoke, 1995).

On Kennedy which has important material on the crises and on Khrushchev:

M. Beschloss, *Kennedy v. Khrushchev: the Crisis Years, 1960–1963* (Faber & Faber, London, 1991).

Nigel Ashton, *Kennedy, Macmillan and the Cold War* (Palgrave Macmillan, Basingstoke, 2002).

There are some interesting articles on the Kennedy years in:

T. G. Paterson (ed.), *Kennedy's Quest for Victory* (Oxford University Press, New York, 1989).

D. B. Kunz (ed.), *The Diplomacy of the Crucial Decade American Foreign Relations during the 1960s* (Columbia University Press, New York, 1994).

Mark White (ed.), (Kennedy: the New Frontier Revisited (Macmillan, Basingstoke, 1998).

The crucial Cold War element in this period is to ensure that books and articles are read that base their analyses on distinguishing between Cold War and Hot War and to realize that the campaign against the Soviet Union and communism on the one hand, and communism's support for and involvement in revolutionary movements on the other, were different from the attempts to avoid the catastrophe of Hot War and settling Us–Soviet disputes. For material relevant to this:

'Eisenhower's Disarmament Dilemma: From Chance for Peace to Open Skies Proposal' in *Diplomacy and Statecraft*, 2 (2001).

Kenneth A. Osgood, 'Form before Substance: Eisenhower's Commitment to Psychological Warfare and Negotiations with the Enemy' *Diplomatic History*, 3 (2000).

On European issues between the two protagonists:

M. Trachtenberg, *A Constructed Peace: The Making of the Europe Settlement 1945–1963* (Princeton University Press, Princeton, 1999).

John Lewis Gaddis, *We Now Know: Rethinking Cold War History* (Clarendon Press, Oxford, 1997).

Wilfred Loth, *Overcoming the Cold War: A History of Détente* (Palgrave, New York, 2001).

On Trans-Atlantic relations:
Pascaline Winant, *Eisenhower, Kennedy and the United States of Europe* (Macmillan, Basingstoke. 1993).

On Eastern European problems:
Christian F. Ostermann, 'The United States, the East German Uprising of 1953 and the Limits of Rollback', Working Paper 11, CWIHP (1994).

Mark Kramer, 'The Soviet Union and the 1956 Crises in Hungary and Poland: Reassessments and New Findings', *Journal of Contemporary History*, 2 (1998).

Alexsandr Stykalin, 'The Hungarian Crisis of 1956: the Soviet Role in the Light of New Archival Documents', *Cold War History*, 1 (2001).

Mark Kramer, 'The Early Post-Stalin Succession Struggle and Upheavals in East-Central Europe: Internal-External Influences in Soviet Policy Making', *Journal of Cold War Studies* 1/1, 1/2, and 1/3 (1999).

On armament:
Andreas Wenger, *Living with Peril Eisenhower: Kennedy and Nuclear Weapons* (Rowman & Littlefield Publishers, Lanham, 1997).

F. Kaplan, *The Wizards of Armageddon* (Simon & Schuster, New York, 1983).

On the Suez Crisis for detail and for the regional origin:
Keith Kyle, *Suez* (Weidenfeld & Nicolson, London, 1991).

W. S. Lucas, *Divided We Stand: Britain the US and the Suez Crisis* (Hodder & Stoughton, London, 1991).

British Documents on the End of Empire, Series B, vol. 4, J. Kent (ed.), *Egypt and the Defence of the Middle East, 1945–1956* (Stationery Office, London, 1998).

British Documents on the End of Empire, Series A, vol. 4, R. Hyam and Wm. Roger Louis (eds.), *The Conservative Governments 1957–1964* (Stationery Office, London, 1998).

On Latin America for the contrasts and similarities between the policies of Eisenhower and Kennedy:
Stephen G. Rabe, *Eisenhower and Latin America: the Foreign Policy of Anti-Communism* (University of North Carolina Press, Chapel Hill, 1988).

Stephen G. Rabe, *The Most Dangerous Area in the World. John F. Kennedy Confronts Communist Revolution in Latin America* (University of North Carolina Press, Chapel Hill, 1999).

S. G. Rabe, 'Controlling Revolutions: Latin America the Alliance for Progress and Cold War Anti-Communism', in T. G. Paterson (ed.), *Kennedy's Quest for Victory* (Oxford University Press, New York, 1989).

A. M. Schlesinger Jr., 'The Alliance for Progress: a Retrospective', in R. G. Hellman and H. J. Rosebaum (ed.), *Latin America: the Search for a New International Role* (Latin American International Affairs Series / Centre for Inter-American Relations, New York, 1975).

For details of the CIA coup in Guatemala:
R. H. Immermann, *The CIA in Guatemala: the Foreign Policy of Intervention* (University of Texas Press, Austin, 1982).

E. Kinzer, and S. Schlesinger, *Bitter Fruit: the Untold Story of the American Coup in Guatemala* (Doubleday, Garden City, 1982).

On the Berlin crises for material not based on archive sources:
H. M. Catudal, *Kennedy and the Berlin Crisis* (Berlin Verlag, Berlin, 1980).

J. M. Schick, *The Berlin Crisis 1958–1962* (University of Pennsylvania Press, Philadelphia, 1971).

And for the earlier origins which conditioned US policy:
David G. Coleman, 'Eisenhower and the Berlin Problem 1953–1954' *Journal of Cold War Studies*, 1 (2000).

On China and the offshore islands:
Robert S. Ross and Jiang Changbin (eds.), *Re-examining the Cold War. US–China Diplomacy 1954–1973* (Harvard University Press, Cambridge, 2001).

Odd Arne Westad (ed.), *Brothers in Arms: The Rise and Fall of the Sino-Soviet Alliance 1945–1963* (Woodrow Wilson Center Press, Stanford, 1998).

G. H. Chang, *Friends and Enemies: the US, China, and the Soviet Union, 1948–72* (Stanford University Press, Stanford, 1990).

On the Cuban Missile Crisis:
See for a record of the Ex-Com meetings:
Ernest R. May and Philip D. Zelikov, *The Kennedy Tapes inside the White House during the Cuban Missile Crisis* (Harvard University Press, Cambridge, 1997)

And for an approach mixing theory and history:
Graham Allison and Philip D. Zelikov, *Essence of Decision* (Longman, New York, 2nd edn., 1999).

For a focus on Cuba and the Soviet perspective:
Alexsandr Furschenko and Timothy Natfali, '*One Hell of a Gamble': Khrushchev, Castro and Kennedy 1958–1964* (Norton, New York, 1992).

J. G. Blight et al., 'Essence of Revision: Moscow, Havana and the Cuban Missile Crisis', *International Security* (1989/90).

Barton J. Bernstein, 'Reconsidering Khrushchev's Gambit—Defending the Soviet Union and Cuba', *Diplomatic History*, 3 (1990).

P. Brenner, 'Thirteen Months: Cuba's Perspective on the Missile Crisis' in James A. Nathan (ed.), *The Cuban Missile Crisis Revisited* (St Martin's Press, New York, 1992).

For details and debate:
James G. Hershberg, 'Before the "Missiles of October", Did Kennedy Plan a Military Strike against Cuba', *Diplomatic History*, 2 (1990).

B. J. Bernstein, 'The Cuban Missile Crisis: Trading the Jupiters in Turkey', *Political Science Quarterly* (1980).

James G. Blight, Joseph S. Nye, and David A. Welch, 'The Cuban Missile Crisis Revisited' *Foreign Affairs*, 1 (1987).

R. N. Lebow, 'The Cuban Missile Crisis: Learning the Lessons Correctly', *Political Science Quarterly* (1983).

R. N. Lebow, 'Domestic Politics and the Cuban Missile Crisis', *Diplomatic History*, 2 (1990).

For details of the early years of the Vietnam conflict:
A. J. Short, *The Origins of the Vietnam War* (Longman, London, 1989).

David L. Anderson, *Trapped by Success: The Eisenhower Administration and Vietnam, 1953–1961* (Columbia University Press, New York, 1991).

Smith, R. B., *An International History of the Vietnam War, 1: Revolution Versus Containment* (1983); 2: The Struggle for South-East Asia, 1961–5 (Macmillan, London, 1985).

John M. Newman, *JFK and Vietnam: Deception. Intrigue, and the Struggle for Power* (Warner, New York, 1992).

Cheng Guan Ang, *Vietnamese Communists' Relations with China and the Second Indochina Conflict, 1957–1962* (McFarland, Jefferson, 1997).

On the US attitudes to the End of the European Empires and the African crises which were important under Kennedy:
M. Kalb, *The Congo Cables: the Cold War in Africa—from Eisenhower to Kennedy* (Macmillan, New York, 1982).

R. D. Mahoney, *JFK: Ordeal in Africa* (Oxford University Press, New York, 1983).

C. Fraser, 'Understanding American Policy towards Decolonization', *Diplomacy and Statecraft* (1992).

Part III, 1963–1971

There a now a number of archival based books on the Johnson administration:
W. I. Cohen and Nancy B. Tucker (eds.), *Lyndon Johnson Confronts the World American Foreign Policy 1963–1968* (Cambridge University Press, New York, 1994).

H. W. Brands, *The Wages of Globalism: Lyndon Johnson and the Limits of American Power* (Oxford University Press, New York, 1995).

Much of this period is dominated by the escalation of the Vietnam War and subsequent US defeat:
Larry Berman, *Lyndon Johnson's War* (Norton, New York, 1989).

Larry Cable, *Unholy Grail: The US and the Wars in Vietnam, 1965–8* (Routledge, New York, 1991).

Lloyd C. Gardner, *Pay Any Price: Lyndon Johnson and the Wars for Vietnam* (Ivan R. Dee, Chicago, 1995).

George C. Herring, *LBJ and Vietnam: A Different Kind of War* (University of Texas Press, Austin, 1994).

Michael H. Hunt, *Lyndon Johnson's War: America's Cold War Crusade in Vietnam, 1945–1965* (Hill & Wang, New York, 1996).

David Kaiser, *American Tragedy: Kennedy, Johnson, and the Origins of the Vietnam War* (Harvard University Press, Cambridge, 2000).

Robert S. McNamara, *In Retrospect* (Times Books, New York, 1995).

David M. Barrett, *Uncertain Warriors: Lyndon Johnson and his Vietnam Advisers* University Press of Kansas, Lawrence, 1993).

Marilyn B. Young, *The Vietnam Wars, 1945–90* (HarperCollins, New York, 1991).

Fredrick Logevall, *Choosing War* (University of California Press, Berkeley, 1999).

Gerard J. de Groot, *A Noble Cause? America and the Vietnam War* (Pearson, Harlow, 2000).

On the Chinese and Soviet sides:
Qiang Zhai, *China and the Vietnam Wars, 1950–75* (University of North Carolina Press, Chapel Hill, 2000).

Ilya Gaiduk, *The Soviet Union and the Vietnam War* (Ivan R. Dee, Chicago, 1996).

On Nixon and Vietnam:
Jeffrey Kimball, *Nixon's Vietnam War* (University of Kansas Press, Kansas, 1999).

William Shawcross, *Sideshow: Kissinger, Nixon and the Destruction of Cambodia.* (Simon & Schuster, New York, 1987, 1st edn., 1979).

For the increasing involvement of the superpowers in the Middle East and how this interacted with the regional and domestic situations:
Yezid Sayigh and Avi Shlaim (eds.), *The Cold War and the Middle East* (Clarendon Press, Oxford, 1997).

G. Golan, *Soviet Policies in the Middle East: from World War II to Gorbachev* (Cambridge University Press, Cambridge, 1990).

I. Kass, *Soviet Involvement in the Middle East: Policy Formulation, 1966–75* (Westview Press, Folkestone, 1978).

W. B. Quandt, *Decade of Decisions: American Policy towards the Arab–Israeli Conflict, 1967–76* (Berkeley, 1977).

M. N. Barnett and J. S. Levy, 'Domestic Causes of Alliances and Alignments: the Case of Egypt, 1962–73' *International Organization* (1991).

Malcolm Kerr, *The Arab Cold War: Gamal 'Abd Al-Nasir and his Rivals, 1958–1970* (Oxford University Press, London, 3rd edn., 1971).

For details of how participants saw the nature of Soviet–American Relations:
Anatoly Dobrynin, *In Confidence* (Random House, New York, 1995).

Dean Rusk, *As I Saw It* (Norton, New York, 1990).

Henry Kissinger, *The White House Years* (Weidenfeld & Nicolson, London, 1979).

For an overview:
Peter G. Boyle, *American–Soviet Relations* (Routledge, London, 1993).

For the opening to China and the problems in Sino–Soviet relations:

Alfred D. Low, *The Sino–Soviet Dispute: An Analysis of the Polemics* (Associated University Presses, London, 1976).

Yang-Kuisong, 'The Sino-Soviet Border Clash of 1969', *Cold War History* 1 (August 2000).

Chen Jian and David Wilson, 'New Evidence on the Sino–American Opening', *Cold War International History Project Bulletin* 11 (Winter 1998).

Odd Arne Westad (ed,), *Brothers in Arms The Rise and Fall of the Sino–Soviet Alliance 1945–1963* (Woodrow Wilson Center Press, Washington, DC, 1998).

On Latin America with the shift in Johnson's policy and its acceptance of overt intervention and the move, continued under Nixon, to favouring dictatorships:
Abraham Lowenthal, *The Dominican Intervention* (Johns Hopkins University Press, Baltimore, 1995).

Walter LaFeber, *Inevitable Revolutions: the US in Central America* (Norton, New York, 2nd edn., 1993).

On the Cold War in other parts of the less developed world:
Matthew Jones, *Conflict and Confrontation in South East Asia, 1961–1965: Britain, the United States, Indonesia and the Creation of Malaysia* (Cambridge University Press, Cambridge, 2002).

Suzanne Cronje, *The World and Nigeria: the Diplomatic History of the Biafran War* (Sidgwick & Jackson, London, 1972).

On the Prague Spring in 1968:
William Shawcross, *Dubček* (Hogarth Press, London, 1990).

Kenneth K. Skoug, *Czechoslovakia's Lost Fight for Freedom* (Praeger, Westport, 1999).

H. Gordon Skilling, *Czechoslovakia's Interrupted Revolution* (Princeton University Press, Princeton, 1976).

James G. McGinn, 'The Politics of Collective Inaction NATO's response to the Prague Spring', *Journal of Cold War Studies* 1/3 (Fall, 1999).

On the problems in Trans-Atlantic Relations focused on France:
F. Bozo, *Two Strategies for Europe: de Gaulle, the United States and the Atlantic Alliance* (Rowman & Littlefield, Lanham, 2001).

On Western Europe and the origins of détente in Europe:
S. R. Ashton, *In Search of Détente* (Macmillan, Basingstoke, 1989).

Josef Korbel, *Détente in Europe* (Princeton University Press, Princeton, 1972).

Gottfried Niedhart, 'Ostpolitik', in Caroline Fink *et al.* (eds.), *1968: The World Transformed* (Cambridge University Press, Cambridge, 1998).

Willy Brandt, 'German Policy towards the East', *Foreign Affairs*, 3 (April 1968).

Part IV, 1972–1980

The essential text for these years is:
Raymond Garthoff, *Détente and Confrontation: American–Soviet relations from Nixon to Reagan* (Brookings, Washington, 2nd edn., 1994).

Memoirs from some key US players are particularly rich in this period. On the Nixon–Ford administrations see:
Henry Kissinger, *The White House Years* (Little, Brown, Boston, 1979).

Henry Kissinger, *Years of Upheaval* (Little, Brown, Boston, 1982).

Henry Kissinger, *Years of Renewal* (Simon & Schuster, New York, 1989).

Richard Nixon, *RN: the Memoirs of Richard Nixon* (Grosset & Dunlap, New York, 1978).

And on the Carter years:
Zbigniew Brzezinski, *Power and Principle: Memoirs of the National Security Adviser, 1977–81* (Farrar-Strauss-Giroux, New York, 1983).

Jimmy Carter, *Keeping Faith: Memoirs of a President* (Collins, London, 1982).

Cyrus Vance, *Hard Choices: Critical Years in American Foreign Policy* (Simon & Schuster, New York, 1983).

On the Soviet side the essential memoirs are:
Anatoly Dobrynin, *In Confidence: Moscow's Ambassador to Six Cold War Presidents, 1962–86* (Times Books, New York, 1995).

Andrei Gromyko, *Memories* (Hutchinson, London, 1989).

While archives on the period are only just opening, there are also a number of good, detailed studies on the Nixon-Kissinger years:
Jonathan Aitken, *Nixon: a life* (Weidenfeld & Nicolson, London, 1995).

William Bundy, *A Tangled Web: the Making of Foreign Policy in the Nixon Presidency* (I. B. Tauris, New York, 1998).

Walter Isaacson, *Kissinger: a Biography* (Faber & Faber, London, 1992).

Tad Szulc, *The Illusion of Peace: foreign policy in the Nixon Years* (Viking Press, New York, 1978).

Richard Thornton, *The Nixon-Kissinger Years* (Paragon, New York, 1989).

But on the Carter administration see especially:
David Brinkley, 'The Rising Stock of Jimmy Carter', *Diplomatic History*, 4 (1966).

Richard Thornton, *The Carter Years: Towards a New Global Order* (Pentagon, New York, 1991).

Valuable studies of Soviet foreign policy include:
Robin Edmonds, *Soviet Foreign Policy: the Brezhnev Years* (Oxford University Press, Oxford, 1983).

Harry Gelman, *The Brezhnev Politburo and the Decline of Détente* (Cornell University Press, Ithaca, 1984).

Adam B. Ulam, *Dangerous Relations: the Soviet Union in World Politics, 1970–82* (Oxford University Press, Oxford, 1983).

More specifically on the theme of détente are:
Mike Bowker and Phil Williams, *Superpower Détente: a Reappraisal* (Sage, London, 1988).

Robert Litwak, *Détente and the Nixon Doctrine* (Cambridge University Press, Cambridge, 1984).

Richard Pipes, *US–Soviet Relations in the Era of Détente* (Westview Press, Boulder, 1981).

Richard Stevenson, *The Rise and Fall of Détente* (Macmillan, London, 1985).

John van Oudenaren, *Détente in Europe* (Duke University Press, Durham, 1991).

Odd Arne Westad, *The Fall of Détente* (Oslo University Press, Oslo, 1997).

But for a focus on European détente:
Kenneth Dyson (ed.), *European Détente: Case Studies in the Politics of East–West Relations* (Pinter, London, 1986).

Vojtech Mastny, *Helsinki, Human Rights and European Security* (Duke University Press, Durham, 1986).

And the Sino–American rapprochement is analysed in:
Robert Ross, *Negotiating Co-operation: the US and China, 1969–89* (Stanford University Press, Stanford, 1995).

On the continuing problems of Indochina:
Jeffrey Kimball, *Nixon's Vietnam War* (Kansas University Press, Lawrence, 1998).

Ben Kiernan, *The Pol Pot Regime: Race, Power and Genocide in Cambodia* (Yale University Press, New Haven, 1996).

On the 1973 war and its aftermath in the Middle East:
Anwar el-Sadat, *In Search of Identity* (Collins, London 1978).

Kenneth Stein, *Heroic Diplomacy: Sadat, Kissinger, Carter, Begin and the Quest for Arab–Israeli peace* (Routledge, New York, 1999).

William Quandt, *Camp David: Peacemaking and Politics* (Brookings, Washington, 1986).

On the Civil War in the Lebanon see:
Farid el-Khazen, *The Breakdown of the State in Lebanon* (Harvard University Press, Cambridge, 2000).

Robert Fisk, *Pity the Nation* (Deutsch, London, 1990).

While on the Iranian revolution and its impact see:
James Bill, *The Eagle and the Lion* (Yale University Press, New Haven, 1988).

Richard Cottam, *Iran and the United States: a Cold War Case Study* (University of Pittsburgh Press, Pittsburgh, 1988).

Shireen Hunter, *Iran and the World* (Indiana University Press, Bloomington, 1990).

Barry Rubin, *Paved with Good Intentions: the American Experience and Iran* (Oxford University Press, New York, 1990).

And on the Cold War's impact on Africa in the 1970s:
Piero Gleijeses, *Conflicting Missions: Havana, Washington and Africa* (University of North Carolina Press, Chapel Hill, 2002).

Norrie McQueen, *The Decolonisation of Portuguese Africa* (Longman, London, 1997).

Robert Patman, *The Soviet Union in the Horn of Africa* (Cambridge University Press, Cambridge, 1990).

On the advances in strategic arms control in these years see:
John Newhouse, *Cold Dawn: the Story of SALT* (Holt, Rinehart & Winston, New York, 1973).

Strobe Talbott, *Endgame: the Inside Story of SALT II* (Harper & Row, New York, 1979).

Part V, 1981–1989

Essential memoirs for these years are:
Mikhail Gorbachev, *Memoirs* (Doubleday, New York, 1996).

Ronald Reagan, *An American Life* (Hutchinson, London, 1991).

Eduard Shevardnadze, *The Future belongs to Freedom* (Sinclair-Stevenson, London, 1991).

George Shultz, *Turmoil and Triumph* (Scribners, New York, 1993).

Margaret Thatcher, *The Downing Street Years* (HarperCollins, London, 1993).

The period of the so-called 'Second Cold War' of 1980–5 is discussed in:
Noam Chomsky, Jonathan Steele, and John Gittings, *Superpowers in Collision: the New Cold War of the 1980s* (Penguin, Harmondsworth, 1984).

Fred Halliday, *The Making of the Second Cold War* (Verso, London, 1986).

William G. Hyland, *Mortal Rivals: Superpower Relations from Nixon to Reagan* (Random House, New York, 1987).

Strobe Talbott, *Deadly Gambits: the Reagan Administration and the Stalemate in Arms control* (Pan, London, 1985).

While on the end of the Cold War in 1985–90 see especially:
Michael Beschloss and Strobe Talbott, *At the Highest Levels: the Inside Story of the End of the Cold War* (Little, Brown, Boston, 1993).

John L. Gaddis, *The United States and the End of the Cold War* (Oxford University Press, Oxford, 1992).

Raymond Garthoff, *The Great Transition: American–Soviet relations and the End of the Cold War* (Brookings Institution, Washington, DC, 1994).

Don Oberdorfer, *The Turn: How the Cold War came to an End* (Jonathan Cape, London, 1992).

On the war in Afghanistan:
George Arney, *Afghanistan* (Mandarin, London, 1990).

Henry Bradsher, *Afghanistan and the Soviet Union* (Duke University Press, Durham, 1983).

Mark Galeotti, *Afghanistan: the Soviet Union's Last War* (Frank Cass, London, 1994).

Thomas Hammond, *Red Flag over Afghanistan* (Westview, Boulder, 1984).

Anthony Hyman, *Afghanistan under Soviet Domination* (Macmillan, London, 1992).

The collapse of communism has generated an enormous literature and remains the centre of intense debate, but on Soviet policy see especially:
Mark Galeotti, *Gorbachev and his Revolution* (Macmillan, Basingstoke, 1997).

Geoffrey Hosking, *The Awakening of the Soviet Union* (Harvard University Press, Cambridge, 1991).

William Watson, *The Collapse of Communism in the Soviet Union* (Greenwood Press, Westport, 1998).

Vladimir Zubok, 'Gorbachev and the End of the Cold War', *Cold War History*, 2 (2002).

While on events in Eastern Europe:
Neal Ascherson, *The Polish August* (Penguin, Harmondsworth, 1981).

David Mason, *Revolution and Transition in East-Central Europe* (Westview Press, Boulder, 2nd edn., 1996).

Michael Waller, *The End of Communist Power Monopoly* (Manchester University Press, Manchester, 1993).

And on the Iran–Iraq War:
John Bulloch and Harvey Morris, *The Gulf War: Its Origins, History and Consequences* (Methuen, London, 1989).

Stephen Pelletiere, *The Iran–Iraq War* (Praeger, New York, 1992).

For the strides taken in European integration in the 1980s, down to the Maastricht Treaty, see:
Alasdair Blair, *Dealing with Europe: Britain and the Negotiation of the Maastricht Treaty* (Ashgate, Aldershot, 1999).

Juliet Lodge (ed.), *The European Community and the Challenge of the Future* (Pinter, London, 1989).

Peter Ludlow, *The Making of the European Monetary System* (Butterworths, London, 1982).

George Ross, *Jacques Delors and European Integration* (Oxford University Press, New York, 1995).

Part VI, 1990–2000

A fascinating overall interpretation of the period is:
Ian Clark, *The Post-Cold War Order* (Oxford University Press, Oxford, 2001) and on Globalization.

D. Held and Anthony McGrew (eds.), *The Global Transformations Reader* (Polity Press, Oxford, 2000).

In general on the US policy in the Post-Cold War years see:
Lester Brune, *The United States and Post-Cold War Interventions: Bush and Clinton in Somalia, Haiti and Bosnia* (Regina Books, Claremont, 1998).

Michael Cox, *US Foreign Policy after the Cold War* (Pinter, London, 1995).

John C. Hulsman, *A Paradigm for the New World Order* (Macmillan, Basingstoke, 1997).

Steven Hurst, *The Foreign Policy of the Bush Administration* (Cassell, London, 1999).

Robert Hutchings (ed.), *At the End of the American Century: America's Role in the Post-Cold War World* (Johns Hopkins University Press, Baltimore, 1998).

William Hyland, *Clinton's World* (Greenwood Press, Westport, 1999).

Anthony Lake, 'Confronting Backlash States', *Foreign Affairs* (March–April l994).

On Russia and the problems of the former USSR:
Leon Aron, *Yeltsin: a Revolutionary Life* (HarperCollins, London, 2000).

John Dunlop, *The Rise of Russia and the Fall of the Soviet Empire* (Princeton University Press, Princeton, 1993).

Anatol Lieven, *Chechnya: Tombstone of Russian Power* (Yale University Press, New Haven, 1998).

Stasys Knezys and Romanas Sedlickas, *The War in Chechnya* (Texas A and M University, College Station, 1999).

Peter Shearman, *Russian Foreign Policy since 1990* (Westview, Boulder, 1995).

Many of the main players are yet to produce memoirs but well worth reading on US policy are:
George Bush and Brent Scowcoft, *A World Transformed* (Knopf, New York, 1998).

James A. Baker, *The Politics of Diplomacy* (Putnam, New York, 1995).

On Russia:
Boris Yeltsin, *The View from the Kremlin* (HarperCollins, London, 1994).

While on South Africa see:
F. W. de Klerk, *The Autobiography: the Last Trek, a New Beginning* (Macmillan, London, 1999).

Nelson Mandela, *The Long Walk to Freedom* (Little, Brown, Chicago, 1994).

German reunification at the start of the decade is the focus of a number of works but see especially:
Stephen Szabo, *The Diplomacy of German Unification* (New York, 1992).

Philip Zelikow and Condoleeza Rice, *German Unified and Europe Transformed* (Harvard University Press, Cambridge, 1995).

On the Balkans conflicts:
Christopher Bennett, *Yugoslavia's Bloody Collapse* (Hurst, London, 1995).

Ivo Daalder, *Getting to Dayton: the Making of America's Bosnia Policy* (Brookings Institution, Washington, DC, 2000).

Tim Judah, *The Serbs* (Yale University Press, New Haven, 1997).

Noel Malcolm, *Bosnia: a Short History* (Macmillan, London, 2nd edn., 1996).

Noel Malcolm, *Kosovo: a Short History* (Macmillan, London, 1998).

While two memoirs on the attempts to settle the Bosnian conflict are:
Richard Holbrooke, *To End a War* (Modern Library, New York, 1999).

David Owen, *Balkan Odyssey* (Victor Gollancz, London, 1996).

On European security:
Clay Clemens, *NATO and the Quest for Post-Cold War Security* (Macmillan, Basingstoke, 1997).

Andrew Dorman, *European Security: an Introduction to Security Issues in Post-Cold War Europe* (Dartmouth, Aldershot, 1995).

William Park and Wyn Rees, *Rethinking Security in Post-Cold War Europe* (Longman, London, 1998).

Trevor Taylor, *European Security and the Former Soviet Union* (Royal Institute of International Affairs, London, 1994).

On East Asia:
Samuel Kim, *North Korean Foreign Relations in the Post-Cold War Era* (Oxford University Press, New York, l998).

Russell Ong, *China's Security Interests in the Post-Cold War Era* (Curzon, Richmond, 2001).

Li Xiaobang, *Interpreting US-China-Taiwan Relations: China in the Post-Cold War Era* University Press of America, Lanham, 1998).

Suisheng Zhao, *Power Competition in East Asia* (St Martin's Press, New York, 1997).

In the Middle East, on the Oslo peace process and its difficulties:
Andrew Buchanan, *Peace with Justice* (Macmillan, London, 2000).

Robert O. Freedman, *The Middle East and the Peace Process* (University Press of Florida, Gainesville, 1998).

George Giacaman and Dag Lonning (eds.), *After Oslo* (Pluto Press, Chicago, 1998).

David Makovsky, *Making Peace with the PLO* (Westview Press, Boulder, 1996).

On conflict in the Gulf:
Said Aburish, *Saddam Hussein* (Bloomsbury, London, 2000).

Andrew and Patrick Cockburn, *Out of the Ashes: the Resurrection of Saddam Hussein* (HarperCollins, New York, 1999).

Lawrence Freedman and Efraim Karsh, *The Gulf Conflict* (Faber & Faber, London, 1993).

Dilip Hiro, *Desert Shield to Desert Storm: the Second Gulf War* (HarperCollins, London, 1992).

And on the changes in southern Africa that accompanied the demise of apartheid:
Walter Carlsnaes and Marie Muller (eds.), *Change and South Africa's External Relations* (Thomson, Johannesburg, 1997).

Chester Crocker, *High Noon in Southern Africa* (Norton, New York, 1992).

Timothy Sisk, *Democratization in South Africa* (Princeton University Press, Princeton, 1995).

Patti Waldmeir, *Anatomy of a Miracle: the End of Apartheid and the Birth of the New South Africa* (Norton, New York, 1997).

Index